UNITED STATES
FOREIGN POLICY MAKING

Process, Problems, and Prospects

WILLIAM H. BAUGH
University of Oregon

HARCOURT COLLEGE PUBLISHERS

Fort Worth   Philadelphia   San Diego   New York   Orlando   Austin   San Antonio
Toronto   Montreal   London   Sydney   Tokyo

Publisher:	Earl McPeek
Executive Editor:	David C. Tatom
Market Strategist:	Steve Drummond
Project Editor:	Travis Tyre
Art Director:	Chris Morrow
Production Manager:	Linda McMillan

ISBN: 0-15-508134-9
Library of Congress Catalog Card Number: 99-72116

Address for orders:
Harcourt, Inc., 6277 Sea Harbor Drive, Orlando, FL 32887-6777
1-800-782-4479

Address for international orders
International Customer Service
Harcourt, Inc., 6277 Sea Harbor Drive, Orlando, FL 32887-6777
407 345-3800
(Fax) 407-345-4060

Address for editorial correspondence:
Harcourt College Publishers, 301 Commerce Street, Suite 3700, Fort Worth, TX 76102

Web site address:
http://www.harcourtcollege.com

Printed in the United States of America

9 0 1 2 3 4 5 6 7 8   016   9 8 7 6 5 4 3 2 1

Harcourt College Publishers

*This book is dedicated to my beloved wife, Cheryl, test audience,
data tabulator, and gentle critic, who combined all the sacrifices
traditional to authors' spouses with loving support throughout the project.*

*It is also dedicated to the memory of my mother, Mary B. Baugh,
who applied the skilled mind of a teacher of English
to many early drafts, whose love was unfailing,
and whose courage in the face of adversity
was a source of inspiration to all who knew her.*

PREFACE

Conceived and written entirely in the post–Cold War era, *United States Foreign Policy Making* is an extensive and critical examination of the process, problems, and prospects of U.S. foreign policy. The overarching theme is the foreign policy problems now confronting the United States differ tremendously in number, character, and potential solutions from the problems faced during the Cold War era; that is, during most of the second half of the twentieth century. Policy-making institutions and processes continue to evolve slowly, although the global context in which we conduct U.S. foreign policy has changed dramatically since 1990, in ways explicitly examined in this book. Half a century ago—in another time of massive change and challenge—American leaders rapidly made huge and far-reaching foreign policy decisions and built, in only a few years, the framework that guided us through more than four decades of the Cold War. Nothing comparable to that experience is happening in today's very different global context of policy. Although we face a multitude of complex new challenges, the United States has yet to develop any comprehensive grand policy to guide its foreign relations into the new century.

United States Foreign Policy Making analyzes new challenges through a systems approach that focuses on the many individuals and organizations who plan and execute policy, the relationships among them, and the ways the system functions. Theoretical perspectives that draw on both classic and contemporary research are integral elements of the text, explicitly discussed, and applied in ways clearly understandable to students. The text illustrates applications that range from historic highlights in the development of U.S. foreign policy to recent and ongoing experiences. This approach provides a strong framework to help students build skills in analyzing historical and contemporary foreign policy actions as well as in anticipating future problems that may develop.

Foreign policy is influenced by a multitude of domestic factors and even more by international factors, all of which must be included in any comprehensive interpretation. Treatment of international factors is an important feature of this book and is strongly slanted toward how these factors influence and may be used by the United States. Determining why policy outcomes frequently differ from expectations and sometimes yield unanticipated or disappointing results is an important concern. Coverage extends to factors whose more thorough study often involves entire courses, including international political economy, international security, development, and the role of public opinion in the foreign policy process.

United States Foreign Policy Making is intended as a comprehensive text for college and university courses in U.S. foreign policy and as a reference for advanced undergraduate and graduate students of political science. Additionally, it is an appropriate supplemental work for international and comparative politics courses in which U.S. actions are considered.

Numerous pedagogical devices are used in this book to facilitate reading and to maximize student learning:

- Brief *foreign policy cases* begin each chapter and are designed to catch students' attention, to provide historical background and context, to illustrate general principles, and to help students apply those principles to contemporary policy problems.

- *Foreign policy boxes* inside the chapters display concise and interesting applications and amplifications that are especially, although not exclusively, suitable for more advanced students.
- *Chronology boxes* summarize key events in history.
- *Bulleted lists* summarize theoretical material and assist in the applications. *Numbered lists* lay out information in a clearly organized and easily readable manner.
- *Boldfaced key terms* draw students' attention to important words and phrases. Each term is boldfaced within the chapters, listed at the end of each chapter, and defined in the glossary at the back of the book.
- *Figures* and *tables* throughout provide current global statistics and communicate ideas about policy issues around the world.
- The *appendix* lists the meanings of the numerous abbreviations and acronyms used in the book and describes the important role these shortcuts play in government usage.
- *Editorial cartoons* offer enduring messages and humor. *Photographs* of important personalities and events play a similar role.

ACKNOWLEDGMENTS

This single-author text bears the imprints of many minds. Scholars too numerous to thank individually have shaped my understanding directly and indirectly (through their writings). Interactions with my students at the University of Oregon over recent years were invaluable in refining the organization and presentation of this material, and many students gave important suggestions for improvement.

I am indebted to Cindy Stormer, former political science editor at Brooks/Cole Publishing Company (with whom this project began) for her insightful help in shaping the original proposal, refining it through reviews, and expanding my understanding of the manuscript development process. After publisher mergers and restructurings, the project landed on the desk of David Tatom, political science executive editor at Harcourt College Publishers, who has been extremely supportive.

The following reviewers provided many valuable ideas that improved the book's organization, content, presentation, and interpretation: Donald A. Sylvan, Ohio State University; B. David Meyers, University of North Carolina at Greensboro; Steve Chan, University of Colorado at Boulder; Larry Elowitz, Georgia College and State University; James Larry Taulbee, Emory University; Melissa A. Butler, Wabash College; Charles Taber, SUNY at Stonybrook; Peter Moody, University of Notre Dame; Louis M. Terrell, San Diego State University; Kim E. Spiezio, Virginia Polytechnic Institute; Roy Licklider, Rutgers University at New Brunswick; Robert McCalla, University of Wisconsin, Madison; Edwin Coulter, Clemson University; Michael G. Schechter, Michigan State University.

Special thanks in particular are due to Susan G. Alkana, freelance developmental editor for Harcourt, who worked very closely with me over the final two years of writing, reviews, and revisions. She was unfailingly encouraging and supportive and kept the occasional necessary chiding gentle. Her editing provided a model for simplifying and clarifying the presentation throughout, and her suggestions were quite helpful. I find it difficult to imagine a better working relationship between writer and editor. I would also like to thank the production team at Harcourt College Publishers in Fort Worth, Texas: Steve Drummond, market strategist; Linda McMillan, production manager; Chris Morrow, art director; and Travis Tyre, project editor.

ABOUT THE AUTHOR

William H. Baugh is associate professor of political science at the University of Oregon, where he teaches U.S. foreign policy and courses on international security and research methodology. After earning degrees in physics at MIT and the University of Rochester, he received his Ph.D. in political science from Indiana University. His interest in issues of war and peace during the Cold War years led to the publication of his first book, *The Politics of Nuclear Balance*, and to several scholarly articles and other writings on deterrence and strategic nuclear balance. His research on the linkages between conventional (non-nuclear) arms transfers and wars among and within developing states of the world continues to evolve. His long-standing interest in U.S. foreign policy has led both to the development of new political science courses and to recent research on the roles that public opinion and belief systems play in shaping and maintaining U.S. foreign policy. He and his wife Cheryl, numerous cats, and a dog reside in the foothills of the Coast Range, outside Eugene, Oregon.

CONTENTS

INTRODUCTION AND OVERVIEW

The greatest questions facing students of U.S. foreign policy at the onset of the twenty-first century are the following:

1. Has the era of U.S. dominance in world affairs ended?
2. Should we care?
3. How should—and how will—the United States respond to the foreign policy problems and opportunities now facing us and those that are likely to face us in the near future?

Let's look at a few brief (if somewhat flippant) answers:

1. Yes. The era of U.S. dominance in world affairs is over, but only in certain ways, which may not be the most important ones. The United States still has greater political influence than any other state, the world's most powerful military, and the largest economy. However, America is increasingly challenged by rising powers, especially in world economics.
2. Yes. We should care because U.S. foreign policy influences individual lives—our own and others'—as well as other countries around the world. American jobs will be gained or lost, depending on the terms of international trade arrangements such as the North American Free Trade Agreement (NAFTA). American diplomats, soldiers, and tourists abroad may become targets of international political terrorists, and such terrorists already have carried out attacks within the United States. American policies of war as well as peacekeeping abroad, such as in Bosnia, can result in the loss of life for American soldiers and can profoundly affect their families.
3. We do not know much yet about how the United States will respond to the problems and opportunities of the new post–Cold War era. This lack of knowledge results from an absence of global vision and grand policy agreement within the foreign policy establishment. Without such agreement, America cannot achieve any broad domestic political consensus or the necessary political follow-through for long-term policy implementation.

Part I: Introduction and Overview introduces the context and major themes of U.S. foreign policy. Included are different viewpoints that people hold toward foreign policy, how policy has evolved from the founding of the country to the present, and where we may be heading as we enter the twenty-first century.

We have just been through a wrenching change in our foreign policy environment. In only a handful of years, since around 1990, the end of the Cold War changed the face of international politics fundamentally and irrevocably. We can date the Cold War period as beginning from Winston Churchill's 1946 speech that first popularized the phrase "Iron Curtain" and ending in the fall of 1990 with the reunification of Germany and the collapse of Eastern European communism. That period spanned forty-four years of intensive and extensive competition around the globe between the United States and the Soviet Union, along with their sometimes fractious allies. Competition with the Soviets dominated U.S. foreign policy for two generations and consumed many lives and several trillion dollars in resources. Appeals to national defense were used to justify not only massive military spending, but almost every other sort of endeavor, including educational improvements, student loan programs, and infrastructure investments such as the interstate highway system. In the cause of containing the spread of communism, the United States engaged in wars and conflicts lasting several years each in Korea (1950–53) and Vietnam (roughly 1963–73), plus many lesser armed clashes and threatened clashes. None of these were great wars, although some exceeded even World War II in certain measures of effort and destruction, such as numbers of bombs dropped. Moreover, the global schism between the United States and the Soviet Union extended to politics, ideology, economics, and even cultural affairs. It involved every other country to some degree.

For any who doubted whether the Cold War had truly ended, the 1991 breakup of the Soviet Union into its ethnically distinct constituent republics settled the issue. Officials from President George Bush on down claimed that the United States had won the Cold War and had emerged as the sole surviving superpower. Such a victory had been a rhetorical goal and declared policy of the United States—what we said we wanted, even if our policies were not really designed to achieve it—for decades. Yet when it came, victory arrived with breathtaking speed, far outstripping most official analyses and expert predictions. The extent to which U.S. policy deserves credit for that monumental political shift is debated, and the question is addressed in Chapter 2. However, the magnitude of the shift is not at issue; the central conflict of international politics during those forty-four years was resolved decisively in favor of the United States and its allies. Moreover, because international politics is both the setting for, and a major determinant of, foreign policies, the United States must now respond to the change and operate in a fundamentally altered political world. Thus, with the end of the Cold War, the preeminent problem facing U.S. foreign policymakers today is how to devise and implement policies appropriate to the new world (dis)order.

Given the magnitude of these issues, it may seem surprising that, while the Cold War was winding down, America's attention was directed much more intensively toward a brewing conflict in the Middle East, which became the Persian Gulf War. Why did the immediate challenges of that conflict absorb more attention during late 1990 and early 1991 than the far greater long-term challenges and opportunities of the Soviet breakup and the end of the Cold War? The reasons will become more apparent in the first several chapters as we explore the Gulf War case and the many factors at home and abroad that are still shaping U.S. foreign policy.

Chapter 1 examines one case that provides a microcosm for the many perspectives and viewpoints from which we can approach the study of U.S. foreign policy. Although many authors present a single viewpoint as the most important—or even the only necessary approach to our subject—each such viewpoint really captures only part of a more complex reality. As we examine different viewpoints on U.S. foreign policy, we can make connections to each of the remaining major parts of the book.

Chapter 2 deals with the continuing and evolving long-term themes of U.S. foreign policy, from the colonial era through the end of the Cold War. Policy themes are viewed as selections made from the available menu of possibilities in our attempt to meet policy goals, subject to a wide variety of domestic and foreign constraints. One particular focus is on the very great changes in U.S. policy from World War II through the end of the Cold War. The major foreign policy orientations of alliance building, nonalignment, neutrality, isolationism, interventionism, and globalism (or internationalism) are introduced and applied to long-term themes. Those motifs include freedom for trade and navigation; early alliance seeking followed by a long period of nonalignment; the early emergence of hemispheric interventionism; *manifest destiny* and the achievement of great power status; decisive intervention in World Wars I and II; the achievement of superpower status, with its corollary of sustained global activism; containment, Cold War, liberal globalist interventionism; preoccupation with the limits of power in the aftermath of the Vietnam War; and the sudden and dramatic end of the Cold War.

Chapter 3 extends the discussion of major foreign policy themes from the end of the Cold War to our present search for a new grand policy that will guide us in the twenty-first century. We examine the great shift since 1990 in the global context of U.S. actions by comparing the early Cold War years (c. 1950), with the early post–Cold War years of the 1990s. Ironically, the sole surviving superpower now has greatly diminished standing relative to the other great powers, a point introduced here and examined more fully in later chapters. As a result, a fundamental foreign policy question facing the United States at the onset of the twenty-first century is "How involved should we be in affairs abroad?" The roles of values and belief systems in shaping foreign policy are examined, including how many contemporary policy debates are polarized between the strongly contrasting positions of internationalism and neoisolationism. The ultimate outcome of those debates is nowhere in sight.

Part II: Who Makes U. S. Foreign Policy and Why It Often Goes Wrong is devoted to system and process. Chapter 4 introduces the systems approach, organizes the involved parties by four zones of relative impact on policy, discusses how they interact, and illustrates how key functions are performed. Chapter 5 introduces the idealized *optimizing* and *satisficing* conceptual-analytic models of decision making. Implications of these competing views of decision making are found in Graham Allison's three models that explain government policy making from different levels of analysis. We then use these and other models to examine the causes of policy failures, an important focus of this volume. Chapter 6 addresses the agencies, groups, and individuals involved in planning and debating policy positions. Chapter 7 examines how different types of feedback enter into the policy process and how citizens—government officials and other actors—may use them to help evaluate the extent of foreign policy success and revise policies to increase success. Feedback is integral to the systems approach, and this coverage is one unique component of the book.

Part III: Tools of Policy expands the treatment of the policy process by providing a detailed examination of the broad but always constrained range of options available to the U.S. government and other foreign policy actors. Chapter 8 begins with the sources and nature of different types of power and the influence that power can bring. Goals in using power and numerous aspects of its application are examined. Chapter 9 begins from the premise that security today involves not just military but also economic, political, societal, and environmental sectors. Dilemmas surrounding security are examined, as are the unconventional military applications increasingly called for by many contemporary policy analysts. In Chapter 10, we interpret procedures and practices for diplomacy as vital channels for international communication and bargaining. Particular emphasis is given to the processes and procedures available to the United States. Chapter 11 examines how domestic and foreign interests interact in the politics of economic issues. We pay particular attention to economic globalization and to how U.S. interactions with the world economy changed during the late twentieth century. In Chapter 12, the development of international cooperation is seen as a response to increasing global interdependence. Three major cases illustrate how intergovernmental organizations, international regimes, and international nongovernmental organizations influence, and provide tools for, U.S. foreign policy.

Part IV: Increasingly Interesting Times: Problems and Prospects classifies and examines types of problems now emerging and selected major specific problems that seem likely. Part IV is organized around three dimensions:

1. Level of development
2. Activity sector at issue (geopolitical, military, economic, societal, and environmental)
3. Time frame.

Level of development is used because of numerous indications that economic structure and processes in upper-middle and high-income states increasingly differ from those in low and lower-middle income economies. A common analytic scheme is employed across fifteen focus cases examined in the last three chapters; it comprises stakes at issue, related U.S. policy themes, perceptions held by others and their relations with the United States, available alternative actions, and future prospects.

Chapter 13 relates the challenges of global development to U.S. foreign policies, international roles, and global standing in the new century. Some thirteen development strategies are assessed. Chapter 14 explores issues that the United States faces primarily in dealings with already developed or nearly developed states. Examples range from realigning global political and military security arrangements for the post–Cold War era, to solving environmental impact problems that often are most severe in the already industrialized states. Chapter 15 explores issues that the United States faces primarily in dealings with developing states. Examples range from the future world order of power distribution and governance, to links between diverse ethnic groups and their former nationals and descendants now in the United States. Chapter 16 concerns issues that bridge the tiers either by unavoidably involving all states or by linking powerful and influential developed states to developing states. Examples range from local and regional peacekeeping to promoting appropriate technologies that help maximize economic development and minimize environmental impact. The Afterword restates the core theme of policy change and relates it to U.S. foreign policy prospects for the twenty-first century.

CHAPTER 1

PERSPECTIVES ON U.S. FOREIGN POLICY: THE UNITED STATES AND THE PERSIAN GULF WAR, 1990–91

⊕ WHO WON THE PERSIAN GULF WAR?

Most U.S. citizens would quickly answer that the United States won by decisively defeating Iraq's military forces and liberating Kuwait. Before casually accepting that view, however, let us look more closely. What does "winning" an international confrontation mean? How do we measure success? Were we clear about our goals? Was there more than one winner and more than one loser? Are there different degrees of winning? Do different parties measure success over different time spans?

Within four months after Iraq invaded Kuwait on 2 August 1990, the United States had organized and led a coalition of more than thirty countries and sent over a half-million troops (its largest foreign military action since Vietnam). In mid-January 1991 the coalition began an intensive five-week campaign of aerial bombardment of Iraq and Iraqi positions in Kuwait. This was followed by a spectacularly quick land campaign in which a substantial portion of the Iraqi military was crushed. Kuwait was freed, and a cease-fire announced in only a hundred hours. Indeed, this was a significant military victory, and President George Bush hailed it as a great triumph and the harbinger of a vague and unspecified "new world order."

In the years after that so-called victory, however, little appeared to have changed in Iraq. From Baghdad, Saddam Hussein continued his oppressive rule. Within weeks of the cease-fire, Iraq's Republican Guard forces, which were never completely encircled and neutralized by coalition forces, played a critical role in Iraq's bloody suppression of rebellions by Kurds in the northwest and Shiites in the southeast—rebellions that had been encouraged by the United States during the previous months of confrontation and war. A UN-sponsored trade embargo continued to keep most Iraqi oil underground and to deny all but essential medical and humanitarian imports. Saddam and his supporters still enjoyed relative luxury while the living conditions of ordinary Iraqi citizens had plummeted. The United States still maintained troops, ships, and aircraft in the region, trying with little success to limit Saddam's oppression of his people, particularly the Kurds and

PHOTO 1.1
At a meeting held on 3 March 1991 (on a captured Iraqi air base in Safwan, Iraq), U.S. General H. Norman Schwarzkopf (seated left), commander of the coalition forces during the Persian Gulf War, and Saudi General Khalid Bin Sultan discuss the terms for a permanent cease-fire.
AP/Wide World Photos.

Shiites. UN inspectors still labored to locate and destroy all of Iraq's weapons of mass destruction and its facilities for building more. During late 1997 and early 1998, Iraq refused to cooperate with UN inspectors of the Special Commission (UNSCOM) when the inspection teams included Americans. By 1999, Iraq's continued raising of obstacles had led to the withdrawal of all UN arms inspectors, and the U.S. had begun bombing selected Iraqi military facilities. Throughout all these developments, however, Iraq continued to be Iran's only serious competitor for regional hegemony.

Did that outcome constitute a great victory for the United States and its allies? Did we accomplish our war goals? Did Iraq?

ASSESSING THE OUTCOMES OF THE PERSIAN GULF WAR

In assessing the outcomes of the Persian Gulf War, let us begin with several general principles:

- Winning should be defined in terms of achieving one's aims and success should be measured against policy goals.

- Foreign policy interactions may have multiple winners. Some situations offer opportunities for all parties to benefit. More confrontational situations still may have multiple winners because some goals are mutually compatible even when one party might not recognize the goals of another.

- Time is a vital dimension when measuring success. One can win in the short term and lose over the long run, or vice versa. One party's goals may be short term while another's are long term. Short-term success followed by long-term loss is one very important form of policy failure.

- Victory has many different dimensions (for example, military, political, economic), encompassing each of those broad classes of policy tools. More than one government has won a war only to lose the political struggles of the peace that followed.

- Hierarchies of policy goals usually exist, from the best imaginable to the least acceptable outcome. If we achieve our minimal aims, we may raise our sights. Thus goals often change over time in response to new situations created by the initiatives of others and by their responses to our actions.

- Finally, not all parties define victory in the same way or in the same time frame. In particular, citizens and rulers may define victory very differently.

Arguably, the United States won a major short-term military victory in the Persian Gulf War by organizing and leading the coalition that deterred Iraq from attacking beyond Kuwait and expelling Iraqi forces from Kuwait. It also achieved a fairly lasting political-economic victory by preserving Western access to the region's oil supplies. However, given the amount of official talk in Washington about ousting Saddam Hussein or encouraging his overthrow, U.S. policy goals were never completely clear and consistent. In particular, early military success in routing Iraqi forces in Kuwait and southern Iraq encouraged some coalition leaders to envision driving onward to Baghdad.

A longer term view suggests that short-term victory was followed by protracted difficulties. It is not farfetched to suggest that U.S. policy goals were fuzzy and contributed to snatching long-term political-economic stalemate or defeat from the jaws of short-term military victory. By failing to dislodge Saddam from power or destroy his most important military forces, the coalition left the seeds of protracted political-military confrontation and years of continued involvement in the region. This was so in part because the Iraqi regime won a long-term political victory simply by surviving. Despite having lost heavily to coalition forces, Iraq retained enough key military units to suppress internal unrest and keep Saddam in power. By the end of 1990, as the coalition built up its forces for war, it probably was politically advantageous to Saddam within Iraq to be defeated by overwhelming outside force rather than to withdraw voluntarily from Kuwait. Ordinary Iraqi citizens, who suffered terribly from both the war and the trade embargo, may not define Saddam's continued rule as a victory.

Interestingly, this conflict appears to have helped produce additional winners in related interactions. U.S. actions on behalf of Kuwait and the other Gulf oil states significantly improved our subsequent relations with the Arab world. In turn, this gave the United States greater influence in promoting a Middle East peace. Despite their fragility, peace agreements between Israel and the Palestine Liberation Organization (PLO) during the 1990s undoubtedly constitute a win for the entire world, especially Palestinian Arabs and peace-minded Israelis.

At least equally interesting today is what the U.S. government was not doing while it was absorbed with the Persian Gulf War. From August 1990 until the spring of 1991 very large shares of government, media, and public attention were focused on the Gulf. Simultaneously, a wave of nationalism and democratization was sweeping across Eastern Europe, and the Soviet Union was collapsing and fragmenting. Those events marked the winding down of the Cold War that had dominated U.S. foreign policy and world politics since the late 1940s. As we explore more fully in Chapter 2, twentieth-century U.S. foreign policy is marked by two great transitions. The first is an acceptance before the end of World War II that we would have a continuing and intensive postwar role in global politics. Second, the end of the Cold War (around 1990) was capped by the Soviet Union's breakup in 1991. In any long-term view of broad scope, the character of global politics in the post–Cold War era far outweighs concerns about any single area like the Persian Gulf. Arguably, had the United States paid more attention to broader concerns during 1990–91, it could have avoided some of today's arguments and uncertainties about appropriate post–Cold War policies.

As we examine key events of the Persian Gulf War in greater detail, keep these principles in mind. We will use this war both to introduce key concepts in the study of U.S. foreign policy and to examine a number of perspectives that different scholars and policy analysts take toward the subject. As we shall see, the Gulf War case demonstrates both how greatly the global context of American foreign policy has changed since 1990 (bringing both new threats and new opportunities) and how that profound change has altered the set of options open to U.S. policymakers.

WHAT HAPPENED IN THE PERSIAN GULF WAR?

At 2 A.M. on the morning of 2 August 1990, some 100,000 Iraqi troops, backed by more than three hundred tanks, rolled across their border into the tiny emirate of Kuwait, at the head of the Persian Gulf. Within six hours, essentially all resistance was crushed. Iraq had seized and annexed Kuwait, which it was later to term its "19th province." The invasion surprised almost everyone, even though it came after months of Iraqi threats against Kuwait. When the CIA reported on 21 July that Iraq had moved some 30,000 troops to the Iraqi border near Kuwait, most analysts had interpreted the move only as a pressure tactic. At various times during 1990, the Iraqi government had demanded that Kuwait forgive as much as $15 billion loaned interest free to support Iraq during the terribly costly 1980–88 Iran-Iraq war, cede some territory to give Iraq direct access to the Gulf, pay $2.4 billion or more in compensation for alleged overpumping of oil from the Rumalia field that stretches across their joint border, reduce oil pumping and support higher OPEC oil prices, and give Iraq $10 billion outright. Alone among U.S. government agencies, the CIA had warned that an invasion seemed imminent—but that assessment did not come until two days before the event.

In one bold stroke, Iraqi dictator Saddam Hussein had seized control of some 20 percent of the world's proven petroleum reserves. Refer to the map of the Persian Gulf region (Fig. 1.1). Almost nothing stood between Iraqi forces and the oil-rich northeastern region of Saudi Arabia, containing another 19 percent. Exiled Iraqis, among others,

FIGURE 1.1

The Persian Gulf Region

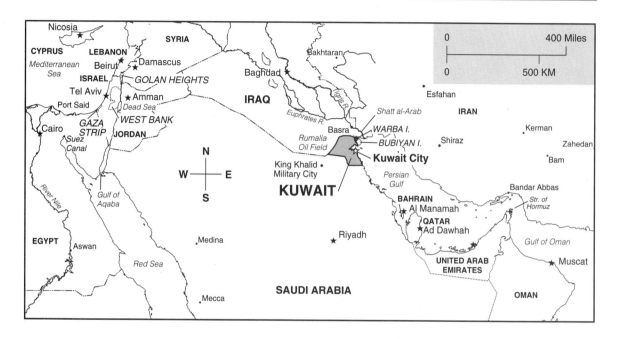

voiced fears that Iraq would indeed invade Saudi Arabia unless actions far stronger than verbal threats were taken. Stock markets reacted sharply. Oil prices immediately rose as traders anticipated that conflict would interrupt oil shipments and lead to future shortages. Within a day, the invasion was condemned by the United States, the North Atlantic Treaty Organization (NATO), the European Communities, the UN Security Council, and in an almost unprecedented joint U.S.-Soviet statement. Yet formal declarations of condemnation had had very little impact in previous international disputes. Most observers believed the annexation of Kuwait was irreversible, and feared further Iraqi military action against Saudi Arabia and other weak Persian Gulf states, such as the United Arab Emirates.

As often happens in such crises, there was immediate confusion about what longer term policy would be adopted. For several days it was not at all obvious that U.S. actions ever would go much beyond solemn diplomatic pronouncements. Consultations moved rapidly, however, and the first U.S. troops were sent to Saudi Arabia only five days after Iraq invaded Kuwait. Many months later it was revealed that the Saudis had first extracted two significant promises from the Bush administration. First, if U.S. troops went in, they would not be recalled precipitously by Washington (as they had been withdrawn from the ill-fated multinational peacekeeping force in Lebanon in 1984). Second, U.S. soldiers would leave promptly upon a Saudi request. The key events are detailed in Chronology 1.1.

Arguments and recriminations filled the days and months following the end of the land war. Critics and officials disputed whether the invasion of Kuwait should have been anticipated and prevented, whether appropriate war goals had been set, and whether a

⊕ CHRONOLOGY 1.1

A Brief Chronology of the Persian Gulf War of 1990–91

1990

July	17	Iraq threatens Kuwait, United Arab Emirates
	19–25	Saudis, Egypt attempt to mediate dispute
	23	Iraqi troops massed along border with Kuwait
August	1	Iraq breaks off talks in Jidda, Saudi Arabia
	2	Iraqi forces invade Kuwait, rapidly seize control
		Invasion condemned by U.S., NATO, EC, others
	3	Invasion condemned by UN; Joint U.S.-Soviet statement
	3–5	U.S. begins consultations with allies
	6	U.S. Sec. of Defense Cheney in Saudi Arabia
	7	First U.S. troops sent to Saudi Arabia
	8	Iraq declares annexation of Kuwait
		Egypt's President Mubarak calls an Arab summit
		Arab leaders approve a joint force in Saudi Arabia
	10	Congress notified of initial U.S. troops in Saudi Arabia
		NATO backs U.S. but bars any direct NATO role
	11–15	Egypt, Morocco, Syria, Pakistan send or commit troops
	16	Soviets provide U.S. with information on Iraqi armaments
	22	President mobilizes U.S. reserves
	28	Kuwait named 19th Iraqi "province"
September		
		Extensive diplomatic maneuvering, signaling
		U.S. negotiates aid from Germany, Japan, Korea, others
	11	First presidential address to Congress
	17	USAF Chief of Staff fired for public talk of war
	19	Emergency defense funds passed in House of Representatives
	23	Saddam threatens attacks on Arab oil fields, Israel
October		
	1	Joint Congressional resolution backs President Bush
	10	Rumors that Iraq seeks a territorial deal
	31	Bush secretly orders doubling of U.S. forces in Gulf; kept secret until after Nov. 6 election

November

11–13	Congressional concerns raised that administration plans to initiate war
22	President Bush visits troops in Gulf theater
29	UN vote authorizes use of force after Jan. 15 deadline
30	Bush offers talks with Iraq; extensive delays follow

December

3–5	Sec. of Def. Cheney, Sec. of State Baker favor attack on Iraq

1991

January

10	Congress opens debate on war authorization
12	Both houses of Congress pass war authorizations
15	UN deadline for Iraqi withdrawal from Kuwait
	President Bush signs written authorization for attack
16	Air war against Iraq begins
17	First Iraqi Scud missiles fired at Israel
19	U.S. sends Patriot antimissile missiles to Israel
22	Iraq begins burning Kuwaiti oil facilities
25	Iraq creates massive Persian Gulf oil spill
26	Major antiwar protests in U.S., Germany
29–31	Iraq attacks Kafji, Saudi Arabia; later driven back

February

8–9	Sec. of Def. Cheney and Gen. Powell visit Saudi Arabia
18	Soviet peace proposal
22	Final U.S. ultimatum demanding Iraqi withdrawal
23	Land offensive begins, with rapid success
27	Cease-fire after 100-hour land offensive
28	Iraq agrees to cease-fire

March

2	UN Security Council approves cease-fire terms, Resolution 686
3	Allied, Iraqi military commanders meet
6	President Bush declares war ended, sets troop pullout
7	Unrest or revolts reported in 15 Iraqi cities
13–27	Numerous cease-fire violations by Iraqi forces
26	Report that Gen. Schwarzkopf "urged" a longer war; rebutted by President Bush and Sec. of Def. Cheney

great deal more might have been achieved with little additional effort. Many questioned whether the whole exercise had accomplished any significant, lasting change. In short, a still-unsettled debate began, questioning whether the apparently decisive victory of February 1991 was not, in longer term reality, at least a partial policy failure.

Although citizens, analysts, and historians no doubt will disagree for years about these issues, the Persian Gulf War provides an excellent vehicle for illustrating many aspects of U.S. foreign policy making and policy execution at the beginning of the post–Cold War era. The United States played myriad more or less simultaneous roles in the Persian Gulf War, and those roles may be viewed and analyzed in a multitude of ways. Many authors argue that one particular approach or viewpoint captures what is essential—for example, political economics for the Marxists and state power for the realists—but the argument in this text is that each approach captures only part of a more complex reality. Some outlooks may be familiar from other cases, have familiar labels, and be associated with recognized political positions. Others may be less familiar, but introduce general principles often found in other applications. We examine eleven viewpoints here, in these three groups: (1) views from the perspective of traditional state-to-state international relations; (2) views from the perspective of the linkages between domestic and international politics; and (3) views involving global and regional perspectives.

VIEWPOINTS FROM THE PERSPECTIVE OF TRADITIONAL STATE-TO-STATE INTERNATIONAL RELATIONS

Most of us—even authors and officials—often are too casual about how we use the terminology of international politics, utilizing words like *nation*, *state*, *people*, and *country* as if they were near synonyms. In what follows, we try to be more precise, because a great deal of important politics lies in the distinctions.

In international political usage, a **state** is a legal entity that has a government, has sovereignty under international law, is identified with some piece of territory, typically has at least de facto control over that territory, and usually is formally recognized by other governments. In contrast, a **nation** is a group of people distinguished primarily by their shared sense of being a distinctive single group. Nations typically share a common ethnic, linguistic, and religious heritage; identify with some piece of territory, although they may not occupy it; and may or may not be formally recognized by other states and nations. Thus, for example, Canada is a single state comprising two major nations, one English speaking and one French speaking, with the latter concentrated in the province of Quebec. Secession of Quebec from the Canadian federation to form an independent **nation-state** (that is, a state with only one significant national group) has been argued for decades, and may yet occur on fairly friendly terms. Indeed, Quebec voters narrowly defeated a secession resolution in 1995. In other examples, we could identify a Jewish nation dispersed around the world before the establishment of the modern state of Israel, and a dispersed Palestinian Arab nation that claims rights to much of the same territory as Israel, and may yet achieve some form of statehood with sovereignty over the West Bank and Gaza. As we shall see, a great deal of contemporary international politics revolves around **nationalism,** the drive of nations to attain independence as recognized states. The intensity of that drive is growing dramatically, often fragmenting existing states.

The Canadian scholar Barry Buzan (1991, 72–77) suggests a fourfold classification that includes the dimension of whether nation or state came first. His *primal nation-state* is exemplified by Hungary, Italy, and Japan, where national identification preceded and helped give rise to statehood. In his *state-nation,* the state comes first and helps promote national cultural identity by generating and promoting uniform language, arts, customs, and law. The United States and Australia are outstanding examples. Buzan's *part nation-state* embraces such instances as North and South Korea, China and Taiwan, Vietnam before 1975, and East and West Germany before reunification in 1990. Here, a clearly self-identified nation is split between two or more states. Finally, his *multination-state* comprises states that contain two or more distinct nations. Sometimes those nations are not significantly spread beyond the state borders, as in Canada and former Czechoslovakia. In other instances, those nations spill across borders into neighboring states.

Iraq clearly is such a multination-state. Britain secured a League of Nations mandate over Iraq after World War I, granting independence in 1932, but establishing state control over three distinct national groups. These groups are the Kurds in the north (who also spill over into Turkey and long have sought independent statehood), Sunni Muslims in the central region, and Shiite Muslims in the southeast, bordering on Shiite Iran. Iraq's national composition made it imaginable that the U.S.-led coalition could exploit Kurdish and Shiite national aspirations to encourage revolt against Saddam Hussein's government. Unfortunately, it also led to the fear that Saddam's defeat could open Iraq to fragmentation and partial absorption by neighbors, thereby removing the only serious obstacle to Iran's hopes of dominating the region.

Traditionally, international politics was seen as primarily involving interactions between states. That view is increasingly challenged as more and more types of nonstate and transnational actors gain international influence; we examine those challenges later, particularly in Chapter 11. Nonetheless, governments usually think first about the actions of other governments. Recognizing this, the **international politics perspective** concentrates on interactions between states and leads us to examine the structure of the international system for its patterns of interaction and for the external influences on government decisions (see Figure 1.2). Thus we focus first on the external or international events that help shape U.S. foreign policy. The Persian Gulf War demonstrates several distinct perspectives that emphasize different aspects of U.S. interactions with other governments and groups of governments.

 VIEWPOINT 1 Countering Aggression

The United States organized an international coalition of governments to counter clear-cut Iraqi aggression against Kuwait.

Despite Iraq's prior complaints, demands, and limited negotiations with Kuwait, almost the entire international community of governments saw Iraq's invasion as an act of **aggression,** an unprovoked attack too severe to be justified by any prior provocation. The near-universality of this view was furthered by Iraqi announcements about plans to annex Kuwait and later news stories about Iraqi actions designed to encourage Kuwaitis to flee their country and Iraqis to settle there. Acts of aggression violate international law, and the UN charter allows the use of force to reverse them. Arguably, every aggression should be opposed on moral grounds (it is wrong), on practical grounds (potential aggressors

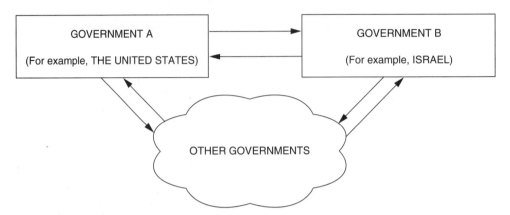

FIGURE 1.2
The International Politics Perspective

Systemic view; emphasis on interactions *between* governments

"Outside" or systemic view emphasizes international system, states as major actors, patterns of interaction, and external influences on the decisions of governments.

should learn that they will be stopped or punished), and on political grounds (friends and allies will doubt our commitments if we fail to support them in times of trouble). International agreements to threaten and use force, however, are serious political decisions, neither easily reached nor lightly taken. One major surprise of the Persian Gulf War was the speed with which those decisions were reached. The governments that eventually took various actions against Iraq had no preexisting alliance or collective security agreement requiring them to counter Iraq's aggression. Despite pious talk about laying the groundwork of a new world order, their deeds were purely ad hoc, addressing only the single case without establishing any new permanent security arrangements. In promoting the coalition, the U.S. government used diplomacy to encourage others to join, and mediated disputes between coalition members. It provided most of the troops and equipment, and played the major role in planning, directing, and carrying out military engagements. All those actions are very traditional enterprises of major powers in international politics. Related important concepts dealt with later in the book include alliances (Chapter 2), collective security (Chapter 9), and diplomacy, bargaining, and negotiation (Chapter 10).

VIEWPOINT 2 Protecting National Interests
The United States acted to protect its own national interests, particularly oil supplies.

Although defensible under international law, U.S. actions in the Persian Gulf War were hardly disinterested and altruistic. Traditionally, states are expected to act to promote their "national" (state) interests, often defined in terms of power, influence, and the ability to continue business as usual. For the United States and other developed states, petroleum is one of the most vital resource inputs to a modern industrial economy. U.S. administrations since the mid-1970s had threatened military action to preserve access to oil, and Iraq presented a credible threat to world petroleum markets. Because the demand for oil is highly *inelastic* (for example, most of us drive our cars just about as far even when the price of gasoline rises sharply), removing Iraqi and Kuwaiti oil from world markets could have caused dramatic price jumps, which were quickly but only briefly seen. Saudi Arabia pumped additional oil to help make up the shortfall and hold prices down, although that was a quid pro quo for U.S. military assistance. Very early in the Gulf crisis, Senator Richard Lugar, ranking Republican on the Senate Foreign Relations Committee, stated in a newsmaker interview that U.S. action against Iraq was justified because "this is our way of life at stake." The U.S. administration, however, quickly moved to justifying its actions by decrying the atrocities of Iraqi dictator Saddam Hussein, who was portrayed (with some accuracy) as the "butcher of Baghdad." U.S. self-interest in the Gulf conflict was also pointed up by the satirical bumper sticker that asked whether Iraq would have been invaded if its major export were broccoli, a vegetable publicly disparaged by President Bush. (See also the discussions of national interests and power, in Chapter 8.)

VIEWPOINT 3 Protecting Clients
The United States acted on behalf of its international clients, notably Saudi Arabia and Israel.

Despite serving its own interests in the Gulf, the United States also acted on behalf of other friendly states. Like protecting one's interests, assisting friendly states is a traditional principle of international politics. In a slightly less positive formulation of this principle, powerful states may assist dependent **client states** out of a sense of duty to support the like-minded, in exchange for assistance in other matters, or for the economic or other benefits derived from having those clients. Thus the United States supports Saudi Arabia to help preserve its oil supply, and Israel to support the only functioning democracy in the Middle East and assuage a large domestic lobby. Early insertion of U.S. troops helped forestall possible Iraqi military action against Saudi Arabia by guaranteeing that any attack would provoke a larger U.S. response. Later, the U.S. diverted substantial resources—up to a quarter of available aircraft sorties, plus coordinated strikes by covert forces on the ground—from the January-February air war against Iraq to locating and destroying Iraqi Scud missiles being launched at Israel and Saudi Arabia. Additionally, batteries of Patriot antimissile missiles were rushed to those states. These anti-Scud actions directly protected Israel and Saudi Arabia, and Israel had long been the de facto ally of the United States and the friendliest state in the region. Additionally, defending Israel protected the coalition by reducing the chance that Israel would intervene directly and alienate Arab coalition members. Saddam Hussein's government had attempted to pass its invasion of Kuwait off as a pan-Arab act and portray coalition moves against Iraq as directed against all Arabs. If a direct attack against Israel had succeeded in provoking an Israeli military response, it could have played into Iraqi goals of turning Arab coalition members against Israel, which was still seen as an enemy by most Arab governments.

VIEWPOINT 4 Pressuring Clients

The United States pressured its international clients, for example when it declined to give Israel the aircraft IFF identification codes necessary to fly into Iraqi airspace while U.S. and coalition forces were conducting operations.

The other side of assisting and protecting friendly governments and client states is pressuring them to take the actions you wish and to refrain from those you oppose. This is another traditional principle of state-centric international politics, and may involve *coercive diplomacy* (see Chapter 8) utilizing some credible threat of force or punishment. During the Gulf war, the United States used diplomatic channels to urge the Israeli government to stay uninvolved, but exerted much more direct pressure by refusing repeated requests for the IFF ("Identify Friend or Foe") codes used on aircraft transponders in the Gulf theater of operations. Without those codes, the Israeli Air Force could not fly over Iraq without risking attack from both Iraqi and coalition forces, while the coalition was flying thousands of attack sorties per day. Thus the United States used significant pressure as well as direct assistance in meeting the Scud missile threat, in its ultimately successful effort to keep Israel from intervening directly in the war.

VIEWPOINTS FROM THE PERSPECTIVE OF THE LINKAGES BETWEEN DOMESTIC AND INTERNATIONAL POLITICS

Carrying out its foreign policy represents the grandest possible scale of political action for a nation-state, yet the political decisions that shape foreign policy usually are influenced as strongly by domestic politics as by international events. U.S. foreign policy thus stands with one foot firmly planted in international politics and the other foot equally firmly planted in domestic "American" politics. Everything we know about either subject area applies to the politics of foreign policies, although the mix varies from issue to issue. Some analysts have attempted to capture this duality in the term **intermestic policies.** Consider Table 1.1, and imagine a continuum extending from purely domestic policies at one end to purely foreign policies at the other. A purely domestic policy would be one that had domestic effects with no impacts abroad. Distributional policies may offer the closest approach to that ideal. Arguably, our domestic system of income tax rates and our rules of access to welfare benefits have no repercussions on foreign states and their citizens. Yet, if we look more closely, income tax structures can influence foreign impressions of the desirability and profitability of investments in the United States. Foreign impressions of our strength also may be influenced by welfare benefits because they can affect the health and education levels of our citizens and their loyalty to the central government.

Turn now to the other end of the continuum in Table 1.1. A purely foreign policy would be one with exclusively foreign impacts and no domestic effects. For the fortunate,

	TABLE 1.1	
	Hypothetical Continuum of Domestic and Foreign Policy Impacts	
Primarily Domestic Impacts	**Intermestic (Domestic and Foreign) Impacts**	**Primarily Foreign Impacts**
Distributional policies	Tariffs	Diplomatic recognition
Tax rates	Immigration	

wars only occur abroad, but even then they always have costs at home in lives and treasure. We might surmise that extending or denying diplomatic recognition to a government has only foreign effects. Yet diplomatic recognition has impacts on at least some of our citizens, for example, the businessperson hoping for an export license or the traveler who will benefit from the availability of consular services in both countries. Thus at both ends of our conceptual continuum, the more closely we look the harder it is to claim that any policy is either purely domestic or purely foreign. *All policies actually are intermestic,* although the mix of foreign and domestic effects varies widely. It should then come as little surprise that those differing mixes in the effects of policies lead to differing mixes of the extent to which domestic and international political considerations determine foreign policies. This point will recur in the chapters of Part II as we study how U.S. foreign policy is made.

Consider briefly a quintessential example of intermestic policy: tariffs. As a tax on imports, a tariff clearly has effects both on citizens of the home country and those of the exporting state. Imagine how an increase in the U.S. tariff on imported automobiles would affect individual citizens here and in Japan, which is by far the largest exporter of autos to this country. Unless the makers and dealers can absorb the increase, the tariff raises the U.S. price of a Japanese car. U.S. citizens wishing to purchase a Japanese auto likely will have to pay more. The price increase may make many people more likely to buy a competing U.S.-made vehicle. U.S. auto companies and their employees, plus everyone along the chains of supply, distribution, and service, would benefit while their counterparts in Japan would suffer. U.S. citizens who really wanted a Japanese car would also suffer a bit. U.S. automakers might take advantage of the forced increase in the prices of Japanese cars to raise their prices and profit margins. In that event, all automobile purchasers in the United States would pay a bit more so that a much smaller set of people benefited. A great deal of politics has always been about large numbers of people paying a little to benefit some few people; the intermestic nature of foreign policy simply adds an international dimension to such political maneuvering.

The intermestic nature of foreign policy also means that we must give as much attention to the domestic sources of foreign policy as to the international sources. As indicated in Figure 1.3, the **foreign policy perspective** concentrates on the decision-making process and the domestic influences upon it. Just as the Persian Gulf War case demonstrates viewpoints that emphasize U.S. interactions with other governments, it also demonstrates several distinct viewpoints that emphasize domestic influences which help shape foreign policy.

FIGURE 1.3

The Foreign Policy Perspective

Inside view; emphasis is on the internal, domestic processes of decision-making, and the interplay between foreign and domestic influences.

GOVERNMENT

(For example, THE UNITED STATES)   POLICIES AND ACTIONS

"**Inside**" **view emphasizes decision-making, how foreign policies are decided, interplay between** *domestic* **and** *foreign* **policies.**

VIEWPOINT 5 Military Interventionism

The United States acted in somewhat traditional ways that called heavily on military and interventionist responses, despite early and unprecedented success in organizing a set of tough international economic sanctions, and despite many calls at home and abroad for more time to let those sanctions work.

Governments and peoples do not change the shape and direction of policy easily, frequently, or rapidly, a fact reflected in the way we often call major policy changes "revolutionary." Making major changes requires significant shifts in people's mind-sets and established patterns of actions, shifts that are even more difficult for great organizations than for individuals. Consequently, U.S. foreign policy usually is characterized by long-term continuity in major themes, as examined in detail in Chapter 2. The Persian Gulf War demonstrated three themes that have distinguished many U.S. actions abroad in the twentieth century: activist interventionism, coercive diplomacy, and the use of military force. Again, these are properties often and traditionally found in the foreign policies of great powers.

Activist interventionism need not necessarily go beyond peaceful diplomacy, while coercive diplomacy requires at least a credible threat that force might be used. Within the first few days of August 1990, the Bush administration settled on an activist approach using coercive diplomacy against Iraq, and over the following weeks used almost every possible diplomatic venue to promote that policy. **Bilateral** (state-to-state) talks, including a visit from Secretary of Defense Dick Cheney, persuaded the Saudi leadership that the seriousness of the Iraqi threat justified accepting U.S. troops on their soil. Other bilateral contacts, all the way up to telephone calls from President Bush, encouraged other governments to join the coalition, and still others to pay much of the cost. **Multilateral** (many-state) contacts were pursued through NATO and, especially, the UN Security Council, where a number of resolutions were obtained authorizing sanctions and, eventually, the use of force.

An early surprise was the wide scope of those UN sanctions and the broad support they received. Almost all Security Council members voted in favor, almost all states joined in their observance, and the sanctions went well beyond statements of condemnation and calls for a return to the status quo antebellum, the condition existing before war. International air traffic with Iraq was suspended and trade was embargoed, excepting only humanitarian food and medical shipments. A further surprise was the effectiveness of the sanctions. International sanctions often suffer from *common pool* or *collective action* problems (see Chapter 12), in which individual governments may decide it is to their private advantage to violate embargoes even when they piously proclaim support. If enough governments make that decision, of course, sanctions become meaningless. That occurred with arms shipments during the Iran-Iraq war, when some thirty states shipped arms to one or even both sides, often while proclaiming support for international efforts to end that supply-limited war by choking off its arms supplies. Perhaps to Baghdad's surprise, the embargoes during the Persian Gulf War were very widely observed. Iraq's many attempts to weaken observance of the sanctions, even including offering free oil to poor states, were generally ineffective. However, it was difficult to choke off trade through Jordan because the Jordanian government was caught between international pressures on one side and, on the other, pressures from its most powerful neighbor, supported by many of Jordan's Palestinian citizens.

Given the scope of the sanctions and the breadth of their support, a debate developed about how soon sanctions would force Iraqi withdrawal from Kuwait. Pursued both internationally and within the United States, that debate still continues. The Bush administration faced the classic problem that both domestic and foreign support for any coalition and any set of sanctions tend to decay over time. The U.S. government acted regularly to mediate disputes between coalition members, even as Iraq sought to inflame them. It was widely recognized that the Bush administration decision in late October of 1990, to double the number of U.S. troops in the Persian Gulf, settled the sanctions issue by shifting over from protecting Saudi Arabia and other weak Gulf states against Iraqi attack to liberating Kuwait by force. That decision, however, was concealed until after the November election and initially was passed off as necessary to pose a credible threat to Iraq. Interestingly, the administration sought a UN Security Council resolution authorizing the use of force weeks before it sought the formal support of the U.S. Congress (in early January 1991, only days before the air war opened).

In retrospect, it seems clear that the Iraqi government always intended to utilize every avenue of delay and deception to exploit any potential weaknesses in the coalition. For example, in the years following war's end, Iraq repeatedly posed obstacles for UN inspectors attempting to locate and verify the destruction of its nuclear program and other weapons of mass destruction. Iraqi tactics included such means as hiding plants, moving production equipment, destroying documents, shuffling weapons from location to location, organizing mass demonstrations against inspections, and physically blocking access to inspectors. Yet the debate still continues whether the coalition would have held together well enough that the embargoes on goods from abroad and sales of Iraqi oil would eventually have forced a withdrawal from Kuwait, and when. A persistent body of opinion holds that the U.S.-led coalition used force too soon. Moreover, those who agree often assert that this was just one more instance of a general U.S. tendency to use force too frequently and too quickly. For more on that tendency, see the discussions of *interventionism* and *liberal internationalism* in Chapter 2, and of *coercive diplomacy* in Chapter 8.

VIEWPOINT 6 Domestic Special Interests

The United States acted to protect domestic special interests, particularly oil companies and industries dependent on inexpensive, plentiful petrochemicals.

As noted in the earlier discussion of intermestic policies, a great deal of politics has always been about large numbers of people paying a little to greatly benefit a few people. A persistent theme in analyses of domestic politics—and not just in the United States—is the tendency of individuals, business firms, trade unions, industry associations, and other interest groups to utilize political processes to seek their own private advantage at the expense of the many. Some analysts argue that protection of moneyed interests is a central, defining feature of U.S. politics. As discussed in Chapter 4, lobbyists for special interests tend to have more influence than ordinary citizens on foreign policy because they are highly informed and on the scene in Washington. Specialization makes possible intimate knowledge of the relevant technical facts and the ways in which those facts can be slanted to favor their clients. Lobbyist specialization extends to detailed information about the channels of action on issues of interest, the status of pertinent legislation and regulation, and personal acquaintance with the legislators and regulators involved. Being on the scene allows up-to-the-minute knowledge and rapid access. The very concept of a military-industrial-congressional complex highlights the intertwined interests of individuals in positions of power. Despite limited moves toward public financing of political campaigns, the development of political action committees (PACs) in recent decades has only increased the dependence of politicians on unions, industries, and their leaders for the contributions essential to running a modern campaign.

Despite the major strides made in increasing the energy efficiency of U.S. homes and industries since the oil scares of the mid-1970s, petroleum is still one of the most critical of strategic materials, needed both as an energy source and as a raw material for the petrochemical industry. At least some oil companies and traders reaped windfall profits in the market fluctuations that followed Iraq's invasion of Kuwait. President George Bush, a former oilman and head of a conservative, probusiness administration, could hardly be expected to be unsympathetic to the needs of the oil and related industries. Thus there should be little surprise in the argument that more than just national interest was at stake in protecting U.S. access to Persian Gulf oil supplies.

VIEWPOINT 7 President versus Congress

There is an ongoing clash between the president and the Congress over who shall control U.S. foreign policy. In the Persian Gulf case, that clash involved (1) presidential ability to manipulate media and the public agenda of policy discussion, (2) presidential reliance on public support in any time of crisis, and (3) arguments growing out of the War Powers Act of 1973.

Congresses have fought with presidents over who controls foreign policy since the early days of the Republic, and no doubt will continue to do so for the indefinite future.

The U.S. president simultaneously holds several demanding roles: that of the ceremonial **head of state,** analogous to the monarch in Britain; usually that of **political party leader;** and that of **head of government,** proposing and shaping policy by directing a huge executive branch that carries out existing policies and proposes new ones. Unlike the prime minister in a parliamentary system, the U.S. president is not a member of the legislature. Indeed, a prime minister is both the political party leader and the person best able to enforce party discipline in parliament. Presidents, however, must lead Congress indirectly. Although it is usually even more true of foreign than of domestic affairs that in establishing policy "the president proposes, the Congress disposes," Congress is never entirely comfortable with that process.

The ways in which presidents lead Congress are explored in more detail in Chapter 4. Two of the most important, both demonstrated during the Persian Gulf War, are shaping the public agenda by manipulating the media, and relying on public opinion to rally around the president in a time of crisis. These phenomena are interrelated. The Bush administration portrayed the Iraqi invasion of Kuwait and the threat posed to Saudi Arabia and other Gulf states as a **crisis,** an *unanticipated* situation with *high stakes* and a *short time* in which to act. Both immediately after the invasion and in the longer term as the coalition built up its forces and the war was fought, the administration had substantial control over media access to information. To some degree, media were even used as channels of disinformation, as when reporters were steered to stories about amphibious assault forces in the Gulf, although the real purpose of those units was simply to pin down Iraqi forces that otherwise could be used elsewhere. When the administration focused on Saddam's atrocities to justify war, refugees from Kuwait were made available to tell their stories of horror. When the air war was launched, film clips of so-called smart precision-guided bombs striking their targets were plentiful, but there was neither discussion nor films of the misses, and little coverage of civilians killed or injured as a side effect. By manipulating media through control of the information available to them, the administration shaped the agendas of both official and public discussions about policy, thus significantly influencing the Congress.

Although it was not until 1933 that a Supreme Court decision formally recognized the president as the chief foreign policy official of the country, it is a well-demonstrated effect that in times of crisis, public opinion tends to rally around the president as the paramount national leader. Modern media greatly facilitate that tendency, and the Bush administration made the most of them. President Bush's public approval rating rose rapidly at the onset of the crisis and eventually reached the unprecedented level of over 90 percent. It also dipped 30 points in the fall of 1990 while Bush was embroiled in a bitter budget dispute with the Congress. Those two shifts demonstrate that public opinion is sometimes volatile. Yet public support gives the president a powerful lever to move the Congress. By January 1991, when President Bush asked the Congress to approve direct action against Iraq by U.S. troops, he had overwhelming public support and an authorizing UN Security Council resolution. Members of Congress who opposed Bush's policy expected immediate trouble with their voters at home.

Believing that President Lyndon Johnson had used information control and public support to hoodwink the Congress into escalating the Vietnam War with the Tonkin Gulf Resolution of 1965, Congress sought to limit the future capabilities of presidents to commit troops without explicit congressional approval by passing the War Powers Act of

1973. No president has formally admitted being bound by the act, but all have grudgingly complied. The 1991 vote regarding troops in the Persian Gulf is but one of several instances in which presidents have been able to bring sufficient pressure on Congress to overcome constraints imposed by the War Powers Act. In particular, once the president has used the commander in chief's authority to send troops, Congress can be blamed for policy failure if it orders those troops withdrawn. Arguments continue, however, about how much power the president should have and how much should be shared with Congress. The War Powers Act of 1973 is discussed more fully in Chapter 5.

VIEWPOINT 8 Domestic Policy Dynamics

The domestic dynamics of policy management are complex. Despite much public and congressional uncertainty about the wisdom of a coalition offensive against Iraqi forces, levels of support were very high once the attack began.

Support for a policy, both from the public and from those charged with carrying it out, is always dynamic, never static. Successful policy management thus requires a delicate sensitivity to the nuances of timing, not all of which always appear to be totally logical. Despite serious public and congressional misgivings about going to war in Iraq, President Bush's public approval ratings reached all-time highs after the air war began on 16 January 1991. Arguably, this is yet another aspect of the public tendency to rally around the president in times of trouble; once policy is set, the people close ranks. Yet, as already noted, the administration chose to conceal the late October decision to double U.S. troop levels in the Gulf until after the November election, at least partly because a few campaigning politicians expressed fears that the United States would attack without giving sanctions enough time to work. Thus it is difficult to escape the arguments that the administration either believed it needed more time to win public opinion over to the attack or was simply indifferent to public opinion, believing the leaders knew best. President Bush had been noted for expressing such elitist views. The onset of the air war saw modest street demonstrations against the administration in liberal centers, but general public opinion was strongly supportive.

Public rallying behind the troops once they have been committed is only one instance of the often complex dynamics of opinion and policy management. The administration was not only concerned that coalition cohesiveness behind sanctions might erode over time. They feared that domestic public support would erode as well, as people saw heavy public expenditures, large numbers of friends and relatives uprooted, and no visible results. Military and political leaders were also concerned that morale among the troops, built up through weeks of intensive on-site training, would decline as months of arduous desert duty dragged on without resolution. Military leaders' advice to the president from the beginning, especially from General Colin Powell, chairman of the Joint Chiefs of Staff, had been that if any troops were sent, he should send large numbers rapidly and avoid a prolonged buildup. It is often remarked that generals are always well prepared to fight the last war without repeating the mistakes previously committed. In urging a rapid buildup and decisive use of troops, military leaders sought to avoid the protracted but indecisive escalation and the slow erosion of public support that characterized the Vietnam War, during which most of the generals of 1990 had first reached officer rank. As explored more fully in Chapter 9, one result of U.S. experience in Vietnam has been an emphasis on *low intensity conflict* (LIC), in which military interventions are planned to be quick, decisive, and relatively low in cost. Thus the dynamics of managing both public opinion and public policy are complex, and we cannot fully evaluate policies without taking time factors into account.

VIEWPOINT 9 Bureaucratic Infighting

There is extensive bureaucratic infighting within the U.S. government for power and influence in managing and executing policy, as was seen in the allocation of the most spectacular fighting roles to army forces, positioning them favorably for later budgetary battles over anticipated defense spending cuts.

Government organizations and agencies have special interests in policy just as unions, corporations, and other group actors do. Indeed, many of those interests are parallel, centering on survival, growth, and preservation of core values and missions. Agencies are set up under initiatives originating most often in the executive branch, less often in the Congress, but beginning with a legislative charter. Within that broad charter, programs are proposed and, upon approval, funded. Despite the common image of "faceless bureaucrats," however, bureau incumbents develop genuine personal interests in their programs' survival and growth. Program continuation means job continuity, of course, and growth means opportunities for promotion, expanded responsibilities, and, one hopes, doing more good. Additionally, as is true in most fields of endeavor, those who do the work tend to develop strong ideas about proper procedures, and may become resistant to change. Agencies often oppose new programs foisted on them by the administration or Congress, if they believe such programs contradict or weaken their *essential missions*. There may be substantial infighting over budgets, both within and between agencies. In the *zero-sum game* of stable or shrinking budgets, when one agency's budget increase must come from another agency's budget cut, such infighting can become particularly intense. One of the enduring ironies of government is that organizations and their **standard operating procedures** are at the same time both essential to accomplish any government action and major sources of resistance to change. The problems these organizational difficulties pose for policy making and policy execution are explored further in Chapter 5.

A major peculiarity of the Persian Gulf War was that it occurred even as the Cold War was winding down and the entire world was beginning to contemplate a new, post–Cold War era. Washington politicians and bureaucrats were no exception, and because Cold War competition with the Soviet Union had helped promote several trillion dollars in defense expenditure, official Washington was divided over what the new era would mean for the Defense Department and military programs in general. Many military officers and defense bureaucrats identified new threats to justify a level of effort approximating what they had come to expect in the past. Opposing them, many citizens and politicians argued that the waning Soviet threat would soon allow defense spending to be slashed and the resulting "peace dividend" to be applied to domestic infrastructure investments, social programs, tax cuts, or at least budget deficit reduction. Thus, even while U.S. armed forces were carrying out their largest deployment since Vietnam and waging a brief war with their latest technology and fighting doctrines, they expected the war to be followed by the deepest budget- and force-level cuts in decades. Every expectation indicated that, by the mid to latter 1990s, it would become impossible for the United States to carry out a Persian Gulf–style buildup because there would not be adequate active and reserve forces, whether in Europe, in the Indian Ocean, or even at home in the United States.

One way to position an agency to defend against budget cuts is to demonstrate spectacular performance of a type that may be needed in the future. It is quite normal for U.S. military leaders to promote a favorable public image by emphasizing successes on the battlefield, as was done during the Persian Gulf War. Concerns about future budget battles added urgency to obtaining missions that offered chances to excel in battle. Images from smart bombs zeroing in on their targets were frequently displayed, as were scenes of Patriot antimissiles destroying incoming Scuds. High success rates for new weapons, such as radar-evading F-117 stealth fighter aircraft and Tomahawk sea-launched cruise missiles, were quoted routinely. Failures were ignored or downplayed, although censorship had its positive side, for example when the numbers of aircraft shot down were concealed to enhance opportunities to rescue downed aviators. Some time after hostilities ended, most of the success rates were downgraded.

Arguably, however, bureaucratic infighting in planning the war went beyond giving each military service the opportunity to test and demonstrate its latest weaponry. The chief generals were army officers, and it is notable that the most spectacular roles in the land war were reserved for army units, which carried out the great "hail Mary" sweep westward and northward to surround and cut off Iraqi forces. Amphibious assault forces, a longtime marine specialty, were utilized only to threaten and pin down certain Iraqi divisions in Kuwait. Other marine forces were assigned the unattractive mission of cooperating with Saudi and Kuwaiti forces in slogging northeastward along the coast. The marines argue in their defense, however, that their troops got off to a faster and more effective start. They liberated Kuwait City a day ahead of schedule, which forced the army units in the West to advance continuously for some forty-eight hours to catch up with the overall battle plan. In these instances we once again see policy being shaped by U.S. domestic politics, in this case politics within the military and between the military services and the remainder of the government. Additional ways in which organizational and bureaucratic politics affect foreign policy making and execution are more fully examined in Chapter 5.

VIEWPOINTS INVOLVING GLOBAL AND REGIONAL PERSPECTIVES

Even as U.S. foreign policy is shaped by domestic politics and traditional state-centric international politics, it is shaped by regional and global politics, the evolving processes through which states and other actors are influenced by concerns about issues of explicitly regional or global scope. This expands the international politics perspective already examined, encompassing broader sets of actors and concerns. They may include any of the following:

1. **Intergovernmental organizations (IGOs),** such as the UN or NATO or the Organization for Security and Cooperation in Europe, whose members are the governments of states;
2. **International nongovernmental organizations (INGOs** or **NGOs)** such as Greenpeace or Amnesty International, which accept individuals (and sometimes organizations) as members;
3. Governments of individual states when they seek to promote policies that impact many or most governments, as the U.S. government did when it sought to utilize its improved standing with Arab governments in the aftermath of the Persian Gulf War to launch a new Middle East peace process in 1991; and
4. **International regimes,** which combine law, regulation, and the practice of interstate and international organizations and individual state governments to regulate selected behaviors. Examples of regimes include the formal international regulation of whaling and the international informal consensus after 1995 to prevent further fragmentation of former Yugoslavia, and particularly of Bosnia-Herzegovina.

Global and regional perspectives thus are defined by the scope of concerns raised, which require action by more than just individual governments, and sometimes by more than just groups of governments. **International security regimes,** for example, focus on arrangements to preserve international order and the safety and security of individual states and governments. The UN and the Organization for Security and Cooperation in Europe represent two very different international security regimes. Yet for decades the UN was virtually paralyzed by U.S.-Soviet confrontation and could act against breaches of the peace only in rare cases when the two superpowers agreed. The Persian Gulf War saw them join in condemning Iraq's aggression. Rapidly improving Soviet relations with the United States were followed in 1991 by the breakup of the USSR. America and other Western powers rapidly established generally friendly relations with almost all the newly independent republics. Russia was broadly seen as the primary Soviet successor state and inherited most Soviet prerogatives, including the veto-wielding Soviet seat on the UN Security Council. These changes, together with general success in managing a large ad hoc coalition during the Persian Gulf War, and far-reaching and intrusive sanctions against Iraqi armaments following the war, have led to calls and predictions for a "new world order." Exactly what that catchy phrase means, however, remains exceedingly unclear.

VIEWPOINT 10 New World Order

The end of the Cold War and the breakup of the Soviet Union produced enormous changes in the global distributions of military, economic, and political power. The ripple effects of those changes continue to this day.

Images invoked by different analysts to describe those momentous movements vary from that of a tidal wave, suggesting rapid and irresistible change, to tectonic shifts, suggesting slow but equally profound, inexorable, and irreversible change. Certainly, the replacement of forty-four years of Cold War by new international concerns may be called a new world order, although the phrase says nothing about what that order will be. Our only certainty is that at least the top and middle of the new international power order will be profoundly different from what we knew for several decades. Many actors will have incentives to explore and exploit the potentialities of their newfound status and freedom of action.

Under these unaccustomed and still-changing circumstances, will the United States provide or dominate or underwrite the world's police force, as it did in the Persian Gulf War? Proponents of such roles often argue, "If not us, who?" Beyond national interest, they argue, lie global interests that can only be addressed by rich and powerful states, whether singly or as coalition organizers and leaders. Opponents often question the moral presumptions of such roles, and they usually argue that the United States no longer can afford them. Instead, critics look toward the establishment of new international security regimes, a concern examined more fully in Chapters 9 and 12. Note that the Persian Gulf War was the first major instance in which the U.S. government actively sought major financial support from foreign governments for a military action, and that immediately after the dramatic 1993 mutual recognition between Israel and the Palestine Liberation Organization, the United States convened a "donors' conference" of governments to solicit aid for the Palestinians. Different types of international power are examined in Chapter 8, and new modes of international cooperation are considered in Chapter 12.

Not all political aftereffects of the end of the Cold War and the breakup of the Soviet Union are positive, however. With the decline of Soviet power, there was no longer an enforcer of order in Eastern Europe. In the late 1980s a wave of nationalism, qualified democratization, and anticommunism swept that region, preceding the 1991 breakup of the Soviet Union. Since then, all of Eastern Europe and the former USSR have been subject to extreme nationalistic pressures. These have been vividly seen in regional fighting over ethnic enclaves in several of the former Soviet republics, the bifurcation of Czechoslovakia, and most tragically in the bloody disintegration of the former Yugoslavia into several republics fighting wars of so-called ethnic cleansing. If the world is fortunate, political leaders will find the will to utilize the new power order to promote effective new international security regimes unhampered by Cold War divisions. The downside risk is clearly demonstrated in former Yugoslavia; ineffective or nonexistent security regimes likely will mean substantial increases in hot wars.

 VIEWPOINT 11 International Cooperation

The United States organized and promoted a coalition effort that was the strongest UN-sponsored security action in decades. Yet extending that precedent to other regions and the future is subject to many limitations and uncertainties.

The coalition action in the Persian Gulf War may be seen as one instance of a newly organized international security regime in action. Beyond the national interests of the United States and other participants, and beyond persistent questions about how successful their efforts were in the long run, the coalition addressed major issues of reversing regional aggression and establishing arrangements to ensure lasting regional security. However, the Persian Gulf precedent does not readily extend over time or to other regions. The coalition was strictly ad hoc, organized after the invasion of Kuwait to deal with that single case. The United States acted first and dominated the coalition from the

MIDDLE EAST PAYOFF FROM THE GULF WAR

UN sponsorship of the Persian Gulf War coalition would have been impossible without improved U.S.-Soviet relations. Cold War confrontation overshadowed all previous Middle East conflicts, usually paralyzing the UN. The two superpowers had long avoided any large-scale introduction of their own troops into the region, in order to prevent a direct clash that might escalate to a major superpower war. Had such confrontation still existed in 1990, U.S. action in support of Kuwait and Saudi Arabia would have provoked automatic Soviet support for Iraq. Yet Iraq received only limited diplomatic support from the Soviets, along with considerable pressure to back down. That pressure was ineffective, however; the Soviets were unable to restrain the Iraqis because they had lost their leverage when they cut off military supplies to Iraq.

In the aftermath of the Persian Gulf War, the United States capitalized on its improved relations with Arab states by working closely with the Soviet Union to organize a broad, many-state, multistage Middle East peace conference aimed at resolving the persistent state of war between Is-

rael and most of its Arab neighbors. Ironically, the Soviets had long proposed such a grand conference, but the United States had opposed it and promoted bilateral negotiations, such as the Camp David accords that led to the 1979 peace treaty between Israel and Egypt. The great conference of 1991 opened in Madrid, Spain, with addresses from leaders of the many states. Its main significance was the political symbolism of those leaders openly listening to the demands of opposing states. Subsequent bilateral negotiations between Israel and Arab states continued and made some progress, most dramatically in the 1993 Israeli–Palestine Liberation Organization agreement for mutual recognition and Palestinian self-rule in Jericho and the Gaza Strip. However, the continuing negotiations were fraught with procedural quibbles, the political significance of which we examine in Chapter 10. Nonetheless, recall that the initial opening for Israeli-Egyptian peace was a 1978 invitation to then Egyptian president Anwar Sadat to address the Israeli Knesset (parliament), where he uncompromisingly presented Egyptian demands.

start. The other four powers with vetoes in the UN Security Council cooperated in varying degrees. Britain and France were very supportive and played limited military roles in the coalition. The Soviet Union was constrained on one hand by internal upheavals that would lead to its breakup in little more than a year, and on the other by its desperate need to maintain good relations with the United States so as to secure Western aid. Thus the Soviets cooperated in condemning the Iraqi invasion of Kuwait, but stayed militarily uninvolved even to the point of cutting off military resupply to Iraq, formerly one of their closest clients in the region. Nonetheless, the Soviets continued to press the Iraqi case for a negotiated (and presumably greatly delayed) solution. China was persuaded to refrain from vetoing the critical Security Council resolutions, partly because the United States continued most-favored-nation (MFN) trading status and largely acquiesced on other issues such as the Chinese crackdown on prodemocracy dissidents. This experience does not bode well for UN solidarity in meeting future security threats because the Security Council is structured to act only on issues about which the five permanent great power members agree.

Moreover, the ability of Gulf War coalition members to sustain agreement after the war was highly questionable. Almost all the forces that fought Operation Desert Storm were quickly returned to their homelands. The United States received little enthusiasm from its former coalition partners when it threatened in the summer of 1992 to take further military action against Iraq if UN weapons inspectors continued to be blocked in Baghdad, or if Saddam Hussein's government continued to attack the Shiites in southeastern Iraq. Western troop levels in the region had been cut to the point that aerial bombardment was the only readily available military option, and its applicability to these problems was questionable. Neither the United States nor other former coalition members wished to return large numbers of troops to the region. Further, the Bush administration, facing a serious reelection challenge, did not want either to risk new troop losses or admit that the great victory trumpeted in 1991 was less than complete and secure.

Highly intrusive rights of on-site weapons inspections under UN auspices may set a precedent for future arms control efforts. Iraq, however, mounted such effective resistance that the inspectors were gone by 1999, and other states have always been extremely resistant to such intrusions on their sovereignty. The difficulties faced in seeking appropriate, successful, and politically acceptable actions after the end of the land war in 1991 point up our lack of experience in such cases and the absence of any effective and truly global arms control regime. These problems are further explored in Chapters 9 and 15.

Recap of the Perspectives and Viewpoints Examined as Applied to the Persian Gulf War

Recall that (1) many authors argue that one or another particular viewpoint captures what is essential, (2) we consider that each viewpoint captures only part of a more complex reality, and (3) each viewpoint may be applied to any number of policy cases.

- Viewpoints from the Perspective of Traditional State-to-State International Relations

  Viewpoint 1: *Countering Aggression*
  The United States organized an international coalition of governments to counter clear-cut Iraqi aggression against Kuwait.

  Viewpoint 2: *Protecting National Interests*
  The United States acted to protect its own national interests, particularly oil supplies.

  Viewpoint 3: *Protecting Clients*
  The United States acted on behalf of its international clients, notably Saudi Arabia and Israel.

  Viewpoint 4: *Pressuring Clients*
  The United States pressured its international clients, as when it declined to give Israel the aircraft IFF identification codes necessary to fly into Iraqi airspace while U.S. and coalition forces were conducting operations.

- Viewpoints from the Perspective of the Linkages Between Domestic and International Politics

    Viewpoint 5:   *Military Interventionism*
    The United States acted in somewhat traditional ways that called heavily on military and interventionist responses, despite early and unprecedented success in organizing a set of tough international economic sanctions, and despite many calls at home and abroad for more time to let those sanctions work.

    Viewpoint 6:   *Domestic Special Interests*
    The United States acted to protect domestic special interests, particularly oil companies and industries dependent on inexpensive, plentiful petrochemicals.

    Viewpoint 7:   *President versus Congress*
    There is an ongoing clash between the president and the Congress over who shall control U.S. foreign policy. In the Persian Gulf case, that clash involved (1) presidential ability to manipulate media and the public agenda of policy discussion, (2) presidential reliance on public support in any time of crisis, and (3) arguments growing out of the War Powers Act of 1973.

    Viewpoint 8:   *Domestic Policy Dynamics*
    The domestic dynamics of policy management are complex. Despite much public and congressional uncertainty about the wisdom of a coalition offensive against Iraqi forces, levels of support were very high once the attack began.

    Viewpoint 9:   *Bureaucratic Infighting*
    There is extensive bureaucratic infighting within the U.S. government for power and influence in managing and executing policy. This was seen in the allocation of the most spectacular fighting roles to army forces, positioning them favorably for later budgetary battles over anticipated defense spending cuts.

- Viewpoints Involving Global and Regional Perspectives

    Viewpoint 10:   *New World Order*
    The end of the Cold War and the breakup of the Soviet Union produced enormous changes in the global distributions of military, economic, and political power. The ripple effects of those changes continue to this day.

    Viewpoint 11:   *International Cooperation*
    The United States organized and promoted a coalition effort that was the strongest UN-sponsored security action in decades. Yet extending that precedent to other regions and the future is subject to many limitations and uncertainties.

POSTWAR REFLECTIONS AND EVALUATIONS

In the aftermath of the Persian Gulf war, as Saddam Hussein continued to rule in Iraq and wreak havoc on opposition and refugee groups, there were ever more questions whether coalition military efforts had been properly directed to secure desired political changes. Of course, it is routine for governments to have postwar second thoughts and recriminations about missed opportunities and misplaced goals, as well as for leaders to disagree with one another and attempt to mislead us about the roles they played. Difficulties of policy making and some techniques for sorting out the record in problematic cases are considered in Chapters 5 and 7.

Long before any opportunities for postwar reevaluations, governments regularly have difficulty in setting goals and maintaining them during conflicts. General H. Norman Schwarzkopf complained later that he received severe and continuing pressure, which he traces to unnamed Washington "hawks," to launch a ground war before he had adequate forces in place, and that the Bush administration's war goals were unclear. Liberation of Kuwait was sought, but there was no clarity on how much of the Iraqi military was to be destroyed, nor on whether Saddam Hussein was individually targeted, although that now appears to have been the case. The history of the Persian Gulf War, like many other cases, suggests that military leaders are often less eager to fight than politicians, and that both groups often are reluctant to use force sufficient to accomplish all their goals. Military commanders, being most familiar with operational details, know best all the things that could go wrong. They are the individuals who stand to lose friends and subordinates and to be blamed if plans go awry.

Governments are always constrained by the action options available to them, as considered in detail in Part III (Chapters 8–12), on the tools of policy. The U.S.-led coalition needed five months to build up its forces in the Persian Gulf before opening the air war, and additional weeks to prepare for the land war. Only limited defensive actions could have been undertaken in the early days of Operation Desert Shield, in the fall of 1990. During those months, troops were being gathered and given on-site training while war plan options were still being developed. After the war, once the bulk of coalition forces was withdrawn, far fewer military options remained for any follow-up action. Thus, when Iraq stonewalled UN weapons inspectors outside the Ministry of Agriculture building in Baghdad in the summer of 1992 and ordered American members of the inspection teams out of the country in 1997, the United States could do little beyond threatening aerial bombardment, and even the eventual bombing required moving some forces back to the region.

One of the most insidious forms of policy failure is that sometimes our present policy choices create our own future problems. In several ways, this appears to have been true in the Persian Gulf War. First, the U.S. government was fully aware long before 1990 that Saddam Hussein was a brutal dictator. Yet because Iraq seemed the only plausible counter to the rise of Iran as a regional power, we pursued generally friendly relations with Iraq during the 1980s. In particular, the U.S. government failed to put significant pressure on Iraq to forestall its invasion of Kuwait, even when the threat had become manifest. After the invasion, there was controversy over whether U.S. ambassador to Iraq April Glaspie had presented U.S. concern about Kuwait in a way that was sufficiently clear, strong, and convincing. Finally and most seriously, it later became clear that, in what Democrats dubbed the Bush administration's "Iraqgate scandal," the United States had provided clandestine aid to Iraq during the 1980s. Those funds, channeled through an Italian bank, had been crucial to Iraq's secret nuclear weapons program. Considering these facts, should we be surprised that Saddam Hussein professed doubt that the United States would act strongly against his invasion of Kuwait?

It is well to remember that policy is almost always developed incrementally, and rarely accomplishes everything we might hope. The clash of domestic interests virtually guarantees that some people will be dissatisfied with whatever policy a government adopts, and the clash of international interests assures frictions even within largely successful coalitions. As developed more fully in Chapter 5, government agencies are constrained either to act by applying their existing procedures or to take time to develop new ones. Both approaches are subject to criticism and dissatisfaction. In practice, all governments regularly operate by making small, incremental modifications to existing policies, to minimize the time and struggle required for bigger changes. Officeholders of all types are subject to powerful incentives to take short-range rather than long-term perspectives, which tends to promote incremental changes and make all implemented policies second best. We should hardly be surprised that the Persian Gulf War demonstrates these effects.

At this remove in history, the Gulf War appears as a singular case that offers only limited and still murky precedents for the future of international politics and foreign policy. It seems unlikely that the same combination of military forces and opportunities will recur. The United States was able to use forces and battle tactics developed for fighting the Soviets on the plains of Europe to fight a desert war of rapid movement and was given five months to build up and train its forces. A rapid and overwhelming military victory in the land war was achieved with very low coalition casualties, but was not exploited to fully cripple the Iraqi military. As a result, Saddam Hussein retained his most important tool for maintaining internal power. Sweeping UN sanctions included a trade and oil purchase embargo and strong provisions to locate, inspect, and dismantle Iraq's programs for nuclear and other weapons of mass destruction. Yet against those sanctions Iraq adopted a strategy of confrontation, evasion, and delay characterized by then House Armed Services Committee chairman (and later defense secretary) Les Aspin as "cheat and retreat." To counter those tactics, the Bush administration—handicapped by dwindling military forces in the region and faced with an uphill reelection battle—adopted a policy that Aspin characterized as "threat and forget." The administration clearly hoped to see Saddam Hussein overthrown in Iraq and evidently targeted him personally in bombing attacks, yet was unwilling to use military force to invade the heart of Iraq. The administration urged Iraqis to rise up and overthrow Saddam's government, but allowed only limited postwar aid to help Kurdish and Shiite groups that briefly seized control in their regions. Predictions that the breakup of Iraq would only further the rise of Iran as a regional power appear to have played a major role in these decisions, and remind us of the old international relations principle that "the enemy of my enemy is my friend." Iraq may have been our enemy when it invaded Kuwait and threatened oil supplies, but it remains a counter to Iranian ambitions. Controversy persists over whether the U.S. government sent sufficiently clear signals to Iraq about its opposition before the invasion of Kuwait.

HOW TO UNDERSTAND AND EVALUATE U.S. FOREIGN POLICY

How do we make sense of a subject on which knowledgeable observers routinely take such diverse viewpoints and that is subject to so many different interpretations? Answering this question takes some time and appropriate analytic tools, which we cover in the next fifteen chapters. We can begin by discerning the overall shape of U.S. foreign policy from its long-term patterns. These form the core subject matter of Chapter 2, in which we begin by examining general policy themes. Although history does not necessarily repeat itself, whether we study it or not, and although it is never sufficient to study only the past, the events of today and tomorrow are always rooted in history. Extending policy themes to the new post–Cold War era and our prospective future is taken up in Chapter 3. We then turn to a systemic approach to the factual matters of what actually *is* and the process matters of *how* policy is decided and implemented. These are examined in Part II, comprising Chapters 4 through 7. Part III, Chapters 8 through 12, deals with the tools of policy that the United States and other governments have available to carry out their policy decisions. Throughout the book we see both how greatly the global context of American foreign policy has changed since 1990, bringing both new threats and new opportunities, and how that profound change has altered the set of options open to U.S. policymakers. In Part IV, Chapters 13 through 16, we expand our consideration of that new global context with a more thorough examination of the issues emerging in the aftermath of the Cold War. There, all the materials developed in previous chapters are applied to examining some of the major foreign policy issues likely to confront the United States in coming years.

KEY TERMS

Aggression

Bilateral (Contrast with *multilateral.*)

Client states

Crisis

Foreign policy perspective (Contrast with *international politics perspective.*)

Head of government

Head of state

Intergovernmental organizations (IGOs)

Intermestic policies

International nongovernmental organizations (INGOs or NGOs)

International politics perspective (Contrast with *foreign policy perspective.*)

International regimes

International security regimes

Multilateral (Contrast with *bilateral.*)

Nation

Nationalism

Nation-state

Political party leader

Standard operating procedure

State

SELECTED READINGS

Ambrose, Stephen E. 1976. *Rise to Globalism: American Foreign Policy 1938–1976.* New York: Penguin Books. A noted historian examines how the World War II experience reshaped U.S. foreign policy toward a sustained and active global role.

Buzan, Barry. 1991. *People, States and Fear, Second Edition: An Agenda for International Security Studies in the Post–Cold War Era.* Boulder, Colo.: Lynne Reinner. Buzan, at pp. 72–77, moves beyond the standard concepts of *nations* and *states* to build a fourfold classification that includes the dimension of whether nation or state came first. His classifications are *primal nation-state* (for example, Japan), *state-nation* (for example, the United States), *part nation-state* (for example, North and South Korea), *and multination-state* (for example, Canada), and have interesting political implications.

Mueller, John. 1994. *Policy and Opinion in the Gulf War.* Chicago: University of Chicago Press.

Neack, Laura, Jeanne A. K. Hey, and Patrick J. Haney, eds. 1995. *Foreign Policy Analysis: Continuity and Change in Its Second Generation.* Englewood Cliffs, N.J.: Prentice Hall.

Schwarzkopf, General H. Norman. 1992. *The Autobiography: It Doesn't Take a Hero.* Written with Peter Petre. New York: Bantam Books. The story of the U.S. commander of American and coalition forces in the 1990–91 Persian Gulf War.

Sifry, Micah L., and Christopher Cerf, eds. *The Gulf War Reader; History, Documents, Opinions.* New York: Times Books. An early compilation of crucial documents and speeches from 1990–91, plus background and opinion pieces.

CHAPTER 2

THEMES IN U.S. FOREIGN POLICY: CONTINUITY AND EVOLUTION

⊕ GEORGE WASHINGTON VERSUS "ENTANGLING ALLIANCES"

A great many people—experts as well as laypersons—believe that George Washington, in his Farewell Address of 17 September 1796, advised the infant United States to avoid "entangling alliances" with other powers. In this they are wrong.

That advice was highly appropriate to U.S. global circumstances of the time, according to the viewpoint of *protecting national interests* as discussed in Chapter 1, but Washington did not use the phrase "entangling alliances." His Farewell Address, however, had deep roots. Political testaments were popular in the eighteenth century, and it was only natural to expect the first president's parting advice to carry great political weight. Washington had been commander in chief of the Continental Army during the American Revolutionary War, later presided over the Constitutional Convention, and was widely called the father of his country. In 1792, when Washington hoped to retire after a single term as president, James Madison advised him to announce that decision in a valedictory address to be published in the newspapers in September, when it could influence people before balloting for presidential electors began. Madison drafted such an address, but in the end Washington yielded to the entreaties of friends to stand for a second term and was unanimously reelected. The basic plan for such an address near the end of his career remained, although other political developments greatly changed its ultimate plan and content. The most critical accomplishments of Washington's first term had been establishing the new federal administration, setting the financial and economic policy course of the infant republic, and deciding on the federal capital. His second term, however, was dominated by foreign policy concerns.

In February 1793, Great Britain, Holland, and Spain joined the German powers fighting against the French Revolution. Britain's blockade of France impinged on U.S. trade, and it was feared that France would demand U.S. assistance under the Franco-American alliance of 1778. During the Revolutionary War, the United States had sought a trade treaty and assistance from France without a political-military connection, ultimately accepting a military agreement that provided money and naval support but no French troops. By the late military operations of the American Revolution, however, the

United States accepted additional French help, and large numbers of regular French troops were sent, crucially assisting the 1781 American victory at Yorktown. However, the infant United States was in no condition to reciprocate in 1793. Its frontiers were surrounded by the North American colonies of England and Spain, and it seemed unlikely that American borders could be defended against joint British-Spanish operations. In those threatening circumstances, President Washington issued a Proclamation of Neutrality in 1793 and went on to negotiate the controversial and unsatisfactory Jay Treaty with Great Britain. Ratification of that treaty in 1795 was difficult, and for a time the House of Representatives threatened to deny funds necessary to carry it out. These domestic and foreign political struggles strengthened Washington's resolve to use his Farewell Address to promote principles that he believed would help protect the United States in the future. He added considerably to James Madison's 1792 draft, then allowed his longtime friend and treasury secretary Alexander Hamilton to rework the entire text. The ultimate address melded the ideas of Madison and Hamilton, who by this time were bitter political enemies. Much of the wording was Hamilton's, although it clearly reflected Washington's thinking. The phrase "entangling alliances" did not appear.

The best known use of that phrase occurred some five years after George Washington's Farewell Address. It came on 4 March 1801, in the first inaugural address of Thomas Jefferson as the third American president, when he called for "peace, commerce, and honest friendship with all nations, entangling alliances with none" (Randall, 1969, 83). Still, Washington had said *similar* things in his 1796 Farewell Address. In the core sections on foreign policy, he made the following points:

> The great rule of conduct for us in regard to foreign nations is, in extending our commercial relations to have with them as little political connection as possible. So far as we have already formed engagements let them be fulfilled with perfect good faith. Here let us stop.
>
> Europe has a set of primary interests which to us have none or a very remote relation. . . .
>
> Our detached and distant situation invites and enables us to pursue a different course. If we remain one people, under an efficient government, the period is not far off when we may defy material injury from external annoyance. . . .
>
> Why forego the advantages of so peculiar a situation? . . .
>
> It is our true policy to steer clear of permanent alliances with any portion of the foreign world. . . .
>
> Taking care always to keep ourselves by suitable establishments on a respectable defensive posture, we may safely trust to temporary alliances for extraordinary emergencies.
>
> . . . it is folly in one nation to look for disinterested favors from another . . .
>
> **(EXCERPTS FROM KAUFMAN, 1969, 27–28)**

This is a clear instance of setting out a **grand policy** or broad policy guidance, by which Washington hoped to influence foreign policy goal setting and responses to many specific problems over a considerable span of time. Grand policy is also referred to as programmatic policy or long-term policy themes. It stands in contrast to **specific policy** or applied policies that deal with single problems at specific points in time. In the 1990s, for example, President Clinton's declaration that economics had become the most important area of U.S. foreign policy presaged a grand policy of promoting economic globalization.

Ratifying the North American Free Trade Agreement (NAFTA) was one specific part of that grand policy.

Note that President Washington proceeds from a clearly expressed worldview that states (he uses the word *nations*) are distinct, sovereign, entirely self-interested entities. He sees American interests and development being promoted by the growth of commerce but imperiled if the infant United States is drawn into the political struggles between stronger European states. Therefore, he encourages commercial and, presumably, diplomatic interaction, but minimal political commitments, and alliances only temporarily in "extraordinary emergencies." In the long term, he foresees a United States strong enough to stand alone against any likely opponent. Modern international relations scholars call Washington's position *realist* as opposed to *idealist*. When Jefferson left the cabinet in 1793 because Washington refused to aid France under our 1778 military alliance, he was acting idealistically, although probably not prudently. (See the discussion of realism and idealism in Chapter 3.)

EVOLVING FOREIGN POLICY THEMES

U.S. foreign policy is built up over time from many specific policies, sometimes formulated to follow grand policies enunciated in advance by political leaders in concrete statements like Washington's Farewell Address. Many other grand policies emerge only incrementally over time. In that case, nobody makes any great statement of broad policy, but more and more specific policies are formulated and implemented until eventually political scientists or historians or journalists discover a broader pattern of action. Many grand policies are built by this process of accretion, which is more frequent than monumental policy statements. Although some grand policies are found in great political speeches and writings, we find much more about specific policies in political speeches and writings, in congressional debates and legislation, in news reports, and occasionally in judicial proceedings. An ongoing interplay between grand and specific policies appears throughout the history of U.S. foreign policy.

In this chapter we examine the evolving and continuing major themes of U.S. foreign policy to see how we arrived at our present global political-economic position and foreign policies. In this we see how two sets of profound changes in foreign policy and in its global context occurred, the first shortly after World War II as the Cold War began, the second around 1990 with the end of the Cold War. Three major sections cover (1) factors promoting foreign policy continuity and evolution; (2) a menu of major types of general foreign policy orientations; and (3) a review of the evolving and continuing major themes of American foreign policy from the colonial era through the Cold War.

First, just as Washington based his advice to minimize foreign alliances on the relative weakness and physical isolation of the early United States, national resources and capabilities constrain possible actions. Because they change only slowly, they exert strong pressures toward policy continuity. Policy evolution is stimulated by powerful long-term factors such as major shifts in global political alignments and economic capabilities, which lead to rises or declines in relative power. Second, the major grand policy orientations of alliance building, nonalignment, neutrality, isolationism, interventionism, and globalism or internationalism are examined. Finally, those orientations are applied to long-term themes that have developed and reoccurred through the history of U.S. policy. Eighteenth- and nineteenth-century motifs include freedom for trade and navigation; early alliance seeking followed by a long period of nonalignment; early emergence of hemispheric interventionism; and "manifest destiny" and the achievement of great power status. Under the U.S. ideology of the "melting pot," people of many nationalities were melded into a single new nation-state, a process that contrasts strikingly with the rapidly growing global problem of interethnic strife today. Twentieth-century motifs in U.S. foreign policy include decisive intervention in World Wars I and II; the achievement of superpower status, with its corollary of sustained global activism; containment, Cold War, and liberal globalist interventionism; preoccupation with the limits of power in the aftermath of the Vietnam War; and the search for a new, post–Cold War policy framework. The last motif is the focus of Chapter 3. To prepare to manage the new world disorder, however, we first need to understand how we arrived where we are today.

FACTORS PROMOTING FOREIGN POLICY CONTINUITY AND EVOLUTION

Foreign policy is shaped by the continuing interplay between two sets of factors, those that encourage continuity and stability and those that stimulate change and evolution. Broadly, constraints and past practice encourage policy continuity, and long-term developments promote policy evolution. Thus, even if there is no explicit statement of grand policy, it is natural to look for recurring patterns in foreign policy. We regularly find tendencies to pursue similar goals by similar means over long periods of time, no matter how unique any individual problem situation may appear as we read about it in the daily newspaper. Long-term patterns in foreign policies are shaped by the constraints of available resources, prior experience, broad policy goals and approaches, and external influences.

Although any individual policy case may be seen as either a win or a loss, longer term regularities of goals and means of action do exist. Some policy problems recur fairly frequently over long periods of time, just as some basketball opponents are tough to play every year. However, speaking of patterns of action or themes of long-term policy goals does not imply that the foreign policy process is *deterministic*. We are not compelled to repeat the past, and neither past failures nor past successes are guaranteed to recur in the future. Policy themes mean only that domestic and foreign constraints, along with human tendencies to act consistently, work both separately and together to produce tendencies toward recurring results. The same means of action are frequently used, for the same reasons, often toward the same end goals, and often with the same resulting policy difficulties.

Forces for continuity usually prevail in the short run. The simplest policy change is no change at all, and inertia is a powerful impediment to change. Treaties, alliances, and legislation all constrain policy to run in existing channels. Bureaucrats do not readily modify existing policies, as suggested by the *bureaucratic infighting* viewpoint examined in Chapter 1. Nor do legislators enact new enabling laws unless presidents and other executives first persuade them to do so, which is a time-consuming political process. That process is often complicated by clashes of *president versus Congress*, as examined in another viewpoint in Chapter 1. Additionally, as we see more fully in Part III (Chapters 8–12), most policy options require lead time to prepare. Just as the United States needed months

DISCOVERING PATTERNS IN FOREIGN POLICY AND BASKETBALL

Finding long-term patterns in foreign policy may be likened to analyzing your school basketball team's performance. Over the course of a season, one expects both wins and losses. Some losses likely will be near misses, in which slightly different play at one or more critical points could have produced a very different outcome. The morning after any given game, sports columnists may enthrall us with detailed, almost play-by-play criticism. Yet, over the course of an entire season, broader general patterns begin to emerge. Those larger, longer term patterns only become apparent when we compare last night's game with last Thursday's game, and last week's games, and so on. Scouts routinely bring back reports about upcoming opponents, so their patterns of play can be analyzed for possible weaknesses, and strategies developed to counter their strengths. As we perform our own similar analysis, we may realize the team cannot run a good full-court press because of players' limitations, that it cannot always react rapidly enough to meet an unexpected change of strategy by an opponent, and that psychological difficulties contribute to mediocre performance against a traditionally strong rival. Conversely, we see that the team plays above its potential when fired up by an enthusiastic home-court crowd, and that it only puts its best efforts into the contests it reasonably expects to win. During the course of a season, fans learn to expect certain strong and successful plays and other weaknesses. Over multiple seasons, the team's approach may change to reflect capability changes due to personnel gains and losses. It also reflects the coach's stable tendency toward particular game strategies. When the coach is replaced, which always happens eventually, game strategy usually changes. Even then, strategy is somewhat constrained in the short run by inherited resources. The new coach must start with an existing roster of players who have established strengths, weaknesses, training, and expectations. In all these ways, long-term patterns in play emerge, influenced by available resources, experience, coaches' styles and intentions, and the external pressures of competing teams with changing capabilities. In analogous ways, long-term patterns in foreign policies are shaped by the constraints of available players and resources, prior experience, broad policy goals and approaches, and external influences.

to mobilize its forces and line up political support for the 1991 air and land wars in the Persian Gulf, what can be done in principle often cannot be done today, or next week, or next month. National capabilities at home and abroad do not change rapidly, so that most external pressures and domestic capacity to meet them are fairly stable. Prior experience is a powerful force for policy continuity; policies that worked in the past likely will be repeated, and policies that failed may become anathema for decades.

Nonetheless, forces for change tend to prevail in the long run. National capabilities usually change only slowly, but they do shift. Eventually, they must respond to such factors as the more rapid growth of an economy that is better managed or better positioned to capitalize on supporting natural resources or an important technological development. Capabilities also respond to important shifts in global political alignments, for example, those produced by the breakup of the Soviet Union and the improvement in U.S.-Arab relations resulting from the Persian Gulf War. The issue of whether such factors will produce an *inevitable* decline in U.S. global influence is taken up under the decline debate in Chapter 11. At the very least, however, evolutionary changes in the relative capabilities of states do require adaptive changes in foreign policies. *Relative capabilities* are crucial. What ultimately matters politically and economically and militarily is not a state's *absolute* power, but how its power and influence (by whatever measures) *compare* to those of others. Such long-term trends continue almost despite the ups and downs of particular short-term developments in any specific international problem area.

Sometimes a specific policy acquires a politically powerful domestic following, becomes virtually fossilized, and is maintained long beyond the point at which objective observers would call for change. An excellent example is U.S. continuation of diplomatic nonrecognition and trade sanctions against Cuba. Diplomatic relations with Fidel Castro's government were broken in January 1961 to protest the expropriation of U.S. landholdings, banks, and industrial concerns, and a trade embargo was imposed in 1962. By the latter 1970s, many Americans believed these measures had seriously hurt the Cuban people without leading to Castro's overthrow, and the time was ripe for diplomatic and trade normalization. However, some 700,000 Cubans emigrated from Cuba in the first years after the 1959 revolution, most of them to the United States, and many of those to Florida. Here they formed a potent interest group, and an especially powerful one in the state of Florida. Beyond their own direct influence, they gained power through natural alliance with anticommunist conservatives. The result was that politicians favorable to policy change did not dare act. Overall support for normalizing relations with Cuba actually declined from the 1970s to the 1990s, among both elites and the general public. Even though nonrecognition and the trade embargo appear to have failed years ago and are condemned by many American allies, there seems little realistic prospect of their reversal while Fidel Castro remains in power.

As one example of how a broad policy area can exhibit both continuity and evolution, consider how changes in global economics in the last quarter of the twentieth century forced the United States to begin coordinating its economic policies with other powers. The U.S. **gross national product (GNP),** the total value of all goods and services produced, has been the world's largest since early in the twentieth century. U.S. global economic dominance was overwhelming in the aftermath of World War II's devastation and a powerful force drawing the United States into managing the world economic system. In the early post–World War II years, U.S. supremacy was so great as to make it a **hegemon,** able virtually to dictate economic policy for the entire world outside the Soviet/communist bloc. Yet as Japan and the states of Western Europe recovered from the war, relying in part on U.S. help in the form of the Marshall Plan and other aid, U.S. economic dominance slowly eroded, until, by 1971, it could no longer use its gold reserves to set global exchange rates. The history of U.S. relations with the other major developed democratic capitalist states can be seen as demonstrating both the *pressuring clients* and *protecting clients* viewpoints of Chapter 1, although all those states were always more allies than dependent client states. In 1975 heads of government of those states held the first in a continuing series of annual summit meetings focused primarily on economic issues. France, Great Britain, West Germany, Italy, Japan, and the United States were represented in 1975. Canada joined the following year, and the European Community has had representation since 1977. In 1986 the conferees agreed to create a *Group of Seven (G-7)* made up of the participating states' finance ministers, intended to strengthen multilateral surveillance of the world economy. Building that new intergovernmental organization exemplifies the *international cooperation* viewpoint examined in Chapter 1. While that cooperation was evolving, the U.S. economy continued to grow, but more slowly than the economies of states such as Germany and Japan. Indeed, by the late 1980s, several years before the breakup of the Soviet Union, the Japanese GNP had exceeded that of the Soviets, long second only to the United States. Such long-term changes are forces for adaptive change in foreign policies. Moreover, because the changes are gradual, resulting policy shifts usually are slow and evolutionary, carried out with minimum possible changes to established practice.

As demonstrated in the global economics example, all "foreign" policies are actually intermestic because they have impacts on people at home as well as abroad. Consequently, they are subject to both domestic and foreign constraints. Domestic factors constraining our foreign policies include natural resources; the size and strength of the productive economy; the size, equipment, and readiness of military and other forms of power; the willingness of the general population to engage in actions overseas; and a host of other factors explored more fully in Part III (Chapters 8–12). Foreign constraints on our foreign policies include the actions, policies, and capabilities of other governments, international organizations, multinational corporations, and other international actors, as well as limitations on our abilities to influence those others. All these constraints represent powerful forces for *continuity* in policy because most of them change only slowly over time. No matter how strongly we are led to focus on dramatic current events, at the grandest scale the world situation seldom looks fundamentally different from its appearance two years earlier, even though we may see significant changes over a span of five or ten or twenty years.

Consider two examples. First, the Cold War and U.S. grand policies to fight it shaped U.S. foreign policy worldwide for more than four decades. The *military interventionism* viewpoint examined in Chapter 1 was prominent. Within that framework, we fought the Korean and Vietnam wars, came close to war in several crises between China and Taiwan, in repeated Berlin crises, and in the Cuban missile crisis. Yet, although these crises and conflicts were intense and absorbing, most failed to produce lasting change in the broader patterns of global relations and U.S. foreign policy. Secondly, consider the Persian Gulf War. In 1990–91, this appeared to be a regional conflict of real importance that required considerable short-term effort. Yet the fact that it occurred and the ways it was dealt with reflected major long-term changes in global relations and U.S. capabilities. Iraq's seizure of Kuwait was important to the United States because of our tremendous post–World War II increase in need for imported oil, and our organization of a great coalition to pursue the Gulf War reflected declining U.S. capabilities to bear the costs of mounting major foreign military actions alone.

Any foreign policy represents a choice of one or more actions from among the set of all alternative possible actions. That set may be quite large, but the choice is always subject to many constraints and is made in the attempt to achieve some set of objectives. At least in the short run, when studying specific policies for particular cases, we routinely examine the available alternatives. Additionally, we examine the policymakers' objectives, the constraints on choices and actions, and—to the extent we can find out about it—the quality of analysis that went into choosing a policy. Imperfections abound, as developed in more detail in Part II (Chapters 4–7). Among them are the following:

- Many choice situations offer few or no really desirable alternatives, forcing the choice of a "least worst" option.
- Domestic and foreign constraints may deny us the policy options we would prefer.
- Useful alternatives may not be recognized.
- We may disagree with decision makers' objectives, whether they are actually achieved or not. Those objectives may be poorly thought out, may be quite short range when we would prefer that they be long range, and may serve personal or institutional ends better than state goals.

Keep these many types of constraints in mind as we examine the menu of the broadest grand policy orientations available.

MAJOR TYPES OF GENERAL FOREIGN POLICY ORIENTATIONS: A MENU

What foreign policy options are available, and have been available, to the United States? At the broadest possible policy level, many analysts suggest there is a fairly small set of general orientations that a state can take in its foreign policy. These may be thought of as the overall shapes or approaches to policy a government pursues, the grandest of grand policies. Dealing with a specific policy problem is then seen as selecting an option within the framework of the broad orientation, subject to all the applicable constraints, and with specific goals in mind. In the history of U.S. foreign policy we find long periods during which one or another of these general orientations applies, even while specific problems come and go. Such long-term policy orientations usually reflect important factors for continuity and widely shared popular notions about state interests, values, goals, self-images, and images of our role in the world. We begin by examining the six general orientations of alliance building, nonalignment, neutrality, isolationism, interventionism, and globalism or internationalism. Those orientations are summarized in Table 2.1.

U.S. foreign policy has evolved over more than two centuries as the country itself has evolved. Primary general policy orientations have included alliance building, nonalignment, and, particularly in the twentieth century, interventionism and globalism. Despite popular beliefs about policy between the world wars, the United States has never been strictly isolationist. There has been a long-term fluctuation between alliance and nonalignment, however, with the latter overcome by globalist alliance building since World War II. A number of specific policy themes have endured for long periods or recurred frequently. For example, freedom of navigation has been a policy goal since colonial times, because we have usually promoted relatively free trade. Interventionism has been a recurring theme since the United States first attained great power status, near the end of the nineteenth century. The Second World War marked a policy watershed, with U.S. emergence into superpowerhood and protracted, often interventionist, internationalism at unprecedented levels of intensity. Containment was sustained as general policy against the Soviet-communist bloc of states through forty-four years of Cold War, even longer than some of our allies might have wished.

Coalition making or **alliance building** is undoubtedly the most frequent of all general foreign policy orientations. By making common cause with other states, governments

---

TABLE 2.1	*Major Types of Grand Policies or General Foreign Policy Orientations*

Coalition Making and Alliance Building

Governments gain strength through agreements to act together with others.
Both formal and informal agreements are possible.
Many forms of cooperation exist: political, economic, military (for example, collective security pacts, military alliances, common markets, secret understandings—ententes).

Nonalignment

Choosing to not form alliances with other states.
May be applied either broadly, to all states, or narrowly.
First used (c. 1950) to mean not siding with either superpower.
"Nonaligned movement" actually is a coalition of developing states.

Neutrality

Strictly, noninvolvement in other states' wars.
May be applied broadly, to all conflicts, as Switzerland does, or narrowly, to a single conflict.
In the 1950s, used to mean nonalignment with the superpowers.

Isolationism

Strictly, minimization of all foreign ties (for example, Japan before its opening to the West in 1854; Cambodia under Pol Pot and the Khmer Rouge, 1975–79).
Commonly (but incorrectly) used to refer to U.S. policy between World Wars I and II.
Aided by the following conditions:
   Economic self-sufficiency
   Social self-sufficiency
   Diffuse structure of world power (no concentrated pressures)
   Physical or geographical isolation
   Absence of external threats.

Interventionism

Forcible interference in locations abroad.
Typically involves military and/or economic actions.
Directing or influencing the affairs of others.
Duration varies from brief incursions to prolonged rule.
Sometimes (and arguably) done for the benefit of those influenced or ruled.
In its extreme form, seizing and ruling colonies (colonialism).

Globalism or Internationalism

Deliberately playing a major world role.
Consciously shaping and maintaining the world order.
Motivations may include both "global interests" and "national interest."

can increase their usable diplomatic, economic, and/or military strength and influence. Agreements may be broad or narrow in scope, involve two members or dozens, and may be either limited or indefinite in duration. The Cold War years provide the most dramatic example of U.S. use of alliances. Beginning in the late 1940s, we forged a globe-girdling series of military, economic, and political agreements designed to help contain Soviet communist expansion. The most crucial of those alliances dealt with Europe, always perceived as central to U.S. security, but their scope extended well beyond purely military concerns. Most important among them was the North Atlantic Treaty Organization, or NATO, begun as a collective security agreement among the United States, Canada, and most of the Western European states. NATO pledged all member governments to come to the aid of any member who was attacked. As part of a Cold War deterrent strategy, NATO promised the Soviets, the Western Europeans, and the people of the United States that any Soviet attack on Western Europe would bring a U.S. response. After the Cold War ended, NATO lived on, as much to preserve transatlantic political ties as military security. By 1999 membership had been expanded to include three formerly communist East European states. Western European security during the Cold War was also promoted by Europe's post–World War II economic recovery, which was itself assisted by U.S. Marshall Plan economic aid. The United States also strongly promoted European joint economic agreements that it did not join, including the European Coal and Steel Community and the European Economic Community, the common market forerunner of the European Union. Later, the United States would join with the major Western European states, Canada, and Japan to form the G-7 (later, G-8) to coordinate global economic policy. These and many other agreements with and among the Western European states that the United States has encouraged in recent decades, whether it has been a member or not, illustrate the great range of coalitions a state may use to promote its interests and policies.

Not all international alliances have as many members, or such broad aims, or so long a lifetime as NATO. Agreements can be strictly *bilateral* (two member), such as the first free trade agreement signed between the United States and Canada in 1989. They may be quite narrow in scope, dealing with a single small issue. They may be quite formal and public, like treaties, or simply a set of unwritten understandings, called an *entente*. For example, Israel has been the closest ally of the United States in the Middle East for decades, yet no part of the U.S.-Israeli relationship was codified in writing until the early 1980s. Keeping agreements secret can encourage many troubles. Many secret agreements existed between the European governments at the outbreak of World War I, specifying who would come to whose aid in the event of an attack by specific third governments. As a result, nobody fully understood the ramifications of any particular attack. When war came, the entire structure collapsed like a house of cards, drawing almost all European governments into the conflict (thus the "World" War). That experience led U.S. president Woodrow Wilson to propose "open covenants, openly arrived at" as one of his famous Fourteen Points for the postwar peace. Nevertheless, no general principle of openness about alliances and other international agreements ever has been established.

Nonalignment properly refers to a policy of *not entering into alliances and coalitions,* although the term has been subjected to a variety of usages and misuses. Governments favored by conditions conducive to isolationism may more easily pursue a nonaligned policy than others (see later). States subject to strong cross pressures from powerful

Photo 2.1

UK prime minister Margaret Thatcher, the first woman and longest-serving prime minister in British history, takes a walk near Aspen, Colorado, on 2 August 1990 with U.S. president George Bush. Their meeting emphasized long-standing U.S.-British cooperation and was supposed to be about the changing face of Europe, but it was redirected toward Iraq's invasion of Kuwait earlier that day; the event that launched the Persian Gulf War.

AP/Wide World Photos.

neighbors may be virtually forced into nonalignment. A notable example is Finland, which lost territory to a major Soviet invasion in 1939. Although democratic Finland survived as an independent state, it never could conduct a fully independent foreign policy in the shadow of its powerful neighbor. Trade dependence born of proximity further limited Finland's independence from the Soviets, who actually forced a change in one elected Finnish government over their trade relationship. Except for states under such strong cross pressures, however, very few governments have applied the concept of non-alignment as broadly as have the Swiss, who deliberately avoid all entangling alliances. During the 1960s nonalignment was used primarily to refer to developing states that chose not to ally with either of the superpowers, the United States and the Soviet Union. The modern "nonaligned movement" is either an oxymoron or an intriguing technical misuse of the term *nonalignment*. In reality, that movement is a loose coalition of developing states, formed to promote common political and economic interests in dealing with the more developed states.

Neutrality properly refers to *noninvolvement in conflicts between other states*. Although usually thought of in a military context, it is equally applicable to diplomatic, economic, and political disputes. States may apply neutrality narrowly, to a single conflict, or broadly, to all. The United States, for example, remained neutral in World War I from 1914 until 1917, and in World War II until 1941. In the latter case, however, early steps little short of war were taken to aid the democracies. Switzerland is the best example of a modern government applying the principle of neutrality broadly. The Swiss remained neutral throughout both world wars and nonaligned afterward. Their recognized neutrality has led to frequent international choices of Geneva or other Swiss sites as locales for international organizations and peace negotiations, including the League of Nations and many of the permanent functional agencies of the UN. Note, however, that the policy of neutrality which kept the Swiss free during World War II while the Axis Powers conquered all the surrounding territory was greatly aided by Switzerland's truly formidable geography, universal military training of males, superb civil defense system, and financial cooperation with Nazi Germany.

Some confusion about the meaning of neutrality arises from the height of the Cold War during the 1950s, when neutrality was widely used to mean nonalignment with the superpowers. The sense of that usage was that the great conflict between democracy and communism was being pursued by means barely short of overt, "hot" war (thus "Cold" War), and that both sides sought alliance commitments. John Foster Dulles, secretary of state (1953–59) under President Eisenhower, went so far as to declare that nonaligned "neutrality" in the Cold War was morally wrong. Nonetheless, Dulles was the architect of Austria's neutralization by treaty in 1955. Austria had been occupied and absorbed by Nazi Germany in 1938 and reestablished in 1945 under Allied occupation. Only in 1955 did the Soviets agree to Austria's full independence, on the condition of its continued neutrality. Austria's enforced neutrality and Finland's constrained nonalignment allowed both states to serve as symbolically unbiased venues for a number of important international negotiations, including the 1969–72 U.S.-Soviet SALT I strategic arms control talks.

Strict **isolationism** means the *minimization of all foreign ties*, and thus automatically includes nonalignment, although it goes much further. There are very few good modern examples. Before its forced opening to the West in 1854, Japan was politically and physically isolated, culturally and economically self-sufficient, almost cut off from contact with the outside world. Within a century of that opening, Japan rose to global prominence, largely by adopting and adapting many of the procedures and technologies of the outside world. China was relatively isolated during its Great Cultural Revolution of 1965–68, when foreign contact, including trade and diplomacy, was deliberately reduced. North Korea remained one of the most inaccessible states from its founding in 1948 throughout the remainder of the twentieth century, with few foreign diplomatic and trade ties and very limited access to foreigners. Thus in the 1990s it was extremely difficult to resolve fears about North Korea's nuclear weapons program, even though the country desperately needed foreign aid to relieve famine. Undoubtedly the most highly isolated modern state, however, was Cambodia, then called Democratic Kampuchea, under the Pol Pot regime of 1975–79. Pol Pot led a group of doctrinaire radical Marxists called the Khmer Rouge. They came to power in 1975 after a long-running civil war and sought to turn Cambodia into an agrarian, socialist state. Foreign trade was cut off, borders were sealed, and foreigners were expelled. Diplomatic relations were severed with essentially all states except China. Urban dwellers were forcibly evicted to the countryside and ordered to farm, leaving the cities largely deserted. More than a million educated individuals and people even remotely connected with the old political order were liquidated. The country's isolation was so complete that it took several years for word of the carnage to leak out by way of refugees and become widely realized. Cambodia's isolation was forcibly ended by a 1978 invasion and the imposition of a puppet regime by Vietnam. Nevertheless, Khmer Rouge forces still controlled territory in northwestern Cambodia beyond Pol Pot's death in 1998.

The rise of modern means of communication and transportation make it very difficult to achieve strict isolation. Moreover, the increasing interconnectedness of the global economy makes isolationism increasingly undesirable. Analysts have suggested a number of conditions that help make isolationism workable; all are clearly seen in the case of Japan before 1854. *Economic self-sufficiency* allows development in seclusion and implies no dependence on others for resources or markets. *Cultural self-sufficiency* allows independence from outsiders for concepts of political and other management. In contrast, for example, the czarist Russian court and government were always highly influenced (including linguistically) by the French. When there exists a *diffuse structure of world power*, states are free of concentrated pressures from nearby great powers and relatively freer to pursue their own courses. *Physical or geographic isolation* helps protect against foreign attack and thus helps make independent and isolationist policies practical. Britain was last successfully invaded in 1066, and Japan's pre-1854 isolation was greatly aided by its island location. In contrast, Poland lacks natural frontier barriers and has suffered centuries of invasion from both east and west. Finally, regardless of the structure of world power, an *absence of external threats* significantly aids isolationism, reducing both the danger of foreign interference and the need or incentive to seek protective alliances. As argued earlier, however, strict isolationism is becoming ever more rare. In addition to modern trends in communication and economics, the rise in the number, sophistication, range, accuracy, and firepower of modern weapons also tend to make true isolationism ever more difficult to achieve.

Interventionism is forcible interference in locations abroad, almost the self-defining opposite of isolationism. Like other broad policy orientations, interventionism may be applied broadly worldwide or narrowly, to particular states, groups, or regions. Although the term conjures images of military expeditions, interventionism often involves economic actions, or military force in support of economic interests. In its extreme form, interventionism becomes **colonialism,** the seizing and ruling of subservient territories. Although such direct rule is almost unheard of today, much of the world's territory was held in great colonial empires well into the twentieth century. In a great movement that peaked between the end of World War II and 1960, most colonies were liberated to become newly independent states, and almost no colonies remain today. In the aftermath of colonialism, however, many analysts see a new form of influence termed **neocolonialism.** This refers to policies that, deliberately or not, tend to keep former colonies economically tied to their previous rulers.

Interventionism short of colonialism involves military incursions or economic muscle to direct or influence the affairs of others, often for fairly brief periods. During

WAS THE UNITED STATES ISOLATIONIST BETWEEN THE WORLD WARS?

Confusion about isolationism usually arises about periods during which grand policy goes beyond nonalignment (not forming alliances) but stops short of strict isolationism (minimizing all foreign ties). The classic example is U.S. policy between the two world wars. Although it had participated in the First World War, the United States never ratified the Versailles peace treaty and never joined the League of Nations that was supposed to ensure the postwar peace. With the onset of the Great Depression in 1929, U.S. trade and economic policy became highly protectionist. Although they recognized that Europeans and others abroad were experiencing terrible conditions, the majority of U.S. citizens found conditions bad enough at home and believed we should stick to our own business, staying out of world affairs. Still, America remained at least somewhat involved abroad. The U.S. economy was already the world's largest, which is why the New York stock market crash triggered worldwide depression. Despite protectionism and a two-thirds drop in international trade, this country remained significant in international economics. Although not in the League, the United States participated in some significant international negotiations, some of which were pathbreaking. Among them were the Washington-London Conferences and Naval Agreements, one of the earliest serious moves toward international arms control and disarmament to control the costs and threats of military spending. They fixed the sizes of the world's three largest navies, those of Great Britain, the

United States, and Japan, in the ratio of 5:5:3, and led to the destruction of a small number of capital ships.

Other American initiatives of the period were less significant. The Kellogg-Briand Pact of 1928 was an idealistic and unrealistic attempt at reforming traditional international relations. Popularly named after the U.S. secretary of state and the French foreign minister who had proposed a treaty outlawing war between the United States and France, and properly known as the Pact of Paris, it condemned "recourse to war for the solution of international controversies." Although the pact outlawed war as an instrument of national policy and ultimately was ratified by sixty-two governments, it proved meaningless because it provided no enforcement mechanism. Indeed, when the U.S. Senate ratified with only one dissenting vote, it rejected any curtailment of America's right to self-defense and insisted that we were not compelled to take action against violators of the treaty. More effectively, the United States proposed the 1924 Dawes Plan for German payment of World War I reparations, which was accepted by Germany and the Allies. Thus, in significant ways, the United States remained active in world affairs between the two world wars and was never strictly isolationist. Nonetheless, many people call U.S. policy during the interwar period isolationist, which is why those calling for a retreat from internationalism in the post–Cold War era are today termed *neo-isolationists.*

the twentieth century, the United States frequently has intervened in Latin America, often on the side of business interests, and less frequently for overtly political goals. For example, in 1983, a moderate Marxist regime on the Caribbean island of Grenada was overthrown by a more radical Marxist faction. President Reagan ordered a U.S. military invasion of Grenada, ostensibly to protect several hundred American students in a Grenadian medical school. Support by other Caribbean regimes was sought and received, but only after the invasion was launched. Whatever the danger to the medical students, who remained unharmed, the invasion allowed the United States to replace a Marxist regime with a more sympathetic capitalist government, at a time when the Reagan administration feared communist penetration into the Caribbean. As in many other cases, this intervention was asserted to be beneficial to those influenced. Yet although interventions sometimes benefit others, that is rarely a strong motivating factor.

Globalism, or **internationalism,** is a sweeping policy of global involvement, a deliberate choice to play a major role in world affairs. Globalism is the antithesis of isolationism. It may involve extensive use of coalitions and alliances, and even intervention. Great powers, such as the United States, may consciously seek to shape the overall world order of political, economic, and military power. Such has been the broad thrust of U.S. policy since the end of World War II. The Soviets used to speak of the "international correlation of forces," by which they meant something of similar scope, and, at least officially, looked toward the eventual global victory of their brand of socialism. Governments and peoples *may* be motivated to globalism by global interests, but there is usually a large element of national interest involved. As we shall see, U.S. globalism since 1945 has been based on a strong belief that the world order had been so profoundly altered by World War II that U.S. *national* security interests now demanded sustained global activism. As we examine the history of U.S. foreign policy, we shall see globalism and other general policy orientations holding over long periods of time, and some policy goals recurring frequently, even as specific policy problems come and go.

KEY FACTORS IN EVALUATING POLICY TRENDS: A RECAPITULATION

Before we review grand policy themes and major specific policies through U.S. history, recall that foreign policy is shaped by the continuing interplay between two sets of factors, one that encourages continuity and stability and one that stimulates change and evolution. Policy continuity is encouraged by the following factors:

- State ("national") interests and capabilities at home and abroad change only slowly.
- Physical constraints prevent many actions from being taken immediately.
- Existing treaties, alliances, and legislation constrain policy to run in existing channels.
- Bureaucratic inertia causes policy changes to require time in which authorities can be persuaded that change is necessary.
- Prior experience encourages reuse of policies that worked in the past and discourages use of those which have failed. Often there is inadequate examination of the circumstances that contributed to those successes and failures.

A different set of factors encourages policy change and innovation:

- State capabilities do change over time in response to long-term economic, resource, technological, and political trends.
- Capabilities respond to important shifts in global political alignments, such as the breakup of the Soviet Union.
- Evolutionary changes in the relative capabilities of states require adaptive changes in foreign policies.

Finally, as states deal with the interplay of these two sets of factors, they work with a fairly limited menu of general foreign policy orientations, including the following:

- Coalition making or alliance building
- Nonalignment
- Neutrality
- Isolationism
- Interventionism
- Globalism or internationalism

Although globalism inherently must be applied globally, the other general foreign policy orientations may be applied broadly worldwide or narrowly, to particular states, groups, or regions. As we quickly review more than two centuries of U.S. foreign policy, watch for most of these orientations and for the ongoing interplay between factors for continuity and factors for change.

Major Events, Orientations, and Goals in U.S. Foreign Policy: Colonial Period Through World War II

History provides many cases and examples for study and is our best laboratory for deriving propositions and testing ideas about how policy works. This section comprises a brief history of the major events in U.S. foreign policy up to the watershed events of the end of World War II and the acceptance of a permanent major global role. Of course, the discussion that follows is necessarily brief because a detailed history easily could comprise an entire thick volume. Although no prior study of American and global history is assumed or required, whatever such work you may have done can be useful in amplifying the treatment here. Each event is related to the general policy orientation or grand policy of the time and to specific policy goals, some of which are found to recur frequently and persist over very long periods of time. Major points are summarized in Chronology 2.1 on pages 50–51.

Colonial Period, Revolution, and the Infancy of Independence

The American Revolution lies far enough in the past for many people to forget that the United States shares with the majority of contemporary independent states a history of prior colonial oppression. The suffering of Great Britain's American colonists may not have been extreme by everyone's standards (and many colonists remained loyal to Britain), but American interests were the same as those of most colonies in later centuries and differed significantly from the mother country's interests. British leaders wanted the colonies to purchase manufactured goods exclusively from Great Britain, and sell to British manufacturers such raw materials and agricultural produce as cotton, tobacco, and timber, including selected old growth trees to provide masts for the Royal Navy. In contrast, the colonists sought economic efficiency through trade with whoever offered advantage, including French colonies in the Western Hemisphere. They also sought domestic manufacturing capabilities to promote economic development. Well before issues about taxation without representation came to the fore, underlying conflicts in economic interest pitted the colonies against Great Britain. The colonists were a rather entrepreneurial lot, little if at all removed from persons ambitious enough to have made the perilous ocean crossing, so it was natural in the long run for them to demand both political and economic freedoms.

The American Revolutionary War and its aftermath demonstrate clearly rational and self-interested policy flip-flops by the infant United States, as well as interesting connections to broader global politics. All of these reflect the viewpoint of *protecting national interests*, as discussed in Chapter 1. Colonial leaders sought foreign alliances and assistance, most notably from France, in fighting the British. France, still more than a decade before its own revolution, aided the colonists largely to create difficulties for its traditional opponent. Britain, in turn, withdrew from the United States in large part because fighting a war against American guerrillas on the other side of the world was difficult, costly, and distracted from greater threats closer to home. Having won its independence, the new United States of America renounced alliances and adopted a policy of nonalignment, clearly reflected in George Washington's 1793 Proclamation of Neutrality in the European war of that time. Nonalignment was ideally suited to promoting U.S. development. All the early nineteenth-century great powers were European, and by staying out of their politics and wars the infant United States could devote its resources to development, secure in the knowledge that the Atlantic Ocean provided a great natural barrier to European adventures in the Western Hemisphere. Was this isolationism? Not really. Recall George Washington's exhortation in his Farewell Address that "in extending our commercial relations to have with [foreign nations] as little *political* connection as possible" (Kaufman, 1969, 27). This was far from true isolationism because the United States, although strongly focused on development issues at home, also vigorously sought free trade abroad to promote that development. Foreign policy themes of (relatively) free trade and (especially) freedom of navigation in support of trade have been maintained almost continuously throughout more than two centuries.

Indeed, so strongly did the young U.S. government believe in freedom of navigation, that the issue helped propel us into the strange and nearly disastrous War of 1812 against Great Britain. U.S. expansion was probably the greatest (but unadmitted) reason behind the decision to declare war. Publicly stated reasons included British blockades of shipping to and from France, and impressment, the British Navy's forcible recruiting of U.S. sailors from ships on the high seas. Declaring war on Britain was an incredibly bold and foolish attack on the world's greatest naval power, for which the United States paid heavily. Britain had over a hundred battleships, while the U.S. Navy consisted of some nineteen smaller vessels. British forces invaded Washington, D.C., and other points, burned the

⊕ **CHRONOLOGY 2.1**

U.S. Foreign Policy: Major Events, Orientations, and Goals (Colonial Period Through World War II)

Time	Major Events	General Policy Orientation	Specific Policy Goals
Colonial Period	Issues of free trade and taxation		Economic efficiency; development
1775–79	Revolutionary War	Alliance seeking (with France)	Independence
1797	Washington's Farewell Address	Political-military nonalignment	Free trade
1812	War of 1812, with Great Britain		Protecting national interests: freedom of navigation
1823	Monroe Doctrine	Hemispheric interventionism	Hemispheric protection-ism with tacit British support
Mid-nineteenth Century	Expansion and consolidation across North America	Nonalignment	Development
1861–65	Civil War	Nonalignment	Preserving the Union; keeping Britain neutral
1898	Spanish-American War	Interventionism	"Manifest Destiny"; great power status
1901	Open door policy (in China)	Interventionism	Expanded free trade
1904	Roosevelt Corollary to the Monroe Doctrine	Hemispheric interventionism	Expeditionary forces; five states occupied
1914–18	World War I		
1914	Outbreak	Neutrality	
1917	U.S. entry as an associated power		Making the world "safe for democracy"

Capitol and the White House, and won almost every battle of the war except the last. American troops briefly captured various points in Canada and won important naval engagements on Lake Erie and Lake Champlain. U.S. troops resoundingly won the last and greatest land battle of the war, on 8 January 1815 at New Orleans. However, communications across the Atlantic were so slow that the battle was fought fifteen days after a treaty of peace already had been signed at Ghent, Belgium. Fortunately for the independence of the United States, the British had much bigger wars to fight in Europe and were willing to withdraw again across the Atlantic. The Treaty of Ghent essentially restored the prewar status, with no gains of territory and no mention of impressments or naval blockades. Nonetheless, the War of 1812 had lasting effects. It helped increase patriotism and bind the United States together into a single nation. Additionally, it pro-

1918	Wilson's Fourteen Points	Collective security through League of Nations (never ratified by the United States)	Reform of the international system
Interwar Period		Nonalignment	Limited foreign involvement
1922	Washington-London Conferences and Naval Agreements		Arms control and disarmament
1928	Kellogg-Briand Pact		Reform: war outlawed (but no enforcement mechanism)
1936	Italy invades Ethiopia	Nonalignment	(No League of Nations action)
1939–45	World War II		
1939	Outbreak in Europe	Neutrality—with a bias toward the democracies	
1941	Lend-Lease (March)	Tacit alliance building	Help preserve Britain
	Atlantic Charter (August)	Informal alliance building	
	Japan attacks Pearl Harbor; United States declares war (December)	Alliance (with Britain, Soviet Union, and others)	Unconditional surrender of the Axis Powers
1945	Victory over Germany, Japan		
1945–50	Development of the Cold War, and of a bipolar world order	Internationalism; alliance-leadership	Confronting the realities of superpower status

moted the rapid rise of manufacturing because goods previously imported were unavailable during the wartime naval blockades.

EXPANSION, DEVELOPMENT, AND GROWTH TO GREAT POWER STATUS

With a few notable exceptions, the remainder of the nineteenth century saw little U.S. activity abroad. Energies were largely devoted to development, expanding and consolidating across the North American continent. In 1823, however, the bold young country embarked on regional interventionism and protectionism, promulgating the Monroe Doctrine, promising to oppose military or political interference by European powers anywhere in the Western Hemisphere. This could be seen as proceeding from both the *countering aggression* and *protecting national interests* viewpoints examined in Chapter 1.

The substantial long-term success of the Monroe Doctrine was due in no small part to its tacit support by Britain and the Royal Navy. In 1861 the United States began refining the political complexion of the country through four bloody years of civil war. By almost every measure, whether of soldiers killed and wounded relative to the total population, general devastation, scorched earth warfare, cruel treatment of prisoners, or expense relative to the size of the economy, this was the most costly war the United States has ever fought. In great contrast to policy in the War of 1812, the Union government bent over backward to avoid giving Britain any excuse to intervene on the side of the Confederacy, submitting to serious violations of sovereignty in incidents at sea. The British populace generally favored the Union cause, although their government favored the Confederacy, partly to ensure access to southern cotton and tobacco, while Union strategy relied heavily on blockading southern ports. Following the Civil War, the country returned to development and westward expansion. Industrial growth, which had been crucial to northern victory, continued apace. And although the industrial revolution came first to Britain, it came even more powerfully to the United States. Here it was bolstered by an abundance of territory, a wealth of natural resources, and a growing and increasingly skilled population.

By the closing years of the nineteenth century, the United States had built itself up to the rank of a great power in industrial capacity and military potential, although the major European powers were far from eager to recognize that stature and accord the upstart Americans comparable political standing. Nonetheless, many in this country recognized it and some began to speak and write of the "manifest destiny" of the United States not only to become a continentwide great power, but to play a major role worldwide. That view became widespread enough to influence the United States to begin exercising its power in foreign interventions in this hemisphere and around the Pacific Rim. Following a highly suspicious 1898 attack on the battleship USS *Maine* in Havana harbor, the United States launched the Spanish-American war, handily capturing the Spanish colonies of Cuba and the Philippines. U.S. troops withdrew from Cuba in 1902, but U.S. and other foreign investments dominated the economy until Fidel Castro's ascendancy in a 1959 communist revolution. Spain was given $20 million for the Philippines after the war, but the United States fought a brutal six-year war against Philippine guerrillas until 1905. Those islands, attacked one day after Pearl Harbor and occupied by Japan during World War II, were eventually liberated by U.S. troops and granted independence in 1946.

The very early twentieth century saw other instances of economic and military interventionism by the newly powerful United States. In 1901, acting together with major European powers, the United States proclaimed an "open door policy" under which several major Chinese ports were forcibly opened to foreign trade. The 1904 Roosevelt Corollary to the Monroe Doctrine proclaimed a U.S. right to intervene in Western Hemisphere states. Under its terms, expeditionary military forces were sent to some nine states over the next few decades, and five of those states were occupied for at least brief periods of time. Most analysts today see those actions as having served primarily the foreign interests of U.S.-based businesses.

WORLD WAR I, WORLD WAR II, AND THE RISE TO SUPERPOWER STATUS

Despite these instances of interventionism, notions of avoiding entanglements in European struggles were still powerful and widespread, and the United States happily adopted

"FOREIGN" POLICY TOWARD INDIGENOUS PEOPLES

Explorers and early colonists found the "New World" of the Americas already populated by indigenous or native peoples. Often those peoples were regarded as obstacles to be swept aside to permit the expansion of farms and settlements and the exploitation of natural resources. Sometimes, notably in Spain's conquest of Latin America and the future American Southwest, natives were targeted for religious conversion. Almost always, they were regarded as inferiors whose exploitation, or even enslavement or extermination, was justified. Europeans who kidnapped Africans for shipment to the Americas as slaves offered similar arguments. Today the history of such actions by the great colonial powers, particularly Britain, France, Spain, and Portugal, is almost universally decried.

The colonists who founded the United States inherited the attitudes and practices of their time toward native peoples. Slavery was already established before independence, posed immediate constitutional problems between slave and free states, and ultimately was the primary cause of the American Civil War. Exploitation of Native Americans persisted through almost two centuries of U.S. independence. Beginning in colonial times, treaties were signed with Native American tribes. Later, under relentless pressure for expansion and development, many such treaties were shamelessly violated by the United States. Tribes were forcibly relocated to reservations in the least desirable areas, often with great loss of life. Deprived of their traditional territories and means of survival, many Native Americans became government dependents. Their children were regularly sent to reservation schools where they were prohibited from speaking their native languages. Native American culture was largely overrun by U.S. culture and the pressures of development. Only in the latter twentieth century did some reversal of these trends begin.

U.S. dealings with Native Americans may be considered a kind of foreign policy. The practice of signing treaties implied recognition of the tribes as sovereign nations. On many occasions, wars were fought between U.S. troops and those nations. Extensive grants of rights, privileges, and territories were made, often under duress and almost always to the benefit of the larger and more powerful U.S. government. Today, the highly exploitative nature of these American policies is widely recognized. Many analysts see parallels to U.S. policies in the developing world, for example, in Central America.

a neutral stand upon the outbreak of World War I in 1914. Few world leaders anywhere realized at its outset how prolonged and devastating the war would prove. Troops sent to the front in August 1914 were told they would be home by Christmas. Understanding of the war's impact grew as the fighting settled into stalemate and attrition. The United States finally entered the conflict in 1917, which decisively shifted the balance of forces in Europe and led to victory and peace in 1918. Yet there was no deep American commitment to sustained global activism. U.S. entry into the most destructive conflict the world had yet seen was touted as helping to "make the world safe for democracy" through a "war to end wars." Yet the long history of U.S. nonalignment with European powers and noninvolvement in European politics still showed in the fact that the United States never signed an alliance with Britain and France, instead fighting on their side as an "associated power." This symbolic protection of American purity was politically costly because no quid pro quo had been obtained before U.S. entry. In his "Fourteen Points" for peace, presented to a joint session of Congress on 8 January 1918, U.S. president Woodrow Wilson sought to lay out a peace proposal that would guide the Allies and appeal to the Central Powers, but also reform the international system in ways calculated to reduce the probability of another similar war. In the postwar peace, Wilson's broad, general reform ideas such as "open covenants, openly arrived at" were largely ignored. Many of his specific proposals, such as redrawing many European borders along nationalistic lines, were implemented. His best known point, "a general association of nations . . . under special covenants" led to the creation of the League of Nations (Chernow and Vallasi, 1993, 988). Arguably, Wilson should have demanded prior agreement to additional points as a price for U.S. entry into the war. In the end, he was incapacitated by a major stroke while campaigning to build public support for ratification of the Versailles peace treaty, and he ended his term as an invalid. We will never know how different the outcome would have been, had Wilson been able to devote his former energy to the cause. More conservative forces prevailed in the Senate, and the United States neither ratified the Versailles treaty nor joined the League of Nations. Separate peace treaties were signed with the European powers in later years, and the United States retreated into an interwar period of nonalignment and limited foreign involvement.

Despite common beliefs to the contrary, those interwar years did not see strict isolationism. Although eschewing foreign alliances and membership in the League of Nations, the United States remained active in international affairs in significant ways, some of which were pathbreaking. (See "Was the United States Isolationist Between the World Wars?" on page 46.) Generally, the interwar period saw the United States turn inward with concern over the Great Depression, trying almost desperately to ignore the early signs of the rising global firestorm that was to bring a second world war.

Signs of the coming conflagration appeared early in the 1930s. Japan invaded Manchuria in 1931. Two years later, Adolf Hitler and his Nazi Party came to power in Germany. Italy's unprovoked 1936 invasion of Ethiopia went unopposed by the League of Nations, despite an impassioned plea from the Ethiopian emperor, Haile Selassie. German remilitarization of the Rhineland in 1936 violated the Geneva peace treaty. U.S. officials, like most foreign leaders, tried to ignore or minimize the implications of these events. Finally, Germany's 1939 invasion of Poland provoked Britain and France to declare war, although major fighting on the continent was delayed until the spring of 1940. Germany then overran the low countries (Belgium, Luxembourg, and the Netherlands) and occupied France in some forty days. Lacking both the means and any serious plan for invading Britain, Germany sought to bring the island nation to its knees through extensive aerial bombardment in what became known as the Battle of Britain. Across the Atlantic, President Franklin Roosevelt and other leaders in his administration believed both that U.S. interests demanded support of the embattled democracies and that we would eventually have to enter the war. More conservative leaders and at least one third of the public opposed that view and sought to keep the country out of European struggles. The famous aviator Charles Lindbergh was a notable speaker for this "America First" movement.

Given strongly divided public opinion, Roosevelt kept the United States officially neutral but sought to increase our preparedness and aid the democracies, especially Britain, by a variety of means short of war. For the first time in U.S. history, a peacetime military draft was instituted in 1940, although initially it was quite limited. In August of that year, Roosevelt met British prime minister Winston Churchill on the cruiser USS *Augusta* to sign the Atlantic Charter. It asserted a sweeping set of democratic principles that already began to look forward to a fundamentally changed postwar world order founded on a transatlantic security regime. The March 1941 Lend-Lease Act allowed arms and equipment to be given by sale, exchange, lease, or direct transfer to any country whose defense the president deemed vital to that of the United States. Britain had already received fifty overage naval destroyers in 1940, vitally needed to keep the shipping lanes open in the North Atlantic battle against German submarines. In exchange, the United States received options to take ninety-nine-year leases on a number of air and naval bases on British territories in the Western Hemisphere. U.S. lend-lease aid from March 1941 through its termination in September 1946 would total $50.6 billion, an amount then greater than the annual federal budget. By initiating a variety of such actions while remaining officially neutral, the U.S. administration engaged in tacit alliance building and laid the groundwork for the eventual wartime coalition that came to be known as the United Nations.

With Japan's 7 December 1941 surprise attack on U.S. naval facilities at Pearl Harbor, Hawaii, domestic opposition to war involvement virtually vanished overnight, and the country turned speedily to mobilization and all-out war production. Historians generally agree there were ample warning signs of possible attack, making the Pearl Harbor raid a classic case in policy failure. American losses—the full extent of which was carefully concealed—and surprise helped mobilize public opinion behind the war effort. Although the United States so distrusted communists that it had not extended diplomatic recognition to the Soviet Union from the time of the Bolshevik victory in 1917 until 1933, it invited the Soviets into the anti-Axis alliance. Spurning the August 1939 Soviet-German nonaggression pact, Germany already had launched a massive invasion of the USSR on 6 April 1941, overrunning most Soviet territory in Europe before being halted by the bitter Russian winter. When the United States made common cause with the Soviets, the old principle that "the enemy of my enemy is my friend" once again prevailed. Nonetheless, U.S.-Soviet wartime relations were always uneasy for both sides, and Congress forced President Truman to cut off aid shipments to the Soviets immediately after the 1945 peace.

The Allies agreed early to the principle of demanding unconditional surrender from the Axis Powers (Germany, Italy, and Japan). Arguably, this was a mistaken political/military strategy that discouraged anti-Hitler German leaders who would have negotiated an earlier peace. Seen in the light of later Cold War division of Germany and repeated U.S.-Soviet crises over the status of occupied Berlin, a negotiated peace that left an intact and non-Nazi Germany might have been far preferable. The demand for unconditional surrender also may have provoked Japan's resistance well beyond the point at which many of its leaders realized the war was lost. Unconditional surrender, however, was a simple and unambiguous goal. It helped the other Allies placate the Soviet Union, which bore the brunt of fighting the Nazis in Eastern Europe and constantly pressed for an earlier and more direct Allied assault on Germany from the west. Unconditional surrender was straightforwardly communicated, readily recognized, easily accepted by the people of the United States, and consistent with widespread beliefs that the Axis governments were genuinely evil. Notions about limited war and negotiated settlements involving give-and-take had much deeper roots in the political consciousness of European powers such as

Britain and France. Their political histories as independent sovereign states stretched back centuries before there was a United States, and involved many less-than-absolute victories. In evaluating U.S. political experience in such matters, recall that our greatest war, the Civil War, ended with the surrender, occupation, and dismantlement of the Confederacy, even though the peace terms imposed were generous. Also recall that World War I ended with harsh reparations and major changes to the map of Europe. However, neither of these cases involved an unconditional surrender.

As World War II developed, Italy overthrew the Fascists and switched sides in 1943, and the Allies obtained devastatingly complete victories over Germany and Japan in 1945. Unlike the First World War, however, World War II was so widespread and destructive that it fundamentally changed the world distribution of power. Most of the prewar great powers were defeated, invaded, or largely reduced to ruin. France was invaded and occupied. Germany industry was virtually destroyed, and the country was occupied and divided. Great Britain remained uninvaded and undefeated, but suffered widespread heavy bombing, and some analysts believe the British economy has never recovered from the combination of wartime damage and war expenditures. Italy was torn by invasion and the post-1943 German occupation of its northern regions. Japan was heavily bombed and occupied. Of all the prewar great powers, only the United States and the USSR emerged relatively strong. Indeed, their strengths so greatly exceeded those of any other surviving states that we began to refer to them as the **superpowers.** The United States suffered casualties far below those of most other belligerents and the invasions only of some of its Pacific island territories. By any measure, the United States emerged from World War II as the world's strongest economic and military power, even without its newly created (though short-lived) monopoly on nuclear weapons. (For more about U.S.-Soviet divisions, see "Soviet Ideology and the Cold War" and "The Late 1940s: Organizing for the Cold War," later in this chapter.)

Consensus both among leaders and the general populace was that the United States now would play an expanded and sustained world role, in great contrast to its post–World War I experience. Whether many people realized how completely the United States would dominate the new postwar environment is debatable. The wartime alliance known as the United Nations made plans for a postwar intergovernmental organization of the same name, which was to help maintain a lasting peace. Other intergovernmental organizations launched during World War II were expected to institutionalize U.S. global involvement. (See Chapter 12 for further details.) Conferees at the New Hampshire White Mountains resort of Bretton Woods in 1944 established new institutions intended to stabilize the postwar international economic order. Bretton Woods yielded agreements creating the International Monetary Fund (IMF) and the International Bank for Reconstruction and Development, commonly called the World Bank. The new UN organization was organized and chartered at a great 1945 San Francisco Conference. Attention in the immediate aftermath of war turned to organizing the occupations of Germany and Japan, and to demobilization. In an America that had only finally built its way out of the Great Depression by rearming for war, widespread belief held that the last soldiers home from the front would not find jobs. But those fears proved groundless. Pent-up consumer demand fueled a postwar economic boom, and the United States built unprecedented prosperity. At the same time, however, it was forced to wrestle with the implications of superpowerhood and world leadership in an environment that rapidly began to appear both challenging and threatening. U.S. responses to that new and profoundly transformed world order are addressed in the following section.

MAJOR EVENTS IN U.S. FOREIGN POLICY SINCE WORLD WAR II

Having emerged into superpowerhood, the United States deliberately embraced a general policy of active globalist internationalism. For decades to come, this was to be supported by a bipartisan consensus in the Congress, almost regardless of what public opinion held, although it was generally supportive. Motivations for globalism varied widely among Americans. There was genuine humanitarian concern for nations that had suffered in the war and now needed assistance for survival and rebuilding, especially in devastated Western Europe. At the other extreme was deep fear of the spread of communism, particularly into war-ravaged states such as France and Italy. Seen from today's perspective, it appears that too much attention had been devoted to winning World War II and too little to planning for a benign and manageable postwar world order. In a provocative 1992 book, Ronald H. Hinckley argues that true consensus never existed either on prewar nonalignment or postwar internationalism. As Hinckley puts that case (1992, 13),

> The [opinion] cleavages identified by researchers since Vietnam (liberal-conservative, unilateral-multilateral or independent-cooperative, and militant-nonmilitant) appear to have existed prior to World War II.
>
> World War II did not change these cleavages; rather, it altered the international order in which the cleavages were to play out.
>
> Each group that so easily embraced [nonalignment] before the war came to embrace internationalism after it. The reason for this consensus was not that internationalism held the answer but because it held every answer, as did [nonalignment] before the war. For the conservatives, the availability of worldwide markets indicated that international involvement would help maintain capitalism and, hence, democracy. For the liberals and timids, the United States could lead the way in building a just and equitable order not only at home but throughout the world through involvement in international organizations and institutions. For the belligerents, internationalism provided independence through leadership and the freedom to use military force if necessary. No one feared that war would result from these internationalist efforts; they felt the opposite.
>
> Internationalism, like [nonalignment] before it, had something for everyone, and the result was a false sense of consensus in international affairs.

That apparent consensus was shattered over Vietnam War policy during the second half of the 1960s. As we will see, neither real nor apparent consensus on U.S. grand policy has yet been reconstructed, even in the aftermath of the Cold War. Major events and policy themes of the post–World War II period are summarized in Chronology 2.2 on pages 60–61.

THE LATE 1940S: ORGANIZING FOR THE COLD WAR

All the essential framework of U.S. foreign policy for the next four decades was established during the last half of the 1940s. Moreover, few elements of that framework had been clearly foreseen. In little more than a year, prevailing positive 1945 attitudes in the United States and Western Europe about having won the war were reversed. Worldviews and desired world orders clashed drastically between the "East," rigorously dominated by the Soviet Union, and the "West," led by Western Europe and, especially, by the United States. East-West relations had always been touchy and suspicious during the war, and rapidly soured after victory over the Axis Powers.

The first major area of controversy was the political future of Eastern Europe, although the bases of contention lay in wartime actions and deep political and ideological differences. Optimistic wartime summit meetings at Potsdam and Yalta had produced agreements calling for political self-determination by European states after they were liberated from German occupation, and had delineated zones of postwar occupation. The Soviets battled the Nazis and their allies from 1941 through 1945, bore the brunt of fighting in Europe, enduring the loss of some thirty million lives and staggering amounts of materiel. They suffered scorched earth warfare across almost all their European territory and paid an enormous price to survive, ultimately emerging with a large army and a significant industrial base. Axis invaders had occupied most Soviet territory in Europe, from their western border eastward almost to the Ural mountains. Occupied territory included the most highly industrialized and heavily populated areas, plus the best Soviet farmland in Ukraine. An analogy would be to picture nearly all the United States east of the Mississippi River ravaged, with the people driven westward. At enormous cost, the Soviets had slogged back across those hundreds of miles, ultimately driving the German armies back through Eastern Europe and into their own heartland. From 1941 until 1944 the Soviets had repeatedly called for the Allies to open a western front on the European mainland, putting pressure on the Germans from both sides in order to reduce demands on the Soviet Union. However, U.S. and British strategy called for wrapping up Axis strength first in peripheral areas, beginning with a push eastward across North Africa, then north across the Mediterranean to Sicily and into Italy, where they were stalemated by a combination of formidable north Italian geography and fierce German resistance. Only in June 1944 was a western front opened, with the invasion of Normandy in northern France. Yet even after that invasion the Soviets still faced the worst of the fighting. The memoirs of Germany's minister of armaments, Albert Speer, an uninspired architect but brilliant manager who kept Germany's war production flowing fairly well despite Allied bombing, make it clear that Germany's Nazi leaders feared the communists more than the Western Allies, and thus maintained greater military effort on their eastern front. Their terrible wartime experience discouraged the Soviets from readily yielding control of the Eastern European territories they had liberated at such great cost.

Additionally, Soviet communist ideology provided easy arguments for ensuring sympathetic and compliant governments in Eastern Europe. (See "Soviet Ideology and the Cold War" on page 62.) After World War II, that ideology was used to excuse the imposition of compliant regimes dominated from Moscow across Eastern Europe. The USSR asserted that it was simply helping those states along the historically inevitable path toward the betterment of their peoples. More cynical Western observers held that Soviet domination of Eastern Europe better served Soviet state interests by controlling buffer states to protect against invasion from the West and by dominating economies that could be harnessed to help rebuild the Soviet Union. Traditionalist analysts who focused on power politics saw a Soviet Union simply behaving as any great power likely would in the circumstances. More pessimistic and fearful observers saw a global communist threat that was, of course, an element of Soviet official ideology. Whichever logic one used to explain it, Soviet domination in Eastern Europe rapidly became evident.

By March 1946, barely ten months after victory had been achieved over Germany, Britain's wartime prime minister, Winston Churchill, traveled to Westminster College in Fulton, Missouri, to deliver one of the seminal speeches of the Cold War. In it he asserted that "from Stettin in the Baltic to Trieste in the Adriatic an iron curtain has descended across the Continent." This was the same Churchill who at an October 1944 meeting with Stalin had semiformally recognized that the USSR would have majority influence in most of the Eastern European states (Churchill, 1954, 198). Since then, however, East-West relations had soured badly as limited and nervous wartime cooperation gave way to animosity and confrontation on every issue. Churchill's "iron curtain" imagery became a Western symbol for Soviet intransigence. In a 1948 speech before a U.S. Senate committee, the influential financier Bernard Baruch asserted that "we are in a Cold War which is getting warmer." He had first used the phrase **Cold War** a year earlier, and its use spread rapidly.

Today it is difficult to have many positive feelings about the Cold War. In the late 1940s, however, most people saw it rather favorably, believing the alternative to be a hot or shooting war. National leaders all the way up to President Harry Truman feared that war with the Soviets easily could erupt at almost any time, over any of a number of flash points. Cold War division of the world into Eastern and Western camps came to dominate U.S. foreign policy from the late 1940s through the 1980s. Because the United States and USSR were by far the most powerful states, it also dominated much of international politics around the world.

All the major elements of U.S. Cold War policy were established by 1950. They are nearly summarized in George Kennan's 1947 article on "The Sources of Soviet Conduct" in the journal *Foreign Affairs*, which proposed a policy of **containment** of Soviet communist expansion. Because Kennan was a State Department official, he published under the pseudonym "X." (Note, however, that *Foreign Affairs* is the premier journal of the U.S. foreign policy establishment.) Originally formulated as a lengthy diplomatic telegram sent from Moscow in 1946, Kennan's proposal rapidly became effective U.S. policy. Containment proposed to block further Soviet expansion by all means short of major war and was based on an assertion that a Soviet Union prevented from imperialist expansion would eventually fail because of the internal contradictions of its own political-economic system. Ironically, this was almost a mirror image of what Soviet Marxist-Leninist ideology asserted about the eventual collapse of the capitalist West. Political scientists and historians still debate the full range of causes for the Soviet Union's collapse and breakup at the end of 1991, but economic failure is prominent on almost every analyst's list. It remains unclear how strongly any Western political leaders believed during the long decades of Cold War that the USSR ever would collapse. Certainly, when collapse did come in the late 1980s, it was startlingly rapid. In recent years, Kennan himself claims to have envisioned that containment would be carried out more by economic means and less by

⊕ CHRONOLOGY 2.2

Post–World War II Themes in U.S. Foreign Policy

1945–50			Emergence into superpower status
			Globalist internationalism
			Opening of the Cold War
			Containment of communism
	1946	5 March	Churchill's "Iron Curtain" speech
	1947	12 March	Truman Doctrine: Aid to fight communism
		5 June	Marshall Plan: Rebuilding Europe
		July	Kennan's "X" article proposes "containment"
	1948	25 February	Soviets consolidate control of Eastern Europe
		24 June–12 July	Berlin blockade and airlift (1949)
	1949	4 April	North Atlantic Treaty Organization (NATO) Treaty
		May	West Germany created from three western zones
		7 October	Soviets declare East Germany a state
			First Soviet nuclear bomb
			Communists win Chinese civil war
1950s			Cold War
			U.S.-Soviet rivalry
	1950	April	NSC-68 secretly establishes militarized containment
			U.S. dominance
			Korean War (1950–53)

military approaches than ultimately was the case. In the event, however, the United States undertook significant moves to implement containment to counter the Soviet challenge, beginning in 1947.

Containment was carried out by the entire range of policy tools, from alliance diplomacy to economics to limited war. Key and typical aspects included the Truman Doctrine of military-economic aid, Marshall Plan economic assistance, firm but limited response to the Berlin blockade of 1948–49, formation of the North Atlantic Treaty Organization (NATO) in 1949 and other defensive alliances ringing the Soviet Union, and limited war to reverse communist aggression in Korea. All but the last came to pass before 1950.

The Truman Doctrine was triggered by Soviet-aided communist insurrections in Greece and the Turkish provinces bordering the Soviet Union. By early 1947, Truman administration officials feared that the Greek government would fall before year's end unless aided, although Turkey was not believed to be in such immediate danger. The

1960s	Decolonization peaks; number of independent states soars
	Rise of a rebuilt Western Europe
	Cuban missile crisis (October 1962); high danger point of the Cold War
	Early stages of the Vietnam War (1963–65)
1970s	End stages of the Vietnam War (1973–75)
	U.S.-Soviet détente, and problems
1972	SALT I Strategic Arms Control agreements
1973	Yom Kippur War in the Middle East
	Preoccupation with the limits of power
1980s	Reagan's defense buildup, and deficits
	Resurgence of the United States
	New debates on the U.S. world role
	Incursions into Grenada (1983) and Panama (1989)
1990s	End of the Cold War
	East European democratization or nationalism
	German reunification
	Collapse and breakup of the Soviet Union
	Nationalistic/ethnic strife
	Realignments; a "new world order"
	New emphasis on international political economy
	Intensified debates on the appropriate U.S. world role

doctrine enunciated on 12 March by President Truman, however, went far beyond assisting Greece and Turkey. It pledged economic and military aid to any government resisting communist aggression, whether by overt attack or subversion. This was a sweeping and global commitment, contrasting dramatically with U.S. nonalignment between the two world wars. Congress formally endorsed the Truman Doctrine by authorizing aid to Greece and Turkey within less than two months, and the president approved an initial appropriation of $400 million on 22 May. Most analysts believe that aid was decisive in maintaining noncommunist governments in Greece and Turkey. However, Greece also benefited when the Yugoslav communist leader, Marshal Tito, cut off Soviet support of

SOVIET IDEOLOGY AND THE COLD WAR

An important factor driving the Cold War was a deep ideological split between the "Western" democratic capitalist bloc led by the United States and the "Eastern" communist bloc led by the Soviet Union. The split hinged on views of the relationships among economics, politics, and citizens, and throughout most of the twentieth century there were deep fears in the West that communism might eventually prevail. Soviet Marxist-Leninist ideology evolved from nineteenth-century analyses by the German socialist Karl Marx, who asserted an inevitable historical progression of sociopolitical orders, ending in communism. The philosophical basis of Marx's analysis was materialism, the belief that everything in the world, including thought, will, and feeling, can be explained only in terms of matter, without reference, for example, to supernatural religious concepts. Marxism's most important analytic concept is *social class*, with one's social class being determined by one's relationship to the means of production. Under *feudalism*, as seen in medieval Europe, a small hereditary noble class owned all property and directed all politics, primarily for its own benefit. Meanwhile, the vast majority of people toiled in abject poverty and with almost no hope of material or social betterment. Technological change and industrialization promoted the rise of a new manufacturing middle class of factory and business owners under *capitalism*. A *class struggle* between owners and workers resulted. The great mass of people might now be forced to move from the country and farming to cities and manufacturing while the benefits of production were still disproportionately enjoyed by a minority. Only with revolution by the working class, or *proletariat*, would wealth be distributed equita-

bly. Eventually and inevitably, workers would recognize this situation and seize the farms, factories, and other means of production through revolution. Benefits would then be distributed equitably, according to the slogan "from each according to his abilities, to each according to his needs." A new political/social/economic order of *socialism* would be established, and eventually the apparatus of the state would be allowed to wither away because it was no longer needed to enforce economic relations. In effect, Marxism argues that politics arises out of and primarily concerns economics.

Lenin modified Marx's analysis by inserting a further stage of *imperialism* in order to explain why the revolution occurred first in Russia and not in the most advanced industrialized states, and why it had not spread. As defined by Lenin, imperialism involved developed capitalist states delaying the revolution by taking advantage of weaker states to overcome the inherent weaknesses in their own system. Under the dictatorship of Joseph Stalin, who dominated Soviet politics from 1922 until his death in 1953, the Soviet Union saw itself as both the vanguard of revolution and an island in a sea of hostile states intent on its destruction. This was not a totally unreasonable view because Britain, France, and the United States had sent military expeditionary forces of moderate size into northern European Russia in 1918 to fight the Soviet Red Army. This background of mutual fear and suspicion helps explain (1) why the Soviet-Western alliance during World War II was both politically surprising and awkward in execution, and (2) why most leaders expected renewed disagreement after the war, leaving both sides fearful of losing the Cold War.

the Greek partisans by closing his country's borders with the Soviet Union as part of his dispute with the Soviet dictator Joseph Stalin.

Marshall Plan aid to rebuild the devastated economies of Western Europe was the most important economic component of containment. In his 1947 Harvard University commencement speech, General George C. Marshall, the wartime army chief of staff and briefly Truman's secretary of state and, later, secretary of defense, proposed a policy directed "not against any country or doctrine but against hunger, poverty, desperation, and chaos. Its purpose should be the revival of a working economy in the world so as to permit the emergence of political and social conditions in which free institutions can exist." The plan, however, originated as much with Truman as with its namesake. Both leaders—and many others—shared the belief that economic recovery in Western Europe was critical to forestall the possibility of communist governments coming to power through free elections, notably in France and Italy, by promising a more effective formula for recovery. Aid was front-loaded to begin at roughly $5 billion the first year and ensure decreasing amounts thereafter. Over $18 billion was distributed over several years, a huge sum for that period. Formally, aid was offered to all European states, including the USSR. The terms were intentionally unpalatable, however, so that the Soviets declined and the Eastern European states declined under Soviet orders. The USSR organized the Council on Mutual Economic Assistance (CEMA) within Eastern Europe early in 1949 as a counter to the Marshall Plan. Aid distributed under the plan achieved everything its proponents could have hoped, contributing decisively to economic and political recovery across Western Europe. That unprecedented economic commitment by the United States deviated just as decisively in the economic sphere from interwar nonalignment as the Truman Doctrine had in the political-military sphere.

During this same period United States and Western European dedication to containment was tested, and the methods to be used in its support were refined, by the first in a long series of German crises. Both Germany and its capital, Berlin, had been divided by the victorious allies into British, French, Soviet, and U.S. zones of occupation (see Figure 2.1). Berlin lay some 90 miles within the Soviet zone, necessitating agreement on corridors for air and land access to the capital's western zones. Those land routes, however, were not guaranteed in the Potsdam Agreement or by the Allied Control Council. As early as 1946, the three western zones of Germany began to be merged administratively, beginning with U.S.-British agreement to combine their zones of occupation. With Cold War tensions growing, the Soviets refused to consider a Western proposal for a four-power agreement to manage Berlin and insisted that Soviet currency be used throughout the city. The United States, France, and Britain rejected the Soviet demand and initiated currency reform in West Berlin on 23 June 1948. On the following day the Soviets clamped a total blockade on all land traffic between Berlin and West Germany. General belief held that the Soviets aimed at nothing less than forcing complete Western withdrawal from Berlin. Rather than risk escalation to major war by a direct military challenge to reopen the land routes, the United States organized and led a Berlin airlift to supply needed food and fuel. No Soviet challenge to the airlift ever developed, probably because few people believed it would be possible to maintain 2.1 million West Berliners by flying in food and coal for winter heating in DC-3s. Yet the airlift succeeded over 321 days, and eventually the Soviets relented and allowed resumption of land traffic. This experience was important and formative for U.S. containment policy. It demonstrated a willingness to devote substantial resources over an extended time to confronting and containing

Soviet expansion, while seeking to avoid triggering a major war. Very significantly for future East-West relations in Europe, it also demonstrated tacit Western recognition of a continuing Soviet sphere of influence in Eastern and Central Europe.

Indeed, both sides were developing and hardening their positions into the protracted divisions we would see for four more decades. In April 1949, some three months before the end of the Berlin airlift, the North Atlantic Treaty was signed by foreign ministers of the United States, Belgium, Canada, Denmark, France, Great Britain, Iceland, Italy, Luxembourg, the Netherlands, Norway, and Portugal. By this mutual defense treaty, the signatories obligated themselves to settle disputes by peaceful means, rearm, and develop their individual and collective capacity to resist armed attack. They also agreed that an attack on any of them would be considered an attack on all, calling for individual or collective resistance under Article 51 of the UN charter. A North Atlantic Treaty Organization (NATO), headed by a council of ministers, was established to integrate defense policies. The treaty was ratified 82–13 by the U.S. Senate on 21 July, and went into effect the following month. Before the end of the Cold War, membership eventually would be extended to include (West) Germany, Greece, Spain, and Turkey. To counter NATO, the Soviets organized a Warsaw Treaty Organization with the Eastern European states in 1955, the same year West Germany was admitted to NATO membership. The NATO alliance would be central to U.S. Cold War policy and was the most lasting and successful of a series of collective defense agreements organized to bind states all around the periphery of the Soviet bloc. NATO would live on as a broader regional security organization after the end of the Cold War, extending loose ties to Russia and membership to some Eastern European states.

Many additional developments during the late 1940s were consistent with, and helped drive, the emergence of containment policy and the division of the world into Soviet and U.S. blocs. By means of a 25 February 1948 coup d'état in Czechoslovakia, the Soviet Union consolidated its political and military control of Eastern Europe. In 1949 the Soviets shocked most people in the West by secretly exploding their first nuclear bomb. The brief period of U.S. nuclear monopoly, never exploited because very few bombs or nuclear-capable bombers were built before the 1950s, was already over. In 1945 General Leslie Groves, army commander of the wartime Manhattan Project that produced the first U.S. nuclear weapons, had predicted it would take the Soviet Union twenty years to duplicate that accomplishment. Scientists knew better. Half what the Soviets needed to know came from the simple fact that U.S. nuclear bombs worked. Part of the second half came from espionage, a fact that helped fuel anti-Soviet paranoia in the 1950s.

Second only to fears of conflict with the Soviets were concerns about China. Chinese communists expelled from the Kuomingtang (Nationalists) in a bloody purge in the late 1920s began a guerrilla war that was to last thirty years. The two sides nominally made common cause against Japanese invaders during the 1930s, but actually devoted greater effort to strengthening foundations for their post–World War II power. The United States aided China's fight against the Japanese, but full-scale civil war resumed after Japan's 1945 defeat. Abundant evidence exists that the Nationalist Chinese government was thoroughly corrupt and unable to win the people's loyalty. High-level American investigative missions concluded during the late 1940s that the United States could do very little to affect the outcome of the Chinese civil war. In 1949 the communists won and proclaimed the Chinese People's Republic in Beijing on 1 October. The Nationalists moved the seat of their government to Taiwan in December 1949. By April 1950, the last pockets of

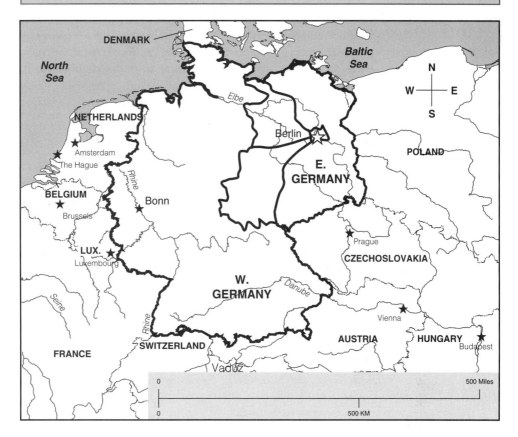

FIGURE 2.1

Occupation Zones in Germany After World War II and Access Routes to Berlin

Nationalist resistance on the mainland were wiped out. The stage was now set for decades of confrontation between the two Chinas. America usually took the side of the Nationalists (Taiwan), and there were continuing fears of open warfare that could involve the United States.

THE 1950S: U.S. WORLD LEADERSHIP, NSC-68, AND THE KOREAN WAR

Cold War divisions and the essential groundwork for containment were well established by 1950. The capstone of those developments came in April 1950 when the Truman administration adopted a key National Security Council strategic planning document designated NSC-68. Drafted primarily by Paul Nitze as head of the State Department Policy Planning Staff, NSC-68 established the framework for military buildup and the primarily military containment of the Soviet Union for decades to come. This was grand policy of a very high order. Although details were implied in legislation brought forward over time by the administration, NSC-68 remained a highly **classified document** (access was restricted to those officially believed to have a "need to know") until 1975 and even its existence was not officially acknowledged. Those privileged to see NSC-68 were instructed with particular emphasis that it "be handled with special security precautions in accordance with the President's desire that no publicity be given this report or its contents without his approval."

Very few planning documents result from as broad a policy review, recommend policy of such grand scope, or have such great and prolonged impact as NSC-68. (The rarity of such events is more fully explored in Part II, especially Chapter 6.) This rather lengthy document begins by contrasting U.S. and Soviet foreign policy goals in harsh terms and tracing the then-current crisis in international relations to the incompatibility of those goals.

> The Kremlin regards the United States as the only major threat to the achievement of its fundamental design. There is a basic conflict between the idea of freedom under a government of law, and the idea of slavery under the grim oligarchy of the Kremlin. . . . The implacable purpose of the slave state to eliminate the challenge of freedom has placed the two great powers at opposite poles. It is this fact which gives the present polarization of power the quality of crisis. . . . The assault on free institutions is world-wide now, and in the context of the present polarization of power a defeat of free institutions anywhere is a defeat everywhere . . .
>
> **(NSC, 1950, 5–9)**

The authors of NSC-68 analyzed four very different grand policy options for dealing with the Soviet threat, as follows: (1) continue existing policies, which, as we have seen, already had launched containment; (2) return to pre–World War II nonalignment; (3) end the Soviet threat by making war against the USSR; and (4) begin "a rapid buildup of political, economic and military strength in the Free World" (NSC, 1950, 54). They recommended option 4 and, implicitly, option 1, stating that "the frustration of the Kremlin design requires the free world to develop a successfully functioning political and economic system and a vigorous political offensive against the Soviet Union" (NSC, 1950, 54). This recommendation was hardly surprising, if seen in light of earlier statements in the report, notably including the following:

> In a shrinking world, which now faces the threat of atomic warfare, it is not an adequate objective merely to seek to check the Kremlin design. . . . This fact imposes upon us, in our own interests, the responsibility of world leadership. . . . Coupled with the probable fission bomb capability and possible thermonuclear bomb capability of the Soviet Union, the intensifying struggle requires us to face the fact that we can expect no lasting abatement of the crisis unless and until a change occurs in the nature of the Soviet system.
>
> **(NSC, 1950, 8–9)**

Note that the first sentence asserts containment is not sufficient, even though in his 1947 "X" article Kennan asserted that containment would ultimately cause the Soviet system to fail. Kennan and Paul Nitze, the principal author of NSC-68, were to clash over other issues, with Nitze typically taking harder policy lines.

Although it was to remain classified for a quarter century, NSC-68 had tremendous impact on U.S. foreign policy. First, given added impetus by North Korea's invasion of South Korea barely over two months after NSC-68 was completed, it effectively made defense spending the top priority in U.S. government budgeting. This was a major reversal from the demobilization push that began immediately after victory in World War II. In real dollar terms, the U.S. defense budget was tripled over two years and roughly stabilized for decades. Second, NSC-68 led to a major buildup of American nuclear (atomic) and thermonuclear (hydrogen) weapons. In the body of the report, although not in its labeled recommendations, was a call for the United States to "produce and stockpile thermonuclear weapons in the event they prove feasible and would add significantly to our net capability" (NSC, 1950, 39). The United States exploded its first nuclear weapons in 1945 and was shocked when the Soviets followed in 1949. Scientists correctly believed it was possible to build thermonuclear weapons that would be far more powerful, and a debate was underway within the Truman administration over whether the United States should proceed with hydrogen bomb research and development. This was yet another issue over which Kennan and Nitze differed, and Nitze's harder line prevailed. The first U.S. thermonuclear device was exploded in 1954.

The third major impact of NSC-68 occurred at home and emphasized the intermestic character of U.S. foreign policy. In calling for the United States and its allies to develop "a successfully functioning political and economic system and a vigorous political offensive against the Soviet Union," the authors went beyond previous speeches and writings about containment to demand a societywide response that would "assure the internal security of the United States against dangers of sabotage, subversion, and espionage." Some analysts (for example, Bliss and Johnson, 1975) argued that desires for internal security extinguished debate over foreign policy because critics of government policy feared being labeled communists. Domestic paranoia culminated during the early 1950s in the McCarthy era (named for Senator Joseph McCarthy, R-Wisc.) of domestic witch-hunts for clandestine communists in government and the arts. In part, those excesses were driven by disillusionment that the great war so recently concluded had not produced a safe new world order and a lasting peace. Political conservatives sought to determine who was responsible for "losing" China to the communists. The domestic search for spies and subversives was heightened by reports, at least partly true, that Soviet espionage had played a role in their nuclear weapons program. Because the United States had won the Second World War so decisively and emerged more powerful than any other state, it was easy for Americans to believe that major postwar problems must result from some sort of betrayal. In reality, as we see in more detail in later chapters, those problems resulted partly from policy mistakes and largely from forces beyond U.S. control.

Fear of communism also contributed to the defense buildup. Because communist official dogma called for world revolution aided by external force, many people feared that at some moment of opportunity massed waves of Soviet nuclear bombers would sweep over the North Pole to attack the U.S. mainland. In actuality, the Soviets never built more than about 200 nuclear-capable intercontinental bombers, while the U.S. bomber arsenal peaked at more than 1,600 in 1958. Only well into the missile age, by the early 1970s, would the Soviets gain the capability to do as much damage to the United

States as could be done to them. Realization of their mutual capability and vulnerability to devastation would then lead both sides to seek stabilizing arms control agreements. In the 1950s and 1960s, however, political thinking was dominated by confrontation, division, fear, and the demands of containment.

Despite widespread fears of the Soviet Union, during the 1950s the United States clearly outmatched the USSR on almost every measure of economic, political, and military power. The United States was the greatest economic power in the world, an essential supporting force behind Western European and Japanese recovery, leader of the dominant voting bloc in the UN, and the virtually undisputed leader of the Western alliance. It is an interesting irony of history and a demonstration of the transitory nature of alliances that within a decade of leading the alliance which had defeated Germany and Japan in World War II and demanded unconditional surrender, the United States promoted the economic recovery, political independence, and limited rearming of both those states. Although Germany was to have no nuclear weapons and Japan's new military capabilities were to be limited and strictly defensive, both became important members of alliances against the new foe.

An unexpected challenge to containment was the outbreak of war on the Korean peninsula in 1950. Korea had been occupied by Japan during World War II and never saw Allied military operations. After Japan's 1945 surrender, the 38th parallel, which roughly divides the peninsula in half, was used as a convenient administrative demarcation point. The United States occupied the south and took the surrender of Japanese forces below the 38th parallel, and the Soviet Union, which had entered the war against Japan only weeks before, occupied the north and took the surrender of Japanese forces north of the 38th parallel. Agreements to create a unified and independent Korea soon fell victim to rising Cold War tensions, just as similar agreements did in Germany and Eastern Europe. By the end of 1948, a Soviet-backed People's Democratic Republic of Korea had been proclaimed in the north, and a U.S.-backed Republic of Korea in the south. These divisions are shown in Figure 2.2 on page 70. North Korea claimed jurisdiction over all Korea; South Korea claimed to be democratic. In a speech on 12 January 1949, Secretary of State Dean Acheson declared that South Korea would be expected to defend itself, backed by "the commitment of the entire civilized world" under the UN charter. Withdrawal of U.S. military forces from Korea was completed in June 1949.

Whether Acheson's speech and the withdrawal of U.S. forces were taken as signals that the United States was not firmly committed to Korean defense is still debated. So are the questions of whether and how strongly the USSR encouraged North Korean aggression. But there is no disputing the fact that massive North Korean forces equipped with Soviet weapons invaded South Korea on 25 June 1950. Two days later an emergency session of the UN Security Council demanded an immediate cease-fire and North Korean withdrawal, and called on UN member governments to "furnish such assistance to the Republic of Korea as may be necessary to repel the armed attack and restore international peace and security in the area." President Truman ordered U.S. air and naval forces into Korea that same day, and land forces three days later. The United States provided the top commanders and the bulk of the UN forces that were to wage the Korean War over the next three years. This was the only major instance in which the United Nations was to take sides in a Cold War dispute between the United States and the Soviets. That choice was made possible in part by U.S. domination of UN voting at that time, and specifically by Soviet absence from the critical Security Council meeting. Soviet delegates were boycotting Security Council meetings to protest UN refusal to recognize the People's Republic of China as entitled to the Chinese permanent (and veto-wielding) seat on the Security Council. Their absence prevented the Soviets from vetoing UN action in Korea, a mistake they would not repeat.

The Korean War was fought in four distinct phases over three years. Along the way, major questions were raised about whether the war goal was to be containment or rollback of communist expansion, and whether the U.S. polity could deal with limited war. Phase 1 was the attempt of UN forces, primarily those of South Korea (ROK) and the United States, to halt the North Korean advance. Lasting from the 25 June attack until 15 September 1950, this phase was nearly lost by the defenders. Their forces were driven down the Korean peninsula into a perimeter of about a 50-mile radius centered on the southeastern port city of Pusan, where they barely sustained a five-week siege. War goals at this time were simply to avoid being overrun, then reverse the North Korean aggression and return to the status quo antebellum, the prewar condition. Phase 2 was a massive UN assault that dramatically turned the tide of battle. In a brilliant but very risky move, UN forces under the command of U.S. General Douglas MacArthur made an amphibious landing at Inchon on the west coast of South Korea on 15 September. Sweeping eastward, they recaptured Seoul in eleven days, cut the North Korean supply lines, and linked up with forces breaking out northward from the Pusan perimeter. North Korean resistance was decimated. MacArthur's UN forces moved north, crossing the 38th parallel on 11 October and capturing the North Korean capital of Pyongyang on 20 October.

Although the shift was not acknowledged, effective war goals had changed. The option of stopping at the 38th parallel had already been bypassed. Another option was to halt and establish a defensive line across the narrowest part of the peninsula, slightly north of Pyongyang. This second option also was quickly dismissed. By continuing northward, UN forces sought to conquer all of North Korea and reunify the country by force, a mirror image of North Korea's initial war goal. Unfortunately, Korea's northern neighbor was the People's Republic of China, whose government had no intention of sharing a border with a U.S.-dominated Korean republic. Chinese warnings from as early as 30 September were widely disregarded in the West. Phase 3 of the Korean War began on 26 October, when Chinese divisions crossed their Yalu River border. A month later they opened a massive counteroffensive against UN troops in the Yalu valley, driving them back to the general vicinity of the 38th parallel in little more than a month. Phase 4 was a war of attrition with relatively little movement, lasting until mid-1953. Armistice negotiations were conducted from 10 July 1951 until 26 July 1953, yielding a truce line angling across the 38th parallel, producing a slight territorial gain for South Korea. No peace has ever been signed. The armistice line remains tense and highly militarized, with periodic armed clashes and recurrent fears of a major North Korean attack. Those fears were heightened when a 1993 U.S. National Intelligence Estimate credited North Korea with possessing two nuclear weapons.

A firm U.S. response in Korea was believed essential to the credibility of containment, and had many other consequences that hardened Cold War divisions between East and West. CIA reports declassified in 1993 reveal estimates that the Nationalist Chinese regime on Taiwan would fall to the communists during 1950, and historians now hold that the Truman administration had been preparing to extend diplomatic recognition to

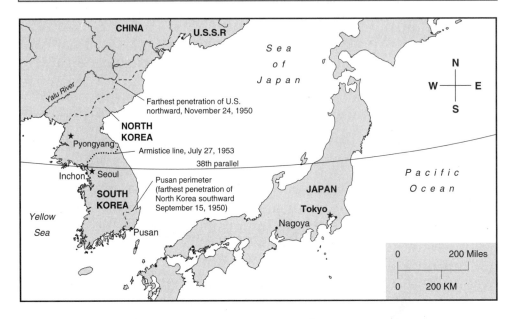

FIGURE 2.2

Korea: Post–World War II Political and Military Divisions

Beijing later that year (Mann, 1993). Recent Chinese scholarly writings assert that Beijing was not prepared to invade Taiwan before 1951. None of these developments were to come to pass, however; with the outbreak of hostilities in Korea, President Truman ordered the U.S. Seventh Fleet to interpose itself in the straits between Taiwan and the mainland to prevent attack by either side. The United States would establish no diplomatic ties with Beijing until 1972, with full diplomatic relations beginning in 1979. American actions in the Korean War are consistent with at least three of the viewpoints introduced in Chapter 1: *countering aggression* of North Korea against the South, *protecting clients* in South Korea and Taiwan, and *pressuring clients* in Taiwan.

The Korean War was the most intense battle in support of containment during the 1950s, and it raised serious problems in the United States about political management of the conflict. **Limited war** may be limited in any or all of the following: goals, area of military operations, amount of force used, and types of military force and weaponry employed. Such limitations were almost never factors in the two world wars, and were unfamiliar to most citizens and many political leaders in the United States. Yet all applied to the Korean War. Except for the brief period of phase 2, war goals were simply to ensure the survival of a pro-Western South Korea. Despite occasional conservative political rhetoric about "rolling back the Iron Curtain," U.S. experience in Korea demonstrated that no such rollback was ever likely to be accomplished by force. The area of military operations was limited to the Korean peninsula and the surrounding waters. Although it was clear that Chinese soldiers and Soviet military supplies flowed across the Chinese-North Korean border, most leaders did not want to risk a much bigger war with China by allowing such actions as the bombing of targets in China. Although newer technologies such as jet fighter aircraft played some role, most of the weaponry and tactics derived from the Second World War. Use of nuclear weapons was never very seriously contemplated. The primary reason, little appreciated by the public, was that the West possessed very few nuclear weapons when war broke out in Korea, and Western leaders believed those weapons had to be reserved to defend Western Europe against possible Soviet attack. Many years later, reports surfaced that during his early 1953 visit to Korea, between his election and inauguration as president, retired general Dwight Eisenhower threatened that nuclear weapons would be used if an armistice was not reached soon.

Nonetheless, the entire war in Korea remained limited in many significant respects. By the time massive Chinese forces intervened to begin phase 3, U.S. public dissatisfaction and leadership disputes over those limitations were major problems. President Truman paid a high political price for removing General MacArthur from command in April 1951, although he had little choice if he was to be the real commander in chief. Despite numerous warnings, MacArthur had continued to challenge or ignore policy guidance from Washington, and he had threatened direct air and naval attacks against China. The Korean War period demonstrated that limited war activated inherent tensions in the U.S. political system over the goals, the means, and the conduct of foreign policy. Some of those tensions are captured in the *president versus Congress* viewpoint. Others exist between the administration and military professionals, and between the public and political leaders, as captured by the *domestic policy dynamics* viewpoint. Beginning little more than a decade later, those same tensions would be seen even more intensely during the Vietnam War. Arguably, managing the response to North Korea's aggression through UN collective security procedures reflected a version of the *new world order* viewpoint appropriate to the early Cold War.

An important manifestation of Cold War fears and East-West competition was missile and space exploration races that began in the late 1950s. Nuclear buildup had led to development of missiles capable of delivering thermonuclear warheads over long distances. Early intermediate-range ballistic missiles (IRBMs) of about 1,500-mile range became operational in the late 1950s, and the first intercontinental ballistic missiles (ICBMs) of up to 5,000-mile range became operational by 1960. An important spinoff from such military programs was rockets capable of launching artificial earth satellites. Today we take hundreds of such satellites for granted, but in the 1950s they became yet another venue for U.S.-Soviet competition. The United States announced plans to launch the first such satellite during the 1957–58 International Geophysical Year. To emphasize the peaceful nature of the program, the political decision was made to utilize a new Vanguard rocket developed outside the military programs. So the world was shocked when, on 4 October 1957, the Soviets announced they had beaten Vanguard and the United States by launching their much larger and heavier Sputnik I satellite. This implied that the Soviets could compete seriously with the United States, and their military missiles could launch heavier warheads. Shock in the American heartland was indicated by newspaper headlines like that in the *Detroit News*, which heralded RED MOON OVER U.S. in 6-inch-high capitals. Fear that the United States really might be falling behind the Soviets led to such reactions as calls for fundamental reforms in education to produce more and better engineers and scientists.

In the 1960 Kennedy-Nixon presidential race, Democrat Kennedy had considerable success by charging the Republican Eisenhower administration, in which Nixon was vice president, with having allowed a "missile gap" to develop, leaving the USSR ahead of the United States in ICBM deployments. Years later we learned that in 1960 an ICBM gap indeed existed—but like the bomber gap of the 1950s, it was in favor of the United States, although the Soviets had more IRBMs. Another and more lasting segment of this high-tech political-military competition for global influence was the race to land the first humans on the moon. Early in his administration (1961–63), President Kennedy persuaded Congress to adopt the goal of landing a man on the moon and returning him safely to earth by 1970. That first landing occurred 20 June 1969, but up to the last moment there were fears that the Soviets would pull another upset surprise. The lunar landing goal was chosen for its very high political salience; sending people to the moon long had been used as a stereotype for a very difficult far-in-the-future, high-technology task. Whatever state succeeded first would gain tremendous prestige. Years later, after the end of the Cold War, we learned that the Soviets had dropped out about halfway through the moon race, partly because of the death of their chief space scientist, but primarily because America could outspend them.

THE 1960s: THE COST OF SUCCESS AND THE VIETNAM WAR

By the beginning of the 1960s, many of the developments set in motion in the first years after World War II were coming to fruition. While America's absolute military power grew, its relative economic and political standing began to decline. U.S. policy had strongly encouraged the growth of strong and secure states in Western Europe and Japan, and we were now called on to begin paying the price of success. With the reestablishment of other major powers, U.S. dominance was unavoidably diminished, and with it the ability to control virtually all aspects of policy in the Western alliance. Western European economies had rebuilt decisively and were booming. A European Economic Community, formed in 1958 with U.S. encouragement, was beginning to coordinate trade policy for the six major continental powers. Numerous analysts had called the 1950s the "American decade," but the same could not be said of the 1960s. Some trade disputes appeared by the early 1960s as the United States and Europe argued over trade barriers such as those that kept U.S. chickens out of French markets. As Soviet and American nuclear arsenals continued to grow, the ability of the United States to launch a nuclear attack against the Soviets without suffering a devastating retaliation steadily eroded. Consequently, the credibility of a U.S. "nuclear umbrella" deterring the Soviets from attacking Western Europe declined as it became less and less believable that the United States would risk a Soviet attack on New York to avenge an attack on Paris. Under President Charles de Gaulle, the French launched a massive program in the early 1960s to develop their own independent nuclear *force de frappe*, or strike force. Over half of all French research and development expenditure for several years was invested in that effort. In 1966 France announced its nearly total withdrawal from NATO military affairs, and the following year NATO headquarters were moved from Paris to Brussels.

Other developments also reduced U.S. world dominance. Most of the great colonial empires that had existed at the onset of World War II, especially those of Britain and France, were being dismantled. Large numbers of former colonies were becoming independent states, most notably in Africa. Part of the effort by former ruling states to maintain good political relations included sponsoring early admission of such new states to the

UN. The result, as the number of independent states tripled within two decades, was rapid growth in the number of UN member states and a fundamental shift in voting blocs in the General Assembly. In the early years after World War II, most UN members were friends or allies of the United States. Now the largest group was nonaligned developing states. Their governments began to see common causes and vote together on development issues that had little relation to the Cold War agendas of the more highly developed powers.

A partial turning point in U.S.-Soviet confrontation occurred with the October 1962 Cuban missile crisis. Most analysts agree that it represents the high-water mark of superpower nuclear war risk, but it soon was followed by the first serious steps toward superpower arms control. These included the 1963 Limited Nuclear Test Ban Treaty and the first agreement to establish a Washington-Moscow "hot line" to help defuse potential crises by keeping top-level communications open. The missile crisis began quietly in mid-October 1962 when U.S. reconnaissance aircraft discovered evidence that the Soviets were building intermediate-range ballistic missile (IRBM) bases in Cuba. Once operational, those missiles would be capable of hitting most of the United States with thermonuclear warheads. Coming early in the age of intercontinental missiles, this move threatened to establish rough U.S.-Soviet nuclear parity by placing the United States under approximately the same risk of missile attack as the Soviet Union, a decade before the United States implicitly accepted such nuclear parity under the 1972 SALT I strategic arms control agreements. The Soviets believed, correctly, that a United States equally at nuclear risk with themselves would be less adventurous around the world and less likely to confront the Soviet Union. Thus introducing missiles into Cuba promised the Soviets major strategic benefits. U.S. domestic political considerations were at least equally serious. Responding to Republican attacks, President Kennedy previously had gone on record that Soviet weapons in Cuba were purely defensive. He perceived that Soviet leader Nikita Krushchev had deliberately lied to him in private assurances that the USSR would not introduce offensive weapons into Cuba, knowing the domestic U.S. political consequences.

Once missiles capable of attacking the U.S. mainland were discovered in Cuba, President Kennedy had to take strong action or be politically dead with both the electorate, gearing up for midterm elections in less than a month, and the permanent bureaucracy. The Soviets argued the Cuban missiles were defensive, intended only to deter U.S. attacks on Cuba (although the announcement came only after the United States revealed the missiles' presence) but could not deny the missiles also could be used against the United States. Key administration and congressional leaders urged an immediate military strike, but Attorney General Robert Kennedy feared it would be perceived abroad as a "Pearl Harbor in reverse." The compromise between the need for immediate strong action and fears about global perceptions of overreaction was to announce the discovery of the missiles and promptly impose a naval blockade. President Kennedy threatened stronger action soon if the missiles were not removed, and he promised that any missile launched from Cuba would require a full nuclear response against the Soviet Union. Plans went forward for a "surgical" air strike against the missiles, but so did diplomatic efforts through multiple channels. Acting so close to its own shores, the United States had many more military options short of nuclear war than the Soviets did. Both sides moved carefully, and an agreement for removal of the missiles was reached only two days before the planned air strike. The United States made a few little-publicized concessions, but the incident weakened Krushchev's power base, contributing to his 1964 ouster. Widespread concern about how close the two superpowers had come to nuclear war soon helped motivate their first limited steps in nuclear arms control, although their arsenals would continue to grow in destructive power until nearly the end of the Cold War.

By the mid-1960s, the Vietnam War joined long-term world political and economic shifts in reducing U.S. global influence and even strained relations with many of America's European allies. Like the Korean War, the Vietnam conflict raised problems about managing limited war, dealing with guerrilla sanctuaries in neighbor states, and achieving clarity about war objectives. Once again we faced questions about whether containment required opposing every possible communist gain for fear that a "domino effect" would spread communism to neighbor after neighbor. Colonial French Indochina was occupied by Japan in 1940, and France attempted to reassert control after Japan's defeat in 1945. But the same communist guerrilla forces that had battled the Japanese occupation turned to driving out the French, finally administering a major defeat at Dienbienphu in 1954. A cease-fire accord divided the country at the 17th parallel, provided for French withdrawal and free elections to determine the country's future governance, and gave control in the north to the communists under Ho Chi Minh. Like the Cold War partitions of Germany and Korea, however, the partition of Vietnam led to two governments, one communist and the other Western and arguably democratic. Fighting in South Vietnam began as early as 1956, with the communist Vietcong aided by North Vietnam and arms from China and the Soviet Union. Large northern army forces were stationed in neighboring areas of Cambodia and Laos, which provided routes for supplies to be smuggled into the South. Fearing that a communist victory would spread from South Vietnam into neighboring states, the United States began gradually escalated support of the South Vietnamese war effort. Military trainers and advisers in the early 1960s were followed by air strikes against North Vietnam in 1964 and a major ground combatant buildup in 1965, peaking at over half a million troops by 1968.

The Vietnam War produced intense political divisions within both the United States and the Western alliance. All the problems of managing limited war that had been so divisive at the time of the Korean War returned even more intensely. War goals were never very clear. Official statements of goals varied from ensuring a democratic Western-oriented South Vietnam, to simply ensuring that the people of the South were allowed to choose their political future. Despite pious declarations about seeking to "win the hearts and minds of the people," the U.S. and South Vietnamese forces never succeeded. Indeed, rural peasants had real grievances against the South Vietnamese government because Vietcong troops extracted lower rice rents than absentee landlords in Saigon. The war effort often relied on uprooting and resettling the peasants to protect them, and destroying the countryside to liberate it. U.S. troops would drive Vietcong forces out of an area only to withdraw and turn it back over to them. News media at home were filled with grisly pictures of civilians burned by napalm bombings. No real progress toward a conclusion of the war could be demonstrated. During the Tet season early in 1968, a major offensive accomplished the Vietcong's paramount political objective by demonstrating that they could not easily be defeated. Given the resulting widespread negative shifts in expectations, U.S. policy turned from buildup and escalation to winding down the war effort and withdrawing from Vietnam. The war would eventually cost the United States alone over 47,000 battle deaths, plus 10,800 "other" deaths. A steadily rising toll of battle without clearly visible progress contributed to a slow shift of domestic public opinion from majority support to majority opposition, with bitter divisions.

THE 1970s: "CONSENSUS" FRACTURES, THE LIMITS OF POWER, AND DÉTENTE

By around 1970, the strong apparent domestic consensus on internationalism after World War II was fractured by many developments, but none more important than the Vietnam War. For conservatives, our involvement in Vietnam had done little to maintain capitalism and democracy. Only the most extreme argued that greater force would win in the end. For liberals, U.S. Vietnam policy was seen not as building a just and equitable order, but as supporting a succession of corrupt dictators and using war tactics that caused tremendous loss of civilian life. By 1972 more Americans supported either withdrawal or greater use of force than continuing administration policy in Vietnam.

Many longtime allies had rejected U.S. policy well before the Vietcong's 1968 Tet offensive. America could no longer dominate Western policy about matters that the allies did not believe vital to their own security. Believing American positions on Vietnam to have been confused and hopeless, they became more willing to question the judgment of the U.S. government in other areas of endeavor. Following years of negotiations, a Vietnam cease-fire was signed in Paris on 27 January 1973. That agreement was fatally flawed by establishing a truce violation commission with equal numbers of communist and noncommunist members and was never effectively implemented, but it gave the Americans a slightly face-saving way out. War continued, however, with the final surrender of the Saigon government coming on 30 April 1975. Those who had questioned U.S. policy on Vietnam, whether friend or foe on other issues, now felt vindicated. Abroad, it was easier to challenge U.S. positions. At home, Americans became almost obsessed with concerns over the limits of political and military power. The Senate took a stand in 1975 that would have been unthinkable a decade earlier, bending over backward to avoid committing military forces to aid the allegedly anticommunist side in the Angolan civil war. Containment now had real limits.

Simultaneously, the United States faced important limits at home, further constraining its foreign commitments and relations. Maintaining large domestic programs without tax increases, while spending additional billions on the Vietnam War, had produced almost unprecedented double-digit inflation. Years of massive foreign economic and military aid had promoted recovery and development in Western Europe and Japan, partly by allowing them to limit their defense burdens. Now those states had become effective competitors to the United States in many markets. Consider the steel industry, long a hallmark of heavy industrialization, as an example. By 1960 steel producers in the United States had begun to suffer from competition with European firms that had all new, post–World War II plants far more efficient than their older counterparts in this country. Today most of the former steel plants in the northeastern United States are closed, giving the region the nickname of the "rust belt." The dominant producers of steel used in the western United States are located in South Korea, which had no such industry at the time of the Korean War.

Other U.S. economic problems also became evident in the early 1970s. Since 1933, the U.S. government had backed its currency by promising to redeem dollars with gold at the fixed rate of $35 per ounce. This practice and the sheer size of the American economy, particularly after World War II, allowed the dollar to be the standard against which all international currency exchanges were made. But decades of selling gold at $35 per ounce had substantially depleted gold reserves, and by 1971 the U.S. government was forced to allow the price of gold to float. (For a fuller discussion, see Chapter 11.) In the fall of 1971, faced with serious public concern about domestic inflation, the Nixon administration imposed wage and price controls (which were conveniently removed before the fall 1972 election) and, without warning, imposed a temporary 10 percent surcharge on all imports. Allies were concerned both about American troubles and U.S. failure to consult them in advance, a difficulty also seen in the diplomatic sphere.

The early 1970s saw important new diplomatic moves by the United States. Another Nixon surprise in the fall of 1971 was the announcement that the president would travel to Beijing early in 1972, ending years without formal contact by extending de facto diplomatic recognition to the People's Republic of China. The Japanese government, which for years had loyally followed the United States in refusing to recognize the People's Republic, was not consulted about this reversal—a slight not easily forgiven. On a more optimistic note, April 1972 saw Nixon travel to Moscow for a summit meeting at which the first Strategic Arms Limitation Talks (SALT I) agreements were signed. SALT I set the first caps on the central strategic nuclear weapons systems of the superpowers. The agreements implied that both sides recognized they had achieved effective rough parity in nuclear capabilities, and established an ongoing regime of institutionalized arms control and limitation which continues to this day. Those agreements were part of a broader policy package called **détente**, after the French term for relaxation of tensions. Other agreements promised consultations to help damp down the potential for conflict escalation elsewhere in the world. Although the superpowers were still serious competitors, their relations had never yet been so cordial.

Seen with more than two decades' additional perspective, it is clear the Soviets sought détente to reduce the terrible economic demands of competing militarily and technologically with the United States. Moreover, the USSR faced other challenges. Although they were communists, the mainland Chinese had rejected Soviet expectations of political control, and in 1960 Soviet aid was terminated and Soviet technicians and advisers pulled out. By the mid-1960s the two countries had fought border skirmishes, and fully one quarter of Soviet military spending went for defenses against the possibility of Chinese attack. Strangely, the West took some time to recognize these developments, which demonstrated that communism was not a monolithic international movement. It did not take nearly so long for the limitations of détente to become manifest. When the 1973 Yom Kippur War broke out between Israel and Egypt, the United States immediately called for a cease-fire. Agreements to consult and limit conflict went by the wayside as the Soviets called for additional Arab states to join in and trounce the nasty Israelis. Only after Israel reversed initial Egyptian gains and threatened to surround the Egyptian Third Army did the Soviets join the United States in calling for a truce. Later reports made it clear the Soviets had threatened Israel with direct intervention. During the remainder of the decade, U.S. relations with the Soviets never returned to their 1972 high. They took a dramatic turn for the worse late in 1979 when the Soviets invaded Afghanistan.

THE 1980S: DEFENSE BUILDUP AND DEBATES OVER THE U.S. WORLD ROLE

U.S.-Soviet relations took a decided downturn in the early 1980s, driven by both external events and domestic politics on both sides. Pro-Soviet leftists had taken power in Afghanistan in a bloody 1978 coup and signed an economic and military treaty with Moscow. Nonetheless, the USSR invaded in 1979 to back a new coup that installed a more strongly pro-Soviet leader. The Soviets were motivated partly by dreams of a year-round warm-water port if they could gain influence in some future revolution in Iran (Afghanistan bordered the USSR on the north and Iran on the south) and partly by fears that Islamic fundamentalism could spread into their heavily Islamic southwestern republics. They encountered prolonged guerrilla war, widely seen as their Vietnam, ending only with a 1988 agreement to withdraw. Throughout that period the United States secretly aided the fundamentalist Islamic guerrillas, who ultimately gained control of most of the country in 1992. The Soviets also faced growing unrest in Eastern Europe. Acting under the so-called Brezhnev Doctrine of the 1970s, which had proclaimed a right to use force to maintain communist regimes in Eastern Europe, the Soviets threatened to invade Poland in 1980 if the Polish government did not impose martial law to stop the Solidarity labor union's demands for democratic reforms. Given the large Polish-American community here, that move also worsened Soviet-U.S. relations.

The year 1980 saw the election of the most conservative Republican president in decades, the former movie actor and California governor Ronald Reagan, ending the troubled four-year administration of Democrat Jimmy Carter. Despite diplomatic triumphs in pushing through the controversial new Panama Canal Treaties in 1978, and in brokering the Camp David agreement that produced a peace treaty between Israel and Egypt after three decades of war, Carter was widely perceived as ineffective. This hinged primarily on two adverse 1979 developments for which the United States had very few good policy options: the Soviet invasion of Afghanistan, and the seizure of American diplomats when a mob encouraged by the fundamentalist Islamic revolutionary government of Iran seized sixty-two American diplomats in the U.S. embassy in Tehran. Reagan campaigned on a platform calling for "supply-side" economics under which tax cuts would stimulate the economy and pay for the tax cuts. Economic stimulus worked to some degree, but new revenues never caught up with the tax cuts and spending increases. Over the next twelve years of supply-side economics under Reagan and his vice president and successor, George Bush, the federal debt quadrupled. This greatly limited the possibility of any later new federal programs.

Reagan also campaigned for a massive defense buildup to end a perceived "window of vulnerability" during which the United States was asserted to be at risk of a Soviet strategic attack. In fact, both superpowers were somewhat vulnerable to a disarming first nuclear strike, but massive technical difficulties probably always made such an attack unfeasible. Nonetheless, Reagan's defense buildups proceeded. One effect was creation of high-technology "smart" weapons that performed fairly decisively in the 1991 Persian Gulf War. The Strategic Defense Initiative (SDI), launched after a surprise 1983 Reagan speech, was particularly controversial. SDI was a many-faceted program to intercept Soviet nuclear missiles and their warheads in flight, perhaps in part through use of space-based interceptors, and was dubbed "Star Wars" by supporters and opponents alike. Even a decade after SDI's initiation, there were major doubts that much of what had been proposed was technically feasible, and many goals had to be scaled back. However, Reagan's defense buildup in general and SDI in particular had deeply alarmed the Soviets, who knew they could not afford to compete. Reports during the 1990s suggested this was all part of a program to win the Cold War by outspending the Soviets, arguably a conclusive demonstration of the superiority of a market economy.

Reagan's campaign rhetoric and official statements called for renewal and a resurgence of U.S. capabilities that would end years of obsession with the limits of power. As is usually the case in Washington, of course, rhetoric somewhat overstated performance. The Reagan-Bush years saw military incursions into Grenada in 1983, as discussed previously, and Panama in 1989. U.S. action in Panama removed a recalcitrant General Manuel Noriega, head of the Panama Defense Forces, from effective dictatorial rule. Noriega was captured, brought to the United States, imprisoned, tried, and convicted of drug trafficking. Later reports made it clear that Noriega had once been a client of the CIA, raising questions about whether our own earlier actions had created a later policy problem. Once again, as so often before in history, a U.S. administration engaged in hemispheric intervention, although there was greater attention to explaining and selling the actions at home and abroad. Both the Grenada and Panama incursions were instances of *low intensity conflict* (LIC; see Chapter 9) for clearly defined and limited objectives, and were interpreted by the administration as successes. LIC typically is characterized by forces limited but sufficient to achieve overwhelming local superiority, used briefly to achieve limited objectives, ideally with low casualties and a quick, decisive result. The amount of attention devoted to LIC in U.S. military thinking during the 1980s, however, suggests the preoccupation with the limits of power that had begun with the Vietnam War still prevailed. Only with the 1991 Persian Gulf War would it be asserted that the Vietnam malaise was ended.

THE 1990S: END OF THE COLD WAR AND BEGINNING OF A NEW WORLD (DIS)ORDER

The key events marking the end of the Cold War began in the mid-1980s and culminated in the breakup of the Soviet Union at the end of 1991. They are summarized in Chronology 2.3. In 1985 Mikhail Gorbachev, youngest member of the ruling Politburo, was chosen general secretary of the Soviet Communist Party, making him the effective head of government and the most powerful single leader in the USSR. Like all Soviet leaders, Gorbachev had risen through Communist Party ranks, the only route to political power since 1917, but he represented a new generation that had matured after the Second World War. After a fairly typical period of consolidating his position, Gorbachev launched a broad set of political and economic reforms in 1987. Those reforms were summarized by their Russian labels: (1) *glasnost* (openness), meaning democratization and expanded freedom to participate in the political process and criticize government, and (2) *perestroika* (restructuring), meaning economic reform through marketlike mechanisms designed to overcome chronic shortages and inefficiencies. The Soviet central-command economic system had depended on massive grain imports for years and was never able to meet many consumer needs. Consider this sign of economic failure: typical Soviet citizens had to wait in queues (lines) for 1,200 or more hours every year simply to purchase

⊕ CHRONOLOGY 2.3

Key Events in the Ending of the Cold War

1985

March — Mikhail Gorbachev chosen Soviet Communist Party general secretary, the most powerful Soviet leadership position.

1987 — Gorbachev initiates a program of economic and political reforms, with expanded freedoms and democratization of the political process, through *glasnost* (openness) and *perestroika* (restructuring).

1989 — First Soviet Parliament since 1918 meets. Although it is still dominated by conservative communists, opponents of government policy have unprecedented freedom to criticize.

Communist leaders and governments are weakened or overthrown in Bulgaria, Czechoslovakia, East Germany, Hungary, and Romania.

4 January — Democratic Solidarity trade unionists sweep the Polish elections, establish a government committed to rapid and radical free market restructuring.

9 November — The Berlin Wall, long a symbol of East-West divisions, is opened. East Germans are now free to travel to the West.

1990 — Bulgaria's communist government falls.

Hungary and Romania hold their first free elections after forty-three years of communist rule.

March — Soviet Parliament repeals the Communist Party's monopoly status.

3 October — Germany is reunified as East Germany joins the Federal Republic. Newly united Germany remains a NATO member and agrees to pay costs of maintaining Soviet troops in the former East Germany until they are withdrawn within four years.

17 November — En route to a Paris summit meeting, President George Bush speaks to 100,000 people in Prague, Czechoslovakia, and hails end of the Cold War.

1991

1 April — Military alliance of the Warsaw Treaty Organization disbands.

21 August — Attempted coup by Soviet hard-liners is defeated after three days. Gorbachev is restored to power, but his program of reformed communism loses ground to forces promoting nationalism and more radical reform. Russian Federation president Boris Yeltsin emerges as the most powerful political leader.

31 December — The Union of Soviet Socialist Republics formally ceases to exist. Its fifteen constituent republics become independent states, with varying degrees of viability. Russian Republic inherits the Soviet UN seat and emerges as the largest and most powerful of the new states.

---

the necessities of life. Such difficulties encouraged chronic alcoholism and workplace absenteeism, further undermining economic productivity. Few in the West understood how desperate the Soviet economic situation was until Gorbachev undertook its restructuring, which came too late. The end of the Cold War and the collapse of the Soviet Union were aided by the fact that most of the new generation of Soviet leaders were unwilling to be as ruthless as their predecessors in preventing collapse. Nonetheless, economic collapse was a very important cause of the Soviet Union's demise.

About the same time he launched internal reforms, Gorbachev made it clear that the Brezhnev Doctrine of the 1970s was canceled, and the USSR would no longer enforce communist orthodoxy in Eastern Europe by force. That profound policy reversal was brought about largely by Soviet internal difficulties and opened the floodgates for rapid economic and political reforms throughout the states that had been dominated by the Soviets since 1945. Beginning in Poland, reform swept through Eastern Europe far more rapidly than the Soviet Union. By 1989 communist governments and old-line leaders were being weakened or overthrown from Bulgaria to Romania. In January 1989 candidates backed by the Solidarity labor union swept to power in free elections in Poland and launched a crash program to convert the country to a free market economy. On 9 November the hated Berlin Wall was breached, and East Germans were again free to travel to the West. (East Germany had erected the wall in 1961 to prevent its citizens traveling to West Berlin, from where they could fly out to the West. Over three million East Germans had emigrated by 1961.) Late in 1989 negotiations began among the two Germanys, the Soviets, and the Western allies, looking toward the possibility of German reunification.

We cannot easily overstate the significance of German reunification in symbolizing the Cold War's end. Maintaining the division of Germany and preventing any great power from arising in Central Europe had been central features of Soviet foreign policy since Hitler's defeat. Like the demise of the Brezhnev Doctrine, the early 1990 announcement that the USSR would accept German reunification clearly signaled the Soviets faced far bigger problems domestically than in Eastern and Central Europe. West German leaders seized the moment by hard and rapid bargaining. Within months the Soviets dropped their opposition to a reunified Germany remaining in NATO, spurred on by several billion dollars in desperately needed hard currency aid. Negotiators agreed to allow Soviet troops stationed in East Germany to remain at German expense for up to four years, saving the Soviet government from trying to find them immediate housing and jobs. Events progressed far more rapidly than almost anyone envisioned, and the reunification of Germany was proclaimed on 3 October 1990. Also during 1990 the Soviet Parliament repealed the monopoly status of the Communist Party, Bulgaria's communist government fell, and Hungary and Romania held their first free elections after forty-three years of communist rule. Nonetheless, Western reports about a wave of democratization sweeping Eastern Europe were a bit optimistic. A more accurate characterization would be a wave of anticommunist nationalism, and the only available leaders with any political or military experience were (allegedly) former communists. En route to a November summit meeting in Paris, President George Bush made an appearance of great symbolic importance, hailing the end of the Cold War before a crowd of 100,000 people in the Czechoslovak capital, Prague. By the end of 1993, a German entrepreneur had proposed building a German Democratic Republic theme park in which people could experience what life had been like in East Germany. Among its other features, visitors would not be allowed to leave until the end of the day.

If the climax of the Cold War's end occurred in 1990 for Europe, it came in 1991 for the United States and for global politics, because of the Soviet Union's breakup into its constituent republics. Even at the beginning of 1991 few analysts foresaw so drastic a development. With East-West confrontation ended in Europe, the military alliance of the Warsaw Treaty Organization disbanded on 1 April. Western fears revived on 19 August, however, when Soviet communist hard-liners attempted to regain power through a coup. Gorbachev was placed under house arrest at his country dacha, and radio and television were censored. Although the defense minister, Marshal Ustinov, was one of the plotters, key units of the military refused to support the coup. Although the vast majority of Soviet citizens remained passive, crucial thousands took to the streets of Moscow, surrounding and protectively barricading the Parliament building in which the Russian Federation president, Boris Yeltsin, took symbolic refuge. The coup might well have succeeded if sufficient force had been used early enough, particularly against Yeltsin. But although Gorbachev had been unable to solve the country's economic problems, four years of *glasnost* had produced a fundamental change in many people's willingness to take political action. The coup collapsed, the plotters were arrested, and Gorbachev was restored to his position.

Effective political supremacy, however, had shifted to Yeltsin. And although Gorbachev had always sought to reform and perfect communism to produce a kinder, gentler Soviet Union, Yeltsin now had little use for either communism or a Soviet Union. Although the provision had meant little during previous decades, the Soviet constitution had always contained a clause allowing republics to secede. This they did, rapidly. With Yeltsin at the helm of a Russian government that took a leadership role, it was decided to disband the Soviet Union. Indeed, several republics had already declared independence in recent years. Just before midnight on New Year's Eve 1992, the Soviet flag was lowered from over the Kremlin in Moscow, and the tricolor Russian flag was raised. The Soviet era had ended, and the Cold War was well and truly over.

The Cold War's end raised the possibility—but not the promise—of a new world order of democracy, peace, prosperity, and increased international cooperation, free of the deep and polarizing divisions of the previous several decades. Yet as the decade of the 1990s wound down toward the end of the twentieth century, the U.S. government had only begun to respond, however haltingly and imperfectly and incompletely, to the new possibilities brought about by the conclusion of the Cold War. Future U.S. global influence and activities still remain unclear *because our future grand policy course is undecided.* Political leaders and analysts are still thrashing around looking for a new "X" article that, like Kennan's 1947 containment proposal, will chart a new grand policy that can hold over several decades. That hope may be too simplistic, however, because the political, economic, and military challenges ahead are highly complex. In the perspective of long-term history, East-West global polarization during the Cold War made world politics much simpler than they usually have been. In the present, we face a new world *dis*order, which is more fully explored in Chapter 3.

SUMMARY

Foreign policies at any point in time can be characterized as either *grand policy* or *specific policy*. Grand policy provides broad policy guidance to influence foreign policy goal setting and organize responses to many specific problems over a considerable span of time. It is also referred to as programmatic policy or long-term policy themes. In contrast, specific policy is much narrower in scope and duration and refers to applied policies that deal with single problems at specific points in time. U.S. foreign policy is built up over time from many specific policies, sometimes formulated to follow grand policies enunciated in advance by political leaders in concrete statements like Washington's Farewell Address. Many other grand policies emerge only incrementally over time, being built through a process of accretion; this is more frequent than monumental policy statements. An ongoing interplay between grand and specific policies appears throughout the history of U.S. foreign policy.

A second ongoing interplay exists between factors that promote policy continuity and those which stimulate policy change and evolution. Policy continuity is encouraged by such factors as the following: (1) state ("national") interests and capabilities at home and abroad change only slowly; (2) physical constraints prevent many potential actions from being taken immediately; (3) existing treaties, alliances, and legislation constrain policy to run in predetermined channels; (4) bureaucratic inertia makes policy changes require time to persuade authorities that change is necessary; and (5) prior experience encourages reuse of policies that worked in the past and discourages use of those that have failed, often without adequate examination of the circumstances that contributed to those successes and failures. A different set of factors encourages policy change and innovation: (1) state capabilities must change over time in response to long-term economic, resource, technological, and political trends; (2) state capabilities respond to important shifts in global political alignments, such as the breakup of the Soviet Union; and (3) evolutionary changes in the relative capabilities of states require adaptive changes in foreign policies.

At the broadest possible policy level, there are some six general orientations a state can take in its foreign policy. These may be thought of as the overall shapes or approaches to policy that a government pursues, the grandest of grand policies. Dealing with a specific policy problem then reduces to selecting an option within the framework of the broad orientation, subject to all the applicable constraints, and with specific goals in mind. Those general foreign policy orientations include the following: (1) *coalition making* or *alliance building*, by which governments can increase their usable diplomatic, economic, and/or military strength and influence by making common cause with other states; (2) *nonalignment*, the opposite of coalition making, a policy of not entering into alliances and coalitions; (3) *neutrality*, which properly refers to noninvolvement in conflicts between other states, whether those conflicts are military, diplomatic, economic, or political; (4) *isolationism*, which strictly involves the minimization of all foreign ties; (5) *interventionism*, which is forcible interference in locations abroad, almost the self-defining opposite of isolationism; and (6) *globalism* or *internationalism*, a sweeping policy of global involvement, a deliberate choice to play a major role in world affairs, the antithesis of isolationism.

Within these sets of constraints and possibilities, American foreign policy has evolved over more than two centuries as the country itself has evolved. The nascent United States used *alliance* with France to obtain much-needed help in its revolutionary war against Britain. By 1793, early in George Washington's second presidential term, the young country had turned to *nonalignment*, choosing the prudent course of staying out of the Europe-centered disputes of stronger powers. In keeping with Washington's advice in his 1796 Farewell Address that we should have "as little political connection as possible" with foreign nations and "trust to temporary alliances for extraordinary emergencies," nonalignment continued as American grand policy through most of the nineteenth century.

There were some interesting exceptions, including aggressive expansion across the North American continent, the War of 1812 declared on England, and the hemispheric protectionist *interventionism* proclaimed in the 1823 Monroe Doctrine, which promised to oppose military or political interference by European powers anywhere in the Western Hemisphere. By the end of the nineteenth century, having mostly avoided conflicts among the great European powers and having built on abundant natural resources at home, the United States had developed to the level of a great power. It also engaged in limited forays into interventionism across the oceans, including the 1898 Spanish-American War, the 1901 Open Door Policy in China, and the 1904 Roosevelt Corollary to the Monroe Doctrine.

Only with its 1917 entry into World War I, three years after its outbreak, did the United States take its first somewhat tentative foray into true *globalism* or *internationalism*. American leaders were correct in believing U.S. entry would be decisive in ending the supposed "war to end wars," but they did not follow through by remaining globally involved. Instead, the United States largely retreated back into nonalignment until World War II. Despite common beliefs about policy between the two world wars, the United States has never been strictly *isolationist*. During the interwar period, for example, the United States was somewhat involved in international diplomacy, including international arms control and disarmament moves. Only during World War II were the foundations laid for long-term globalist internationalism, based on new expectations about vastly increased U.S. stature in the postwar world. The Second World War marked a policy watershed, with U.S. emergence into superpowerhood and protracted, often interventionist, internationalism at unprecedented levels of intensity. *Containment* was sustained as general policy against the Soviet-communist bloc of states through forty-four years of Cold War, even longer than some of our allies might have wished. Recently the U.S. government has begun to respond, however haltingly and imperfectly and incompletely, to the great changes brought about in the global context of foreign policy since the late 1980s by the conclusion of the Cold War. The great question as the twenty-first century dawned was whether the United States would continue its large-scale internationalism or retreat into a new form of nonalignment sometimes called "neo-isolationism." In Chapter 3 we examine more fully the challenges the new world disorder poses for U.S. foreign policy.

KEY TERMS

Classified documents 630
Coalition making and alliance building 630
Cold War 630
Colonialism 631
Containment 631
Détente 632
Glasnost 635
Globalism or internationalism 635
Grand policy 635
Gross national product (GNP) 635

Hegemon 636
Interventionism 637
Isolationism 637
Limited war 638
Neocolonialism 639
Neutrality 639
Nonalignment 640
Perestroika 640
Specific policy 642
Superpowers 643

SELECTED READINGS

Blight, James G., and David A. Welch. 1990. *On the Brink: Americans and Soviets Reexamine the Cuban Missile Crisis*, 2d ed. New York: Noonday Press. When secret records of the Executive Committee deliberations during the 1962 crisis were declassified in the 1980s, and as surviving major participants began joint meetings around the twenty-fifth anniversary of the crisis, Blight and Welch played major roles in publicizing those materials.

Gilbert, Felix. 1961. *To the Farewell Address: Ideas of Early American Foreign Policy.* Princeton: Princeton University Press.

Hinckley, Ronald H. 1992. *People, Polls, and Policymakers: American Public Opinion and National Security.* New York: Lexington Books.

Inch, Edward S. 1992. *Clearer Than the Truth: NSC-68 and the Metaphoric Construction of World Visions.* Ph. D. dissertation, University of Washington.

Kennan, George F. 1947. "The Sources of Soviet Conduct." (Written under the pseudonym "X.") *Foreign Affairs 25*, 4 (July): 566–82.

McCullough, David. 1992. *Truman.* New York: Simon & Schuster. A superb biography of the president who saw the United States through the crucial decisions that set America's course for the Cold War during the period 1945 to 1953. Historians today rank Truman as one of our greatest presidents, chiefly because of his ability to make decisions. McCullough demonstrates that those decisions were never easy.

NSC (National Security Council). 1950. *A Report to the National Security Council, NSC-68, April 14, 1950.* Declassified on 27 February 1975 by Henry A. Kissinger, Assistant to the President for National Security Affairs.

Robinson, James. 1992. *Reason of State: The Origins Of NSC 68.* Ph. D. dissertation, Johns Hopkins University.

Spanier, John W., and Steven W. Hook. 1998. *American Foreign Policy Since World War II*, 14th ed. Washington, D.C.: CQ Press.

Steel, Ronald. 1995. *Temptations of a Superpower.* Cambridge, Mass.: Harvard University Press.

CHAPTER 3

A New World Disorder:
Into the Twenty-First Century

⊕ A New World Disorder

In 1996 Democratic president Bill Clinton's bid for a second term was contested by Republican senator Bob Dole. Clinton decisively led all opinion polls by midyear. Dramatic and increasingly desperate moves by Dole—including resigning from the Senate during the summer and campaigning nonstop for the last ninety-six hours before Election Day—failed to dent Clinton's lead. In October, with only fourteen minutes left in the second and final televised so-called debate between the two candidates, moderator Jim Lehrer of the Public Broadcasting System plaintively asked the audience, "Does anybody have a foreign affairs question?" There were no takers.

Foreign affairs seemed not to be a major concern of those "average Americans" in that San Diego auditorium. Opinion researchers discovered that in 1996 most U.S. citizens were more satisfied with their lives and more optimistic about the future than a few years earlier. What does their apparent lack of foreign policy interest indicate for us today?

Several interpretations are possible. One is that with the Cold War over, the entire world can relax, and the United States is safe to turn its attention inward to domestic issues and politics. Another view is that almost everyone wants to relax, even though we really should not because of new and ongoing problems that lack the high threat levels of U.S.-Soviet confrontations. The most plausible interpretation, however, combines (1) the natural desire to relax from the rigors of the Cold War with (2) the U.S. failure to develop any new grand policy to direct foreign affairs after decades of Cold War and containment. Numerous political leaders and policy analysts have tried to follow in George Kennan's footsteps and write the next "X" article that would shape foreign policy for decades. Thus far, all have failed. For example, Harvard political scientist Samuel Huntington's 1993 *Foreign Affairs* article "The Clash of Civilizations?" produced a firestorm of reaction. In his piece, Huntington argued that future great international political clashes would occur between "civilizations" defined along regional, racial, ethnic, linguistic, and religious lines, such as Islam and the Slavs. In another example, the Clinton administration's carefully orchestrated 1993 attempt to advance "enlargement" of the sphere of market economy democracies as the cornerstone of U.S. foreign policy and the successor to containment fell on deaf ears. Opinion surveys during the 1990s decisively indicated that key components of enlargement, such as promoting democratic governance and assisting developing market economies, ranked near the bottom on people's lists of very important foreign policy goals. Moreover, this was true of both the general public and the policy-making and opinion-leading elites. (See, e.g., Rielly, 1999.)

The U.S. government has only begun to respond, however haltingly and imperfectly and incompletely, to the great changes since the late 1980s caused by the conclusion of the Cold War. Future U.S. global influence and activities remain unclear *because our future grand policy course is undecided.* The hope of finding a new grand policy as powerful and as lasting as containment may be too simplistic, however, because East-West global polarization during the Cold War made world politics much simpler than they usually have been across the long term of history. In the present, we face a new world *dis*order because the political, economic, and military challenges ahead are more numerous and more complex than those of the early Cold War period. The alternative to a new grand strategy is muddling through with incremental changes to past policies. Unfortunately, as we examine in Chapter 5, policy making usually is incremental but seldom is optimal. Incremental policy changes are especially inappropriate responses to fundamental changes, and the end of the Cold War was the second of the two greatest twentieth-century global changes in U.S. foreign policy. (The first was the choice of ongoing internationalist involvement during and after World War II.)

FOREIGN POLICY AFTER THE COLD WAR

In this chapter we see dramatic evidence that the foreign policy problems now confronting the United States differ tremendously in number, character, and possible solutions from the problems faced during the Cold War era, that is, during most of the second half of the twentieth century. We extend the viewpoints discussed in Chapter 1 and the policy themes approach of Chapter 2 to examine U.S. foreign policy prospects for the twenty-first century. Three major sections cover (1) the new challenges posed by the emerging post–Cold War world order; (2) the geopolitical, military, economic, societal, and environmental properties of the new global context within which foreign policy is played out; and (3) the roles of normative considerations and belief structures in shaping appropriate new policies.

First, we find the United States unavoidably and increasingly interacting in a global arena limited by major constraints and filled with powerful competitors. The decline of American global economic dominance or hegemony exemplifies the dramatic increases in constraints and competition since the early Cold War years. For example, fluctuations in international financial markets now drastically affect U.S. exports, and we struggle to retain world leadership in cutting edge technologies such as semiconductor design. These and related economic developments are examined more fully in Chapter 11. Second, the geopolitical context of foreign policy has changed fundamentally since the end of the Cold War, best dated around 1990. The world economic context has changed fundamentally since 1975, with rapid globalization of markets and production. It has changed even more since 1990 as most of the formerly communist states have begun converting to market economies. Military and societal contexts have mostly followed the geopolitical, undergoing rapid and fundamental change. The environmental or ecological context began changing on a globally significant scale about a century ago. Finally, part of the un-ending political debate about foreign policy inevitably involves **normative considera-tions** about what is to be considered "good," and exactly whose good we should consider. The foreign policy stands one takes depend crucially on one's fundamental values or be-lief system. Views about the nature of international politics and the appropriate world role of the United States have important consequences for policy. Such considerations are crucial to the ongoing debate over continued globalist involvement versus neo-isolationism. The chapter closes with two contrasting visions of U.S. foreign policy for the new century, commonly termed *internationalism* and *neoisolationism.*

NEW CHALLENGES IN THE POST-COLD WAR ERA

Around the world, leaders and publics alike were surprised by how rapidly and profoundly political changes swept over Eastern Europe and the Soviet Union at the end of the 1980s. Their surprise was accompanied by a profound sense of relief. With the Cold War ended, fears of East-West war and of a devastating U.S.-Soviet nuclear exchange almost vanished. Those fears had driven defense planning and spending for decades, and the dis-appearance of overwhelming threat led to rapid policy changes. Before anyone had much time to analyze appropriate future alternatives to policies and programs that had been de-veloped to wage the Cold War, officials in Washington and other capitals expected major cuts in defense spending. In doing so, they failed to see how new demands were arising. The U.S. government, which had spent several trillion dollars over forty-four years fight-ing the Cold War, now had great difficulty agreeing to give a few billion in economic aid to help Russia make the transition to democratic governance and a market economy. In-stead, Washington acted as a broker in organizing multinational efforts, and states such as Germany pledged more than the United States to aid Russia. Defense has always been more politically popular than development, of course, and support for foreign aid of all types had been declining in public opinion polls for years. Important national interests still get attention, though; the Senate quickly agreed to a Bush administration request for several hundred million dollars to help the Russians dismantle nuclear weapons.

Few analysts foresaw the new problems that soon arose from the increased number and independence of newly sovereign governments. With the lifting of Soviet domina-tion, Eastern European states became fairly independent. Some, like Czechoslovakia and Yugoslavia, fragmented, and the Soviet Union itself split into fifteen autonomous states. At the same time, U.S. attention began to turn from defense to economic problems at home and abroad. Leaders were quicker than publics to perceive that the Cold War was truly over and major policy shifts now were appropriate. In the fall 1990 Chicago Coun-cil on Foreign Relations national survey, 66 percent of decision-making and opinion-leading elites but only 25 percent of the general public agreed with the statement that "The Cold War is over and we can now trust the Russians" (Rielly, 1991, 37). The survey statement was poorly worded, however, in that it combined an issue of fact about the end of the Cold War with an issue of trust and evaluation about U.S.-Russian relations.

DID THE UNITED STATES, OR THE WEST, WIN THE COLD WAR?

This rhetorical question easily evokes a political debate along ideological lines. Conservatives see a competition won by the universal appeal of Western democratic political ideals and free market capitalist economics, backed up by policies of hardheaded military and political persistence and a willingness to outspend the Soviets. By 1993 the term of choice in political discourse both East and West had become *market* economics, not *capitalist*, thus blurring old ideological distinctions. Liberals may admit the appeal of Western democratic and free market theories while questioning how well we have applied either, and they are likely to see the Cold War as a competition lost by Soviet inefficiency and ultimate economic collapse. Certainly, few Soviet political changes resulted directly from U.S. actions. President George Bush (R, 1989–93), always seen as a specialist in foreign rather than domestic policy, argued that the United States had won the Cold War, and he claimed some of the credit for his administration. In reality, the Cold War simply ended during his watch. Insofar as the United States was responsible, most of the critical actions took place over several decades, and the most important framing decisions were taken before the end of 1950.

The more we learn about conditions during the closing years of the Soviet Union, the clearer it becomes how great a burden Cold War competition with the United States had imposed. During President Gerald Ford's administration (R, 1974–77), estimates of the Soviet percentage of GNP devoted to defense were doubled from previous CIA estimates, at the urging of political conservatives. As better data became available in the 1990s after the Soviet collapse, relatively objective historians redoubled those estimates. Evidently, a quarter or more of Soviet GNP was spent on defense for decades; the U.S. share peaked at 10 percent under the Eisenhower administration in the 1950s, and in later decades ran closer to half that level. As we see in Chapter 11, most economists agree that military spending stimulates development somewhat less than spending in the civilian sector. Thus very high Soviet defense spending over decades reduced resources otherwise available for promoting long-term economic growth. By the latter 1980s Soviet GNP had fallen below that of Japan. Meanwhile, America's larger economy allowed the United States to outspend the Soviets on defense with less effort. The United States really may have won the Cold War by spending the Soviets into the ground. Political scientists and historians undoubtedly will debate these issues for years, aided by the steadily increasing availability of data from the former Soviet Union. Interesting as those debates are, however, the United States is faced with enough difficult problems in the post–Cold War environment that political, military, and economic leaders may well agree that it matters very little today whether the United States won the Cold War or the Soviet Union lost it.

Unquestionably, the end of the Cold War and the breakup of the Soviet Union produced enormous changes in the global distributions of military, economic, and political power, with ripple effects likely to continue for years. Images evoked by different analysts to describe those momentous movements vary from tidal waves, suggesting rapid and irresistible change, to tectonic shifts, suggesting slow but equally profound, inexorable, and irreversible change. Although the United States emerged into the 1990s

CARTOON 3.1

A wave of clashes between the opposing forces of globalization and fragmentation has been seen in Bosnia, Liberia, Rwanda, and Somalia. Such new internal wars lack the ideological component common to the civil wars that occurred during the Cold War era, and they most often occur in failed states, in which anarchy invariably follows the collapse of a central government.

as the sole surviving superpower, its nuclear military preponderance is seen today as irrelevant to most likely conflicts, and its dominance of conventional military power, international production, and international finance was increasingly challenged. It may seem ironic that the end of the Cold War left the United States with reduced global influence. However, Cold War allies no longer require support to contain the Soviet challenge, and consequently are less likely to conform their behavior to U.S. wishes.

Peace leaves us all free to compete, and in international politics and economics there are terribly few rewards for past actions. The United States now faces problems from diminished military and, more important, economic capabilities relative to those of other great and rising powers. Many such problems were clearly foreshadowed as early as the 1960s and 1970s. As we move further into a highly competitive post–Cold War era, the United States must find answers to many difficult questions, including the following: How strongly and how widely should we promote democracy and market economics, and how much are we willing to devote to those efforts? What are the demands of defense and security in the new environment? How are we to remain competitive in an era of profound global economic changes? Can increasingly intense ethnic and nationalistic strife be managed, and how? How strongly and how widely should we support human rights abroad?

As the twenty-first century approached, the greatest unsettled question about U.S. foreign policy was what grand policy—if any—would be adopted for the new post–Cold War era. Would that policy be proclaimed in a few crucial statements and actions, or emerge only incrementally over time through the accretion of small policy acts? Certainly, the latter course prevailed throughout the 1990s. Even then, it was unclear whether the United States would maintain its post–World War II commitment to strong internationalism or retreat toward the nonalignment some analysts called **neoisolationism.** Highly respected voices were heard on both sides of that debate, which is more fully examined in the section "Two Visions of Future Foreign Policy," near the end of this chapter. Even if the post–World War II internationalist consensus was only apparent and fractured during the Vietnam War (see Hinckley, 1992, 9–14), it was importantly motivated by the Soviet communist threat. Moreover, post-1945 internationalism was made easier by American global hegemony, and U.S. dominance was much eroded by 1990. Could American democratic and economic theory provide new rallying points for sustained globalism in the new era? Throughout the 1990s these questions remained unanswered, and those looking for a new grand policy remained unsatisfied. Almost all analysts agree, however, that U.S. foreign policy will be shaped by, and must respond to, its global context or environment, which has been profoundly changed by the end of the Cold War. We turn next to an examination of those global changes and how they are likely to shape American foreign policy themes in the future.

POST-COLD WAR CHANGES IN THE GLOBAL CONTEXT OF U.S. FOREIGN POLICY

To gain further understanding of the constraints and opportunities that will bear on U.S. policy choices across broad classes of problems and major regions of the world, we next examine the geopolitical, military, economic, societal, and environmental properties of the emerging global environment. Key points are summarized in Table 3.1. To emphasize how different today's world is from that which faced top decision makers of the mid-twentieth century, the Cold War context of the 1950s at the peak of U.S. global hegemony is contrasted with the vastly different world at the onset of the twenty-first century.

GEOPOLITICAL CONTEXT

Global geopolitics during the 1950s were characterized most notably by U.S. hegemony in essentially every sphere of activity—diplomatic, economic, military, and political—and by the intensive and extensive worldwide competition we came to know as the Cold War. The United States had emerged from World War II with the world's largest economy and minimal war damage. Even before the war's end, American leaders had sought to bind the country into permanent internationalist global activism by playing a pivotal role in building new international institutions including the UN, IMF, and World Bank that would force the United States to stay involved. Driven by the American worldview, global politics was fairly rigidly polarized. Both East and West characterized the world as divided between "our" good guys and "their" bad guys. There was a small "neutralist" movement that we would today call nonaligned, but most of the colonial empires built during the nineteenth century remained, and the number of independent international actors was relatively small. At its 1945 founding, the United Nations had only fifty-one members despite numbering almost every sovereign state among its members.

In the prevailing United States—and Western—Cold War view, communism was the primary global opponent, the Soviet Union was its most important manifestation, and military security was paramount over economic, political, societal, and environmental security. Opponents and issues thus were highly predictable, although conflicts might arise in far-flung locations. Communist challenges almost anywhere in the world were perceived as important enough to demand serious responses. Nonetheless, there was some recognition of the realities of usable power. For example, repeated crises over access to West Berlin led to Western posturing and the 1948–49 Berlin airlift to counter the Soviets' Berlin blockade, but never to a direct attack against Soviet troops. Similarly, the West recognized that Soviet and Warsaw Pact invasions of Hungary and East Germany in 1956 and of Czechoslovakia in 1968 could not be countered militarily because those states lay firmly within the USSR's sphere of military influence. The U.S. grand policy of containment drove Western policy and led to the creation of a globe-girdling system of long-term, fixed alliances. Although these were primarily military in character, the United States also strongly promoted its alliance partners' economic development through such means as the General Agreement on Tariffs and Trade (GATT), Marshall Plan reconstruction aid, and the functional precursors of European economic union. Creating and staying active in a universal security organization had been important U.S. policy goals during and after World War II, but calls for UN security actions regularly were paralyzed by East-West confrontation. Despite U.S. hegemony, America and the West were genuinely afraid of the global communist political and economic threats. They worried about whether the democracies could survive and whether market economies could triumph over command economies.

By fifty years after the end of World War II, most aspects of the global geopolitical context had changed dramatically. Although the U.S. economy still was the world's largest and was performing quite well, American dominance of global markets and of world trade and financial policy was shrinking toward that of first among near equals. U.S. military preeminence remained, although the political salience of nuclear weapons had declined fairly seriously. With the end of the Cold War, America's ability to lead and dominate policy for a major fraction of the world's great powers was seriously undermined. Western European members of NATO, for example, no longer feared a Soviet invasion, and by the mid-1990s NATO had become a vehicle for the Europeans to keep the United States engaged on their continent. Cold War political simplicity had given way to a much more complex and nuanced multipolar view that recognized the often differing interests of states and was reminiscent of nineteenth-century European politics. On everybody's part, this was entirely consistent with the *protecting national interests* viewpoint examined in Chapter 1. Views of "good guys" versus "bad guys" across all issues had given way to "gray guys" who might be friendly regarding one issue and hostile about another. Opponents had become more uncertain and changeable. Governments could become adversaries over issues arising from diverse causes, including old international animosities, nationalism, and religious extremism. Although NATO continued with

TABLE 3.1
Post-Cold War Changes in the Global Context of U.S. Foreign Policy

Early 1950s Cold War Context	Context at the Onset of the Twenty-First Century
Global Geopolitical Context	**Global Geopolitical Context**
Bipolar rigidity; "Good guys versus bad guys"	Multipolar complexity; "gray guys"
Small number of independent states: 51 original UN members in 1945	Increasing numbers of independent states —185 UN members by 1995
Military security paramount	Economic security paramount; U.S. dominance challenged; militarily number 1, but not economically
U.S. dominant, pursuing containment	
Communism as the primary opponent	Uncertain and changeable opponents; nationalism/religious extremists/others
Predictable opponents and issues	
Long-term, fixed alliances	Ad hoc coalitions
UN paralyzed	UN viable but weak
Concerns:	Concerns:
—Market victory over command economies	—Future U.S. global standing
—Survival of the democracies	—Spreading market economies
	—Promoting democratic governance
Global Military Context	**Global Military Context**
Global security concerns primary for United States	U.S. domestic security concerns primary
High defense budgets	Declining real dollar defense budgets
Concerns:	Concerns:
—Soviet military power	—Instability in the former Soviet republics
—Deliberate Soviet attack	—Horizontal proliferation of nuclear weapons
	—International political terrorism
	—Regional thugs
	—Drug traffickers
Global Economic Context	**Global Economic Context**
Relatively separate "national" economies	Rapidly developing global economic "net"
United States the global economic hegemon	Challenges from Japan, China, Europe
U.S. dollar the global standard currency	Currency fluctuations, "baskets"
U.S. economic power assumed	G-8; global policy coordination required
Founding of IMF, World Bank, first GATT	Final GATT; WTO formed
Concerns:	Trading blocs forming; NAFTA, EU
—Postwar recovery and development	Concerns:
—Building institutions for economic stability	—U.S. "twin deficits" in federal dudget and international trade
	—Heightened concerns about development

TABLE 3.1

(continued)

Early 1950s Cold War Context	Context at the Onset of the Twenty-First Century
Global Societal Context	**Global Societal Context**
Optimism about progress and the future	Concern about problems of change
Distinct nation-states	Integration versus fragmentation
National media	International media: CNN, satellites, cable television, Internet
Dawn of the Television Age	
Early freeways	Widespread freeway networks
First jet airliners	Widespread air travel and air transport
Primarily national communication nets	Global communication nets
Global Environmental Context	**Global Environmental Context**
Human impact seen as bounded	Human impact seen as massive and growing
Very limited environmental consciousness	Growing environmental consciousness
World population about 2.5 billion in 1950	World population 5.78 billion in 1996; projected 6.86 in 2010, 7.60 in 2020
Concerns:	Concerns:
—Per capita income	—Per capita income
	—Environmental costs of development
	—Species extinctions
	—Global warming
	—Deforestation

expanded membership and somewhat redirected purpose, the old pattern of fixed alliances mainly gave way to ad hoc coalitions organized to deal only with specific problems, such as Iraq's 1990 invasion of Kuwait, and disbanded afterward. No longer paralyzed by East-West confrontation, the UN was freed to become a viable security organization but was weak and easily overextended.

Whereas the policy debates of the early 1990s focused heavily on the post–Cold War decline of U.S. global influence, by the latter 1990s many observers had begun to say that many important international collective actions required U.S. leadership and participation and otherwise would not go forward. Prominent examples included the ups and downs of Israeli-Palestinian peace negotiations in 1993 and 1998, the 1994 restoration of democracy in Haiti, the 1995 Dayton peace accords for Bosnia and their subsequent peacekeeping forces, and the 1998 Northern Ireland peace accord.

In the new post–Cold War world, economic security is the paramount concern of the United States and most other governments. Removing fears of East-West military competition freed attention and resources for other arenas of activity. Additionally, important economic and technological changes already have promoted substantial globalization of markets. Political independence and economic development well may be mutually supportive. The number of independent states has quadrupled since 1945, most notably because of the breakup of the old colonial empires, beginning with freedom for India and Pakistan in 1947 and peaking in Africa around 1960. By 1995 the United Nations had grown to 185 member states. Politically, mushrooming numbers of newly independent states had long eroded U.S. and Western dominance in the UN. The United States and its closest allies occasionally have to rely on Security Council vetoes to protect their core interests in today's UN. Building on the lessons of European and Japanese recovery from the ravages of World War II, many states (for example, Brazil, Singapore, South Korea, and Taiwan) have aggressively pursued economic development. Others, like China and India, are growing toward becoming what many predict will be major economic powers early in the twenty-first century. In light of these developments and of the breakup of the Soviet Union, the most important U.S. concerns for the beginning of the twenty-first century have become our future global standing, encouraging the spread of market economies, and promoting democratic governance.

MILITARY CONTEXT

By almost all measures, the United States was the dominant world military power throughout the Cold War, challenged only by the Soviet Union. Although the Soviets broke America's nuclear monopoly in 1949, their nuclear weapons delivery systems did not gain true global reach until the 1960s. Despite a protracted war without victory in Vietnam, U.S. planners usually remained confident of our ability to win regional wars against any opponent except the USSR. In the Middle East and elsewhere, we carefully avoided direct combat with the Soviet military, fearing escalation to global war and attacks on the American homeland. Although always worried about potential Soviet breakthroughs, the United States led almost every major advance in military technology, including nuclear bombs, thermonuclear weapons, intercontinental ballistic missiles, multiple independently targetable missile warheads, supersonic jet fighters, and laser-guided smart munitions. Although sometimes serious technological competitors, as with their air superiority fighters, the Soviets opted out of races for intercontinental bombers in the 1950s, human moon landings in the 1960s, land-based ICBM defense in the 1970s, and space-based missile defense in the 1980s. Only after the end of the Cold War did we realize how draining such military technology competitions had been on the Soviet economy.

Although George Kennan later stated that he had intended containment to utilize a balance from across the entire range of policies, its implementation involved heavy military and only mild economic emphasis. U.S. Cold War policies made global security paramount and defined it primarily in military terms. Internationally, we feared Soviet military power generally and direct Soviet attack particularly. Secondarily, we feared Soviet military attack on others, and Soviet economic and political subversion of weaker states. Domestically, defense became the justification for a wide range of programs, raising concerns in some quarters about high defense budgets and the manipulation of political processes for individual and corporate gain.

The end of the Cold War and the disappearance of the Soviet threat have fundamentally altered the global military context faced by the United States. Instead of a single primary opponent, we now face many and more varied threats, although all are less severe. These include (1) regional wars due to instability in many of the former Soviet republics and Eastern Europe; (2) "horizontal" proliferation of nuclear weapons to additional states, possibly aided by such instabilities; (3) international political terrorism, possibly aided by increased availability of nuclear materials, biological and chemical weapons, and missiles; (4) ambitious regional thugs like Iraq's Saddam Hussein; (5) drug traffickers whose operations some politicians seek to counter by military means; and (6) the possible rise of ambitious and aggressive new superpowers. Because this broad and relatively uncertain constellation of potential military threats lacks the political salience and simplicity of Cold War anticommunism and containment, it has been difficult to build a large constituency among either politicians or ordinary citizens to combat it. Plans to oppose the rise of any new superpower were decisively quashed during the Bush administration. Despite the localized pain of military base closings, the post–Cold War U.S. military has been notably downsized and real (after inflation) military budgets have been reduced. Worries about the twin deficits in the federal budget and international trade have played an important role. Defense hawks fret that the multiplicity of threats in the more complex new world order requires a substantial continuing defense effort; doves argue that the end of the Cold War removes the major justification for large military budgets. By 1998 concerns about declining military readiness led to some increases in the real defense budget. Still, concern has shifted from the global communist threat to the primacy of threats to American domestic security, giving pride of place to economic rather than military threats.

ECONOMIC CONTEXT

Emerging from World War II with the world's largest economy and minimal war damage, the United States entered into a period of economic hegemony difficult to imagine in today's world. Continued strength and U.S. economic dominance were articles of faith. The dollar was the world's standard currency, backed by gold at $35 per ounce. America played key roles in founding the great postwar global economic institutions, including the IMF, World Bank, and the GATT process that ultimately led to the World Trade Organization decades later. These institutions were promoted to ensure global economic stability and the economic health of our allies, and to forestall state financial instabilities like the runaway inflation that ravaged Germany in the 1920s and another global depression like that of the 1930s. Marshall Plan reconstruction aid for Europe helped set the stage for U.S.-European economic competition in later decades, but grew out of deep concerns about democracy's future if we failed to assist Western Europe's recovery from the ravages of World War II. Building institutions to secure global economic stability took some time, and economies remained relatively separate and "national" in character during the early post–World War II years.

More than fifty years later, U.S. economic hegemony has been eroded substantially, although we still have the world's largest economy. That erosion stems not from absolute U.S. decline, but from the growth of others and the globalization or interpenetration of economies. Indeed, world economic history shows that the United States has been forced to coordinate its economic activity with the rest of the world increasingly since about 1970. (For a much fuller discussion, see Chapter 11.) European recovery and economic union created a formidable trading bloc that is becoming ever more unified. Japan's post–World War II recovery led it to surpass the Soviet GNP before 1990. Some analysts think that China's rapid industrialization, building on its great size and abundant resources, may give it the world's largest GNP by 2020. Foreign dollar holdings exceeded U.S. capabilities to redeem them in gold at $35 per ounce in 1960, and by 1971 we were forced to terminate such redemptions and float the price of gold on international markets. The dollar remains one of the most important international currencies, but powerful traders such as OPEC governments now often price their products according to a "basket" of major currencies, of which the dollar is only one. In the latter years of the twentieth century

Japan and some other governments regularly chided the United States for its "twin deficits" in the federal budget and international trade. In 1986 leaders of the most highly developed market economy democracies established the Group of Seven (G-7) to help coordinate their economic policies. The Russian Federation was given formal observer status during the 1990s and offered full formal membership in 1998. This created the G-8 and gave Russia equal status with the major developed democracies, except on issues of international finance. With the final GATT agreement in 1994 having given way to the World Trade Organization, conservative economists fear the United States will lose even more control over its international trade. Some observers fear the world will be divided into a few powerful competing economic blocs. They cite as evidence (1) the North American Free Trade Agreement (NAFTA), encompassing Canada, Mexico, and the United States; (2) President Clinton's April 1998 call for a Western Hemisphere–wide free trade area encompassing all thirty-four states in the hemisphere except Cuba; and (3) the European Union's economic and currency union, begun at the end of the 1990s.

The rise of new economic powers to major status and the rapid industrialization of many developing states have combined with technological advances in communication and transportation to stimulate an unprecedented globalization of markets. As Robert Reich (1991) described, the relatively free flow of most factors of production except labor across state borders has undermined old notions of separate "national" economies. Instead, we see a developing global economic "web" of activity whose very nature limits any single government's control. (These ideas are more fully explored in Chapter 11, where data are presented to help trace changes in the U.S. economy and its global role since the end of World War II.) Increases in the number of significant economic players combine with the growing number of independent states and the 1990s surge in adoption of market economics around the world to heighten the international focus on strategies for development. For the first time in human history, concerns are being raised worldwide about how much of the world's burgeoning population can enjoy the benefits of substantial development in a manner that is sustainable over the long term.

SOCIETAL CONTEXT

Despite the rigors of the Cold War, 1950s Western society was characterized by widespread optimism about a future that promised almost unlimited progress. Fascism had been defeated in the previous decade. World War II was followed by an economic boom in the United States, and economic recovery was advancing in Western Europe. Global hegemony, challenged only by the Soviet Union, contributed to American optimism. Despite the early stages of functional integration in Western Europe, nation-states remained fairly distinct entities, and international penetration of most developed societies was relatively limited. Colonial empires around the world were being liquidated, and new peoples were beginning to experience political independence and sovereign statehood. They, too, tended to expect progress. International health programs organized through the UN already had made great progress in eradicating some of the chronic major diseases common in less developed areas, and life expectancies were rising. Television was becoming widespread in highly developed states, but communication networks and media still were primarily national in character and reach. Transportation speeds and volumes were advancing with the early automobile freeways and the beginnings of rapid growth in the airline industry, then just beginning to fly jet airliners.

By the end of the Cold War and as the end of the twentieth century approached, many of these factors had changed, with profound effects on societies and their international environment. Most significantly, continuing and accelerating technological changes had transformed transportation and communications, facilitating the creation of truly global markets and communication networks. Media reported events from around the world by satellite transmission, cable television, and 24-hour news networks like CNN. This allowed the U.S. government to control what information Saddam Hussein received about coalition military movements by way of CNN during the Persian Gulf War. It also stimulated public desires to "do something"—even if few practicable options existed—about humanitarian outrages in distant locations such as Bosnia or Kosovo or Somalia. Widespread freeway networks, air freight, and overnight mail services such as Federal Express had revolutionized the speed at which many businesses could be conducted. Transportation developments also increased and speeded the mobility of individuals, from ordinary citizens to international drug couriers and political terrorists. One intriguing outcome of the revolution was rising doubt that governments could control media coverage of any future war because miniature cameras and direct satellite uplinks easily could be smuggled almost anywhere.

Such changes have made societies more open—and more vulnerable—to foreign penetration than ever before. Rapid communications and the rise of computers combine to make truly worldwide, 24-hour-per-day markets possible. Economic globalization depends on rapid communication and transport but undermines the comfortable national economies of only a generation or two before. For example, the rapidity of the declines in value against other currencies experienced by the Mexican peso in 1995 and the Indonesian rupiah in 1997–98 would have been unimaginable before the rise of today's 24-hour global currency market. The net result of such changes has been to decrease the sense that any society is stable and secure against outside threats. The confident optimism of the 1950s about progress and the future has decreased, and fears have arisen about whether all changes really represent progress. Concerns have risen about the domestic impacts of change in the international environment and the ways in which international activities are conducted. Once-distinct nation-states now are more connected with the outside world and thus more severely penetrated by global economics, world politics, international political terrorism, and so on. In some cases, concerns about external penetration and pressures may encourage regional integration, as in the European Union. In other cases, however, they may stimulate a retreat to older ethnic and religious values and points of reference. In extreme cases, they help encourage nationalistic regional and civil wars. The clash between the opposing forces of globalization and fragmentation pervades contemporary societies and, inevitably, their foreign policies.

ENVIRONMENTAL CONTEXT

Issues of sustainable development and environmental degradation were almost unseen and unconsidered in the early Cold War years. World population reached about 2.5 billion in 1950, and human impact on the planet generally was perceived as minimal and bounded. Environmental consciousness was extremely limited. Few people had examined the implications of ever-expanding natural resource use, forthcoming increases in population, or the environmental costs of real increases in standards of living for the majority of those billions living in developing states. Nor were resource extraction industries immune to such shortsightedness. We know, for example, that the planet's supply of oil and natural gas was created millions of years ago and is strictly finite. In the 1950s, however, petroleum-based industries relied on having always discovered new reserves faster than demand grew. They ignored the facts that demand was growing exponentially and even stable production could not be sustained forever. In the exuberance of that time, almost everyone expected new technologies, perhaps nuclear power or breeder reactors, to solve any future energy shortage. Indeed, natural gas distribution companies in the midwestern United States installed free gas mantle yard lights upon request in suburban front yards to build year-round demand for gas and increase their sales. Governmental regulations at that time allowed such utility companies a fixed rate of return on their capital investment. Increased sales volume required more equipment and thus more investment, so the fixed rate of return increased total profits. This instance, at least, demonstrates an environmental shortsightedness partly cured by subsequent changes in domestic regulation of utility industries.

The late years of the twentieth century saw significant growth in environmental consciousness around the globe, driven by ever more obvious signs that growing and developing human populations were running into serious headroom limitations. Despite the inevitable environmental exploitation problems, conventional wisdom perceptions have changed, and human impact on our planet is now widely seen as massive and growing. World population more than doubled from 1950 to 1996, when it reached 5.78 billion. Reasonable projections place world population at 6.86 billion in 2010 and 7.60 in 2020. Despite ever-present biases to plan for the short term, most governments already have expressed serious concerns about the environmental costs of development. Increasingly, they are joining in the search for methods to develop their economies in sustainable ways and thereby limit deforestation, species extinctions, and global warming. For one notable example, see the discussion of the emerging global warming regime in Chapter 12.

Environmental problems are part of the context in which all governments must operate because most of them occur in physical and biological systems that unavoidably affect more than one government. In one environmental arena after another humans still are learning how great their impacts already have been, how much those impacts have occurred in only the last century or even the last few decades, and how seriously those impacts threaten to grow in the early twenty-first century despite our current tentative efforts to limit them. Such concerns form an important part of the political context for all governments and a significant set of constraints on our future actions. Although most of these concerns are quite new in history, we can be confident that the United States and other governments will have to take them into account in future policy planning.

WHAT DO THESE CHANGES IN GLOBAL CONTEXT IMPLY FOR U.S. FOREIGN POLICY?

The many and dramatic post–Cold War changes in the global context or environment within which U.S. foreign policy must be carried out mean that new problems must be faced. A number of specific problems that either surfaced during the 1990s or may be foreseen are examined in detail in Part IV (Chapters 13–16). Some new policy tools may be available to help deal with those problems, and certain older tools may be subject to new constraints. Tools potentially available to implement policy solutions are examined in Part III (Chapters 8–12), along with ways in which the changing global context may constrain their use. Broadly, America likely will remain the world's greatest economic, military, and political power at least into the early years of the twenty-first century, although in each of these areas its power *relative to* other states has decreased and likely will continue to decrease. This limits U.S. capability to go it alone in most arenas of international activity.

Faced with reduced relative power, a significantly changed international environment, a host of new and different problems abroad, and the disappearance of the foe that had dominated more than four decades of Cold War policy, the United States entered the 1990s with a suddenly widened range of foreign policy possibilities. As the twenty-first century approached, no new grand policy had gained widespread acceptance, and an intensive policy debate continued. Inertia encouraged continuity, perpetuating old policy themes and maintaining existing institutions built to fight the Cold War. Contrastingly, new opportunities presented by the changed international environment encouraged innovation, through the pursuit of policies previously hoped for but ruled out by Cold War confrontations and resource limitations. Part of the grand policy debate was between continued globalist internationalism and a less active, more nonaligned approach often termed neoisolationism. Many variations on these general approaches have been proposed. Debates exist within each camp over how intensively the grand policy should be pursued, that is, how globalist or how nonaligned the United States should be in the new century. We should not be surprised that an important part of that policy debate is over normative issues, the "goods," "bads," "shoulds," and "oughts" of applied foreign policy. Because the policy stands of both officials and ordinary citizens are strongly shaped by their beliefs on such matters, the next section is devoted to normative considerations and belief structures.

NORMATIVE CONSIDERATIONS AND BELIEF STRUCTURES

Policy choices are shaped not only by internal possibilities and capabilities and by external pressures and opportunities, but also by our own values and perceptions of the world and of our global role. Values encompass normative considerations about both the goals or ends we seek and the policy tools or means we believe are appropriate. Whether we accept international moral issues as an important component in shaping U.S. foreign policy depends crucially on how we think about policy choices and the role we assign, consciously or unconsciously, to values. Policy goals and means we decide are appropriate to reach them also are influenced by our perceptions of the world outside our country and beliefs about how the international system works. The combination of values and perceptions may lead to fairly stable patterns in the types of goals and means we approve, so that we can predict a citizen's or an official's stand on some new issue by knowing his or her past belief patterns.

Within the last generation, scholars have identified a small number of important dimensions of such patterns or **belief structures.** A generation or more ago, many analysts believed a single dimension of isolationism versus internationalism captured the important differences between individuals' thinking on the grand themes of foreign policy. Contemporary studies identify more complex and nuanced belief structures. In the next several subsections, we examine these different aspects of how normative considerations and belief structures bear on foreign policy choices. Inevitably, they will influence the debates over appropriate policies for the twenty-first century. We then examine what contemporary research tells us about how well informed or logical the public is about foreign policy choices. Lastly, because people always deal with the world as they perceive it, we examine how citizens' and officials' perceptions about the motivations driving our opponents critically shape the policy solutions they consider to be possible.

TO WHAT DEGREE SHOULD MORALITY SHAPE FOREIGN POLICY?

Normative considerations are views about what is to be considered "good," and exactly whose good we should consider. This includes "shoulds" and "oughts" about the goals or ends of foreign policy, and the means considered acceptable to implement policy. For a great power such as the United States, state goals could vary from reaching full employment at home and a favorable foreign trade balance, to promoting democracy and free market capitalism abroad, to working with other governments and agencies in eliminating major diseases like smallpox around the world. The process of deciding policy is fundamentally political, and a significant part of that unending debate is deciding what the goals of policy ought to be. Among the broad, general questions raised are the following: Should U.S. foreign policies evince moral properties and seek the good of others as well as our own advantage? Should we pursue purely self-interested policies designed to maximize our interests, leaving others to their own devices? Does the good of others necessarily conflict with our good? Is it even possible to separate U.S. interests fully from those of other governments and peoples around the globe? These are clear examples of broad normative questions. One example of their application to specific policy problems is to ask whether the United States should have cared enough in 1995 about Bosnian peace to send American troops to help implement the Dayton peace accord. Where each of us comes down on such issues depends crucially on our fundamental values or belief system, including our views of the nature of international politics and of the world role of the United States. Strictly speaking, every goal becomes a norm or standard for evaluating policy performance, although people often tend to equate normative considerations with moral deliberations.

Accepting one or another of the viewpoints discussed in Chapter 1 has a strong normative component. The viewpoints of *protecting national interests*, *protecting clients*, and *pressuring clients*, all of which proceed from the traditionalist perspective of state-to-state international relations, involve putting our interests ahead of others. So does the *military interventionism* viewpoint. The *countering aggression* viewpoint may be more altruistic. The *new world order* and *international cooperation* viewpoints, which inherently take global and regional perspectives into account, identify our good as inherently bound up with the good of others around the globe.

Throughout history, U.S. foreign policy frequently has included a significant moral component, appearing more frequently and more strongly than in the policies of many other states. This has been expressed sometimes through nonalignment and neutrality and in other periods through activist interventionism. For examples, recall our survey of the history of U.S. foreign policy, and focus on the dominant general policy orientations and specific policy goals during several of the major periods summarized in Table 2.1.

Through the first three quarters of the nineteenth century, nonalignment and international freedom of navigation served the interests of this weak but rapidly developing state while it was physically isolated from the European centers of world power. Yet freedom of navigation was treated as virtually a moral principle. The young United States went so far as to assert hemispheric protectionism in the 1823 Monroe Doctrine, although it lacked the power to enforce that doctrine without tacit British support. At the 1914 onset of the First World War, America proclaimed a neutrality that was both principled and self-serving. U.S. entry into the war in 1917 was predicated on making the world safe for democracy, and in the postwar peace negotiations we sought to reform the international system. Much the same sequence was followed regarding the Second World War, except the deliberate decision to remain actively involved in postwar global leadership reflected an intent to finish the job, avoiding the failures produced by nonaligned withdrawal after World War I.

Some analysts have argued that the moral component of U.S. foreign policy is a double-edged sword, lending strength in some situations but weakness in others. As Michael Elliott (1995, 45) put it,

> Only America . . . professes to run its foreign policy on moral lines. Sometimes this is disastrous: Americans were so keen to keep their hands away from grubby compromise that they stayed disengaged from the search for a solution in Bosnia for far too long. . . . Yet precisely because America *does* adopt a moral tone at the start of issues, its vote in favor of any particular endgame carries weight.

In this view, taking moral stands may lead sometimes to inappropriate action and at other times to inappropriate inaction, yet may also yield additional bargaining power in dealing with other governments. Taken together with the fact that the United States is the world's sole surviving superpower and the only state with truly global reach to assist or counter the actions of other governments, this known tendency to take stands based on enduring moral principles sometimes yields major bargaining leverage.

Normative considerations are integral elements of the political process of policy determination at many levels. As more fully set out in Chapters 4 and 5, policy is determined incrementally through a complex political process that involves many individuals and agencies. Each individual has personal goals and distinct ideas about what is best for the country, and therefore both personal and policy interests to protect and advance. Much the same is true of government agencies. Thus policy determination is an ongoing multilevel game of strategy among those individuals and agencies. Looking abroad, that game is over how the United States will conduct its foreign dealings, what means will be employed, and toward what ends. Domestically, the game concerns more mundane but vitally important issues such as which individuals and organizations will reap political and financial credit and how wealth will be created or shifted between individuals and groups and regions of the country. Because policy choice is a political process, changes normally occur only in small steps for which adequate support can be found, however temporarily. Policies are invariably subject to further struggle and change, and appeals to moral principles in shaping policy probably are based on anticipated advantage and preexisting party identifications more often than on genuine belief.

MORAL APPROVAL AND DIPLOMATIC RECOGNITION

Not all states assign moral considerations as important a role as the United States does in determining foreign policies. Two diametrically opposed positions exist about extending diplomatic recognition to other governments. The **moral approval** position, often avowed by the U.S. government, holds that diplomatic recognition implies at least some degree of approval. Consequently, recognition becomes a good for which a political price may be extracted. During the years when coups d'état were common in Latin America, for example, the United States usually withheld recognition of the new rulers until after they publicly promised to hold free elections at a date certain. The opposing **de facto recognition** view is that diplomatic recognition implies only our realization of who actually wields power and that we need to be able to

carry on business with that government. In this view, recognition is not believed to express approval of any government or of the way it came to power. These two conflicting positions were clearly demonstrated in differences over recognizing the new People's Republic of China (PRC) after the communists came to power in 1949. Despite being the closest ally of the United States, Great Britain held to the de facto recognition position and opened relations with the PRC in 1950. The United States—partly because of the onset of the Korean War—held to the moral approval position, interposed its forces between the Chinese mainland and Taiwan to prevent any PRC attack on the Chinese Nationalists (Republic of China), and did not open any formal diplomatic ties with Beijing until 1972. (See also the section on the 1950s in Chapter 2.)

REALISM VERSUS LIBERALISM IN FOREIGN POLICY CHOICES

Transcending their use in political arguments over policy, normative questions have been examined throughout the history of political theory. They concern issues about which people of goodwill honestly may disagree, and on which arguments will persist forever. It is often said that they have no fully satisfactory answers, or that answers are right only if and when policies prove successful. We often settle normative questions by appealing to broad belief structures or styles of policy, which usually have long histories. One major example is the ongoing debate between realism versus idealism (or liberalism) in international politics. Although new applications and the evolution of ideas through continuing scholarship have led to refined versions of these belief structures, currently termed *neorealism* and *neoliberalism*, their fundamental concepts remain essentially unchanged. Those concepts are summarized in Table 3.2, which draws heavily on a recent and detailed examination of the contemporary debate by David Baldwin (1993, 4–8).

Table 3.2 reflects summaries of the assumptions of two major schools of thought, said by many to encompass and divide the entire community of opinion about the nature of international politics and its implications for applied policy. Each school suggests a model of how international politics functions, implicitly identifying the important actors and realms of activity, and the values or goal functions sought. Neorealists are the

TABLE 3.2

Assumptions and Debates Between Neorealism and Neoliberalism

Focal Point of Debate	Neorealist Assumptions	Neoliberal Assumptions
Nature and consequences of international anarchy	The international system is anarchical, raising concerns about state survival.	The international system is anarchical, but growing interdependence constrains state behavior.
International cooperation	Possible, but difficult to achieve and maintain, and dependent on state power.	Possible, not as difficult to achieve and maintain, or as dependent on state power as neorealists believe.
Relative gains versus absolute gains	Greater concern with relative gains; that is, who will gain more, or who wins in a win-lose outcome.	Greater concern with absolute gains, that is, whether all parties gain something, a win-win outcome.
Priority of state goals	Security issues predominate, especially military security, relative power, and state survival.	Political-economic issues predominate.
Intentions versus capabilities	Capabilities emphasized (worst-case analysis).	Intentions emphasized (likely case analysis).
Institutions and regimes	Neoliberal claims about the significance and efficacy of international regimes and institutions are questionable.	International regimes and institutions have become significant and mitigate the effects of international anarchy.

contemporary successors of the realists. They are practitioners and prophets of what is often still called **realpolitik** (the German term) and reasonably may be translated as power politics. The **realists** were exemplified by the late Hans Morgenthau, author of the classic international relations text of the middle twentieth century, whose central dictum was that governments seek their state interest defined in terms of power. Realists saw states as the most important actors in a fundamentally anarchical international system. States thus needed to maximize their power relative to all possible opponents, on all dimensions of power, including military, economic, and diplomatic or political influence. Referring to the focal points of Table 3.2, realists believe that morality stops at the water's edge and is defined strictly in terms of state interests. In an international anarchy that constantly threatens state survival, cooperation with other states requires a careful balance of interests and is subject to continual shifts of policy stands and political alignments. Expectations that other states will seek their own advantage require constant attention to security issues and relative gains by different actors. Because coalitions are subject to change at any time, governments need to be more concerned with the capabilities of other states than with what is known about current intentions. Given such concerns and the general belief in international anarchy, realists have little faith in the ability of international institutions and regimes to constrain the actions of governments, and therefore undertake only limited efforts to build such institutions. Probably the best exemplar of the realist position in recent U.S. politics has been Henry Kissinger, presidential national security adviser and later secretary of state under Presidents Nixon (1969–74) and Ford (1974–77), and subsequently a widely read political writer and columnist. Most realists supported using U.S. troops in the Persian Gulf War of 1990–91 because they saw vital American interests in that region, not the least of which was the oil supply. (Recall the *protecting national interests* viewpoint of Chapter 1.) Few realists supported sending troops to Bosnia to enforce the 1995 Dayton peace accords because they did not perceive vital U.S. interests to be at stake.

In contrast to the realist position, idealists or **liberals** recognize international anarchy but stress opportunities and methods for limiting and overcoming that anarchy. These include the growing ability of international institutions and regimes to constrain governments' freedom of action, and the resultant opportunities to craft win-win outcomes in which all parties receive absolute gains. In reality, contemporary neorealists and neoliberals do not form monolithic opinion blocs, and they generally recognize some validity in each other's points. Their analyses are more detailed and nuanced than the stereotypes of the realist and liberal positions set out earlier, but still reflect important differences in their beliefs about the emphases and possibilities of the modern international arena. In outlook or worldview, neorealists remain more Hobbesian and Machiavellian than neoliberals, more pessimistic, and less inclined to assert international moral imperatives that would challenge the sovereignty of nation-states. Most idealists supported sending American peacekeeping troops to Bosnia in 1995, but many idealists hoped to give economic sanctions more time to work against Iraq before liberating Kuwait by force in 1991.

MILITANT INTERNATIONALISM VERSUS COOPERATIVE INTERNATIONALISM

Although scholars of belief structures do not completely agree on either the research methodologies they employ or the resulting dimensions they identify, many analysts accept an interesting scheme found by Eugene Wittkopf (1990, 1994, 1995). Using data from the quadrennial national surveys sponsored since 1974 by the Chicago Council on Foreign Relations (CCFR), he used factor analyses to locate patterns among the responses by large numbers of individuals to questions about U.S. foreign policy. Wittkopf then attempted to identify the substantive meaning of the attitude clusters found. He distinguished the two dimensions of (1) support for or opposition to militant internationalism (MI), and (2) support for or opposition to cooperative internationalism (CI). **Militant internationalism** involves strongly activist and sometimes unilateral policies around the world, of the sorts often prescribed by realists, including alliances, military aid, use of American troops abroad, and foreign interventions. **Cooperative internationalism** involves activism of types often prescribed by idealists, emphasizing economic aid, diplomacy, multilateral action in cooperation with others, and strengthening international cooperative institutions such as the United Nations. Because a person may support or oppose on either dimension, we can distinguish four distinct attitude clusters that have proved remarkably stable over time. Most importantly, they transcend the end of the Cold War, and thus can be expected to influence debates over future policy. They are summarized, along with Wittkopf's own descriptive titles and labels, in Table 3.3.

TABLE 3.3		
Attitude Clusters Determined by Wittkopf's Belief Dimensions of Cooperative Internationalism and Militant Internationalism		

	Oppose Militant Internationalism	**Support Militant Internationalism**
Support Cooperative Internationalism	**Accommodationists (Idealists)** Politically liberal Most highly educated	**Internationalists** Politically moderate
Oppose Cooperative Internationalism	**Isolationists**	**Hardliners (Realists)** Politically conservative Least highly educated

Notes: Compiled from a number of Wittkopfs' publications (see 1990, 1994, 1995) and the author's work with Chicago Council on Foreign Relations survey data (see, for example, Rielly, 1999). Notes on political orientation and education level indicate tendencies found across most of the surveys (every four years, 1974–1998).

Wittkopf's most important finding implies an underlying stability in the ways people think about foreign policy. Through successive waves of analyses carried out across the end of the Cold War as additional years of CCFR data became available, he continued to identify only two principal components or factors emerging: cooperative internationalism (CI) and militant internationalism (MI). The survey items and scales (groups of related questions) associated with each factor changed somewhat over time, however, in response to major international developments. Remember that CI and MI are dimensions of policy action, and an individual may support or oppose actions that lie along either or both dimensions.

Whereas earlier scholarly views included only an isolationism-internationalism dimension, Wittkopf's two dimensions yield four different attitude clusters, which he considers to be distinct belief structures. In his usage, **isolationists** oppose both cooperative internationalism (CI) and militant internationalism (MI), thus rejecting most forms of active international involvement. This is not strict isolationism involving the rejection of all foreign contacts, but is similar to U.S. nonalignment after independence and between the two World Wars. **Internationalists** support both CI and MI, accepting an active international role employing both conciliatory and coercive strategies. This approach was exemplified by the "bipartisan foreign policy" paradigm widely held and followed from World War II until the Vietnam War. These results could be derived from the old single-dimensional isolationism-internationalism view. What Wittkopf's analysis adds is the other two attitude clusters, in which one type of internationalism is embraced while the other is rejected. He suggests that these attitudes first emerged in the 1970s, driven particularly by events surrounding the Vietnam War. **Accommodationists** support CI and oppose MI. Thus they accept conciliation, negotiation, and cooperation while rejecting the use of force. During the 1980s, for example, they supported détente with the Soviets because they did not see communism as a great threat. **Hard-liners** take the opposite position, opposing CI and supporting MI. As Wittkopf himself puts it, "accommodationists and hard-liners also are internationalists, but they are *selective* internationalists; they differ about *how* the United States should be involved in world affairs, not *whether* it should be involved" (1994, 5–6; Wittkopf's emphasis).

The accommodationist-hardliner split may be seen as both measure and metaphor for the post-Vietnam polarization over U.S. foreign policy often found among both decision-making elites and the general public. Earlier scholars simply may have failed to carry out the correct analyses to identify these two attitude clusters. It seems more likely, however, that Wittkopf is correct, and that they first emerged in the 1970s. In either event, we must contend with them today. Although Wittkopf found the general public to be fairly evenly distributed across the four attitude clusters in Table 3.3, elites typically are more internationalist. These findings that belief structures are multidimensional undermine the apparent broad consensus of the early Cold War years on a bipartisan foreign policy. Even if true bipartisanship existed during the early Cold War years—a proposition increasingly challenged by such scholars as Ronald Hinckley (1992)—today's multidimensional belief structures make it much difficult to achieve sufficient agreement to undertake major new policy initiatives. This adds complexity to policy making and contributes importantly to slowing U.S. adaptation to the new post–Cold War international environment. In practice, every president now must build a supportive coalition from scratch for every major foreign policy initiative, and the resulting coalitions have dramatically different political makeups for different issues. President Clinton, for example, had to rely mostly on Republican congressional support to ratify NAFTA in 1993, had strong Democratic support for sending troops to Bosnia in 1995, and (only after strong lobbying) broad bipartisan support for ratifying NATO expansion in 1998.

IS THE PUBLIC WELL INFORMED AND LOGICAL ABOUT FOREIGN POLICY?

A major question regarding the role of public opinion in determining foreign policy either directly or indirectly is whether members of the public are either well informed or logical. Mid-twentieth century officials and scholars, such as Converse (1964), generally believed that foreign policy attitudes among the general public are disorganized and underdeveloped, uninformed, volatile, and therefore dangerous and subject to manipulation. Much contemporary research on political attitudes, however, involves approaches that are domain specific and focus on connections between general and specific concepts within any given policy domain. (*Domains* may best be understood here as the geopolitical, military, economic, societal, and environmental sectors examined earlier in this chapter.) These approaches suggest that individuals' foreign policy belief structures have fairly complex hierarchical structures that help them make logical policy choices consistent with their value systems (see, e.g., Hurwitz and Peffley, 1987). Thus people may be poorly informed about the facts of foreign events, but if confronted with some new foreign policy development salient enough to attract their attention, they can use limited new information to take positions logically consistent with their core values.

These newer approaches allow us to resolve an apparent major paradox. Many opinion surveys demonstrate that people typically are quite poorly informed about the factual details of international politics. Queries about geographical locations or names of faction leaders, let alone about how the protagonists view the issues, often show only confusion. How, then, can people form policy views that are rational in the sense of deriving reasonably and logically from fundamental values? The key to the answer lies in the work of Hurwitz and Peffley, who found a fairly detailed three-level hierarchical constraint model of foreign policy attitudes. In their work, confirmed by the author's research on the Chicago Council on Foreign Relations (CCFR) data, individuals' core values (e.g., ethnocentrism) predict their general postures (e.g., isolationism), which, in turn, predict their positions on specific issues (e.g., support for trade protectionism) (see, e.g., Baugh, 1995). Such hierarchical structures are consistent with the schema theory literature in psychology that assumes individuals to be **cognitive misers** who use their older or more general information to interpret newer or more specific information, due to their limited capabilities for dealing with new information.

A problem **schema** consists of information about a class of problems to which it applies and information about their solutions. Within a policy domain, beliefs are then expected to show a *vertical* structure from general concepts to specific policy positions, a proposition backed up by a good deal of empirical research. Thus, for example, someone whose core values included very strong ethnocentrism, a belief that U.S.-style democracy and nominally free market capitalism is the best political-economic system, would be led (at least during the Cold War years) to a general policy position of strong anticommunism. In turn, that general position would lead to specific policy positions opposing recognition of Fidel Castro's Cuban government or lifting the embargo on trade with Cuba. A different individual whose core values were more ideologically liberal and less ethnocentric could be led to a general posture of promoting democracy abroad and from that stand to a specific policy position opposing generous trade terms with China, to protest Chinese domestic human rights abuses and their imprisonment of prodemocracy dissidents. Much additional information supports the existence of such belief system hierarchies. Findings of hierarchically structured belief structures apply as much to decision-making elites as to the general public, and demonstrate another side of the role of values in shaping foreign policy. For example, Jervis (1976) argued that the general beliefs of diplomats and other experts strongly affect their interpretations of foreign policy events.

In examining contemporary policy problems and disputes, it is important to remember the various ways in which values influence policy choice. Many of the still unresolved disputes about how U.S. foreign policy should be framed for the post–Cold War era raise distinctly normative issues. Is it proper to intervene abroad by force on behalf of human rights? When, where, and under what circumstances should we intervene? Is such action right even if a legitimately elected and recognized government opposes our intervention in its country? All of these questions applied to Liberia during the mid-1990s. Would we answer these questions differently about interventions to secure peace than interventions to secure human rights? Is it ever right to impose peace by force, over the objections of the combatants? If so, how great a price in lives and treasure should we be prepared to pay? These questions were raised regarding Bosnia, before the 1995 Dayton peace accords and regarding Kosovo when "ethnic cleansing" intensified in 1999. Additionally, as discussed in the introductory case of Chapter 7, many of these questions were raised when President George Bush sent U.S. troops to Somalia in January 1993, nearly at the end of his term. Starvation in Somalia may have presented a good case for the virtues of humanitarian intervention, but nobody wanted to pay the price of long-term success.

When we examine contemporary policy problems and disputes in Part IV of this book, remember the ways in which values influence policy choices, and the distinctly normative issues raised by cases like those just considered.

IDEOLOGY AND PERCEPTIONS OF MOTIVATION

Any use or threat of power implicitly depends on the *perceptions* held by key decision makers about their prospective target. Conciliatory proposals will be dismissed if hearers believe the speakers to be implacably warlike. Threats of serious harm will be dismissed if hearers believe the threateners to be weak, spineless, and unlikely to carry out their threats, even if capable of doing so. Such misperceptions have received some attention from political scientists (see, e.g., Jervis, 1976). In cases that may not be as infrequent as we could wish, deep-rooted political ideologies or worldviews may fundamentally shape perceptions. William Zimmerman (1974) distinguished three different positions advocated in U.S. interpretations of Soviet policy during the Cold War years. Those three positions reflect dramatically divergent worldviews about the role of ideology in shaping an adversary's actions. In order of decreasing importance assigned to ideology, Zimmerman called them "essentialist," "mechanistic," and "cybernetic" views. As with many classification schemes, think of the three types as points along a continuum. There is some correlation with political ideology: **essentialists** tend to be conservative realists, **cyberneticists,** liberals. Generally, essentialists are most likely to prescribe force, and cyberneticists are most likely to prescribe accommodation. Most importantly for our purposes, even though Zimmerman used those types to examine U.S. interpretations of Soviet actions, they are equally applicable to Chinese interpretations of U.S. actions, Rwandan interpretations of Burundian actions, and so on.

The **essentialist** view assigns great importance to official and formal ideology as a shaper of an adversary's actions. Thus essentialists described Soviet foreign policy behavior as "flowing logically from the nature of totalitarianism," so that "it is not what the country . . . does but what it is that is the source of conflict" (Zimmerman, 1974, 91). During the nuclear strategy debates of the 1980s, there was a very high correlation between those who assigned great importance to Soviet communist revolutionary ideology and those who advocated major strategic weapons building programs to counter a dire Soviet threat. Notable among public figures who have espoused essentialist views are the once exiled Soviet writer Alexander Solzhenitsyn (from 1974 to 1994) and John Foster Dulles, secretary of state through most of the Eisenhower administration. Some years ago the political scientist Ole Holsti studied Dulles's public utterances over several years. When the USSR made moves that threatened U.S. interests, Dulles interpreted them as exactly what one would expect from godless communists out to take over the world. But when they made apparently conciliatory moves, such as announcing reductions in their troop levels in East Germany, Dulles interpreted them as actions reluctantly taken during temporary weakness by godless communists who were still out to take over the world.

The **mechanist** or **mechanistic** approach may best be described as a traditional realist or power balance political view. Mechanists perceive foreign policy behavior as based primarily on the interests of a government as a world power. A notable interpretation of Soviet foreign policy from this perspective was George F. Kennan's famous 1947 *Foreign Affairs* "X" article setting out the concept of containment policy. From a mechanist viewpoint, for example, the Soviet Union's desire to control Eastern Europe after World War II stemmed much more from desires for a protective buffer zone against attack from the West than from desires to spread communism. Henry Kissinger and Zbigniew Brzezinski, political scientists and presidential national security advisers to Presidents Nixon and Carter, respectively, evinced variants of the mechanist perspective.

Finally, the **cybernetic** or **cyberneticist** view holds that we may be able to evoke desired responses from adversaries by carefully sending appropriate signals calculated to appeal to leaders (or that faction within a government) willing to work with us. Of Zimmerman's three viewpoints, this one assigns the least importance to ideology. As he notes,

> A cybernetic or organismic imagery of a state's foreign policy . . . not only (a) presupposes a reactive propensity on the part of those who act in the name of the state. It also presupposes that (b) external events have an impact on attitudes and produce structural adaptation, and that (c) attitudinal divergence and political conflict are persistent attributes of the political process even within rigidly hierarchical command systems. (1974, 96, 99)

For example, during the Cuban missile crisis the Kennedy administration received two very different letters from Soviet premier Nikita Khrushchev. One was blustery, uncompromising, and formal, and the other was informal and filled with expressions of concern about the threat of a devastating nuclear war. Correctly assessing the first letter as having been drafted by Soviet bureaucrats and the second by Khrushchev personally, Kennedy's people responded only to the second and more favorable letter. In doing so, they appealed to Khrushchev and those in his government who wanted to resolve the crisis through dialogue. In effect, the cyberneticist seeks to apply a "golden rule" of exhibiting the kind of behavior sought from others.

Clearly, individuals holding different worldviews according to Zimmerman's classification likely will prescribe very different policies for the same problem. Consider the case of arms control. Cyberneticists stress possibilities for arms control through such means as building verification mechanisms to allow a mutually cooperative solution to the fear that others will build new arms. Mechanists may favor arms control, but place greater stress on bargaining from a position of strength. They may urge confrontation and contemporary versions of brinkmanship in times of heightened international tension. Finally, essentialists typically hold that arms control is a bad idea. They may argue for new arms programs to counter a multitude of perceived threats. We can often determine which of these worldviews public officials hold by examining their public acts and statements. Sometimes substantial shifts in the political center of gravity occur from one administration to another. Thus, for example, most Reagan and Bush administration officials were essentialist or mechanist, whereas Clinton administration officials ranged from mechanist to cyberneticist. When President Reagan gave his famous speech labeling the Soviet Union as an "evil empire," his rhetoric was purely essentialist. At other times he spoke in much more moderate, mechanist terms, but continued to appoint essentialist second-tier officials. After taking considerable flack about some of his more liberal and cyberneticist early appointments, President Clinton turned to more moderate, mechanist officials.

TWO VISIONS OF FUTURE FOREIGN POLICY

The most fundamental foreign policy question facing the United States at the onset of the twenty-first century is "How involved shall we be abroad?" In turn, policy debates at this most basic level often are oversimplified into two strongly contrasting, polar positions. The most-used labels are internationalism versus neoisolationism, with the latter denoting a "new" isolationism that would move back from post–World War II foreign activism to something more resembling prewar nonalignment and limited foreign involvement. Alan Tonelson (1998) uses the labels "active" versus "passive" foreign policy. Still other authors, no doubt thinking of the debate discussed in the section "Realism and Liberalism in Foreign Policy Choices" here, refer to idealism versus realism. Whatever labels they choose, people are at least implicitly taking some stand on this controversy whenever they suggest actions—or inaction—in any specific case.

Advocates of the internationalist view encourage different versions of the globalist international involvement that has characterized U.S. foreign policy since World War II. Their prescriptions assign high importance to global and regional perspectives and are consistent with the *new world order* and *international cooperation* viewpoints examined in Chapter 1. They see such involvement as supporting important U.S. interests that frequently coincide with the interests of others. With many variations, they prescribe continued worldwide activism involving different combinations of promoting democracy and market economies, development, human rights around the world, and international cooperative action. For example, one of the broadest internationalist positions is that of James Huntley (1998). He proposes that we follow the collapse of Cold War competition between the democracies and communism by maintaining and extending the new peace through building "pax democratica," an integrated intercontinental federal community of democracies modeled on such institutions as NATO and the European Union. Huntley's new vision for world federalism draws importantly on U.S. constitutional experience, but would advance cooperative endeavors well beyond what many internationalists propose. Most American internationalists, for example, see U.S. interests extending around the globe and want to preserve a high degree of U.S. independence while still enhancing global cooperation.

The opposing neoisolationist camp also includes many variations on its world vision. Central tenets are that American interests should rank first and may best be served by reducing past levels of U.S. international activism, acting abroad more selectively, and leaving more international problems to be dealt with by others. Members of this camp strongly accept the *protecting national interests* viewpoint of Chapter 1. Alan Tonelson (1998) calls this "minding our own business in foreign affairs." Like others in this camp, he believes the diminished relative capabilities of the United States on the world stage make it illogical to engage in far-flung interventions. Tonelson argues that America today is curiously reluctant to use what power it does have, and that, for example, being the only superpower is a much better protector of U.S. citizens abroad than is international law. He argues that American ideas of democratic governance and market economics are our most powerful influences on the world. Thus we would be better off directing our attention homeward toward the continued working out of our own great experiment, building a more perfect union.

It is strikingly clear that these two camps differ importantly in their fundamental assumptions about the present and proper positions of the United States in the world, and about the normative questions discussed in the previous section regarding appropriate goals and acceptable means to achieve them. An analogy that captures some of the differences between the two camps is to compare usable U.S. global power to a glass of water. With inevitable variations, almost everyone agrees that the glass is not as full as it was in 1945 or 1950. For internationalists, the glass remains at least half full; we can make up the difference through international cooperation, and the future is full of promise. Contrastingly, for the neo-isolationists the glass is half empty; we should conserve what remains by looking out for our own interests first, and the future is rife with challenges. The differences can be completely resolved only if one view gains ascendancy. It seems more likely, however, that in the classic processes of U.S. politics, these views will coexist and compete for some time. We should expect to find them in policy debates both general and specific, including the contemporary and near-term policy problems examined in Part IV of the book (Chapters 13–16).

SUMMARY

The U.S. government has only begun to respond, however haltingly and imperfectly and incompletely, to the tremendous global changes since the late 1980s caused by the conclusion of the Cold War. Future U.S. global influence and activities remain unclear, however *because our future grand policy course is undecided.* Political leaders and analysts are still searching for a new post–Cold War grand policy that can hold over several decades. That hope may be too simplistic, however, because the political, economic, and military challenges ahead are highly complex. The end of the Cold War about 1990 and the 1991 breakup of the Soviet Union produced enormous changes in the global distributions of military, economic, and political power, with ripple effects likely to continue for years. Now and in the foreseeable future, we face a new world *dis*order.

United States foreign policy will be shaped by, and must respond to, its profoundly altered global context or environment. Geopolitically, the single opponent and bipolar rigidity of the Cold War years have been replaced by multipolar complexity. Today there are more potential threats over more different types of issues, involving more governments and other actors. Militarily, domestic security concerns now overshadow international security, and real dollar military spending is lower. Nonetheless, the world faces particular concerns about nationalistic instabilities leading to civil wars, and the proliferation of nuclear, biological, and chemical weapons. Economically, America's global hegemony has passed, and the U.S. economy may not remain the world's largest beyond the year 2010. Increasingly, global economic policy must be coordinated with others. Societally, dramatic increases in the speed of global communications and transport have promoted the globalization of cultures, along with economies and military threats. There is a great clash between forces for integration and forces for fragmentation. Finally, as population and human impacts on the physical world have grown, environmental consciousness has risen dramatically, although not necessarily enough yet to avoid serious environmental degradation over the next few decades.

Policy choices are shaped not only by internal possibilities and capabilities and by external pressures and opportunities, but also by our own values and perceptions of the world and of our global role. Values encompass normative considerations about both the goals or ends we seek and the policy tools or means we believe are appropriate.

Throughout history, U.S. foreign policy has often included a very strong moral component, expressed sometimes through nonalignment and neutrality and in other periods through activist interventionism and internationalism.

Realism and idealism are two important and opposing broad sets of beliefs. Realists see states as the most important actors in a fundamentally anarchical international system. States thus need to maximize their power relative to all possible opponents, on all dimensions of power. By contrast, idealists or liberals recognize international anarchy but emphasize the growing ability of international institutions and regimes to constrain governments' freedom of action, and the resultant opportunities to craft win-win outcomes. These two opposing belief structures have survived across the end of the Cold War.

Numerous contemporary researchers find that the foreign policy opinions of both the general public and decision-making elites are structured by two fundamental dimensions, termed militant internationalism (MI) and cooperative internationalism (CI). MI involves strongly activist and sometimes unilateral policies around the world, including alliances, military aid, use of American troops abroad, and foreign interventions. CI involves activism emphasizing economic aid, diplomacy, multilateral action in cooperation with others, and the strengthening of international cooperative institutions such as the United Nations. These two dimensions have survived across the end of the Cold War.

People may be poorly informed about factual details of foreign policy problems yet still use their limited information to form specific policy positions that logically reflect their core values and beliefs. In hierarchical structures of foreign policy attitudes, one's core values (e.g., ethnocentrism) constrain and predict one's general postures (e.g., isolationism), which in turn predict positions on specific issues (e.g., support for trade protectionism).

Citizens and officials may hold widely varying perceptions of the motivations that drive other governments. The essentialist view assigns great importance to official and formal ideology as a shaper of an adversary's actions. In the mechanist view, foreign policy behavior is perceived to be based on a government's interests as a world power. Finally, the cybernetic view holds that we may be able to evoke desired responses from adversaries by sending appropriate signals.

The most fundamental foreign policy question facing the United States at the onset of the twenty-first century is "How involved shall we be abroad?" In turn, contemporary policy debates at this most basic level often are polarized between two strongly contrasting positions, termed *internationalism* and *neoisolationism*. Advocates of the internationalist view encourage different versions of the globalist international involvement that has characterized U.S. foreign policy since World War II. With many variations, they prescribe continued worldwide activism to promote different combinations of democracy and market economies, development, human rights around the world, and international cooperative action. The opposing neoisolationist camp holds, with many variations, that American interests should rank first and may best be served by reducing past levels of U.S. international activism, acting abroad more selectively, and leaving more international problems to be dealt with by others. We can expect these two sets of views to coexist and compete for some time in the battles to determine U.S. policy in the twenty-first century.

In Part II, we see those views at work in the process of making and executing U.S. foreign policy.

KEY TERMS

Accommodationists or idealists

Belief structures

Cognitive misers

Cooperative internationalism (Contrast with *militant internationalism*)

Cybernetic or cyberneticist (Compare with *essentialist* and *mechanist* views)

De facto recognition (Contrast with the opposing *moral approval position*)

Essentialist (Compare with *mechanist* and *cybernetic* views)

Hard-liners or realists

Internationalists

Isolationists

Liberals or idealists (Contrast with *realists*)

Mechanist or mechanistic (Compare with *essentialist* and *mechanist* views)

Militant Internationalism

Moral approval recognition (Contrast with the opposing *de facto recognition position*)

Neoisolationism

Normative considerations

Realists (Contrast with *liberals*)

Realpolitik (See also *realists*)

Schema

SELECTED READINGS

Beschloss, Michael R., and Strobe Talbott. 1993. *At the Highest Levels: The Inside Story of the End of the Cold War.* Boston: Little, Brown.

Brown, Seyom. 1994. *The Faces of Power: Constancy and Change in United States Foreign Policy from Truman to Clinton.* New York: Columbia University Press.

Brzezinski, Zbigniew. 1993. *Out of Control: Global Turmoil on the Eve of the 21st Century.* New York: Columbia University Press. Observations by President Jimmy Carter's national security adviser, a notable Columbia University political scientist and in-and-outer.

Holsti, Ole R., and James N. Rosenau. 1994. "The Post-Cold War Foreign Policy Beliefs of American Leaders: Persistence or Abatement of Partisan Cleavages? In Eugene R. Wittkopf, ed., *The Future of American Foreign Policy*, 2d ed. (pp. 127–47). New York: St. Martin's Press. Holsti and Rosenau draw on data from their Foreign Policy Leadership Project survey of elites in presidential election years beginning in 1976. In 1992, their first post-Cold War survey, they find high levels of bipartisan agreement on such general questions as the structure of the post-Cold War international system, but substantial differences between Democrats and Republicans on more specific issues, such as appropriate post-Cold War U.S. roles and goal priorities.

Rosecrance, Richard, and Arthur A. Stein, eds. 1993. *The Domestic Bases of Grand Strategy.* Ithaca, N.Y.: Cornell University Press.

Wittkopf, Eugene R. 1994. "Faces of Internationalism in a Transitional Environment." *Journal of Conflict Resolution 38*, 3 (September): 376–401.

Wittkopf, Eugene R., ed. 1994. *The Future of American Foreign Policy*, 2d ed. New York: St. Martin's Press. The end of the Cold War, around 1990, made new flexibility in U.S. and global policies imaginable. Many previously unimaginable policies were proposed, and this volume provides an excellent survey. Today, many of those ideas have been rejected outright or considerably toned down.

WHO MAKES U.S. FOREIGN POLICY AND WHY IT OFTEN GOES WRONG

How is U.S. foreign policy made? Who makes it? Where is it made? What determines the relative importance of the various individuals and groups involved? Given that all foreign policies are really intermestic, as discussed in Chapter 1, how does the interplay of different foreign and domestic influences determine the policy stands ultimately taken? Is there truly an ongoing, systematic process of policy making that we can learn about and use to help predict future policies? What are the major viewpoints about how governments, their component agencies, and other international actors make and execute policy? Why do organizations have their own parochial priorities that often interfere with policies laid down by the top leadership? Why does every new administration tinker with the governmental organization charts, and does it really improve the policy process? Should the United States seek to do good through its policies, or simply try to serve national interests? If the processes for making policy are imperfect, can we ever hope to get the ultimate results we seek? How successful are U.S. foreign policies, on average? How do we evaluate the degree of success achieved and revise policies to more fully achieve our goals? These and related questions are the subjects of Part II, which deals with the *process* of policy making, rather than with the long-term themes and more specific policy goals introduced in Chapters 2 and 3.

U.S. foreign policy is not an esoteric and difficult subject; its perceived complexity lies mainly in the fact that it is multifaceted. It involves many different actors—individuals, organizations, interest groups, government agencies, international organizations, foreign governments, and others—who have widely varying types and degrees of influence. To make sense of it, we need sets of guiding principles. The following are several such sets (see Chapters 1, 2, and 3):

- The eleven different viewpoints on our subject introduced in Chapter 1 suggest the difficulty of the understanding and the interpretation engendered by our subject's complexity.

- The limited menu of six basic foreign policy orientations was introduced in Chapter 2.
- Those six orientations were used in Chapters 2 and 3 to examine the historical development of U.S. foreign policy to date.
- Constraints on policy imposed by dramatic changes in the international environment at the end of the Cold War were reviewed in Chapter 3.
- Numerous aspects of normative considerations that affect policy choice from among the available options were examined in Chapter 3.

The U.S. government has only begun to respond to the tremendous global changes caused by the conclusion of the Cold War, as we have seen (particularly in Chapter 3). If future U.S. global influence and activities remain unclear because our future grand policy course is undecided, we are experiencing a major policy planning failure. Understanding why this is happening is a major goal of Part II.

In it, we build more principles to guide our interpretation of U.S. foreign policy by focusing on who makes policy, where, and how. We apply the general systems approach to policy making as we seek to gain improved capabilities for predicting future policy outputs, or at least, the range of likely actions. Another goal is to explain why policy often seems to produce suboptimal outcomes. Along the way, each chapter provides numerous case examples of policy making and its problems.

Chapter 4 organizes foreign policy actors by four zones of relative influence:

1. The president and key advisers
2. The executive branch and specialized advisers
3. Congress, political parties, special interest groups, and the media
4. The public, judicial branch, and international influences.

Clashes of interest and policy receive specific coverage. We take a systems perspective that follows Anatol Rapoport in defining systems according to their parts or members, relationships among those members, and system process or function. Actors are organized into the four zones of influence according to their statutory responsibility, their access to information (partly implied by that responsibility), and their share of attention or span of control. Those zones help us translate the broad, abstract guidance of the systems approach into concrete applications of the general criteria of members, relationships, and functions. In particular, we focus on the actors: who they are, what they do, why some have more influence than others, and how policy ideas move among them. Their policy roles are considered in detail, as are the limitations on them. Particular consideration is given to the ongoing struggle between the president and the Congress for control of foreign policy and to the impacts of public opinion and foreign policy on each other.

Chapter 5 examines two idealized conceptual-analytic models for how decisions are made: *optimizing* and *satisficing*. Whereas an optimizer examines every alternative and chooses the best one, a satisficer examines only some alternatives and chooses the first one good enough to meet a given set of minimum criteria. Limitations on decision-making time, available information, and cost/benefit ratios all push toward satisficing. Implications of these competing views of decision making are seen in Graham Allison's three models of government policy decision making as viewed from different levels of analysis: the government as a whole ("rational actor" or unitary government), the organizations within that government ("organizational process"), and individuals within the government ("governmental politics"). The life cycle of organizational charters, procedures, and growing inertia is considered in light of Morton Halperin's concept of "organizational essences," the widely held internal concepts of an agency's major mission. Examples of all these aspects of policy making are considered, along with related problems such as cross pressures on cabinet secretaries from their agencies and the president, ongoing clashes between Congress and the president over foreign policy management, "filtering" to reflect only favorable information up the chain of command, and the essential impossibility of full, comprehensive problem anticipation. The characteristics and effects of crises, problems of ideology, and difficulties posed by limited governmental and public attention spans are considered. The chapter also discusses problems that arise from *institutional design* and uses the example of the War Powers Act of 1973.

Chapter 6 builds on Chapters 4 and 5 and examines the agencies, groups, and individuals involved in planning and arguing policy positions and options. First, the need for intelligence and the agencies that gather and interpret it are discussed. Interagency procedures for preparing national intelligence estimates (NIEs) are examined in detail. The chapter also examines why long-range policy analysis and grand policy planning are carried out in remarkably few places in the U.S. foreign policy system and by remarkably few people. The broad sampling includes the increasingly influential National Security Council staff, policy planning staffs in the Department of State and Department of Defense, policy research organizations that support the Congress, think tanks and policy study contractors (known around Washington as "beltway bandits"), lobbying organizations for both public and private interests, and in-and-outers (individuals who move frequently between government positions and careers in industry or academia). Reasons for policy failures and suboptimal results are examined in light of the models introduced in Chapter 5.

Chapter 7 examines how different types of feedback enter into the foreign policy process. We see both (1) how the government may use feedback to help evaluate the degree of success and revise policies to more completely achieve desired goals and (2) how citizens may use feedback information channels to evaluate how well government officials, procedures, and policies succeed. We first examine where citizens, government officials, and other actors in the foreign policy process may locate current U.S. foreign policy. Different types of feedback are then classified according to the speed with which they make information available. Finally, we examine the relative effectiveness of the different feedback sources in the success of policy and policy making and in revising policies to approach goals better.

CHAPTER 4

THE ACTORS WHO MAKE U.S. FOREIGN POLICY AND THEIR RELATIVE INFLUENCES

FOREIGN AND DOMESTIC INFLUENCES IN ACTION: ENDING THE PERSIAN GULF LAND WAR

One of the most intriguing questions about the Persian Gulf War is this: Why did the U.S.-led coalition terminate the land war after a hundred hours, limiting the scope of its military victory and setting the stage for Saddam to retain enough of his best forces to ensure his continued rule? At the hundred-hour mark, coalition forces had not completely encircled and neutralized elite Iraqi Republican Guard units. Within weeks of the cease-fire, the Republican Guard played a critical role in Iraq's bloody suppression of rebellions by Kurds in the northwest and Shiites in the southeast—rebellions that had been encouraged by the United States during the previous months of confrontation and five weeks of aerial warfare. Having failed to dislodge Saddam from power or destroy his most important military forces, the coalition left the seeds of protracted political-military confrontation and years of continued involvement in the region. Undeniably, the spectacularly quick land campaign crushed a substantial portion of the Iraqi military and freed Kuwait. President George Bush was correct in hailing this as a victory—but victory was only part of the truth.

Some of the explanation lay with the desire of Bush administration leaders to manage media coverage, packaging war and victory attractively to portray this as a big U.S. win. Commanding general H. Norman Schwartzkopf was later to say that those officials "really knew how to package an historic event" when they decided to end the land war at a hundred hours despite the fact that they "understood that some (Iraqi) tanks would get away and had decided to accept it."

More of the explanation lay in U.S. interactions with other key members of the UN Security Council. Minutes of meetings not released until several years later reveal that Security Council consensus began to disintegrate even before the opening of the land war. Some members were unhappy that the air war included targets throughout Iraq. Others believed the militarily expedient decision to surround Iraqi forces by a great sweep through Iraq blurred the council mandate to liberate Kuwait. The most telling episode, however, was the "highway of death," on which coalition aircraft devastated Iraqi forces fleeing north as Kuwait was liberated. Even British support for continuing the land war began to crumble on the fourth day as pictures of the carnage were widely and rapidly disseminated on CNN (Moore, 1996, 8–9). Faced with the possibility of being left to continue the war alone, the United States backed down and agreed to a cease-fire at the salient point of a hundred hours—even though we had adequate forces in place to continue the war and had never really needed the military support of other coalition members. The political need to maintain the coalition and the economic need for others to finance military operations now outweighed other military-strategic considerations to a degree unseen during decades of Cold War.

That ending of the Persian Gulf land war demonstrates the interplay of domestic and foreign influences in shaping U.S. foreign policy, and the way in which the spin, or presentation, that policy decisions and their results are given at home and abroad gained in importance as rapid global communications evolved during the late twentieth century. Recall that CNN first became accepted as a major global news organization during the Persian Gulf War. Most importantly for this chapter, however, the Gulf War case demonstrates how foreign governments and publics sometimes play important roles among the many actors who determine U.S. foreign policy.

HOW POLICY IS CONCEIVED AND EXECUTED

In this chapter we examine how U.S. foreign policy is conceived and executed by a very large and complex sociopolitical system. Because that system spans the globe and is made up of a huge number of individuals, groups, and organizations, we seek to build skills for understanding how it works. Each of the three major sections of the chapter addresses a part of that task. Those sections cover (1) how to apply a generalized systems approach to studying the making of U.S. foreign policy; (2) key actors, divided into four zones according to their relative influence on foreign policy; and (3) the dynamics of how policy ideas and influence flow between zones. Even though the United States has not settled on a new post–Cold War grand policy, the profound changes in the global context of foreign policy since 1990 already have led to changes among the actors making policy, and in their interrelationships and relative power.

The U.S. foreign policy system shares the following four defining criteria of all systems: (1) members, (2) relationships between them, (3) methods of functioning to perform certain tasks, and (4) some degree of predictability. The system primarily processes information. It receives inputs about the actions of others, generates policies and actions as outputs, and receives feedback in the form of information about the effects our actions have on others and the international environment. Such feedback then can be used to adjust policies to approach desired outcomes more closely. By directing our attention to identifying the members, relationships, and functions of the foreign policy system, the systems approach gives us a useful general tool for interpreting how policy is made in particular substantive areas and how it may be made in dealing with some new problem that has just surfaced. It also helps us focus on those functional limitations that contribute to policy failures and less-than-optimal outcomes.

PHOTO 4.1
Aerial view of the "Highway of Death" on which Iraqi forces fleeing the city in every available vehicle were intercepted by allied air forces and destroyed (1 March 1991). International revulsion toward such scenes built pressure within the UN Security Council to end the land war (an untimely decision that allowed Saddam Hussein to retain power).
AP/Wide World Photos

We organize information here about the major actors in the system, the relationships between them, and some of their functions by placing those actors into four zones of decreasing relative influence on foreign policy. Any particular actor's zone of influence is determined by these three interrelated considerations: (1) responsibility deriving from constitutional or statutory authority, (2) access to needed information, and (3) share of time and attention available to devote to foreign policy. In the systems perspective, classifying foreign policy actors into zones of influence tells us both what individuals, groups, and organizations make up the system and a good deal about the relationships among them. The section on the dynamics of how policy ideas and influence flow between zones of influence extends our examination further into the ways in which the system functions.

A SYSTEMS APPROACH TO THE STUDY OF U.S. FOREIGN POLICY MAKING

The system through which U.S. foreign policy is made and carried out is large and complex, in the sense that it spans the globe and is made up of a huge number of individuals and many organizations. The three branches of government are involved in widely varying degrees, with their importance and influence decreasing in the sequence executive, legislative, and judicial. Some individuals in key roles, such as the president, the national security adviser, and the chairman of the Joint Chiefs of Staff receive considerable publicity and come to mind readily, as do key organizations like the Departments of State and Defense. Many more key individuals, however, like foreign policy specialists serving on the National Security Council staff or in a congressional committee office, may be almost unknown outside Washington. A first look at the manual of government organization charts may be quite daunting. Digging out the details of how some specific policy was decided and implemented may seem at first a formidable task, and the detailed study of foreign policy sometimes may appear rather esoteric.

DEFINING AND IDENTIFYING SYSTEMS

Daunting as its study may appear at first, there really is a **system** by which U.S. foreign policy is made and executed, and it meets all the criteria for a *system* as that term is understood by social scientists. The system concept originated in engineering but has been applied by researchers in fields ranging from accounting to zoology. A simple set of four criteria for recognizing and describing a system, derived from the work of Anatol Rapoport, is given in Table 4.1.

First, any system is composed of a set of components, parts, elements, or **members.** An oil refinery, for example, is a large and complicated physical system made up of piping, retorts, storage vessels, cracking towers, and so on. The human circulatory system is a biological system composed of elements that include the heart, arteries, veins, lungs, and so on. The U.S. foreign policy-making system is a complex social and political system. The members who make it up, and whose actions are indispensable to its functioning, include individuals as well as groups or organizations. Key individuals may be well known and frequently in the public eye, as the president always is, the secretary of state may be, and top military commanders often are in times of conflict. General Schwartzkopf, for example, was extremely visible in briefings and interviews during the Persian Gulf War. When he retired from the army later in 1991, he left the inner circles of policy but joined the ranks of famous former officials and carefully rationed his lucrative public appearances. Other key individuals may know one another but almost never attract public attention outside Washington. Examples could include a presidential friend who offers vital but secret political advice, or the intelligence analysts who deciphered what Iraq's 1990 military deployments in the Kuwaiti desert meant about Iraqi battle strategy. Key groups involved in foreign policy making are usually organizations, often quite large ones. They range from the Congress, especially its Armed Services and Foreign Relations or Foreign Affairs Committees, to special interest groups such as the National Association of Manufacturers or the Veterans of Foreign Wars, which can field well-paid and highly informed lobbyists.

Second, any system has a network of **relationships** or **connections** between its members that binds them together into a functioning unit. The oil refinery's elements are connected by its piping and control wiring. So are the human circulatory system's elements, although blood vessels are its piping and nerve bundles are its wiring. Relationships in the foreign policy system are connections between human individuals and groups, including legal, organizational, political, and personal ties. The president can command obedience

TABLE 4.1		
System Criteria and Sample Applications to U.S. Foreign Policy		

	Criteria for a System	Sample Applications to U.S. Foreign Policy
System Structure	1. A system is composed of components, parts, elements, *Members*.	Individuals: President, Secretary of State Groups: National Security Council staff, House Foreign Affairs Committee
	2. *Relationships* or *Connections* exist between the members of the system.	Formal: Organization chart lines of responsibility Informal: Personal friendship; policy agreement
System Function	3. The system *Functions* so as to perform certain tasks or produce certain products or outputs.	Negotiating the reduction of Japanese non-tariff barriers to trade; fighting the Persian Gulf War.
System Use for Prediction	4. Past or present *states of the system* may be used to *predict* future states.	Decisionmakers change operating styles and policy stands rarely and slowly. Themes or action tendencies, for example, interventionism, tend to be maintained for long periods of time and over many policy cases.

from a soldier by virtue of constitutional authority as commander in chief. Beyond authority, a president who is a true leader will win that soldier's obedience out of patriotism, personal respect, and affection. Many other important connections exist beyond those shown on organization charts. An individual in any bureau has superiors who must be obeyed, but usually has at least some loyalty to the agency. Organizational loyalty may be self-interested because members usually benefit when their agencies flourish, but it also typically includes a belief that one is helping perform necessary and beneficial functions. All these types of relationships are part of the total system because they influence the ways in which it functions. Indeed, informal relationships are sometimes more important than formal ties. Many administrations have seen cases in which an official's feud with a counterpart in another agency stems more from personal animosity than policy disagreement. Such feuds can seriously influence policy execution, even though both officials owe loyalty to the same administration. Together, system membership and the set of relationships between members are sometimes called the **structure** of the system. Changes to that structure represent changes to the **institutional design** of the foreign policy system, that is, the structure of members and relationships established by the Constitution, legislation, executive orders, and case law.

Third, any system **functions** so as to perform certain tasks or produce certain outputs. Indeed, if a system had no significant functions, we probably would care little about it. An oil refinery produces useful petrochemicals such as gasoline and lubricating oils. The human circulatory system moves blood from the lungs to individual cells and back again, bringing oxygen and nutrients and removing waste products. The foreign policy system has a wide range of products or functions or actions taken, ranging from diplomatic messages sent or received to formal policy announcements to the waging of war. Usually some notion of **stability** is associated with the systems viewpoint. Systems are expected to achieve more or less of an equilibrium and to function in much the same way over time. Again, if this were not the case, we might find little utility in the systems approach. Equilibrium within living systems is a familiar concept in our own bodies. Exercise raises heart rate and blood pressure, but they tend to return to the same resting levels. If we sustain a long-term exercise program, our heart rate and blood pressure will not rise as much when exercising and will fall to lower levels at rest. Those changes, however, occur only slowly and over an extended time. Similar expectations hold for policy making. Most changes within the foreign policy system are small and incremental. This year's committee procedures, for example, will be much like last year's. Despite major emphasis on change, governmental organization charts in the Clinton administration looked much as they had in the Bush and Reagan administrations before it. Additionally, systems tend to be made up of **subsystems,** and to be subsystems of still larger systems. For example, a lung may be considered a system for exchanging gases into and out of liquid, but it is also an element of the circulatory system, which in turn is part of a larger system known as an individual human being. Sometimes we are interested in a particular subsystem of the foreign policy system. For example, parts of several cabinet departments are included among the elements of the subsystem that deals with foreign trade agreements.

Fourth and finally, we can use our knowledge of the structure and past functioning of a system to gain insight into its likely future performance. Arguably, this **predictability** criterion is redundant and already implied by the combination of the previous three criteria. Systems analysts use the term *state of the system* to refer to a snapshot describing all the significant variables, essentially everything important about the membership, connections, and functioning of the system at one instant. If we know the system's structure and its state at one moment, we should be able to *predict* its state at any future time. This is more readily applied to an oil refinery than to the foreign policy system, however, because the refinery is far simpler and there is much less disagreement about which are its important variables. Nonetheless, the general principle applies that the more we know about the structure and past functioning of the foreign policy system, the better we can predict what is likely to occur in future. Even if we cannot make exact predictions with high confidence—which often is the case—it is valuable to be able to predict a range of likely outcomes. At a very large or macro scale, the long-term policy themes discussed in Chapters 2 and 3 demonstrate sustained stable operation of the foreign policy system. At much smaller or micro scale, most officials maintain fairly stable policy stands and operating styles over time. No policy is continued forever, of course. Still, instances of stable functioning give us a base from which to begin prediction, after which we can focus on forces that may compel change.

RECAP OF RAPOPORT'S FOUR CRITERIA FOR RECOGNIZING AND DESCRIBING A SYSTEM

- *Members:* Any system is composed of a set of components or parts or elements or members. The U.S. foreign policy-making system is a complex social and political system comprising individuals as well as groups or organizations.

- *Relationships* or *connections:* Any system has a network of relationships or connections between its members, which binds them together into a functional unit. Relationships in the foreign policy system are connections between human individuals and groups, including legal, organizational, political, and personal ties.

- *Functions:* Every system operates so as to perform certain tasks or produce certain outputs. The foreign policy system has a wide range of products or functions or actions taken, ranging from diplomatic messages sent or received to formal policy announcements to the waging of war.

- *Predictability:* We can use our knowledge of the structure and past functioning of a system to gain insight into its likely future performance. Arguably, this criterion is redundant and already implied by the combination of the three criteria just described.

USING THE SYSTEMS APPROACH TO GUIDE OUR STUDY OF FOREIGN POLICY

The foreign policy system is a *sociopolitical* system, one made up of human beings and human political and social groups and organizations. It is also a **living system,** in the sense used by James G. Miller (1978) and other researchers in the Society for General Systems Research, because it is made up of living beings and itself has many of the properties of a living organism. Miller identifies seven levels of living systems, each of which consists of multiple systems that are subsystems of the next higher level. Those levels are cell, organ, organism, group, organization, society (in our terminology, *nation*), and the supranational system (in our terminology, the *international* or *global system*). All living systems have physical existence, are composed of matter and energy, are organized by information, and satisfy the four system criteria of elements, relationships, functions, and predictability. In making and executing foreign policy, Miller's top five levels of living systems are of interest because they characterize members of the foreign policy system. They include individuals (organisms), groups (made up of individuals), organizations (made up of individuals and groups), and society (the nation-state, made up of individuals, groups, and organizations). We might think of the U.S. foreign policy system as a subsystem of what Miller calls a society, although it also receives inputs from elements of the supranational or international system.

The most important property of living systems for our purposes is that they are organized by information and they process information. Any government can be considered an enormous information processing system, in the specific sense that it must process enormous quantities of messages and data, and in a more general sense that is conceptually diagrammed in Figure 4.1. Even if we knew nothing about how a government carries out its information processing, if we had the necessary access we could observe a tremendous input flow of information. Included would be details about such things as varied as diplomatic messages and visits; data on trade, customs, immigration, and tourism; intelligence gathered about the economic capabilities and military deployments of other governments; and so on. Information processing outputs also would be voluminous, including every single government policy and action. Among them we would expect to find formal statements, diplomatic messages, officials' answers to journalists'

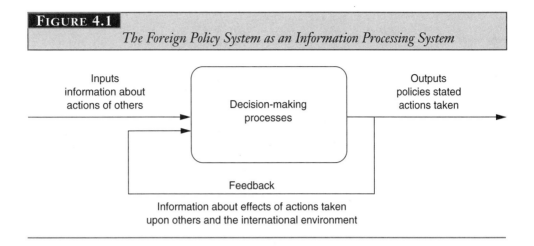

FIGURE 4.1

The Foreign Policy System as an Information Processing System

questions, government agency purchase orders, instructions to negotiators, orders to military commanders, and so on. Finally, we expect **feedback** to exist. At least some input information concerns measures of how well policies are working, which can be used in adjusting those policies to more closely approach the desired outcomes.

The existence and use of feedback is crucial to success in foreign policy, as it is in a great range of other endeavors. Uses of feedback in controlling system behaviors abounds in our daily lives. An automobile cruise control system, for example, uses a speed sensor to tell whether the vehicle is above or below the set target speed, and the engine control computer orders less or more fuel sent to the engine as needed. When we exercise to excess, numerous bodily signals urge us to stop and recover. If you doubt how important and pervasive feedback is in daily life, try shaving or putting on makeup without looking in a mirror, or writing your class notes without looking at the paper.

Nothing about the abstract conceptual treatment diagrammed in Figure 4.1 guarantees that we will find any of the foreign policies adopted by the U.S. government appropriate to the country's domestic and international circumstances. We may not agree that the system functions well or quickly enough or by acceptably moral means. Nonetheless, the existence of feedback implies that the system *can exhibit learning behavior.* Information about policy mistakes and failures can be used to modify future actions in the same or similar situations; information about policy successes causes those actions to be reinforced and repeated. All living systems have this capability for learning behavior. Although we cannot guarantee appropriate system responses or outputs, it is generally true that living systems which correctly evaluate their environments, learn, and utilize feedbacks to adjust their behaviors will survive, or at least maximize their chances of survival.

ACTORS AND THEIR INFLUENCES ON FOREIGN POLICY

Applying the criteria discussed in the previous section, systems may be described by means of their members, the relationships between them, and the details of how they function. We begin our scrutiny of the U.S. foreign policy system by simultaneously examining its members, their interrelationships that determine policy influence or impact, and some aspects of their functioning that affect policy influence. Following an idea originated by Roger Hilsman (1967, 541–44), we divide the actors in the system according to four zones of relative influence. This notion relies partly on a piece of the conventional wisdom in U.S. politics, to the effect that foreign policy making is much more hierarchical than domestic policy making. Hilsman described only three zones and referred to them as "the concentric rings of decision making," without ever being very clear about what principles put some actors into one zone and others into another zone.

In Figure 4.2 on page 128, the actors are placed into four zones based on the following three interrelated principles that determine relative influence or impact on foreign policy:

- *Responsibility* for an area of endeavor and constitutional or statutory *authority* to act.

- *Access to needed information* often comes automatically with authority, but officials are not always given all the information they should receive. A great deal of information flows along unofficial links, and officials usually build personal networks for gathering information.

- *Available share of time and attention* that an actor can afford to devote to a specific problem or to foreign policy in general. Officials and others with multiple areas of responsibility and many demands upon them can alleviate the time crunch by employing staff specialists to advise them and by delegating responsibilities, but real limits still exist.

The next several subsections are devoted to a zone-by-zone consideration of foreign policy actors. In each case, we examine responsibilities, access to information, and share of attention available for foreign policy in order to determine why that actor belongs in one zone of relative policy influence rather than another (see Figure 4.2).

In the zone-by-zone discussion that follows, do not try to infer how much influence any particular official or agency has by the number of words that appear here. You already know a good deal about some of the most important foreign policy actors, for example, the president or the secretary of state. Relatively more may be said here about foreign policy actors with whom you are likely to be less familiar. Examples include staff members who support key congressional committees and foreign policy think tanks that employ important in-and-outers. The key indicators of relative influence are the zone to which an actor is assigned and what is said about that actor. In zone 2, for example, clear distinctions are made among senior foreign policy departments, junior foreign policy departments, and domestic agencies with foreign policy interests.

ZONE 1: THE PRESIDENT AND KEY ADVISERS

Very few officials see U.S. foreign policy from a comprehensive viewpoint. Those in zone 1 should come closest because they have the broadest scope of authority, can command access to the widest range of information, and either can devote most of their time to

Roger Hilsman: The Career of an In-and-Outer

Roger Hilsman is an excellent example of an **in-and-outer,** an individual whose career involves a number of alternations between periods working in government and times working in academia, business, or policy think tanks. (See also "Zone 2: The Executive Branch and Specialized Advisers" later.) Hilsman graduated from West Point in 1943 and served four years in the army. Thereafter his career alternated between government and academia. After earning a Ph.D. degree he worked in London and Frankfurt on NATO planning (1950–53), returning to posts as research associate and professor at Princeton (1953–56). He next devoted five years to studies on post–World War II military policy and foreign relations for the Library of Congress and Johns Hopkins University. In 1961 he joined the Kennedy administration as director of the State Department's Bureau of Intelligence and Research, traveling to crisis areas and reporting to the secretary of state. He was much involved with U.S. policy for South Vietnam, recommending techniques for dealing with guerrilla warfare and winning popular support. His association with Vietnam continued during 1963–64 as assistant secretary of state for Far Eastern affairs. Splitting with President Lyndon Johnson over Vietnam policy, Hilsman left government in 1964, returning to academic life at Columbia University and writing about policy making. In a 1968 *Foreign Affairs* article, he recommended deescalating the Vietnam War and implementing the withdrawal policy that became known as Vietnamization (see Findling, 1989, 238–39).

foreign policy or can command the largest support staffs to help overcome conflicting demands for their time. Officials in the other zones usually have more tightly circumscribed authority and reduced access to information. Most actors outside the government have even less authority and access. These concepts are further explored in the decision-making models examined in Chapter 5.

In most administrations the president is the first official whom citizens think of when foreign policy issues are raised. Under the U.S. Constitution, the president is both *head of state*, the ceremonial representative of the entire country, and *head of government*, who leads the entire executive branch of the U.S. government, through which all federal policy is implemented. Under the Constitution, the president also is commander in chief of American military forces. These broad powers and responsibilities exceed those of any other official, making the president the most powerful of all U.S. government officials. In principle, those powers imply that the president should be able to command access to every bit of information anywhere throughout the government. All these considerations combine to make the president preeminent in determining U.S. foreign policy.

Preeminence does not mean absolute control, however. Presidents do not rule as monarchs, but must lead and cajole and persuade in an ongoing political process. The noted scholar of presidential power, Richard Neustadt, whose work strongly influenced President Kennedy at the outset of his administration, argues that presidents cannot merely order things done, but must make them happen. He tells the story that when longtime politician Harry Truman contemplated career military man Dwight Eisenhower assuming the presidency, Truman said, "He'll sit here, and he'll say, 'Do this!

FIGURE 4.2

Actors and Their Relative Influence in Shaping U.S. Foreign Policy

Influence increases toward the center, based on the principles of statutory authority to act, ability to command access to necessary information, and share of attention that can be devoted to foreign policy issues.

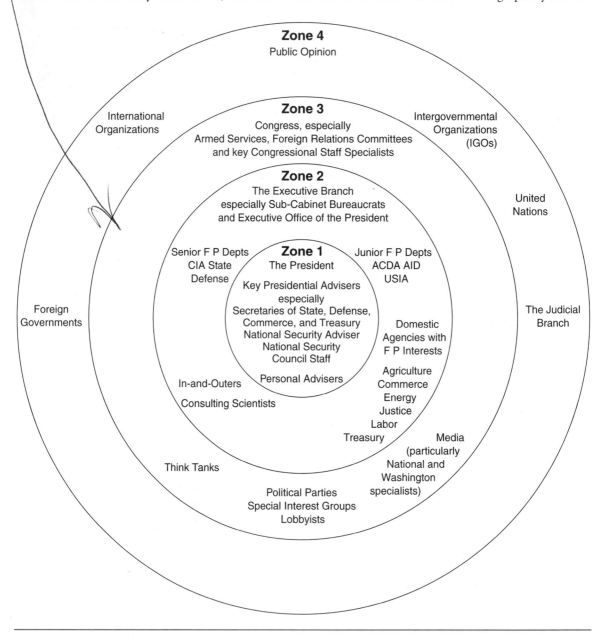

Do that!' *And nothing will happen.* Poor Ike—it won't be a bit like the Army. He'll find it very frustrating" (1990, 10; Neustadt's emphasis). The military ethos says that soldiers follow orders from their superiors in a rigid hierarchy. In contrast, politicians and government officials tend to dispute hierarchies and follow their own agendas. The result, as we see more fully in Chapter 5, is that presidents must struggle endlessly to impose their will on the executive branch, let alone the Congress.

Additionally, presidents have only finite time, which must be very carefully rationed. Time constraints preclude their examining all possible information. Limitations on time and what business theorists call **span of control,** the number of individuals whom one person can supervise effectively, mean that most presidential responsibilities must be delegated. Even most of the business of seeing that those delegated responsibilities are carried out falls to others. The responsibility buck may stop with the president, as Harry Truman's famous desk sign THE BUCK STOPS HERE asserted, but the president must rely on a host of others to advise about, plan, and execute policy, and those others do not always cooperate.

Several officials are traditionally considered senior and most influential among those who advise and serve the president. They are the same officials most concerned with foreign policy: the secretary of state, the secretary of defense, and, since about 1969, the president's national security adviser. The Department of State was the first executive department created, in 1789. It is charged with carrying out diplomatic activity and maintaining contacts with other governments worldwide. The Defense Department was created only after World War II, in 1947, by combining the former Departments of War and Navy. Cabinet secretaries heading these departments have broad responsibilities, though necessarily narrower than those of the president. They work full time in areas central to foreign policy and can command a very wide range of information. As issues of international trade and finance arise more frequently and become ever more important to U.S. foreign policy, the secretaries of commerce and treasury increasingly become top advisers to the president.

Issues of foreign policy and national security typically resist compartmentalization and overlap departmental jurisdictions, creating a pressing demand for interdepartmental coordination. The secretaries of state, defense, and treasury, like other cabinet members, supervise huge agencies and are under severe cross pressures. Presidents want their cabinets to impose the presidential will on the agencies on behalf of the administration, but cabinet secretaries are pressed from below to advocate agency positions to the president and the rest of the administration. For such reasons, no less a figure than vice president of the United States Charles G. Dawes (1925–29, under Calvin Coolidge, and otherwise as unknown as most holders of that office) once stated, "The members of the cabinet are a president's natural enemies." More recently, the problem of cabinet officers pressuring presidents on behalf of their agencies was demonstrated by Caspar Weinberger, Ronald Reagan's first secretary of defense (1981–87). Weinberger came to Washington with the nickname "Cap the Knife" for his budget-cutting prowess as a high official when Reagan was governor of California. Within little more than a year, however, Washington insiders decided the new secretary of defense had been taken captive by the admirals and generals because he pressed hard for defense spending increases substantially beyond the already large ones Reagan advocated and obtained. This problem of clashes between presidents and their high officials is further examined in Chapter 5.

Under the constitutional doctrine of **executive privilege**, a president is entitled to strictly confidential consultations with close advisers and exempt from being required to disclose information to congressional inquiries or the judiciary. The doctrine has its roots in the earliest presidential cabinets, but is not frequently invoked. Most claims of executive privilege are made to protect confidential diplomatic or military undertakings, or private discussions and debates between presidents and their very closest aides. A president's need for strictly confidential discussions and advice about alternative policies is obvious. The courts have rejected efforts by several presidents since Eisenhower to claim absolute and unconditional privilege, although they support most claims of executive privilege. Such claims are weakest when criminal charges are being brought against a president, as they were against Richard Nixon prior to his 1974 resignation.

The National Security Act of 1947 created a National Security Council (NSC) to "advise the President with respect to the integration of domestic, foreign, and military policies relating to the national security." It is the principal forum for examining issues of foreign and national security policy that require presidential decisions. Statutory members include the president as chairperson, the vice president, and the secretaries of defense and state. Statutory advisers to the NSC include the director of Central Intelligence (known in Washington as the DCI, and also head of the Central Intelligence Agency—CIA) and the chairman of the Joint Chiefs of Staff (JCS). Most presidents have added at least some other officials to the NSC either permanently or temporarily, depending on their personal inclinations and the policy issues under consideration. Presidents Truman and Eisenhower made relatively little use of the NSC. During the Kennedy administration (1961–63), however, a permanent supporting staff for the NSC was institutionalized. The director of that staff has usually held the post of assistant to the president for national security affairs. Hereafter, we follow the common Washington usage of NSA, for national security adviser to the president, whenever it will not cause confusion with the National Security Agency. Like any government official, the NSA serves at the pleasure of the president and could be fired at any time, although such changes are rare in most administrations. However, the NSA's charter covers all of national security, subject only to whatever limitations the president sets. It has always been difficult to distinguish between national security and foreign policy, particularly during the Cold War years. The NSA's broad responsibilities overlap and encompass those of the secretaries of state and defense, giving the position tremendous potential power. By the time of the Nixon administration (1969–74), the NSA had become second only to the president in determining U.S. foreign policy.

Nixon's NSA gained influence for both personal and institutional reasons. He was Henry Kissinger, an already noted Harvard University professor of government who had advised Nelson Rockefeller, among other Republican officials. Kissinger brought a powerful intellect and realpolitik perspective, along with substantial political skills, to his new role. He worked well with Nixon and deserved at least as much credit as Presidents Nixon and Ford (1974–77) for the major changes in U.S. foreign policy during their administrations. Institutionally, the NSA had the advantages of running a small department, organizationally located in the Executive Office of the President (making it relatively immune to congressional prying), and physically located in the White House basement. Many NSAs have had daily access to the president, including giving the president a daily briefing on national security issues. Secretaries of state, in contrast, are located many blocks away, have a large agency to supervise, and must request appointments with the president.

Kissinger made the most of these institutional advantages and soon was recognized by Washington insiders as the real foreign policy power in Nixon's administration. His role was convincingly demonstrated when foreign leaders visiting Washington began requesting meetings to discuss policy issues with Kissinger, rather than with William Rogers, Nixon's secretary of state until 1973. In that year Kissinger became the only person ever to hold the offices of both NSA and secretary of state simultaneously. Later he was forced to give up the former role for legal reasons. It was determined that one individual could not be both a cabinet secretary and a member of the Executive Office of the President because members of the latter are less subject to congressional scrutiny, making it unclear what the Congress can and cannot demand to know. Institutionalization of the presidency and the accompanying growth of the Executive Office of the President is further discussed later under zone 2. Almost all of Kissinger's successors as NSA have been less public figures, and President Reagan, who had six different NSAs, made a determined effort to downgrade the post. Nonetheless, it remains highly influential. Interestingly, after having served as NSA and secretary of state in the Nixon and Ford administrations, Kissinger himself decided that the secretary of state should be the president's primary foreign policy adviser. However, his deputy and successor as NSA to Presidents Nixon, Ford, and Bush, General Brent Scowcroft, later said (1981, 40) that Kissinger "never really moved over to the State Department [and] was never in a true sense of the word a Secretary of State."

Reflecting the tendency for economic and military dimensions of national security to converge and bring increased emphasis to global economic issues in the aftermath of the Cold War, newly inaugurated President Bill Clinton created a National Economic Council (NEC) as an executive branch advisory body by an executive order signed 25 January 1993. The NEC was intended to parallel the NSC in importance, coordinating national economic policy in the same way the NSC seeks to coordinate foreign and security policy. This reflected President Clinton's emphasis on and expertise in economic policy in preference to foreign policy. Investment banker Robert E. Rubin had already been named the previous month to head the NEC. Early reports indicated that the NEC would place special emphasis on monitoring U.S. trade competitiveness and curbing the export of industrial technologies in which the United States was thought to have an advantage. By late in Clinton's second term, it remained unclear whether the NEC would acquire the direct presidential access, supporting staff, and policy impact that have characterized the NSC. Conceivably, it could provide an important mechanism for coordinating policy among the half-dozen nominally domestic cabinet departments with foreign policy interests that are primarily economic in character. Although the NEC does not stem from a congressional mandate like the one that established the NSC, remember that the NSC gained real influence only after President Kennedy institutionalized its support staff by executive order.

A further and perhaps somewhat surprising category of presidential advisers in the most influential zone 1 is *personal advisers*. These are individuals known to and trusted by the president as personal friends, often going back many years. Usually they have no official government position, although President Kennedy appointed his brother and former campaign manager Robert as attorney general in order to have his highly skilled political advice close at hand and in the cabinet. (The Congress later made such appointments of relatives illegal.) Presidents seek personal advisers more for friendship and reality checks than for any specialized expertise. A longtime friend who has no government position and no personal stake in policy can be highly influential when virtually everyone the president sees wants something. Personal advisers may have no government experience. For example, one close friend and adviser of President Nixon was Robert Abplanalp, who became a millionaire by inventing the valve used on aerosol spray cans. Occasionally, however, scandals have resulted when presidential friends have proved to have personal financial interests in some government policy.

ZONE 2: THE EXECUTIVE BRANCH AND SPECIALIZED ADVISERS

Although zone 1 officials come closest to seeing U.S. foreign policy from a comprehensive viewpoint, almost all of U.S. foreign policy is carried out, and much of it is planned, in zone 2. Top-level diplomacy directly involving individuals from zone 1 is the most notable exception. In Chapter 6 we examine several of the few places where broad policy studies are conducted. Zone 2 comprises the entire executive branch of the U.S. government, to the extent that it deals with foreign policy, plus high-level consultants called in for specialized advice. Individuals and groups in zone 2 have narrower areas of responsibility and authority than those in the most central zone, but they have the detailed and specialized operational knowledge unique to people who deal with particular problems on a daily basis. Within their areas of authority, they can command almost all relevant information held by the government. Relative to zone 1 officials, they are more likely to be involved with day-to-day operations than with main issues, and that tendency increases as we move down the organizational hierarchy. Included in zone 2 are (1) a set of senior foreign policy departments (State, Defense, and Central Intelligence), (2) a junior set of departments created during the Cold War with more limited responsibilities (Arms Control and Disarmament Agency, Agency for International Development, United States Information Agency), (3) nominally "domestic" agencies that have some foreign policy interests (Agriculture, Commerce, Energy, Justice, Labor, Treasury), and (4) specialized consultants. The large number of these agencies reflects a fact we see more fully in Chapter 5: lines of authority and responsibility tend to be fragmented and overlapping.

The executive branch is an enormous **bureaucracy,** a great hierarchical structure of bureaus and subagencies with responsibility and authority funneling down from the president through cabinet secretaries and undersecretaries to the individuals and groups who carry out most policy actions. Few people get warm feelings when they hear the term *bureaucracy*, but organization theorists argue that it is one of the great inventions of civilization. Bureaucracies organize the means to carry out tasks that must be dealt with uniformly, frequently, and in great quantity. Most federal employees spend their entire careers in such agencies, as do most officials below the highest levels. No more than a few thousand officials lose their positions and are replaced by new appointees when there is a change of administration, and only a fraction of those appointments requires Senate confirmation. Those highly desirable appointive positions are listed in a congressional publication shortly after each presidential election; Washington insiders call it the "Plum Book." Policy stands previously taken by new appointees provide important symbolic signals about policies that a new administration may seek to adopt. Nonetheless, agencies are self-interested, and career officials are concerned both about their agencies' interests and their own progress. These considerations make the federal bureaucracy not just the channel through which policy must be implemented, but a source of tremendous policy continuity, inertia, and resistance to change.

A partial response to bureaucratic inertia by presidents in the last two thirds of the twentieth century was the institutionalization of the presidency reflected in creation and expansion of the Executive Office of the President. Beginning with President Franklin D. Roosevelt's election in 1932, the federal government became activist first at home, to combat the Great Depression, and then abroad, to fight World War II and the Cold War. One result was a several-fold expansion in the number of government agencies and employees. The Executive Office was created by Roosevelt under authority of the 1939 Executive Reorganization Act. As a subset of the executive branch, it is intended to be more responsive than other bureaucracies to presidential wishes and control, and less driven by its own institutional prerogatives and agendas. Like most government reorganizations, this one under Roosevelt was as much a matter of rearrangement as creation. It moved the already existing Bureau of the Budget out of the Treasury Department and created a new White House office. The former managed budgetary matters and the rest of the president's legislative program, and the latter provided an organizational home for the president's personal assistants and their staffs. Like the rest of the federal government, the Executive Office has grown significantly since 1939. Names of included offices and councils have changed considerably over time, and the list changes a bit with every new administration. Through more than four decades, however, the Executive Office has strengthened the president's hand as chief policy planner and administrator by making many of the top presidential assistants more independent of the remaining executive branch. For example, the only source within government of sufficient budgetary expertise to challenge what is now called the Office of Management and Budget (OMB) is the Congressional Budget Office (CBO). As a part of the Congress, however, the CBO cannot command the same level of access to data from federal executive branch agencies as the OMB can.

Within the executive branch, the Departments of State and Defense, together with the Central Intelligence Agency (CIA), are considered the senior agencies dealing with foreign policy. This seniority mirrors their representation in the inner circle of presidential advisers, and derives from the breadth of their responsibilities and the crucial role they play in planning and conducting foreign policy. Just as the Department of State manages diplomatic activity, the Defense Department has charge of planning and conducting the whole range of military activities. The Central Intelligence Agency was created in 1947 by the same National Security Act that established the National Security Council. CIA succeeded the wartime Office of Strategic Services, and was sought by President Truman in part to give him a source of intelligence gathering and analysis independent of the military establishment and the State Department. The CIA head, designated director of Central Intelligence or DCI, has overall charge of the complex and contentious process of determining what is likely to happen in the world. See also the discussion of how National Intelligence Estimates (NIEs) are made, in Chapter 6. As you will read in more detail in Chapter 5, subordinating agency biases to central control is a major motivation behind most presidential moves to reorganize the government.

Several departments and agencies created during the Cold War years are considered the more junior foreign policy departments, both because they are newer and because their areas of responsibility are narrower than those of State, Defense, and CIA. The United States Arms Control and Disarmament Agency (ACDA) is rare because it was originated more to limit the Cold War than to fight it. ACDA was created by congressional action led by Senator Hubert Humphrey and signed into law on 26 September 1961 by President John F. Kennedy. Supporters sought greater emphasis on controlling the intensive U.S. arms competition with the Soviet Union. ACDA was the only independent government agency in the world with the sole responsibility of formulating and implementing arms control policy. It always had a special and relatively independent status, and Congress mandated that ACDA's director serve as the president's principal adviser on arms control issues. ACDA's four primary activities were officially described as follows:

> The Agency conducts studies and provides advice relating to arms control and disarmament policy formulation; prepares for and manages United States participation in international negotiations in the arms control and disarmament field; disseminates and coordinates public information about arms control and disarmament; and prepares for, operates, or directs, as needed, U.S. participation in international control systems that may result from United States arms control or disarmament activities. (Office of the Federal Register, 1993, 751)

By Washington standards, ACDA is a tiny agency, housed within the two-block-square State Department building, and never numbering more than 200 to 400 persons. Different administrations have alternately blessed and cursed ACDA, and the agency's political fortunes have ridden a figurative roller coaster of fluctuating presidential support. Immediately after concluding the 1972 SALT I strategic arms limitation agreements with the Soviets, for example, President Nixon purged large numbers of ACDA officials. President Carter was criticized by Senate conservatives for appointing Paul Warnke, a notably dovish arms control advocate, to head ACDA. Four years later, President Reagan took liberal flak for appointing Kenneth Adelman, a young, hard-line conservative to the post, and critics argued that ACDA's top leadership had ceased striving for arms control. Through all such shifts, however, the agency continued playing a crucial role in the interagency process of approving U.S. arms control proposals.

A major battle over ACDA's future arose in the spring of 1993, when the new Clinton administration seriously considered abolishing the agency and folding its responsibilities into the State Department (*New York Times*, 21 April 1993). That proposal raised a more general issue often faced in government, namely, whether any specific area of policy concern (in this case arms control) can receive adequate attention without an independent agency power center to promote those concerns. In the aftermath of the Cold War, and with major agreements signed on eliminating intermediate-range nuclear forces (INF) in 1987, on reducing conventional forces in Europe (CFE) in 1990, on deep cuts in intercontinental strategic weapons (the START I Treaty in 1991 and START II in 1993), and on banning chemical weapons in 1993, there is general agreement that today's greatest arms control task is curbing the spread of nuclear arms and other "weapons of mass destruction" to additional governments. Of concern are the so-called *NBC weapons*, for nuclear, biological, and chemical weapons, together with long-range delivery systems such as missiles and strike aircraft. Arguments for reorganizing ACDA out of existence included the belief that the new challenges required reorganization.

Concerns about weapons proliferation were mirrored in the Defense Department by the appointment of a new assistant secretary, and in the State Department by a existing comparable position. ACDA defenders argued that both Defense and State have other missions with higher priority than arms control that often conflict with arms policy. The Defense Department is partly in the business of selling arms abroad, and in the early 1990s, the State Department was preoccupied with problems in Bosnia and Russia. During the 1980s, Defense promoted a Reagan administration "reinterpretation" of the 1972 Anti-Ballistic Missile Treaty that would have allowed space-based testing of Strategic Defense Initiative components, and State attempted to deny the existence of Pakistan's nuclear weapons program to keep that country eligible for U.S. military aid. ACDA officials opposed administration decisions in both those cases, keeping the issues under continuing review (see Resor and Rhinelander, 1993, and Smith and Krepon, 1993). These examples demonstrate why an independent agency can best promote a set of interests, a view clearly held by the Congress when ACDA was established. After several years of these arguments, President Clinton announced on 18 April 1997 a plan under which ACDA would be fully integrated into the State Department within one year, and USIA within two years. The agencies were given four months to prepare specific plans for the transition.

The United States Information Agency (USIA) operated for decades as an independent agency administering the foreign information and cultural programs of the United States. Although officially called "public diplomacy," many of these activities are more directly known as psychological warfare and propaganda, the systematic, widespread propagation and promotion of ideas and policies. *Propaganda* sometimes is true, but the term generally has a pejorative connotation. Recent usage often substitutes the broader and less emotionally loaded term *spin*, the interpretation of events in ways most favorable to oneself. USIA was established in 1953 and renamed the International Communication Agency from 1978 to 1982, before reverting to its original name. Its best known programs are the Voice of America, which broadcasts a variety of programs known for their candor and objectivity, and the Fulbright exchange scholarship program, which has supported the exchange of thousands of students and faculty between the United States and countries worldwide. One principal stated USIA objective is to "bring about greater understanding between the people of the United States and the peoples of the world." Activities include round-the-clock radio broadcasts in some forty languages, television programs, distribution and showings of documentary, feature, and newsreel films, and distribution of leaflets, pamphlets, news bulletins, and related propaganda materials. The USIA employs Americans and foreign nationals in more than a hundred countries and operates many information centers and libraries abroad, some of which have become targets for anti-U.S. demonstrations.

The Agency for International Development (AID) is sizable and has enjoyed a less controversial history than ACDA. AID is a semi-independent agency functioning as part of the United States International Development Cooperation Agency (IDCA) in directing economic and technical assistance programs to foreign states. Created by Congress in the 1961 Act for International Development, AID replaced the former International Cooperation Administration. AID was created particularly to implement President

Kennedy's (U.S.-Latin American) Alliance for Progress program, but its operations became worldwide. Those operations grew increasingly important as competition intensified with the Soviets and other communist states to help less developed states progress, partly in hopes of gaining their political allegiance. Thus AID may be seen as having administered the economic component of containment policy. Although military aid outweighed economic aid during the 1950s, all administrations during the 1960s and 1970s stressed economic aid programs. AID's role was reduced during the 1980s by substantial Reagan administration and congressional budget cuts, at the same time that military aid was greatly increased. AID administers developmental loans and grants, investment surveys and guarantees, and developmental research, reaching more than a hundred countries. The agency head has a dual role as chief of the operating agency (AID administrator) and IDCA director. Each AID program, of course, has its own supporting organization.

The intermestic nature of policy produces some foreign policy interests on the part of cabinet departments charged with nominally domestic concerns. Among affected agencies are the Departments of Agriculture, Commerce, Energy, Justice, Labor, and Treasury. Unlike the State Department, many of these agencies deal with major sectors of the economy that affect substantial domestic constituencies of workers, traders, and businesses. The United States is the world's largest exporter of food, and the Department of Agriculture seeks to promote foreign sales of U.S. food products, such as the grain long needed by the Soviet Union. When President Carter canceled grain sales to the Soviets in 1980 as one way to punish them for invading Afghanistan, many American farmers were upset, and Department of Agriculture officials protested. The Commerce Department seeks to promote exports, especially of U.S. manufactured goods. Like Agriculture, Commerce must be deeply concerned with trade barriers and incentives affected by multinational negotiations to which the U.S. government is a party, such as the World Trade Organization (WTO) and the North American Free Trade Agreement (NAFTA). The United States is the world's largest oil importer, and the Energy Department faces complex interactions among world oil prices, the oil reserves and income needs of individual foreign governments, and domestic interests that differ sharply between regions. Governments with limited reserves and south-central oil-producing states at home benefit from high oil prices; northeastern oil-consuming states at home and most foreign governments with large oil reserves prefer lower oil prices. The government of Saudi Arabia, for example, long supported lower world oil prices because it had been demonstrated that they produce fewer U.S. moves toward conservation and energy independence.

The Justice Department becomes involved in foreign policy when crime reaches across international borders. For example, drug trafficking from Central and South America has been a major problem in recent years. Late in 1989 U.S. troops invaded to seize the Panamanian dictator General Manuel Noriega, who had been indicted by two federal grand juries on drug charges. Subsequently convicted here, Noriega remains in a U.S. prison to this day. Labor Department interests generally intersect with but may oppose those of Commerce. Export trade is generally favored by domestic labor organizations because it supports American jobs. However, organized labor was a major source of opposition in 1993 to ratification of the North American Free Trade Agreement (NAFTA), which brought the United States into a free trade area with Canada and Mexico. Their concern, subsequently proved out by events, was that many U.S. jobs would be moved to

Mexico in search of lower wages. Finally, the Treasury Department has a compelling interest in worldwide monetary policy. If the value of the dollar declines against foreign currencies, it encourages U.S. exports by making it less expensive for foreigners to buy our products. If domestic interest rates fall, purchase of U.S. securities is less attractive to foreigners. Because most of the huge federal debt is in fairly short-term bonds, it must be refunded regularly. If foreigners decrease their bond purchases, the federal debt absorbs more of the domestic dollars available for investment, removing them from the private money market that supports domestic economic growth. In these sorts of ways, many agencies whose primary mission appears on the surface to be domestic turn out to have important foreign policy interests. Those interests have grown over the past several decades as economies around the world have become ever more globalized. The end of the Cold War has only compounded the change, by shifting concern from military security to economic security.

Two somewhat related groups of individuals in zone 2 remain to be examined; they are the consulting scientists and specialists, and the in-and-outers. In an age when governments may be seriously affected by highly technical matters, the need for specialized advice is obvious. Most government agencies have substantial expertise available in-house, yet outsiders may still be preferred for political reasons because they have no agency position to defend. If such consultants are imposed by outside decree and truly have no agency biases, however, agencies may be intimidated. Many such advisers are in-and-outers, people whose careers involve a number of alternations between periods working in government and times working in academia, business, or policy think tanks. (See, for example, the earlier box about Roger Hilsman.) Such individuals may be sought as officials or expert advisers or members of special study commissions. Their desirability for such roles stems from and is enhanced by their specialized nongovernmental experience. All too frequently, businesspeople limit their terms of government service because their pay and benefits are far below what they can receive in the private sector. This is one reason why there is often a good deal of turnover in high-level appointive positions on a four-year cycle, even when a sitting president wins reelection.

Many in-and-outers serve in government posts whenever their party holds the presidency, and find homes in policy study organizations in the interim years. This is particularly true for those several thousand appointed positions at the very top of the government hierarchy. Conservatives criticized President Jimmy Carter for choosing too many liberal appointees from among the ranks of the Atlantic globalist Trilateral Commission. After Carter lost to Republican Ronald Reagan in 1980, many former Carter administration officials took positions with the Brookings Institution, a liberal Washington policy analysis think tank, and many former members of the conservative Heritage Foundation were appointed to posts in the new Reagan administration. Less than two weeks after George Bush won the 1988 presidential election, the Heritage Foundation sent his transition planning team some two thousand résumés of individuals it wanted considered for those top posts. Such personnel movements are routine and reflect the fact that most of the top managers of U.S. foreign policy come from a fairly small elite, geographically centered in the Boston-New York City-Washington, D.C. axis. Members of that elite, especially the in-and-outers and the organizations with which they affiliate, form an effective shadow government in waiting, similar to but less formal than those common in parliamentary systems like that of Great Britain. Within the past two decades, policy think tanks like the

Brookings Institution and the Heritage Foundation have proliferated around Washington, becoming more active and increasingly partisan. Washington insiders, of course, are fully aware of the partisan and ideological leanings of such organizations. Their role in the policy planning process is further considered in zone 3 and in Chapter 6.

Although many special advisers and study commissions are simply political exercises to permit leaders to claim that something was done, others have substantial policy impact. Often they have broad authority to command access to information relevant to their inquiries and can concentrate full-time attention on their charge. Typically, they are backed up by supporting investigative staffs. For example, after the space shuttle *Challenger* blew up on 28 January 1986, a blue-ribbon special commission was appointed to determine the cause and recommend needed changes in the National Aeronautics and Space Administration (NASA) to reduce the chance of any recurrence. Like most special commissions, it became known by the name of its chairperson, William P. Rogers. As a Washington lawyer and former secretary of state (under President Nixon), Rogers knew the ways of administration and was respected within the government. Vice chairman was Neil Armstrong, the first man to set foot on the moon and thus the most prestigious of astronauts. He had previously eschewed any government service after leaving the astronaut corps, shunned publicity and lived quietly as a professor of aeronautical engineering at the University of Cincinnati. Another member of the Rogers Commission was the brilliant and iconoclastic Caltech physicist Richard P. Feynman. After more than a year of investigation and hearings, the commission issued a report recommending a number of management and procedural changes within NASA. The Rogers Commission report had significant impact not just on NASA, but on the entire U.S. space program. Over the next decade, exclusive reliance on the space shuttle system for satellite launches was phased out. Excessively optimistic plans for the numbers of shuttle launches and turnaround time between launches were revised. The military services were encouraged to shift from the shuttle to unmanned rockets to launch their satellites. Private firms were encouraged to enter the space launch business. The U.S. government began retreating from exclusive management of space technology that had been most highly developed in this country, and facilitated its internationalization. Telecommunications firms that had relied on NASA for satellite launch began to contract with government agencies or private launch firms in France, Japan, and China. Within the next decade, plans were well advanced to launch a new international space station beginning in the late 1990s. Those plans, of course, reflected the political decisions to deemphasize international competition in space, build new political ties in the post-Cold War era and into the new century, and distribute the substantial costs over more parties.

ZONE 3: CONGRESS, POLITICAL PARTIES, SPECIAL INTEREST GROUPS, AND THE MEDIA

Why are Congress, the political parties, and special interest groups, all clearly important players in the political process, not placed in a more central zone of influence? The Congress, after all, has certain unique powers, including the Senate's power to ratify treaties and the House of Representatives' power to originate bills appropriating money to run the government. Although it is less true today than in the past, none of the actors in zone 3 can command the same degree of access to information as members of the executive branch. Nor can they readily specialize as much as the actors in zone 2. Below the very highest levels, members of the executive branch tend to have highly subdivided and specialized responsibilities. By virtue of that specialization, they become expert to a degree that Congress members cannot equal. Within their areas of responsibility, executive branch bureaucrats can command ready access to needed information. Congress members may not even be aware that relevant information does or should exist. They often can be stalled or deflected from attempts to obtain critical details that an administration would prefer to keep confidential.

Members of the Congress must be generalists, dealing with a multitude of issues. Individual members develop interest concentrations and expertise, usually reflected in their committee assignments. Some members gain national reputations for their specialized abilities, for example, Senator J. William Fulbright of Arkansas during the 1950s and 1960s on foreign policy, Senator Sam Nunn of Georgia during the 1980s and 1990s on defense issues, and Representative Dan Rostenkowski of Illinois during the 1980s and 1990s on finance and taxation. Even those members, however, still must deal with the full range of issues before the Congress. Their solution is to build specialized abilities within the staffs of committees and individual members' offices. The majority of staff within any Congress member's office deal with constituent interests. Their tasks include discussing specific concerns with individuals and delegations, pursuing inquiries through the bureaucracy to determine why a constituent's Social Security check is late, and the like. A few staffers, however, specialize on issues pertinent to their Congress member's particular interests and committee assignments. When Senator Edward Kennedy (D-Mass.) served on the Senate Foreign Relations Committee, for example, he had a full-time foreign policy specialist on his staff. Specialized staffers may serve in committee positions, or may even work for several members. Defense specialist Robert Sherman, for example, first directly served three liberal young Democrats on the House Armed Services Committee in the 1970s, later held staff positions for that committee when Democrats held the majority in the House, worked for Representative Les Aucoin of Oregon, and moved to an ACDA position in 1993 after Aucoin narrowly lost a Senate race. Such career moves are typical for congressional staffers.

Elections are an additional factor reducing the foreign policy influence of Congress members relative to that of executive branch officials. Top officials hold office at the pleasure of their president and lower level bureaucrats usually have Civil Service career security, but Congress members must constantly think about their next primary and the next federal election. Traditionally, about 95 percent of incumbents who run again are reelected, although most work quite diligently to achieve it. With the luxury of six-year terms, senators usually can confine their reelection worries to the last two of those years, leaving them freer to adopt foreign policy stands based on national and global interests rather than home state preferences. Serving only two-year terms, members of the House of Representatives are constantly running for reelection. The pressures of an impending general election contest (or, worse yet, a primary fight) are powerful forces directing attention to the district and to constituent desires—and away from national and global issues, except to the extent that they impinge directly on the district. Fears about election impacts usually keep presidents from submitting controversial measures to the Congress in even-numbered years. President Carter took a risky step in forwarding the controversial Panama Canal Treaties for Senate ratification in 1978, and several senators who supported those treaties paid a price. In the 1990s public dissatisfaction with government in general seems to have played a large role in increasing congressional turnover and promoting a nationwide movement to set term limits for political offices, including those of senators and representatives. Voters elected 110 new members to the House of Representatives in 1992, the largest such group in more than four decades. Many were elected to seats vacated by retiring incumbents, however, and such retirements soared during the 1990s. Only time will demonstrate whether new members conduct business much differently than their predecessors. Presidents have been limited to a maximum of eight years in office since the Twenty-Second Amendment was ratified in 1951, a limitation that may increase their extensive reliance on staff and advisers for expertise. Term limits for Congress members work strongly against developing the sorts of expertise that take a long time to build up, and demonstrated, for example, by Senators Fulbright and Nunn or Representative Rostenkowski, and tend to increase congressional reliance on staff specialists. All these considerations work to reduce congressional influence on foreign policy in favor of the president and the executive branch bureaucracy.

As the twentieth century wound toward its close, Congress generally was less concerned about foreign policy than during the Cold War. Foreign policy concerns were less often front-burner issues, so Congress members tended to become even more responsive to domestic electoral pressures. To this was added the post–Vietnam War breakdown of previous consensus—whether it had been real or only apparent—on a "bipartisan foreign policy." Although these were not the only causes, they contributed to increasingly harsh partisan division in the Congress and in Washington politics generally during the 1980s and 1990s. Previously, especially during the first two decades after World War II, the majority and minority leaders of crucial congressional committees had been especially important managers of consensus. Congressional standing (permanent) committees central to foreign policy concerns include the House and Senate Armed Services Committees, the House Foreign Affairs Committee, and the Senate Foreign Relations Committee. Important committees with less frequent and pervasive foreign policy impact include the standing Appropriations Committees, the Select Committees on Intelligence, and the various standing committees that deal with the concerns of the nominally domestic federal agencies. Because a great deal of expertise resides within the committee staffs, much vital behind-the-scenes interaction takes place among staff members, federal bureaucrats in zone 2, and lobbyists.

Lobbyists represent and advocate special interests. The term originated in the 1830s, based on the tendency of such advocates to populate the lobbies of Congress, the White House, and executive branch offices in hopes of buttonholing officials and legislators. By having specialized representatives tracking their interests on the scene, lobbying organizations tend to be much better informed than members of the general public. Although they cannot command the same official access to information as bureaucrats, members of Congress, and congressional staffers, they often receive restricted inside information from sympathizers at all levels in government. Lobbyists can be highly influential in shaping policy. Given the ability to specialize full time, they are among the best informed people in Washington within their areas of interest. Backed up by the often substantial resources of sponsoring organizations, they can receive serious attention from Congress members eager for campaign support funds. Cynical observers argue that dispensations of political action committee (PAC) campaign funds by lobbyists are legal bribes to

Congress members dependent on such support to win reelection. Hundreds of organizations hire lobbyists and maintain offices in Washington to help them obtain sympathetic treatment—and often more tangible benefits—from government. They span an enormous range of interests. Businesses, for example, are represented by the National Association of Manufacturers (NAM), labor is represented by the American Federation of Labor-Congress of Industrial Organizations (AFL-CIO), and they took opposing stands on the 1993 ratification of NAFTA. K Street is filled with the offices of organizations representing foreign countries. Following the 1996 election, serious charges were raised that foreigners, notably including Indonesian businesspeople, and foreign governments, most notably the Chinese, had tried to buy influence with political campaign contributions laundered through lobbyists.

The major political parties play a complex and changing role in foreign policy, and their policy stands altered significantly over the last two or three decades of the twentieth century. Like the larger special interest groups, they maintain sizable organizations in Washington and throughout the country. Policy specialists track legislation and federal regulation and perform many of the same advocacy functions as lobbyists. Unlike special interest groups, however, major political parties represent extremely broad coalitions of interests. Although there is some validity to common stereotypes that Democrats are liberal and prolabor and Republicans are conservative and probusiness, both traditional major parties cover very broad ideological ranges, with substantial overlap. Partly because of their ideological breadth and intersection, U.S. political parties do not play nearly as major a role as parties in most parliamentary systems. In Britain, for example, the identifications of one party (Labour) with working-class interests and another party (Conservative or Tory) with business and finance interests are far more comprehensive than party sympathies in the United States, and the legislative programs of the two parties differ much more. Strong party loyalty is crucial in a parliament, where the government can stand or fall on a single roll-call vote. Nomination for reelection may be withheld from members who fail to support their party's leadership on an important vote. In the U.S. Congress the only strict party-line votes are those electing the leaders of the two houses, and the penalties for defection on key votes are uncertain and variable. If the U.S. political system featured party loyalty comparable to Britain's, the president and administration would craft their legislative program and, provided their party had a majority in the Congress, that program would sail smoothly through the approval process.

Whereas parliamentary governments fall if they lose a legislative majority, the United States has often had **divided government,** under which one party holds a majority in Congress while the other party holds the presidency. Many opinion polls in the last two or three decades of the twentieth century showed majorities of the public preferring divided government, apparently in hopes of limiting the ability of either party to do too much mischief. Republicans held the presidency for 28 of the 48 years from the end of World War II through 1992, and Democrats held majorities in the House of Representatives throughout that period except for 1953–55, and in the Senate except for 1953–55 and 1981–87. Republicans regained majorities in both houses of Congress in 1994, although they were unable to win back the presidency in 1996. Party majorities in Congress are somewhat misleading, however, because there is often little policy cohesion within either party.

Divided government forces most presidents to build congressional coalitions across party lines to pass their programs, and exacerbates the weakness of American political parties. If voters' loyalties are sufficiently undisciplined to elect divided governments, presidents cannot readily cajole uncooperative Congress members by withholding party or administration support for their reelection. We can discern some regularities in the parties' foreign policy positions, but defections have plagued presidents increasingly in recent decades, beginning with splits over Vietnam War policy. Defections over treaty ratifications have been especially troublesome. Carter could not hold his southern Democrats to support the 1979 SALT II arms control treaty, which was eventually withdrawn from consideration for ratification. Clinton needed more Republican than Democratic votes to win House approval of the NAFTA treaty in 1993. The latter case is more fully examined in Chapter 11, but demonstrates some of the changes that have overtaken the political parties as concerns about economic security have grown. Prior to the 1970s, many Democrats and many of the labor unions that usually supported them were strongly internationalist and encouraged lowering tariff barriers to trade, and Republicans generally supported higher, more protectionist tariffs. The United Automobile Workers union (UAW) held a typical pro–free trade view. But their view shifted as foreign automobiles gained an ever-increasing share of the U.S. market and American automakers responded by downsizing their companies and increasing the offshore content of their products. Losing members as factories closed, the UAW became more concerned with job security and retraining programs than wage increases. The once pro–free trade UAW became strongly protectionist, supporting import quotas and higher tariffs. A large majority of today's congressional Democrats supports protectionist policies, and a slim majority of Republicans favors free trade. Similar policy realignments on other issues have helped limit the impact of the political parties on foreign policy. The Congress remains a disparate group of individuals, lacking unity along party or almost any other lines. This leaves presidents and their administrations with difficult coalition-building tasks, but may actually increase their policy influence relative to the Congress.

Policy **think tanks** are organizations dedicated to full-time policy analysis and advocacy. They are a particularly interesting zone 3 group, combining features of special interest groups and political parties. Some, like the Carnegie Endowment for International Peace or the Worldwatch Institute, deal almost exclusively with foreign or intermestic policy issues. Others, like the Brookings Institution and the Heritage Foundation, deal with a mix of foreign and domestic policy issues. The majority of think tanks deals primarily with domestic issues and is of little interest to us here. Like interest groups, think tanks seek to educate citizens and government officials, although more to improve government as they define improvement than to convert people to their cause. Like interest groups, think tanks also link government and the public, although different segments of the public. Most think tanks focus on the politically active community of intellectuals interested in policy, rather than on citizens with similar interests. Like political parties, think tanks advocate both general and specific policies, but usually in lower key and less overtly politicized ways. As noted earlier, policy think tanks have proliferated around Washington since World War II and especially since the Kennedy administration (1961–63). The number of openly partisan think tanks has increased considerably since the advent of political action committees (PACs). Washington insiders, of course, are fully aware of the partisan and ideological leanings of such organizations. Think tanks originate from a tradition of apolitical reform and provide a substantial body of expertise as well as a home away from government for in-and-outers. Many are highly regarded for their expertise, for example the Brookings Institution for its economic studies. The role of think tanks in the policy planning process is further considered in Chapter 6.

Media include newspapers, magazines, radio, television, and the Internet. They provide channels for widespread dissemination of news, interpretation, and opinion. Hilsman, writing in 1967, placed media in the least influential zone. Since then, however, the direct and indirect roles of media in shaping U.S. foreign policy have grown dramatically. We have lived for some time in a television age, in which astute politicians take maximum advantage of their coverage. Political effects range from the benign to the pernicious. When President Kennedy was assassinated in 1963, several days of almost nonstop television coverage promoted national healing and helped dispel fears of a broader threat or conspiracy. Additionally, the political use of media can be highly educational. Major events during President Nixon's precedent-shattering 1972 trip opening ties with the People's Republic of China were carried live via still-new satellite television relays, carefully scheduled to occur at times convenient to viewers in the United States. That coverage helped sell a major policy change to the public while doing Nixon's reelection chances a world of good. At other times, election campaigns degenerate into sound bites and media may be used by government to manipulate public opinion. Cable News Network (CNN) coverage of the 1991 Persian Gulf War was watched even by government leaders and made CNN a serious news competitor to the three established broadcast networks. However, coalition military authorities allowed media access only to selected activities, both to manage public opinion at home and to disinform Iraqi authorities. Coverage of U.S. marines poised for an amphibious assault on the Kuwaiti coast perpetrated a bluff, keeping several Iraqi divisions immobile when they might have helped repel the main coalition strike overland. Reporters were kept uninformed about the great westward shift of troops and supplies prior to the main assault (the "Hail Mary" play), and could say only that a great deal of movement was occurring.

Persian Gulf War experience illustrates one of the major limitations on media's influence in shaping foreign policy: journalists themselves can be manipulated by government officials. More importantly, the media devote only limited attention to foreign affairs, and their coverage is spotty. Major international news may be the stuff of headlines in flashy instances like the Israeli–Palestine Liberation Organization (PLO) peace agreement of 1993, but relegated to the back pages when it concerns detailed and technical issues like Ukraine's hesitancy to follow through on its 1991–92 agreements to ship all its nuclear weapons to Russia for dismantling. Except in times of war or crisis, the vast majority of television and other media coverage is devoted to celebrities, sports, other entertainment, and local news. Only a small minority of media professionals play any significant and ongoing role in the foreign policy process.

A few reporters and columnists are as highly informed in specialized and technical areas as any lobbyist in zone 3. Apart from deliberate leaks of information, they cannot command all the information available to a congressional staffer in zone 3 or a bureaucrat or in-and-outer in zone 2. Nonetheless, the analyses of some reporters and columnists are so cogent that they are closely followed in Washington, both inside and outside government. Consider several examples: Hedrick Smith, long a foreign affairs columnist for the *New York Times*, authored two best-selling books about Russia and its people and became

THE INTERNET AND FOREIGN POLICY

The Internet and its graphically oriented World Wide Web experienced explosive growth during the 1990s. Politicians, officials, and ordinary citizens still struggle to comprehend its potential. Optimists see a tremendous advance in communication, freedom, and access to information. Pessimists see threats to privacy and power structures and widespread access to bad information, whether "bad" is defined as pornography or as organizing manuals for grassroots political activism. Electronic mail, documents, and pictures can be sent worldwide almost instantaneously and at low cost. These capabilities tremendously accelerate the globalization of business and of financial markets. As we see in more detail in Chapter 11 and later, this has both desirable and undesirable effects on different groups of people. Within the United States, businesses heavily dependent on information retrieval already have been revolutionized. Lawyers, for example, already are dispensing with rooms of law books because they can conduct faster, more comprehensive, and more accurate research through online services like Westlaw.

The Internet appears to have widely varying potentials for influencing foreign policy and the ways in which it is conducted. Currently, Internet and Web availability are largely restricted to the wealthiest and most developed countries. With appropriate support, that might be broadly extended to developing states to help them leap-frog past some earlier stages of communications technology. Citizens already connected can use the Internet as a rapid channel for lobbying and gathering information. They have rapid access to many sites maintained by major newspapers and newsmagazines, government agencies, think tanks, lobbying organizations, businesses, political parties, and international organizations like the United Nations. From these they can download such items as the president's daily schedule, the secretary of state's speech yesterday before the Washington Press Club, the text of a newly signed treaty, the list of accessions to the Climate Change Convention, and a lobbying organization's ratings of Congress members. Except for limitations imposed by stages of development, international reach is almost as easy as domestic. Lobbying organizations use the Internet both to recruit and to inform members, and to organize campaigns. (See the case of Amnesty International in Chapter 12.) Whether the Internet will become a force for the international spread of democracy, however, remains unclear. For example, China's government requires that all Internet connections be run through its service provider and imposes severe penalties on any Chinese who connect through offshore links. By these means, they hope to block their citizens' access to such so-called subversive sites as the *New York Times* or the *Washington Post*.

an independent journalist. *Time* magazine correspondent Strobe Talbott learned enough about strategic arms and U.S.-Soviet arms control negotiations to author several books about those negotiations and the people who conduct them, and was appointed to a high Defense Department post in the Reagan administration and the second highest post in the State Department in the Clinton administration. Leslie Gelb, a political scientist with two years' experience in academia and nine in government, became a foreign and military policy columnist for the *New York Times* from 1973 through 1977. Joining the Carter administration as director of the State Department's Bureau of Politico-Military Affairs in 1977, Gelb returned to the *Times* after Carter left office, actually switching jobs with his predecessor (Marquis, 1977). Individuals this influential, however, are a distinct minority among the large journalistic community.

ZONE 4: THE PUBLIC, JUDICIAL BRANCH, AND INTERNATIONAL INFLUENCES

The group and individual actors in zone 4 have less influence on U.S. foreign policy than those in the three central zones for two interrelated primary reasons: limited access to information and limited share of attention. Those actors may be divided into the following three groups: (1) the general public, particularly as represented by public opinion polls; (2) the judicial branch of government; and (3) all international actors, including foreign governments, international organizations, and intergovernmental organizations such as the United Nations. Of these three groups, only the judicial branch has any formal authority to command access to information.

The general public presents a set of apparent contradictions. A generation ago, political scientists believed public opinion about politics in general and foreign policy in particular was both uninformed and unstructured. Although initially it appears paradoxical, today we believe public opinion about foreign policy to be uninformed but highly structured. Every study asking ordinary citizens factual questions about foreign affairs finds their knowledge level disturbingly low. For example, even during Nixon's détente with the Soviets and Reagan's defense buildup, few people understood many of the critically determinative details either of the negotiations themselves or the weapons they concerned. Despite such findings, however, other studies show that most people have stable and highly structured belief systems. From *core values*, such as their beliefs about ethnocentrism or the validity of war as a policy tool, they make reasonable extensions to *general principles* like militarism or anticommunism. Then from their general principles they draw logical conclusions about *specific policies* like recognizing Castro's government in Cuba or agreeing with Russia about nuclear disarmament or granting most-favored-nation (MFN) trading status to China. The thought processes involved are examined in the section of Chapter 3, "Is the Public Well Informed and Logical About Foreign Policy?"

Even if individuals have logically and consistently structured belief systems, though, few citizens spend enough time to become and remain well informed about foreign affairs, and all are dependent on government and the media for most of their factual information. Because ordinary citizens have only limited and indirect access to foreign policy information, they are ripe for manipulation. Foreign policy is commonly considered to be led by an elite of politicians, bureaucrats, and others with sufficient direct interests to be well informed. A good picture of that elite is given by the set of opinion leaders surveyed in the quadrennial Chicago Council on Foreign Relations surveys, as shown in Table 4.2. The individuals in that table, together with the groups from which they were selected, encompass most of the domestic actors already discussed here in zones 2 through 4. These are precisely the people to whom most citizens look for information about what is happening in world affairs and guidance regarding how they should think about those events. Looking to such actors for interpretations is consistent with the *cognitive miser*

TABLE 4.2

Opinion Leaders in the U.S. Foreign Policy Elite
As surveyed by the Gallup organization for the Chicago Council on
Foreign Relations (1990)

Category	Number	Individuals and Roles Selected for Interviews
Congress: House	28 Personal Interviews	Chairers of Committees on Agriculture; Appropriations; Armed Services; Banking, Finance, and Urban Affairs; Budget; Energy and Commerce; Foreign Affairs; Government Operations; House Judiciary; Intelligence; Interior and Insular Affairs; Science Space and Technology; Ways and Means; and Select Committee on Hunger. Chairers of 24 major subcommittees of those 15 committees. Speaker of the House.
Congress: Senate	22 Personal Interviews	Chairers of Committees on Agriculture, Nutrition and Forestry; Appropriations; Armed Services; Banking, Housing and Urban Affairs; Environment and Public Works; Finance; Foreign Relations; and Judiciary. Chairers of 16 major subcommittees of those 8 committees. President of the Senate Pro Tempore.
Administration	24 Personal Interviews	Assistant Secretaries from White House Office; Office of Management and Budget; National Security Office; Office of the U.S. Trade Representative; Departments of Agriculture, Commerce, Defense, Energy, Justice, State, Transportation, and Treasury; Agency for International Development; Nuclear Regulatory Commission; U.S. International Trade Commission; and Veterans Administration.
Business	63 Phone Interviews	Vice presidents in charge of international affairs, chosen from among the top 200 industrial corporations in the Fortune 500 list and the *Corporate 1000 Yellow Book* of managers of the leading 1000 listed U.S. companies.
Media	27 Personal	Television news directors, network newscasters, and radio news directors from major networks.
	15 Personal	Newspaper editors and columnists from major newspapers. Foreign news editors from the three primary wire services.
	15 Personal Interviews	Editors from 15 major news magazines and the following foreign affairs magazines: Foreign Affairs; Foreign Policy; World Politics; Orbis; and International Studies Quarterly. All respondents selected based on extent of their involvement with international news.
Labor leaders	32 Personal	Presidents selected from among the largest 50 labor unions. Vice President of the International Division, U.S. Chamber of Commerce.
Educators	62 Phone	Presidents and faculty who teach in the area of foreign affairs, selected from a list of 60 major universities.
Religious leaders	47 Phone	Leaders representing all faiths, proportionate to the number of Americans who follow each faith.
Special interest groups	22 Phone	Presidents of large special interest groups relevant to foreign policy, including trade and professional organizations, think tanks, and foreign policy research and action organizations.
Private foreign policy organizations	20 Phone	Presidents of major private foreign policy organizations, including think tanks and foreign policy research and action organizations.

theory examined in Chapter 3, because it is reasonable to expect these people to be well informed. Citizens may select among such sources according to their already established personal and political preferences. Accepting interpretations of fact and guidance about desirable policies from people you trust can be a rational way to reach a consistent set of foreign policy beliefs without having to take the trouble to become informed in detail.

The judiciary are placed in Zone 4 because they rarely become involved in U.S. foreign policy. When they do, however, their role is highly significant, for they are the arbiters of disputes not only between the public and government, but between the executive and legislative branches. For example, the president was not legally declared the chief foreign policy official of the country until a 1933 Supreme Court ruling in the case *U.S. v. Curtis-Wright Export Corporation*. Congress had passed legislation allowing the president to prohibit sales of arms abroad for cause. Under terms of that law, President Roosevelt barred shipments to belligerents in the Chaco War in South America. Curtis-Wright Export Corporation sold machine guns in violation of that ban and was taken to court by the Justice Department, losing on appeal. In its ruling, the Supreme Court declared that the president had the power to prohibit the sale because of his role as chief foreign policy officer, plus specific enabling legislation. In other rare cases, the courts have been called on to settle clashes between the president and Congress, although they are usually very reluctant to become involved.

A major case that went to the Supreme Court began with President Carter's sudden and rather unexpected 1978 announcement that the United States would upgrade its ties with the People's Republic of China. Moving beyond maintaining liaison offices in the respective capitals, the two governments would establish full diplomatic relations, complete with an exchange of ambassadors. The United States agreed to downgrade its ties to the Republic of China on Taiwan to less than full diplomatic relations, a condition insisted on by Beijing with all foreign states, and to sever its mutual defense treaty with Taiwan. Carter duly provided Taiwan with the one-year notice of U.S. withdrawal required under that treaty. Conservatives in the Senate were outraged, calling this a betrayal of our longtime anticommunist allies on Taiwan. Under the Constitution, of course, the Senate must consent to the ratification of treaties. Limited historical precedents exist on both sides of the issue of whether the Senate must also consent to terminating a treaty. After a somewhat lengthy debate, a "sense of the Senate" resolution claiming for itself a consenting role in the termination of treaties was approved on a preliminary vote. However, no final vote was ever taken, so the Senate technically did not place itself in conflict with the president. Several of the more conservative members filed suit in the federal courts challenging Carter's action. A divided Court of Appeals, on the merits, held that presidential action was sufficient by itself to terminate treaties (*Goldwater v. Carter*, 617 F.2d 697 [D.C.Cir.][en banc]). Upon appeal, the Supreme Court vacated that decision and instructed the trial court to dismiss the suit (444 U.S. 996 [1979]). Four justices found the matter a nonjusticiable political question, once again demonstrating reluctance to rule on clashes between the president and Congress. Although no Supreme Court ruling bars future litigation on this issue, it appears likely that the political question doctrine or some other rule of judicial restraint will leave the matter to be resolved politically.

The *international actors* placed in zone 4 include foreign governments; international nongovernmental (NGOs), whose members may include individuals across state borders, as in Greenpeace; and intergovernmental organizations (IGOs), whose members are the governments of states, as in the United Nations. The only formal roles international actors have in the U.S. governmental process stem from the principle that treaties ratified by the United States are considered the law of the land just as surely as is domestic legislation. International actors have only very limited access to information. They devote attention primarily to their own interests, although their representatives in this country and their U.S. specialists at home help overcome that limitation by tracking intersections between their concerns and those of the United States. When foreign and U.S. interests clash, the competition automatically limits foreign influence here. However, many foreign governments have learned to play the U.S. domestic side of intermestic policy quite well. For example, in addition to the usual meetings with the president and leaders of the administration and Congress, almost every U.S. visit by an Israeli prime minister includes meetings in New York City with leaders of major Jewish organizations, urging them to lobby the U.S. government in support of Israel's policy. Given a substantial number of Jewish voters in this country and the fact that many of them can be influenced by those organizations, such lobbying is potent. Clearly, there is a connection between the facts that (1) there are far more Jews than Muslims among the American populace, and (2) U.S. policy has long been dominantly pro-Israel in Middle East conflicts.

Many other governments have learned to lobby the United States. Some do so directly by hiring Americans or sending their own lobbyists to Washington, and those individuals properly belong in zone 3. In May 1993, for example, it was announced that Mexico would spend $30 million lobbying for congressional approval of the North American Free Trade Agreement (NAFTA). Other governments lobby less directly. For example, when Chinese prime minister Zhu Rongji visited Washington in April 1999, he publicly failed to persuade President Clinton to support China's entry into the World Trade organization. (The administration feared congressional concerns about Chinese nuclear spying and giving China permanent most-favored nation trading status.) Zhu then toured major U.S. cities and spoke before business groups, touting significant Chinese concessions on long-fought trade-access issues. Major corporate political donors began bombarding the White House with requests to take a second look at Zhu's proposals, which played into major policy disagreements within the administration. Clinton capitulated, arranged another round of trade talks, and promised "strong support" for China's accession to the WTO in 1999.

The United Nations is a special case among international actors. As the United States emerged from World War II, the new UN was envisioned as a vehicle for overcoming mistakes made after the First World War. The United States would be intensively involved in this new intergovernmental organization, which symbolized our hopes for an enduring world order conducive to Western democracy and would have effective means for maintaining the peace. Most member states were U.S. friends or allies, and we led the dominant voting bloc during the early UN years. Unfortunately, the new world organization was never designed to keep peace among the five great powers endowed with veto-wielding permanent seats on the Security Council. Once Cold War global politics was polarized around the two superpowers, every dispute immediately took on an East-versus-West dimension. This usually paralyzed the UN, with the notable exception of the Korean War. With the end of the U.S.-Soviet competition that characterized the Cold War, the UN suddenly became free to realize its full potential, but that potential remains uncertain. The Western democracies no longer dominate the General Assembly. By the end of 1997 the UN had 185 member states, more than four times the number of independent sovereign states in the entire world in 1945. By far the largest group of states today is nonaligned developing states. Their issues tend to be polarized along the North-South axis between the (mostly Northern Hemisphere) developed states and the (mostly equatorial and Southern Hemisphere) developing states. Although those issues have long been with us, they were long overshadowed by the Soviet threat, at least as seen from the United States. Reflecting its hopes for the UN role in the post–World War II world, as well as the lack of any other capable sponsor, the United States paid most of the UN budget in the early years and still pays about one quarter. This is a source of frustration to some political conservatives, who see little return for the expense, distrust the UN, and fear it could set real limits on U.S. sovereignty.

THE FLOW OF POLICY IDEAS AND INFLUENCE BETWEEN ZONES

Our review of the positioning of foreign policy actors into four zones of relative influence already has covered much about their specific powers and duties. Recall that actor assignments to zones are based on their statutory authority to act, access to information, and share of attention available to devote to foreign policy. Those assignments also represent an application of the first two criteria for a systems perspective on the foreign policy system: identifying the members and the relationships between them. We turn now to examining the flow of policy ideas between zones, an important application of the third systems criterion, focusing on the dynamics of how the system functions. As we do so, remember the following key points developed in the previous section as we examined the four zones of relative influence:

- Very few officials see U.S. foreign policy from a comprehensive viewpoint. Those in zone 1 come closest.
- Most officials are much more involved with day-to-day operations than with main issues. That tendency increases as we move down the organizational hierarchy.
- Throughout the U.S. foreign policy system, lines of authority, responsibility, and influence tend to be fragmented and overlapping.

ZONE 2: THE SOURCE FOR MOST NEW POLICY IDEAS

Executive branch actors in zone 2 are the primary sources of ideas, information about policy alternatives, and policy recommendations. Those actors include the people involved at high levels in day-to-day foreign policy operations in departments like State and Defense. Unlike the president and most presidential advisers in zone 1, they can devote full time to their areas of expertise. Leaders in zone 1 usually select from among policy options prepared in zone 2. And although those leaders occasionally lay down broad policy outlines, they rely on actors in zone 2 to work out most of the details and implement policies. Zone 2 is also the source of most ideas that flow outward. One truism of American politics is that "The president proposes, the Congress disposes." Not just the federal budget, but almost every major piece of legislation is sent up to the Congress by the president. That legislation is drafted by federal bureaucrats in zone 2, particularly in the Executive Office of the President. Special interest groups in zone 3 also propose policies, sometimes persuading members of Congress, the federal bureaucracy, and even presidents. Interest groups can win on economic issues if their desires do not conflict with established policies of the federal agencies. Occasional media representatives become as highly informed about specialized matters as anyone else in zone 3, but media usually respond to and publicize policy alternatives rather than initiating them. One notable exception occurred in 1977 when the highly respected CBS news anchor, Walter Cronkite, interviewed Egyptian president Anwar Sadat. Cronkite unexpectedly asked Sadat about his willingness to travel to Israel if that would promote the cause of peace. Sadat answered affirmatively, and the Israeli government seized the opportunity. Although he only reiterated established Egyptian positions, the symbolic message that Sadat made a state visit to Jerusalem on 9 November 1977 was what mattered. He incurred the wrath of most other Arab governments and of Islamic fundamentalists, who would assassinate him in 1981. Sadat's Jerusalem visit, however, opened the door to a formal peace treaty between Israel and Egypt, signed 26 March 1979 after intensive 1978 negotiations mediated by President Carter at the Camp David, Maryland, presidential retreat (see Chapter 10).

CRISES AND RALLYING AROUND THE PRESIDENT

Public opinion about foreign policy is usually formed as a *response* to presidential action, especially in a time of crisis. Charles Hermann's three conditions for crisis are reviewed in Table 4.3. High threat, short decision time, and surprise are the antitheses of the conditions of routine decision making under which bureaucracies thrive. Indeed, as we see more fully in Chapter 5, the vast majority of decision-making situations is routine. One way in which organizations attempt to avoid crises is through *contingency planning*, developing alternatives to be applied on a "what-if" basis. Unfortunately, it is almost impossible to anticipate every contingency. When crises do occur, the instinctive response of most citizens is to look for leadership from the president as chief foreign policy officer. The same conditions that make a few decision situations into crises also attract great attention to those cases. Decision making under crisis has been much studied, partly because of fears that leaders often make wrong decisions under pressure. Crises tend to produce greater centralization of decision making, which helps speed action. Responses to crisis, however, tend to be less innovative and more bellicose than actions taken under less pressure and after greater deliberation. Unfortunately, the term *crisis* is casually applied to myriad situations that meet only one or two of Hermann's criteria. A useful exercise for you is to test any alleged crisis against those criteria. Additionally, detailed examination of specific cases often raises ambiguities. Frequently some official in government did anticipate what developed, only to have that analysis rejected in the processes of policy planning and review.

Rallying of public opinion around the president in times of crisis frequently produces brief increases in presidential popularity, even in the event of foreign policy "losses" for the country. Table 4.4 shows changes in public approval of the way the president is carrying out the duties of office, measured across the onset of a number of crises and other major events. Some of those cases are clear foreign policy victories for which the president deserves at least some of the credit. In the 1978 Camp David summit, President Jimmy Carter undertook to mediate a Middle East conflict most analysts considered almost impossible, and he deserves enormous credit for the peace agreement achieved. Despite being a clear foreign policy win for Carter, however, Camp David netted him only

TABLE 4.3	
	Conditions for Crisis Decision Making

High threat to important interests; **high stakes** at issue

Short decision time in which to select what actions are to be taken

Surprise, or little advance anticipation

Source: Compiled from the research of Charles Hermann, 1972, 14.

a 13 percent increase in approval rating. He gained 29 percent in approval in 1979–80, starting from the low 30s, when he responded strongly to the Soviet invasion of Afghanistan and the Iranian seizure of diplomats in the American embassy in Tehran. Rises in the polls in such cases of clear foreign policy losses or great challenges for the United States often seem to indicate public approval of firm presidential action.

Unfortunately, presidents can use the expectation of public trust and the rally effect to mislead and manipulate. Richard Nixon campaigned in 1968 with the promise of a "secret plan" for ending the Vietnam War, and he claimed that divulging details would only help the enemy undermine that plan. After the war, Nixon's own national security adviser and secretary of state, Henry Kissinger, revealed there never was any secret plan beyond muddling through in the war effort and relying on the gullibility of U.S. voters. In the absence of a consensus, presidents also can use inconsistency in public opinion to argue against changes in policy.

Although public support may change rapidly in response to new developments, it can give the president a powerful lever to move the Congress. President Bush's approval ratings ranged as high as 90 percent after the first firm response to Iraq's invasion of Kuwait in 1990, as well as during and immediately after the 1991 Persian Gulf War. By the time Bush asked Congress to approve direct action against Iraq by U.S. troops in January 1991, he also had an authorizing UN Security Council resolution. Members of Congress who opposed his policy believed they were in immediate trouble with their voters at home. Such leverage can be fleeting, however, because public opinion can shift fairly rapidly. By the end of 1991 the spring victory in Kuwait and Iraq no longer seemed so decisive, attention had shifted to domestic economic troubles, and Bush's approval ratings had slipped to as low as 47 percent. Ultimately, Congress members who had opposed the Persian Gulf War suffered little at the polls in November 1992. In great contrast to Bush's leverage early in 1991, Washington insiders generally believed throughout most of 1993 that President Bill Clinton was hampered by having won election with only a plurality, 43 percent of the popular vote in a strange three-way contest. After Clinton finally demonstrated his ability to use all the powers of the presidency to win the NAFTA debate in November 1993, analysts began revising those estimates.

IMPACT OF PUBLIC OPINION ON FOREIGN POLICY

Despite the ability of presidents to manipulate public opinion, and despite public expectations of presidential leadership, public opinion *can* change foreign policy. Such change only comes slowly, however. The most notable case of recent decades is the Vietnam War.

TABLE 4.4		Changes in Presidential Popularity with the Onset of Crisis or Major Problems	
		Percentage change in respondents approving of the job the president is doing	

President	Year	Event	Change
Franklin Roosevelt	1941	Pearl Harbor bombed; War declared on Japan, Germany	+12
Harry S Truman	1947	Announcement of the Truman Doctrine	+12
	1950	Firm and rapid response to invasion of South Korea	+ 9
Dwight Eisenhower	1954	Indo-China peace agreement; U.S. stays out, for now	+11
John Kennedy	1962	Cuban Missile Crisis	+12
Lyndon Johnson	1967	U.S. bombs Hanoi; Six-Day War in Middle East	+ 8
Richard Nixon	1973	Vietnamese peace signed; U.S. withdraws troops	+16
Gerald Ford	1975	U.S. intervenes in Cambodia to free Mayaguez crew	+13
Jimmy Carter	1978	Camp David summit: Egyptian-Israeli peace agreement	+13
	1979	U.S. diplomats taken hostage in Tehran; Soviets invade Afghanistan; Carter invokes sanctions	+29
Ronald Reagan	1983	U.S. intervention in Grenada; Major U.S. troop losses in Lebanon peacekeeping (announced simultaneously)	+ 7
George Bush	1991	Opening of the air war against Iraq (change in one week)	+20

Public opinion was always divided about the war, but slowly shifted from an overwhelming majority supporting the administration in the early 1960s to a near majority opposing by the late 1960s. A seminal event affecting public opinion was the great Tet guerrilla offensive of 1968. Although U.S. military authorities were correct in their assessment that they had stopped the enemy's best effort, the North Vietnamese and Vietcong were correct in their political judgment that they had demonstrated U.S. inability to defeat them by all the force employed to that date. After Tet, U.S. policy shifted decisively from indefinite escalation to reducing the American force commitment and finding a way out. Vietnam is the outstanding case demonstrating that no administration can resist public opinion indefinitely. It also vies with the Persian Gulf War case for top honors in demonstrating media influence in shaping public opinion about foreign policy issues.

How can public opinion change foreign policy? All the channels used for other political causes are available, including direct appeals to members and staffers in Congress and the administration, and indirect appeals through special interest groups that maintain lobbyists. Nonetheless, American politics scholars hold that foreign policy concerns *usually* do not decide national elections. William Schneider (1997, 35–36) argues that President Bill Clinton "knows two great political truths about foreign policy." From Lyndon Johnson's Vietnam War experience he learned that "foreign policy can destroy you." In contrast, George Bush's experience of losing the 1992 election after soaring to 90 percent approval two years earlier during the Persian Gulf War demonstrates that "foreign policy cannot save you." Clinton's 1992 campaign strategists certainly must have hoped that this was true because their in-house slogan was "It's the economy, stupid." Collectively, these lessons suggest that presidents will tend to be politically wary of foreign policy.

Conventional scholarly wisdom long has held that ethnic groups can expedite consensus policies, but not reverse them. By the 1990s, however, the ethnic politics of so-called hyphenated Americans was gaining strength. Examples of long standing, such as the American Jewish lobby in support of Israel, already have been mentioned. In the 1990s, however, the breakup of the Soviet Union helped give impetus to intermestic ethnic politics. The Baltic states of Estonia, Latvia, Lithuania, which had large exile populations living in America, regained their independence. Indeed, many of those Baltic Americans began moving back to their countries of origin. The same happened with others of the former Soviet republics. Ethnic clashes within those republics only added to the pressures. By 1996 the Clinton reelection campaign had even designated a staffer for outreach to Albanian Americans (Glastris, 1997).

Political scientists have found that constituency views convert Congress members much more effectively on domestic issues like civil rights and social welfare than on foreign policy issues. This could result both from congressional deference to the administration and from the general public's limited information and lack of time to track foreign affairs. Another possible channel for changing policy is through elections, but that path is slow and imperfect. Our most frequent federal elections, to the House of Representatives, occur only in alternate years, with the vast majority of incumbents being returned to office. When we elect a senator or representative, are we voting for a delegate expected to echo our views slavishly, or an honest person expected to do his or her best for the country (or at least the district)? How do we resolve situations in which a Congress member differs from the majority of constituents on only one major issue? How should a member vote when district opinion includes a large and vocal minority? These are all fundamental questions in democratic voting theory, and none have easy solutions that satisfy all citizens.

ROLE OF POLITICAL IDEOLOGY

On relatively rare occasions, political ideology seems to be a prime determinant of congressional voting. When it does, it appears that policymakers act on their own deeply held views. Appeals may be made to public opinion, but the links between constituents' views and Congress members' votes and reelection usually seem to move too slowly for the issue at hand. To examine the role of ideology, let us begin with the ideological spectrum shown in Figure 4.3. The great majority of voters and members of Congress are moderates, lying in the middle of that spectrum. Progressively fewer are found as we move either left or right of center. In general, those toward the left end are more accepting of big government and regulation, and those toward the right end seek smaller government and deregulation. These are generalities, of course, and the major political parties have members and officeholders spanning a wide range. For example, there are many conservative Democrats and a number of liberal Republicans. Additionally, a politican may have conservative views on some issues and liberal positions on others. In a European parliamentary system like that of France, we would find many parties across the spectrum, each fairly narrow in its range of beliefs. Partly because of the very wide range of beliefs among citizens belonging to a U.S. political party, it is common for special interest groups to rate

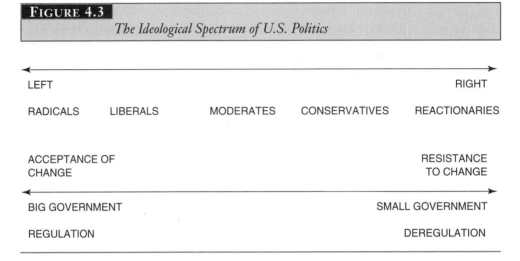

FIGURE 4.3

The Ideological Spectrum of U.S. Politics

Congress members on agreement or disagreement with their particular legislative agenda. Typically, this is done by selecting ten or twelve critical votes on which the group has taken positions during the last Congress. The selected votes often attract little public attention because they concern amendments about whether the group's issue even gets into a final bill. Interest groups then rate Congress members according to their percentage agreement with the group's stands on the selected critical votes. For example, the conservative Americans for Constitutional Action might give a liberal Congress member a rating of 20 percent, and the liberal Americans for Democratic Action might give the same member an 80 percent approval rating.

Using a computational procedure called *unfolding analysis*, political scientists including Carnegie-Mellon University's Keith Poole have used such ratings from dozens of interest groups across the entire ideological spectrum to produce overall ideological orderings for the Senate and House of Representatives. The resultant orderings give a picture of how individual members fit into the ideological spectrum of the larger body, based on their views across a wide range of issues. None of this says that an individual member cannot hold a liberal position on one issue and a conservative position on another. Most members, however, have fairly consistent ideological positions across the range of issues they must decide. Two such orderings for the U.S. Senate are given in Tables 4.5 and 4.6, each for a year in which an ideologically polarized issue had to be decided.

Certain regularities are immediately apparent in Tables 4.5 and 4.6 on pages 156 and 157. Listings begin with the most liberal senators at the top of the first set of columns and end with the most conservative at the bottom of the second. Although there were changes in membership, senators still in office six years later were almost all within ten positions of their previous locations. Senators may become as much as twenty positions more conservative in the last two years of their terms, but they almost always return to similar ideological positions if reelected. The votes reported in both tables concerned strongly emotional issues and show very high correlations with ideology. In 1972 the United States and the Soviet Union signed the SALT I strategic arms limitation agreements, which included an Anti-Ballistic Missile (ABM) Treaty limiting both sides to very small ABM forces, and a five-year executive agreement effectively capping U.S. and Soviet strategic missile arsenals at then-existing levels. That ABM Treaty is still in force, and the SALT I executive agreement began a sequence of agreements now continued with the Soviet successor states. The Nixon administration argued that it was justifiable to allow the Soviets more intercontinental ballistic missiles (ICBMs) and more missile-carrying submarines because the United States had multiple-warhead missiles carrying larger numbers of warheads than the Soviets, plus more submarines on station. But allowing larger numbers to the Soviets did not sit well with conservatives. They worried about what would happen when the Soviets installed multiple warheads on their land-based missiles, which had larger payload capacities than their U.S. counterparts. (Dealing with that very development was a major motivation behind Reagan administration defense spending increases only a decade later.) Led by Washington senator Henry M. Jackson, a strongly prodefense Democrat, conservatives brought forward an amendment to the bill ratifying the SALT I agreements, stating that

> [T]he Congress recognizes the principle of United States-Soviet Union equality reflected in the anti-ballistic missile treaty, and urges and requests the President to seek a future treaty that, inter alia, would not limit the United States to levels of intercontinental strategic forces inferior to the limits provided for the Soviet Union. (York, 1973, 273)

Regardless of how its military significance may have been perceived, and despite its often very weak relationship to truly sound measures of the strategic "balance," in this instance numeric equality clearly was perceived by many in the Senate as a *politically salient* measure of nuclear parity. Jackson and the conservatives prevailed. As shown in Table 4.5, taking the most liberal senator (Edmund Muskie of Maine) as position 1 and the most conservative (Carl Mundt of South Dakota) as position 100, the most liberal twenty-four senators opposed the Jackson Amendment. There was only one yes from the most liberal third of the Senate, and only four no votes among the most conservative half, with the last no from Senator Cooper of Kentucky at position 60. A line drawn between positions 38 and 39 (Senators Hatfield and Randolph) yields only six deviations on each side from a perfect ideological split. Given traditions of conservative fear of the Soviets and liberal support for arms control, the issue was important and emotionally charged for both sides, and an ideological split was reasonable.

An even more emotional and ideologically polarized issue was ratification of the new Panama Canal Treaties in 1978. The canal's construction was an American engineering triumph of the early twentieth century. After midcentury, however, the canal's clouded political history and quasi-colonial U.S. perpetual rights "as if sovereign" within a 10-mile-wide zone across Panama raised increasing problems with Latin American and developing states. On 22 January 1903 the United States had signed a treaty with Colombia allowing it to dig a canal across the Isthmus of Panama, then a Colombian province. Colombia proceeded to reject the treaty. With U.S. support, Panama declared independence on 3 November 1903. Her independence was recognized by President Theodore Roosevelt three days later, and a new treaty was signed on 18 November. Although U.S. payments for use of the canal had been raised over the years, the near-colonial administration of the Canal Zone became decreasingly popular throughout the region, particularly after decolonialism peaked in the 1960s. Negotiations looking toward eventual Panamanian control were begun during the Johnson administration, continued under

TABLE 4.5
1972 Senate Ideological Ordering, with Jackson Amendment Votes

Senator	State	Party	Vote	Senator	State	Party	Vote
Muskie	ME	D	N	Bible	NV	D	Y
Hart	MI	D	N	Bentsen	TX	D	Y
Kennedy	MA	D	N	Cannon	NV	D	Y
Mondale	MN	D	N	Aiken	VT	R	N
Nelson	WI	D	N	Weiker	CT	R	N
Cranston	CA	D	N	Spong	VA	D	Y
Hughes	IA	D	N	Scott	PA	R	Y
Williams	NJ	D	N	Smith	ME	R	N
Eagleton	MO	D	N	Packwood	OR	R	Y
Harris	OK	D	N	Cooper	KY	R	N
Tunney	CA	D	N	Long	LA	D	Y
McGovern	SD	D	N	Cook	KY	R	Y
Gravel	AK	D	N	Beall	MD	R	Y
Case	NJ	R	N	Saxbe	OH	R	Y
Hartke	IN	D	N	Griffin	MI	R	(None)
Mansfield	MT	D	N	Taft	OH	R	Y
Burdick	ND	D	N	Roth	DE	R	Y
Ribicoff	CT	D	N	McClellan	AR	D	Y
Stevenson	IL	D	N	Gambrell	GA	D	Y
Symington	MO	D	N	Fong	HI	R	Y
Humphrey	MN	D	N	Bellmon	OK	R	Y
Proxmire	WI	D	N	Talmadge	GA	D	Y
Bayh	IN	D	N	Sparkman	AL	D	Y
Pell	RI	D	N	Miller	IA	R	Y
Inouye	HI	D	Y	Jordan	NC	D	Y
Church	ID	D	N	Young	ND	R	Y
Moss	UT	D	N	Allen	AL	D	Y
Metcalf	MT	D	N	Byrd	VA	I	Y
Javits	NY	R	N	Jordan	ID	R	Y
Brooke	MA	R	N	Dominick	CO	R	Y
Pastore	RI	D	Y	Allott	CO	R	Y
Magnuson	WA	D	Y	Baker	TN	R	Y
Schweiker	PA	R	N	Dole	KS	R	Y
Percy	IL	R	Y	Edwards	LA	D	Y
Mathias	MD	R	N	Gurney	FL	R	Y
McIntyre	NH	D	Y	Ervin	NC	D	Y
Montoya	NM	D	Y	Stennis	MS	D	Y
Hatfield	OR	R	N	Eastland	MS	D	Y
Randolph	WV	D	Y	Buckley	NY	C	Y
Fulbright	AR	D	N	Hruska	NE	R	Y
Jackson	WA	D	Y	Brock	TN	R	Y
McGee	WY	D	Y	Bennett	UT	R	Y
Stafford	VT	R	Y	Cotton	NH	R	Y
Stevens	AK	R	N	Curtis	NE	R	Y
Chiles	FL	D	Y	Tower	TX	R	Y
Anderson	NM	D	Y	Thurmond	SC	R	Y
Pearson	KS	R	Y	Fannin	AZ	R	Y
Hollings	SC	D	Y	Hansen	WY	R	Y
Boggs	DE	R	Y	Goldwater	AZ	R	Y
Byrd	WV	D	Y	Mundt	SD	R	(None)

TABLE 4.6

1978 Senate Ideological Ordering, with Panama Canal Treaties Votes

Senator	State	Party	Vote	Senator	State	Party	Vote
Kennedy	MA	D	Y	Percy	IL	R	Y
Metzenbaum	OH	D	Y	Huddleston	KY	D	Y
Clark	IA	D	Y	Pearson	KS	R	Y
Culver	IA	D	Y	Bumpers	AR	D	Y
Sarbanes	MD	D	Y	Hodges	AR	D	Y
Pell	RI	D	Y	Sparkman	AL	D	Y
Cranston	CA	D	Y	Ford	KY	D	N
Bayh	IN	D	Y	Deconcini	AZ	D	Y
Hathaway	ME	D	Y	Stone	FL	D	Y
Reigle	MI	D	Y	Hollings	SC	D	Y
Muskie	ME	D	Y	Packwood	OR	R	Y
Williams	NJ	D	Y	Cannon	NV	D	Y
Leahy	VT	D	Y	Morgan	NC	D	Y
Glenn	OH	D	Y	Chiles	FL	D	Y
M. Humphrey	MN	D	Y	Talmadge	GA	D	Y
Abourezk	SD	D	Y	Bentsen	TX	D	Y
Javits	NY	R	Y	Long	LA	D	Y
Nelson	WI	D	Y	Schweiker	PA	R	N
McGovern	SD	D	Y	Bellmon	OK	R	Y
Case	NJ	R	Y	Baker	TN	R	Y
Durkin	NH	D	Y	Danforth	MO	R	Y
Matsunaga	HI	D	Y	Stevens	AK	R	N
Ribicoff	CT	D	Y	Nunn	GA	D	Y
Eagleton	MO	D	Y	Zorinsky	NE	D	N
Hart	CO	D	Y	Dole	KS	R	N
Inouye	HI	D	Y	Johnston	LA	D	N
Stevenson	IL	D	Y	Domenici	NM	R	N
Moynihan	NY	D	Y	Griffin	MI	R	N
Haskell	CO	D	Y	Thurmond	SC	R	N
Brooke	MA	R	Y	Hayakawa	CA	R	Y
Jackson	WA	D	Y	Stennis	MS	D	Y
Anderson	MN	D	Y	Schmitt	NM	R	N
Gravel	AK	D	Y	Lugar	IN	R	N
Magnuson	WA	D	Y	Allen	AL	D	N
Byrd	WV	D	Y	Young	ND	R	N
Mathias	MD	R	Y	Eastland	MS	D	N
McIntyre	NH	D	Y	Bartlett	OK	R	N
Burdick	ND	D	N	Byrd	VA	I	N
Hatfield	MT	D	Y	Wallop	WY	R	N
Weicker	CT	R	Y	Roth	DE	R	N
Church	ID	D	Y	Helms	NC	R	N
Proxmire	WI	D	Y	McClure	ID	R	N
Stafford	VT	R	Y	Tower	TX	R	N
Biden	DE	D	Y	Goldwater	AZ	R	N
Randolph	WV	D	N	Scott	VA	R	N
Melcher	MT	D	N	Laxalt	NV	R	N
Hatfield	OR	R	Y	Hansen	WY	R	N
Heinz	PA	R	Y	Curtis	NE	R	N
Chafee	RI	R	Y	Garn	UT	R	N
Sasser	TN	D	Y	Hatch	UT	R	N

Presidents Nixon and Ford, and finalized under President Carter. The new agreements provided for gradual Panamanian takeover of the canal and withdrawal of U.S. troops, all to be completed by the end of 1999. Liberals supported the changes because they believed they would improve U.S. foreign relations in the region. Additionally, the canal was vulnerable both to nuclear war and guerrilla attack. The largest modern warships and tankers cannot transit the canal, making it less vital to U.S. security than it was during World War II. Many conservatives still opposed giving up a symbol of U.S. technological prowess when there was no legal reqirement to withdraw, a virtual "we stole it fair and square" attitude.

Ratification of the Panama Canal treaties produced unusually close public attention to two key Senate votes, one on 16 March 1978 approving a treaty guaranteeing the area's neutrality beginning in the year 2000, and a second vote on 18 April ratifying the turnover of the canal to Panama on 31 December 1999. When ratifying a treaty, the Senate debates and passes a bill called an *instrument of ratification*, in the same manner as other bills. In this case, the Senate added some thirty conditions to the instrument, effectively revising the treaty. Such action is highly unusual, but the Panamanians accepted the Senate's conditions, recognizing they would lose even more by insisting that negotiations be reopened. Opponents of the treaty conducted unusually active lobbying. Conservative opposition groups organized grassroots efforts in the states of vulnerable senators like Nebraska's conservative Democrat, Edward Zorinsky. Table 4.6 reports votes on 18 April, and the fit to ideology is even tighter than for the 1972 Jackson Amendment. A line drawn between positions 68 and 69 yields only five no votes above and five yeses below. Only four senators among the most liberal two thirds voted no. Among the most conservative twenty-seven, only California's maverick Hayakawa voted yes. Almost all senators voted their consciences, that is, according to their personal political ideologies, without regard to home state preferences. Zorinsky was able to vote no, but had promised President Carter his support if absolutely necessary. He still lost the next election.

Dramatic evidence of how strongly politicians may feel about such ideologically polarized issues appeared nearly seventeen years after the Panama Canal Treaties were ratified. In January 1995 President Clinton withdrew the nomination of Robert Paster to be U.S. ambassador to Panama. Senator Jesse Helms (R-N.C.), archconservative chairman of the Senate Foreign Relations Committee, strongly opposed Paster because he had worked on the Panama Canal Treaties negotiations, which Helms called a "giveaway" of the canal. Paster's previous association with the treaties ran headlong into a "litmus test" on Helms's part. Of course, Washington insiders do not carry around printed ideology listings like Tables 4.5 and 4.6. Nonetheless, they usually have accurate mental images of legislators' and bureaucrats' ideological leanings. If we can identify issues that tap fundamental emotional and political values, knowing lawmakers' overall ideological positions can be a powerful predictive tool.

CONGRESSIONAL HEARINGS, LEAKS, AND WHISTLE-BLOWERS

Sometimes, congressional hearings are very powerful tools to publicize ideas and shape policy. Officially, Congress passes legislation to solve problems. Congressional committees and subcommittees hold hearings to determine whether specific problems exist and what might best be done through legislation to solve them, and to answer similar questions about draft legislation sent up to the Congress by the executive branch. The most important question about any hearing is always who is called to testify. Hearings can be opportunities to bring out the views of the best qualified experts on every side of an issue, making the published committee report a mine of information for students, scholars, and interested citizens. Alternatively, hearings can be manipulated by committee chairs to present extremely biased interpretations by suppressing some views and promoting others. Whether biased or not, the information brought out in hearings may attract media attention, converting public, administration, and even congressional opinion. Thus hearings become another means for Congress members and staffers to influence actors in the other zones, either directly or indirectly through public opinion. This sometimes leads to hearings on what appear to be unlikely subjects for the committees or subcommittees involved. For example, in 1978 the dominant conservative majority on the House Armed Services Committee believed U.S. land-based ballistic missiles were becoming vulnerable to a Soviet first strike and was blocking exposure of more liberal views contesting that judgment. Hearings to publicize the views of the committee's more liberal members had to be held by an unlikely subcommittee on which they held a majority, the Subcommittee on Intelligence and Military Application of Nuclear Energy (1978).

Another tactic that can influence policy makers is the **leak,** a deliberate sharing of restricted or classified information outside official channels in hopes of changing policy. Leaks have become an important channel for Washington policy wars since several highly publicized leaks during the Vietnam War. Indeed, Richard Nixon resigned the presidency rather than be impeached and convicted for his efforts first to organize and then to cover up the burglary of Democratic Party National Headquarters in the Watergate building. The burglars had been called the "plumbers" because their task was to locate and stop leaks regarding Vietnam policy. A particularly notorious case was the leaking of the secret Pentagon Papers analyzing the Vietnam war effort. Political scientist and CIA analyst Morton Halperin, who oversaw their drafting, was thought by some to have been involved when those papers were passed to the *New York Times*. When President Bill Clinton appointed Halperin to the new post of assistant secretary of defense for democracy and human rights in 1993, it provoked a firestorm of conservative protest in the Senate, and the nomination was withdrawn in early January 1994. Few leaks generate so much publicity as these cases, however. Most originate in zone 2 and go to members of Congress, congressional staffers, or special interest groups and media representatives in zone 3.

Leakers and media members tend to be synergistic, and leaks have little policy impact without publicity. If media pick up on a leak, coverage can help generate public pressure on the administration. Sympathetic Congress members and lobbyists can arrange publicity through press releases and hearings. On a number of occasions, leaks have uncovered mistakes and illegal activities, for example, abuses in Pentagon contract cost overruns. This can involve the special category of **whistle-blowers,** government employees who expose illegal activities, often to congressional investigators. All too often, though, bureaucrats are able to retaliate against leakers and whistle-blowers. One celebrated case of retaliation in the 1980s involved A. Ernest Fitzgerald, the Pentagon whistle-blower who exposed cost overruns on the giant C-5A transport aircraft. Moreover, legitimate policy disagreements exist within any administration. Sometimes those whose ideas and interpretations have lost out in the regular policy-making processes employ leaks to prolong their policy battles. When those losers are correct, the public benefits. More often, the process of making policy decisions is unnecessarily complicated and prolonged. Since

THE PROBLEM OF PAST PRESIDENTS

Finding useful and rewarding roles for past presidents presents a difficult task for them and the nation alike. No higher political offices remain to seek. Only a few past presidents have been willing to accept lower offices, and we never have settled the role of "elder statesperson." Living past presidents have been relatively rare throughout most of U.S. history, although that may be changing because of lengthening life expectancies and several recent one-term presidencies. Presidents typically come to power in middle age or later. The stresses of office exact a fearful toll, and few live for decades after leaving office. Many have died in office, as did Franklin Roosevelt. Others, like John Kennedy, have been assassinated. Very few past presidents remain truly public figures and maintain public policy roles, although there are some exceptions. Richard Nixon, the only president to resign from office in the face of certain impeachment and conviction (in 1974), lived out his last two decades in New York City. From there, he maintained extensive ongoing contacts at the highest policy levels, and wrote a series of books that partially rehabilitated his political image as a foreign policy expert. Upon his death in 1994, most politicians, from President Clinton on down, ignored Nixon's 1974 disgrace and lauded his accomplishments. The most notable of those, of course, were the 1972 foreign policy moves of opening effective diplomatic relations with China and signing the first strategic arms control agreements with the Soviets. In a very different postpresidential career, after Jimmy Carter lost his 1980 reelection bid he went on to build a solid reputation as an international peacemaker and mediator, and a builder of houses for the homeless through Habitat for Humanity. His Carter Center presidential library in Atlanta was established as a center for international peace activities. Among currently living former presidents, Carter has maintained the most presidential role and the highest national and international visibility, including frequent foreign trips to serve as a peace negotiator or neutral observer. Finally, in a very rare event, the five then-living past presidents (Nixon, Ford, Carter, Reagan, and Bush) joined President Clinton in 1993 in publicly endorsing the North American Free Trade Agreement (NAFTA). Their endorsement was echoed by all the then-living former secretaries of state.

the Vietnam war era, leaks have become more and more common, simply another means to ensure that policy is never completely settled.

SUMMARY

U.S. foreign policy is conceived and executed by a large and complex sociopolitical system that spans the globe and is made up of a huge number of individuals and large organizations. That foreign policy system shares the following four defining criteria of all systems: members, relationships between them, functions by which it performs certain tasks, and some degree of predictability. The system primarily processes information. It receives inputs about the actions of others, generates outputs of policy and action, and receives feedback in the form of information about the effects of actions taken on others and the international environment. That feedback is used to adjust policies to more closely approach desired outcomes. Information about the major actors in the system, the relationships between them, and some of their functioning may be organized by placing those actors into four zones of decreasing relative influence on foreign policy. Placements of actors into those zones are based on three interrelated principles determining their relative influence or impact on foreign policy: (1) responsibility deriving from constitutional or statutory authority; (2) access to needed information; and (3) share of time and attention available for foreign policy.

By directing our attention to identifying the members, relationships, and functions of the foreign policy system, the systems approach gives us a useful general tool for interpreting how policy is made in particular substantive areas and how it may be made in dealing with some new problem that has just surfaced. It also helps us focus on those functional limitations that contribute to policy failures and less-than-optimal outcomes. Among those limitations are the following: (1) Very few officials see U.S. foreign policy from a comprehensive viewpoint. Those in zone 1 come closest. (2) Most officials are much more involved with day-to-day operations than with main issues. That tendency increases as we move down the organizational hierarchy. (3) Throughout the U.S. foreign policy system, lines of authority, responsibility, and influence tend to be fragmented and overlapping.

Actors in zone 1 are the most influential, and consist of the president as preeminent foreign policy official, together with top presidential advisers. Those advisers include the secretaries of state and defense, the president's national security adviser, the National Security Council staff, and personal advisers used by the president for nongovernmental reality checks. Zone 2 comprises all foreign policy actors throughout the executive branch of the U.S. government, plus high-level consultants called in for specialized advice. Much of U.S. foreign policy is planned, and most foreign policy is carried out, in this zone, except for top-level diplomacy directly involving individuals from zone 1. Particularly important roles are played by the Executive Office of the President and three senior foreign policy agencies, the Departments of Defense and State and the Central Intelligence Agency. Many nominally domestic departments have foreign policy interests that are increasing with the globalization of economies. Also included in zone 2 are specialized consultants and in-and-outers whose careers alternate government service with periods in academia, business, or policy think tanks.

Zone 3 comprises actors who have intense policy interests but cannot devote full time to foreign policy and/or cannot command as good access to information as those in the more central zones. Key actors include the Congress, especially congressional staff specialists and the committees on armed services, foreign affairs, and foreign relations; plus political parties, special interest groups, lobbyists, and media. Congressional staffers, lobbyists, and national and Washington specialists among the media may develop great foreign policy expertise. Although a few foreign policy specialists in media are highly informed and influential, all media suffer from limitations on available time and access to information, and are subject to government manipulation. Zone 4 comprises public opinion, the judicial branch, and all foreign actors. Public opinion is generally not well informed and lacks quick and direct channels to influence foreign policy. However, ordinary citizens have logical and consistently structured opinions, are able to assimilate new information, and are capable of forcing eventual policy change. The judicial branch of government is only rarely involved in foreign policy, notably to resolve clashes between the executive and legislative branches. The influence of international actors is usually limited by their attention to their own interests, although many foreign governments have learned to play the U.S. domestic side of intermestic policy rather well. A particularly intricate intermestic relationship exists between the UN and U.S. politics.

Executive branch actors in zone 2 include the people involved at high levels in day-to-day foreign policy operations and are the primary sources of ideas, information about policy alternatives, and policy recommendations. Congress generally deals responsively with proposals by the president and legislation drafted in the executive office of the president. Public opinion is usually formed as a response to presidential action, especially in times of crisis. Foreign policy is changed only slowly and incrementally by public actions through normal political channels such as lobbying and elections. Presidents have significant powers to manipulate public and Congress alike by controlling media and other access to information. Congress members may utilize publicity through the hearings process to shift policy by changing public and governmental views. Occasional issues tap fundamental emotional and political values in public and government alike. Legislators generally follow their consciences on such issues, so that knowing lawmakers' overall ideological positions becomes a powerful predictive tool. Over the past two decades, executive branch actors have turned increasingly to deliberate leaks of restricted or classified information in hopes of changing policy by influencing public and congressional opinion. The multitude of actors and modes of affecting policy ensure that policy is never completely settled. Profound changes in the global policy environment since the end of the Cold War already have led to changes among the actors making policy, and in their interrelationships and relative power. Globalization of economics and the rising importance of international trade, for example, have moved the secretaries of commerce and treasury into the central zone of influence when economic security is at stake.

The remaining three chapters in Part II allow us to extend the systems approach by examining in greater detail how the foreign policy system functions. In particular, they deal with the processes by which U.S. foreign policy is formulated and carried out, and reasons why policy goals are so seldom fully realized.

KEY TERMS

Bureaucracy	Members
Divided government	Predictability
Executive privilege	Relationships or connections
Feedback	Span of control
Functions	Stability
In-and-outer	Structure
Institutional design	Subsystem
Leak	System (See also *living system*.)
Living system	Think tanks
Lobbyists	Whistle-blowers
Media	

SELECTED READINGS

Bennett, W. Lance, and David L. Paletz, eds. 1994. *Taken by Storm: The Media, Public Opinion, and U.S. Foreign Policy in the Gulf War.* Chicago: University of Chicago Press. Provocative pieces by major scholars concerning the links between public opinion and foreign policy, and how the U.S. government strongly manipulated Gulf War coverage.

Graber, Doris A. 1997. *Mass Media and American Politics,* 5th ed. Washington, D.C.: CQ Press.

Hermann, Charles F. 1972. "Some Issues in the Study of International Crisis." In Charles F. Hermann, ed., *International Crises: Insights from Behavioral Research* (pp. 3–17). New York: Free Press.

Holsti, Ole R., and James N. Rosenau. 1984. *American Leadership in World Affairs: Vietnam and the Breakdown of Consensus.* Boston: Allan & Unwin.

Page, Benjamin I., and Robert Y. Shapiro. 1992. *The Rational Public: Fifty Years of Trends in Americans' Policy Preferences.* Chicago: University of Chicago Press.

CHAPTER 5

MODELS AND PROBLEMS OF POLICY DECISION MAKING

VIETNAM: POLICY FAILURE AND THE LIMITS OF POWER

The Vietnam War presents a classic case of U.S. foreign policy gone wrong. Over nearly a decade of fighting, the United States alone suffered more than 47,000 battle deaths, plus 10,800 "other" deaths, only to see South Vietnam conquered by indigenous guerrillas and the army of communist North Vietnam in 1975. That defeat and the policy battles which preceded it produced intense political divisions within this country, contributed to reducing U.S. global influence, and even strained relations with many of America's European allies. Containment policy failed in Vietnam, and ebullient post–World War II optimism about American hegemony was jolted. The rest of the 1970s and much of the 1980s would be spent in debates over the limits of U.S. power. Our Vietnam policy had been strongly disputed both inside and outside government at the time, yet it had been continued on the premise that more of the same would win in the end. How could we have gone so wrong?

As discussed in "The 1960s: The Prices of Success and the Vietnam War" in Chapter 2, communist guerrilla forces that fought against Japan's World War II occupation of colonial French Indochina later turned to driving out the French. After suffering a major defeat at Dienbienphu in 1954, the French withdrew and accepted a cease-fire accord that divided Vietnam at the 17th parallel. As in the Cold War partitions of Germany and Korea, this partition led to two governments, one communist and the other Western and only arguably democratic. Fighting in South Vietnam began as early as 1956, with the communist Vietcong supported by North Vietnam and aided by Chinese and Soviet arms shipments. Fearing a communist victory would spread from South Vietnam into neighboring states in a domino effect, the United States began a first phase of gradually escalated support for South Vietnam's forces. Military trainers and advisers in the early 1960s were followed by air strikes against North Vietnam in 1964 and a major ground combatant buildup in 1965, peaking at over a half-million troops by 1968. Nonetheless, no real progress toward a conclusion of the war could be demonstrated.

Worse was to come. Early in 1968, during the three-day Tet festival celebrating the arrival of the lunar new year, the communists launched an all-out, countrywide offensive.

Although it failed to topple the Saigon regime, that offensive accomplished the Vietcong's paramount political objective by demonstrating that they could not easily be defeated. Widespread negative shifts in expectations resulted, and U.S. policy turned from buildup and escalation to a second phase of winding down the war effort and withdrawing from Vietnam. A steadily rising toll of battle without clearly visible progress already had contributed to a slow shift of domestic public opinion. The Tet offensive jolted opinion from majority support to majority opposition, although bitter divisions remained. After a fragile and fatally flawed peace accord was signed in Paris on 27 January 1973, most U.S. troops left Vietnam. That peace was never truly implemented, and the South Vietnamese surrendered to the communists on 30 April 1975.

At least in its early stages, the war in Vietnam was a guerrilla conflict, although North Vietnam later fielded full-scale conventional units. U.S. policy for fighting a guerrilla war relied on the dubious and poorly developed theory that we would eventually win if we could kill perhaps ten enemy soldiers for every battle death we suffered because North Vietnam and the Vietcong could not sustain such a loss rate and keep replacing soldiers. (See, for example, McNamara, 1995, 177.) In the event, this proved untrue, and every U.S. escalation was at least matched by the enemy. However, believing it to be true even in the face of mounting evidence to the contrary, U.S. leaders kept escalating troop levels until the 1968 Tet offensive. Only then did President Lyndon Johnson reject the military commanders' requests for additional troops and decree that we must begin reducing our force levels and seeking a way out. More than a quarter century later, Robert S. McNamara, who served as secretary of defense for seven years under Presidents Kennedy and Johnson while the fateful escalation decisions were being made, wrote of his belief that had Kennedy not been assassinated in 1963, he would have pulled us out of Vietnam:

> Having reviewed the record in detail, and with the advantage of hindsight, I think it highly probable that, had President Kennedy lived, he would have pulled us out of Vietnam. He would have concluded that the South Vietnamese were incapable of defending themselves, and that Saigon's grave political weaknesses made it unwise to try to offset the limitations of South Vietnamese forces by sending U.S. combat troops on a large scale. I think he would have come to that conclusion even if he reasoned, as I believe he would have, that South Vietnam and, ultimately, Southeast Asia would then be lost to Communism. He would have viewed that loss as more costly than we see it now. But he would have accepted that cost because he would have sensed that the conditions he had laid down—i.e., it was a South Vietnamese war, that it could only be won by them, and to win it they needed a sound political base—could not be met. Kennedy would have agreed that withdrawal would cause a fall of the "dominoes" but that staying in would ultimately lead to the same result, while exacting a terrible price in blood. (McNamara, 1995, 96)

Vietnam is certainly not history's only example of a major policy mistake carried out over years with tragic consequences. But this one was made in the United States, and it profoundly affected U.S. foreign policy for the rest of the twentieth century. Policy only occasionally goes this seriously wrong, but it quite often misses the goals to which we aspire. In Vietnam, the U.S. government—or at least a decisive enough majority of key decision makers to set policy—started with a flawed theory of the conflict, unclear war goals, and inadequate intelligence about the enemy's capabilities. They then chose and sustained a policy well beyond its early signs of failure and in the face of mounting evidence that conditions in the field had never been conducive to that policy's success.

WHY WE STUDY HOW POLICY IS MADE

Many authorities urge us to study the lessons of history so we can avoid repeating the mistakes of the past. Yet neither the conditions of our past failures nor our past successes are likely ever to be exactly duplicated. This is truer today more than ever, given that the foreign policy problems now confronting the United States differ so greatly in number, character, and possible solutions from the problems faced during the Cold War era. A better plan for understanding why policy often goes wrong and for reducing the likelihood of such failures in the future is to *study how policy is made*. When we do so, we find that the reasons for policy failures, whether great or small, may be grouped into three grand categories. First, the *inherent nature of the decision-making situation* may limit options and prevent policy optimization. Second, the *approach taken to deciding* may lead to suboptimal results. Finally, the *design of the institutions* through which decisions are made may be flawed. The first category of difficulties is fundamentally unchangeable, and the second may be extremely difficult to change. Chances for bringing about improvements in policy decision making are greatest when dealing with the third category. Examining how policy is made, so we can better determine whether one or another of these causes of policy difficulties applies to any particular situation, is the focus of this chapter.

The four major sections of this chapter address (1) an initial survey of ten reasons why policy often "goes wrong" in the sense of failing to accomplish our maximum goals; (2) two conceptual and analytic models for how decisions are made, called **optimizing** and **satisficing**; (3) three generalized models for how decisions are made within governments, collectively termed the Allison models after the political scientist who first wrote extensively about them; and (4) several additional problems that affect foreign policy decision making. First, the earlier chapters of this book already revealed a number of reasons for policy failures, which are briefly reviewed, summarized, and generalized, with examples. Second, everything that government does is carried out by government agencies, which are enormous organizations. Our search for the causes of policy failure therefore turns to general principles of decision making by individuals and organizations. We first consider models of synoptic or optimizing or "rational" decision making, and "satisficing" decision making. Under optimizing, an individual or a government agency would examine all possible alternatives and determine the one best. Under satisficing, by contrast, one would examine enough alternatives to find one good enough to meet minimal criteria for acceptability. We will find that real-world limitations on decision-making time, available information, and cost/benefit ratios all drive policymakers strongly toward satisficing.

Third, as Graham Allison reminds us, both citizens and officials tend to approach decision situations with largely implicit conceptual models that shape our views and interpretations. Such models are information filters and inevitably affect the content of our analyses, but they also point out reasons for policy difficulties. Allison studied three analytic models that present perspectives on policy decision making from different levels of analysis: the government as a whole ("rational actor" or unitary government); the organizations within that government ("organizational process"); and individuals within the government ("governmental politics"). We discuss how the bases of those models lie in the optimizing and satisficing models. Allison's Model I assumes **unitary governments** that optimize by following the postulates of rational action, but it cannot answer questions about effects at lower levels of analysis within the government. If we meet all the assumptions, this model works well in assessing the impacts of global level, government-to-government interactions. Model II emphasizes **organizational processes** and sees government actions as organizational outputs arrived at through a process of competition for leadership group approval. Available options provided by programs and standard operating procedures tremendously constrain all government actions, and a host of other organizational processes help cause policy failures. Model III emphasizes the **governmental politics** of interplay between key individuals, each with his or her personal history, goals, priorities, past policy stands, and network of connections—both positive and negative—to others throughout government. Each of these considerations limits the possibilities for fully comprehensive, optimizing decision making, and thus limits the chance of completely successful policy.

In the fourth section of this chapter we address four other problems that affect foreign policy decision making. These include the following: (1) *Crises* distort decision making in many ways, including focusing leaders' attention on time pressures and tending to reduce policy innovation. (2) Widely held internal concepts of an agency's major mission, which Morton Halperin calls *organizational essence*, encourage members to fight to preserve missions they believe essential, and resist assignments that would shift effort elsewhere. This strongly affects the life cycle of organizational charters, programs, and procedures, and encourages policy inertia. (3) In *information filtering*, individuals fall victim to temptations to slant or distort the information they report upward in ways intended to please their bosses. (4) Finally, we consider problems which can arise from *institutional design*, the *structure* of members and relationships established in the U.S. foreign policy system by the Constitution, legislation, executive orders, and case law. As a major example, we consider the War Powers Act of 1973, an early post-Vietnam War expression of the battle between Congress and the president for control of U.S. foreign policy.

WHY DOES POLICY OFTEN GO WRONG?

Far more often than anyone would like, foreign policy suffers failures of some degree, ranging from the disappointment of not achieving everything hoped for, to complete frustration and defeat. In the most benign policy failures, outcomes are merely suboptimal. More severe failures produce embarrassment, formidable new policy problems, and even full-blown crises. Such severe problems have the fascination of disaster, and thus tend to receive far more attention, and more detailed examination, than milder policy failures. Regrettably, the history of U.S. foreign policy since World War II offers many policy failures for our study.

Consider the following examples: (1) In 1950 the U.S. failed to predict both the 30 June North Korean invasion of South Korea and China's massive 26 November counteroffensive after MacArthur's brilliant 15 September Inchon landing and drive north to the Yalu. Arguably, better prediction could have allowed the North Korean attack to be deterred, or a strategy adopted that would not have provoked Chinese entry into the war. (2) The nonexistent U.S.-Soviet intercontinental ballistic "missile gap" that played so prominent a role in the 1960 presidential campaign resulted from faulty intelligence estimates, as did subsequent U.S. overreaction in missile building during the early 1960s. (3) In April 1961 U.S.-trained anti-Castro Cuban exiles invaded their homeland at the Bay of Pigs, carrying out an operation planned by the CIA under the Eisenhower administration and simply carried forward by the new Kennedy team. Confounding official U.S. expectations, the Cuban people rallied against the invasion rather than against Castro's government. Denied promised American air cover, the invaders were ignominiously defeated, imprisoned, and eventually ransomed back. (4) In a striking demonstration of intelligence failure, Iran's 1979 revolution, which brought Islamic militants to control of that region's natural hegemon, occurred after four major revisions within less than one year in the National Intelligence Estimate about probable events in Iran. (5) The Iran-contra affair less than a decade later involved a complex scheme to sell arms secretly to Iran, channeling the proceeds to anti-Sandinista contra rebels in Nicaragua in violation of U.S. law. The Reagan administration hoped for help from nonexistent Iranian "moderates" to secure the release of U.S. hostages held by Islamic militants in Lebanon. (6) Finally, looming over all such policy frustrations is the fact that the U.S. government—and virtually everyone else—failed to predict the implosion, collapse, and breakup of the Soviet Union, with the attendant end to forty-four years of Cold War.

Policy failures often have extremely serious consequences in lives and treasure. Certainly, this is true of the failures on the list just cited. Those consequences give plentiful motivation for seeking out the causes of policy failures and identifying ways to limit their occurrence in future. Earlier chapters have already revealed some reasons for such failures, including the following:

- *Short-term goals:* Decision making usually is driven more by the need to solve some immediate problem than by striving after a long-term goal. There may be a pressing political need to do something, even though everyone understands that the something is far from a complete and final solution. For example, as we saw in Chapter 4, the desire to keep the Gulf War coalition from fragmenting led to the land war's end after a hundred hours, with little regard for that decision's long-term implications in Iraq.

- *Politics of the possible:* Policy decisions are determined more often by political considerations about what is possible than by concerns about what might be optimal, morally right, or maximally desirable. Consider the 1947 reorganization that created the Department of Defense. Although a centralized organization was created under the defense secretary, each armed service retained its independent organization. A fully integrated general staff was considered better but politically unacceptable, because Nazi Germany had used that organizational model.

- *Distributed policy making:* Policy making is often distributed rather than centralized. Policies thus bear small imprints from each of many minds. Although this practice may offer many opportunities to fine-tune policy, it often works against comprehensive and long-range planning. This problem has been particularly severe in the State Department.

- *Competitive intelligence:* Intelligence gathering can become competitive, and intelligence estimation usually is competitive. In particular, as examined in Chapter 6, the National Intelligence Estimate (NIE) process encourages an interagency struggle for primacy in a battle of interpretations. In the optimistic view, competition improves the product. Far too often, however, competition leads to endless footnotes in NIEs, each intended to protect an agency from recriminations if the estimate proves wrong. Recall the *bureaucratic infighting* viewpoint discussed in Chapter 1.

- *Competitive overlap:* Agencies regularly battle over Washington turf and influence, seeking authority and the control of necessary policy support functions. For example, competition between the president and Congress for policy control led to the simultaneous creation of the executive branch Office of Management and Budget and the legislative branch Congressional Budget Office. Competition between agencies is exemplified by the Defense Department's 1993 moves to create offices dealing with traditional State Department concerns about democracy and human rights. Although the best policy may win out in the end, such competition may be wasteful and inefficient, directing substantial energy to inter-agency squabbles. Again, recall the *bureaucratic infighting* viewpoint.

- *Dual roles:* Some officials have dual roles with overlapping and conflicting responsibilities. For example, the director of central intelligence (DCI) is both (1) chief of the central intelligence agency (CIA) and (2) overall head of the national intelligence community. Although an NIE is supposed to reflect the DCI's professional judgment based on all inputs, agency pressure exists to support CIA views.

- *Reward structures:* Federal agencies may fail to train and reward their employees for long-range orientation and for focusing on policy rather than operations. The State Department's Foreign Service Officer (FSO) program is notorious for such failings.

- *Size:* Sheer size may make comprehensive management of some agencies exceedingly difficult. The classic case is the Department of Defense.

- *Turnover:* The few thousand top officials who change with presidential administrations tend to have much shorter tenure than the career civil servants and military officers comprising most of the upper and middle-level bureaucracy. This discourages long-term planning and implies that continuing agency concerns receive more consistent long-term attention than administration wishes that top officials attempt to impose. An interesting contrast existed between the United States and the former Soviet Union, where many top Soviet officials had extended tenure in office. Andrei Gromyko, for example, spent almost his entire career from 1939 on as a diplomat, serving as foreign minister from 1957 to 1985 despite other top leadership shakeups.

- *Wrong choices:* Finally, and for a great many reasons, leaders may receive good advice but fail to act on it.

This list of reasons for policy failures is far from comprehensive. Some receive further consideration in this and the next two chapters, as do additional problems. Many of those problems should remind us of viewpoints from the perspective of linkages between domestic and international politics, discussed in Chapter 1. Some problems are inherent in the policy-making process and unavoidable. Others arise from difficulties in institutional design, and can be modified by changes in law and organization. Still others arise from the institutional ethos, values, and practices within particular agencies, and may be changeable by retraining the individuals involved. Additional problems are understood but still considered preferable to their alternatives. This is the logic underlying the fundamental U.S. constitutional principle of checks and balances, which guarantees a certain amount of conflict in governance. As we begin to look deeper for the causes of policy failures, we might do well to remember an observation of Winston Churchill before the House of Commons (11 November 1947):

> Many forms of government have been tried, and will be tried in this world of sin and woe. No one pretends that democracy is perfect or all-wise. Indeed, it has been said that democracy is the worst form of Government except all those other forms that have been tried from time to time.

In the spirit of Churchill's statement, we will find that many policy failures arise not from the concept of democracy, but from imperfections and unavoidable difficulties in the organizations and procedures we construct to implement democracy.

For policymakers, a fundamental goal in seeking the causes of policy failures is to correct problems whenever possible, in order to be more successful in the future. For us as students of foreign policy, an equally fundamental goal in examining policy failures is to improve our abilities to predict the future course of policy events. By better understanding the causes of policy failures, we can better distinguish between those causes that are changeable and those that are politically immutable. Knowing that crucial difference, we can better focus our efforts if we wish to change policy, better accept what we cannot change, and enjoy greater confidence and success in predicting the outcomes of future policy problems. Following the systems perspective outlined in Chapter 4, we seek to understand how the foreign policy decision-making system functions and why it often operates in ways that lead to policy failures. Referring to the system as conceptually diagrammed in Figure 4.1, we examine the inner workings of the decision-making information processor, looking for the functional reasons why some policies have not succeeded. That analytic focus on *how* and *why* things happened in various types of past cases distinguishes the systems approach from the purely historical approach of replaying *what* happened in particular cases. The systems approach provides a framework that focuses on process rather than description, and invites us to apply that framework in analyzing future cases.

TWO CONCEPTUAL/ANALYTIC MODELS FOR DECISION MAKING: OPTIMIZING AND SATISFICING

We begin with concepts of decision making by individuals because foreign policy decisions are made either by key individuals or, more often, by organizations consisting of many individuals. Although organizations have their own influences on the ways people make decisions, as discussed in the next section, the ways in which individuals think also have important influences on how groups operate. We consider two opposing major models for individual decision making: optimizing and satisficing. Key properties of these two models are summarized in Table 5.1.

Models of individual decision making were at issue in theories of psychology and business management long before they attracted the attention of political scientists. Both optimizing and satisficing assume that the act of decision is a choice from among some set of alternatives. Such a choice, of course, may be a complex combination of many actions to be carried out in sequence over time. The crucial difference between these two models concerns how many alternatives are considered before choosing. The optimizer examines every alternative and chooses the one best. But how does an optimizer identify that one best alternative? The identification process is *assumed* or postulated. This is the axiomatic, formalized part of this model, often called rational choice. The assumptions, of course, are reasonable. Moreover, models built on this model for choice have enjoyed considerable success in modern economics and in the study of voting behavior. Drawing on the work of Anthony Downs, the rational choice axioms can be summarized as follows:

- *Decisiveness:* Faced with a set of alternatives, a rational actor always can make a choice.
- *Consistency:* Faced with the same set of alternatives, a rational actor always makes the same choice.
- *Ranking:* Alternatives are ranked by *preference* or *indifference*, that is, given any two alternatives, A and B, either A is preferred to B, or B is preferred to A, or each is considered equally desirable, so the chooser is indifferent between them. Any number of alternatives may be ranked in this manner by making pairwise comparisons, comparing one new alternative at a time to items on the already-ranked list. When the process is complete, either a single alternative or a set of two or more tied alternatives heads the ranking. Different individuals may have different preference orderings over the same set of alternatives.
- *Transitivity:* Given any three alternatives A, B, and C, it is *assumed* that if A is preferred to B, and B is preferred to C, then A is preferred to C. This property is necessary to prevent preference cycles (A preferred to B, B preferred to C, but C preferred to A) that would not leave a clearly most preferred choice.
- *Choice:* A rational actor always chooses the highest ranked alternative.

Having examined all alternatives, an optimizer thus chooses either the single item at the top of the list, or one of several items tied in top place. Our optimizer is *synoptic,* in the sense that he or she examines every alternative. The option chosen need not be attractive; it may be simply the "least worst" of a bad set. Optimizers cannot be said to win a fundamentally unwinnable situation, only to do as well as possible under the circumstances. Not all optimizers rank the same set of alternatives identically because preference orderings are individual and determined by the goals and values of the individuals. Political scientists and economists usually call this decision-making model the *rational actor* model, but that label simply assumes one among many different possible definitions of rationality. Whether good or bad, however, that label has stuck and is widely used. A more descriptive label might be *purposive actor* because optimizers choose with a goal in mind.

TABLE 5.1 Properties of Optimizing and Satisficing Models for Individual Decision Making	
Optimizing Model	**Satisficing Model**
Also called *synoptic* Rational actor Purposive actor	Also called *successive limited comparisons*
Decision logic: Examine *all* alternatives, Pick the *one best* alternative.	Decision logic: Examine *some* alternatives, Pick the first alternative *good enough* to meet some set of minimum criteria
Optimizing; focus on *long-range* goals.	Adaptive; focus on *short-range* goals.
Policy change is movement toward goals (goods), in search of a desired end state.	Policy change is movement away from present bads, seeking solution to some current problem.
Axiomatic, formalized model. Normative and predictive because it prescribes what an individual should choose, given a set of alternatives and a set of preferences (values).	Process predictive only, because it describes the process by which choice will be made.
Compatible with a government by planning; utopian.	Compatible with a history-bound government by crisis; only demonstrated problems are capable of stimulating policy change.

Because all alternatives are examined, this model for choice suggests the most efficient possible movement toward ultimate, long-range goals. This is utopian, and conducive to governance by informed and enlightened central planning, provided the goals set are informed and enlightened. The optimizing model is *normative*, in that it prescribes what choice an individual *should* make, given the set of alternatives and that individual's values. It is also *predictive* because we know what choice should result if we know the alternatives and the chooser's preferences.

A satisficer, in contrast to an optimizer, examines only *some* alternatives, and selects the first one *good enough* to meet some set of minimum criteria. In the words of Herbert A. Simon, "satisficing involves choosing an alternative that meets or exceeds specified criteria, but that is not guaranteed to be either unique or in any sense the best" (1987, 243). Simon was the first social scientist to use the term *satisficing* as he sought to answer the question, "How simple a set of choice mechanisms can we postulate and still obtain the gross features of observed adaptive choice behavior?" (1956, 129). All the *living systems* mentioned in Chapter 4 exhibit adaptive choice behavior. In particular, individuals, groups, organizations, governments, and societies do so, and policy making is adaptive behavior. Satisficing often involves short-range adaptation, focused on solving current problems. It then becomes more a process of moving away from some present bad than toward some eventual good. This model tells us less than the optimizing model because it predicts only the process of choice, not what that choice should be. Policy shifts made by satisficers may be large or small, but will not be optimal in the synoptic sense.

Satisficing neither requires nor prohibits **incrementalism,** under which governments modify existing policy as little as possible and only in response to problems that have grown severe enough that they no longer can be ignored. However, satisficing assumes overt choice, whereas incrementalism does not require it. Under incrementalism, policy movement over time will almost surely be a series of fits and starts, proceeding jaggedly from point to point rather than smoothly from start to eventual goal. Some analysts have termed this method "successive limited comparisons" because no policy shift is permanent and none is based on a comprehensive evaluation of options. Precisely because satisficing cannot guarantee optimal policy, it may be more likely than optimizing to require the later readjustments characteristic of incrementalism.

Why might officials satisfice rather than optimize? Primarily because many limitations make optimizing difficult, time consuming, and costly. Determining all possible alternatives takes time and effort. In a crisis, there may not be enough time and enough help, or stress may cause people to perceive there is not enough time. Not all necessary information may be available quickly and readily. Gathering information is costly, and the stakes in some choice situations may not be high enough to justify the cost of determining every option. Moreover, the options may not hold still long enough for a complete enumeration. The optimizing model assumes an essentially static set of alternatives, but real-world options are in continual flux. Finally, real-world goals often are more complex than the optimizing model may suggest, and officials often have entire hierarchies of goals they would like to achieve. For example, in the October 1962 Cuban missile crisis, President Kennedy wanted above all to get Soviet nuclear-armed missiles out of Cuba. He also wanted to do so without major war, before the fast-approaching November elections, without making significant public concessions to the Soviets, preferably without giving a quid pro quo by withdrawing U.S. missiles from Britain, Italy, and Turkey—and so on. All these considerations suggest that optimizing is an extremely difficult ideal to realize, and fundamental limitations push everyone toward satisficing.

The pressures that push us all toward satisficing in daily life also affect individuals, groups, and agencies within government. Not only does determining all possible alternatives take time and effort, one must persuade others to accept that those alternatives really are possible. Cost/benefit ratios for information gathering are very real considerations. Not all information will necessarily be available immediately, so that options either worked out in advance or quickly definable are more likely to be selected. When crises occur, they often promote a sense that doing almost anything is preferable to waiting. Time pressures are exacerbated by the fact that real-world political and military options may be as short lived as the market availability of a specific used car. Stress causes decision makers to become less innovative and more than ordinarily concerned about time limitations. A frequent bureaucratic response is to make only incremental changes to an existing contingency plan. For example, when President Kennedy wanted plans for a surgical air strike to destroy Soviet missiles in Cuba during the 1962 missile crisis, Pentagon officials simply added the missile bases to a contingency plan for attacking Cuban military targets. (There were also organizational and operational considerations, which are discussed in the next section.) If a group must concur on policy, the desire for consensus

SATISFICING IN DAILY LIFE

Everyday personal decision making readily demonstrates pressures to satisfice. If we need a new pen for note taking, the cost/benefit ratio hardly justifies examining every model available in the bookstore. Instead, we probably review the stock only until we find a good enough pen. Judicious use of our time suggests that such small choices in daily life are satisficed.

What about bigger, less frequent choices? Imagine that you have decided to purchase your first automobile. Only a used car can meet budget limitations, but you may have numerous other choice criteria. You want a certain minimum mileage per gallon; definite styles and makes are preferable for your lifestyle image; a few colors are completely unacceptable. This narrows things down to a million or so cars in the United States, many of which are probably for sale. Few of them are likely to be nearby, however, and searching for an acceptable used car can take time, effort, and money. This is a huge

pressure to satisfice by confining your search to cars that are conveniently close. If you find nothing acceptable soon, you can always look further afield later. Whatever mix of bulletin board ads, newspaper ads, magazines, used car lots, and so on that you peruse, any realistic search strategy means that at least some potential vehicles will go unexamined. Additionally, the options keep changing. The car you find today, almost exactly what you had in mind except that it is yellow, may be sold to somebody else tomorrow. A price you found just a little too high may be paid by another buyer. With luck, the auto you ultimately purchase will prove quite acceptable, but the process you followed to select it probably will look much more like satisficing than optimizing.

A useful exercise is to consider some other choices—large and small—that you have made in your life. Ask whether optimizing or satisficing better describes your decision process, and be able to explain why.

may lead to **groupthink** (Janis, 1972), in which participants find it difficult to challenge the first reasonable proposal raised. Political realities of frequent elections and limited terms of office tend to work against long-range planning. Being able to point to some action taken before the upcoming election may appear far more important than establishing something expected to last for decades. President Kennedy feared that if he did not get the Soviet missiles removed from Cuba in October it would cost the Democrats dearly in the midterm congressional elections in November. Politicians not only face such pressures to act quickly for short-range goals, but also have little expectation of being in office when the long-term consequences of their actions must be faced.

Finally, as political scientist Vincent Ostrom has suggested, satisficing may be the automatic result of limited information, which may be unavoidable in the long term. The late Buckminster Fuller pointed out that the amount of knowledge held by the human race has increased *exponentially*, that is, the rate of increase is itself increasing. We know much more today about many more things than ever before, and knowledge increase is accelerating. How can we have fully comprehensive long-term policy planning when the long term will see options not presently known? Our world today has been shaped profoundly by discoveries unforeseen even a few decades ago. Consider two examples, antibiotics and microelectronics. Penicillin, discovered in 1928 and first purified in 1941, was the first of a large group of antibiotic agents that have revolutionized the treatment of bacterial infections. Now augmented by genetically engineered synthetic antibiotics, they can defeat previously intractable infections and diseases, and have saved countless lives. Transistors, announced in 1948 by Bell Telephone Laboratories, were the first solid-state devices to replace vacuum tubes, which were larger, more fragile, and produced much more heat. Many discrete (single) transistor applications are now accomplished by integrated circuits combining up to millions of transistors on a single silicon chip. These devices have made possible a host of developments that significantly impact not only our lives as individuals, but the lives of nation-states. Integrated circuits provide the memory and central processing units for the desktop and laptop computers on which most of us now do our writing and data processing. They make possible the on-board computers that manage engines and emissions systems of modern automobiles, permitting nearly 1960s levels of performance with several times the gasoline mileage and a tiny fraction of the emissions. They also make possible the miniaturized guidance computers for intercontinental ballistic missiles. Developments of such new technologies are notoriously difficult to foresee. Arthur C. Clarke, the science fiction writer usually credited with conceiving the idea of synchronous earth satellites, is one of the better futurists of this century, yet in the stories he wrote during the 1950s the computers of galaxy-hopping spacecraft run on vacuum tubes.

The tremendous difficulty, or even fundamental impossibility, of predicting what new technologies may be developed in the future seems decisive in ruling out fully comprehensive long-range policy planning. This implies that in the long range we are forced to satisfice. It is only the last in a fairly long list of practical and political considerations that have similar effects. A useful exercise is to determine how closely the decision making in some specific case of foreign policy making meets the requirements for optimizing, and the question is raised in cases throughout this chapter. In the next section, however, we turn to three analytic models presenting perspectives on policy decision making from different levels of analysis.

THREE MODELS OF DECISION MAKING WITHIN GOVERNMENTS

The three so-called **Allison models,** after Harvard University political scientist Graham Allison, are conceptual models of how decisions are made within governments. Officials do not choose these models or use them in making their decisions. However, any particular official's personal beliefs about how policy is made usually are closer to one or another of these models than the others. We can use these models to help gain understanding of foreign policy decision making.

Allison's fundamental premise is that all analysts of foreign affairs, whether laypersons or professionals, think about problems of foreign and military policy by using *largely implicit* conceptual models of how governments function in making policy. Because the models tell us how the foreign policy decision-making system functions, they unavoidably affect the *content* of our thinking. Models or theories about how the world works become effective *information filters*, specifying the sorts of questions that are important, what types of indicators we should watch, and implicitly what things we can ignore. When we begin to analyze any system, we choose some appropriate **level of analysis,** essentially the smallest independent member of the system. For many systems, we can make more than one such selection, so that we effectively choose a viewpoint to take on the system.

The three Allison models span three different levels of analysis: the government as a whole (Model I, "rational actor" or unitary government); the organizations within that government (Model II, "organizational process"); and individuals within the government (Model III, "governmental politics"). Thus each model assumes a different level of smallest significant detail in the structure of the foreign policy system. The three models are ordered from highest to lowest level, adding additional detail to the system's structure as the level of analysis becomes finer. Each model leads us to ask certain questions in studying a decision-making case, and to ignore other questions.

As in any application of theory, we seek to accomplish the three functions of *description, explanation,* and *prediction,* that is, describing what happens, explaining why it happens that particular way, and predicting what likely will occur in future. Like many other analysts, Allison concludes that we must use all three models, or work at all three levels of analysis, to obtain a complete treatment of any policy case. We might visualize each model as a snapshot that captures only part of a complex total picture. As we examine those models, however, keep in mind Allison's assumptions that most of us normally believe *one* of these models to be most nearly correct and complete, and we do not normally examine our beliefs. Allison did not invent any of the three models, but pulled together a large literature, combining themes about individual and group decision making and drawing heavily from the business decision-making literature. He then applied these ideas to political science concerns about governmental decision making, using the 1962 Cuban missile crisis case as a specific application.

MODEL I: RATIONAL ACTOR OR UNITARY GOVERNMENT

In this first model, we assume a government is a single (unitary) optimizing actor choosing from among available options according to the axioms of rational choice discussed earlier. Referring to the conceptual diagram in Figure 4.1, government is viewed as if it were a large "black box." Without looking at the internal structure of that box, we postulate that it processes information according to the rules of optimizing rational action. Information is received, including information about available options. All options are ranked, a rational choice is made, and that choice yields a policy. Except for the rational choice assumption, the internal structure or decision-making mechanisms of government are ignored. Because our level of analysis is the government as a whole, no consideration is given to internal governmental disagreements or struggles over the determination of policy, and the unitary government is assumed to choose in the same manner as an individual optimizer. *Governmental action is seen as a choice from among possible options.* The unitary government is seen as seeking to achieve particular goals, exactly as an optimizing individual would, by evaluating options according to their consequences or costs and benefits, and using those evaluations to rank options for choice.

Any model we use to analyze government decision making biases our subsequent analysis. Our model leads us to ask certain questions when studying a specific policy problem and to ignore other questions. Questions appropriate under the unitary government model include the following: What is the nature and background of the policy problem at hand? What other governments are involved? What alternatives are available to us immediately, and over time? What alternatives do other actors or opponents have? What costs and benefits are associated with the alternatives? What international systemic (external) pressures exist on us and others? What observations do we have about past actions, and what other information do we have to help evaluate how our opponents will rank their options? At least some administrations can be seen clearly asking such questions. President Nixon asked his staff to prepare detailed lists of U.S. options, with their associated costs and benefits but without a final policy recommendation because he reserved that choice to himself.

Every model has inherent strengths and weaknesses in application. Among the benefits of this model are the following: It stresses the interaction between governments and between their goals. It implicitly stresses the role of international power (see also Chapter 8). Rational actors are predictable; if we know the options available to another government and know that government's preference ordering, we can predict what should occur. This unitary actor model is useful when we have little or no information about the internal workings of a government, as in the case of the Chinese People's Republic during the 1950s and 1960s. Options available to other governments, and the external pressures on them, are reasonably observable and knowable. Unless we have information about those governments' preference orderings, however, we must fall back on estimating what our preference ordering would be in the same circumstances. Over time, however, we can infer the preference ordering of another actor by observing what it does in different circumstances because it is impossible to make any move without revealing something about your preferences.

Remember Allison's premise that everyone uses *largely implicit* conceptual models of how governments function in making policy. Most of us regularly use language which implies that nation-states are at least unitary, if not necessarily rational, actors. Consider the prevalence of news reports with statements like "China has shipped missiles to Iran" or "Russia has denounced Ukraine's action." We do not usually say, "The decisive group at the core of the Chinese government has decided to sell missiles abroad." Having one paramount decision maker, dictatorships may have an easier time than democracies in appearing to be unitary actors. In reality, most studies of dictatorships reveal at least some internal struggles over policy. Nonetheless, the existence of a dictator probably simplifies external estimation of a preference ordering. Finally, the unitary government model is useful in crisis situations when time limitations make it difficult to carry out a full evaluation of another government's internal decision process.

Applications of the unitary government model abound, and it is often employed in first cut initial analyses that will later be further detailed. When Allison applied this model to questions regarding the 1962 Cuban missile crisis, it explained quite well why the Soviets would introduce nuclear missiles into Cuba. First, preventing attacks on Cuba was the Soviets' publicly announced goal, although the announcement did not come until after the United States revealed the presence of the Soviet missiles. Once the highly vulnerable surface-mounted missiles became operational, fear that they would be launched under attack (the "use it or lose it" syndrome) probably would deter the United States from launching or sponsoring any further attacks on Cuba, as it had done in the 1961

Bay of Pigs invasion. Second, from a broader, global perspective, the Soviet move would have established rough nuclear parity. Soviet nuclear missiles in Cuba would have placed the United States under approximately the same risk of missile attack as the Soviet Union, a decade before the United States implicitly accepted nuclear parity under the 1972 SALT I strategic arms control agreements. The Soviets were always concerned about the "international correlation of forces," by which they meant the overall world order of political, economic, and military power. They believed, correctly, that a United States at nuclear risk equal to their own would be less adventurous around the world and less likely to confront the Soviet Union. Thus the Cuban missile introduction promised the Soviets big strategic benefits. What the unitary government model cannot explain, however, is why the Soviets made one critical mistake: their missile installations were not camouflaged, which allowed U.S. aerial reconnaissance to discover the missiles in time to threaten attack before they became operational. To answer that question, we must examine the case from another perspective, at a lower or more detailed level of analysis.

Model II: Organizational Process

Organizational processes are unavoidable because everybody in government is part of some organization, and every government action is carried out through such organizations. Thus *every government action can be seen as an organizational action.* We therefore must pay serious attention to how those organizations influence the making and execution of foreign policy. Without necessarily denying the importance of points raised by the unitary actor model, we open up the black box of Model I and add some detail about the internal workings of government. The additional structure added to our previous conceptual diagram, Figure 4.1, is shown in Figure 5.1. Government is now seen as composed of a number of agencies, which are huge organizations, plus a leadership group. The agencies are cabinet departments, and the leadership group primarily consists of the cabinet and the executive office of the president. Our level of analysis is now organizations within the government.

The life cycles of governmental agencies have tremendous influence on organizational behavior. When a new agency is created by authorizing legislation it receives a **charter** specifying the general functions it is to perform. That charter is further interpreted by devising a series of *programs* to carry out those functions. Each year an agency budget must be prepared and melded into the draft federal budget submitted to Congress by the president. Officials of programs that receive funding create and staff *offices* and other lower levels of internal organization. Considerable political maneuvering may occur at every stage of this process, and in every budget cycle. Eventually, funded programs and offices prepare repertoires of **standard operating procedures (SOPs)** to ensure that all their employees carry out needed functions correctly. SOPs are imperative for large organizations that must ensure their operations are performed consistently, frequently, in many places, and by employees not all of whom are rocket scientists.

Citizens' feelings about bureaucracies often are less than warm and fuzzy because the same SOPs needed for consistent performance also become constraints on what is possible. Organization theorists tell us that bureaucracy is one of the great inventions of

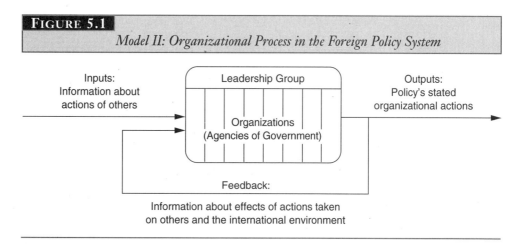

FIGURE 5.1

Model II: Organizational Process in the Foreign Policy System

our civilization, but most people's images of bureaucracies include delay, indecision, red tape, and rigidity. Management decisions are required to do anything outside the SOPs. If an action must be performed by many employees, any agency usually needs time to develop new procedures and train people to execute them. It probably is impossible to anticipate every possible variation on any procedure, but the attempt to do so often makes procedure manuals thick in both bulk and syntax. Military training manuals provide the ultimate stereotype of inflexible SOPs and dense explanations. For example, one navy manual contained the following gems of instruction:

> There are two man overboard procedures: a peacetime man overboard procedure, and a wartime man overboard procedure. . . . The peacetime man overboard procedure is for use only in time of peace. . . . The wartime man overboard procedure is for use only in time of war.

Although this example may seem extreme, it also illustrates the difficulty of writing entirely comprehensive instructions. Does "time of war" include peacekeeping, police actions, and undeclared wars?

Each agency has its *turf* or areas of responsibility assigned by its charter and further specified by approved and funded programs. Within those areas of responsibility, only a fairly inflexible menu of actions is available, at least in the short run. In the perspective of this model, *governmental action in the short run is largely determined by present programs and SOPs.* These are the only actions for which people are trained, equipped, and prepared. The effective result is satisficing rather than optimizing because the range of options is extremely limited. Agencies are not prepared to carry out every alternative the leadership group can envision. We do what we can now, risking a possible return to the problem later. For example, when President Ford asked for a marine landing in Pol Pot's Cambodia in 1975 to free the crew of the seized American-flag freighter *Mayaguez*, Pentagon planners added sites thought to house the prisoners to a contingency plan for attacking Cambodian military targets. This was their quickest and simplest way to develop operational procedures, requiring only minimal change to existing maps, orders, and contingency training.

Just as governmental action in the short run is largely determined by current SOPs and programs, *governmental action in the long run is strongly affected by organizational charters, goals, and programs.* Both the internal survival dynamics of organizations and interagency competition cause this. Imagine that you work for a government agency. You find your work rewarding and believe it serves the public good. If your program was expanded, you could do more good, and your own opportunities for advancement, higher pay, and increased responsibility would expand. You have a personal stake in the survival and growth of your agency and believe the country also would benefit. This is a powerful dynamic working toward the expansion of government programs. Although soaring deficits in the 1980s led to budgetary stringencies and a shrinkage of government programs in the 1990s, the expansion dynamic can be seen in widely accepted models of government budgeting since World War II. Authors such as Davis, Dempster, and Wildavsky (1966) found it easy to predict budgets over time using a model in which this year's budget equals last year's budget times an inflation factor slightly greater than one, plus an adder for new programs, and an error term. This is consistent with accounts from within many organizations. Officials assume that everything being done now will continue, and then they seek to add new programs. If agencies are forced to contract, they struggle to preserve those programs perceived within the organization as essential (see the section "Organizational Essence" beginning on page 189).

Intense competition to solve policy problems often exists between agencies, and government organizations are extremely protective about their turf. New policy problems tend to be factored out among competing organizations, each claiming those parts of the problem that fall within its areas of responsibility. Power is thus fractionated rather than centralized, and each organization responds more to its own parochial priorities than to anybody's concept of the common good. Avoiding or working out disagreements takes time. Very similar concerns arise between different units within an agency. These considerations exemplify the *bureaucratic infighting* viewpoint discussed in Chapter 1. Agencies compete for funding, using every available political channel, including appeals to the president, the public, interest groups, and key members and committees of Congress. Interest groups and Congress members also share strong interests with particular agencies whose survival and health ensures their own continued power and influence. Because different agencies tend to have particular domestic constituencies, we should recall the *domestic policy dynamics* viewpoint discussed in Chapter 1.

Like the unitary actor model, the organizational process model leads us to ask certain questions when studying a specific policy problem, and to ignore or slight other questions. Questions appropriate under this model include the following: What organizations, and what components of organizations, make up the government? Which ones traditionally act on a problem of the type at hand, and with what relative influence? What programs, repertoires, and SOPs do they have available for making information available to key decision makers, for generating policy alternatives, and for implementing alternative courses of action?

The organizational process model emphasizes the tremendous importance of available options in constraining possible actions. It highlights important domestic political influences on foreign policy decision making. It helps explain observed budgetary phenomena, many of the motivations that drive individuals working in government agencies, and interagency fights over turf and influence. Among other applications, it directs us to ask the sorts of organizational questions that allow an explanation of the Soviets' failure to camouflage their Cuban missiles. The Soviet Strategic Rocket Forces, charged with building the new bases, had never operated outside Soviet territory. Having had no need to camouflage construction in progress, they never developed a procedure to do so. Nobody happened to think that it might be advisable to do things differently in Cuba, 90 miles off the Florida Keys.

MODEL III: GOVERNMENTAL POLITICS

Although governmental actions genuinely are organizational outputs, key individuals in critical positions can have great influence in deciding those actions. Model III takes our level of analysis down to those key players in vital positions. In so doing, it clearly exemplifies the *domestic policy dynamics* viewpoint discussed in Chapter 1. Without denying either the external influences highlighted by the unitary governmental model or the organizational influences emphasized by the organizational process model, the governmental politics model adds finer detail. Each key individual has personal goals and interests in policy issues, responds slightly differently to the stakes involved, and has a prior history of policy stands that may impact current issues. Each also has some organizational position and commitments, plus personal ties to other key players within and outside government. Those various commitments and connections constitute a network of action channels through which one can influence policy, and the individual power of these players determines their personal impacts on policy. Governmental action, as seen in this model, is the *resultant of a political bargaining process* among the key players. Even if all those individuals were optimizers, the decisions resulting from their bargaining and coalition building would not likely be optimal for the country. Seen from a national level, decision making will be a satisficing process of settling on the first alternative to gain support from a winning coalition. Shifts in coalitions will help assure that problems will be revisited. The additional structure added to our previous conceptual diagrams, Figures 4.1 and 5.1, is shown in Figure 5.2.

Perceptions and priorities held by key players in government are highly individual and may or may not agree with our perceptions of reality or our concepts of the general good. For ambitious officials, the most important consideration in dealing with any specific policy problem may be whether the solution advances their personal power in government or their chances of winning higher office through election or appointment. Many key players derive immense pleasure from the games of politics and governmental decision making and engage in them while maintaining friendly personal relations with their opponents. Others take defeats very personally and maintain lasting feuds. Thus links of personal friendship or animosity between key players often are as important as the lines of formal responsibility shown on organization charts. Knowing and, ideally, liking an individual in a critical position in another agency can do wonders to facilitate interagency coordination. Players usually care intensely about the rules of their interactions, which determine formal and informal aspects of the paths to power, the range of acceptable decisions and actions, and the sorts of moves acceptable under different circumstances.

Even though individuals carry policy stands and histories with them, the *roles* or *organizational positions* they occupy often press them to change some of their positions to

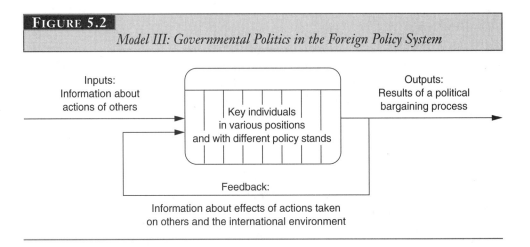

FIGURE 5.2

Model III: Governmental Politics in the Foreign Policy System

conform with the demands of a new position, agency, or administration. This is summed up in Allison's famous aphorism, "Where you stand depends on where you sit." Regardless of personal preferences, your policy stand on a specific issue may be determined by your job. An international trade official in the State Department during 1993, for example, aware that President Clinton favored the North American Free Trade Agreement (NAFTA) with Canada and Mexico, would neither casually nor publicly voice personal doubts about whether NAFTA was a good deal for U.S. workers. Officials who go public with doubts about policies already decided by the administration risk losing their jobs. Seldom are officials able to build personal power bases strong enough to afford them true and lasting independence. One outstanding exception was J. Edgar Hoover, the first director of the Federal Bureau of Investigation, who served from 1924 until his death in 1972. He ran his agency with an iron hand, was obsessively anticommunist, and orchestrated the systematic harassment of people he considered dissenters, such as Dr. Martin Luther King, Jr. Hoover also used his agency's investigative capabilities to build secret files on political leaders and their associates, accumulating such great personal power that presidents including John Kennedy and Lyndon Johnson did not dare fire him, even for direct (but nonpublic) insubordination.

When we analyze a specific policy problem, the governmental politics model directs our attention to the following sorts of questions: What are the existing action channels for this sort of problem? Which players in what positions will be centrally involved in deciding on and implementing a solution? How are the pressures of their jobs, personalities, and past policy stands likely to affect the central players on this issue? What deadlines will tend to force a resolution? Where are foul-ups likely because of organizational inadequacies, clashes of position, or personal conflicts? Will the coalition that wins the policy decision remain united throughout its implementation, especially if the policy runs into difficulties? This model adds important detail about domestic politics to our views of foreign policy making. It helps explain the roles of key individuals and the reasons why they sometimes appear to be working at cross purposes contrary to the interests of the government as a whole (because they are). In this way, it helps explain why policy actions sometimes appear irrational from a nation-state or unitary government perspective.

Model III helped Allison answer one of the bigger questions of the Cuban missile crisis: Why did the Kennedy administration choose a naval blockade of Cuba as its first major action when an immediate military strike against the missiles had a higher probability of destroying them before they were fully operational? This question cannot be answered well using either Model I or Model II. The answer hinges on crucial points regarding the key individuals involved, their histories of previous interactions, the political stakes they had in different possible actions and outcomes, and national history. President Kennedy had gone on record that Soviet weapons in Cuba were purely defensive. Once missiles capable of attacking the U.S. mainland were discovered in Cuba, he had to take strong action or be politically dead with both the electorate and the permanent bureaucracy. Worse yet, Kennedy previously had received private assurances from Soviet leader Nikita Khrushchev that the USSR would not introduce offensive weapons into Cuba. He perceived that Khrushchev had deliberately lied to him, knowing the domestic U.S. political consequences. (The Soviets argued that the Cuban missiles were defensive, intended only to deter U.S. attacks on Cuba, but could not deny the missiles also could be launched against the United States.) Kennedy, already perceived as weak by Khrushchev after their disastrous 1961 Vienna summit meeting, knew he had to respond forcefully or be pressed even harder by the Soviets in future interactions. Key administration and congressional leaders focused on global military security concerns urged an immediate military strike. Attorney General Robert Kennedy, however, was a key political adviser who had the president's ear and served in the cabinet because his brother trusted him and his past advice. He also was one of the more politically liberal figures in the administration, less inclined than others toward the use of force, and feared that an immediate strike would be perceived abroad as a "Pearl Harbor in reverse." In such policy stands, President Kennedy's closest advisers reflected their agency interests and political histories. The compromise between the need for immediate strong action and fears about global perceptions of overreaction was to announce the discovery of the missiles and the prompt imposition of a blockade, threatening stronger action soon if the missiles were not removed.

DESCRIPTION, EXPLANATION, AND PREDICTION

Because the three Allison models approach policy decision making from different levels of analysis, they accomplish the tasks of description, explanation, and prediction quite differently and have distinctly different strengths and weaknesses. Model I, the rational actor or unitary government model, describes policy as a choice made by the government as a single actor from among the available alternatives. Choice is explained as selection according to the axioms of rational choice, after evaluating all possible alternatives and selecting the one best. Great predictive capability results because knowledge of the alternatives and the chooser's preferences allows us to say what option should be selected. This is clearly optimizing decision making, but subject to all the limitations on optimizing, including the difficulties of learning all the alternatives and expecting them to remain available. Model II, the organizational process model, describes policy as an organizational output and explains that output as the resultant of a battle between agencies to win approval from the top leadership group. Model III, the governmental politics model, describes and explains policy as the resultant of a political bargaining and coalition-building process among key decision makers throughout the government. Decision making under

Models II and III is satisficing because the first alternative to win the support of a winning coalition of agencies or individuals becomes policy.

As one proceeds from Model I to Model III, detailed data requirements increase and the specificity of predictions decreases. Each model captures part of the totality of decision making, at a different level of detail or resolution, and we can use these models to help gain understanding of foreign policy decision making. Always remember that these are conceptual models of how decisions are made within governments. Officials do not use these models in making their decisions, although one model may best describe their personal beliefs about how policy is made. Thus, for example, officials whose internal models of decision making closely resemble Model III are likely to pay particular attention to their networks of contacts.

FURTHER PROBLEMS IN FOREIGN POLICY DECISION MAKING

We turn next to several additional problems in foreign policy decision making. They include the impacts of crises on decision makers' behavior, internally held images of organizations' essential missions, filtering of information as it flows up the management hierarchy, and problems of institutional design.

DECISION MAKING UNDER CRISIS

Following the research of Charles Hermann and as mentioned in Chapter 1, analysts typically define *crisis* as an unanticipated situation with high stakes and a short time in which to act. These conditions are the antithesis of circumstances conducive to the *routinized* decision making on which bureaucracies thrive. Recall from the organizational process model that any bureaucracy is prepared to carry out a small set of basically similar procedures whenever needed. If an unanticipated situation arises and procedures for it do not already exist, the organization is at least temporarily stymied. The short decision time characteristic of crises precludes taking the usual lengthy path to develop new procedures and train people to execute them.

Crises have the fascination of calamity, and people often casually label situations meeting only one or two of Hermann's conditions as crises. All three conditions promote social scientists' interest in true crises. High stakes mean that crises really can make differences in politics and in people's lives. Unanticipated situations imply at least some degree of failure in policy making because the problem was not foreseen and contingency plans were not prepared. Short decision times promote stress and encourage decision making that deviates from normality, even to the point of being in some degree irrational.

After the Cuban missile crisis of 1962 and spurred on by fears accompanying the nuclear age, studying and planning for crisis management became a growth industry among political scientists, other analysts, and government. **Crisis management** refers to all means of controlling crises, keeping the decision making as normal as possible, maintaining or even improving lines of communication, and limiting the escalation of violence. Research findings from studies of the outbreak of World War I and other crises indicate that decision making under crisis suffers from serious problems not found in less

ORGANIZATIONAL AND GOVERNMENTAL POLITICS IN ACTION: U.S. WAR AID TO ISRAEL

An excellent example of an internal U.S. government policy clash well explained by the organizational politics and, especially, governmental politics models concerns U.S. military aid to Israel during the very intense 1973 Yom Kippur War. The case illustrates actions unexplainable by a unitary government model, with well-intentioned leaders of government agencies competing for presidential policy approval as predicted by the organizational politics model, but also feuding and waging the sort of policy battle described by the governmental politics model. It presages the emergence of issues about energy supplies and regional power balances that have taken on increased importance in the post–Cold War world. As seen from abroad, which is perhaps the closest we can come to a unitary government view, the U.S. leadership appeared indecisive, irrational, changeable, and burdened by problems of presidential control.

In 1967, fearing imminent attack from Egypt, Israel launched a preemptive war against its Arab neighbor states Egypt, Jordan, and Syria. In fierce fighting during what became known as the Six Day War, Israel conquered substantial territory, taking the Golan Heights from Syria in the north, East Jerusalem and the West Bank from Jordan in the east, and the Gaza Strip and the Sinai peninsula from Egypt to the southwest, all the way to the Suez Canal. Many observers expected Israel would offer to trade most of the conquered territories back in exchange for diplomatic recognition, formal acceptance of Israel's right to exist, and peace. Unfortunately, those hopes failed on both sides.

On the morning of Saturday, 6 October 1973, following six years of very limited war along the new frontiers, Syrian and Egyptian armies attacked Israel in force. This occurred on Yom Kippur, the Day of Atonement, holiest day in the Jewish calendar. Most Israelis, including many

members of their heavily reserve-dependent armed services, would be at home with their families or in synagogue at prayer. Syria attacked on the Golan Heights. Simultaneously, Egyptian forces attacked across the Suez Canal in force and began driving the Israeli armies back into the Sinai. Failure to predict these attacks represented stunning intelligence failures for both Israel and the United States. Only the day before, the CIA had reported war as unlikely, dismissing observed troop movements as maneuvers and precautionary steps. Rather than calling for an immediate cease-fire, President Nixon hoped that a battlefield stalemate would leave neither side with a decisive advantage, thus creating a foundation for negotiation. The Soviets, however, called for additional Arab states to join in attacking Israel, which violated agreements with the United States to consult and limit conflict. Within hours Israel was engaged in two of the greatest tank battles in history; one on the Golan Heights against Syria and the second in the Sinai desert against Egypt. Losses were heavy, and the usage of war materiel phenomenal. By the third day of the Yom Kippur War, Israel had lost a thousand men, more than in the entire 1967 war, and nearly a third of its tanks. With the Soviets airlifting 700 tons of military materiel daily to Egypt and Syria, Israel appealed to the United States, her primary supplier, for desperately needed tanks, ammunition, and antitank missiles. Without such supplies, Israel faced the serious prospect of defeat on both fronts.

A major policy battle followed within the Nixon administration (Nixon, 1978, 920–28). Secretary of State Kissinger advocated rapid and massive resupply of Israel, a friend and de facto ally that had been attacked first and was in serious trouble. Helping Israel would demonstrate the value of U.S. commitments, express

(continued)

(continued)

opposition to the use of war as a policy instrument by the Arabs, and counter Soviet aims to destabilize the region. Kissinger was opposed by Secretary of Defense James Schlesinger, who sought to avoid antagonizing Arab oil exporters and advocated a strategic view in which energy supplies were of greater concern than Israel's future. Nixon accepted Kissinger's recommendation. On 9 October he ordered Kissinger to inform Israel that the United States would replace all their losses, and to work out the logistics for doing so. In answer to Nixon's query the next day, Kissinger replied, "Defense is putting up all kinds of obstacles." Schlesinger worried that letting Israeli El Al transport planes land at U.S. military bases would offend the Arabs, and he relented only if the Israeli planes would first land in New York to have their tail markings painted over. Nixon considered it "unthinkable that Israel should lose the war for lack of weapons while we were spraying paint over Stars of David" and ordered Kissinger to "Tell Schlesinger to speed it up." Two days later, Nixon learned that plans to resupply Israel were still bottlenecked, this time over issues of insurance for private transport aircraft flying into the war zone. He concluded that avoiding further delay justified using U.S. military aircraft, and asked Kissinger to convey that decision to the Pentagon and have them prepare a plan. The Defense Department responded with a plan to send only three C-5A transports to Israel, arguing that more planes would provoke stronger Arab and Soviet reactions. Nixon (1978, 927) describes his reaction as follows:

> I called Schlesinger and told him that I understood his concern and appreciated his caution. I assured him that I was fully aware of the gravity of my decision and that I would accept complete personal responsibility if, as a result, we alienated the Arabs and had our oil supplies cut off. I said if we could not get the private planes, we should use our own military transports. "Which-

> ever way we have to do it, get them in the air, *now*," I told him.

> When I was informed that there was disagreement in the Pentagon about which kind of plane should be used for the airlift, I became totally exasperated. I said to Kissinger, "Goddamn it, use every one we have. Tell them to send everything that can fly."

Although President Nixon's initial resupply order came on 9 October, the United States airlift to Israel did not begin until 13 October, the eighth day of the war. Within four days, the airlift was moving 1,000 tons per day. Israel had already begun to turn the tide of battle on its own, and the new supplies helped its armies make impressive gains on the battlefields. Only after Israel reversed initial Egyptian gains and threatened to surround the Egyptian Third Army did the Soviets join the United States in calling for a truce. Later reports made it clear that the Soviets had threatened Israel with direct intervention. A somewhat tenuous truce was arranged between Israel and Egypt on 24 October, although a truce with Syria was to wait until 1974.

From abroad, the U.S. government appeared indecisive, although there is legitimate room for disagreement about which policy would have been optimal. Israel survived the war, but Arab members of OPEC embargoed oil shipments to the United States. As the organizational politics model suggests, Kissinger and Schlesinger fought to win Nixon's policy approval. Each presumably acted in what he believed were the country's best interests, advancing his agency's view of the threats and possibilities inherent in the situation. Yet, as Neustadt (1990) details in other cases, the presidential action first chosen was not carried out immediately. Instead, having lost the initial policy decision, Schlesinger found repeated excuses to drag his agency's heels in implementing that policy. As the organizational politics model might suggest, operating procedure issues about

(continued)

(continued)

disguising Israeli aircraft and insuring private aircraft became ways of delaying action. People at the operating level may even have believed they were doing the right thing by raising such issues. Moreover, Kissinger and Schlesinger had feuded before, about other issues. Each was a brilliant analyst with a strong ego and big ambitions. (Kissinger never downplayed his role in Nixon and Ford administration foreign policy. Schlesinger later had the dubious distinction of being fired from cabinet positions by both Republican and Democratic presidents: Gerald Ford ended Schlesinger's career as secretary of defense in 1975 and Jimmy Carter fired him from the post of secretary of energy in 1979.) The governmental politics model reminds us about the importance of such individual-level considerations. One very important reason for policy failures is when responsible officials disagree and deliberately *choose not to carry out policies* determined by their peers and superiors. As noted by Jonathan Daniels (1946, 31–32), an aide to President Franklin Roosevelt,

> Half of a President's suggestions, which theoretically carry the weight of orders, can be safely forgotten by a Cabinet member. And if the President asks about a suggestion a second time, he can be told that it is being investigated. If he asks a third time, a wise Cabinet officer will give him at least part of what he suggests. But only occasionally, except about the most important matters, do Presidents ever get around to asking three times.

In 1973 President Nixon had to ask at least four times to get military resupplies to Israel.

stressful circumstances. This is exactly opposite to the better than normal decision making that we might wish for when stakes are high. Beginning with parts of the 1972 détente package, the United States and the Soviet Union devoted considerable thought to measures designed to defuse tensions in times of international crises. **Contingency planning,** the systematic evaluation of "what could we do if . . . ," can help keep adverse high-stakes developments from becoming crises by reducing both the surprise factor and the response-planning time. Unfortunately, it seems impossible in principle to anticipate every contingency.

Concern that top-level decisions leading to the outbreak of World War I in 1914 were irrational led Robert North and his colleagues at Stanford University to undertake during the 1960s a major investigation of crisis decision making. The then-recent Cuban missile crisis also helped stimulate their study. Collectively known as the *1914 Studies*, that investigation involved detailed content analysis of all available written messages between heads of state and other top government leaders of the states that shortly became embroiled in war, for the several months leading up to August 1914. Because work was begun fifty years after war broke out, the last document classification limits had expired. Those written records are believed to be fairly complete because most critical messages in 1914 were written, whereas many today would be transmitted electronically as voice or text. Moreover, there was good reason to think that something strange occurred in the decisions leading to World War I. Examination of the messages showed that almost every one of the top decision makers shared the three perceptions that (1) there was an intense competition in arms building between the major European powers (an "arms race"), (2) which would lead to war if not checked, (3) but could only be stopped if their opponents backed down. When held by all the key decision makers, these conditions obviously are incompatible. Weapons building continued and accelerated, becoming the stereotype of arms racing, and war ultimately broke out.

Realization of their danger placed the key decision makers under increasing stress as the summer of 1914 wore on. North and his colleagues found a number of behavioral patterns associated with that stress, which they have generalized to other crises. These patterns have been confirmed in many other historical and laboratory studies.

- As stress increases in crisis situations, time will be perceived as increasingly important, and planning horizons will become more short run. Thus crises drive decision makers further away from optimizing toward satisficing, and as crises intensify we find more and more messages specifically address time constraints.

- Decision makers in a crisis will perceive their own alternatives as more restricted than those of their adversaries, and will perceive their allies' alternatives similarly restricted. This finding is fascinating because it is objectively impossible. Both sides to a conflict cannot have fewer alternatives than their opponents. Crises thus promote illogical thinking, which makes optimizing impossible, and may greatly intensify conflict.

- There is an analogous dynamic or *time-dependent* finding: As stress increases, decision makers in a crisis perceive that their own range of alternatives is decreasing while their adversaries' range of alternatives is increasing. This finding also is objectively impossible.

- The higher the stress in a crisis situation, the more communications channels are overloaded, the more stereotyped the messages become, the more improvised or extraordinary communications channels are used, and the more messages are sent within coalitions rather than between them. Message traffic always increases in crises. Employing unusual communications channels is a logical response to overloading of the normal channels. For example, a crucial message about Soviet willingness to settle the 1962 Cuban missile crisis was passed in conversation between a Soviet UN diplomat and ABC television reporter John Scali. Messages within coalitions during crises often involve repeated assurances that the coalition will hold together. This is a reasonable concern, but leaders require increasing assurance as stress intensifies.

Good communication can help defuse crises, and one well-known mechanism for crisis communication is the Washington-Moscow "hot line" established in 1963. It provides for rapid transmission of hard copy in the originator's language between the two capitals, and has been used many times to help prevent potentially explosive situations from escalating through misunderstanding. An excellent example occurred during the 1973 Yom Kippur War. U.S. officials wanted to scramble several fighters from an aircraft carrier in the eastern Mediterranean to take reconnaissance photographs of the Syrian battlefront, but were concerned that officers on nearby Soviet ships would interpret the flights as U.S. intervention on Israel's side against Syria, a Soviet client. The solution was a hot line message to Moscow, specifying in advance the timing and nature of the flights.

ORGANIZATIONAL ESSENCE

The concept of *organizational essence* was introduced by Morton Halperin and two co-authors in a 1974 Brookings Institution book. *Essence* refers to widely held ideas within an organization about the nature of its essential missions and capabilities (Halperin et al., 1974, 28). Members of the organization believe that performing those missions is the essence of the organization, its fundamental and defining purpose. Such notions may not be spelled out in the organization's charter or in any of its formal programs. They may not even be written down. Usually, they are transmitted informally by word of mouth, but are perpetuated and strongly influence the actions of organization members because they are widely accepted. Views of the essential missions determine what programs the agency will fight hardest to preserve and expand, and which career tracks are most advantageous. Agencies sometimes refuse new programs that members think would deflect attention and resources away from essential missions.

Widely shared internal views of essential missions have their positive side. They can promote a sense of purpose and focus. They encourage government agencies to emulate the classic business advice that successful firms concentrate on what they do well. They help the agency present a united front in dealing with other agencies, the Congress, and the executive. On the negative side, those views discourage agency responsiveness to their "market," the executive branch and citizenry. They also are a powerful conservative force, perpetuating the organizational rigidity and inertia about which President Franklin Roosevelt complained. Having served as assistant secretary of the navy from 1913 to 1920 in Woodrow Wilson's administration, Roosevelt once described trying to change something in the navy as like punching a featherbed; you could exhaust yourself without making any lasting impression.

Throughout decades of Cold War, the U.S. Air Force saw its essential mission as flying penetrating bombers into Soviet airspace to drop nuclear bombs. This view made the Strategic Air Command (SAC) the hot career track. Fighter commands bought aircraft large enough to carry nuclear bombs and equipped them with aerial refueling gear that gave them the potential (with supporting tanker aircraft) to reach the Soviet Union. Commands with other missions, such as the Military Air Transport Command, became career backwaters.

Every agency is characterized by widespread acceptance of one or several essential missions. When several exist, they divide the organization into camps that may fight intensively for resources. Agencies may even resist new missions that will compete with those already established. For example, the navy has long been split among four essential missions. Naval flyers, called the brown-shoe navy, promote carrier-based air units. Advocates of more traditional sea power, the black-shoe navy, emphasize surface ships. Submariners prefer attack submarines. All three groups have the general mission of controlling the surface and subsurface of the seas against potential enemies. The fourth group operates the "boomers" or missile submarines, whose distinctly different mission is to sail away and hide from everyone for the duration of their cruise, preserving a highly secure deterrent force of nuclear missiles. When the Kennedy administration sought to expand the missile submarine program in 1960–61, navy leaders responded that it was a "national program," meaning that traditional navy programs should not be reduced to fund it. Additionally, no senior naval officers seem ever to have identified with the transport mission. Like running boomers, transport lacks the panache of combat.

ORGANIZATIONAL ESSENCE IN ACTION
The U.S. Air Force and Penetrating Bomber Aircraft

The notions of organizational essence and essential missions easily explain the long U.S. Air Force struggle to maintain penetrating bombers into the missile age and beyond the end of the Cold War. For decades, they were believed necessary for the essential mission of flying into Soviet airspace to drop nuclear bombs. B-52 heavy intercontinental bombers, last built in 1962, have been sustained through continuing upgrades, with 120 still operational in 1994. Plans in the 1960s called for replacing the B-52s with the supersonic B-70, but only two prototypes were built. One crashed after a midair collision while filming publicity pictures for General Electric, the builder of its engines. The other last flew in 1969. The B-70 program was canceled in 1967 due to high costs and worries about the ability of high-altitude bombers to penetrate steadily improving air defenses.

Next came the B-1, which was originally intended to cruise subsonically and approach its target in a very low-altitude supersonic dash, using terrain-following radar to fly beneath defenses. But extensive development work revealed that airframes strong enough to survive the stresses of supersonic low-altitude flight would weigh so much that they would have a negligible range and payload capacity. Performance requirements were relaxed, but the Carter administration canceled the B-1 program in 1977. Over strenuous air force opposition, Carter proposed to equip Boeing 747 jetliners with large numbers of cruise missiles. Those jets could have cruised to points

just outside Soviet airspace, then released two dozen or more cruise missiles each. About the size of a submarine torpedo, such cruise missiles use terrain-following radar in low altitude subsonic flight and are very hard to defend against, especially in quantity. Carter's scheme probably would have worked, but was strongly resisted by the air force and never implemented. The Reagan administration substituted 100 simplified B-1s as part of its major defense buildup. Designated the B-1B, those aircraft were plagued by cost overruns and operational difficulties. After several crashes, only 94 remained operational by 1994. The next penetrating bomber, the subsonic B-2 stealth, was designed to be exceedingly difficult to detect on radar. It, too, suffered huge cost overruns and heavy production cutbacks. In the 1990s, well after the end of the Cold War and the breakup of the Soviet Union, the need for penetrating bombers was maintained. Doing so had passed beyond an essential mission into the realm of maintaining existing procedures and equipment; if the aircraft existed, missions would be found. B-52s and B-2s saw operational service in spring 1999 during sorties against Serbia and Serbian forces in Kosovo. For the B-2, it was its first combat. However, both flew at relatively high altitudes (well above the range of most Serbian surface-to-air missiles), and the B-52s launched stand-off cruise missiles, a move reminiscent of President Carter's proposed use of 747s in the mid-1970s.

Different camps within agencies may fight especially hard to preserve their essential missions if funding is being cut. Thus we should expect particularly intense infighting as the Defense Department and other agencies struggle to adjust to reduced post–Cold War budgets. Members tend to favor policies that raise the importance of their organizations *as they define those organizations*. Agencies fight hardest for capabilities to perform their perceived essential missions and to maintain sole control of those missions. Agencies also may resist taking on duties their members believe detract from essential missions, as the State Department resisted the transfers of the United States Information Agency (USIA) and Agency for International Development (AID) during the 1990s. New missions may be accepted if they are expected to generate new funding and freedom to expand essential missions, or if refusal might lead to curtailment of essential missions. Usually, though, agencies forgo new functions and capabilities not accepted as part of their essential missions or necessary to protect those missions, even when changing technologies make important new activities possible. After World War II, for example, the army supported spinning off its air corps into an independent air force, fearing that flying would come to dominate the army and change its fundamental role of ground combat. Ironically, helicopters became highly integrated into army fighting doctrine by the time of the Vietnam War, only two decades later. In all these ways, organizational concepts of essential missions promote continuity and the extension of existing programs while encouraging resistance to change, restructuring, new missions, or redistribution of resources. Organizational essences thus reduce adaptability and amenability to management by national authorities, decreasing the range of available options and diminishing our chances of optimizing policy.

INFORMATION FILTERING

Information filtering is the distortion of information as it is "interpreted" by each individual involved in transmitting it up the organizational hierarchy. The noted political scientist Gordon Tullock was the first to discuss such filtering in his book *The Politics of Bureaucracy* (1965, 137–41). Part of the filtering problem is *unintentional* distortion. We see this in the childhood game in which each participant whispers a message into the ear of the next person in line, only to find that the accumulation of small errors leads to a final message seemingly unrelated to the initial one. *Summarizing* produces another form of filtering. High officials have extremely limited time to deal with any one problem, so they typically work with summaries, and even the most skilled and honest summarizers lose something in preparing issue briefs. The most severe form of filtering, however, is *deliberate distortion*. This occurs because individuals often promote their own interests, stakes, and agendas, and because most people usually want to tell their bosses what they think the bosses want to hear. Pressures to curry political favor can be extremely strong, and can encourage withholding or modifying particular facts or estimates because they contradict known user preferences regarding policy or outcomes.

A particularly severe case of widespread and protracted filtering occurred during the Vietnam War, concerning the reporting of postbattle body counts. This grisly figure of merit derived from the belief, noted early in this chapter, that North Vietnam and the Vietcong could not sustain the war if U.S. and South Vietnamese forces killed about ten guerrillas for every soldier they lost. Commanders thus placed great emphasis on body counts as a measure of performance. Knowing this, the guerrillas devoted considerable efforts to removing their dead before retreats. Commanders in the South knew this, too, and inflated the figures from the field in hopes of compensating for bodies removed. Combined with the natural tendency to overstate counts so as to look good, this practice meant that the numbers announced by top commanders and used by Washington planners had only one relationship to reality: systematic inflation. Officials working from inaccurate data cannot plan accurate and appropriate policies. Worse yet, the problem is compounded when inaccuracies overstate the effectiveness of present policy because they encourage continued inadequate actions.

Top officials can help minimize filtering by promoting an organizational ethos that stresses accuracy, accountability, responsibility, and sound planning based on sound data. Additionally, leaders in government, business, tax collection, and a host of other activities can devise reporting systems designed to force people to report accurately what they would rather disguise. (This approach is further considered in Chapter 7.) In the diplomatic arena, it may be easier to appoint ambassadors personally trusted by the administration than to devise methods to make every ambassador report accurately. Indeed, part of staffing any organization at every level is to try to be aware of individuals' biases. This hardly should be a surprise. In everyday life we regularly encounter individual prejudices and learn how much of what any given person tells us about particular subjects should be believed. One reason few secretaries of defense have really run the Pentagon is that they are outsiders, while the military ethos promotes mutual support among officers. Information filtering is an aspect of organizational behavior and politics that is almost impossible to eradicate. Because filtering encourages planning based on inaccurate data, it adds to the list of reasons why policies often fail.

POLICY PROBLEMS ARISING FROM INSTITUTIONAL DESIGN

Some major foreign policy problems arise directly from *institutional design*, the structure of members and relationships established in the U.S. foreign policy system by the Constitution, legislation, executive orders, and case law. Institutional design establishes channels and procedures for policy making, and designing institutions and procedures presents an unending struggle toward finding the best balance between different and competing operational problems. Typically, some problems are built into the system. We may tinker with institutional design, seeking to minimize policy-making problems such as those induced by crises, organizational essence, and information filtering, but we will never fully eliminate them. Changes to institutional structures and procedures almost always are politically controversial and are almost never settled either quickly or permanently. Checks and balances between different units and branches of government are a fundamental part of U.S. constitutional structure, designed to prevent the tyranny of any branch over the others and the people. Yet those checks and balances guarantee a certain amount of internal conflict over policy.

One policy result of constitutional checks and balances is continuing battles between presidents and Congress for primacy in managing foreign policy, demonstrating the *president versus Congress* viewpoint discussed in Chapter 1. A major example that has shaped U.S. foreign policy for more than a quarter century and demonstrates Neustadt's concern about the *weakness* of the modern presidency is the **War Powers Act of 1973** (Public Law 93-148). Passed in the same year the Vietnam peace accords were signed, the act was part of the reaction to widely perceived abuses of presidential power during that war. Presidential initiatives as military commander in chief often have been defended on grounds of the need for fast response in the nuclear age. President Lyndon Johnson, however, utilized information control and public support to hoodwink the Congress into escalating the Vietnam War with the Tonkin Gulf Resolution of 1965. That resolution gave the president approval "to take all necessary measures to repel any armed attack against the forces of the United States and to prevent further aggression." Although the precise meaning of those words was intensely debated as the Vietnam morass worsened, the Johnson administration continued to treat it as the functional equivalent of a declaration of war. By the War Powers Act, Congress sought to limit the future capabilities of presidents to commit troops without explicit congressional approval.

The presidential-congressional clash of powers is clearly framed by two crucial provisions of the Constitution. Article I, Section 8, states that "the Congress shall have power . . . to declare war"; Article II, Section 2, specifies that "the President shall be Commander in Chief of the Army and Navy of the United States." With the virtual disappearance of formal declarations of war since World War II, the latter constitutional provision has come to dominate. The power to station troops around the world as part of containment policy, and to commit them to battle, became the power to wage war without a congressional declaration. Military interventions by U.S. troops in wars as large as Korea and Vietnam, as well as in many lesser instances, were justified by a succession of presidents as falling within their powers as commander in chief, without declarations of war. After Vietnam, Congress sought to reverse that development, although intense controversy continues over whether the War Powers Act has accomplished that aim.

What does the act specify? The president may deploy troops abroad without prior congressional approval in the form of a declaration of war or otherwise, but only if necessary to protect U.S. troops or citizens, or after finding that the United States is threatened with attack. The president must consult with Congress "in every possible instance" before taking action, and report to Congress within forty-eight hours about the circumstances and actions taken. Clearly, this leaves the president an opening not to consult in advance, and most presidents have used it. Consultation has varied from none to limited, often taking the form of discussions with key congressional leaders. In about half the relevant cases, Congress has been informed in advance, but only after the president decided to act. No president has formally admitted being bound by the act, but all have grudgingly complied with the reporting requirement. These provisions give the president ample powers to take the initiative, and in the early stages of military engagements, Congress is allowed only a rather passive role. Other provisions, however, permit Congress to restrict the continued deployment of troops. Congress has only a negative sanction until sixty days after initial troop deployment, but a positive sanction afterward. Within those sixty days, Congress can pass a concurrent resolution *prohibiting the continuation* of troop deployment, and that resolution cannot be vetoed by the president (but see later). After sixty days, Congress must pass a concurrent resolution to *allow* continued troop deployments. The president is allowed a further thirty days to withdraw troops by declaring that time necessary to their safe withdrawal. Although its positive sanction may appear to give Congress considerable power, the president is free to blame Congress for policy failure if it orders the troops withdrawn.

President Nixon vetoed the War Powers Act, saying in part that the sixty-day limit and concurrent resolution provisions "purport to take away, by a mere legislative act, authorities which the President has properly exercised under the Constitution for almost 200 years" and that "the only way in which the constitutional powers of a branch of government can be altered is by amending the Constitution." Nixon was already greatly weakened by the Watergate scandal that would lead to his resignation a year later, however, and Congress passed the act over his veto on 7 November 1973. Intense debates over the meaning and effect of the bill have continued ever since, and they have not just been divided along liberal-conservative lines regarding "handcuffing the president." Liberal Democratic senator Thomas Eagleton of Missouri, one of the act's originators, ultimately decided that "it gives the President and all of his successors *in futuro* a predated 60 day unilateral war-making authority." Conservative Republican senator Barry Goldwater of Arizona joined him, complaining that "the President is no longer prohibited from initiating original actions" because "this language puts into law language that is not contained in the Constitution." Later, at least part of the War Powers Act was thrown into constitutional limbo by a Supreme Court decision. Ruling on 23 June 1983 on an obscure emigration case, the Court invalidated a half-century-old congressional practice of blocking executive action by **legislative veto** after having already delegated authority to the president. A legislative veto occurs when Congress provisionally authorizes the president to take action, subject to ultimate legislative approval. The War Powers Act runs afoul of that ruling because it grants the president authority to deploy troops but reserves a congressional right to reverse such deployment decisions. Those portions of the act that require presidential reports to Congress and prohibit keeping troops deployed beyond sixty to ninety days without a congressional declaration of war or approval of extended deployment remain intact. Although most authorities presume that the 1983 ruling applies, the Supreme Court has never considered the War Powers Act directly.

Thus far, applications of the War Powers Act better demonstrate the concerns of its detractors than the plaudits of its supporters. In 1991, seeking approval for offensive operations in the Persian Gulf, President Bush brought sufficient political pressure on Congress to overcome constraints imposed by the act, as discussed in Chapter 1. In 1993, in contrast, President Clinton rushed to announce a date by which U.S. troops would be withdrawn from Somalia, before Congress moved to compel that withdrawal. Perhaps the most important case in which the act has appeared to interfere with effective U.S. policy making concerns the use of U.S. troops as peacekeepers in Lebanon in 1982–84. They were first sent to Beirut from 25 August to 10 September 1982 to oversee the evacuation of PLO guerrillas. After the massacre by Lebanese Christian militia of Palestinian refugees in areas controlled by Israeli troops, and the assassination of the Lebanese president, they returned on 29 September, joining French and Italian troops in a multinational peacekeeping force. When the first marine was killed by shellfire the next day, Illinois liberal Republican senator Charles Percy urged invocation of the sixty- to ninety-day withdrawal rules of the War Powers Act. The Reagan administration denied that the act applied, but submitted the required reports to Congress. Almost a year of negotiation ensued, ultimately leading to congressional approval to keep the troops in Lebanon for eighteen more months, until March 1985. Practical political problems in applying the act were evident throughout those negotiations. If Congress forced a quick pullout, Reagan could blame them for failure to accomplish the peacekeeping mission. Given any firm deadline for a U.S. pullout, the competing militias could simply wait to resume fighting.

CARTOON 5.1

Whether or not to build missile defense systems is a divisive political issue and presents tough decision-making problems. Proponents argue that every opportunity to defend our people against attack must be pursued. Opponents fear that such buildup will stimulate enemies to spend more on offensive capabilities.

Reprinted with special permission of King Features Syndicate.

Congress thus lacked strong options for constraining Reagan's actions. U.S. troops never had either the mandate or the power to disarm the militias. Unfortunately, it was almost inevitable that one faction or another in that many-sided civil war would perceive the Americans as favoring their opponents. On 23 October 1983, suicide truck bombers killed 241 marines and 58 French troops in Beirut. President Reagan, who had ordered U.S. troops into Lebanon over the objections of the Joint Chiefs of Staff, initially stood firm and asserted that withdrawing the troops would lead to collapse of the Lebanese government. In early February 1984, however, he abruptly reversed himself and ordered U.S. troops out, ending further debate about applicability of the War Powers Act. Withdrawal responded more to domestic political pressures over U.S. casualties than to either the unfeasibility of their mission or the constraints imposed by the War Powers Act. This case, like other applications of the act, clearly demonstrates that many conflicting pressures bear upon every institutional design question.

SUMMARY

Foreign policies regularly suffer failures for many reasons. Degrees of failure range from disappointment over not achieving everything hoped for, through embarrassment, frustration, formidable new policy problems, and full-blown crises, to utter defeat. The reasons examined in this and preceding chapters may be grouped into three grand categories. First, the inherent nature of the decision-making situation may limit options and discourage policy optimization. Second, the approach taken to deciding may lead to suboptimal results. Finally, the design of the institutions through which decisions are made may be flawed. Because the foreign policy problems confronting the United States have changed greatly in number, character, and possible solutions from the problems faced during the Cold War era, contemporary policy failures are most likely to arise because institutions and procedures have not caught up to changes in the global policy context and new demands on the United States. The ill-fated Somalia peacekeeping effort of 1992–95, for example, demonstrates such a procedural lag on the part of the Department of Defense, government leaders, and the American public. (See introductory case in Chapter 7.)

Early in this chapter we examined two idealized conceptual-analytic models for how decisions are made: optimizing and satisficing. Whereas an optimizer examines every alternative and chooses the one best, a satisficer examines only some alternatives and chooses the first one good enough to meet some set of minimum criteria. Pressures of limited information, decision urgency, and the cost/benefit ratios of gathering more information all encourage decision makers to satisfice. Real-world options keep changing, while analysts and officials must persuade others about which options are even possible. Incremental decision making is encouraged when politicians and even many high military officials may not be active in their positions long enough to pay the full price for their decisions. Long-range, fully comprehensive knowledge is impossible because unforeseen and unforeseeable options will become possible. In addition to these structural aspects, human failings also influence the nature of decision-making. For all these reasons, policy decisions are satisficing decisions, not necessarily bad, but also not optimal.

Beyond the pressures to satisfice, the most intractable problems in foreign policy decision making are those stemming from the inherent nature of the decision-making situation. Sometimes no good options exist. Even true optimizers cannot win a fundamentally unwinnable situation, but only do as well as possible given the available options. Because we cannot anticipate and prepare contingency plans for every eventuality, at least some crises will occur. Under the stress of crisis conditions, systematic but illogical changes in decision makers' perceptions distort decision making. Time is perceived as increasingly important. Planning horizons become increasingly short run. Alternatives are perceived as more restricted than those of adversaries. The range of alternatives is perceived to be decreasing while adversaries' ranges of alternatives increase. Communications channels become overloaded, and messages become more stereotyped. More improvised and extraordinary communications channels are used, and more messages are sent within coalitions than between them.

Problems arising from the inherent nature of the approach to decision making often are nearly as intractable as those stemming from the nature of the policy situation, although in principle such problems are somewhat amenable to human action. All the pressures toward satisficing already summarized help produce incremental policy changes, in which there is not even an attempt to produce permanent and optimal policies. Government actions are usually responsive and reactive to problems rather than proactive and innovative, anticipating and heading off problems. This is the *politics of the possible*, in which the need to be seen doing *something* about a problem outweighs doing the *best* thing. Policies must be sold to the bureaucrats who must implement them, and to the public that pays for them and votes for leaders. Neither the bureaucracy nor the public is usually receptive to sweeping change. Responsible officials will not always accept and act on good advice, and the information and advice they receive are not always good. In particular, organizations are self-interested, and *information filtering* systematically distorts data moving up the organizational hierarchy.

As Graham Allison reminds us, all analysts of foreign affairs, whether laypersons or professionals, think about problems of foreign and military policy by using largely implicit conceptual models of how governments function in making policy. The three so-called Allison models (unitary government, organizational process, and governmental politics) are conceptual models of how decisions are made within governments. Officials do not choose these models or directly use them in making their decisions. However, any particular official's personal beliefs about how policy is made usually are closer to one or another of these models than the others. We can use these models to help us understand foreign policy decision making. The models are information filters that inevitably shape the content of our analyses, but that also point out reasons for policy difficulties.

We have the best chance of reducing or eliminating problems in foreign policy decision making that stem from particular aspects of institutional design, the structure of members and relationships designed into the policy system by humans through the Constitution, legislation, executive orders, and case law. Such structures are always changeable in principle, although the politics of change may be exceedingly difficult. All the decision making models examined in this chapter speak to these issues. The framers of the U.S. Constitution saw checks and balances within government as necessary to prevent dictatorship and were willing to pay the price in inefficiency. Part of that price, however, is continuing struggle between presidents and the Congress for foreign policy primacy. Some applications of the War Powers Act, for example, clearly have encouraged policy failures. Interagency turf and budget battles might be reduced by changes in organizational design, for example, by a truly unified general staff in the defense department. Eliminating overlapping dual roles for officials, like those of the director of Central Intelligence and head of the CIA, could reduce agency biases on central decisions. Through appropriate legislation and restructuring, we might loosen or break up the "iron triangle" of military forces, defense contractors, and Congress members supporting their mutually intertwined interests, and close the "revolving door" of officials leaving government to lobby for interests they previously regulated. Failures to train and reward for long-range orientation could be reduced through appropriate programs backed at the highest levels. Agencies too large to be managed effectively could be restructured.

In sum, there are myriad reasons for suboptimal policies and policy failures. Only some of those reasons are changeable, even in principle. Few can be changed easily. We will continue living indefinitely with almost all these problems. Given that policies often are suboptimal, where and how are those policies made? How do we determine how well policies are working, to be able to correct failures and improve effectiveness? The answers form the subject matter of the next two chapters.

KEY TERMS

Allison models

Charter (See also *standard operating procedures.*)

Choice (See also *consistency, decisiveness, ranking,* and *transitivity.*)

Consistency (See also *choice, decisiveness, ranking,* and *transitivity.*)

Contingency planning

Crisis management

Decisiveness (See also *choice, consistency, ranking,* and *transitivity.*)

Governmental politics (Compare with Allison's unitary government— Model I— and organizational process— Model II—models.)

Groupthink

Incrementalism

Legislative veto

Level of analysis

Optimizing

Organizational process (Compare with Allison's unitary government— Model I— and governmental politics— Model III—models.)

Ranking (See also *choice, consistency, decisiveness,* and *transitivity.*)

Satisficing

Standard operating procedures (SOPs)

Transitivity (See also *choice, consistency, decisiveness,* and *ranking.*)

Unitary government or rational actor (Compare with Allison's organizational process— Model II— and governmental politics— Model III—models.)

War Powers Act of 1973

SELECTED READINGS

Adler, David Gray. 1988. "The Constitution and Presidential Warmaking: The Enduring Debate." *Political Science Quarterly 103* (Spring): 1–36.

Allison, Graham T., and Philip Zelikow. 1999. *Essence of Decision: Explaining the Cuban Missile Crisis,* 2d ed. New York: Longman. Allison's 1971 classic remained in print for more than a quarter century and was widely influential. This new edition draws on substantial newer scholarship and considerable amounts of fresh information that became available on both the U.S. and Soviet sides after the twenty-fifth anniversary of the 1962 missile crisis, and, especially on the Soviet side, after the end of the Cold War.

Fisher, Louis. 1995. *Presidential War Power.* Lawrence: University Press of Kansas.

Hilsman, Roger. 1990. *The Politics of Policy Making in Defense and Foreign Affairs: Conceptual Models and Bureaucratic Politics,* 2d ed. Englewood Cliffs, N.J.: Prentice Hall.

Hybel, Alex Roberto. 1993. *Power over Rationality: The Bush Administration and the Gulf Crisis.* Albany: State University of New York Press.

Janis, Irving L. 1982. *Groupthink: Psychological Studies of Policy Decisions and Fiascoes,* 2d ed. Boston: Houghton Mifflin.

Wilson, Heather. 1994. "Missed Opportunities: Washington Politics and Nuclear Proliferation." *The National Interest 34* (Winter): 26–36.

PAUL NITZE AND NSC-68

Long-range policy analysis and grand policy planning are carried out in remarkably few places in the U.S. foreign policy system, by remarkably few people. Indeed, as former Director of Central Intelligence Robert Gates describes it (1998), for most people in Washington, "Long range planning is a week from Thursday." As the organizational process and governmental politics models discussed in Chapter 5 point out, government agencies primarily carry out routine tasks, and most officials are busy managing those agencies. Because the highest officials, such as the president, must attend to current problems, policy innovations and grand policy planning usually come from officials just below the very top level, and from their support staffs. One particularly notable individual among that small group of grand policy planners is Paul Nitze, an in-and-outer whose government service spanned fifty years. In a memoir of his years dealing at high levels with foreign policy, defense, and arms control matters, Nitze (1989, ix) observed that "for almost five decades I have played some role in the affairs of state, working with others to bend what might otherwise have been called the 'inevitable trends of history.'" Most importantly, he was principal author of the crucial National Security Council Cold War planning document NSC-68, discussed in the section of Chapter 2 on the 1950s.

Drafted primarily by Nitze as the State Department's director of policy planning and adopted in 1950, NSC-68 was the capstone of grand policy for the Cold War, and it set the framework for defense buildup and the primarily military containment of the Soviet Union for decades to come. Very few planning documents result from as broad a policy review. Very few recommend policy of such grand scope or have so great and prolonged impact. NSC-68 effectively made defense spending top priority in U.S. government budgeting and led to a major buildup of American nuclear (atomic) and thermonuclear (hydrogen) weapons. It called for "a vigorous political offensive against the Soviet Union" and a society-wide response that would "assure the internal security of the United States against dangers of sabotage, subversion, and espionage." In this last recommendation, it helped launch the McCarthy era of domestic witch-hunting for clandestine communists hiding in the government and the arts. By recommending to continue the policies that had already launched containment, as well as a "rapid buildup of political, economic, and military strength in the Free World" (NSC, 1950, 54), the report implicitly saw containment by itself as insufficient. This was one of many issues on which hardliner Nitze would clash with George Kennan, author of the already-famous 1947 "X" article proposing containment. In the body of the report, although not in its labeled recommendations, was a call for the United States to "produce and stockpile thermonuclear weapons in the event they prove feasible and would add significantly to our net capability" (NSC, 1950, 39).

Secretary of State General George C. Marshall returned from a conference of foreign ministers in Moscow in late April 1947, convinced the Soviets would pose many difficulties for the United States for years to come. On his first day back in Washington, Marshall called George Kennan to his office and asked him to establish and head the new Policy Planning Staff (PPS). Kennan requested Paul Nitze as his deputy, but that appointment was blocked by Undersecretary (and later Secretary of State) Dean Acheson, who had tangled with Nitze on policy issues during World War II. Nitze continued working in the State Department's Office of International Trade Policy, having frequent contact with Kennan. By late 1949 the two seriously disagreed about whether the United States should develop a hydrogen bomb. Nitze, who supported that development, replaced Kennan as head of PPS. Kennan went on an extended fact-finding tour of Latin America and then left government to join the Institute for Advanced Study at Princeton (Talbott, 1988, 45, 53). Through all the years since, PPS has remained a very small unit within the Office of the Secretary of State. Its direct reporting line to the secretary, and the fact that most members of the group are political appointees, reflect its importance.

By the time he became director of policy planning on 1 January 1950, Nitze was already a distinguished in-and-outer. Born in 1907 to an upper-crust banking family, he attended prestigious schools and made a successful career in investment banking. In June 1940 his New York boss, James Forrestal, was asked to become a special administrative assistant to President Franklin Roosevelt, who was then seeking to build ties with the business community to bolster the anticipated war effort. Forrestal would go on to become secretary of the navy (1944–47) and the first secretary of defense (1947–49). Within weeks of reaching Washington, Forrestal asked Nitze to join him. Nitze served in a variety of high-level government posts during World War II, mostly working on economic problems. In the fall of 1944 he was assigned to assist in organizing and conducting the U.S. Strategic Bombing Survey, initially as one of its directors and later as its vice chair. A few years later he would be instrumental in the formation of the Marshall Plan for postwar European economic recovery.

Shortly after Nitze became director at PPS, NSC-68 was triggered by the secret Washington debate about whether to build a hydrogen bomb. As Nitze later wrote (1989, 91),

> [Secretary of State Dean] Acheson accepted my suggestions [about bomb development], but as might have been expected he had trouble persuading Secretary of Defense [Louis] Johnson. Though Johnson fully endorsed working on the H-bomb, he objected to the idea that it be developed in conjunction with a review of our basic national security policy, probably because he knew that such a review would undermine his credibility by exposing critical deficiencies in our military posture. But if he wanted Acheson's backing for the H-bomb, his only choice was to acquiesce in the policy review. It was the necessary price.

PHOTO 6.1

Paul Nitze (shown here in 1960) was principal author of the crucial National Security Council Cold War planning document NSC-68. His long career as an in-and-outer included periods of high-level government service spanning fifty years.

AP/Wide World Photos.

Nitze's account surely demonstrates the interplay of agency positions and key players emphasized in the *organizational process* and *governmental politics* models, discussed in Chapter 5, and the *bureaucratic infighting* viewpoint introduced in Chapter 1. He continues (1989, 93),

> While the AEC [Atomic Energy Commission] began serious work on building an H-bomb, a [joint] State-Defense group was formed to examine the national security implications of the President's decision. The group had no chairman. Secretary Acheson and Secretary Johnson had joint responsibility. On the State Department side, since the study involved matters of long-range policy, the Policy Planning Staff was responsible for the staff work.

Intense work on NSC-68 went on from mid-February 1950 until early April, when the final report was submitted to the National Security Council. Given Secretary of Defense Johnson's opposition to the study, Nitze was particularly concerned that the Joint Chiefs of Staff appoint a reasonably unbiased representative to work with PPS. He later expressed real satisfaction with the appointment of Major General Truman "Ted"

Landon, who was then the air force member of the Joint Strategic Survey Committee. Writing NSC-68 fell almost entirely to PPS. Although Nitze is considered the primary author, he later insisted (1989, 94) that "practically everyone on the staff participated in one way or another to make it a joint effort from start to finish." This is reminiscent of the distributed policy making discussed in Chapter 5. In this instance, however, it did not detract seriously from the final document's unity of focus. Relatively few individuals were even aware of the study, and giving a number officials some input may have helped win them over and ensure broader political support.

Winning acceptance took serious political maneuvering. Nitze arranged with General James H. Burns, Secretary Johnson's deputy for politico-military affairs and chief contact with PPS, for Johnson and Acheson to be briefed on 22 March. Johnson arrived in a rage, refused even to sit down, and stormed out asserting that "I won't have anything to do with this conspiracy," even after Acheson told him,

> You and I are supposed to deliver this report and these are the people we've appointed to do the staff work for us. I can't understand why you won't let yourself be briefed on what they've done. After all, the report is going to be yours and mine, not theirs. We're the ones who are going to have to sign this document. (Nitze, 1989, 95)

Nitze quotes Burns as then saying "I've kept my secretary advised. He agreed to this meeting and now he humiliates me this way. I'm going to have to resign." With some difficulty, Burns was dissuaded from resigning, and work on NSC-68 went forward. Secretary Johnson opposed the policy review because he expected it would recommend a major defense buildup, when he adamantly wanted to hold the military budget to $13 billion. Nitze's estimated cost, kept out of NSC-68 on Acheson's recommendation, was $40 billion. Within two years of the onset of the Korean War in 1950, the U.S. defense budget tripled, to around Nitze's estimated level. (Note that those 1950-era dollars were worth much more than today's dollars, and the buildup represented a tripling of real-dollar expenditures, returning defense spending to World War II levels.)

In the end, Louis Johnson was outmaneuvered. The final report was circulated near the end of March while he was in Europe attending a meeting of NATO defense ministers. Secretary of State Acheson, the three military service secretaries, and each of the Joint Chiefs of Staff promptly endorsed the report. As Nitze describes it (1989, 95),

> When Johnson returned he greeted what amounted to a fait accompli. He could have lodged a dissenting opinion, but he would have looked foolish doing so given the endorsements . . . already received. Johnson . . . knew when he was beaten; in this instance he tried to make the best of the situation by adding his approval of the report and by recommending that Mr. Truman accept it.

Johnson and Nitze's policy battles exemplify the intense commitment to their agencies and their personal policy views that the organizational process and bureaucratic politics models examined in Chapter 5 predict.

President Truman did not officially approve the recommendations of NSC-68 until September 1950, several months after the outbreak of the Korean War, by which time they already were operative policy. For decades afterward, particularly once knowledge of the planning document became more widespread, debates raged over whether containment needed to be pursued in so highly militarized a fashion, or whether an approach closer to Kennan's would have proved better for the country and the world. Nitze's government service in later years would include periods of time as secretary of the navy (1963–67, arguably his highest appointment), deputy secretary of defense (1967–69), member of the U.S. delegation to the first U.S.-Soviet Strategic Arms Limitation Talks (SALT I) (1969–73), assistant secretary of defense for international affairs (1973–76), chief negotiator of the Intermediate Nuclear Forces (INF) treaty (1981–84), and President Reagan's special adviser on arms control (1984–88).

WHAT IS POLICY AND WHERE AND HOW IS IT MADE?

In Chapter 2 we examined the differences between grand policy, which is broad policy guidance intended to influence foreign policy goal setting over a considerable span of time, and specific policy, or applications that deal with single problems at specific points in time. As the bureaucratic process and governmental politics models introduced in Chapter 5 suggest, government agencies spend most of their time and effort making and implementing specific policies. Only small units are regularly engaged in long-range or grand policy planning. The more common process of determining policy for specific cases often is slow moving because it usually involves small inputs from many persons. In turn, the large number of inputs suggests that most policy is not so much *planned comprehensively* as *made*, evolving incrementally. Reflecting on his years in high-level foreign policy posts, Roger Hilsman (1967, 3) observed that *policy making is politics.* He went on to say this:

> We assume that what we call the "decisions" of government are in fact decisions—
> discrete acts, with recognizable beginnings and sharp, decisive endings. We like to
> think of policy as rationalized, in the economist's sense of the word, with each step
> leading logically and economically to the next. . . . The reality, of course, is quite
> different. Put dramatically, it could be argued that few, if any, of the decisions of
> government are either decisive or final. Very often policy is the sum of a congeries
> of separate or only vaguely related actions. On other occasions, it is an uneasy,
> even internally inconsistent compromise among competing goals or an incompat-
> ible mixture of alternative means for achieving a single goal. There is no systematic
> and comprehensive study of all the implications of the grand alternatives—nor can
> there be. A government does not decide to inaugurate the nuclear age, but only to
> try to build an atomic bomb before its enemy does. (1967, 5)

Another Washington official at the middle levels of government once observed that "policy is like a river," his metaphor for the fact that a suitably placed individual may contribute something to the policy stream, but cannot hope to have much personal impact on its grand flow patterns. Additionally, Paul Nitze and others have reflected that the number of qualified individuals interested in helping make policy far exceeds the number of suitable government positions available. By implication, we must look beyond laments about the passing of great leaders when we seek to explain policy failures.

This may appear counter to what we have seen about NSC-68, which clearly was grand policy. It is also an unusually rare case. Few policies are nearly so grand, and most have narrower scope, lesser impact, shorter duration, and fewer different specific applications. According to Nitze himself, a moderate number of officials had inputs to NSC-68. Getting it adopted clearly involved a political struggle, which was more between individuals (as predicted by the governmental politics model) than between agencies (as predicted by the bureaucratic process model). We see this in the fight waged by Nitze and his bureaucratic allies to circumvent Louis Johnson's opposition and win the official endorsements needed to forward the report to President Truman. In turn, Johnson's opposition, based primarily on his views of national and Defense Department needs as reflected in the size of the defense budget, is entirely consistent with his agency position (promoting Defense Department concerns, as predicted by the governmental politics model) and prior experience (concern with limiting the defense budget, consistent with his banking background and the governmental politics model). Implementing the recommendations of NSC-68 required actions by many officials, agencies, and the Congress. Moreover, the report did not emerge from a vacuum. It never could have been adopted had it not expressed a generally supported broad policy consensus, although its early adoption at the highest policy levels was contested. The whole experience of the early Cold War groundwork, from Churchill's "Iron Curtain" speech through the Truman Doctrine, Marshall Plan, and Berlin airlift, was background. Thus even adopting so grand a policy blueprint as NSC-68 can be seen as part of an incremental process of policy building.

As with Paul Nitze and Louis Johnson, policymakers often have widely divergent concerns, different goals, distinct ideas about what is best for the country, and conflicting interests to protect and advance. Competition for policy-making positions is intense, and instances such as NSC-68 are rare. Few among the successful individuals can expect to have great and distinctively visible personal impact on the policies adopted. The processes of developing and deciding foreign policies are ultimately political and carried out through the entire range of means devoted to other political processes. Because politics almost never produces complete consensus, there will always be policy disagreements. And because the policy process is political, changes normally occur only in small steps for which majority support can be found, however temporarily. Indeed, many specific policies never receive enough visibility to receive or require majority support. Policies are invariably subject to further struggle and change. Moreover, given how greatly the foreign policy problems now confronting the United States differ from those faced during the Cold War era, and given that we have not yet settled on a new grand policy, we may anticipate years of unusually intense struggles over both short- and long-term policies.

Certain individuals, groups, and agencies consistently are more involved in making foreign policy than are others. The two major sections of this chapter cover (1) the gathering and interpretation of information to produce intelligence needed for policy planning, and (2) how policy—especially long-range policy—is made in six key locations within and outside government. Those six are intended to be illustrative rather than comprehensive, although they include most of the very important players at this level. Do not try to infer how much influence any particular group or agency has by the number of words that appear here. The six key locations examined are (1) the highly influential National Security Council (NSC) staff; (2) the Department of State, including its Policy Planning Staff, NSC's traditional rival; (3) the Department of Defense; (4) three important congressional support agencies, the Congressional Budget Office (CBO), Congressional Research Service (CRS), and General Accounting Office (GAO); (5) think tanks and policy study contractors (the Washington so-called "beltway bandits"); and (6) special interest groups for both public and private interests, lobbyists, and the "in-and-outers" who move frequently between government positions and careers in industry or academia. Although we discussed many reasons for policy failures in Chapter 5, some new suggestions emerge from the examinations here.

INFORMATION GATHERING, THE INTELLIGENCE COMMUNITY, AND NATIONAL INTELLIGENCE ESTIMATES

Mei Yao-ch'en: When confronted by the enemy respond to changing circumstances and devise expedients. How can these be discussed beforehand?

Reply: [I]f the estimates made in the temple before hostilities indicate victory it is because calculations show one's strength to be superior to that of his enemy; if they indicate defeat, it is because calculations show that one is inferior. With many calculations, one can win; with few one cannot. How much less chance of victory has one who makes none at all.

—SUN TZU, VERSE 28, AS QUOTED BY PRADOS (1986, VII)

Essential prerequisites for policy planning include gathering data about the actions and intents of others, as well as about the effects of our policies, and then analyzing and interpreting the stream of incoming information. Broadly, these tasks are performed by the national **intelligence community,** a large functionally defined group of analysts and officials in a number of executive branch agencies and departments with overlapping interests and global reach. From the perspective of the foreign policy system as an information processing system, conceptually diagrammed in Figure 4.1, the intelligence community is one of its most important *subsystems*. Specialists distinguish between **information,** which is unevaluated material, and **intelligence,** which is the product after received information has been processed. In a major review of U.S. intelligence activities triggered by the failures of Vietnam War policy as discussed at the outset of Chapter 5, the Church Committee (1976) defined intelligence as "the product resulting from the collection, collation, evaluation, analysis, integration, and interpretation of all collected information." Given the intelligence community's size and diversity, the bureaucratic politics model correctly predicts that all the traditional sorts of bureaucratic maneuvers will be used to advance the views and standings of particular agencies.

Exact figures on the size and budget of the intelligence community are difficult to ascertain. The Clinton administration initially planned large cutbacks in the intelligence budget, but evidently came to agree with DCI James Woolsey that new tasks for the intelligence community required maintaining its budget at Cold War levels. Late in 1993 congressional leaders sent President Clinton a letter asking for public release of the size of that budget. The CIA alone was estimated in 1988 to have 16,500 to 20,000 employees in the Washington, D.C., area, with an annual budget approaching $1.5 billion. Other estimates placed CIA as merely 15 percent of the intelligence community, with upward of 150,000 intelligence employees and an annual budget of around $6 billion (Dumbrell, 1990, 144–45). Later estimates placed the total U.S. intelligence budget at about $28 billion, roughly 10 percent of the current defense budget. These public estimates are so imprecise because some elements of the intelligence community are exceedingly secretive, as we see in more detail later. Let us therefore review the principal agencies making up that system, drawing extensively on the summary provided by Fain et al. (1977, 24–25), updated for recent developments:

> The intelligence community is an administrative apparatus composed of specialized agencies with roles circumscribed by both statute and policy control. Some elements have evolved somewhat independently (such as the Department of Defense, the State Department, and the CIA) and have overlapping jurisdictions and capabilities. This framework exists and is encouraged to promote a "healthy competition" and "diversity of views" among the various elements of the community. Presided over in theory by a "director of Central Intelligence" and subjected to continuing review by four different coordinating bodies, plus the president's own staff, the various intelligence agencies are supposed to unify on matters of supreme importance.

The four principal operating elements of the intelligence community, discussed later, are as follows:

- Central Intelligence Agency (CIA)
- State Department Bureau of Intelligence and Research (INR)
- Department of Defense and the Defense Intelligence Agency (DIA)
- National Security Agency (NSA)

U.S. withdrawal from Vietnam in 1973 precipitated several years of intensive analysis of intelligence failures and abuses. In 1975 alone, three major investigations were initiated, first by a presidential commission chaired by Vice President Nelson A. Rockefeller, then by two congressional committees headed by Senator Frank Church (D-Idaho) and Representative Otis Pike (D-N.Y.). All three groups issued voluminous reports, of which the Church Committee report proved the most influential (Johnson, 1983, 176). The latter 1970s, which political scientist Loch Johnson termed a "season of inquiry," produced the first real public look at the hidden intelligence functions of government, and yielded some reforms in organization and oversight. It also produced major controversies over whether and how the intelligence community could be overseen and controlled, and over whether the inquires helped or hobbled U.S. intelligence capabilities. (We leave discussion of the special problems of covert and quasi-military operations until Chapter 9.) At least some analysts believe the post-Vietnam, post-Watergate reforms have worked quite well, preventing military control of the intelligence community and ensuring direction by the president and senior cabinet officers (See, for example, Breckinridge, 1986, 312–14). Controversy remains about the relative powers of Congress and the executive, as examined in Chapter 5. We turn next, however, to some enduring problems of intelligence, and to the process of reaching official intelligence estimates.

THE CENTRAL INTELLIGENCE AGENCY

Although originally envisioned as the central unit advising the NSC on intelligence activities and coordinating those activities, the CIA—aided by bureaucratic struggles fought by early directors—became both the major operating intelligence agency and an independent collector and producer of intelligence.

> Established in 1947, the CIA was to correlate and evaluate foreign intelligence relating to the national security, to recommend to the NSC methods for the coordination of intelligence, and to perform those services that the NSC determined could be more efficiently accomplished centrally. It was authorized "to perform such other functions and duties as the NSC may from time to time direct," language often interpreted to authorize covert action. Police, subpoena, law enforcement powers, and internal security functions were forbidden. (Fain et al., 1977, 24)

As noted in Chapter 5, the director of Central Intelligence's (DCI's) mandated dual role creates a fundamental conflict between responsibilities as head of an agency (the CIA) and as overall chief of the intelligence community and process. The National Security Act of 1947 is vague about the DCI's duties, which has long complicated the task of exercising overall management and coordination of the intelligence community. Because CIA was a producer, the DCI was led to defend its output, and thus lost the ability to claim impartiality. Moreover, CIA's two primary analytic competitors, the DIA and INR (see later) each report to cabinet secretaries. Although the DCI reports to the president and the president is the ultimate intelligence customer, few agency directors are willing to fight bureaucratic battles with the president, so CIA may actually be disadvantaged by the different reporting lines. Only with the post-Vietnam intelligence restructuring of the mid-1970s and beyond did the DCI receive explicit full authority for the management and coordination role. Authority came in a series of public executive orders issued by Presidents Ford, Carter, and Reagan. The DCI did not even obtain control of the overall intelligence budget until 1976, twenty-nine years after the agency's creation. That control is still subject to adjustments by the Office of Management and Budget (OMB), with ultimate appeal to the president.

The DCI is assisted by a deputy director of Central Intelligence (deputy DCI or DDCI) and a National Foreign Intelligence Board (NFIB), the most recent in a series of such management boards. Like the DCI, the deputy DCI is appointed by the president, subject to Senate confirmation. Although the deputy has authority to act for the DCI if the latter is absent or disabled, the precise division of duties between the two posts is largely subject to the DCI's pleasure. That division became controversial in the case of questions about how much Robert Gates knew about the Iran-contra affair while serving as deputy to DCI Robert Casey during the Reagan administration. The NFIB was originated by a 1978 executive order of President Carter, and restructured during the Reagan administration to deal with analytical and substantive issues, including final approval of National Intelligence Estimates and resolution of interagency disputes. The NFIB is chaired by the DCI, and includes the DDCI as vice chair and CIA representative, the directors of the Defense Intelligence Agency (DIA) and National Security Agency (NSA), the assistant secretary of state for Intelligence and Research (INR), the assistant director of the FBI (Intelligence Division), the assistant secretary of energy for defense programs, and the special assistant to the secretary of the treasury (national security). Representatives of the military services and the Defense Department's specialized intelligence offices attend as observers. Additionally, a National Foreign Intelligence Council (NFIC) has membership largely paralleling that of the NFIB, but including the military services, the Defense Department's specialized reconnaissance offices, and senior representatives of the secretary of defense, attorney general, secretary of commerce, and the assistant to the president for national security affairs. The NFIC sets priorities and allocates intelligence resources, dealing more with management than operational and analytical issues (see Lowenthal, 1992, 105–12).

OTHER MAJOR INTELLIGENCE AGENCIES

State Department Bureau of Intelligence and Research (INR)

INR is devoted to assessing rather than collecting intelligence. It manages the State Department's external research and provides departmental policy guidance for intelligence operations conducted by other agencies. Unlike most other elements of the intelligence community, INR is a Washington organization without field operatives. Some 200 of its roughly 320 staff members are foreign affairs or intelligence analysts, and the remainder provide clerical, administrative, and other support. INR's three major sections are Current Analysis (INR/CA), Assessments and Research (INR/AR), and Coordination (INR/C).

Department of Defense and the Defense Intelligence Agency (DIA)

The DIA supports the Joint Chiefs of Staff and the secretary of defense with in-house intelligence assessments, and coordinates Defense Department participation in national intelligence. DIA was created in 1961, early in the Kennedy administration, under Secretary of Defense Robert S. McNamara, following numerous official recommendations over the previous several years. Each of the armed services maintains sizable intelligence organizations and conducts its own cryptography. All services participate in producing national intelligence, but each specializes in the weaponry of its counterpart services abroad. A semiautonomous program of some interest within the Defense Department is the Program for Overhead Reconnaissance, which operates satellite reconnaissance programs for the entire intelligence community under the general direction of the DCI and the assistant secretary of defense for intelligence (Watson et al., 1990, 156).

National Security Agency (NSA)

NSA is the most secret of all U.S. intelligence agencies. Indeed, Washington wags declare that the initials stand for "No Such Agency." It monitors foreign communications and other signals for analysis by other agencies and is responsible for protecting the security of U.S. communications. An early secretary of defense, Louis Johnson, created the Armed Forces Security Agency (AFSA) on 20 May 1949. After review, its name was changed to the NSA later in the Truman administration (24 October 1952), but few other changes were made, and NSA still reports to the secretary of defense. The NSA Act of 1959 codified already established procedures and helped assure NSA's independence when it made the agency "exempt from having to provide any information concerning its mission and activities or the names, numbers, or ranks of its employees" (Watson et al., 1990, 388). Despite personnel reductions in recent years, NSA remains the largest U.S. intelligence agency.

Intelligence units of the Federal Bureau of Investigation (FBI), Treasury Department, and Energy Department also have formal roles in the intelligence community, contributing specialized foreign intelligence on matters falling within their jurisdictions. They are joined by staff elements of the Office of the Director of Central Intelligence. Because the intelligence community is composed of so many quasi-independent agencies, the bureaucratic process model predicts substantial internal disagreement, and it occurs frequently. Even if consensus can be achieved, there is still the problem of potential clashes between the "reality" uncovered by the intelligence and assessment process and the desires of top policymakers. In his testimony before the Pike Committee (1976, 26 January, 13–14), one of the most important post-Vietnam intelligence review groups, John Huizenga labeled this "a natural tension between intelligence and policy," saying,

> [T]he task of the former is to present as a basis for the decisions of policymakers as realistic as possible a view of forces and conditions in the external environment. Political leaders often find the picture presented less than congenial. . . . Thus, a DCI who does his job will more often than not be the bearer of bad news, or at least will make things seem disagreeable, complicated, and uncertain. . . . When intelligence people are told, as happened in recent years, that they were expected to get on the team, then a sound intelligence-policy relationship has in effect broken down.

NATIONAL INTELLIGENCE ESTIMATES

National Intelligence Estimates (NIEs) are documents that are supposed to embody the intelligence community's thorough assessment of the situation in a particular state or region or substantive area and project probable future developments and appropriate courses of action. Although prepared for use at the highest levels of government, NIEs represent the considered opinion of the entire intelligence community. Major differences of opinion are common, and the attempt to project future developments often ends with a very wide range of disagreement. Differing views will be reflected in the text and in footnotes of the NIE document (Fain et al., 1977, 43). NIEs have been prepared for widely varied topics; examples from the 1970s include whether the Soviets were attempting to achieve a first strike potential with their ICBMs, and whether the shah of Iran would be overthrown by revolution. Projections about such crucial topics as aspects of the U.S.-Soviet strategic balance were prepared at many different times over the years, to reflect changing physical, technological, and political conditions.

The director of Central Intelligence (DCI) is the president's principal foreign intelligence adviser and is officially responsible for each NIE, which is supposed to reflect the DCI's judgment about known (and knowable) facts and probable developments. The production of NIEs is a responsibility of the National Intelligence Council (NIC), which is a staff element under the executive director of the CIA and subordinate to the deputy director for requirements and evaluation, intelligence staff. Created in 1980, the NIC now consists of eight national intelligence officers (NIOs), each responsible for producing NIEs regarding a particular geographic area. Each NIO is the director of Central Intelligence's (DCI's) senior staff officer and deputy for national intelligence for an assigned area of substantive responsibility. Within that area of expertise, the NIO manages the production of estimates and interagency intelligence and is the principal contact between the DCI and intelligence customers below cabinet level. Additionally, the NIOs provide national-level substantive guidance to other members of the intelligence community, and interface with defense intelligence officers to obtain their input to national intelligence questions. All NIEs are reviewed by the NIC for quality, assisted by four generalist NIOs-at-large.

In preparing and using NIEs, officials must be concerned with a host of actual and potential problems. Political scientist Robert Jervis (1985, 113–14), noted for his studies of perception and misperception in international politics, has suggested several inherent *limitations on what is knowable* that often lead to incorrect conclusions even when there are no organizational difficulties and the intelligence process is not politicized. Our still incomplete and imperfect understanding of human behavior means the world is not yet a very predictable place. Many situations are interactive, with state actions being based at least partly on leaders' predictions of what other governments will do. Even area specialists have difficulty in acquiring all the state-specific and situation-specific information that might be needed to predict events. Finally, deliberate deception further complicates our understanding. The Soviet Union was notorious for its programs of "disinformation." Still other problems reflect inherent *limitations in the nature of analysis.* A fundamental tension exists between consensus building and competitive analysis. When a group must produce one joint product, the desire for consensus may produce "groupthink" (Janis, 1972), in which participants find it difficult to challenge the first reasonable agreement reached. Analysts may go along with the first winning coalition in order to be included in the final report. Additionally, dissenters expose themselves to much higher levels of individual accountability. (See Woodrow Wilson School, 1988, 28–29.)

Beyond such limitations, basic questions to be faced in intelligence estimation include the following:

- *Timeliness:* Does the estimate reflect the latest available information? How long will it stay timely? Was it prepared and presented in time to have an appropriate bearing on policy decisions?

- *Completeness:* Recognizing that truly complete information is only theoretically possible, in part because other governments will strive to limit access to data about their actions and intent, how closely is the ideal of completeness approached within the available time and with available resources?

- *Precision:* Are the conclusions replicable? Given the same data, will the same conclusions always be reached?

- *Accuracy:* Are the alleged facts correct? Do the projected events actually occur?

- *Relevance for action:* Does the NIE raise and answer the questions essential to making policy decisions about projected actions?

Additional potential problems include the following:

- *Bias:* Estimates may be biased to reflect the perspective or interests of the department primarily responsible for their preparation, or of the CIA itself. Such biases could take many forms, including cultural and experiential bias, promoting particular types of actions (diplomatic, military), relying mainly on particular agencies, or advancing the interests of one foreign government in preference to another. Organizational rearrangements may inadvertently exacerbate such difficulties. One example of such an institutional design problem was the 1973 shift from an Office of National Estimates to a system of eleven national intelligence officers (NIOs), each with staff responsibility to the DCI for intelligence collection and production activities in a geographical or functional specialty. This increased the problem of agency bias because each NIO was primarily identified with a single agency (Fain et al., 1977, 44). Interagency disputes that were previously reflected in the NIE drafting process might then surface only after the draft was completed and circulated.

- *Filtering:* As implied by the discussion of information filtering in Chapter 5, particular facts or even completed estimates may be withheld because their conclusions and predictions contradict known user preferences regarding policy or outcomes. Here again, information may be distorted in transmission by being "interpreted" by each transmitting individual (see Tullock, 1965, 137–41).

- *Direct pressure:* Estimators may be pressured to reach specific answers or types of solutions, or to avoid others. Pressures at the individual and personal level may be exceedingly slippery to document and maddeningly difficult to expose.

Examples of all these types of problems are quite readily found, given the period of intensive analysis of intelligence failures and abuses that followed U.S. withdrawal from Vietnam in 1973. At the grandest level, we now know that data on hand in Washington would have permitted a realistic assessment of U.S. Vietnam War policies. Yet although the intelligence-*gathering* system worked, accurate estimates were not presented or were not acted on or were revised to reflect the desired improvement in the war situation, often referred to as "light at the end of the tunnel" (Hoopes, 1969). Political pressures on the preparers of NIEs can be very heavy-handed. During the Nixon administration, an assistant to Secretary of Defense Melvin Laird informed DCI Richard Helms that a paragraph in the draft NIE on Soviet strategic forces contradicted Laird's public position. The offending paragraph began as follows:

> We believe that the Soviets recognize the enormous difficulties of any attempt to achieve strategic superiority of such order as to significantly alter the strategic balance. Consequently, we consider it highly unlikely that they will attempt within the period of this estimate to achieve a first-strike capability . . .

Helms then deleted the nettlesome paragraph. Later, in a move that demonstrated how reaching agreement on an NIE is actually a bureaucratic battle over ideas, the paragraph was restored as a footnote by the State Department representative on the U.S. Intelligence Board (Fain et al., 1977, 47).

Why is there so much argument over NIE paragraphs and footnotes? As the bureaucratic process model discussed in Chapter 5 suggests, they project each agency's prevailing view into the policy battle while simultaneously helping protect agencies against recriminations for any subsequent policy failures. Individual officials also have strongly held views to advance and reputations to protect, as the governmental politics model suggests. Top officials like Laird may want the bargaining leverage of a supportive NIE to help them impose their will on agencies that have their own internal agendas and essential missions. NIEs typically are classified, meaning that access is restricted to persons with arguable "need to know" and the appropriate level of security clearance. Simply having access may be a sign of bureaucratic power. In the Laird versus Helms case, for example,

Laird surely expected high defense officials in charge of preparing strategic force level and budget plans to have access, so that controlling the content of an NIE about Soviet intent was crucial to imposing his desires on those officials' policy recommendations.

Gaining and acting on accurate assessments of the capabilities and intent of other governments are thus subject to a wide variety of misfires. These range from difficulties in obtaining sufficient data, through interpretation disagreements exacerbated by all the forces of bureaucratic politics, to the all-too-frequent unwillingness of leaders to accept unwelcome messages. Moreover, throughout the intelligence gathering and assessment process the questions asked, the data accepted, and the interpretations placed on those data will all be influenced by beliefs about the way the foreign policy system functions. In 1993 Senator Daniel Patrick Moynihan of New York proposed legislation to abolish the CIA, arguing that the CIA and the broader intelligence community failed to capture the central event of the late Cold War, the gradual implosion of the Soviet Union. Less drastic proposals have been made to transfer some CIA assets and responsibilities to the Departments of Commerce, State, and Treasury, the Drug Enforcement Agency, the Environmental Protection Agency, and the FBI.

POLICY MAKING IN SPECIFIC AGENCIES AND ORGANIZATIONS

If all goes well, the intelligence community yields a stream of information vital to effective policy planning, including data about the actions and intents of others, and about the effects of our own policies. We next examine how policy—especially long-range policy—is made in six key locations within and outside government. Although those six include most of the very important players at this level, their selection is intended to be illustrative rather than comprehensive. As we noted earlier, do not try to infer the relative influence of any particular group or agency from the number of words that appear here. The six key locations examined are as follows:

- The National Security Council (NSC) staff, which is highly influential
- The Department of State, including its Policy Planning Staff, NSC's traditional rival
- The Department of Defense
- Three important congressional support agencies, the Congressional Budget Office (CBO), Congressional Research Service (CRS), and General Accounting Office (GAO)
- Think tanks and policy study contractors (the Washington "beltway bandits")
- Special interest groups for both public and private interests, lobbyists, and "in-and-outers."

This sequence follows the order in which these different groups appear in the zones of foreign policy influence diagrammed in Figure 4.2.

THE NATIONAL SECURITY COUNCIL STAFF

Casual and misleading shorthand usage often fails adequately to distinguish between the **National Security Council (NSC)** and the NSC *staff*. As noted in Chapter 4, the council was created by the National Security Act of 1947 to "advise the President with respect to the integration of domestic, foreign, and military policies relating to the national security." It is the principal forum in which cabinet-level advisers examine issues of foreign and national security policy that require presidential decisions. By statute, the council consists of only four people: The president as chair, the vice president, and the secretaries of defense and state. Several lesser officials with broad advisory roles, plus additional temporary and permanent members, are added based on presidential preferences and the issues under consideration. The president has complete discretion regarding how the NSC is used, the frequency of its meetings, the breadth and seriousness of issues to be considered, and whether it produces final solutions or only a set of options for ultimate presidential decision. As Christopher Shoemaker (1991, 21) notes in his excellent study, "The NSC has no institutional cohesion, little corporate memory, and no life beyond that which the president gives it."

Nonetheless, most presidents since Kennedy have used the National Security Council intensively. As the Tower Commission (1987, I–3), appointed by President Reagan to investigate the Iran-contra affair, aptly stated, "There are some functions which need to be performed in some way for any president." Those functions are the domain of the NSC staff, which provides at least some institutional cohesion and corporate memory. The same National Security Act of 1947 that created the NSC stipulated that "the Council shall have a staff headed by a civilian executive secretary who shall be appointed by the President." The beginnings of the NSC staff during the Truman administration were very modest: an executive secretary and a staff of three professionals, expanding to fifteen over two years. Divided into loose groupings of staff members, consultants, and secretariat, that staff served primarily administrative functions for the council. The post of special assistant to the president for national security affairs (NSA) was not created until 1953, under President Eisenhower. (In Washington usage, this post is abbreviated as NSA. Context normally keeps it from being confused with the National Security Agency.) The NSA did not supplant the post of NSC executive secretary, still mandated by law, but institutionalized a consulting role previously filled by informal presidential friends and advisers. Only in later administrations would the NSA be given effective charge of the NSC staff. Initially, a cooperative relationship was forged because mutual convenience dictated that the NSA needed staff support, and the NSC staff and executive secretary needed an advocate with close access to the president.

President Truman, who wanted no rivals in managing foreign policy and saw the legislation creating the NSC as an attempt to mandate collegial policy making, kept the NSC strictly limited to an advisory role and rarely attending its meetings. Although the staff was suitably minimal and administrative in character, it still sank firm institutional roots. President Eisenhower created the post of NSA and raised the prestige of the NSC by chairing most NSC meetings himself, making decisions there. Despite a recommendation from the 1953–55 second Hoover Commission on government reorganization that the NSC staff should "evolve ideas," the staff remained primarily administrative, providing support, coordination, and policy supervision. Neither Eisenhower nor his NSA,

Robert Cutler, wanted the NSC staff to intervene between the president and his cabinet. Only during the Kennedy administration did the NSC staff begin to gain real influence and become institutionalized as a distinct center for policy making. Growing influence was mirrored by a growth in staff size; both soared in the Nixon administration. Table 6.1 traces the fluctuations in numbers of NSC staff members over time.

The relatively small NSC staff may be surprising, given the very broad scope of NSC responsibilities. Certainly, it gives new meaning to Paul Nitze's observation that the number of qualified individuals far exceeds the number of policy-making posts. Many critics have argued that staff resources are inadequate to cover all major issues or to study any of them in sufficient depth. Of course, many of the size fluctuations recorded in Table 6.1 resulted from the desire of each new administration to design its staff organization. Recent administrations have increased the size of the NSC staff to reflect new foreign policy problems (See the discussion of the staff's 1998 organization later in this chapter). Scholars and practitioners alike generally agree that the NSC staff must adapt and be organized in accord with each president's preferred working style. Members are recruited to achieve balance among the executive departments and agencies and the private sector. Many are in-and-outers with broad experience in national security affairs. They tend to be relatively young and well connected at a number of levels throughout the government. Indeed, some analysts see their connections as paths directly to the White House, via personal contacts. As Shoemaker (1991, 44) suggests, "A departmental officer, or even an individual outside the government, with an idea that has not surfaced through normal departmental channels, calls or visits an NSC acquaintance, who may then propose the idea at the policy level."

Shoemaker (1991, 22) identifies seven "vital functions that the NSC Staff has periodically performed." With some shifts of emphasis, these have continued through subsequent administrations. Listed in order of increasing controversy, which is also the approximate chronological order in which they were first undertaken, they are as follows:

- Administration
- Policy coordination and integration
- Policy supervision and monitoring
- Policy adjudication
- Crisis management and planning
- Policy formulation
- Policy advocacy

At least once, the NSC has moved beyond these seven functions into ill-fated policy implementation; see the later discussion of the Iran-contra affair. Shoemaker's first four are *process* functions dealing largely with how the NSC operates under normal (noncrisis) conditions as part of the policy process. The last three are *substantive* functions dealing more with what policies are adopted. Under normal conditions, there is sufficient time for department and agency staffs to be fully involved in decision making, with the NSC staff playing various facilitative roles. Controversial or not, none of these seven NSC staff functions is completely free from the possibilities of deliberate or unintended bias.

Systems of NSC staff organization adopted to implement these different vital functions have been shaped not only by the preferences of individual presidents, but also by

	TABLE 6.1 *Approximate Numbers of NSC Staff Under Different Presidents*				

President	Approximate NSC staff size	President	Approximate NSC staff size
Harry S. Truman	6	Gerald R. Ford	95
Dwight D. Eisenhower	12	Jimmy Carter	38
John F. Kennedy	10	Ronald Reagan	92
Lyndon B. Johnson	9	George H. W. Bush	134
Richard M. Nixon	100	William J. Clinton	177

continuing reflection and experience, particularly the numerous official reviews of the intelligence function since the mid-1970s. by 1998, that organization had come to consist of the following entities (CQ, 1998, 25–28):

- *Assistant to the President for National Security Affairs (NSA)*, two deputy NSAs, three special assistants, two executive assistants, and two administrative assistants.
- *Executive staff*, consisting of the statutory NSC executive secretary; personal staff supporting the executive secretary; a legal affairs adviser; and special assistants for legislative affairs, speechwriting (called "strategic planning"), and public affairs—all of whom have supporting secretaries or adminstrative assistants.
- *Staff directorates.* Eleven functional directorates cover democracy, human rights, and humanitarian affairs; intelligence programs; international economic affairs; global issues and multinational affairs; Gulf War illnesses; defense policy and arms control; nonproliferation and export controls; systems and technical planning; records and access management; the White House situation room; and the White House Communications Agency. Seven geographical directorates cover Africa, Asia, Central and Eastern Europe, Europe, Russia/Ukraine/Eurasia, the Near East and South Asia; and Inter-American affairs.

Administration has always been a function of the NSC staff, and clearly was intended by the 1947 National Security Act. Administration encompasses such tasks as ensuring that papers are prepared, duplicated, and distributed on time, and that secure files are maintained. These may appear to be mundane clerical tasks, but managing that flow of official paper means directing the idea stream processed by the NSC. It is relatively uncontroversial and normally has been a duty of the NSC executive secretary. Two other duties in managing the idea stream—preparing meeting notes and summary documents, and preparing the agenda for NSC meetings—are potentially more influential and controversial because they could introduce bias. In the post-Watergate era, official Washington is permeated by widespread reluctance to tape-record meetings or even to have verbatim transcripts prepared. Typically, NSC staff members take notes at meetings and later transcribe them into summaries for the president and other interested parties. Notes usually are taken by the staff member charged with responsibility for the subject area under consideration. This helps ensure an interested and informed treatment, but also raises the specter of intentional or unintentional bias. Other note-taking problems will be familiar to every student who has ever attended a lecture: Attention may wander. Too much material may be presented too quickly, causing a crucial point to be missed, after which one scrambles to catch up. Personal beliefs may cause shades of meaning to be distorted toward an individual preference, or toward what the note taker expected.

Many of the same problems can affect agenda setting. Generally, the NSA is responsible for preparing the agenda for NSC meetings, an apparently innocuous task that has great potential for influence. As in other areas of politics, the power to set the agenda for deliberations may go a long way toward determining their outcome. In much the same way that the president's chief of staff has enormous influence over which individuals and groups receive time with the president, the NSA, with NSC staff support, plays a gatekeeper role determining which issues reach the president and NSC for consideration. Presidents have only finite available time and attention, an unavoidable limitation that places them somewhat at the mercy of their handlers. While this will not prevent deliberations about an issue the president is determined to have discussed, it may well prevent a president from learning about some lesser issue or about a viewpoint held somewhere in the lower levels of government.

Policy coordination and integration build on note taking and agenda setting, and are subject to many of the same potential biases. *Coordination* is the management of information exchange, in which the NSC staff acts as an interagency channel. It begins with the collection of concepts, policies, and proposals for NSC consideration. Issue papers that present (often opposing) views are collected, redundancies are excised, and issues needing resolution are identified. Staff members ensure that all relevant agencies and officials are made aware of the pending NSC consideration, understand the issues, have an opportunity to comment, approve or have their disapprovals noted, and are given early opportunities to resolve disagreements. Like administration, this coordination function clearly was intended by the 1947 National Security Act. Little or no substantive input is required. Ideally, the staff serves as an honest broker of policy ideas and helps ensure that valid but unpopular alternatives are included among those given full examination. Washington belief holds that the NSC staff usually have been successful in coordination, but the function is open to the same biases of emphasis, interpretation, and prior positions as note taking. Judgment is importantly involved in deciding which agencies and officials are relevant, as suggested by the bureaucratic process and governmental politics models. Staff members must decide how much interagency coordination an issue merits. Clearing an issue with an agency that lacks an important interest only invites delay while officials struggle to develop a position on an item distant from their agency's central concerns and expertise. Failing to clear an issue with an agency whose officials do perceive an important interest, however, can provoke intense bureaucratic struggle. Overcoordination also increases the chances for sensitive or classified materials to be leaked.

Policy integration is a small but significant step beyond policy coordination, and involves reducing diverse and often conflicting views to a single brief document. This function is even more subject to potential bias than those already considered, but it is essential if the NSC process is to facilitate presidential decision making. Issues raised for top-level decision by the president and NSC commonly are presented in lengthy position papers prepared in the originating department or agency. Other departments then weigh in with papers presenting their positions. Issues that can be resolved at lower interagency levels never reach the NSC or the president. Only difficult issues rise to the top, but the sheer volume of position papers still would overwhelm any president. Conflicting positions must be summarized as completely and fairly as possible, and the results distilled into a one- or two-page document, which is all the president will have time to study. The potential for bias to creep into these integrated summary papers is obvious. Subtle choices of pejorative adjectives, omission of a critical point without which an argument will be unclear, sequencing that presents a preferred choice advantageously, and other such tricks, even unintentionally, may skew the decision taken.

Policy supervision and monitoring ensure that a policy is carried out, once decided on, but are distinct from the operational direction and conduct of operations. Every policy decision must be implemented by one or more departments, and simply ordering them to act is insufficient. As Richard Neustadt (1990) has so eloquently written, presidents cannot merely order something done, but must persuade government departments to carry out the desired action, using all their powers to reward or punish as necessary. As the bureaucratic process model reminds us, departments have particular stakes in taking or obstructing action, whereas the more balanced perspective of the NSC staff leaves them well placed to supervise policy implementation and keep the president and cabinet-level officers apprised of developments. *Monitoring* is an instance of using feedback to help ensure that policy achieves the desired results, a subject further explored in Chapter 7. Policy decisions also may not be fully and correctly implemented because they are misunderstood, overlooked in the press of other work, or demand expertise beyond that available in the operative location. Ideally, monitoring would expose all such failings in time for corrective action. Unfortunately, that ideal seldom is met.

Policy adjudication is the last of the four NSC process functions. Closely related to policy supervision and monitoring, it refers to resolving disputes that arise about what a policy decision means or how it should be implemented. It may seem surprising that the meaning of a presidential decision could be unclear. However, critics have charged that NSC staff often are unclear in communicating policies and the rationales behind them to the rest of the government. Worse yet, policy decisions may not even be communicated in writing. As Shoemaker (1991, 33) notes, "because of the omnipresent fear of leaks, even clearly written presidential documents conveying the president's decisions *are not usually made available* to the action officers in the implementing departments who are charged with acting upon those decisions" [emphasis added]. Instead, oral instructions are given, but they are notoriously imprecise and subject to later confusion. Disputes easily arise. Moreover, presidential decision documents rarely give detailed instructions on how policy is to be implemented, thus raising further occasions for disputes. NSC staff who have established that they know the president's desires and operating style are uniquely well positioned to resolve such disputes. They then can clarify the president's intent, resolve interdepartmental disputes about meaning, and settle implementation issues without having to go back to the president or the NSC itself. Ideally, an implementation monitoring committee chaired by NSC staff is established by the decision document or by the NSC staff itself. As with policy coordination and integration, opportunities for bias abound, and the NSC staff will be more effective policy adjudicators when they have built a reputation for fair and evenhanded dealings.

Crisis management is the first of the three substantive functions, and one in which the NSC staff have unique organizational advantages. Recall that crises involve high stakes, short decision time, and surprise, and that crisis management was briefly discussed in Chapter 5. Politicians, bureaucrats, and analysts throughout (and beyond) government tend to agree with Zbigniew Brzezinski (1987, 95), a noted Soviet specialist and President Carter's NSA, that "crisis management must stay in the White House." High stakes ensure that the president will be involved. Surprise only obtains when nobody anticipated events and made contingency plans in advance. Finally, short decision time plays straight to the natural advantages of the NSC staff because it routinely deals with the bureaucracy on the president's behalf, cuts across departmental lines of organization, and is used to summarize issues and action options for presidential decisions. As a relatively small group within the executive branch, housed close to the president and enjoying quick access, the NSC staff can react quickly, interface with the highest levels of government, and remain outside the glare of publicity.

In the more structured administrations, trusted advisers to the president will already be on the NSC. It is then natural for the president to turn to the NSC to form a crisis working group, as Presidents Ford and Carter did. In turn, the NSC will turn to its staff for detailed support in reaching out to tap needed expertise throughout the government, and in summarizing and presenting action options. Additionally, the NSC staff are well positioned to supervise policy and provide rapid feedback to the president about results. The tendency for decision making to become more centralized under crisis implies increased NSC staff power over the federal bureaucracy, which may facilitate implementation of chosen policies. However, insider reports suggest that it has been difficult to get people, even NSC staffers, to focus much attention on anticipating and planning ahead for high-stakes contingencies that could produce crises.

Policy formulation is an end to which essentially all NSC staffers aspire. However, as the bureaucratic process and governmental politics models predict, this function provokes criticism from others in government, chiefly in executive branch departments, who believe they should formulate policy. NSC staff freedoms in this regard depend crucially on the president's operating style. Zbigniew Brzezinski, having served as President Carter's NSA, distinguished between presidents who use "secretarial" and "presidential" systems in managing national security policy. Secretarial style (after cabinet secretaries) vests responsibility for most policy development in the federal departments, whereas presidential style involves the president intimately in policy management and keeps most policy development in the White House. Almost of necessity, presidential-style management implies a major policy formulation role for the NSC staff.

Unlike the vast majority of the federal bureaucracy, the NSC staff largely changes with each new president. Those positions are among the few thousand "plum" appointments made by each incoming administration. Although many staffers are drawn from government departments, their period of White House service involves a vast increase in power and influence, with concomitant improvements in long-range career prospects. Because they owe their primary political loyalty to the president, the chief executive can expect them to be attuned to presidential operating style and goals. This expectation of direct presidential support adds to the NSC staff's independence of the bureaucracy and contributes to its strengths in policy formulation. Its chief disadvantages are its small size, with the attendant limitations in depth; lack of continuity from one administration to the next; and ongoing clashes with the State Department over long-range policy planning (about which we say more in the next section).

Policy advocacy is the next step beyond policy formulation, and the most controversial among the vital NSC staff functions. Those who object to policy formulation by NSC staff object even more strongly to staff members advocating the formal adoption of their proposals. Potential clashes arise between arguing one's personal views versus coordinating departmental views and honestly representing them. Advocacy is most effectively pursued by staffers working within the committees of the NSC, where they can best contribute to long-range planning. Advocacy also may be pursued through the positions presented in summary papers, through recommendations forwarded and argued by the NSA, and occasionally in arguments presented directly to the president.

Policy implementation is a major step beyond advocacy and clearly was never originally intended as an NSC function. Nonetheless, President Ronald Reagan's NSC took that step in the Iran-contra affair. This involved a complex scheme to sell arms secretly to Iran, channeling the proceeds to anti-Sandinista contra rebels in Nicaragua. Iranian so-called "moderates," whose very existence now appears doubtful, were then supposed to help secure the release of U.S. hostages held by Islamic militants in Lebanon. Congress had passed legislation prohibiting the Defense Department, CIA, or any other government agency from providing military aid to the contras during the period December 1983 to September 1985. The NSC was used to supervise covert aid because it was not specifically mentioned in the legislation. Initially, the NSC raised private and foreign funds for the contras; later they progressed to diverting profits from the Iranian arms sales. After reports in Lebanese newspapers revealed the deal late in 1986, President Reagan's national security adviser Robert Poindexter resigned, and NSC staffer Colonel Oliver North was fired. A special prosecutor later brought charges against most of the major figures in the scandal. Most, including North, were convicted, although many of the convictions were overturned on appeal because of immunity agreements concerning prior testimony in hearings conducted by the U.S. Senate. The roles of President Reagan and Vice President Bush remain unclear. Both claimed to have been uninformed about the details of the Iran-contra affair, and some reports contradicted their claims. Officials long have sought **plausible deniability** for covert operations, meaning that they—either personally or on behalf of the U.S. government—could claim no knowledge of an operation and reasonable people could say that the disclaimer might be true. If Reagan's and Bush's denials are true, the NSC and NSA undertook a major foreign policy initiative with no higher supervision nor approval.

THE DEPARTMENT OF STATE

Should the State Department be the primary location for planning U.S. foreign policy? Should the secretary of state be the primary foreign policy officer after the president? Newly elected presidents routinely say "yes" to both questions, yet just as routinely turn to the National Security Council and the NSA, as discussed in the previous section. Thus the Department of State is the traditional rival of the NSC staff for primacy in policy planning. Henry Kissinger, undoubtedly the most powerful NSA to date and the only one ever to serve simultaneously as secretary of state, later echoed those newly elected presidents, writing (1979, 30) the following:

> I have become convinced that a President should make the Secretary of State his
> principal adviser and use the national security adviser primarily as a senior administrator and coordinator to make certain that each significant point of view is heard.
> If the security adviser becomes active in the development and articulation of policy,
> he must inevitably diminish the Secretary of State and reduce his effectiveness.

Still, presidents continue to turn away from the State Department. Interestingly, many in Washington say that Kissinger never really became a secretary of state, and his tenure in office was marked by the resignations of many discouraged foreign service officers (FSOs). A few years later, President Jimmy Carter, praised for his analytic skills but often criticized for involving himself too deeply in policy minutiae, complained that he "rarely received innovative ideas from [the State Department] staff about how to modify existing policy in order to meet changing conditions" (1982, 53). Leslie Gelb, the journalist who headed the political-military affairs section at State during Carter's administration, later asserted that "recent Presidents have probably concluded sometime during their first year that they cannot trust anyone in the State Department below the Secretary" (1983, 286).

Given the prominence of the State Department Policy Planning Staff (PPS) in preparing NSC-68 in 1950, these complaints may seem surprising. Considering *organizational essence* (see Chapter 5), however, they make sense. Since its founding in 1947, PPS has remained a very small unit within the Office of the Secretary of State, operating outside the department's regular channels. By 1992 it consisted of a director, three deputy directors (two of them career incumbents), a senior adviser, and four GS-15 grade staff members. Its importance is reflected by its direct reporting line to the secretary of state, and the fact that most of the group are political appointees. Yet it is normally not staffed with career foreign service officers (FSOs), placing it at a disadvantage in internal dealings with a department whose essential career track has always been that of the FSO.

Beyond this organizational or institutional design problem, why has the Department of State not worked well in policy generation, causing a succession of presidents to turn elsewhere? Part of the difficulty lies with the department's demoralization during the McCarthy "red scare" era of the early 1950s. Conservatives seeking someone to blame for the general reverse that turned World War II victory into Cold War fears and competition, and particularly seeking parties responsible for "losing" China to the communists, claimed to find them in the State Department. Many career officials, particularly "old China hands," were driven out of government, not to be rehabilitated until the mid-1970s. Thereafter, the department ran scared and self-paralyzed. It was natural for presidents to turn elsewhere and for other policy power centers—most notably the NSC and the NSA—to arise. Additionally, as previously discussed, those new power centers had all the organizational advantages of placement in the Executive Office of the President.

These factors still are not sufficient to explain persistent State Department difficulty in innovating policy. Organizational and operational issues are at least equally important. Simply put, the State Department's methods of conducting business work against policy innovation. This is one instance of an organizational problem in decision making, as discussed with the bureaucratic politics model in Chapter 5, and it bears brief examination here so that we may better understand how the department makes policy. Shoemaker (1991, 42) argues that "the most important weakness is the State Department's inability to formulate meaningful long-range policy that integrates foreign concerns with domestic political realities. This important deficiency stems both from the structural makeup of the department and from historical proclivities of the Foreign Service." Much power within the department lies in bureaus responsible for geographical regions. Gelb (1983, 287) insists that FSOs "neither by training nor by disposition are gifted or even interested in the formulation of policy." Instead, embassies around the world are closely tied to headquarters in a "management by cable" system, referring to the telegram network linking each embassy to its corresponding regional desk officer in Washington. Faced with desk officers tracking their every act, embassy staff tend to refer even minor problems to Washington for resolution. This builds workload to the point that desk officers and their immediate superiors must concentrate on solving immediate problems and have little time to devote to long-range policy. Having fallen into such habits, they cannot readily break them, and officials promoted up the chain of command tend to carry those habits along.

Policy then becomes the slow accretion of small measures taken without reference to any grand vision. The small PPS is not enough to change this overall pattern, particularly because it is seldom populated with FSOs who are accepted throughout the department because they have shared the common experiences of postings abroad.

Typical noncrisis policy making in the state department is responsive rather than innovative and reactive rather than proactive, and the department only incrementally extends existing programs. Consistent with the bureaucratic politics model, FSOs seek to run their agency's programs, not the administration's program. Distributed policy making rules: Many individuals have a small part in drafting policy, and the ultimate results bear small imprints of many hands and minds. Long-range impacts of policy changes receive little consideration. Bureaucrats spend quite a bit of their time responding to concerns raised elsewhere in the organization and which—like it or not—fall within their areas of responsibility. Most requests for policy changes never go near the policy planning staff.

THE DEPARTMENT OF DEFENSE

Under the topic of defense department impact on foreign policy, most texts devote space almost exclusively to covering the department's organization. Given the sheer size of the defense establishment, there are implicit expectations that it must have profound policy impact. The question whether the foreign policy uses of military power, which include threats much more frequently than actual combat, are *originated by* the defense department rarely receives adequate consideration. Certainly, the department employs more people than any other agency of government. In 1990, before post–Cold War downsizing began, the United States had slightly over 2 million uniformed personnel on active duty and about 1 million civilian employees. By 1996 active duty forces had been cut to about 1.47 million. Like defense staffing, the defense budget is enormous. At the end of the Cold War, it was second in federal spending, behind only entitlement programs such as Medicare and Social Security. By the mid-1990s, cuts dropped that share below 20 percent of the federal budget, to third place, after interest on the federal debt. That huge defense budget and work force, distributed over the entire country, supported a politically potent **"iron triangle"** of military forces, defense contractors, and Congress members throughout the Cold War years. The military services needed Congress to provide funding and contractors to develop and build weapons. Contractors needed business and could provide good postretirement jobs to reward military officers who helped them get business. Congress members wanted military bases and contracts to provide jobs in their districts. This is a clear example of the *domestic special interests* viewpoint introduced in Chapter 1. Cuts in defense spending reduced the size of the pot, but the iron triangle incentives remain in place.

Beyond sterile arguments of the "size implies impact" sort, analysts of policy planning and defense department policy impact regularly have raised questions about whether civilian control can be made to work. Despite the primacy accorded the notion that military officers ultimately report to civilian superiors—the chairman of the Joint Chiefs of Staff to the secretary of defense, the air force chief of staff to the secretary of the air force, and so on—the only secretary of defense widely believed to have made the department obey his will is Robert S. McNamara, under Presidents Kennedy and Johnson in the 1960s. McNamara, fresh from serving as the young and dynamic president of Ford Motor Company, brought to the defense secretary's Office of Program Analysis and Evaluation (PAE) a group of brilliant analysts soon dubbed the "whiz kids." That office related to the secretary of defense in much the same way the NSC staff relates to the president, with close and direct reporting lines and great independence from the established bureaus. McNamara introduced a new integrated planning and budgeting scheme known as Planning, Programming, and Budgeting System (PPBS), designed to link procurements more closely to defense missions. In this he had some success, although certain decisions, such as requiring the air force and navy to agree on one design for a new fighter-bomber aircraft, ultimately proved unsuccessful. Difficulties in imposing civilian control on the department should remind us of the *bureaucratic infighting* viewpoint introduced in Chapter 1, and of the *bureaucratic process* model discussed in Chapter 5.

In his brief and uncomfortable tenure as secretary of defense during the first year of the Clinton administration, Les Aspin initiated significant reorganization and reanalysis within the department. Another of the whiz kids, Aspin was elected to the House of Representatives from Wisconsin at the age of thirty-two and served more than two decades before resigning to assume the defense post. Initially a critic of the armed services, Aspin had become more a critic of military spending and had risen to be the highly regarded chair of the House Armed Services Committee. Aspin was Senator Sam Nunn's only serious challenger as the Congress member most knowledgeable about military affairs. Unfortunately, although Aspin's entire previous life could be seen as excellent preparation to be secretary of defense, his operating style was more that of an academic or think tank analyst than the leader of a great bureaucratic organization. This rapidly led to frictions with the uniformed services and the White House. President Clinton, who had opposed the Vietnam War and never served in the military, needed a defense secretary whose credibility with the military would win support for administration programs. This, Aspin could not deliver. In December 1993 he was eased out, with everybody claiming for the record that he stepped down at his own request.

Despite his unhappy departure from the defense secretaryship, Aspin initiated two major moves that have had some profound impact on defense policy and defense policy making. The first was a "bottom-up review" intended to "define the strategy, force structure, modernization programs, industrial base, and infrastructure needed to meet new dangers and seize new opportunities" in the post–Cold War era. Completed by September 1993, the review began with an assessment of the new political-military era, moved to devising a suitable defense strategy, then constructing force "building blocks" to implement that strategy, aggregating them into an overall force structure, and finally building a multiyear defense plan. Although this may appear a very logical process, nothing of the sort was done during the Cold War decades, and the notion of building programs up from operating-level inputs rather than imposing them downward by Pentagon directives also is highly unusual in the defense department (see Aspin, 1993). Aspin's other major move was to propose reorganization of the Office of the Secretary of Defense, roughly the defense secretary's analogue of the Executive Office of the President, to streamline its operations and focus attention on new missions required in the new era. Under the part of that reorganization proposal later enacted, the general counsel and officials handling public and legislative affairs function more like the executive staff to the head of a large corporation. Four undersecretaries replace more than two dozen officials previously reporting to the secretary. They are responsible for defense policy, personnel and readiness, financial management, and technology and hardware (Office of the Federal Register, 1998, 173–74).

CONGRESSIONAL SUPPORT ORGANIZATIONS

In recent decades, several organizations supporting the legislative branch have gained importance and influence in analyzing and shaping policy. Today these include the Congressional Budget Office (CBO), Congressional Research Service (CRS), and the General Accounting Office (GAO). The birth and death of a fourth congressional support organization, the Office of Technology Assessment (OTA), are chronicled later. Collectively, these organizations represent the largest governmental organizations for policy planning and assessment outside the executive branch. During the 1970s congressional support services of all types grew and were reorganized. CRS was guaranteed independence and its staff were increased and upgraded; the CBO and OTA were created; the GAO's program evaluation capabilities were strengthened; and numbers of committee and members' personal staff were increased. Those staff increases were important, facilitating interaction among committees, members' personal offices, and the support organizations, and allowing greater specialization by all involved.

Congressional support organizations perform an eclectic mix of functions combining historical research, information generation, policy option generation, and policy impact assessment of the sort examined in Chapter 7. They have become effective policy consultants and think tanks reporting to the Congress. Their general roles include analyzing policy, locating and organizing information, evaluating the success of programs, and specifying available options and their probable impacts. Thus they shape policy by establishing the menu of possibilities from which ultimately political choices must be made by Congress and the executive. The principal products of the three surviving organizations are nicely summarized by Verdier (1992, 253):

- CBO does the budgeting, forecasting, and policy analysis. It is grounded firmly in the discipline of economics; it does what economists do.

- CRS is more eclectic in terms of disciplines. It provides information and responses to congressional questions, with products that have evolved from factoids to broader frameworks.

- GAO is also evolving, from accounting to program evaluation, but its signature products still bear the stamp of its accounting tradition ("accuracy, independence, and objectivity").

Congressional support organizations provide substantial in-house expertise and a full-time staff of highly qualified analysts, helping to overcome time and knowledge limitations for Congress members and their staffs. They are important tools helping to reduce Congress's inherent disadvantages relative to the president and the federal bureaucracy. (Recall the *president versus Congress* viewpoint introduced in Chapter 1 and Congress's placement in influence zone 3 in Chapter 4.) Although they cannot fully substitute for an administration's ability to command access to information, they make Congress independent of the administration's experts, forecasts, and interpretations. Typical policy applications include using CBO numbers to challenge the trade and income projections in the president's budget, CRS studies to discern grand policies from the utterances of high officials, and GAO studies to evaluate whether new weapons systems perform to their design specifications.

The Congressional Budget Office

The **Congressional Budget Office (CBO)** is the youngest of the three congressional support organizations, created by the Congressional Budget Act of 1974. In a town in which assured access to information carries significant political power, the CBO guarantees Congress its own budgetary and economic information, regularly used in making policy and in challenging executive branch numbers. In the words of assistant director for budget analysis James L. Blum (1992, 227), "CBO is not just a budget office that estimates the cost of legislative actions, but also is a policy analysis office that helps shape the content of legislation." Its mission, providing economic and budgetary information in support of the congressional budget and legislative process, is narrower than those of the other support organizations. However, the federal budget affects almost all government activities and has major impact on the national economy, so CBO's subject matter is extremely broad.

CBO's major functions are budgetary assistance to the Congress, economic analysis, and policy analysis. These are carried out by a combination of informed judgments and advanced quantitative analyses, including modeling and computer simulations. CBO is the only legislative branch unit that makes economic forecasts and projections, although it does not maintain its own econometric model of the national economy. More than 60 percent of its staff have college and graduate training in economics. Major products include (1) annual economic, budget, and deficit projection reports to the House and Senate Budget Committees (created by the same 1974 act that originated the CBO); (2) annual analyses of the president's budget, which typically predict higher deficits or lower surpluses; (3) program analyses requested by the Congress, normally published; (4) cost estimates for legislative bills; and (5) "scorekeeping" for spending and revenue legislation. CBO program analyses present and analyze alternatives without recommendations. Blum (1992, 221) characterizes their report writing style as "on the one hand, . . . on the other hand, . . ." CBO's program analysis is properly a subject for Chapter 7, on feedback policy evaluation. However, it also deserves a place here as a source of policy ideas because many alternatives are enacted into law after CBO has brought them to congressional attention. Its continuing influence and credibility rest on a reputation for unbiased and authoritative analyses.

The Congressional Research Service

The **Congressional Research Service (CRS)** is the oldest and second largest of the congressional support organizations, housed both physically and organizationally within the Library of Congress (LC). CRS is the only LC department whose sole purpose is providing information and policy analysis to the Congress. Its statutory roots go back to the creation of a Legislative Reference Service (LRS) in 1914. Permanently established as a separate department in the LC by the Legislative Reorganization Act of 1946, the LRS was renamed the CRS and guaranteed complete research independence and maximum practicable administrative independence by 1970 amendments to that act. By statute, there are stringent constraints on CRS publication for noncongressional use. If you want to see CRS research, your Congress member must make a request on your behalf, although many students and faculty receive marvelous cooperation. With the Congress as its only official client, CRS emphasizes quality, timeliness, nonpartisanship, and confidentiality. Its analysts are among the most talented in Washington, and it has earned a reputation for extremely rapid and insightful work of very high quality. CRS analysts serve as consultants to Congress members and their staffs and are closely involved in the legislative process, an involvement that nurtures and requires confidential relationships. Nonpartisanship is vital to the survival of an organization serving a body as highly politicized as the Congress. Although CRS does not formally make legislative or policy recommendations, its studies and evaluations of options are extremely influential. Past CRS foreign policy studies include such products as detailed background briefs on the 1980 Falkland Islands war and the Persian Gulf War, and detailed studies of strategic missile basing and arms control options during the mid-1980s.

Under the 1970 amendments to the LRA, CRS has a very broad charter. Some excerpts follow:

> It shall be the duty of the Congressional Research Service, without partisan bias . . . upon request, to advise and assist any committee of the Senate or House of Representatives and any joint committee of Congress in the analysis, appraisal, and evaluation of legislative proposals . . . or of recommendations submitted to Congress, by the President or any executive agency, so as to assist the committee in—
>   (A) determining the advisability of enacting such proposals;
>   (B) estimating the probable results of such proposals and alternatives thereto; and
>   (C) evaluating alternative methods for accomplishing those results; and, by providing such other research and analytic services as the committee considers appropriate for these purposes, otherwise to assist in furnishing a basis for the proper evaluation and determination of legislative proposals and recommendations generally . . .

The CRS thus has a broad mandate to prepare and analyze policy alternatives, evaluating them by whatever criteria its analysts may propose. Although the Congress responds at least as much as the bureaucracy to incentives that normally cause policy to evolve incrementally, CRS analysts are free to propose criteria that would allow long-term policy optimization. The numbers of such proposals and the proportion accepted, however, are not publicized. Although the bulk of what CRS produces remains qualitative analyses, increased capabilities for quantitative analyses were built during the 1980s. As a result, CRS analysts increasingly use such tools as computer simulation and econometric models, for example, in forecasting developments in major sectors of the economy. Since the 1970s, a rising reputation, advanced analytic techniques, and intensive involvement in congressional policy making have combined to make CRS positions desirable to the best people coming out of top graduate programs.

Like the CBO and GAO, the CRS provides substantial in-house expertise and a full-time staff of highly qualified analysts and thereby is an important tool helping to overcome Congress's inherent disadvantages in dealing with the president and the federal bureaucracy. Regional experts track developments in sensitive regions such as the Middle East and former Yugoslavia. Similarly, substantive experts track developments on topics of concern, such as trade patterns or nuclear proliferation. Numerous ongoing summary reports are regularly updated for new developments. Thus, for example, if a congressional staffer calls for a report on the current situation in Bosnia or Kosovo or regarding Indian-Pakistani nuclear proliferation, something close to the desired product is already available. Sometimes CRS analysts are asked to help interpret an administration's foreign policy intentions. For example, Stanley Sloan (1991) tried to figure out what the "new world order" meant to President George Bush, who used the phrase frequently but never defined it and confessed having problems with "the vision thing." Similarly, Mark Lowenthal (1993) assembled information about a coordinated set of speeches in September 1993 by President Clinton and his top foreign policy officials. At the time, Clinton was trying to launch "enlargement" of the sphere of market-economy democracies as grand policy to succeed containment, and critics charged that his administration lacked any grand foreign policy.

Its single-client relationship and the restrictions on noncongressional publication give CRS little public visibility and a fairly low profile within the broader policy community. CRS impacts on policy are indirect, being mediated by the Congress and congressional staff. Compared with many think tanks and other policy organizations, there is little internal competition and a strong interdisciplinary focus. Given the fragmentation of congressional committee responsibilities and expertise, that interdisciplinary emphasis is probably salutary. By 1990 the CRS had a staff of 864, an annual budget of $46 million, and was processing more than 500,000 information requests from Congress each year, two thirds of them answered within one day. The most important CRS products are topical *Issue Briefs*, summary analysis documents of ten to fifty pages on each of the 350 to 450 issues facing the Congress in any particular session. In Washington usage, **brief** most often is a verb meaning to present a summary of pertinent information, usually in person. Secondarily, a brief is a document presenting such a summary. A typical CRS *Issue Brief* presents a one-page executive summary, defines the issue, traces its development, analyzes its causes, presents alternative solutions, describes any major bills in the area, presents a chronology of developments, and gives supporting references to additional reading. Regular CRS publications include a quarterly *Guide to CRS Products* and a monthly *Update* (Robinson, 1992). By the late 1990s, many CRS reports had been published on various Internet Web sites.

The General Accounting Office

The **General Accounting Office (GAO)** is another nonpartisan agency of the Congress, created by the Budget and Accounting Act of 1921 to "investigate, at the seat of government or elsewhere, all matters relating to the receipt, disbursement, and application of public funds." Because every government activity requires expenditures, this charge can be interpreted very broadly, including program evaluation to determine whether government funds have purchased—or can purchase—the intended performance capabilities. In yet another example of the continuing struggle between Congress and the presidency for control of policy, that same 1921 act created in the executive branch a U.S. Bureau of the Budget, now the Office of Management and Budget (OMB), to assist the president in planning and budgeting programs. OMB carries out for the executive branch functions very similar to those that GAO carries out for the Congress and is not discussed further here.

GAO practice has evolved and broadened over the years, passing through three distinct eras. (1) Through World War II, it concentrated on reviewing the validity of government contracts and conducting detailed audits of individual vouchers for government expenditures. Wartime spending caused a severe overload, and (2) beginning in 1950 the audit functions were given over to the various government departments. GAO shrank in size, hired accountants rather than clerks, and focused on prescribing accounting practices and checking the adequacy of federal government financial management practices and controls. (3) GAO's modern era began with the appointment of Elmer Staats as comptroller general in 1966. An economist with thirty years of service in the Bureau of the Budget, Staats instituted new analytic approaches tied to the Planning, Programming and Budgeting System (PPBS) initially introduced to the Defense Department under Robert McNamara during the Kennedy administration. Backed by legislation in 1970 and 1974, new program evaluation and policy analysis functions were added and later melded into an interdisciplinary organization capable of performing a range of activities including audits, management reviews, evaluations, and other studies (see Havens, 1992). Today's GAO employs some five thousand persons. One guarantee of its independence is that its chief, the comptroller general, is appointed by the president, with Senate confirmation, for a nonrenewable fifteen-year term.

Like CBO's program analysis, GAO's audit, management review, and evaluation functions are properly subjects for Chapter 7, on feedback policy evaluation. Yet GAO also deserves a place here because it contributes to the policy-making process by providing evaluations whose recommendations often are enacted into law. Numerous defense studies in the 1980s included reviewing how problems in the B-1 bomber's avionics system impaired its ability to perform assigned strategic missions, assessing the performance of the navy's Aegis guided-missile cruisers, and studying the systemic causes of contract overpricing and cost overruns. An even broader study examined operational implications of the mismatch between fleet composition and the overall maritime strategy the navy was supposed to carry out under the Reagan administration's plans for a 600-ship navy. All GAO reports not classified for security reasons are available to the media and public, and such reports regularly are the subjects of news stories. Increasingly during the 1980s, Congress began requesting or mandating specific audits and reviews, which now consume the bulk of GAO resources. The GAO remains broadly respected for its capability and objectivity, and its recommendations continue to be sources of policy innovation, subject to executive branch adoption or congressional legislation.

THINK TANKS

Where do in-and-outers go when they are out of government? With increasing frequency, they find new institutional homes in think tanks dedicated to full-time policy analysis. Indeed, with the rapid growth in numbers of such organizations since 1970, there now are more policy analysis positions in think tanks than in government itself. For in-and-outers whose careers involve a number of alternations between periods working in government and times working in academia, business, or policy analysis organizations, a Washington think tank presents the attraction of staying much closer to the corridors

POLITICS, TECHNOLOGY, AND FUTURISM
The Rise and Fall of the Office of Technology Assessment

The Office of Technology Assessment (OTA) was created in 1972 to serve as a distant early warning line for new technologies. Its subject matter made its charter broader and vaguer than those of other congressional support organizations. In establishing OTA, Congress sought long-range, objective analysis and expressed the wish to "equip itself with new and effective means for securing competent, unbiased information concerning the physical, biological, economic, social, and political effects" of emerging, difficult, often highly technical issues. Given increasing economic globalization, the inherently global and technical nature of most environmental problems, and the increasing role of technology in daily life, Congress's aims in establishing OTA appear entirely reasonable and its subsequent demise may seem puzzling. As we saw in Chapter 5, however, one important reason for policy failures is that humans cannot forecast the future very well. That fundamental limitation was reflected in the OTA legislation, which read in part as follows:

> The basic function of the Office shall be to provide early indications of the probable beneficial and adverse impacts of the applications of technology and to develop other coordinate information which may assist the Congress in carrying out such function, the Office shall: (1) identify existing or probable impacts of technology or technological programs; (2) where possible, ascertain cause and effect relationships; (3) identify alternative technological methods of implementing specific programs; (4) identify alternative programs for achieving requisite goals; (5) make estimates and comparisons of the impacts of alternative methods and programs; (6) present findings of completed analyses to the appropriate legislative authorities;

(7) identify areas where additional research or data collection is required to provide adequate support for the assessments and estimates described in paragraph (1) through (5) of this subsection; and (8) undertake such additional associated activities as the appropriate authorities . . . may direct.

OTA was founded in the belief that rational thinking and futurist analytic techniques could be used to anticipate the effects of new and expanding technologies, helping set policies to avoid bad effects and optimize resource use. Assessments were OTA's main product, and, like CBO and GAO studies, had significant policy impacts when Congress adopted them into legislation. The greatest analytic difficulty was that the methods of futurism are difficult to specify precisely. Early OTA hopes of finding that much of the needed information and analysis already existed in academia were not fulfilled. As procedures were developed, OTA would assemble an expert advisory panel representing diverse attitudes and interests for each assessment. Meeting several times during each study, the advisory panels guided OTA's analysts, oversaw their approach, ensured that all concerns and factions were addressed, and conducted expert technical reviews. By 1990, 140 people were doing analytic work, and fifty or more assessments were published annually. With a permanent employment ceiling of 143, however, many of the analysts were temporary employees, government contractors, and individuals temporarily detailed by executive branch agencies. After an initial concentration, the proportion of staff analysts with final degrees in engineering, physics, biology, and other "hard" sciences dropped to about one third. Correspondingly, the numbers of those with final

(continued)

(continued)

degrees in political science, law, economics, and other social and policy sciences rose (Carson, 1992).

By statute, general governance was provided by a Technology Assessment Board composed of six senators and six representatives. Chosen by the leadership in each house, and representing both major parties and their major factions, the board met about every six weeks. Surprisingly, this arrangement seemed to work well, and the board avoided political polarization. A more limited guidance role was played by a Technology Assessment Advisory Council of distinguished private citizens with diverse occupations, which met semiannually. Although OTA was permitted to make policy recommendations to Congress, it rarely did so, primarily because few of the complex issues assessed had a single dominant solution. Instead, OTA assessment reports tended to have an "if . . . then" character: if an important objective is this, then a suitable option is. . . . As with products of the other congressional service organizations, such assessments were not complete specifications of policy, but menus of options and consequences from which political choices could be made. Programs during OTA's later years included (1) security, space, and strategic trade; (2) energy and environment; (3) health and health policy; and (4) science, industry, and competitiveness. Of these four, the first is the most highly international in character, the third most domestic, and the other two strongly intermestic. OTA's products thus heavily involved areas of foreign policy significance.

After a twenty-three-year run of providing Congress with nonpartisan analytical advice on the complex highly technical issues that increasingly affect American society and the world, OTA closed its doors on 29 September 1995. In a move little noticed by the public, part of the late 1994 congressional-presidential budget deal withdrew all funding except for a skeleton closeout staff. Republicans had gained control of both houses of Congress in the 1994 elections—somewhat narrowly, but with a distinctly conservative tilt —and had pledged to reduce the size of government. Anticipating such a victory, they had stalled congressional budget action until after the election. In the resulting difficult debate over passing a budget late in 1994, the Clinton administration and congressional Democrats had higher priorities than fighting to preserve OTA.

Considering the increasing prominence of technology issues in foreign policy, shutting down OTA appears extremely shortsighted. By the time of President Clinton's June 1998 trip to China, for example, one major issue (particularly between Democrats and Republicans) was whether Bush and Clinton administration agreements allowing U.S. satellites to be launched on Chinese rockets constituted a dangerous transfer of missile technology. It seems incontestable that two important contributing factors in OTA's demise were the facts that its products were more esoteric than those of the other congressional support organizations, and that Congress is not deeply into long-term planning.

of power and the people who inhabit them, and thus more current on policy issues, than would be possible in business or academia. The growth of think tanks is an important development because they offer alternate routes to policy influence for the large numbers of qualified individuals seeking policy impact. Additionally, think tanks are fertile recruiting grounds for government offices such as congressional staffs, and provide training for individuals who may later seek civil service jobs. Numerous academically trained analysts have moved to Washington and followed the think tank route into eventual government positions.

Think tanks are not-for-profit, nominally (although, in as we see in some cases, decreasingly) nonpartisan research institutes or centers or foundations or organizations. The usage *"think tanks"* became common during the Kennedy administration, although several other terms were previously applied and the earliest such organization, the Russell Sage Foundation, was chartered in 1907. Think tanks bring together semipermanent and visiting experts to conduct research on policy issues and share that knowledge with policymakers and the public. They focus more on the politically active community of intellectuals interested in policy than on ordinary citizens with similar interests. These thinkers are members of the policy elite and direct their messages primarily to other members of that elite, in and out of government. Briefly examined in Chapter 4, the policy elite is a large community of informed individuals with policy interests, often with some policy experience, and often holding government positions or hoping for future government policy roles. Think tank analysts tend to be academics of one type or another (individuals with advanced postgraduate training, former academics, or academics on temporary assignment) or individuals with policy-relevant experience in government or the military. Former politicians are more likely to be found in interest groups, partly because they are more numerous, more visible, larger, richer, and generally more powerful over a broader range of issues than think tanks.

Washington think tanks have tripled in number since 1970 and the post-1974 boom in political action committees (PACs). Although PACs were first organized in the 1940s, their numbers grew rapidly after the 1974 election reform legislation, which limited individual campaign contributions and set guidelines for PACs. By 1988 there were more than four thousand PACs, many representing special interest groups and others representing large liberal or conservative political coalitions. This PAC proliferation has contributed to a *convergence* between analysis and activism, with many think tanks taking on more of the characteristics and activities of interest groups and political parties. All three types of organizations seek to educate citizens and government officials, although think tanks traditionally seek knowledge more to improve government as they define improvement rather than education to convert people to their cause. Think tanks, interest groups, and political parties all lie at the interface between government and public and seek to connect the two groups, although the involved "publics" differ.

One driving force behind the convergence of analysis and activism arose from the American conservative political movement. Following Richard Nixon's narrow loss to John Kennedy in the 1960 presidential election, conservatives moved to take control of the Republican party. Their candidate was Senator Barry Goldwater (R-Ariz.), the most conservative major party presidential candidate in some decades, who was duly nominated but overwhelmingly defeated in 1964. Many conservatives believed one reason for Goldwater's defeat and the generally poor success of conservative causes during the 1960s was the lack of a well-known and widely respected intellectual footing, backed up by analysis centers of the sort already actively supporting liberal causes. The Brookings Institution, for example, founded in 1927, is highly regarded for its economic studies and has long been seen as almost a "shadow government" for Democratic in-and-outers when their party lost the presidency.

One answer from conservatives, and a model for the think tank boom and the convergence between analysis and activism, was the Washington-based Heritage Foundation. Founded in 1973 and now well known and fairly respected, the foundation has played exactly the sort of analytical and policy role envisioned. It provided an intellectual underpinning for conservative causes and it proposed many officials for the Reagan and Bush administrations. Deviating greatly from the original think tanks' nonpartisan ideal of apolitical reform, the Heritage Foundation's stated purpose is to engage in "research to provide recommendations on critical public issues which serve the principles of free enterprise, limited government, individual liberty, and a strong national defense." This list, of course, is composed of key conservative symbolic, even iconographic, phrases and in itself constitutes a broad policy outline. The foundation clearly supports projects it expects will aid that conservative agenda, and only publicizes results that do. Over 40 percent of its support comes from individual contributions, an unusually high proportion, suggesting that many contributors see the foundation as virtually a political action committee.

Traditionally, think tanks advocate both general and specific policies, but usually in lower key and less overtly politicized ways than political parties and PACs. As the Heritage Foundation example suggests, however, there are close relations among the three phenomena of the rise of PACs, increasing numbers of think tanks, and convergence of think tank analysis and activism. Washington insiders, of course, are fully aware of the partisan and ideological leanings of such organizations. Consider, for example, the in-and-outers Frank Gaffney and Strobe Talbott. In a 1989 review of Talbott's book about Paul Nitze, *Master of the Game*, Gaffney said in part,

> Mr. Talbott is a chronicler of contemporary arms control efforts who writes didactically and for partisan effect. . . . The contents of this book and the timing of its release made transparent Mr. Talbott's political agenda: He evidently hoped to provide ammunition to those seeking to deny President Reagan a new mandate on the grounds that in its first four years, the administration had dreadfully botched U.S.-Soviet relations and set back the cause of arms control. . . . Mr. Reagan is reviled as an incompetent dolt. . . . Mr. Talbott lionizes State Department officials determined to advance personal agendas at odds with that of the president they serve. . . . I believe history will . . . prove [Talbott] wrong . . . [and will judge] Mr. Nitze's most estimable accomplishments to be those that the author derides and those on which he lavishes praise to be among Mr. Nitze's least valuable contributions.

In interpreting this passage, consider the following: Strobe Talbott was a senior reporter for *Time* magazine and had written several generally well-received books. A political liberal and longtime friend of President Clinton, he went on to serve as assistant secretary of state and a high-level personal adviser to Clinton. Paul Nitze was the subject of the introductory case in this chapter. Principal author of NSC-68 and generally considered a hard-liner, Nitze later became a strong advocate of arms control and served as chief negotiator of the Intermediate Nuclear Forces (INF) treaty (1981–84). Frank Gaffney is a political conservative who served as a high defense official in the Reagan administration. At the time of this review, he was director of the Center for Security Policy in Washington and a senior fellow of the conservative Hudson Institute. The governmental politics model discussed in Chapter 5 leads us to expect strong policy differences between individual in-and-outers, whichever their current phase. Moreover, as the tone of Gaffney's review suggests, partisanship runs high and individuals may view another person, as well as his or her policy positions, with derision and even contempt.

Because the majority of think tanks include foreign policy as at least part of their agendas, many such organizations are potentially relevant to our subject. Table 6.2 summarizes a number of characteristics of twenty-three leading think tanks. This list is merely a sampling, consisting of the think tanks with foreign policy interests from among the thirty discussed in the appendix to James Allen Smith's 1991 book, *The Idea Brokers*, the only definitive recent study of think tanks. With more than a thousand think tanks and related organizations active today, even the widely used *Access Resource Guide* to organizations and research centers concerned with international security and peace (Seymore, 1992) presents only a sampling, albeit a much larger one.

Some think tanks are heavily involved and quite influential in the areas of foreign and defense policy, perhaps in part because those areas are intensely interesting to many social scientists. Of the 30 organizations in Smith's sample, 8, or slightly over one quarter, deal exclusively in foreign policy, and another half have some foreign policy interests. Some of these think tanks or their predecessor organizations were founded as early as 1910, although 11 of the 23 in Table 6.2 were founded since 1970 and 6 since 1974. Of the 23, only 6 are *not* headquartered in Washington, D.C., and one of those (RAND Corporation) also maintains a large Washington office. Permanent research staffs vary from zero at the Center for National Policy, which acts mainly as a convener of conferences among policy makers, to more than 135 at the Heritage Foundation. Many think tanks supplement their permanent resident staffs with grant-supported adjunct researchers elsewhere, for example at universities. Many offer unpaid or lowly paid temporary positions for interns, which can be marvelous learning opportunities for students with political and policy interests. Several of the think tanks in Table 6.2 have loose ties to academic institutions, and several were founded by former elected or appointed government officials. RAND Corporation even maintains an excellent graduate program offering a doctorate in public policy analysis. Ideological orientations of these organizations range from extremely liberal to extremely conservative, with several being tied fairly closely to one of the major political parties. Their degrees of objectivity and impartiality also vary widely.

Think tanks rely on diverse mixes of funding from six basic sources: corporation gifts, endowments, foundation grants, government research contracts, individual bequests or contributions, and sales of publications. Corporate underwriting often supports the more conservative groups, and those studying business and economics. Some of the older and larger think tanks have substantial investment incomes from endowments by early benefactors. The Carnegie Endowment and the Twentieth Century Fund are foundations in their own right. Other think tanks have been heavily supported, particularly during their formative years, by grants from such other major foundations as the Ford Foundation and the German Marshall Fund. A few think tanks rely partly on government research contracts; RAND Corporation, at 80 percent, is the extreme case on this list. Some rely heavily on gifts or membership fees from individuals; at 43 percent, the Heritage Foundation leads that category. Almost all think tanks, and especially the smaller ones, rely at least somewhat on income from sales of publications.

Think tanks distribute their messages through many channels. All such organizations publish research results, position papers, and, to a lesser degree, the scholarship of others. Their publications include important and highly regarded periodicals, such as *The American Enterprise, Brookings Review, The Defense Monitor, Foreign Policy, Policy Review, The Washington Quarterly, World Policy Journal*, and *World Watch*. Users, of course, need to remember the institutions' ideological and issue preferences. Other publications include major book series, reports on issue-oriented conferences, monograph series such as those from RAND, sporadic survey results, and occasional papers. Many such publications are issued in continuing series available by subscription.

Think tanks frequently hold conferences focused on particular issues. In turn, those conferences often generate attendance fees and create publication opportunities. All such channels serve the general purpose of educating members of the policy elite. Think tanks provide a ready source of expert advice that government agencies and others can tap, and a "talent bank" (the Nixon administration's usage) that can both supply and absorb in-and-outers. Policy analysts regularly provide expert testimony before congressional committees and engage in direct lobbying of politicians and policy-making officials. Additionally, policy analysts often are involved in educational outreach through public speaking and electronic media appearances. Demand for immediate analysis and commentary has grown in step with the development of instant remote television reporting and the proliferation of networks and channels. (Whether quality analysis can be maintained under such conditions remains in dispute.) Additionally, many think tanks now produce video reports and even regular television programs, for example, the Center for Defense Information's weekly *America's Defense Monitor*.

Some measure of the enormous talent reserve available in think tanks may be gained by examining the brief and incomplete list of noted analysts in Table 6.2. (An interesting exercise is to check those names against library bibliographic sources.) The list includes political scientists such as Bruce Bueno de Mesquita, Jeane Kirkpatrick, Seymour Martin Lipset, Thomas Mann, Michael Novak, Norman Ornstein; Nobel Prize–winning economists Gunnar Myrdal and Milton Friedman; other noted economists including Otto Eckstein, William Niskanen, Herbert Stein, and Lester Thurow; retired military officers such as Rear Admiral Gene LaRocque and Colonel William J. Taylor; scholar-activists such as Richard Barnet and Marcus Raskin; and a host of others.

Many of those analysts have played important policy roles in one or more administrations. Donald Rumsfeld and Caspar Weinberger were secretaries of defense under Presidents Ford and Reagan, respectively. Lawrence Korb and Richard Pearle were assistant secretaries of defense under President Reagan. Jeane Kirkpatrick and Madeline Albright were U.S. permanent representatives to the United Nations under Presidents Reagan and Clinton, respectively, and Albright went on to become secretary of state in Clinton's second term, the first woman to hold that post.

Many of these people have made significant contributions to the development of theory and practice in specialized policy areas. For example, the late Herman Kahn, founder of the Hudson Institute, was a major figure in the 1960s wave of nuclear deterrence theorizing. A decade later, John Steinbruner made major contributions differing strongly from

TABLE 6.2

A Sampling of Leading Think Tanks with Foreign Policy Interests

Organization	Year Begun	Location; Staff Size	Institutional Affiliation	Major Sponsorship; Political Ideology	Sample Products; Major Clients	Noted Affiliated Analysts
Exclusively Foreign Policy Interests (8 organizations)						
Carnegie Endowment for International Peace	1910	Washington; 20 scholars		Foundation, $85 million endowment; nonpartisan liberal	*Foreign Policy;* study groups, roundtables	Geoffrey Kemp, Dimitri Simes
Center for Defense Information	1972	Washington; 24		Public contributors, Paul Newman; liberal, supports defense spending cuts	*Defense Monitor;* television	Gene LaRocque (rear admiral, retired)
Center for Strategic and International Studies	1962	Washington; 50 senior residents, 100 staff plus adjuncts	Georgetown University (loosely) until 1987	Foundations (40%) corporations (35%), individuals (10%) endowment (5%)	*Washington Quarterly; Washington Papers Issues Series; Panel Reports*	G. Fauriol, Walter Laqueur, Edward Luttwak, Col. William Taylor
Institute for International Economics	1981	Washington	Former Brookings, Carter administration	German Marshall Fund, initially	Book-length studies	C. F. Bergsten, William R. Cline, I. M. Destler
Overseas Development Council	1969	Washington; 14 informational staff plus interns		Foundations, corporations, international development banks	Biannual *Agenda*, policy focus papers, meetings, congressional staff forum on third world issues	Richard Feinberg, Cathryn Thorup
World Policy Institute	1982, reorganized	New York; 5 informational staff		Individuals, publication sales	*World Policy Journal;* surveys, briefings	
World Resources Institute		Washington; 80 plus researchers			WRI *Guides to the Environment;* Cooperation with UN	
Worldwatch Institute	1975	Washington; 30		Publications	*World Watch; State of World*	Lester Brown

(continued)

(continued)

	TABLE 6.2	A Sampling of Leading Think Tanks with Foreign Policy Interests (continued)				
Organization	**Year Begun**	**Location; Staff Size**	**Institutional Affiliation**	**Major Sponsorship; Political Ideology**	**Sample Products; Major Clients**	**Noted Affiliated Analysts**
Some Foreign Policy Interests (15 organizations)						
American Enterprise Institute for Public Policy Research (AEI)	1943; reorganized 1960	Washington; 47 scholars plus adjuncts and interns	Originally a business research group	Corporations (50%), foundations (35%); conservative	*The American Enterprise* (bimonthly); 40–50 books annually, previously, *Public Opinion, Regulation, AEI Economist*	Jeane Kirkpatrick, Irving Kristol, Michael Novak, Norman Ornstein, Herbert Stein, Richard Pearle, B. Wattenberg
Brookings Institution	1916; reorganized 1927	Washington; 40–50 senior researchers, plus visitors and research assistants	–	$100 million endowment; publications, conferences, grants and gifts; liberal	*Brookings Review*; frequent books and study reports	Lawrence Korb, Thomas Mann, Charles Schultze, J. Steinbruner
Cato Institute	1977	Washington; 5 adjuncts		Libertarian (classical liberal)	*Cato Journal, Policy Reports*, op-ed pieces, 10 books annually	David Boaz, Peter Ferrara, William Niskanen
Center for Budget and Policy Priorities	1981	Washington; 23		Field Foundation	Autonomous defense budget project	Gordon Adams, R. Greenstein
Center for National Policy	1981	Washington; no residents	Organized by Ed. Muskie, Democratic leaders	Centrist Democrat	Off-record policy seminars, publications	Madeleine Albright, Otto Eckstein, Stanley Hoffman, Lester Thurow
Ethics and Public Policy Center	1976	Washington		Pro-Western values	Books, seminars, conferences	E. W. Lefever, George Weigel
Heritage Foundation	1973	Washington; 135		Individuals (43%), foundations (25%), corporations (13%) endowment (13%); conservative	*Policy Review*; books, monographs, over 200 publications annually	Roger Brooks, Stuart Butler, Kim Holmes

A Sampling of Leading Think Tanks with Foreign Policy Interests (continued)

Organization	Year Begun	Location; Staff Size	Institutional Affiliation	Major Sponsorship; Political Ideology	Sample Products; Major Clients	Noted Affiliated Analysts
Hoover Institution	1919	Stanford, California; 120 informational staff	Formally independent but Stanford governance	Conservative or libertarian	Essays, books, scholarly publications	B B de Mesquita, Milton Friedman, S. M. Lipset, Edward Teller
Hudson Institute	1961	Indianapolis, Indiana; 18 senior residents		Lilly Endowment, government contracts; conservative	Books, reports	Herman Kahn (founder, died 1983)
Institute for Contemporary Studies	1972	San Francisco; 25		Conservative Republican	Reagan campaign research (1970s); publications	Edwin Meese, Donald Rumsfeld, Caspar Weinberger
Institute for Policy Studies	1963	Washington	Transnational Institute, Amsterdam	Deweyan scholar-activists, artists	Films, writings, videotapes	Richard Barnet, Marcus Raskin
Joint Center for Political and Economic Studies	1970	Washington; 50	Howard University; Metropolitan Applied Research Centers	Focus on issues affecting African Americans	Guide to Black Politics	Kenneth Clark, Frank Reeves, Eddie Williams
Progressive Policy Institute	1989	Washington; 11	Former Democratic Leadership Council	Liberal Democratic		Will Marshall, Robert Shapiro
RAND Corporation	1948	Santa Monica, California; (very large)	RAND Graduate School	Government contracts (80%); foundation grants	Reports, notes, papers; over 250 publications annually	
Twentieth Century Fund	1911	New York; 20 New York staff; scholars		foundation; $41 million endowment	6–10 books/year; reports; papers	Jean Gottmann, Fred Hirsch, Gunnar Myrdal

Data are tabulated largely from Smith (1991, appendix on "Leading Think Tanks," 270–94), with updates by author.

A THINK TANK POLICY INITIATIVE
Origins of the Strategic Defense Initiative ("Star Wars") Program

The recommendations of think tanks often significantly impact policy, for good or ill. Consider the origins of the Strategic Defense Initiative (SDI), popularly known as Star Wars. In a project spun off from the Heritage Foundation and headed by retired army lieutenant general Daniel O. Graham (1982), an organization called High Frontier published a book-length proposal calling for a comprehensive program of military and industrial exploitation of outer space, including a major strategic defense mission organized in layers of ground-based and space-based missile interceptors. A major doctrinal underpinning of the project was the goal of ending reliance on nuclear deterrence (always referred to as MAD) and substituting strategic defense (labeled "Assured Survival").

The noted prodefense nuclear physicist Edward Teller later pitched many of the same ideas to President Reagan, who surprised even many high officials of his own administration by a 23 March 1983 television address calling for study and definition of "a long-term research and development program to begin to achieve our ultimate goal of eliminating the threat posed by strategic nuclear missiles," and calling on "the scientific community" to "give us the means of rendering these nuclear weapons impotent and obsolete" (Cannon, 1983). Administration officials then scrambled to organize what became a multibillion dollar program that never yielded a space-based missile defense, and ultimately was redirected in the early 1990s to within-atmosphere tactical missile defense.

Kahn. Some think tanks are characterized by one dominant analyst, like the Center for Defense Information's Admiral Gene LaRocque. Other and larger think tanks, like the American Enterprise Institute, the Brookings Institution, and the Hoover Institution, have plentiful stables of notables.

In sum, think tanks offer an alternate Washington home for a large and highly talented group of analysts and in-and-outers, within which they can devote themselves full time to policy studies and advocacy. Consequently, think tanks have become an important source of policy ideas that may be taken up elsewhere in the system and eventually implemented.

SPECIAL INTEREST GROUPS, LOBBYISTS, AND IN-AND-OUTERS

Just as many in-and-outers regularly find out-of-government homes in think tanks, others, particularly out-of-office politicians, find new homes as lobbyists for special interest groups. For example, J. William Fulbright of Arkansas served thirty years in the Senate, wrote the 1946 act bearing his name and providing for the exchange of students and teachers between the United States and foreign countries, and chaired the Senate foreign relations committee from 1959 to 1974. In that position he strongly criticized U.S. military interventions abroad, including the Vietnam War, and held many open hearings to educate the public and reassert the Senate's role in long-range policy formulation. After losing the 1974 Democratic primary to then-governor Dale Bumpers, who charged that he had lost touch with the folks at home, Fulbright stayed on in Washington—perhaps suggesting that Bumpers was correct—and became a highly paid lobbyist.

Although special interest groups and their lobbyists often focus more on domestic than foreign issues, do not infer from the relatively brief mention here that these actors are unimportant in the foreign policy process. The increasingly intermestic character of contemporary concerns—enforced by growing international economic interdependencies—ensures that we cannot ignore special interest groups, which are discussed under influence zone 3 in Chapter 4. Like think tanks and political parties, interest groups lie at the interface between public and government and seek to educate the public to their positions. Their focus is on both the general public and the policy elite, with the public receiving more attention from interest groups than from think tanks. Lobbying methods, of course, span the entire range utilized by the think tanks, although interest groups emphasize personal contacts more than scholarly research. The same post-1974 growth in PACs that encouraged the proliferation of think tanks has stimulated interest groups even more strongly. Because interest groups are much more interested in policy support and advocacy than in policy research and planning, they are more a force for the adoption of specific policies than a source of policy innovation.

SUMMARY

Given how greatly the foreign policy problems now confronting the United States differ from those faced during the Cold War era, and given that we have not yet settled on a new grand policy, we may anticipate some years of unusually intense struggles over both short- and long-term policies. This chapter deals with some of the most important places and processes to watch.

Perhaps surprisingly, long-range policy analysis and grand policy planning are carried out in remarkably few places in the U.S. foreign policy system, by remarkably few people. This actually makes sense because, as the *organizational process* and *governmental politics* models point out, government agencies primarily carry out routine tasks, and most officials are busy managing those agencies. The highest officials, such as the president, must attend to current problems, and policy innovations and grand policy planning usually come from officials just below the very top level, and from their support staffs. Only small units are regularly engaged in long-range or grand policy planning. The more common process of determining policy for specific cases often is slow because it usually involves small inputs from many persons. In turn, the large number of inputs suggests that most policy is not so much planned comprehensively as constructed piecemeal through a political process, evolving incrementally.

The two major sections of this chapter cover (1) the gathering and interpretation of information to produce intelligence needed for policy planning, and (2) how policy—especially long-range policy—is made in six key locations within and outside government.

Essential prerequisites for policy planning include gathering data about the actions and intentions of others, as well as about the effects of our own policies, and then analyzing and interpreting the stream of incoming information. Specialists distinguish between information, which is unevaluated material, and intelligence, which is the product after received information has been processed. Broadly, the gathering and analysis tasks are performed by the national intelligence community, a large functionally defined group of analysts and officials in a number of executive branch agencies and departments with overlapping interests and global reach. From the perspective of the foreign policy system as an information processing system (see Figure 4.1), the intelligence community is one of its most important subsystems.

The U.S. intelligence community is headed by a director of Central Intelligence (DCI), who also manages the Central Intelligence Agency (CIA). Other major components of that community include the State Department's Bureau of Intelligence and Research (INR), the Defense Department's centralized intelligence agency (DIA) and the intelligence organizations of the individual armed services, the communications-monitoring National Security Agency (NSA), and units of the Federal Bureau of Investigation (FBI), Treasury Department, and Energy Department that contribute specialized foreign intelligence. The intelligence community's collective current knowledge about the situation in some specific country or region, or about a particular topic, along with estimates of projected future developments, is often summarized in an official National Intelligence Estimate (NIE). Intelligence gathering and assessment is a complex bureaucratic process reflecting the beliefs of analysts in the many agencies involved, and often ends with unresolved major disagreements.

In recent decades, one of the most important groups analyzing and shaping policy has been the National Security Council (NSC) staff. Under the National Security Act of 1947, the NSC consists of only four people: the president as chair, the vice president, and the secretaries of defense and state, plus several statutory advisers and additional temporary and permanent members added based on presidential preferences and the issues under consideration. The president has complete discretion regarding how the NSC is used. Most presidents since Nixon (1969–74) have assigned major roles to the NSC support staff, and appointed an assistant to the president for national security affairs (NSA) to head that staff. Beginning with Henry Kissinger under Presidents Nixon and Ford, and bolstered by close and regular presidential access and by independence from other federal agencies, many NSAs have been second only to the president in shaping foreign policy. Major NSC staff functions, in order of increasing controversiality, include administration, policy coordination and integration, policy supervision and monitoring, policy adjudication, crisis management and planning, policy formulation, policy advocacy, and (rarely) policy implementation.

In great contrast to the NSC staff's small unit, highly centralized policy making directly under the president, and despite the existence of a small Policy Planning Staff (PPS) reporting to the secretary of state, policy making in the State Department is far more distributed than centralized. It is characterized by regional geographical foci, managing by cable, referring all problems to Washington headquarters, and tending to focus on small, cumulative measures rather than any grand policy vision. Questions about policy making in the Department of Defense tend to revolve around whether the politically potent "iron triangle" of military forces, defense contractors, and Congress members forged during the Cold War years can be limited (recall the *domestic special interests* viewpoint), and whether civilian control can work effectively (recall the *bureaucratic infighting* viewpoint and the *bureaucratic process* model).

In recent decades, several organizations supporting the legislative branch have gained influence in analyzing and shaping policy. These include the Congressional Budget Office

(CBO), the Congressional Research Service (CRS), and the General Accounting Office (GAO). These support organizations perform an eclectic mix of functions combining historical research, information generation, policy option generation, and policy impact assessment of the sort examined in Chapter 7. They provide substantial in-house expertise and a full-time staff of highly qualified analysts, helping to overcome limitations on Congress member and staff time and knowledge. (Recall the *president versus Congress* viewpoint.) Although they cannot fully substitute for an administration's ability to command access to information, they make Congress independent of the administration's experts, forecasts, and interpretations. In effect, they have become policy consultants and think tanks reporting to the Congress. General roles include analyzing policy, locating and organizing information, evaluating the success of programs, and specifying available options and their probable impacts. Thus they shape policy by establishing the menu of possibilities from which ultimately political choices must be made by Congress and the executive.

Outside government, many policy ideas are generated in think tanks, which are nominally nonpartisan research institutes, centers, foundations, or organizations, all dedicated to full-time policy analysis. Mostly located in Washington, their numbers have tripled, to more than a thousand since 1970. Think tanks offer alternate, nongovernmental routes to policy influence and a convenient Washington home to in-and-outers during their "out" phases. They also provide fertile recruiting grounds for government offices such as congressional staffs, and training for individuals who may later seek civil service jobs. Many openly partisan and ideologically driven think tanks have been founded since 1970, deviating greatly from the original think tanks' nonpartisan ideal of apolitical governmental reform. Ideological orientations of these organizations range from extremely liberal to extremely conservative, with several being tied fairly closely to one or another of the major political parties.

Like think tanks, political parties and interest groups lie at the interface between public and government and seek to educate the public to their positions. Their focus is on both the general public and the policy elite, with lobbyists attending particularly to politicians and officials.

In the next chapter, we turn to the use of policy feedback (1) by government to help evaluate and revise policies to achieve desired goals and (2) by citizens to evaluate how well government officials, procedures, and policies succeed.

KEY TERMS

Brief	Intelligence community
Congressional Budget Office (CBO)	Iron triangle
Congressional Research Service (CRS)	National Intelligence Estimates (NIEs)
General Accounting Office (GAO)	National Security Council (NSC)
Information	Plausible deniability
Intelligence	

SELECTED READINGS

Andrew, Christopher. 1995. *For the President's Eyes Only: Secret Intelligence and the American Presidency from Washington to Bush*. New York: HarperCollins.

Berkowitz, Bruce D., and Allan E. Goodman. 1991. *Strategic Intelligence for American National Security*. Princeton. N.J.: Princeton University Press.

Kessler, Ronald. 1992. *Inside the CIA: Revealing the Secrets of the World's Most Powerful Spy Agency*. New York: Pocket Books.

Lowenthal, Mark M. 1992. *U.S. Intelligence: Evolution and Anatomy*, 2d ed. Westport, Conn.: Praeger.

Smith, James Allen. 1991. *The Idea Brokers: Think Tanks and the Rise of the New Policy Elite*. New York: Free Press.

Wise, David. 1995. *Nightmover: How Aldrich Ames Sold the CIA to the KGB for $4.6 Million*. New York: HarperCollins.

CHAPTER 7

FEEDBACK: EVALUATING AND CORRECTING POLICY

⊕ PAINFUL POLICY FEEDBACK IN SOMALIA

In January 1991 the central government of the northeastern African state of Somalia collapsed after twenty-one years of one-person rule. Rival factions led by regional warlords plunged the country into civil war, and Somalia became a new and painful instance of what analysts call a **failed state.** By 1992 the combination of banditry, civil war, and drought combined to create conditions threatening some 1.5 million people with starvation. Sufficient food either was grown or shipped into Somalia to feed all its people, but warlords and bandits hoarded, stole, and prevented its effective distribution. Due to the intense factional fighting, the UN secretary-general declared in July 1992 that Somalia was a country without a government. In a development unimaginable before the age of globe-girdling television, world concern was heightened by graphic media coverage of starving Somalis.

The U.S. government offered assistance, driven in part by enthusiasm about a new world order made imaginable by the recent end of the Cold War. Additional motivations included humanitarian belief that something ought to be done, and practical knowledge that the United States had the power to do it. In December 1992 the UN accepted President Bush's offer to send troops to safeguard the delivery of food to starving Somalis. U.S. troops came ashore with abundant media fanfare on 9 December. They brought sufficient strength to stop the violence, along with organizational skills to manage food distribution. There was virtually no fighting because the Americans generally negotiated the advance withdrawal of the various warlords' large forces and heavy weapons before advancing into new areas. Peaceful flows of food and relief supplies followed quickly, and living conditions for average Somalis rapidly began to improve.

Unfortunately, the longer term potential outcomes of the Somalia exercise had not been well thought through. The American troop presence created four new possible outcomes. First, those troops could remain indefinitely as protectors and food distributors. Second, they could find somebody else, perhaps the United Nations, to take over those tasks. Third, they could strive to disarm the warlords to prevent renewed civil war, and then engage in nation building to establish new political institutions capable of creating a stable Somali government. Finally, they could give it all up as a hopeless cause, withdraw, and allow the preintervention chaos to reemerge. Within less than two years all four approaches were tried.

Intermestic considerations were important. By the time he sent in U.S. troops, President Bush had lost the 1992 election and knew he would not be in office to select one of those longer term policy options and face the consequences. On 4 May 1993 the United States turned command of the relief effort over to the UN, which began negotiations among rival factions in hope of establishing an interim government. U.S. troops remained, and some attempts were made to disarm the Somali factions. In particular, U.S. and UN troops attacked the forces of the strongest warlord, General Mohammed Farah Aidid. Although the Clinton administration denied details of their assignment, the elite Delta Force clearly was sent to Somalia in 1993 to capture General Aidid but came up empty-handed, losing eighteen soldiers in the process. Televised images of the body of a U.S. soldier being dragged through the streets of Mogadishu by Aidid's troops brought a storm of calls for prompt withdrawal, and even centrist U.S. politicians questioned the Somalia operation. President Clinton rushed to set a "date certain" for that withdrawal before Congress compelled it under the War Powers Act. Months of effort had yielded U.S. casualties, squabbles about the effectiveness of UN command, but no capture of General Aidid. Facing rising domestic and congressional dissatisfaction with the Somalia efforts, President Clinton canceled attempts to capture Aidid, launched a new diplomatic initiative, and pledged complete withdrawal of U.S. troops within six months. The last UN peacekeeping troops withdrew early in 1995, with little lasting change in conditions in Somalia.

U.S. experiences in Somalia may demonstrate the fundamental intractability of many post–Cold War international political problems, as well as the difficulties the UN faces in creating institutional peacekeeping and nation-building capabilities that it was not allowed during the Cold War. Those experiences also demonstrate an intricate intermestic relationship between the UN and U.S. politics. Liberals tend to support the UN, seeing it as a vehicle of hope and a foundation for building a truly international peacekeeping capability. Conservatives tend to view the UN as inefficient and ineffective and to resent encroachments on U.S. sovereignty. Extreme conservatives fear the UN as a first step toward a world government that would overwhelm U.S. freedom and identity. Cynics question whether the UN has the organization and gumption to mount a seriously contested military operation in the cause of peacemaking. All these concerns came into play in domestic reaction to the Somalia adventure. By the end it appeared that U.S.-UN relations concerning regional conflicts would prove difficult for years to come.

For the United States, the Somalia debacle represents the worst possible misuse of policy feedback. Recall from the discussion of the systems approach in Chapter 4 that using feedback entails using information about how well policies are working to help adjust those policies to best achieve our desired outcomes. This is as crucial to success in foreign policy as it is in a tremendous range of other endeavors, great and small, in daily life. Nonetheless, feedback is unlikely to salvage defeat from victory when policies have been inadequately planned or when wrong conclusions are drawn from the information received. Both problems applied in Somalia.

Fresh from his November 1992 reelection defeat, President George Bush sent troops into Somalia on an apparently open-ended mission, knowing his successor eventually would have to find an **exit strategy** or way to bring the troops home. This was clearly inadequate policy planning because no evidence indicates that the details and risks of later stages of the operation were considered. The new Clinton administration then revised and expanded the mission of American troops in Somalia. Feedback about the results—the deaths of eighteen American soldiers in the ill-fated attempts to capture General Aidid —then triggered hasty policy changes. Those changes showed a lack of U.S. willingness to pay the costs of producing lasting change through nation building because some losses were inevitable if we were ever to disarm the warlords and build a new and stable political structure. The policy reverses of 1993 clearly illustrate the *president versus Congress* viewpoint introduced in Chapter 1. They also demonstrate the struggle between internationalists and neoisolationists to shape post–Cold War grand policy, as discussed in Chapter 3. President Clinton rushed to salvage what he could in Somalia before Congress compelled him to bring American troops home. Thereafter, fear of suffering even small losses became known in Washington as the "Mogadishu factor" and seriously limited troop deployments abroad.

Ideally, policy feedback leads to more effective policy and to achieving our goals. However, it cannot make a failed policy successful unless we have adequate advance policy planning and are willing to follow through and pay the price of success.

FEEDBACK IN THE FOREIGN POLICY PROCESS

This chapter examines how different types of feedback enter into the foreign policy process, including (1) how the government may use feedback to help evaluate the degree of success and revise policies to more completely achieve desired goals and (2) how citizens may use feedback information channels to evaluate how well government officials, procedures, and policies succeed. These evaluative uses of feedback are more important today than ever because the United States confronts foreign policy problems dramatically different from those faced during the Cold War era, although policy-making institutions and processes continue to evolve only slowly.

How successful is U.S. foreign policy making, on average? How successful can it be? Answering these questions constitutes a global effectiveness assessment of the complete foreign policy system. Before we can make that judgment we must answer two other questions. First, we need to identify current policy. Then we must ask how well it works. Considering the manifold difficulties in reaching fully comprehensive and optimal policy making, how do policymakers evaluate the degree of success achieved and revise policies to attain desired goals more completely? Evaluating success and revising policy closes the loop in the foreign policy system conceptually diagrammed in Figures 4.1, 5.1, and 5.2 as a *purposive control system*. That feedback loop is an integral part of a system designed to meet deliberately chosen goals, and correctly utilizing information about policy effects is imperative if policies are to succeed. Setting foreign policy goals, however, is an extended political process. It draws on people's fundamental values and beliefs about how international politics does and should operate, as discussed in Chapter 3. Determining goals, evaluating policy, assessing its impacts, and making adjustments to achieve the desired effects typically are both slow and incomplete.

As developed in Chapters 5 and 6, some problems in the foreign policy process are *inherent in the nature of all foreign policy interactions*, and ultimately unavoidable. Other problems, also inescapable, are *intrinsic to particular cases*. Still other problems inhere in the *approaches taken to decision making*, and are exceedingly resistant to change. Some of those decision-making problems arise from aspects of *institutional design* in the foreign policy structure we have built. These are potentially changeable, although improvements may be extremely difficult, time consuming, and politically costly. Additional problems exist in the *inputs to the system* because our information about the international environment is usually imperfect and incomplete. *Interpretations* of that information are always subject to some degree of bias. Rigidity and a host of other *organizational difficulties* affect policy choice and implementation. Yet, despite all such limitations in the policy process, feedback received and correctly utilized offers the *possibility* of adjusting policies so we have a better chance of eventually achieving the ends we seek.

This chapter is devoted to that policy feedback process. Its three major sections cover (1) where citizens, government officials, and other actors in the foreign policy process may locate current U.S. foreign policy in statements and actions; (2) the various types, uses, and limitations of foreign policy feedback in correcting and improving policy; and (3) how different types of feedback may be used by officials and citizens in assessing overall policy success.

First, because policy may take many forms, including official statements, formal messages, legislation, and both public and secret actions, we begin by examining the many ways in which U.S. foreign policy and its myriad changes are revealed. Although some sources of information about current policy are limited to those who make and execute policy, others are available to ordinary citizens. Second, one way to classify different types of feedback is according to the speed with which they make information available. **Real-time feedback** is built into the policy process and immediately available, primarily to officials. Information takes longer to become available through **intermediate-time feedback,** but may be at hand quickly enough to influence current policies. Several intermediate-time channels require making information public. **Post hoc** (or after-the-fact) **feedback** becomes available only well after the relevant events, but often is valuable in assessing the quality of policy making and the effectiveness of policies adopted. Most such information is available to the public. Finally, we assess how much help different sources provide in judging policy and policy making, and in revising policies to approach goals more closely.

WHERE DO WE FIND CURRENT POLICY?

Like the law, U.S. foreign policy grows incrementally as the product of a multitude of actors, each with limited powers and moderately specific areas of responsibility. Unfortunately for us, foreign policy is not nearly so conveniently collected as law. Law can be found in great sets of bound volumes, constantly revised and extended to reflect new legislation, court rulings, and administrative regulation. In the mid-1990s, law books began to be replaced by superior computer-searchable databases, such as Lexis and Westlaw. Foreign policy also is partly determined by legislation, case law, and administrative regulation, but determining foreign policy is even more a political process than determining the law. Like lawyers, the creators of foreign policy seldom give up easily, making the

CARTOON 7.1

Policy feedback does not always provide the most preferred messages. At the 1995 Bosnia peace accords in Dayton, Ohio, the Clinton administration promised that U.S. troops would accomplish their peacekeeping mission within a year. Instead, the Peace Implementation Force (IFOR) was succeeded by the Stabilization Force (SFOR) and numerous other organizations. Five years later (the end of the twentieth century), knowledgeable observers had concluded that maintaining peace in that ethnically fractured region would require international peacekeepers indefinitely.
Macnelly/Tribune Media.

policy process protracted and any result changeable. However, we have no great databases of foreign policy.

Current policy, its implications, and its changes may be revealed in many different ways. Obviously, officials have access to formal policy documents to the extent their responsibilities allow. Others who seek information about policy outputs study both the statements and the actions of officials at all levels. At first it may seem surprising the policy establishment is so incestuous that everybody follows what everybody else is saying. In this era of leaks, however, even high officials regularly read the papers to see what the major Washington columnists write about them and about what the rest of the government and the policy establishment are doing. Lobbyists, interest group analysts, and interested citizens cannot command the same access to government information as qualified officials, but they regularly follow some of the same public sources. In the balance of this section, we examine a number of those sources available outside the government. Because officials and key nongovernment actors follow them, our examination reveals not only where we may look for information, but also part of the foreign policy system itself.

Policy is partly what qualified officials say it is. The president may announce an important policy change through a televised address to the nation from the White House Oval Office, via an address before the Congress or the General Assembly of the United Nations, or by means of a speech to a group of civic or business or union leaders. A more problematic channel for policy information, much used in the last two decades, has been officials speaking with journalists "on **background**." This means that reporters can use the information but may not name the source. Opportunities for bias are obvious: Readers must rely on the correspondents' reputations and draw their own conclusions. President Nixon's national security adviser and secretary of state, Henry Kissinger, was notorious for frequent backgrounding. Policy specialists such as lobbyists follow the public speeches of lesser officials nearly as closely as those of the president. From 1975 through 1990, the Department of State regularly published a series of releases entitled *Current Policy*, in which almost all entries were transcripts of speeches by officials. The successor publication, entitled *Dispatch*, continued extensive coverage of official speeches. Currently, the department publishes official speeches on its Web page at www.state.gov. Their inclusion demonstrates (1) the importance that successive administrations attach to such speeches, (2) the expectation that followers of policy will want to know what has been said, and (3) the reason higher officials must clear all official speeches and obtain approval and assurance that they conform to current policy.

Failure to clear speeches may incur severe penalties. On 17 September 1990, early in the Operation Desert Shield phase of the Persian Gulf War, Secretary of Defense Richard Cheney fired air force chief of staff General Michael J. Dugan for unauthorized remarks to reporters from the *Washington Post, Los Angeles Times*, and *Aviation Week and Space Technology* magazine. General Dugan told the journalists, who had been invited to join him on a one-week tour of Saudi Arabia, that members of the Bush administration had accepted advice from sources in Israel about "the best way to hurt Saddam Hussein." Stories based on his remarks included comments about deliberately targeting Hussein, his family, and senior Iraqi commanders in heavy bombing raids (Gersh, 1990). The journalists were said to be surprised at Dugan's dismissal because virtually all the information published except his remarks about the Israeli connection had been expressed previously by other officials who spoke on background. Nor was General Dugan inaccurate; he simply spoke too openly at the wrong time for administration and global political sensitivities. Because the general spoke some four months before the opening of the air war against Iraq, when the Bush administration had yet to obtain UN and congressional authorizations to use offensive force, his remarks were considered premature, embarrassing, and likely to promote opposition to a forthcoming policy change.

Policy is revealed less frequently today by *what policymakers write* than by what they say. Encouraged by the ease and speed of modern transportation and electronic communications media, this effect became far more pronounced in the second half of the twentieth century. Verbal communications can be captured and preserved with increased ease and accuracy, and the rise of television is only part of that communications revolution. Nonetheless, most major policy agreements are reduced to written form, and public writings remain important sources of policy information. The journal *Foreign Affairs*, for example, regularly features articles by heads of government and foreign ministers of major states. Officials and other policymakers, such as members of Congress, often use writings to present analyses of present policies and proposals for change. Occasionally those proposals become the bases for new policies. An outstanding example is George Kennan's

TREATY NEGOTIATION HISTORIES AS POLICY SOURCES
Reinterpreting the Anti-Ballistic Missile Treaty

In one notable case, the negotiating history of a treaty played a prominent role in the political process more than a decade later. In 1985 the Reagan administration "reinterpreted" the 1972 Anti-Ballistic Missile (ABM) Treaty, hoping to allow space-based testing of Strategic Defense Initiative (SDI) missile defense components. The treaty had set a limit of 200 ABMs per side, divided between two sites, and a 1974 protocol halved that limit to a single site of no more than 100 ABMs per side. Additionally, any space-based ABM activities appeared to most readers to be prohibited by Article V, Section 1 of the treaty, which states, "Each Party undertakes not to develop, test, or deploy ABM systems or components which are sea-based, air-based, space-based, or mobile-based" (Barton and Weiler, 1976, 369). On 6 October 1985 then national security adviser, Robert C. McFarlane, casually announced on the television interview program *Meet the Press* that testing and development of ABM systems based on "new physical principles" was "approved and authorized by the [ABM] treaty" (*Department of State Bulletin*, 1985, 33).

The reinterpretation announced through this unorthodox channel rested on a complex argument involving several interrelated treaty provisions. The crucial point was that systems based on "other physical principles" are never explicitly mentioned anywhere in the body of the treaty. They appear only in the associated Agreed Interpretation D, which concerns deployment and not development or testing. Administration officials argued that the reinterpretation, prepared by Judge Abraham Sofaer for the State Department, was justified by the detailed negotiating history of the treaty as falling within the negotiators' intent. That view was devastated by Senator Sam Nunn (D-Ga.) in a 1987 series of three Senate speeches (Nunn, 1987) and by former ambassador Raymond L. Garthoff (1987) in a Brookings Institution monograph later that year. Nunn based his analysis on personally reading the classified negotiating record. He went on to threaten that if the administration did not back down, the Senate would in the future demand minute study of the complete negotiating record of every treaty before ratification, lest another administration years later decide the treaty meant something quite different from what the Senate understood. Had the Reagan administration's reinterpretation prevailed, it would have set an important precedent further shifting the balance of foreign policy-making power from the Congress toward the president. Here again we see the *president versus Congress* viewpoint in action.

1947 "X" article recommending containment of Soviet expansionism. Note, though, that Kennan and the editors of *Foreign Affairs* agreed his position as a State Department official justified publishing the article under a pseudonym. Even that action might have provoked retaliation against Kennan, had his views not already been widely known and supported within the State Department and throughout the higher levels of the administration. Some written policies adopted by the executive branch may receive little or no publicity. In extreme cases, even their existence may be kept secret, as happened with NSC-68 for decades.

Treaties and *legislation* are undeniable written expressions of policy. Moreover, the legislative process of hearings and debates generates voluminous and detailed records of policy alternatives and the ways in which details are thrashed out. With those records, we can trace ideas back to their originators and follow the development of important policy concepts. Given the incremental nature of policy making, however, tracking policy development can be a protracted and detailed task. Additionally, legislative histories are unavailable for interesting but highly secret areas such as the CIA budget and so-called black programs for some advanced military developments, for example, the F-117 "Stealth" fighter aircraft. (**Black programs** are considered so sensitive that they receive no publicity and are kept out of published budgets, with details being revealed only to a few select members of Congress.) The *negotiating histories* of treaties often are classified and rarely receive much publicity beyond contemporary journalists' reports and later allegations in the memoirs of participants. In a notable exception, the negotiating history of the 1972 Anti-Ballistic Missile Treaty played an unusually prominent role in the political process during the mid-1980s.

Treaties and legislation form bridges between official statements and policy actions, but the range of *actions* that demonstrate policy is extremely broad. Any combination of the policy tools examined in Part III (Chapters 8–12) may be used. No matter what is said or written, actions conclusively demonstrate operational policy. Nonetheless, as we saw in some detail in Chapter 5, there are many reasons for discrepancies between actions *intended* and actions *taken*. From time to time, policy is implied through **tacit bargaining,** that is, actions taken that demonstrate what is desired and intended, without formal announcements or negotiations. A milder form of tacit bargaining utilizes public announcements without formal negotiation, but with clear expectations of appropriate reciprocation. For example, following the end of the Cold War, the United States, the Soviet Union, and (after 1991) Russia made a series of moves to reduce symbolically the hair-trigger readiness of their strategic nuclear forces. Those moves included standing down U.S. nuclear-equipped bombers that had been kept on high alert for more than two decades, ready to take off within minutes of receiving attack orders. In an age when intercontinental nuclear missiles also could be launched within minutes and reach their targets in half an hour, deactivating the bombers was only a symbolic act. Still, it reduced tensions and gave visible proof that the governments involved no longer feared and expected war. As seen in more detail in Chapter 10, such *symbolic acts* may be exceedingly important. Other notable examples include President Nixon's 1972 trip to China, Egyptian president Sadat's 1977 Jerusalem visit, and the handshake between Israel's prime minister Yitzhak Rabin and the Palestine Liberation Organization's Yasir Arafat at the 13 September 1993 White House signing ceremony for the first Israeli-PLO accord.

Policymakers' memoirs seldom are available quickly enough to give much information about current policy, although they may be mines of information about processes and infighting over previous policy development. Far too often they are self-serving retroactive attempts to promote the writer's importance, role, and policy views. Unfortunately, although interest in the contents of such memoirs tends to rise with the uniqueness of the information conveyed, our inability to cross-check the information also rises with its very uniqueness. Solutions to these problems are at best imperfect. We can compare with alternate sources when possible; examine evaluations and publication reviews by recognized scholars; seek other cases and points of objective information to test the writers' veracity; and sometimes compare an individual's writings in office and out of office. Occasionally, such writings are voluminous. Roger Hilsman, for example, compiled both a modest academic publication record before entering government service and wrote extensive public and academic literatures after leaving government. In examining the voluminous works of retired officials such as Henry Kissinger and Richard Nixon, we must ask how much change in what they say and write over time results from honest evolution of thought and how much stems from the desire to rewrite history.

Students and citizens alike may be daunted by the large numbers and serious limitations of sources for information about current policy. A useful exercise, however, is to utilize library resources to locate a policy statement or otherwise determine current U.S. policy on some selected point. Many fairly specific source suggestions are included in the previous paragraphs, and others appear in the source citations throughout this volume. In the next section we turn to the many sources of feedback used in the processes of policy formulation and correction, some of which are publicly available to help us evaluate past policy making.

TYPES AND USES OF FEEDBACK

Utilizing feedback means using detected and evaluated information about the results of present policy to help control the results and achieve desired outcomes. Scholars using the systems approach discussed in Chapter 4 have characterized the requisites of direct control of policy as director, detector, and effector, or guidance, evaluation, and control. **Directing** or **guiding** is the process of goal setting and policy determination. **Detecting** or **evaluating** is the process of measuring the results achieved. **Effecting** or **controlling** is the process of adjusting and revising policy to more closely approach targeted outcomes (see Dunsire, 1985). Controlling foreign policy and evaluating its success are subject to several large problems, including the sheer size and complexity of the system and the absence of commonly accepted measures of success and failure.

The foreign policy system links multitudes of individual and organizational actors in a dense network of formal and informal interrelationships, as seen in Chapters 5 and 6. The large number of actors, agencies, programs, and procedures leads to conflict over policies and responsibilities, inertia that limits innovation, and momentum that tends to keep present policies on track. Officials want to protect turf and prerogatives. New programs are not easily launched, and programs under way are not easily deflected to revised paths. Although private sector programs often are evaluated according to their profitability, the public sector lacks any readily corresponding criterion of success. Instead, the foreign policy arena regularly sees intense political arguments over conflicting policy choice criteria, as suggested in the section of Chapter 3 on normative considerations and belief structures. For example, the Carter administration strove to increase the importance of human rights abroad in shaping U.S. policy, only to be reversed by the Reagan administration. Later, officials early in the Clinton administration spoke of helping expand democracy around the world, only to have Republican leaders decry such foreign entanglements after they gained control of the House and Senate in the 1994 midterm elections.

Some use of feedback always inheres in foreign policy processes. In examining different types of feedback that may be used to help assess and manage U.S. foreign policy, we ask questions such as the following:

- What is the nature of the feedback?
- What type of information is provided, from what sources?

TABLE 7.1		
Time Frame and Sources of Foreign Policy Feedback		
Real Time	**Intermediate Time**	**Post Hoc**
Intelligence gathering	Treaties and legislation	Officials' memoirs
Official interviews, speeches, and writings	Congressional oversight	Historical studies
Diplomatic exchanges	Trial balloons	Case studies
Negotiations	Investigative journalism	Declassified documents
Top-level or summit meetings	Think tanks	Legal proceedings
Monitoring of public opinion	Interest and watchdog groups	
	Leaks	
	Whistle-blowers	
	Programmed internal reviews	
	Economic and other indicators	

- When does the information become available?
- How is that information used, and through what action channels?
- How quickly does using that feedback produce policy modifications?
- How reliable and unbiased is the information provided?

In this section we consider some twenty-one types of foreign policy feedback, categorized according to how rapidly information becomes available (see Table 7.1).

Like any classification scheme, that of Table 7.1 oversimplifies matters. More realistically, a continuum extends from instantly available real-time information to post hoc data, that is, data that become available only years after the events. Real-time feedback is built into the policy process and immediately available, primarily to officials. In the middle of the continuum is the largest category, intermediate-time feedback. This information becomes available over a span of days, weeks, or months, often before policies have been completely determined and usually before they have been fully carried out. Several intermediate-time channels require making information public. Post hoc (or after-the-fact) feedback becomes available only well after the pertinent events, but still may be useful in assessing the quality of policy making and the effectiveness of policies adopted. Most such information is available to the public. Policy evaluators generally use post hoc data, and their recommendations may have broad long-term effects.

The ways policy choices are made received considerable attention in Chapters 5 and 6. We devoted particular concern to the ways short-term considerations often overpower longer term concerns, raising questions whether our own short-term policy goals necessarily serve our long-term interests. In the remainder of this section, however, we examine the types of policy feedback set out in Table 7.1 more fully. For each type, attention is focused on the nature, strengths, and weaknesses of the information for guiding, evaluating, and controlling U.S. foreign policy.

REAL-TIME FEEDBACK

Real-time information about the effects of policy becomes available immediately, even as policy is being decided and implemented. Immediate use of such information is an important part of the policy determination process. Real-time feedback occurs across the entire range of policies, and its immediacy sometimes helps avoid political battles over whether and how the information should be used (although such battles are frequent). Six real-time information sources are introduced next in order of decreasing breadth of issues and activities covered before being examined in greater detail. Information received through these sources remains largely within the institutional structures of government, entering the public domain only indirectly through media activities and later releases via intermediate-time and post hoc feedback.

1. *Intelligence* gathering of all types is continuous. In actuality, of course, most types of information are subject to some delays in transmission and analysis. Some messages are so sensitive that they must be hand carried and then await the attention of top officials. Intelligence inputs may be received when the specialized analyst best capable of processing certain information is off duty. Finally, processing speed varies with the information's political salience.

2. *Official interviews, speeches, and writings* are essential sources of information and commentary on current policy and were discussed in the previous section, "Where Do We Find Current Policy?" Officials and other foreign policy actors follow them even more closely than ordinary citizens do.

3. *Diplomatic exchanges* produce a similar, essentially continuous flow of information. Meetings between high officials may yield vital information about how our opposite numbers perceive and value different policy options, and occasionally such meetings promote important breakthroughs. For example, earlier secret meetings in Norway between top Israeli and PLO officials paved the way for their breakthrough agreement signed in Washington in September 1993.

4. *Negotiations,* once undertaken, produce a continuous give-and-take of argumentation, positions taken, and concessions made or received. Meetings occur somewhat sporadically, as needed. In our increasingly interdependent world, however, negotiations all the way up to some summit meetings, such as annual gatherings of the leaders of the G-8 developed market-economy states, are being institutionalized as elements of the permanent policy-making structure.

5. *Summit meetings* between heads of state or government are the highest possible level of official meetings, but rarely produce new agreements. Instead, summits usually are carefully choreographed in advance, with top leaders ceremonially signing agreements worked out in advance by their subordinates. The 1993 Washington ceremony between Israeli and PLO leaders (see introductory case in Chapter 8) exemplifies this tendency. In rare contrast, President Nixon and then-Soviet general secretary Brezhnev settled some important final details of the 1972 SALT I arms control agreements in Moscow only hours before signing the formal documents. Thus summit meetings sometimes provide vital negotiating opportunities.

6. Intensive *monitoring of public opinion* about current policy and policymakers, by news media, politicians, and other actors, became a significant part of U.S. foreign policy in the last half of the twentieth century. As noted in Chapter 1, emphasizing Iraqi aggression and human rights abuses rather than Iraq's threat to oil supplies was a crucial part of Bush administration strategy for mobilizing public opinion to support the Persian Gulf War. Some authorities argue that following public opinion closely makes foreign policy more democratic, although others hold that it makes for erratic policy.

Intelligence

Ideally, the intelligence process provides comprehensive, ongoing, real-time information about the actual effects of our policies on others. Gathering data about the actions and intents of other international actors, as well as about the effects of our policies, and then analyzing and interpreting that stream of incoming information, are essential prerequisites for informed policy planning. For the intelligence thus generated to provide useful feedback, it must to the maximum possible extent be timely, complete, precise, accurate, relevant for action, and unbiased. Yet none of these goals is easily attained, and probably none is ever completely achieved. Actors and procedures involved in intelligence gathering and interpretation were examined in some detail in Chapter 6, in which we saw examples of problems regularly found in attempting to achieve these goals, such as the intense bureaucratic battles over ideas that occur frequently within the intelligence community. As noted there, specialists distinguish between *information*, which is unevaluated material, and *intelligence*, which is the product after received information has been processed and interpreted for its meaning. Incoming information arrives continuously, but converting it into intelligence may take some time. Major evaluative products like National Intelligence Estimates (NIEs) are produced only sporadically.

During the Cold War decades, the largest share of U.S. intelligence efforts was devoted to the Soviet Union. Beginning early in the 1990s, there was serious debate over how extensive U.S. espionage and other intelligence efforts needed to be, following the Cold War's end and the Soviet Union's breakup. Arguments that the end of the Cold War should allow U.S. intelligence programs to be scaled down implicitly assume that efforts should be proportional to the threats faced. Optimists saw the danger of major nuclear war drastically diminished, and called a large intelligence establishment—especially one focused on the former Soviet Union—a Cold War relic. Pessimists of one type saw a more complex world in which the activities of increasing numbers of increasingly independent actors must be tracked. Instead of dealing with the centrally controlled Soviet Union, for example, the United States suddenly needed to negotiate with Belarus, Kazakhstan, Russia, and Ukraine over intercontinental ballistic missiles on their territory and the START strategic arms control agreements.

A storm of official protest arose over the 22 February 1994 arrest of CIA official Aldrich Ames, who eventually admitted having spied for the Soviet KGB since 1985 and then having spied for its Russian successor agency. The Ames case well may reflect bureaucratic tendencies to continue business as usual despite the breakup of the Soviet Union, and deep disagreements between factions inside the Russian government about how closely to cooperate with the United States. Widespread concerns that intelligence agencies on both sides were continuing Cold War procedures quickly gave way to statements that spying is part of business as usual, even between friendly governments. Indeed, the Pollard spy case of the 1980s demonstrated that Israel had spied on the United States despite decades of de facto alliance and massive U.S. aid.

Pessimists of another type, not so inclined to perceive that Cold War activities still continue, view the United States as already enmeshed in a much more complex, more interdependent world in which its former hegemony has been forever lost. They tend to see U.S. maintenance of the best possible position in this new world order as critically dependent on effective intelligence, but with a new emphasis on economic activities. Their view stresses a need for large amounts of information about previously underexamined actors and activities, whether that information is obtained through espionage or more common intelligence means. Some authorities have even called for the U.S. government to engage in industrial espionage, a perhaps surprisingly widespread activity among developed states.

Intelligence as policy feedback is thus vital but subject to a host of difficulties. Questions about how much effort should be directed toward intelligence, and toward which targets, have only gained intensity in the post–Cold War era. An important peculiarity of intelligence is that *using the information gathered reveals that we know it*, and thus provides important feedback to our opponents. Sometimes the benefits of using information must be weighed against the costs of revealing our knowledge, which might include compromising the identity (or worse) of an agent or source within another government. During the Second World War, for example, the British government permitted massive German bomber attacks against several major cities to proceed against only normal resistance, rather than mount a more focused defense and risk revealing that it had broken the German high command's radio codes.

Official Interviews, Speeches, and Writings

These essential sources of information and commentary on current policy were discussed earlier. Sometimes they reveal policy in a very timely manner. At other times they play important roles in the policy process, making a crucial argument in an ongoing policy debate through a public channel, or floating a trial balloon (see later). In all such uses they provide information that can be used to revise policy.

Diplomatic Exchanges

Diplomatic exchanges of messages and other communications are primarily means by which governments and other international actors *signal* their concerns, wishes, and intentions to one another. In principle, such exchanges provide the U.S. government with an important source of information not always available as quickly or completely through other channels. Elaborate rituals and rules of diplomatic procedure and precedence have been developed over the last several centuries principally to ensure that messages really do get through and are understood as intended (see Chapter 10 for more details). Just as we use diplomatic channels to inform and persuade others, the normal workings of diplomacy yield a continuing flow of messages from outside the U.S. government. Unlike much of what emerges from the intelligence community, however, these are official messages that other governments want the U.S. administration to receive. The chief caveat in interpreting such messages is that they are very unlikely to tell all.

In times of crisis, diplomatic channels may be used to convey messages of the greatest urgency and import, with profound impacts on policy. After Israeli troops halted the

Egyptian advance in the 1973 Yom Kippur War, then broke through and began to surround the Egyptian Third Army, Soviet diplomats threatened direct Soviet intervention. Because both the United States and the USSR had long sought to avoid using their own troops in the Middle East and risking a direct U.S.-Soviet confrontation, those threats gave increased urgency to U.S. efforts to promote a cease-fire. The Nixon administration ordered a heightened state of defense readiness (referred to as "Defcon Three") to signal the intensity of U.S. concern. Within days, this complex of moves, signals, and countermoves yielded superpower agreement to pressure their clients into a cease-fire.

Afterward, U.S. Middle East policy was seriously reevaluated, for two major reasons. First, we had never come closer to direct U.S.-Soviet conflict in the region. Second, Egypt's limited success before being forced back by Israeli forces demonstrated that the long-term regional balance of power was shifting, and Israel could no longer survive indefinitely in a state of war with all its immediate neighbors. The U.S. government began moving toward dealing more evenhandedly with Israel's enemies and increased its efforts toward a lasting peace in the region. Although a comprehensive peace has yet to be achieved, considerable progress has been made, notably including the 1979 Israeli-Egyptian peace treaty and the 1993 Israeli-Palestine Liberation Organization (PLO) peace agreement.

The vast majority of diplomatic messages is routine and unlikely ever to enter public knowledge. Truly momentous messages are infrequent and may remain secret for many years. Only long after the events will those messages be declassified or discussed in the memoirs of involved but now-retired officials. If such information enters the public information stream quickly, it is often through leaks and disclosures by whistle-blowers. In one of the most celebrated and exceptional leaks, the *New York Times* began on 13 June 1971 to publish a massive classified government document compilation and study of U.S. involvement in Vietnam, called the Pentagon Papers. A Supreme Court ruling on 30 June of that year affirmed the right of the *Times* and the *Washington Post* to publish the documents under the protection of the First Amendment. That single case did a great deal to establish leaks as a major action channel.

Knowing that diplomatic messages are used for feedback, governments must be exceedingly careful to send correct messages, carefully designed to convey what is really intended. This is not always easy because senders must anticipate how recipients will interpret their messages. Initial communications often must be followed by a sequence of clarifications, a phenomenon regularly seen in public announcements about domestic policy. The wrong message, or the right message wrongly phrased, may reap only trouble. One highly publicized case concerned U.S. signals to Iraq shortly before Iraq's 1990 invasion of Kuwait. Only days before the attack, U.S. ambassador April Glaspie met with Iraqi dictator Saddam Hussein to express American concern about Iraqi pressures on Kuwait. One version of events holds that she stated the case so weakly, Saddam interpreted her to mean the United States would not stand in his way. Other officials held that Glaspie was made a scapegoat after the fact, and Saddam correctly heard her message but believed U.S. threats were no more than a bluff. Other evidence supports the second interpretation; late in 1990 there were many signs that Saddam disbelieved what most informed observers in the West interpreted as clear signs of the coming U.S.-led invasion. As noted in Chapter 5, policy failures may result from leaders receiving good advice but failing to act on it.

Negotiations

International negotiations are a specialized subset of diplomatic exchanges, and thus are subject to the same general strengths and weaknesses. Feedback automatically occurs in the messages that are part of the negotiating process, as well as in cross checks on those messages through other channels such as intelligence. Negotiations are more formalized than some other types of exchanges, sometimes involve other actors besides governments, and often include elaborate sequences of positions taken only in hopes of evoking some desired response. A dance of adjustments takes place. Ultimate agreements, if any, are reached through slow and mutual steps toward some ultimate common ground. Negotiators usually can be presumed to want eventual agreement, but only on terms favorable to their side. Negotiations cannot be conducted without a continuing flow of information, but it must be interpreted in the intertwined contexts of ongoing negotiations and continuing relations outside the immediate negotiations. Additionally, most negotiations are two-level games in which the external talks with foreign actors are mirrored by internal bargaining within the governments to determine what messages their negotiators should convey (see Chapter 10).

Top-Level or Summit Meetings

Summit meetings between heads of state and/or government usually are tightly scripted ceremonial occasions. Only occasionally do they allow a special type of negotiation in which the highest authorities make major policy shifts to reach important agreements. Nonetheless, even ceremonial meetings may provide important feedback by enabling leaders to develop personal ties with their opposite numbers. As in all negotiations, one must be careful to convey the right signals. The 1961 U.S.-Soviet summit meeting in Vienna, for example, was disastrous. Reports said that Soviet Premier Nikita Khrushchev emerged believing President John Kennedy to be weak and vacillating, and that Kennedy was badly shaken by Khrushchev's belligerence and intransigence. Impressions formed at that meeting probably encouraged Khrushchev to take the major risk of introducing Soviet nuclear missiles into Cuba the following year. In turn, the perceived need to overcome those impressions left Kennedy at a disadvantage with the October 1962 onset of the Cuban missile crisis, and added pressure for him to take an early strong stand.

On rare occasions, high officials establish a rapport enabling them to reach breakthrough agreements, only to have the accords rejected by their governments. On 16 July 1982, Paul Nitze, heading the U.S. delegation to the intermediate nuclear forces (INF) negotiations with the Soviets, took a carefully prearranged private "walk in the woods" outside Geneva with his opposite number, Yuli Kvitsinskiy. As Nitze (1989, 375) later related,

> My instructions directed me to explore with my opposite number any possibility
> of significant movement on issues of interest to us. I was not authorized to commit
> the government to any change in the U.S. position as set forth in my instructions.
> I saw no way of exploring the possibility of significant Soviet movement without
> at least indicating the U.S. movement I personally thought commensurate with the
> movement I was soliciting from them. . . . I did not think a "step-by-step" exchange
> of concessions was likely to be the best path. . . . I came to the conclusion that the
> best hope . . . was to explore informally with Kvitsinskiy a joint package entailing

concessions by both sides leading to a mutually acceptable final outcome. Such a package could be developed without commitment by either side and no element would be agreed unless all elements were agreed, thereby protecting each side's formal negotiating position. . . . I recognized that, while I was authorized to probe for real movement on the issues, the explorations that I had in mind would be seen by some in Washington as going beyond my instructions.

At the time, the United States officially supported the "zero-zero option" of worldwide elimination of INF missiles, a position eventually adopted in the 1987 INF treaty. The Soviets officially claimed that zero-zero called for their unilateral disarmament because only they then had such missiles in Europe. Kvitsinskiy agreed with few changes to Nitze's proposals setting fairly low and balanced limits, but both governments subsequently rejected their agreement. After hearing nothing from the Soviets about the tentative accord for more than seven weeks, the Reagan administration instructed Nitze to say nothing more about it, and to disavow the accord if the Soviets brought it up. The administration, and evidently Nitze himself, feared the Soviets would interpret the walk in the woods proposal to be a new U.S. negotiating stand, then propose splitting the difference between that and the Soviet bargaining position. Subsequently, in another private meeting, Kvitsinskiy relayed to Nitze his instructions to renounce their previous agreement. After the United States began introducing new INFs into Europe late in 1983, negotiations were broken off by the Soviets for more than two years.

Monitoring of Public Opinion

Intensive *monitoring of public opinion* about current policy and policymakers, by news media, politicians, and other actors, became a significant part of the foreign policy system in the last half of the twentieth century. Drawing on scientific polling techniques developed around the time of World War II by political and other social scientists, pollsters today can obtain representative samples of national or regional opinion on specific issues, politicians, or developments within hours. Since John Kennedy's successful 1960 presidential campaign, politicians have used these techniques not only to learn how much the public cares about which issues, but to tune their presentations to whichever issues matter most to particular audiences. By the time of President Carter's 1980 loss to Ronald Reagan, limited exit polling at selected key precincts could tell us by noon on Election Day who would win. Polling told the Clinton campaigners in 1992 that the public cared more about the state of the economy than about President Bush's foreign policy leadership during the Persian Gulf War.

Opinion polling about current policy issues obviously is timely and has the potential to influence policy change. Arguably, following public opinion closely emphasizes intermestic effects and makes foreign policy more democratic and more responsive to the citizenry. However, critics charge that it is prone to stimulating overreactions, making policy erratic and too rapidly changeable. Somalia, discussed earlier, is a case in point. After the deaths of eighteen American soldiers in Mogadishu provoked a firestorm of public protest, politicians with at least one eye on the polls rushed to demand policy change. President Clinton could have argued to public and politicians alike that casualties were part of the price we had to pay for an important humanitarian and nation-building mission, but he chose not to do so. In this and later instances, critics charged that he governed too much by polls and too little by principle or any grand policy vision. (Of course, as we have seen, the entire country lacks any single grand vision for post–Cold War policy.) Another indicator of the importance of public opinion is found in Bush administration strategy for mobilizing public opinion to support the Persian Gulf War, emphasizing Iraqi aggression and human rights abuses rather than Iraq's threat to oil supplies.

INTERMEDIATE-TIME FEEDBACK

Intermediate-time feedback ranges from nearly real time to very protracted, occupying the large middle range of the continuum introduced earlier and summarized in Table 7.1. This information takes a while to become available, but it may be at hand in time to influence current policies. Many different actors and institutional structures in the foreign policy system produce and process intermediate-time feedback. In contrast to real-time feedback, this information does not always remain within the institutional structures of government, and several intermediate-time channels require making information public. Post hoc feedback used to adjust current and future policies based on examinations of the past generally takes much longer to become available.

Treaties and Other Legislation

These essential sources of information about current policy were discussed earlier. They are included here because they reveal essential U.S. commitments and standards for foreign policy conduct. As such, they establish part of the background that officials and other foreign policy actors must know. At least some received information will concern how legislatively established policies are working. For ordinary citizens, treaties and other legislation have the advantage of being published and readily available. However, they identify only part of formal foreign policy. They tell us nothing about such policy sources as secret agreements, classified documents, and understandings between officials.

Congressional Oversight

Congressional oversight is the broad process of supervision to ensure that actions by the president and executive departments follow the laws of the land. It derives from the Constitution's vesting of "all legislative powers herein granted" in the Congress, and "executive power" in the president, although both grants are subject to significant qualifications. Congressional oversight is simultaneously one of the checks and balances programmed into the U.S. Constitution and a form of internal government operational review. Congressional oversight is also an essential tool in the Congress's ongoing battle with the president and the executive branch for control of foreign policy, according to the *president versus Congress* viewpoint introduced in Chapter 1.

Oversight occurs in two quite different forms: public hearings and secret proceedings. As we noted in Chapter 4, congressional hearings sometimes are powerful tools to publicize ideas and shape policy. Officials and nationally recognized experts may be called before standing or special committees of the Congress, and their testimony normally is published. Secret proceedings, such as those established by law for managing the intelligence community and the use of U.S. troops abroad, provide internal information largely kept within the government. As with the real-time feedback sources previously discussed, however, that information sometimes is revealed on a timely basis through leaks and investigative journalism. Oversight procedures for managing troops abroad, established by the 1973 War Powers Act, are discussed in Chapter 5.

Having the sole authority to levy taxes and appropriate funds gives the Congress significant inherent power. Yet full publicity about the more sensitive aspects of foreign policy and intelligence easily could undermine policy objectives and endanger agents abroad. How are these conflicting objectives reconciled? Legislation developed from the mid-1970s to 1980 established permanent select committees on intelligence in each house of Congress. Executive Order 12333, which finalized the reorganization of the national intelligence effort and was signed by President Reagan in 1981, formally recognized the congressional role and ordered departments and agencies to cooperate "with the Congress in the conduct of its responsibilities for oversight of intelligence activities" (Breckinridge, 1986, 73). Each select committee includes representatives from the committees dealing with appropriations, the armed forces, and foreign affairs. Information about sensitive intelligence activities, particularly including covert operations, is conveyed to members in strict secrecy, and in especially sensitive cases, only to selected senior members. Feedback about the policies exists in securing this limited and highly constrained form of congressional approval.

Critics charge that members of the select committees may be coopted by their special access to information; that is, they may be drawn into cooperating with the administration by fear both of damaging the country and of losing their personal access to the information if they publicize misguided policies or abuses of process. A 1995 case demonstrates the dilemma posed to a member of such an oversight committee who learns secret information about a serious abuse of process. Representative Robert Torricelli, a senior Democratic member of the House Select Committee on Intelligence, publicly released classified information that linked a Guatemalan colonel who had worked for the CIA, Julio Roberto Alpirez, to the killings in Guatemala of an American innkeeper and a guerrilla leader married to an American lawyer. Although he had long been staunchly anticommunist on matters relating to Cuba, Torricelli joined with other members of the committee in writing President Clinton, asking that as much as possible of the record of intelligence dealings with Guatemala be declassified and appending a list of dozens of atrocities committed by Guatemalan forces. The Republican speaker of the House, Newt Gingrich, moved to have Torricelli expelled from the committee on the grounds that national security required him to keep silent about what he had learned (Lewis, 1995). Although Gingrich's move was blatantly political, it raised the argument that members of the select committees have promised to respect the classification of information, even though they have no direct control over how any particular piece of information is classified. Torricelli argued that violations of law properly subject to committee scrutiny well may have occurred. Colonel Alpirez was reportedly present at the torture interrogation of the American innkeeper, Michael DeVine. Lacking evidence of a political motive for DeVine's killing, the U.S. Justice Department found no case for prosecuting the colonel under U.S. law. Arguably, however, if DeVine knew about drug dealing by the Guatemalan military and the CIA withheld that information from the Justice Department, the CIA officials involved would be guilty of obstruction of justice.

Some months after the initial publicity, the validity of Torricelli's charges gained new public support. John Deutsch, appointed director of Central Intelligence in 1995, announced in a classified briefing to the Congress in September that he had dismissed the former Latin American Division and Guatemala Station chiefs, and had disciplined eight other officials for concealing Colonel Alpirez's abuses. He stated, "a common theme is lack of candor" and "there is no evidence that there was a conspiracy not to inform

Congress, (but) the essential facts are that Congress was not kept informed as required by law." Taking a more critical view, Senator Robert Kerrey (D-Nebr.), vice chair of the Senate Select Committee on Intelligence, asserted, "there was a violation of U.S. law . . . an intentional effort to withhold information from and to mislead the Congress" (Risen, 1995).

Even if there is no intent to conceal information, misunderstandings well may occur over whether senators and representatives on the select committees have been fully informed. One such case occurred regarding the U.S. mining of Nicaraguan ports in 1984, which was part of a program to interdict arms supplies from the Sandinista government of Nicaragua to insurgents in El Salvador. Such mining could be held to be in violation of international law. The House Select Committee on Intelligence was briefed early in 1984, but various circumstances delayed the Senate committee's briefing until the end of the first quarter of the year. When the mining became public knowledge and controversial, some senators disavowed any knowledge of it, although it had been reported (Safire, 1984). Senators had been told of the general program to limit the movement of war supplies from Nicaragua to the Salvadoran insurgents, and they may have interpreted the mining as a logical part of what they had already approved. Reportedly, only one senator reacted to the mining and requested additional information. Breckinridge (1986, 80–81) suggests that the fragmented attention span of legislators dealing with many concerns and subject to frequent interruptions during committee hearings may have contributed to this misunderstanding. At the very least, cases such as these suggest the congressional oversight system has very serious limitations as a feedback process for controlling policy.

Trial Balloons

Trial balloons, or announcements of potential policies intended to gauge reaction before they are put into force, have become common in U.S. politics. Trial balloon flights can be useful in obtaining feedback about the responses a proposal is likely to evoke from Congress, officials, the public, and other governments. Their use is usually viewed cynically, however, because a proposed policy that evokes significant protest may be disavowed within days. Often some scapegoat waits in the wings to be sacrificially fired for being "responsible" for the "mistaken" policy announcement. At their worst, trial balloons suggest government by opinion poll, without regard to what unpopular but principled policy might be best. Trial balloons cannot be floated too frequently because any administration that habitually shifts policies will be charged with vacillating. For example, the Clinton administration often was criticized for rapid policy shifts under fire, both at home and abroad but particularly regarding foreign policy, and especially its policy on the civil war in Bosnia before the 1995 Dayton peace accords.

Investigative Journalism

Investigative journalists may react quite rapidly to some policy developments, giving their policy feedback an almost real-time character to which some policymakers respond before final policy is set. (Recall the comment earlier that everyone in the Washington policy establishment follows what everybody else is saying.) Many cases require extended time for investigation, however, delaying any journalistic impact on policy. Public disclosure is inherent in this type of feedback, which leads many decision makers to consciously coopt and enlist journalists in the policy process, as discussed in Chapter 4. "Journalists" here means investigators working in any media, including radio, television, newspapers, magazines, and books. At the long end of the time-to-publication continuum, tending toward strictly post hoc evaluations, investigative journalism includes historical case studies, biographies, and officials' memoirs. (See the section on post hoc feedback later.) Taking somewhat less time to reach publication are the results of the type of investigative journalism—still, often protracted—that yields one or more stories in a newspaper or newsmagazine. A classic domestic politics example is Woodward and Bernstein's *Washington Post* series uncovering how the Nixon administration organized and tried to cover up the 1972 Watergate break-in of Democratic Party headquarters. Indeed, the Watergate break-in was conducted by a covert unit dubbed the "Plumbers," from their original assignment to stop leaks that had included the release of the Pentagon Papers about Vietnam war policy. The CIA-Alpirez case in Guatemala, discussed earlier, provides a good foreign policy example in which investigative journalism was crucial to unearthing abuses. Such stories regularly involve investigation of matters that government agencies and officials would rather conceal, and often rely on assistance from leaks and whistle-blowers.

At the short end of the time-to-publication continuum, nearing real-time influence on decision makers are *political columnists.* Those who specialize in foreign policy are worth particular consideration. These reporters cultivate high-level access channels and are often sought out by officials who either want to promote or oppose current policy. Their writings are regularly followed, and sometimes feared, by Washington insiders. Although few can be considered in-and-outers, some have experience in government service. For discussion of journalists who are genuine in-and-outers, such as Leslie Gelb and Strobe Talbott, see Chapter 4.

Another example is William Safire, who served four years as a high-level speechwriter in the Nixon White House before joining the *New York Times* as a political columnist with an essentially unrestricted portfolio. Ever the witty conservative and endowed with a true gift for wordplay, Safire often focuses on domestic politics. He won a 1978 Pulitzer Prize for exposing the unorthodox banking practices that forced the resignation of Bert Lance, Jimmy Carter's budget director. He is noted for clear, fearless, and unambiguous predictions, which almost inevitably have their misses. However, in late 1988 he correctly called the fall of the Berlin Wall, which was opened about a year later. In another important foray into foreign policy, some of Safire's early 1989 columns reportedly enraged the West German government by helping reveal that state's complicity in building a Libyan poison gas factory (Shapiro, 1990, 62).

In evaluating the writings of such columnists as policy feedback sources, both we as citizens and government officials as decision makers need to keep certain limitations firmly in mind. Despite specialization, expertise, and well-placed sources, reporters and columnists lack the detailed day-by-day information access enjoyed by actors in the first two zones of policy influence. Political and other biases sometimes become glaringly evident. Beyond his Republican conservatism, for example, William Safire is staunchly pro-Israeli to a degree that would do a Likud member of the Knesset proud. In contrast, Boston-based *New York Times* columnist Anthony Lewis is consistently liberal. He may be expected, for example, to support arms reductions, peaceful resolution of conflicts, and the promotion of human rights while eschewing almost any use of force. If we keep their biases and prior experiences in government (if any) firmly in mind, however, such columnists at their best reveal important inside details of the policy process. They may then serve as important generators and publicizers of alternative policy ideas and an important check on government.

Foreign policy columnists are but one specific instance of the broader species known as political *pundits*. Nimmo and Combs (1992, xix) define punditry as follows:

> [A]n ancient practice whose traditions are chronicled in the Holy Bible, countless sacred and secular texts, volumes of history, works of fiction, and philosophical tomes. It is a practice whose currency and vitality fill today's newspapers, news-magazines, radio programs, and television productions. It has carried several labels: prophesy, revelation, gossip, fortune-telling, reporting, interpretation, analysis, and opinion leadership are but a few. It consists of commenting on events, reports of events, and the people who make them.

Examining this phenomenon in detail could occupy a major segment of an entire course on media politics. Much has already been written about the rise in the 1990s of highly in-fluential, and almost exclusively conservative, punditry via so-called talk radio. This phe-nomenon should remind us that pundits vary tremendously in the extent to which they investigate their subjects in depth, offer us proof of what they assert to be "facts," are open and honest about their assumptions, and set out clear and convincingly logical steps lead-ing to their conclusions. Those of us interested in foreign policy would be well advised to confine our attention to those few pundits who emphasize investigation and analysis, and who avoid interpreting events by forcing them into preconceived ideological frameworks. Undoubtedly the modern pundits best able to provide useful feedback are those who reg-ularly follow foreign affairs and actively pursue investigative journalism.

Think Tanks

Policy think tanks are not-for-profit, nominally (although decreasingly) nonpartisan, research institutes, centers, foundations, or organizations dedicated to full-time policy analysis (see details in Chapter 6). Because policy studies and recommendations are the primary products of think tanks, it is natural to expect some of that output to provide use-ful feedback about the efficacy and efficiency of present policies. The great strengths of such organizations are their specialization and expertise, and their analysts' experience. As noted in Chapter 6, think tanks now have more policy posts than government itself and frequently attract in-and-outers during their out-of-government periods. The ma-jority of analysts are members of the policy elite and direct their messages primarily to other members of that elite, in and out of government. Most of their recommendations are published in some form, however, and can be obtained by informed members of the public. See Table 6.2 for a list of numerous examples of think tanks that deal with foreign policy interests.

As always, of course, we must beware of biases. The partisan affiliations of former officials and the general ideological leanings of particular think tanks are well known. Whether analysts have risen above such biases in any particular case may be arguable. If we keep those biases as firmly in mind as we would when reading political columns, how-ever, think tanks can serve as important generators and publicizers of alternative policies and procedures.

Interest and Watchdog Groups

Like think tanks, interest groups are nominally nonpartisan not-for-profit organizations. Some, such as the Council on Foreign Relations, the Foreign Policy Association, and the

Trilateral Commission, clearly focus on foreign policy, and some perform watchdog functions tracking particular activities. In comparison with think tanks, interest groups are more likely to have dispersed national memberships and somewhat less likely to have either large full-time staffs or single, central locations. Like think tanks, the primary product of foreign policy interest groups is policy studies and recommendations, which may be important sources of feedback about the efficacy and efficiency of present policies. In common with think tanks, the great strengths of these organizations are their specialization and expertise, and their lobbyists' and analysts' experience. Again, like think tanks, many of their recommendations are published in forms obtainable by informed members of the public, but we must beware of biases. Some of these organizations have enormous influence in shaping foreign policy.

Consider the case of the Council on Foreign Relations, the New York–based organization that publishes the journal *Foreign Affairs*, easily the most influential of all foreign policy journals. Recall that George Kennan's "X" article launching the Cold War policy of containment was published in there. The council's membership is so rich with influential in-and-outers that Dye and Zeigler (1989, 79) called its "connection with policy . . . so pervasive as to make it a quasi-governmental organization." Its influence became dramatically evident during the Vietnam War era when the policies it proposed were repeatedly adopted by both Democratic and Republican presidents—military intervention and later deescalation, both under Lyndon Johnson, and slowly phased withdrawal under Richard Nixon. Prominent council members who helped shape war policy during Lyndon Johnson's administration included Secretary of State Dean Rusk, National Security Adviser McGeorge Bundy, Director of Central Intelligence John McCone, and Undersecretary of State George Ball, the only major opponent of war policy within the administration. After dramatically escalating the numbers of U.S. troops in Vietnam and shifting their role from advisers to direct ground combat in 1965, Johnson directed the creation of a "senior advisory group on Vietnam." That group was unofficial and consisted mainly of private foreign policy specialists, but twelve of its fourteen members belonged to the council. Eventually, mainly under George Ball's urging, the group restudied U.S. policy and foresaw what became the nearly devastating North Vietnamese and Vietcong Tet offensive in February 1968 (see the opening case of Chapter 5). Seen by U.S. prowar hawks as the last gasp of the communist offensive and by antiwar doves as the beginning of defeat, that offensive provoked a drastic reexamination and reversal in the U.S. position. In meetings of the senior advisory group, Ball's position won the conversions of key hawks, including council members C. Douglas Dillon (treasury secretary), Cyrus Vance (later Jimmy Carter's secretary of state), Dean Acheson (once Harry Truman's secretary of state), and McGeorge Bundy. In a dramatic nationally televised address five days after the group presented its recommendation, Johnson announced that the United States would begin reducing its commitments in Vietnam, and that he himself would not seek reelection.

The senior advisory group was then disbanded and reconstituted as the "Vietnam Settlement Group." Its recommendations eventually became the basis of the January 1963 Paris peace agreement reached under the Nixon administration. The Carter administration (1977–81) was strongly influenced by the council's post–Vietnam War studies recommending foreign policies aimed at reducing nuclear proliferation and conventional arms sales, promoting human rights abroad, and reassessing relations between developed and developing states. Indeed, the council (and the interlocking U.S.-British-German Trilateral Commission) provided many members of Carter's top foreign policy team.

Along with Vance, council members included Vice President Walter Mondale, National Security Adviser Zbigniew Brzezinski, Secretary of Defense Harold Brown, Treasury Secretary Michael Blumenthal, UN Ambassador Andrew Young, and ACDA (United States Arms Control and Disarmament Agency) director and chief arms control negotiator Paul Warnke. Following the Soviet invasion of Afghanistan begun in 1979–80, the Carter administration shifted to a harder line on U.S.-Soviet relations, presaging early Reagan administration policy. In these instances, it thus appears the advice of the Council on Foreign Relations has been decisive both in shaping U.S. foreign policy *and in later revising it.* Arguably, this implies that the council, substantially consisting of past, present, and future officials, provided valuable feedback that helped in revising policies. Equally arguably, it implies the council's advice sometimes was wrong because some policies it advised were later drastically modified.

Leaks and Whistle-Blowers

As discussed in Chapter 4, a particularly intriguing type of feedback is the leak, a deliberate sharing of restricted or classified information outside official channels in hopes of changing policy. A special subcategory of leakers is whistle-blowers, government employees or others who expose illegal activities, often to congressional investigators. Leaks and whistle-blowers have become increasingly important since the Vietnam War era, and they can be enormously helpful tools of investigative journalism. They can furnish inside information that otherwise might never be revealed, providing an important protection against abuses of power. In cases like the Pentagon Papers, significant policy changes have resulted.

Important as they may be, however, leaks and whistle-blowers have major drawbacks as feedback sources. Coverage is spotty and unpredictable. A critical individual must first gain access to trenchant information and then decide to release it. Normally, officials never publicly criticize policy, even if they oppose it within government channels. A notable example at the highest level was provided by the memoirs of Robert McNamara, secretary of defense under Presidents Kennedy and Johnson through much of the Vietnam War, a conflict often called "McNamara's war" at the time. Nearly three decades after he left the Defense Department in 1968 to head the World Bank, McNamara (1995) wrote, "we were wrong, terribly wrong" in Vietnam policy even though administration planners "acted according to what we thought were the principles and traditions of this nation." Yet McNamara did much more than keep his policy disagreements confined within the administration; he remained silent for decades thereafter. In interviews after the publication of his memoirs, McNamara espoused the singular doctrine that a cabinet officer owes virtually permanent obedience and silence to a president, saying, "Every cabinet officer must do as the president says, or get the hell out. And if he gets out, my view is that he cannot attack the president from outside the cabinet, essentially using the power given to him by the president" (Alter, 1995, 52).

McNamara's position seems extreme, but it points out one severe limitation of relying on leaks, whistle-blowers, and the writings of officials for policy feedback. We cannot determine who will decide to speak out about what policy problem, nor when. Unlike such polities as Britain and Japan, the United States has no well-developed tradition of officials resigning to protest the adoption of a policy they have opposed, or to take symbolic responsibility for a failed policy. Resignations on principle are almost unheard of in Washington. One rare and notable exception was the resignation of President Jimmy

Carter's secretary of state, Cyrus Vance, protesting the 1980 decision to attempt a military rescue of U.S. diplomats held hostage in Teheran, Iran. That attempt failed, although there is some opinion that a larger and better planned expedition could have succeeded. Vance, however, announced his resignation only after the mission failed, and he minimized opportunities to publicize his disagreements with administration policy.

Unpredictable and spotty coverage is not the only serious limitation of relying on leaks, whistle-blowers, and official writings. Legitimate policy disagreements exist within any administration, and leaks may simply become outlets for those who wish to prolong the policy battle after their ideas and interpretations have lost out in the regular policy-making processes. Despite their operational experience and access to inside information, such individuals may be biased to promote particular causes, exaggerate their personal importance, or revise the historical record. With the explosive growth of the Internet, leaks (and, unfortunately, rumors) can be spread worldwide very rapidly. Staff members may use that capability to whipsaw their organizations over policy debates they have lost, and recipients face an ever-increasing volume of information to try to check.

Programmed Internal Government Reviews

Programmed internal reviews may provide systematic feedback on how well a particular agency or bureau functions. Such reviews may be thorough and objective, and be carried out either by auditing departments within the agencies themselves or by government examining agencies such as the Congressional Budget Office (CBO) and the General Accounting Office (GAO), both discussed in Chapter 6. In this latter case, reviews are still internal to the government, although participants well may view them as adversarial processes. CBO and GAO have built particularly strong reputations for their nonpartisanship and objectivity. The objectivity of internal audit departments may be more suspect, on grounds that they naturally want to promote the agency of which they are a part, and they are more subject to agency pressure than external reviewers.

More and bigger limitations exist in relying on programmed government reviews for policy feedback. It is far easier to test for compliance with procedures than to examine the soundness of the policies that led to establishing those procedures. There can never be enough internal reviews to locate every problem or abuse, and legitimate questions arise about the relative resources devoted to policy execution and policy checking. Consider the analogy to auditing individuals' tax returns: most returns receive only cursory checks unless those reveal problems because exhaustive checking of every return would cost more than it yielded in increased payments. However, these practices rest on the knowledge that most people in the United States are fairly law abiding about their taxes. Analogously, audits of government agencies start from the assumption that most officials and employees are trying to do what they perceive as right actions consistent with existing policies. Even in the best of circumstances, however, internal government reviews are too infrequent to provide a major and comprehensive source of feedback about policy effectiveness. Finally, reports of internal reviews may receive little public exposure, unless they are picked up by alert journalists or politicians.

Economic and Other Quantitative Reports and Indicators

Some activities lend themselves readily to quantitative (numeric) *indicators* or *figures of merit* that can be used to measure policy effectiveness. The best quantitative measures provide objective indications of policy impacts over time, which can be extremely valuable feedback. Some of these measures are so commonly used that they regularly appear in news reports. One example is the consumer price index (CPI), which measures inflation by comparing the current cost of a standard "basket" of necessities including food, clothing, and housing against what those goods cost at an earlier reference time. Another example, much simpler to compute, is the U.S. monthly international trade deficit, the amount by which total imports exceed total exports. (We leave the dangers of almost always running a trade deficit for consideration in Chapter 11.) If government policy correlates with slower growth in the CPI and lower international trade deficits, we are likely to consider those policies more successful than the policies in force during periods in which the CPI or the trade deficit rise—even if we cannot readily build a causal chain connecting a policy change to a shift in one of those indexes. Indicators of economic performance, trade, military strength, and so on, usually take considerable time to compile and refer to some particular past instant or period. Only a few indicators, such as major economic measures for the last month, quarter, or year, are available fairly rapidly.

Unfortunately, not all policies lend themselves to such easily countable measurement. If we consider it important to promote respect for the United States abroad, how is "respect" to be measured? Although it turns out that such indicators can be computed, the results often are complex enough to be better understood by academics than by politicians and members of the general public. We might measure international respect for the United States by developing a scheme for coding the statements and actions of diplomats and international leaders according to how much friendliness, policy cooperation, or hostility they express toward the United States, its government, and its people. An index combining and averaging such measures over some span of time could be compared from year to year to see whether this measure of "respect" rose or fell. Once this scheme was developed, we could use it to test how the United States was viewed by a single government, by all states in a region, or by the entire global polity.

Consider another nonobvious measure of policy effectiveness. Suppose we wanted to test the effectiveness of U.S. Middle East policy by asking whether there had been a reduction in the probability of a new war in that region. Scholars of international cooperation and conflict have assembled data on the international flows of armaments, the occurrence and severity of armed conflicts, and the conflictfulness or cooperativeness of international events over time. An "event" in this usage is any action taken by a government, an official, or other important international actors. Through the statistical process known as regression, such data sets allow us to estimate how much a certain rise in cooperative events or fall in arms transfers predicts a reduction in the probability of new war, relative to established historic behavior patterns globally or in a particular region. Unfortunately, neither our "international respect" measure nor such "probability of war" measures lends itself to a fifteen-second newscast sound bite or a two-sentence newspaper paragraph. Thus neither officials nor the general public are likely to pay much attention. These examples, therefore, identify two major problems of quantitative policy indicators: not everything of interest is readily countable, and not all good measures have sufficient political salience.

Political **salience** (which might be defined as political impact, noticeability, or effectiveness) often conflicts with soundness of measurement. During the Cold War years when the United States and the Soviet Union mutually feared (usually at some very low level of expectation) a devastating strategic nuclear missile exchange, great political significance was attached to notions of the strategic nuclear "balance" between the superpowers. One crude but popular measure was to compare how many nuclear-tipped missiles the two sides had. A better comparative measure was the relative numbers of nuclear missile warheads, the actual explosive devices deliverable. Yet the number of missiles plus intercontinental bombers was so simple, readily countable, and politically salient that, when ratifying the 1972 SALT I Strategic Arms Limitation Treaty, Congress required that all future agreements include numerically balanced ceilings. In actuality, that requirement failed to take account of the facts that the Soviets had more intercontinental missiles but far fewer bombers than the United States, and the Soviets had larger missiles capable of carrying more warheads. The most accurate strategic balance measures are outcome or effects measures that state how much damage of what types could be done in a particular type of attack. The complexity of such measures, however, reduces their political salience. The most thorough nuclear exchange models require lengthy runs on very large computers, and the details behind their assumptions probably are fully understood only by people working with them full time. Even so, by late in the Carter administration, the annual posture statement by the secretary of defense assigned major importance to an effect measure of how many intercontinental missile warheads each superpower would expect to have after riding out a "first strike" sneak attack (Brown, 1980, 87).

A further problem of quantitative policy indicators is that activities easiest to count tend to be examined more fully than activities that do not lend themselves readily to counting. In any quantitative measure of policy effectiveness, the devil truly lies in the details. To be able to make good use of such measures over time to test for policy effectiveness, we must always ask what assumptions underlie the measure. If we are willing to take the time and trouble, we often can design measures that really tell us what we want to know about policy impacts.

POST HOC FEEDBACK

Post hoc or after-the-fact feedback becomes available only well after the relevant events have transpired, but still helps us to assess the quality of policy making and the effectiveness of policies adopted, and to suggest changes for the future. Five post hoc data sources are examined in this section. All information from these sources is in the public domain.

1. *Officials'* and other insider *memoirs* are often biased and self-serving, frequently being written years after the events. Some, however, appear quite soon after the authors leave office. For example, General H. Norman Schwarzkopf's autobiography was published in October 1992, barely a year after he retired from the army and nineteen months after he directed the Persian Gulf land war.

2. *Historical studies* may cover a considerable span of time or compare the handling of different policy problems.

3. *Case studies* feature in-depth examination of particular policy problems or periods, although neither type appears until years after the events examined. Relevant documents and interview opportunities seldom are available immediately, and researchers need time to locate and study documents, conduct interviews, and evaluate and integrate the information obtained.

4. *Declassified documents*, often vital to historical research, only become available years or even decades after their composition. Included are formerly secret or classified information made public through "sunset" or freedom-of-information laws.

5. Finally, trials and other *legal proceedings* may reveal seldom seen parts of the policy process and enforce public accountability on officials.

Information from each of these sources may provide valuable insights into problems and successes of policy making, yet each is subject to major limitations. By the time documents and studies become available, the international situation and perhaps even our policy-making structure may have changed so fundamentally that the lessons of the past no longer apply. Coverage is inevitably spotty, so the cases about which we gain newly detailed information may have little in common with our most pressing current international problems. Finally, all post hoc feedback is subject to severe biases on the part of officials and individual historians, and currently popular views among scholars, who regularly go through waves of fashion in reinterpreting the lessons of the past.

Officials' Memoirs

Memoirs written by retired officials or by in-and-outers during their "out" periods offer the promise of insider information about how policy was made and executed, both in general and in particular crises or cases of interest. Their "you are there" quality may be entrancing and absorbing. They may help motivate and inspire future leaders. Such reports may yield details unavailable through any other channel about actions, motivations, the sequence of idea formulation and revision, personal interactions among officials, and their responses. Because of that uniqueness, we are almost forced to make some use of official memoirs if we are to gain a comprehensive picture of the ways in which policy is formulated and executed. Yet, as sources of policy feedback, officials' memoirs are plagued by severe difficulties.

Memoirs are timed for the convenience of authors, appearing in print months to decades after the events described, and always after the authors have left office. The timing of General H. Norman Schwarzkopf's autobiography, for example, appeared calculated both to promote the general's political prospects and to capitalize on his wartime experience before it faded too much from public memory. In great contrast, the Vietnam War memoirs of Secretary of Defense Robert McNamara, discussed earlier, appeared fully 20 years after the fall of South Vietnam, and 27 years after McNamara left office. Memoirs of in-and-outers who aspire to higher office may be particularly self-serving. Consider, for example, the 1998 publication of Richard Holbrooke's memoir on Bosnia, entitled *To End a War*. Holbrooke, architect of the 1995 Dayton peace accords for Bosnia, was well known in Washington as an extremely effective diplomat, tough, hard to deal with, shamelessly self-promoting, and a leading contender to be a Democratic secretary of state someday. His book was praised for its account of "how Clinton was dragged [by Holbrooke] into exerting leadership on Bosnia," and is unflattering about foreign policy making at the highest levels of the Clinton administration (see Hoagland, 1998).

When two or more former officials disagree in their memoirs about what happened or why, there are generally no cross checks for accuracy. How are we to decide which author is more truthful, and whether any such writer is entirely honest? Retired officials are subject to fully understandable temptations to present versions of the historical record that emphasize the importance of their contributions and the correctness and ultimate superiority of their personal policy visions. Over the two decades after he resigned the presidency in disgrace in 1974, Richard Nixon wrote a number of books in which he not only presented his analyses of world politics, but sought to revise history's view of his accomplishments. When disputes arise over what really happened in some previous administration, many of the participants will be conveniently dead. These difficulties lead to arguments that may endure among historians for centuries; yet we still examine officials' memoirs for clues unavailable through any other source.

Historical and Case Studies

Historical and case studies provide unique types of feedback, best suited to evaluating specific ways of organizing to make decisions, or helping us avoid repeating past mistakes if similar situations arise in future. Of course, whether new situations are fundamentally similar to past experiences is always open to debate. Historical studies may cover policy developments regarding a particular activity, such as the globalization of economics, over a considerable span of time. Alternatively, they might concern overall U.S. foreign relations with a single region, such as the Middle East. Comparative historical studies might contrast policy relations with two or more different states, for example, to determine why in 1997 the United States supported NATO membership for the Czech Republic, Hungary, and Poland, but not for other Eastern European states. Case studies generally involve detailed examination of a single problem, state, or time point.

Consider one particularly important comparative policy study. In his classic 1972 book, *Victims of Groupthink*, Irving L. Janis contrasted how the Kennedy administration organized itself for top-level decision making in the disastrous 1961 Bay of Pigs Cuban invasion and the far more successful 1962 Cuban missile crisis. In the first case, Janis's introduction to Chapter 5 described how U.S.-trained anti-Castro Cuban exiles invaded their homeland in April 1961, only to find that the Cuban people rallied against the invasion rather than against Castro's government. Denied promised U.S. air cover, the invaders were ignominiously defeated, imprisoned, and eventually ransomed back. Janis cites this as an example of groupthink, under which officials eager to make a decision uncritically accepted the first plausible option raised. The incoming Kennedy team had accepted and carried forward operational plans prepared by the CIA under the Eisenhower administration, without subjecting those plans to any serious reexamination. No doubt influenced by that failure, they took a very different organizational approach to the 1962 missile crisis. Kennedy directed a secret ad hoc Executive Committee of the National Security Council (dubbed the ExComm) that brought together top officials and area specialists while largely ignoring bureaucratic lines of command. To help avoid groupthink, the president gave the ExComm tasks and then deliberately left its meetings, to prevent biasing their discussions by his reactions to the options raised.

As sources of policy feedback, historical and case studies remain subject to severe limitations. Except for what we may ourselves undertake, we have little or no influence on which cases are examined or how long after the events occurred. Vital information may remain unavailable for decades after the events of interest. Unconventional ideas may face serious barriers to acceptance and publication because historians and political scientists go through waves of currently fashionable thought. Historical and case studies are unlikely ever to provide comprehensive coverage; but their greatest limitation as sources of policy feedback is insufficient timeliness.

Declassified Official Documents

All governments restrict access to some information they classify as secret, hoping to keep others from learning either what they are planning or how much they know about the plans of those others. Great Britain's 1911 Official Secrets Act even makes it a crime to *receive* information if reasonable grounds exist to believe the information being communicated is unauthorized (Plamondon, 1994, 46). In the United States, there are many levels of security classification according to information's importance and sensitivity. Elaborate procedures are in place for investigating and "clearing" individuals for access at different levels, and for the secure storage of classified data. Access to such information requires not only the proper level of clearance, but also a "need to know" specific facts.

Critics of this system raise many arguments. It is too easy for officials to err on the side of excessive classification. Even collections of open-literature data have been classified, on the ground that collectors with access to classified information would select only the best unclassified data. During the early years of the Cold War, and particularly during the McCarthy era of the 1950s when many people feared government subversion by domestic communists, security classification ran rampant. In more recent years, substantial amounts of older classified information have been declassified and released. One notable instance was the 1975 release of the crucial 1950 defense strategy plan, NSC-68, as discussed in Chapter 2. Security classification tends to inhibit innovation because if one does not know a piece of information exists, one can never make a crucial connection between that datum and other facts at hand. In policy circles, access to classified data is a sign that one is connected and influential. In conducting one study of arms control negotiations, the author found that officials believe that persons with access to classified data would reject the use of open-literature data, even when comparisons showed only minor differences.

Releases of once classified information can be valuable resources in evaluating past policy making and policy execution. The key drawbacks are that such releases concern only the past and may be highly selective. Many governments keep some information classified for up to fifty years after the events covered, almost guaranteeing that key decision makers will be deceased before any embarrassing revelations reach publication. In the United States, some information can be gained through the Freedom of Information Act, although that information is still subject to government censorship before release. These channels for gaining information are important tools for historians, but as sources of policy feedback are subject to all the constraints affecting historical and case studies.

Consider the possible utility of the **Freedom of Information Act (FOIA)** to persons seeking information about previously secret government actions. Originally passed in 1966, the act rests on the presumption that open governance and widespread access to information are in the public interest. Government agencies are required to make information available on request unless it falls within one or more of nine stated exempt categories, and may choose to release records even though they are covered by an exemption. The first exemption, however, is national security, covering documents classified pursuant to a presidential executive order. Other exemptions that might limit access to information of interest to scholars and citizens interested in foreign policy making cover personnel rules that are predominantly internal in nature, and internal memoranda that would convey information about an agency's decision-making process (but not the factual contents of documents concerning how some particular decision was made). Agencies are required to respond to an initial request within ten working days and to an appeal within twenty working days, although delays are common (*The Quill*, 1991). Over the decades since the FOIA's passage, thousands of court cases have refined its interpretation. Following a 1973 Supreme Court case concerning an agency refusal to release documents on the ground that they were classified, Congress amended the act to allow a district court judge to review requested documents *in camera* (privately) to determine whether they are properly classified. As one reviewer concluded, "If any trend in the litigation under the FOIA can be discerned, it seems to favor restricting rather than freeing information. Decisions affirm that there is no constitutional right to know involved, rather the availability of information is a matter of legislative discretion" (Plamondon, 1994, 60).

Perhaps the greatest limitation on using the FOIA is a variant on the old saying that to ask a reasonable question one must know half the answer. Requesters must "reasonably describe" the records sought in sufficient detail that a government employee can locate them. The Electronic Freedom of Information Act Amendments of 1996 (E-FOIA, 1996) extended rights of access to electronic records. As computer capabilities mushroom and more and more organizations eschew printed materials in favor of CD-ROMs, this already is becoming an important access channel. The Clinton administration moved rapidly to declassify substantial amounts of material, notably including Energy Department materials on nuclear weapons programs. Although fascinating to historians and activists, however, many declassified documents are decades old, and likely to have only the most limited bearing on present policies. This feedback channel is subject to all the constraints affecting historical and case studies.

Legal Proceedings

Fairly rarely, but more frequently than a generation ago, trials and other legal proceedings reveal seldom seen parts of the policy process and enforce public accountability on officials. Motions to produce or suppress specific information may be argued, sometimes raising issues of executive privilege, the constitutional doctrine that a president is entitled to strictly confidential consultations with close advisers (see Chapter 4). More rarely, former officials may be tried for crimes committed while in office. In either case, judicial proceedings become a feedback channel to the public and the policy establishment about policy itself and, more significantly, abuses of the policy process. Information thus revealed may lead to significant changes, although debates regularly ensue about whether they are improvements. Such legal proceedings offer only occasional glimpses into parts of the policy process. Trials often occur only years after the events and may drag on through appeals for additional years. Choices to undertake either motions or trials are highly political.

Consider, for example, the Iran-contra case, which arose during the Reagan administration (see Chapter 6 for details). Two years after the scandal first broke in 1986, Judge Gerhard Gessell ruled on several motions regarding the case against former NSC staffer Colonel Oliver North. North's indictment for lying to Congress during its investigation of the affair was allowed to stand. He had argued that, because he was doing what President Reagan wanted and the president is the chief foreign policy official, he was immune from prosecution. Judge Gessell ruled that the president could have ordered North not to testify, claiming executive privilege. But he did not, so North could be tried for lying to Congress. Additionally, because North violated a law—signed by the president—prohibiting aid to the contras at that time, he could be tried for that violation. Ultimately, North was convicted of lying to Congress, but his conviction was overturned on appeal because of immunity agreements concerning his congressional testimony. He went on to become a popular speaker for conservative causes and made an unsuccessful run for the U.S. Senate from Virginia.

USING FEEDBACK TO ASSESS OVERALL POLICY SUCCESS

On balance, how much help do the different feedback sources provide in assessing policy processes and policy success, and in revising policies to approach more closely the goals sought? Whether this question is posed about feedback that is inherently part of the policy process or about sources by which both officials and members of the general public may judge the overall effectiveness of foreign policy, three great limitations apply. First, neither any single source, nor all of them in combination, necessarily provide comprehensive coverage of all the information that should be assessed. Second, only real-time feedback is relatively prompt, and then only if everything works as it should. Finally, no matter what the source of information, we must always be on guard against bias.

These limitations recall the "imaginary ideal machine for making policy" (IIMMP) that John Lovell (1985, Chapter 2) devised as a thought experiment to demonstrate how far reality falls short of ideal capabilities. Lovell's hypothetical IIMMP was perfect and comprehensive in detecting problems, instantaneous and undistorted in transmitting information, and able to use feedback for instantaneous self-correction. In reality, of course, Lovell noted that human limitations in foreign policy decision making lead to spotty coverage and fragmentary detection of problems; bias and rigidity in coding of information; delay, distortion, and lost information in transmission; and thus to feedback that is imperfect in detection and correction of errors. In the less-than-perfect real world, we may decide the Kennedy administration did well to learn as much at it did from its 1961 Bay of Pigs invasion mistakes by the time of the 1962 Cuban missile crisis.

Many cross checks are possible between different feedback sources, but essentially no absolute standards of truth are available. We must always beware of being taken in by a falsehood or incomplete truth that attracts us, either because of what it asserts or who makes the claim. We may have greater confidence in some authorities than others, or in alleged "facts" asserted by more than one source. Yet a system in which high officials have been demonstrated to lie publicly tends to produce at least some paranoia in the best of us. Each of us, whether an official or an ordinary citizen, must somehow reach a balance between trust and wariness in interpreting the available information.

Similar problems affect both government and private users of policy feedback. Even the most objective evaluation research about foreign policy takes place within an inevitable political context. The policies being evaluated are legislative and bureaucratic decisions resulting from a complex intermestic political process involving all the actors discussed in Chapter 4. Feedback generated by policy evaluation must compete for political attention like any other decision input. Incremental policy changes complicate the evaluation process because effects are best judged when policies are stable over long periods. Evaluations are usually commissioned by officials of the agency under study. They may deliberately bias the information they give evaluators in hopes of obtaining desired conclusions. Additionally, officials often are free to bury the resulting report, and can always put their spin on any release to the public or Congress. The political sensitivities of program managers may reduce their receptivity toward any evaluation and limit their cooperation with study procedures. In the end, they may dismiss evaluators' findings as inconclusive and deny any need to act on them. Typically, the legitimacy of official program goals and strategies is assumed, as are long-term strategies of incremental reform. Evaluators often gear their recommendations to what appears reasonable and feasible for the agency. When social scientists participate as outside consultants in evaluations, they hold important but often unexamined views about their appropriate role in designing and revising programs, and about the results likely to be achieved. Significant widespread assumptions within the program evaluation community include the following: (1) Prescribed reforms will improve performance through incremental changes and without requiring any drastic restructuring. (2) Decision makers will heed the evaluators' evidence and will act on it. Unfortunately, the experience of recent decades suggests that both assumptions are wrong.

Less widely realized is the complication that evaluation, by its nature and assumptions, makes implicit political statements. Although the origins of program evaluation are reformist, its political implications tend toward pro-establishment orientations. Some policies and programs are assumed to be problematic and, thus, suitable subjects for study, although the conventional wisdom holds others to be unchallengeable. Programs subjected to serious evaluations most often are new, expanding, and lack powerful established constituencies. Interestingly, one Government Accounting Office study found the ratio of numbers of evaluative studies to budget size among federal departments to be highest for the State Department and lowest for the Department of Defense, almost inverse to budget size (Starling, 1984, 290).

The nature, major strengths, and major weaknesses of the twenty-one classes of feedback examined in this chapter are summarized in Table 7.2. Important distinctions should be made regarding the users and availability of those different classes of feedback. Only real-time feedback is widely available for rapid use in policy processes, and it is directly available primarily to zone 1 and 2 actors involved in policy making and policy execution. Wider public availability of such information comes only through indirect channels and may be considerably delayed. Journalists, for example, may write about information that the directly involved actors choose to release. Pundits may write in hopes of changing current policy, either by directly influencing decision makers or through indirect channels like public opinion, Congress, or the bureaucracy. In general, the longer the time a feedback channel requires, the more its use tends toward revising the foreign policy system and processes, rather than toward revising any one specific policy. Even some intermediate-time feedback, such as congressional oversight, is directly available only to official participants. However, most intermediate-time feedback and all post hoc feedback is almost equally available to everyone, including citizens informed enough to seek it. Yet real-time feedback is most likely to be comprehensive, and we cannot be certain that all the details of foreign policy making will ever become public.

SUMMARY

In this chapter we examined how different types of feedback enter into the foreign policy process. This includes (1) how government agencies and officials may use feedback to help evaluate the degree of success and revise policies to more completely achieve desired goals, and (2) how citizens may use feedback information channels to evaluate how well

Time Frame and Source	Nature of Feedback	Major Strengths	Major Weaknesses
Real Time			
Intelligence gathering	Impact of policies on targets	Measures effects; comprehensive; ongoing	Never *entirely* timely, complete, precise, accurate, relevant for action, and unbiased
Official interviews, speeches, and writings	Public information about current policy; commentaries that are part of the policy debate; comments given "on background"	Timely; expose part of the policy process; involve citizenry	Not comprehensive; background comments are anonymous and may be biased and self-serving
Diplomatic exchanges	Signals about other actors' concerns, wishes, and intentions	Ongoing; timely; broad coverage	Rarely complete or totally honest; require great caution; may require clarifications
Negotiations	Responses of others to our proposals and positions	Feedback is inherent in the negotiation process, and essential to it	Limited substantive coverage; rarely completely honest; interpretation is vital
Top-level or summit meetings	Messages from top leaders; views of ultimate decision makers	Views of top leaders; personal ties; rare breakthroughs	Infrequent; limited agendas; great care and clarity required
Monitoring of public opinion	Opinion polling about current policy and policymakers by news media, politicians, other actors	Timely; arguably democratic; potential to improve policy responsiveness; intermestic	Prone to stimulating overreactions, making policy erratic
Intermediate Time			
Treaties and legislation	Published U.S. commitments	Establish standards for part of U.S. foreign policy conduct; publicly available	Shows only part of formal policy; shows nothing of informal and secret policies
Congressional oversight	Congress reviews executive actions; checks and balances	Increases accountability; may make information public	Ethical dilemmas of secrecy versus larger duties; questions about full information, coopting
Trial balloons	Information to policymakers about likely reactions by public, others to possible policies	Precommitment feedback	Can only be used infrequently; may actually signal vacillation
Investigative journalism	Information about policy failures, hidden aspects and problems of policy	Essential check on government; often very timely	Political biases; spotty coverage; political coopting by sources

(continued)

Time Frame and Source	Nature of Feedback	Major Strengths	Major Weaknesses
Think tanks	Alternative policies and procedures; reviews	Policy expertise; experience; specialization	Ideological biases; special interests
Interest and watchdog groups	Supervision and investigation of selected activities	Expertise; specialization; inside ties to influence	Limited focus and coverage; isolation of insiders; institutionalization of errors
Leaks	Inside information about problems with policies in force or under consideration	Inside information, operational experience	Biases, special interests; unpredictable coverage
Whistle-blowers	Inside information about problems or illegalities with policies in force or under consideration	Inside information, operational experience	Biases, self-glorification, causes to promote; unpredictable coverage
Programmed internal government reviews	Systematic review of an agency, bureau, or function	Thoroughness, objectivity	Limited frequency; biases toward minimal change
Economic and other quantitative reports and indicators	Quantitative indexes of policy effects	Ongoing time series; can provide objective measures of effects	Limited number of measures; not all activities measured; aggregation hides some problems; not all good measures are politically salient
Post Hoc			
Officials' memoirs	Policy and procedural review and recommendations	Inside information on process; operational experience	Biases, self-glorification, causes to promote
Historical studies	Policy and procedural review, possibly with recommendations	Long-term view; may be comparative	Slow, spotty coverage, post hoc
Case studies	Policy and procedural review, possibly with recommendations	In-depth examination	Slow, spotty coverage, post hoc
Declassified documents	Details of past policy making and policy execution	Inside information; crucial decision documents	Only available long after the events; unpredictable coverage
Legal proceedings	Motions to produce or suppress information; trials for violations of law	Publicize seldom seen parts of the policy process; enforce public accountability	Far from comprehensive: Choices are highly political: may occur years later

government officials, procedures, and policies succeed. Such evaluative uses of feedback are more important today than ever because the United States confronts foreign policy problems dramatically different from those faced during the Cold War era, although policy-making institutions and processes continue to evolve only slowly.

Evaluating success and revising policy closes the loop in the foreign policy system conceptually diagrammed in earlier chapters as a purposive control system. Feedback correctly used can help us evaluate and improve not only specific policies, but the policy-making process itself. The three major sections of this chapter devoted to the policy feedback process cover (1) where citizens, government officials, and other actors in the foreign policy process may locate current U.S. foreign policy; (2) the various types, uses, and limitations of foreign policy feedback in correcting and improving policy; and (3) how different types of feedback may be used by officials and citizens in assessing overall policy success.

Current foreign policies are not nearly so conveniently compiled as the law. Foreign policy is derived partly, like law, from legislation, case law, and administrative regulation, but determining foreign policy is considerably more of a political process. Current foreign policy may be revealed in many different ways. Qualified officials announce and refine policy through interviews, speeches, and writing. They may speak with journalists on background.

Policy is revealed less frequently today by what policymakers write than by what they say, an effect encouraged by the ease and speed of modern transportation and electronic communications media. Treaties and legislation are undeniable written expressions of policy. Morcover, the legislative process of hearings and debates generates voluminous and detailed records of policy alternatives and the ways in which details are settled. No matter what is said or written, actions conclusively demonstrate operational policy. From time to time, policy is implied through tacit bargaining, that is, actions taken that demonstrate what is desired and intended, without formal announcements or negotiations. Policymakers' memoirs seldom are available quickly enough to give much information about current policy, although they may be mines of information about processes and infighting over previous policy development.

Some use of feedback always inheres in foreign policy processes. Utilizing feedback means using detected and evaluated information about the results of present policy to help control the results and achieve desired outcomes. Scholars of the systems approach discussed in Chapter 4 have characterized the requisites of direct control of policy as follows: Directing or guiding is the process of goal setting and policy determination. Detecting or evaluating is the process of measuring the results achieved. Effecting or controlling is the process of adjusting and revising policy to more closely approach targeted outcomes. Controlling foreign policy and evaluating its success are subject to several large problems, including the sheer size and complexity of the system and the absence of commonly accepted measures of success and failure. Although private sector programs often are evaluated according to their profitability, the public sector lacks any readily corresponding criterion of success. Instead, the foreign policy arena regularly sees intense political arguments over conflicting policy choice criteria.

One of many ways to classify different types of feedback is according to the speed with which they make information available. Real-time feedback is built into the policy process so that information about the effects of policy becomes available immediately, even as policy is being decided and implemented. For example, immediate use of intelligence and diplomatic massages is an important part of the policy-making process. Real-time feedback occurs across the entire range of policies, making information directly available primarily to zone 1 and 2 actors involved in making and carrying out policy. Such information enters the public domain only indirectly through media activities and later releases through other channels.

Information takes days, weeks, or months to become available through intermediate-time feedback. Still, information often is at hand before policies have been completely determined, and may be available quickly enough to influence current policies before they have been fully implemented. The most significant channels of intermediate-time feedback are treaties and legislation; public and secret congressional oversight procedures; investigative journalism; and economic and other performance indicators.

Post hoc (or "after-the-fact") feedback becomes available only well after the relevant events have transpired, but still helps us to assess the quality of policy making and the effectiveness of policies adopted, and to suggest changes for the future. All such information is in the public domain. Notable examples include officials' and other insider memoirs, historical studies, and declassified documents.

Each type of policy feedback has serious problems, which may be summarized in three great limitations. First, neither any one source, nor all of them in combination, necessarily provides comprehensive coverage of all information that should be assessed. Second, only real-time feedback is relatively prompt, and then only if everything works as it should. Third, we must always be on guard against bias, in any source of information. Human limitations in foreign policy decision making lead to spotty coverage and fragmentary detection of problems; bias and rigidity in coding of information; delay, distortion, and lost information in transmission; and thus to feedback that is imperfect in detection and correction of errors. Although many cross checks are possible between different feedback sources, we have essentially no absolute standards of truth. Despite all the channels through which feedback eventually becomes public knowledge, we cannot be certain that all the details of foreign policy making will ever come out.

KEY TERMS

Background	Failed state
Black programs	Freedom of Information Act (FOIA)
Congressional oversight	Intermediate-time feedback (Compare with
Detecting or evaluating (Compare with	*real-time feedback* and *post hoc feedback*.)
directing or guiding and *effecting or*	Post hoc (or after-the-fact) feedback
controlling.)	Real-time feedback
Directing or guiding	Salience
Effecting or controlling	Tacit bargaining
Exit strategy	Trial balloons

SELECTED READINGS

Acheson, Dean. 1969. *Present at the Creation.* New York: W. W. Norton. As secretary of state (1949–52) under President Truman, Acheson played a key role in the development of containment policy.

Fromkin, David. 1995. *In the Time of the Americans: FDR, Truman, Eisenhower, Marshall, MacArthur —The Generation That Changed America's Role in the World*. New York: Knopf.

Holbrooke, Richard. 1998. *To End a War*. New York: Random House. The inside story of the 1995 Dayton peace accords for Bosnia, by their chief architect, who is also a very savvy political self-promoter and a notable in-and-outer.

Hoopes, Townsend. 1969. *The Limits of Intervention: An Inside Account of How the Johnson Policy of Escalation in Vietnam Was Reversed*. New York: D. McKay Company.

Moynihan, Daniel Patrick. 1998. *Secrecy: The American Experience*. New Haven: Yale University Press. In his fourth term, Senator Moynihan suggested that CIA failures to predict the end of the Cold War and the breakup of the Soviet Union were grounds for abolishing the agency. As bureaucratic politics would lead us to expect, that idea gained little resonance with either the public or Congress. In this book Moynihan argues that compartmentalization of secret information within U.S. government departments intensified the Cold War and raised its costs for the United States.

TOOLS OF POLICY

If you were a policymaker, what would you recommend in a foreign policy crisis? What would you do differently in a noncrisis situation? As seen in Chapter 5, decision makers tend to perceive their environment and options differently and to behave quite differently in crises. Limited decision time is part of our definition of crisis, but it is only one among many constraints upon decision makers. According to the unitary government model, policy action is a choice from among available alternatives, and availability is an overriding constraint. Differences in resources, planning, and investment, cause some governments to have more options than others, and any government will have different options at different times. The organizational process model points out how our alternatives as circumscribed by organizational programs, repertoires, and standard operating procedures, essentially the set of actions already planned and prepared for. The governmental politics model adds still more constraints upon policy decision, based on the personalities, goals, and past experiences of government officials.

In Part I we examined the *setting* of U.S. foreign policy in its domestic and global contexts. In Part II we examined the *processes* by which U.S. foreign policy is made and some of the ways in which limitations within those processes may produce policy failures. Part III (Chapters 8–12) adds detail to the policy process by examining the tremendous range of options available to the U.S. government, other governments, and important nongovernmental actors. These are the *tools of policy*.

Every selection made must appear on the great menu of conceivable choices. Not every option will be equally desirable for economic, moral, operational, or political reasons. Not every alternative will be equally feasible. Still, recognizing every option and including it on the menu reduces the chance that a good possibility may be overlooked, and thereby increases the probability of effective policy choice. Typical policies are complex because they involve the use of many tools in combination and, frequently, in stages over time. Goals can be pursued through many means, and policies often call for escalating the intensity of action over time until desired results are achieved. Effective policy must be credible to all parties and must be planned in light of the probable responses of other actors. Outcomes almost can never be guaranteed. Power and influence have dynamic as well as static aspects, and many policy options are critically affected by timing. Although we may speak of diplomatic, economic, and military tools of policy, and each may be employed toward political ends, these classes overlap severely.

Given that the nature of world politics is still largely state-centric, there is some emphasis in these chapters on tools that are available to the governments of states. Nonetheless, important nonstate actors also are considered, including regional trading blocs, cartels, the international monetary system, along with interstate and international economic, functional, political, and security organizations, and international regimes. Given how dramatically the foreign policy problems now confronting the United States differ in number, character, and possible solutions from the problems faced during the Cold War era, we should expect important changes in the importance and potential usefulness of different types of power.

Concerns about the menu of policy tools are not simply abstract. Consider the Persian Gulf War case from Chapter 1. Some options were fairly quickly available to the United States, including official statements condemning the Iraqi invasion of Kuwait, diplomatic consultations with other governments directly and through the United Nations, economic sanctions against Iraq, and shows of military force. Many other important options were not immediately available. Coalition actions required time to explore other governments' concerns and organize agreements. Major military actions required considerable time to move forces into place, train them, and develop detailed operational procedures. Among important constraints on U.S. action were the time required to organize a coalition, the time to mobilize and apply military force, and the need to solicit contributions toward the enormous expense of military operations. Moreover, that last constraint is itself a reflection of two broader and constraining long-term global developments: increasing economic interdependence and decreasing U.S. dominance. In Part III we examine not only the menu of policy tools, but also how different policy instruments apply to notable historical and contemporary policy problems and to the problems often associated with using those policy tools.

Policy options and constraints on their use are concerns not only for government officials, but for interested citizens. Both groups need to understand the boundaries of what is *possible* before they can accurately assess foreign policy *effectiveness*. Knowing the broad and detailed menu of options helps us determine whether decision makers have failed to recognize a potentially valuable action. Discerning the nature and variety of constraints helps us realize why certain actions occur often and others only rarely and why some events proceed rapidly but others slowly. Normative concerns often lead us to believe the United States should pursue certain goals abroad or that some means of pursuing those goals are acceptable but other means should be proscribed. If we plan to measure the actions of officials, programs, agencies, and administrations against such criteria, we owe them an informed understanding of the limitations under which they have selected options and designed their policies. Understanding the available tools of policy is vital to strengthening our own capabilities for comprehending and appreciating past and present policies, to imagine more appropriate and more effective policies for the future, and to strengthen our own predictive aptitudes.

In Chapter 8 the attributes that make states (and nonstate actors) powerful are classified as either (1) natural—those things one has by accident of location, such as a rich resource endowment or a protective geography, or (2) synthetic—those things one acquires by policy choice, such as a large army, a developed economy, or a loyal voting bloc in intergovernmental organizations.

Social-psychological aspects, such as charismatic leadership or the political allegiance of allies and citizens, is an important subgroup of synthetic power attributes. Both actual and potential power must be considered, taking into account conversion and mobilization potential as well as existing forces. The U.S. role in World War II provides an important example. Power includes, but goes far beyond, military force. Beyond the ability to prevail in military and diplomatic conflicts and to overcome obstacles, power includes the ability to influence others and to alter the probable outcomes of policy interactions. Power in its many aspects can be used to assist or to oppose, coerce, or deny the goals that opponents seek. Usable power of virtually every variety tends to decline with distance from one's homeland, although the decline is not so great for nuclear weaponry. Extrapolations of the Persian Gulf War example (see Chapter 1) include the following:

- Force is usable only when rapidly available.
- Unmobilized force can be nothing more than a threat.
- Threat only works if it is both credible and perceived as credible.

Chapter 9 begins from the premise that security is far more than military in character. Security involves both the physical state or condition of *being* secure and the psychological perception of *feeling* secure. It inherently involves economic, political, societal, and environmental aspects as well as the more traditional military concerns. Since the 1970s, and particularly since the end of the Cold War, security increasingly has come to be seen as international rather than just national in scope. The post–Cold War international threat environment includes such problems as linked state and international economic disruptions, environmental cleanup, "leakage" of nuclear weapons and technology from former Soviet states, and the proliferation of weapons of mass destruction to additional, and possibly rogue, states. The concept and pursuit of security are surrounded and permeated by many dilemmas, apparent contradictions, and inherent and unavoidable clashes of interest. A number of such dilemmas concerning security in general and deterrence in particular are examined. For example, actions taken in search of any form of security—military or otherwise—actually may imperil it or another form of security. One instance would be that arming to meet every possible challenge may lead to bankruptcy. Military instruments of policy today include unconventional means such as covert operations, coercive diplomacy, and low-intensity conflicts, as well as more conventional warfare, police, and collective security operations. The inducements, uses, and difficulties of arms transfers (sales, aid, and gifts) are considered, as are the growing problems of rising levels of military technology in developing states and the recent tremendous growth in licensed production of modern weaponry. We examine cross pressures inherent in institutionalized arms control; the same major powers that seek to limit the "horizontal" proliferation of nuclear and other high-technology capabilities seek expanded markets for many of those same capabilities, thereby promoting regional proliferation. Ironically, the end of the Cold War and the virtual disappearance of fears about a superpower nuclear exchange have left a new world disorder in which small and regional conflicts are increasingly likely.

Chapter 10 introduces procedures and practices for diplomacy that are interpreted as important channels for international communication and bargaining. We give particular emphasis to the processes, procedures, and mechanisms available to the United States.

Negotiations consist of three stages: preliminary contacts about negotiating, development of procedures, and substantive bargaining. Bargaining tactics are considered in detail. Possible outcomes of negotiation include failure, continuation, tacit agreements, treaties, executive agreements, and more complex combinations. Negotiations are examined as multilevel processes in which intergovernmental talks may occur at several levels. Usually they are accompanied by position-setting bargaining within each government, and between the negotiators and their home governments over the details of negotiating positions. Examples are drawn from major arms control negotiations. We examine trends in negotiations, including the increase in numbers of executive agreements, mainly on functional matters; summit meetings and shuttle diplomacy, facilitated by rapid transportation; and the difficulty in keeping negotiations secret, given the encouragement of leaks by modern communications media.

Chapter 11 is devoted to the intermestic politics of economic issues, the broad area in which politics and economics intersect, commonly called international political economics. The chapters opens with the debate over whether the United States is in decline relative to other world powers, examined in light of the impact of economic globalization on national economies and national futures. The emerging world economy rewards different groups of individuals very differently, both in the United States and abroad, depending on whether their skills are globally competitive. Connections are made to issues crucial to developing states and to the mobilization of economies (see Chapter 8). Major international political economic (IPE) developments since World War II examined in this chapter include the growing role of the state, the increasing globalization of economics, and the consequent increase of international penetration into the economies of individual states. The United States is not immune from these effects. We examine reasons for the decline of U.S. political-economic hegemony, including America's "twin deficits" in the federal budget and in international trade. Economic "tiers" and the older but still frequently used terminology for classifying levels of development are discussed. We explore theories and problems of global trade, including comparative advantage, single-product economies, neocolonialism and dependency, tariffs and other forms of protectionism, multinational corporations, and regional trading blocs and cartels. The development of the contemporary system of international monetary exchange is described, as are some of its difficulties, including global debt and the special difficulties of states such as Mexico that struggle to service large foreign debts while attempting to confront major fluctuations in foreign trade and exchange rates.

In Chapter 12 we address how increasing global interdependence has encouraged the development of interstate and international economic, functional, political, and security organizations. All international activity that involves the U.S. government and its citizens in collaboration with other international actors, such as intergovernmental organizations, international nongovernmental organizations, and international regimes, is collective action. Consequently, it is subject to all the dilemmas and difficulties of collective action that are widely studied by political scientists. Chapter 12 examines the processes, perspectives, and prospects of the many different types of international collective action organizations with which the government and citizens of the United States work. We place special emphasis on how they interact with the United States and how they may be used as tools of policy by the government, by citizens, and by other major actors within the political system. Three major types are examined in depth, with contemporary cases:

1. The members of intergovernmental organizations (IGOs) are governments of states, and different IGOs deal with economic, functional, political, and security problems.
2. International regimes combine law, regulation, and the actions of interstate and international organizations and individual state governments to create international norms. They thereby influence and manage selected behaviors. Regimes may be created at the urging of particular governments or by the joint action of many governments under the auspices of an IGO, as seen in the UN Framework Convention on Climate Change.
3. International nongovernmental organizations (NGOs) bring groups of individuals, businesses, and other organizations together across government lines to pursue common interests. They often lobby and may even take stands against particular governments.

CHAPTER 8

POWER AND INFLUENCE: A MULTIFACETED INTERPRETATION OF TRADITIONAL POLITICAL CONCEPTS

WHY THE ARAFAT-RABIN HANDSHAKE OCCURRED AT THE WHITE HOUSE

On 13 September 1993, in a ceremony televised worldwide from the south lawn of the White House in Washington, D.C., Palestine Liberation Organization (PLO) chairman Yasir Arafat and Israeli prime minister Yitzhak Rabin signed an historic peace agreement. Their accord provided for limited Palestinian autonomy in the Gaza Strip and Jericho, the latter lying within the Israeli-occupied West Bank territories. It established procedures and timetables for further Israeli withdrawals and for working out the remaining unresolved peace issues. Twenty-six years after Israeli conquered those occupied territories in the 1967 Six Day War, an Israeli government finally would begin trading land for peace. Many observers expected that if the 1993 agreement ever were fully implemented, it would lead to the creation of a Palestinian state. Major stakes were involved for the parties at that signing ceremony, which was an occasion of high drama. After the signatures, President Clinton as host stage-managed a ceremonial handshake between Chairman Arafat and an obviously uncomfortable Prime Minister Rabin. But why was the ceremony held at the White House?

In 1991, beginning shortly after the Persian Gulf War, the United States had capitalized on its improved relations with Arab states and worked closely with the Soviet Union to organize a broad, multilateral Middle East peace conference in Madrid, Spain. Subsequent initiatives by the United States and other parties continued a peace process intended to finally resolve the persistent state of war between Israel and most of its Arab neighbors. Sporadic bilateral negotiations between Israel and various Arab states followed. Yet the agreement signed in Washington by Arafat and Rabin was worked out in a lengthy series of secret meetings in Oslo between top Israeli and PLO officials, facilitated by Norwegian diplomats. Although it remained active in the ongoing peace process begun at Madrid, the United States played essentially no role in reaching the Oslo agreements. Why, then, were they signed at the White House?

The Oslo accords were signed in Washington partly because of America's history of support for Israel and U.S. involvement in the Middle East peace process, but primarily

PHOTO 8.1

Palestine Liberation Organization chairman Yasir Arafat (center) shakes hands with
a visibly uncomfortable Israeli prime minister Yitzhak Rabin (with President Clinton
looking on) after signing the framework Mideast peace agreement called the Oslo
Accords. The signing ceremony was held on the South Lawn of the White House on
13 September 1993, symbolizing both an American commitment to Mideast peace and
the continuing U.S. power and influence in the post–Cold War world.
AP/Wide World Photos.

because of the global power and influence of the United States. As the sole superpower
after the end of the Cold War and the Soviet Union's 1991 breakup, the United States
was foremost among the great powers witnessing the signing and informally guaranteeing the Oslo agreements. As Israel's longtime de facto ally and strongest foreign supporter, the United States had greater potential than any other state either to reward Israel
for following through on the Oslo accords or to punish delays and deviations. Symbolic
U.S. backing for the agreements was an important tactic to help ensure their success. That
Rabin's government, Arafat's PLO, and other major governments interested in the Middle East peace process all wanted to hold the ceremony in Washington is a testimonial

to U.S. power and influence in the post–Cold War world. It also gives evidence that the nature of power and influence changed in the late twentieth century, for America and for the wider world.

PERSPECTIVES ON POWER AND INFLUENCE

Power often suggests military instruments of policy and the use of force. In reality, power in world politics is a much broader concept, better suggested by the term *influence*. This is ever more true as economies become increasingly globalized and modern transportation and communications technologies shrink time and the physical world. The following ruminations of noted Harvard University political scientist Karl Deutsch (1967, 232, 233, 236) about power a generation ago still ring true:

> Politics consists in the more or less incomplete control of human behavior through voluntary habits of *compliance* in combination with threats of probable *enforcement*. In its essence, politics is based on the interplay of these two things: habits and threats.
>
> Enforcement consists of the threat or the use of rewards or punishments. In practice, punishments are used more often . . . (and) are usually cheaper. . . . Punishments may deter some transgressors from repeating their offense, but it is more important that they deter others from following their example.
>
> Power, put simply and crudely, is the ability to prevail in conflict and to overcome obstacles.

Power includes, but goes far beyond, military force, and its political purpose is that partial control of human behavior of which Deutsch speaks. Power has many forms, is based on many factors, and applies in varied ways to different situations. Power always has limits, but it extends beyond the ability to prevail in military and other conflicts and overcome obstacles, to include the ability to influence others and alter the probable outcomes of policy interactions. We may speak of power in the abstract, but translating power into active influence requires evaluating many factors. Political scientists and politicians love to think, talk, and write about power, yet they regularly are quite vague about what power is and how it works to produce influence. Moving to dispel some of that vagueness, this chapter is organized according to some ten perspectives from which we can analyze the nature and operation of power and influence. Those perspectives are far more complementary than conflicting. Each captures a different aspect of the nature or workings of power and influence, and we often have to consider more than one perspective at once. Although many analysts will argue that one particular perspective captures what is truly important, the argument here is that each captures only part of a complex reality. This is exactly parallel to the argument about perspectives and viewpoints on U.S. foreign policy in Chapter 1. The power perspectives examined in this chapter are summarized in Table 8.1.

As we consider these different perspectives, keep in mind that every tool or channel of action available to policymakers may be classified according to the type, quantity, and other characteristics of power involved. Officials have many policy tools to use, as reviewed in this and the next four chapters. *The purpose of utilizing any type of power or exercising any*

TABLE 8.1		
Perspectives on Power and Influence		

Perspective	Attributes or Values	Key Concepts and Terms
Source and Nature of Power		
Source of power	Natural, synthetic (including social-psychological)	Sources of power
Type of action	Military, diplomatic, economic, political	Action channels
Mobilization potential	Presently available, potential	Mobilization
Dynamics and balance	Dynamic (changing), static (continuum)	Balance, rate of change
Goals in Using Power		
Assistance/opposition	Assistance–opposition (continuum)	General goals
Coercion/persuasion	Coercion, persuasion continuum	Hard versus soft power
Techniques of Power Application		
Severity	Extent to which each option is utilized; degree of violence (continuum)	Escalation
Timing	What is to be done when?	Escalation
Coercive diplomacy	Credible force potential plus seven other supporting conditions	Credible force potential
Range of usability	Short range–long range (continuum)	Viability; strength versus distance

type of influence, however, is always to assist in achieving policy goals. In examining these aspects of power, consider that every policy represents a complex choice combining several actions to be taken. Each action is drawn from among the many policy tools available, combined according to their times of availability and their contribution to solving the policy problem at hand. Actions are chosen subject to pressures and constraints that range from physical limitations to political realities, further constrained by our own normative, political, and other criteria for policy selection. Common sense tells us to choose appropriate policy tools, but all too often we must settle for the best available options, even if they are not entirely appropriate. In turn, of course, this may contribute to policy failure.

Perspectives on power and influence are grouped into three major sections in this chapter, followed by their application to a major case. First, the *sources and nature* of different kinds of power are examined. Natural, synthetic (created), and social-psychological power attributes are examined, along with combined forms, mobilization of potential power, and the dynamics and balance of power in flux. Power may be exercised through military, diplomatic, economic, and political action channels. Indeed, the next four chapters are devoted to more detailed examinations of the possibilities and problems of military, diplomatic, economic, and international cooperative tools of policy, respectively.

Second, we turn to *goals in using power*. Two dimensions are considered, one a continuum of assistance and opposition, the other a continuum of coercion and persuasion. Third, we examine several aspects of *techniques of power application*. They include severity and timing of action, escalation, coercive diplomacy, and range of usability.

Finally, these frames of reference are employed in examining the future of U.S.-European relations in light of the Bosnian civil war, the 1995 Dayton peace accords, and subsequent events. The need for continuing Bosnian peacekeeping arrangements is but one example of how different the foreign policy problems confronting the United States today differ from the problems faced during the Cold War era, that is, during most of the second half of the twentieth century.

SOURCES AND NATURE OF POWER: NATURAL AND SYNTHETIC FORMS

Let us begin from the perspective that **power attributes**—those things that cause us to consider their possessors, whether states or nonstate actors, to be "powerful"—may be classified as either natural or synthetic, depending on whether they occur naturally or are created according to deliberate policy choices by human decision makers. As we shall see, a sort of continuum is involved because many power attributes partake of both properties. **Natural power attributes** involve strengths that actors have by fortunate accident of location, such as a rich resource endowment or a protective geography. **Synthetic power attributes** involve those strengths that actors can acquire only by choice, such as a large army or a loyal voting bloc in intergovernmental organizations. Synthetic power often requires natural power attributes for support. For example, natural resources help underpin a developed economy. Synthetic power attributes also include **social-psychological aspects,** such as charismatic leadership or the ability to command the political allegiance of allies and citizens. In each category, more of any attribute almost always (but not invariably) translates to greater potential and usable power.

NATURAL ATTRIBUTES OF POWER

Natural attributes of power inevitably involve aspects of geography and the natural resources that are ruled in or out by political boundaries. In the latter twentieth century, after OPEC oil price wars in the 1970s and the Persian Gulf War in 1990–91, almost everyone thinks of petroleum as the epitome of natural resources that convey economic power, and therefore, political power. The most fundamental input to any modern industrial economy is energy, and states lacking needed energy sources are open to manipulation by others who possess them. Rapid oil price increases during the 1970s brought about a tremendous shift of wealth from industrialized oil consumers such as the United States and Western Europe to relatively undeveloped oil exporters such as Saudi Arabia and Iraq. The U.S. government suddenly became much more solicitous of OPEC governments, such as that of Saudi Arabia, which urged price moderation on more militant regimes, such as that of Iraq, which sought more rapid price rises to maximize their incomes.

Oil resources can be translated into tangible power, made manifest when such states as Iraq and Iran import enormous quantities of modern weapons. Although neither was a modern industrialized state, Iran and Iraq were able to fight a protracted and costly war (1980–88) limited primarily by their ability to purchase outside military supplies from some thirty states. Moreover, their mutual dependence on oil exports to purchase arms sometimes led each to attack the other's oil terminals and shipping in the Persian Gulf. Those attacks, in turn, motivated the United States and others to intervene to protect freedom of Gulf navigation. Such interventions, along with relatively ineffective international embargoes on arms shipments and the exhaustion of the combatants eventually helped yield a cease-fire.

Natural resources also can be translated into major political influence. A notable example involves Japan, which depends on imports for some 95 percent of its energy needs. After the 1967 Mideast war, Arab governments pointed this dependence out to the Japanese government, which promptly reversed its formerly pro-Israeli policies. France, previously Israel's largest foreign military supplier, made a similar change for the same reason. France and the other major Western European states are even more dependent on Mideast oil imports than the United States. Fully expecting another Mideast war (which occurred in 1973) and fearing that war could leave them on the wrong side from their Arab oil suppliers, the French government abruptly canceled all military sales to Israel, even stopping delivery of ships already paid for. In turn, the French cutoff led the United States to assume the major role in supplying Israel, and encouraged the Israelis to expand their own military industry, including arms exports to help defray development costs.

All types of natural resources contribute to a state's power by supplying inputs to its economy and making it independent of coercion from foreign suppliers. During the nineteenth century the young United States benefited from vast reserves of space to populate, rich farmland to cultivate, coal for fuel, iron and other metals to mine for basic industrial inputs, forests to yield lumber for building, and so on. The United States also benefited from an abundance of other natural power attributes, including physical isolation that helped provide protection from major foreign powers; long seacoasts with excellent natural ports to facilitate shipping and great rivers that ease transport to the interior; and a relatively mild climate that helps facilitate agricultural production and eases almost every other form of economic activity.

If you doubt the value of such attributes, compare U.S. experience with that of less fortunately endowed states. European great powers of the nineteenth and early twentieth centuries sought foreign colonial empires at least partly because they were running out of space and natural resources at home. Germany, for instance, openly demanded *lebensraum*, or living space. Britain enjoys the military benefit of being an island state that was last successfully invaded in 1066, and Japan's island location greatly aided its pre-1854 isolation. Harsh climate has always made Russian agricultural production marginal, and has led almost all of Canada's population, which is quite small relative to its enormous land area, to settle within 200 miles of the U.S.-Canadian border. Before the achievement of majority rule in South Africa, landlocked black-ruled states in the interior were severely constrained by the fact that their only land links to the outside world ran through white-ruled South Africa.

Several other natural attributes of power are geopolitical. Following Mackinder's dictum, it was believed that location in the center or heartland of Europe conveyed the advantage of short internal lines of communication and (military) supply, lending natural advantage to states like Germany. Studies by Lewis Richardson (1960) and others indicate that, other things being equal, states that share borders with fewer neighbors are less likely to become involved in interstate wars. Other natural barriers beside seacoasts help protect against invasion. Poland's lack of natural barriers on its frontiers has contributed to centuries of invasion from both east and west, leading to many imposed changes in those frontiers, but even Nazi Germany found the prospect of invading Switzerland unprofitable. Control of navigational chokepoints can be extremely valuable. Fortifying the Rock of Gibraltar helped Britain control all access between the Atlantic Ocean and the Mediterranean Sea. Controlling the Straits of the Bosporus has given Turkey disproportionate strength over Russia because those straits are the only route from Russia's only warm water ports, on the Black Sea, to the Mediterranean and thence to the world's deep oceans.

SYNTHETIC ATTRIBUTES OF POWER

Synthetic power attributes are acquired by making decisions and carrying out acquisition programs, often over prolonged periods of time. Nonetheless, synthetic attributes of power are not entirely independent of natural attributes. For example, possessing adequate raw materials and energy supplies greatly facilitates any government's decision to build a modern industrial economy. The biggest losers in the oil price wars of the 1970s were developing states dependent on imports of both energy and manufactured goods. Technological developments and policy decisions may drastically alter the value of natural resource power attributes. Although this point is further developed later, the example of Arab oil is obvious. Massive petroleum reserves were unimportant until the industrial revolution made them useful, and serious oil markets also depended on consumer states making technology choices to invest heavily in internal combustion engines.

Among the classic examples of synthetic power attributes are economic development, industrial capacity, and military strength, which are traditionally closely linked with one another and with foreign perceptions of state strength. Important parts of those interrelationships are covered in several later chapters. Chapter 11 includes a review of major global economic changes since World War II. Dramatic shifts in U.S. relations to the increasingly globalized economy have occurred since the mid-1970s, giving impetus to President Clinton's declaration that economics has become the most important post–Cold War area of U.S. foreign policy. Chapter 13 is structured according to development as a defining dimension, and includes a detailed review of the pros and cons of some eleven major development strategies.

An important class of synthetic power attributes is **infrastructure,** the fundamental systems on which growth and development depend. Traditionally, these include such systems as transportation, energy generation and transmission, and communications. They profoundly influence economic development, technology choices, and population movements, and are strongly shaped by policy choices. Thus, for example, government backing for the first transcontinental railroad opened up the West to white settlement and development, and building the interstate highway system beginning in the 1950s vastly increased citizen mobility, shifted goods transport away from railroads, and stimulated a burgeoning trucking industry. Today, building the information superhighway of high-speed digital data links promises to speed our movement into the postindustrial information age. As we undergo a third industrial revolution, manufacturing capacity and economic development no longer are synonymous. Data examined in Chapter 13 suggest that since the 1980s the wealthiest states have been building postindustrial economies, moving from reliance on heavy industry to combinations of in-person services, high technologies, and information services as their economic cornerstones.

Through most of the twentieth century, however, heavy industrial capacity was seen correctly as providing the base for building a large military establishment. Military forces, in turn, convey tangible state power in very traditional terms, as offensive and defensive capability. Soviet experience in World War II provides a notable example combining natural and synthetic attributes of power. Acting on these premises about the uses of industrial and military power, and correctly perceiving itself to be a pariah state in a hostile world, the Soviet Union embarked in 1928 on a series of five-year plans for heavy industrial development. These were designed to force rapid movement into modern economic and military strength, and early stages of that development began to pay off after Germany's devastating 1941 invasion. Despite enormous losses and the invasion of vast western territories, the Soviets rallied, held on, and battled back. They first used their vast land area to absorb and slow the German attack, then let the bitter Russian winter weaken their attackers. Finally, drawing on an industrial base larger than Germany's for weapons production and on their huge population to build armies vastly outnumbering their German attackers, they began the long, slow battle back across the western Soviet Union and Eastern Europe to eventual victory.

This case demonstrates an important distinction between forces in being and potential forces after mobilization, which is explored more fully later. Just as industrial capacity or the wealth to buy advanced weaponry abroad is required to underpin military might, a highly developed consumer economy requires an industrial base that, given time, can be converted to military production. Such was the case for the United States in World War II.

Rather than building heavy industry or military might, states may choose to promote general economic growth and focus their efforts on forefront technologies expected to lead the way into the next generation of economic strength. In principle, developing states may leapfrog over present technologies, minimizing the total investment required to reach modernity. Thus, for example, in parts of the developing world satellite communications bring telephone and television to previously isolated rural areas without anyone ever building land lines. States also may choose to promote the development of advanced education and workplace skills in their populations to build a base for raising the general level of economic activity. Governments also may engage in **industrial policy,** sponsoring economic programs in which the public and private sectors coordinate their efforts and investments to develop or promote new industries and technologies. Thus, for example, Japan's Ministry of International Trade and Industry (MITI) coordinates policy between industrial combines to promote Japanese penetration of foreign markets.

Industrial policy and other forms of direct government involvement in business planning traditionally have been viewed with suspicion in the United States. Opinion has grown since the 1980s, however, that such policies may be required to retain competitiveness and technological leadership in an increasingly internationalized economy. One notable case of contemporary U.S. industrial policy is SEMATECH, the Semiconductor Manufacturing Technology Consortium. Organized in 1987, the consortium brought together archrival semiconductor manufacturing firms whose leaders were convinced that they had to work together to recapture a market for large-scale integrated circuit chips, which was being lost to Japan. Driven partly by Defense Department concerns about its growing dependence on foreign-supplied components for advanced weaponry, Congress voted in 1987 to provide the relatively modest subsidy of $100 million per year to SEMA-TECH, with the fourteen consortium members providing the same. Funds were to go toward building and running a chip plant, providing research grants to equipment suppliers, and buying their equipment for testing. There is general agreement that the U.S. position in semiconductor manufacturing rebounded handsomely after SEMATECH's founding, although there was strong disagreement about how much credit the consortium deserved, and its political fortunes fluctuated. SEMATECH was founded late in the Reagan administration, but a hostile Bush administration regularly tried to cut off funding. The Clinton administration saw the consortium as "a model for Federal consortiums funded to advance other critical technologies," and some leaders in other industries have called for comparable undertakings (Hafner, 1993). At the very least, SEMATECH increased communication between chip manufacturers and suppliers of chip-producing equipment, helping to remove the greatest bottleneck to advanced generations of integrated circuits.

A final, vital synthetic power attribute is *organization*. The more effective our institutional design, the more our government is capable of recognizing and solving problems quickly and efficiently. As we saw in earlier chapters, some government agencies—and some governments—are more effective and innovative than others. Similarly, some systems of economic organization are more effective than others, making more goods and services available to more people more efficiently. In the great Cold War contest between American-style market economics and Soviet-style central command economics, the latter failed badly. While the United States continues to refine its economic system incrementally, with all the intermestic interest politics that implies, many developing states today can choose their type of economic system. Eastern European and post-Soviet states generally have chosen to replace command economies with market economies, reflecting a major policy victory for the United States and its allies.

SOCIAL-PSYCHOLOGICAL ATTRIBUTES OF POWER

Social-psychological attributes are special types of synthetic power, pertaining to social cohesiveness, political stability, and public confidence in government. These cannot necessarily be built to order as directly and readily as military forces. A state in which there is a single dominant nation, leading to a widespread sense of being "one people," is best able to act in a cohesive and coordinated manner when meeting external challenges. This important advantage is partly natural, deriving from the background of the people living in the area, and partly synthetic, deriving from the way political boundaries have been drawn. (Nationalism, of course, provides a powerful motivation to define those boundaries along ethnic-nationalistic lines.) States riven by internal nationalistic disputes, as seen in extreme form in former Yugoslavia, are unlikely to be able to coordinate their actions toward outside powers. Although a classic theory of international politics holds that governments can rally their people by directing their attention to an external enemy, the historical evidence is mixed. States subject to frequent changes of government, whether peaceful or violent, will be less able to pursue long-term programs either at home or abroad than more stable states. For example, extremely frequent peaceful changes of government since World War II have contributed to a widespread sense both at home and abroad that Italy is weak and irresolute. The United States, in contrast, long has enjoyed fairly high social cohesiveness, high political stability, and fairly high public confidence in government, even if the last declined in the 1990s. As noted in Chapter 1, Barry Buzan (1991, 72–77) classifies the United States as a *state–nation*. After the American Revolution, predominantly English colonists built a state that helped promote national cultural identity by generating and promoting uniform language, arts, customs, and law as it expanded across the continent. Although the assimilation of such peoples as Native Americans, Hispanics, and the descendants of slaves brought from Africa remains highly imperfect, huge waves of immigrants came to these shores to "become Americans," and that movement continues.

Public confidence in both the capability and policies of government—a widespread sense within their populations that government leaders are competent and well motivated, and what might be called a sense of followership—contributes greatly to any state's ability to carry out policy. Moreover, social-psychological attributes of power clearly extend to the cost tolerance of peoples, their willingness to endure hardships for state causes. Compare, for example, attitudes in the United States during World War II with the Vietnam era. Following Japan's 1941 attack on Pearl Harbor, a U.S. neutralist movement that had enjoyed the confidence of up to a third of the population vanished almost overnight. Throughout the war, even though nobody believed government to be infallible, there was almost universal belief that the Axis Powers were genuinely evil, and their utter defeat and unconditional surrender were imperative. Along with those beliefs came a willingness to pay the prices of victory, through conscription and military training, dead and wounded soldiers, disruptions of family life, government deficits, and drastically reduced availability of consumer goods. Those World War II costs were far higher to the United States than comparable Vietnam War costs, but public disposition to bear them was much higher. During our long involvement in Vietnam (1961–73), the steadily mounting toll of battle without visible progress toward a clearly identifiable goal contributed to a slow but inexorable shift of domestic public opinion from majority support to majority opposition, with bitter divisions.

All the components of nationhood and nationalism discussed in Chapter 1 can contribute to public cohesiveness backing state policy. Governments sometimes use open appeals to the uniqueness and value of national culture in unifying their people. Charles de Gaulle, president of France from 1959 to 1969, regularly appealed to French *grandeur* and historic world role to justify such policies as building an independent nuclear strike force. Contemporary French governments legislate against corruption of the French language by foreign terms like *le hot dog*. American presidents regularly refer to "our free market economy" and "the American way of life" in appeals for public support.

Although social-psychological attributes of power sometimes can be encouraged by government actions, they cannot be built quickly. Only long-term programs can socialize a population, stabilize a political system, build a sense of common culture and nationalism, or create a favorable image of leadership. Moreover, the success of such programs is always debatable. The United States enjoys a high level of political stability, drawing on more than two hundred years of political history. Yet this country began with a fairly homogenous population and benefited from many abundant natural components of power, as discussed earlier. The founders consciously sought to create a new political entity that would avoid the problems which drove many of them from Europe. Nonetheless, the

United States endured a protracted revolution (1775–83), an early period of upheaval extending from tentative unification under the Articles of Confederation (sent to the states by the Continental Congress in 1777 and ratified in 1781) until the adoption of the present Constitution in 1789, and fought the devastating and protracted Civil War (1861–65). Despite increasing emphasis in recent years on cultural diversity and recapturing our roots, there remains a widespread sense that the people of the United States are one people, "Americans," even if hyphenated Americans. In notable contrast, through more than seven decades of rule (1917–91), communists failed in their attempt to create the "new Soviet man." During the Second World War, Soviet internal propaganda relied primarily on appeals to the Russian nationalism of the dominant ethnic group. Even before the Soviet Union's breakup at the end of 1991, nominally Soviet citizens demonstrated greater loyalties to their individual republics and ethnicities. Ethnic fragmentation continues today as Russia and many other former Soviet republics are plagued by secessionist movements.

COMBINED POWER ATTRIBUTES

Some power attributes *combine* natural and synthetic aspects. No synthetic aspect is under absolute government control because the efforts of many individuals must be coordinated toward a common goal, and because underlying natural power attributes may be essential. However, the combination of natural and synthetic aspects is particularly obvious in certain cases, such as population. Control programs may be designed to limit population growth in the interest of maximizing development, as in contemporary China, or to promote growth for its military potential, as in Nazi Germany. A large population implies the potential for many workers and soldiers, yet can be a double-edged sword. It is more a liability than an asset if people are untrained, multiplying rapidly enough to absorb all or most economic growth, or cannot adequately be housed, clothed, and fed. India's large population (and 752 person per square mile population density) is a problem because of its high growth rate and widespread poverty. At the other end of the population density scale (7 persons per square mile), Canada pays cash bonuses for having children. The early United States actively encouraged population growth and immigration to develop its abundant resources. As the economy matured in the twentieth century, however, undeveloped space became rare, urban population densities rose, and concerns about environmental pollution and natural resource depletion appeared. Protecting standards of living for present citizens gained increasing support.

Alliances are among other power attributes that combine natural and synthetic aspects. States form alliances to gain effective synthetic power. Those possessing useful power will be attractive alliance partners, whether their power is natural, as in critical location, or synthetic, as in economic or military strength. Thus, for example, NATO could not adequately plan to defend Western Europe against the Soviet threat without finding a formula for incorporating West Germany. That formula had the additional benefit to both East and West of ensuring that Germany would not become a nuclear power. Additionally, state borders often are adjusted to ensure ethnic cohesiveness, as were those proposed in the 1995 Bosnian peace settlement mediated by the United States. Less frequently, state borders are adjusted to ensure military viability. This is a vexing issue in Middle East peacemaking, where conservative factions argue that Israel cannot be militarily secure if all the territories conquered in 1967 are returned to Arab control.

TYPES OF ACTION CHANNELS

Any complete specific policy usually involves combining and coordinating many different actions. Although such a complete policy often is complex enough to have considerable overlaps, it is helpful to distinguish military, diplomatic, and economic channels of action. Additionally, each type of action usually has some political meaning and motivation. In developing the broad menu of possible foreign policy tools, the next three chapters are devoted to military, diplomatic, and economic tools, respectively. Each class or channel of actions, however, is considered in the broader context of the types of policy concerns to which it is best suited. One of the most important uses of this perspective about action channels is to remind ourselves not to overlook possible options when developing a menu for policy choice in any specific case.

MOBILIZING POTENTIAL POWER

Both *actual* and *potential* power must be considered, taking into account conversion and mobilization potential as well as forces in being. **Actual power** is immediately available in such forms as active duty military forces, diplomatic weight sufficient to sway a vote in the United Nations, or economic strength sufficient to manipulate an international currency market. **Potential power** requires time to prepare, after which it may or may not be actualized. Examples include mobilizing reserve troops, converting a civilian economy to wartime production, developing a highly trained modern work force or a new technology, and exploiting a previously untapped natural resource.

U.S. mobilization for World War II provides an outstanding example of the military potential provided by a modern developed economy, given sufficient time. The United States began conscripting men into the armed forces even before Pearl Harbor. After war was declared against the Axis Powers, conscription and military training were accelerated. Factories previously devoted to consumer goods were rapidly converted to military production. Auto factories were changed over to produce tanks and aircraft. Steel production capacity previously used for building stoves and refrigerators was diverted to military uses. Gasoline was rationed east of the Mississippi River, although that rationing reflected distribution costs more than any true petroleum shortage. Throughout the U.S. economy, machine tools and engineering and manufacturing expertise were diverted from civilian to military production.

Given that the United States started with the world's largest and most highly developed economy, and was never invaded or bombed to interrupt production, its capacity to build military machinery was simply enormous. The case is clear in Table 8.2 (see page 297), which reports the percentages of the world's total combat munitions produced by the main belligerents from 1938 through 1943. Remember that these are percentages of an ever-increasing total, so different states' shares of that total are far more significant than their absolute production. Thus, for example, the Soviet *share* dropped throughout the period even though *absolute* Soviet production rose every year. The large German and Soviet shares in 1938 reflect the fact that they had begun rearming before the other European powers. Nazi Germany had a time window of about two years during which its earlier start gave significant military advantage over Britain and France (and probably the Soviet Union). After that time, British arms production would catch up with Germany's capacity. Worse yet for Germany, its naval buildup was about five years behind its production of land weapons and aircraft, and Hitler's war plans had no margin to redress that imbalance. Britain's share tripled from 1938 to 1940 as it geared up military production. Its later start on major military development ultimately left Britain with newer technologies —notably including radar—than Germany. United States and Italian shares dropped from 1938 to 1939, not because of absolute cuts but because other states were increasing military production more rapidly. As the world's largest civilian economy was converted to war production, the U.S. share doubled from 1940 to 1941, and the next year it doubled again. By 1943 the United States alone was producing fully 40 percent of the world's combat munitions. Moreover, the United States then was building all the arms it could use at the fronts and had as many men under arms as were believed necessary to fight the war to ultimate victory, expected about 1947. Some in Washington questioned whether production of civilian consumer goods should be increased somewhat because it was now possible. Limits were continued, however, in the belief that increased consumer production might undermine morale at the fronts. In turn, continued restrictions helped build consumer demand that fueled a postwar economic boom.

Comparing UN to Axis shares of world total production demonstrates how sensitive Axis plans were to timing. In particular, Nazi Germany counted on knocking France and Britain out of the war early, so it was a serious mistake to attack the Soviet Union in 1941 without first defeating Britain. Japan's Pearl Harbor attack was intended to neutralize the U.S. Navy's Pacific Ocean capability. In turn, this would have permitted Japan to consolidate its conquest of Southeast Asia and the South Pacific, securing vitally needed supplies of petroleum and rubber. The Japanese admiral in charge of the attack reportedly declared the war lost when he learned the U.S. aircraft carriers were not caught in port. In 1938 the Axis Powers enjoyed a 60:40 advantage over their eventual opponents, but by 1939, the year the war opened in Europe, that advantage had dropped to 55:45. By 1942 the first full year of the United States in the war, that position of Axis advantage had reversed to 36:64, and by the next year it had slipped even further, to 30:70. From a strategic perspective based solely on military production capacity, the outcome of the war was a foregone conclusion by 1942 or 1943, even though vicious fighting dragged on into 1945. Lest this seem too deterministic, however, note that unexpected major developments could have skewed this analysis. Hitler's Germany regularly sought breakthrough weapons through new technologies, and produced the first jet combat aircraft and the first guided missiles (V-1 "buzz bomb" cruise missiles and V-2 ballistic missiles fired across the English Channel into Britain). A major motivation behind the U.S. Manhattan Project to produce nuclear bombs was fear that Germany would acquire them first, a development that could have drastically altered the war. In the event, even though Germany had been the world center for vanguard physics in the 1920s and 1930s, Nazi racism and practice drove out many of the leading scientists, who went on to build the bomb for America.

The strategic perspective on potential power in World War II, of course, assumed a prolonged war in which all parties had time to mobilize and reach their full potential. Certain other international power competitions, particularly over economics, also have that prolonged character. What counts then is not so much the stocks of power capabilities on hand at the outset, but the cumulation of flows over time to produce eventual preponderant strength. The outcomes of still other conflicts are determined much more by initial stocks on hand or forces in being. Such was the logic of U.S.-Soviet nuclear

TABLE 8.2						
Translating Economic into Military Power: Combat Munitions Output of the Main Belligerents in World War II (1938–1943) as Percentages of World Total						

Nation-State	1938	1939	1940	1941	1942	1943
United States	6	4	7	14	30	40
Canada	0	0	0	1	2	2
Britain	6	10	18	19	15	13
Soviet Union	27	31	23	24	17	15
TOTAL UNITED NATIONS	39	45	48	58	64	70
Germany plus Conquests	46	43	40	31	27	22
Italy	6	4	5	4	3	1
Japan	9	8	7	7	6	7
TOTAL AXIS POWERS	61	55	52	42	36	30
WORLD TOTAL	100	100	100	100	100	100

Source: Deutsch, 1967, 236, reporting data from Knorr, 1956, 34. Published by permission of the *Journal of Internal Affairs* and the Trustees of Columbia University in the City of New York.

Note: Combat munitions are the equipment and explosives used to prosecute a war, including aircraft, army ordnance and signal equipment, naval vessels, and related equipment.

confrontation during the Cold War when any strategic nuclear exchange would have occurred between missiles, bombers, and submarines already deployed. To an extent this was also the logic of U.S. and coalition superiority in the 1990–91 Persian Gulf War. Although months were required to mobilize forces, update training, and move weaponry and support equipment into position, the sophisticated weapons already had been developed and built during the Reagan defense buildup of the 1980s, and the battle tactics largely had been developed for NATO's defense of Western Europe.

DYNAMIC CHANGES AND POWER BALANCES

The case of the Axis Powers in World War II is a pointed reminder about the importance of *dynamics* in power measurement. Essentially, this means directing attention to any pattern of change, determining whether one's power is shifting *relative to* that of one's competitors and whether such shifts are favorable or unfavorable. Many analysts direct attention to power *balances*, which tend to shift over time unless carefully managed. As implied in the previous section, mobilizing potential power is intimately connected with dynamic change in power balances. Serious power imbalances generally cannot be maintained in the long term. For example, Israel's greatest incentive to seek peace with its Arab neighbors is that its greater mobilization, productivity, and military sophistication cannot indefinitely outweigh the significantly larger populations, land areas, and long-term economic potential of neighboring Arab states.

In this post–Cold War era we are likely to think more about economic than military balances. Here, too, dynamics and time trends are important, and the relative gains debate reappears (see "Realism versus Liberalism in Foreign Policy Choices" in Chapter 3). Analysts struggle to extrapolate from what we know today to estimate the long-term economic potential of states. Backed by its huge dynamic population and substantial natural resources, China is engaged in economic takeoff into industrialization and beyond, as correctly foreseen years ago. Yet a closer look reveals a distinctive regional pattern in which the advance is being led by China's southeastern coastal provinces, and there is far less development in the vast interior. Some specialists even forecast a fragmentation of China, should tight central political control ever be relaxed. Nigeria evidences a much less successful economic forecast. One of Africa's largest and most populous countries, with significant reserves of oil and other natural resources, Nigeria was expected to flourish after attaining independence in 1960. Instead, after a hard-fought civil war in 1967–70, democratic governance gave way mostly to periods of brutal military rule. Nigeria's rulers appear to have enriched themselves rather than their country, and by the early 1990s only twelve states ranked lower in per capita income.

Analysts must consider many types of trends when forecasting the long-term relative economic standing of states. Policies feasible and even helpful in the short run may not be sustainable over time, again directing attention to balances. Thus, for example, the United States needed to borrow about half the total federal budget during World War II to pay for the war effort. The federal budget peaked at 45 percent of gross domestic product in 1944. Economists divide, however, over whether a budget deficit can be sustained indefinitely. Moreover, just as budget deficits continue to build government debt, sustained trade deficits promote a continuing shift of wealth abroad. In assessing U.S. world standing and future prospects at the end of the twentieth century, the 1900s saw increasing attention being paid to the "twin deficits" in government budget and foreign trade. These issues are further explored in Chapter 11.

Note that the power which attaches to particular attributes depends on other factors and may change over time. In his best-selling 1987 book, *The Rise and Fall of the Great Powers: Economic Change and Military Conflict from 1500 to 2000*, British-born Yale University historian Paul Kennedy makes a highly lucid and literate case for the inevitability of eventual great power decline. In examining the growth and decline of powerful states over the long sweep of history, Kennedy starts from the realist perspective that *relative power* rather than absolute power counts in international politics. Leaders are always more concerned with how their state ranks compared to possible rivals than how it compares with its own standing, say, a decade or two ago. Yet the relative strengths of leading states never remain constant, primarily because technological changes and organizational breakthroughs lead to different growth rates between different societies. Natural power endowments of states strongly influence their abilities to develop and exploit new technologies. For example, the rise of Atlantic Ocean trading after 1500 benefited states like Britain, Portugal, and Spain because of their relatively advanced economies, maritime experience, and coastal access. Later, the development of steam power gave advantages to states endowed with the requisite coal and metal resources. Still later, substantial petroleum reserves benefited the United States during the ascendancy of petrochemical industries and of the internal combustion engine.

New technologies may drastically change the significance of natural power attributes. For example, the separation afforded by two great oceans benefited the developing

United States, but that advantage is increasingly negated in the missile age. That was the greatest message of Sputnik I in 1957; if the Soviets could orbit a satellite around the earth, intercontinental nuclear missile capability could not be far behind. This is only one of many instances in which decisions to acquire synthetic power attributes change the value of natural resource attributes. Building new political-economic institutions also may change the value of natural resources, as seen when OPEC and its key member states manipulate world oil prices by expanding or constricting their crude oil pumping.

GOALS IN USING POWER: ASSISTANCE AND OPPOSITION

One concern always raised at least implicitly when considering using any type of power to support policy is our *purpose* or intent. Power may be used either to *assist* or to *oppose* or *coerce* others, or to *deny* opponents their goals. This is yet another dimension on which a continuum exists. It ranges from all-out support to milder support, through neutrality to mild opposition, and on to all-out opposition. Such continua are easily visualized for any type of power, whether diplomatic, economic, or military. As we see later, a close connection exists between these purposes for utilizing power and the notion of escalation. A useful exercise is to consider any foreign policy problem, such as a conflict in which one or more sides seek U.S. support, and list some of the types of actions that might belong at different points along that continuum of support or opposition.

COERCION AND PERSUASION

Another perspective that combines purposes for utilizing power with the means employed is the distinction between "hard" and "soft" power, as discussed by Joseph Nye (1990, 31 ff.). Nye is an excellent contemporary example of an in-and-outer. A Harvard political scientist, he served as assistant secretary of defense for international security affairs early in the Clinton administration, returning to Harvard in 1995 to become dean of the Kennedy School of Government.

Hard, or **command, power** is the ability to coerce and compel others, bending them to our will, usually by using tangible power resources such as military and economic might. **Soft,** or **cooptive, power** is the ability to attract rather than command others, persuading them to join us in seeking the same goals. A continuum of behavioral possibilities exists here, as with many of the other perspectives on power examined in this chapter. Nye himself suggests the following major points on that continuum: command power, coercion, inducement, agenda setting, attraction, and cooptive power (1990, 267). The first behaviors form a clear sequence with decreasing degrees of force employed, and tend to rest on tangible hard synthetic power such as military and economic strength. The latter three behaviors also form a clear sequence with decreasing coercion and usually rest on soft power resources. For example, anyone who has ever served on a committee recognizes the power of agenda setting, in which the chairperson may declare by fiat or appeal to authority what issues will be discussed in what sequence. Informal agenda setting may be almost equally powerful. For example, forcefully and effectively arguing a position early in discussion may cause others to refrain from presenting alternative views later in the deliberations because they now expect that their positions will be seen as unrealistic. (If so, this is an example of groupthink in action; see Janis, 1972.) Moving on across the continuum, being attracted to the positions of others clearly represents a greater degree of cooptation than being shut off through agenda setting.

Relationships between behavior types and underlying resource types may be still more subtle. In Nye's terms,

> The distinction between hard and soft power resources is one of degree, both in the nature of the behavior and in the tangibility of the resources. Both types are aspects of the ability to achieve one's purposes by controlling the behavior of others. Command power—the ability to change what others *do*—can rest on coercion and inducement. Co-optive power—the ability to shape what others *want*—can rest on the attractiveness of one's culture and ideology or the ability to manipulate the agenda of political choices. . . . [However,] countries may be attracted to others with command power by myths of invincibility, and command power may sometimes be used to establish institutions that later become regarded as legitimate. (1990, 267; Nye's emphasis)

Thus sometimes hard power may stem from soft power resources, and vice versa. Nye and many other analysts predict that the United States must rely increasingly on soft power in the future, both because of the waning of the world hegemony it enjoyed early in the Cold War and because the disappearance of the former Soviet threat removed one of the major pressures on other governments to accede to U.S. wishes.

TECHNIQUES OF POWER APPLICATION

We turn now from issues about the goals of power utilization to practical techniques for applying power. It should come as no surprise that such techniques have received a great deal of attention in the policy literature. We begin with severity, timing, and escalation, which are inextricably intertwined. Foreign policy acts of any type may be applied at different levels of intensity or severity, and may be increased in a controlled manner over time until they are just sufficient to accomplish our goals. Second, we examine the intriguingly named concept of coercive diplomacy, and some criteria for judging its likelihood of success. Third, we examine the range of power usability. Effectiveness usually declines sharply with distance, depending on the specific type of power and its application.

SEVERITY, TIMING, AND ESCALATION

Severity, unsurprisingly, refers to how much available power will be utilized, from the least manageable bit to everything obtainable. Many factors affect that choice. They include the quality of past relations with the target of our action, which may predispose us either toward leniency or harshness, and the target's anticipated response. Ethical norms, such as those concerning "just wars," suggest that force should be proportionate to the stakes involved, never greater. **Timing** refers to the availability of options, many of which require advance planning (see earlier). **Escalation** involves the controlled increase of severity over time, with results monitored by feedback, until a level sufficient to accomplish policy goals is reached.

This notion of escalation effectively assumes that one's applicable power exceeds that of any adversary. Although the United States often has enjoyed such an advantage, it cannot always be guaranteed. Escalation first gained widespread public attention during the Vietnam War, especially the period 1965–68. Throughout those years, war leaders argued that increasing the numbers of U.S. troops, expanding their range of operations and severity of actions, and extending and intensifying the bombing of North Vietnam eventually would impose casualties that Vietcong and North Vietnamese forces could not long sustain, so the tide of battle would turn. Such predictions never were fulfilled. That bitter experience helped give escalation a bad reputation that persists today, at least in the United States. Nonetheless, escalation is a fundamental notion about any use of power, applicable as much in the economic and diplomatic spheres as in the military arena.

The escalation concept was first advanced in Herman Kahn's 1965 book, *On Escalation: Metaphors and Scenarios.* This was a polemic in a major dispute regarding nuclear conflict, a controversy now both partly settled and seen as much less relevant in the post–Cold War environment. The dispute concerned whether a nuclear war could be kept limited and, if so, whether we should prepare operational plans for limited nuclear options (LNOs). From an organizational politics perspective, limited nuclear war could never be a policy option unless operational plans were prepared in advance. Military planning from the early period of U.S. nuclear monopoly (1945–49) at least through the adoption in 1960 of the first single integrated operational plan (SIOP) for the conduct of all U.S. forces in a strategic nuclear war called for a single massive attack against an "optimum mix" of "high priority military, industrial and government control centers" (Rowen, 1975, 225). Effectively, this was a plan for all-out nuclear and conventional war. Kahn called this spasm or insensate war, referring to it in public talks as a "wargasm." In the late 1950s, however, the world began to enter the missile age, and fears of a (then nonexistent) "missile gap" between the United States and the Soviet Union played a prominent role in the 1960 presidential campaign. Realization was dawning that thermonuclear-armed intercontinental ballistic missiles (ICBMs) were beginning to make even the United States vulnerable to massive nuclear attack. Kahn argued the case for LNOs partly by constructing a conceptual "ladder" of escalation steps that started with actions far short of an all-out thermonuclear exchange.

Kahn's escalation ladder is important to us today, quite independent of our historical experiences in Vietnam and the LNO debates, because its lower steps present a formula for the *graduated use of power.* It moves from ostensible crisis to spasm war in 44 steps; the first 20 steps are given in Figure 8.1, and several key points are evident. There is a distinct *severity sequence* in which actions become more intense in both effort required and impact on the target. *Many types of actions* are employed together and/or in escalatory sequence, including political, diplomatic, and economic gestures, even though Kahn's overall focus is more on the use of military force. Different types of action must often be combined, for example using diplomatic channels to convey threats of economic or military escalation or proposals for a settlement.

We can build other useful escalation ladders by constructing hypothetical sequences, either of increasingly severe uses of some specific class of actions, or (more realistically in any particular case) of combined types of actions. Diplomacy, for example, regularly features extremely fine graduations of behavior calculated to send highly precise signals. Suppose our government wanted to indicate its disapproval of another state's action. A private communication from a low-level official to his or her counterpart would indicate

FIGURE 8.1	
	The Lower Steps of Herman Kahn's Conceptual Ladder of Escalation

(No Nuclear Use Threshold)

	20. "Peaceful" Worldwide Embargo or Blockade
	19. "Justifiable" Counterforce Attack
	18. Spectacular Show or Demonstration of Force
	17. Limited Evacuation (approximately 20 percent)
INTENSE	16. Nuclear "Ultimatums"
CRISES	15. Barely Nuclear War
	14. Declaration of Limited Conventional War
	13. Large Compound Escalation
	12. Large Conventional War (or Actions)
	11. Super-Ready Status
	10. Provocative Breaking Off of Diplomatic Relations

(Nuclear War Is Unthinkable Threshold)

	9. Dramatic Military Confrontations
	8. Harassing Acts of Violence
TRADITIONAL	7. "Legal" Harassment—Retortions
CRISES	6. Significant Mobilization
	5. Show of Force
	4. Hardening of Positions—Confrontation of Wills

(Don't Rock the Boat Threshold)

SUBCRISIS	3. Solemn and Formal Declarations
MANEUVERING	2. Political, Economic, and Diplomatic Gestures
	1. Ostensible Crisis

(Disagreement—Cold War)

Source: Herman Kahn, *On Escalation: Metaphors and Scenarios* (New York: Praeger, 1965, p. 39). Reprinted by permission of the Hudson Institute.

the mildest concern. Making one's expression of concern public, for instance by talking with a reporter, indicates greater importance. So do the same steps if taken by a higher level official. Wordings used are carefully calculated to express precise shades of meaning and intensity of concern. Thus, the sequence, "we are somewhat concerned," "we are concerned," "we are deeply concerned," "we regret," "we deeply regret," "we deplore," "we condemn" expresses steadily increasing intensity. A formal meeting between diplomats has greater symbolic importance than an informal encounter, no matter how carefully the latter may be prearranged. In cases considered extremely important, ambassadors may be called before host government officials and rebuked or asked to account for their governments' actions. Recalling an ambassador to the home capital "for consultations" is a signal of extreme displeasure, and effectively lowers the official level of diplomatic contacts for some time. A useful exercise is constructing similar escalation ladders for other classes of actions.

HERMAN KAHN'S ESCALATION LADDER AND THE CUBAN MISSILE CRISIS

Consider how Herman Kahn's escalation ladder for the controlled increase of severity over time could be applied to the 1962 Cuban missile crisis. Growing out of the background of U.S.-Soviet Cold War competition and the previous year's humiliating Bay of Pigs invasion, ostensible crisis was reached when New York's senator Kenneth Keating and others began charging that the Soviets were introducing nuclear missiles into Cuba. The administration's first major public comment came with President Kennedy's televised address announcing discovery of the missiles, pledging that the United States would bring about their removal, and announcing a "quarantine" line would be established by naval blockade. By combining a solemn declaration with a hardening of will, that address jumped up to steps 3 and 4 in Kahn's ladder. Within days, the United States moved up two more steps, through military mobilizations and attendant shows of force. Establishing the blockade could be seen either as a debatably "legal" harassment, step 7 on Kahn's ladder, or a harassing act of violence, step 8. Great care was taken, however, to reduce the chance that shots would be fired. At the same time, extensive diplomatic efforts went on out of public view in hopes of working out a solution. Had the narrowly averted "surgical" air strike against the missiles been carried out as planned, it would have represented at least a dramatic military confrontation (step 9). That would have risked further escalation, which could have occurred in tit-for-tat fashion between the two sides. The negotiated solution avoided such escalation, and all actions stayed below Kahn's "nuclear war is unthinkable" threshold.

COERCIVE DIPLOMACY

Coercive diplomacy seems at first glance to be one of the stranger phrases to emerge from the academic and policy communities in recent decades. It appears almost contradictory, suggesting the application of force to a fundamentally peaceful activity. The phrase originated with Stanford political scientist Alexander George and gained currency from his book *The Limits Of Coercive Diplomacy: Laos, Cuba, Vietnam* (George, Hall, and Simons, 1971). Remembering the discussion of escalation in the previous section, we can position coercive diplomacy on a simplified conceptual continuum of peaceful and violent actions, diagrammed in Figure 8.2.

On this continuum from strict peace to extreme violence, coercive diplomacy falls between completely peaceful diplomacy and limited war. As Alberto Coll reminds us, the world has never enjoyed total peace, although we may envision taking entirely peaceful actions. Nor does total war really exist because no state has ever taken every imaginable action in war. Nonetheless, there is a meaningful distinction between major war and limited war. The latter may be may be limited in any or all of the following: goals, area of military operations, amount of force used, and types of military force and weaponry employed. Such limitations were almost never factors in the two world wars, and were then unfamiliar to most citizens and many political leaders in the United States. However, the Korean, Vietnam, and Persian Gulf wars were limited in all these ways; the limitations were the subject of domestic political debates.

FIGURE 8.2		
A Conceptual Continuum of Peaceful and Violent Actions		

Strict Peace			Extreme Violence
Peaceful Diplomacy	Coercive Diplomacy	Limited War	All-Out War

Coercive diplomacy extends from peaceful diplomacy to limited war, overlapping and including both. Its one indispensable prerequisite is that *usable and believable options to use force must exist*, although coercion need not always require *military* force. Even though Alexander George focused on the use of military force, coercion may take the form of diplomatic and economic pressures. After the end of the Persian Gulf land war in 1991, for example, continuing severe economic sanctions including a strict international trade embargo often exerted the strongest pressures on Iraq to comply with UN inspections of its *weapons of mass destruction* (see Range of Usability later in this chapter). During the Indonesian financial crisis, conditions attached to 1998 International Monetary Fund loans were one of the strongest pressures for domestic economic and political reforms.

Alexander George et al. (1971) discussed eight conditions believed to facilitate coercive diplomacy and argued that the probability of success increases as more of those conditions are met. As summarized and slightly regrouped in Table 8.3, their logic is straightforward. We cannot coerce without having usable options with which to apply some form of force. Attempts to coerce will be ineffective if our adversary does not believe (1) that such options exist and (2) we have the political will to use them. We should be clear about our objectives, not only to plan appropriate actions, but also to communicate our goals accurately at home and abroad. Moreover, one rarely wins everything sought, so policymakers need to be clear individually and within the administration about acceptable terms for a settlement. We need to be strongly enough motivated to apply the threatened force, should that prove necessary, and to pay the requisite prices in lives, treasure, and political influence. If our adversaries fear escalation more than we do, it will help induce them to capitulate. This is possible only if we possess more of those believable force options than our opponents (a condition not explicitly discussed by George), and if we are more strongly motivated to employ them. Finally, in the U.S. political system, any but the briefest uses of force abroad must enjoy adequate domestic political support from Congress and the public.

George et al. induced these conditions from detailed studies of the 1962 Cuban missile crisis, the Vietnam War, and anticommunist conflict in Laos before and during that war. Their book was an early entry in the post–Vietnam War wave of rethinking the limits of power. Their case studies can be extended to a larger set spanning some thirty years, as shown in Table 8.4. In each case, "Y" indicates a criterion was met, "?" that its attainment was doubtful, and "NEG" that the condition favored the adversary of the United States. We contrast the Persian Gulf War and Vietnam War cases, leaving the others as exercises for you.

The U.S. response to Iraq's invasion of Kuwait in 1990, which ultimately led to the 1991 Persian Gulf War, unequivocally met most of George's criteria. Most observers

TABLE 8.3	
Criteria for Successful "Coercive Diplomacy"	

Usable and *Believable* Military or Other Force Options
  (The Only *Necessary* Condition)

Clarity of Objectives
  Objectives We Seek
  Settlement Terms We Will Accept

Motivation
  Strong Motivation
  Stronger Motivation Than Our Opponents

Sense of Urgency to Achieve Our Objectives

Opponents' Fear of Escalation
  Note: Implies We Have Greater Usable Force Than Our Opponents

Adequate Domestic Political Support

Source: Alexander George et al., 1971. George's eight criteria have been reorganized and comments added.

judge that coercive diplomacy worked in the Persian Gulf case, although some thoughts to the contrary are discussed in Chapter 1. Here we restrict our attention to the early phase of that confrontation, in the fall of 1990. Usable U.S. military options existed. The major buildup required weeks for troop and equipment movements, but soldiers were flown into Saudi Arabia within a week of the invasion. Even though strong military options existed, doubt remains about whether Iraqi dictator Saddam Hussein believed the United States and others would use those options against him. It would be months before all the elements were in place to force Iraq from Kuwait, but that goal was clear from the outset. So, too, was the goal of preventing Iraqi forces from pushing further south and west into Saudi Arabia or one of the weak smaller Gulf coast states. Indeed, this was the overriding short-term goal. Between 1990 and 1991 some lack of clarity emerged about goals and terms of settlement, notably about whether the U.S.-led coalition really sought Saddam's overthrow or would support internal groups that revolted. There was very strong motivation in the United States and the developed Western world generally to take action preserving access to petroleum supplies. Nonetheless, our propaganda emphasized other justifications, such as very real Iraqi human rights abuses. It remains debatable whether we were more strongly motivated than Saddam, and whether he feared the very real potential of the United States and the coalition it built to escalate the conflict far beyond Iraq's capabilities. A strong sense of urgency in the fall of 1990 arose from fears, already noted, about Saudi vulnerability to Iraqi invasion. Finally, there was very strong domestic support in the United States and most other coalition member states. President Bush's popularity reached levels higher than those of any previous president, and many congressional opponents of Persian Gulf action kept silent for fear that voters would retaliate at the polls.

George argued that success is more likely as more of his eight criteria are met, and comparing the Gulf War and Vietnam cases tends to support his position. Even during the

TABLE 8.4

George's Criteria Applied to Several Cases of Attempted U.S. "Coercive Diplomacy"

Criteria	Cuban Missile Crisis 1962	Vietnam War Early Period c. 1965–6	Vietnam War Late Period c. 1967–8	Seizure of the *Mayaguez* 1975	Iran Hostage Seizure 1979–81	Grenada Invaded 1983	Panama Invaded 1989	Iraq Invades Kuwait 1990
1. Military Options	Y	?		Y	?	Y	Y	Y
2. Clarity of Our Objectives	Y	?	?	Y	Y	Y	Y	Y
3. Settlement Terms	Y	?	?	Y	Y	Y	Y	Y
Motivation								
4. Strong	Y	Y	?	Y	Y	?	?	Y
5. Asymmetric	Y	?	NEG		NEG	Y	?	?
6. Opponents Fear Escalation	Y	?		?		?	?	?
7. Sense of Urgency	Y	?		Y	?	Y		Y
8. Domestic Support	Y	Y	?	Y	Y	Y	Y	Y

1965–68 period of major U.S. buildup, the only criteria clearly met in the Vietnam War were strong motivation and generally strong domestic support. Major questions exist regarding every other criterion. As war costs accumulated without unambiguous progress toward a clearly identifiable goal, domestic public opinion shifted slowly but inexorably from majority support to majority opposition, remaining bitterly divided the whole time. The 1968 Tet offensive then precipitated a major policy reversal and marked a watershed in the war's conduct. U.S. losses in the 1968–73 period actually exceeded those before 1968, and in that latter period of the war we never clearly enjoyed advantage on any of George's criteria. Instead, there was fairly strong motivation to get out, reflecting an asymmetry in favor of North Vietnam and the Vietcong. U.S. and South Vietnamese military options no longer looked reasonable, sense of urgency was almost reversed, and our opponents could not fear the escalation that we had renounced. On the remaining criteria, U.S. advantage is questionable at best. Every use or consideration of military action since Vietnam has raised questions about our willingness to use force and pay the price in casualties. One response has been a rise in attention to so-called *low-intensity conflict,* which receives fuller consideration in the next chapter.

RANGE OF USABILITY

Usable power *of almost any variety* tends to decline with distance from one's homeland. This notion was examined and applied to defense issues by noted economist, Quaker, and peace activist Kenneth Boulding, who wrote of a loss of strength gradient (1962, 78–79). However, the more descriptive term **strength/distance function** (or SDF) is used here. As Boulding put it, "[W]e have some concept of a space or field within which the conflict takes place, we have a concept of the location of the parties within this space, some place within the conflict space where the party is at home, and we also have a concept of a cost of transport of competitive power through the conflict space."

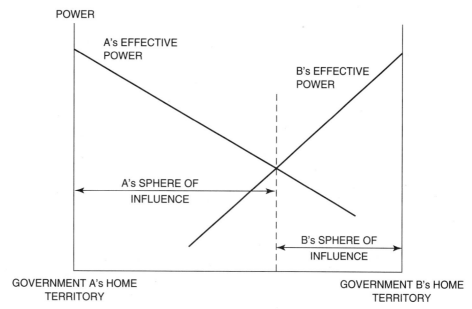

FIGURE 8.3

Strength/Distance Function for a World Without Long-Range Weapons of Mass Destruction

POWER

A's EFFECTIVE POWER

B's EFFECTIVE POWER

A's SPHERE OF INFLUENCE

B's SPHERE OF INFLUENCE

GOVERNMENT A's HOME TERRITORY

GOVERNMENT B's HOME TERRITORY

In a system in which governments possess no long-range weapons of mass destruction, effective or usable power, both military and economic, declines with distance from its base in a manner described by the strength/distance function (SDF). As one moves further and further away from Government A's homeland, eventually a point is reached at which Government B's power equals A's. Beyond that point, B's effective power will exceed A's. Although it may be difficult to locate that point precisely, the fact that it must exist underlies the traditional concept that the world is divided into spheres of military and economic influence. Such a system rests on the critical assumption that the SDF is fairly steep, so each government is viable on its home territory. In the economic analogue of this system, costs of transport contribute to dividing the world into marketing territories within which producers can undersell outside competitors.

Power is assumed to be at its peak on one's home territory, and to grow weaker as the distance over which that power must be projected increases. The decline of competitive power with distance is then measured by the strength/distance function. As one's effective power becomes ever weaker with distance, eventually a point is reached at which it falls below that of some other party. In principle, this explains a classic idea of traditional international relations, according to which the entire world is divided into *spheres* of *influence*. Within each sphere a single government is dominant, as sketched in Figure 8.3. This simple system rests on the critical assumption that the SDF is fairly steep.

Why does usable power decrease with distance from one's homeland? Consider first the military dimension of power; comparable issues regarding economic power are taken up in the next subsection. Washington insiders call the movement and use of military force abroad **power projection.** It requires time and effort, often including considerable difficulties in coordinating the logistics of transport. Very few aircraft have intercontinental range without aerial refueling or intermediate airfields for staging. Transporting tanks overseas by air is so difficult and expensive that it cannot be carried out on a large scale; the largest U.S. military transport aircraft, the C-5A, can carry only two modern main battle tanks. Large numbers of troops and their supplies still are often moved by sea, which is a very slow but relatively inexpensive. The greater the distances over which forces must be moved, and the more rapidly it must be done, the greater are the time and money costs incurred. Moreover, troops and weapons en route are subject to attack and attrition by defenders, particularly as they near their targets.

The decline of power projection capability with distance was clearly demonstrated in studies of U.S. capability to counter a hypothetical Soviet invasion of Iran after the 1979 Iranian revolution. Washington planners commissioned those studies out of concern that postrevolutionary instabilities might offer an opportunity for Soviet intervention, perhaps at the putative invitation of one faction in an internal Iranian power struggle. The USSR was found to enjoy significant advantages of location, which would have allowed troops and armor to be brought in both overland from Soviet-occupied Afghanistan (bordering Iran) and by air from Afghan and southwestern Soviet airfields. With only limited naval forces in the region, the United States would have had to transport forces from home and Western Europe. The studies projected that, by maximum effort including stripping its European forces, the United States could land over a period of 16 to 30 days perhaps a quarter of the troops and one tenth of the armor that the Soviets could bring to bear (Burt, 1980, 4; Middleton, 1980).

The great twentieth-century shift in power projection capabilities may be described in the language of Boulding's concept of **viability.** If a state cannot be absorbed or destroyed as an independent decision-making center, it is said to be **unconditionally viable.** A state that could be absorbed or destroyed is said to be only **conditionally viable,** and its opponent to be dominant. If it would not be advantageous for the dominant government to destroy its rival, the rival has **secure conditional viability.** Finally, if attack would "pay off" but the dominant government still refrains, the weaker state has **insecure conditional viability** (Boulding, 1962, 58–59). During portions of the 1950s and 1960s, for example, the U.S. strategic nuclear superiority over the Soviet Union was so great as to make a devastating American first strike theoretically possible. (Only a few members of the extreme right-wing fringe believed such an attack should be undertaken, however.) During that period, the USSR was insecurely conditionally viable, and the United States had secure conditional viability. The strategic doctrine of mutual assured destruction (or MAD), widely but not universally accepted since the SALT I U.S.-Soviet arms control agreements of 1972, assumes a deterrent system that is stable because each party has secure conditional viability. In such a system, the assurance that initiating war would not pay is provided by a deterrent force believed to be capable of surviving any foreseeable attack.

Viability is closely related to the strength/distance function introduced earlier. As diagrammed in Figure 8.3, each government has at least secure conditional viability within its sphere of influence. Government A enjoys unconditional viability at its homeland, where Government B's effective power is negligible. Iran in 1980 clearly lay much more within the Soviet than the U.S. sphere of influence, just as Cuba lay well within the U.S. sphere during the 1962 missile crisis, provided that only conventional weapons were considered. Soviet introduction of nuclear missiles into Cuba created a crisis, as seen from the United States, precisely because it threatened to replace U.S. nuclear dominance with mutual secure conditional viability. Similarly, close location and the enormous power differentials contributed to an SDF strongly favoring the United States in its many Latin American interventions, as recently as those in Grenada (1983) and Panama (1989). Political will to take advantage of one's sphere of influence remains vital, however. Cuba, for example, was just as much within America's sphere of influence during the disastrous Bay of Pigs invasion attempt of 1961 as during the 1962 missile crisis.

Balance and advantage are more ambiguous in occasional cases in which the focus of action is near the boundary between spheres of influence. Such boundaries are fuzzy wherever we believe the effective power of two or more actors to be nearly comparable. Inevitable small uncertainties in power measurement then become more significant, and speed of mobilization and readiness for action gain importance. Timing and surprise then may overcome small disadvantages according to many measures of power balance.

Consider the example of the 1982 Falklands Islands war between Britain and Argentina. On 2 April of that year Argentina invaded and seized control of the tiny British dependency, located some 350 miles off the southern Argentinean coast, and which Argentina had long claimed under the name of the Malvinas Islands. Britain pursued diplomacy and economic sanctions without success, but, perhaps to the surprise of the Argentine government, rapidly mobilized a substantial naval task force and threatened to retake the islands by force. The proposed theater of operations lay in the fuzzy zone where spheres of influence met, thousands of miles from Britain but only hundreds of miles off the long Argentine coast. That location caused genuine uncertainty about British success until the recapture of the Falklands was nearly completed. In such ambiguous situations of close balance, other factors may gain great importance, and critical technologies and tactics were important factors in the Falklands war. Argentina used French-built Exocet cruise missiles to devastating effect when British ships came close to the islands, and there were some (unsubstantiated) fears that Argentina had a few nuclear weapons. Britain bombed island airfields to force Argentine aircraft to fly from the mainland, and kept most of its ships far enough east of the islands to place those aircraft at the limits of their range. Additionally, Britain's sinking of the cruiser *General Belgrano* early in the conflict and with great loss of life persuaded the Argentine navy to spend the rest of the war in port, removing a submarine threat to British ships.

How do **weapons of mass destruction (WMD),** carried by long-range delivery systems, affect patterns of viability and spheres of influence? The analysis to this point has rested on the assumption that the SDF was fairly steep. Militarily, this means that all but extremely small and weak states will be unconditionally viable or at least securely conditionally viable in their core home territories. Now consider the impact of weapons of mass destruction, the so-called **NBC weapons,** for nuclear, biological, and chemical weapons. When mated with long-range delivery systems such as missiles and strike aircraft, NBC weapons dramatically raise the level of destructiveness. At the very least they shift the conceptual SDFs of Figure 8.3 upward, eventually to such heights that no state

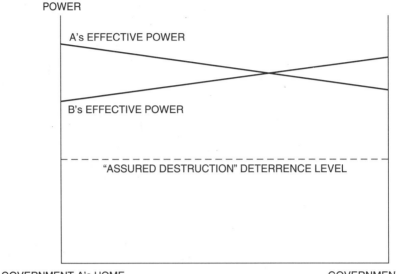

FIGURE 8.4

Strength/Distance Function for a World with Long-Range Weapons of Mass Destruction

POWER

A's EFFECTIVE POWER

B's EFFECTIVE POWER

"ASSURED DESTRUCTION" DETERRENCE LEVEL

GOVERNMENT A's HOME TERRITORY

GOVERNMENT B's HOME TERRITORY

In a system in which governments possess weapons of mass destruction and the long-range means to deliver them to targets, such as strategic nuclear missiles, effective power declines only slowly with distance. This is so primarily because of the very great losses to be suffered even if only a tiny fraction of attackers is able to penetrate defenses. Because no government is unconditionally viable, strategic nuclear weapons do not divide the world into spheres of influence, although such spheres still may be defined by conventional (non-nuclear) and tactical nuclear weapons. According to mutual assured destruction doctrine, governments should refrain from initiating attack so long as the destruction they would expect to suffer in retaliation would exceed some maximum acceptable level. In the economic analogue of such a world, costs of transport would be very low relative to all other costs, so that suppliers had the potential to sell competitively anywhere.

would enjoy unconditional viability. More seriously, the combination of increased power of individual weapons with long-range delivery systems leads to a much slower decline of usable power with distance. Enormous losses can be suffered if even a tiny fraction of attackers penetrates defenses. The slope of the SDF thus becomes much shallower, leading to the situation diagrammed in Figure 8.4.

Here the SDF is fairly flat, and each government can project great power deep into the other's home territory. If each side's power exceeds some critical deterrence level, a regime of *mutual assured destruction* (MAD) may exist. "Assured destruction" is the presumed ability to absorb an attack with confidence that sufficient forces will remain to mount an overwhelming retaliation. In such situations we expect rational would-be attackers to be deterred. It is a misnomer to call this "assured" destruction, of course, because it cannot be guaranteed. "Expected" destruction would be more accurate, and even then deterrence depends on would-be attackers evaluating the situation rationally. If both sides have such a capability, the regime is one of mutual secure conditional viability. Because no government is unconditionally viable, weapons of mass destruction such as strategic nuclear weapons do not divide the world into spheres of influence, although such spheres still may be defined by conventional (non-nuclear) and short-range tactical nuclear weapons.

At this point we run headlong into a major contemporary defense dilemma. Ideal stable security traditionally has been believed to require unconditional viability in the home territory. Now, modern weapons of mass destruction threaten to deny even the most powerful states that degree of viability. Middle-level powers may be encouraged to develop nuclear weaponry for short-term advantage and to do as well as they can long term in such a system. As Boulding put the traditional idea, "[F]or national defense as a system to possess any kind of equilibrium and for nations to be unconditionally viable under a system of national defense, each nation must be able to preserve an area of peace within its critical boundaries, even if it has to maintain this area of peace by fighting wars outside it" (1962, 267).

Weapons of mass destruction coupled to long-range delivery systems threaten to deprive every state of that core zone of peace. In a crucial development for international politics at the turn of the twenty-first century, it has become possible, if not probable, that no more than one state can be unconditionally viable at any given time—and then only if it has a monopoly on the highest military technology. Although Boulding's condition can be met today with conventional weapons, intercontinental nuclear weapons without any adequate defense imply the loss of even conditional viability, unless a deterrent system can be maintained. In the aftermath of the Soviet breakup, there are now few concerns about a superpower nuclear exchange. By far the greater concern today is NBC weapons in the hands of smaller powers. Given such weaponry, small and regional powers have the potential to cause real damage to the United States and other great powers. More likely, however, such capabilities could extend the reach and severity of regional wars. Note Boulding's use of the phrase "unconditionally viable *under a system of national defense*" (emphasis added). His solution for this problem was to move away from state-based national defense toward international security arrangements.

Given NBC weaponry and long-range delivery systems, rogue states willing to violate international behavior norms are a much greater danger than in the past. Iraqi launches of chemical weapons on missiles during the Iran-Iraq war, and of 200-mile-range Scud missiles with conventional explosive warheads against Israel and coalition forces during the Persian Gulf War, present only a tiny foretaste of what is already possible. As UN inspection teams in the 1990s uncovered more and more information about the breadth and depth of Iran's nuclear weapons program, it became ever clearer how an ambitious government endowed with significant natural resources can purchase sufficient destructive capability to threaten every power in the region, and even the regional forces and interests of extraregional great powers. In this context, the reported response of the Indian military chief of staff to a question about what he had learned from the Persian Gulf War is instructive: "Never fight the United States without nuclear weapons" (Aspin, 1992, 9).

Viability and SDFs for Economic Power

Economic viability is analogous to military viability, and usable economic power declines with distance in ways quite similar to military power, for many of the same reasons. Transporting goods requires time, effort, risk, and expense, just as does transporting troops or tanks. Manufactures in transit typically remain on shippers' inventories, delaying payment and incurring holding costs until delivery, and are subject to both damage and delay. Reconsider Figure 8.3 as representing a hypothetical world with two producers whose potential profit (selling price minus costs of production and transport) declines with distance. If products are identical, producers seek to maximize their sales, and buyers purchase without bias, the market will be divided according to distances. Each producer will be unconditionally viable in its home market and will capture all the market from its home base out to the point at which it cannot undersell competitors and still make a profit. Note that this division of the market into spheres of influence does not assume that all producers have equal costs of either production or transport. Given this example, we should not be surprised to find that studies by such scholars as Bruce Russett indicate that most states trade heavily with their near neighbors. Canada, for example, is the largest trading partner of the United States.

This pattern is true around the world, with a few notable exceptions. Uneven distribution of critical resources is the biggest anomaly, and heavy petroleum shipments from areas such as the Middle East to developed economies such as the United States, Western Europe, and Japan are the outstanding example. Political divisions also produce exceptions. There was relatively little trade between Eastern and Western European states when the Soviet Union dominated Eastern Europe, although increases in east-west European trade helped signal the winding down of the Cold War. There was little trade between Israel and the neighboring Arab states throughout their decades of alternating hot and formal war. Infrastructures and trading patterns laid down during colonial times also have proved durable exceptions to the general pattern of trade with near neighbors. In contemporary Africa, for example, former British colonies tend to trade extensively with each other and with Britain, and former French colonies tend to trade heavily with each other and with France. The logic of such patterns is straightforward: trade ties were built during colonial times, and the former colonial language eases communication and tends to be the common language of business.

If transport costs somehow could be made very low relative to other costs, the resulting world with very flat economic SDFs would give suppliers the potential to sell competitively anywhere. This situation could be represented by Figure 8.4. The economic "nuclear powers" of such a world would be states able to undercut other producers in their home markets. Defenses exist in such forms as tariffs, quotas, and severe import inspection regulations. Counters to some of those defenses also exist, for example, dumping goods in selected markets below cost to drive indigenous producers out of business. Given such a situation, governments well might negotiate to divide territory into markets by agreement. Tariffs and similar trade barriers promote just such divisions, whereas free trade areas encourage their breakdown. Restricting trade to specified areas effectively establishes zones of secure conditional economic viability. As we see in Chapter 11, however, the increasing internationalization of business is rapidly undermining the very concept of national industries and national markets. In effect, this undercuts the notions of location and homeland that are key underlying assumptions of viability and SDFs.

APPLIED POWER PERSPECTIVES: THE UNITED STATES, EUROPE, AND BOSNIA

Let us now apply the many perspectives on power examined in this chapter to a contemporary case of significant magnitude and consequence: recent and future relations between the United States and the Europeans, with particular emphasis on France, NATO, and the Bosnian war in former Yugoslavia. On 5 December 1995, French foreign minister Hervé de Charette announced his country would resume active participation in NATO's military wing nearly three decades after then–French president Charles de Gaulle withdrew his country from the alliance's military command structure and ordered U.S. forces to leave France. Effectively, de Charette's announcement meant that France's position within NATO would become very close to that of Spain, which is fully involved in all NATO military planning but does not place its forces under alliance command in peacetime (Cohen, 1995). The announcement came during a meeting of foreign and defense ministers in Brussels, Belgium, devoted mainly to formally approving NATO's largest operation to that date the dispatch of some 60,000 troops—20,000 of them American—to enforce a tenuous U.S.-brokered peace in Bosnia. French visions of European emancipation from U.S. military and political leadership had foundered during more than three years of inability to end the Bosnian war, so de Charette's announcement had profound implications for the future of U.S.-European relations.

As discussed in Chapter 2, Soviet and American nuclear arsenals grew rapidly during the 1960s, increasing superpower nuclear vulnerability and undermining credibility that a U.S. "nuclear umbrella" could continue to deter attack against Western Europe. When the superpowers gained global reach extending deep into each other's heartlands, their SDFs became much flatter and they lost unconditional viability. With the United States becoming at best securely conditionally viable, the notion that we would retaliate directly against the Soviets to avenge an attack on France became less and less credible. Under President de Gaulle, France struggled to remain an independent great power in the nuclear age, and launched a massive program in the early 1960s to develop its own independent nuclear *force de frappe*, or strike force. That force of fighter-bombers, and later intermediate-range ballistic missiles, was quite small compared with the Soviet arsenal, but it had enough penetration capability against Soviet defenses to maintain mutual secure conditional viability. France had the additional advantage that any Soviet land attack would first have to cross West German territory, where NATO planned to make its stand. As the *force de frappe* came on line, France announced in 1966 its nearly total withdrawal from NATO military affairs, and the following year NATO headquarters were relocated from Paris to Brussels. Opting out of NATO's military wing while remaining an alliance member for political purposes served the cause of French independence and Gaullist notions of French *grandeur*. Additionally, ordering U.S. forces out of France protested America's role in Vietnam.

French actions were consciously designed to assert an independent great power position in the world, only one step below the two superpowers. Policy independence went along with a long independent political and cultural history and a veto-wielding permanent seat on the UN Security Council. Developing the *force de frappe* without U.S. help comparable to that given to the British during their nuclear development was a major assertion of French economic capacity and technological capability. Although France was indeed overmatched by the superpowers on most measures of power, it retained a large and well-educated population and labor force, fairly large land area close to other European markets and ocean transport, mild climate and substantial agricultural production, and a highly developed modern industrial economy. Thus France's independent political and military course built on considerable natural and synthetic power attributes. Moreover, so long as Germany remained divided into eastern and western zones, France remained the largest political and economic force in Western Europe and, until British entry, in the Common Market. These advantages were used to extract a high price for that British entry: renunciation of special trade ties to the commonwealth.

When dramatic developments at the end of the 1980s brought an abrupt end to the Cold War, major governments around the world were forced to recalculate their policies under radically revised situations, and none more than the Europeans. After German reunification in 1990, France no longer had the largest economy in Western Europe. With the USSR's breakup and formal fragmentation at the end of 1991, the Soviet threat that had been central to NATO planning and European politics since the end of World War II effectively disappeared, although fears of Russian ultranationalism would resurface within only two years. No longer was Western Europe menaced by a power so great that it could only be countered with aid from the other superpower across the Atlantic. Consequently, the United States lost quite a bit of its ability to influence the Europeans, and they gained political maneuvering room and independence.

Leaders of the (then) twelve member states of the European Community met at Maastricht, the Netherlands, 9–11 December 1991 and signed treaties on monetary and political union to create what has been known since 1994 as the European Union (EU). Building on decades of post–World War II functional cooperation, the Maastricht agreements looked toward eventual unification of Scandinavia and (at least) Western Europe. A common currency was launched for some states by 1999, although Britain and Denmark were allowed to opt out. The range of policy issues in which the EU would have a voice was increased. A leading role in social policy was assigned, except in Britain. Increased aid was pledged for Greece, Ireland, Portugal, and Spain, the four poorest member states. Powers of the 567-member European Parliament were slightly increased. The Maastricht agreements also sought to establish common foreign policies for the member states and laid the groundwork for a common defense policy. In the optimistic Europeanism of late 1991 and early 1992, French officials actively suggested that the end of the Cold War and the emergence of the EU should lead Europe to adopt a defense structure more independent of NATO, embodied in the Western European Union (WEU).

Why did that not happen? Because of the Bosnian civil war. From the onset of major fighting in former Yugoslavia in April 1992 until the U.S.-brokered peace accords were signed in Dayton, Ohio, in November 1995, there was continued friction between the United States and its European allies within and outside NATO. Over those forty-three months a succession of plans and negotiations under the auspices of the EU, NATO, the

Organization for Security and Cooperation in Europe (OSCE), WEU, UN, and individual governments, plus NATO airstrikes, UN arms embargoes, and sizable UN peace-keeping forces on the ground, all failed to bring peace. Ultimately, only the United States had the combination of political will and military muscle to coerce a peace agreement among the major combatants and make it work.

This has profound implications for the relative power and influence of the United States and the European Union for some time to come. Clearly, the United States has the military forces and power projection capability to take an active role in Europe. Its active duty armed forces in 1996 were second only to China's, and at the beginning of 1995 it had over 137,000 active duty troops assigned to western and southern Europe. Perhaps more important, few states exceed U.S. military technologies, and then only for a few selected weapons. For example, the United States buys Harrier "jump jets" from Britain for its marines because they are the world's best short-takeoff high-performance jet fighter. On balance, as amply demonstrated in the Persian Gulf War, U.S. forces are widely equipped with the latest in high-performance military technologies. Additionally, those forces are backed up by substantial airlift and sea transport capabilities. Decades of preparing for possible war with the Soviet Union in Europe left a formidable U.S. military force. Downsizing due to budget stringencies and the widely (if perhaps incorrectly) perceived lack of post–Cold War need for large forces in being nonetheless left the United States able to project considerable force into Eastern Europe.

Even more interesting is the U.S. political muscle evidenced in the 1995 Bosnian peace accords. In effect, the United States engaged in coercive diplomacy not only with the Bosnians, Bosnian Serbs, and Croats, but also with its European NATO allies. Over the previous several years those allies had criticized the United States for limiting its participation to air strikes while Britain, France, and other states had peacekeeping troops on the ground. Additionally, both the Bush and Clinton administrations had been criticized for their reluctance to become involved in Bosnia, particularly when U.S. troops were engaged in humanitarian relief and even some nation building in their ultimately fruitless Somalia undertaking (see the opening case in Chapter 7). During the summer of 1995, U.S. aircraft assigned to NATO extensively bombed Bosnian Serb forces who were besieging Sarajevo and other key points in Bosnia. This helped break the Serbian advantage in artillery and revised the balance of power in favor of the Bosnian-Croation federation. Croatia particularly benefited, and was able to retake much territory previously lost to the Bosnian Serbs. This helped put severe pressure on the Serbs to participate in peace talks. At the same time, U.S. diplomatic cajolery combined with the relentless toll of more than three years of military, territorial, and population losses persuaded the Bosnians to settle for a smaller share of (formerly their own) territory. U.S. diplomats who had once airily announced that they "don't do maps" designed a territorial division along ethnic lines and sold it to the parties. They also proposed and sold a NATO military presence carefully labeled a "peace implementation force." This appellation was chosen to emphasize that the force was to help implement a peace agreed on by the parties and then depart, neither remaining indefinitely as peacekeepers nor engaging in nation building.

The 1995 announcement of France's return to NATO's military structure implied recognition that the United States would continue to have a central role in European defense and military planning for the foreseeable future and that any European military force would evolve within NATO rather than outside. Dominique Moisi, deputy director of the French Institute for International Relations, stated, "The fact is that, militarily, we have depended on NATO and our margin of independence has been negligible. But our margin of political influence on NATO was also negligible before today" (Cohen, 1995). This suggests that French leaders sought to maximize French power and had come to believe that an expanded role within NATO now served that end. Despite French foreign minister de Charette's call for "a European pillar of defense" within NATO and for the Western European Union to become "the European pillar of the Alliance," few observers considered such developments at all likely (Cohen, 1995). Seen in light of the previous forty-three months of wrangling, announcing the peace implementation force meant the United States had procured the agreement that Europeans were unable to generate. This implies that the United States maintains a political reach far more consequential than its military compass, even though the former relies significantly on the latter. Given years of European inability to concert effective action in Bosnia, the peace agreement and NATO implementation force also seem to imply that U.S. power is not in decline relative to Europe. Recall also Michael Elliott's words quoted in Chapter 3, that "precisely because America *does* adopt a moral tone at the start of issues, its vote in favor of any particular endgame carries weight" (1995, 45).

How does this case stack up against the various power perspectives discussed in this chapter and summarized in Table 8.1? The United States continues to enjoy many natural power attributes and to lead the world on many synthetic power attributes, including overall military capability and force projection capability. It compares very favorably with any of the European states, and even with the EU as a whole, on essentially all power measures. Perhaps more interestingly, this case suggests that U.S. social-psychological-political leadership of NATO will continue beyond the Cold War. Every type of action channel was employed in Bosnia, including bombing raids, negotiations and diplomatic pressure, economic embargoes and incentives, and political support and punishments. U.S. military actions utilized forces already in being and deployed in Europe for the bombing raids, and even most U.S. troops in the peace implementation force came from Germany. Dynamically, the United States gained influence relative to the Europeans, and managed the power shifts in Bosnia quite effectively in pressuring the Bosnian Serbs to settle. U.S. goals included assisting the Bosnians, generally thought to have the superior moral ground, and opposing those seeking territorial gains, most notably the Bosnian Serbs. (No side, however, was free of all offenses.) In the Dayton negotiations and events in the run-up to those talks, tactics employed included a combination of coercion and persuasion, utilizing both hard and soft power. For example, the settlement relied crucially on all sides being exhausted by horrible losses in more than three years of war, and promised territorial stability and peace. As sometimes happens in diplomacy, the settlement promised mutually incompatible results to the different parties: a form of unification to the Bosnian Muslims and effective autonomy to the Croats and Bosnian Serbs.

Lurking behind U.S. coercive diplomacy regarding the Bosnian settlement were the threats that the United States and NATO could escalate, and that our withdrawal would allow a return to further bloody fighting. The Dayton peace accords seemed clearly to signal that U.S. influence still extended not only across the Atlantic to Western Europe, but onward into Eastern Europe. Similar thoughts would recur in 1997–98 regarding NATO expansion into Eastern Europe. Analysts of the Bosnian peace are likely to credit the United States with goals beyond its own direct interests. Peace and security in Europe continue to be seen as vital to U.S. security, and the fear of a wider Balkan war was cited by President Clinton as one important reason for sending U.S. troops to Bosnia. To be sure, domestic political considerations also played an important role. The Bosnian peace implementation force was undoubtedly the riskiest undertaking yet for a president previously severely criticized for foreign policy failings because renewed fighting or serious U.S. casualties could have led to new charges of ineptitude. Yet the move came near the end of a highly successful foreign policy year for President Clinton. Earlier in 1995 he had helped facilitate an extension of the 1993 Israeli-PLO peace accord. Visits to Britain, Ireland, and Northern Ireland en route to the Paris signing of the Bosnian accords were themselves sufficient to trigger a new British-Irish step in peace negotiations for Northern Ireland, where all sides praised his even-handedness. Suddenly, President Clinton seemed to have grasped the full potential of his office to influence foreign relations, and the Europeans seemed most pleased.

SUMMARY

Power includes, but goes far beyond, military force, and its political purpose is the partial control of human behavior. Power always has limits, but it extends beyond the ability to prevail in military and other conflicts and overcome obstacles, to include the ability to influence others and alter the probable outcomes of policy interactions. Power attributes—those things which cause us to consider their possessors, whether states or nonstate actors, to be "powerful"—may be classified as either natural or synthetic, depending on whether they occur naturally, as do petroleum reserves or a climate favorable to agriculture, or result from deliberate policy choices by human decision makers, such as large standing armies or highly educated populations. Social-psychological attributes are a special type of synthetic power, pertaining to social cohesiveness, political stability, and public confidence in government, and cannot necessarily be built to order as directly and readily as military forces. Although a complete policy often is complex enough to have considerable overlaps, it is helpful to distinguish military, diplomatic, and economic channels of action. Additionally, each type of action usually has some political meaning and motivation, both at home and abroad. Both actual and potential power must be considered, taking into account conversion and mobilization potential as well as existing forces. The dynamics of power measurement and balance direct attention to whether one's power is shifting relative to that of one's competitors and whether such shifts are favorable or unfavorable.

Power is always directed toward some goal. It may be used either to assist or to oppose or coerce others, or to deny the goals that opponents seek. Another perspective on purposes for utilizing power is the distinction between the hard power to command others, and the soft power to coopt others, persuading them to join us in seeking the same goals. Severity, timing, and escalation in the use of power are inextricably intertwined. Severity refers to how much of the power available will be utilized, from the least manageable bit to everything obtainable. Timing refers both to what options are available when, and to the role of time sequence in escalation. Escalation is the staged increase of action severity over time, monitored by feedback, until a level sufficient to accomplish desired policy goals is reached. The closely related concept of coercive diplomacy extends in severity from peaceful diplomacy to limited war, overlapping and including both.

Although seven other conditions are considered favorable to successful coercive diplomacy, its one indispensable prerequisite is that usable and believable options for the use of force must exist, whether the force be diplomatic, economic, or military.

Usable power of almost any variety tends to decline with distance from one's homeland. This explains both the concept of economic and military spheres of influence, along with their attendant political influence, and the economic tendency to trade primarily with near neighbors. In Kenneth Boulding's usage, a state that cannot be absorbed or destroyed as an independent decision-making center is said to be unconditionally viable. A state that could be absorbed or destroyed is said to be only conditionally viable, and its opponent to be dominant. If it would not be advantageous for the dominant government to destroy its rival, the rival has secure conditional viability; and if attack would "pay off" but the dominant government still refrains, the weaker state has insecure conditional viability. The concepts of viability and the decline of usable power with distance apply equally well in the realms of defense and economics. Because no government is unconditionally viable against nuclear weapons coupled to long-range delivery systems, weapons of mass destruction do not divide the world into spheres of influence, although such spheres still may be defined by conventional (non-nuclear) and tactical nuclear weapons.

The next four chapters are devoted to broader, deeper, more detailed examinations of the possibilities and problems of military, diplomatic, economic, and international cooperative tools of policy, respectively. Each set of policy tools, however, is considered in the larger context of the types of concerns to which it is best suited. Given how dramatically the foreign policy problems now confronting the United States differ in number, character, and possible solutions from the problems faced during the Cold War era, we should expect important changes in the importance and potential usefulness of different types of power.

KEY TERMS

Actual power (Compare with *potential power*.)

Coercive diplomacy

Escalation

Hard power or command power (Compare with *soft power*.)

Industrial policy

Infrastructure

Natural power attributes (Compare with *synthetic power attributes*.)

NBC weapons (See also *weapons of mass destruction—WMD*.)

Potential power (Compare with *actual power*.)

Power attributes (See *natural, synthetic*, and *social-psychological types*.)

Power projection

Severity of action

Social-psychological power attributes

Soft power or cooptive power (Compare with *hard power*.)

Strength/distance function

Synthetic power attributes (Compare with *natural power attributes*.)

Timing

Viability (Different types are listed here in order of decreasing viability.)

    Unconditional viability

    Conditional viability

    Secure conditional viability

    Insecure conditional viability

Weapons of mass destruction (WMD)

SELECTED READINGS

Boulding, Kenneth E. 1962. *Conflict and Defense: A General Theory.* New York: Harper & Row.

George, Alexander L. 1991. *Forceful Persuasion : Coercive Diplomacy as an Alternative to War.* Washington, D.C.: United States Institute of Peace Press

———. 1994. *The Limits of Coercive Diplomacy.* Boulder, Colo.: Westview.

Johnson, Robert H. 1994. *Improbable Dangers: U.S. Conceptions of Threat in the Cold War and After.* New York: St. Martin's Press.

Kahn, Herman. 1965. *On Escalation: Metaphors and Scenarios.* New York: Praeger.

CHAPTER 9

SECURITY, SECURITY DILEMMAS, AND MILITARY INSTRUMENTS OF POLICY

FREEMAN DYSON AND THE ⊕ "TWO COMMUNITIES" PROBLEM

In his 1984 book *Weapons and Hope*, Freeman Dyson suggested a fundamental problem of perception that affects the whole gamut of political decisions about security issues. Dyson was well qualified to do this because he was a brilliant physicist often consulted by the U.S. government on nuclear weapons policy issues, but maintained numerous important friendships within the peace activist community. This gave him a foot in each camp, the defense policy establishment and its opponents, and he wrote during a time of intense military and arms control policy debates. In 1984 the Reagan administration defense buildup was in full swing, the Strategic Defense Initiative for missile defense had been launched only the previous year, and the world was—unbeknownst to almost all the principal parties—only about six years from the end of the Cold War.

The perceptual problem Dyson described involves many aspects of styles of thought and action but hinges on which of two broad sets of issues an individual considers to be the more significant and tractable. This is described in other sources as the "two communities" problem (Baugh, 1989). In effect, Dyson asserts that the two communities talk past each other when arguing security issues, each ignoring whatever validity the other's arguments may possess.

Dyson writes of the two "worlds" of the "warriors" and the "victims." "Warriors share a common language and a common style" (Dyson, 1984, 4). Whatever their differences of political position or specific policy recommendations, they seek to apply the tools of objective factual analysis to help produce incremental improvements in world conditions. This outlook leads naturally to questions about the state and management of political and military balances. For example, the question, "Will the United States have adequate military forces to meet potential Asian region nuclear challenges in the early twenty-first century?" is meaningful to warriors. Victims, however, tend toward a personalistic, anecdotal, nontechnical, and humanistic style of argument. They are likely to focus strongly on the human tragedy of war and to seek revolutionary rather than incremental change. Those holding that outlook naturally raise questions about reforming the international system and disarming nuclear weapons.

CARTOON 9.1

The War Department was created by act of Congress in 1789 and originally had jurisdiction over the navy. As part of the post-World War II defense reorganization in 1947,
the War Department (and departments of the Navy and Army Air Force) became the
Department of Defense. "Defense" sounds much better in peacetime than "war," and
the new department's name was a significant signal to the post-Cold War world that
global internationalism would demand large standing military forces.
© Sidney Harris.

Dyson worries that the two communities speak different languages and consequently
regard each other's concerns as irrelevant to the "real" problems. His concept provides a
metaphor for an undeniable difficulty that plagues security studies: fundamental disagreements on the questions we should be asking, and even more on the methods we should
adopt to answer them. Thus *"security"* means very different things to different people, and
resolving the differences is intensely political. For Dyson's warriors, taking a traditional
realist perspective, security primarily meant national or state security, to be defended by
state actions in a fundamentally anarchic world. Appropriate actions included building
intercontinental nuclear missiles to deter attack, and defensive antimissiles to help ward
off attack if deterrence failed. For Dyson's victims, in contrast, security was both more individual and more global in scope, and was threatened by state actions. For them nuclear

missiles increased the chance of war, even if by miscalculation or accident, and made any possible war more terrible, potentially harming all the world's people. The fact that actions taken in search of security may actually reduce it is one of many dilemmas surrounding security.

WHAT IS SECURITY AND HOW DO WE ATTAIN IT?

What is **security**? Dictionaries speak of a state or sense of safety or certainty, and of freedom from anxiety, danger, doubt, and so on. Such definitions raise the important distinction between the physical state or condition of *being* secure and the psychological perception of *feeling* secure. Although we may both be and feel secure, it seems clear that we may have either without the other. Moreover, it seems unlikely that we can ever be totally secure and free from all anxiety and doubt. At the international level, even an *unconditionally viable* state (see Chapter 8), capable of surviving any conceivable attack, still could be attacked by an irrational opponent. At the individual level, each of us sees at least small conflicts between risk and opportunity in everyday life. Often we cannot be certain of receiving an "A" in our most interesting college courses; drivers face small risks of injury or death to pursue convenient transportation; and we cannot win a great new job without applying and facing the risk of rejection. Thus, even at the individual level, it is impossible to gain absolute security by totally eliminating risk. The same result holds at every higher level of organization, all the way up to the international system. This is only one of many dilemmas or apparent contradictions that surround and permeate the concept and pursuit of security.

Not the least of those dilemmas is the fact that scholars and analysts never have reached general agreement on any simple definition of the term *security*. In an excellent and broad-ranging examination of security issues, the Canadian scholar Barry Buzan devotes two pages to surveying thirteen authors' quite disparate attempts to frame such a definition (1991, 16–17). Kenneth Boulding's different degrees of nation-state *viability*, discussed in Chapter 8, also define different types or degrees of security against military or economic threats. Whenever so many different definitions exist, even if not all of them conflict, we should anticipate two things: First, the subject is many faceted and probably quite important; and, second, we need to be careful and precise about what we mean when discussing it.

Thoughts about security in the realm of foreign policy often turn first to the vague but frequently mentioned concept of national security. Decision makers regularly invoke national security but rarely define it, even though it is a stock phrase of the Cold War period and of political realism. Usually **national security** refers to what properly should be called *state* security, and even many analysts who take broad approaches to security studies retain a state-centric approach. This view is entirely consistent with the realist perspective on international politics, which emphasizes the pursuit of state interests defined in terms of power. During the Cold War era in the United States and the Western world generally, national security referred almost exclusively to state security, survival, and the protection of power interests around the world. The perceived global communist threat was to be countered and contained primarily by military means. National security became the all-purpose justification for policy choices as diverse as tripling the defense budget after the outbreak of the Korean War in 1950, proceeding from nuclear to thermonuclear bomb development in the early 1950s, carrying out anticommunist witch-hunts at home during the McCarthy era of the 1950s, devising and building intercontinental ballistic missiles, and constructing the interstate highway system. Security thinking in the United States revolved particularly around nuclear weapons and deterrence strategy, and drove security thinking throughout the developed world.

During the Cold War, most security specialists within the academic community focused primarily on military aspects, and many participated in government as in-and-outers. Even the interdisciplinary "peace science" movement, well enough developed by 1957 to support the newly founded *Journal of Conflict Resolution*, still directed much of its attention to military aspects of security. Conflicts were to be resolved, reduced, or avoided by compiling and analyzing data about wars and other conflicts, allowing scholars to determine the patterns by which arms competitions and other disputes escalated to violence and might be controlled. Practical policy advice included methods for crisis management (see Chapter 5) and for institutionalizing arms control. Only a rather small set of academics and activists interpreted peace studies to mean studying the workings of peace or actively waging peace through such means as direct citizen action, and they were marginalized by both the political and academic establishments.

Beginning slowly in the last quarter of the twentieth century and gaining impetus particularly since the end of the Cold War, academic and other analysts increasingly have come to see security as international rather than just national in scope, and have challenged the exclusively military treatment of security issues. One reflection of that change, and also an outlet for studies embracing the new viewpoint, is the journal *International Security*, founded in 1975. The new and broader viewpoint is typified by the work of Barry Buzan (1991, 19–20), who identifies the following five major sectors in which the security of human collectivities is affected by human activities:

- *Military security* is the traditional focus of security studies, embracing not only the interplay between states' armed offensive and defensive capabilities, but also their perceptions of each other's intentions.

- *Political security* concerns the organizational stability of states, including their systems of governance and the ideologies to which they appeal for legitimization.

- *Economic security* involves the access to natural and financial resources and to markets necessary to maintain acceptable levels of individual welfare and state power.

- *Societal security* concerns the maintenance of national cultural, ethnic, linguistic, and religious identity and traditional practices, presumably with some allowance for necessary evolution and adaptation to external conditions and developments.

- *Environmental security* involves maintaining local, national, and planetary biospheres as the vital life support system for all human endeavors.

In this chapter we examine the many aspects of security in the contemporary world and what they imply about U.S. foreign policy problems and policy tools for solving them.

The five major sections of this chapter cover (1) explications of the five major security sectors just sketched; (2) an examination of the new international threat environment as the twentieth century gives way to the twenty first; (3) dilemmas that plague contemporary security policy; (4) unconventional responses for unconventional times, an examination of military policy instruments not already discussed here or in Chapter 8; and (5) an exploration of the benefits and drawbacks of arms transfers.

We find first that security always has been a core concern in political theory and applied policy. Second, we examine how the end of the Cold War has changed the international context of foreign policy in ways that greatly alter the set of security concerns facing the United States. Broadly, military security concerns now focus on more but smaller conflicts, often of new kinds. Economic security concerns have grown as economic globalization progresses and former U.S. dominance is reduced. Political and societal security concerns have grown in number and increasingly cause military and economic conflicts. Environmental security never appeared on government policy radar screens during the early Cold War, but now is increasingly recognized by most governments, and has begun to force changes in U.S. foreign and domestic policies. Third, we explore how a number of inherent limitations constrain how thoroughly we can meet our security concerns. Fourth, we examine a number of unconventional military instruments of policy that are receiving attention in the post–Cold War era. Finally, we explore why arms transfers are a double-edged policy instrument, by examining the incentives to sell or give arms to others and the problems they create.

THE FIVE MAJOR SECTORS OF SECURITY CONCERNS

Buzan (1991: 21–23) argues powerfully the neorealist insight that the anarchic structure of the international system—by which he means that government resides in the units of the system rather than in any central authority—is the primary political context for international security. From this he derives three major conditions which that anarchy imposes on the concept of security. First, "states are the principal referent object of security because they are both the framework of order and the highest source of governing authority." In addition to this sociopolitical centrality, states control larger amounts and more potent forms of military power than any other type of actor in the international system. This explains the dominance of concern about "national" security. Second, external threats will always be important enough to national security that "international security" is "best used to refer to systemic conditions that influence the ways in which states make each other feel more or less secure." Finally, "if security depends on either harmony or hegemony, then it cannot be lastingly achieved within anarchy," implying that "under anarchy, security can only be relative, never absolute." In this view, international anarchy implies that states are and likely will remain the most important actors affecting security. To that extent, Buzan's analysis is state centric, even though it extends well beyond the traditional arena of military security. Most other analysts share his focus on states as the most important international actors for security concerns.

Almost as important as the question "What is security?"—and inextricably intertwined with it—is the question "Whose security?" Buzan, for example, examines security questions at levels of analysis starting with individuals, moving up through states, regional security complexes, interregional complexes, and ending with the global (international) security complex. There are powerful arguments for adopting broad interpretations of security regarding both (1) spheres of activity and concern, and (2) levels of analysis, or the individuals and groups affected. In particular, the rising density of actors and interactions in the international system implies a rapid increase in security interdependencies. More types of human activities in more locations have more widespread effects than ever before. The end of the Cold War has done more than renew concern about old types of violence like the ethnic conflicts that have torn apart states like Rwanda and the former Yugoslavia. It also has heightened concerns about new types of violence stemming from such activities as the spread of nuclear capability from former Soviet republics to rogue states. Environmental problems and the security challenges they pose become ever more severe as population increases cause densities to rise, industrialization spreads and increases quantities of emissions, and thresholds of irreversible change are approached or crossed. Increasing internationalization of corporations and trade raises economic security questions for more and more individuals and states across the whole spectrum of wealth, making economic security arguably our greatest concern as we enter the twenty-first century.

MILITARY SECURITY

Military security, of course, is the traditional focus of security studies and cannot be ignored in the contemporary world. It embraces not only the interplay between states' armed offensive and defensive capabilities, but also their perceptions of each other's intentions. In the aftermath of the Cold War, attention has shifted from superpower nuclear arms control and management to issues in the use and management of violence on a smaller scale but with broader worldwide application. Such actions include covert operations, coercive diplomacy, low-intensity conflicts (LICs), larger conflicts that are conventional in the sense that they do not involve the use of nuclear weapons, and peacemaking, humanitarian relief, peacekeeping, peace enforcement, nation building, and police actions. Many such actions may be collective security operations conducted by multiple governments.

Other issues of concern include the inducements, uses, and difficulties of arms transfers (sales, aid, and gifts), the growing problems of rising levels of military technology in developing states, and the recent tremendous growth in licensed production of modern weaponry. Institutionalized arms control is subject to severe cross pressures. The same major powers that seek to limit the "horizontal" proliferation of nuclear and other high-technology capabilities to additional states seek expanded markets for many of those same capabilities, thus promoting regional proliferation. Ironically, as we discussed in Chapter 3, the end of the Cold War and the virtual disappearance of fears about a superpower nuclear exchange have left a new world order in which small and regional conflicts are increasingly likely.

POLITICAL SECURITY

Political security concerns the organizational stability of states, including their systems of governance and the ideologies to which they appeal for legitimization. Recall the earlier attention, especially in Chapter 5, devoted to the ways in which policy "goes wrong." Certain types of policy problems tend to arise from the institutional structures we have built to formulate and execute policy, and we cannot eliminate all such policy problems. Inherent tensions will always exist, for example, between the desire for time to reflect on policy choices and the need for prompt actions. Even the most stable governments exhibit some such problems, and any organizational and governmental instabilities compound these difficulties by an order of magnitude. A government in upheaval, whether by revolution from within or attack and penetration from without, is inherently insecure and unstable. At a less extreme level, some governments clearly enjoy greater political stability (and thus, security) than others.

Superior institutional design contributes tremendously to superior political stability and greater political security. Political scholars generally consider the U.S. Constitution and the political system evolved under it to be among the world's great success stories in institutional design, responsible in no small part for the prolonged political stability this state has enjoyed. That constitution has endured, adapted, and evolved through more than two centuries of profound change, including continentwide growth, vast increase and dispersion in population, economic development through and beyond the industrial revolution, and broad political emancipation and extension of civil rights well beyond what was foreseen by the Founders. If you doubt the ability of institutional design to contribute to political stability and security, compare the stability the United States has enjoyed under its essentially two-party system (not directly specified in the Constitution) with the recurrent instability suffered by such multiparty states as contemporary France or Italy.

Ideology also can either promote or undermine political security. Political stability itself may be highly and widely valued within a population, and inculcated through educational systems. If widely shared ideology generates a widespread sense that most citizens agree about major social and political issues, it contributes powerfully to stability and concerted national purpose. In some societies, political security becomes positively associated with societal security based on national cultural identity and uniqueness. In other societies, instability, upheavals, coups, and frequent government restructurings may become part of the prevailing political ethos. Marx wrote about the inevitability of a proletarian (working-class) revolution against the owners of the means of production, and most communist governments have devoted considerable effort to persuading their peoples that they were involved in ongoing revolution. In the Soviet Union during the 1920s and 1930s, with no other communist state in the world, there was a widespread and well-founded sense of being surrounded by a hostile world. That situation, certainly not conducive to political security, helped provide legitimization for the Soviet dictator Joseph Stalin's brutal internal purges and paranoia about the outside world. Cambodia under Pol Pot during the 1970s and North Korea during the 1990s provide even more aberrant examples of paranoid extreme isolationism.

ECONOMIC SECURITY

Economic security involves the access to natural and financial resources and to markets necessary to maintain acceptable levels of individual welfare and state power. It thus is closely related to many of the aspects of both natural and synthetic power discussed in Chapter 8. States must either possess or have reliable access to needed economic inputs in order to maintain adequately developed economies. Otherwise, no government can be certain of keeping its economy productive, or even of being able to feed, clothe, and house its people.

Cuba provides a poignant contemporary example of how economies rapidly can devolve to lower levels when access to vital economic inputs is interrupted. Isolated from most Western Hemisphere trade by U.S.-sponsored embargoes, the Cuban economy depended for decades on Soviet subsidies, especially oil shipments and sugar purchases (Cuba is the world's largest exporter of sugar). As the Soviet economy began to collapse in the late 1980s, Kremlin leaders were compelled to drastically curtail subsidies to the East European and Cuban economies. Cuba lost both cheap Soviet oil and the foreign exchange subsidy of above-market prices for its sugar. By the mid-1990s, many medical supplies were extremely limited. Gasoline was in such short supply that electrical power generation was curtailed, private automobiles were parked, even buses ran only irregularly, and the government hailed the import of tens of thousands of Chinese-built bicycles as a great step forward in transportation. Ironically, the loss of foreign exchange needed to import fertilizer began to push Cuba toward world leadership in developing sustainable organic agriculture.

Governments traditionally seek secure access to a number of *strategic raw materials* required to maintain industrial—and especially military—production. The United States today depends on more than twenty such materials, and such dependencies often influence policy positions quite strongly. Consider the example of chromite and other ores that yield the metallic element chromium, a strategic material seldom given much public attention. Chromium's most important use is as a hardening additive in steel. Moreover, chrome plating is almost universally used on the balls and rollers in bearings, and most machinery—whether for civilian production or military use—requires such bearings. Chromite ore is found in even fewer places than petroleum; the two largest world sources are Zimbabwe and Russia. In 1965 Zimbabwe was the self-governing British colony of Southern Rhodesia, and its white minority government declared independence from Britain. Two years later the UN imposed mandatory sanctions against that government, which over a span of years withstood world diplomatic pressure, economic sanctions, guerrilla attacks, and a right-wing assault. A black majority government finally came to power and was recognized by Britain in 1980 as the independent state of Zimbabwe. During the intervening years, however, the United States violated UN trade sanctions and, under a congressional mandate known as the Byrd amendment, continued to purchase its chromite ore from Rhodesia rather than depend on imports from the Soviet Union.

For heavily export-dependent states like Japan, *secure access to markets* can be almost as important as energy and raw material inputs because significant curtailment of a major market such as automobile sales to the United States would produce economic dislocations at home. The most violent forms of state action to control markets, of course, are warfare and imperialistic colonization. Securing markets was one factor in Japan's World War II attempt to establish its "Greater Southeast Asia Co-Prosperity Sphere" through conquest. In the aftermath of that war, formal colonial rule gradually ended worldwide. With Namibia's independence in 1990, all former colonies of Western European powers had become independent states. However, many analysts charge that the imperial system of exploiting colonies has been succeeded by **neoimperialism,** under which developed states control and seriously retard the economic development of weaker states, using unfair trading practices and exploiting the weakness of controls over international business corporations. This is the greatest of all economic security issues for many governments on both sides of the economic development divide. Developed states want trading agreements that secure raw material supplies as economic inputs, and markets for their manufactured goods or agricultural exports. In the short run, developing states seek fair export market prices, which are often difficult to obtain when exports are dominated by one or two crops or raw materials. In the longer run, such states usually seek to increase their independence by building capabilities to supply more of their own needs, which threatens the established markets of more developed economies.

Governments also may pursue economic security through industrial policy, as discussed in Chapter 8. This involves coordinating public and private sectors' economic efforts and investments to develop or promote new industries and technologies targeted to retain competitiveness and technological leadership in an increasingly internationalized economy. For many developed states, domestic action for economic security now also involves social policy to ameliorate the individual and regional impacts of *deindustrialization*, the devolution of industrial sectors displaced by more efficient foreign competition. (See the example about the American steel industry.) Deindustrialization is only partly a result of economic development into a postindustrial information age. As discussed in Chapter 13, data suggest that since the 1980s the wealthiest states have been shifting from reliance on heavy industry to combinations of in-person services, high technologies, and information services as their economic cornerstones.

SOCIETAL SECURITY

Societal security concerns the maintenance of national cultural, ethnic, linguistic, and religious identity and traditional practices, presumably with some allowance for necessary evolution and adaptation to external conditions and developments. Societal security thus considerably overlaps economic security, political security, and social-psychological attributes of power (see Chapter 8). For the United States, the dominant national culture has long emphasized individual economic, religious, and political freedoms, progress, and upward economic and social mobility while deemphasizing societal responsibilities to assist individuals in attaining those ends. Much progress has been made in recent decades toward incorporating women and minorities in the advance toward those ideals, although a great deal remains to be done.

Probably the greatest societywide security threat faced by the United States as we enter the twenty-first century is economic. The post–World War II economic boom helped millions of families move into the middle class and enjoy levels of material prosperity unknown to their forebears. Today, however, despite a general economic "boom" and low unemployment levels, internationalization of economics has increasingly stalemated middle-class real wage gains. This development, explored in detail in Chapter 11, threatens to split U.S. society into haves and have-nots to a degree not seen (except for the institution of slavery) since the early years of independence. Nonetheless, there remains a widespread sense that U.S. citizens are one people, "Americans," which was long the goal of immigrants who came to these shores seeking a better life. In a nation largely consisting of immigrants and their descendants, recent years have seen increasing emphasis on cultural diversity and recapturing our roots. Tolerance of varied religious practices is probably increasing, and the dominance of Christianity has never extended to an official state church, even when religious tenets like those against birth control were enshrined in law. English, the language of the colonial power and many early settlers, has always

DEINDUSTRIALIZATION AND ECONOMIC SECURITY: THE LATE AMERICAN STEEL INDUSTRY

A notable example of deindustrialization is the steel industry in the so-called rust belt of the northeastern United States. At the end of World War II, the United States dominated world steel production, but failed to aggressively modernize its facilities. European steel makers had to completely rebuild their facilities, and they wisely chose to purchase the most modern and efficient equipment. By the early 1960s their costs of producing steel and shipping it across the Atlantic were lower than U.S. producers' costs at home. U.S. steel exports withered and domestic production for the home market began to decline.

In subsequent decades, competitive steel production spread first to Japan and then to other newly industrializing states of South Asia, notably South Korea. By the late 1980s executives of steel-intensive businesses like heating and air-conditioning contractors on the U.S. West Coast would say that their choices were to use Korean steel or go out of business because they could not bid competitively. Factories in the former centers of U.S. steel production, like Pittsburgh, Pennsylvania, and Youngstown, Ohio, were shut down and abandoned, leading to heavy unemployment and drastic cuts in average incomes throughout the region.

Surviving U.S. steel producers today are largely limited to marketing specialty steels. In this instance, economic security in an increasingly global economy has become a very personal issue for many thousands of American families.

been dominant, although not officially prescribed by law. In recent years, a movement to make English the official language has gained force among conservatives, concerned that multilingualism—particularly driven by a rapidly rising Hispanic population—undermines national cohesiveness.

National cohesiveness built on national cultural, ethnic, linguistic, and religious identity clearly is an extremely important social-psychological component of state power (see also Chapter 8). Despite the contemporary economic threat and racial divisions never resolved since the abolition of slavery, the United States remains more cohesive and thus more favored than many states today.

Compare, for example, our northern neighbor. As noted in Chapter 1, Canada is a single state comprising two dominant nations, one English speaking and one French speaking, with the latter concentrated in the province of Quebec. Despite strong efforts since the 1960s to make bilingualism and biculturalism work in federated Canada, divisions remain intense. A November 1995 Quebec referendum to begin making the province an independent nation-state nearly passed. English-speaking Canadian politicians and citizens mounted a large last-minute campaign to convince French-speaking Québecois that the federation genuinely wanted them. Polls showed that a majority of Canadians, English and French speaking, supporters and opponents of secession, expected both nations to suffer economically if the federation fragmented. Québecois support for independence dropped in the last days before the vote, but secession advocates immediately promised new referenda campaigns. Quebec vividly demonstrates how intensely economic security and societal security can clash.

Although Czechoslovakia split fairly peacefully into the Czech Republic and Slovakia in 1992, regrouping according to societal identities can produce extreme violence. The breakup of former Yugoslavia led, among other clashes, to the Bosnian civil war (1992–95) and NATO action against the Serbs in Kosovo in 1999. (See the discussions of Bosnia in Chapters 8 and 15.)

ENVIRONMENTAL SECURITY

Environmental security involves maintaining local, national, and planetary biospheres as the vital life support system for all human endeavors. Environmental problems are quintessential *common pool* problems, in which the activities of a large number of members are unavoidably linked by physical processes. As explored more thoroughly in the opening case of Chapter 12, common pools tend to suffer from a characteristic set of problems. Physical systems are no respecters of international boundaries, and force different states into common pools which they must manage in order to solve their interrelated environmental problems. For example, industrial burning in the U.S. Midwest creates acid rain that affects southeastern Canada, and industry in Ontario similarly affects the New England states. This problem has forced the United States and Canada to negotiate methods for reducing acid emissions. Physical systems usually have an inherent *carrying capacity* without suffering degradation, but exceeding that capacity may cause irreparable damage. Fish, for example, may support substantial commercial landings year after year, but overfishing can destroy a productive fishery or even wipe out a species.

Holding down the human usage of physical systems to their natural carrying capacity requires political solutions that limit all users. In turn, this creates usage rights that must be managed by the political system, and may even be marketed between potential users. For example, because rivers can absorb and process a certain quantity of sewage with its attendant biological oxygen demand, governments may regulate sewage quantities discharged, and discharge rights may be sold by one municipality with excess capacity to another with inadequate capacity. Holdouts who refuse to accede to political management arrangements may still exploit the system or even cause irreparable harm. Thus, for example, Japanese refusal to join international conventions limiting whaling has contributed to endangering several species of whales. In the absence of adequate political regulation, people confronted with a physical system in decline have incentives to exploit the resource while it still exists, which only accelerates the decline. Several fisheries have suffered this fate in recent decades, giving states added impetus to extend their claims of exclusive fishing rights to 200 miles offshore.

Whenever political systems limit activity and assign rights, concerns arise about what distributions are equitable and whether particular individuals or states benefit at the expense of others. Some environmental issues concern equitable division of the costs of environmentally friendly technology, with developing states seeking needed assistance from (or, from another perspective, seeking to exploit) more developed states. We examine the case of international efforts to limit the release of chlorofluorocarbons (CFCs) in Chapter 14.

THE NEW INTERNATIONAL THREAT ENVIRONMENT: SECURITY PROBLEMS AT THE BEGINNING OF THE TWENTY-FIRST CENTURY

As we examined in Chapter 3 and summarized in Table 3.1, the global geopolitical, military, economic, societal, and environmental contexts of U.S. foreign policy today are vastly different from those of the Cold War era. U.S. perceptions and concerns about security, military and otherwise, have been profoundly affected. These changes influence which concerns are identified as likely threats, and which military policy means are considered appropriate to deal with those threats. Changes in the perceived threat environment and in military forces and roles are summarized in Table 9.1.

Shaped by widely shared perceptions about the world and the geopolitical context it imposed, U.S. perceptions of the Cold War threat environment were dominated by cognitions of a single primary Soviet communist threat. U.S. survival, and probably that of democracy worldwide, were at stake. The threat was overt, known, and deterrable through the use of nuclear weapons. It was widely believed—although less so among officials than ordinary citizens—that a strategic nuclear war was possible, even if quite unlikely. Although a global threat was perceived and regularly responded to, U.S. defense planning gave particular attention to Europe, always considered vital to American security. Thus NATO was primary among the alliances designed to implement containment. Fear of a nuclear exchange led to apprehension that any conflict could escalate out of control, and motivated extensive and serious study of crisis management techniques.

Aspin (1992, 6) saw the Persian Gulf War as a defining event, "the first crisis of the post-Soviet world." Instead of a single, Soviet, threat there were diverse threats of new kinds, smaller but more complex and nuanced, harder to understand and manage. These included an aggressive regional power acting as a model for other would-be aggressors, environmental and potentially nuclear terrorism, and nuclear potential made manifest. Arguably, none of these threats could be predicted very far in advance and none were deterrable, at least by forces on the U.S. mainland. Although U.S. survival was never at stake, U.S. interests and lives were, directly in terms of Western access to Middle Eastern oil, and indirectly in what lessons each case would set for future incidents around the world. Confrontations in the new threat environment contain little risk of escalation to major nuclear exchanges. Instead, they include risks like covert attacks by diverse states and groups, civil and international wars fueled by ethnic absolutism, and nuclear terrorism not only by rulers like Saddam Hussein, but by international terrorist groups that gain access to nuclear materials. Threats will be dominantly local and regional rather than global, and ill defined to those not following the local issues on a detailed and continuing basis.

During the Cold War, U.S. military forces and roles were designed and directed primarily to implementing containment and meeting the global Soviet and communist threat(s). High-technology weaponry dominated U.S. planning, not only in forms like ICBMs, but in bombers and air superiority fighters designed to penetrate Soviet airspace. This was a way to use engineering and production capabilities as a substitute for the personnel that we valued more highly. Beyond the possibilities of nuclear exchanges, wars were expected to involve attrition, as in Korea and Vietnam. In such cases, U.S. productive capacity would allow us eventually to outproduce and wear down any enemy. Because

> ### TABLE 9.1
>
> *The Changing (Primarily Military) Security Environment for the United States*

Old (Cold War) World	New (post–Cold War) World
Threat Environment	**Threat environment**
Single (Soviet) primary threat	Diverse threats
American survival at stake	American interests and lives at stake
Known	Unknown
Deterrable	Nondeterrable
Strategic use of nuclear weapons	Terrorist use of nuclear weapons
Overt	Covert
Europe centered	Regional, ill defined
High risk of escalation	Little risk of escalation
Military Forces and Roles	**Military Forces and Roles**
Attrition warfare	Decisive attacks on key nodes
War by proxy	Direct involvement
High-tech dominant	High-, medium-, low-tech mix
Forward deployed	Power projection
Forward based	U.S. based
Host-nation support	Self-reliant

Source: Aspin, 1992, 21, greatly revised, reordered, and amended.

containment was implemented through a set of globe-girdling alliances, it required forces and allies close to the Soviet periphery. We thus relied on forward deployment of forces and forward basing of soldiers and equipment, which in turn needed extensive host country support. Where the Soviets and Chinese aided indigenous forces in civil and guerrilla wars, the United States typically aided established local governments, effectively fighting the communists by proxy. Military force sizes, training, and weapons design and procurement were all designed with these considerations in mind.

Most of those considerations have changed in the post–Cold War world, and U.S. military security planning needs to change with them. Acceptance of foreign military bases has declined steadily in the postcolonial era. Even regimes very friendly to the United States have demanded base closures, reduction in base sizes, visible signs of joint or local sovereignty, and ever-higher compensatory payments. As a result, the United States has come to rely more and more on its own forces based at home and on means for their rapid movement abroad in power projection. Sometimes troops are augmented with weapons and supplies prepositioned abroad near areas of possible need, either in friendly states or at some of the few remaining U.S. bases abroad, such as Diego Garcia in the Indian Ocean. Proxy wars are seen as unlikely; foreign military operations of interest to the United States in the future will almost always involve U.S. forces directly. Tactically, military operations will aim at decisive attacks on key nodes of opposition forces, utilizing a broad mix of technologies appropriate to the task.

In the Persian Gulf War, for example, coalition forces led by the United States won a quick and decisive victory (but for its early termination) in the land war with almost no casualties because they had effectively paralyzed Iraq's war-fighting capability. A wide variety of techniques, from high tech to low tech, was utilized to achieve this end. Bombs and missiles were directed particularly at Iraqi power stations, radar installations, and military installations, effectively severing Iraqi lines of command and control. Generals in Baghdad knew more about what was happening at the front from CNN telecasts than from their own forces. Cruise missiles and radar-evading stealth fighter-bombers were used to attack the most heavily defended targets. Aging subsonic B-52 bombers were used in high-altitude massed bombing raids on Iraqi tanks in the desert, and to drop leaflets informing Iraqi soldiers why they should surrender promptly, and how to do so.

The dramatically changed security conditions that Aspin saw in the post–Cold War world are reflected in many of the cases already discussed in Chapter 8 and thus far in this chapter. We now examine two other security problems in which those changed global conditions play prominent roles and demonstrate the broadening of security concerns beyond their purely military aspects. These interrelated issues are the major environmental security problem of nuclear and chemical cleanup and the threatened leakage of nuclear materials from the former Soviet Union. Finally, we examine how the end of the Cold War and the virtually disappearance of fears about a superpower nuclear exchange have left a new world order in which small and regional conflicts have become increasingly likely.

ENVIRONMENTAL CLEANUP

The environmental costs of more than four decades of Cold War ultimately may come to be seen as even greater than the monetary costs. General Secretary Mikhail Gorbachev's program of political openness, or *glasnost*, during the last years of the Soviet Union, the USSR's subsequent breakup, and post–Cold War reductions in secrecy on both sides of the world all contributed to the revelation of industrial and nuclear pollution on a scale previously unimagined.

Pollution is particularly acute in Russia and the European former Soviet republics. Under the direction of a single-party government obsessed with secrecy and fears of outside attack, the Soviet command economy relied on growth through building heavy industry at all cost, and defense planning revolved around matching and surpassing American nuclear and missile capabilities. Russia's continent-spanning vastness, pervasive secret police, restrictions on individual movement, and strictly enforced secrecy all helped keep word about environmental accidents from spreading. Compiling any comprehensive picture of environmental problems under those conditions would have been exceedingly difficult.

The April 1986 nuclear reactor explosion at Chernobyl, Ukraine, was kept secret except in the immediately affected area for several days, until Swedish scientists publicly announced that they had detected fallout from the explosion. Spring crops throughout much of Eastern and Northern Europe were too heavily irradiated for human consumption, and some 50,000 square miles were contaminated by radioactive material released in the disaster. However, the incident did lead Gorbachev to expand *glasnost*, removing many restrictions on the Soviet press and people. Subsequently, Soviet officials admitted the 1957 chemical explosion of a nuclear waste storage site near Chelyabinsk, Russia, long suspected in the West. That blast dispersed some 80 tons of radioactive waste into the atmosphere and forced the evacuation of more than 10,000 people (Stanglin, 1992, 44).

Nuclear power and weapons projects may not even have been the worst polluters. Soviet industries across the entire economy polluted shamelessly because there were no incentives to do otherwise. Under command economics, central planners assigned quotas for the quantities and types of goods to be produced and the channels for distribution. Efficiency was believed to result from large-scale production, so powerful state monopolies arose and built gigantic production complexes that overtaxed local environments. Plant managers were expected to meet production quotas however they could, but there were no incentives for efficiency and no restrictions on dumping wastes. This system lacked the efficiency incentives that exist in a market economy, for example, to produce with the least possible energy input in order to minimize costs. Relentless political pressure for industrialization and economic growth pushed aside most concerns about environmental damage.

A confidential report prepared by the Russian Environment Ministry for the 1992 Earth Summit at Rio de Janeiro stated that the military-industrial complex had "operated outside any environmental controls." That report also noted that the "frenetic pace" of relocating industrial plants and equipment east to the Ural mountains and Siberia to escape the German invasion in the early 1940s, and often back to European Russia after the war, created a "growth-at-any-cost mentality" (Stanglin, 1992, 43). By the early 1990s some 70 million former Soviet citizens in 103 cities breathed air polluted with at least five times the allowed levels of dangerous chemicals. Alexi Yablokov, science adviser to Russian president Boris Yeltsin, stated in 1992 that a nuclear submarine sank near Novaya Zemlya in the early 1980s, its reactor never recovered. He also claimed that some 920,000 barrels of oil, nearly 10 percent of total production, were spilled daily. To speed pipeline construction, builders were permitted to install cutoff valves every 30 miles instead of every 3, so that any break spills ten times the oil that would otherwise be lost. One pool of spilled oil in Siberia has been reported as 6 feet deep, covering an area 4 by 7 miles. Because the rivers feeding the Aral Sea were diverted, it is now evaporating, raising local temperatures as much as three degrees and releasing enough salt and dust to increase particulate matter in the planet's atmosphere by 5 percent. By 1992, pollution and indiscriminate clear-cutting were causing Siberian forests, which absorb much of the world's carbon dioxide, to disappear at a rate of 5 million acres annually, a heavier rate of loss than that of the Brazilian rain forests (Stanglin, 1992, 43).

Nor was the Soviet Union alone in suffering environmental pollution from industrialization and nuclear weapons and power projects. Cold War paranoia, the unfamiliarity of new nuclear technologies, and the urgency of weapons development led to environmental carelessness and abuse in the United States as well. Here, too, secrecy helped hide the magnitude and severity of the problems for years. A 1995 Energy Department report to the Congress estimated that cleaning up radioactive waste left over from decades of American nuclear weapons production would cost $230 to $350 billion. The decontamination of more than 80 facilities in 30 states would take decades, with most of the work to be completed by the year 2035 but other work extending until 2070. The Hanford Reservation near Richland, Washington, would see the most costly cleanup, estimated at $48.7 billion. Built in 1943 by the Army Corps of Engineers and Du Pont Corporation to supply weapons-grade plutonium for the Manhattan Project, Hanford grew from an initial three reactors to nine by 1964. Over succeeding decades, the fortunes of the works fluctuated with Cold War developments. By 1971, as the United States approached the first strategic arms control agreements with the Soviet Union and demand for new plutonium dropped, all but one reactor had been shut down. That last reactor, the N-Reactor, was operated until 1988, then shut down because of a combination of safety concerns and beliefs that the approaching end of the Cold War would terminate demand for new plutonium.

Hazardous chemicals and radioactive wastes produced during thirty-five years of plutonium production at Hanford were disposed of in a number of ways. Waste was dumped into the soil, injected into deep wells, released into the air in gaseous form, or held in storage tanks located only a few miles from the Columbia River. Environmental Protection Agency data indicate that more than 100 million gallons of toxic liquids were dumped during the 1940s and 1950s, and it is conservatively estimated that some 750,000 gallons of high-level nuclear waste has leaked from single-shell storage tanks. Liquid discharges have raised the water table as much as 75 feet under some parts of the reservation, and contaminated at least 120 square miles of groundwater (Steele, 1991). Other radioactive materials injected into deep wells are now thought to be moving through groundwater toward the Columbia River. Cleanup work envisioned at Hanford includes dismantling the nine mothballed reactors and burying their cores, entombing a massive plutonium processing plant in concrete, and draining and capping more than 170 underground waste storage tanks (Hebert, 1995). The weapons plant cleanup proposal assumes construction of a centralized underground disposal site for high-level nuclear wastes, also required for spent power reactor fuel. However, no such site had been approved by 1995, much less built. Under a federal government program, intensive investigations of a proposed site at Yucca Mountain in southwestern Nevada had been under way for some years, but were being vigorously contested by activists and the state of Nevada.

In the United States as in the former Soviet states, cleaning up environmental pollution from nuclear weapons programs pits environmental security against economic security. The Energy Department's budget for cleanup and environmental restoration ran about $6 billion annually in the early 1990s. Cleanup of soil and groundwater at the Nevada bomb test site was not even planned, because officials do not believe any available technology would succeed within acceptable cost (Hebert, 1995). Although these problems faced in the United States are serious, however, they are orders of magnitude less severe than those in the former Soviet Union. The Bush administration quietly secured congressional approval of a half-billion dollars to help the former Soviets dismantle and dispose of nuclear weapons under terms of the START agreements, and by 1994 that amount had been raised to $1.2 billion. However, post-Soviet environmental cleanup is another matter because it would be many times more expensive and protracted, would require international financing, and seems to lack the apparent urgency.

NUCLEAR "LEAKAGE" FROM THE FORMER SOVIET STATES

A different, and perhaps more immediately dangerous, form of nuclear pollution is the leakage of weapons-grade plutonium and enriched uranium, and perhaps even functioning nuclear warheads themselves, from former Soviet states into unauthorized hands.

This is one of the most critical nuclear proliferation threats the world faces at the onset of the twenty-first century.

Nuclear scientists were among the most favored of Soviet state employees. Fear that economic desperation in post-Soviet states might drive at least a few of them to work for international political terrorists or rogue governments like those of Iraq or Libya has led to quiet U.S.-Russian joint efforts to find them alternative employment. Similar desperation could drive weapons plant employees or local military commanders to sell nuclear materials to wealthy foreigners. By 1995, for example, several small shipments of smuggled Russian plutonium had been intercepted in Germany and Hungary. On 10 August 1994 German police seized 12 ounces of Russian plutonium-239, in a Munich sting operation against three Spaniards and a Colombian who had offered 4 kilos (about 8.8 pounds) of weapons-grade plutonium for $250 million in cash. The quantity seized is more dangerous than might first appear. The U.S. Natural Resources Defense Council has estimated that a nuclear bomb with the explosive yield of 1,000 tons of dynamite, about a tenth the yield of the Hiroshima bomb, could be built with only 1 kilo of plutonium, one eighth the amount that the International Atomic Energy Agency (IAEA) uses as its threshold (Masland, 1994, 30).

Moreover, although public worries about nuclear terrorism usually focus on bombs, other applications for the same amount of nuclear material could cause far greater loss of life. For example, plutonium is so highly toxic that the 12 ounces seized in Munich could poison the entire water supply of a major city or be used to seed a devastating "dirty bomb" that would use conventional high explosives to disperse plutonium in the air. To put these quantities of plutonium into perspective and demonstrate how small an amount of leakage could be deadly, consider that reliable estimates at the end of 1993 placed total world stocks of plutonium (fissionable and nonfissionable isotopes, but all highly toxic) at 1,100 tons, and of highly enriched uranium at the equivalent of 1,700 tons of weapons-grade material (Albright et al., 1995, 318).

Economic pressures on civilian scientists and other employees of the former Soviet nuclear weapons program are particularly clear and severe, and probably worse than those facing military personnel. Russia's huge Atomic Energy Ministry, known as Minatom, was once estimated to have a million employees. As essential workers in a critical defense industry, they received favored treatment. Ordinary Russians called them "the chocolate eaters" because they were pampered with comfortable housing and abundant food in an economy plagued by constant shortages.

But by 1994 the country's three thousand top nuclear scientists were being paid less than Moscow bus drivers, and at highly irregular intervals. According to U.S. intelligence sources, workers at the major weapons production and assembly plants, where plutonium is prepared for warheads, routinely steal precious metals but are strip-searched for radioactive material. In the dozens of nuclear research institutes and laboratories, however, security is much more lax or has broken down. By using trace differences in isotopic composition as a type of nuclear fingerprint, scientists often can trace radioactive materials like plutonium to a specific plant or even a single reactor. U.S. sources using such techniques believed the plutonium in the 1994 Munich seizure came from a submarine-research reactor or a plant preparing isotopes for civilian use, and suspected that a senior laboratory technician stole the material. If so, it would fit the pattern of the man who carried about 6 pounds of highly enriched uranium out a Minatom lab earlier that year, only to be caught trying to sell it on the black market (Masland, 1994, 32).

Given the tremendous pressures on individuals to sell nuclear materials and the pull of a moderate but immensely wealthy international market, how can the United States and other governments best respond? Sale of nuclear material is but one of the manifold severe problems Russia faces today, and may not receive the attention it warrants. Like the rest of those problems, it arises largely from internal economic upheaval, political confusion, and universal uncertainty about Russia's future. Applicable control techniques are essentially those of traditional espionage, undercover police work, and use of informants. One German expert asserted in 1994 that "the European market consists almost entirely of undercover policemen" (Masland, 1994, 32). To some extent, outside powers can require Russian cooperation as a price for economic aid and technological assistance. In turn, Russia gains leverage to demand such assistance from the fact that the rest of the world cannot afford to let it fail.

As discussed in Chapter 3, the end of the Cold War and the virtual disappearance of fears about a superpower nuclear exchange have left a new world disorder in which small and regional conflicts are more, rather than less, likely. Cases like the disintegration of former Yugoslavia into ethnically based civil war, Russia's bloody suppression of Chechen separatists, and the autonomous region Abkhazia's revolt against the Republic of Georgia demonstrate that the collapse of overwhelming Soviet power has allowed many ancient hatreds to manifest themselves in wars for which the world lacks any established and effective means to create and enforce peace. The disappearance of the Soviet Union as its single dominant foe and only serious challenger leaves the United States exactly as President George Bush described it: the sole surviving superpower. Unfortunately, there is neither official nor public agreement about what that should imply in the policy arena. Although the U.S. unquestionably remains a military superpower, its economic standing is coming under increasing challenge. Nor is this a new concept. In the latter 1960s, shortly before he joined the Nixon administration as its chief architect of foreign policy and without foreseeing the end of the Cold War, Henry Kissinger wrote that the world was becoming politically multipolar while remaining militarily bipolar.

America is now free to scale back the efforts it devoted to countering the USSR and refocus its efforts on other struggles, notably those of maintaining leadership and competitiveness in international economics. With the end of the Cold War, a widespread consensus grew rapidly within the United States, holding that defense spending *had to be cut* to reduce the federal budget, and *could be cut* because the great threat of more than four decades had vanished. Additionally, the defense budget was increasingly shifted during the 1980s from long-term commitments to funds requiring annual congressional renewal, making defense funds *easier to cut* than entitlements. This rationale for cutbacks was persuasive despite the pains they caused in local districts, and despite questions about whether U.S. military forces would require resources at something approximating the old levels to deal with a new and poorly understood set of global threats. 1990s budget cutting undoubtedly gained some of its persuasiveness from the fact that no clear and comprehensive vision of U.S. global policy emerged to replace containment and Cold War. Nonetheless, by the late 1990s Congress and the Clinton administration had agreed to raise real-dollar defense budgets. In looking ahead, we should remember that enormous costs and resources were required to fight limited wars in Korea, Vietnam, and the Persian Gulf.

With the collapse and breakup of the Soviet Union, security threats are seen as most likely to arise from rogue states, horizontal nuclear proliferation to unstable minor powers, and regional conflicts. The era of east-west Cold War polarization tended to concentrate superpower attention on problems in the developing world. Today, many analysts fear that problems within and among distant weak states, particularly in Africa, are increasingly neglected. To the extent that the leaders of such states perceive that the great powers will ignore their actions, inhibitions against aggression will be reduced. In a world that has always had moderate numbers of shooting wars each year, most of them small by U.S. standards, America must reevaluate how much attention it should pay such conflicts.

Evidence already exists that the numbers of armed conflicts classified as major by the Uppsala Conflict Data Project have declined only slightly since the end of the Cold War. In 1993 and 1994, none of these conflicts was a classic interstate war over some dispute about government or territory. Rather, these were conflicts between parties within states, about half over government and half over territory, although several wars had interstate aspects. (Many were *new internal wars;* see Chapter 15.) The 1994 conflict most costly in human lives was the genocidal massacres of Tutsi and other Hutu by Hutu extremists in Rwanda. These data suggest that the end of the Cold War has seen neither global peace nor a worldwide increase in wars within or between developing states. Nonetheless, the nearly complete lack of international response to the slaughter in Rwanda suggests that much work remains for peacemakers and peacekeepers, and that the United States must decide the level and nature of its involvement in such efforts.

DILEMMAS OF CONTEMPORARY SECURITY POLICY

It has become commonplace among analysts to speak and write of "the security dilemma." As suggested earlier, however, the concept and pursuit of security are surrounded and permeated by many dilemmas, apparent contradictions, or unavoidable clashes of inter-est. We are forced to adapt to many of these difficulties, just as we have to live with the ir-reducible limitations of decision-making systems examined in Chapter 5. Two of those dilemmas were discussed earlier: First, complete, perfect security is impossible to achieve. Therefore, security analysis is slanted toward dealing with specific threats. Even at the in-dividual level, it is impossible to gain absolute security by totally eliminating risk. Second, actions taken in search of any form of security—military or otherwise—actually may im-peril it or another form of security. The very measures taken in hopes of reducing risk may only increase it. Arms purchased by one government to protect against perceived threat from a neighbor may raise fears within that neighboring government which trig-ger countering increases in arms. In turn, that increase can trigger a response, and the two states may engage in a back-and-forth ratcheting up of arms levels. This pattern of arms competition is a common enough phenomenon in history that political scientists have studied it extensively. Scholars refer to it as an *action-reaction process* (ARP), although it is more popularly known as an "arms race."

Barry Buzan (1991, 271) distinguishes between at least two types of "defense dilem-mas" that involve contradictions between national security and the pursuit of military de-fense. His first type involves tradeoffs between devoting resources to defense or to other societal objectives. This is a problem of *opportunity costs*, in which spending limited re-sources on one policy goal constrains opportunities to spend on alternatives. Economists traditionally call this the "guns versus butter" problem. For example, much of the severe inflation experienced in the United States during the 1970s can be traced to basic economics of the Vietnam War policy begun under President Lyndon Johnson, who hoped to pursue the war without having to curtail his Great Society program of domestic welfare expenditures. Defense spending was raised substantially without either increasing taxes or reducing domestic spending, but the result was inflation and increased federal debt. Another type of defense dilemma obtains when the very nature of defense preparations threatens survival or other core values. The difference between these two types of defense dilemma is a matter of (severe) degree, with nuclear deterrence providing the outstanding example of the second type (see the section titled "Environmental Cleanup" earlier).

Let's look at five other dilemmas that affect security in general, and four dilemmas concerning deterrence.

FIVE ADDITIONAL DILEMMAS OF SECURITY

States are the major sources of both threats to individuals and security for individuals.

Analysts commonly refer to the duty of states to protect their citizens against both external and internal threats. The Preamble to the U.S. Constitution refers to the need to "provide for the common defence" and "insure domestic tranquility." However, providing protections against one type of threat may endanger individual security in some different arena of activity. Our least fortunately endowed citizens suffer if social welfare expenditures are cut in order to raise defense spending to meet perceived military threats from outside. States differ widely in how they define the delicate line between outlawing political and other activities subversive to the state, and suppressing legitimate and needed political protest. Domestic police services are needed to make citizens secure in their persons and property by protecting them from lawless individuals or groups, but how much intrusion on individual liberty and privacy is required to carry out those police functions? At what points do state activities such as data collection and dissemination, wiretaps, mail openings, surveillance, searches, and seizures of property move beyond legitimate and necessary tools of police protection, and become tools that help the state oppress its people and suppress dissent?

Consider one reasonably benign example. Air travelers in the United States have been required since the 1970s to submit at least to metal detector searches of their persons and x-ray searches of their baggage, in hopes of preventing armed hijackings or bombings of airliners. States faced with higher incidences of political terrorism, as in Western Europe, require far more rigorous aircraft security measures. Most citizens view such measures as small sacrifices of individual privacy and dignity that are worth enduring to protect everyone against a few violent individuals and radical groups. However, such small measures may evoke genuine fear that they could cumulate over time and become opening wedges for far more intrusive and repressive measures. Given the historical experience of regimes such as Hitler's Germany, Stalin's Soviet Union, or Saddam Hussein's Iraq, it is clear that some governments move beyond protecting citizens to dominating and controlling every aspect of individual life, often in the name of protecting national security against external enemies.

Security planning is subject to severe logical and practical
contradictions between violent means and peaceful ends.

Attempting to assure security often involves the seeming contradiction of threatening or using force in order to create or maintain peace. Coercive diplomacy, discussed in Chapter 8, illustrates the problem. If the attempted coercion fails, doctrine requires that violence follow. Even cases in which we believe that coercive diplomacy has worked, like the Cuban missile crisis of 1962, often involve tremendous risk. Coercive diplomacy at its most successful can yield **deterrence,** under which policy goals are accomplished without requiring the use of violence, but deterrence also involves risk. Some analysts use "deterrence" to refer to a *policy;* others refer to the (hoped for) *outcome* of that policy. In a policy process sense, deterrence requires posing a sufficient threat to key values that our opponent becomes convinced that the costs and risks of aggression (or whatever other action we oppose) outweigh the possible benefits. To obtain our desired outcome, we must be both able and willing to carry out threatened actions. In extreme cases, however, those actions could result in our own destruction. Mutual assured destruction (MAD) strategic nuclear doctrine called for a massive U.S. nuclear strike against Soviet cities and infrastructure in response to a sufficiently large Soviet first strike against the United States. That retaliatory strike would be undertaken in full knowledge that enough Soviet missiles probably would survive to inflict even further damage in return, so both societies would suffer levels of destruction they deemed unacceptable.

Power is sought by some to achieve state security in an anarchic world, although
others see such pursuits as the primary source of international insecurity.

What Buzan (1991, 271) calls the power-security dilemma involves interactions between the struggle for power and the struggle for security, and the fact that observers and even policymakers may have difficulties distinguishing between the two. Indeed, the two sides of this dilemma frame opposing general theories about the nature of world politics. Ironically, both groups focus on struggles for security, but they proceed from fundamentally different explanations for insecurity. The first group, which includes the realist school, right-wingers, and Marxist-Leninists, believes that conflict originates from hostility and direct, conscious competition among states. International politics is thus seen as a struggle between states seeking security by promoting their interests defined in terms of power. The second group, which includes the idealist school and liberal or social democrats, believes that conflict originates from particular state behaviors (such as action-reaction processes) and patterns of relations in the international system, in which both conflict and hostility may be unintended. The important struggle for this group is systemic, with states and multistate organizational actors seeking international security by limiting violent state activities. During the Cold War, for example, the first group urged the United

States to build more strategic nuclear arms, and the second group urged more U.S.-Soviet arms control.

Both arming decisions and disarming decisions are subject to a prisoners' dilemma *structure of motivations (see Chapter 12), in which individually risk-averse choices by governments will always be to develop new weapons and to refrain from disarming.*

Governments are under powerful cross pressures to arm and to refrain from arming, and to disarm and to refrain from disarming. *Incentives to arm* include hopes of deterring attack by building up military strength; desires to obtain a more favorable war outcome, should war occur; aspirations to increase national prestige, diplomatic weight, and international bargaining leverage; promoting the vested interests of domestic military-industrial-legislative complexes; reacting to another government that is seen as a "pacer" of one's own bureaucratic behavior; solving new technological puzzles; and hopes of achieving a "strategic breakout" or massive upward shift in relative military capability.

Disincentives to arm include both the real costs incurred and the social opportunity costs of giving up the chance to devote resources to alternative public and private goods. An additional disincentive may be skepticism based on the observation that massive increases in military spending, weapons quantities, and levels of available destructive-ness since World War II have not been accompanied by increases in perceived security. Rather, the great increase in felt security within the major powers since 1990 derives from massive political-economic change brought about by the end of the Cold War. *Incentives to disarm* are largely the same as the disincentives to arm, with the possible addition of a greater concern for our stewardship of the planet as the heritage of generations yet unborn.

In considering possible *disincentives to disarm*, however, we find another dilemma and a structure of cross pressures that closely resembles the impulses affecting decisions about the development and deployment of new weaponry. That structure may be represented as an archetypal mixed-motive game of strategy known as "the prisoners' dilemma." Consider the choice situation when each of two governments must decide whether to develop or refrain from developing some new type of weapon that engineers and scientists have conceived. Each government's risk-averse strategy is to proceed with the new development. Refraining represents a risky strategy. If one government refrains while the other proceeds, and the new weapon proves significant, the developer might gain a major strategic advantage. Fear of such an eventuality, which would be the worst possible outcome for the loser, tends to drive both governments toward development. Yet this is very much a mixed-motive game, and its central dilemma is that if both governments pursue the development strategy dictated by individually risk-averse rationality, they will find themselves at the jointly worst outcome: both develop, and the costs and risks of war increase. A jointly preferable outcome, under which both would be better off, is for both to refrain from developing the new weapon.

An entirely comparable structure of incentives and disincentives exists when the two governments must choose between reducing or maintaining present stocks of weapons. If neither elects to reduce arms, the status quo obtains. Arms competition continues, and whatever dangers inhere in the present situation continue indefinitely, and quite likely into new areas of competition over time, given the prisoners' dilemma logic of development. Depending on the details of arms control agreements and the actions of third parties, the jointly optimal outcome probably is for both sides to reduce arms. Yet this is still a mixed-motive game, and a highly imbalanced situation might result if one side reduced while the other did not. Such a situation probably could not arise without either cheating by one side or a major—and perhaps ill-conceived—unilateral arms reduction, but could cause a major shift in relative power.

Although parity is the minimum politically acceptable force level,
its precise definition is often disputed for reasons of both clarity and politics.

One route to overcoming the prisoners' dilemma in arming and disarming decisions lies through institutionalized arms control, with carefully established mechanisms to "verify" each party's continuing compliance with the agreements. Setting allowable arms levels often becomes quite complex, however, because governments usually are happy to accept superiority but unwilling to accept even slight relative disadvantage, and different governments have chosen different force compositions or mixes of weapons types. This was a major issue for the United States and the Soviet Union during the Strategic Arms Limitation Talks (SALT) from 1969 into the 1980s. The Soviets had placed major emphasis on ICBMs while the United States built proportionally more bombers and ballistic missile submarines. *Numerically equal quantities* proved to be so politically salient a formula that the SALT negotiators had to develop elaborate formulas that, for example, lumped bombers together with MIRVed missiles as carriers of multiple warheads.

FOUR DILEMMAS CONCERNING DETERRENCE

Deterrence is a strategy intended to convince an opponent that the costs and risks of aggression or other actions contrary to our desires outweigh any benefits likely to be gained. Although often thought of as a product of the nuclear age, deterrence is an ancient political-military-economic concept and a very general approach to dealing with opponents. Like security, deterrence is fraught with dilemmas, four of which we examine here.

There is a widespread belief in the effectiveness of deterrence, although
we cannot strictly either prove or disprove that deterrence ever has worked.

If deterrence fails, active hostilities result. If deterrence works, peace results. Yet a peace we observe could have arisen from other causes. A would-be attacker may have been prevented not by our steps aimed at producing deterrence, but by internal moral, political, logistical, or other restraints. To assert, for example, that U.S. nuclear deterrence policy worked because there was never a nuclear exchange with the Soviet Union is to commit the logical fallacy called the "affirmation of the consequent." Seeing an outcome that *could have* resulted from successful deterrence does not tell us it actually *did* result from deterrence. Even when the United States held a reasonable nuclear first-strike capability against the Soviet Union, based on far larger numbers of intercontinental-range bombers roughly from the mid-1950s and larger numbers of intercontinental ballistic missiles until the mid-1960s, it refrained from attacking. This may have occurred because the United States was deterred by actual or perceived Soviet nuclear capabilities. More likely, it occurred because Soviet conventional military power held Western Europe hostage (Holloway, 1984, 27–28), or simply because it was believed such an attack would be contrary to fundamental U.S. values or an excessive response to Soviet provocation.

Logically, there are circumstances under which deterrence should not work.

If a deliberate attack occurs, deterrence has failed, regardless whether the attack was rational or irrational according to cost-benefit analysis. Moreover, it is not clear that the retaliation called for under deterrence theory is always—or, perhaps, ever—rational. As but one example, suppose the United States were attacked with nuclear weapons, but responding in kind would exceed the threshold that would plunge the world into a "nuclear winter" during which particulate matter in the atmosphere primarily from burning would block sunlight, precipitating a season of widespread freezing and crop failures. A U.S. nuclear response would then be irrational in that it would cause even greater suffering at home than would otherwise be experienced, and immoral in that it would inflict suffering on millions of innocent people around the globe.

If you are self-deterred and your opponent is not, then deterrence has failed.

There is a high degree of faith, particularly in official Washington circles, that deterrence usually works. If we share that faith, we can join Donald Snow (1986) in directing our greatest concern about possible deterrence breakdown toward the management of crises with serious escalatory potential. Deterrence could succeed because of uncertainties on both sides about their own and each other's capabilities and about the other side's actual intent. There is serious reason to expect that political needs to avoid being seen failing to respond when attacked may override well-founded beliefs that retaliation would be irrational. The other side of this problem, closely related to the logical situations examined in the previous paragraph, is inappropriate self-deterrence.

Deterrent systems based on nuclear weapons might help stabilize regional politics.

Vertical nuclear proliferation, or growth in the sizes of existing nuclear arsenals, long has been almost universally seen as bad. It is no longer a problem for the major nuclear powers nor for some of the minor nuclear powers. A greater threat, still growing in the aftermath of the Cold War, is **horizontal nuclear proliferation,** or the spread of nuclear capability to additional states (or, worse yet, nonstate actors). As seen earlier, the threat of leakage of nuclear technology and materials from former Soviet republics is particularly severe, although there has been some success in forging international agreements to prevent such transfers. However, the end of the Cold War has rekindled an old debate about the merits of systems of mutual nuclear deterrence. A few scholars have held that nuclear weapons are so destructive that possessors can never use them. Nuclear weapons states then are paralyzed; even rough nuclear parity within a dispute dyad produces mutual deterrence, leading to peace.

The logical problem just discussed notwithstanding, supporters of this view usually point to the fact that the United States and the Soviet Union never fought a nuclear war. They then argue that nuclear weaponry can help stabilize other, more regionalized dispute sets. If so, then some nuclear proliferation could be benign. A possible example involves the Indian subcontinent, where India and Pakistan have fought several wars over the disputed province of Kashmir. The significance of India's underground test of a "peaceful nuclear explosive" in the 1970s was not lost on Pakistan, which turned during the 1980s to developing a countering "Islamic bomb." Indian and Pakistani rounds of underground nuclear tests in 1998 fueled fears worldwide of a new regional nuclear arms race, aggravated by missile capabilities to deliver warheads up to several hundred miles. In the sympathetic and optimistic minority view, these mutual nuclear developments will help reduce the probability of serious Indian-Pakistani conflict in the future. (See also the opening case of Chapter 16.)

For the foreseeable future, advanced strategic nuclear weaponry also provides some level of deterrence against the proliferation of mass destruction capabilities to additional states. It has been argued, for example, that U.S. threats of nuclear retaliation convinced Iraq to refrain from mounting chemical warheads (which it possessed, and had used against Iran during their 1980–88 war) on the missiles it launched against Israel and coalition forces during the Persian Gulf War.

RECAPPING THE SECURITY DILEMMAS

Dilemmas of Security

1. Complete, perfect security is impossible to achieve. Even at the individual level, it is impossible to gain absolute security by totally eliminating risk.
2. Actions taken in search of any form of security—military or otherwise—actually may imperil it or another form of security.
3. States are the major sources of both threats to individuals and security for individuals.
4. Security planning is subject to severe logical and practical contradictions between violent means and peaceful ends.
5. Power is sought by some to achieve state security in an anarchic world, whereas others see such pursuits as the primary source of international insecurity.
6. Both arming decisions and disarming decisions are subject to a prisoners' dilemma structure of motivations, in which individually risk-averse choices by governments will always be to develop new weapons and to refrain from disarming.

7. Although parity is the minimum politically acceptable force level, its precise definition is often disputed for reasons of both clarity and politics.

Dilemmas of Deterrence

1. There is a widespread belief in the effectiveness of deterrence, although we cannot strictly either prove or disprove that deterrence ever has worked.
2. Logically, there are circumstances under which deterrence should not work.
3. If you are self-deterred and your opponent is not, then deterrence has failed.
4. Deterrent systems based on nuclear weapons might help stabilize regional politics.

SEEKING SECURITY THROUGH POLICY CHOICES

The dilemmas sketched here present a mix of logical difficulties, apparent contradictions, and inherent and unavoidable clashes of interest. The examples used to illustrate them cover a range of post–World War II and contemporary foreign policy problems, a number of which remain unsolved and likely will demand considerable attention as we move into the twenty-first century. Some of those dilemmas encourage the use of military force; others constrain it. Collectively, they help define the context of worldwide searches for security pursued through a wide variety of policy instruments. Broadly, every policy tool discussed anywhere throughout Part III of this text can be interpreted as an instrument through which the United States and other actors in the global arena attempt to attain security in one or more of the five activity sectors discussed here, that is, military, political, economic, societal, and environmental security.

A number of military instruments of policy already have been discussed in Chapter 8 and thus far in this chapter. These include the following: (1) Escalation, the staged increase of action severity over time from peaceful to increasingly violent until a level sufficient to accomplish desired policy goals is reached. This notion, of course, applies to all types of activities, not just military actions. (2) Coercive diplomacy, in which a credible threat of violence forms an essential part of a process aimed at persuasion, and often must be implemented. (3) Low-intensity conflict, which received brief consideration in Chapter 8. (4) Arms competitions, briefly considered earlier in connection with action-reaction processes. (5) Deterrence, both nuclear and conventional. These instruments span most of the conventional uses of military power. In addition, some important constraints on the use of military power were discussed in Chapter 8. Among them are the availability of natural resources and production capacity; the degree of and potential for mobilization, and the speed with which further mobilization can be achieved; and the range over which power projection is feasible.

The next section discusses a variety of less conventional military instruments of policy, reviewed in conjunction with constraints and problems associated with their use. The examination begins with covert operations, a more detailed look at low-intensity conflicts, and police, peacekeeping, peacemaking, nation building, and collective security operations.

UNCONVENTIONAL RESPONSES TO UNCONVENTIONAL TIMES: MILITARY INSTRUMENTS OF POLICY FOR THE POST-COLD WAR ERA

In terms of both demand—the types of threats seen thus far in the post–Cold War era—and supply—substantial cuts in real defense spending, troop levels, and numbers of military bases after the Cold War—military operations today are more likely than ever to be unconventional. Threats and possible military responses are examined later. Despite extensive cutbacks, however, the military-industrial-congressional complex remains a potent group actor in U.S. politics, encouraging maintenance of large military forces and defense expenditures.

COVERT OPERATIONS

Dictionaries use terms like *concealed*, *hidden*, *disguised*, or *surreptitious* to define the adjective *covert*. We would thus expect **covert military operations** to be concealed or disguised, hidden from examination by our own or the world's media, formally disavowed in the world of international politics. In practice, an operative bureaucratic criterion often has been plausible deniability, meaning the U.S. government should be able to claim it had nothing to do with an operation, and the possibility of that claim being true should be imaginable.

Why would a government want to pursue covert operations? First, because they represent a form of limited war. (On the conceptual continuum of peaceful and violent actions plotted in Figure 8.2, covert operations would span the range from coercive diplomacy through limited war.) During the 1950s U.S. military security doctrine turned increasingly to reliance on nuclear weapons at the same time our nuclear monopoly was being eroded. The doctrine of limited war allowed some possibility of responding to perceived threats around the world by means short of "going nuclear," and covert operations were part of that doctrine. They were thought to be particularly appropriate for situations in which only limited threats existed, or in which threats did not directly affect vital U.S. interests. The relatively successful case about covert operations in Afghanistan is discussed later in this chapter.

Covert operations also appeared desirable because they often involved messy, unpleasant operations from which decision makers wished to distance themselves, including torture, political assassinations, and cooperation with violent and unsavory elements of foreign societies. Many of those threats that did not directly affect vital U.S. interests lay in developing states of Africa, Asia, and Latin America. When Cold War grand strategy called for containing communist expansion around the world, it was all too easy to support any government that claimed to be anticommunist, no matter how corrupt or repressive it was. The cynical might say of a nominally anticommunist and pro-American dictator that "He's a bastard, but he's *our* bastard." Naturally, this did little to endear the United States to the people of such countries. All too often, covert operations supported by the United States ended up being directed against nationalists who opposed the dictators, whether or not the rebels really were communists.

Is there anything good to say about the possibility of covert operations in the post–Cold War era? Arguably, secrecy could benefit both the United States and friendly governments in certain circumstances. Consider a hypothetical example regarding the international trade in illegal drugs. The United States is an extremely tempting target for drug producers and smugglers. Funded by our enormous relative wealth and facilitated by relatively ineffective drug laws and great freedom of movement both within the country and across its frontiers, their product is in great demand here. The immense sums of money involved also neutralize much opposition to drug operations within foreign countries. Drug money provides improved standards of living to peasant farmers and minor operatives, allows the bribing of officials at all levels, and funds large quantities of sophisticated weaponry to intimidate or kill any opponents unwilling to be bribed. Officials of a government sympathetic to U.S. hopes of reducing the drug traffic might be willing to entertain a covert operation against drug operations on their territory. In this case, plausible deniability would assist in protecting both governments against blame and reprisals, and would particularly help shield sympathetic host country officials.

LOW-INTENSITY CONFLICT

In theory, **low-intensity conflict (LIC)** calls for military action falling somewhat short of limited war and characterized by (1) quick entrance followed by (2) decisive results and (3) quick exit with (4) minimal losses. Several U.S. military interventions in the Western Hemisphere since the early 1980s often are cited as examples of LICs. They include the October 1983 invasion of Grenada (with token participation by forces from six other Caribbean states), and the December 1989 invasion of Panama to depose General Manuel Noriega and arrest him on charges of racketeering and drug trafficking. The narrowly averted invasion of Haiti planned for September 1994 to return democratically elected President Jean-Bertrand Aristide to power would have been another example. However, military strongman General Raul Cedras agreed at the last moment to relinquish power, although only after learning that planes carrying U.S. paratroops had taken off from their base in Georgia (see the opening case in Chapter 15 for further details). One extrahemispheric example of a LIC is the December 1992 U.S. intervention in Somalia. Although begun as a humanitarian and peacekeeping mission, it was later, briefly, and unsuccessfully extended to a peacemaking and nation-building undertaking (see the opening case of Chapter 7 for further details).

Motivations for adopting LICs go beyond the universal desire to achieve policy objectives at minimal cost. U.S. inclinations toward LIC are usually considered to be part of the reaction to the bitter losses of the Vietnam War a generation ago. Normally, LICs are undertaken only in situations believed to satisfy all or most of Alexander George's criteria for successful coercive diplomacy (see Chapter 8, and Table 8.3). Usable military options must be geared to quick entrance and exit, with superior strength that will help assure a decisive result. Such operations are designed to ensure speed and success through locally overwhelming force that will deter opponents and produce justifiable fear of escalation. Efforts usually are directed toward ensuring clarity of objectives and settlement terms, and communicating them unambiguously to opponents. Ensuring adequate domestic political support is a prime reason for adopting LIC doctrine because it is thought that quick and decisive action evokes enthusiastic support (or at least grudging

SUCCESSFUL COVERT OPERATIONS IN AFGHANISTAN

Arguably one of the most successful covert operations ever was U.S. aid to rebels fighting the Soviet Union in Afghanistan during the 1980s. In a bloody 1978 coup, pro-Soviet leftists took power in that largely Islamic state, only to be themselves deposed by another Soviet-backed coup in December 1979. The new and more strongly pro-Soviet leader called for further aid, and the USSR responded by airlifting in substantial numbers of troops and supplies. A protracted guerrilla war ensued between Soviet forces and fundamentalist Muslim rebels called the Muhajadeen.

As in some other guerrilla wars, well-armed troops with heavy armor controlled the urban areas and helicopter gunships could rain destruction on rural villages, but the guerrillas could melt away into the hills. Soon Soviet troops feared to move outside the major cities except in heavily armed convoys, or even to leave their fortified compounds at night. Parallels to the U.S. experience in Vietnam were regularly drawn, and conservative forces in the Reagan administration sought to help the rebels turn Afghanistan into "the Soviets' Vietnam." Their most effective tool in that effort was the hand-portable "Stinger" surface-to-air antiaircraft missile, with which a Muhajadeen guerrilla having only minimal training could shoot down a Soviet helicopter. With tacit approval from the Pakistani government, Stingers and other supplies were smuggled across the rugged mountains separating Afghanistan from Pakistan, carried on the backs of humans and pack animals. Soviet losses eventually reached a reported 15,000 troops killed, and the war became a terrible drain on the already reeling Soviet economy. Morale deteriorated badly. Internal Soviet ethnic divisions became a factor because military leaders were afraid to send soldiers conscripted from the Muslim southwestern republics, for fear they would desert to the Muhajadeen.

Faced with mounting economic and political problems at home and an essentially stalemated conflict in Afghanistan, the Soviets appeared to give up, withdrawing the last of their troops on 15 February 1989. Not publicly admitted, however, was the secret U.S.-Soviet deal that made that withdrawal possible. By 1989 the United States was on relatively good terms with the Gorbachev government in Moscow (which was to be relatively helpful in dealing with the Persian Gulf War later that year), and wanted to relieve pressures on the USSR. To secure Soviet withdrawal, the United States promised to cut off its clandestine supplies to the rebels. In effect, both superpowers agreed to back off and the let the various Afghan groups fight their own war unaided. Many in the West were surprised when the leftist government in Kabul survived for more than three years. After the Soviets withdrew, numerous Muhajadeen factions began fighting against one another as much as against the central government, and a fairly comprehensive rebel victory was not achieved until 28 April 1992.

Nonetheless, the period of clandestine U.S. aid should be considered a fairly decisive covert operation. Although it did not overthrow the government in Kabul, and probably never could do so while the Soviets backed that government with sufficient firepower, it produced a protracted no-win stalemate for the Soviets, and could have been continued indefinitely. Still, by the latter 1990s, Western fears rose that arms sent to help the Muhajadeen fight the Soviets would find their way to Islamist rebels fighting friendly governments.

acceptance), whereas prolonged action and ambiguous results allow domestic political resistance to build. This is particularly true of congressional resistance, fear of which drives every modern administration toward LICs and away from more prolonged military commitments abroad.

Arguably, low-intensity conflict is only a new name for old U.S. interventionism, as seen particularly in the Western Hemisphere, well into the twentieth century. (Recall the *military interventionism* viewpoint of Chapter 1, and see the discussion of grand foreign policy orientations in Chapter 2.) To the extent that Senator Thomas Eagleton of Missouri, one of the originators of the War Powers Act of 1973, was correct in his ultimate decision that the act was a mistake that "gives the President and all of his successors *in futuro* a predated 60 day unilateral war-making authority," the War Powers Act provides a powerful incentive toward LICs (see Chapter 5). Moreover, even if military action should extend beyond sixty to ninety days, the president remains free to blame Congress for policy failure if it orders the troops withdrawn.

There is some debate about exactly what constitutes "low intensity" in the amounts and types of force employed, numbers of troops involved, and casualties suffered by our own forces, by opponents, and by civilians. Typically, U.S. attention focuses almost entirely on American losses. Keeping low-intensity conflicts quick and decisive requires using U.S. military advantages in weapons sophistication, firepower, and mobility to achieve at least locally overwhelming superiority of force. In Panama, U.S. military casualties were quite light, given unexpectedly fierce resistance from some elements of the Panamanian military, but hundreds of Panamanian civilians died in bombings and cross fires. The invasion of Grenada is said to have been unnecessarily complicated by the desire of every element of the U.S. armed forces to have a role; that lesson was learned and avoided in planning for the Panama and Haiti operations. It seems clear that "low intensity" will continue to depend on who makes the measurement. U.S. officials likely will continue to demand overwhelming American superiority, and to regard conflicts not involving nuclear weapons or very large conventional forces to be LICs.

PEACEMAKING, HUMANITARIAN RELIEF, PEACEKEEPING, PEACE ENFORCEMENT, NATION BUILDING, AND POLICE ACTIONS

Certain military activities even less traditional than covert operations and low-intensity conflicts have gained enormously in importance since the end of the Cold War. They form a diverse group sometimes called other military operations (OMO) and formerly called operations other than war (OOTW). That group includes peacemaking, humanitarian relief, peacekeeping, peace enforcement, nation building, and police actions, as well as disaster relief, noncombatant evacuation, and drug interdiction, which are dealt with in the following section. William J. Durch (1993a, 5) provides a useful categorization of the many types of peace actions, arrayed across the dimensions of (1) amount of force used or threatened, and (2) degree of consent obtained from host or target governments. That scheme is reproduced in Figure 9.1.

Peacemaking is the process of negotiating agreements to accomplish such ends as stopping armed hostilities, defusing a threatened military clash, repatriating displaced

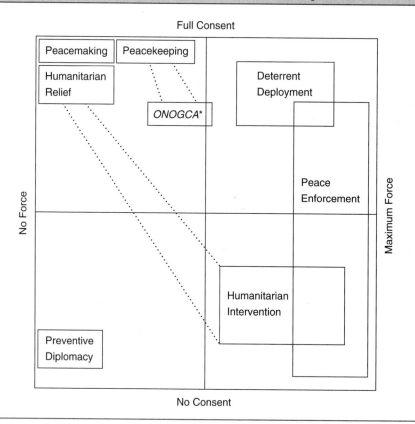

FIGURE 9.1

Level of Host (Target) State Consent and
Use or Threat of Force in Peace-Related Field Operations

*United Nations Observer Group in Central America.

Source: William J. Durch, "Introduction," in William J. Durch, ed., *The Evolution of UN Peacekeeping: Case Studies and Comparative Analysis* (New York: St. Martins Press, 1993)

peoples, addressing the root causes of sustained disagreements, and laying the groundwork for a more amicable future. Nominally, such efforts are peaceful and require the participation of all affected parties. However, any of the negotiating tactics examined in Chapter 10 may be employed, including at least the threat of force and the promise of reward. The results of peacemaking may range from treaties that endure for many years, to armistice agreements that nobody expects will hold without on-site peacekeeping, which may be included in cease-fire agreements.

Humanitarian relief missions typically involve providing food, shelter, medical services, and other supplies after wars and natural disasters, and may include assisting in the repatriation of prisoners and displaced peoples. Such relief may be coordinated through such intergovernmental organizations as the UN but provided by any of a host of international nongovernmental actors such as the Red Cross, Doctors to the Rescue, and charitable religious organizations. Although fundamentally peaceful, humanitarian relief missions do not always enjoy full consent from all parties in target countries. Conditions of anarchy and war often require that such missions be protected by armed peacekeepers, as seen in U.S./UN efforts to ensure adequate distribution of food throughout Somalia in 1993–95 (see the opening case of Chapter 7).

Peacekeeping means keeping a peace already made, building confidence through measures that aid wary states or factions in defusing potential new hostilities and evolving toward eventually living in peace, *provided that all parties want to keep the peace.* In the run-up to the 1967 Middle East war, for example, Egypt ordered UN peacekeepers to leave the Sinai. Israel had never allowed peacekeepers on its side of the border, but interpreted the Egyptian demand as a prelude to invasion, making it one of a number of signs that led Israel to attack preemptively. Peacekeeping operations may involve **unarmed military observer missions,** first employed in the Balkans in 1947. Such missions can help keep a cease-fire peaceful by overseeing and reporting on the conflicting parties' behavior and helping resolve violations before they escalate into local battles. Some operations involve **armed peacekeeping missions,** first employed in the Sinai in 1956. Armed peacekeepers generally are authorized to fire only in self-defense, partly because they almost always are outgunned by the parties they monitor. Whether armed or not, international peacekeepers can accomplish such varied tasks as (1) verifying compliance with agreements to separate troops and to demarcate and respect borders, (2) helping provide security, administration, food, shelter, and other supplies to sustain and stabilize life, (3) verifying for all parties that agreements to neutralize weapons, disarm, or relocate forces are kept, (4) monitoring the repatriation of displaced peoples and their property, and (5) organizing and monitoring elections to verify their freedom and accuracy. U.S./NATO operations in Bosnia following the 1995 Dayton accords involved all these types of actions. Peacekeeping forces often are drawn from politically neutral states, which was particularly true during the Cold War. Because their assignments require great tact and circumspection, troops usually receive special training for peacekeeping.

Peace enforcement moves beyond the limitations of peacekeeping by involving military operations of many types designed to impose peace on would-be combatants. This can—and often must—involve disarming the combatants, thus bringing about peace by removing the wherewithal to continue making war. Consequently, peace enforcement rarely enjoys full consent and may involve substantial and sustained use of force, with significant casualties. After the United States began moving beyond peacekeeping into peace enforcement in Somalia and lost eighteen soldiers killed in raids intended to capture the warlord General Mohammed Farah Aidid in 1993, domestic political pressures mounted and led to the 1994 U.S. pullout (refer to the opening case of Chapter 7). A slightly milder and more consensual, if rarer, variant of peace enforcement is **deterrent deployment,** in which international military forces are strategically placed to signal their ability and intent to counter some threatened aggression. Such deployments are made with the consent of the threatened party and may involve considerable force capability.

Both peacekeepers and peace enforcers face special difficulties in dealing with multisided civil wars like that which raged for years in Lebanon. U.S. troops landed in Lebanon on 25 August 1982 to oversee the evacuation of Palestine Liberation Organization guerrillas from Beirut, then besieged by Israeli forces that had invaded Lebanon the previous April. This was seen as a peacekeeping mission, and the United States had strongly encouraged Israel to let the PLO forces leave Lebanon for North Africa. Following the massacre of hundreds of Palestinian civilians in the Sabra and Shatila refugee camps in southern Beirut by Lebanese Christian militia in September, Israel yielded to plans for an international peace force comprising French, Italian, and U.S. troops. The first U.S. marine was killed by shellfire in Beirut on 30 September, only one day after landing. Larger losses were to follow. The first authoritative calls for withdrawal came after the U.S. embassy in Beirut was devastated by a car bomb on 18 April 1983. Such calls intensified after suicide truck bomb attacks killed 241 U.S. and 58 French troops the following October. On 7 February 1984 President Reagan ordered U.S. marines withdrawn from Beirut to ships offshore, from which they could hardly conduct any peacekeeping operations. The crucial problem in Lebanon was the many-party nature of the civil war, involving major groups of Christians, Muslims, and Druze, plus numerous splinter groups. The truck bomb attacks, for instance, were blamed on pro-Iranian Muslim fundamentalists. Because there were so many different warring parties, it was all too easy for any one of them to interpret U.S. actions as favoring some opponent.

Nation building may be part of a comprehensive program including either peacekeeping or peace enforcement to maintain stability, depending on the circumstances. It involves actively working to create new political, social, and economic infrastructures in the affected area. Although often considered to be a particularly military undertaking, nation building may involve substantial amounts of economic aid, farming and manufacturing demonstration projects, building of roads, bridges, and schools, and other undertakings employing significant numbers of U.S. and allied civilians. Depending on the circumstances of the case, nation building is a very large step beyond peacekeeping or peacemaking. Within the framework of other military operations, however, nation building often is considered to be a particularly military undertaking. Maintaining stability may require that peacekeepers remain at work, and peacemaking may still be under way. Additionally, many of the necessary building activities are thought to be particular strengths of military engineer forces. Being trained not only in rapid and large-scale construction, but in carrying out such activities while subject to adverse conditions of bad weather, supply difficulties, and even military attack, such forces are especially prepared to work in settings that lack stable civilian governance.

Police actions are military actions of diverse types undertaken to enforce international law or treaties, and may range in size from brief actions by small units up to fairly sizable and prolonged wars. Of all the types of actions considered in this section, they potentially involve the greatest use of force and least consent from targeted states. The only such action conducted under UN auspices during the Cold War years was the Korean War, which lasted three years and cost the United States alone more than 33,000 battle deaths.

DISASTER RELIEF, NONCOMBATANT EVACUATION, AND DRUG INTERDICTION

A second group of other military operations, often considerably less violent than police actions, peacekeeping, peacemaking, and nation building, consists of disaster relief, noncombatant evacuation, and drug interdiction. U.S. aid to the Kurds beseiged in northwestern Iraq after the Persian Gulf War provides one example. *Disaster relief* operations frequently involve military forces for many of the same reasons that military engineering forces are employed in nation building. They are trained in rapid mobilization and operations under adverse weather and supply conditions, and disaster relief often involves both construction activities and the need to establish security in affected areas. Such operations may involve both National Guard and active or reserve military forces, either at home or abroad. *Noncombatant evacuation* might be considered a variant of peacekeeping, also involving the risk of combat to protect civilians. As suggested in the hypothetical example discussed earlier, however, *drug interdiction* easily can shade over into covert operations and involve large-scale violence. Although there are natural political temptations to utilize any available and reasonably appropriate policy instrument, and to meet the drug threat with force, drug interdiction is not a mission much sought by the U.S. military. Still, establishing secure containment lines and interdicting infiltrators remain traditional military missions, and it is tempting to consider their analogues in dealing with the drug trade. Politicians seem to find those analogues appealing; President Bush devoted considerable rhetoric to a the so-called war on drugs, although the methods utilized seemed unchanged from past practice, and the results were inconclusive.

COLLECTIVE SECURITY

Collective security agreements are regional or even global cooperative undertakings to protect the military security of some number of states either by waging war or by taking military steps designed to prevent war. In its narrow sense, collective security extends only to member states. This may be thought of as the teen gang theory of security, under which an attack against any one member is considered to be an attack against all which demands a coordinated response from all members. In the broader sense of collective security, a group of states can extend aid to an outside state or nation. Both types of aggregated action are envisioned under the United Nations Charter, which effectively recognized that the world was not ready for a unified global police force in 1945. During the Cold War years, that unreadiness combined with East-West polarization to require that all security or peacekeeping operations taken under UN auspices be arranged ad hoc by some subset of the UN membership. Both the Korean War and the Persian Gulf War were such ad hoc undertakings. Because NATO was designed to protect Western Europe against Soviet attack, its original charter prohibited operations outside its membership area, and had to be modified to permit out-of-area operations such as sending the 1995 "Peace Implementation Force" to Bosnia.

In the aftermath of the Cold War, some liberal and globalist analysts envision a UN freed from its old polarization between communists and anticommunists, able to serve as a global collective security agency in disciplining aggressors. Other analysts, exemplified by some on the right wing of U.S. politics, fear that the development of any UN military capability will be the opening wedge of a world dictatorship, or at least of the subordination of U.S. interests to those of outsiders. Still others take a more traditional realist stance and oppose the notion of global collective security arrangements because it would restrict the freedom of individual states to pursue their own interests and to decide whether and how to involve themselves in each particular case. For the time being, political conservatism and inertia are likely to leave the traditionalist group in the ascendancy, and collective security operations will remain ad hoc. Certainly, developments following the Persian Gulf War of 1990–91 have not put any global collective security flesh on the bones of President George Bush's "new world order." Thus proposing or choosing to participate in collective security agreements or operations remain options on the policy menus of the United States and the governments of other individual states, and of already existing organizations like NATO, the Organization for Security and Cooperation in Europe (OSCE), or the Organization of American States (OAS).

ARMS TRANSFERS: THE DOUBLE-EDGED SWORD

Arms transfers comprise *sales*, *aid*, and *gifts* from producer states to recipient states. Additionally, and increasingly in recent years, they also comprise *licensed production* in consumer states under authorization from the developer states. In addition to these channels through which arms transfers occur, we can distinguish a number of important categories along a continuum of destructive capabilities. The vast majority of arms transfers lie at the least destructive end of that continuum, and are termed *conventional arms transfers* to distinguish them from everything else. At the most destructive end are weapons of mass destruction, comprising the so-called NBC (for nuclear, biological, and chemical) weapons. In the middle are high-technology and so-called smart weapons, typically utilizing modern electronic and computer technology to improve the accuracy of individual weapons enormously over that of conventional versions. Examples include bombs and missiles that seek out the spot from a laser designator beam held pointed on a target to achieve a direct hit, and terrain-following cruise missiles. Some authorities suggest that the extremely high accuracy and low *collateral damage* (to persons and objects other than the target) achievable by smart weapons will allow them to replace their nuclear alternatives. This view is compatible with the position of John Mueller (1988), who holds that the enormous destructiveness and political salience of nuclear weapons has since 1945 rendered them unusable, and thus politically irrelevant. An unfortunate corollary of this view is that smart weapons may increase the probabilities that tensions sometimes will escalate to war.

Arms transfers today are more than just a set of military and security tools on the menu of foreign policy options. As we shall see, powerful arguments exist that *this sword is double edged because arms transfers create at least as many problems as they solve.* Transfers occur primarily between developed states and from developed to developing states, although licensed production often takes place in newly industrialized states. In the early years after World War II, arms transfers from the United States consisted primarily of obsolete and surplus weaponry, which were still desired and largely unavailable in the developing world. Levels of sophistication in transferred arms began to rise dramatically during the 1960s. Today, the most advanced weaponry available regularly is sold, at least to highly favored client states. Indeed, the sophistication and firepower of weapons transferred are excellent indicators of the recipients' political importance to their suppliers. Moreover, although arms transfers in the 1950s were intended almost exclusively to serve the producer states' political and military goals abroad, today they are shaped at least as much by their domestic economic and foreign trade goals.

Conventional arms transfers declined rapidly between 1987 and 1991, as the Cold War ended, but stabilized thereafter. The United States remains the world's largest exporter of conventional arms, a position it has held for decades. According to a Defense

Department report, the United States made 44.8 percent of all weapons sales agreements in 1990.

The U.S. real dollar volume of major conventional arms transfers (CAT) rose by more than one fifth after the Persian Gulf War, declining slightly by 1994. However, the Soviet Union's collapse and breakup dropped Russia, its major successor state, to fifth place by 1994, and contributed greatly to raising the U.S. share of the CAT market to over 58 percent by 1994. Ironically, through much of the Cold War, the five permanent members of the UN Security Council (Britain, China, France, the Soviet Union, and the United States) led the world in arms sales (Anthony et al., 1995, 493–4).

Although arms transfers serve both military and economic ends, as we shall see, those great power arms sales are a clear signal that the military aspect dominated security concerns during the Cold War. Additionally, Germany's rise to fourth place by 1990 and second place by 1994 reflects one aspect of its role as the dominant economy in the emerging European Union. Israel ranked sixteenth for the 1990–94 period, with arms exports of $367 million, far below the arms imports of any of the major Arab states. Total world CAT exports dropped by some 30 percent over that half decade. During the 1990–94 period, Japanese CAT imports dropped significantly, and Germany's imports dropped as its exports grew rapidly. Many Arab states increased their arms purchases substantially in the aftermath of the 1990–91 Persian Gulf War. The tailing off of Afghan purchases reflects the completion of Soviet withdrawal on 15 February 1989, and the achievement of rebel victory on 28 April 1992.

INCENTIVES, DISINCENTIVES, AND USES OF ARMS TRANSFERS

States engage in arms transfers for numerous and varied reasons, and many of the incentives to do so are domestic. Costs of the latest and most sophisticated weapon systems have risen steadily for decades. Selling some top-line weapons abroad lowers unit costs by allowing the fixed expenses of developing new weaponry and setting up manufacturing lines to be recovered over a larger production run. Producing larger numbers may even lower the variable cost per unit by achieving economies of scale. Longer production runs also help even out the always irregular levels of employment in defense industries, maintaining a pool of expertise that represents a genuine resource. Additionally, sustaining some minimum number of healthy defense contractors allows at least the possibility of competition to keep costs down, and should help promote innovation. Thus, for example, the U.S. government decided some years ago to grant financial aid to Lockheed Corporation when it approached bankruptcy.

The post–Cold War defense environment, however, has already seen waves of layoffs and mergers driven by the downsizing of defense procurements. In turn, this provides yet another incentive for defense contractors to seek out sales opportunities abroad. States with some military development and production capabilities may export their less sophisticated products to earn foreign exchange for purchasing more sophisticated equipment abroad. Thus, for example, Israel is a major exporter of arms, using the profits to support its development efforts. Despite that thriving industry, Israel cannot afford to develop all of its own top-line weaponry. It still imports air superiority fighters from the United States, and in 1994 canceled its program to develop such a fighter, after investing billions of dollars in the program. In a variation of this strategy, China buys little military technology abroad, but sells large quantities of simple arms to help pay for a development program that has yielded its own nuclear and thermonuclear arms, all the way up the so-phistication ladder to small numbers of ICBMs and ballistic missile submarines. In the early 1990s the United States was very concerned about Chinese sales of relatively simple missile technology to Iran. Other domestic reasons also may lead states and industries into arms transfers. In the 1980s Brazilian automobile manufacturers turned their truck production capabilities to making armored personnel carriers (APCs) because essentially the same technologies were involved and they perceived the APC market to be less vola-tile than the truck and automobile market. Brazil rapidly became one of the world's ma-jor producers of light armored vehicles.

Beyond their domestic utility, arms transfers remain potentially useful tools of for-eign policy. Whether as sales or gifts, transferred arms may help support and protect friends and allies while transferring some of the collective burdens of defense to them. There are at least some instances of states giving military aid to tip the scales of battle in favor of clients and thus securing military victories for allies or proxy states. In the Per-sian Gulf War, U.S. movements of Patriot antimissile batteries to Israel were part of a campaign to keep Israel from attacking Iraq and possibly splitting some Arab states away from the U.S.-led coalition. Military assistance is regularly given with stated—and, per-haps, real—intent to preserve the peace by deterring a client's opponents. Arms transfers are a bargaining tool that may win concessions in negotiation. Moreover, although ini-tially it appears somewhat paradoxical, it has even been argued that we should provide arms to both sides in some conflicts in order to raise their perceived security levels and gain leverage to be used in bargaining for lasting peace. The Middle East provides a notable example; in negotiating the Camp David accords that led to the 1979 Israeli-Egyptian peace treaty, President Carter promised additional arms to both sides. He also promised nuclear power reactors to Egypt, probably fully realizing that Congress would never authorize their transfer.

Many disincentives for conventional arms transfers remain. It has become almost a matter of "received wisdom" that they increase the probability of interstate conflict. The usual argument is that such transfers increase military capability, which in turn is interpreted by opponents as hostile intent, leading to a variety of conflict behaviors, and possibly to an action-reaction process in arms transfers. With the breakup of the So-viet Union, the probably of such arms spirals dropped dramatically. During the Cold War years, however, the U.S. and USSR found themselves supplying competing client states in several regions, notably including Israel versus the Arab states and India versus Pakistan.

Transfers of sophisticated weapons raise the difficulty and cost for even the strongest states to project power into the vicinity of well-armed smaller powers. For example, in 1986 the United States launched a series of air raids against Libya, nominally in response to that radical state's purported role in the bombing of a West German disco heavily fre-quented by U.S. service personnel. However, those raids never attempted to penetrate far inland against Libya's substantial defenses, and were very carefully designed to first knock out Libyan coastal radars and antiaircraft missiles. Another disincentive for arms trans-fers is that they may exacerbate the impact of any subsequent shift in alliances. Iran, for example, purchased billions of dollars worth of sophisticated U.S. aircraft and other late-model weaponry over a span of many years. Following the 1979 revolution, American weapons previously sold to the shah helped make the newly radicalized Iran one of the most powerful states in the Persian Gulf area and a potential regional hegemon. Optimistic hopes that Iran lacked the expertise and spare parts to maintain systems such as advanced fighter aircraft were dispelled during the 1980–88 Iran-Iraq War. A final disincentive is that arms transfers may absorb funds a developing state would be better off devoting to internal economic development.

The dramatic rise in *licensed production* abroad over the last decade or so serves both the developers' incentives to transfer arms and the producer-recipients' desires to minimize costs while improving their military capabilities. It also promotes producer development through technology transfer and the building of indigenous production capacity and skills. Developing states thus may see licensed production or joint production deals as channels for acquiring improved technologies, gaining design and manufacturing information, and building labor skills. The originators of the designs and technologies involved, however, may have good reason over time to fear their transfer because information gained through military joint or licensed production deals may facilitate inroads on civilian markets to which they carry over. In the early 1990s, for example, such concerns were raised regarding a joint U.S.-Japanese program to produce a new high-performance fighter aircraft in Japan. Many knowledgeable observers in the United States feared the Japanese could use technologies transferred through this program to compete with the United States in the lucrative international market for civilian airliners, long dominated by American firms but already facing increasing competition from the joint English-French Airbus consortium.

ARMS PROLIFERATION PROBLEMS

Although arms transfers are encouraged by substantial numbers of both domestic and foreign incentives, most of the disincentives considered thus far lie in the foreign relations domain. Practical politics thus may suggest that domestic incentives will prevail and tip the policy scales in favor of continued arms transfers. Unfortunately, such transfers likely will exacerbate several types of arms proliferation problems. In the 1980s the greatest concerns usually were (1) the growth or vertical proliferation of U.S. and Soviet nuclear stockpiles, augmented by continuing qualitative improvements in accuracy and firepower within ceilings set through arms control agreements and (2) horizontal nuclear proliferation through which states like Israel, Pakistan, Iran, and Iraq acquired or sought nuclear weapons. Vertical proliferation can be addressed through bilateral or regional arms control. For example, through negotiations begun in 1969, the United States and the Soviet Union reached a series of agreements setting ceilings on their strategic nuclear weapons and associated delivery vehicles. Agreements shortly before the collapse of the USSR continued and extended with the Soviet successor states (notably, Belarus, Kazakhstan, Russia, and Ukraine) have led to actual reductions in weapons quantities, with careful procedures for observing and "verifying" the destruction of significant numbers of missiles and the dismantling of their thermonuclear warheads. In this instance, a continuing arms control and reduction process has been created and institutionalized.

If Mueller is correct about the irrelevance of nuclear arms, however, reversing vertical proliferation by reducing their numbers ought to be relatively straightforward. Limiting horizontal proliferation is another matter entirely. The case of France in the 1960s, already discussed in Chapter 8, clearly demonstrates how governments may conclude that they must possess nuclear weapons to be seen as serious international powers. The attempt by the major nuclear powers and most other states to limit horizontal nuclear proliferation by means of the Nuclear Nonproliferation Treaty (NPT) of 1968 is discussed in the opening case of Chapter 16. Regrettably, the very same major powers that seek to limit the horizontal proliferation of nuclear and other high-technology capabilities seek expanded markets for many of those same capabilities, and thereby promote regional proliferation.

Those same monetary and political incentives that encourage horizontal nuclear proliferation act even more powerfully to promote the proliferation of other advanced capabilities in high-technology weaponry and weapons of mass destruction, areas in which the special stigma associated with nuclear weapons is absent. For instance, in the 1980s it was discovered that a (West) German firm had built a chemical plant at Rabta, Libya, allegedly for fertilizer production but actually for nerve gas and other chemical weapons ingredients. Perhaps even more worrisome than transfers driven by greed and political concerns are *transfers of weapons-applicable high technology that occur inadvertently as a natural result of normal economic activity*. For example, microchips make possible tiny navigational receivers that can receive and process signals from the Pentagon's system of navigational earth satellites, translating that information into a three-dimensional position accurate to within a few feet. Given that technology, it is now possible to build a cruise missile much simpler than U.S. versions that rely on complex digitized terrain maps and terrain-following radar. Thus low-cost precision-guided weapons may shortly come into the hands of rogue states such as Iran, Iraq, and Libya.

Another development of substantial concern, not the product of any single state's deliberate transfer policies, is the combination of smart weapons and weapons of mass destruction with effective long-range delivery systems such as advanced strike aircraft and ballistic missiles. Just as the development of nuclear weapons and intercontinental ballistic missiles gave the United States and the Soviet Union the capability to strike deep into each other's heartlands virtually free of any defense, thus depriving them of unconditional viability, similar capabilities threaten to extend the reach and destructive capability of regional powers tremendously. The Scud-B missiles fired by Iran against Israel and Saudi Arabia in 1991 had only a fraction of the destructiveness potentially available. There is good reason to believe that Saddam refrained from using chemical weapons in the Persian Gulf War for fear of chemical or nuclear retaliation by the United States. However, Iraq used missiles and chemical weapons against Iran during their 1980–88 war. Given that history, and how close Iraq came to losing that war, can we be certain that Saddam would not have used nuclear warheads if they had been available? A nuclear strike against U.S. troop concentrations during the 1991 war well might have been expected to produce such high casualties that public revulsion would have compelled an American pullout. Extending similar scenarios around the world clearly indicates why there is so much concern about the potential for NBC weapons on ballistic missiles in the hands of rogue or pariah states. Even if never used, such weaponry could hold the promise of potent political blackmail.

CONTROLLING HIGH-TECH WEAPONS PROLIFERATION

As was the case in dealing with nuclear proliferation, controlling the horizontal proliferation of other types of advanced weaponry requires developing specific, targeted institutions. One notable example is the Missile Technology Control Regime (MTCR), begun in 1987 and now including as members the nuclear weapons states Britain, France, and the United States, plus Austria, Canada, Finland, Germany, Iceland, Italy, Japan, New Zealand, Norway, Sweden, and Switzerland. The MTCR aims at promoting non-proliferation of ballistic missile technology in nonmember states, concerning itself with states such as China, India, North Korea, and the former Soviet republics that produce missiles having a greater destructive capacity than the Scud-B. More specifically, MTCR regulations originally limited the transfer of missiles with a 500-kilo (about 1,100-pound) payload capable of traveling more than 300 kilometers (about 186 miles). In 1993 those regulations were extended to limit the transfer of all missiles intended to be armed with weapons of mass destruction, including NBC weapons. The logic of MTCR regulations is that potential supplier states agree to cooperate in preventing the spread of selected technologies by adjusting their export controls and by bringing pressure to bear on other actual or potential exporters. At best, this control undertaking is fraught with potential leaks and loopholes. China caused some of the greatest concerns in the mid-1990s. Despite having signed the NPT in 1992 and vowing in 1994 to abide by the MTCR, the Beijing government had violated the Limited Nuclear Test Ban Treaty of 1963, sold uranium to India, and sent weapons technology to Pakistan and missiles to Iran.

SUMMARY

Security involves both the physical state or condition of being secure and the psychological perception of feeling secure, but scholars and analysts have failed to reach general agreement on any simple definition of the term. Traditionally, political scientists and foreign policymakers focus on the vague concept of *national security*, which properly should be called *state* security, and on the military dimension of security. That approach is consistent with the primarily militarized interpretation of containment policy practiced by the United States during the Cold War. However, beginning slowly in the last quarter of the twentieth century and gaining impetus particularly since the end of the Cold War, academic and other analysts increasingly have come to see security as international rather than just national in scope, and have challenged the exclusively military treatment of security issues.

Following the usage of the Canadian political scientist Barry Buzan, we examined five major sectors in which the security of human collectivities is affected by the activities of humankind: military, political, economic, societal, and environmental. Important post-Cold War changes worldwide now require the U.S. to be concerned about security in all five sectors.

Although analysts commonly speak and write of "the security dilemma" as if there were only one, the concept and pursuit of security are surrounded and permeated by many dilemmas, apparent contradictions, or inherent and unavoidable clashes of interest. We are forced to adapt to many of these difficulties, just as we have to live with the irreducible limitations of decision making. Seven of the more important dilemmas of security are examined in this chapter. Additionally, we discuss four dilemmas associated with deterrence.

Broadly, every policy tool discussed anywhere throughout Part III of this text can be interpreted as an instrument through which the United States and other actors in the global arena attempt to attain security in one or more of the five activity sectors discussed here. Escalation and coercive diplomacy are among the military instruments of policy discussed in Chapter 8, along with a number of important constraints on the use of military power. Arms competitions and deterrence are discussed in this chapter in connection with security dilemmas. Together with low-intensity conflict (LIC), these instruments span most of the conventional uses of military power. A variety of less conventional military instruments of policy is discussed in conjunction with the constraints and problems associated with their use. Those instruments include covert operations, low-intensity conflicts, and peacemaking, humanitarian relief, peacekeeping, peace enforcement, nation building, police actions, and collective security operations. Arms transfers (sales, aid, and gifts), together with the recent tremendous growth in licensed production of modern weaponry, serve many ends and are subject to many difficulties, including raising the levels of military technology in developing states. Institutionalized arms control is subject to severe cross pressures. In particular, the very same major powers that seek to limit the horizontal proliferation of nuclear and other high-technology capabilities to additional states seek expanded markets for many of those same capabilities, thereby promoting regional proliferation.

In evaluating security problems at the onset of the twenty-first century, U.S. perceptions of the international threat environment have changed markedly from those of the Cold War era. The geopolitical context of the Cold War years was dominated by anti-communism, containment, and activist interventionism, as discussed in Chapter 3. It was widely believed—though less so among officials than ordinary citizens—that a strategic nuclear war was possible, even if quite unlikely. U.S. military forces and roles were designed and directed primarily to implementing containment and meeting the global Soviet and communist threat(s). Like the geopolitical context that shapes them, almost all these perceptions and policies have been drastically modified or reversed in the post–Cold War world. Military security concerns in the late 1990s tended to center on new problems like cleaning up nuclear and chemical damage to the environment caused by Cold War industrial and military programs, preventing the leakage of nuclear materials from the former Soviet republics to rogue states and international political terrorists, and controlling the drive by such rogue states as Iraq to develop weapons of mass destruction. Ironically, the end of the Cold War and the virtual disappearance of fears about a superpower nuclear exchange have left a new world disorder in which small and regional conflicts are increasingly likely.

The search for security in various forms is also the prime motivation behind use of the other policy instruments examined in the remaining three chapters of Part III. Chapter 10 is devoted to the relatively peaceful techniques of diplomacy, bargaining, and negotiation. These tools for conflict resolution also may form the opening wedge of coercive diplomacy.

KEY TERMS

Arms transfers	Deterrence
Collective security agreement	Deterrent deployment
Covert [military] operations	Economic security

Environmental security

Horizontal nuclear proliferation (Compare with *vertical nuclear proliferation.*)

Humanitarian relief

Low-intensity conflict

Military security

Nation building

National security

Neoimperialism

Peacekeeping

Armed peacekeeping mission

Unarmed military observer mission

Peacemaking

Peace enforcement

Police actions

Political security

Security

Societal security

Vertical nuclear proliferation (Compare with *horizontal nuclear proliferation.*)

SELECTED READINGS

Buzan, Barry. 1991. *People, States and Fear: An Agenda for International Security Studies in the Post–Cold War Era*, 2d ed. Boulder, Colo.: Lynne Reinner. Buzan was instrumental in spreading the notion that security is many faceted, embracing not only military, but political, economic, societal, and environmental sectors.

Durch, William J., ed. 1993. *The Evolution of UN Peacekeeping: Case Studies and Comparative Analysis.* New York: St. Martin's Press.

Dyson, Freeman J. 1984. *Weapons and Hope.* New York: Harper & Row.

Jordan, Amos A., William J. Taylor, and Michael J. Mazarr. 1999. *American National Security: Policy and Process*, 5th ed. Baltimore: Johns Hopkins University Press.

Romm, Joseph J. 1993. *Defining National Security: The Nonmilitary Aspects.* New York: Council on Foreign Relations.

Schraeder, Peter J., ed. 1992. *Intervention in the 1990s: U.S. Foreign Policy in the Third World*, 2d ed. Boulder, Colo.: Lynne Reinner.

SIPRI (Stockholm International Peace Research Institute). Annual. *SIPRI Yearbook* [Year]: *Armaments, Disarmament, and International Security.* Oxford: Oxford University Press.

Snow, Donald M. 1999. *National Security: Defense Policy in a Changed International Order*, 4th ed. New York: St. Martin's Press.

CHAPTER 10

DIPLOMACY AND NEGOTIATION

PRESIDENT JIMMY CARTER HAMMERS OUT A MIDDLE EAST PEACE AT CAMP DAVID

In 1978 President Jimmy Carter and his top foreign policy team brought Israeli prime minister Menachem Begin, Egyptian president Anwar Sadat, and their top advisers together at the isolated and highly secure presidential retreat at Camp David, Maryland, outside Washington. Their goal was to advance the slow and difficult Middle East peace process they had inherited from the Nixon and Ford administrations. Their setting guaranteed that all parties could be isolated from ordinary daily political concerns, allowing an unusually intense focus on the single policy goal of regional peace. That focus also was lengthy; the major participants engaged in full-time bargaining for thirteen days, 5–17 September.

President Carter and his team of advisers were not optimistic about their chances of success, and realized that such a summit meeting without progress would be a political liability. Nonetheless, they believed that Carter needed a breakthrough toward lasting peace to avoid joining several of his predecessors in facing a new Arab-Israeli war. Those stakes demanded a serious effort, and President Carter was willing to take the political risk. To the surprise and delight of most of the world, the negotiators achieved much more than simple progress. After nearly two weeks of uninterrupted bargaining, they emerged smiling, with a breakthrough framework agreement for an Israeli-Egyptian peace treaty. After further negotiation, the promised treaty was signed in Washington on 26 March 1979.

The Camp David accords did not arise out of a vacuum; an already long-running Middle East peace process had laid substantial groundwork. During the Nixon and Ford presidencies, Henry Kissinger had negotiated two Israeli withdrawals from large parts of the Sinai desert taken from Egypt in the 1967 Six Day War. Moreover, the Carter administration came to office at the beginning of 1977 with a plan, proposed in a 1975 Brookings Institution study group report entitled *Toward Peace in the Middle East*. Recall from Chapter 6 that Brookings is a highly regarded Washington policy think tank with strong ties to the Democratic Party. Indeed, Carter's national security adviser, Columbia University political science professor Zbigniew Brzezinski, had been a member of the distinguished sixteen-member Brookings study group. That group concluded that the previous incremental approach of small steps designed to reduce tension and move the parties gradually toward a comprehensive settlement was no longer feasible. They argued that to avoid a dangerous stalemate it was imperative that "peacemaking efforts should henceforth concentrate on negotiation of a comprehensive settlement, including only such interim steps as constitute essential preparations for such a negotiation." They proposed a "package" of agreements on borders, the nature of a Palestinian entity, and a regime for Jerusalem, to involve all affected states and important external guarantors, including the United States (Brown, 1994, 338–39).

Following the Brookings recommendations, Carter's administration enlisted the Soviet Union in a joint call, issued 1 October 1977, for a reconvened Geneva conference on Middle East peace, to involve all the affected regional parties. Egypt's Sadat and Israel's Begin immediately reacted negatively, Sadat because he recently had ended Egypt's status as a major Soviet client and feared bringing the Soviets back into the peace process, and Begin because he feared the U.S.-Soviet statement envisioned Palestinian statehood. Meanwhile, an extremely secret dialogue began behind the scenes between the highest levels of the Begin and Sadat governments, exploring the possibilities of direct and substantial agreements between their two states. That secret dialogue grew out of Begin's decision to share Israeli intelligence information with Sadat about a Libyan terrorist plot to assassinate him (Drell and Dan, 1979), and Sadat's historic visit to Israel on 9 November 1977 (see Chapter 4). Recognizing an opening, the Carter administration shifted its efforts away from a potential new Geneva conference and toward offering American "good offices" to promote peace through three-way U.S.-Egyptian-Israeli talks. Begin and Sadat both visited Washington in late 1977 and early 1978, and in the summer of 1978 Carter invited both leaders to join him in a three-way summit at Camp David to work out the peace agreement they all wanted. Begin and Sadat both accepted immediately and unconditionally (Brown, 1994, 344).

The Camp David meetings involved rare high-stakes, high-risk diplomacy. Extended and continuous talks were directly mediated by President Carter and his top advisers, including Vice President Walter Mondale, Secretary of State Cyrus Vance, and National Security Adviser Zbigniew Brzezinski. Historic animosities and personal tensions were so high that only two face-to-face sessions were held between Begin and Sadat, each of whom threatened at least once to leave Camp David. Carter and his team engaged in prolonged shuttle diplomacy between the parties and held working sessions with Begin's and Sadat's representatives in Carter's cabin. The Americans then held their own late-night planning sessions, seeking ideas for a breakthrough. Later reports said that Carter and his officials barely slept four hours nightly, but at the end they had brokered unprecedented agreements that few people inside or outside government had anticipated (Jimmy Carter, 1982, 327–403).

Two documents were signed at the White House on 17 September 1978 by the trio of leaders, Begin and Sadat as parties and Carter as witness. Both were "framework agreements" that set guidelines for final agreements to be reached through further negotiations. The "Framework for Peace in the Middle East" set principles for negotiating "autonomy" and a "self-governing authority" for the primarily Palestinian inhabitants of the West Bank and Gaza. The "Framework for Conclusion of a Peace Treaty Between Egypt and Israel" was more specific, stipulating the key points of agreement on the Sinai, to become the core of a peace treaty to be worked out within three months (Brown, 1994,

345–46). That treaty was duly concluded and signed the following spring, although the futures of Israeli-Palestinian peace and of Jerusalem were still contentious issues two decades later. (See also discussions of the Israeli-Palestinian case in Chapter 16 and the introductory case of Chapter 8.)

The Camp David negotiations involved skillful use of tactics calculated to encourage agreement. A substantial literature about such tactics now exists within the business, social science, and government communities. The negotiation process for those accords demonstrates a number of features of diplomacy and of international negotiation that we examine in this chapter and encounter in other cases. Important bargaining tactics included offering American "good offices" to facilitate negotiation and mediate differences; isolating the parties to prevent distractions and information leaks; negotiating at the summit level to make policy changes and concessions easier; negotiating continuously to maintain focus and encourage movement; using "shuttle diplomacy" to carry ideas back and forth when direct meetings between the parties threatened to become too explosive; and maintaining complete secrecy so the results could be presented and defended as a complete package. The negotiations arose from considerable preliminary work, and yielded a framework agreement pledging an ongoing negotiation process and outlining its goals. In comparing Camp David with other instances of diplomacy and negotiations, however, we should remember that these talks were unusual in their intensity, the importance of the stakes involved, the summit level of the negotiators, the singular focus they achieved, the isolation of the proceedings, their length, and—most importantly—their profoundly significant outcome. Most of diplomacy and foreign policy negotiation is much more routine, with notably lower stakes and consequences. Nonetheless, these are vital tools of policy.

DIPLOMACY AND NEGOTIATION AS TOOLS OF FOREIGN POLICY

Diplomacy and negotiation have become even more important in the aftermath of the Cold War. We now have important interactions with many more independent states, both because of the breakup of multiethnic states such as the Soviet Union and former Yugoslavia, and the independence of former Soviet satellites such as Hungary and Poland. Ethnically based conflicts have torn several former states apart, as seen in the breakup of former Czechoslovakia, and threaten others, as in the Russian-Chechen war. As international economics becomes ever more globalized, international agreements about trade and finance increase in number and importance. The decline of U.S. relative strength and global dominance has led us to seek to accomplish more through international cooperation, as in the Persian Gulf War coalition. Such agreements take considerable effort to initiate and even more work to maintain. The number, importance, and difficulty of diplomatic activities and international negotiations have increased apace with such changes in the global context of foreign policy.

Diplomacy is the process of conducting international relations, especially *communication*, between governments and other international actors. Above all else, it is a process of *signaling* others regarding the issues we care about, how much we care, and what we are prepared to do about it. Peaceful diplomacy comprises the nonviolent end of the conceptual continuum of peaceful and violent actions diagrammed in Figure 8.2, although the threat and possibility of violence are always implicit—and often explicit—in diplomatic exchanges. War and other forms of violence short of war are almost always part of the menu of policy options. However, we should never forget that diplomatic discussions, negotiations, and similar actions comprising the peaceful end of the action continuum do not necessarily either imply or produce policy agreement. Successful communication is important because failure may be fatal to large numbers of individuals, and occasionally to a government. Consider, for example, the lingering controversy, referred to in Chapter 7, about whether U.S. Ambassador to Iraq April Glaspie failed to convey to Saddam Hussein how seriously her government would react to an invasion of Kuwait. Other interpretations of what in any event appears to be a major U.S. policy failure suggest that Glaspie was inadequately instructed by her superiors, or that those officials had incorrectly assessed intelligence about Iraqi mobilization, capabilities, and intent.

The great majority of diplomatic exchanges is routine and peaceful, just as the majority of bureaucratic agency decisions is routine. Following the research of Charles Hermann as mentioned in Chapters 4 and 5, political scientists typically define crises as unanticipated situations with high stakes and a short time in which to act, conditions antithetical to the routinized decision making on which bureaucracies thrive. Hermann illustrated this situation with a conceptual cube of decision-making situations, defined by three dimensions: seriousness of threat, available time to take action, and degree of advance anticipation. Only one of the cube's eight corners corresponds to true crises, and the opposite corner (low threat, long decision time, anticipated problems) characterizes routinized decision making. The remaining six corners describe situations less than true crises, even if casual observers often misidentify them. In an exactly parallel manner, the vast majority of international actions is routine and peaceful. This includes most diplomatic exchanges; the small subset that attracts most of our attention consists of exchanges in which the stakes and possibilities for violence are high.

In this chapter, we examine diplomatic procedures and practices as important channels for international communication and bargaining. Particular emphasis is given to diplomatic tools of policy available to the United States. The two major sections of the chapter cover (1) institutions for diplomacy, and (2) international negotiation. First, we examine how elaborate diplomatic procedures have been developed over the last five centuries to help keep extraneous concerns from blocking essential communication. This regularization and codification of diplomatic procedures has occurred largely since the development of the modern state system. Second, we discuss negotiations as multilevel interactions within governments as well as between them. Intergovernmental talks normally are accompanied by position-setting bargaining within each government, and between the negotiators and their home governments, over the details of negotiating stands. The three stages through which negotiations are arranged and conducted are (1) contacts about deciding to negotiate, (2) development of arrangements and formal procedures, and (only then) (3) substantive negotiations. Bargaining tactics are considered in detail, building on Thomas Schelling's classic treatment. Possible outcomes of negotiation include failure, continuation, tacit agreements, treaties, executive agreements, and more complex combinations. Examples are drawn from major arms control negotiations. Trends in negotiations are examined, including the increase in numbers of executive agreements, mainly on functional matters; summit meetings and shuttle diplomacy, facilitated by rapid transportation; and the difficulty of keeping negotiations secret, given the way modern communications media encourage leaks.

INSTITUTIONS FOR DIPLOMACY

Elaborate diplomatic procedures have been developed over the last five centuries to help prevent extraneous concerns from blocking essential communication. Emissaries have been used between social groups since the earliest days of recorded human history, but the regularization and codification of diplomatic procedures have occurred largely since the development of the modern state system, codified at the Congress of Vienna in 1815. Those procedures began with ambassadors and other individual emissaries. Until the fifteenth century, formal communication or negotiation between states was almost entirely *bilateral* (two party) and conducted either by direct correspondence between heads of state or by special ambassadors appointed for particular missions. By the mid-sixteenth century, several states had established permanent representatives in foreign states. One of the first powers to do so was Venice, which in 1496 appointed two merchants as its representatives in London because the journey to England was considered "very long and very dangerous" (Chernow and Vallasi, 1993, 768). Recall that the number of significant independent states was then quite small, and mostly confined to Europe. By the end of the seventeenth century, permanent **legations,** or foreign-posted diplomatic ministers with supporting staff, were widely used throughout Europe. Titles and status had not yet been regularized, however, and agents below the level of ambassador often were corrupt. After the Congress of Vienna, a system of diplomatic ranks was adopted that supported the establishment of a professional diplomatic service as a branch of the public administrative service in each state. Subsequently, as the number of states grew and modern transport and communications vastly speeded and multiplied interstate contact, diplomatic services grew apace.

Formalizing diplomatic procedures and personnel allowed states to place increased reliance on diplomacy as a policy tool they could utilize to promote accurate and reliable official communication under circumstances often strained by competing claims and desires. Along with channels of communication, diplomatic services provided personnel and contacts for negotiations and interstate bargaining. A body of international law grew from both actual practice and interstate agreements formalized as treaties, and gave rise to international legal institutions. Still, the greatest number of international institutions continues to be *functional*, arising from the need to coordinate activities that almost everybody agrees need to be regulated to ensure the necessary infrastructure and procedures for international communication, travel, commerce, and so on (see the section on coordination of functional activities in Chapter 12). The great majority of international negotiations concerns such relatively routine functional matters, even though high-stakes situations such as peace negotiations attract far more attention.

The growth of international contacts and negotiations has been driven by vast increases in the number of independent states since World War II, greater internationalization of economics, and improvements to international transport and communications. In turn, that growth has encouraged more attention to international negotiation, and to the tactics states and other international actors employ to promote their policy goals in such venues.

Studying diplomatic language and bargaining tactics can be amusing because they differ significantly from ordinary, everyday usage. For example, when a diplomatic press officer says the principals met and had "a full and frank exchange of views," it means they met, stated the respective official positions of their governments, and agreed on absolutely nothing. Diplomats have traditionally relied on strict rules of etiquette and employed precise language and meaning, so even serious threats could sound polite. Because diplomacy is about communication and signaling, it is understood that *absolutely no statement or action happens without meaning.* It is said that Prince Metternich, the Austrian statesman and arbiter of post-Napoleonic Europe, upon learning of the death of the French diplomat Talleyrand in 1838, mused, "I wonder what he meant by that." Much of the ritual, formalism, and *politesse* of diplomacy has been eroded in the twentieth century, to be replaced by the sort of crudity suggested by the image of Soviet premier Nikita Khrushchev pounding his shoe on the lectern of the UN General Assembly. Nonetheless, learning the language of diplomacy and the ways in which bargaining tactics are used to send signals to other governments still can be useful, helping us to decode governmental statements and other actions, extract their real meaning, and improve our understanding.

The earliest instances of permanent **missions,** or legations established by one state in the capital of another, date from the fifteenth century. Such missions included an ambassador or other primary agent plus supporting staff members, and growth in the numbers of such missions led to the establishment of a professional **corps of diplomats.** Those diplomats' general tasks included obtaining information about the capabilities and intent of the host government and people, safeguarding and promoting the military and political interests of their home governments, and lobbying to extend trade and commerce. Numbers of diplomats were relatively few because the international system was still small. Only twelve well-defined sovereign states existed in Europe in 1648, when the end of the Thirty Years' War left Germany split into small principalities and kingdoms. The international system grew in membership and complexity over the ensuing centuries. The number of states increased, trade and commercial interdependencies multiplied, the industrial revolution became advanced in England by about 1760 and subsequently in other states, and scientific knowledge and technology grew among advanced economies. Consequently, the number of issues of mutual interest to advanced states grew apace and led to changes in patterns of diplomatic activity. Bilateral negotiations tended to give way to *multilateral* (more-than-two-party) conferences and institutions, particularly specialized functional institutions like the International Telecommunications Union (ITU) and the Universal Postal Union (UPU).

Early multilateral conferences most often were peace negotiations, but after the Franco-Prussian War of 1870–71, governments began sending delegates to conferences on the codification of international law, such as the 1899 and 1907 conferences at The Hague, Netherlands. **International law** or the *law of nations* is the body of rules considered legally binding in international relations, comprising both the *customary rules and usages* to which states have given express or tacit consent, plus the provisions of ratified *treaties* and *international conventions*. Thus, in effect, international law is whatever a sufficient number of sufficiently influential states agree among themselves to accept, and it is always subject to varying numbers of nonadherents. One of the most often referenced international conventions is popularly known as the Geneva Convention, formally the Geneva Convention of 1864 for the Amelioration of the Condition of the Wounded and Sick of Armies in the Field. Twelve of sixteen states whose representatives met in Geneva that year adopted and signed the convention, which provided for the neutrality of medical personnel of armed forces, the neutrality of civilians who voluntarily assist them, and the use of a red cross as an international symbol to mark medical personnel and supplies. That 1864 Convention, its subsequent revisions, and allied treaties such as the Hague Convention for naval forces and the Prisoner of War Convention have been signed but not always ratified by almost all states and their dependencies. They are widely but not universally observed.

PROTOCOL: GREASING THE WAYS OF DIPLOMACY

The rituals and procedures of diplomacy often appear arcane to the uninitiated, but all serve one fundamental purpose: preventing extraneous concerns from blocking essential communication. Because diplomacy is about signaling others, great importance attaches to issues such as the relative rank or seniority of diplomats.

Consider the situation when the United States and the People's Republic of China agreed in 1972 to establish liaison offices in each other's capitals. Although this was still short of full diplomatic relations, the importance that both governments accorded the agreement was clearly indicated by the distinction and seniority of the individuals appointed as their first liaison officers. China sent Huang Hua, who would later become foreign minister, to Washington, and the United States sent to Beijing David K. E. Bruce, who previously had served at different times as U.S. ambassador to France, the Federal Republic of Germany, and Britain.

In 1815 the Congress of Vienna established a classification of diplomatic *ranks*. The highest grade is ambassadors, papal legates, and papal nuncios, the latter two representatives of the Roman Catholic Holy See and the Vatican microstate. Normally an ambassador is the chief of mission, highest ranking among a state's permanent staff in a foreign capital. Second in rank are minister plenipotentiary and envoy extraordinary, individuals normally appointed for specific, nonrecurring functions, such as a set of negotiations. Minister plenipotentiary literally means "a minister full of power." Third in rank are ministers or ministers resident. Lowest rank is that of chargé d'affaires, literally "a person in charge of business." If a government calls its ambassador home nominally "for consultations," which is usually a sign of serious disapproval of something the host government has done, its **embassy,** which is the ambassador's official residence or offices in the host state, often is left under the supervision of a chargé d'affaires. Turning it over to the lower ranking official is another sign of disapproval. The chargé still performs most of the ambassador's routine functions, although usually with reduced latitude for innovative or politically salient actions.

Diplomatic **precedence** is based on rank and seniority, to avoid arguments over whose government is more powerful or more important or better liked by the host government. Procedures bearing on seniority and its recognition were fixed in international law at the Congress of Aix-le-Chapelle in 1818. Thus, for example, when diplomats of equal rank march into a room as a group for ceremonial functions, they enter in order of their length of service as appointees to the particular host government. For some years before the 1979 Sandinista revolution, the Nicaraguan ambassador to the United States was considered the senior member, or *dean*, of the Washington diplomatic corps by virtue of his thirty years' service in this country, and he would lead the assembled ambassadors into state dinners. Similarly, rank and precedence determine seating at diplomatic functions; hosts are expected to conform to such principles so that nobody can read political significance into the practices of the host government. Domestic politics, of course, are not subject to such stringent procedures, and analysts may search behaviors such as seating patterns for political clues, particular to relatively closed societies. Sovietologists regularly used to study pictures of the Kremlin leadership atop Lenin's tomb for the May Day parade, reading closeness to the general secretary of the Communist Party as a sign of political favor.

IMMUNITY, NONINTERFERENCE, AND EXTERRITORIALITY

Immunity and noninterference probably are the most important principles of diplomatic procedure. The doctrine of **diplomatic immunity** grants diplomats exemption from search, arrest, or prosecution by the governments to which they are accredited. They are to be allowed communications and transportation without interference, a practice with deep roots in history and almost universally recognized as essential for diplomats to properly carry out their duties without fear of reprisals. As far back as the ancient Indian Mahabarata, it was said "the king who slays an envoy sinks into hell with all his ministers."

In the event of an abuse of these privileges, a government may declare a diplomat **persona non grata,** literally unwelcome, and ask that he or she be recalled. Such requests usually arise as responses to inappropriate political actions by diplomats, rather than from violations of local law. For example, diplomats might violate the principle of *noninterference* (see later) by involving themselves in the host country's internal affairs, or abusing their positions by engaging in espionage. A mild but frequent and therefore frustrating abuse, never the subject of serious retaliation, occurs when diplomats ignore traffic and parking laws. The problem is particularly acute in Washington and in New York, where many diplomats accredited to the UN reside. By 1991 the Soviet Union owed more than $3 million in parking fines for more than 65,000 Washington tickets issued to automobiles bearing diplomatic plates.

In an extreme case involving some violation far beyond the scope of diplomatic behavior, such as murder, host governments may ask that a diplomat be stripped of diplomatic status and thus made subject to arrest and trial. However, sending governments are not required to grant such requests. Just such a case occurred in 1996, when Georgian diplomat Gueorgui Makharadze was accused of killing an American teenager while driving drunk in the District of Columbia. Protracted negotiations with the government of Georgia followed. Eventually the diplomat, who had been recalled, was stripped of immunity by Georgian president Eduard Shevardnadze, extradited to the United States, tried, convicted of involuntary manslaughter, and imprisoned here (Janelle Carter, 1997).

The principle of **exterritoriality** refers to the exemption of diplomats, along with their families and staffs, residences, and archives, from the jurisdiction of the states in which they reside and to which they are accredited (Freeman, 1994, 140). To allow diplomats to operate independently and effectively, these aspects of jurisdiction are temporarily suspended. In theory, such suspensions can be lifted, although this is rare in practice, because diplomacy relies so heavily on mutual respect and mutual extension of such privileges. In this era of international political terrorism, there also are fears that strong action against foreign diplomats in any state may provoke retaliation against our diplomats in some other state.

Like any other principle in diplomatic practice, exterritoriality usually works because almost all governments honor it almost all the time. Although embassies usually have guards, they are few in number and incapable of defending against any sufficiently determined assault. In the event of actions against an embassy, one must rely on the host government for protection. Sometimes host governments allow—or even organize—demonstrations against embassies as a form of policy protest. In a few cases, embassies have been seized by terrorist groups, sometimes provoking counterassaults by SWAT teams.

The seizure of the U.S. embassy in Teheran, Iran, on 4 November 1979, which began some four hundred days of captivity for more than fifty diplomats, was a clear violation of the duty of host governments to protect diplomats and diplomatic property. The mob that stormed the Teheran embassy could only have been stopped by massive police action, and had been whipped into a fury against the United States by a speech given the previous day by the religious leader Ayatollah Khomeini. In that same year, a mob clearly organized and aided by the Soviet-backed revolutionary government in Afghanistan invaded the U.S. embassy in Khabul, ransacking it and killing the American ambassador. Still, such incidents remain exceedingly rare.

The principle of exterritoriality also can cause an embassy to become a place of refuge for political dissidents, although that right is limited. An unusual example involved Cardinal József Mindszenty, Roman Catholic primate of Hungary. Hungary had joined Germany in World War II, and was captured by Russian troops in 1944–45. Following a brief postwar republic, communists gained political control in 1947. A strong anticommunist, the cardinal was arrested late in 1948 and tried for treason and illegal monetary transactions. He was convicted and imprisoned until 1955, when he was released but kept under close watch. In late October 1956 major public uprisings challenged the communist governments in Hungary and East Germany. A short-lived democratic republic was proclaimed in Hungary, and the rebels freed Cardinal Mindszenty. On 4 November, Soviet troops invaded to restore communist rule, and the cardinal fled to the U.S. embassy for refuge, which he refused to leave unless the Hungarian government rescinded his conviction and sentence. He remained there for some fifteen years as a living symbol of resistance to communism.

Noninterference with diplomats as they go about their business in host countries is another important principle of diplomacy, frequently subject to some kinds of violations. Governments regularly provide diplomatic "cover" to spies, giving them diplomatic passports and nominal diplomatic assignments. Everyone understands that a certain amount of spying goes on, but if it becomes too widespread and invasive, action may be taken. People may be expelled when spying is particularly egregious. In 1983, for example, France suddenly and dramatically expelled about one third of all Soviet diplomats. Because diplomacy is about signaling, governments often engage in tit-for-tat retaliation to express their displeasure, and the Soviets did so in the French case. If we expel a diplomat for spying, we probably can expect one of our diplomats to be expelled for spying, regardless of guilt or innocence. The Soviet Union, which severely limited the movements of its own citizens within their country, refused to let Americans drive automobiles anywhere in the USSR, and usually limited U.S. diplomats to movements within 25 miles of Moscow, allegedly for fear of spying. In retaliation, the United States imposed comparable restrictions on Soviet diplomats' travel around Washington and UN headquarters in New York City. All such limitations, of course, violate the principle of noninterference.

The principle of noninterference is supposed to be bidirectional. Not only are states to let accredited diplomats carry out their proper functions unimpeded, but those diplomats are expected to avoid any interference in the internal politics of host states. Official discussions normally are expected to be confined to government personnel. Diplomats regularly explain and defend their governments' policies to members of the foreign public through such channels as public addresses and media interviews. However, established international law and customary practice dictate that diplomats are to refrain from direct appeal to foreign publics to pressure their governments about specific policies, and from engaging in political acts such as advising or subsidizing political parties, organizations, or subversive insurgent groups, distributing covert propaganda, training secret police forces in techniques for suppressing human rights, and the like.

Like many rules, this side of noninterference is rather frequently violated. As the ease of modern communications and transportation help make foreign policy increasingly intermestic, the number of such violations increases. Recall this rather mild example mentioned in Chapter 4: Prime ministers or presidents of Israel visiting the United States often move beyond meetings with the U.S. president and leaders of the administration and Congress to travel to New York City and address major Jewish organizations. Those addresses, nominally explanations of Israeli policy, often are thinly disguised appeals for those organizations to pressure the administration and Congress to support Israeli policy. Given the size of the American Jewish community and the widespread sympathy for Israel among non-Jews in the United States, such lobbying often has been quite effective.

What happens to contacts between governments if diplomatic relations are broken? Severing formal relations is a powerful political act, taken only rarely and usually to protest severe violations of normal diplomatic, economic, or political practice. Even then, circumstances and functional ties may require that some contacts be maintained between governments. Citizens of each country may remain within the other, and diplomatic properties remain. Normal practice is to turn management of those properties and dealings about government and citizen interests over to diplomats of another country, often one seen to be politically neutral in whatever dispute prompted the rupture. Even after formal relations are broken, contacts normally are available through other channels, such as continuing mutual membership in the United Nations. Consider, for example, U.S.-Cuban relations. After diplomatic relations with the Castro government were broken in January 1961 to protest the expropriation of U.S. landholdings, banks, and industrial concerns, the former U.S. embassy became the U.S. **Interests Section,** managed by Swiss diplomats. Many American interests remain within or linked to Cuba. Substantial numbers of U.S. citizens trace their ancestry to Cuba, have family there, and/or came to these shores as refugees from Castro's regime. Proximity and human ties ensure the continued existence of interests that both governments must work together to manage, even when they find it politically distasteful.

For example, during the 1960s Cuba was a popular destination for airline hijackers motivated less by politics than by greed, and Cuba initially offered them a haven. Eventually the Cuban government agreed in behind-the-scenes negotiations to try hijackers under harsh Cuban laws and return seized aircraft promptly. Commandeering aircraft is illegal under international law, and Cuban authorities doubtless feared harsh U.S. action if agreements were not reached to end the wave of hijackings. From time to time new incidents call public attention to the U.S. Interests Section in Havana. When Cuban air force MIG-29 fighters over international waters shot down two U.S.-based civilian aircraft flown by a Cuban exile group on 24 February 1996, two of President Clinton's first actions were to order formal protests, presented first to Cuban officials in Havana by diplomats of that Interests Section and later by U.S. ambassador to the UN Madeleine Albright to her Cuban counterpart.

FUNCTIONS OF DIPLOMATS

Diplomats on station perform a number of significant functions:

- *Symbolic representation* of their home government is an important corollary of having diplomats in place, and extends beyond mere attendance at ceremonial and state occasions. Every action taken by a diplomat or by a host government toward that individual has symbolic importance, probably is intended to send a message, and certainly will be so interpreted.

- Diplomats *gather information* both overtly and, to some degree, covertly. It is important not to overemphasize the covert aspect, however; 90 percent of the information gathered by the CIA is open and unclassified. Nonetheless, an officer on station may be able to gather the information more readily than an analyst back home in Langley, Virginia, the CIA headquarters, and can put it into the perspective of actual on-site experience.

- Drawing on their in-country experience, diplomats may offer expert *advice*.

- Diplomats sometimes participate in *policy making*.

- Diplomats sometimes take part in *negotiations* with the host government. Both the policy making and negotiation roles have been much diminished, however, by the speed of modern communications and transport.

The late Buckminster Fuller, best known for inventing the geodesic dome, once wrote about how diplomats and negotiators before the twentieth century were given great responsibility and very wide latitude for policy change because they had to be able to act, and it could take weeks for messages to flow back and forth between them and their governments. Today, however, coded radio messages travel at the speed of light, messages too secret even to risk decoding can be flown in secure pouches by couriers halfway around the world in a day, and diplomats can return home for consultations just as quickly. Consequently, today's diplomats usually operate on very short leashes, with limited responsibilities and little freedom of movement in negotiation. Instead, specially appointed negotiators have become the norm—and their freedom of policy movement also is quite constrained.

- Another important function of diplomats is *protection of their nationals*. Although U.S. citizens are subject to the laws of the countries in which they travel, they can appeal for assistance from U.S. diplomats in the event they encounter legal problems. The ability of diplomats to assist is more limited than people sometimes realize, but in many cases diplomats can help ensure fair and humane treatment of arrested citizens, and help arrange quick resolutions to simple problems.

- On a more positive note, diplomats in place regularly help *promote trade and commerce* with foreign states, through such actions as helping facilitate introductions and contacts between businesspeople and officials on both sides, and arranging for representation at trade shows and scientific or technological meetings and exhibitions.

In their communication function, diplomats serve a number of purposes. They may exchange official government views with host government officials, and attempt to gain further information about their hosts' desires and intentions. They may attempt to persuade those officials to adopt new policy positions, although they face many constraints in such attempts, as we see in the next section, on negotiation. At other times, diplomats may engage in discussions purely to make propaganda, stall negotiations, and feign interest in particular issues. Finally, because every action taken either by a diplomat or by a host government has symbolic importance, the ease with which diplomats are allowed to carry out all these functions rises and falls in step with the general tenor of relations between the sending and host governments.

INTERNATIONAL NEGOTIATION

Once a government has decided to seek negotiations on some set of issues, it embarks on a process that may be terminated abruptly at any time, but usually involves three distinct stages, as follows:

- *Preliminaries*, or contacts about deciding to negotiate.
- *Process*, or working out the procedures for conducting negotiations.
- *Bargaining*, the actual substantive negotiations.

Specific activities in these stages are outlined in Table 10.1. Although we often phrase discussion throughout the remainder of this chapter in terms of two sides or governments in bilateral negotiations for simplicity, all the points covered apply equally well to multilateral negotiations involving three or more parties, some of which may be nongovernmental actors. The points developed here usually are illustrated with specific historical cases, but read those cases only as illustrations. Since about 1960, social scientists have developed a considerable literature analyzing the processes of negotiation in a systematic and generalizable way. (For an excellent survey, see Hopmann, 1995.) In so doing, they have begun to move the study of negotiation beyond sets of ad hoc case studies and excessively simplifying assertions such as claims that every negotiation is unique, that diplomacy is an art form, or that only experienced diplomats who develop subjective understandings of that art form can master the negotiating process. As you read the following sections, look for the systematic and generalizable features of negotiating processes, and think

PHOTO 10.1

U.S. secretary of state Madeleine Albright, the first woman to head the state department and the highest ranking female government official in U.S. history, meets with Syrian president Hafez Assad in the presidential palace in Damascus on 12 September 1997. Secretary Albright faced the very difficult diplomatic task of trying to help Israel and Syria restart peace talks.

AP/Wide World Photos.

about other applications in everyday life and domestic politics as well as in carrying out foreign policy.

STAGES OF NEGOTIATION

Preliminaries actually are talks about holding talks, which we may call the "who" of negotiation. Typically, these begin with exploratory contacts from one government or other actor to another suggesting the possibility that they negotiate or encourage other parties to bargain, perhaps with their mediation. If initial contacts are sufficiently encouraging, further talks help define the substantive scope and context for negotiation. This is a time for deciding how many and which parties will be involved, whether one or more parties will play the roles of sponsor or mediator, and whether the meetings will be open or closed. The context or global situation of the talks may influence these decisions quite strongly.

TABLE 10.1
Stages of Preparation and Negotiation

Stage 1: Preliminaries: Contacts about Deciding to Negotiate

Talks about holding talks

Context

Substantive scope

The "who" of negotiation

> Exploratory contacts
> Decisions to proceed toward negotiations
> Bilateral versus multilateral meetings
> Open versus closed meetings
> Situation or context: Normal, stressful, or crisis
>> Available time: Open ended, or subject to deadline or ultimatum?
>> Mediator, or only direct participants?

Stage 2: Process: Working Out the Procedures for Negotiations

Talks about procedures

Rules of the game

The "how" of negotiation

> Location: Symbolically neutral? Fixed site or rotating sites? Isolated?
> Parties' representation, size and composition of delegations
> Languages, interpretation, translation, and record keeping
> Publicity or secrecy; media coverage

Stage 3: Bargaining

Talks about substantive issues

The "what" of negotiation

> Multilevel game involving negotiators, home governments, substantive arena, back
> channels, summit meetings, media, and public opinion (see Figure 10.1)
> Presentation of positions (initial objectives), revisions, draft text
> Symbolic acts or signals
> Wide variety of bargaining tactics
> Many possible outcomes

For example, negotiations to resolve a confrontation in which armies stand ready to launch hostilities may be organized much more rapidly than talks to reduce the emission of CFCs. A high degree of stress or sense of crisis usually speeds arrangements, and may lead to a deadline or ultimatum limiting the time available for negotiation.

Preliminaries can take years, if the context does not demand rapid action and the parties want a long time to think out the implications of negotiating. Timing also may have enormous symbolic importance, as nobody wants to be seen to be cooperating with an intransigent foe or seeking negotiations out of weakness. All these aspects are demonstrated by the case of the first U.S.-Soviet Strategic Arms Limitation Talks, or SALT I. Although formal negotiations ran from 1969 until agreements were signed in 1972, the first serious preliminary contact occurred in 1965. President Lyndon Johnson held a brief summit meeting with Soviet president Alexi Kosygin in a high school gymnasium (the best available space) in Glassboro, New Jersey, symbolically located halfway between Washington and New York City, where Kosygin had come to address the UN General Assembly. At their talks, Johnson first broached the idea of negotiations to begin reducing the danger of nuclear war between the superpowers. Limiting their central strategic weapons systems would move far beyond the tightly restricted arms control agreements previously reached, and it took the two sides three years to reach an understanding on opening such negotiations. As is often the case, those understandings were reached in secret and included a date for a joint public announcement. Unfortunately, that agreed date fell one day after the Soviet Union and other Warsaw Pact states invaded Czechoslovakia to overthrow the liberal communist regime of Alexander Dubcek and replace him with a leader more sympathetic to Moscow. U.S. leaders, reluctant to be seen cooperating with the Soviets on anything at such a time, canceled the SALT announcement. It took another year to restore that agreement to negotiate, and the talks finally opened in 1969.

The **process** stage consists of talks about procedures, the "how" of negotiations. Parties must establish the rules of the game, working out the mechanics and logistics of the negotiations that they have agreed in principle to pursue. This can involve prolonged haggling over symbolic issues, which may even lead to stalemate, breakdown, and shelving of the proposed negotiations. An enormous number of practical issues must be resolved at this stage, and many of those questions may have profound impact on how the ultimate negotiations proceed and whether they succeed. How many representatives of what types and ranks will participate for each party? How will they be seated? What languages will be spoken, and what arrangements will be made for translation, simultaneous interpretation, and maintaining records of the negotiations? Will talks be conducted publicly or in secret? Will any media coverage be allowed, and will the parties periodically make public statements about progress, either jointly or separately? Where will talks be conducted, and for how long at a time?

The SALT talks of 1969–72 again demonstrate many of these aspects. It was agreed that sessions would be held in rounds of varying length depending on results and the nature of discussions at that point. The two sides would return to their respective capitals between rounds, after fixing a time for the next round. Rounds were held alternately in Helsinki, Finland, and Vienna, Austria, two symbolically neutral cities with good accommodations, conveniently close to Moscow. Negotiations would be entirely secret, with no announcement until their ultimate conclusion with hoped for agreements. This provision was generally observed by both sides, except for a major leak in Washington about halfway through, when it was revealed the two sides were working on a treaty of indefinite duration severely limiting antiballistic missile (ABM) systems, and a five-year executive "interim agreement" capping numbers of ICBMs, SLBMs, and SSBNs (submarines carrying SLBMs). The Soviets were furious about that leak, and there was no repetition. In contrast, the 1973–79 SALT II negotiations were so badly riddled by leaks that almost every term of the ultimate 1979 package was revealed a full year ahead by *New York Times* reporter Richard Burt (1978) in a *Foreign Affairs* article. This permitted strong domestic political opposition to build within the United States to *specific* details of the planned agreements well before the Carter administration could present SALT II as a package, and contributed strongly to its downfall.

Many symbolically important issues must be confronted at the process stage. One that might appear arcane at first blush is seating arrangements. However, symbolism is vital to diplomacy, and sitting at the same table with diplomats implies that they represent an independent and legitimate government or other international actor, and thus constitutes a degree of formal recognition. Arrangements vary for managing negotiations between parties who deny each other diplomatic recognition. Delegates to one unsuccessful mid-1980s peace conference regarding the many-sided civil war then raging in Lebanon represented so many mutually antagonistic factions that they were seated at seven separate tables in a conference center on symbolically neutral Cyprus. This seating arrangement and the fact that several factions considered it a major concession merely to listen to a speech by the elected president of Lebanon foreshadowed the eventual failure of the conference. Arrangers of the Paris negotiations that eventually produced the 1973 Vietnam peace agreement argued for an entire year before working out the compromise that almost all delegations would be seated alphabetically at a great round table, and representatives of the Vietcong and the South Vietnamese government would use small side tables on opposite sides of the circle.

Who sits where at a conference table has implications about individual conferees' ranks and the relative importance of the governments they represent. Delegates to bilateral talks usually sit at a long rectangular table, with representatives of each party literally on their *side* of the table. Heads of delegations sit across from each other at the center, and seating on each side is in order of decreasing rank toward either end, with officials sitting across from their substantive opposite numbers. Staffers usually sit behind those they assist. To avoid any pride of position, multilateral talks often assign space to delegations in alphabetical order by state name at a round table.

STRUCTURE AND INFLUENCE: THE MANY LEVELS OF INTERNATIONAL NEGOTIATION

Only if the preliminary and process stages are successfully concluded do negotiations ever reach the substantive **bargaining** stage. This is the "what" of negotiation, getting down to the issues that justify all the prior work, in hopes of achieving some agreement. As in the theory of exchange that underlies much of economics, no two parties are likely to reach agreement unless each of them feels at least a little better off afterward. Moreover, diplomats are as likely as the bargainers in economic theory to seek as much as they can while giving up as little as possible. They therefore engage in a negotiation game that entails as much calculated drama and posturing as the stereotypes of haggling in a bazaar or over the purchase of a new car. In reality, international negotiations typically involve a *many-level game of strategy* (see Chapter 12) that takes place through several different channels between governments (and/or other types of international actors) and simultaneously within those governments or organizations. This situation is outlined in Figure 10.1.

A great deal more is obviously going on in Figure 10.1 than simply the formal talks between working negotiators at the center of the diagram. Horizontal links represent formal and informal bargaining and other interactions between the two governments, occurring

FIGURE 10.1

*Levels of Influence and Channels of Action
in International Negotiation*

Negotiation occurs at multiple levels, both within and between governments.
Authority and influence increase toward the top of the diagram.
Leaks to the media and public may occur from any party at a higher level.

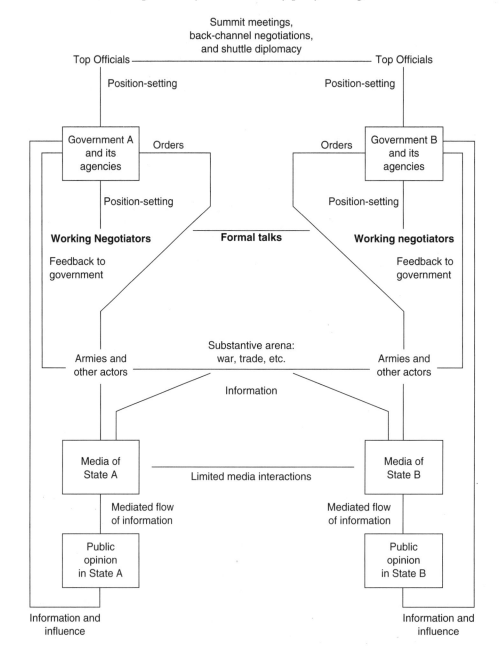

at four distinct levels. Vertical links represent either flows of information up and down or bargaining between different levels within each government.

Normally, negotiations only take place when there are substantive issues to settle, and sometimes the most important bargaining moves take place in the substantive arena rather than the meeting room. What happens in negotiations may depend critically on developments on the battlefield or in the customs inspection warehouse, and cannot proceed in ignorance of those developments. Governments constantly issue orders to their armies, trade officials, and other actors, who in turn provide a flow of information back to their respective agencies. Actions taken in the substantive arena may signal a government's true intent much more faithfully than anything said by negotiators. In turn, instructions to negotiators may be adjusted to reflect approval or disapproval of recent developments in the field. Thus, for example, during the Paris Vietnam peace talks of the late 1960s and early 1970s, whenever either side made major military advances, the other side canceled the next session of the peace talks. Those talks, however, particularly for the communists, were intended more to create the illusion of bargaining and progress than to produce a peace agreement; all sides hoped to win real victory on the battlefield.

Official working negotiators are engaged not only in a game of bargaining with their counterparts in the formal talks, but also in an ongoing *position-setting* game with their home governments to determine their instructions and bargaining limits. Often the negotiators are outranked by other officials at home who take a serious interest in the subject at hand and are deeply involved in determining policy positions. Because modern modes of communication and transport allow governments to keep negotiators on very short leashes (as noted earlier), the place to look for real policy movement in negotiations usually is in each government's internal struggle to shape its negotiating positions. Unfortunately for us as critical observers, much of the internal struggle may remain secret for decades.

The position-setting game may extend upward from agencies to the very highest officials. Sometimes those top officials and heads of government become personally involved in negotiations at summit meetings, in settling the most sensitive of issues, in so-called back-channel talks, and in shuttle diplomacy. These channels may parallel, supplement, and even overshadow formal and public negotiations. **Summit meetings** normally are ceremonial meetings between heads of state or government, at which they sign and formally recognize agreements worked out in advance by negotiators within their administrations. Sometimes such meetings provide symbolic backing for settlements devised by others, as when President Clinton hosted a signing ceremony on the White House south lawn for the 1993 Israeli-PLO agreement (see the opening case of Chapter 8). Occasionally, summits provide a venue for negotiating sensitive issues that demand the political clout of the highest officials. When President Nixon traveled to Moscow for his 1992 summit meeting with Leonid Brezhnev, negotiations for the SALT I strategic arms control agreements proceeded simultaneously between the presidents in Moscow and between the regular SALT negotiators in Helsinki, Finland, and some issues were settled only at the last moment. The dramatic diplomatic opening represented by President Richard Nixon's 1972 trip to Beijing and other points in the People's Republic of China was arranged at secret meetings between Secretary of State Henry Kissinger and his Chinese counterparts, and those meetings, in turn, had been set up by lower ranking officials with Pakistani assistance.

Kissinger and his North Vietnamese counterpart, Le Duc Tho, engaged in prolonged secret **back-channel negotiations** over the eventual 1973 Vietnam peace agreement, throughout much of the period when formal multiparty negotiations were being conducted by lower level officials in Paris. Back channels often are kept secret, but, like summits, they offer opportunities to resolve disputes by involving officials high enough to have broad powers to grant concessions and commit to agreements. **Shuttle diplomacy** often involves officials at those same levels serving as mediators or brokers who propose solutions and carry ideas and responses back and forth between parties otherwise too deeply estranged to negotiate formally over a conference table. Notable examples include the Middle East shuttle diplomacy of two secretaries of state, Henry Kissinger under Presidents Nixon and Ford in dealings between Israel and Egypt, and Warren Christopher under President Clinton in dealings between Israel and Syria. Like summit meetings, such shuttle diplomacy has become more frequent in recent decades because of the ease and speed of modern air transportation. After his retirement in February 1996, Richard Holbrooke, who had brokered the 1995 Dayton accords for Bosnian peace, recalled having traveled to four Balkan countries in one day.

Media and public opinion provide additional channels of interaction and influence within and sometimes between governments. Media often receive regular flows of information from governments, from armies or other actors in the substantive arena, and from their direct coverage of such substantive interactions as wars. They also may receive leaks from officials at every level. In turn, media filter and process that information for distribution to the public, and thereby help shape public opinion. Reporters may have some direct interactions with their foreign counterparts and with foreign officials. Sometimes such contacts create additional channels for international negotiation, particularly when the stress of crises drives officials to seek unconventional channels for communication. A celebrated case occurred during the 1962 Cuban missile crisis when a Soviet diplomat passed an important message to the Kennedy administration through ABC television reporter John Scali at the United Nations. Sometimes governments seek to influence the outcome of negotiations by taking actions designed to sway public opinion and thereby bring pressure to bear on an opposing government. The North Vietnamese and Vietcong, for example, correctly believed that continued losses would shift U.S. public opinion from majority support of the war effort to majority opposition.

Formal international negotiations typically open with presentations of each party's initial positions and, at least by implication, initial objectives. Negotiators may read formal statements and present written copies of their positions. Typically, parties start out far apart. After some period of discussion and argument, they may move slightly closer to their opposite number's position, then announce that they can move no further without new instructions from home. The internal domestic game of policy setting then becomes paramount until it is time to send the negotiators back. Bargaining thus involves an alternation of primary focus between the international talks and the domestic policy-setting game, although the latter never completely stops. If international negotiations are to succeed, the parties must move toward some eventual common position, taking however many steps are necessary. Often it helps to seek agreement on some general principle, on a limited matter, or on the general form an agreement might take. Frequently, negotiators present their positions in the form of draft text for a proposed agreement. They may utilize a wide variety of bargaining tactics, as discussed in more detail later, including symbolic acts or signals.

POSSIBLE OUTCOMES OF NEGOTIATIONS

Negotiations yield many different sorts of outcomes, as summarized in Table 10.2. Even after the parties have decided to negotiate and have worked out the logistics and other arrangements, there is no guarantee of success. They may find little or no common ground, or too little flexibility to revise their positions to reach agreement. Thus some talks produce no agreement, either on substantive matters or even on meeting again. Different sides may seek fundamentally incompatible goals and may not yet have decided that they prefer compromise and agreement to the status quo. Quite often, talks are recessed and continued later. This allows delegates who have achieved some success to return to their capitals, engage in the domestic negotiation about bargaining positions, and return to the talks with new instructions. Sometimes, announcements that talks will be recessed and continued at a later time mask a real breakdown, so that the key to distinguishing genuine recesses from breakdowns is whether or not the parties set a date for resuming talks. Even then, governments sometimes halt negotiations for purely propagandistic purposes, feigning reasonability when they actually seek to dictate terms by victories on the battlefield or in the warehouses of international trade rather than to settle differences through negotiations in conference centers.

If agreements are reached, they may take one (or more) of several forms. Although an **understanding** or **entente** is relatively informal and often unwritten, it may guide serious policy for years. One example is the de facto alliance between Israel and the United States, only partly reduced to writing in the early 1980s. **Executive agreements** are formal, written accords between the executives or heads of government of two or more states. Often considered as treaties in all but name, executive agreements usually are not formally ratified like treaties. A notable exception for the United States is that Congress passed legislation over President Nixon's veto requiring that all arms control agreements be approved by Congress. The tremendous growth in international functional arrangements since World War II has led to a concomitant increase in numbers of executive agreements.

Treaties are formal agreements between the governments of sovereign states or organizations of states. They are the source of most international law, and probably the form of international agreement that ordinary citizens think of first. Treaties have existed since the earliest states. Records survive of Mesopotamian treaties from before 3000 B.C., and many treaties are mentioned in the Old Testament. Treaties usually deal with the rights and obligations of states, but sometimes grant specific rights to private individuals, much like private interest legislation in the U.S. Congress. Some states consider treaties to be part of the law of the land and binding on all individuals. In the United States, for example, the Supreme Court has held that a ratified treaty abrogates (that is, supersedes and nullifies) any state or federal law in conflict with it. The designation *treaty* is ordinarily applied to the most important formal agreements; less important accords may be denoted conventions, acts, declarations, or protocols. An agreed revision to some part of a treaty, for example, is often called a *protocol*. The ancient Greeks and Romans utilized

TABLE 10.2	
Possible Outcomes of Negotiation	

No Agreement
Talks produce neither agreement nor willingness to continue meeting.

Continuation
Talks are recessed, giving time to go home to report and receive new instructions.

Normally, a date is set for the next meeting.

Sometimes continuation announcements mask a real breakdown.

Agreement Is Reached
Agreements take several major forms:

　　Understanding or entente, often unwritten

　　Executive agreement

　　Treaty

　　　Agreement is reached

　　　Text is initialed by the negotiators

　　　Formal signing ceremony

　　　Ratification; may impose changes, reopen negotiations

　　　Deposition of signed copies for formal storage and reference

　　　Registration with the United Nations

　　　Entry into force; date or conditions normally stipulated in the treaty text

　　Convention, act, declaration, protocol

elaborate ceremonies to emphasize the sanctity of treaties, and many current treaty practices have classical antecedents. The major substantive types of treaties are *political*, dealing with such issues as alliances, war and peace, cessions of territory, and modifications to boundaries; *commercial*, governing matters such as navigation, fisheries, seabed resources, tariffs, and monetary exchange; and *legal*, concerning issues such as patent and copyright protection, or the extradition of criminals.

Treaties pass through a number of distinct stages from negotiation to entry into force, as follows:

- When negotiators reach agreement, they *initial* the treaty text, literally placing their initials on every page of draft material to provide a permanent record of exactly what terms everyone accepted.

- Neat final archival copies are then prepared for a formal *signing ceremony*. This is an opportunity for the involved heads of government to endorse the treaty by their presence and statements as well as by their signatures.

- Most states have procedures for *ratification* of a signed treaty. Ratification under the U.S. Constitution requires approval by two thirds of the Senate.

- Once ratified by all parties, copies of treaties are formally *deposited* in one or more locations where they are kept secure and may be consulted if any question about their contents arises. Members of the United Nations are required to *register* their treaties with the UN, and may not invoke an unregistered treaty before a UN agency.

- If not otherwise specified, a treaty *enters into force* when instruments (documents) of ratification are exchanged. However, a treaty may specify a date of entry into force, or stipulate that it enters into force when certain specific states or some number of states has ratified.

U.S. negotiators ordinarily are Department of State officials, operating under the executive authority of the president. However, special negotiators have become more common in the post–World War II era of greater technical specialization and rapid international transportation. Top officials may take personal roles in negotiations on brief occasions, either to deal with the most important and sensitive issues when other parties seek assurances of sufficient administration interest to carry agreements through ratification, or to restart movement when negotiations have stalled.

Signing a treaty implies a significant level of recognition that a foreign government holds at least de facto power regarding some matter of mutual interest and can be trusted to carry out the terms of the agreement. What can be done when we want two governments that do not formally recognize each other to accede to a treaty? This problem really does come up occasionally, and faced the United States, Britain, and the USSR when they sought to gain worldwide acceptance of the 1968 Nuclear Nonproliferation Treaty (NPT). The three great power sponsors of the NPT particularly wanted both East Germany and West Germany to sign, some five years before the two halves of (then) divided Germany extended mutual diplomatic recognition in 1973. The formula devised was to have three equally authentic original copies of the treaty, one each kept in Washington, London, and Moscow. States could accede to the NPT by signing in any of the three sponsors' capitals. Thus East Germany signed in Moscow, West Germany in London and Washington, and especially eager governments anxious to offend none of the sponsoring great powers signed in all three locations.

When ratifying a treaty, the Senate actually debates passage of a bill called an *instrument of ratification*, which may provide opportunities to interpret and effectively revise the treaty. In the instrument ratifying the 1978 Panama Canal Treaties, for example, the Senate included numerous provisions asserting U.S. rights not specified in the treaty. In principle, such changes could reopen the entire negotiation process, requiring a new agreement and new signatures. In 1978 the Panamanian government realized the Senate bill was the best deal it could get, and accepted the U.S.-imposed conditions.

In normal international practice, states are considered bound by the terms of *unratified* treaties they have signed, unless they specifically state or legislate renunciation of all or part of the treaty terms. An important instance concerns U.S. practice regarding strategic arms control. The SALT II treaty, extending and continuing the 1972 SALT I accords, was signed in Vienna by U.S. and Soviet representatives on 18 June 1979 after some seven years of negotiation. It was approved by the Senate Foreign Relations Committee but withdrawn from the Senate by the Carter administration in December 1979. Even before the Soviets invaded Afghanistan that month, administration ability to muster the two-thirds vote to ratify appeared dubious, and worsening U.S.-Soviet relations doomed the ratification effort. Both sides continued to observe almost all the terms of the unratified SALT II treaty from 1979 until the first Strategic Arms Reduction Treaty (START I) was signed in Moscow by Presidents Bush and Gorbachev on 31 July 1991. Although the Reagan administration announced in the early 1980s that the United States would violate selected SALT II terms in ways calculated to offset alleged Soviet violations, all such violations remained limited relative to the terms that both sides continued to observe. In the latter 1990s both the United States and Russia observed the terms of the START II treaty, and even implemented some follow-on measures, even though only the United States had ratified.

States are generally considered to have rights under international law to **abrogate** a treaty—that is, cancel their agreement and withdraw from the treaty—if continued observance would threaten their "supreme national interests." It has become common practice in recent decades to specify such rights explicitly in treaties. For example, when the United States established full diplomatic relations with the Chinese People's Republic in 1979, both sides understood that the United States would withdraw from its mutual defense treaty with the Republic of China, the government of Taiwan. Accordingly, the Carter administration gave Taiwan its formal one-year notice of withdrawal, as required under that treaty. This raised a firestorm of protest from conservative senators, who filed suit directly in the Supreme Court arguing that because the Senate must ratify treaties negotiated by the executive branch under the president's direction, a comparable two-thirds vote should be required to withdraw from a ratified treaty. Historical precedents are fewer and more mixed than one might expect. Nonetheless, in 1979 the Court ruled in *Goldwater v. Carter* that terminating the treaty was within the president's authority because at the time of ratification the Senate had not written any role for itself into the termination process spelled out in the treaty. Barring the adoption of such a practice by the Senate, it appears that the executive retains effective authority to abrogate treaties. This is one of those rare but vital instances in which the courts play an important role in shaping the foreign policy process.

Like other such instances since the landmark 1936 *United States v. Curtis-Wright Export Corporation* ruling that declared the president to be the chief foreign policy officer of the country, the 1979 case was decided largely on narrow procedural grounds. The possibility thus remains that some future Senate may decide to reserve explicit rights to approve any withdrawal when writing an instrument of ratification, which would open the door to battles both with the president and the international parties to the treaty.

TACTICS FOR BARGAINING

Once the parties have worked their way through the preliminary and process stages, they may employ a large arsenal of tactics in bargaining. Although there is no guarantee of success and agreement is unlikely unless it is *Pareto optimal* (that is, at least one party is made better off and no party is made worse off), all parties have incentives to bargain effectively so as to obtain the best agreement they can. Some bargaining tactics thus involve concealing one's real preferences, whereas others involve trying to structure the negotiations to position oneself advantageously. Many such tactics were described in a classic article by Thomas Schelling (1960), and the tactics discussed here are summarized in Table 10.3.

TABLE 10.3
Some Tactics for Negotiation

Bargaining Agents
Utilized to strengthen positions and restrict one's ability to make concessions.

Precommitment
Strengthen one's position by publicly committing to a specific strategy.
Drastically raises the political costs of backing down or changing strategy.
Leaves one's opponent the last clear chance to back down and avoid escalated conflict.

Intersecting Negotiations
Linkages may make some concessions easier—or harder.
Familiarly known in legislative politics as *logrolling*.

Secrecy versus Publicity
Public moves are harder to reverse than moves taken in secret.
Secrecy makes it easier to group gains and losses into attractive packages overall.
Holding negotiations in private at remote locations tends to increase flexibility.

Appeals to Principle and Precedent
Appeal to previous actions and agreements as patterns.
Strongly tied to *salient points* arrived at because of obviousness or equity.
May involve raising stakes through *issue escalation*.

Casuistry
Mask concessions by appealing to general principles.

Bargaining Chips
Acquire goods for the purpose of later bargaining them away for offsetting concessions.
Chief problem is that the bargaining chips acquire their own constituencies.
Combine features of salient points, precommitment, and bureaucratic politics.

Threat and Promise
As in *coercive diplomacy* and *deterrence*, threats are crucially dependent on *credibility*.
Maintaining credibility requires that threats sometimes be carried out.
Credibility also requires *proportionality* to the stakes at issue.

Compensation
Direct savings
Direct payments
Side payments (bribes)

Manipulation of the Mechanics of Negotiation
Cancellations
Walkouts
Continuous negotiations
Deadlines
Manipulation of timing within and between negotiations
  Exploit an opponent's impatience for closure.
  Exploit an opponent's transitory weakness.
  Build "momentum" by agreeing on small points before tackling larger issues.

Tacit Bargaining
Bargaining through actions and the reciprocation they evoke rather than through talks.

Arbitration, Adjudication, and Good Offices
Rely on the *good offices* and facilitation of third powers, often neutral on the issue at hand.
Normally, any party can veto submission to *binding arbitration* or *adjudication*.
Only issues on which one can afford to lose are submitted to arbitration or adjudication.

Schelling's most fundamental bargaining principle is that *we gain bargaining strength by restricting our own flexibility to change positions and make concessions.* Thus bargaining agents do more than extend the executive's ability to engage in many negotiations simultaneously. By claiming limited flexibility to change positions, they shift an important part of the negotiating responsibility away from the site of international talks and back to the domestic struggle over bargaining positions and the amount of flexibility that will be allowed. Agents' limited flexibility also helps leave their opposite numbers the last clear chance to achieve agreement through concessions. A more extreme use of bargaining agents is to disavow what they have negotiated, claiming that they have exceeded their instructions. This occurred with the Vietnam peace talks during the Nixon administration. Secretary of State Henry Kissinger returned from Paris late in 1972 with a draft agreement, saying, "peace is at hand." After consultations with conservative advisers, however, Nixon repudiated the agreement and ordered further intensive bombing of North Vietnam, only to accept essentially the same agreement early in 1973. This case suggests the major problem of Schelling's principle: gaining bargaining strength by limiting our flexibility presumes that we seek only to win, whereas flexibility to move away from preferred positions or to find new ways of addressing problems is generally considered essential to resolving conflicts. (See, for example, Druckman and Mitchell, 1995.)

Precommitment locks one into a strategy announced in advance. As with bargaining agents, precommitment strengthens one's bargaining position by limiting flexibility, leaving the other party the last clear chance to reach agreement or avoid escalated conflict by backing down. The classic game of "chicken" is based on precommitment. In its stereotypical form, chicken involves two teens with hot cars driving straight toward each other on a deserted road. Whoever swerves first loses face and is declared to be chicken. If both drivers swerve at the same time, nobody loses face, but if neither swerve, both die. We can win this game of strategy only by convincing our opponent that we will never swerve first, or that we cannot swerve at all. The first option operates on our opponent's psychology, perhaps through raising our stakes by bringing a large number of supporters so we would lose more face by swerving first, or by boasting loudly about how we will never swerve, or by drinking or otherwise appearing to lack complete control of our faculties. The second option operates on our opponent's factual knowledge. In one variant, we demonstrate our clever steering wheel locking mechanism to all those present, then pitch the steering wheel out the window as we set the car in motion.

Governments and politicians also can play chicken by raising the costs they would suffer by changing course. A classic example concerns President Kennedy's strategy in the 1962 Cuban missile crisis. After the United States discovered that Soviet missiles had been secretly introduced into Cuba, and after the initial U.S. response had been planned, the president precommitted to achieving U.S. goals. He announced on worldwide radio and television that his government would take steps to ensure the withdrawal of the missiles, beginning with the establishment of a naval "quarantine" (read "blockade") around Cuba. Having promised results so publicly, and with midterm congressional elections only one month away, Kennedy knew that backing down would be very politically costly. Soviet leaders also knew this. Faced with a relatively weak position confronting U.S. military forces only a few hundred miles from their home bases, and not wishing to escalate the conflict, they backed down and agreed to withdraw the missiles. Although sometimes portrayed as a pure chicken game, however, this interaction was neither a total victory for the United States nor a total defeat for the Soviets. Although it was little publicized, the U.S. government gave assurances to the Soviets that it would neither attack nor sponsor indirect attacks against Cuba in future, and would withdraw its own intermediate-range ballistic missiles (IRBMs) from Turkey. These concessions allowed Soviet leaders to claim at home that they had achieved their "real" goal of protecting Cuba.

Intersecting negotiations occur when parties negotiate about more than one topic simultaneously, creating opportunities to trade concessions in one set of talks for offsetting concessions in another. In domestic legislative politics and ordinary committee meetings we know this as *logrolling*. Even if not explicitly stated, it reduces to "You vote for my bill and I will vote for yours." In international politics we also know intersecting negotiations under the rubric of *linkage*, the deliberate creation of ties between substantively unrelated negotiations. Although logrolling may have a history of general success, however, linkage does not. The United States regularly tried to assert linkage in dealings with the Soviet Union, but Kremlin leaders resisted with fairly consistent success. Indeed, the Soviets were highly skilled in arguing that being at loggerheads in one set of talks carried absolutely no implication that we could not reach agreement in another.

Consider some examples of attempted linkage. Several U.S. administrations tried with little success to link improvements in U.S.-Soviet relations to increased emigration of Soviet Jews to Israel. The Soviet Union had continued a long and sorry Russian tradition of anti-Semitism, adding the requirement that would-be émigrés repay the Soviet government huge sums for societal investments in their education and training. Despite continuing U.S. pressures, studies have indicated little correlation between Soviet Jewish emigration and either the quality of U.S.-Soviet relations or the overall volume of U.S.-Soviet trade. In an interesting reversal of the usual diplomatic linkage pattern, the Nixon administration correctly concluded that the Soviets were too interested in signing the 1972 SALT I agreements to back out in protest over U.S. bombings of Hanoi in North Vietnam.

Secrecy and *publicity* also influence negotiations by affecting one's flexibility to change positions and make concessions. As with precommitment, moves taken in the glare of publicity are difficult to reverse. Secret moves may be much simpler to implement, and may have the opportunity to prove themselves valuable before domestic opponents can stymie their implementation. Perhaps more importantly, secret negotiations may more readily lead to packages in which concessions in some areas are offset by gains in others, while still leading to an attractive agreement overall. Secrecy then operates similarly to intersecting negotiations.

We mentioned earlier the stark contrast between generally effective secrecy in the 1969–72 SALT I negotiations and repeated leaks in the 1973–79 SALT II talks. President Nixon was able to present the SALT I package as one that was desirable to the United States even though the Soviets were favored in certain aspects, such as being allowed larger numbers of ICBMs (which already existed). President Carter, by contrast, faced repeated leaks about SALT II terms that allowed his opponents to build strong grassroots opposition to selected specific terms of the new treaty well before it was signed and ready for ratification.

Unfortunately for the causes of secret or intersecting negotiations, leaks have become pervasive since the Vietnam War era. One of the few ways to ensure secrecy today may be the complete *isolation* of negotiators, which is feasible in cases of fairly brief, concentrated talks. Simulation experiments demonstrate increased negotiator flexibility when talks are held in private at remote locations, and talks held under such conditions show a stronger impact on bargainer behavior than do suggestions made by mediators (Druckman, 1995). As discussed in the opening case of this chapter, the 1978 Camp David accords are one notable example of isolated negotiations that yielded agreement. Another is the 1995 Bosnian peace agreement brokered by Undersecretary of State Richard Holbrooke, held on the secure grounds of a U.S. Air Force base at Dayton, Ohio. One Balkan leader complained about that isolation, asking plaintively, "What do they think I am, a monk?"

Agreements regularly appeal to *principle* and *precedent*. Just as jurists mask the judicial creation of new law by asserting that their present rulings are rooted in past decisions, negotiations that break new ground often cite established and accepted general principles as justification. Governments and negotiators appeal to past actions as established precedents, both to save effort and to avoid charges that they seek to overturn settled matters. In more than two decades of arms control negotiations, for example, the United States and the Soviet Union accepted and continued understandings worked out early in the SALT I talks. Even U.S. failure to ratify SALT II did not derail the continued use of many points previously agreed on. Early agreement was reached on counting missile launchers rather than missiles themselves because launchers, such as in-ground ICBM silos, were easily counted by noninvasive "national technical means of inspection" such as spy satellites. Once SALT I had been agreed on, its counting rules were automatically continued into the SALT II negotiations. When negotiators wanted to find ways to take multiple warhead missiles into account, they were fitted into the preexisting counting rules by instituting new categories subject to sublimits within the overall limits.

Appeals to principle and precedent are strongly related to **salient points** arrived at in bargaining because of their obviousness or because they appeal to equity norms. Something is salient because it is noticeable, prominent, conspicuous, or stands out from the rest. In military usage, a salient is that part of a battle line that projects farthest toward the enemy. Salient points are so ubiquitous that we tend to accept them unconsciously, so looking for salient points in daily life is a useful exercise. If something is to be divided between two parties, for example, the first split that usually comes to mind is equal shares, because it satisfies a basic equity norm. Consider also the widespread furor over the arrival of the year 2000—a highly salient number in a society using base-10 numbers— even though strong arguments indicate that the twenty-first century should be counted from 1 January 2001.

If you doubt the significance of salient points in international politics, examine an atlas and note how many international boundaries lie either in rivers, which are militarily salient because they are natural barriers to movement, or in lines of longitude or latitude, which have no physical existence but are readily verified. Indeed, U.S. claims to what today is the southern half of British Columbia were once expressed in the political slogan "54-40 or fight," after the line of latitude 54 degrees 40 minutes north of the equator. The choice of salient points for their obviousness suggests an element of groupthink (see Janis, 1972), in that the point chosen is not necessarily best in terms of efficiency or equity, but because it is likely that large numbers of people will think of it first or accept it as the first adequate suggestion.

Examples of salient points in foreign policy abound. Consider three:

1. By 1970 Nixon administration officials had concluded that domestic opposition could be contained so long as the weekly average of U.S. soldiers killed in Vietnam did not exceed one hundred, a grim but fairly accurate conclusion about a figure of merit for evaluating policy success.

2. When U.S. and Soviet negotiators in SALT I capped ABM programs, they allowed each side two sites, one to protect the national capital and one to protect a missile field. This avoided having to destroy completed sites; Moscow was defended by an operational ABM system, and the United States stopped work on the least advanced of the two sites it was building. The Soviets never built an ABM site at a missile field, and after the U.S. Senate refused to fund a site to protect Washington, D.C., the two sides agreed in a 1974 protocol to the 1972 ABM Treaty to limit each side to one ABM site, still the lowest number that would avoid having to scrap operational systems.

3. In December 1983 the Soviets walked out of the intermediate nuclear forces (INF) talks and refused to set a date for the next negotiating session of the strategic arms reduction talks (START), to protest the U.S.-NATO decision to deploy new INF in Europe to counter Soviet introductions of SS-20 missiles to Europe. When the two sides finally resumed strategic arms negotiations early in 1995, they were carefully labeled "new" talks, so nobody could lose face over returning to the suspended "old" talks.

Appeals to principle may include *issue escalation*, in which one party raises negotiating stakes by appealing to broad general principles. This tactic can increase the saliency of an otherwise straightforward issue dramatically, making concessions far more difficult. Prior to Argentina's April 1982 invasion, Britain's government leaned toward giving the Falklands Islands to Argentina, despite the opposition of the some 1,800 residents, almost all ethnically British. But the invasion challenged deeply ingrained British notions of great power status, and thereafter the government of Prime Minister Margaret Thatcher interpreted the Falklands case as clear international aggression. Perhaps not so incidentally, her firm response lifted Thatcher's government from declining popular approval to easy reelection. The Falklands war cost Britain over $2 billion immediately, and dramatically increased long-term costs to maintain a continuing strong military presence on the islands. Beyond the lives lost, it would have been far less costly to have paid each Falklands resident a million dollars to relocate to Britain or Australia. Once the issue had been framed as one of international aggression and British world power standing, however, flexibility for compromise was lost. Often, all that is necessary to stymie negotiating progress is for some major domestic actor in one party's homeland to escalate the issue by framing it in broader terms.

Consider the example of U.S.-Cuban relations, characterized since 1959 by an absence of diplomatic relations and a U.S.-sponsored trade embargo. Suggestions for improved relations have been made fairly regularly, both on humanitarian grounds because the embargo makes the lives of ordinary Cuban citizens much more difficult, and on practical grounds because Cuba's proximity to the United States regularly creates refugee problems. Just as regularly, however, those suggestions have been shot down when political conservatives and Cuban exiles in the U.S. have framed the issue in terms of anticommunism and fears that Cuba would export revolution in this hemisphere. Although past Cuban actions suggest those fears are not entirely groundless, simply raising them has always been enough to stop U.S. government movement toward improved relations, and evidently to harden official Cuban positions as well.

Casuistry is one of the most intriguing bargaining tactics, if perhaps one of the more cynical. Schelling speaks of masking concessions by appealing to general principles. Dictionary definitions speak of subtle but misleading or false reasoning. Others call casuistry creative lying, and a popular contemporary synonym is "spin doctoring." Casuistry is based on the principle that whoever controls the language controls the debate. In an era when policymakers and citizens all suffer from information overload, the shorthand description of a policy proposal strongly shapes popular perceptions.

Searching out uses of casuistry in daily life and politics is an interesting and often amusing exercise, and examples of casuistry in the politics of foreign policy abound. For instance, when the Reagan administration sought to reverse the Carter administration's emphasis on human rights in U.S. foreign policy, the Department of State announced in 1984 that in official reports on the status of human rights worldwide, the word *killing* would be replaced by the phrase "unlawful or arbitrary deprivation of life." President Reagan also renamed the MX missile the *Peacemaker*, echoing the Colt .45 revolver of a century earlier. During 1997's annual debate over renewing "most-favored nation" (MFN) trade status for China, the Clinton administration attempted to defuse the issue by substituting the phrase "normal trade relations," or NTR, which is more accurate because all but a half-dozen states have MFN status (Baker, 1997).

Governments regularly engage in casuistry when they deny making some exchange when there really is a quid pro quo. In October 1990, relatively early in the Persian Gulf War, the government of France sought the release of some three hundred French citizens and diplomats being held in Iraq or Kuwait. France had a long history of strong trade ties with Iraq, and had expressed more sympathy with Iraq than most Western governments, including talking up possible compromises. Saddam Hussein announced the "unconditional" freeing of those French citizens. The following week, the French government announced it would comply with a new Iraqi demand for a planeload of desperately needed medical supplies, not prohibited under UN sanctions, to repay Iraq's costs of providing air transport to the French evacuees. Once again, two governments had conspired to use casuistry in denying that political bargaining and exchange had taken place.

Casuistry also has been labeled *doublespeak*, a term originated by George Orwell in his famous dystopian *1984*. In his 1989 book *Doublespeak*, William Lutz provided the explanation that doublespeak is "language that pretends to communicate but really doesn't. It is language that makes the bad seem good, the negative appear positive . . . language that avoids or shifts responsibility," language used to mislead and deceive and to obfuscate the truth. Among Lutz's juicer examples are these: President Jimmy Carter labeled the failed 1980 raid to free the Teheran embassy hostages an "incomplete success." The 1983 intervention into Grenada, conducted almost entirely by U.S. armed forces, was officially attributed to the "Caribbean peace-keeping forces," and involved not an invasion but a "pre-dawn vertical insertion." On 4 March 1987 President Reagan both denied and admitted participation in an arms-for-hostages deal with Iran, in which the United States sold arms to Iran to induce that government to persuade radicals sympathetic to Iran to free American hostages in Lebanon. Reagan said, "A few months ago I told the American people I did not trade arms for hostages. My heart and my best intentions still tell me that's true, but the facts and evidence tell me it is not."

These sorts of doublespeak involve behaviors any of us can watch for in daily life, but their pervasiveness tends to numb perception and make us unaware of the abuse. We have grown inured to the excesses of advertisers touting "genuine imitation leather" and "real counterfeit diamonds," and using words like *new, improved, better,* and *fresh* that evoke positive responses while providing little or no information.

As political scientists are fond of saying in other contexts, *language matters.* The flip side of casuistry as spin doctoring to make light of troubles is that affairs labeled serious tend to become serious. U.S. media promptly labeled the 1979 Teheran diplomatic hostage seizure a crisis, helping to firm up Iranian intransigence and ensure that American politicians treated it as a crisis. The ABC television news program *Nightline* was launched in 1979 as a late-night report entitled "The Iran Crisis: America Held Hostage." U.S. officials may have learned something from the Iran case, however. On 10 August 1990, eight days after invading Kuwait, Iraq suddenly and explicitly prohibited foreigners, including some 3,600 U.S. citizens, from leaving Iraq or Kuwait, and told diplomats in Baghdad that their embassies in Kuwait City should be closed. Prior to the invasion of Kuwait, resident foreigners had been able to obtain exit visas within one day, and until the Iraqi announcement, visitors were routinely allowed to depart. State Department officials took great care to avoid using the term *hostage.* Even thirty-eight Americans who had been brought to Baghdad from Kuwait and were being held under armed guard in a hotel were described as being "sequestered" rather than held hostage. A senior White House official was quoted to the effect that "It was a very conscious and deliberate decision not to turn these people rhetorically into hostages because then they become hostages" (Kamen, 1990).

Bargaining chips are goods or powers acquired with the specific intent of bargaining them away later in return for offsetting concessions. In principle, this could work, although it seems to imply that one be must richer than one's opponent to avoid being outspent by an adversary who buys more chips. A larger problem arises directly from bureaucratic politics: insofar as bargaining chips are products of government programs, they acquire their own constituencies and become difficult to give up (see Chapter 5).

Modern cruise missiles provide a notable example. When the SALT I agreements capped numbers of ICBMs, SLBMs, and SSBNs, the Nixon administration immediately proposed new strategic weapons programs in all the unconstrained areas. These included the new B-1 intercontinental bomber, the new MX ICBM (only the numbers of ICBMs were then limited), the new Trident SLBM, to be carried on the new Ohio-class SSBNs, and new long-range cruise missiles. Essentially small pilotless aircraft, cruise missiles had been the subject of relatively unsuccessful development during the Eisenhower administration in the 1950s. With modern electronics, the sorts of inertial guidance platforms then well developed for ballistic missiles, and new terrain-following radars, cruise missiles offered the promise of delivering conventional or nuclear warheads over hundreds of miles to within 50 feet of their targets. Flying at subsonic speeds 50 to 100 feet above ground, they were extremely difficult to intercept, even with then-speculative "lookdown, shoot-down" capabilities. These characteristics made them very scary to the Soviets as they contemplated defending their western territories against hundreds of cruise missiles launched from Europe, and thus made them an attractive bargaining chip for the United States and NATO. As development proceeded with great success, however, those properties also made cruise missiles highly attractive to U.S. defense planners. In the end, U.S. negotiators insisted on allowing cruise missiles under the SALT II and subsequent arms control agreements. What really had been intended as a bargaining chip ended up as a significant weapon in the U.S. arsenal and has seen significant use in instances such as the Persian Gulf War.

In a contrasting example, bargaining chips were highly effective in the 1983 U.S.-NATO introduction of Pershing IRBMs and ground-launched cruise missiles into Europe. Although the Soviets had earlier introduced SS-20 modern IRBMs to Europe and rejected the Reagan administration "zero-zero option" of eliminating all IRBMs, they later accepted that option in the 1987 Intermediate Nuclear Forces (INF) Treaty, which broke new ground by eliminating U.S. and Soviet INFs worldwide.

Threat, *promise*, and *compensation* are traditional, fairly straightforward and obvious bargaining tactics. Threat and promise are the negative and positive faces of the same process. Threat of damage or reprisal is integral to coercive diplomacy and deterrence, and promises of subsequent actions are essential to any exchange that offers benefits to two or more negotiating parties. Compensation may take the form of direct payments between parties or direct savings, for example, by reducing costs of arming through arms control negotiation. A common but less openly discussed form of compensation is bribes, casuistically termed **side payments** by political scientists because they occur outside the formal framework of negotiated exchange. Such payments are considered a normal part of doing business in many societies, however, which can pose problems for U.S. businesses prohibited by law from paying bribes. One Japanese prime minister lost office in the 1980s over having demanded bribes for government contracts with U.S. aircraft manufacturers.

If threats are to believed, they must be carried out at least occasionally. This is perhaps even more essential to coercive diplomacy than to deterrence, but neither can succeed unless one has a credible capacity to carry out the actions threatened. During the coalition buildup phase of the Persian Gulf War, Saddam Hussein kept insisting publicly that the United States would never attack. Did this mean that he misread the post-Vietnam limitations of the U.S. military, expected the coalition to fragment, or expected somebody, perhaps the French or Soviet governments, to pull a diplomatic solution rabbit out of the hat at the last moment? An intriguing alternative to these possibilities is that he correctly assessed the situation but concluded that the best counter to a threat he could not overcome was to deny its credibility. By the time the air war opened, many observers had concluded that Saddam's chances of maintaining support or acquiescence from the Iraqi people were higher if his forces suffered defeat in war than if he ordered withdrawal from Kuwait without a fight. The scorched-earth action of blowing up Kuwaiti oil wells before the land war began seems to indicate that by that time Saddam expected the coalition to carry out its threat and expel his forces from Kuwait.

Effective, credible threats also require *proportionality* to the stakes at issue. This concept is fundamental in the traditional theory of *just wars*. Examples abound to demonstrate that no state can threaten all-out war in response to some relatively minor provocation and expect to be believed.

Consider the nuclear strategic doctrine called "massive retaliation" during the 1950s. In a speech before the Council on Foreign Relations on 12 January 1954, Secretary of State John Foster Dulles set out the basis of a new policy that would "depend primarily upon a great capacity to retaliate instantly by means and at places of our own choosing" (*New York Times*, 1954). Widely interpreted as a statement that the United States would respond to any Soviet provocation around the world by launching a major nuclear strike against the Soviet Union, massive retaliation policy miserably failed the test of proportionality. Indeed, the policy was bankrupt at its core, a point realized in some quarters even when massive retaliation was enunciated. The United States might credibly threaten such retaliation in the event of a threat to a core interest, presumably including a major Soviet move against Western Europe, but U.S. behavior had already demonstrated in Korea and Indochina that the threat would not be implemented to counter a Soviet move against a low-stakes peripheral target.

Manipulating the mechanics of negotiation involves actions we may associate more readily with domestic labor negotiations than international bargaining. Upon examination, however, we find that tactics such as deadlines, cancellations, walkouts, continuous negotiations, and manipulation of timing within and between different sets of talks are used in many types of bargaining. *Deadlines* often are invoked in domestic bargaining, as when a strike is called to occur shortly after the old labor contract expires, but deadlines also are fairly common in international negotiations. For example, some agreements expire unless they receive periodic review and reauthorization. A notable example was the required 25-year review and renewal of the Nuclear Non-Proliferation Treaty (NPT) in 1995. Another form of deadline is an ultimatum requiring specific action by a fixed time, as when the United Nations demanded that Iraq withdraw from Kuwait by 15 January 1991.

Yet another form of deadline is the *fixed timetable* for accomplishing some function. This is familiar in U.S. legislative politics, where many state constitutions fix the timetable of legislative sessions. Uninformed readers of the legislative record might marvel at the enormous amount of legislation passed on the final day before the constitutionally mandated adjournment. In reality, legislative leaders faced with numerous required budget bills still uncompleted on the final day simply pull the plug on the official clock, continue for another day or two until essential business is finished, then plug the clock back in and adjourn. Exactly the same procedure was followed in the 1985 ten-year review conference for the (then) Conference on Security and Cooperation in Europe, where Soviet intransigence had delayed completion of mandated human rights reviews.

Cancellation of scheduled negotiating sessions and *walkouts* from meetings are tactics for signaling one's disapproval of an opponent's actions, or of lack of progress in the talks themselves. Examples abound both in domestic labor negotiations and in international conferences. The 1973 Soviet walkout from the INF talks, mentioned earlier, illustrates an important weakness of walkouts: if you break off negotiations to protest some point but fail to gain the concession sought, you lose face if you return for further talks. Walkouts are a form of precommitment and send a signal so strong that one cannot afford to use it for less than the most important issues.

Continuous negotiations occur with some frequency domestically, but only rarely in international politics. Typical domestic cases involve labor negotiations in which the union agrees to continue working beyond the contract's expiration, provided that negotiations continue without letup and appear to be making progress. The bleary-eyed negotiators often stumble out in front of cameras the next morning to announce a tentative agreement. Similar continuous negotiations are fairly rare between governments. Notable examples include the 1978 Camp David Israeli-Egyptian peace agreements, discussed in the opening case of this chapter, and the 1995 Dayton Bosnian peace accords.

Timing of proposals or other moves within negotiations may be chosen either to strengthen one's bargaining position or to improve the odds of reaching agreement. A sound idea may be salable at one time but unsalable at another, depending on other conditions. Thus, for example, partition of Bosnia to end its 1992–95 civil war was unacceptable when the 1993 Vance-Owen proposal was raised, but effective partition was central to the Dayton peace accords in 1995 after events had shifted all the parties' hopes and capabilities. If an opponent is eager to reach agreement, delaying and obstructionary tactics may *exploit impatience* to produce greater gains. Typical ploys include haggling over minor details, evading closure on major points, and introducing new and unexpected topics. For decades, Soviet negotiators were noted for taking hard-line stands in bargaining with the United States and remaining absolutely intransigent until convinced that we would never agree to their terms.

Proposals may be timed to *take advantage of an opponent's transitory weakness, or even of one's own limitations.* For example, the United States rarely ratifies high-profile controversial treaties in even-numbered years, when one third of the Senate is up for reelection. More than once during the 1970s, U.S. administrations used the difficulty of getting arms control treaties ratified during election years to pressure the Soviets toward earlier agreement, although with little success. Careful negotiators may seek to build a sense of *momentum* about reaching agreements, by manipulating agendas to facilitate early agreement on small points and general principles, then appealing to what has already been accomplished as a sign that the process should move forward to more significant and more difficult issues.

A final but extremely important negotiating tool is tacit bargaining (introduced in Chapter 7). Tacit bargaining takes place through actions and the reciprocation they evoke rather than through formal talks. In this case, we allow our actions and public statements to communicate what we seek and what we are willing to do to obtain it. In some instances, this can help bring public and international pressure to bear on governments. A classic formulation of applied tacit bargaining is Charles Osgood's (1962) proposal for graduated reciprocation in tension reduction (GRIT). In presenting a scheme for U.S.-Soviet nuclear disarmament a decade before SALT I, Osgood called for a sequence of highly publicized unilateral moves by each side, to be continued as long as responsive moves sufficient to avoid any serious disadvantages to either side were taken. In the early 1990s President Bush's announcement that nuclear bombers were being taken off standby alert and joint U.S.-Soviet announcements that they were retargeting their strategic nuclear missiles away from each other's cities, are reminiscent of Osgood's GRIT, which has also been applied to defusing other types of confrontations. Tacit bargaining has several virtues that make it an acceptable approach in many situations: (1) it minimizes investment in the trappings and preliminaries of formal negotiations and (2) it may help parties reach agreement even though they may at first find it difficult to deal face to face.

TACIT BARGAINING IN PERSONAL BUSINESS

At the risk of a digression from foreign policy, my favorite personal example of tacit bargaining is domestic and individual rather than international. While attending graduate school, I had occasion to move back into an apartment complex where I had previously lived. A suitable apartment was about to be vacated, but had been occupied by the same family for five years and needed thorough cleaning and repainting. This was agreed, and a move-in date was set. Upon moving in, I found everything in good condition except the bathroom, which had indeed been re-painted, but unsuccessfully. The new color was an off-mustard, and failed to cover the underlying paint, with a result far less attractive than before. I reported this to the rental agent and was told the bathroom would be repainted the following week, but nothing happened. For several months, once or twice a month, I would report the need for repainting to either the resident manager or the rental agent and be assured it would be taken care of promptly. Still, nothing happened. Finally, one month I made no telephone call, but also did not send the rent check. Ten days passed without incident. Then one night I returned from work and walked in to find —sniff, sniff—the smell of fresh paint! The bathroom had been beautifully repainted. I wrote out the rent check and mailed it the next morning. Neither I nor the management ever said another word about these events, but we had bargained.

ARBITRATION, ADJUDICATION, AND GOOD OFFICES

Governments and agencies of international governmental organizations (IGOs) like the United Nations frequently offer assistance and facilitation in negotiation, called **good offices.** They may call on the parties to come together, provide a meeting place and other logistical support, offer suggestions for settlement, proffer peace inspection and enforcement forces, supply economic and military aid and other enticements as rewards, and engage in considerable arm-twisting to encourage agreement. The United States used many of these tactics in the 1978 Camp David talks, and all of them at the Dayton, Ohio, conference leading to the 1995 Bosnia settlement, presided over by Assistant Secretary of State Richard Holbrooke with occasional visits by Secretary of State Warren Christopher. Governments and agencies also may offer their services as *arbitrators*. Less frequently, governments agree to submit a dispute to *adjudication*, for example, by the International Court of Justice (hereinafter, the ICJ) at The Hague. The fundamental limitation on arbitration and adjudication as means for resolving disputes in international relations is analogous to their application to domestic disputes between individuals or firms: governments normally submit to binding arbitration or adjudication only those issues on which they expect to win or believe they can afford to lose. The ICJ's jurisdiction between states is limited to disputes concerning treaty interpretation, questions of international law, breaches of international obligation, and reparations due. Cases may be brought before the ICJ if all parties agree, which is a major constraint.

In 1986, for example, the U.S. government disregarded an ICJ finding that it had violated Nicaragua's sovereignty under that country's Sandinista government by mining the harbor of Managua and supporting rebellion by antigovernment contra guerrillas. In that same year, the United States vetoed a UN Security Council resolution ordering a halt to aid to the contras.

A dispute also may be brought before the ICJ if all parties have made advance formal declarations accepting the court's jurisdiction. Many states have made such declarations, but frequently with restrictive conditions. The United States excludes all disputes concerning domestic matters from ICJ jurisdiction, and reserves the right to decide what is domestic. In an era of increasing internationalization of economics and increasingly intermestic foreign policies, this is a major reservation.

FITTING BARGAINING TACTICS TO POLICY GOALS

Which of the dozen types of bargaining tactics summarized in Table 10.3 are most important for purposes of policy making and international negotiation? The answer depends strongly on our goals. If we wish to win as much as possible by following Schelling's principle of increasing our bargaining strength through limiting our own flexibility, we should use bargaining agents, precommitment, publicity, perhaps bargaining chips (although they are quite situation dependent), and certain manipulations of negotiating mechanics, such as cancellations, walkouts, and deadlines. To promote agreement, we could employ positive linkages (in the logrolling sense) between intersecting negotiations, secret talks to allow flexibility, appeals to salient points, threats, promises, side payments in some situations, offers of compensation, continuous negotiations in some circumstances, and agenda manipulations designed to produce a sense of momentum toward agreement. If we seek agreement in an unfriendly political climate in which it would be difficult to open negotiations, or perhaps if we doubt our ability to obtain ratification of a treaty, we could employ tacit bargaining. In selling agreements to the public and the Congress, we well might employ casuistry, appeal to offsetting gains and concessions in intersecting negotiations, emphasize gains in a package of terms arrived at in secret, and frame agreements and our political efforts to sell them in ways that appeal to broadly accepted principles and precedents.

BARGAINING CONTEXTS

The *context* or *setting* of a set of negotiations seriously influences which bargaining tactics will be appropriate, and expectations about the type and likelihood of agreement. Consider first a fundamentally supportive context in which all parties are presumed to have essentially compatible objectives, so that we can presume eventual agreement. Talks within the framework of one of the UN functional agencies, for example, presume the parties already have a recognized need for and history of cooperation. Moreover, functional agencies regularly deal with matters on which the very structure of the situation gives states an incentive to cooperate. For example, governments may need to agree on the regulation of a common pool resource such as a fish species that migrates between their territorial waters and international waters, lest it be overfished and a renewable resource destroyed. Such situations offer win-win possibilities and are termed *positive-sum games*, in that they are strategic interactions in which all parties may be able to benefit. Negotiations then can be relatively low key and unhurried. Each issue can be seen as merely a single play in an iterated game of strategy, in which the temporary gains of acting exploitatively now would be paid for manyfold over years of subsequent negotiations. Such technical matters present problem-solving situations, so that negotiators operate within a framework that presupposes agreement to be possible and desirable, simply a matter of working out details, even though the parties still have somewhat differing interests (see Hopmann, 1995, 25–28.) Problem-solving talks thus often begin with a sharing of technical data, research analysis, and interpretations, with a view toward arriving at a common understanding of the facts that must underlie agreement.

Similarly, talks within the framework of a major alliance or treaty association such as NATO or the European Union, although they may involve the highest political and economic stakes, still occur within a context of prior agreement and commitment. Thus, for example, arguments at the 1997 NATO summit about whether to expand membership by taking in some Eastern European states occurred in the context of shared beliefs about the vital importance of maintaining a viable alliance.

Situations in which the parties have *essentially incompatible objectives* present far more difficult problems and demand bargaining more than problem solving. Unlike the positive-sum game of technical agreement, negotiators here face what may initially appear to be a *zero-sum game* like chess or poker, in which one can win only what is lost by another party. Territory, for example, always belongs to somebody, a genuinely zero-sum situation—unless parties can agree to shared access for essential purposes. Even when such solutions are possible, bargaining situations always involve using tactics like those summarized in Table 10.3 to induce agreement. So long as one or more parties believe they can accomplish their objectives by means other than negotiation, as on the battlefield or through unfettered trade competition, diplomatic bargaining cannot bring about a settlement.

Dealing with situations of essentially incompatible objectives requires a two-stage process, *first persuading all parties to want an agreement*, then bargaining over details. The Bosnian civil war provides a clear example. All factions, and especially the (Muslim) Bosnian government, were unwilling in 1992–93 to accept partition of the country into Muslim, Croat, and Bosnian Serb regions. By 1995, after NATO bombing and Croat attacks had reversed many Bosnian Serb gains and Bosnian Muslims realized they would never get a better deal, that partition became acceptable, and the details were hammered out in Dayton with U.S. facilitation and pressure. Bargaining contexts characterized by essentially incompatible objectives almost always require significant developments in the substantive arena (see Figure 10.1) before formal talks can yield agreement. Thus, when initial objectives are essentially incompatible, bargaining tends to occur first in the substantive arena, and only later in formal talks.

VERIFICATION

Verification is the institutionalized process of confirming that another party is abiding by the terms of an agreement. It is more a mechanism of agreement available to negotiators than a bargaining tactic. Although publicized particularly in the context of strategic arms control agreements, verification is applicable to many types of agreements. In the 1970s U.S. and Soviet SALT negotiators based verification on means that neither side could prevent the other from employing, such as reconnaissance satellites used to count missile silos, and termed these "national technical means" of inspection. By the late 1970s it had become clear that this formula had been pushed about as far as possible, and U.S. negotiators began devising cooperative means for verification, such as opening silo doors at predetermined times so satellites passing overhead could count the missiles therein. By the mid-1980s negotiators had faced the fact that some matters could only be verified with real confidence by on-site inspectors, and that principle was implemented in the 1987 Intermediate Nuclear Forces (INF) Treaty and the subsequent START strategic arms treaties.

Like any intelligence operation, verification involves probabilities rather than certainties. Because the INF and START Treaties involve destroying weapons already built and counted, negotiators believed that only on-site verification would confirm those destructions with adequate confidence. Accepting on-site verification implies considerable loss of secrecy and sovereignty, so governments are reluctant to agree and instances are rare. Victory in the Persian Gulf War allowed the UN to appoint a Special Commission to supervise and verify Iraq's destruction of weapons of mass destruction and programs for their development and manufacture (see the geopolitical focus case in Chapter 15). Experience in Iraq now makes it clear that even on-site verification by an overwhelmingly superior power can never locate all proscribed activity with complete certainty.

BARGAINING TACTICS AND THE CITIZEN

Knowing the procedures for international negotiations and the bargaining tactics discussed here should help citizens interpret the true status of interactions between governments and other international actors at any given time. It is a useful exercise to examine any press report regarding either domestic or international negotiations to determine the context or situation, the stage of negotiations, and the tactics being employed. Is the problem at hand technical or functional, within an essentially supportive problem-solving context? Or is it a bargaining situation in which interests fundamentally conflict and a win-win solution is impossible? Although secrecy can limit available information, ask yourself what the negotiators have decided thus far. Even if not all the needed information is available directly, we often can find knowledgeable published analyses by skillful and well-informed analysts whose biases and political predispositions are known. Understanding the concept of casuistry helps alert us to spin that needs to be decoded, even while diplomacy retains its own peculiar language. If you suspect spin, try rephrasing what official spokespeople say into simpler, more direct, and less flattering language. As with any other activity, you will build skill and understanding through practice.

SUMMARY

The number, importance, and difficulty of diplomatic activities and international negotiations have increased apace with the deep and lasting changes in the global context of foreign policy since the end of the Cold War.

Diplomacy is the process of conducting international relations, especially communication between governments and other international actors. Above all else, it is a process of signaling others regarding the issues we care about, how much we care, and what we are prepared to do about it, and it is understood that absolutely no statement or action happens without meaning. The great majority of diplomatic exchanges is routine and peaceful. To help keep them that way, fairly elaborate diplomatic procedures have been developed over the last five centuries to help prevent extraneous concerns from blocking essential communication. Both the language and procedures of diplomacy sometimes appear arcane or amusing, but understanding them helps greatly in deciphering foreign policy actions. International contacts and negotiations have multiplied manifold since World War II, driven by vast increases in the number of independent states, increased internationalization of economics, and improvements to international transport and communications. In turn, that growth has encouraged increased attention to international negotiation, and to the tactics states and other international actors employ to promote their policy goals in such venues.

Diplomats on station perform many functions, including symbolic representation of their home government; gathering of information both overtly and, to some degree, covertly; offering expert advice based on their in-country experience; helping offer protection to their nationals; and helping to promote trade and commerce. Less frequently, they participate in policy making and in negotiations with the host government.

Governments and other international actors regularly seek negotiations over many issues, setting in motion a process that may be terminated abruptly at any time, but usually involves three distinct stages. Preliminaries are talks about whether or not to hold talks, typically beginning with exploratory contacts. The process stage consists of talks about procedures, working out the mechanics and logistics of the negotiations that the parties have agreed in principle to pursue. This stage sometimes involves prolonged haggling over symbolic issues. Only if the preliminary and process stages are successfully concluded do negotiations ever reach the substantive bargaining stage. A many-level game of strategy then ensues, taking place through several different channels between governments (and/or other types of international actors) and simultaneously within those governments or organizations. In addition to formal talks between working negotiators, governments may interact and influence negotiations through top-level back-channel and summit meetings, through shuttle diplomacy by high officials, through moves in the substantive arena of interest, and through somewhat indirect channels involving media and public opinion. To understand the negotiations completely, we must examine all those channels. Because modern modes of communication and transport allow governments to limit negotiators' freedom to change positions, the place to look for real policy movement in negotiations usually is in each government's internal position-setting struggles to shape its negotiating positions. Unfortunately for us as critical observers, much of the internal struggle may remain secret for decades.

Negotiations yield many different sorts of outcomes. They may be broken off or otherwise terminate with no agreement, either on substantive matters or even on meeting again. More frequently, talks are recessed and continued later. The key to distinguishing genuine recesses from breakdowns is whether or not the parties set a date for resuming talks.

If agreements are reached, they may take one (or more) of several forms. Although an understanding or entente is relatively informal and often unwritten, it may guide serious policy for years. Executive agreements are formal, written accords between the executives or heads of government of two or more states. Often considered as treaties in all but name, executive agreements usually are not formally ratified like treaties, but are increasingly used for international functional arrangements. Treaties are formal agreements between the governments of sovereign states or organizations of states, and are the source of most international law.

Once the parties have worked their way through the preliminary and process stages, they may employ a large arsenal of tactics in bargaining. Which of the dozen types of bargaining tactics discussed here are most important for policy making and international negotiation depends strongly on whether we wish to maximize our own bargaining strength, maximize the chance of agreement, or promote agreement when the political climate is unfriendly at home or abroad. In problem-solving situations all parties are presumed to have differing interests, but essentially compatible objectives. Reaching agreement then is fundamentally a technical matter. In bargaining situations the parties have essentially incompatible objectives and diplomatic bargaining cannot bring about a settlement so long as one or more parties believe they can accomplish their objectives by actions in the substantive domain, as on the battlefield or through unfettered trade competition. Such situations require a two-stage process, first persuading all parties to want an agreement, then bargaining over details. Knowing the procedures for international negotiations and the bargaining tactics discussed in this chapter should help citizens interpret the true status of interactions between governments and other international actors at any given time.

One important substantive area often involving negotiations is international political economics, variously described as the broad area in which politics and economics intersect, or as the politics of intermestic economic issues. In Chapter 11, we turn to a number of issues and policy tools within that area.

KEY TERMS

Abrogate	Legation
Back-channel negotiations	Mission (See *legation*.)
Bargaining	Noninterference
Bargaining chips	Persona non grata
Casuistry	Precedence
Corps of diplomats	Precommitment
Diplomacy	Preliminaries
Diplomatic immunity (See also *exterritoriality*.)	Process
	Salient points
Embassy	Shuttle diplomacy
Executive agreement	Side payments
Exterritoriality	Summit meetings
Good offices	Treaty
Interests section	Understanding or entente
International law or the *law of nations*	Verification
Intersecting negotiations	

Selected Readings

Druckman, Daniel, and Christopher Mitchell, special eds. 1995. *Flexibility in International Negotiation and Mediation. The Annals of the American Academy of Political and Social Science*, Vol. 542, November. Thousand Oaks, Calif.: Sage Periodicals Press.

Fisher, Roger. 1997. *Getting to Yes : Negotiating an Agreement Without Giving In*, 2d ed. London: Arrow Business Books. An excellent small manual on applied bargaining.

Kissinger, Henry. 1994. *Diplomacy*. New York: Simon & Schuster.

Schelling, Thomas C. 1960. "An Essay on Bargaining."

Schelling, Thomas C. *The Strategy of Conflict* (Chapter 2). Cambridge, Mass.: Harvard University Press.

Steigman, Andrew L. 1985. *The Foreign Service of the United States: First Line of Defense*. Boulder, Colo.: Westview Press.

CHAPTER 11

INTERNATIONAL POLITICAL ECONOMY AND ECONOMIC POLICY TOOLS

INTERNATIONAL POLITICAL ECONOMY AND THE DEBATE ABOUT U.S. DECLINE

International political economy (IPE) is the broad area in which politics and economics intersect, or the politics of economic issues. Much of domestic politics always has been about economics, so it should come as no surprise that a good deal of international politics also revolves around economic issues. What is new is the breadth and depth of international penetration into domestic economies. The internationalization of economics since World War II, and especially in the last quarter of the twentieth century, already has created a truly global economy and fundamentally changed the ways in which individuals and states relate to that economy. Nor is the United States immune to those changes, despite being the global hegemon on almost every measure of economic, military, and political power at the end of World War II. This is why the late 1980s saw an intense debate about whether the United States is in decline as a global power, and whether such a decline is inevitable.

Consider the following story of comparative political economy as related by the economist Walter Russell Mead (1990):

> Fifty years ago, the United States was the wonder of the world: a rare combination of Canada, Saudi Arabia, and Japan. We had enormous quantities of strategic minerals, the largest oil reserves in the world, vast stocks of food, and the most dynamic industrial economy of any nation.
>
> At the end of World War II, other advantages were added to these. We were the only major country whose economy and infrastructure had not been destroyed by the war. No one else had a merchant marine capable of handling such a flow of goods in international trade. We had accumulated an enormous gold reserve. We had the best equipped army in the world and an unchallengeable navy and air force. We enjoyed an atomic monopoly, made all the more useful by our demonstration that we possessed the will to use the bomb.
>
> These weapons have fallen from our hands. Our oil production is no longer adequate for our own uses. World markets in minerals and food are glutted. Our industrial economy has lost its supremacy—it is, at best, first among equals. We now owe foreigners more than Argentina, Brazil, and Mexico combined; Germany and Japan can set the value of the dollar.

This is the road to Argentina. . . .

Fifty years ago, Argentina was part of the First World. It was a European society with living standards comparable to those of Canada and France. Today it is part of the Third World. . . .

The future does not have to be this bleak. But we will have to change the way we think about foreign policy.

[T]o avoid a fate like that of Argentina, the United States will need to stop gloating about winning the Cold War and start to assess, soberly, its place in the global economy.

How bleak is our collective future? Is the United States in decline? If so, is that decline inevitable, or reversible by the right policies? To find answers we must first discover how IPE works. Mead's story about Argentina's global economic slippage should warn us that international economics seriously affects the relative global standing of states, and also seriously impacts their citizens. The U.S. loss of the global economic hegemony that it enjoyed after World War II, and the increasing global penetration of all economies, now strongly impact each one of us.

EFFECTS OF IPE ON U.S. FOREIGN POLICY

International political economics is an activity area in which the United States is unavoidably and far more strongly affected today than during the early Cold War years. The end of the Cold War has only intensified dramatic changes in U.S. interactions with the world economy that began in the mid-1970s. We discussed important changes in the global economic context (and other contexts) of American foreign policy since 1990 in Chapter 3. Like international law, international organization, or diplomacy, international political economics is so huge a subject that entire courses are devoted to it at major universities. Comprehensive coverage is impossible in one chapter. Rather, we seek here to learn enough about IPE to understand the outlines of (1) how the United States operates in the international economy, (2) why this country is now so strongly penetrated by outside economic developments that President Clinton declared economics the primary U.S. foreign policy concern after the Cold War, and (3) what economic tools of foreign policy are available to the United States.

In the major sections of this chapter, we (1) flesh out the implications of Walter Russell Mead's story by examining the debate over U.S. political-economic decline; (2) cover how IPE works and how it affects the United States; (3) examine economic "tiers" and older but still frequently used terminology for classifying levels of development; and (4) study some policy tools for managing international political economics.

THE DECLINE DEBATE AND BEYOND

We begin by examining and expanding on the perspectives of three noted authors concerning (1) the case for decline, (2) the case against decline, and (3) the impact of economic internationalization on national economies and national futures.

THE CASE FOR INEVITABLE DECLINE

As mentioned in Chapter 8, historian Paul Kennedy made a highly lucid and literate case that great powers eventually must decline in his best-selling 1987 book, *The Rise and Fall of the Great Powers: Economic Change and Military Conflict from 1500 to 2000*. Kennedy examines the growth and decline of powerful states over the long sweep of history, taking the realist perspective that relative power rather than absolute power counts in international politics.

The relative strengths of leading states never remain constant, primarily because technological changes and organizational breakthroughs cause different societies to experience different growth rates. Natural power endowments of states strongly influence their abilities to develop and exploit new technologies. For example, substantial petroleum reserves benefited the United States during the ascendancy of petrochemical industries and of the internal combustion engine.

Availability of critical resources may combine with other accidents of history to give great advantage to particular states, and to the growth of particular industries, at certain times. For example, neither automobiles nor the assembly line were invented in the United States, but Henry Ford developed both to permit mass production at popular prices. Production line work was mind-numbingly repetitious, but raised workers into the middle class within a generation. Driven by Ford's organizational innovation and sustained by growing wealth, the United States became the first state to enjoy mass private ownership of automobiles. The vast majority of automobiles ceased to be rare and expensive craft objects. Auto building flourished in the American Midwest, initially drawing on the experience and technology of wagon builders who had prospered there supporting westward expansion. Later, it concentrated in and around Detroit, Michigan, which offered easy lake access to coal and Minnesota iron as basic inputs, plus a central delivery location on the national railroad net and relative to the national population distribution. The industrial strength built there proved crucial to America's World War II mobilization.

The aircraft industry also started in the American Midwest and drew on many of the same technologies as auto builders, but concentrated in southern California by the end of World War II. Modern aircraft are much more complex than automobiles, requiring considerably more labor. Transport of manufacturing inputs is relatively less important because far fewer units are produced, and the end product is self-transporting. Aircraft manufacturers thus were free to locate plants to obtain other advantages, and mild southwestern weather offered both lifestyle and manufacturing conveniences. Situating plants in California provided large spaces and weather favorable to aircraft testing, outdoor storage, and even some outdoor major assembly.

Building on such considerations of location and resource availability, Kennedy argues that over the long term there is a very significant correlation between productive and revenue-raising capabilities and military strength. It is more than simple **mercantilism** (maximizing exports and minimizing imports) to argue that wealth usually is required to build and maintain military power, and that military power often is needed to acquire and protect wealth. Great powers usually are strong both militarily and economically. However, great powers in relative decline instinctively tend to spend more on military security to protect their wealth, standing, and foreign commitments. This compounds their long-term dilemma, by diverting resources that otherwise could be invested in economic growth and technological advance. Note that the *multiplier effect*—the tendency of an additional dollar spent to add more than one dollar to the GNP because every recipient spends most of the amount received—is slightly higher for monies spent in the civilian economy than in the military economy. Although the U.S. military, like other employers in this country, spends more on salaries than on any other factor of production, military hardware cannot produce anything else, whereas at least some spending by civilian sector employers goes for items such as machine tools that increase long-term productive capacity. Unlike lathes and robot welders, tanks and missiles cannot produce additional goods. Thus, all other things being equal, a society that invests more in its civilian economy should expect greater long-term growth in productive capacity. Internationally, studies indicate that states with greater numbers of alliance commitments experience lower long-term economic growth, with noticeable effects over less than twenty years.

Over the long term, most states' power tends to follow a time course almost like a life cycle, although there usually are noticeable time lags between trends in relative economic strength and changes in military and territorial influence. Historically, the sequence often looks like this: an economically expanding power may prefer to become rich rather than spend heavily on armaments. Examples include Britain in the 1860s, the United States in the 1890s, and Japan and China today.

By perhaps a half century later, priorities have altered. Economic expansion brings with it overseas obligations in the form of dependence on foreign markets and sources of raw materials, along with military alliances, perhaps foreign military bases and, until the latter twentieth century, colonies. Continuing technological and organizational change now help other powers expand economically at a faster rate. Because they wish to extend their influence, the world has become more competitive. Market shares are being eroded, there is competition for raw material resources, and military threats abroad have increased. Pessimistic observers begin to talk of decline, and patriotic statespeople call for renewal. A great power may find its sense of security lower, despite higher defense spending than a generation or two earlier. Other powers have grown faster and are becoming stronger, so the world environment appears less secure. Shifting more resources away from economic productivity and into defense simply compounds the problem, except perhaps in response to very short-term threats.

Eventually, the great power must curtail something in order to synchronize its aspirations with its reduced capabilities. This may take many forms, including lowering military investment, curtailing foreign military and alliance commitments, seeking "burden sharing" from other alliance members, and surrendering control of selected market types or market areas. For example, neither Britain nor France ever regained its prewar status after World War II. Both liberated their colonial empires, Britain fairly readily and beginning with independence for India and Pakistan in 1947, France only after a bitter struggle over Algerian independence, ending in 1962. Britain gave up attempting to maintain a naval presence east of the Suez Canal, and by the 1960s was purchasing many of its major weapons systems from the United States.

Writing before the breakup of the Soviet Union, Kennedy foresaw a gradual shift in shares of total world product and total world military spending away from the five largest concentrations of strength to many more states. More immediately, he forecast a three-level distribution of world power, consisting of (1) a dominant "pentarchy" comprising the United States, the USSR, China, Japan, and Western Europe; (2) the "four tigers," or newly industrializing countries (NICs) of Asia: South Korea, Taiwan, Singapore, and Hong Kong; and (3) the rest of the world, consisting of developing states. Within the pentarchy, global productive balances were already beginning to change. The United States and Western Europe enjoyed roughly equal productive and trading muscle. Japan and the Soviet Union were at about two thirds the U.S. level, but with Japan growing faster and already about to overtake the Soviet GNP. Last but growing fastest was China. Kennedy's predictions were generally confirmed over the next decade, except that collapse and breakup dropped the Soviet Union and its successor states to the third level. Knowledgeable Russians today look longingly at South Korea as a model for economic development.

Kennedy's rather general predictions give us at least sketchy explanations for some major political-economic phenomena of the latter 1980s and early 1990s. The Soviet Union retreated from the Brezhnev Doctrine under which it had asserted the right to control Eastern Europe, and those states were allowed to follow independent political paths *because the Soviets no longer could afford to maintain control*. After forty-five years of Soviet "socialist" domination, Eastern European states rapidly overthrew old communist regimes and turned in varying degrees to market economics. Yet as recently as 1980, the Soviets had planned military intervention if Poland failed to impose martial law to control the Solidarity labor movement.

During the latter 1980s, faced with a GNP already slipping below that of Japan, the Soviet Union under President Mikhail Gorbachev desperately searched for a new economic formula through *perestroika* (restructuring). It also sought to reduce military spending by withdrawing from the draining Afghan war and by inviting new arms control agreements with the United States, especially one that would avoid a competition in "Star Wars" antimissile defenses predicted to cost $60 billion or more. The Soviets also searched for *rapprochement* (improved relations) with Beijing, because roughly one quarter of their military spending had been directed toward the threat of war with China.

As the Soviet Union broke up, its former republics became nominally sovereign states seeking political and national independence even as they sought solutions to the USSR's economic collapse. By the time of that political breakup, the Soviet command economy had devolved into chaos. GNP actually dropped for several consecutive years before and after the breakup, an almost unprecedented decline for a modern developed state. Cities and regions had begun ignoring central economic directives, bartering essential goods and services or insisting on payment in hard foreign currencies. Soviet economic desperation in the latter 1980s was far greater than suspected in the West at the time. Today we understand far better why Soviet leaders pushed as hard as they did for arms control agreements and other cost reductions.

Kennedy's analysis and predictions also help explain recent major developments affecting Western Europe and the United States. Despite deep attachment to their respective centuries-old independent histories and cultures, and regardless of continuing arguments over the details, both Britain and France have cast their political and economic lot with integration and the European Union. This development was foreshadowed on a smaller scale by such past enterprises as the joint Anglo-French Concorde supersonic transport aircraft and Airbus Industries' joint development of modern jet airliners. In the United States, we see continuing concerns about the need to reduce overseas military spending, reduce our foreign trade deficit (the amount by which imports exceed exports), and encourage allies such as Japan and the Europeans to bear more of the costs of regional and global military security. Additionally, we saw precedent-shattering reliance on foreign contributions to pay most of the costs of the Persian Gulf War. At the very least, these developments indicate that the United States today cannot undertake independently all the things it did only a few decades ago. Even if we do not read such events as indicators of decline, they appear discomfortingly close to Kennedy's image of a great power suffering reduced relative capabilities.

THE CASE AGAINST INEVITABLE DECLINE

Three years after Paul Kennedy's book made the best-seller lists, Harvard University political scientist Joseph S. Nye, Jr., published *Bound to Lead: The Changing Nature of American Power.* To Kennedy's pessimistic observer talking of decline, Nye is the patriotic statesman calling for renewal. His fundamental argument is that things are not as bad overall as some signs make them appear, and by exaggerating past U.S. world dominance, "declinists" find it overly easy to portray a diminished American present. In this, of course, Nye is absolutely correct. Given the degree of U.S. ascendancy immediately after World War II on virtually every measure of power, plus the peculiar circumstances in which we had achieved that dominance, there was almost nowhere to go in the long term but relatively downward. Moreover, Cold War containment policy promoted eventual competitors by rebuilding Japanese and Western European economic capacities, taking on the major burdens of collective defense, and encouraging European economic union.

Nye admits many negative developments that other analysts interpret as decline. Important economic sectors such as consumer electronics and automobiles have suffered strong foreign penetration. The household savings rate dropped from 8 percent in the 1970s to 5 percent in the 1980s. By 1995, it dropped to 3.5 percent, and it went negative in the first quarter of 1999. Persistent federal deficits subtracted another 3 percent from effective national savings rates. With gross investment staying roughly constant, reductions in savings were replaced by massive capital imports. This foreign borrowing combined with a persistent trade deficit—driven partly by increasing dependence on imported oil as world oil prices soared, and partly by a wave of consumer imports beginning in the 1980s—to transform the United States into the world's largest debtor in absolute terms. Still, the phrase, "in absolute terms," is significant. In 1994 the public debt of the United States stood at $4.693 billion, and GNP was $6.727 billion, making the national debt about 70 percent of one year's GNP. Many other states have debt burdens far higher relative to national product. Moreover, that 70 percent ratio compares quite favorably to banking industry standards that allow individuals to spend between two and three times their annual gross incomes to purchase a house.

Nye cites a number of positives to counter the negatives of decreasing savings, growing foreign debt, and increasing foreign economic penetration. During the 1980s the U.S. economy grew on average 2.5 percent annually, above its historical average of 2 percent over the last century. Manufacturing productivity rose by 3.5 percent per year during the 1980s, and production per worker remained higher than in Germany and Japan. The United States remained in the forefront of many high-technology industries, including aircraft, biotechnology, chemicals, and computers. Many of those trends continued

SURRENDERING LEADERSHIP IN A CUTTING-EDGE INDUSTRY
The Case of Aircraft

Cutting-edge industries based on the newest and most advanced technologies traditionally are expected to lead to spin-offs in other fields, thus contributing both directly and indirectly to economic prowess. The earliest successful aircraft were developed in the United States, and helped give commanding leads in aircraft development, technology, and production. Although occasionally and briefly outperformed by competitors, American aircraft accomplished most of the technological firsts and overwhelmingly dominated both military and civilian markets for decades. Only in the last quarter of the twentieth century did that dominance begin to unravel. In the 1970s an Anglo-French consortium developed the Concorde, which became the only civilian supersonic transport (SST) after the United States and, later, the Soviets withdrew from SST competition. The Concorde never has been an economic success, but some experts have argued in recent years that both high SST costs and upper atmosphere pollution from SSTs could be cured by newer technologies. Despite some government encouragement in the 1980s during the Reagan administration, nobody appears ready to take up those challenges. On a more mundane but higher volume front, by the 1980s the European Airbus Industries consortium had developed airliners competitive with the latest U.S. designs, and began making inroads in sales to American airlines. By the late 1990s Airbus Industries was the world's second largest producer of commercial aircraft, the only serious competitor to U.S.-based Boeing.

Also in the 1980s U.S. firms essentially withdrew from producing small general aviation single- and twin-engine planes. Previously, American manufacturers had enjoyed at least 95 percent of the world market for such aircraft. This change, however, occurred not because of lower foreign prices or superior foreign technology, but because manufacturers feared enormous product liability lawsuits over manufacturing flaws that might not become manifest for twenty years. Their fears were triggered by a national wave of product liability lawsuits in our already litigious society. U.S. aircraft manufacturers did not even abandon this market because of any actual large liability awards, but because they feared the magnitude of their *exposure* to possible lawsuits and the *potential* costs of defending against them.

Individuals or small firms wishing to purchase a plane like the two-seat, 90 mile-per-hour Cessna 150 in which a generation of pilots learned to fly were forced to choose between buying used planes or building kit aircraft that could be licensed as "experimental." This market segment, at least, provides concrete evidence that many Americans today seek risk elimination to an unrealistic degree and are far too eager to find someone else to blame for every loss. Almost total world market dominance was surrendered over an issue curable through product liability reform. A cure by policy change finally came in the form of 1994 legislation limiting the time period of liability after manufacture, and the U.S. general aviation industry began a slow recovery.

well into the 1990s while Japanese and Western European economic growth rates faltered. However, Nye does not adequately acknowledge that the United States already faces and will continue to face serious challenges in all those cutting-edge industries.

Beyond taking a more optimistic view of U.S. leadership in key industries, Nye attacks Kennedy's economics head on, arguing that defense effort has decreased, not increased, as concerns about decline have grown. Indeed, defense spending was capped at 10 percent of GNP during the 1950s by order of President Eisenhower, fell to 6 percent of GNP during the 1980s despite Reagan administration increases in absolute dollar defense spending, and had fallen to 4.5 percent by 1994. Writing after the appearance of his book, Nye also argued (1990b) that Iraq's 1990 invasion of Kuwait undermined the view that the world had entered an era in which economic power had replaced military power, and that U.S. success in organizing collective action against Iraq demonstrated continuing leadership potential. At this point, however, Nye's argument sounds much like Mead's contention that the United States must change the way it conducts foreign policy. Nye suggests we must replace the hard power of command coercion with the soft power of cooptation and persuasion. (See also the section on coercion and persuasion in Chapter 8.)

ECONOMIC GLOBALIZATION, NATIONAL ECONOMIES, AND NATIONAL FUTURES

Is the entire debate about the decline of the U.S. decline moot because rapid globalization of economics is undermining the very notion of an "American" economy? That is one major implication of Robert Reich's 1991 book, *The Work of Nations: Preparing Ourselves for 21st-Century Capitalism.* A major political economist and notable in-and-outer, Reich trained at Dartmouth, Yale Law School, and Oxford, served in the Ford and Carter administrations, on the faculty of Harvard's Kennedy School of Government, and as labor secretary in the first-term Clinton administration, where he gained the opportunity to deal firsthand with policies regarding economic standing and productivity.

In his book, Reich focuses on the global trend of economics increasingly becoming international or transnational in character, vastly increasing the foreign penetration of national economies regardless of what governments desire. Reich then moves to a more micro-level analysis than Kennedy or Nye, examining how economic internationalization affects various classes of individuals quite differently, depending on their work roles. His analysis has profound and unsettling implications for all nation-states, for the future world role of the United States, and for individuals' hopes that American citizens will continue to see advances like those enjoyed since World War II, with standards of living rising with each succeeding generation.

In his introduction, Reich challenges what he terms "the national idea," noting,

> We are living through a transformation that will rearrange the politics and economics of the coming century. There will be no *national* products or technologies, no national corporations, no national industries. There will no longer be national economies, at least as we have come to understand that concept. All that will remain rooted within national borders are the people who comprise a nation. . . . Each nation's primary political task will be to cope with the centrifugal forces of

the global economy which tear at the ties binding citizens together—bestowing
ever greater wealth on the most skilled and insightful, while consigning the less
skilled to a declining standard of living. (Reich, 1991, 1; emphasis in original)

In terms reminiscent of Nye, Reich contrasts optimistic visions of new jobs, new firms,
new patents, and increasing foreign investment, with pessimistic views of closed manufacturing plants, huge trade deficits, and growing foreign debt. Whether we are becoming better off or worse off, and where we are heading, he says, depends on who we mean
by "we."

Reich uses the metaphor of a boat to describe the traditional—and now outdated—
image of a national economy. Despite obvious differences between individual incomes
and quality of accommodations, most of us still share the view that we are all moving together in the same boat, rising or falling along with our national economy. That economy
and that boat have been visualized as being commanded by political leaders such as the
president and the chair of the Federal Reserve Board, business leaders typified by the
chief executives of major American corporations, leaders of organized labor, investors
such as mutual fund managers and venture capitalists, and a diverse group of entrepreneurs and scientific-technical specialists. The metaphor is readily extended to a world flo-
tilla of distinct national economic boats sailing on the same ocean, some more rapidly
than others, with the lead position occasionally changing hands, and with some need for
international coordination to prevent collisions. National economic growth and a flourishing economy are seen as benefiting each individual in our boat to greater or lesser degree, as we all rely on our country's economic strength. In turn, that strength depends on
how effectively the country develops, mobilizes, and governs its resources, including all
the types of resources discussed in Chapter 8. Unfortunately, Reich continues (1991, 5),
"this vision's clarity and soothing comprehensibility are its only virtues," for in today's
world it is wrong.

The view of distinct and relatively isolated national economies is outdated because
modern communications and transportation allow almost every factor of production to
be moved rapidly and almost effortlessly across nation-state borders. Information travels
at the speed of light via wires, cables, computer networks, radio, and satellite transmission
links that interconnect telephones, fax machines, and computers. Information conveyed
may include negotiations, agreements, contracts, designs, engineering drawings, bids and
proposals, orders and confirmations, data about trades and any number of other activity
measures, observations, test results, and other feedbacks about the conduct of business.
Money also flows at the speed of light because people need merely send a message transferring title to an asset or moving sums between accounts. This has created an international market in currencies, capable of moving with breathtaking rapidity, as evidenced
when international trades cut the value of the Mexican peso by half in a matter of days
early in 1995. A substantial amount of trading on today's stock and other financial exchanges is automated, carried out between computers programmed to buy or sell when
price movements exceed selected margins. The notion that people who process all sorts
of information may work at home and interact electronically with their counterparts
around the world is no longer the stuff of science fiction.

Although not movable at electronic speeds, many physical factors of production also
travel much more rapidly than ever before. Courier services regularly transfer small packages across the United States or the Atlantic Ocean overnight, and air freight carries

fairly large shipments nearly as rapidly. To be sure, it remains more economical to ship larger, heavier, and less valuable items by slower and less expensive means, but today we move more goods over greater distances than ever before. Compared to the costs of production, shipping costs are lower than ever before. Within the United States, for example, the year-round availability of almost every type of fresh produce throughout the country relies on a system for rapid shipping almost entirely developed since World War II. During the latter 1980s, General Motors concluded it was less costly to ship Cadillac Allante bodies from an Italian coach builder's factory to this country by air than by sea, because they would spend less transit time as expensive inventory items before being mated to their chassis to complete salable automobiles.

The ease and speed of information transfer and the growth of fast and relatively inexpensive transport of goods have facilitated the decentralization of production because the movement of subassemblies from numerous manufacturing points to final assembly is readily coordinated. They also have made possible the system of "just in time" inventory control, pioneered in the Japanese auto industry, under which subcontracted suppliers deliver parts only hours before they are needed, reducing assemblers' inventories and handling. All of these developments share a chicken-and-egg relationship with their supporting and enabling technologies, and combine with important political changes to facilitate the internationalization of production. It becomes difficult to say precisely whether technologies have been developed to enable new forms of economic endeavor, or whether activities made possible by new technologies almost always are pursued. Probably both are true, and both have contributed to profound economic changes.

After World War II, the United States undertook a far more active role in the management of international economics than ever before. To facilitate the rebuilding of European industrial and general economic strength and thereby help support containment of Soviet expansion, Washington strongly promoted functional integration through such venues as the European Coal and Steel Community. At the same time, the U.S. government reversed stands it took between the two world wars, now supporting lower tariffs and increased international trade. In the late 1950s we strongly encouraged formation of the European Economic Community. And, of course, recent years have seen significant growth in regional customs unions and free trade arrangements such as expansion of the EEC into the EC and ultimately the EU, the U.S.-Canadian Free Trade Agreement later expanded to include Mexico under NAFTA, and finalization of the World Trade Organization to succeed the post–World War II interim arrangements called the General Agreement on Tariffs and Trade (GATT). Increasing international trade, made easier by all these developments, has made it far simpler for markets to cross borders and for production to be spread over multiple states, effectively internationalizing production. Design and development activities may take place wherever the requisite skills are found, and subassemblies may be built wherever costs—notably labor costs—are lowest.

Workers themselves are the least movable factor of production. Reich (1991, 8) argues that workforces are "the only aspect of a national economy that is relatively immobile internationally." With infrequent exceptions, like Germany's import of foreign "guest workers" from relatively poorer states like Spain to fuel its economy during boom times, or the flow of Mexican immigrants to the United States, workers usually remain in the states where they have citizenship. By contrast, even whole factories and their equipment are movable. A California food processing plant that freezes vegetables for the U.S. market may be shut down and its equipment moved south of the border to take advantage of lower Mexican wages, made even more attractive by NAFTA and the precipitous drop of the Mexican peso against the dollar in 1995.

In the face of such developments, as industry after industry internationalizes, it becomes less and less meaningful to think of a purely "American" economy, or American corporations, technologies, and products. Only the American people and work force remain. Similar phenomena are occurring around the world in every other economy. As the global economy develops, "national" success consists increasingly of maximizing the value of the skills and capabilities which a state's citizens can contribute to that economy and the ease with which they are linked to the emerging global market.

Thus the answer to the questions whether we are becoming better off or worse off, and where we are heading, are that "we" are no longer all in the same boat. The optimistic view that globalization is wonderful applies for precisely those individuals whose skills and services are becoming more valuable in the emerging world economy. Unfortunately, they are only a minority. The pessimistic view applies to the majority, whose skills either are subject to replacement by lower cost foreign substitutes (as is true for many U.S. citizens) or are stagnating in value (as is often true in low-income developing states). Classifying which jobs fit into each category is perhaps the most interesting part of Reich's analysis.

Types of Work: Reich's "Three Jobs of the Future"

Reich eschews the usual methods used by the U.S. Bureau of the Census and countless others to classify jobs by (often implied) socioeconomic status. Instead, he classifies jobs according to a small number of broad categories that describe both the nature of the work performed and its competitiveness in the emerging global economy. The results, summarized in Table 11.1, are not always comforting.

Routine production services involve repetitive or similar steps that yield a stream of identical or similar products, whether those products are made from metal, plastic, fabric, or data. They include the sorts of jobs traditionally classified as blue collar: labor and assembly-line work, often gritty and seldom glamorous. However, they also include tedious and repetitive high-tech jobs, such as stuffing components into electronic circuit boards, assembling and testing computers, and manufacturing integrated circuits. Moreover, many jobs traditionally thought of as white collar are also routine production services, including most clerical positions and routine supervisory jobs such as line managers and clerical supervisors. The crucial element is that routine production services *consist of routine and standardized operations*, whether they involve making physical objects, keying data into computers, conducting clerical operations, repetitively checking the quality of subordinates' work, or enforcing standard operating procedures.

In-person services are those that cannot be provided without direct customer contact to deliver a product or service. Like routine production services, they involve repetitive and standardized operations. Their essential difference is that they are nonexportable because they must be carried out face to face, although the individuals who perform them may be employed by multinational firms. Such jobs comprise the rapidly growing service economy, and include all types of retail sales, repair services, restaurant servers, janitors, child-care providers, and the like. Wages tend to be low, hours often are limited and irregular, and benefits usually few or nonexistent. Pay normally is an hourly wage strictly based on the time worked. Service workers usually are closely supervised, as are their immediate supervisors. Some service jobs, such as child care in the provider's home, may be

TABLE 11.1

Reich's "Three Jobs of the Future" and Distribution
of Job Types in the United States (circa *1990*)

Job Type	Percentage of U.S. Work Force	Time Trend
1. Routine Production Services **Product: Streams of metal, fabric, data** Repetitive tasks Blue-collar jobs Routine supervisory jobs Standard procedures, codified rules	25%	Shrinking
2. In-Person Services **Product: Non-exportable services** Providing services requires direct contact with customers	33%	Growing
3. Symbolic-Analytic Services **Product: Ideas, solutions to problems** Problem-identification Problem-solving Brokering	20%	Possibly growing
Resource production and extraction: farmers, **miners, loggers, etc.** **Product: Resources grown, managed, harvested** **Job type: Primarily routine production services**	5%	Stable or shrinking
Government employees, government-financed **workers, and regulated industries** **Job type: Primarily routine production** **and in-person services; some** **symbolic-analytic**	17%	Stable or shrinking

Source: Compiled from Reich, 1991, Chapter 14.

carried out independently and escape such close supervision. Only a limited number of in-person service jobs, such as registered nursing, involve high levels of responsibility, judgment, problem solving, and pay. Even RNs, however, perform routine operations, many of which are now being assigned by hospitals to other workers with less training and lower wages.

Symbolic-analytic services are the most creative of what Reich calls the "three jobs of the future." Symbolic analysts deal in problem identification, problem solving, and strategic brokering of many types. Their products are ideas, solutions to problems, and brokered agreements. These products require manipulating symbols, which may include streams of data, writings, design drawings, logical and legal arguments, systems of equations, and the like. Symbolic analysts may describe themselves as architects, lawyers, engineers of all types, research scientists, consultants of many varieties, advertising or public relations executives, real estate developers, writers and editors, systems analysts, and so on.

Each symbolic analyst applies a particular set of analytic tools plus accumulated experience to convert reality into some set of abstract images, manipulate those images to solve the problem at hand, and then convert the images back into a real-world plan of action. Usually those analytic tools are learned in colleges and, often, graduate and professional schools, which teach law, business management, medicine, computer science, filmmaking, accounting, international finance, architecture, mechanical engineering, and countless other specialties.

Symbolic analysts may be employees, but often form professional partnerships with others in their specialty. Their incomes may fluctuate over time, but always depend far more on the creativeness and innovation of the solutions generated than on hours worked, which may be long and fluctuating. Beyond their periods of formal schooling, symbolic analysts often spend lengthy periods gaining practical work experience and building their professional reputations before they acquire recognition and the high incomes that may accompany it.

Reich's three jobs of the future are very differently rewarded because they are very differently valued in the emerging global economy. Increasing mobility of goods and the information needed to coordinate and manage production means that routine production services may be traded around the globe and must compete with foreign providers even in the U.S. market. Labor-intensive production can be moved to locations offering the least costly workers possessing adequate skills.

In the last quarter of the twentieth century such moves have played major roles in the decline of once flourishing American industries like steel and automobiles, and in the general decline of unionized labor. U.S. steel producers have lost much of their domestic market to European and Asian competition, resulting in many plants closing and others surviving only by shifting production to more lucrative specialized steels. By the 1990s the American automobile industry had rallied to improve product engineering and build quality, but had lost nearly half of its domestic market. United Automobile Workers union membership stood at about half its pre-1970 peak. Foreign automakers had begun to find it less costly overall to open plants in the United States, both to reduce U.S. import tariffs and to take advantage of relatively lower American labor costs.

Nor are such movements of manufacturing labor confined to these shores; Japanese firms now routinely export routine production work to less expensive locations throughout Asia. Such shifts have tended to reduce the number of highly paid union workers, substituting nonunion laborers at lower pay and benefits. Unions have been forced to bargain for job security rather than higher wages and benefits, a holding action at best. By 1990 routine production services accounted for only about one quarter of U.S. jobs, and that share was shrinking.

The in-person services sector has been growing rapidly, and accounted for one third of U.S. jobs by 1990. Like routine production services, these jobs usually require only a basic education, perhaps a high school diploma plus some vocational training and on-the-job experience. Hours are often more limited and irregular, and many such jobs pay only minimum wage. Low educational requirements and high competition keep wages for this work low. Educational limitations cause many workers displaced from higher paid routine production jobs to enter this sector.

Only symbolic-analytic services tend to be well paid, because their products are easily transportable and their creativity makes them globally competitive. Like routine production services, but unlike in-person services, they can be traded worldwide and must

CARTOON 11.1

The information revolution began in the last decades of the twentieth century, driven by computer advances and networking, and strongly stimulated economic globalization. New capabilities to move information worldwide almost instantaneously encouraged firms to downsize and move many jobs abroad, wherever necessary skills could be utilized at the least expense.

compete in international markets. How successfully providers compete determines their remuneration, and depends on how creative, clever, original, and innovative they are. Although symbolic analysts may gain great success at early ages and lose out later if their creativity flags with age, they are the one group that is well rewarded in the new global economy. By 1990 such work represented about 20 percent of U.S. jobs, with perhaps some slow growth. Moreover, *this is the one group likely to determine the overall economic future of any state's economy.* Whether the United States vanquishes its foreign competitors or is vanquished by them depends on whether its symbolic analysts are more innovative, create and master the cutting-edge technologies of the future, and organize routine production and in-person services in ways that meet or beat foreign competition.

Two remaining job types retain fairly static or slowly shrinking shares of the U.S. work force. These groups are distinguished by being largely sheltered from global competition. By 1990, 5 percent of U.S. workers dealt in *resource production and extraction.* They are the farmers, miners, and loggers who grow, manage, and harvest or extract produce or resources. Almost all such work entails routine production, although there is some specialized management and scientific research. The final job group is *individuals who work directly for governments* at all levels, in government-financed jobs, or in industries regulated by government. A limited number of symbolic analysts is included, for example, the government policy analysts we discussed in Part II. However, most government work involves routine production services, especially clerical work, and in-person services that range from advice about tax forms to physical therapy at veterans' hospitals. Government service was a growth category in the United States in the 1960s and 1970s, but decades of federal deficits and state voter tax revolts have reversed that trend. By 1990 government and protected industries had shrunk to about 17 percent of the U.S. workforce. The federal deficit reduction movement that took hold in the mid-1990s seems destined to shrink government employment even further.

Government's share of the workforce also is shrinking because of the trend since the 1970s to reduce government regulation of industries. Arguably, opening industries to market competition encourages greater efficiency and gives consumers better products and services and/or lower costs. If so, the cost almost always is lost jobs and lower wages. Often, both workers and consumers suffer greater market instability. The deregulation of the U.S. airline industry since the 1970s offers a case in point. Deregulation probably has helped hold down the real cost (after inflation) of vacation travel while substantially boosting the number of passengers. But it has led to waves of airline mergers and bankruptcies, constant shuffling of flights, frequent service movements in and out of smaller city markets, elaborate many-tiered fare systems that vastly increase passenger uncertainty and decision costs, large fare increases for business travelers who must book flights on short notice, and the virtual end of our previous freedom to make last-minute changes in air travel plans.

The Global Web

Reich asserts that products are more and more international composites from the "global web" of the internationalized economy. Indeed, in 1990 more than half the value of U.S. imports and exports consisted of transfers of goods and services within international corporations (Reich, 1991, 114). One excellent example of an internationalized composite product is a nominally "American" General Motors compact car, the Pontiac LeMans (c 1990). Although sold in this country under an American badge, it was assembled in South Korea. As becomes clear in Table 11.2, one cannot accurately say the car was "built" in South Korea; purchasers actually made a whole series of complex international transactions.

Table 11.2 demonstrates the high mobility of both routine production services and symbolic-analytic services. Their outputs can be produced around the world, eventually to be coordinated and combined into a single global composite end product, in this instance a small automobile. Production is coordinated from General Motors corporate headquarters in Detroit, a location dictated by historical development rather than necessity. Several distinct levels of routine production services are involved, each carried out in a state whose workers can perform the work with the requisite degrees of skill and precision. The most advanced, precise, and difficult machining is done in Japan. Less demanding steel production, body fabrication, and final assembly work is carried out in South Korea, and readily fabricated small components come from a variety of locations around the Asian Pacific Rim. Data processing can be performed wherever labor costs for the

TABLE 11.2
Products as International Composites from the Global Economic Web

Example: Pontiac LeMans compact car from General Motors, *circa* 1990.

$10,000 paid to General Motors distributes as follows:

Amount	Spent In	To Purchase	Work Type*
$3,000	South Korea	Routine labor and final assembly	RP
1,750	Japan	Advanced components (Engine, transaxle, electronics)	RP
750	Germany	Styling, design engineering	SA
400	Taiwan, Singapore, and Japan	Small components	RP
250	Britain	Advertising and marketing services	SA
50	Ireland and Barbados	Data processing	RP
3,800	United States	Strategists in Detroit	SA
		Lawyers and bankers in New York	SA
		Lobbyists in Washington	SA
		Insurance and health-care workers	RP
		General Motors shareholders (mostly in United States, but increasingly in foreign nationals)	

*RP = Routine production services
 SA = Symbolic-analytic services
Source: Data from Reich, 1991: 113.

required routine skills are lowest, because inputs and outputs can be transmitted electronically. Symbolic-analytic work, including product planning, styling, design engineering, advertising, marketing services, and legal and financial services, can be assigned to locations where the necessary high skills—some of which may be unique—are available at competitive prices.

HOW INTERNATIONAL POLITICAL ECONOMY AFFECTS YOUR LIFE

International political economy matters to each of us at two levels: individually and as members of collectivities ranging from firms to communities to our country to international organizations and regions. Economic globalization will do much to determine whether we prosper as individuals. Whether enough of us become and remain competitive in that global economy will determine whether the United States prospers. The discussion of the previous sections should establish that the United States faces some types of relative decline as a world power and inevitable major adjustment to changes in its global economic environment since the end of World War II. The perceived relative strength of different state economies determines rates of exchange between their currencies, which in turn changes the costs of imported goods. Thus, when the dollar is strong relative to other major currencies, consumers in this country can buy imported goods more readily. At the same time, domestic producers suffer from increased foreign competition, and the strong dollar hurts our exports by raising foreign costs for our goods. Shifts in international currency exchange rates impact consumers most heavily in industries dominated by foreign-made products. In the United States today, those markets include such products as cameras, consumer electronics like radios and televisions, motorcycles, shoes, and textiles. Exchange rate shifts have somewhat less impact on markets in which American producers still challenge imports, such as aircraft, automobiles, and computers.

The internationalization of economics that Robert Reich terms the development of a global web, in which products are increasingly becoming composites of work performed in many states, implies that *economic isolationism is no longer a viable policy option*. Production of such basic goods as automobiles already is extensively international in character. Moreover, the United States depends heavily on imports, both of raw materials and of advanced components. Oil is merely the best known of many strategic resource inputs for which the United States is far more dependent on imports than it was at the end of World War II. American defense contractors today depend on imports for a number of vital advanced components, such as flat panel displays built in Japan. As discussed by Reich and in the earlier section here, different classes of individuals will be very differently impacted by these developments, depending on whether their work is globally competitive. In this we see explanations for the stagnation of real incomes across the American middle class since the 1970s and for the fact that the American labor movement, which gained real power only in the late 1930s, has declined precipitously in only two generations. Indeed, whereas one third of U.S. workers belonged to a union in 1960, that fraction had dropped to 16 percent by 1990, and with that decline went much of the power of workers to demand middle-class wages for routine productive services.

How IPE Works and How It Impacts the United States

Preserving good standards of living for large numbers of U.S. citizens, and preserving a major economic role for the United States in a world of increasing economic internationalization, will depend on mastering the tools of international political economy in ways that make as many citizens as possible globally competitive. Taking that perspective, we devote much of the remainder of this chapter to examining those policy tools. We begin, however, with some examination of the processes of international political economics and their impact on the United States.

Growing Role of the State in Economics

Despite some persistence of the myth that government and business are largely separated in the United States, the twentieth century has seen marked intensification of government's role in economics. This was true well before post–World War II internationalism, and was driven particularly by responses to the Great Depression of the 1930s. Government began regulating securities markets and banks to prevent further crashes, bailing out failing banks to preserve the confidence of both small customers and major investors, and creating an economic safety net to protect the poor and unemployed. Cold War defense spending regularly was considered economic pump priming, so that defense contracts for their districts were highly prized by Congress members. Early in the 1960s Congress accepted the notion that budget deficits to support public spending today could pay dividends in economic growth tomorrow, making up the deficits by future growth in tax collections. Economic management through government fiscal (budget income and outgo) and monetary (interest rates and money supply) policies grew, bringing with it ongoing tension between maintaining tolerably low levels of both inflation and unemployment.

Thus far, other governments have done much more than the United States to create close partnerships between government and business geared toward promoting economic growth. Still, many such steps have occurred since the founding of this country, and their pace has quickened in recent decades. Rapid early growth was stimulated by government acquisition of vast territories, such as the Louisiana Purchase and the conquest of California from Mexico. The building of transcontinental railroads was stimulated by government grants of money and of vast tracts of land along the right of way, and was vital to opening up the West to settlement and development. The 1960s Apollo program to land men on the moon was intended not only to create a highly salient victory in Cold War competition with the Soviets, but also to yield technological spin-offs that would promote growth and leadership in emerging industries. Sematech, the joint government-industry venture to bolster the U.S. semiconductor industry, was created in 1987, mirroring similar ventures in a variety of industries already carried out so successfully by the Japanese (see discussion in Chapter 8).

Although the United States has been slower to adopt a broad industrial policy than other highly developed states, it has moved increasingly toward a national economic strategy involving mobilizing resources, promoting critical industrial sectors, protecting at least some home markets, and aggressively seeking to open foreign markets to U.S. goods. Such moves by this and other governments have created an increasingly competitive international environment in which every state capability is mobilized toward success in the global economy.

The military and political power of any state derives primarily from its economic strength. International markets are organized under political agreements reached between states, so legal arrangements that create or limit economic opportunities and raise or lower profits ultimately are determined by the global power of the governments which negotiate them. For the United States, economic policy and economic involvement on a world scale were elements of post–World War II internationalism as vital as promoting the United Nations, creating NATO, or fighting the Korean War. Analysts who foresee the division of the world into three great trading blocs (of Europe, the Americas, and Asia) envision moves that governments will take in the belief they are essential to economic survival. The reluctant advance of major Western European states with centuries-long sovereign histories, like Britain and France, toward economic and monetary union demonstrates the strength of international economic pressures. As we examine the major IPE developments since World War II, we see both the rise and the retreat of U.S. global economic hegemony, in terms starkly reminiscent of the decline debate (see summary of these developments in Chronology 11.1).

DOMINANCE AND COMPETITION: MAJOR IPE DEVELOPMENTS SINCE WORLD WAR II

Many crucial U.S. decisions that laid the groundwork for sustained internationalism—and for U.S. international economic dominance—were taken well before the end of World War II. Even before the 1945 San Francisco Conference organized and chartered the United Nations, conferees at the New Hampshire White Mountains resort of Bretton Woods in 1944 established new institutions intended to stabilize the postwar international economic order. Bretton Woods yielded agreements creating the International Monetary Fund (IMF) and the International Bank for Reconstruction and Development, commonly called the **World Bank.**

The IMF's main purpose is to stabilize international monetary exchange by making short-term loans to governments experiencing a current account deficit in their balance of payments. (See the discussion of such accounts accompanying Table 11.3.) IMF loans normally are used to support the value of a state's currency, contingent on required austerity programs involving reduced government spending and restrictions on the money supply. Such measures typically produce national economic slowdown, higher unemployment, and lower inflation, all intended to ease pressures on the value of the currency by discouraging imports and encouraging exports. Their domestic effects have made such policies controversial in international development circles, where many see the IMF as enforcer for a conservative U.S. financial community. In the 1940s trade deficits were widely believed to signal excessive domestic consumption, which should be cured by adjusting the domestic economy to make it more competitive globally.

Although both the IMF and World Bank became operational in 1946, the year before the Marshall Plan was launched, the World Bank had relatively little impact on early post–World War II reconstruction. Eventually the bank received an allocation of $10 billion and authority to borrow additional funds in world capital markets. By the 1960s requests from developing states produced over $1 billion in new loans annually. Like IMF loans, World Bank loans have been controversial in development circles because debt service—payments of interest and principal—reduces net funds available for development (see Chapter 13).

As we discussed in Chapter 2, the outlines of Cold War global political divisions emerged clearly by 1947, barely two years after World War II. That year also saw the opening of concurrent conferences to create two additional major international economic institutions, the first General Agreement on Tariffs and Trade (GATT) and an International Trade Organization (ITO). From 1947 until 1994, extending through some eight rounds of protracted negotiations, GATT was the primary international trade organization. GATT proved fairly effective as a forum for negotiating reductions in tariffs and some other barriers to trade, and yielded significant decreases in world tariffs. For example, U.S. tariffs had fluctuated between 30 percent and 45 percent of the value of dutiable imports between 1890 and 1935. By 1955 they had been cut to 15 percent and by 1970 to 12 percent (Pastor, 1980, 96–98).

The ITO, however, languished for decades. The U.S. government objected that the 1947 agreement restricted American actions while creating exceptions for other states, and President Truman refused to submit the treaty for Senate ratification. Although signed but unratified treaties normally are considered binding, the ITO never become operational. The similar World Trade Organization (WTO) came into force in 1995, following ratification of the final GATT agreement in 1994. Concerns that the WTO will restrict U.S. freedoms of action persist in some quarters. U.S. acceptance in 1994 of a global trade organization believed unacceptable in 1947 is yet another sign of waning U.S. global economic hegemony, but also a sign of growing international cooperation.

With the opening of the Cold War came serious changes in U.S. plans for the new global economic order. Early post–World War II plans had called for keeping Germany and Japan occupied and marginalized. Now their rapid economic recovery was promoted and they were groomed for major roles in the developing system of anticommunist alliances. Marshall Plan aid was extended. Integrated European economic institutions were encouraged. In the U.S.-promoted constitution adopted 3 May 1947, Japan renounced the right to wage war, the emperor gave up claims to divinity, and the Diet became the sole lawmaking authority. With the onset of the Korean War in 1950, the United States initially relied heavily on its troops in Japan, and increasingly sought to integrate Japanese bases into its regional defense planning. In 1951 the U.S. and forty-eight other noncommunist states signed a peace treaty under which Japan regained full sovereignty as of 28 April 1952, and the first U.S.-Japan Defense Treaty was signed.

The 1950s saw the intensity peak of the Cold War, and the opening of what some have called the 1958–70 heyday of U.S. hegemony (Lairson and Skidmore, 1993, 76). The Treaty of Rome, signed on March 1947 by Belgium, France, (West) Germany, Italy, Luxembourg, and the Netherlands, called for creation of a European Economic Community (EEC; later the Economic Community or EC; still later the European Union). The EEC was strongly encouraged by the United States, partly through conditions on Marshall Plan aid, as a means of promoting European anticommunist economic strength and unity. Begun as a **tariff union** that would slowly eliminate tariffs and other trade restrictions between member states while establishing common tariffs on imports from nonmembers, the EEC eventually grew to take in most of Western Europe and Scandinavia and provided much of the political/organizational base for the European Union. By early 1959 fourteen European states including Great Britain had agreed to accept full **convertibility** of their currencies. Convertibility meant those currencies could be freely traded for gold and other foreign currencies, although gold was not used internationally for convertibility after 1971.

Both currency convertibility and fears that future EEC tariff walls would limit external trade encouraged heavy investment in Europe by U.S. corporations from 1958 on, launching a fifteen-year period of rapid multinational corporation (MNC) growth. For the United States, that period combined economic dominance with growing worries about eventual loss of hegemony. In many ways, such a change would be an inevitable by-product of successful postwar containment policy. Having determined that European security was essential to blocking Soviet expansion and preserving American security, U.S. policymakers promoted Western Europe's reconstruction and its functional and economic unification. This created a bulwark against communist advances from within and without, and a stark contrast between the living standards of ordinary citizens on the two sides of the Iron Curtain. Simultaneously, however, it promised eventual serious economic competition from a major region of highly developed, unified, and up-to-date economies.

⊕ CHRONOLOGY 11.1

Key Events in the Development of International Political Economy (1945–1998)

Year	Key Events
1944	Bretton Woods Conference creates IMF and World Bank
1945	Founding of the United Nations; end of World War II
1946	IMF and World Bank become operational
1947	Beginnings of the Cold War; first GATT; rapid recovery for Germany and Japan promoted
1948	
1949	NATO Treaty signed
1950	Korean War opens
1951	Japanese peace treaty, constitution, and U.S.-Japan Defense Treaty signed
1952	
1953	Korean War ends
1954	
1955	
1956	
1957	
1958	U.S. encouragement of EC opens age of MNC growth; beginnings of balance of payment worries
1959	
1960	Foreign-held financial liabilities first exceed U.S. gold supply
1961	
1962	Trade Expansion Act empowers president to negotiate lower tariffs
1963	Kennedy round of GATT opens
1964	
1965	Major U.S. buildup begins in Vietnam
1966	
1967	Kennedy round of GATT concluded
1968	
1969	
1970	
1971	U.S. actions become more unilateral; gold price floated; temporary 10 percent import surcharge
1972	
1973	First oil price shock (rises triggered by Yom Kippur War); end of MNC growth era; Vietnam peace
1974	

1975	Fall of South Vietnam; France, West Germany, Great Britain, Italy, Japan, and United States begin economic summits
1976	
1977	
1978	Second oil price shock
1979	
1980	
1981	Reagan's "supply-side economics" begins; budget deficit soars, quadrupling federal debt in a decade
1982	
1983	
1984	
1985	
1986	Uruguay found of GATT negotiations (its eighth) opens; Group of Seven (G-7) established
1987	
1988	
1989	U.S.-Canadian Free Trade Agreement, effective January, to eliminate all tariffs and duties by 1999.
1990	Persian Gulf War—opening phases (Desert Shield); end of the Cold War; German reunification
1991	Persian Gulf War—closing phases (Desert Storm); Soviet Union disbanded; Maastricht Treaty signed
1992	
1993	North American Free Trade Agreement (NAFTA) between Canada, Mexico, and United States ratified
1994	NAFTA takes effect; final GATT agreements ratified by United States, create World Trade Organization (WTO)
1995	WTO takes effect; balanced-budget forces gain support (but not balance) in Congress
1996	U.S. trade deficit reaches $114.2 billion, highest since 1988
1997	
1998	President Clinton proposes first balanced federal budget since 1969, and Western Hemisphere free trade area

Fulfillment of that promise proceeded rapidly. By 1958, the very year the EEC began operations, the United States began facing worries about its balance of payments. In 1960 foreign-held dollar liabilities first exceeded the total U.S. gold supply. Since 1933 the U.S. government had backed its currency by promising to redeem dollars with gold at the fixed rate of $35 per ounce. The dollar was the primary standard of international exchange and confidence in its value was still high, but if that confidence faltered, an all-out run no longer could be met. By the early 1960s the French government under President

Charles de Gaulle demonstrated its lack of confidence in the dollar by demanding sizable settlements in gold. Trade disputes began between the United States and the EEC. In one early case, European tariffs limited the import of U.S. chickens.

U.S. firms increasingly went multinational and established European operations in order to get a toehold inside the Common Market's tariff wall and avoid curtailment of their export markets. The 1962 Trade Expansion Act empowered the president to negotiate lower tariffs, launching the five-year Kennedy round of GATT bargaining, which yielded substantial tariff cuts but did little to improve the U.S. trade balance.

After the mid-1960s, the determination of President Lyndon Johnson's administration to maintain his Great Society program of development and poverty reduction at home simultaneously with the Vietnam War effort fueled rising inflation and put increasing pressure on the trade balance (see Figure 11.3.). For the first time since a one-year 1951 spike driven by the post–World War II boom, consumer price inflation in 1969 exceeded 5 percent.

Observers during the 1970s looked back on a 5 percent inflation rate with nostalgia, but in the 1960s and early 1970s the international economic situation of the United States was perceived as turning serious. By the summer of 1971 President Nixon decided that interlinked domestic and international economic problems were grave enough to justify unilateral actions breaking U.S. policy away from previous global norms. In a series of sensational pronouncements, Nixon decreed a domestic wage and price freeze to help limit inflation, a 10 percent tariff surcharge on all imports, and the floating of gold prices in international exchange. Allies were not consulted. For the first time since 1933, the U.S. government refused to redeem dollars with gold, and the price of gold was allowed to fluctuate in international markets. After being prohibited since 1933, American citizens were again allowed to own gold in forms other than jewelry and old coins. Gold prices rose rapidly, eventually peaking around $800 per ounce before settling into the $200 to $400 range.

Nixon's actions were highly intermestic. Beyond attacking domestic inflation and the foreign trade imbalance simultaneously, they contributed mightily to one of the great American political comebacks. In the spring and summer of 1971, knowledgeable political analysts and pollsters saw any of a half-dozen Democratic contenders as likely to defeat Nixon's 1972 reelection bid. However, Nixon complemented his economic actions with his fall 1971 announcement and February 1972 trip to Beijing and Shanghai, effectively reopening diplomatic relations with the People's Republic. The China opening was followed by his April trip to Moscow to sign the first Strategic Arms Limitation Talks (SALT I) Treaty with the Soviet Union. By the fall elections of 1972, Nixon could claim these major international relations successes, and point to the continuing wind-down of the Vietnam War, which ultimately led to a peace treaty early in 1973. He relaxed wage and price controls a few months before the election, making it possible to claim strong action and some success on the economic front, although only the gold float truly produced lasting change. By mid-1972, the election outlook between Republican Nixon and eventual Democratic presidential nominee Senator George McGovern had been completely reversed from one year earlier. This dramatic change of fortunes makes Nixon's insistence on the Watergate break-in of Democratic Party headquarters, which would eventually lead to his downfall and resignation in disgrace in 1974, highly ironic. It also should remind us how strongly international and domestic politics and economics are now linked. (See also the section on the 1970s in Chapter 2.)

The remaining major IPE development of the early 1970s was the first oil price shock, triggered by the 1973 Yom Kippur War. When war broke out between Israel and Egypt, the United States immediately called for a cease-fire. Within days, however, massive military resupply shipments flowed to Israel to counter Soviet arms shipments to Egypt and Syria. Arab petroleum-exporting states joined in embargoing oil exports to the United States and the Netherlands, arguing they had been too strongly pro-Israeli. This move helped unify the Organization of Petroleum Exporting Countries (OPEC) behind price increases and common pricing, and first brought OPEC to public attention in the United States.

For most of the next year, news media here were filled with stories about gasoline shortages. Many localities imposed alternate-day (odd and even license plate number) gasoline rationing. In 1974 the federal government imposed a uniform national speed limit of 55 miles per hour, not relaxed until 1995; this was intended to reduce fuel consumption by improving vehicle fuel efficiency and (although not admittedly) by discouraging travel through making it take longer. (Because setting speed limits had always been accepted as one of the powers reserved to the states, Washington decreed it would deny federal highway funds to states that did not adopt the new, lower limit.) Additional legislation began setting minimum fuel efficiency standards, a program that has now had considerable effect, more than doubling the fuel efficiency of our national vehicle fleet since the mid-1970s.

Although U.S. public concern may have focused more on gasoline's availability than its price, the domestic crude oil price rapidly followed international markets, doubling from 1973 to 1974 and continuing to climb slowly. A second oil price shock occurred in 1978–79. Crude oil prices climbed tenfold from 1973 to 1981, profoundly affecting economies around the world (see Figures 11.2 and 11.3.) Petroleum is vital both to developed and developing states. It provides energy inputs to transportation, manufacturing, home heating, and electric power generation, along with raw material inputs to chemical manufacturing processes from plastics to pharmaceuticals. Price rises made energy conservation a hot topic, rapidly increased demand for smaller, more fuel-efficient automobiles, and eventually led to building code changes mandating better insulated homes and offices. Such changes drove down prices of older cars and houses and intensified demand for energy-saving products like insulation and timer-controlled heating thermostats. Municipalities thinned out the asphalt coatings used for road repair and began replacing mercury-vapor street lamps with more efficient sodium-vapor bulbs, changing the color of nighttime America. Critics reminded us that U.S. citizens used about twice as much energy per capita as Western Europeans generally considered to enjoy comparable standards of living.

Although energy price rises had profound impacts in developed states like the United States and Western Europe, they affected developing states even more severely. Most developing states must import both energy and manufactured goods, and export primarily agricultural products and raw materials. Most suffer from the *terms of trade problem*, in which their exports suffer cyclical price fluctuations while manufactured imports slowly inflate in price. Oil price jumps benefited the few developing states fortunate enough to be energy exporters (e.g., Mexico and Angola), but most developing states now faced massively increased costs for energy imports, further compounding their development difficulties.

As shown in Figure 11.3, oil prices began a sharp drop in the mid-1980s, down to about half their 1981 peak. This eased the difficulties of energy price rises, but like most such major movements, it had several causes. First, demand declined because of government-mandated energy conservation programs and the adjustments of market economies to the new price structure. Secondly, OPEC exporter states often sold below unified official prices because they wanted higher market shares and faster payoffs from their oil reserves. Finally, some foresighted OPEC states with large oil reserves, most notably Saudi Arabia, deliberately manipulated supply. By pumping more and raising world oil supplies, they sought to drive prices down just enough to discourage major customers—especially the United States—from pursuing energy efficiency strongly enough to decrease long-term oil markets. Although there is a partisan aspect in which Republicans generally support existing oil producers and Democrats are more likely to support conservation measures, both federal support and general public interest in energy conservation and alternative supplies like solar, geothermal, and wind power declined notably after the price spikes of the late 1970s. Auto industry observers find that whenever the real price of gasoline falls, interest in larger vehicles rises. In the 1990s middle-class Americans had made trucks and sport utility vehicles the growth segments of the industry, and conservationist critics noted that gasoline prices were three times higher in Europe and Japan.

Many IPE trends that first drew serious public attention during the 1970s have continued and drastically worsened since. From 1977 through 1980 the Carter administration wrestled with the second oil price shock and with inflation that topped 13 percent in 1980. President Carter lost the election of 1980 in a landslide to Ronald Reagan, who used the campaign question "Are you better off than you were four years ago?" to great effect. Reagan's administration touted supply-side economics that encouraged deregulation (a movement begun during President Carter's term) and federal tax cuts to stimulate business. In theory, benefits to business and the rich would "trickle down" to everyone, and increased tax collections eventually would pay for the tax cuts. Defense spending was increased significantly (another movement begun under President Carter). By many measures, such as soaring stock markets, the Reagan years produced the longest economic boom in U.S. history. Trickle down never worked well, however, and wealth shifted upward to the rich. Businesses from book publishing to television underwent waves of mergers and leveraged buyouts financed by fundamentally worthless "junk bonds," and millions of Americans were downsized out of their jobs as companies strove to become leaner and more competitive. Partly driven by rising entitlement payments like Medicare and Social Security, cumulative federal debt quadrupled in a decade, setting the stage to make balancing the federal budget a major concern in the 1990s and beyond.

The world economy was becoming increasingly global and increasingly competitive, and its penetration of state economies was growing. In 1975 heads of government of the major developed capitalist states began annual summit meetings focused primarily on economic issues. Representatives of France, Great Britain, West Germany, Italy, Japan, and the United States met that year, Canada joined in 1976, and European Community representation began in 1977. In 1986 the conferees agreed to create a Group of Seven (G-7) made up of the participating states' finance ministers to strengthen multilateral surveillance of the world economy. This became the Group of 8 in 1998 when Russia was given permanent but somewhat limited status; see details in the Chapter 14 economic sector focus case on page 553. U.S. participation in these developments reflected limited retreat from the economic unilateralism of the early 1970s, growing recognition of lost economic hegemony, and dawning understanding that global political-economic developments now demanded greater cooperation and policy coordination.

As the 1980s gave way to the 1990s, IPE tilted strongly toward the growth of free trade areas. A U.S.-Canadian free trade agreement took effect in January 1989, designed to lead to the virtual elimination of tariffs between the two states. It was considerably broadened by adding Mexico under the North American Free Trade Agreement (NAFTA), ratified in 1993. The concluding GATT agreements were ratified by the United States in 1994, creating the World Trade Organization (WTO).

ECONOMIC INDICATORS AND
U.S. ECONOMIC ACTIVITY

To develop a more detailed and nuanced understanding of how the interaction of domestic and international economics has come to impact the United States, we turn in this section to analyzing the terminology of international trade accounts and deficits, and examining time trends of a number of important variables and indicators of economic activity.

Washington's Twin Deficits:
The Federal Budget and International Trade

Economists insist that *the balance of payments always balances.* Meanwhile, political pundits of the 1990s decried Washington's twin deficits in the federal budget and international trade. How can we reconcile these statements? The economists are right about the balance, but to make sense of the subject we must understand which of several "balances" is referred to in any particular news report. Several of the most important accounts in the international balance of payments are defined, and their interrelationships are summarized, in Table 11.3.

The *merchandise trade balance* is the amount by which exports exceed imports. *Exports* include all tangible goods produced in the United States and sold abroad, and *imports* are tangible goods produced abroad and sold in the United States. Exports generate credits on our trade balance; imports generate debits. In 1997 U.S. merchandise imports exceeded exports by $198.1 billion, leaving a negative merchandise trade balance. Trade involves much more than merchandise, however. *Services* include intangibles like transport costs for goods, people, and data, along with insurance, banking, and consulting. (Recall symbolic-analytic services, as summarized in Table 11.1.) In 1997 U.S. exports of services exceeded imports of services by $87.7 billion. The *trade balance* includes both merchandise and services. In 1997 the favorable services trade balance helped offset the unfavorable merchandise trade balance, leaving a trade balance of −$110.2 billion, still highly unfavorable. After falling below $31 billion in 1991, the trade deficit began to climb again, exceeding $110 billion in 1997. In 1996 the trade deficit with Japan fell to $47.7 billion, while deficits with all other major trading partners of the United States rose. The 1994 trade deficit with China reached a record $39.5 billion, the highest trade gap the U.S. had

TABLE 11.3

Accounts in the Balance of Payments (1997 U.S. Values, $ Billions)

Account	Description	1997 U.S. Values, $ Billions		
		Credits	Debits	Balance
1. Merchandise				
Exports	Tangible goods produced in United States and sold abroad	679.3		
Imports	Tangible goods produced abroad and sold in the United States		877.3	
Merchandise Trade Balance	(Exports minus imports)			−198.1
2. Services	Intangible items such as transport costs			
Exports	for goods, people, and data; insurance;	258.3		
Imports	banking; consulting; see also Table 11.1.		170.5	
Services Trade Balance	(Exports minus imports)			87.7
Trade Balance	Merchandise and services (1 + 2)	937.6	1,047.8	−110.2
3. Investments				
Income	Investment earnings to citizens from foreigners	241.8		
Payments	Investment earnings paid to foreigners		247.0	
Investment Income Balance				−5.3
4. Government				
Exports	Government sales of goods and services abroad			
Imports	Government purchases from abroad			
Aid	Foreign aid expenses abroad less receipts			−39.7
Government Balance				
5. Balance on Current Account	Sum of 1 through 4; a very frequently used summary measure of U.S. international transactions			−155.2
6. Capital Account	Long- and short-term actual investments			
Exports	of either U.S. resources abroad or		478.5	
Imports	Foreign assets in the United States	733.4		
7. Official Reserves	Federal Reserve holdings of foreign exchange and gold, used in transactions with other central banks and interventions in foreign exchange markets		1.0	
8. Statistical Discrepancy	Sum of statistical adjustments for measurement errors and to balance overall credits and debits			−99.7

Sources: For descriptions, see Lairson and Skidmore, 1993, 15–17. For values, see *Economic Report of the President, February 1999*, 444–7, and the U. S. Bureau of the Census, 1998, 786–7.

ever had with any state other than Japan. By 1998 the U.S. trade deficit with China exceeded that with Japan in some months.

Investment income comprises earnings on investments paid to citizens by foreigners, and *investment payments* are similar earnings paid to foreigners. Once again, the balance is credits (income) minus debits (payments). In 1997 U.S. citizens and firms paid $5.3 billion more to foreigners on their investments than was received from foreigners on the investments of American citizens. Finally, the *government balance* consists of government sales of goods and services abroad, government purchases from abroad, and the net of foreign aid expenses abroad less receipts.

A frequently used summary measure of U.S. international transactions is the *balance on current account*. It is the sum of the merchandise trade balance, services balance, investment income balance, and government balance. For 1997 it was −$155.2 billion. The balance on current account is analogous to the balance between an individual's income and expenses. When we spend more than we earn, we must borrow the difference, whereas, if we earn more than we spend, we can save and invest the difference. The *capital account* records investment exports, which are long- and short-term actual investments of U.S. resources abroad, and imports, which are actual investments of foreign resources in the United States. An amount approximating the deficit on current account must be borrowed in the form of foreign investment. This happens in a multitude of ways, from foreign governments and individuals buying government bonds to Japanese firms buying Rockefeller Center in New York or motion picture studios in Hollywood.

Two additional balances complete the main accounts in the balance of payments. *Official reserves* are holdings of foreign currencies and gold by the Federal Reserve for use in transactions with other central banks and interventions in foreign exchange markets, usually to support the international exchange value of the dollar or the currencies of friendly governments. Finally, the *statistical discrepancy* is the sum of statistical adjustments for measurement errors and to balance overall credits and debits; it often reaches several billion dollars.

You should now be ready to use the terminology of accounts in the balance of payments to better understand the content of news reports that often become far too casual in their treatment of balances. In the next several pages, we use this terminology and plots of key economic indicators since the end of World War II to illustrate how the position of the United States in international political economics has evolved and contemporary difficulties have developed, especially since the mid-1970s.

Budget Deficits and Cumulative Federal Debt

Figure 11.1 shows the movements of the merchandise trade balance, balance on current account, annual federal budget deficit, and cumulative federal debt since 1945. It is immediately obvious that those movements have been far greater since the early 1970s than ever before. The U.S. merchandise trade balance was modestly positive—up to $10.12 billion in 1947—every year from World War II through 1970. It has been negative every year since then except 1973 and 1975, and reached −$197.95 in 1997. The balance on current account has followed a similar, although usually somewhat less negative, path. The annual federal deficit ran around half the budget during World War II, ending at −$47.6 billion in 1945 and −$15.9 in 1946. Thereafter, the federal budget ran small surpluses or deficits of less than $13 billion until 1968. There were no surpluses, however, after 1969 until

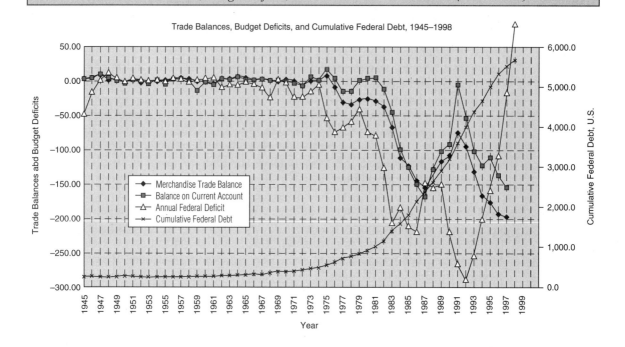

1998. In the mid-1970s the budget deficit grew significantly, reaching $68.4 billion in 1977, crossing $100 billion in 1982 and $200 billion in 1983, and peaking at $290.4 billion in 1992. Through much of the 1980s, the budget deficit tracked the merchandise trade balance but exceeded it by around $100 billion. In 1987–89, the deficit dropped slightly and trade balances rebounded dramatically, although the deficit nearly doubled from 1989 to 1991, and trade balances deteriorated in the early 1990s.

Large budget deficits year after year have increased the cumulative federal debt phenomenally since World War II, and higher interest rates since the inflation-prone 1970s have exacerbated the effect by increasing the cost of refinancing existing bonded debt. The gross federal debt of the United States in 1945 was $260.1 billion, and for decades it grew only slowly. It passed $300 billion in 1962, and $400 billion in 1971. From 1970 to 1990, debt growth approximated an exponential curve in which the rate of increase itself constantly increased. Federal debt passed $500 billion in 1975, $600 billion in 1976, $700 billion in 1977. It exceeded $1 trillion in 1982, $2 trillion in 1986, $3 trillion in 1990, $4 trillion in 1992, and $5 trillion in 1996. During the Reagan and Bush presidencies (1981–93) it more than quadrupled. In 1995 interest on the public debt ($332.4 billion) was exceeded in federal budget share only by Social Security payments ($362.2 billion) and ranked ahead of Health and Human Services ($303.1 billion) and Defense Department ($259.6 billion) expenditures.

By the time President Clinton took office in 1993, public and congressional opinion had begun to coalesce around moving to balance the federal budget. This huge task could not be accomplished overnight or without pain. President and Congress eventually settled on achieving a balanced budget by 2002. A booming economy actually helped the United States achieve a balanced federal budget in 1998 by raising federal revenues. Balancing the budget, however, only stops the growth of debt. Note in Figure 11.1 that the rate of rise in cumulative debt decreases slightly after 1992 and more after 1996. After 1993 the struggle to balance the budget led to real cuts in many government programs and placed exceedingly tight constraints on President Clinton's desires to launch new undertakings like the AmeriCorps service program and college student aid.

Many analysts, especially those of conservative political persuasions, lay much blame for the federal budget deficit on programs like Social Security and Medicare, called *entitlements* because recipients are legally entitled to payments by virtue of *being* retired, sick, or disabled. As health care improved dramatically throughout the twentieth century, costs and life expectancies rose apace. Today's U.S. population has much higher fractions of elderly and retired citizens than two or three generations ago, and the fastest growing population segment is people over eighty-five. Under the broad conceptions of state power considered in Chapter 8, healthy and long-lived citizens are desirable. However, they also are expensive. By the election of 1996, a bipartisan near-consensus had formed around the notion that entitlements would have to be "reformed" (casuistry for "reduced") to keep the system solvent beyond the early twenty-first century, particularly as the post–World II baby boomers began retiring en masse. Politically, cutting entitlements is even more difficult than cutting defense spending, which was substantially reduced in real, after-inflation terms in the early 1990s.

Trade Deficits: The Effect of Oil Prices

Consider now the second of the twin deficits, international trade. As we already noted, the United States has suffered seriously negative merchandise trade balances since 1975. Rising petroleum prices are not enough to explain this, although they did have serious impacts. Consider the time trends of crude oil prices and the merchandise trade balance shown in Figure 11.2. The first oil price shock of 1973–74 was followed by merchandise trade deficits beginning in 1976. The second and much larger oil price shock of 1979–81 was followed by large merchandise trade deficit increases only after 1982, by which time oil prices had begun to drop. Only between 1988 and 1993 does the merchandise trade deficit seem to correlate closely with crude oil price movements. The overall inflation rate, however, does follow oil prices moderately closely after 1973; see Figure 11.3.

A better understanding of the impact of oil prices can be gained by examining U.S. petroleum production and imports (see Figure 11.4). Total petroleum usage rose steadily until 1973 when the first oil price shock produced a sharp break. Growth then resumed until it peaked in 1978, at the time of the second price shock. In the meantime, domestic production topped out at 11.3 million barrels per day in 1970 and began to decline thereafter. The difference could only be made up by oil imports, which rose rapidly after 1970. Sharp drops in total use after the two price shocks came at the expense of imports, and domestic output remained quite stable near 10 million barrels per day until 1987. Declines in domestic output after 1985 reflect both the gradual depletion of domestic petroleum reserves and the fact that extracting the remaining domestic oil became less economically feasible as prices dropped. Once again, gaps between domestic production and total use had to be filled by imports. The most interesting aspect of Figure 11.4,

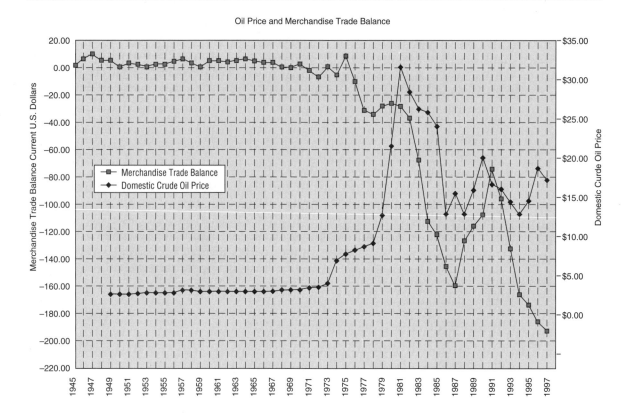

however, is that by 1987 total U.S. petroleum usage had stabilized around 17 million barrels per day. Although it is easy to argue that much more energy could be conserved, stabilization of petroleum consumption reflects the impact of more than fourteen years of government policy adjustments and individual and industrial microeconomic adjustments. As in many other cases, policy change has been incremental, somewhat time consuming, not necessarily optimally efficient, but eventually at least moderately effective.

Policies affecting oil imports and energy conservation are extremely intermestic, involving a host of actors at home and abroad. Domestically, those policies involve decisions by government, industry, and individuals. Consider a sampling. Federal government moves since 1973 have included cutting speed limits, offering insulation tax credits, and beginning a strategic petroleum reserve, although all these policies were later modified or canceled. Many industrial firms have developed more energy-efficient production techniques and adopted the same sorts of insulation and heating practices used by homeowners faced with rising utility bills. Local governments, sometimes with federal and state financial help, have sponsored rebate programs to encourage replacement of water heaters with newer, better insulated models. Individual citizens have adopted strategies that include buying more fuel-efficient autos, improving home insulation, and turning

FIGURE 11.3

Domestic Crude Oil Price and Overall Inflation Rate (1945–1998)

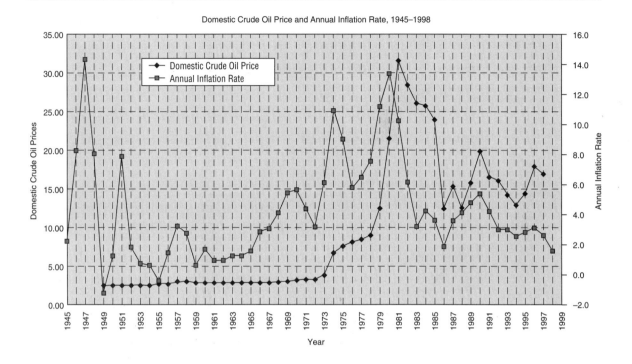

Domestic Crude Oil Price and Annual Inflation Rate, 1945–1998

down furnace and water heater thermostats. Internationally, government has jawboned petroleum-exporting states to encourage price moderation, floated numerous trial balloons about going to war to protect access to oil supplies, and at least in the case of the Persian Gulf War, carried out the threat. Despite the vital need for petroleum in any modern industrial economy, however, oil price increases are cannot fully explain Washington's twin deficits.

Trade Deficits: A Nation of Consumers

Considered in light of the decline debate we discussed earlier, the merchandise trade balance plotted in Figure 11.1 has turned negative primarily because over the last generation the United States has become a nation of consumers and has lost its competitive producing edge in many important industries. We already have seen instance after instance. Televisions no longer are produced in the United States; nor are VCRs or 35 millimeter cameras, yet more American households own such devices than ever before. Foreign automobiles that were rarities in 1945 form an absolute majority of new cars in the western United States today. Undeniably, business decisions such as U.S. airlines buying planes from Airbus Industries rather than from domestic producers like Boeing hurt our merchandise trade balance. Yet the negative shift in that balance arises primarily from the cumulation of millions of individual decisions to buy that new imported camera or VCR or automobile, compounded by the inability or unwillingness of domestic

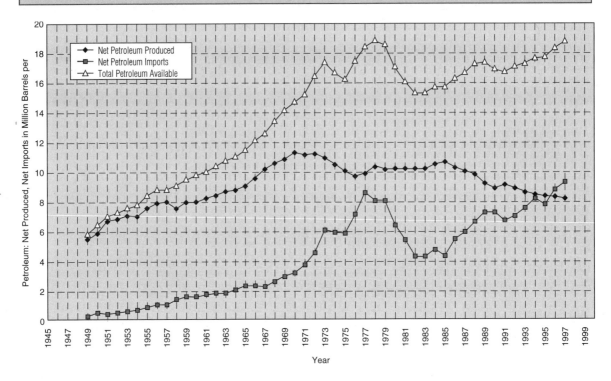

FIGURE 11.4

Petroleum: Net Produced, Net Imports, and Total Available (1945–1997)

producers to engineer and produce sufficiently competitive products to win those sales. Finally, sales losses to foreign producers are compounded when domestic firms export jobs into the global economic web as they strive to compete in a world of firms using similar tactics.

The post-1970 consumerist wave has profound effects. Many American consumers today enjoy unprecedented levels of affluence, with larger homes and more possessions than any previous generation. This may be wonderful for those so blessed, but not all citizens partake of this plenty because inequality in wealth has increased. The remaining effects of this consumerism, including aspects of IPE involving the country as a whole, are uniformly bad. Consumer affluence and acquisitiveness have been fueled by great increases in consumer debt and by reductions in individual savings, which increase competition for investment funds in an already busy capital market. Continued over decades, such trends strongly promote national decline.

Because the balance of payment always balances, the merchandise trade deficit must be financed, just as the federal budget deficit must be financed by issuing federal bonds to investors at home and abroad. Foreign loans and other investments appear as imports in the capital account and help offset the current account deficit. Growth of government-bonded indebtedness and consumer debt in the form of credit card balances and bank loans has been accompanied by another sort of borrowing: the sale to foreign investors of

JAMES MICHENER ON CONSUMERISM AND DECLINE

In a 1996 book the prolific author James Michener used terms strongly reminiscent of Paul Kennedy to compare the potential fate of consumerist America to the decline of Spain after its discovery of gold in the New World. Sixteenth-century Spain ruled the Iberian Peninsula and much of central Europe, including Austria and the Netherlands. Its naval power was rivaled only by Britain and Portugal. In Michener's view (1996, 81–83), the discovery of gold in its Mexican and Peruvian colonies contributed strongly to Spain's decline from first- to third-rate power within one century. Gold shipments from the Americas flooded Spain's economy with unearned wealth. Prices of basic necessities soared. Spaniards now bought goods rather than make them, and the trades and industries that had made their country great fell into disuse. Much of the new wealth was consumed in foreign wars. In contrast, England and France experienced no gold bonanza, and underwent slower, more orderly, sustained economic and productive growth. In Michener's analysis (1996, 83),

> The gold and silver mines that we have discovered are the factories of Japan, Korea, Taiwan, Hong Kong, Singapore, and Mexico. They make the consumer goods our once famous factories no longer bother with. Like sixteenth-century Spain, we buy the goods we want from abroad and allow our bold peasantry to languish without jobs. We are able to purchase so much from abroad because our tax system has constantly enriched our upper classes so that they can afford the foreign goods.

assets ranging from land to skyscrapers to collector automobiles built in Detroit's 1960s heyday. Pessimists see this as the selling of America, including natural resources like land and accumulated synthetic assets built up through centuries of high industrial productivity. Like deficit spending, resource sell-offs cannot be sustained indefinitely. Additionally, government debt and increased domestic debt both stimulate higher interest rates. Government bonds mature and must be refinanced in periods ranging from a few months to a decade. This requires keeping rates high enough to attract new buyers and prevent the needed funds from flowing to other markets in, say, Europe or Asia. High interest rates make new investments in improved productivity more difficult and tend to push inflation up and employment down. To a degree unimaginable in the late 1940s, U.S. money managers today, both government and private, must calculate their actions in a global market.

The movements of the prime interest rate charged by U.S. banks, average unemployment rate, annual inflation rate in the consumer price index, and annual federal deficit for 1945 to 1996 are plotted in Figure 11.5. Like the other economic indicators examined in earlier figures, these show much larger movements since 1970. The only notable exceptions to this rule are the inflation spikes of 1947 and 1951. Like the unemployment peak accompanying the 1949–50 recession, these reflect postwar adjustments to a new world order and surging consumer demand after wartime restrictions were lifted and soldiers returned home. Over the following two decades we can see indications of the continuing and relatively unsuccessful struggle to find a policy combination that would keep both

FIGURE 11.5

Prime Interest Rate, Average Unemployment, Annual Inflation Rate, and Annual Federal Deficit (1945–1998)

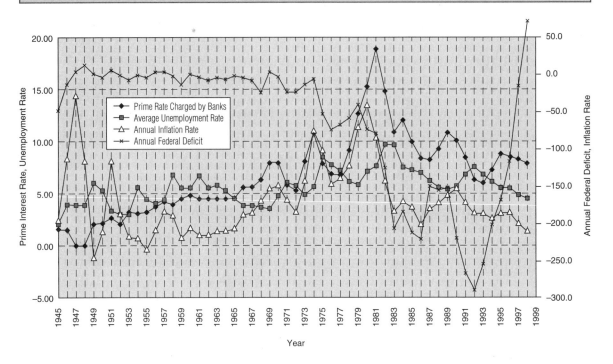

inflation and unemployment low simultaneously. From 1972 on, note how most movements of inflation and prime interest rates occur together. Both spiked upward after the two oil price shocks. The prime rate, which banks charge their preferred business customers, peaked just below 19 percent in 1981. This meant comparable rates on secured loans for items like automobiles and home mortgages, and credit card rates that approached 30 percent. Although ordinary citizens who had money to invest could earn 16 percent in money market funds, auto loans tended to grow longer and home sales virtually collapsed. In the recession of the early 1980s, overall unemployment nearly reached 10 percent in 1982 and 1983, and double to triple that rate among African Americans. The 1990s saw generally improving economic indicators except for soaring federal budget deficits. After 1990 the prime rate fell below 10 percent, annual inflation rates stayed below 5 percent, reaching 1.6 percent in 1998. Unemployment dropped to 4.5 percent in 1998 after peaking at 7.4 percent in 1992. These improved trends continued throughout the 1990s, despite foreign markets that suffered stagnation and exchange-rate crises.

It now should be obvious that the management of modern economies is difficult, complex, highly intermestic, and extremely interactive internationally. Full employment tends to drive prices up as producers operate at or near capacity, so that managing unemployment involves tradeoffs with inflation. Expanding the money supply tends to drive down interest rates, which makes it more difficult to carry out the continuously required refinancing of federal (and other) debt. Lower interest rates at home may discourage increasingly needed foreign investment, and encourage our citizens to invest abroad. Lower interest rates also may encourage citizens to buy more, which well may include more imports that worsen our merchandise trade balance. Supporting a high value for the dollar in foreign exchange markets makes U.S. exports more costly and also encourages imports. But allowing the dollar to weaken may undermine foreign confidence in U.S. economic leadership. The smarter leaders of major oil exporting states, such as Saudi Arabia, consciously keep petroleum prices just low enough to discourage major energy conservation moves by the U.S. government and American industries. These situations are far removed from the characteristics of the American and international economic environments of the late 1940s and 1950s. Just as producers today are caught up in Reich's worldwide economic web, each of us is unavoidably involved in the global economy.

ECONOMIC TIERS: THE UNITED STATES, THE DEVELOPED WORLD, AND THE DEVELOPING WORLD

How do we classify the United States and other states in the global economy? The end of the Cold War has outdated the terminology still widely used. For decades it was common to speak of the First, Second, and Third Worlds. The **First World** consisted of developed states with market (capitalist) economies. Today's best examples are the G-7 states, but the First World certainly includes the United States, Canada, Western Europe, Scandinavia, Japan, Australia, and New Zealand. The **Second World** comprised developed states with command economies, and generally was considered to include the Soviet Union and Eastern Europe, particularly East Germany, Poland, Czechoslovakia, and Hungary, the most developed Soviet satellite states. A **command economy** is one in which central planners dictate what is to be produced, in what quantities, where, by whom, and how it is to be distributed.

The **Third World** was everybody else except the First and Second Worlds, lumped into the largely undefined category "developing states." More honestly if less politically acceptably, in the 1950s these were termed the *less developed countries*, or *LDCs*. Like Third World, however, that term obscures their enormous diversity. These states have many different types of economies, from pure market to (rarely, today) pure command and every degree of mix in between. They vary enormously in state and per capita income, patterns of wealth distribution, degrees of development, and future prospects.

Since the oil price boom, the highest per capita incomes usually have been in one or another of the Persian Gulf states, such as Kuwait or Qatar. Even when rulers absorb enormous fractions of state wealth, ordinary citizens may enjoy substantial largesse. In Saudi Arabia, for example, foreigners can be hired for most labor, and citizens have come to expect levels of benefits that rulers curtail only at the risk of social upheavals.

At the other end of the economic scale, substantial numbers of people in states like India are born, live out their lives, and die in the streets without ever enjoying proper housing. Third World states have diverse political histories, from long independence in Thailand and Liberia to the much more common experience of having been colonies of European powers until the 1960s or even later. Many of these states suffer from intense cultural divisions between modernists and traditionalists. Many also suffer extreme ethnic divisions between their nations and states, a problem exacerbated where former colonial powers split nations by drawing arbitrary state boundaries for their own convenience.

Some authors also distinguished a **Fourth World** subgroup of states with very limited development and even poorer future prospects. Sometimes termed the *least developed states*, they lie primarily in a band across equatorial Africa, which saw mass starvation in the 1980s. Also included in the Fourth World are some of the more physically isolated states of southern Asia, such as Afghanistan, Bangladesh, Laos, and Nepal.

Although the term *Third World* is still widely used, the old terminology suffers from three major problems. Most important is the disappearance of the Second World, which self-destructed because command economies failed. Shortly after the Soviet Union allowed the Eastern European states to overthrow their old communist regimes, its own fifteen constituent republics became sovereign states. In varying degrees, they adopted democratic governments and market economies. China, greatest of the few remaining communist states, adopted most of the features of market economics and by the 1990s enjoyed real GNP growth of 10 or more percent annually. Secondly, the old terminology offers no adequate classification for the most rapidly developing states, commonly called the newly industrializing countries, or NICs. Notable examples include Singapore, South Korea, and Taiwan, which have enjoyed rapid and sustained growth in recent decades. These states grew wealthy through manufacturing based on cast iron and steel technologies since the 1950s, and now are well advanced in electronics. Although their per capita incomes and living standards are not yet at First World levels, that cannot be many decades away. Finally, the old terminology fails to account for the enormous differences among Third World states.

The simplest alternative to the old terminology is to classify states as either First Tier or Second Tier. On the assumption that almost all economies today are either fully market or of mixed character with some strong market elements, classification focuses simply on level of development. **First Tier** states are highly developed, members of the former First World. The **Second Tier** comprises all developing states, although this elides the questions of degree and speed of development, and how to classify the NICs and other rapidly developing states such as Brazil. Arguably, the least developed states, which have received special consideration from some international lenders, could be designated as Third Tier. The old and new terminologies are summarized in Table 11.4. If economics is now the most important arena of foreign policy, then the two-tier system *is* the post-Cold War new world order.

Levels of development are used as an organizing framework for examining present and likely future U.S. foreign policy problems in Part IV (Chapters 13 through 16). Very broadly, those problems might be summarized as (1) meeting the problems posed by the global economy so as to remain a First Tier state through the twenty-first century, while (2) promoting peace, democracy, human rights, and market economy development in Second Tier states. Some major characteristics of First Tier states or communities strong enough to be considered economic superpowers are summarized in Table 11.5.

POLICY TOOLS FOR MANAGING INTERNATIONAL POLITICAL ECONOMICS

International political economy encompasses both a major set of policy concerns and a set of policy tools for dealing with them. As noted earlier, the management of modern economies is difficult, complex, highly intermestic, and extremely interactive internation-

TABLE 11.4	
Economic Tiers: Old and New Terms for Major Levels of Economic Development	

Old Terminology	New Terminology
First World Developed, market economy states; mainly U.S. and major allies	**First Tier** Developed states, almost all with market economies; G-7 and others
Second World Developed, command economy states; mainly Soviet Union and Eastern Europe	
Third World Developing states, with many types of economies	**Second Tier** Developing states, increasingly with market economies, but still with many mixed economies
Fourth World Least developed (and most disadvantaged) states; not a universally recognized term.	

ally. IPE affects nation-state power and security as deeply and as pervasively as do more traditional military matters, and is perhaps the ultimate set of intermestic issues. For example, as we have seen, setting U.S. federal standards for automobile fuel economy is more a foreign policy than a domestic policy move.

Many political economy policy tools available to U.S. administrations already have been mentioned. Domestic actions, many of which interact and some of which have strong international impacts, include the following:

- Management of the money supply available for investment through manipulation of bank *reserve requirements* (regulating what percentage of loans must be backed by readily available reserved "liquid" assets).

- Regulation of credit availability through putting pressure on interest rates by changing the *discount rate* at which the Federal Reserve loans to member banks. If the Federal Reserve raises the rate, banks must charge more for loans, and less money will be borrowed.

- Management (however imperfect) of the interrelated rates of inflation and unemployment, particularly through monetary policies and job creation and training programs.

- Manipulation of tax rules and incentives to encourage desired behaviors, for example, capital gains tax reductions and investment tax credits targeted to encourage more investments that promote building productive capacity.

- Regulations reducing energy usage and, thus, oil imports, ranging from vehicle fuel efficiency standards to speed limits to promotion of effective mass transit systems to building code changes that encourage better insulation.

TABLE 11.5			
Comparative Properties of First-Tier Economic Superpowers (1997)			
State or Group	Gross Domestic Product in trillions	Population in millions	Gross Domestic Product per Capita in dollars
United States	$7.17	268.0	$24,896
Japan	2.68*	125.7	21,321
European Union	6.58*	375.2	17,542

*1995 estimates

Source: Compiled from World Almanac, 1998.

Many of these tools are utilized by state and local governments, as well as at the federal level. Building codes, for example, commonly are enacted and enforced by cities, counties, and states. Yet the federal government can influence building codes significantly by such mechanisms as setting minimum standards for homes to be financed by the Federal Housing Administration.

Like domestic actions, IPE policy tools available to the United States internationally are numerous and diverse. They include the following:

- *Loans, grants,* and other forms of *aid* to support allies, cement regional peace agreements, and promote democracy, market economies, human rights, and other policy goals abroad.
- Coordinated international *buying and selling of currencies* to support and stabilize the exchange value of the dollar and the currencies of friendly states.
- Actions to reduce tariffs and settle trade disputes through intergovernmental organizations like the WTO.
- *Regional free trade agreements,* such as NAFTA.
- *Nontariff barriers* to trade, such as the elaborate Japanese import inspection rules and agricultural import specifications so strongly decried by the United States.
- *Boycotts,* or refusals to deal in certain goods or with certain states.
- *Embargoes,* or refusals to trade with certain states, accompanied by pressures on others to comply.

As we saw in the brief discussion of automobile import tariffs in Chapter 1, tariffs usually raise consumer prices and government revenues and generate higher profits for protected domestic producers. Tariffs are the most important form of **protectionism,** policies designed to protect domestic producers from foreign competition. Tariffs tend to reduce domestic producers' incentives to lower production costs and create innovative product improvements. During the 1990s considerable attention was focused on nontariff barriers to trade, which have similar effects. The Clinton administration pressured Japan about such barriers in market segments like cellular telephones and automobile service parts, with some success.

INTERMESTIC POLITICS AT WORK
The Case of Gasohol

Political economics always involves both economics and politics, and politics long has been termed the authoritative allocation of value. Thus it often is instructive to follow the money to see who benefits. Consider the case of fuel conservation. Most gasoline-fueled vehicles can run fairly successfully on gasohol, a mix of gasoline with up to 10 percent ethanol, an alcohol commonly distilled from corn. For some years the federal government subsidized gasohol production, on the grounds that it replaced some oil imports with readily available domestic agricultural produce. However, accounting for total energy usage in production and consumption, gasohol is less efficient than refining petroleum into gasoline. It well might be argued that the gasohol program had political value abroad as a message to oil producers. However, it was continued primarily because it yielded substantial income to midwestern farmers and agribusiness combines, and thus was strongly supported by their Congress members. Producers benefited and consumers paid more both in taxes and at the gasohol pump. Once again, we find political economics that is strongly intermestic and affects various domestic actors quite differently.

The United States occasionally has employed unilateral trade restrictions such as import surcharges and trade embargoes like the one imposed against Cuba for decades after 1960. International commitments like those to the WTO increasingly restrict such unilateral moves. Under the Helms-Burton act of 1996, U.S. citizens were given authority to sue in U.S. courts any foreign firms doing business with Cuba if that business involved assets seized by the Cubans from those American citizens without compensation. Many such seizures and nationalizations occurred in the early 1960s. Although President Clinton delayed implementation of the most controversial portion of the act, numerous foreign governments, including major U.S. allies like Britain and Canada, termed this a *secondary boycott* in restraint of trade, began passing countering legislation, and threatened actions through the WTO.

Only certain IPE policy tools span between tiers. Currency exchange actions, for example, most often involve First Tier states. U.S.-led action to support the value of the Mexican peso in 1995 is one recent exception notable both for its size and its effectiveness. Foreign aid of all types, in contrast, results almost exclusively from First Tier-to-Second Tier efforts. In order to understand more fully how IPE policy tools operate, the remainder of this section discusses additional aspects of international economics, particularly theories and problems of global trade and how they interact with the U.S. economy.

DIFFICULTIES IN MANAGING MARKETS: MULTINATIONAL CORPORATIONS AND CARTELS

Many authorities see multinational corporations (MNCs), which underwent rapid growth during the fifteen-year period from 1958 to 1973, as a new type of international actor more powerful than the governments of most states. Indeed, many Second Tier governments would be thrilled to enjoy GNPs equaling the annual sales of a corporation such

NONTARIFF BARRIERS TO TRADE: AMERICAN APPLES REACH TOKYO

An illustrative example of nontariff barriers is provided by a large Washington State farm that succeeded in exporting apples to Japan in the 1990s. On-site visits from Japanese inspectors were required at numerous stages of apple growth and preparation for shipment. Chemical pesticide use was strictly regulated. A quarter-mile-wide pest-free barrier zone was required around the orchards. Yet despite requirements far more stringent than those imposed by the U.S. Department of Agriculture for domestic consumption and export, the farmers were able to grow the apples, ship them across the Pacific, have them accepted by Japanese customs officials, and make a profit. The apples sold out almost immediately, at prices half those of Japanese-grown competitors, because Japanese consumers long have paid the price for policies strongly protecting domestic agriculture against import competition.

as General Motors or a major oil company. The MNC boom, particularly in European investments by firms headquartered in the United States, was encouraged by freer currency convertibility and fears that future EEC tariff walls would limit external trade. Most *direct foreign investment* (DFI) during the MNC boom was American. By the early 1970s the book value of U.S. investments abroad was $86 billion, and U.S. firms produced $172 billion worth of goods abroad, compared with only $43.5 billion produced at home for export (Gilpin, 1975, 15).

This distribution presaged the strong offshore job shift seen in the 1990s, although the reasons were somewhat different. The MNC boom also benefited from the last years of U.S. global economic hegemony and the attendant strength of the dollar as the dominant international currency. By the 1990s American concern had shifted to the growing role of foreign-headquartered MNCs absorbing once great firms in the United States. As one example, British Petroleum bought Mobil Oil in the mid-1990s and continued its business under the somewhat casuistic name BP.

Many of the same analysts who study the growth and influence of MNCs decry their tremendous power relative to governments. It seems intuitively obvious that a Second Tier state may be disadvantaged compared to an MNC that provides badly needed jobs and can do much to set the global price of exports from its one- or two-product economy. Some authorities see MNCs as a form of neo-imperialism, which dominates and retards the economic development of weaker states, creating new dependencies by using unfair trading practices and exploiting the weakness of controls over international business corporations. The intuitively obvious is not invariably true, however. States with coveted resources may enjoy considerable leverage over MNCs. When Marxist rebels gained control of the former Portuguese colony of Angola on the oil-rich portion of the West Africa coast in 1976, Gulf Oil Corporation officials were delighted to continue pumping oil and paying royalties to the new government despite a civil war that continued for years. Petroleum, of course, is a special case because it is highly concentrated in select areas and vital to most economies, especially the most developed ones. We should not be surprised that petroleum is the one product for which exporters have been able to manage a fairly effective **cartel,** or international organization fixing prices and allocating export quantities.

Successful commodity producer cartels are aided by several conditions, including the following:

- *Price inelasticity of demand* means that consumers and their governments will not or cannot reduce purchases much in response to price increases.
- Coordinating action is easier and the dropout problem is reduced if there are few producers.
- Shared values and experiences also may make coordination easier between producer governments.
- Consumer resistance to price increases may be reduced by small purchases, indifference, and even sympathy with the producers.
- Intermediaries may buffer between producers and consumers, smoothing out short-term price fluctuations and slowing the impact of large increases.
- Finally, cartels are strengthened if they can absorb short-term losses in hope of long-term gains.

Even OPEC, the most successful twentieth-century cartel, cannot meet all these conditions. Headquartered in Vienna, the Organization of Petroleum Exporting Countries was created in September 1960. It attempts to set world oil prices by controlling production, as well as advancing its members' interests in trade and development dealings with First Tier oil-consuming states. By the mid-1990s OPEC consisted of Algeria, Gabon, Indonesia, Iran, Iraq, Kuwait, Libya, Nigeria, Qatar, Saudi Arabia, the United Arab Emirates, and Venezuela. These dozen states, six of which border the Persian Gulf, include most of the world's major oil exporters. Some significant oil producers export relatively little. Britain, for example, benefited from the development of large North Sea oil fields in the 1970s, but exports little. Iraqi oil exports were fully embargoed from 1990 until late in 1996, when the UN finally allowed limited sales for humanitarian needs.

Oil demand has proved to be fairly inelastic with price, although sufficiently rapid increases somewhat depress demand. Consumer resistance to price increases seems not to have been high. Intermediaries, notably the firms that purchase crude oil and refine it into gasoline, heating oil, lubricants, and other products which they distribute to retailers, serve to buffer cost fluctuations and often delay price increases. Despite these favorable conditions, however, OPEC has had only limited success in maintaining uniformly high prices. States with the largest petroleum reserves can afford to pursue long-term policies like those of Saudi Arabia, pumping enough oil to hold world market prices below levels that would exceed the limits of price inelasticity and trigger stringent energy conservation programs, particularly in the United States. Other member states with smaller reserves often seek higher prices and volumes to generate capital as rapidly as possible, seeking some mix of filling the rulers' coffers and promoting rapid industrialization and development to sustain them after the oil is exhausted. Examples include Iraq before the Persian Gulf War and Iran before the 1979 revolution.

CAMERAS AND RICE: TWO STUDIES IN COMPARATIVE ADVANTAGE

States engage in international trade because their productive capabilities differ, due to complex combinations of developed design and manufacturing skills and technologies, natural resource endowments, economic and political history, and a host of other reasons. The theory of **comparative advantage** asserts that states should export those goods they produce most efficiently and import goods which they produce less efficiently. Indeed, in a two-party trade, both can benefit even if one is absolutely less efficient in producing all the types of goods traded. This is a powerful theory that implies that everyone can live better by engaging in international trade. (However, it does not explain why states commonly import and export goods of the same type.)

Consider comparative advantage in the simplest possible situation, two states and two products. We first examine a hypothetical trading situation between Japanese cameras and U.S. rice. From humble beginnings copying European and American designs during early post–World War II reconstruction, Japanese firms (most notably Canon and Nikon) went on to become world leaders in camera design, technology innovation, and manufacture. By the 1980s they had driven almost every European and U.S. competitor out of business by building the best products and selling them at reasonable prices. Japan enjoyed so much comparative advantage that it had become the primary source of cameras, and photographers the world around had very few alternative sources.

During the same time frame, the United States had built on its industrial strength and huge resources of arable land in temperate climes to become the world's most efficient agricultural producer. By the time the Soviet Union began importing huge quantities of grain and sending annual delegations of farmers to study American agricultural methods, the fraction of farmers necessary to feed the United States had shrunk to only a few percent of the population.

This situation is ripe for international trade because each party is so efficient that it has an absolute advantage in producing a good which the other probably wants. For purposes of illustration we relax Japanese dominance in camera manufacture a bit, to create a situation in which each state produces both cameras and rice (see Table 11.6).

There is no trade in the first case. In one year, a single worker in Japan produces 250 cameras or 150 tons of rice, and a single worker in the United States produces 100 cameras or 300 tons of rice. Thus, assuming no differences between comparable products from one or the other state, Japan has an absolute efficiency advantage in building cameras and the United States has an absolute advantage in producing rice. If 100 workers are employed in each industry in both countries, Japan produces 25,000 cameras and 15,000 tons of rice annually, compared with 10,000 cameras and 30,000 tons of rice produced annually in the United States. The productivity ratio of cameras to tons of rice is 5:3 in Japan and 1:3 in America. Total annual production in this two-state "world" is 35,000 cameras and 45,000 tons of rice.

In the second case in Table 11.6, decision makers in the two countries specialize in producing their advantaged good. Each year 200 Japanese workers build 50,000 cameras and 200 American workers produce 60,000 tons of rice. Annual output in the two-state world rises by 15,000 cameras and 15,000 tons of rice. Those increases suggest the possibility of trading Japanese cameras for U.S. rice, leaving consumers on both sides better off.

TABLE 11.6	
Cameras and Rice: A First Study in Comparative Advantage	

Situation 1: Each state has absolute advantage in making one product

	Case 1: No trade					Case 2: Total product specialization		
			Productivity					
State and Product	**Output per Worker-Year**	**Number of Workers**	**Annual Output**	**Ratio, C:R**		**Number of Workers**	**Annual Output**	**Gains of Specialization**
Japanese cameras	250 units	100	25,000	Japan:		200	50,000	
Japanese rice	150 tons	100	15,000	5:3				
U.S. cameras	100 units	100	10,000	USA				
U.S. rice	300 tons	100	30,000	1:3		200	60,000	
Total camera production			35,000				50,000	15,000
Total rice production			45,000				60,000	15,000

Case 3: One possible trade at the ratio of availability (5 cameras per 6 tons of rice)

	Output per Worker-Year	**Number of Workers**	**Annual Output**	**Less Exports**	**Plus Imports**	**Net Supply**	**Before Trade**	**Gains of Trade**
Japanese cameras	250 units	150	37,500	10,000		27,500	25,000	+10%
Japanese rice	150 tons	50	7,500		12,000	19,500	15,000	+30%
U.S. cameras	100 units	50	5,000		10,000	15,000	10,000	+50%
U.S. rice	300 tons	150	45,000	12,000		33,000	30,000	+10%
Total camera production			42,500			42,500	35,000	+10%
Total rice production			52,500			52,500	45,000	+10%

The third case in Table 11.6 details one of a potentially infinite number of possible trades. Any such case is based on two decisions: how much is produced and how much is traded. For simplicity, we eliminate currency exchange questions by assuming simple barter exchange of goods. The amounts produced are determined by assigning workers at rates intermediate between those of the no trade and total specialization cases. In Japan, 150 workers build 37,500 cameras and 50 workers produce 7,500 tons of rice annually. In the United States, 50 workers build 5,000 cameras and 150 workers grow 45,000 tons of rice each year. Total production of each good is 10 percent higher than without trade, but lower than under total specialization. Assume the two states trade at the *ratio of availability* of goods that would be produced under total specialization, 5 cameras per 6 tons of rice. The 10,000 Japanese cameras buy 12,000 tons of U.S. rice. Comparing net supply (annual output minus exports plus imports), each state has more cameras and more rice (with increases ranging from 10 percent to 50 percent) than without trade. Consumers on both sides are better off. Different decisions about production, amounts traded, and price would result in different rates of gains of trade.

Now consider comparative advantage in the more difficult and less obvious situation when one state has absolute advantage in making both products, as detailed in Table 11.7.

Again, we examine a hypothetical trade situation involving cameras and rice, and work through the same three cases as in Table 11.6. Here, however, we consider Japan and Vietnam as producers and consumers. With the same worker productivity for Japan as in Table 11.6, assume a Vietnamese worker could produce one fifth as many cameras or half as much rice annually as a corresponding Japanese worker. The productivity ratio of cameras to tons of rice is still 5:3 in Japan and is 2:3 in Vietnam. Total annual production in this two-state "world" is 30,000 cameras and 22,500 tons of rice.

In the second case in Table 11.7, decision makers in the two countries decree specialization in producing the goods at which they are most efficient. Two hundred Japanese workers build 50,000 cameras, and two hundred Vietnamese workers produce 15,000 tons of rice. Annual camera output in the two-state world rises by 20,000, but rice production falls by 7,500 tons. Still, it remains possible for both sides to benefit from trade, although the range of possibilities is narrower than in Table 11.6, and the gains of trade will be smaller.

Case 3 in Table 11.7 involves one possibility, trading at a rate between the two states' productivity ratios, 3.9 cameras per 3 tons of rice. Japanese producers use 130 workers to build 32,500 cameras per year and 70 workers to grow 10,500 tons of rice. Vietnam assigns 20 workers to build 1,000 cameras and 180 workers to grow 13,500 tons of rice. Japan then purchases 5,000 tons of Vietnamese rice with 6,500 cameras. Comparing net supply (annual output minus exports plus imports), each state has more cameras and more rice than without trade, and consumers on both sides are better off. Different decisions about production, amounts traded, and price would result in different rates of gains of trade. Gains are much more modest than in Table 11.6, except for a 50 percent increase in camera availability in Vietnam. However, most Second Tier states would be delighted to see Vietnam's 13 percent increase in rice supply, and most First Tier states would consider Japan's 3 percent and 4 percent gains significant.

Thus the theory of comparative advantage predicts that First Tier and Second Tier states can benefit by trading both within and between tiers. Most states usually export any particular good to many states, import other goods from many states, and often export and import the same goods with other states. Exceptions to these generalizations include (1) situations of uneven resource endowments, such as oil and mineral deposits and arable land for farming; (2) political divisions, like those between North and South Korea today and Eastern and Western Europe during the Cold War; and (3) trading infrastructures carried over from former colonial powers, still seen in contemporary Africa.

If the theory of comparative advantage says that advantageous trade possibilities exist, will the trades occur? Not necessarily. In addition to the exceptions already noted, states may have many reasons for choosing to protect favored industries. Japanese rice is a notable example. Beyond its role as a diet staple, rice is extremely important in Japanese culture. Claims that domestic Japanese rice is different from imports protect both the culture and the notoriously inefficient but politically powerful farmers. This is a classic example of nontariff barriers to trade.

Global Debt and Contemporary Monetary Exchange: Process and Problems

As this chapter's final example of IPE policy tools and problems, we examine the linked topics of global debt and contemporary monetary exchange, taking Mexico as a case in

TABLE 11.7	
Cameras and Rice: A Second Study in Comparative Advantage	

Situation 2: One state has absolute advantage in making both products

<table>
<tr><td colspan="6" align="center">Case 1: No trade</td><td colspan="3" align="center">Case 2: Total product
specialization</td></tr>
<tr><td rowspan="3">State and
Product</td><td rowspan="3">Output
per
Worker-Year</td><td rowspan="3">Number
of
Workers</td><td colspan="2" align="center">Productivity</td><td rowspan="3">Number
of
Workers</td><td rowspan="3">Annual
Output</td><td rowspan="3">Gains &
Losses of
Specialization</td></tr>
<tr><td>Annual
Output</td><td>Ratio,
C:R</td></tr>
<tr></tr>
<tr><td>Japanese cameras</td><td>250 units</td><td>100</td><td>25,000</td><td>Japan:</td><td>200</td><td>50,000</td><td></td></tr>
<tr><td>Japanese rice</td><td>150 tons</td><td>100</td><td>15,000</td><td>5:3</td><td></td><td></td><td></td></tr>
<tr><td>Vietnamese cameras</td><td>50 units</td><td>100</td><td>5,000</td><td>Vietnam</td><td></td><td></td><td></td></tr>
<tr><td>Vietnamese rice</td><td>75 tons</td><td>100</td><td>7,500</td><td>2:3</td><td>200</td><td>15,000</td><td></td></tr>
<tr><td>Total camera production</td><td></td><td></td><td>30,000</td><td></td><td></td><td>50,000</td><td>20,000</td></tr>
<tr><td>Total rice production</td><td></td><td></td><td>22,500</td><td></td><td></td><td>15,000</td><td>−7,500</td></tr>
</table>

Japanese domestic cost of rice:
  5/3 = 1.667 cameras per ton
Vietnamese domestic cost of rice:
  2/3 = 0.667 cameras per ton

Japanese domestic cost of cameras:
  3/5 = 0.6 tons of rice per camera
Vietnamese domestic cost of cameras:
  3/2 = 1.5 tons of rice per camera

Case 3: One possible trade in which each state buys goods in which it is disadvantaged and price is set
between the two states' productivity ratios, at 3.9 cameras per 3 tons of rice

	Output per Worker-Year	Number of Workers	Annual Output	Less Exports	Plus Imports	Net Supply	Before Trade	Gains of Trade
Japanese cameras	250	130	32,500	6,500		26,000	25,000	4%
Japanese rice	150	70	10,500		5,000	15,500	15,000	3%
Vietnamese cameras	50	20	1,000		6,500	7,500	5,000	50%
Vietnamese rice	75	180	13,500	5,000		8,500	7,500	13%
Total camera production			33,500			33,500	30,000	12%
Total rice production			24,000			24,000	22,500	7%

point. Mexico today is a sizable and fairly rapidly industrializing state, although plagued by inflation, unemployment, and major economic fluctuations. It is perhaps the most urbanized of the Second Tier states; in 1996, 71 percent of its growing population of around 96 million lived in urban areas. Rugged topography and limited rainfall always hindered Mexican development, but prospects brightened with the discovery in the 1970s of what may be the world's largest oil reserves, estimated at 50.8 billion barrels in 1995. After oil prices soared in the mid-1970s, Mexico became a large producer and exporter of petroleum and natural gas.

Major problems followed. The Mexican government borrowed heavily in international money markets to finance numerous major projects, intending to promote rapid development and pay off the loans using its huge stream of oil revenue. When oil prices dropped dramatically in the early 1980s, there was apprehension that Mexico would

default on (be unable to repay) its debt. International bankers feared that defaults by Mexico and Brazil could shatter confidence throughout the international lending market and even disrupt major firms like the U.S.-based Citibank, which had made major loans to Mexico. As in many similar—if less severe—situations, the short-term solution was **debt rescheduling.** Loan terms were rewritten to allow smaller payments over a longer time.

Having solved the immediate problem, however, Mexico continued its previous actions. With a low savings rate at home, much development was financed by foreign investors. Severe corruption existed throughout the essentially one-party government. Presidents regularly enriched themselves while in office and squirreled millions away in foreign banks to support an affluent retirement. Inflation and unemployment were chronic. By 1993, when years of inflation had pushed the price of bread above 1,000 pesos, a new peso was decreed with a thousand times greater value. Foreign investors were promised high interest and a fixed-exchange-rate peso, but the Mexican government could not keep those promises without curbing domestic spending. Its failure or inability to do so eventually meant that the peso had to be **devalued,** reducing its supported value against foreign currencies. Traditionally, devaluation promotes exports by making them less expensive in foreign currencies, and discourages imports by making them more expensive for your own citizens.

Devaluation undermined investors' confidence in their Mexican holdings, triggering a rash of sales that dramatically drove down the value of the peso in January 1995. Nor was Mexico the only state affected; its interdependence with other economies led many global investors to bail out of all emerging markets, driving down values from the Thai bhat to the Argentine peso. Mexico's peso had traded around three to the dollar for several years, but fell rapidly to a low of 6.35 by the end of January. Many analysts feared a collapse of the peso's value and a default on Mexican bonds. The Clinton administration devised a plan for the United States to cosign a package of $40 billion in loans to Mexico to stop the run and stabilize the peso. Congress, however, newly controlled by Republicans after the 1994 election, showed little sign of approving loan guarantees. Opponents argued that Congress would be bailing out wealthy investors and pension funds that had gambled and lost on junk bonds issued by the Mexican government. In actuality, millions of present and future retirees would be the chief losers in any pension fund setback.

President Clinton then found previously unclaimed authority to lend up to $20 billion to Mexico to keep it from defaulting on government-issued bonds, and his commitment broke the political logjam. The U.S. loan became the cornerstone of an international package that included $17.5 from the International Monetary Fund, the largest IMF loan ever, and eventual commitments from major European governments. Mexico agreed to strict financial conditions similar to those of many IMF loans, and put up $7 billion annually in oil earnings as collateral to guarantee the U.S. loan. The peso rose to 5.75 to the dollar as soon as the package was announced (Sanger, 1995), eventually settling around 5 to the dollar. In the end, the United States loaned Mexico $12.5 billion, which was repaid early with $560 million interest in slightly under two years, by which time international investors had returned to Mexican markets and offered more attractive rates (Sanger, 1997a).

Who won in this case? Who lost? What lessons does it hold for us today? Certainly, restoring stability meant that international financial markets won, as did all the governments, firms, and individuals around the world investing and borrowing in them. President Clinton won an important and risky political victory, confounding his opponents by finding a way around a reluctant Congress and ultimately seeing the loan paid off early. Senator Alfonse D'Amato (R-N.Y.), a harsh critic of Clinton, had warned, "you'll never see [the $12.5 billion] again" (Sanger, 1997a). *New York Times* columnist Thomas Friedman (1995a) termed the peso affair the "first postmodern economic crisis" which "hit [Mexico] with a financial neutron bomb" so powerful that "all the buildings have been left standing but the people have been financially devastated."

Mexican reliance on foreign funds to finance development was nothing new, although the sheer amount of such investment probably was. Undeniably new was the speed with which the globalized investment economy moved. Using worldwide telecommunications and electronic fund transfers, investors today can move funds at the speed of light. More seriously, panicked reactions can spread more rapidly than ever, which is why the Clinton administration was so concerned about the time needed to persuade Congress to act when some opinion polls showed more than 80 percent of the general public opposed to a Mexican bailout.

In many respects, ordinary Mexican citizens were the chief losers. Relative to 1993, prices of all imported goods, which had included many U.S. agricultural products, nearly doubled. Friedman (1995a) quotes a peasant woman, living in a shack on the fringe of Mexico City, who cannot buy meat anymore because "Mexico is now different—now we are poor." Doubling the prices of imported cars and cameras lowers the living standards of middle- and upper-class citizens, but the greatest impact of devaluation falls on the poor. The only respect in which Mexican peasants and workers gain is that a cheaper peso makes it much more attractive for foreign firms to transfer work to Mexico—which often means jobs lost by U.S. workers.

The peso crisis of 1995 serves to remind us that during the last quarter of the twentieth century all markets became increasingly global and capable of reacting almost instantly, and none more so than money markets. International market fluctuations now have profound and differential effects on states and peoples half a world away from the principal parties. A Mexican official in 1995 lamented that markets now outweighed nations. Moreover, both poor people and the wealthy may be affected, but often quite differently. Ordinary citizens who may never own a bond can suffer profound disruptions to their lives and standards of living. The 1995 run on the peso is somewhat reminiscent of the run on U.S. banks early during the Great Depression of the 1930s, which prompted President Franklin Roosevelt to declare a bank holiday and initiate measures to restore the confidence of small investors. Most of the parties in 1995 had large investments that ultimately were stabilized, albeit with nontrivial losses. The solution was ad hoc, partly arranged through existing institutions like the IMF and consultations within the G-7, pointing out the lack of a fully functioning global political-economic system capable of managing problems of this magnitude. Institutions and practices of that system are still evolving, and this promises to be an area of serious policy concern for the twenty-first century.

SUMMARY

International political economy (IPE) is the broad area in which politics and economics intersect, or the politics of economic issues. It encompasses both a major set of policy concerns and a set of policy tools for dealing with them. Because political economy always involves both politics and economics, at home and internationally, IPE affects each of us both individually and as members of collectivities ranging from firms to communities to our country to international organizations and regions. The end of the Cold War has only intensified dramatic changes in U.S. interactions with the world economy that began in the mid-1970s, and the United States is unavoidably and far more strongly affected today. Rapidly advancing economic globalization will do much to determine whether we prosper as individuals.

Whether enough of us become and remain competitive in that global economy will determine whether the United States prospers. Clearly, the United States faces some types of relative decline as a world power, and inevitable major adjustment to changes in its global economic environment. The broad and deep international penetration into domestic economies is the outstanding IPE development since World War II, having occurred primarily in the last quarter of the twentieth century and having already created a truly global economy.

The United States is not immune to IPE changes. The late 1980s saw an intense debate about whether the United States is in decline as a global power, and whether such a decline is inevitable. Paul Kennedy made a strong case for the inevitability of eventual great power decline, examining the growth and decline of powerful states over the long sweep of history from the realist perspective that relative power rather than absolute power counts in international politics. Over the long term, most states' power tends to follow a time course similar to a life cycle.

Three years after Kennedy, Joseph S. Nye, Jr., published a rebuttal. His fundamental argument is that things are not as bad overall as some signs make them appear, and that by exaggerating U.S. world dominance in the past, declinists find it overly easy to portray a diminished American present.

Yet the entire debate about U.S. decline probably is moot because the rapid internationalization of economics undermines the very notion of an "American" economy, as argued by Robert Reich. The old view of distinct and relatively isolated national economies is outdated because modern communications and transportation allow almost every factor of production—except workers themselves—to be moved rapidly and almost effortlessly across nation-state borders. Thus the answer to the questions whether we are becoming better off or worse off, and where we are heading, are that "we" are no longer all affected the same way. The optimistic view that globalization is wonderful applies for precisely the minority whose skills and services are becoming more valuable in the emerging world economy. The pessimistic view applies to the majority, whose skills either are subject to replacement by lower cost foreign substitutes (as is true for many U.S. citizens) or are stagnating in value (as is often true in low-income developing states).

Many analysts of the 1990s decried Washington's twin deficits in the federal budget and international trade. Federal budget deficits resulted primarily from a combination of (1) growing entitlement programs like Social Security and Medicare, (2) large tax cuts during the Reagan and Bush presidencies of 1981–93, when the cumulative federal debt more than quadrupled, and (3) dramatic increases in interest rates, partly driven by the international trade deficit and exacerbated by the need to refinance growing debt. An economic boom and dramatic government policy changes began balancing the federal budget (but not eliminating accumulated debt) at the end of the 1990s. The international trade deficit arose primarily from a combination of (1) dramatic "shocks" in world petroleum prices, and the fact that (2) the United States has become a nation of consumers, which meant dramatically cut savings rates, an increasing reliance on imports, and a loss of its competitive producing edge in many important industries. The trade deficit problem has not been solved.

Classifying the United States and other states in the post–Cold War global economy requires modifying the widely used terminology of First, Second, Third, and sometimes Fourth Worlds. The simplest alternative is to focus exclusively on level of development and classify states as either First Tier or Second Tier. First Tier states are highly developed, members of the former First World. Second Tier comprises all developing states, although this elides the questions of degree and speed of development, and how to classify the newly industrializing countries.

Political economy policy tools available to U.S. administrations include the following types of domestic actions, many of which interact and some of which have strong international impacts: (1) management of the money supply available for investment through manipulation of bank reserve requirements; (2) regulation of credit availability through putting pressure on interest rates by changing the discount rate at which the Federal Reserve loans to member banks; (3) management of the interrelated rates of inflation and unemployment, particularly through monetary policies and job creation and training programs; (4) manipulation of tax rules and incentives to encourage desired behaviors; and (5) regulations reducing energy usage and, thus, oil imports. Additionally, many types of international actions are possible both unilaterally and through intergovernmental organizations such as the International Monetary Fund (IMF), the World Trade Organization (WTO), and the Group of Seven (G-7). International political economy tools potentially available to U.S. adminsitrations include the following types of actions, many with strongly intermestic impacts:

1. Loans, grants, and other forms of aid
2. Coordinated international buying and selling of currencies to support and stabilize the exchange value of the dollar and the currencies of friendly states
3. Actions to reduce tariffs and settle trade disputes through intergovernmental organizations like the WTO
4. Regional free trade agreements, such as NAFTA
5. Tariffs and nontariff barriers to trade
6. Boycotts, or refusals to deal in certain goods or with certain states
7. Embargoes, or refusals to trade with certain states, accompanied by pressures on others to comply

Many authorities see multinational corporations (MNCs), which underwent rapid growth from 1958 to1973, as a new type of international actor more powerful than the governments of most states. The MNC boom, particularly in European investments by firms headquartered in the United States, was encouraged by freer currency convertibility and fears that future EEC tariff walls would limit external trade. Most direct foreign investment (DFI) during the MNC boom was American, but by the 1990s, American concern had shifted to the growing role of foreign-headquartered MNCs absorbing once-great firms in the United States.

States engage in international trade because their productive capabilities differ, due to complex combinations of developed design and manufacturing skills and technologies, natural resource endowments, economic and political history, and a host of other reasons. The theory of comparative advantage asserts that states should export those goods they produce most efficiently and import goods that they produce less efficiently. Indeed, both parties to such an exchange can benefit even when one is absolutely less efficient in producing all the types of goods traded. Although everyone can live better by engaging in international trade, comparative advantage does not explain why states commonly import and export goods of the same type. The general late-twentieth century global trend has been toward freer trade, both through tariff-lowering agreements like GATT and through regional free-trade areas in Europe and North America (NAFTA).

Mexico's 1995 peso value crisis reminds us that, since the 1990s, all markets have become increasingly global and capable of reacting almost instantly, and none more so than money markets. International market fluctuations now have profound and differential effects on states and peoples half a world away from the principal parties, and some lament that markets now outweigh nations. Mexico's experience demonstrates both the burdens of foreign debt and the volatility of contemporary monetary exchange. The solution highlights the lack of a fully functioning global political-economic system capable of managing problems of this magnitude. IPE institutions and practices continue to evolve, and IPE promises to be among the most serious areas of policy concern for the twenty-first century.

KEY TERMS

Cartel

Command economy

Comparative advantage

Convertibility

Debt rescheduling

Default

Devalue

First Tier

First World

Fourth World

In-person services (Compare with *routine production services* and *symbolic-analytic services*.)

International political economy (IPE)

Mercantilism

Protectionism

Routine production services (Compare with *in-person services* and *symbolic-analytic services*.)

Second Tier

Second World

Symbolic-analytic services (Compare with *in-person services* and *routine production services*.)

Tariff union

Third World

World Bank

SELECTED READINGS

Bernstein, Michael, and David E. Adler, eds. 1994. *Understanding American Economic Decline.* Cambridge: Cambridge University Press.

Esty, Daniel C. 1994. *Greening the GATT: Trade, Environment, and the Future.* Washington, D.C.: Institute for International Economics.

Friedman, Thomas L. 1999. *The Lexus and the Olive Tree: Understanding Globalization.* New York: Farrar Straus Giroux.

Isaak, Robert A. 1995. *Managing World Economic Change: International Political Economy,* 2d ed. Englewood Cliffs, N.J.: Prentice Hall.

Kenen, Peter B., ed. 1994. *Managing the World Economy: Fifty Years After Bretton Woods.* Washington, D.C.: Institute for International Economics.

Kennedy, Paul. 1987. *The Rise and Fall of the Great Powers: Economic Change and Military Conflict from 1500 to 2000.* New York: Random House.

Lairson, Thomas D., and David Skidmore. 1997. *International Political Economy: The Struggle for Power and Wealth,* 2d ed. Fort Worth, Tex.: Harcourt Brace.

Nye, Joseph S., Jr. 1990. *Bound to Lead: The Changing Nature of American Power.* New York: Basic Books.

Reich, Robert B. 1991. *The Work of Nations: Preparing Ourselves for 21st-Century Capitalism.* New York: Knopf.

Sandholtz, Wayne, Michael Borrus, John Zysman, Ken Conca, Jay Stowsky, Steven Vogel, and Steve Weber. 1992. *The Highest Stakes: The Economic Foundations of the Next Security System.* New York: Oxford University Press.

Toffler, Alvin. 1980. *The Third Wave.* New York: Morrow.

CHAPTER 12

INTERNATIONAL COLLECTIVE ACTION IN U.S. FOREIGN POLICY

THE TRAGEDY OF THE COMMONS AND INTERNATIONAL COLLECTIVE ACTION

Picture a group of cattle grazing peacefully on a modest grassy field. Now imagine that field located in the heart of a city. Although strange to today's eyes, this scene would have been routine two to three centuries ago in Europe and colonial America, when locales we know today as great cities often qualified as towns by modern standards. Boston Common is a typical example. Today it is a manicured park with concrete walkways, benches, and lawns for warm-weather relaxation, filling a somewhat irregular space about two blocks by three, bounded by streets laid down as mere paths centuries ago. In colonial times it was a grassy field termed a "common" because it was owned by the community as a whole and available for use by all citizens. Outdoor meetings might be held on the common, and the local militia trained there. Citizens also were allowed to graze cattle on the common, and the problems raised by those grazing rights went on to become an archetypal example of the interlinked political and environmental problems facing people within and between towns, cities, and nation-states. The case became an archetype because the same structure occurs in many present-day interactions in which we must use political processes to manage resources and physical systems.

In a classic 1968 article, Garret Hardin called this archetypal problem the **tragedy of the commons,** and his label has stuck. The "tragedy" arises because the common is successful and survives only when its use is strictly limited. Grazing a small number of cattle on the common works well; the grass may be close cropped, but it survives wandering hooves and continually regrows. The common's physical boundaries limit its grazing capacity, however, and if too many cattle graze there they will chew the grass to the ground, trample it, and even kill it. As in many other environmental systems, this physical resource can sustain only a certain amount of use. When grazing is kept below that limit, the common can be sustained indefinitely. But what process will keep usage within those limits? Imagine that Farmer Jones has been running one cow on the common. He reasons that if he adds a calf, it will mature and provide additional milk and later beef for his family, or eventually be sold at a profit. If enough citizens share his reasoning, they may run so many cattle that the common's grazing capacity is exceeded and the common is destroyed. Worse yet, some individuals who understand that danger and expect the common to be destroyed may rush to graze as many cattle as possible, seeking to extract as much wealth from the common resource as they can before the end. If that happens, individual greed accelerates resource destruction which everyone believes undesirable, even if they believe it is inevitable. This, then, is the ultimate tragedy of the commons.

Preventing the destruction of the common requires keeping usage within sustainable bounds, either by every user's recognizing the resource's fragility and tacitly cooperating, or by all usages being regulated to decide who gets to graze how many cattle. The latter approach is more likely to succeed, and such regulation is a political problem. Regulating grazing on the common exemplifies the large class of **collective action problems,** in which governments try to limit and coordinate their citizens' individual activities so that society as a whole benefits. A major contemporary international collective action problem, examined in depth later in this chapter, involves the United States and most other governments acting under the auspices of the United Nations to limit global warming.

THE NEED FOR AND MAJOR TYPES OF INTERNATIONAL COLLECTIVE ACTION

Dramatic post–Cold War changes in the global context in which we conduct U.S. foreign policy have profoundly altered the number, character, and possible solutions to foreign policy problems confronting the United States. One result is an increased need for American collaboration with others in international collective action. Declines in U.S. power relative to other major powers have reduced our ability to "go it alone" in major military or economic endeavors. We see this in the Persian Gulf War, Bosnian peacekeeping arrangements, and international financial management through such organizations as the G-8. Although U.S. leadership remains important, it is often easier and more politically acceptable at home and abroad to use collective arrangements to ensure the political and societal security of others. Most environmental problems, hardly recognized fifty years ago, inherently require international collective action. This is clearly demonstrated in the evolving global warming regime (see later in this chapter). The end of the Cold War, which opened the former Soviet Union and its former Eastern European satellite states to global examination, helped emphasize the need for remediation of widespread severe environmental damage.

All international activity in which the U.S. government and its citizens collaborate with other international actors, as in intergovernmental organizations, international regimes, and international nongovernmental organizations, is collective action. Consequently, it is subject to all the dilemmas and difficulties of collective action. Only the scale and types of activities and the size and types of actors involved differ from the original tragedy of the commons: world regions or the entire globe instead of Boston Common, global warming or whaling or peacekeeping rather than cattle grazing, usually governments and other international actors instead of citizens.

Some of those international actors may be able to utilize every type of policy tool discussed in this part of the book, including diplomacy, economic aid, coercion of many types, and military force. Every policy tool covered in this chapter, however, inherently and unavoidably requires the United States to work collectively with others. Nonetheless, cooperation in dealing with one issue almost never implies cooperation on every issue, and separate cooperative arrangements usually are required for each issue area. So long as the United States and other parties all benefit, they can agree to deal with one specific issue at a time—even when their particular interests on that issue are not identical. In the global warming negotiations, for example, major industrial producer states such as the United States generally want small cutbacks in carbon dioxide emissions, for fear of stagnating their economies. Contrastingly, small island states that fear rising sea levels want immediate deep cuts.

In this chapter we examine the processes, perspectives, and prospects of different types of international collective action organizations with which the government and citizens of the United States work. Special emphasis is placed on how they interact with the United States and on how they may be used as tools of policy by the government, by citizens, and by other major actors within the U.S. political system. We analyze intergovernmental organizations, international regimes, and international nongovernmental organizations in depth with contemporary case examples.

INTERGOVERNMENTAL ORGANIZATIONS (IGOs)

The members of intergovernmental organizations (IGOs) are governments of states, and different IGOs deal with economic, functional, political, and security problems. These entities range in scope from nearly universal organizations such as the United Nations, to selective and regional organizations such as the Organization for Security and Cooperation in Europe (OSCE) and the European Union (EU). Substantively, they range from large interest groups such as the Organization of Petroleum Exporting Countries (OPEC), to regional trading organizations such as the North American Free Trade Area (NAFTA), and security organizations such as the North Atlantic Treaty Organization (NATO). IGOs also include many functional organizations such as the International Telecommunications Union (ITU). The number and diversity of these examples should suggest the importance of IGOs in U.S. foreign policy. Among those just named, the United States is a member of OSCE, NAFTA, NATO, and the ITU and has extremely important interactions with OPEC and the EU over major issues.

INTERNATIONAL REGIMES

International regimes are very large systems (in the sense of system introduced in Chapter 4) created by treaties and actions, and may include specialized intergovernmental organizations. Regimes combine law, regulation, and the actions of interstate and international organizations and individual state governments to create international norms and thereby influence and manage selected behaviors. For example, a formal regime regulates whaling internationally. Much less formally, an international consensus between the U.S. and major European powers evolved after the 1995 Dayton peace accords, dedicated to preventing further fragmentation of former Yugoslavia in general and of Bosnia-Herzegovina in particular. International security regimes are a particularly important type, focused on a major traditional concern, preserving international order and the safety and security of nations, states, and governments. Three quite different examples are the Security Council and related organizations of the UN, the Organization for Security and Cooperation in Europe, and the ongoing Middle East peace negotiations. Permanent regimes may be created by treaty, either at the urging of particular governments or by the joint action of many governments under the auspices of an IGO, as seen in the UN Framework Convention on Climate Change. As these examples illustrate, the U.S. government also is a major player in many international regimes.

Views of exactly what constitutes a regime vary enormously, even though regimes have attracted much scholarly work in the past two decades. The regime level of analysis falls between the broader study of international structures and the narrower study of formal organizations. Regime analysts presume that state actions are influenced by norms but are still consistent with state interests (Haggard and Simmons, 1987, 492). In Stephen Krasner's (1983) definition, which has won wide acceptance, a regime comprises "implicit or explicit principles, norms, rules and decision-making procedures around which actors' expectations converge in a given area of international relations." The most restricted definition treats regimes as "multilateral agreements among states which aim to regulate national actions within an issue-area" (Haggard and Simmons, 1987, 495). By any definition, regimes are examples of international collective behavior and tend to facilitate such cooperation, although regimes are not necessary for cooperation.

Ad hoc regimes to manage particular problems expected to be limited in time and scope may be created when a few governments stimulate international collective action to promote policies that impact many governments. The Persian Gulf War and its aftermath have involved at least three such ad hoc regimes. First, the U.S. government organized a broad coalition under UN auspices to prosecute the war. The Gulf War coalition regime involved authorizing resolutions and supporting sanctions voted by the UN Security Council and the U.S. Congress, troops or financial support provided by some thirty governments, and a coordinating military planning and command structure. Shortly after the war, that entire regime was largely dismantled. After the cease-fire, new, smaller regimes were created under UN auspices to manage weapons destruction and other postwar activities in Iraq. These involved more authorizing resolutions, troops and experts from numerous governments, and command and procedural arrangements. Most of these were still operating late into the 1990s. One of these regimes, the UN Iraq-Kuwait Observation Mission (UNIKOM), is examined in detail later in this chapter. Finally, the United States sought to utilize its improved standing with Arab governments in the aftermath of war to launch a new Middle East peace process in 1991. That peace negotiation process, involving many governments, may be considered either a new regime or an updating of the regime under which earlier peace negotiations were conducted.

Regimes create new pressures and opportunities that alter the interests and preferences of governments and other international actors. Consequently, they modify interactions between governments in ways that make cooperation more likely. A regime that encourages others to take actions we desire may be an important tool of U.S. foreign policy, whereas a regime that presses for actions we seek to avoid may create serious pressure on the United States. Both effects are apparent in the global warming case that will be presented later in this chapter.

INTERNATIONAL NONGOVERNMENTAL ORGANIZATIONS (NGOS OR INGOS)

International nongovernmental organizations (NGOs or INGOs) are fundamentally different from IGOs and international regimes. These organizations bring groups of individuals, businesses, and other organizations together across government lines to pursue common interests, often lobbying and even taking stands against particular governments. Thus they can offer channels for U.S. citizens to directly influence foreign policy. Many NGOs, such as Greenpeace or Amnesty International, accept individuals as members and have state organizations and local chapters. Frequently they operate as interest groups raising individual consciousness and pressuring governments on behalf of broad international goals such as limiting practices that threaten species extinction, ending nuclear testing, and eliminating human rights abuses worldwide. NGOs pursuing aims compatible with particular aspects of U.S. foreign policy, such as the International Red Cross, may receive approval and support from the U.S. government. Those pursuing aims at odds with U.S. foreign policy may exert serious pressure on citizens, the Congress, the bureaucracy, and the administration.

Three major cases demonstrating these very different channels of international cooperation and supported to different degrees by the U.S. government and people are examined in this chapter. They are as follows:

- Peacekeeping under the auspices of the United Nations, perhaps the best known intergovernmental organization, in the early aftermath of the Persian Gulf War.
- The Climate Change Convention (treaty) with its associated global warming regime, as an example of an important international regime.
- The major international nongovernmental organization Amnesty International.

The first is a classic case of UN peacekeeping, broadly supported by many governments although carried out by relatively few, limited in area and scope, but of longer duration than originally anticipated. It was a logical follow-up to American efforts to liberate Kuwait. The second, the Climate Change Convention, demonstrates the U.S. government and the majority of other states around the world building a new regime to deal with a major global problem. Earth's climate is an obvious and enormous **common pool**, a distinct physical system that, like Boston Common, poses collective action problems. Finally, Amnesty International is an important NGO that focuses the efforts of individual citizens around the globe on advocating prisoner rights outside those advocates' own countries. Although Amnesty criticizes the United States for such actions as imposing the death penalty, its support for imprisoned political dissidents in states such as China helps build broader global support for some important American foreign policies.

Important global political developments make it likely that we will see all three of these forms of international cooperation increasingly often in the post–Cold War world. Each form of cooperation has characteristic strengths and understandable weaknesses. Fortunately, their problems are rather well known and well studied in the political science literature. In the balance of this chapter we use both theory and case studies to examine those strengths and weaknesses and to build understanding for the future.

CHARACTERISTICS AND PROBLEMS OF COLLECTIVE ACTION

Intergovernmental organizations, international regimes, and international organizations often are valuable tools of policy for the governments, organizations, and individuals forming them. Although they are subject to particular types of problems and almost never are under the complete control of any single actor or government, they provide vital means for planning and carrying out collective action. Consider again the need to manage Boston Common to keep cattle grazing within sustainable limits. City legislation could establish regulation and enforcement by higher authority. Alternatively, organization for collective action could come from below, by grazers forming an association and agreeing to allocate and enforce grazing rights. In this case, however, the association might need to persuade the city to assign it authority. Otherwise, it could be powerless to act against individuals who ignored grazing rules and assignments. Political scientists refer to such individuals as **free riders, defectors,** or **holdouts** from collective action agreements. They are people (or, internationally, governments and other international actors) who decline to participate in collective action, usually because they value their private gain above the common good.

Regulation of the common grazing resource, whether imposed from above or organized from below, provides the means to limit or prevent holdouts. However, several other activities are crucial to managing and maintaining the common. These include determining maximum sustainable levels and limiting total grazing to within those levels, carrying out any needed maintenance such as replanting and fencing, and providing whatever usage reporting and policing are required to ensure compliance. The city government or grazing association may decide to charge for permits or otherwise tax users to pay the costs of regulation, maintenance, and policing.

Regulation converts grazing cattle on the common from a universal right into a limited privilege, with usage rights conveyed by grazing permits. Necessary decisions about which citizens are allowed to run how many cattle raise questions about equity and individual advantage. Typically, prior grazing becomes an important determinant of allowed future use. Because grazing permits convey usage rights essential to the money-making business of cattle raising, they may become commodities salable to the highest bidder. Such commodity sales are found in many other common pool and collective action situations. In New York City, for example, permits to operate taxicabs have been strictly limited for decades and sell for tens of thousands of dollars. In the 1997 global warming talks at Kyoto, the United States argued strongly (but unsuccessfully) that targeted levels of greenhouse gas emissions should be considered rights, with states that fall below their target emissions levels allowed to sell some emissions rights to others. See "How Greenhouse Gases Produce Global Warming" on page 476.

THE PRISONERS' DILEMMA IN INTERNATIONAL COLLECTIVE ACTION

Many collective action situations involve the interaction structure called the **prisoners' dilemma.** In such situations, individuals who pursue goals intended *either* to maximize

ECONOMIC INSIGHTS ON COLLECTIVE ACTION

Since the 1960s the Public Choice Society has brought together a diverse group of scholars interested in how societies decide the classic allocation questions of who gets what, where, when, and how. The society, composed largely of economists and political scientists, is well known for applying economic concepts to political decisions. Collective action problems are fundamental to this concern, and the public choice approach has much to tell us about international collective action.

To economists, a *good* is the product or result or consequence of any activity. Some goods are things, the tangible results of design, engineering, development, and routine production, such as toasters or automobiles. Other goods are ideas, the results of symbolic analysis (see Chapter 11) such as political campaign plans, architectural designs, legal research documents, or courtroom arguments. *Private goods* are those that individuals can possess as property, whether toasters, house designs, or lawyers' arguments. Moreover, the consumption of most private goods by one person reduces the amount left for others. For example, you and your neighbor cannot simultaneously drive, or individually own, the same automobile. Much of economic analysis is devoted

to the study of private goods. Classically, in market economics individuals seek to sell their products as expensively as possible and purchase goods they need as inexpensively as possible. As the price of goods rises, providers usually are willing to supply more and consumers are forced to demand less. The equilibrium amount at which every good produced is sold is determined by the intersection of the supply-versus-price and demand-versus-price curves. If only private goods exist, the entire society benefits when individuals seek to maximize their private utility by acquiring as much as possible of the goods they desire.

The common plot of ground considered in Garret Hardin's "The Tragedy of the Commons" is one example of a *common pool* or *collective* or *public good*. Collective or public goods benefit many individuals at once. They are characterized always by jointness of supply and questions about whether individuals may opt out of the affected group, and often by nonexclusiveness or nonexcludability. *Jointness of supply* means a good is not private; if supplied to any member of the affected group it must be made available to all. Unless regulated, the common is open to unrestricted grazing by any citizen's cattle. Na-

(continued)

their individual benefit *or* to minimize their individual risk end up worse off than if they had cooperated with others. The story that gave its name to such situations concerns two burglars arrested but awaiting formal charges. Police are confident the pair have committed major burglary, but the police have only enough evidence to anticipate convictions for petty theft unless at least one miscreant can be persuaded to confess. Having cannily kept the two crooks apart, police then present to each separately the following proposition: We know you did the major crime, but confess and we'll go easy on you. If your partner confesses and you don't, we'll throw the book at you. Each prisoner then faces a set of alternatives that could look like this: If I confess, I get either one year in prison if my partner doesn't confess or four years if he does. But if I don't confess, I could get two years if my partner doesn't confess and six years if he does. The exact potential prison terms are

(continued)

tional defense is a jointly supplied good usually characterized by *nonexcludability* or *nonseparability*, in that the government cannot readily defend some residents of a city from such perils as nuclear terrorists without defending all residents. Certain other defense department activities may offer *separable* or *excludable* benefits. For example, some U.S. citizens might opt not to be evacuated from a foreign state torn apart by riots like those that afflicted Albania in the spring of 1997.

Boston Common lends itself more readily than defense to excludability because regulations could require a grazing permit for each cow. A cattle-owning citizen with grazing alternatives could elect to opt out of the grazing management regime. Opting out of nonexcludable collective goods is far more problematic. For example, the government cannot easily allow citizens who disagree with military policy to withhold that portion of their federal taxes that supports the Department of Defense, because extending such holdouts to any federal program to which a citizen might have or claim objection would paralyze government.

In reality, many goods have *externalities* that make them more public than private. Externali-

ties are costs or benefits created by one producer but borne or enjoyed by others. From the contemporary perspective that all physical production depletes material resources, absorbs energy, and produces waste ranging from solid matter to global warming, all consumable physical goods involve externalities. It often is quite difficult to measure or price externality costs and benefits. For example, if I plant a beautiful garden my neighbors and even passersby also get to enjoy the view, but if I burn the garden trimmings others may choke on the smoke that blows beyond my fence. A very helpful externality for the young United States during the nineteenth century was provided by the British navy, without which the Monroe Doctrine probably would have been unfeasible. Policing the high seas protected British colonial possessions and international trade (a collective good) on which Britain was far more dependent than was the young United States. In the process Britain almost unavoidably protected U.S. shipping and helped deter Western Hemisphere interventions by other European powers, providing as an externality the collective good of protection to all Western Hemisphere states.

---

not crucial. What is critical is a structure in which each prisoner is encouraged to confess both by the hope of obtaining the best possible personal outcome (here, one year in prison) and the desire to avoid the worst possible personal outcome (here, six years in prison). Collectively, the burglars would be better off if neither confesses (four person-years in prison) and worst off if both confess (twelve person-years). Yet, if both seek individual over collective good, they end up worse than they could have by coordinated action.

Many international interactions have the same underlying structure as the prisoners' dilemma, although usually with more than two parties. If enough governments refuse to commit troops to peacekeeping in a regional conflict, for example, no action may be taken, allowing conflict to escalate and ultimately demand far more costly action. Only after the 1995 Dayton peace accords did the United States lead NATO and Russia in decisive action to stop ethnically based bloodshed in Bosnia. Earlier Bosnian peacekeeping attempts by various combinations of European powers proved inadequate in scope and intensity. In a larger instance from the formative stages of World War II, failure to agree on early collective action was disastrous. Both Britain and France were strong enough individually to intervene and reverse Germany's violations of the Versailles Treaty, such as remilitarization, at least as late as the mid-1930s. Such action well could have ended German expansionism, and might even have deprived the Nazi government of domestic political support it needed to retain power. However, neither France nor Britain wanted to act alone, they were unable to agree to act together, and they and others paid a vastly higher price to defeat Nazi Germany in the 1940s.

The prisoners' dilemma is one example of what political scientists call a **game of strategy,** one much studied because it occurs in so many real-world situations. Games of strategy have several necessary characteristics, as follows:

- Two or more players involved are involved in an interaction.
- Each player must select from two or more possible alternative actions.
- The outcome of the interaction is jointly determined by the choices made by all the players.
- Every outcome has certain payoffs—costs and benefits—to each player. The payoffs may favor one player and penalize another, but no single player can determine the outcome.

Overcoming or transcending the prisoners' dilemma usually requires either that the parties conspire to modify the characteristics or structure of their interaction, or that they modify their strategies for interacting within that structure. If the two arrested burglars somehow manage to communicate, they change the structure of their interaction. They can share their analyses of the situation and pledge loyalty. Perhaps they have discussed the chance of the dilemma in advance. If they belong to a crime family that punishes defections, neither is likely to confess. In international politics, unfortunately, there are few to no Mafia-like enforcers, especially against major powers. For example, the United Nations supported an ad hoc coalition to punish Iraq for invading Kuwait in 1990, but was unwilling in the latter 1990s to use force to compel Iraqi compliance with inspections of its weapons of mass destruction, and clearly was not prepared to enforce Chinese pledges regarding Hong Kong's special status after that former British colony was returned to Chinese sovereignty in 1997.

The second route to overcoming the prisoners' dilemma is for parties to reexamine the interaction structure, searching for strategies that will encourage better outcomes. If parties recognize that they will interact repeatedly in the future, fear of punishment through future defections by others often deters their defection now. Similar actions result if each party analyzes the situation *as if* their interaction will recur in the future. Each of the arrested burglars may realize that word will spread about any defection now, drastically reducing the chances of finding another partner in the future. Similarly, officials usually figure that reneging on any alliance commitment, even if it appears desirable in some particular case, reduces their future credibility to other governments. Researchers including Robert Axelrod (1984) have found in experiments that the most effective strategy for repeated play of the prisoners' dilemma is *tit-for-tat,* cooperating if an opponent cooperates and defecting if an opponent defects. A tit-for-tat strategy is strengthened by taking the initiative in cooperating, and by quickly returning to cooperation after using defection to punish. If direct negotiation is unavailable, such moves allow highly effective *tacit bargaining* (see Chapters 7 and 10), using actions to demonstrate what is desired and intended and what one is willing to risk or pay to get it.

PROBLEMS AND PROMISES OF INTERNATIONAL COLLECTIVE ACTION

International collective actions take place in common pool settings that range geographically from regions to groups of states with particular characteristics to the entire world's people. Such collective actions are carried out through many different types of groups and organizations, notably including the IGOs, international regimes, and NGOs already mentioned. Required collective action may involve more than just individual governments and, sometimes, more than just groups of governments. Notable common pools requiring collective action include physical, political, and economic types. *Physical common pools* encompass resources and the environment, and regional military security. For example, preventing whale extinctions and managing global warming require management regimes of global scope, whereas NATO deals mainly with the physical security of a group of contiguous European states. Coalitions exemplify *political common pools.* The European Union, for example, is one such coalition with a regional membership and focus; its primary concerns bridge between politics and economics. The resource cartel OPEC, together with its customers, forms an important example of an *economic common pool.*

The tragedy of the commons offers us several important general insights into the characteristics and problems of international collective action, and some solutions, as follows:

- Many common pools have absolute limits, for example, the maximum number of cattle that can be grazed on Boston Common or the minimum proportion of participating governments required for a regional peacekeeping force to succeed.

- Where such limits exist, regulation is more likely than altruistic cooperation to yield success. The problem lies in preventing free riders who seek to enjoy benefits without helping to cover costs, and holdouts who opt out of arrangements that may require universal membership for success.

- In the international arena, there usually is no higher authority to set and enforce rules upon governments. Thus in any given common pool or issue area the number of governments that agree to cooperate or accept regulation must be large enough to ensure success.

- The number of activities for which governments accept regulation is growing, but each new international cooperation agreement is ad hoc, specific to a new type of behavior. Nonetheless, actions that work in one case may help in another, so a repertoire of methods is built up over time.

- Regulation may turn usage rights into valuable commodities that can be bought and sold internationally, as with rights to emit greenhouse gases or other pollutants.

- Any distribution of rights and privileges through political processes raises questions about bias, favoritism, and influence.

Similarly, the prisoners' dilemma offers us additional general insights into the characteristics and problems of international collective action, and their solutions, as follows:

- The dilemma occurs when particular interactions (1) offer benefits to all governments for cooperation, (2) offer the possibility of greater benefits to particular governments that refuse to cooperate (i.e., defect), but (3) end up leaving everyone worse off than they could have been by cooperating.

- One way to overcome the temptation to defect is to change the dynamics of the interaction, for example, using negotiation to convince all parties that cooperation is more beneficial than defection.

- Agreeing on regulation either from within or from without is one important way to change the dynamics of the interaction and overcome the dilemma. For the crooks in the original prisoners' dilemma, joining the Mafia would be accepting outside regulation against confessing. In the international community, regulation must be built from within by agreement.

- Another way to overcome the dilemma is to view the interaction as if it is not isolated, but part of a continuing series of interactions over the same and other matters. Cooperation now can be rewarded by cooperation in the future, and conversely.

- In solving either the prisoners' dilemma or the tragedy of the commons, regulation means that all parties negotiate and accept formal arrangements to promote and require cooperation.

Look for these points in the balance of this chapter as we examine major international collective action organizations and functions, and several major cases. Despite the dilemmas and difficulties of achieving international cooperation, the already existing body of cooperative international arrangements has broader scope and impact than most people realize.

THE GROWING NEED FOR INTERNATIONAL COLLECTIVE ACTION

International collective actions are increasing in frequency and importance, both for the United States and globally. The numbers of such actions grew substantially after World War II, but important global social and political developments drove the rate of increase significantly upward as the twenty-first century approached. The near quadrupling in the number of independent states since 1945 created more potential for both conflict and cooperation, with myriad interests to be reconciled and coordinated. Increasing interdependence, especially economic globalization as discussed in Chapter 11, heightens pressures to coordinate such activities as trade and currency exchange. Faster and easier movements of goods and people, especially by air, generate new opportunities for undesirable movements of drugs, terrorists, and diseases, virtually mandating new and coordinated international control measures. Huge increases in world population, typically highest among developing states, dangerously increase total human impact on the global environment, from arctic warming to whaling. Population increases virtually guarantee additional pressure on natural and political common pools, generating or worsening environmental and governance problems solvable only through coordinated international action.

Additional developments make international collective action both more attractive and more necessary to the United States today than at the end of World War II. For some forty-four years the Cold War stimulated the grand policies that gave overall coherence to U.S. foreign policy. The Cold War also gave the United States the political, economic, and military leverage needed to dominate the international institutions, such as NATO, designed to manage it. The Cold War's end diminished that leverage by lowering the stakes and decreasing the urgency of following America's policy lead. Western European governments, for example, are much less likely to conform their defense policies to the wishes of leaders across the Atlantic when they no longer believe their survival to be at stake.

Perhaps more importantly for the United States, the decline of post–World War II hegemony decreases every type of American leverage over other governments and makes collective action ever more attractive. *Soft power* (attracting rather than commanding others, persuading them to join us in seeking the same goals; see Chapter 8) now may be more desirable than *hard power* (coercing and compelling others, using tangible power resources such as military and economic might) because the latter is unavailable or has become too expensive. Following the Persian Gulf War, for example, there were questions about why American troops did not continue on to Baghdad. The United States, however, was the coalition leader of a group of allies fighting the war. When breakdown threatened the supporting political consensus, the United States conceded to its allies and stopped the fighting. The political goal of maintaining consensus clearly overcame the military and political goal of eliminating Saddam. Moreover, we solicited other governments for most of the war costs.

Inability to maintain U.S. dominance of international economic institutions began to appear by the early 1970s, and by 1985 coordinated action through such institutions as free trade areas and the Group of Seven gained appeal. By the latter 1990s political leaders spoke openly of China as an emerging superpower likely to overtake the American economy early in the next century. Concerns like these are broader and more fundamental than the details of solving current major problems such as chronic budget and trade deficits. They address what global standing is imaginable and feasible for this country in the twenty-first century. Increasingly, our more attractive alternative futures require active U.S. involvement in intergovernmental organizations and regimes.

MAJOR INTERNATIONAL COLLECTIVE ACTION FUNCTIONS

The government and citizens of the United States work with many different international collective action organizations. The three major types of such organizations, discussed earlier, are intergovernmental organizations (IGOs), international regimes, and international nongovernmental organizations (NGOs or INGOs). In this section we examine several of the important activities or functions that may be carried out through such organizations, including (1) coordination of functional activities; (2) international political forums; (3) peacemaking, humanitarian relief, peacekeeping, peace enforcement, nation building, and police actions; and (4) international law. Each type of organization may carry out multiple functions, although they often specialize.

COORDINATION OF FUNCTIONAL ACTIVITIES

Functional activities are those that almost everybody agrees need to be regulated to ensure the necessary infrastructure and procedures for international communication, travel, commerce, and so on. Typically they are regulated by autonomous specialized intergovernmental organizations (IGOs) or international organizations with their own memberships and organs. Functional IGOs usually are affiliated with the UN through formal relationships or working agreements. Cooperation over functional activities occurs because (almost) nobody has interests that would be served by *not* cooperating. Most functional activities are so widely understood to be necessary that they have relatively limited political salience and controversy and usually receive little public attention. For example, the Universal Postal Union (UPU) was formed in 1875 to regularize arrangements for states to mutual recognize one another's postage and receive international mail. A few governments, like that of North Korea, may want to discourage contact with the outside world. Others may want to limit communication from particular states, like China from Taiwan. Most governments, however, consider international mail desirable for citizens and businesses and recognize the value of agreements to set rates and recognize each other's postage.

Another functional organization managing common pools with relatively limited controversy is the International Telecommunications Union (ITU), which establishes regulations for radio, telegraph, telephone, and space radio communications. Like many functional organizations, it regulates matters that serve all users, such as setting technical standards that help ensure that one state's telephone system can receive signals from another's. Broadcasting involves a physical common pool with potential conflicts of interest because radio or television signals do not stop at international borders. Thus the ITU allocates frequencies so that, for example, Canadians do not broadcast TV signals at the frequencies used by U.S. police agencies for field radio communications.

INTERNATIONAL POLITICAL FORUMS

International collective action organizations provide important forums in which political issues can be debated and publicized. Indeed, such forums are much more widely known than the activities of functional organizations such as the International Telecommunications Union. Undoubtedly, the agencies and organs of the United Nations provide the most familiar of such political forums. Having grown from 51 members at its founding in 1945 to 185 by its fiftieth anniversary, and with only a handful of states holding out as nonmembers, the UN easily qualifies as humankind's closest approach yet to a universal world political organization. A speech before the General Assembly is the closest most leaders can come to addressing all the earth's peoples, and an appeal to the Security Council often is one of the first steps taken to resolve the threat or actuality of war. The UN also provides a symbolically neutral location for delicate and off-the-record political contacts between adversaries. We can see all the tactics of negotiation discussed in

A HIGH-TECH FUNCTIONAL CONCERN: ALLOCATING SLOTS FOR SYNCHRONOUS EARTH SATELLITES

A somewhat controversial International Telecommunications Union (ITU) responsibility involves allocating synchronous satellite positions because states around the world increasingly rely on satellite relay of radio, telephone, television, and other electronic signals. This usually is accomplished through so-called synchronous satellites placed some 22,000 miles above the equator, where their orbital speed exactly balances earth's gravity to maintain stable altitude. Making exactly one revolution around the earth daily, they appear to be parked above a fixed point on the equator. In reality, position control is less than perfect, so satellites wander a bit and must be nudged back into position periodically by onboard gas jets. Consequently, a block of space must be reserved for each satellite to allow those wanderings without collisions. The ring of space at 22,000 miles above the equator is thus a physically determined common pool with finite capacity and all the other problems associated with such pools. If unlimited numbers of satellites are launched, collisions eventually will reduce them to rubble. Worse yet, the rubble could virtually destroy the resource because no new synchronous satellites could be launched without an enormously expensive cleanup in advance. One aspect of solving this common pool problem is stunningly clear: just as the number of cattle grazing on Boston Common must be limited, orbital slots must be limited in number.

In the early days of earth satellites, roughly from 1957 through the 1960s, the pool was uncrowded. Few states possessed adequate knowledge and resources to develop and launch satellites, and even they had very few. But knowledge soon spread, potential uses and traffic volume mushroomed, and new players entered the pool. Competition for scarce orbital allocation slots threatened to become serious. The political answer was to develop an international regulatory regime because unrestricted launches imperiled both old and new satellites, along with their users and applications. Both physical limitations and political considerations then came into play. Technological advances may improve guidance, thereby reducing wandering and diminishing the required size of allocations, allowing more slots, but the number of slots will remain finite. Moreover, older satellites will continue to need their allocated spaces so long as they remain in service. Other technological advances regularly increase new satellites' bandwidth and number of channels, adding to their information transmission capacity—but the number of slots still remains finite.

Political controversy regarding orbital slots revolves primarily around state development. Because orbital slots are a limited physical resource, are they part of the inalienable heritage of all humans? Does every state have an equal right to access, regardless of present wealth and technology level? Should slots be allocated on a first-come-first-served basis, giving preference to states that developed and first used the technology? Should volume of usage receive preference? Should slots be reserved for presently developing states to use in the future? Should space be allocated by population rather than level of technological advancement? Can developing states be accommodated by promising them channels on present and future satellites? Should we expect that future technological advances will increase the numbers of channels and improve navigation to safely allow smaller slots and more satellites to accommodate developing states? Resolving issues like these typically involves lengthy negotiations and more compromise than principle. Thus far, the ITU's international allocation regime has leaned toward the rights of prior users and expectations of future capacity improvements.

Chapter 10 there. Other regional (e.g., the Organization of American States) or functionally defined (e.g., the G-8 major economic powers) IGOs play similar but more bounded roles in facilitating intergovernmental contacts. UN forums have played important roles in establishing major new regimes, such as the global warming regime discussed later in this chapter. NGOs also provide important, typically specialized, international forums. Because of its great international influence and many IGO and regime memberships, the United States is an important participant in many international political forums, which often provide useful venues for pursuing foreign policy contacts, negotiations, and formal policy statements.

PEACEMAKING, HUMANITARIAN RELIEF, PEACEKEEPING, PEACE ENFORCEMENT, NATION BUILDING, AND POLICE ACTIONS

The concepts of peacemaking, peacekeeping, peace enforcement, police actions, and nation building were examined in detail in Chapter 9. Recall that these diverse activities vary enormously in the amount of force employed and the degree of consent obtained from target governments (see Figure 9.1 on page 350). International governmental organizations (IGOs) may perform or coordinate any of these activities, often through their specialized functional agencies. The UN, for example, has organized peacemaking and peacekeeping operations that report to the Security Council. International regimes may be organized to carry out some of these activities in particular instances or regions, as the UN organized a regime to search out and destroy Iraq's weapons of mass destruction after the Persian Gulf War. International nongovernmental organizations (NGOs or INGOs) normally are limited to nonviolent operations, such as humanitarian relief missions. The International Red Cross provides one such example.

The Cold War's end terminated U.S.-Soviet polarization that had often paralyzed peace actions during the UN's first forty-five years. Thus the door was opened to expanded peacekeeping and related activities. Unfortunately, as William Durch (1993a, 2) points out, "[T]he [United Nations] can only be asked to do as much or as little as its members are willing to agree on and pay for. The difficulty of late is that they have been agreeing much more readily than they have been paying."

Durch's trenchant comment should remind us that international peace actions are collective attempts to attain collective ends, and all the problems of collective action apply. Because there is no standing universal enforcer, each instance must be dealt with ad hoc. Coalitions must be negotiated and the nature and scope of action decided. If an issue is taken to the UN Security Council, for example, the council must decide whether to rule on it. If force is authorized, member governments willing to participate must be found. Force levels, numbers and types of forces from each contributor, channels of command, assessments to pay for the action, and scope of authorized actions all must be negotiated. Some nonparticipating members may hold out and refuse to pay their assessments, and, as the 1994 U.S. pullout from Somalia reminds us, participating members can always decide to withdraw. In general, as the costs, severity, and duration of action increase, cooperation decreases and the likelihood of pullouts increases. Internationalism calls for engaging in all these varieties of cooperative peace actions, as the United States has done many times over the decades since World War II. Given the increased demand for peace actions since the end of the Cold War, an important contemporary question is how involved the United States will be in the future.

INTERNATIONAL LAW

International law is the evolving cumulative product of agreements and practices that states and other international actors have built over time, working individually and through international governmental organizations, and sometimes establishing new international regimes to regulate specific types of activities. Like international political economics, international law is so huge a subject that entire courses are devoted to it at major universities. Like international regimes, international law is at different times and in highly variable combinations both a tool of U.S. foreign policy and a constraint on U.S. policy options. Unlike domestic law, international law has no regular enforcers, although weaker states sometimes are punished for violations. Also unlike domestic law, there is no universally recognized legislative body empowered to create new law, although institutions and procedures exist for making, interpreting, and executing rules. Substantively defined bodies of international law, such as the law of the sea or the laws of war, deal with common pools and suffer all their difficulties.

According to Article 38 of the Statute of the International Court of Justice, the three major sources of international law are, in order of importance, (1) international conventions or treaties, (2) custom or accepted usage, and (3) general principles of law accepted by civilized nations. Secondary sources include the judicial decisions of international courts and the writings of legal scholars.

Despite its severe limitations, international law performs a growing number of useful functions for governments (primarily) and other international actors (secondarily). It establishes a body of expectations about normal behavior in the global arena. It sets standards against which new governments may be measured and, hopefully and eventually, to which they can be socialized. It encompasses procedures for communication even during crises, when such interchanges may provide the best hope of avoiding escalation. (See the discussion of diplomatic institutions in Chapter 10.) It includes the international agreements and administrative rules under which functional policy coordination operates. (See the discussion of international regimes earlier.) International law remains highly state centric, focused particularly on issues of territory and nationality. Recent international actions regarding human rights, however, represent significant expansions in the positivist direction. Moves to apply the Universal Declaration on Human Rights to the specific actions of states toward their citizens, as in the case of China's repression of political dissidents, represent—or at least threaten—significant inroads on state sovereignty. Some of the more powerful actors in this arena are not governments, but NGOs; see the specific case of Amnesty International later. The United States has never had a completely supportive attitude toward the growing body of international law. Congressional conservatives particularly see it as an infringement on sovereignty, which it must be to succeed.

ILLUSTRATIVE CASES

The remainder of this chapter discusses three major cases demonstrating very different forms of international cooperation, supported to different degrees by the U.S.

government and people: (1) UN peacekeeping in the early aftermath of the Persian Gulf War, (2) the Climate Change Convention with its associated global warming regime, and (3) the major international nongovernmental organization Amnesty International. Each case is distinct and involves details beyond the general theories set out earlier. Nonetheless, those theories give us an organizing framework to begin understanding these individual cases themselves, the lessons we should draw from them, and the significance of these different types of international collective action for U.S. foreign policy.

UN PEACEKEEPING AFTER THE PERSIAN GULF WAR

Organizing international collective peacekeeping action through international governmental organizations demonstrates several lessons of the tragedy of the commons. Like grazing rights on Boston Common, local, regional, and international peace are collective goods because most governments and people benefit from peace, but no single government can ensure peace. Security regions may be considered common pools because conflicts between two states often spill over and affect other states through expanding war, economic disruptions, and refugee movements. Indeed, we may consider that peacekeeping involves overlapping common pools: One pool includes the immediate combatants and the local interests of larger outside powers, but is part of a larger regional or global pool.

In principle, peacekeeping activities benefit almost the entire international community by limiting violent conflict, and harm only those who believe their interests are served by war. Peacekeeping, of course, is most often conducted by outside powers to protect their own interests in the region and prevent conflict from spreading outside. Regulation in this case typically means formal arrangements through the UN Security Council to organize and manage peacekeeping missions. Equity issues arise mainly in the fact that multilateral international peacekeeping depends on participation by numerous governments to preserve impartiality and political neutrality in appearance and reality.

Post–Gulf War peacekeeping also demonstrates the core lesson of the prisoners' dilemma. If too many governments hold out and decline to act, thinking that their likely costs of peacekeeping outweigh their potential benefits, collective inaction may allow regional violence to escalate and spread outside the region, ultimately causing far greater losses to everyone. Government leaders may choose to avoid participation because they perceive only limited benefits; because of domestic political pressures regarding costs, casualties, or the interests affected; or out of blatant (if, perhaps, unadmitted) desires to free ride. Maintaining a fair peace between Iraq and Kuwait is, after all, in the interests of almost all states, in and out of the region. In the United States, domestic disagreements over peacekeeping efforts usually are part of the ongoing struggle between the president and Congress for foreign policy control, typically expressed in the form of congressional limitations under the War Powers Act on how long U.S. troops may be used. Such limitations were applied, for example, in Lebanon in the 1980s, Somalia in 1993–94, and Bosnia in 1997–98.

Peacekeeping is one of the more moderate steps discussed earlier. Three distinct UN actions begun shortly after the Persian Gulf War involve different activities and different degrees of force. (1) A UN Special Commission (UNSCOM), a special-purpose IGO of limited duration but still operating more than six years later, was empowered to locate and destroy Iraq's non-nuclear weapons of mass destruction and the systems to deliver them to targets. Coordinated responsibility for locating and destroying nuclear weapons and facilities was delegated to the International Atomic Energy Agency, one of the many UN functional agencies. Together, these arrangements were designed to neutralize Iraq's widespread and highly redundant nuclear weapons program, along with its chemical weapons, ballistic missiles, and laboratories and factories dedicated to their development and production. The Special Commission's work punished Iraq by destroying weapons and weapons development facilities, and attempted to protect potential future victims from further Iraqi aggression. It probably is best classified as an instance of peace enforcement, although with no significant use of military force (which undoubtedly complicated the UN inspectors' difficult tasks in coping with Iraqi subterfuge and overt resistance). (2) Humanitarian relief operations for Kurds in northern Iraq—who had rebelled, only to be crushed by Saddam's remaining forces—were carried out with substantial military forces from the United States and a few other countries, along with a small and largely symbolic UN constabulary. These actions were organized with the approval of the UN Security Council. (3) The United Nations Iraq-Kuwait Observation Mission (referred to herein as the Mission or UNIKOM) was pure peacekeeping, an initially unarmed military observer mission to verify demarcation of, and compliance with, the Iraq-Kuwait border. UNIKOM is the focus of this section.

Circumstances that call for peacekeeping vary tremendously, and the UN has no standing military forces. For these two reasons, each UN peacekeeping mission, including its mandate, organization, forces, and logistics, is a unique ad hoc arrangement designed to deal with one specific situation. Thus, even though some procedures are common to different peacekeeping operations, each such operation deserves separate study. When we examine real and potential peacekeeping situations, we need to study (1) the affected area—its history and political, military, economic, societal, and legal characteristics, (2) the UN resolutions authorizing action, including their specific mandates and restrictions, (3) the forces deployed—who they are, how many people are involved, their armaments and potential power, their rules of engagement, and how the peacekeeping force will be managed, and (4) what arrangements have been made for providing needed logistical support.

The characteristics and history of the post–Persian Gulf War setting are discussed in Chapter 1. Here we examine one small part of the international arrangements made to stabilize the situation and ensure regional security after the U.S.-declared cease-fire of 27 February. On 3 April 1991, some five weeks later, the UN Security Council passed Resolution 687 (1991). It reaffirmed the earlier economic sanctions and arms embargo against Iraq, offered a formal cease-fire on Iraq's acceptance of the resolution's terms, declared a demilitarized buffer zone (DMZ) extending 10 kilometers (about 6.2 miles) into Iraq and 5 kilometers into Kuwait from the official Iraq-Kuwait border, and created UNIKOM to be a UN observer force in that DMZ (see UNRes687). Iraq formally accepted these terms on 6 April 1991 (Goshko, 1991).

The UNIKOM peacekeeping mission's mandate was to monitor the 125-mile-long DMZ and the 25-mile-long Khawr'Abd Allah waterway, which together form the Iraq-Kuwait border. Within those areas, UNIKOM was to deter boundary violations through its presence and its surveillance of the DMZ and to observe any hostile action mounted from the territory of one state against the other. Humanitarian missions were carefully eschewed; responsibility for refugee relief was assigned to the UN High Commissioner for Refugees and the Red Cross. Initially, UNIKOM's observers were unarmed; the Mission's original mandate granted neither authority nor capacity to take actions to prevent military personnel or equipment from entering the DMZ. Instead, UNIKOM could only monitor (observe) and report on proscribed military activity. Responsibility for maintaining law and order in the DMZ remained with the governments of Iraq and Kuwait, and their police were allowed only sidearms. Obviously, UNIKOM lacked the power and authority to force compliance with UN terms. Compliance depended on genuine desires to keep the peace and potential embarrassment over detected violations, backed up by the deterrent potential of the UN and other powers such as the United States to take stronger actions.

In the absence of dedicated UN standing forces, neither Security Council resolutions calling for "immediate deployment" nor pressing needs in the field can bring any peacekeeping force into existence overnight, yet neither does it emerge from a vacuum. We may divide the process into major stages of initial planning, on-site deployment planning, setup and deployment, and actual operations. Each stage may be facilitated by drawing on prior planning, experience, and troops already trained and available. Initial planning for UNIKOM proceeded rapidly because the potential need for such a mission had been foreseen at least as early as the air war in February. Resolution 687 (1991) requested the secretary-general to submit to the Security Council within three days a plan for UNIKOM's immediate deployment. A sketchy plan was submitted only two days later, on 5 April, and approved by the council on 9 April in Resolution 689 (1991). Working out detailed logistical and budgetary details required two more weeks. On-site deployment planning began when a UNIKOM advance party consisting of the first commander and a dozen borrowed UN headquarters staffers arrived in the area on 13 April and prepared the structural deployment plan. Deployment took about three more weeks, with the Mission wholly dependent on U.S. Army logistical support, but UNIKOM was fully deployed by 6 May, just over one month after the original authorizing resolution. The DMZ officially came into existence on 9 May, after UNIKOM had monitored the withdrawal of military forces still in the zone. The Mission's full observation responsibilities then began. Security during the setup phase was provided by five infantry companies drawn from relatively nearby UN peacekeeping forces in Cyprus and Lebanon, which were withdrawn by the end of June 1991. UNIKOM's operational arrangements combined patrol and observation bases, temporary observation points in areas of particular activity or where roads or tracks entered the desert DMZ, ground and air patrols, investigation teams, and liaison with the regional parties. The DMZ was divided into three sectors, each with a headquarters and six observation posts/patrol bases.

Peacekeeping usually requires that all parties desire help in implementing a peace to which they have agreed. In the Persian Gulf War case, Iraq's agreement with most ceasefire conditions was limited and grudging. Saddam's government regularly used so-called **salami tactics,** endlessly pushing just a bit beyond what the rules allowed, and, if not stopped, pushing just a bit further. (The logic behind the term *salami tactics* is that what is lost at each step is only a tiny slice of the salami, and therefore not worth fighting over, but eventually the whole salami is gone.) Given Iraq's very limited cooperation, all post–Gulf War UN missions relied to an unusual degree on the implied deterrent threat of great power military action to support Security Council resolutions and the missions established to implement them. Given Iraq's blatant aggression against Kuwait in 1990, one might have expected armed peacekeepers in UNIKOM. But unarmed personnel no doubt seemed appropriate for an observation mission. Arms were not allowed until almost two years later, after Iraq had piled up a record of violations. Security Council Resolution 806 (5 February 1993) expanded UNIKOM's tasks to allow limited physical action to prevent or redress small violations of the boundary or DMZ. Resolution 806 came in response to a series of Iraqi incursions into the Kuwaiti side of the DMZ and unauthorized retrievals of property from Kuwaiti territory, and raised the mission's authorized strength. By the late summer of 1991, disguised bands of Iraqi soldiers regularly entered the DMZ to raid weapons caches and dig up land mines, for which their government paid cash rewards. UNIKOM recorded numerous casualties and often was asked to help evacuate the injured to hospitals (Durch, 1993b, 266). The secretary-general's report in early April 1993 proposed reinforcing the military observers with one mechanized infantry battalion; although approved by the Security Council on 13 April, that battalion was not fully deployed until January 1994.

UNIKOM's forces peaked at 1,440 in June 1991, never reaching authorized levels of 300 military observers and 3,645 total personnel. By the fall of 1994 the Mission included 243 observers, 881 troops and support personnel, and 80 international and 130 local civilian staff. Observers numbered fewer than one per 4 square miles. After some rotations of forces, 4 states had troops in UNIKOM, and they and 28 other states (including France, Russia, the UK, and the United States) each had 2 to 15 observers in place. The 1994 Mission costs totaled roughly $68.6 million, with two thirds paid by the government of Kuwait and the remainder assessed to UN member states (UNIKOM, 1994). Three fatalities had been incurred. UNIKOM also assisted other UN missions in Iraq and Kuwait, providing technical support to the Iraq-Kuwait Boundary Demarcation Commission until its dissolution in May 1993 and to the UN office facilitating the return of Kuwaiti property from Iraq; movement control of all UN aircraft operating in the area; and assistance in relocating Iraqi citizens from the Kuwaiti side of the border, a task completed in February 1994. Violations observed through 1994 were primarily of three types: minor ground incursions by small groups of soldiers, military aircraft overflights, and police carrying weapons other than sidearms. The vast majority of violations during the first two months were air and ground incursions into the DMZ by Kuwaiti or allied forces.

What operational lessons does this case teach regarding the future of peacekeeping endeavors like UNIKOM as elements in U.S. foreign policy? UNIKOM functioned as intended, verifying the separation of forces and compliance with the Iraq-Kuwait border. However, it suffered from initial disorganization and appeared to need both better advance planning and higher cost effectiveness. As William Durch (1993b, 267) summarized,

> UNIKOM is doing the job it was sent out to do, but its early weeks were far more disorganized than they needed to be. Operational plans were drawn up in the field, as observers and initial equipment began to arrive and stack up, reflecting the basic lack of planning capacity at UN Headquarters. The delays in establishing habitable field accommodations illustrate an outmoded supply system that has no reserves and no stockpiles, as well as a seemingly counterproductive requirement for committee approval of any novel expenditure over $40,000.

The organization and its member states can draw on more than fifty years' experience in mounting peacekeeping missions when planning and executing new missions. Yet even with transfers from other nearby UN peacekeeping forces, UNIKOM required about a month to reach operational status. Its forces barely exceeded a third of authorized levels and military observers were less than one fifth of total personnel, numbers that might lend support to congressional conservatives who decry UN waste and inefficiency.

UNIKOM's mandate was constrained to limit its geographical area and avoid entangling humanitarian missions, and UN reluctance to deploy an armed force in the DMZ before 1993 appears to reflect well-reasoned political judgment. Historically, unarmed observer forces usually have been used where armed forces would be too sensitive politically, as between Iran and Iraq after their 1980–88 war. Although Iraq's aggression against Kuwait undoubtedly justified UN military forces in the DMZ, the zone then might have become a haven for thousands of unhappy Iraqis, creating a new population of UN dependents unwelcome either in their homeland or in Kuwait. With only unarmed observers in the DMZ, potential Iraqi refugees knew they would not be protected against reprisals. Although this UN limit on UNIKOM's role may seem cynical from a human rights standpoint, it was realistic in light of limited UN capabilities. Once it became clear that UNIKOM would not exercise a military role, however, Iraq began violating UN requirements in numerous ways, including weapons-gathering incursions, failures to dismantle police posts on Kuwaiti territory, and maintaining posts closer to the border than allowed (Durch, 1993b, 268).

The UN tried to carry out UNIKOM's mission without bias, as it usually does. Thus using observers but not troops from major combatants like Britain, France, and the United States made political sense, although it probably did nothing to improve Iraq's limited and grudging cooperation. Although more than 33 states contributed personnel to UNIKOM at one time or another, the 4 states that had troops on duty in the fall of 1994 (Argentina, 50; Austria, 12; Bangladesh, 775; Denmark, 44) were typical Cold War "usual suspects" for such duty, states which had remained relatively nonaligned. Resolution 689 (1991) implied that UNIKOM could exist indefinitely, requiring review but not reauthorization every six months. This mission soon appeared very open ended, illustrating the slow growth of demands that now exceed available resources for UN peacekeeping. Note that some peacekeeping operations, like those in Cyprus and Lebanon, continue for decades, typically well out of the U.S. news limelight. Indeed, UNIKOM enjoyed almost no publicity in the United States, whereas more unusual and more salient missions such as the UN Special Commission on weapons of mass destruction regularly appeared in news reports.

When obvious impartiality is important, peacekeeping under the auspices of the UN may be a useful tool for U.S. foreign policy. It also helps meet peacekeeping needs where the United States has interests but the Congress and public are reluctant to commit troops. Despite quibbles—not entirely unjustified—about UN bureaucracy and inefficiency, peacekeeping usually is relatively inexpensive, particularly when measured against the potential costs if hot wars resume. Concerns about UN inefficiencies have been high among conservatives in the U.S. Congress in recent years and played a major role in the 1996 U.S. decision to veto a second term for Secretary-General Boutros Boutros-Ghali. Acting entirely alone, the United States forced another choice, which fell to the highly regarded Kofi Annan of Ghana, who had headed UN peacekeeping operations from 1993 through 1995. Nonetheless, by 1997 there was concern that despite Annan's evident intent to reform UN administration and his desire to expand UN peacekeeping capabilities, Washington policymakers were leaning more toward ad hoc peacekeeping arrangements through coalitions outside the UN. One notable example was the NATO peacekeeping force arranged under the 1995 Dayton accords for Bosnian peace.

THE CLIMATE CHANGE CONVENTION AND THE EVOLVING GLOBAL WARMING REGIME

Organizing international collective action to control climate change demonstrates many of the lessons of the tragedy of the commons. First, it involves a physical common pool resource—global climate—that may be irreparably harmed if there are too many hold-outs. Unlike the maximum number of cattle that can be grazed on Boston Common, there is no clear absolute limit to world temperature, although we can predict serious damage to many states and people from only small increases. Like any international regime, the United Nations Framework Convention on Climate Change (hereinafter, UNFCCC)—some 165 governments by 1997, including the United States and the other most developed states—is organized from below by member states just as the common's cattle farmers might organize to regulate grazing. Unlike those farmers, however, UNFCCC member states cannot appeal to some higher sovereignty to recognize their regulatory authority and coerce holdouts. Instead, they must rely on such tools as compensating political and economic trades, moral suasion, public embarrassment of hold-outs, and eventually convincing others of the logic of cooperation. The United States has raised the issue of making emissions quotas tradable, just as grazing rights on the common might be traded if allowed by the regulators. Finally, many developing states raise equity issues when they ask to be exempted from cutbacks in greenhouse gas emissions while they pursue rapid development. The climate change case also demonstrates two key lessons of the prisoners' dilemma. Regulation means formal arrangements through the UNFCCC to promote but not compel cooperation. Defecting (holding out) may lead to collective disaster in the long run but gain for the holdouts in the short run.

The Climate Change Convention demonstrates how the U.S. government and the majority of other states around the world are building a new regime to deal with a major problem in the common pool that is the global environment. International regimes were introduced earlier in this chapter, with brief mention of the UNFCCC. That convention is a notable example of a regime as work-in-progress, having been developed mostly since 1990, especially since the 1992 UN Earth Summit in Rio de Janeiro, and likely to continue evolving for some time to come. Although no regime is ever under the complete control of any one government, working within regimes which promote cooperation sought by the U.S. government—as this one does—can be vital to U.S. foreign policy.

Dealing with climate change involves global interactions among science, technology, and politics as they influence a very large and highly complex natural system, in the sense of "system" discussed in Chapter 4. Human activities, particularly the production of so-called greenhouse gases by the burning of fossil fuels, have grown in scope to create significant long-term effects planetwide. Earth's climate is an obvious and enormous common pool; global warming affects each of us and is affected by the sum of all our individual actions, regardless of our awareness or desires. This is one instance in which science and technology have made new human behaviors possible, with some benefits and some seriously undesirable—and unexpected—effects. Because the natural system involved spans the globe, complex and difficult international politics are unavoidable in

HOW GREENHOUSE GASES PRODUCE GLOBAL WARMING

This is a case in which science and technology have made new human behaviors possible, only to discover later that physical processes link with those behaviors to create seriously damaging effects worldwide. Solutions then require both technology and politics.

Ultimately, the sun is the source of all energy on earth, ranging from direct heat input to the stored energy in fossil fuels formed from vegetation that lived millions of years ago. As our planet evolved, a fairly stable temperature range was reached, and the life-forms we know today all evolved to live within that range. For global average temperature to remain stable over the long term, the earth must radiate away as much energy as it absorbs from the sun. Our atmosphere stores and distributes heat, preventing the tremendous dayside-to-nightside temperature fluctuations seen on other planetary bodies such as earth's airless moon. Most solar energy arrives as short-wavelength radiation, some of which is reflected away by the atmosphere, although most passes through to the surface. There again some is reflected away, but much is absorbed, converted to heat, and radiated as long-wavelength infrared radiation. In turn, most of that radiation is absorbed by airborne water vapor and **greenhouse gases,** so called because they help absorb and trap surface infrared radiation in much the same manner as greenhouse windows. The most important such gases are carbon dioxide (CO_2), methane (CH_4), and nitrous oxide (N_2O). Occurring naturally, they make up less than one tenth of 1 percent of our atmosphere, which is mainly oxygen (21 percent) and nitrogen (78 percent). Yet, although fairly rare, the greenhouse gases are crucial to life as we know it. Without them, the earth's surface would average about 54 degrees Fahrenheit colder than today (see UNFCCC, 1999, 2).

Unfortunately, with greenhouse gases as with many other necessities, there can be too much of a good thing. For example, space probes tell us that the atmosphere of Venus traps so much heat that temperatures average hundreds of degrees, hot enough to melt lead. Earth's present equilibrium temperature will change if crucial determining factors, such as the chemical composition of the atmosphere, change. Human life and all the other life-forms on which we depend are closely matched to present earthly conditions, but our activities now threaten to raise earth's temperature balance by significantly increasing greenhouse gases. Chief culprits are agriculture, burning of fossil fuels, and deforestation. Cattle, for example, release surprisingly large amounts of methane as a digestive by-product. (Space scientists have even suggested searching for atmospheric methane as a potential indicator of life on other worlds.) Burning petroleum and products refined from it, for purposes such as transportation, electric power generation, and heating, releases large amounts of carbon dioxide. Deforestation affects the greenhouse gas balance both by releasing carbon dioxide through widespread burning and by removing vast stands of trees that otherwise would absorb CO_2, store the carbon, and release vital oxygen to the atmosphere.

Carbon dioxide seems clearly to be the most important greenhouse gas resulting from human actions. It is estimated (UNFCCC, 1997, 2) that if emissions continue growing at current rates, atmospheric carbon dioxide will double from pre-1850 levels (that is, before widespread industrialization, although the industrial revolution began first in Britain around 1760) by 2030 and triple by 2100. Freezing emissions at current levels would postpone CO_2 doubling to 2100. Climate models predict that changes would continue for centuries after atmospheric gas concentrations stabilized, and it is estimated that emissions would have to be cut to perhaps 30 percent of present levels for concentrations to stabilize

(continued)

(continued)

eventually at double the present level. The unsettling implication is that human activities have already made irreversible changes in our planet, not just in localized areas but globally.

In the 1950s Walt Kelly's comic strip character Pogo paraphrased Oliver Hazard Perry's War of 1812 dispatch by declaring, "We have met the enemy, and he is us." Human populations and population densities and the technologies that produce greenhouse gas emissions all grew exponentially (that is, with an ever-increasing rate of increase) throughout the twentieth century. Developing states, typically those with the fastest growing populations, now often seek growth by applying the same offending techniques used earlier by the already developed states. Currently, states of the industrialized North, with about 20 percent of world population, use about 80 percent of global resources. Technologies developed mostly over the last 150 years—and largely in the twentieth century—have combined with rapid population growth to make human environmental impact global.

Such an outcome hardly could have been foreseen during the founding years of the United States. Images commonly held by citizens then, from merchants to politicians to homesteaders, were of subduing a vast, rich, undeveloped, and essentially indestructible land with almost unbounded potential. Humans were few and faced daunting challenges in developing the land. Clearing forests was seen as good because it yielded both arable farmland and timber for building; homesteaders on the great plains built sod houses only because there was no local timber. Today, as legal struggles continue about cutting the few remaining old growth forest areas of the Northwest, some people look to histories of the forests that originally covered such states as Michigan and Wisconsin, noting that none survive. Environmentalists today strive to inculcate principles that humanity must give up subduing nature and begin finding ways to live with its lands, if people are to survive in the long run and

enjoy good living conditions in even the fairly short run.

Even small increases in global average temperatures can create serious problems for people in many regions of the world. Weather almost certainly will be affected as rainfall and evaporation patterns change. In turn, these affect freshwater resources vital to individuals, industry, and agriculture. Farming seems likely to suffer some regional dislocations that easily could lead to food shortages in some areas. Rising sea levels threaten not only extensive coastal flooding, but possible increases in severe storms. Economies, settlements, and health seem likely to experience numerous impacts, both direct and indirect.

By the latter 1990s a scientific consensus was emerging that global warming is likely to run between 1.5 and 4.5 degrees Celsius (2.7 to 8.1 degrees Fahrenheit) over the next century. Some authorities also believe that past greenhouse gas emissions have already added about 0.5 degrees C (0.9 degrees F) since 1850 (UNFCCC, 1999, 2). Mean sea level is expected to rise 15 to 95 centimeters (5.9 to 37.4 inches), threatening widespread flooding and other damage, particularly to a number of island states already barely above sea level. Climate zones could be shifted 150 to 550 kilometers (93 to 342 miles) northward in middle-latitude regions, dislocating the associated ecosystems and agricultural regions (UNFCCC 1997, 1).

As in many other systems having serious impacts on humans, the science of global warming is disputed, both because of genuine scientific disagreements and because many individuals, firms, and governments have huge stakes in maintaining business as usual—a classic case of exploiting an endangered common pool. Much of the science is quite new, making honest disagreements more likely and dishonest disagreements easier. Clearly, there is a wide range of uncertainty in quantitative scientific estimates of global warming, although there no longer is much dispute that temperatures are rising.

dealing with global warming. Understanding physical processes requires the physical sciences, but changing human behaviors to reduce or eliminate the bad effects is the province of political and behavioral science.

Manifold political problems face those trying to deal with global warming, partly because the physical processes take many years and their effects persist far beyond the terms in office, or even the lifetimes, of politicians and bureaucrats. Even if we could drastically cut greenhouse gas emissions tomorrow, the warming trend would continue for centuries. Dealing with climate change is thus a genuine instance when politicians need to plan now for impacts not only on today's children, which politicians usually love to do, but on generations of the descendants of today's children. In the absence of regulation, ecological damage can occur much more rapidly than we can either gain adequate understanding of the consequences or build sufficient political support to take action. For example, by the late 1990s there was genuine concern that Indonesia, seeking rapid development and endowed with only a fledgling environmental movement, could destroy most of its rich rain forest within another decade. Yet despite environmental threats of such tremendous magnitude and great duration, and notwithstanding ever-present worries about common pool exploitation and holdouts, governments may be responding more rapidly than cynical political scientists would have expected. For a brief history of the evolution of the UN Framework Convention on Climate Change and its associated regime through 1998, see Chronology 12.1.

Faced with scientific consensus that global warming is a real threat, but with many unknowns about its severity, timetable, and possible solutions, most members of the UN committed in 1992 to a **framework convention** (treaty), whereby they agreed to do something sometime in the future, and established procedures for working out what and when. In any such framework agreement, the devil truly is in the details, which are difficult to work out because not all governments have identical interests. Nonetheless, we should avoid excessive skepticism; widespread international acceptance of the 1992 agreement and subsequent steps to actualize a global climate change regime represent serious accomplishments. The convention indicates broad international recognition of a serious problem and establishes expectations that detailed procedures will be developed to deal with that problem. It sets the "ultimate objective" of stabilizing "greenhouse gas concentrations in the atmosphere at a level that would prevent dangerous anthropogenic (human-induced) interference with the climate system." This nonspecific objective recognizes that it may take another decade of scientific work, another generation of supercomputers, and considerable political-scientific bargaining to resolve current uncertainties. Nonetheless, the convention's objective remains meaningful, regardless what atmospheric concentration of greenhouse gases is ultimately accepted as dangerous. It directs that "such a level should be achieved within a time-frame sufficient to allow ecosystems to adapt naturally to climate change, to ensure that food production is not threatened and to enable economic development to proceed in a sustainable manner" (UNFCCC, 1999, 3).

In the absence of an international government with power to compel cooperation, political solutions to international physical system problems like climate change must proceed by coordinating action, building agreement that a problem exists, and creating expectations that the future will bring improvements in knowledge and steps toward an ultimate solution. Thus, in common with other international regimes, the UN Framework Convention on Climate Change creates expectations about international "behavioral norms" about how individual governments and their citizens should act. In particular, the convention reflects an emerging consensus that all states need to reduce greenhouse gas emissions significantly and soon, and that the biggest producers—including the United States—should act first. International educational efforts by scientists, activists, and interested governments did much to make the convention possible, and an agreement to "turn the corner" by reducing and then ending the increase of greenhouse emissions represents an important first step.

Turning the corner is often a political first step to later and much more far-reaching agreements. Such was the case, for example, in the 1972 U.S.-Soviet SALT I strategic arms-capping agreement, and in the Clinton administration's agreements with Congress to balance the federal budget by the year 2002. New international bodies like the 1991–95 Intergovernmental Negotiating Committee (see Table 12.1) were created to further the convention's definition and implementation. In hard bargaining within that committee, negotiators from some 150 countries set a strict deadline to have a treaty agreed on by the 1992 Earth Summit, and they completed their draft in fifteen months. The climate change regime will continue to develop for some time, as additional agreements defining concrete actions to be taken within the framework convention are hammered out. The convention already places governments under what political scientists call "cross-level" pressures, from above and outside by agencies of an international regime created under UN auspices, and from below and inside by their own citizen-activists and established interest groups.

Very intense bargaining over the details of concrete actions was evident at the Third Conference of the Parties (COP-3) under the UNFCC, held in Kyoto, Japan, 1–12 December 1997. This produced the first set of mandated action requirements to begin meeting the goals of the framework convention. Governments took dramatically different stands on what reductions in greenhouse emissions should be mandated, depending on their differing state interests and expectations regarding anticipated climatic and other impacts of warming (see Table 12.1). In October 1997 President Clinton announced a U.S. bargaining position for Kyoto proposing that greenhouse gas emissions be reduced worldwide to 1990 levels by 2010 and developing states be required to bear a share of the burdens of accomplishing those reductions. Most environmentalists termed the proposed reductions wholly inadequate, whereas industry advocates called them ruinously excessive and announced plans for an advertising campaign aimed at U.S. abrogation of the previously ratified convention. Advocates for developing states denounced the burden-sharing requirement as unfair and too great a restriction on their legitimate aspirations for higher standards of living.

As often happens in major multiparty negotiations, many important issues were finessed at Kyoto. After serious fears that no agreement would be reached, the United States retreated significantly from its October 1997 position. Thirty-eight developed states agreed to cut their aggregate greenhouse gas emissions to 5.2 percent below 1990 levels between 2008 and 2012. That overall target would be met by cuts varying among states, including the European Union, 8 percent; United States, 7 percent; and Japan, 6 percent.

No agreement was reached for emissions reductions by developing states, and working out details for possible trading of emissions rights was left for the November 1998 Fourth Conference of the Parties. Supporters called the Kyoto Protocol an historic,

⊕ CHRONOLOGY 12.1

Highlights in the Evolution of the United Nations Framework Convention on Climate Change and Its Associated Climate Change Regime Through 1998.

Date	Event
Late 1980s	A series of intergovernmental conferences on climate change begins.
1988	The UN Environment Program and the World Meteorological Organization establish the Intergovernmental Panel on Climate Change (IPCC) to assess the state of existing knowledge about the climate system and climate change; environmental, economic, and social impacts; and possible response strategies.
1990	First IPCC Assessment Report released and confirms the science used to study climate change. This report strongly influences subsequent negotiations on the convention. Second World Climate Conference calls for a framework treaty on climate change.
December	UN General Assembly approves start of climate change treaty negotiations.
1991 February	First of five major sessions of the Intergovernmental Negotiating Committee for a Framework Convention on Climate Change (INC/FCCC), continuing through May 1992. In hard bargaining, negotiators from some 150 countries set a strict deadline to have a treaty agreement by the 1992 Earth Summit and to complete that work in fifteen months.
1992 9 May	Adoption of the UN Framework Convention on Climate Change (in New York).
June	Convention opened for signatures at the UN Earth Summit, held in Rio de Janeiro, Brazil; many governments sign, including the United States, on 12 June.
15 October	United States ratifies the Convention.
1994	The convention enters into force on 21 March.
1995 February	INC/FCCC is dissolved after its eleventh and final session; thereafter, the Conference of Parties (COP) becomes the convention's ultimate authority.

significant, and necessary step on the long path to limiting global warming, although numerous environmentalists called the planned emissions reductions woefully inadequate. Opponents decried U.S. concessions and doubted our national capability and willingness to make the sacrifices needed to meet the 2012 target. An economic boom already had contributed to a 12 percent increase in American CO_2 emissions since 1990, and it was estimated the United States would need to reduce consumption of gasoline, natural gas, and the coal burned to make electricity by some 30 percent below levels expected to be consumed in 2012. (See, for example, Smeloff and Branfman, 1998.) Clearly, such reductions would mandate real changes in technologies and lifestyles. Opponents also challenged the failure to require reductions by developing states, noting that before long they would produce half the world's CO_2 emissions. Because the U.S. Senate already

March–April	First Conference of the Parties (COP-1), held in Berlin, Germany. Parties agree to begin negotiations to yield an agreement on climate change in the post-year-2000 period, to be adopted at the 1997 Kyoto conference. Ad Hoc Group on the Berlin Mandate is created for those negotiations.
1996	First greenhouse gas inventories filed by parties (33 developed states).
July	Second Conference of the Parties (COP-2), held in Geneva, Switzerland.
December	Negotiating session in Geneva.
1997	First greenhouse gas inventories due from developing states. By this year, some 165 parties (governments) had acceded to (signed) the convention.
28 July–7 August	Negotiating session in Bonn, Germany.
20–31 October 1–12 December	Third Conference of the Parties (COP-3), held in Kyoto, Japan. After hard bargaining, 38 developed states agreed to cut emissions by 2012 to 5.2 percent below 1990 levels. That overall target would be met by cuts varying among states, including European Union, 8 percent; United States, 7 percent; and Japan, 6 percent. No agreement was reached regarding cuts by developing states. Working out details for possible trading of emissions rights was left for a November 1998 meeting. US Senate ratification appeared dubious.
1998	Fourth Conference of the Parties (COP-4), held in Buenos Aires, Argentina.
2–18 November	Delegates made only modest progress, agreeing to set 2000 as the deadline for developing a global mechanism for policing reduced emissions of six major greenhouse gases. They also decided to allow (1) industrialized states to gain credits through a "clean development mechanism" by financing clean-air projects in developing states; (2) states to trade emission allowances with one another; and (3) developed states to gain credit by helping other developed states reduce emissions

Source: Data compiled from UNFCC, 1999, *USIA Electronic Journal*, 1997, and other sources referenced in this section.

had passed a resolution admonishing the Clinton administration not to agree to any treaty that did not require limitations on greenhouse gas emissions by developing states, ratification appeared doubtful.

The Fourth Conference of the Parties (COP-4), held at Buenos Aires on November 2–13, 1998, produced only modest progress. After a week of civil servants bickering, higher-ranking political officials arrived and began to cut some deals. Delegates set 2000 as the deadline for creating a global mechanism to police reduced emission of six major greenhouse gases. In small steps toward the U.S. position favoring emission reductions credits (opposed by major European governments), it was agreed that industrialized states could gain credits through a "clean development mechanism" by financing clean-air projects in developing states; that states could trade emission allowances with one another;

TABLE 12.1	Interests and Positions of Important Groups Prior to the Third UNFCCC Conference of the Parties (December 1–11, 1997), Which Yielded the Kyoto Protocol

Group	Interests and Positions
European Union	Supported binding targets and timetables for emissions reductions by developed states, taking a stand tougher than that of the United States. Internally, the EU's poorer members argued for higher emissions quotas within any future overall EU target; richer members who would have to make compensating reductions in their emissions objected.
Non-EU developed states (notably Australia, Canada, Japan, New Zealand, Norway, Switzerland, and the United States)	Generally supported a more flexible approach to limiting greenhouse gas emissions than did the EU, including emissions rights salable from states below their quotas to states over their quotas. In the United States, the Clinton administration retreated from more ambitious earlier stands and proposed the less ambitious goal of stabilizing greenhouse gas emissions levels, partly because the sustained economic boom of the mid-1990s had raised U.S. emissions substantially.
Industrialized Central and Eastern European states, and former Soviet Union	Major greenhouse gas emitters are fearful of the monetary and economic recovery costs of implementing stringent emissions quotas. However, the difficulties of their transitions from command to market economies so badly disrupted production that emissions were expected to remain below 1990 levels through 2000, rising sharply thereafter.
Developing States	Many worked through the Group of 77 to develop common positions on emissions reductions and financial and technological transfers, but their state interests often diverged. China and some others have huge coal reserves they want to exploit for development; states with great forests want to limit demands to maintain those forests as carbon sinks for global benefit; newly industrializing countries (NICs) worry about being subjected soon to emissions-reduction targets; many African states focus on their multifaceted vulnerability.
Association of Small Island States (AOSIS)	Strongly supported rapid action to reduce emissions because its members are particularly vulnerable to sea-level rises.
OPEC	Concerned about the impact on their economies if other states reduced their petroleum use. In particular, OPEC states with very large oil reserves, like Kuwait and Saudi Arabia, emphasized scientific uncertainties and argued that the convention process should move slowly.
Business Groups	Energy-intensive firms worried about negative economic impacts of the convention; many in the insurance sector saw their firms vulnerable to losses associated with increased storms and other effects of climate disruption, and clean energy firms see new market opportunities.
Environmental Groups	Mostly from developed states, environmental groups have been active supporters of the convention process worldwide since its inception.
City Governments	Many city governments around the world have been extremely active in the climate change movement, making plans considerably more ambitions than those of their state governments. Urban governments often operate energy and transport utilities, and the governments of great cities may have substantial impact on emissions in their locales.

Source: Data compiled primarily from United Nations Climate Change Secretariat (UNFCCC), "A Brief History of the Climate Change Convention," 1997a. http://www.unfccc.de/fccc/conv/hist.htm (31 March 1997), and later updated.

CARTOON 12.1

The 1992 UN Framework Convention on Climate Change is organized by member states (165 governments by 1997, including the United States) and cannot appeal to some higher sovereignty to be heard. Instead, it must rely on moral persuasion and public embarrassment of holdouts to effect cooperation. The Association of Small Island States (AOSIS) supports rapid action to reduce greenhouse gas emissions because its members are particularly vulnerable to sea-level rises caused by global warming.

Toles © 1997 *The Buffalo News*. Reprinted with permission of Universal Press Syndicate. All rights reserved.

---

and that developed states could gain credits by helping other developed states reduce emissions (Rotella, 1999). These developments were thought to materially improve the chances of U.S. Senate ratification of the 1997 Kyoto Protocol. Resolving intergovernmental conflicts of interest under the UNFCCC may take many years. The stakes for everyone—as both local and global citizens—are enormous, however, and the politics somewhat new, quite fascinating, and well worth following as the climate change regime develops.

AMNESTY INTERNATIONAL: CITIZEN ACTION THROUGH AN NGO WITH CLOUT

Amnesty International differs in almost every respect from peacekeeping under UNIKOM and limiting global warming under the UNFCCC international regime. As an international nongovernmental organization, Amnesty's members are individual citizens of many countries, and they cooperate in lobbying governments on behalf of human rights in general and the rights of all prisoners. This is truly *grassroots citizen action*, designed to influence governments by nonviolent actions somewhat beyond their control. It is surprisingly effective.

Amnesty International also demonstrates some lessons of the tragedy of the commons. Although not dealing with a physical common pool like regional peacekeeping or global warming, Amnesty asserts that human rights, and prisoner rights in particular, are indivisible worldwide, and thus exist in a global political common pool. Somewhat analogously to international regimes or the common's cattle farmers organizing to regulate grazing, Amnesty organizes action from below. In order to persuade governments to cooperate, Amnesty must rely even more than international regimes upon lobbying tools such as moral suasion, public embarrassment of holdouts, and eventually convincing people of their logic. The fundamental equity issue they raise is worldwide observance of human rights at a uniformly high standard. The only international regulation to which Amnesty can appeal is the slowly developing body of international law on human rights as found, for example, in the UN's Universal Declaration of Human Rights.

The chief lesson of the prisoners' dilemma for this case is that some governments expect to benefit by abusing human rights, and thus may hold out from signing a treaty, resolving an international dispute that has led to human rights abuses, or yielding to international pressure about an internal abuse case. The most repressive regimes probably are correct in calculating that allowing full human rights could hasten revolution. Thus governments face choices between perceptions of their own interests and international interests; and in such clashes they are subject not only to pressures from within and from other governments and intergovernmental organizations, but also internationally organized citizen action as exemplified by Amnesty.

Amnesty International undoubtedly is the world's best known NGO. It was initiated by British lawyer Peter Benenson in 1961 after he read about two Portuguese students sentenced under the Salazar dictatorship to seven years' imprisonment for raising their glasses in a toast to freedom. Benenson published a newspaper appeal that stimulated more than a thousand offers of support for an international campaign on behalf of human rights. Within one year the fledgling organization had taken up 210 cases, sent delegations to four states to argue on behalf of prisoners, and organized branches in seven states. By 1997 Amnesty had become the world's largest international voluntary organization dealing with human rights, with over 1.1 million members and supporters in more than 150 states and territories, and organized sections in more than 50 states and territories. The distribution of those country sections still reflects the organization's British and Western origins; of the 57 sections in 1999 (with separate English and French branches in Canada and separate Flemish and French branches in Belgium), only one (Slovenia) was in Eastern Europe or the former Soviet republics (see Table 12.2). Amnesty is democratically governed internationally and within the many sections. Its International Secretariat in London includes over 290 paid staff and 90 volunteers from over 50 states (Amnesty International, 1996a, 1999).

Amnesty International has since its inception emphasized principles of strict impartiality and neutrality in the international protection of human rights. Members speak and

Region	Number of Sections	Region	Number of Sections

TABLE 12.2

International Distribution of Amnesty International Country Sections (1999)

Region	Number of Sections	Region	Number of Sections
Africa (except north)	7 Benin, Cote d'Ivoire, Ghana, Nigeria, Senegal, Sierra Leone, Tanzania	**Australia and New Zealand**	2 Australia, New Zealand
The Americas: North	5 Canada (2), Costa Rica, Mexico, United States	**The Caribbean**	2 Bermuda, Puerto Rico
The Americas: South	9 Argentina, Brazil, Chile, Colombia, Ecuador, Guyana, Peru, Uruguay, Venezuela	**Europe and Scandinavia**	20 Austria, Belgium (2), Denmark, Finland, France, Germany, Greece, Iceland, Ireland, Italy, Luxembourg, The Netherlands, Norway, Portugal, Slovenia, Spain, Sweden, Switzerland, United Kingdom
Asia	9 Bangladesh, Hong Kong, Japan, South Korea, Mauritius, Nepal, Philippines, Taiwan, Thailand	**Middle East and North Africa**	3 Algeria, Israel, Tunisia

Total: 57 sections (including Flemish and French branches in Belgium and English and French branches in Canada), plus International Secretariat in London.

Source: Data compiled from Amnesty International, 1999.

act only on cases outside their own countries. However, they are free to advocate abolition of the death penalty at home, pressure their own governments to ratify international human rights treaties, lobby against returning refugees to states where they might face persecution, and participate in local human rights education programs. The four main parts of Amnesty's mandate are based on the UN's Universal Declaration of Human Rights (1948), as follows:

- Seeking the release of prisoners of conscience (i.e., individuals imprisoned solely for their beliefs, color, sex, ethnicity, language, or religion, and who have neither used nor advocated violence).

- Working for fair and prompt trials for all political prisoners.

- Opposing the death penalty, torture, and other cruel, inhuman, or degrading treatment or punishment of any prisoners.
- Ending "disappearances" and "extrajudicial" executions that occur arbitrarily, illegally, and without trial.

Since the end of the Cold War, Amnesty has begun to move beyond campaigns on behalf of prisoners into slightly broader areas of human rights concerns. Newer targets of Amnesty's efforts include (1) abuses by opposition groups, including hostage taking, torture and killings of prisoners, and other arbitrary killings; (2) asylum seekers at risk of being returned to countries where they might be held as prisoners of conscience, tortured, executed, or "disappeared;" and (3) individuals forcibly exiled for nonviolent expression of their beliefs or because of their ethnicity, sex, color, or language. All these areas of concern are logical extensions of Amnesty's basic focus on prisoners.

Amnesty International's activities explicitly challenge state sovereignty and interfere in what governments normally consider their internal affairs. Its activities are based on these three fundamental assumptions:

- Human rights transcend interstate boundaries, as recognized in the United Nations Universal Declaration of Human Rights, which every UN member state is formally obligated to observe.
- State laws often violate international human rights standards.
- Civil and political rights are essential to all societies at every stage of development, so there can be no double standard that excuses some human rights abuses by developing states.

Note that the third assumption seriously challenges the Bush and Clinton administrations' assertions about "engagement" with China, according to which the United States can use trade with China as a way of leading China to improve the rights of its citizens.

Recognizing that its resources do not permit actions on behalf of every prisoner who may be a victim of some miscarriage of justice, Amnesty focuses on the more narrowly defined types of cases set out in its mandate. Cases are dealt with on a strictly individual basis; Amnesty does not "rate" or "grade" governments' human rights records in any manner like that which Congress requires of the U.S. Department of State. Amnesty employs a multifaceted approach to pressure governments on behalf of human rights. Individual letters and other contacts with governments are the most frequent action channel. The United Kingdom (British) headquarters sends the bimonthly publication *Amnesty* to all individual members worldwide, and each issue contains information needed to write on behalf of six victims of human rights abuse. "Urgent action" notices are issued irregularly, whenever somebody is in imminent danger of torture, execution, unfair trial, and so on. They are sent to a network of individuals who have committed to respond to a specific number of cases annually, and they contain addresses and suggestions for appeals. In this electronic age, they can be received by fax and e-mail, as well as regular "snail" mail.

Amnesty also organizes several three- to six-month campaigns each year to focus attention on human rights in specific states (mid-1990s examples include the Sudan and

Indonesian actions in East Timor), and occasional theme campaigns (e.g., on women as victims of human rights abuses). In addition to direct appeals to abusing governments, Amnesty members lobby their own governments to pressure abusers, seek to persuade the media to publicize abuses so as to build international awareness and bring additional pressure on home and abusing governments, and organize occasional symbolic events. As an NGO, Amnesty's funding comes strictly from contributions by members and the public, so it depends on no government. Like many nonprofit organizations, however, it employs professional fund-raisers.

Consistent with the goal of strict independence from governments, Amnesty selects its own cases and gathers and cross-checks all its own information. Sources include fact-finding missions, interviews with prisoners, meetings with government officials, letters from prisoners and their families, reports from legal experts, government bulletins, newspapers and journals, and transcripts of broadcasts. Independence has paid off with an international reputation for accuracy, fairness, and impartiality. Note, however, that the more repressive a society, the more difficult it is to gather information using Amnesty's open methods, and the lower the likelihood of significant impact. With that caveat in mind and remembering that not every case ends successfully, Amnesty's record of successes is still impressive, suggesting that international grassroots citizen action can have significant impact. Since its 1961 inception, Amnesty has investigated more than 44,000 cases and completed its action on some 93 percent (admittedly not all successfully). Nor are Amnesty members the only human rights campaigners in all the cases they take. Still, the impact of an Amnesty campaign is suggested by the following excerpt from a letter written by a former prisoner of conscience in the Dominican Republic:

> When the first two hundred letters came the guards gave me back my clothes.
> Then the next two hundred letters came and the prison director came to see me.
> When the next pile of letters arrived, the director got in touch with his superior.
> The letters kept coming and coming: three thousand of them. The President was informed. The letters still kept arriving and the President called the prison and told them to let me go. (Amnesty International, 1996a, 8)

Amnesty's annual reports have become an important tool for gaining media attention to further publicize the cause. For example, the 1996 *Annual Report*, covering the year 1995, detailed human rights abuses in 146 states, including many of those in which Amnesty maintains sections. Sixty-three governments were cited for actual or possible extrajudicial executions; 49 for "disappearances"; 85 for jailing prisoners of conscience; and 114 for torturing or mistreating detainees, including 54 countries in which detainees died. Armed opposition groups in 41 states were cited for deliberate and arbitrary killings, torture, and hostage taking. The United States was cited for executing 56 prisoners during 1995, the highest number since executions resumed in 1977. Extensive use of torture and ill treatment by law enforcement agents was reported in Mexico. Patterns of impunity for human rights violators were reported throughout Latin America. Prominent Chinese dissident Wei Jingsheng was given a fourteen-year prison sentence despite international condemnation. (Wei later was freed and moved to the United States in 1997 in a deal worked out when Chinese president Jiang Zemin's state visit to the United States was being arranged.) Instances of torture were detailed against both the Israeli General Security Service and the Palestinian Authority. Similar human rights abuses in every region of the world were enumerated (Amnesty International, 1996b). Nonetheless, it seems fairer to charge the persistence of abuses to the enormity of the problem rather than to Amnesty's failure.

What sort of role may Amnesty International play in U.S. foreign policy? Clearly, as an NGO, Amnesty has no direct role in U.S. governmental action. Indeed, Amnesty regularly criticizes such U.S. domestic actions as death sentences. Yet Amnesty's campaigns for prisoners' rights may serve U.S. policy interests in many states around the world. The United States is not alone in championing human rights causes internationally at the same time some of its domestic actions are criticized by human rights activists. In confronting issues like trade and political relations with China, however, the U.S. government seems squarely caught in conflicts between its official human rights principles and its trade interests and hopes of influencing China's government on other issues. Those conflicts are exacerbated by genuine disagreements about whether we can best influence China's political future through "engagement," contact, and continued favorable trade terms or through confrontation and pressure. In the longer term, however, we should see Amnesty International as an example of how international direct citizen action now forms part of the international system's evolution beyond strict and unlimited state sovereignty. That evolution appears likely to progress in the post–Cold War global political environment.

SUMMARY

All international activity in which the U.S. government and its citizens collaborate with other international actors, as in intergovernmental organizations, international regimes, and international nongovernmental organizations, is collective action. Consequently, it is subject to all the dilemmas and difficulties that affect collective action in other political and social settings, from couples and families to organizations and governments. Governments and some other international actors may be able to utilize every type of policy tool discussed in this section of the book, including diplomacy, economic aid, coercion of many types, and military force, but every policy tool covered in this chapter inherently and unavoidably requires the United States to work collectively with others. Moreover, cooperation in dealing with one issue almost never implies cooperation on every issue. Still, dramatic post–Cold War changes in the global context of U.S. foreign policy have profoundly altered the number, character, and possible solutions to foreign policy problems confronting the United States. One result is an increased need for American collaboration with others in many types of international collective action.

This chapter discusses the processes, perspectives, and prospects of different types of international collective action organizations with which the government and citizens of the United States work. Special emphasis is placed on how they interact with the United States, and on how they may be used as tools of policy by the government, by citizens, and by other major actors within the U.S. political system. Three major types are examined in depth, with contemporary cases: (1) The members of intergovernmental organizations (IGOs) are governments of states, and different IGOs deal with economic, functional, political, and security problems. IGOs range in scope from nearly universal organizations such as the United Nations, to selective and regional organizations such as the Organization for Security and Cooperation in Europe (OSCE) and the European Union (EU). Substantively, they range from large interest groups such as the Organization of Petroleum Exporting Countries (OPEC), to regional trading organizations such as the North American Free Trade Area (NAFTA), and security organizations such as the North Atlantic Treaty Organization (NATO). IGOs also include many functional organizations such as the International Telecommunications Union (ITU). (2) International regimes are very large systems created by treaties and actions and may include specialized intergovernmental organizations. Regimes combine law, regulation, and the actions of interstate and international organizations and individual state governments to create international norms and thereby influence and manage selected behaviors. Permanent regimes may be created by treaty, either at the urging of particular governments or by the joint action of many governments under the auspices of an IGO, as seen in the United Nations Framework Convention on Climate Change. (3) International nongovernmental organizations (NGOs or INGOs), such as Greenpeace or Amnesty International, accept individuals as members and often have state organizations and local chapters. Frequently they operate as interest groups raising individual consciousness and pressuring governments on behalf of broad international goals such as limiting practices that threaten species extinction, ending nuclear testing, and terminating human rights abuses worldwide.

Our theoretical perspective for examining such activities is built on two archetypes of political interaction: the tragedy of the commons and the prisoners' dilemma. From them we draw several important general insights into the characteristics and problems of international collective actions. Three major cases demonstrating very different forms of international cooperation and supported to different degrees by the U.S. government and people then are examined. They include (1) UN peacekeeping in the early aftermath of the Persian Gulf War, particularly the United Nations Iraq-Kuwait Observation Mission (UNIKOM), which verified the separation of forces along the border; (2) the United Nations Framework Convention on Climate Change (UNFCCC), part of a major evolving regime dedicated to limiting global warming; and (3) the major international nongovernmental organization Amnesty International. Important global political developments make it likely that we will see all three of these forms of international cooperation increasingly often in the post–Cold War world.

These different types of international collective actions take place in common pool settings, distinct systems in which collective action problems tend to occur. Notable common pools requiring collective action include physical, political, and economic types. They range geographically from regions to groups of states that have particular characteristics to the entire world's people. Within them collective actions are carried out through channels that sometimes involve many governments. Physical common pools include resources and the environment, and regional military security. For example, preventing whale extinctions and managing global warming require management regimes of global scope, whereas NATO deals mainly with the physical security of a group of contiguous European states. Coalitions exemplify political common pools. The European Union, for example, is one such coalition whose concerns bridge between politics and economics. The resource cartel OPEC, together with its customers, forms an important economic pool. Regimes to manage common pools often face the problems of free riders who seek to enjoy benefits without helping to cover expenses, and of holdouts who opt out of regimes that may require universal membership for success.

International collective actions are increasing in frequency and importance, both for the United States and globally. The numbers of such actions grew substantially after World War II, and important global social and political developments significantly increased the need for international cooperation as the twenty-first century approached. The number of independent states increased dramatically after 1945. Global interdependence increased, especially economic globalization as discussed in Chapter 10. This was facilitated by faster and easier movements of goods and people, especially by air, which also generated new opportunities for undesirable movements of drugs, terrorists, and diseases. World population increased substantially, dangerously increasing total human impact on the global environment. The United States lost the leverage the Cold War had given it over other states that needed American help. Finally, the decline of post–World War II U.S. hegemony reduced our capabilities to deal with major problems alone. As a result of all these developments, our more attractive alternative futures increasingly require active U.S. involvement in intergovernmental organizations and regimes, and American citizens are increasingly active in international nongovernmental organizations.

KEY TERMS

Collective action problem

Common pool

Defectors

Framework convention

Free riders

Functional activities

Game of strategy

Greenhouse gases

Holdouts

Prisoners' dilemma

Salami tactics

Tragedy of the commons

SELECTED READINGS

Haggard, Stephan, and Beth A. Simmons. 1987. "Theories of International Regimes." *International Organization 41*, 3 (Summer): 491–517.

Hardin, Garrett. 1968. "The Tragedy of the Commons." *Science, 162:* 1244. The classic article that labeled an entire class of problems.

Hardin, Garrett, and John Baden, eds. 1977. *Managing the Commons.* New York: Freeman.

Karns, Margaret P., and Karen A. Mingst, eds. 1990. *The United States and Multilateral Institutions: Patterns of Changing Instrumentality and Influence.* Boston: Unwin Hyman.

Krasner, Stephen, ed. 1983. *International Regimes.* Ithaca, N.Y.: Cornell University Press. An excellent collection edited by the author of the most popular definition of regimes.

Ostrom, Elinor. 1990. *Governing the Commons.* Cambridge: Cambridge University Press. Ostrom, long interested in exceptions to Garrett Hardin's conclusions about the tragedy of the commons, reviews the conditions under which a commons can be saved or destroyed without either centralized coercion or complete privatization.

Rapoport, Anatol, and Chammah, Albert M. 1965. *Prisoner's Dilemma: A Study in Conflict and Cooperation.* Ann Arbor: University of Michigan Press.

PART FOUR

INCREASINGLY INTERESTING TIMES: PROBLEMS AND PROSPECTS

In Part IV we apply all the principles of Parts I–III to assessing the foreign policy issues that face the United States today and may be reasonably foreseen as we move into the twenty-first century. Many contemporary and foreseeable problems are profoundly different from those on the U.S. foreign policy agenda as recently as 1990. Dramatic post–Cold War changes in the global context of foreign policy have significantly altered not only our foreign policy problems, but also our menu of available policy tools. Unfortunately, even in this time of rapid change, policy-making institutions and processes continue to evolve only slowly. Forward-looking contingency planning is one way to solve such institutional limitations.

Futurism in any form is always more art than science. If we shirk the task because of its difficulty, we lose any opportunity to anticipate problems and to deal with them early (when they usually are most easily solved). Policy then becomes purely reactive, as we endlessly respond to other actors' initiatives with little hope of building bases for long-term stability and progress. This is a foolish approach because history is replete with situations in which early moderate actions could have mitigated or eliminated later disasters. One chilling instance is the failure of the democracies to oppose early Axis aggressions before 1939.

At other times we invest years, lives, and treasure in unsuccessful policies, only to end by accepting terms once thought intolerable. Such was the case in the Vietnam conflict, from which the United States suffered serious consequences. From the early 1960s to the mid-1970s, our Vietnam involvement generated deep rifts both within the American polity and between the United States and most of its allies—rifts that persisted well beyond the 1975 communist victory. Yet, scarcely twenty years later, U.S. businesspeople were building commercial ties with Vietnam, American tourism was growing, and full diplomatic relations had been established with the still communist Vietnamese government. Undeniably, the end of the Cold War helped make a reconciliation with Vietnam possible. Still, it would be far preferable if we could more effectively separate solvable from intractable policy problems before investing years, lives, and treasure.

Many of the reasons for policy failures—or perhaps more accurately, failures of policy vision—lie in our processes for making and executing policy. Nonetheless, policymakers have many tools to use in making more effective decisions. Moreover, citizens have tools for more effectively predicting future policy concerns, understanding available options as well as their advantages and disadvantages, recognizing whether the policies chosen are likely to prevail, and promoting good choices. Building all of these skills is a major objective of this book.

We can never anticipate every specific future policy problem, but Part IV examines and classifies *types* of problems that we can confidently expect to face because we already see them emerging. We also examine some major specific problems that seem likely and make links to a number of policy problems that are set out in cases previously examined. Chapter 13 introduces three dimensions which organize Part IV:

1. *Level of development* increasingly defines different sets of problems faced by the United States. Here, states are categorized according to the four World Bank levels of gross domestic product (GDP) per capita: low, lower middle, upper middle, and high. Numerous indicators demonstrate that economic structure and processes in upper-middle and high-income states increasingly differ from those in low- and lower-middle income economies; this is an important part of the argument for using development as an organizing dimension. Thus we classify low- and middle-income economies as Second Tier and high-upper-middle-income economies as part of, or rapidly approaching, the First Tier (see terminology introduced in Chapter 11 and summarized in Table 11.5).

   We review some eleven strategies for promoting development, including the following: industrialization; rapid capital accumulation; mobilization of underemployed workers; centralized economic planning by an economically active state; direct foreign aid (economic grants, loans, and military assistance); foreign trade; foreign direct investment; technical assistance; isolated self-development; regional integration; and commodity producer cartels. In each case, discussion covers the process involved, the major strengths asserted, major weaknesses and critiques raised, and what can be discerned from available evidence to date about the effectiveness of the strategy and the balance between its advantages and disadvantages. Although development indicators and strategies usually focus on states, nonstate actors are included whenever appropriate.

2. *Activity sectors at issue* are discussed according to the geopolitical, military, economic, societal, and environmental contexts of U.S. foreign policy in the post–Cold War era (see Chapters 3 and 9). Changes in that global context are profound. Because changes inevitably affect specific foreign policy issues facing the United States, they already affect all our lives and will influence them more strongly in the future.

3. *Time frame* has several aspects, including how soon a particular issue is likely to become serious, how long it is likely to remain serious, and the longevity of its consequences. Current problems already appear large enough on political radar screens for at least some policymakers to demand action. Although policies may not yet have been adopted, and those already adopted may not be optimal, current issues typically are more easily dealt with than longer term concerns. Other problems may be anticipated in the short term, and still others not until the medium

or long term. Unfortunately, the further we try to look ahead, the more uncertain all attempts at prediction become. Some problems anticipated today will never develop; others not yet foreseen surely will arise. How likely any particular issue is to arise, and how long it may persist, must be evaluated on systemic and logical grounds. Finally, a set of elements for evaluating U.S. policy interests across all actors and cases is proposed here. The discussion includes stakes at issue, relevant policy themes, perceptions held by other actors, their past relations with the United States, and available alternative actions and policy tools. This evaluation scheme is intended to be applied after the case background has been established by using the system perspective of actors, relationships, function, and predictability introduced in Chapter 4.

Table P4.1 summarizes the organization of the final three chapters. In it, many of the more important U.S. foreign policy problems evident by the latter 1990s or reasonably foreseeable in the early twenty-first century are classified by development tiers and issue sectors.

Focus cases are typical of each tier and issue sector and receive somewhat greater attention, except for a few that are given detailed treatment in earlier chapters. We link each of these focus cases explicitly to U.S. policy concerns and generalize to the larger issue category. More recently, particularly during the 1990s, those primary areas of concern have expanded to include cross-tier environmental issues whose inherently global common pool character unavoidably links between the tiers. Arguably, the United States should raise the priority it assigns to issues in a few additional cells of Table P4.1. To take only one instance, almost all contemporary military conflicts occur within and between Second Tier states. Viewed in combination with the post–Cold War world's increased opportunities for ethnic conflict, this suggests increased needs for peacekeeping, peace-making, and nation building.

Chapter 14 is devoted to issues the United States faces primarily in its dealings with already developed or nearly developed states. It is entirely reasonable to expect quite different policy issues with First Tier states than Second Tier states. Interactions with developed states are likely over such needs as realigning global political and military security arrangements for the post–Cold War era, deciding on required defense spending levels and the composition and missions of twenty-first century military forces, coordinating international economic policy and managing global markets, and solving environmental impact problems that often are most severe in the already industrialized states. Over the longer term, jockeying for position within the First Tier and for movement into the First Tier seems likely because of widely varying resource endowments and rates of economic growth. Some issues will take explicitly political forms, such as calls in the 1990s for a permanent (and veto-wielding) Japanese seat on the UN Security Council.

Exemplary issues discussed in this chapter include the following:

- In the geopolitical sector, domestic political concerns played a large role in shaping the Clinton administration's push for NATO expansion into Eastern Europe, despite the risk of damaging U.S.-Russian relations.

- In the military sector, future U.S. missions, force levels, and budgets are intensely debated and linked to the question of whether the United States should act to ensure that it remains the single superpower indefinitely.

TABLE P4.1

Classifying U.S. Foreign Policy Concerns by Development Tiers and Issue Sectors

---

NOTE: Boldfaced issues are archetypal focus cases given extended treatment in appropriate chapters.

Sector	First Tier (Developed) and Near First Tier (see Chapter 14)	Second Tier (Developing) (see Chapter 15)	Cross-Tier Issues (see Chapter 16)
Geopolitical	**NATO expansion:** organizational and mission realignments UN Security Council: expansion Future U.S. global standing The decline debate	**Aftermath of the Persian and Gulf War** Future of global power Future world order Promoting democracy and human rights abroad	**Promoting democracy and human rights** Does democracy promote peace? Resource supply and distribution Relations with Russia and Eastern Europe Islamic radicalism Korean security, unity
Military	**Missions, force levels, and the future of superpower status** Single superpower debate B-2, other major weapons Precision-guided munitions Missile Defense Systems versus the ABM Treaty Post–Cold War role and management of the CIA	**New Internal War and Peace-keeping in Bosnia** (see also Chapter 8) Implementing START arms control with Russia New demands for peacekeeping, peacemaking, and nation building Solving "new internal wars" (civil and interstate wars)	**Middle East peace** Nuclear proliferation Terrorism: especially nuclear, biological, chemical Arms control (e.g., land mines, chemical weapons) Comprehensive Nuclear Test Ban Helping failed states
Economic	**Coordination with the G-8 and other highly developed economies** Expanding membership, powers; future U.S. role European Union and the Maastricht Treaty Future trading blocs Specific trade issues (e.g., access to Japan's home markets) Promoting market economies worldwide The twin deficits in the United States: budget and international trade	**Potential rise of China**	**Promoting development** (see also Chapter 13) Do market economies promote the right types of development?
Societal	**The U.S. decline debate** (see also Chapter 11) Ownership and control of assets and resources	**Illegal immigration** Future composition of the polity	**Humanitarian political asylum**
Environmental	**Ozone depletion** Distributing costs of environmental cleanups and improved technologies	**Sustainable development** Appropriate technologies What is a fair share of aid? Resource dependencies: oil and other strategic materials	**Global warming** (see also Chapter 12) Deforestation (also linked to global warming) Species extinctions Distributing solution costs

- In the economic sector, international coordination through such mechanisms as the G-8 will be needed for the indefinite future. Although the Russian Federation has enjoyed full formal membership since 1998 and its political inputs are needed on many issues, Russia remains far from the economic equal of the most advanced industrial states (the original G-7).

- In the societal sector, western governments want to foster fragile democracies in Russia, Eastern Europe, and elsewhere.

- In the environmental sector, agreements to end the adverse environmental impact of chlorofluorocarbon (CFC) production and thereby reduce upper-atmosphere ozone depletion exemplify a class of problems on which the already developed states can do the most to limit adverse impacts worldwide.

Chapter 15 discusses issues the United States faces primarily in its dealings with developing states and other actors interested in development. Interactions with developing states are likely over specific local issues, development assistance, resource needs, and links between their ethnic groups and their former nationals and descendants now in the United States. Notable issues for both the short and long terms include the future world order of power distribution and governance. Exemplary issues discussed in this chapter include the following:

- In the geopolitical sector, persistent problems with Iraq years after the 1990–91 Persian Gulf War raise serious questions about policy failures, the difficulty of reigning in pariah states and would-be regional hegemons, and global failures to develop broadly successful mechanisms for ensuring international security.

- In the military sector, the end of the Cold War removed some important constraints against regional conflicts, often ethnically based, that threaten others in their regions and draw in greater powers. This need for First Tier states to promote peacemaking in such regional conflicts was seen intensely in the Bosnian civil war (see Chapter 8).

- In the economic sector, rapid growth in such states as China and India has given rise to concerns about whether new economic and military superpowers may arise early in the twenty-first century and whether the United States should take steps to discourage such developments. Continuing balance-of-trade issues surround the growth of new producers, such as China.

- In the societal sector, China is only one of many states in which the U.S. and other governments have serious human rights concerns.

- In the environmental sector, we seek appropriate technologies to help promote sustainable, rapid, and efficient development while discouraging developing states from adopting highly polluting technologies previously used—and now partly superseded—in now developed economies. Issues for First Tier states often center around their dependencies on Second Tier resources. For Second Tier states, receiving effective development aid in equitable amounts is a critical issue.

Chapter 16 is devoted to issues that bridge between the tiers either by unavoidably involving all states or by linking powerful and influential developed states to less powerful and less influential developing states. Solving cross-tier problems requires the

United States to interact with states in both the First and Second Tiers. Such issues include local and regional peacekeeping, most global environmental problems, ensuring needed resource supplies while minimizing the effects of their unequal distribution around the planet, and promoting the most appropriate technologies to simultaneously maximize economic development while minimizing environmental impact. One major cross-tier problem concerns how First Tier nuclear weapons states (the United States, Great Britain, and France) respond to Second Tier states such as India that seek recognition as nuclear weapons states under the 1968 Nuclear Non-Proliferation Treaty originally intended to help prevent their acquiring such weapons. Other exemplary issues discussed in this chapter include the following:

- In the geopolitical sector, the United States and its major developed allies have yet to agree on how (and how vigorously) to promote the spread of democratic governance, market economies, and economic development.

- In the military sector, regional peacemaking that links between the tiers is most notably seen in the still unsettled Middle East.

- In the economic sector, many issues remain unresolved about how best to promote development (see Chapter 13).

- In the societal sector, many First Tier states are torn between humanitarianism and self-interested protectionism (or even xenophobia) when faced with demands for political asylum or mass immigration.

- Global issues in the environmental sector are both intense and long lasting. Two important (and related) problems are global warming, as discussed in Chapter 12, and deforestation.

Level of development (First Tier, Second Tier) is not the only dimension on which the types of foreign policy problems presently confronting or likely to confront the United States can be organized. Another author might organize such problems—even the same set of problems examined here—according to regions of the world, perhaps emphasizing regional similarities. Many regional patterns, however, are captured by levels of development. Yet another author might organize foreign policy problems strictly according to their nature or the applicable types of tools, similarly to what is described here according to the five activity sectors (geopolitical, military, economic, societal, and environmental). However, the sorts of, say, economic interactions the United States has with First Tier states are substantially different from those with the Second Tier. As suggested in these descriptions, America generally deals with quite different First Tier, Second Tier, and cross-tier sets of problems.

Development is at least one of the most important dimensions for classifying foreign policy problems, and arguably the single most important. Population growth steadily yields more mouths to feed, increasing pressures to deplete and possibly destroy all sorts of natural resources, including minerals from antimony to zinc, animal and fish stocks, wilderness areas, water, arable farmland, and building space. All natural resources exist in common pools and are subject to similar problems that include difficulties in establishing political regulation and pressures to overutilize limited assets. The desires of almost all peoples to improve their standards of living only exacerbate these problems by increasing political pressures for economic growth and industrialization.

For example, the Soviet Union was always torn between investing in heavy industry to build for the future and spending to satisfy current consumer desires. Despite decades of five-year plans for industrial development, consumer goods slowly gained ground, with vodka production as the interim fix. Some authorities now believe China's leaders are promoting rapid economic growth at least partly out of fear that their people will otherwise demand political reform. One result of growth pressures is global warming, which is already leading to international political action (see Chapter 12).

The common pool nature of such problems means that the United States has no good options to remain uninvolved. American industries and automobiles contribute measurably to global warming. Moreover, as the Clinton administration noted in 1995, China's environmental impact will be much greater if most of its citizens acquire automobiles built with yesterday's technology. In similar ways, people's desires for more goods and comforts—which we in this country are used to considering as natural—lead to other common pool problems in diverse areas such as agriculture, energy systems, food distribution, goods transportation, and water supply. Development inevitably creates pressures on natural resources and generates requirements for improved technologies. In turn, those pressures can lead to political—and other—conflicts, and thus to foreign policy problems. Even if we had no regard for the living conditions of other human beings around the planet, the United States could not avoid international dealings in such issues as deep ocean mining, fisheries depletion, global warming, petroleum supplies, and water rights.

Development also may lead to military conflicts when ambitious governments like Saddam Hussein's Iraq choose aggression and territorial seizures as their route to greater power and prosperity. Industrial growth and development often advance military as well as civilian technologies; the extreme cases of the 1990s saw fears of Iraqi and Libyan chemical weapons and North Korean nuclear weapons. Development and industrial progress thus may both motivate and support actions against other states and raise another class of problems for U.S. foreign policy. Finally, development is important because it supports long-standing American goals of promoting democratic governance and market economies. As discussed in Chapter 11, there is now widespread agreement that democratic governments best promote free markets, which in turn are widely believed to encourage the fastest and most efficient economic growth.

All these reasons justify using development as one defining dimension for organizing foreign policy problems. We classify such problems to promote our understanding through simplification, to analyze the lessons of past occurrences, to better anticipate future issues, to comprehend classes of potentially applicable solutions, and to prepare improved contingency plans.

How should we evaluate U.S. policy interests in specific states and regions and the types of substantive issues that are part of the process of formulating foreign policy? Arguably, the answer can be separated from the issue of how large a role U.S. interests should play in determining policy. In Chapters 14, 15, and 16, the following elements are used to evaluate U.S. policy interests across all actors and cases:

- Stakes at issue
- Relevant U.S. policy themes
- Perceptions held by other international actors and their relations with the United States

- Available alternative actions and policy tools
- Future prospects and concerns

Normally, we establish the initial background and structure of the problem by making the key identifications of the systems approach as introduced in Chapter 4; that is, the actors, the relationships between them, the way the system functions, and how that information allows us to predict future developments. The five-element scheme introduced here then helps us develop and analyze the case more fully.

Agreeing on the *stakes at issue* may be the most difficult task because it cannot be accomplished without agreement on the grand policy themes being pursued. Without such accord, policy becomes strictly ad hoc and reactive, driven by improvised responses to events initiated by others. The Bush administration took only a few days in 1990 to decide that Iraq's invasion of Kuwait justified a strong U.S. military response, although both the Bush and Clinton administrations took almost three years to decide the September 1991 overthrow of Haiti's first democratically elected president, Jean-Bertrand Aristide, justified a military response (see the opening case in Chapter 15). Both administrations, however, were justly criticized for lacking any overall strategic vision. The military liberation of Kuwait and the barely averted invasion of Haiti to restore President Aristide were justified on grounds of supporting independence and democracy, but those justifications rang hollow. Almost everyone realized that the speed with which Operation Desert Shield was mounted derived from desires to protect Persian Gulf oil supplies, and the slow response to President Aristide's overthrow stemmed from disagreements over the value of Haitian democracy to the United States. Consensus on what matters and how much it matters is always fundamental to deciding what actions can be justified.

Relevant policy themes genuinely matter. Long-term themes reflect important and broadly shared values and can facilitate policy consensus. Appeals to long-standing principles can help decision makers sell policies, in the same way that jurists seek precedents in law and previous rulings for legal decisions that actually break new ground. Action in Haiti could be justified on grounds of notions about the right to freedom that trace back to our own revolutionary war, and before, to the origins of English common law. Defense of Saudi Arabia and the later liberation of Kuwait could be justified on antiaggression lines that trace back at least to Wilson's Fourteen Points at the time of World War I. Additionally, the Bush administration argued that if UN prohibitions against aggression were to have substance, they must demand a reversal of Iraq's naked aggression against Kuwait. None of this necessarily implies that the themes cited in support of any particular policy action are the real reasons. Cynics could argue that the Persian Gulf War followed a long line of U.S. armed interventions to guarantee desired resources. Still, long-term themes cited in support of any policy are important in the political process.

So, too, are the *perceptions held by other international actors* particularly when they are governments of allied and friendly states. Many authorities believe that unilateral U.S. persistence in policies not supported by others is ultimately hopeless. America's Vietnam War policy, for example, seriously harmed our relations with important allies. Arguably, the United States never would have sent large numbers of troops to the Persian Gulf if important allies and friends had opposed. UN approval for military action was sought even before U.S. congressional approval, although that was partly a domestic political tactic to ensure congressional acquiescence. Similarly, U.S.-led intervention in Haiti officially was a UN action. Even situations about which the United States cares enough to act unilaterally become considerably more manageable when other states cooperate. Their support expands the list of conceivable policy options and frees us from worrying about whether going it alone in one matter will lead to retaliation or reduced cooperation in the future. The United States might well have acted in Haiti and in the Persian Gulf even with the disapproval of its major allies, but their support unquestionably facilitated U.S. action, even to the extent of paying the full cost of the Gulf War.

Other international *actors' relations with the United States* have important influences on our options. In the long term, we share values as well as interests in broad geographical areas and classes of problems with friendly and allied states. In the short term, we may share interests in specific cases and areas with a variety of states and other international actors. Shared values tend to imply common, grand policy visions and thereby facilitate agreement on appropriate actions. A history of allied and cooperative action also tends to build a shared sense of responsibility to assist the other government. Such facilitation may dramatically augment our capabilities and add many important policy options to the menu of possibilities. In the Persian Gulf War, for example, military bases in Saudi Arabia were vital in providing the United States power projection capability to mount major Persian Gulf military actions. Another factor vital to U.S. and coalition success was cooperation from the Soviet Union, which only recently had become relatively friendly after decades of Cold War.

Available alternative actions and policy tools are exceedingly important determinants of U.S. interests, both directly and indirectly. Although it may seem cynical, it certainly is politically expedient to decide that situations offering no reasonable leverages to the United States are not vital to American interests. More directly, as noted earlier, favorable perceptions and cooperation from other states often add many valuable policy options. Often, important conflicting interests must be prioritized. For example, the Mideast policy of the United States throughout the Cold War was shaped by the Washington perception—often fairly openly stated—that the United States had more at stake in avoiding direct confrontation with Soviet troops—because it possibly could escalate into global war—than it had in the Middle East in general and Israel in particular. Thus, although Israel was an important client state and de facto ally, the sending of American troops into a Mideast conflict never was considered a serious option. Only in the 1970s and later were U.S. troops involved in clearly defined peacekeeping supervisory and inspection roles on the Israeli-Egyptian frontier.

U.S. *future prospects and concerns* in any specific case should become apparent as we apply the previous four elements. Inevitably, the balance between stakes at issue, policy themes, perceptions held by others, their relations with the United States, and available policy options will vary with the specifics of the case as we struggle to define U.S. interests. Our task is greatly simplified if there is broad agreement upon the grand policy themes to be pursued. Applications to particular cases then will be decided more rapidly because there will be less controversy. Our fundamental problem today is failure to reach any single grand policy vision for the post–Cold War era. Until we settle on a new world vision, U.S. foreign policy will remain largely ad hoc and reactive, primarily driven by improvised responses to events initiated by others. Arguably, this is a sad condition for the world's single surviving superpower, particularly when we face a growing list of foreign policy challenges.

The end of the Cold War permitted contradictory developments in global politics and in U.S. foreign policy. The simplifying lens of East-West competition was removed, and this freed perceptions to embrace important policy concerns in other sectors beyond the previously dominant arena of military security. At the same time, removing the pressure of superpower competition allowed new issues to arise. Many American citizens believed the post–Cold War era—notably defined by what it was not—allowed them to retreat into a neo-isolationism that permitted decreased attention to world affairs. In reality, the old world order driven by fears of superpower nuclear confrontation has been replaced by a new world order that is still neither fully defined nor fully understood. It is already clear, however, that the typically smaller risks of the new era are far more numerous and occur in many more realms of human activity. The frequency, variety, and number of locations of foreign policy concerns and confrontations have risen apace. Although no single menace threatens to blow us away overnight as the prospect of nuclear war among the superpowers might have, the cumulative effect of the perils we face today could be just as deadly. Consequently, the early years of the twenty-first century promise to be extremely challenging and distinctly interesting. We should remember, however, that when people in Chinese society expressed the wish, "May you live in interesting times," it was meant as a curse.

CHAPTER 13

DEVELOPMENT AND THE GLOBAL CONTEXT OF U.S. FOREIGN POLICY

THE CLINTON ADMINISTRATION AND "ENLARGEMENT": DEVELOPMENT MATTERS, BUT SOME DEVELOPING STATES ARE MORE IMPORTANT THAN OTHERS

William Jefferson Clinton was inaugurated as the 42nd president of the United States on 20 January 1993. Because his expertise and prior experience lay largely in domestic politics, he had campaigned primarily on domestic and economic issues. (A well-publicized sign in Clinton campaign headquarters proclaimed, "It's the economy, stupid.") In its early months, the new administration was strongly and rather frequently criticized for not paying enough attention to foreign policy and for lacking any clear conceptual foreign policy framework. Thus, critics said, the Clinton administration had difficulty sorting out how to deal with both inherited and new problems. Among those problems were maintaining good relations with post–Soviet Russia, peacekeeping in Bosnia (see Chapters 8 and 15), peacekeeping in Somalia (see Chapter 7), and restoring democracy in Haiti (see Chapter 15). The administration's domestic political standing and American leadership abroad both required a serious response to those criticisms.

The Clinton administration's response finally came eight months after the inauguration. In a carefully orchestrated series of speeches delivered over the week of 20–27 September 1993, four of the highest foreign policy officials of the United States—President Clinton himself, Secretary of State Warren Christopher, Assistant for National Security Affairs Anthony Lake, and UN Ambassador Madeleine Albright—set out their intellectual framework for guiding foreign policy. As noted in Chapter 7, policy is partly what qualified officials say it is, and this set of officials was unusually prominent. Only the secretary of defense might reasonably claim to outrank any of them on foreign policy issues. Their speeches were delivered before diverse but prominent audiences and stressed the same basic themes, often in exactly the same language. Clearly, their set of speeches was intended to respond to administration critics by offering a definitive statement of post–Cold War U.S. foreign policy. As summarized by the Congressional Research Service's Mark Lowenthal (1993, 2–8), the core themes were as follows:

- *Central purpose of U.S. foreign policy:* As stated by Secretary of State Christopher, "to ensure the security of our nation and the economic prosperity of our people—and to promote democratic values," and at another point, "to protect American interests."

- *Engagement versus isolation:* All four speakers supported engagement, the continuation of post–World War II globalism or internationalism. Although some critics had called for reduced international involvement after the Cold War, continued globalism was justified on grounds of (1) U.S. economic interests in a global economy, and (2) U.S. security, which could be threatened by reversals in the currently favorable international situation.

- *Primacy of economics:* Under the Clinton administration, domestic concerns—especially economic ones—were to have primacy and would tend to limit involvement abroad. The president noted that "daunting economic and political pressures" were forcing many governments "to focus greater attention and energy on . . . domestic needs and problems." Pursuit of globalism would require and build on domestic economic "self-renewal."

- *Peacekeeping:* New, stricter criteria would be applied to U.S. involvement. Generally, these would encourage acting only where stakes were high, objectives were clear, the parties had agreed on a cease-fire, financial and human resources were available, and an end point or exit strategy was identifiable.

- *Enlargement:* Under this new policy, clearly intended to succeed the Cold War grand policy of *containment,* the United States would seek to expand the number of states that are democratically governed and have market economies.

Some of these core themes responded to criticisms over then-current difficulties; for example, the point about stricter criteria for involvement in peacekeeping operations reflected the new administration's difficulties in finding either success or an exit strategy in Somalia. Others, notably continued globalism and the primacy of economics, reflected realistic reassessments of America's position in a fundamentally changed post–Cold War world. Globalism or engagement, of course, had been maintained at least since World War II, although the administration now considered it necessary to defend continuation. Protecting American interests is a very traditional policy goal, no doubt accepted by every foreign policy official. Note, however, that different officials interpret protecting American interests very differently, and those interests need not always be served at the expense of others. After 1993 the Clinton administration generally followed the first four themes on this list.

Consider now the final point, the proposed new policy of enlargement. As noted in Chapter 3, enlargement never seemed to "sell" decisively. Opinion surveys during the 1990s indicated that both the general public and policy-making and opinion-leading elites ranked key components of **enlargement,** such as promoting democratic governance and assisting developing market economies, near the bottom on lists of very important foreign policy goals (see, e.g., Rielly, 1995 and 1999). Critics charged that the Clinton administration never made concerted campaigns to win either public or congressional support of enlargement. Nonetheless, the characteristics of enlargement as outlined in 1993 remain significant for contemporary and future U.S. foreign policy. As defined by Anthony Lake, enlargement was to have four components, as follows (Lowenthal, 1993, 6):

- Strengthening the core community of free market economies, which will provide the base for enlargement.
- Fostering and consolidating democracies and free markets where possible, but especially in "states of special significance and opportunity."
- Countering the aggression of and attempting to liberalize states hostile to democracy and free markets.
- Pursuing a "humanitarian agenda" via aid and efforts to see democracy and market economies expand to "regions of greatest humanitarian concern."

Note well those "states of special significance and opportunity." Together with "strengthening the core community," and read in the context of the core purpose of protecting U.S. interests, this meant that enlargement would be applied selectively to the states and regions considered most important to American economic and political security. National Security Adviser Lake said the United States must help democracy and market economies "expand and survive in . . . places where we have the strongest security concerns and where we can make the greatest difference." He identified target states as those "with large economies, critical locations, nuclear weapons, or the potential to generate [flows of] refugees" into the United States or friendly states. He specifically identified Russia and Ukraine among the former Soviet republics, emerging democracies in Central and Eastern Europe, the Asian-Pacific region, and the Western Hemisphere (Lowenthal, 1993, 7). This is almost identical to lists of the states and regions that most concerned the United States during the Cold War. The United States would be selective in applying enlargement, but what was new?

The primary change since the Cold War was the drastically changed global context of U.S. foreign policy, discussed in Chapter 3, and particularly shaped by the breakup of the Soviet Union and the decline of U.S. hegemony. Lowenthal (1993, 11–12) called the concept of enlargement "the key intellectual component [of] the emerging Clinton foreign policy," but criticized it on several important grounds, as follows:

> The main problem with the enlargement concept is the dearth of details as to what the United States is willing to do in terms of programs and policies to see that these four steps [summarized above] come to fruition. There are no recommendations for specific actions or statements of U.S. willingness to accept some levels of risk, to pay some price and to exert some leadership to foster enlargement. Indeed, the concept seems to be isolated to some extent from possibility of active U.S. engagement, given the various caveats that are raised about limiting or "picking and choosing" among involvements.

Cold War containment entailed numerous specific programs that committed the United States to globalist activism in very concrete terms. Among these were the United Nations, the International Monetary Fund, the Truman Doctrine, the Marshall Plan, and NATO, all implemented during the late 1940s. Without specific proposals and action to create new major programs, enlargement fell victim to a criticism that dogged much of President Clinton's foreign policy: interesting ideas without sufficient follow-through. This repeated the troubles Clinton's predecessor and the first post–Cold War president, George Bush, experienced with what he termed "the vision thing" and defining the "new

PHOTO 13.1

Former Philippines president Corazon Aquino meets with a political science class at the University of Oregon in 1997. The widow of a politician assassinated in 1983 for opposing the dictatorial rule of longtime (1966–86) president Ferdinand Marcos, Mrs. Aquino led a popular grassroots prodemocracy movement against him in 1986 and won, laying the groundwork for significant development in her country and a peaceful democratic transition of power at the end of her term, with substantial assistance from the United States.

Photo by Jack Liu for the University of Oregon. Reprinted by permission of the photographer and Mrs. Aquino.

world order." U.S. foreign policy remained largely reactive to events initiated by others, with ad hoc individualized responses to specific problems and no consciously initiated new grand policies. That lack of a new grand policy vision limits our ability to shape events on the world stage, and thus qualifies as our grandest foreign policy problem as we enter the twenty-first century.

FUTURE FOREIGN POLICY PROBLEMS

As we examine contemporary and probable future foreign policy problems in this and the next three chapters, keep several key points in mind. Some we discussed much earlier, and most are illustrated by the Clinton administration speeches of 1993 and the failure of enlargement to win broad support.

- The global context of U.S. foreign policy changed dramatically around 1990, with the end of the Cold War. With the breakup of the Soviet Union, America is the sole surviving superpower. The threat of global nuclear war has receded, but the number and diversity of smaller challenges has multiplied dramatically (see Chapter 3).
- U.S. world dominance is much reduced today from the levels enjoyed shortly after World War II, even though we remain the world's greatest economic and military power. Consequently, U.S. foreign policy must proceed through much more cooperative means than during the mid-twentieth century (see Chapters 9 and 11).
- Development—how best and how much to promote it—is one of the larger and more difficult problems facing the United States and other developed economies today, and likely the one that will involve us with the greatest number of other states around the world.
- The United States faces rather different sets of problems in dealing with developed (First Tier and near–First Tier) states than with developing (Second Tier) states. Yet another set of problems requires simultaneous interactions with both First and Second Tier states. (This provides the organizing logic for Chapters 14 through 16; see also the introduction to Part IV.)

In this chapter we begin examining U.S. foreign policy prospects within the post–Cold War global context that likely will continue well into the twenty-first century. In Chapter 3 we examined the geopolitical, military, economic, societal, and environmental properties of that global context. There, we found the United States to be unavoidably and increasingly interactive in a global arena that is both its sphere of action and its major set of constraints and competitors. As exemplified by the decline of American global economic hegemony examined in Chapter 11, constraint and competition both have increased dramatically since the early Cold War years. In the remaining major section of this chapter, we direct attention to the many and varied strategies available for promoting development, a central topic for First Tier–Second Tier interaction. We examine eleven tools for promoting development and mobilizing economies: industrialization; rapid capital accumulation; mobilization of underemployed workers; centralized planning by an economically active state; direct foreign aid in the forms of economic grants, loans, and military assistance; foreign trade; foreign direct investment; technical assistance; isolation in self-development; regional integration; and commodity producer cartels. We investigate the arguments of the proponents and opponents of each strategy, along with historical performance to date.

DEVELOPMENT STRATEGIES

What strategies for promoting development appear on the menu of policy options? How has the United States used them in the past, and what promise do they hold for the future? Development economics is an important subset of international political economics;

consider it in the context of Chapter 11, where we explored the changing nature of global economics and the growing constraints on U.S. economic actions.

In his foreword to the World Bank's *World Development Report 1997*, the bank's president, James D. Wolfensohn, asserts,

> [D]evelopment requires an effective state, one that plays a catalytic, facilitating role, encouraging and complementing the activities of private businesses and individuals. Certainly, state-dominated development has failed. But so has stateless development—a message that comes through all too clearly in the agonies of people in collapsed states such as Liberia and Somalia. . . . History and recent experience have . . . taught us that development is not just about getting the right economic and technical inputs. It is also about the underlying, institutional environment: the rules and customs that determine how those inputs are used. . . . [A]lthough there is an enormous diversity of settings and contexts, effective states clearly do have some common features. One is in the way government has played by the rules itself, acting reliably and predictably and controlling corruption. (World Bank, 1997a, iii)

A central concern for First Tier–Second Tier interaction is which development strategies are best, for whom, what they may cost in money, natural resources, and environmental damage, and who should contribute what and how much. Table 13.1 lists most of the world's independent states according to their gross national product (GNP) per capita in 1995. They are grouped into the World Bank's four income categories: low, lower middle, upper middle, and high. Additionally, Table 13.1 includes the 23 states that form the Organization for Economic Cooperation and Development (OECD). Members of this IGO pledge to work together to promote their own economies, to extend aid to underdeveloped states, and to contribute to the expansion of world trade. All 23 OECD members are high-income, unquestionably First Tier states. However, whether all 51 high-income states should be considered First Tier members on grounds of their advanced economies is debatable. Bahrain, Brunei, Qatar, and the United Arab Emirates all enjoy high per capita GNPs because of oil exports but lack significant industry. Liechtenstein and Monaco are tiny states made wealthy by significant roles in international finance. As we see later, there are growing indications that economic processes in low- and lower-middle income states are increasingly different from those in upper-middle and high-income economies. This provides a basis for classifying low- and middle-income economies as Second Tier and upper-middle income economies as part of or rapidly approaching the First Tier.

Through more than two decades of its annual World Development Reports, the World Bank has used GNP per capita as its primary criterion to classify economies and broadly distinguish stages of economic development. Yet, although the bank is fundamentally an economic institution, its policymakers long have recognized that growth is not synonymous with development, and both growth and development involve more than economics. Indeed, recent World Bank annual reports contain numerous measures of socioeconomic development, including wealth, life expectancy of newborns, adult literacy, economic growth and inflation, and the kind of economic environment that countries face. Human resources indicators are intended to show the rate of progress in social development and include measures of population growth, labor force participation, income distribution and inequality, malnutrition, access to health care, school enrollment ratios, and gender differences in adult literacy. Sustainability measures address human impacts on the environment and include deforestation, land use patterns, freshwater withdrawals, carbon dioxide emissions, energy use, urbanization, and areas of protected habitat. Finally, economic performance measures present information on economic structure and growth, foreign investment, external debt, and degree of integration into the global economy.

This broad understanding of the nature of development is applied in assessing the diverse development strategies examined in the eleven subsections that follow (see summary in Table 13.2). Included are concepts advanced by authorities and experts in both tiers over the entire post–World War II period. Their proposals span the political spectrum from conservative to radical. Discussion in each case covers the process involved, the major strengths asserted, major weaknesses or critiques raised, and what we can discern from available evidence to date about the effectiveness of the strategy and the balance between its advantages and disadvantages. Many strategies can be complementary, so realistic development programs both within the Second Tier (e.g., isolation in self-development, commodity producer cartels) and across tiers (e.g., foreign direct investment, technical assistance) often involve mixes of several policy tools, in the same manner as most U.S. foreign policies.

In assessing alternative development strategies here and in the following subsections we apply and update the approach used by the noted political economist Amartya Sen (1983) in his 1982 presidential address to the Development Studies Association, comparing appropriate empirical indicators with growth in GNP per capita for selected states and economic groups of states. Several key indicators are summarized in Table 13.3, based on World Bank data for states with populations of 10 million or more. States are ordered by increasing 1995 GNP per capita and subdivided into the four World Bank income categories. Sen (1983, 746) also observed that the first four strategies summarized in Table 13.2 "have been among the major strategic themes pursued ever since the beginning of" development economics.

Consider first an important large-scale trend apparent in the data of Table 13.3. As measured by gross domestic product (GDP) per capita in states for which sufficient data are available, *the rich are getting richer much faster than the more fortunate poor, and the less fortunate poor are getting poorer.* All high-income states experienced large GDP per capita increases from 1980 to 1995. The only upper-middle income state to experience a decline was Saudi Arabia, due to declining oil prices. The only lower-middle income states to experience declines in GDP per capita from 1980 to 1995 were Algeria, Syria, and Venezuela, all oil-exporting states that suffered from severe oil price fluctuations that began in the mid-1970s. Finally, although some low-income states made impressive gains, the majority suffered declines in GDP per capita. Among the gainers, only Sri Lanka enjoyed an increase comparable to those of most high-income states. This is a disquieting pattern for people who seek widespread development out of desires for equitable distribution of world income. Additionally, as we see in examining different development strategies, other evidence in Table 13.3 suggests that upper-middle income and high-income economies have passed beyond industrialization and are now evolving into new economic types for which conventional lessons of the past do not apply. However, we might do well to heed Sen's advice (1983, 746):

TABLE 13.1	
Economies Classified by World Bank Income Categories	

Note: States are ordered alphabetically within each income group.

Low-Income Economies (63) [1995 GNP per capita less than U.S. $766]

Afghanistan	Central African Republic	Guinea	Mongolia	Sri Lanka
Albania	Chad	Guyana	Mozambique	Sudan
Angola	China	Haiti	Myanmar	Tajikistan
Armenia	Comoros	Honduras	Nepal	Tanzania
Azerbaijan	Congo	India	Nicaragua	Togo
Bangladesh	Côte d'Ivoire	Kenya	Niger	Uganda
Benin	Equatorial Guinea	Kyrgyz Republic	Nigeria	Vietnam
Bhutan	Eritrea	Lao PDR	Pakistan	Yemen, Republic
Bosnia and Herzegovina	Ethiopia	Liberia	Rwanda	Zaire
Burkina Faso	Gambia, The	Madagascar	São Tomé and Principe	Zambia
Burundi	Georgia	Malawi	Senegal	Zimbabwe
Cambodia	Ghana	Mali	Sierra Leone	
Cameroon	Guinea-Bissau	Mauritania	Somalia	

Lower-Middle Income Economies (65) [1995 GNP per capita U.S. $766–3,035]

Algeria	Ecuador	Kiribati	Panama	Syrian Arab Republic
Belarus	Egypt, Arab Republic	Korea, Democratic People's Republic	Papua New Guinea	Thailand
Belize	El Salvador	Latvia	Paraguay	Tonga
Bolivia	Estonia	Lebanon	Peru	Tunisia
Botswana	Fiji	Lesotho	Philippines	Turkey
Bulgaria	Grenada	Lithuania	Poland	Turkmenistan
Cape Verde	Guatemala	Macedonia, FYR	Romania	Ukraine
Colombia	Indonesia	Maldives	Russian Federation	Uzbekistan
Costa Rica	Iran, Islamic Republic	Marshall Islands	Slovak Republic	Vanuatu
Cuba	Iraq	Micronesia	Solomon Islands	Venezuela
Djibouti	Jamaica	Moldova	St. Vincent and the Grenadines	West Bank and Gaza
Dominica	Jordan	Morocco	Suriname	Western Samoa
Dominican Republic	Kazakhstan	Namibia	Swaziland	Yugoslavia, FR

(continued)

It was argued by development economists that neoclassical economics did not apply terribly well to underdeveloped countries. This need not have caused great astonishment, because neoclassical economics did not apply terribly well anywhere else.

INDUSTRIALIZATION

Rapid industrialization is a traditional development strategy that has been promoted by both communists and capitalists. It is intended to encourage growth of new industries,

TABLE 13.1

Economies Classified by World Bank Income Categories (continued)

Upper-Middle Income Economies (30) [1995 GNP per capita U.S. $3,036–9,385]

American Samoa	Chile	Hungary	Mayotte	Slovenia
Antigua and Barbuda	Croatia	Isle of Man	Mexico	South Africa
Argentina	Czech Republic	Libya	Oman	St. Kitts and Nevis
Bahrain	Gabon	Malaysia	Puerto Rico	St. Lucia
Barbados	Greece	Malta	Saudi Arabia	Trinidad and Tobago
Brazil	Guadeloupe	Mauritius	Seychelles	Uruguay

High-Income Economies (51) [1995 GNP per capita U.S. $9,386 or more]

Andorra	Cyprus	Iceland	Monaco	Spain
Aruba	Denmark	Ireland	Netherlands	Sweden
Australia	Faeroe Islands	Israel	Netherlands Antilles	Switzerland
Austria	Finland	Italy	New Caledonia	United Arab Emirates
Bahamas, The	France	Japan	New Zealand	United Kingdom
Belgium	French Guiana	Korea, Republic	Northern Mariana Is	United States
Bermuda	French Polynesia	Kuwait	Norway	Virgin Islands (U.S.)
Brunei	Germany	Liechtenstein	Portugal	
Canada	Greenland	Luxembourg	Qatar	
Cayman Islands	Guam	Macao	Reunion	
Channel Islands	Hong Kong	Martinique	Singapore	

High-Income OECD Members (as of 12/31/96: 23) [G-7 States in Boldface]

Australia	Finland	**Italy**	New Zealand	Switzerland
Austria	**France**	**Japan**	Norway	**United Kingdom**
Belgium	**Germany**	Korea, Republic	Portugal	**United States**
Canada	Iceland	Luxembourg	Spain	
Denmark	Ireland	Netherlands	Sweden	

Source: Query to World Bank 1997b; World Bank 1997a.

especially strategic ones that support others, serve as springboards to further development, and supply growth markets. Goals also include raising standards of living, building work force skills, and diversifying markets to reduce overall economic vulnerability of one- or two-product economies such as those primarily based on agriculture or resource extraction. The Soviet Union applied this approach internally, through a series of five-year plans that assigned top priority to heavy industry, such as steel and heavy machine production. Early payoffs included the ability to withstand the German onslaught in World War II and, by the middle of that war, outproduce Germany in arms and munitions. On the other side of the political divide, early Cold War U.S. strategy, including the Marshall Plan, strongly promoted reindustrialization in Europe and Japan. This strategy represented a substantial reversal of Allied plans late in the war and shortly after victory to occupy the defeated Axis powers and keep postwar Germany weak, demilitarized, and deindustrialized. As these examples suggest, rapid industrialization can be promoted both by developing states from within and by developed states through outside aid.

Heavy industry is not always appropriate to a particular state's resources or prior development, however, and it strongly influences available work force skills and channels for product distribution and use. For a time during the 1960s many developing states wanted steel plants and state airlines, although neither was economically efficient. China's

TABLE 13.2

Summary of Properties of Different Strategies for Development

NOTE: Strategies may be complementary.

Strategy	Process	Major Strengths	Major Weaknesses
Industrialization	Encourage growth of new industries, especially strategic ones that support others and serve growth markets	Raises standards of living; diversifies markets, reducing overall economic vulnerability	Sometimes inappropriate industries for a given state's resources; frequent pollution problems
Rapid Capital Accumulation	Encourage capital retention to build a body of funds for investment	Supports industrialization and infrastructure development	Denies some short-term benefits to populace, in hope of bigger long-term payoff
Mobilization of Underemployed Workers	Create new jobs; train peasants, women, and others with limited previous employment to fill them	Raises standards of living; promotes infrastructure and general development	Social restructuring, dislocation; social upheavals; weakening of traditional society
Centralized Economic Planning by an Economically Active State	Features of both market and command economies; often state control of major strategic industries	Efficiency; rapid and strategic development	Supported industries not always most efficient; prone to pork barrel politics
Direct Foreign Aid Economic Grants	Grants of funds for specific purposes and projects	Short term: stabilization, disaster relief. Long term: infrastructure building to promote development	Grants may be tied to purchases from special interests in donor state; new forms of dependence are created
Direct Foreign Aid Loans	Loans for specific purposes and projects	Typically, infrastructure building to promote development	Debt service absorbs part of productivity increase
Direct Foreign Aid Military Assistance	Grants of funds, new and surplus equipment, in-country training, advanced training in United States	Protect and stabilize state; free funds for investment; promote regional defense	May protect repressive governments, help maintain a military that absorbs other funds better used for development

(continued)

attempted 1957–60 "Great Leap Forward" was an economic and social disaster. Initiated by Mao Ze-dong and intended to revitalize all sectors of the economy, the plan emphasized decentralized labor-intensive industrialization exemplified by the construction of thousands of backyard steel furnaces instead of large mills. Much of the steel produced was of such poor quality that it proved unusable. Additional aspects of Chinese central planning were wildly unrealistic. Poorly contrived communization of agriculture contributed to a meager harvest in 1959 and mass starvation. GNP dropped seriously and Mao was forced to turn government administration over to Liu Shaoqi and Deng Xiaoping.

TABLE 13.2			
Summary of Properties of Different Strategies for Development (continued)			
Strategy	**Process**	**Major Strengths**	**Major Weaknesses**
Foreign Trade	Encourage imports and/or exports	Imports diversify markets and raise standards of living; exports earn investment capital and promote industrialization	Imports cost investable capital; terms of trade problem; unorganized labor easily exploited
Foreign Direct Investment	Jobs are created, technology transferred; local goods substitute for imports; demonstration effect increases efficiency and productivity; market access improved	Jobs provide training and raise standards of living; investment promotes new industries	Foreign control; extraction of exorbitant profits; social restructuring; dependence
Technical Assistance	Consultation, training, demonstration projects; benefits expected to trickle down throughout the economy	Labor force skills increased; skills transfer to other jobs that support new and growing industries	Productivity increases restrict fraction of population in agriculture, thus restructure and stratify social classes; fertilization and pollution problems
Isolation in Self-Development	Limit all foreign involvement in development	Preserves local political control and culture; limits limits foreign extraction of resources	Slower development than otherwise could be realized
Regional Integration	Any or all of the following: free trade area, customs union, common market, monetary union (common currency), tax system merger, shared budgets	Offset one state's weaknesses by the strengths of others; gain strength to compete with major actors in global markets	Submergence of state cultures and histories into new and larger entities
Commodity Producer Cartels	Concert action to control markets through supply restrictions and common pricing	Stabilizes income streams and predictability; avoids cutthroat economic competition; may raise income realized from resource extraction	May not maximize income realized from resource extraction

After further extreme policy fluctuations that included the 1966–76 Cultural Revolution, Deng introduced widespread market-oriented restructuring of the Chinese economy during the 1980s.

Strategies of rapid industrialization are consistent with the notion of economic "take-off" popularized by Walt Rostow in his 1960 book *The Stages of Economic Growth*, which strongly influenced official thinking in the United States for many years. In Rostow's view, once an economy that had been idling along at subsistence level passed through the takeoff stage it would embark upon continued self-sustaining development leading to eventual developed status. The crucial takeoff stage might be aided by many of the strategies examined in this section, including rapid industrialization. Ironically, the Soviets

TABLE 13.3

Development Indicators for States with 1995 Population of Ten Million Persons or More

Note: States are ordered by increasing GNP per capita and divided into World Bank income categories.
Figures in italics indicate data estimated from years or periods other than those specified.
Weighted averages are weighted by population.

Country Name	GNP Per Capita Current U.S. Dollars 1970	1980	1995	% Growth 1980–95	1970	GDI Percent GDP 1980	1995	Industry Value Added Percent GDP 1970	1980	1995
Low-Income States [1995 GNP per capita less than U.S. $766]										
Weighted Average			430			24	32		32	38
Excluding China and India			290				20			25
Mozambique			80			22.5	*60*		30.9	*12*
Ethiopia			100			*9*	17.2		*12*	*10*
Tanzania			120			*29*	31.0			17.2
Nepal	180	140	200	42.9	6.0	18.3	23.5	11.5	11.9	22.4
Burkina Faso	80	250	230	−8.0	11.6	17.0	*22*	24.5	22.0	27
Madagascar	170	460	230	−50.0	9.9	15.0	10.8	16.3	16.1	13.5
Bangladesh	100	160	240	50.0	11.3	14.9	16.6	8.7	15.9	17.6
Uganda			240		13.3	6.0	16.4	13.7	4.5	14.0
Vietnam			240				27.1			30.1
Nigeria	170	1,180	260	−78.0	14.8	22.2	*18*	13.8	40.3	53.3
Yemen, Republic of			260				*12*			27
Cambodia			270		12.5		*19*			14.4
Kenya	130	450	280	−37.8	24.4	29.2	19.2	19.8	20.8	16.9
India	110	250	340	36.0	17.1	20.9	24.5	21.9	25.9	29.0
Ghana	250	430	390	−9.3	14.2	5.6	18.6	18.2	11.9	15.8
Angola			410				27.3			59.1
Pakistan	170	300	460	53.3	15.8	18.5	18.7	22.3	24.9	24.4
Zimbabwe	320	760	540	−28.9	20.4	18.8	*22*	36.3	33.7	*36*
China		290	620	113.8	28.5	35.2	40.5	38.3	48.5	48.4
Cameroon	180	700	650	−7.1	16.0	21.0	14.5	18.6	23.5	23.3
Côte d'Ivoire	270	1,290	660	−48.8	22.5	26.5	13.2	23.4	20.4	19.7
Sri Lanka	180	280	700	150.0	18.9	33.8	25.1	23.8	29.6	25.1
Lower-Middle Income States [1995 GNP per capita U.S. $766–3,035]										
Weighted Average			1,670							36
All Middle-Income States			2,390				25			*35*
Egypt, Arab Republic	230	540	790	46.3	13.9	27.5	16.9	28.2	36.8	21.1
Uzbekistan			970				*23*			*34*
Indonesia	80	500	980	96.0	15.8	24.3	37.8	18.7	41.7	41.5
Philippines	220	690	1,050	52.2	21.3	29.1	22.5	31.7	38.8	32.1
Morocco	260	990	1,110	12.1	18.5	24.2	21.0	27.0	30.9	33.2
Syrian Arab Republic	360	1,540	1,120	−27.3	13.8	27.5		24.9	23.3	
Kazakhstan			1,330				22.0			30.1
Guatemala	360	1,200	1,340	11.7	12.8	15.9	*17*			*19*
Ecuador	290	1,370	1,390	1.5	18.2	26.1	18.7	24.6	38.1	36.4

(continued)

TABLE 13.3

Development Indicators for States with 1995 Population of Ten Million Persons or More (continued)

| Country Name | GNP Per Capita | | | | | GDI | | Industry Value Added | | |
| | Current U.S. Dollars | | | % Growth | | Percent GDP | | Percent GDP | | |
	1970	1980	1995	1980–95	1970	1980	1995	1970	1980	1995
Romania			1,480			39.8	25.7			40.2
Algeria	360	2,080	1,600	−23.1	36.5	39.1	32.0	41.5	53.7	46.5
Ukraine			1,630							41.8
Colombia	330	1,210	1,910	57.9	20.2	19.1	20.0	27.6	31.6	*32*
Belarus			2,070				25.2			34.6
Russian Federation			2,240			22.4	25.0			*38*
Peru	520	1,050	2,310	120.0	15.5	29.0	16.8	31.6	42.0	37.6
Thailand	210	720	2,740	280.6	25.6	29.1	43.1	25.3	28.7	39.8
Turkey	340	1,940	2,780	43.3	14.0	18.2	24.9	20.1	22.2	30.6
Poland			2,790			26.4	17.0			39.4
Venezuela	1,250	4,410	3,020	−31.5	32.9	26.4	15.9	39.3	46.4	38.3
Upper-Middle Income States [1995 GNP per capita U.S. $3,036–9,385]										
Weighted Average			4,260			25	21		47	37
South Africa	740	2,300	3,160	37.4	30.4	28.3	18.3	39.8	50.0	31.4
Mexico	730	2,660	3,320	24.8	21.3	27.2	15.3	29.4	32.7	25.7
Brazil	450	2,190	3,640	66.2	20.5	23.3	21.9	38.3	43.8	36.5
Czech Republic			3,870				24.7		62.7	*39*
Malaysia	390	1,800	3,890	116.1	22.4	30.4	40.6	25.2	37.8	43.2
Hungary		2,060	4,120	100.0	33.6	30.7	22.8			33.3
Chile	830	2,160	4,160	92.6	19.2	24.6	27.4	40.2	37.3	
Saudi Arabia		14,600	7,040	−51.8	11.9	21.7	*20*	69.3	80.5	
Argentina	1,210	2,890	8,030	177.9	24.4	25.3	18.3	42.3		30.7
Greece	1,170	4,680	8,210	75.4	28.1	28.6	18.7	49.4	48.2	*36*
High-Income States [1995 GNP per capita U.S. $9,386 or more]										
Weighted Average			24,930			23	21		37	*32*
Korea, Republic of	270	2,330	9,700	316.3	24.4	32.0	37.1	28.7	40.4	*43*
Spain	1,100	5,690	13,580	138.7		23.2	21.5			
United Kingdom	2,210	8,580	18,700	117.9	19.6	16.9	16.0	46.8	43.5	*32*
Australia	3,100	11,210	18,720	67.0	27.2	25.4	22.7	39.0	36.4	*28*
Italy	1,990	8,000	19,020	137.8	27.4	27.0	18.5		39.0	31.0
Canada	3,840	11,040	19,380	75.5	21.8	23.6	18.9	40.5	40.2	*27*
Netherlands	2,580	12,970	24,000	85.0		22.2	22.0		32.2	
Belgium	2,660	12,950	24,710	90.8	22.7	21.8	17.9		34.1	
France	2,980	12,680	24,990	97.1	26.9	24.2	17.7		33.7	*27*
United States	4,960	12,820	26,980	110.5	18.1	19.9	*16*		33.5	*26*
Germany			27,510				21.5			
Japan	1,940	10,390	39,640	281.5	39.0	32.2	29.0	46.7	41.9	*38*
World (weighted)			4,880			24	23		38	33

Source: Query to World Bank 1997b; World Bank 1997a, Tables 1, 12, 13.

clearly intended their own—and, arguably, their allies'—takeoff through heavy industrialization, although Rostow's book was subtitled *A Non-Communist Manifesto*. Rostow's prescription held the political attraction that development aid, although it might have to be intense, could be brief.

Rapid industrialization often has been wasteful of resources, unsustainable in even the moderately long term, and severely polluting. During the 1990s, after the liberation of Eastern Europe from Soviet domination and the breakup of the USSR, the outside world learned how extreme these problems had been behind the Iron Curtain. In other regions, many developing states today argue that prior environmental abuses by now-developed states entitle them to their own period of rapid but wasteful and polluting growth. Environmentalists and many others—especially those with the advantage of living in developed states—worry about irreparable environmental damage. See, for example, the discussion in Chapter 12 of disparate views and goals among major groups of states parties to the Climate Change Convention. The U.S. position that developing states should join the major industrialized states in making significant reductions in emissions of greenhouse gases has been particularly controversial. Even before the December 1997 Kyoto conference, the U.S. Senate already had passed a resolution admonishing the Clinton administration not to agree to any treaty that did not require limitations on greenhouse gas emissions by developing states.

How well has industrialization, rapid or otherwise, worked as a development strategy? To test the impact of industrialization on development, consider value added by industry as a percentage of gross domestic product (GDP). Among the 22 low-income states in Table 13.3, the six top performers in growth of GDP per capita from 1980 to 1995 range from Sri Lanka (+150 percent) to India (+36 percent). Indeed, the other eight states for which sufficient data exist to compute GDP change suffered *negative* growth, up to 78 percent for Nigeria, an extreme case of an oil-rich state driven into general poverty by a succession of corrupt dictators. Among all low-income states (weighted by population), value added by industry rose from 32 to 38 percent over this period. That result, however, is distorted by China (48.4 percent in 1995) and India (29.0 percent in 1995). The other four of the most successful six fall around or even below the 25 percent average for the group with China and India excluded. All six, however, raised their industrial share of GDP significantly from 1970 to 1995; most dramatic was Bangladesh, from 8.7 to 17.7 percent.

Perhaps most tellingly, most of the states that suffered large declines in GDP per capita from 1980 to 1995 also showed significant declines in their industrial share of GDP over the same period and from 1970 to 1995. Nigeria is the most notable exception, but suffered from its own unique combination of rich petroleum reserves and severe and exploitative mismanagement. Thus evidence from both the successful and unsuccessful ends of the low-income group of states suggests that promoting industrialization may help raise their GDP per capita.

A similar pattern appears among lower-middle income states. Thailand (+280.6 percent), Peru (+120.0 percent), and Indonesia (+96.0 percent) experienced the highest growth in GNP per capita from 1980 to 1995, and all three were above the group weighted average industrial share of GDP in 1995 and experienced significant industrial growth since 1970. The three least successful states in this group were Venezuela (−31.5 percent), Syria (−27.3 percent), and Algeria (−23.1 percent), all oil-exporting states that suffered from severe oil price fluctuations which began in the mid-1970s. (See the figures and discussion of oil prices in Chapter 11.)

Quite different phenomena appear among upper-middle and high-income states. They enjoyed more rapidly rising GDP per capita than low-income and lower-middle income states while simultaneously reducing the share of industry in their economies and enjoying fewer economic fluctuations—a mostly attractive set of outcomes, if only for those states. Both groups show notable *declines* in the industrial share of value added to GDP from 1980 to 1995. This suggests they have been building postindustrial economies, moving from reliance on heavy industry to some combination of service and information or symbolic-analytic services as their economic cornerstones; see the discussion of such shifts in the United States in Chapter 11. Among these states only the Republic of Korea raised its industrial share of GDP over the periods 1970 to 1995 and 1980 to 1995. The single state among these groups to suffer a decline in GDP per capita from 1980 to 1995 was Saudi Arabia, whose economy is critically dependent on oil exports.

Overall, it appears that promoting industry helps raise GDP growth among low-income and lower-middle income states. Upper-middle income and high-income states—notably including the United States—have passed beyond that stage and are now reducing their industrial sectors. Whether this suggests that some other strategy would more effectively promote development among lower income states remains to be determined.

RAPID ACCUMULATION OF INVESTMENT CAPITAL

Like most other development strategies, investing in industrialization requires foreign and/or indigenous funds, and industrialization often has been promoted by encouraging capital retention within developing states to build funds for investment. The United States traditionally has encouraged such efforts. Increasing the pool of available capital surely will encourage investment and thereby promote economic growth, although there are no guarantees about how the money will be invested. Many policies may promote growth of a domestic investment capital pool, although not all such policies will be welcomed by ordinary citizens. Higher interest rates and favorable tax treatment of interest earnings help promote domestic savings, but so does restricting the availability of consumer goods. Tariffs and other import-limiting strategies help keep capital at home, but reduce the variety of goods available for purchase and tend to protect inefficient domestic industries. Laws often limit how much money citizens may take abroad. Investment tax credits may encourage entrepreneurs. A variety of laws may discourage foreign investors from taking their profits home and encourage local reinvestment, but the same legislation may drive some foreign investors away. In a multitude of such ways, policies to promote the growth of an indigenous investment capital pool have quite diverse impacts, not all of which necessarily encourage immediate economic growth.

Probably the most extreme modern example of draconian measures to preserve domestic capital for investment was Romania under the communist regime of Nicolae Ceausescu (1965–89). Imports were drastically curtailed and the best Romanian products and produce were exported to earn foreign exchange in hopes of paying off the country's external debt. The Romanian people were forced to live in relative poverty. Preserving oil primarily for export led to energy conservation so severe that people had to wear overcoats indoors. Energy consumption doubled almost immediately after Ceausescu was over-thrown, executed, and replaced by a more liberal government in late 1989.

To test the impact of investment on development, consider the relationship between growth of GNP per capita and gross domestic investment (GDI) as a percentage of gross domestic product (GDP), using the data of Table 13.3. Among low-income states the weighted average GDI was 24 percent in 1980 and 32 percent in 1995, although only 20 percent if China and India are excluded. China seems a notable case in which investment (GDI up from 28.5 percent in 1970 to 35.2 percent in 1980 and 40.5 percent in 1995) led to growth in GDP (up 113.8 percent from 1980 to 1995).

Of the six low-income states that experienced gains in GDP per capita over that period, only Bangladesh and Pakistan were below the group average in GDI, and made significant increases since 1970. Côte d'Ivoire and Madagascar saw GNP per capita fall nearly 50 percent from 1980 to 1995, with drops in 1995 GDI to 13.2 and 10.8 percent, respectively. Weighted average GDI for lower-middle income states in 1995 was 25 percent, higher than the 20 percent average for most lower income states, about the same as India's 24.5 percent, although notably below China's 40.5 percent.

Of the three lower-middle income states highest in GNP per capita growth from 1980 to 1995, Thailand, Peru, and Indonesia, all but Peru were significantly above group and world average GDI in 1980 and 1995. Peru's GDI nearly doubled from 1970 to 1980, then dropped back down to nearly its 1980 level. Within this group, Venezuela, Syria, and Algeria suffered 1980–95 losses in GDP per capita. Both such states for which we have the data, Venezuela and Algeria, also had severe and moderate drops, respectively, in GDI from 1970 to 1995. Thus far, both the successes and the failures among the low-income and lower-middle income states seem consistent with the traditional wisdom of development economics: investment strongly encourages development.

As we found on examining value added by industry, however, the results for upper-middle and high-income states differ from those for the less wealthy states. Weighted average GDI shares for these groups were 25 percent and 23 percent in 1980 and 21 percent in 1995, as compared to the world averages of 24 percent and 23 percent in those years.

Among upper-middle income states, GDI shares declined from 1970 to 1995 in South Africa, Mexico, Hungary, Argentina, and Greece, yet all saw gains in GDP per capita from 1980 to 1995. GDI shares increased from 1970 to 1995 in Brazil, Malaysia, Chile, and Saudi Arabia. Argentina saw this group's largest 1980–95 GDP per capita gain (177.9 percent), yet its 1970–95 GDI share fell (24.4 to 18.3 percent). Malaysia saw the group's second largest 1980–95 GDP per capita gain (116.1 percent) and had the largest 1970–80–95 GDI increase (22.4, 30.4, 40.6 percent). Saudi Arabia's GDI share rose and fell slightly (11.9, 21.7, 20 percent), but GDP per capita fell 51.8 percent from 1980 to 1995. This was the only upper-middle income state to experience a GDP decline, un-doubtedly influenced by declining oil prices.

Among high-income states, all of which experienced large GDP per capita increases from 1980 to 1995, only South Korea increased its GDI share from 1970 to 1980 and 1995. As with industrialization, the evidence about capital accumulation suggests that upper-middle and high-income economies are evolving into new types for which the conventional lessons no longer apply.

MOBILIZATION OF UNDEREMPLOYED WORKERS

An important thesis of conventional development theories was that the less developed states significantly underutilized their labor capability and potentially improvable work skills of their people. The United States traditionally has encouraged worker mobilization programs, supporting some with direct grants and technical assistance. In principle, large gains might be realized by bringing jobs to the people or vice versa, by increasing worker productivity, and by raising education levels, particularly through training for literacy and more specific job skills.

Of course, the results of such programs may not be uniform either within or between states. India, the world's second most populous state with about 940 million people in 1997, was 51 percent illiterate (65 percent of women, 35 percent of men) yet had educated the world's second largest pool of trained scientists and engineers (Tharoor, 1997, 7–8; World Bank, 1997b). The nuclear bomb programs of China and India illustrate how large developing states with limited overall development may concentrate resources to produce dramatic progress in salient high-technology sectors. Moreover, development disparities between regions or social groups may lead to serious political unrest. China's government, for example, aimed to develop the entire country fairly uniformly when tractors were first widely introduced in agriculture in the mid-1970s. That goal of uniform development was relaxed when marketlike reforms were introduced in the 1980s, and every work unit became free to produce almost whatever it wanted to, provided it could be sold at a profit. By the mid-1990s, the heavily exporting southeastern coastal provinces like Guangdong were developing much more rapidly than the more isolated interior provinces, leading to potentially dangerous discontent in the interior, massive rural migration to the cities in search of jobs, and some locally serious employment.

China's introduction of tractors exemplifies the type of program that can significantly enhance worker productivity with relatively low investment. Subsequently, using traditional labor techniques appears inadequate. However, limited need in particular economic sectors may mean that programs to increase the output of individual workers generate unemployed "surplus" workers, at least in the short run. Classical economics argues that, in the long run, such displaced workers find other work, possibly in other locations. In the short run, though, individual lives are severely disrupted, particularly when retraining and relocation programs are inadequate. China and South Korea are two notable high-growth performers with vastly different political systems that have strong records of labor-utilizing economic growth over the past several decades. Specialists have extensively studied and praised their labor mobilization efforts. During the 1980s and 1990s, of course, China's has become much more a market economy than before.

To test the success of labor mobilization in promoting development, let us examine several indicators tabulated in Table 13.4. Labor forces normally grow as populations increase, so increases in labor force size tell us little about mobilization without adjusting for population growth. The 1980–95 labor force growth weighted for population was 35.7, 29.2, 45.6, and 17.2 percent for low-, lower-middle, upper-, and high-income states, respectively. For the same four groups, population-weighted average annual population growth rates from 1990 to 1995 were 1.7, 1.4, 1.7, and 0.4 percent, respectively. Among low-income states excluding China and India, the weighted rate was 2.4 percent. China's rate was 1.1 percent and India's 1.8 percent, reflecting the fact that both governments,

TABLE 13.4   Labor Mobilization Indicators for States with 1995 Population of Ten Million Persons or More

States are ordered by increasing GNP per capita and divided into World Bank income categories

(continued)

Country Name	Labor Force* 1995	% Labor Growth* '80-95	% Labor Force in Agriculture 1970	1980	Illiteracy Fem 1995	Total 1995	Urban % of Population 1970	1980	1995	Urban % Increase '80-95	Fem % Labor 1995	Fem % Incr. '70-95	Mineral % of Exports 1980	PCs per 1,000 1995
Low-Income States [1995 GNP per capita less than U.S. $766]														
Weighted	1,433,690,870	35.7	73			34					41	1		
Excluding China and India			72			46					41	1		
Mozambique	8,470,604	26.7	86.2	84.3	76.7	59.9	5.7	13.1	37.9	24.8	49.2	0.3	5.1	
Ethiopia	25,425,294	50.2	91.2	86.1	74.7	64.5	8.6	10.5	13.4	2.9	38.8	−1.9	7.4	
Tanzania	15,188,508	59.7	90.0	85.8	43.2	32.2	6.7	14.8	24.4	9.6	49.5	−0.4	4.7	
Nepal	10,055,390	43.2	94.4	95.3	86.0	72.5	3.9	6.5	13.7	7.2	40.5	1.1		
Burkina Faso	5,428,027	35.9	92.0	92.1	90.8	80.8	5.7	8.5	27.2	18.7	46.4	−1.1		0.0058
Madagascar	6,467,860	49.9	84.4	84.9			14.1	18.3	26.7	8.4	48.8	1.7	6	
Bangladesh	59,887,704	46.6	81.4	73.9	73.9	61.9	7.6	11.3	18.3	7.0	42.2	0.0		
Uganda	9,477,078	43.2	89.9	89.2	49.8	38.2	8.0	8.8	12.5	3.7	52.8	3.7		0.5257
Vietnam	36,924,156	44.3	76.6	73.2	8.8	6.3	18.3	19.2	20.8	1.6	50.2	2.1		
Nigeria	44,142,624	49.5	70.9	54.6	52.7	42.9	20.0	27.1	39.3	12.2	36.1	−0.6	96.9	
Yemen, Republic of	4,610,392	85.5	70.4	69.8			13.3	20.2	33.6	13.4	27.2	−4.1	0.1	
Cambodia	4,958,949	50.3	79.0	75.7			11.7	12.4	20.7	8.3	54.4	−1.9		
Kenya	12,788,733	64.1	85.7	82.6	30.0	21.9	10.3	16.1	27.7	11.6	48.1	−1.9	33.4	0.6745
India	398,412,032	33.0	70.6	69.7	62.3	48.0	19.8	23.1	26.8	3.7	32.1	−1.9	0.4	1.2912
Ghana	7,956,778	56.3	60.5	61.5	46.5		29.0	31.2	36.3	5.1	51.8	0.9	0.4	1.1714
Angola	4,958,981	42.8	78.4	76.5			15.0	21.0	32.2	11.2	47.5	0.6	78	
Pakistan	46,288,960	58.3	58.8	61.8	75.6	62.2	24.9	28.1	34.6	6.5	28.5	5.0	7.1	1.195
Zimbabwe	5,030,614	59.8	76.8	73.6	20.1	14.9	16.9	22.3	32.1	9.8	45.7	0.5	1.5	2.997
China	709,283,392	31.7	78.3	75.6	27.3	18.5	17.5	19.4	30.3	10.9	46.0	2.0	16.3	2.1641
Cameroon	5,409,799	48.7	85.2	73.0	47.9	36.6	20.3	31.4	44.9	13.5	37.3	0.7	30.7	
Côte d'Ivoire	5,009,196	52.6	75.6	64.8	70.0	59.9	27.4	34.8	43.6	8.8	34.2	2.0		
Sri Lanka	7,515,801	38.5	55.3	52.1	12.8	9.8	21.9	21.6	22.4	0.8	35.7	8.7	17.9	1.1041
Lower-Middle Income States [1995 GNP per capita U.S. $766–3,035]														
Weighted	418,898,152	29.2	41			18					40	2		
All Middle-Income States			38								38	2		
Egypt, Arab Republic	20,951,278	46.3	51.8	61.2	61.2	48.6	42.2	43.8	44.8	0.9	31.1	2.7	64.2	
Uzbekistan	9,287,419	43.9	42.6	38.4			36.7	40.8	41.6	0.8	46.2	−1.8		
Indonesia	88,665,952	51.4	66.3	58.9	22.0	16.2	17.1	22.2	34.3	12.1	40.6	4.8	71.9	3.7483
Philippines	28,259,180	49.9	57.9	52.3	5.7	5.4	33.0	37.5	53.4	15.9	36.6	1.6	0.7	11.4007
Morocco	10,281,105	47.6	57.6	56.0	69.0	56.3	34.5	41.0	49.0	8.0	35.1	1.6	4.8	1.6832
Syrian Arab Republic	3,994,398	61.2	50.2	38.7	44.2		43.4	46.7	53.1	6.4	26.9	3.4	77.1	0.0682
Kazakhstan	8,095,664	15.1	26.9	24.4			50.3	54.0	59.8	5.8	47.3	−0.3		

	GNP	1	2	3	4	5	6	7	8	9	10	11	12
Guatemala	3,778,705	59.3	53.8	51.4	44.4	35.5	37.4	41.5	4.1	26.1	3.7	1.1	2.8185
Ecuador	4,232,767	66.3	39.8	11.8	9.9	39.5	47.0	58.4	11.4	26.3	6.2	63.1	3.9209
Romania	10,703,728	-1.9	34.8			41.8	49.0	55.4	6.4	44.4	-1.3		5.2882
Algeria	8,627,966	77.9	36.0	51.0	38.4	39.5	43.4	55.8	12.4	24.3	2.7	98.5	3.0402
Ukraine	25,787,574	-2.4	24.7			54.6	61.7	70.3	8.6	48.8	-1.4		5.6256
Colombia	15,588,772	68.5	38.5	8.6	8.7	57.2	63.9	72.7	8.8	35.7	10.7	2.8	16.2312
Belarus	5,371,191	5.5	25.7			43.9	56.5	71.2	14.7	48.1	-1.7		
Russian Federation	77,252,488	1.7	16.0			62.5	69.8	72.5	2.7	48.6	-0.7		17.6551
Peru	8,675,580	60.1	40.4	17.0	11.3	57.4	64.6	71.8	7.2	28.6	4.7	20.3	5.9494
Thailand	33,801,828	38.7	70.9	8.4	6.2	13.3	17.0	20.2	3.2	47.0	-0.4	0.1	15.3236
Turkey	27,843,138	48.7	70.7	27.6	17.7	38.4	43.8	69.9	26.1	35.7	0.2	1.4	12.4748
Poland	19,310,752	4.3	38.9			52.3	58.2	64.7	6.5	45.8	0.5	13.2	28.4878
Venezuela	8,388,668	65.1	14.8	9.7	8.9	72.4	83.3	92.8	9.5	33.3	6.2	94	16.6577
Upper-Middle Income States [1995 GNP per capita U.S. $3,036–9,385]													
Weighted	171,273,488	45.6		31	14					34	5		
South Africa	16,186,896	47.9	17.3	18.3	18.2	47.8	48.1	50.8	2.7	37.4	2.3	6.8	26.5335
Mexico	35,835,692	62.5	36.6	12.6	10.4	59.0	66.3	75.3	9.0	31.6	4.7	66.8	26.135
Brazil	71,156,160	48.6	36.7	16.8	16.7	55.8	66.2	78.2	12.0	35.2	6.9	1.8	12.9949
Czech Republic	5,569,321	4.7	13.1			52.0	63.6	65.4	1.8	47.3	0.0		53.2121
Malaysia	8,030,418	51.7	40.8	21.9	16.5	33.5	42.0	53.7	11.7	36.8	3.1	24.7	39.7496
Hungary	4,758,992	-7.0	18.4			48.5	56.9	64.7	7.8	44.0	0.7	4.8	39.1619
Chile	5,560,943	45.6	20.9	5.0	4.8	75.2	81.2	85.9	4.7	32.1	5.7	1.3	37.8284
Saudi Arabia	6,255,591	126.3	44.6	49.8	37.2	48.7	66.8	78.7	11.9	12.3	4.6	99.2	24.5714
Argentina	13,509,670	26.2	13.0	3.8	3.8	78.4	82.9	88.1	5.2	30.7	3.1	3.5	33.4384
Greece	4,409,807	17.3	31.2			52.5	57.7	65.2	7.5	36.3	8.4	15.6	
High-Income States [1995 GNP per capita U.S. $9,386 or more]													
Weighted	393,548,906	17.2		9	2					42	3		
Korea, Republic of	21,576,370	38.8	37.1	3.3	2	40.7	56.9	81.3	24.4	40.5	1.8	0.3	120.8
Spain	16,626,961	19.1	18.5			66.0	72.8	76.5	3.7	36.2	7.8	4	81.6
United Kingdom	29,145,640	8.2	2.6			88.5	88.8	89.5	0.7	43.1	4.3	13.1	186.2
Australia	9,085,236	34.8	6.4			85.2	85.8	84.7	-1.1	42.6	6.1	11.1	275.8
Italy	24,906,474	10.4	12.6			64.3	66.6	66.3	-0.3	37.7	4.8	5.7	83.7
Canada	15,482,434	27.0	6.7			75.7	75.7	76.7	1.0	45.2	5.6	14.5	192.5
Netherlands	7,108,137	25.9	5.6			86.1	88.4	89.0	0.6	39.9	8.5	22.2	200.5
Belgium	4,132,406	4.8	3.0			94.3	95.4	97.0	1.6	40.1	6.2		138.3
France	25,732,148	8.0	8.3			71.0	73.3	72.8	-0.5	44.2	4.0	4.1	134.3
United States	133,132,032	21.2	3.5			73.6	73.7	76.2	2.5	45.6	4.0	3.7	328
Germany	40,481,316	8.1	6.9			79.6	82.6	86.6	3.9	41.7	1.7	3.8	164.9
Japan	66,139,752	15.6	19.6			71.2	76.2	77.6	1.4	40.5	2.6	0.4	152.5
Maximum				53	2								328
World (weighted)					2					40	2		328

*These weighted averages are for states in this table only.

Source: Query to World Bank 1997b; World Bank 1997a, Tables 1 and 4.

particularly China's, have aggressive programs to limit population growth. Traditionally, it was believed that population growth rates would decline as income and life expectancy rose and people realized they could have even richer lives with fewer children. Population growth rates are notably lower among most high-income states, especially those of Western Europe, none of which exceeded 1 percent. Differences in population growth rates are not large enough to explain the greater labor force growth among upper-middle income states as compared with lower-middle income states, suggesting the former must be doing something more effective in mobilizing people into jobs.

Another traditional expectation is that industrialization, coupled with the introduction of mechanization and chemicals to agriculture, will free people from farm work to seek other jobs. Thus the percentage of the labor force in agriculture becomes an important indicator of modernization. Indeed, it is one of the most dramatic indicators of differences between the four income groups of states, whose agricultural labor force percentages in 1980 were 73, 41, 31, and 9 percent, respectively. No state showed an increase from 1970 to 1980, and decreases were largest among middle-income states. Programs to teach reading and writing are fundamental to building skills needed in most nonfarm jobs, so reduction of illiteracy becomes another important indicator of potential labor mobilization. Total 1995 adult illiteracy averaged 34 percent among low-income states, 18 percent among all middle-income, and 14 percent for upper-middle income states. Female adult illiteracy is often substantially higher in low-income states, a gender differential that greatly decreases as income rises, although it does not appear to be linked to substantial increases in female participation in the labor force.

The urban share of population is another important indicator of modernization because displaced farm workers are freed—or forced—to move to cities to seek work, and industries typically require the support of infrastructure and suppliers most readily found in cities. Urbanization was already far advanced by 1970 in most states of lower-middle income or above. Low-income states had much lower 1970 urbanization, and most experienced dramatic rises by 1995. An intriguing indicator of the nature of a state's economy is the mineral share of exports. Higher rates generally indicate less developed economies heavily dependent on extractive industries, with oil coming most readily to mind. Interestingly, heavily oil-dependent exporters may be found in all but the high-income group. Examples include Nigeria (96.9 percent), Algeria (98.5 percent), and Saudi Arabia (99.2 percent). A final indicator of modernization tabulated in Table 13.4 is the number of personal computers (PCs) per thousand people. Higher numbers seem likely to indicate higher levels of wealth, education, and connectedness to the emerging global information economy. Highs for the four income groups in 1995 are Zimbabwe (3), Poland (28.5), the Czech Republic (53), and the United States (328, or nearly one for every three people of all ages).

CENTRALIZED ECONOMIC PLANNING BY AN ECONOMICALLY ACTIVE STATE

Centralized economic planning and intensive government involvement in the economy have characterized many developing states since the 1950s, although fewer since the global ascendancy of market economics in the 1990s. During the Cold War, the United States opposed command economies because the communists prescribed them; today, we oppose them perhaps even more strongly on the ground that command economies collapsed in the Soviet Union and its Eastern European satellites. Sen (1983, 11) notes that "development economics was born at a time when government involvement in deliberately fostering economic growth, and industrialization in particular, was very rare, and when the typical rates of capital accumulation were quite low." India's first prime minister, Jawaharlal Nehru, embraced the goal of a "socialist pattern of society" in 1954, seven years after independence (Tharoor, 1997, xi). By the 1960s India had adopted stringent controls on goods imports and money outflows, seeking to encourage self-sufficiency by developing and promoting indigenous industry. As Tharoor (1997, 28–29) put it,

> The ideas of Fabian socialism captured an entire generation of English-educated Indians; Nehru was no exception. In addition, the seeming success of the Soviet model—which Nehru admired for bringing about the industrialization and modernization of a large, feudal, and backward state not unlike his own—appeared to offer a valuable example for India. Like many others of his generation, Nehru thought that central planning, state control of the "commanding heights" of the economy, and government-directed development were the "scientific" and "rational" means of creating social prosperity and ensuring its equitable distribution. Self-reliance was the mantra: the prospect of allowing a Western corporation into India to "exploit" its resources immediately revived memories of the British East India Company, which also came to trade and stayed on to rule.
>
> In India, one of the lessons we learn from history is that history too often teaches the wrong lessons.
>
> [Nehru's] . . . socialist economics . . . [were] disastrous, condemning the Indian people to poverty and stagnation and engendering inefficiency, red-tapism, and corruption on a scale rarely rivaled elsewhere.

Outside the United States, many other First Tier governments have seen centrally planned command economies as the most efficient route to Second Tier development. (Many of the same governments argued that the costs and controversies inherent in multiparty democratic governance were similarly inefficient and wasteful of resources.) Market-oriented economists reply that unfettered competition aids consumers by driving prices down and stimulates development because producers innovate to improve quality and features and thereby win business away from competitors. Proponents of state activism argued that central management promotes rapid development through the most efficient use of resources, targeting the development of strategic industries that build infrastructure and job skills and have synergistic effects throughout the economy. Command economies often featured state control of major strategic industries like energy, military production, and steel. Unfortunately, state industries often lose efficiency by being insulated from market pressures. Far too often they become hotbeds of favoritism and pork barrel politics. In the worst cases, state industries and state allocation of business to factories owned by rulers retard development by directing fortunes into the private accounts of dictators, as in Zaire under Mobutu or Nigeria under a long series of military dictators.

Comparative qualitative data about planning and state activism are difficult to locate. The three top-growing states among the low-income group in 1995, Sri Lanka, China, and Pakistan, also were the top three in 1982. However, they demonstrate different degrees of state effectiveness and later implemented profound economic strategy changes. Sri Lanka's government maintains active government intervention in fields from health to education to food consumption, and since 1982 has moved from the middle of the low-income pack to the very borderline of lower-middle income. China had extensive government management of the economy for decades during which specific policy goals fluctuated, as already discussed. Since the 1980s, however, China has pursued a largely laissez-faire market economy and enjoyed soaring growth. Pakistan has slightly outperformed India in recent years, but often has been cited as an example of the harm that can arise from government meddling. In the 1990s India began, albeit slowly, to become more involved in the global economy. Generally, U.S. government officials and business leaders consider such involvements favorable.

DIRECT FOREIGN AID: ECONOMIC GRANTS, LOANS, MILITARY ASSISTANCE

Direct foreign aid is one of the oldest classes of development tools, actively promoted at different times both by developed states—notably including the United States—and by associations of developing states, such as the group that issued a formal call for a new international economic order (NIEO) under which developed states would devote 1 percent of GNP to development assistance. Direct foreign aid is discussed here in the three major classes of economic grants, loans, and military assistance. **Grants** are gifts of funds for specific purposes and projects, including such diverse purposes as training and educational facilities and programs, demonstration projects, dam and road construction, and so on. In the short term, grants may include disaster relief and promote the stabilization of lives and governments, both necessary preconditions to development. In the long term, grants may significantly assist development by helping build infrastructure and labor force skills. Cold War competition for political influence extended to development grants, and recipient states sometimes encouraged such competition to drive up aid amounts. Unfortunately, such grants also can be used to create new forms of dependence.

All these effects were seen with Egypt's Aswan high dam, built from 1960 to 1970. When the United States and Britain canceled their participation in 1956, the Soviets were eager to step in because they gained political influence—and dependence on other forms of Soviet assistance—that lasted at least through Egypt's 1973 Yom Kippur war with Israel. Finally, in a little realized intermestic aspect of development grants, purchase funds usually are "tied," for example by requirements that equipment be purchased from firms in the granting state. The real shift of government funds then is not abroad but to domestic industries.

Direct foreign aid *loans* are given for specific purposes and projects, often for infrastructure building to promote general development. Aid sometimes takes the form of government loan guarantees that actually subsidize private domestic lending institutions. As with grants, there may be tied purchases and other special interests. Political conditions may connect lenders with rather dubious clients. The biggest problem with loans, however, is that they must be repaid. Debt service—payments of interest and principal—reduces the benefits of development and creates new forms of dependence. The other side of this coin is that lenders live in fear of default by the biggest debtors, which may give them substantial power to demand "rescheduling" in which payments are delayed or reduced. In the 1980s, for example, Citibank had to renegotiate substantial Mexican loans when declines in oil prices reduced the Mexican government's ability to pay, and the banking community lived in fear that defaults by Brazil and Mexico could bring the whole international lending system to its knees.

Military assistance may include grants of funds, gifts of either new or surplus equipment, loans for purchases on favorable terms, training programs in-country, and advanced training in the United States. At its best, military assistance promotes development by helping protect the recipient state, stabilize its government against threats from within and without, free indigenous funds for investment, and promote regional security. At its worst, military assistance protects corrupt rulers and repressive governments and encourages regional instabilities. Critics charge that funds spent on the military could be more productively invested in other forms of development assistance, many developing states spend too far much of their limited funds on the military, indigenous military forces all too often become involved in domestic struggles for power, and in extreme cases foreign military assistance facilitates coups d'état. Today's widespread concern about balances of trade leads to ever-greater pressure for foreign military sales. Moreover, desires to spread weapons development costs over bigger production runs encourage domestic pressures that weapons sales and gifts be increased. For both these reasons, the United States in the early 1960s began deemphasizing gifts of its obsolete surplus weaponry in favor of selling newer weapons and even models specially developed to appeal to export markets.

Despite the history of the Marshall Plan, direct foreign aid generally has been poorly understood and politically unpopular among U.S. voters. Most citizens realize neither how small the foreign aid share of the federal budget is nor the extent to which tied aid assists domestic lenders and industries. Nonetheless, foreign assistance has declined further in popularity since the end of the Cold War. It is reasonable to expect both that all forms of direct aid will continue to be important internationally and that U.S. domestic political battles over such aid will persist. Unless future administrations more effectively make the case for foreign aid within the broader case for international engagement, those battles will intensify.

FOREIGN TRADE

Foreign trade is a politically "natural" development strategy for the United States because it conforms to our free market ideology. For years, the United States has strongly supported expanded free trade areas, both regionally and at home. Intensification of that support during the 1990s only strengthened the attractions of free trade as a development strategy. Foreign trade may be encouraged by many policies, including tariff reductions, export promotion, free trade areas, and cooperation in the international standardization, reduction, and elimination of tariffs and nontariff barriers to trade. Imports diversify the goods available in domestic markets and thereby raise citizens' standards of living. They may also support indigenous industries and encourage them to innovate, both to meet competition and to take advantage of newly available materials and technologies. Exports earn capital that can be used for industrialization and other forms of development. Unfortunately, inevitable tensions exist between imports and exports. Broadly, consumers want more imports while governments and local industries want increased exports. Imports cost investable capital and detract from indigenous industries that might promote development by producing the same or substitute goods. Exports of manufactures encourage local industries to build more factories and hire and train more indigenous workers.

Unfortunately, many developing states suffer severely from the **terms of trade problem.** Over the long term, prices of manufactured goods usually inflate slowly while agricultural and raw material prices fluctuate widely because suppliers enter or leave the market, new oil or mineral deposits are discovered, or crop yields vary with rainfall cycles and weather extremes. States whose one- or two-product economies are tied to exports of agricultural produce and raw materials thus face the dilemma of importing manufactured goods at slowly increasing prices while their export incomes ebb and flow and do not necessarily average out to long-term increases. Since the dramatic oil price rises of the mid-1970s, single-product exporting states that lack energy resources have faced the double blow of dramatic jumps in energy costs plus ever-increasing costs of manufactured goods, exacerbated by the manufacturers' energy cost increases. Among petroleum exporting states, the winners have been those states blessed with both large reserves and good management, such as Saudi Arabia. Even upper-middle income Mexico ran into trouble in the 1980s when oil prices dropped.

Another major critique of foreign trade as a promoter of development arises from its impact on labor. As states industrialize and farm workers move to cities seeking new and more lucrative work, unorganized labor is easily exploited. Workers may not know enough to be able to protect themselves from abuses in hours, wages, and working conditions if there is no strong history of industrial labor organization and if education levels are not high enough to yield widespread awareness of other states' labor histories. Such problems may occur whether the investment that supports industrialization is indigenous or foreign.

FOREIGN DIRECT INVESTMENT

Like foreign trade, foreign direct investment is a politically "natural" development strategy for the United States because it conforms to our free market ideology. Foreign direct investment may supplement or even exceed foreign aid as a means for stimulating industrialization and modernization. Proponents argue that such investment has both direct and "trickle down" benefits. Directly, jobs are created, and the workers who fill them gain skills. Less directly, wages low on the world scale still may be high by local standards, putting more funds into circulation, raising local living standards, and driving prevailing local wages upward by example and competition. Thus benefits trickle down to others not directly involved in the firms that receive foreign investment. Technology is transferred from developed to developing states and finds its way into additional firms and industries. Imports are substituted by indigenous production, improving the developing state's balance of trade. Improved production techniques raise efficiency both by demonstration and, in free markets, by driving out less efficient competitors. Exports may gain access to new markets abroad.

Critics argue that such benefits cost too much and create new problems. Foreign direct investment brings with it at least some degree of foreign control. The trickle down of benefits may be too little and too slow. Exorbitant profits may be extracted and exported, effectively draining wealth from developing states, even if that wealth was previously unrealized. Creating new jobs at dramatically higher wage levels can bring social restructuring and create cleavages between the more and less fortunate workers. New dependencies are created as states count on foreign investments and compete to gain them. Many of the benefits and difficulties of foreign direct investment are shared with technical assistance programs.

TECHNICAL ASSISTANCE

Technical assistance programs long have been a mainstay of U.S. foreign aid. They encourage development through education and training in techniques of farming and production at all levels of technology. Their fundamental premise in comparison with other types of aid programs is summed up in the adage that giving people fish feeds them one day at a time while teaching them to fish feeds them for a lifetime. As with direct foreign investment, there are strong expectations that technical assistance yields demonstration effects and trickle down of techniques and benefits. However, technical assistance is more likely to involve simple technologies taught to large numbers of individuals. Three examples spanning the technology range from high to low are the Atoms for Peace program, the Green Revolution, and the Peace Corps. Of these, the Peace Corps is probably best known both at home and abroad.

Atoms for Peace was begun in the 1950s under the Eisenhower administration and aimed to assist states in developing peaceful nuclear research and nuclear power programs. It clearly exemplifies high-technology, low-volume technical assistance, suited primarily to the more advanced developing states. By contrast, the Green Revolution demonstrates medium technology combined with very wide application. The term *green revolution* refers mainly to dramatic increases in cereal-grain production in many developing states since the late 1960s. Researchers in Mexico began in the mid-1940s to develop genetically improved wheats that were broadly adapted, short stemmed, disease resistant, and converted fertilizer and water into very high yields. The resulting improved seeds helped boost Mexican wheat production, avert famine in India and Pakistan, and earn the 1970 Nobel Peace Prize for U.S. plant breeder Norman E. Borlaug, who led the Mexican wheat team.

The Peace Corps exemplifies low-technology, wide-application technical assistance. Established in 1961 by executive order of President Kennedy and approved by Congress as a government agency housed in the State Department, the corps sends volunteers to more than sixty states for one- to two-year periods. There they engage in widely varied programs, typically at village level. Some volunteers have helped villagers build schools and have taught languages, mathematics, or science. Others have assisted in building wells and irrigation systems for local fields. Still others have provided vocational training and employed business experience to teach management and public administration. Proponents of the Peace Corps argue that it shows individual Americans in the best possible light, thus building global support for the United States while promoting grassroots development. Perhaps the best indicator of success is that volunteers still are sought by many states more than thirty-five years after the corps was founded.

Technical assistance programs are not without critics, however. The biggest downside potential of Atoms for Peace was demonstrated in 1974 when India exploded a nuclear device built with plutonium produced in Canadian-built research reactors previously thought incapable of such production. Productivity increases in agriculture inevitably restrict the percentage of the population in farming, thus restructuring social classes and possibly leading to social stratification. The Green Revolution is credited by many as essential to avoiding widespread famine deaths as populations grew. Nonetheless, others attack it as encouraging monoculture crops that reduce biological diversity and may be susceptible to future diseases or pests. The hybrid wheat strain developed by Borlaug's team required higher than previous levels of fertilizer, thus raising dependence on petro-chemical fertilizers. When the world price of oil began to soar in 1973–74, fertilizer prices rose apace. Many farmers in India and Mexico could not afford to fertilize their hybrid wheat and lost most or even all of their crop. In later years, additional questions were raised about the environmental impacts and long-term sustainability of agriculture dependent on high levels of chemical fertilizers. Thus, in the long term, the Green Revolution began to take on some aspects of tragically inappropriate technology.

ISOLATION IN SELF-DEVELOPMENT

One dramatic alternative to direct foreign aid, trade, foreign direct investment, and technical assistance is self-development in relative isolation. This policy has never been directly encouraged by the United States. A number of states, among them India, have tried this approach, but their experiences have contributed strongly to the 1990s trend away from isolated self-development.

China has undergone radical policy shifts toward and away from self-development in isolation. Its laissez-faire market phase of the 1980s and 1990s is one extreme, and its opposite occurred during the Great Cultural Revolution (1966–76). Intended by Mao Ze-dong to mobilize urban Chinese youth to restore revolutionary zeal and prevent development of Soviet-style bureaucratized communism, the Cultural Revolution turned violent and caused a 12 percent drop in industrial production from 1966 to 1968. Schools were closed and young people encouraged to join Red Guard units that persecuted Chinese teachers and intellectuals, promoted Mao's cult of personality, and then began factionalizing and turning on each other. Eventually Mao ordered the Army to stem Red Guard factionalism while promoting their radical goals. During this period China's external diplomatic and trade relations were drastically curtailed. Within a decade, however, most Chinese had come to see that period of isolation as counterproductive to development.

By the mid-1990s most authorities in both the First and Second Tiers had concluded that the price of isolation is cutting one's people off from the progress enjoyed, admittedly in varying degrees, by other states. Success in isolated development certainly requires significant resources, including energy, raw materials, space, and arable farmland, so this strategy can never be appropriate for all states. Proponents of isolation argue that it facilitates political and cultural security by insulating a state against penetration by foreign values and control. Opponents argue the price is the sort of poverty and backwardness seen in extreme form in North Korea, one of the most isolated and impenetrable states of the late twentieth century. North Korea notably lacks the resources for significant development on its own, and by the late 1990s was facing mass famine and appealing for international food aid.

REGIONAL INTEGRATION

Regional integration has a long history as a development strategy, and the United States has promoted it in Western Europe since the end of World War II. Regional integration takes numerous forms. Many involve functional integration as employed in Western Europe over decades, while others are only now beginning to be applied. Free trade areas eliminate internal tariffs on sales between their members. Customs unions establish common external tariffs on imports from all outside states. Common markets provide for free internal movements of labor and capital. Monetary unions provide for common currency. In more highly integrated regions, tax systems and even government budgets can be merged. Yet, many difficulties must be faced, so that there are very few successful instances of such regional integration. Benefits often accrue to the most developed member states and cost the least developed. Although it may promote economic security, regional integration challenges the societal security of member states and must overcome formidable obstacles in national pride and accumulated grievances from the past.

Contemporary Europe provides the best example of pressures that both encourage and impede regional integration. Beginning in 1958 and preceded by earlier steps of narrower functional integration, the European Common Market (later the Common Market, now the European Union) established a free trade area, customs union, and common market. Fully eliminating internal barriers to trade, however, took decades. Moving to monetary union in the late 1990s under the Maastricht Treaty not only raised the hackles of national pride but required stringent fiscal policies to control inflation. Thus far, Western Europe demonstrates the most fully realized regional integration, going far beyond regional free trade agreements like NAFTA.

COMMODITY PRODUCER CARTELS

Commodity producer cartels, international organizations that fix prices and allocate export quantities, offer the promise of enhanced market power to states that are major agricultural or natural resource exporters. As a major importer of such products, the United States often has acted to discourage producer cartels. From the wealth produced through regulation of export prices and quantities, cartels offer the promise of enhanced development, but those promises seldom have been fulfilled.

As we discussed in Chapter 11, successful commodity producer cartels are aided by several conditions. Price inelasticity of demand means that consumers and their governments will not or cannot reduce purchases much in response to price increases. Coordinating action is easier and the dropout problem is reduced if there are few producers. Shared values and experiences also may make coordination easier between producer governments. Consumer resistance to price increases may be reduced by small purchases, indifference, and even sympathy with the producers. Intermediaries may buffer between producers and consumers, smoothing out short-term price fluctuations and slowing the impact of large increases. Finally, cartels are strengthened if they can absorb short-term losses in hope of long-term gains.

Petroleum is the one commodity that best meets these conditions and for which exporters have been able to manage a fairly effective cartel. However, even that cartel, OPEC, has suffered from internal divisions over pricing strategy as member states regularly have pumped oil beyond their quotas and sold below official prices. Partly as a result, and partly because of consumer price resistance and economic fluctuations, oil prices have fluctuated significantly, and OPEC was unable to sustain the price peaks of 1981–85. Lacking petroleum's vital role as energy source and raw material for the chemical industry, other commodity producers have had notably less success with cartels. Most authorities today suggest that states heavily dependent on commodity exports should diversify rapidly, by applying as many of the other strategies discussed here as possible.

A SUMMARY OF DEVELOPMENT STRATEGIES

Unfortunately, there is no single magic bullet for development. Realistic policies likely will involve combinations of several of the strategies discussed here, chosen to be appropriate to the human and material resources and the current economic structures of particular states. As economic globalization sweeps around the world, it should provide not only pressures to develop and join the global economy but opportunities to utilize new international ties in facilitating development. This is an optimistic view, of course. Pessimists see global economic divisions continuing to widen. Nonetheless, already developed states such as the United States have a number of options to employ in facilitating development around the globe if they choose to continue and intensify that policy goal, which can be supported on grounds of equity, humanity, and practical politics.

SUMMARY

Four key points frame our examination of U.S. foreign policy prospects within the post–Cold War global context that likely will continue well into the twenty-first century. (1) The global context of U.S. foreign policy changed dramatically around 1990, with the end of the Cold War. With the breakup of the Soviet Union, America is the sole surviving superpower. The threat of global nuclear war has receded, but the number and diversity of smaller challenges has multiplied dramatically. (2) U.S. world dominance is much reduced today from the levels enjoyed shortly after World War II, even though we remain the world's greatest economic and military power. Consequently, U.S. foreign policy must rely much more heavily upon cooperative means than during the mid-twentieth century. (3) Development—how best and how much to promote it—is one of the larger and more difficult problems facing the United States and other developed economies today, and likely the one that will involve us with the greatest number of other states around the world. (4) The United States faces rather different sets of problems in dealing with developed (First Tier and near–First Tier) states than with developing (Second Tier) states. Yet another set of problems requires simultaneous interactions with both First and Second Tier states. This provides the organizing logic for the next three chapters.

Issues of sustainable development and environmental degradation were almost unseen and unconsidered in the early Cold War years. Human impact on the planet generally was perceived as minimal and bounded, and environmental consciousness was extremely limited. Few people had considered the implications of ever-expanding use of natural resources, forthcoming increases in population, or the environmental costs of real increases in standards of living for the majority of those billions of people living in Second Tier states. The late years of the twentieth century have seen significant growth in environmental consciousness around the globe, driven by ever more obvious signs that growing and developing populations are running into serious headroom limitations. Most environmental problems occur in global common pools, making them part of the context in which all governments must operate. In one such pool after another humans still are learning how great their impacts already have been, how much those impacts have occurred in only the last century or even the last few decades, and how seriously those impacts threaten to grow in the early twenty-first century despite our current tentative efforts to limit them. Such concerns form an important part of the political landscape for all governments and a significant set of constraints on future U.S. actions.

Development is at least one of the most important dimensions for classifying foreign policy problems, and arguably the single most important. Population growth steadily yields more mouths to feed, increasing pressures to deplete and possibly destroy all sorts of natural resources. The common pool nature of such problems means the United States has no good options to remain uninvolved. Development also may lead to military conflicts when ambitious governments like that of Saddam Hussein's Iraq see seizures as the route to greater power and prosperity. Industrial growth and development often contribute to military as well as civilian technologies. Finally, development is important because it supports long-standing American goals of promoting democratic governance and market economies. There is now widespread agreement that democratic governments best promote free markets, which in turn are widely believed to encourage the fastest and most efficient economic growth.

Unfortunately, there is no single magic bullet for development. Development strategies examined in this chapter include industrialization; rapid capital accumulation; mobilization of underemployed workers; centralized economic planning by an economically active state; direct foreign aid as economic grants, loans, and military assistance; foreign trade; foreign direct investment; technical assistance; isolated self-development; regional integration; and commodity producer cartels. Discussion in each case covers the process involved, the major strengths asserted, major weaknesses or critiques raised, and what we can discern from available evidence to date about the effectiveness of the strategy and the balance between its advantages and disadvantages. Many strategies can be complementary, so realistic development programs both with and without cross-tier links often involve mixes of several policy tools, in the same manner as most U.S. foreign policies.

KEY TERMS

Enlargement
Grants

Terms of trade problem

SELECTED READINGS

Crush, Jonathan. 1995. *Power of Development.* London: Routledge.

Tisch, Sarah J., and Michael B. Wallace. 1994. *Dilemmas of Development Assistance: The What, Why, and Who of Foreign Aid.* Boulder, Colo.: Westview.

United Nations Development Program. [Annual]. *Human Development Report.* London: Oxford University Press.

World Bank. [Annual]. *World Development Report* [Year]. Washington, D.C.: The World Bank.

World Bank. [Annual]. *World Development Indicators* [Year] *on CD-ROM.* Washington, D.C.: The World Bank.

Zimmerman, Robert F. 1993. *Dollars, Diplomacy, and Dependency: Dilemmas of U.S. Economic Aid.* Boulder, Colo.: Lynne Reinner.

CHAPTER 14

FIRST TIER AND NEAR FIRST TIER: THE DEVELOPED AND NEARLY DEVELOPED WORLD

⊕ A BRIEF CONTEMPORARY TRADE DISPUTE

In midafternoon on Thursday, 16 October 1997, an unexpected flare-up in a U.S.-Japanese trade dispute produced threats that the majority of Japanese container ships would be barred from U.S. ports and Japanese ships already in those ports would be detained (Sanger, 1997b). Those actions would have halted most American imports from Japan (except automobiles, carried on specially equipped ships) and most U.S. exports to Japan, notably including agricultural produce carried back on the same container ships. Acting under a 1920 law giving it such authority over all ships moving through U.S. ports, the Federal Maritime Commission voted to order the Coast Guard to bar and detain ships after Japan's three largest shipping companies, apparently on orders of their government, had refused to pay $4 million in accumulated fines. Those fines, of $100,000 per ship entering a U.S. port, had been imposed by the commission starting the previous month, after the U.S. government charged the Japanese government with defaulting on earlier agreements to liberalize port procedures. At issue was American shippers' insistence that the Japan Harbor Transport Association, a politically powerful private group representing stevedores and terminal operators and widely believed to have organized crime ties, was imposing freight handling rules so strict as to constitute nontariff barriers to trade. The Maritime Commission's order was a very serious big gun action that threatened to disrupt billions of dollars in shipping and wreak severe economic hardships on both countries.

The commission's ruling came without prior consultation, completely surprising top Clinton administration officials. Although it was a legal zone 2 agency action (see Figure 4.2 and the accompanying discussion), it threatened extreme escalation of a serious dispute in an area so important and sensitive that it normally would be dealt with at the highest levels by zone 1 officials. The very same day, those officials began to take control. An unnamed senior administration official noted that President Clinton had authority to overrule the commission on national security grounds, but probably would not. A meeting of the president's National Economic Council was convened at the White House to review proposals already on the negotiating table. Undersecretary of State Stuart Eizenstat stepped in on Friday to lead the American negotiating team. At a joint press conference later that day, Eizenstat and Japanese ambassador Kunihiko Saito announced tentative agreement in principle on a solution which would give American shippers the same access to Japanese ports that the Japanese enjoy in the United States, although there were "still a few details to be worked out," which both men characterized as minor (Crutsinger, 1997). Under the accord, Japan agreed to create an alternative system for foreign carriers to negotiate for stevedores to unload their ships. Eizenstadt said he believed "meaningful reform" in Japanese port practices could result. President Clinton hailed the tentative deal in a statement issued in Argentina, where he was completing a four-nation South American trip. Federal Maritime Commission Chairman Howard Creel announced the commission would meet again on Monday to review details of the completed agreement and, if no problems were raised and the $4 million fines were paid, would permanently drop its threatened ban on Japanese ships.

Of course, any agreement in principle must be tracked to see whether it results in the agreed actions, and long-term follow-up regarding any promised procedural changes always is advisable. The prompt announcement and high level at which this accord was reached demonstrate the importance both governments attached to the issue, but did not guarantee real change. Eleven days after the commission's original vote, an agreement was signed promising new Japanese port procedures and reducing the accumulated fines to $1.5 million. Almost a year later no real progress had been made in reforming Japanese port practices, while appointments of commissioners to the Federal Maritime Commission were stalemated by partisan bickering between Democratic president Bill Clinton and the Republican-led senate and by shipping industry pressures for deregulation (Sansbury, 1998). This stubborn dispute exemplifies the sorts of sensitive specific trade issues faced by the United States in dealing with other developed states now and in the years ahead.

INTERACTING WITH ALREADY DEVELOPED STATES AND REGIONS

This chapter is devoted to issues the United States faces primarily in its dealings with already developed states (see summary in Table 14.1). Some controversies involve the United States with single states, as the one just described involved tough negotiations over opening Japan's domestic markets to more American goods and thereby helping reduce our trade deficit. Any of the many negotiating tactics discussed in Chapter 10 may be applied in such cases. Other issues are unavoidably multilateral, for example, coordinating international economic policy among the most developed states through the G-8. Here, negotiating tactics must be adjusted to facilitate coordinated collective action of the sorts discussed in Chapter 12.

As set out in the introduction to Part IV, this chapter is organized according to the five activity sectors of geopolitical, military, economic, societal, and environmental contexts of U.S. foreign policy in the post–Cold War era. Focus cases are typical of each tier

TABLE 14.1	
U.S. Foreign Policy Concerns with First Tier (Developed) *and Near-First Tier Actors, Classified by Issue Sectors*	

Note: Boldfaced issues are archetypal focus cases given extended treatment.
Shaded areas denote traditional areas of primary U.S. concern.

Sector	Contemporary and Foreseeable Policy Issues
Geopolitical	**NATO Expansion** Organizational and Mission Realignments UN Security Council Expansion Future U.S. Global Standing The Decline Debate
Military	**Missions, Force Levels, and the Future of Superpower Status** Missile Defense Systems vs. The ABM Treaty Single Superpower Debate Post–Cold War Role and Management of the CIA B-2, Other Major Weapons Precision-Guided Munitions
Economic	**Coordination with the G-8 and Other Highly Developed Economies** Expanding Membership and Powers Future U.S. Role Specific Trade Issues, e.g., Access to Japan's Home Markets Promoting Market Economies Worldwide The "Twin Deficits" in the United States Federal Budget and International Trade European Union and the Maastricht Treaty Future Trading Blocs
Societal	**The U.S. Decline Debate (see also Chapter 11)** Ownership and Control of Assets and Resources
Environmental	**Ozone Depletion** Distributing Costs of Environmental Cleanups and Improved Technologies

and issue sector and receive somewhat greater attention, except for a few given detailed treatment in earlier chapters. Each focus case is explicitly linked to U.S. policy concerns and generalized to the larger issue category. The three shaded cells of Table 14.1 indicate traditionally primary areas of U.S. foreign policy concern: geopolitical, military, and economic issues with other First Tier states. In Chapter 15 we address issues the United States faces primarily in its dealings with developing states. Finally, for issues that bridge between the tiers either by involving the entire world or by linking powerful and influential developed states to less powerful and less influential developing states, see Chapter 16.

According to the definitions introduced in Chapter 13, the First Tier consists largely of World Bank high-income states, with upper-middle income states forming a near–First

Tier group. These are distinctly different—and evolving—types of economies than those in the Second Tier (low-income and lower-middle income groups). States with large and highly developed economies have obvious weight in affecting global economic issues. Moreover, such economies enable military prowess because their scale allows raising and maintaining substantial military forces and either purchasing sophisticated weapons or acquiring the technology to build them. Very few low- or middle-income economies are large enough to allow the investment necessary to compete with First Tier states; the nuclear weapons programs of China, India, and Pakistan are notable exceptions.

The United States today and in the future faces quite different policy issues with First Tier states than with Second Tier states, even though almost all our foreign relations have been profoundly affected by post–Cold War changes in the global policy environment. Relations between high-income and upper-middle income states increasingly revolve around expanding trade, changing economic interactions, and rivalry to remain in or move into the upper reaches of the First Tier. Widely varying resource endowments and rates of economic growth imply significant changes in economic strength over time. Over the long term, we should anticipate considerable jockeying for position. We also should anticipate trade disputes and other forms of competition and maneuvering for influence with significant governments and other actors in both tiers (for example, oil exporters). Interactions with high-income states are likely over such needs as realigning global political and military security arrangements for the post–Cold War era, deciding on required defense spending levels and the composition and missions of twenty-first century military forces, coordinating economic policy to manage global markets and to promote development, and solving environmental impact problems that are most severe in already industrialized states. Some issues will take explicitly political forms, such as calls in the 1990s for permanent (and veto-wielding) German and Japanese seats on the UN Security Council.

ARCHETYPAL FOCUS CASES

We examine five focus cases in this chapter, each selected as typical of its tier and issue sector. Each is discussed according to the five-point framework described in the introduction to Part IV: stakes at issue, relevant U.S. policy themes, perceptions held by other actors and their relations with the United States, available alternative actions and policy tools, and future prospects and concerns. Cases given extended treatment in this chapter include the following:

- In the *geopolitical sector*, domestic political concerns played a large role in shaping the Clinton administration's push for NATO expansion into Eastern Europe, despite the risk of damaging U.S.-Russian relations. Although initial expansion was approved by NATO in 1997 and ratified by the U.S. Senate in 1998, it remained controversial, and the possibility of further expansion was even more contested.

- In the *military sector*, future U.S. missions, force levels, and budgets are intensely debated. The 1990s saw real defense budgets decrease while international threats increased in number and changed in character. Meanwhile, the hoped for post–Cold War "peace dividend" went largely into reducing the federal budget deficit.

- In the *economic sector*, international economic coordination through such mechanisms as the G-8 group of highly developed economies will be needed for the indefinite future. Political considerations and the desire to foster fragile Russian democracy press for arrangements that increasingly integrate the Russian Federation into the G-8.

- In the *societal sector*, we briefly consider the debate over the decline in U.S. economic and global political standing (see also Chapter 11).

- In the *environmental sector*, agreements to end chlorofluorocarbon (CFC) production and thereby reduce upper-atmosphere ozone depletion exemplify a class of problems on which the already developed states can do the most to limit adverse impacts.

Some additional contemporary and foreseeable issues are discussed following the geopolitical, military, and economic focus cases.

GEOPOLITICAL SECTOR FOCUS CASE: NATO EXPANSION

NATO's survival and growth beyond the Cold War era were political surprises not clearly foreseen in the early 1990s, and continue to generate policy challenges. Founded in 1949, the North Atlantic Treaty Organization (NATO) played a primary role in U.S. Cold War containment policy. It became the most lasting and successful of the collective defense agreements organized to bind states all around the periphery of the Soviet bloc. The original North Atlantic Treaty was signed by the foreign ministers of the United States, Canada, and ten Western European governments (Belgium, Denmark, France, Great Britain, Iceland, Italy, Luxembourg, the Netherlands, Norway, and Portugal). Signatories obligated themselves to settle disputes by peaceful means, rearm, and develop their individual and collective capacity to resist armed attack. They also agreed that an attack on any of them would be considered an attack on all, calling for individual or collective resistance under Article 51 of the UN charter. Defense policies were integrated—although not without some major exceptions and political squabbles—under a new organization headed by a council of ministers. During the long course of the Cold War, NATO membership slowly expanded to include four additional Western European governments: Germany (initially West Germany), Greece, Spain, and Turkey. Until about 1990, NATO's fundamental goals were well described by the epigram of Lord Ismay, NATO's first secretary general (1952–57), that its central purpose was to keep the Americans in Europe, the Soviets out, and the Germans down (Millar, 1998).

The Cold War's end included the overthrow of communist regimes across Eastern Europe, reunification of Germany, and the breakup of the Soviet Union. Serious questions about NATO's future promptly surfaced. Knowledgeable analysts of the early 1990s predicted massive reductions in troop levels, particularly American troops in Europe. As the military wing of the Warsaw Treaty Organization was disbanded in 1991, others questioned whether European security required any continued U.S. involvement. In the optimistic Europeanism of late 1991 and early 1992, French officials actively suggested that the end of the Cold War and the emergence of the European Union should lead Europeans to adopt a defense structure more independent of NATO, to be embodied in the Western European Union (WEU). Unsurprisingly, early U.S. responses were almost instinctive calls to maintain the alliance and redefine NATO's purpose. Organizational politics predicts such calls, which were echoed by the NATO organization. Yet, by the mid-1990s, many European leaders had made major political turnarounds and were calling for continuing and reinvigorating NATO in order to keep the United States engaged in Europe. The turning point came as terrible ethnically based slaughter in the Bosnian civil war gave particular urgency to those calls. Ultimately, only the United States had the combination of political will and military muscle to coerce a fragile peace agreement among the major combatants and make it work. After forty-three months of plans and negotiations under the auspices of many European organizations including NATO itself, a Bosnian peace agreement was reached in the November 1995 Dayton accords. American troop commitments proved essential to winning European participation.

Subsequently, the Clinton administration began a very strong push for **NATO expansion,** under which some newly democratizing Eastern European states would become NATO members and the sphere of NATO security guarantees would be expanded. Initial European enthusiasm was minimal at best. By NATO's July 1997 Madrid Summit, however, remaining major questions were down to how many new members, which states, and when. France urged immediate membership for Romania and Slovenia, and U.S. leaders openly promised them later consideration. In the end, the U.S. position prevailed: the Czech Republic, Hungary, and Poland were invited to begin accession talks, and other new memberships were deferred for later decision. NATO heads of state and government agreed to review the issue at their 1999 meeting. In the meantime, a Protocol of Accession was signed by foreign ministers at their fall 1997 meeting, with ratification or parliamentary approval procedures in allied states completed in time for NATO's fiftieth anniversary in April 1999.

Interestingly, public enthusiasm within potential new NATO member states was somewhat mixed. When citizens eligible to vote were asked in November 1996 polls conducted for the European Commission how they would vote on a referendum to join NATO, respondents in favor (and, in parentheses, uncertain) were as follows: Romania, 76 percent (8 percent); Poland, 65 percent (14 percent); Slovenia, 39 percent (21 percent); Hungary, 32 percent (17 percent); and Czech Republic, 28 percent (25 percent). Twenty to 25 percent of those interviewed gave no response. Opposition to NATO membership usually was quite a bit less than uncertainty, and ranged from a low of 3 percent in Poland to a high of 23 percent in Hungary (European Commission, 1997, Text Figure 11).

What drove the United States to promote NATO's continuation and expansion, Western European governments to initially oppose and later accept it, and Eastern European governments to seek membership? What do these events portend for future U.S. foreign policy problems in Europe and possibly in other regions? As with most major political developments, the motivations underlying and surrounding NATO expansion are complex and somewhat contradictory. We have already identified the major actors, their key relationships, and part of the NATO system's function, as suggested by the systems approach introduced in Chapter 4. In expanding our analysis and assessing these questions we now use the five-point framework for analyzing U.S. interests introduced earlier.

STAKES AT ISSUE

NATO expansion affects many top-level interests of the United States and most European governments, whether NATO members or not. Regionwide concerns include broad, long-term arrangements for Eastern European security, driven by fears of more Bosnia-style civil wars and the possibility of resurgent Russian nationalism. When Russian ultra-nationalists like Vladimir Zhirinovsky call for reabsorbing the "near abroad," it gives reason for concern even in the larger former Soviet republics like Ukraine, and certainly in their smaller neighbors. Their concerns are mirrored by Russian Federation anxieties that NATO, feared as a relic of the Cold War, will push superior military capability all the way to Russia's borders. In turn, this raises U.S. and European concerns about future relations with Russia.

For the West, NATO expansion provides highly visible support and encouragement to new democracies. Full costs of meeting the security commitments of NATO expansion and bringing Eastern European military forces up to NATO standards have not been determined. The pace of expansion seems to evince a desire to add NATO members while it is politically feasible and worry about costs later, an attitude reminiscent of Germany's leaders at the time of its 1990 reunification. This may be politically astute provided that, in both the German and NATO cases, expansion is genuinely desirable but long-term monetary costs are high. Finally, there were fascinating intermestic stakes in appealing to Americans who trace their roots to Eastern Europe and in President Clinton's desires to find an issue area in which he could demonstrate foreign policy leadership to build his historic legacy.

RELEVANT U.S. POLICY THEMES

NATO's continuity and vital importance to European and global security have been important U.S. policy themes since early Cold War days, and the alliance long has been at the core of U.S.-European relations. Supporting NATO expansion expressed themes of promoting democracy, stability, and regional security. At home, strengthening, reaffirming, and expanding NATO recalled the heady post–World War II days of bipartisan foreign policy, at a time when partisan divisions in the American government had grown notably sharper, more bitter, and much more frequent. Thus NATO expansion offered a promising area for President Clinton and the post-1994 Republican congressional majority to cooperate. Cold War worries often led the United States to call every non-communist government democratic. Today we have opportunities to support states that are genuine emerging democracies, including some with pre–World War II histories of democratic governance. By supporting them we also help promote successful conversion from command to market economies.

PERCEPTIONS HELD BY OTHER ACTORS AND THEIR RELATIONS WITH THE UNITED STATES

Numerous Eastern European governments seek NATO membership, both from fear of a resurgent Russia and desires to strengthen economic, military, and political ties with the West. Ethnic communities within the United States that trace their ancestry to Eastern

European states strongly support NATO expansion. This is particularly true for the Baltic states (Estonia, Latvia, and Lithuania), which pose a particular sore point for Russia. The Baltics were overrun and forcibly made Soviet republics early in World War II. Thereafter, American presidents throughout the Cold War annually proclaimed "Captive Nations Day" in memory of Baltic independence. Soviet absorption efforts included imposing the Russian language and settling large minorities of ethnic Russians in the Baltic states. After independence, some of those minority Russians began to suffer discrimination and fear for their future. Baltic state membership would bring NATO to Russia's western border, so Russian fears that NATO expansion is a new form of containment are most intense regarding the Baltics. Already agitated by the Soviet breakup and Russia's decline from superpower status, followed by a shaky conversion to democracy and severe difficulties in converting to a market economy, many Russians saw NATO's advance toward their borders as unwarranted.

Some analysts saw the extension of NATO membership as a less expensive alternative to incorporating Eastern European states into the European Union. Despite the uncertain—and probably high—costs of NATO expansion, the experience of German reunification suggests that economic integration would be considerably more expensive. A major factor slowing Germany's overall economic growth since 1990 has been the enormous costs of bringing eastern Germans up to western German standards of living, replacing and modernizing inefficient eastern factories, and beginning to clean up decades of East German environmental pollution. Comparable costs reasonably may be expected across all of Eastern Europe. It is notable that the economies of Poland, Hungary, and the Czech Republic are the most developed and furthest advanced toward market structure within their region.

AVAILABLE ALTERNATIVE ACTIONS AND POLICY TOOLS

Prior to the 1997 Madrid Summit, NATO's expansion options could be grouped broadly into the following categories: (1) large and rapid expansion; (2) limited but rapid expansion, with or without promises to take in more members later; (3) expansion accompanied by other steps designed to save political face and lessen fears in Russia; (4) delay; and (5) cancellation. The July 1997 decisions mixed limited but prompt expansion with political olive branches for Russia and calculated ambiguity about additional memberships later. This meant political victories for the Clinton administration at home and within NATO, at the risk of damaging future relations with Russia. Stephen Sestanovich (1997, 164) argues strongly that, by the mid-1990s, U.S. "policy toward Russia [was] derivative of choices and calculations that have nothing directly to do with Russia" and that President Clinton's actions were strongly driven by intermestic considerations, asserting,

> In defining his position on [NATO expansion], the president faced a vastly more serious problem than whether he might please or displease Polish-Americans (and others). He had to take a stand at a time when *his handling of foreign policy had become a glaring—and, some of his advisors were obviously telling him, potentially fatal—political weakness.* . . . The issue . . . offered the administration an opportunity to present itself

as the defender of foreign policy bipartisanship in pursuit of traditional American goals. (Sestanovich, 1997, 169–170; emphasis in the original)

FUTURE PROSPECTS AND CONCERNS

NATO enlargement threatens a worsening of Russian relations with the United States and Europe, in both the short and long terms. Arguably, more is at stake in maintaining good relations with the world's number two nuclear power and encouraging democracy and market economic conversion in the core state of the former Soviet Union than in any other European concern. In the eyes of many analysts, the Clinton administration persisted and prevailed over strongly voiced Russian objections because officials knew that Russia could not stop NATO expansion. Unfortunately, this was only the latest and most severe of a number of ways in which the U.S. government ceased working as harmoniously with the Russians as in the early 1990s. Russia was offered limited concessions that did not alter the fundamental fact of NATO expansion. Vague promises were made about keeping nuclear weapons out and restricting troop levels in the new member states. Russia's status was upgraded from that of formal observer at G-7 economic meetings to full participant in what was billed in 1997 as the "Summit of the Eight." In 1998 full formal membership was offered, creating the G-8 and giving Russia equal status with the major developed democracies, except on issues of international finance.

Ambiguity about adding additional NATO members in the future suggests that there will be recurring waves of argument over subsequent expansion. Such arguments may intensify both internal NATO arguments and confrontations with Russia. Pending the operational absorption of new members into NATO's structure, we should anticipate battles over the costs of converting their equipment, training, and procedures to conform with NATO standards, and real difficulty in organizing NATO's response to any major new regional security crisis.

The NATO expansion case exemplifies an important class of future foreign policy problems and some recurring problematic features. Serious political and military security issues remain to be worked out as we move further into a new post–Cold War world order. The economic component of such issues is stronger than ever before. European unity has significant spillover effects on economic and monetary union under the European Union. NATO expansion was the centerpiece of U.S. foreign policy during the second Clinton term, but domestic political concerns shared importance with international and regional European political and security concerns. Finally, as in the Bosnia and Kosovo cases, continuing active American engagement appears to be necessary to make security agreements—even with other major developed states—happen.

NATO expansion entails other debates about *NATO's future missions* and the *organizational realignments* necessary to accomplish them. Expansion requires reequipping Eastern European armies with weaponry and supplies compatible with those of long-term NATO members. Perhaps even more importantly, it requires developing compatible plans, standard operating procedures (SOPs), and training. Detailed costs have yet to be reliably estimated, but appear to be substantial. Raising funds and apportioning burdens thus will be difficult and likely expand long-standing U.S.-European contention. Clearly, NATO's mission no longer is to protect Western Europe against Soviet and Warsaw Pact attack.

But exactly what threats NATO is to counter on behalf of former Warsaw Treaty Organization states remains extremely vague. NATO, however, is no stranger to vagueness. War plans that called for using tactical nuclear weapons in West Germany to halt a Soviet invasion always had a certain ring of incredibility. Nonetheless, for decades NATO's deterrence of Soviet attack relied in part on deliberate ambiguity regarding when and under what conditions the alliance would "go nuclear." Additionally, NATO participation in Bosnian peacekeeping and peacemaking under the 1995 Dayton accords, and later actions in Kosovo, were major departures from previous rules that prohibited actions outside member states. Deciding on NATO goals, needed organizational revisions, operational planning, equipment, and training no doubt will occupy member governments for some years to come.

Other Geopolitical Issues

Concerns about America's future global standing and about expanding the veto-wielding permanent membership of the UN Security Council have global geopolitical scope but are rooted in economic strength. We outlined the decline debate regarding long-term U.S. global political-economic strength in Chapter 11. Informed analysts continue to disagree about the severity and inevitability of decline, although most concur that U.S. hegemony in world political, economic, and even military matters never again will be as great as during the early post–World War II years. With the all-enveloping Soviet threat perceived during the Cold War gone, many authorities see U.S. influence waning as other states gain military strength and become richer, more developed, and more populous. If the United States continues to gain economic strength slowly while other states grow more rapidly and move into the high-income First Tier, long-run American *relative* decline is inevitable. Although Henry Kissinger took considerable flak for writing in 1968 that America could not remain the most powerful state in the world forever, by thirty years later his insight was widely accepted. This implies a geopolitical influence shift of profound importance to U.S. foreign policy.

One political consequence of this long-term shift in influence has been agitation to expand the veto-wielding permanent membership of the UN Security Council beyond the original five great powers (China, France, Russia, the United Kingdom, and the United States) to include others of the richest and most powerful states, notably Japan and Germany. Such demands do not require absolute decline of the original five great powers, only that additional states begin to attain comparable power—especially economic power—and political influence.

Consider the case today for Germany and Japan. Despite an economic slowdown that intensified in the late 1990s, Japan had the world's second largest economy and had surpassed the United States in GDP per capita (see Chapter 13, especially Table 13.3). Upon reunification in October 1990, Germany's GDP immediately became the largest in Europe, and Germany quickly supplanted France as the most influential member of the Economic Community. By 1994, after the Soviet Union's breakup and subsequent economic reforms and disruptions, Germany's GDP was roughly twice that of the Russian Federation. Many Germans and Japanese believe that permanent Security Council membership would suitably reflect the world influence their countries already have achieved, particularly in political-economic matters. Some analysts also have argued that higher status recognition would encourage Germany and Japan to take more active political roles in, and contribute more resources to, global security and development programs. This issue promises to gain importance as we move into the twenty-first century. In the longer term, as additional states such as India gain power and influence through development, their governments likely will make similar demands.

MILITARY SECTOR FOCUS CASE: MILITARY MISSIONS, FORCE LEVELS, AND THE FUTURE OF SUPERPOWER STATUS

Many military issues are more intensely intermestic than geopolitical issues, even though both sets originate in (1) policy adjustments to the end of the Cold War, and (2) decline in relative U.S. global dominance. Soviet decline and breakup created a possibility that would have fascinated realpolitik practitioners of the nineteenth century: as the sole surviving superpower, the United States could adopt policies to actively oppose any challengers and thereby sustain U.S. hegemony indefinitely. More broadly, the end of the Cold War created uncertainty and disputes about appropriate future American grand policy, roughly at the same time the decline debate raised questions about U.S. ability to afford and maintain its past strong role. Consequently, much attention has been devoted to questions such as the following:

- What military threats should the United States be prepared to counter, and how?
- Which new weapons systems should be purchased in what quantities? Should we sell them to foreign states? If so, under what conditions?
- What troop levels are appropriate to meet likely threats while remaining affordable?
- Which military bases should be closed or "realigned" (reassigned to other forces and functions)?
- How much can superior advanced technologies such as precision-guided weapons substitute for large numbers of troops?
- How many of the threats we are likely to face are unconventional and must be met by new means?
- How great an intelligence effort, and of what type, is required in the new era?
- How should U.S. efforts and programs be integrated with those of other governments and IGOs to increase effectiveness and reduce costs?

All these questions are closely related to the geopolitical issue of how broad and engaged a global role the American government expects to play in the new century. When it emerged from the Cold War as the world's sole surviving superpower, should the United States have acted to preserve its status into the indefinite future by opposing the rise of new superpowers? Is such a result feasible? If so, should we pursue it today and into the twenty-first century? These questions frame one policy debate of truly grand scope, closely linked to the broad task of evaluating potential military threats and then sizing and structuring forces to meet those threats. Uncertainty inevitably accompanies risk assessments and contingency planning and complicates our responses. For essentially peaceful governments, planning and structuring military forces is akin to insurance against the downside risks of international politics. We examine this case using two time-point snapshots of future-oriented strategic planning: the 1992 single superpower debate and a 1997 global strategic reassessment. In this context the distinction between strategy and tactics may be analogized to our use of grand and specific foreign policies; **strategic planning** deals with long-range goals and large-scale programs to achieve them, whereas **tactical planning** deals with procedures for fighting specific battles. Although most potential future military threats to the United States seem likely to arise from Second Tier states, the case appears in this chapter because any emergent superpower would automatically be a contender for First Tier status.

The single superpower debate arose in 1992, the last year of the Bush administration, and became public only a year after the Persian Gulf War and barely more than a year after the demise of the Soviet Union. Its meteoric rise and decline are well chronicled in a series of incisive articles by *New York Times* reporter Patrick E. Tyler (1992a–h). In two 17 February stories (1992a, b), Tyler sketched seven scenarios for potential foreign conflicts that might draw U.S. forces into combat over the next decade. Those scenarios were contained in a classified document summarizing the Pentagon's first detailed military planning for the post–Cold War era. Called the *Defense Planning Guidance*, the document usually is produced every other year for internal Defense Department use. This version's preparation was overseen by Paul D. Wolfowitz, undersecretary of defense for policy (Tyler, 1992d, A14). Wolfowitz, a conservative in-and-outer who was once an assistant professor of political science at the University of Chicago, first was called to government service after writing a brilliant and influential 1970 paper examining the technical flaws of launching ballistic missiles upon warning of an incoming attack.

Publication and subsequent public examination of the *Defense Planning Guidance* resulted from a major leak of classified materials, as has happened in numerous cases since the Vietnam War era. As Tyler describes it (1992a, A8), seventy pages of planning documents

> . . . were made available to the *New York Times* by an official who wished to call attention to what he considered vigorous attempts within the military establishment to invent a menu of alarming war scenarios that can be used by the Pentagon to prevent further reductions in forces or cancellations of new weapons systems from defense contractors.

Those seven hypothetical scenarios covered six regional conflicts including a new Iraqi invasion of Kuwait and Saudi Arabia, and a Panama coup threatening access to the Panama Canal. Assaults on U.S. forces by nuclear, biological, or chemical (NBC) weapons were considered possible under all six regional scenarios. The seventh scenario, emergence of a new expansionist superpower, envisioned the possibility that by the year 2001 a single state or coalition would arise "to adopt an adversarial security strategy and develop military capability to threaten U.S. interests through global military competition" (Tyler, 1992b, A8). All seven scenarios were considered to be illustrative rather than either predictive or exhaustive.

As Tyler's source no doubt envisioned, public release of the Pentagon planning scenarios evoked considerable public and congressional criticism, and the plan caught flak from both ends of the political spectrum. Liberal defense leaders like Wisconsin

Democrat Les Aspin, then chairman of the House Armed Services Committee, pressed for details of the underlying analysis. Other critics were openly skeptical of the assumption that the United States had to be prepared to fight two major regional wars simultaneously, an argument that had flared periodically since the Kennedy administration in the early 1960s (Tyler, 1992c). Right-wing neo-isolationists attacked the plan, with Republican Patrick Buchanan calling it "a formula for endless American interventionism in quarrels and war when no vital interest of the United States is remotely engaged" (Tyler, 1992f). By the time of Tyler's 11 March article (1992g), only three weeks after the original release, high Pentagon and White House officials were mounting a tactical withdrawal, announcing the previously leaked version never had received final approvals. In his final article on the subject (1992h, on 24 May), Tyler reported that Defense Secretary Cheney had just approved a revised draft that had been circulated for four weeks, in which collective action with other governments was emphasized.

In the terms of Figure 4.2 and its accompanying discussion, a study by high zone 2 officials has been attacked by others in zones 2 and 3, and the issue was resolved by being booted upstairs to zone 1 officials. Earlier language stating that "our first objective is to prevent the re-emergence of a new rival . . ." was replaced with the following: "Our most fundamental goal is to deter or defeat attack from whatever source. . . .The second goal is to strengthen and extend the system of defense arrangements that binds democratic and like-minded nations together in common defense."

The Bush administration's rejection of active measures to preserve single superpower status was continued under President Clinton, although occasional calls to reconsider were heard, typically reflecting concern about major Chinese growth in the future. In the National Defense University (NDU) *Strategic Assessment 1997*, the emphasis was on major regional threat "flashpoints." Several had been included in the 1992 set: new Iraqi aggression in the Persian Gulf, a North Korean attack on the South, and Russian attacks into their "near abroad" of former Soviet republics like Ukraine or the Baltic states. Others were new: Iranian disruption of oil shipments through the Straits of Hormuz; Chinese blockade or attack on Taiwan; breakdown of the Arab/Israeli peace process; strife within former Yugoslavia; a new humanitarian crisis in central Africa; or nuclear war between India and Pakistan (Binnendijk and Clawson, 1997, xiv). Some of those options reflected developments during the previous five years; in 1992 peace processes had not been far enough advanced either in Bosnia or the Middle East to worry greatly about their breakdown.

The 1997 NDU *Strategic Assessment* was not quite as high level and official a study as the 1992 *Defense Planning Guidance*. NDU is a unit of the Department of Defense, charged with educating senior military and governmental officials on issues related to national strategy, security policy, resources management, and warfare in the information age. *Strategic Assessment 1997* was prepared by zone 2 experts at NDU's Institute for National Strategic Studies (INSS), with help from a few outside consultants from comparable institutions. Because INSS is an in-house Pentagon policy study unit, its products are carefully labeled to indicate that they do not present adopted official policies.

STAKES AT ISSUE

At its worst, the emergence of a new superpower could threaten global war or a prolonged new cold war. (Remember that when the term *cold war* was first used in the late 1940s, it was considered a vastly preferable option to hot war, at a time when Truman administration officials greatly feared war with the Soviet Union.) Tyler's leaked Pentagon planning documents included a 4 February 1992 memo from David S. C. Chu, assistant secretary of defense for program analysis and evaluation, acting on behalf of Defense Secretary Richard Cheney, Chu instructed the secretaries of the military departments to use the draft scenarios in preparing each service's spending plans for 1994–99. This, of course, was the political concern of Tyler's source. Preparing to counter any emergent superpower could be extremely costly and involve the United States in serious disagreements with important allies.

Writing five years later, the NDU/INSS group concluded that the present (military) security environment is far more complex than in earlier eras. Their analysis assumed that three mostly post–Cold War revolutions have transformed the nature of the global security environment. First, a geostrategic revolution has reshaped once bipolar relations among the major powers, with the U.S. pole now much the strongest. Ideology is no longer a divisive force, and even nationalism is tempered by desires to build world markets. Second, the information technology revolution provides ever-expanding and previously unimagined access to information, supporting the trend toward more open societies. Third, under the governmental revolution, the sphere of state control is shrinking. In most developed states, power is devolving to regional and local governments and to the private sector, further reinforcing the trend toward pluralistic societies.

Building on those three key assumptions, the NDU/INSS group foresaw three broad classes of potential threats. (1) Potential "theater-peer" competitors unable to challenge U.S. interests around the globe still may be able to challenge them in areas close to their borders. This makes sense, in light of the rising sophistication of weapons sold internationally, increasing tendencies to sell the latest or recent models of weapons systems such as F-16 jet fighters, and the sale of former Soviet weapons and technologies to states with questionable intent, such as Iran. Even a superpower now can be outgunned in local areas. For example, U.S. bombing raids into Libya in 1986 carefully kept close to the coast and first knocked out radar and antiaircraft missile sites, all because of the fear of sophisticated Libyan air defenses. Also, American air strikes against a terrorist training base in Afghanistan in August 1998 relied exclusively on cruise missiles, to minimize the danger of pilots being shot down. (2) Rogue states such as Iran, Iraq, and North Korea may instigate major regional conflicts. (3) International political terrorists and internally troubled states or failed states (see the introductory Somalia case in Chapter 7) pose additional problems (Binnendijk and Clawson, 1997, xii). The dangers of terrorist attacks, particularly if they should involve NBC weapons, need little further comment. Failed states typically have seen governments collapse in the face of civil war, are torn apart by ethnic, regional, and nationalistic strife, or both. Notable examples from the 1990s include Somalia and former Yugoslavia. Few such situations pose direct threats to U.S. interests unless they should escalate into wider regional wars. Instead, they involve U.S. values, particularly if the United States adopts broader goals of promoting stable and peaceful democracies worldwide.

RELEVANT U.S. POLICY THEMES

The single superpower debate undoubtedly is the grandest of debates over future military requirements, force levels, and budgets. It is a major aspect of the still larger geopolitical

A POLITICAL HOT POTATO: DEFENSE BASE CLOSURES

The 1990s saw troop reductions and real dollar (after inflation) cutbacks in U.S. military spending, although defense budget increases began late in the decade. Setting military force levels and budgets involves profoundly intermestic policies because those decisions have tremendous impact on armed forces personnel, defense contractors, localities with large military bases and defense plants, and the Congress members who represent those districts. Indeed, military cutbacks are so politically salient that the Congress sought to insulate itself from retaliation over needed cutbacks during the 1990s by creating an independent Military Base Closure and Realignment Commission. The commission was empowered to investigate and recommend closures or "realignments," meaning partial closures, shifts of troops, and changes in functions and in which armed service would perform them. The administration next had a limited opportunity to make changes. Congress then was required to vote the entire list of recommendations up or down, without opportunities to logroll (see *intersecting negotiations* in Chapter 10) over revisions and amendments. Military service worries about impending post–Cold War cutbacks—accompanied by jockeying for favorable positions—can be traced back at least to the 1990–91 Persian Gulf War, as mentioned in Chapter 1.

debate over whether the United States will remain deeply engaged in global politics in the wake of the Cold War. Neo-isolationists prescribe a return to earlier, simpler, less involved days, despite growing global interconnectedness and vastly larger U.S. responsibilities in international institutions than existed prior to World War II. In a manner reminiscent of Allison's bureaucratic politics Model III, individual actors' stands on these issues often reflect their general political and ideological views as well as their positions in the organization charts of the armed services, defense contractors, or policy analysis groups. Disagreements about potential threats and the size and types of forces needed to meet them thus tend to reflect both differences in (1) worldview and preferred political/military approaches, and (2) real interests involving separable private benefits. An important constraint on policy choice was the growing 1990s pressure to reduce the federal budget deficit. It rapidly became apparent that the long-sought "peace dividend" from ending the Cold War would go mostly into deficit reduction rather than to social programs, although hope remained alive within the left wing, creating another pressure against any move to stabilize or increase military spending.

PERCEPTIONS HELD BY OTHER ACTORS AND THEIR RELATIONS WITH THE UNITED STATES

Most U.S. allies were not enthusiastic about the single superpower proposal. In particular, the 1992 controversy arose when the more independent European major powers, such as France, were agitating for a reduced American role in European security arrangements. Opponents of the United States, and such rising powers as India, were strongly opposed. China's leaders complained strongly for several years about U.S. intentions to contain their country's rise to global prominence.

AVAILABLE ALTERNATIVE ACTIONS AND POLICY TOOLS

Both the 1992 and the 1997 studies were examinations of policy alternatives. The policy debates turned on issues of values, appropriate goals, and whether each study group had overlooked or discounted some promising options. In such debates, multiple and redundant action channels almost always exist. Arguably, the single superpower goal could have been stopped in Congress in 1992, at the point when funds had to be voted to retain or initiate programs, without the necessity of the February leak.

FUTURE PROSPECTS AND CONCERNS

Both the 1992 and 1997 studies involve problems of broad military policy for the new era and offer useful insights into the policy-making process. The types, frequency, and severity of military threats abroad that the United States may face in the post–Cold War era remain important unsettled issues. How they will be met and whether we need to act alone also remain unresolved, and events like the Persian Gulf War offer little guidance. It is intriguing that both the 1992 and 1997 studies used ten-year time horizons. Although notably longer than many Washington planning horizons, ten years is less than the development time for most new major weapons systems, let alone their probable operational life. The information technology revolution identified by the INSS analysts may suggest that ten years is a long time to predict anything in today's world. So long as we have action channels with such long lead times, however, we have little choice but to try.

Other Military Issues

Some military issues hinge less closely on post–Cold War grand policy and U.S. global standing than on the size of the overall defense program, the degree of reliance on advanced technologies, and the role assigned to negotiated solutions to military threats. Consider, for example, the interaction between advanced missile defense systems and international arms control. One of the few foreign policy differences between President Clinton and Senator Dole during their 1996 election contest was that Clinton opposed, whereas Dole supported, programs to develop and deploy more effective short- to medium-range interceptors of ballistic missile warheads. The Reagan-era Strategic Defense Initiative (SDI; popularly called Star Wars) had sought to counter Soviet weapons with a widespread defense against intercontinental ballistic missiles. Early visions were of a multilayer defense including exotic space-based lasers and antimissile missiles. Later goals involved less exotic land-based interceptors, but the ICBM defense task proved too large and expensive, particularly when the United States began reaching new strategic arms control agreements with the Soviets during the late 1980s. Less than a decade later, some defense scientists argued that technologies studied under the SDI could be applied to defend American cities and military installations from a light attack by ballistic missiles carrying nuclear, biological, or chemical (NBC) warheads.

By the latter 1990s it was increasingly imaginable that such an attack could be launched by terrorists, an emerging and aggressive power, or rogue military officers in a disorganized state, perhaps Russia. Defense might employ improved versions of ground-launched missiles such as the Patriots deployed in Israel and Saudi Arabia during the Persian Gulf War. More advanced and speculative technologies might include tiny unguided interceptor rockets launched in vast numbers, ground-based lasers, and extremely rapid-fire guns like the navy's Phalanx system.

Such antimissile systems well may be technically feasible, and the task of defending against a light attack is far more practicable than countrywide defense against the massive Soviet attack feared during the Cold War. Yet a huge political obstacle with much wider ramifications remains: deploying almost any significant ballistic missile defense would violate the 1972 SALT I ABM Treaty, threatening the future of other broad international arms control agreements. The antiballistic missiles (ABMs) of around 1970 were so problematic as to be unworkable on a large scale, and informed estimates suggested a cost-benefit ratio that favored building more offensive missiles equipped with multiple warheads to overwhelm any defense (Chayes and Wiesner, 1969). Consequently, in 1972 when the United States and the Soviet Union reached a five-year interim agreement capping strategic offensive missiles, they also signed a permanent ABM Treaty limiting each side to no more than a hundred ABM interceptors in two sites. A 1974 protocol to the treaty reduced that limit to one such site per side. Because any major antimissile deployment would violate this limit, leading antimissile proponents urge abrogating or modifying the ABM Treaty; arms control proponents oppose any modifications. In July 1998 a commission chaired by former secretary of defense Donald Rumsfeld decided that rogue states such as Iran or North Korea could develop the capability to attack the United States with missiles carrying weapons of mass destruction within five years, not the fifteen years predicted in the Clinton administration's November 1995 National Intelligence Estimate (Heilbrunn, 1998). By that time, the Clinton administration already had yielded to critics and promised a limited antimissile deployment by the year 2000.

An important quasi-military issue for the post–Cold War era concerns future needs for and methods of intelligence gathering and covert operations. This is debated both within the United States and between America and its major allies. Although many government agencies take part in the intelligence function, during the 1990s internal debates centered around the CIA. Many government officials and many citizens perceived that Cold War covert operations had become politically inappropriate, often harming foreign civilians and producing political embarrassment and military fiascoes. Intelligence generated even bigger disagreements. Quite amazing satellite reconnaissance systems were developed during the Cold War. Capable of distinguishing from orbit whether an individual in the open was in military or civilian dress, such systems are marvelously suited to identifying and counting missiles and other military hardware. Unfortunately, however, they are ill suited to identifying the less obvious capabilities of an opponent, and even less attuned to determining an opponent's intentions. Consequently, hard-liners who see a post–Cold War world with more—although smaller—threats call for increasing intelligence budgets and shifting relative importance toward **human intelligence,** that is, information gathered by agents in place (spies) rather than by remote technical means such as electronic intercepts or satellite imagery. Their opponents decry past CIA failures and excesses and argue that the end of Cold War fears should allow major cuts in intelligence budgets and even the elimination of the Central Intelligence Agency. By the mid-1990s the Clinton administration had quietly begun raising the budget for human intelligence, but contention on these issues undoubtedly will persist for some time.

Transfer of important technology to potential rivals is both a military and an economic concern and likely to grow in importance. Foreign sales of increasingly sophisticated weaponry help the U.S. balance of trade and spread development costs over larger production runs. However, purchasers may "reverse engineer" the products to adopt features for their own later domestic production, and today's friend may become tomorrow's well-armed opponent. In 1998 a major flap arose over possible transfer of earth satellite technology to China. After an accident destroyed the space shuttle orbiter *Challenger* in 1986, the U.S. government began encouraging commercial firms to turn to private industry and foreign states for satellite launch services. Both the Bush and Clinton administrations approved commercial satellite launches on Chinese missiles, with some safeguards intended to limit the chances for technology theft. As economics increasingly becomes the most important foreign policy arena, such issues can only increase in number, and they have both economic and military consequences.

ECONOMIC SECTOR FOCUS CASE: COORDINATION WITH THE G-8 AND OTHER HIGHLY DEVELOPED ECONOMIES

The U.S. economy has been the world's largest since early in the twentieth century. It was overwhelmingly superior in the aftermath of World War II's devastation, when global economic dominance powerfully encouraged U.S. engagement in managing the world economic system. Supremacy made the United States a true hegemon in the early post–World War II years, able virtually to dictate economic policy for the entire noncommunist world. Over time, as Japan and Western Europe recovered from war, helped in part by the U.S. Marshall Plan and other aid, U.S. economic dominance slowly eroded. By 1971 American gold reserves were insufficient to stabilize global exchange rates. Although economic coordination among the major developed democracies can be traced back to the late 1940s, that coordination has become ever more a negotiation among equals since 1975. In that year, heads of government of the major developed capitalist states held the first of what unexpectedly became a continuing series of annual summit meetings focused on both economic and political issues. France, Great Britain, West Germany, Italy, Japan, and the United States were represented in that 1975 summit. Canada joined the following year. The European Union (formerly the European Community) has been represented since 1977, albeit still as a less-than-equal partner. In 1986 the conferees agreed to create a **Group of Seven (G-7)** made up of the participating states' finance ministers, intended to strengthen multilateral surveillance of the world economy. While these institutions were evolving the U.S. economy continued to grow, but more slowly than the economies of such states as Germany and Japan. By the late 1980s, several years before the breakup of the Soviet Union, the Japanese GNP had exceeded that of the Soviets, long second only to the United States.

The need for coordination among the top First Tier economies and the creation of the G-7 were driven by the decline of U.S. hegemony and the increasing globalization of economics, as discussed in some detail in Chapter 11. Four specific events in the early 1970s helped trigger the first G-7 summit:

- The Bretton Woods monetary system, set up in 1944 and based on fixed exchange rates and the convertibility of the U.S. dollar into gold, collapsed after that convertibility was ended in 1971. The institutions set up at the Bretton Woods conference, the IMF and World Bank, tried but failed to set up needed reforms.

- The European Community's first enlargement, in which Britain, Denmark, and Ireland joined the original six members, brought Western Europe's largest economies under one organizational umbrella.

- Western governments failed to agree on how to respond to the embargo of oil shipments to the United States and the Netherlands that was ordered by Arab OPEC states after the 1973 Yom Kippur Israeli-Arab war.

- Finally, the OPEC embargo helped start an economic recession among OECD member states, with inflation and unemployment rates rising sharply (see Hajnal, 1995). (In Figure 11.3, note that the first big jump in the U.S. domestic inflation rate, although still far below the levels reached in the early 1980s, came in 1974.)

Collectively, these developments demonstrated the failure of previous institutional arrangements and stimulated the development of newer systems for economic coordination. Economic globalization also drove a parallel growth in European political and functional economic integration. This integration was reflected in many institutions and political actions, with its high point thus far being the 1992 Treaty of European Union (Maastricht Treaty), which promised three "pillars" of (1) structure, rooted in the treaties of Paris and Rome as modified by the Single European Act, (2) common foreign and security activities, including the possibility of an eventual common defense system, and (3) justice and home affairs activities. By the latter 1990s the structural pillar was most advanced, and justice and home affairs cooperation were most distant. For purposes of the present case, economic cooperation under the first pillar is most essential.

The result of these diverse political and economic pressures was a sometimes delicate dance involving on one hand economic rivalries among the greatest economic powers and, on the other, needs to coordinate international trade, development, and economic policy toward each other and the entire world. By one view, the economic institutions urged by the U.S. government during and immediately after World War II to help ensure continued American engagement abroad helped create a new world order, only imperfectly foreseen by their creators, in which newer institutions were required.

G-7 summits quickly took on roles extending beyond economics to politics. Their precedent-setting first political pronouncement, on aircraft hijackings, came at the 1978 fourth summit. At their June 1996 Paris summit, shortly after the bombing of a U.S. military complex in Saudi Arabia, the G-7 presidents and prime ministers backed a package of antiterrorism proposals (a topic whose roots trace back to their 1984 summit) that included broadening extradition treaties, controlling firearms imports and exports, and controlling money laundering. Dealing also with the Bosnian civil war, they threatened new economic sanctions unless Radovan Karadzic, an indicted war criminal, resigned as president of the Bosnian Serb republic. Nonetheless, it is worth noting that European NATO members had made it clear a year earlier that they would not send troops to Bosnia to help enforce the 1995 Dayton peace accords unless the United States sent American troops.

Lairson and Skidmore (1993, Chapter 13) divide international economic relations of the mid- and latter twentieth century into three major periods. (1) During the decade of the 1930s and up to World War II, competitive urges overcame cooperative efforts. The strains of the Great Depression led states to erect high protectionist tariff barriers and form economic blocs in vain hopes of preserving domestic production and employment. International trade plummeted and political tensions rose. Existing international economic institutions were weak and no states came forward to exercise leadership. (2) During World War II, however, the Roosevelt and Truman administrations determined that the United States needed to remain intensively engaged in the postwar world. They sought to ensure that engagement by building new and stronger international institutions such as the IMF, World Bank, and GATT. Remembering the harsh lessons of the 1930s, and helped by U.S. hegemony and leadership and the close postwar security ties rapidly built among America, Western Europe, and Japan to fight the Cold War, world leaders ushered in a new era of international economic cooperation from about 1947 to 1973. Protectionism declined rapidly, and international trade and investment soared, particularly during the 1960s. (3) As developed in Chapter 11 (see particularly Table 11.3 and the associated discussion), the period since 1973–75 has been more volatile, with cooperation more balanced by competition. By the early 1970s global economic growth had outdistanced U.S. ability to continue dominating global economic markets and policy, and to continue backing the dollar with gold at $35 an ounce. The oil price shocks of 1973 and 1978 demonstrated the downside risks of economic interdependence. Still, the economic interdependence that Robert Reich (1991) characterized as a global web continues to grow today.

STAKES AT ISSUE

Numerous and significant forces encourage international economic cooperation. Broadly, the economic, technological, military, environmental, societal, and political dimensions of power are becoming ever more tightly interconnected. The oil crises and massive debt requirements of the 1970s and 1980s stimulated unprecedented growth in financial markets for equity, debt, and foreign exchange. An electronic and computer revolution in communications facilitated the growth of global 24-hour financial markets. World trade increased dramatically. All these developments contributed to the establishment of Reich's "global (economic) web." The sheer size of international flows in money and goods have stimulated new efforts toward cooperation. At the firm and industry level these have included efforts to share research and development costs and to moderate high-technology competitions. Internationally, they have included building or expanding trading blocs and striving to manage the newly floating exchange rates and to coordinate macroeconomic policies (Lairson and Skidmore, 1993, 95–96)—hence the increasingly important role of the G-7. By 1990 more than half of all world trade passed through the European Community.

Just as numerous and significant forces encourage international economic cooperation, other forces scarcely less powerful work against it. Despite growing international collaboration in many fields of endeavor, and notwithstanding Europe's ever-hesitant advance toward monetary and political union, the traditional realist model of sovereign states operating in an anarchic world still holds much truth and appeals to many people, particularly nationalists. The intermestic side of foreign policy reminds us that nation-states seldom are fully unified on international economic policy because any decision usually benefits some individuals and groups more than others. Consider, for example, the diverse interests found in the automobile import tariff example discussed in Chapter 1. Consider also **free trade areas,** such as NAFTA, within which states agree to allow goods and services to move freely without tariffs. In general, such areas benefit producers who are competitive within the newly created market area, damage those who are not, and expand the range of consumer choices. Free trade areas also may lead to significant international job shifts. Finally, international economic cooperation may be hindered because states want the benefits of expanded exports while still protecting their home markets. Probably all states are guilty of this to some extent, but the outstanding contemporary example is Japan.

RELEVANT U.S. POLICY THEMES

Intensive and continuing U.S. international economic engagement is strictly a post-1944 development that became an important part of postwar globalism. Beginning shortly after World War II, the United States also promoted European functional integration through the creation of such new organizations as the European Coal and Steel Community and EURATOM. Economic revival was promoted by the Marshall Plan, begun in 1947. By 1950 German and Japanese revival was promoted as part of the Cold War effort to contain communism. From 1957 on, European economic union was promoted. For some years the standard American formula was that the United States accepted some economic disadvantages of European political integration because of the greater political advantages of such unity (Hillenbrand, 1994, 176). By the 1990s it had become acceptable to question those advantages. After the mid-1970s the United States became more independent and self-interested in international political economics while slowly recognizing the increased need to coordinate our actions with those of other First Tier governments. In the aftermath of the Cold War, some authorities and about a third of American citizens, usually termed neo-isolationists, call for reducing foreign engagement, economic and otherwise.

PERCEPTIONS HELD BY OTHER ACTORS AND THEIR RELATIONS WITH THE UNITED STATES

Are all the G-7 states appropriate coordinators of the highest level global economic activity? Some analysts would drop the states with the smaller economies from the group. Britain, France, and Germany undeniably are the largest Western European economies,

PHOTO 14.1

Members of the G-8 economic summit pose for photographers before beginning their formal session in Birmingham, England, on 17 May 1998. From left front (counter-clockwise) Italian prime minister Romano Prodi; president of the European Commission Jacques Santer; their host, British prime minister Tony Blair; Russian president Boris Yeltsin; U.S. president Bill Clinton; French president Jacques Chirac; German chancellor Helmut Kohl; Canadian prime minister Jean Chrétien; and Japanese prime minister Ryutaro Hashimoto.

AP/Wide World Photos.

but Italy is hardly as powerful. Similarly, Canada's economy long has been dominated by that of the United States. Arguably, full economic unification under the European Union would make separate memberships by Britain, France, Germany, and Italy unnecessary. Other analysts would add China and India, largely on grounds of their long-term economic potential. Although both remained in the World Bank's low-income group in 1995, their huge populations and rapid economic growth may make them major international players within a decade or two. Indeed, given China's more stringent population control measures, India could even become the world's most populous state early in the twenty-first century. The case for Brazil is its rapid industrialization and economic growth; by 1995 it had emerged as the second most powerful Western Hemisphere state, after the United States, and accounted for half the GNP of South America (Friedman, 1995b).

Russia is a special case, notably as the major survivor state of the Soviet Union and potentially a democratic state with a large developed economy in the long term. Connections with the G-7 began to be forged as soon as the Cold War began to wind down. Soviet president Mikhail Gorbachev sent letters to the host presidents of the 1989 and 1990 summits that were discussed and commented on by the leaders and reflected in summit documents. Gorbachev visited London during the 1991 summit, where he met G-7 leaders individually and collectively, discussed in detail plans for Soviet economic and political reform, and worked out the final details of the START strategic arms reduction treaty with President Bush. Only a month later, Gorbachev was the target of an abortive coup that led to the demise of the Soviet Union and to his replacement as national leader by Boris Yeltsin. Yeltsin attended the 1992 Munich Summit, at which President Bush first floated the idea of welcoming Russia into an expanded "G-8." Instead, observer status was offered. In 1997 President Clinton finessed the issue by simply terming the meeting the "Summit of the 8." The case for immediate Russian membership, despite its 1995 World Bank classification among the lower-middle income states, rested on the country's large size and population, high skill levels, former superpower status, nuclear weapons holdings, and the desire to promote nascent democracy and market economics in this most significant of the formerly communist states. At the 1998 summit, held 15–17 May in Birmingham, England, the Russian Federation was accorded full membership status, and the group was formally renamed the **G-8**. The former G-7 states, however, remained free to meet without Russia in certain circumstances (e.g., when the primary focus was global finance).

AVAILABLE ALTERNATIVE ACTIONS AND POLICY TOOLS

The United States is under strong domestic and international cross pressures regarding coordinating economic policy through the G-8. On the one hand, since the 1970s when we passed beyond the era of U.S. global economic dominance, we have been forced to cooperate with other major economic powers. On the other hand, that cooperation binds us ever more tightly into a system that we strongly influence. The neo-isolationists notwithstanding, going it alone seems not to be a viable option. Today, as during the 1940s, the lessons of the 1930s urge us to pursue international cooperation because everyone will prosper.

FUTURE PROSPECTS AND CONCERNS

The great importance of the G-8 arises from the pressure to coordinate policy because of ever-increasing economic globalization. Moreover, the G-8 long has been led into explicitly political decisions. Managing the economic and political forces at work seems beyond the scope of any smaller body. The United States, like every other member, must struggle to achieve balance between incentives to cooperate and pressures to defect and seek single-state advantage. Given the rate at which economic globalization has proceeded and generated pressures for political globalization, the long-term balance appears to lie with cooperation.

Other Economic Issues

Rapidly advancing globalization of economics is leading inevitably to a comparable globalization of formerly individual state ("national") economies, as discussed by Robert Reich (1991) and in Chapter 11. Two related and particularly important pressures result on the United States and other First Tier states: to gain economic strength through trading blocs and to increase efficiency by merging some economic functions across state borders. In effect, both pressures encourage larger actors in a global economy that rewards efficiencies of scale. NAFTA and the European Union are major contemporary examples of free trade areas intended to benefit all their member states by easing the wider flow of goods and services among them (see also the section on regional integration in Chapter 13). Some analysts foresee much of the world dividing into three great trading blocs: Europe, the Americas, and South and East Asia (see, e.g., Nye, 1992). They also predict that such divisions are fundamentally disadvantageous to the United States in the long term.

For European Union member states, a major issue of the latter 1990s involved extending functional economic integration by converting to a single currency, the Euro, under the terms of the 1992 Treaty of European Union (widely known as the Maastricht Treaty). That common currency was expected to lower the accounting and currency conversion costs of interstate trade within the EU, further easing the flow of goods within the union's existing free trade area. Opposition originated in government and public concern about the fiscal austerity required to meet stability conditions for implementing the single currency, and the societal and cultural losses entailed in giving up established centuries-old currencies. Austerity measures that cut budgets, raise interest rates, and increase unemployment to reduce inflation seldom are popular, and monetary union implies a serious loss of state autonomy in establishing monetary policy.

The Euro also has societal and cultural impacts beyond that loss of autonomy because giving up established state currencies directly attacks cherished symbols of statehood. Many Americans are fiercely patriotic and protective of national symbols, as evidenced, for example, by repeated attempts to pass a constitutional amendment outlawing flag burning. But remember that the United States has a much shorter history than many European states, and a large proportion of Americans are descendants of people who immigrated within the last 150 years. By contrast, states such as Britain and France have been independent for many centuries. This translates into a strong sense of historical continuity and makes it difficult to give up the British pound sterling or the French franc, which long have been major international currencies.

As in the case of G-8 economic coordination, the United States is under strong domestic and international cross pressures regarding the EU and the Euro. On the one hand, European functional and economic integration strengthens governments that have been important allies for prolonged periods and have been thought vital to American security. On the other hand, strengthening their economic capabilities and coordination makes them more competitive with the United States in an ever more integrated world. The potential GDP of the EU has been estimated as comparable to that of the United States, and economic disputes between the United States and the EU and its forerunner organizations go back to the early 1960s and have become both more frequent and more severe. Additionally, EU common tariff barriers have created strong pressures on U.S. firms to expand into Europe, furthering the development of multinational corporations (MNCs) and the globalization of markets and economies.

Dealing with other First Tier economies is likely to remain an important long-term U.S. concern well into the twenty-first century, raising issues in many forms. Trade competition clashes with the need to cooperate with other G-8 states in managing the global economy. If encouragement of market economies worldwide is to become a major feature of post–Cold War policy, it will be greatly facilitated by cooperation among governments of the largest and most developed economies. Trade disputes over specific product types and market sectors, typified by the shipping dispute discussed in the opening of this chapter, seem likely to continue and even become more frequent as economics rises in importance in every country's foreign policy. Other major economic actors have chided the United States many times for its twin deficits in government spending and international trade. Nonetheless, Japan's is not the only government to strongly resist measures that would improve the U.S. international trade deficit by reducing their exports here or increasing American penetration of their home markets.

SOCIETAL SECTOR FOCUS CASE: THE U.S. DECLINE DEBATE

We examined the arguments over whether the United States is in decline either absolutely or relatively, and whether such decline is inevitable, in some detail in Chapter 11. They are reviewed here because global standing is exceedingly important to future American diplomatic and political influence, and to its bases in economic and military capabilities. Moreover, the decline debate is about societal security because it involves fundamental national self-images. This is so both internationally regarding how we see ourselves in comparison to others, and domestically when we consider who benefits and who suffers from economic globalization.

Decline primarily involves comparisons and interactions with other First Tier states because development is prerequisite to great power status. The United States, global hegemon on almost every measure of economic, military, and political power at the end of World War II, is hegemon no longer. Although America undeniably is the sole surviving superpower, the relevance of military power is questioned today as it never was during the Cold War. Of course, only when the great powers are militarily secure can a president declare that economics is the primary issue area for U.S. foreign policy. By the 1990s the United States saw continuing concerns about the need to reduce overseas military spending, reduce its foreign trade deficit, and encourage allies such as Japan and the Europeans to bear more of the costs of regional and global military security. Additionally, we saw precedent-shattering reliance on foreign contributions to pay most of the costs of the Persian Gulf War. At the very least, such developments indicate that the United States today cannot undertake independently all the things it did only a few decades ago. Even if we do not read these events as indicators of decline, they appear discomfortingly close to Paul Kennedy's image of a great power suffering reduced relative capabilities.

Yet the entire debate about U.S. decline may be moot because the rapid internationalization of economics undermines the very notion of an "American" economy, as argued by Harvard economist Robert Reich. The old view of distinct and relatively isolated national economies is outdated because modern communications and transportation allow almost every factor of production to be moved rapidly and almost effortlessly across nation-state borders. The United States is compelled to change and adapt for the same reasons that European former great powers move toward economic union. By the latter 1990s, helped by a booming economy, great progress had been made on reducing the federal budget deficit. Progress on the other of the twin deficits, in international trade, has not been so rapid. If long continued, it leads inevitably to loss of American control of assets built up in this country over our entire prior history. In some analysts' view, globalization undermines national identity, which is yet another form of decline. Usually, however, this charge is leveled against the United States by foreigners because under globalism our massive economy promotes the penetration of their markets by American consumer goods.

ENVIRONMENTAL SECTOR FOCUS CASE: OZONE DEPLETION

Most individuals using spray underarm deodorants in the 1960s and 1970s did not realize that their actions contributed to an emerging global environmental problem. By the 1980s, however, the chemicals previously used to power such sprays had been changed, and by the 1990s important international agreements had been reached to begin phasing out the offending gases. Those actions were driven by concerns about depleting the earth's protective atmospheric layer of ozone. This is an environmental common pool problem technically related to global warming, which we examined in depth in Chapter 12. Like global warming, ozone depletion is a physical problem in which certain human actions anywhere in the world eventually affect the entire globe. Worldwide application of solutions requires political agreement that can be reached only through international cooperation. Some incentives exist to hold out and exploit a failing common pool, although diplomats may be able to craft offsetting incentives to cooperate.

Ozone is an oxygen molecule containing three atoms of oxygen (O_3) rather than the usual two found in most earth-surface-level chemistry (O_2). Electrical discharges produce small quantities of ozone, which is why you may smell its sharp odor during lightning storms or near an electrostatic dust precipitator or other device that produces a high-voltage discharge. Ozone is useful as a deodorant, and is used in clearing fire-damaged buildings of smoke odors, yet it is poisonous, a breathing irritant, and can be fatal if inhaled in large quantities. Naturally produced ozone is found in the earth's atmosphere in a layer 20 to 40 kilometers (12 to 25 miles) above the surface. At that altitude it is highly beneficial, filtering harmful ultraviolet (UV) rays from sunlight and protecting surface life from harmful levels of UV radiation. However, ozone is not stable and is destroyed by contact with such natural gases as nitrogen (80% of the atmosphere at sea level), hydrogen, and chlorine. This is where the older underarm deodorant sprays come in.

One of the major culprits in ozone depletion is chlorofluorocarbons, or CFCs. Ironically, CFCs were developed during the 1930s specifically to have all the properties of an ideal chemical: immensely stable and inert to reactions with other chemicals, thus harmless to humans and the environment, nonflammable and nontoxic, and inexpensive to produce and store. Their first big application was as the working fluid in refrigeration systems—initially refrigerators, later air conditioners in homes and automobiles—where they replaced poisonous ammonia. It was only decades later that scientists began to discover that CFCs were not inert under the very low pressure and high radiation conditions of the upper atmosphere, and CFCs released at the surface eventually would migrate to the upper atmosphere. For example, surface releases occur from aerosol sprays using CFC as a propellant or auto air-conditioner hose bursts. By the 1970s satellite data indicating a hole, or thinning of atmospheric ozone over Antarctica stimulated further experiments that proved CFCs could break down and release chlorine, which in turn would destroy ozone. Scientists began to realize the release of CFCs was primarily responsible for ozone depletion in the upper atmosphere, which in turn allows increased penetration by ultraviolet light that can cause blindness and skin cancers. This presents a classic environmental common pool case with several important properties (see also Chapter 12): an activity anywhere in the world (here, CFC release) affects people everywhere, the activity exists primarily in developed states, and holdouts anywhere against regulation present a serious threat. In 1987 twenty-four states, including all members of the European Community, agreed to reduce their CFC use by at least 30 percent by 1999, and by 1995 non-CFC refrigerants were beginning to come into use in the United States. Developing states have sought technical and monetary assistance in adopting these more expensive technologies. Some authorities in developed states question whether such assistance would force them to subsidize other states' technological and economic development at a pace more rapid than would otherwise occur.

STAKES AT ISSUE

The stage was now set for a major environmental problem. CFCs are but one of a series of related chemicals, collectively dubbed **ozone-depleting substances (ODSs).** Various ODSs have been used as aerosols, foaming agents, refrigerants, fire extinguishers, and solvents. In the upper atmosphere a molecule of the simple refrigerant CFC 11 lasts on average 74 years; a molecule of the fire extinguishant Halon 1301 for 110 years. Under intense ultraviolet radiation, the CFC gives up a chlorine radical, which breaks down an ozone molecule (O_3) to produce an oxygen molecule (O_2) and chlorine monoxide (ClO). Eventually, the ClO releases a free chlorine radical, which then can attack another ozone molecule (Environmental Management Bureau, 1994, 7). As stratospheric ozone is depleted, more ultraviolet radiation, especially the harmful UV-B, reaches the earth's surface. There it contributes to global warming through additional direct absorption as heat, much of which is reradiated to be trapped in the atmosphere by greenhouse gases. Increased UV radiation also damages crops, raising food costs and contributing to malnutrition; accelerates damage to building materials, especially plastics; increases urban pollution by reacting with emissions such as oxides of nitrogen to produce smog; and creates serious direct human health risks. Among dangers to health are respiratory problems, immune system suppression, increased eye problems such as cataracts and glaucoma (potentially leading to blindness), and increases in serious skin cancers.

RELEVANT U.S. POLICY THEMES

Solving global environmental problems through international agreement is a very recent theme in U.S. foreign policy. One early precedent may be found in post–World War II UN programs to eradicate a number of major diseases worldwide. We may confidently predict that needs for international environmental agreements will only increase in the twenty-first century. Controversies almost certainly also will increase. Pessimists see the management of environmental threats as raising the costs of Second Tier development and creating incentives for some First Tier states to sell off older, polluting technology to Second Tier states. Optimists see opportunities to promote development with newer and less polluting technologies while stimulating science and technology in First Tier states. If the United States were to make a major commitment to promoting development worldwide, it would raise the chances of implementing both development and improved technologies, helping to avoid the intensification of environmental problems as Second Tier states seek development with older technologies. One example is the suggestion that the United States would itself benefit directly by sharing techniques for building low-pollution automobiles with China, because of the enormous size of the Chinese market and the expectation that they will build massive numbers of cars beginning early in the twenty-first century.

PERCEPTIONS HELD BY OTHER ACTORS AND THEIR RELATIONS WITH THE UNITED STATES

As in the global warming case, the chief agreement and implementation problems remain holdout governments, arguments about equitable distributions of effort and costs between First and Second Tier states, and technical disagreements about extending controls to cover all damaging activities (here, types of ODSs). Major First Tier producers generally have been quite cooperative, although technical concerns and high conversion costs occasionally are impediments. The Russian Federation, for example, was the only developed state that failed to end Halon production on 1 January 1994 (UNEP, 1994, 6). Many Second Tier states have joined the agreements to phase out ODS production and use, although progress has lagged in some cases even when substitutes are available and cost effective, offering rapid payback of investment. This may suggest a lack of needed investment capital, and some developing states have suggested that First Tier states seeking rapid progress should help them fund newer technologies. Finally, as in any problem with technological origins, some technical details remain to be solved. In this case, they usually involve the development of new alternatives to ODS usage.

AVAILABLE ALTERNATIVE ACTIONS AND POLICY TOOLS

Reversing ozone depletion involves both technical and political difficulties. It is one of a class of problems in which a technology chosen to support economic growth and improve human living standards, and developed with every expectation that it would have only benign human and environmental impacts, is later discovered to have side effects so serious that they overwhelm its benefits. At the extremes, some people respond to such dangers by opposing any new technology, and others refuse to consider possible problems. By the 1980s, however, there was no significant scientific disagreement that serious ozone depletion already had occurred. Nor was there significant scientific disagreement about its causes, or the dangers of increased UV radiation to humans and other surface life, or the need to eliminate the causes of ozone depletion and allow natural restoration of the ozone layer. Because ozone-depleting substances played essential roles in many consumer products and, more importantly, in many industrial processes, the technical problem reduced to finding alternative substances and processes. Persuading or compelling consumers, industries, and governments to take the necessary steps is a political problem, however, and the global common pool nature of ozone depletion means that a solution ultimately requires international cooperative action.

As with most environmental problems, solutions are highly intermestic, and actions at many levels can contribute to halting and reversing ozone depletion. Individuals can search for alternative products that minimize ODS usage, from stick or roll-on deodorants to fast foods packaged in cardboard rather than plastic foam containers. Producers can modify industrial processes, for example, by using alternative foaming agents and refrigerants. Governments can encourage adoption of newer, non-ODS technologies by offering tax incentives and discourage older technologies by mandating their phaseout over time, requiring recovery of ODS from scrapped appliances and equipment, and even banning ODS production. Unfortunately, the costs of implementing such measures create incentives for those with vested interests to hold out, exploit the common pool a while longer, and pass economic and environmental costs on to others. Industries may resist expensive requirements to scrap their old equipment, purchase new machinery, and retrain their workers. Some consumers may resist new technologies that raise their costs or decrease their options. Certain ODS uses, such as CFCs to propel inhalants like asthma medications, have no quick, easy replacements. In the end, the inherently global nature of the problem implies that no one nation-state's actions can end ozone depletion.

In this case, however, international cooperative action made huge strides before the end of the twentieth century. Agreement was facilitated by strong scientific consensus and by the fact that ODS production and use were far greater among First Tier than Second Tier states, making this more a First Tier than a cross-tier problem. Agreements usually involved first reducing production and use of a particular class of ODSs to percentages of a base year level, then later completely phasing out production. Stages of agreement up to the mid-1990s are summarized in Chronology 14.1.

Several notable points are evident. Reaching scientific consensus on the nature and scope of an environmental problem takes time, and translating such a consensus into widespread diplomatic agreement takes even longer. Thus, signing the Vienna Convention in 1985, only four years after UNEP began negotiations, was a considerable accomplishment. Presaging the 1992 the UN Framework Convention on Climate Change (see Chapter 12), the Vienna Convention established a framework for cooperation in research, environmental monitoring, and information exchange. This strengthened essential groundwork and anticipated the 1987 Montreal Protocol. However, the protocol and its subsequent rounds of amendments all require ratification by enough states to have the necessary global impact, raising the classic common pool problem of holdouts.

FUTURE PROSPECTS AND CONCERNS

Scientists agree that natural processes eventually will heal the earth's ozone layer, provided ODS releases are eliminated or at least drastically reduced. By the latter 1990s, international agreements to that end already were well advanced in many states, including the major ODS producers, and rapid progress had been made on phasing out many of the worst offending chemicals. Scientific, technical, and political problems remaining in the short and intermediate term are well understood. The scientific and technical problems

⊕ **CHRONOLOGY 14.1**

Key Events in the Development of the Ozone Depletion Control Regime

Date	Action	Key Provisions
1981	As scientific consensus grows, the United Nations Environmental Program (UNEP) begins negotiations to develop multilateral protection of the ozone layer.	
1985	**Vienna Convention for the Protection of the Ozone Layer** signed in March	Established a framework for cooperation in research, environmental monitoring, and information exchange
1987	**Montreal Protocol on Substances that Deplete the Ozone Layer** signed in September by 24 governments, including the United States, Japan, USSR, EC, and EC-member countries	Base year 1986 CFCs frozen by 1989; reduced 20% by 1993 and 50% by 1998 Specified Halons frozen by 1986 Required scientific and technical assessments at least every four years
1989	Montreal Protocol enters into force on 1 January	
1990	**London Amendments** to the Montreal Protocol signed in June	CFC reductions deepened to 50% by 1995 and 85% by 1997. Halon reductions set at 50% by 1995 and 100% by 2000. Other substances added, with base year 1989 Other fully halogenated CFCs to be cut 20% by 1993, 85% by 1997, and 100% by 2000 Carbon tetrachloride to be cut 85% by 1995 and 100% by 2000 Trichloroethane and methyl chloroform to be frozen by 1993, cut 30% by 1995, 70% by 2000, and 100% by 2005. Nonbinding elimination of HCFCs by 2020–40.

(continued)

include continuing measurement of ozone depletion and its environmental impacts; the search for other offending chemicals and mechanisms of ozone depletion and, possibly, regeneration; and the search for more benign alternative chemicals and industrial processes. Although research and action take time, technical prospects are excellent. It appears that elimination of all but minute amounts of ODS usage for a few purposes is feasible within the next few decades, offering the prospect of full recovery of the ozone layer within the twenty-first century. The political problems remain those of reaching agreements on ever-lengthening lists of different types of ODSs, winning all the significant offenders and holdouts over to agreement, and policing observance of agreements to ensure that neither governments nor individuals succumb to short-term economic incentives to continue ODS releases. Such monitoring requires endless attention

1991	By April, 68 states representing over 90% of global CFC and Halon production had ratified the Montreal Protocol.	
	Complete assessment of CFC, Halon, trichloroethane, carbon tetrachloride, and HCFCs.	Led to agreement upon accelerated phaseouts in the 1992 Copenhagen Amendments to the Montreal Protocol
1992	Supplemental Atmospheric Science, Technology, and Economic Assessment.	Reported atmospheric consequences of methyl bromide
		Technical and economic consequences of reducing methyl bromide's uses and emissions.
	Copenhagen Amendments to the Montreal Protocol	Tightened 100% phaseouts of CFCs to 1996, Halons to 1994, other CFCs to 1996, carbon tetrachloride to 1996, trichlorethane and methyl chloroform to 1996
		Set base year 1989 for HCFCs, to be frozen by 1996, cut 35% by 2004, 65% by 2010, 90% by 2015, and 100% by 2030
		HBFCs to be eliminated by 1996. Methyl bromide to be frozen at base year 1991 by 1995
	London Amendments entered into force on 8 October	
1994	Copenhagen Amendments had been ratified by 34 Parties, entered into force on 14 June. As of 30 September, the Montreal Protocol had been ratified by 139 states, and the London Amendments had been ratified by 93 states.	

Source: Compiled primarily from United Nations Environmental Program (UNEP), 1994: 16–19.

to details that may receive little public attention. International cooperative action in this instance is off to a good start, remains very much in process, will require continuing attention and much additional work, but has prospects for high success over the long term.

Summary

This chapter discusses issues the United States faces primarily in its dealings with already developed states and interstate organizations such as the European Union and the G-8. Some controversies involve the United States with single states; others are unavoidably multilateral. The chapter is organized according to the five sectors of geopolitical, military, economic, societal, and environmental contexts of U.S. foreign policy in the post–Cold War era. According to the definitions introduced in Chapter 13, the First Tier consists largely of World Bank high-income states, with upper-middle income states forming a near–First Tier group. These are distinctly different—and evolving—types of economies than those in the Second Tier (low-income and lower-middle income groups).

States with large and highly developed economies have obvious weight in affecting global economic issues. Moreover, such economies enable military prowess because their scale allows raising and maintaining substantial military forces and either purchasing sophisticated weapons or acquiring the technology to build them. Very few low- or middle-income economies are large enough to allow the investment necessary to compete with First Tier states, although the nuclear weapons programs of China, India, and Pakistan are notable exceptions.

Generally, the United States today and in the future faces quite different policy issues with First Tier states than with Second Tier states, even though almost all our foreign relations have been profoundly affected by post–Cold War changes in the global policy environment. Relations between high-income and upper-middle income states increasingly revolve around expanding trade, changing economic interactions, and rivalry to remain in or move into the upper reaches of the First Tier. We should anticipate trade disputes and other forms of competition and maneuvering for influence with significant governments and other actors in both tiers (for example, oil exporters). Interactions with high-income states are likely over such needs as realigning global political and military security arrangements for the post–Cold War era, deciding on required defense spending levels and the composition and missions of twenty-first century military forces, coordinating economic policy to manage global markets and to promote development, and solving environmental impact problems that are most severe in already industrialized states. Some issues will take explicitly political forms, such as calls in the 1990s for permanent (and veto-wielding) German and Japanese seats on the UN Security Council.

Focus cases given extended treatment in this chapter include NATO expansion; military missions, force levels, and the future of superpower status; coordination with the G-8 and other highly developed economics; the U.S. decline debate; and ozone depletion. The NATO expansion case exemplifies an important class of future foreign policy problems and some recurring problematic features. Serious political and military security issues remain to be worked out as we move further into a new post–Cold War world order. The economic component of such issues is stronger than ever before. European unity has significant spillover effects on economic and monetary union under the European Union. NATO expansion was the centerpiece of U.S. foreign policy during the second Clinton term, but domestic political concerns shared importance with international and regional European political and security concerns. Finally, as in the Bosnia case, continuing active American engagement appears to be necessary to make security agreements—even with other major developed states—work.

The types, frequency, and severity of military threats abroad which the United States may face in the post–Cold War era remain important unsettled issues. How they will be met and whether we need to act alone also remain unsettled, and events like the Persian Gulf War offer little guidance. The single superpower debate, undoubtedly the grandest of debates over future military requirements, force levels, and budgets, is part of the still larger debate over whether the United States will remain deeply engaged in global politics in the wake of the Cold War, or whether it will attempt to return to earlier, simpler, less involved days despite growing global interconnectedness and vastly larger U.S. responsibilities in international institutions than existed prior to World War II. An important constraint on policy choice was the growing 1990s pressure to reduce the federal budget deficit. It rapidly became apparent that the long-sought "peace dividend" from ending the Cold War would go mostly into deficit reduction rather than to social programs, although hope remained alive within the left wing, creating another pressure against any move to stabilize or increase military spending.

The importance of the G-8 lies in the pressure to coordinate policy because of ever-increasing economic globalization. Moreover, the G-8 long has been led into explicitly political policy decisions. Managing the economic and political forces at work seems beyond the scope of any smaller body. The United States, like every other member, must struggle to achieve balance between incentives to cooperate and pressures to defect and seek single-state advantage. Given the rate at which economic globalization has proceeded and generated pressures for political globalization, the long-term balance appears to lie with cooperation. The United States is compelled to change and adapt for the same reasons that European former great powers move toward economic union.

Although research and action take time, technical prospects for halting and reversing ozone depletion are excellent. It appears that elimination of all but minute amounts of ozone-depleting substance (ODS) usage for a few purposes is feasible within the next few decades, offering the prospect of full recovery of the ozone layer within the twenty-first century. This is primarily a First Tier problem because the heaviest ODS producers and users are in the First Tier. The political problems remain those of reaching agreements on ever-lengthening lists of different types of ODSs, winning all the significant offenders and holdouts over to agreement, and policing observance of agreements to ensure that neither governments nor individuals succumb to short-term economic incentives to exploit the common pool by continuing ODS releases. Such monitoring requires endless attention to details that may receive little public attention. International cooperative action in this instance is off to a good start, remains very much in process, will require continuing attention and much additional work, but has prospects for high success over the long term.

Key Terms

Free trade area	NATO expansion
G-7 or Group of Seven	Ozone-depleting substances (ODSs)
G-8 or Group of Eight	Strategic planning
Human intelligence	Tactical planning

Selected Readings

Binnendijk, Hans A., and Patrick L. Clawson, eds. 1997. *Strategic Assessment 1997: Flashpoints and Force Structure*. Washington, D.C.: National Defense University, Institute for National Strategic Studies.

Gregg, Robert W. 1993. *About Face? The United States and the United Nations*. Boulder, Colo.: Lynne Reinner.

Lincoln, Edward J. 1993. *Japan's New Global Role*. Washington, D.C.: Brookings Institution.

CHAPTER 15

SECOND TIER: THE DEVELOPING WORLD

🌐 RESTORING DEMOCRACY UNDER ATTACK IN HAITI

Is it important to the United States that weak neighboring states be democratically governed? If so, how much should we be willing to sacrifice in lives and treasure? These questions arose poignantly during the early 1990s in the case of Haiti. The poorest state in the Western Hemisphere, Haiti lies only a few hundred miles from the U.S. mainland and comprises 10,695 square miles, forming the western third of the island of Hispaniola. The Dominican Republic occupies the eastern two thirds of the island, and Cuba lies to the west. Visited by Columbus in 1492, Haiti became a French colony from 1697 and attained independence in 1804 following a rebellion led by a former slave. After a period of political violence, the United States occupied Haiti from 1915 to 1934, but did relatively little to promote long-term development. From 1957 to 1986 Haiti was ruled and exploited by the Duvalier family dictatorship. The last of the Duvaliers fled in 1986, after which there were five governments by mid-1990. In that year, Father Jean-Bertrand Aristide became Haiti's first democratically elected president. He had been an activist Roman Catholic priest with enormous popularity among the poor but little sympathy for and little following among the former ruling elites. President Aristide's political difficulties were compounded by Haiti's lack of any tradition of democratic governance. Having taken office in February 1991, he was arrested by the military and expelled from the country only seven months later.

Aristide's overthrow raised questions about what the United States and other world powers should and would do to restore Haiti's fragile infant democracy. If democracy was expected to flourish worldwide after the Cold War, any attack on a fledgling democracy, either from within or without, automatically was serious. Despite this principle and Haiti's closeness to the United States, however, Aristide's overthrow received much slower and less intensive action than Iraq's invasion of Kuwait in the Persian Gulf War only one year earlier. Cynics asserted that this demonstrated how much more important oil supplies were than democracy in American—and other people's—value systems. U.S. self-interest in the Gulf conflict was satirized by the bumper sticker SUPPOSE IRAQ'S MAIN EXPORT WERE BROCCOLI, questioning whether Iraq would have been invaded if its major export were the vegetable so publicly disparaged by President Bush.

Initial U.S. and UN responses to the overthrow of President Aristide involved slowly tightening trade and other sanctions on Haiti. These aggravated the island state's grinding poverty, already the worst in the hemisphere, but failed to break the ruling junta's resolve. Junta members and well-connected wealthy individuals suffered little and could obtain most goods on the black market. Gasoline, for example, was smuggled overland from the Dominican Republic in barrels. On 23 June 1993, nearly two years after Aristide's overthrow, the UN imposed a worldwide oil, arms, and financial embargo on Haiti. That embargo was suspended a few months later when the junta agreed to President Aristide's return to power on 30 October, but the military effectively blocked his return. After renewed sanctions failed to produce further movement, on 31 July 1994 the UN Security Council authorized an invasion of Haiti by a multinational force to restore democracy and return the elected president to power. Only on 18 September, with U.S. troops already en route, did military leaders agree to step down. Former President Jimmy Carter, already in Haiti leading a top-level peace delegation, brokered an agreement under which thousands of American troops began arriving the next day and stayed for some months as peacekeepers. Aristide was restored to office on 15 October, and a UN peacekeeping force took over responsibility for Haiti in March 1995. President Aristide transferred power to his elected successor, René Préval, on 7 February 1996. This was Haiti's first peaceful transfer of power and considered particularly crucial to the prospects for continuing democracy. The last U.S. combat troops left Haiti in April 1996. In February 1997 the UN voted to remove its last one thousand peacekeepers, leaving three hundred international police force trainers in Haiti.

President Aristide's restoration came thirty-seven months after his overthrow but only three months after the UN authorized the use of force to return him to power. This case should remind us that trade and other sanctions usually work only very slowly and typically penalize ordinary citizens of target states far more severely than the leaders and elites who could bring about policy change. Against a sufficiently intractable foe, only force or a believable threat of force will prevail. (Recall the discussion of coercive diplomacy in Chapter 8.) U.S. and UN leaders clearly sought to avoid paying a high price to restore Haitian democracy, and left Haiti to face more than three years under resurgent dictatorship. This experience does not bode well either for future efforts to succor fledgling democracies or for giving such a goal a high priority in U.S. foreign policy for the post–Cold War era. Nonetheless, the Haiti case exemplifies an important class of political problems likely to confront the United States fairly frequently in its dealings with developing states.

INTERACTING WITH DEVELOPING STATES AND REGIONS

This chapter is devoted to issues the United States faces primarily in its dealings with developing states and other actors interested in development. Interactions with developing states are likely over specific local issues, political support for democratic governments, development assistance, resource needs, and links between their ethnic groups and their

TABLE 15.1	
U.S. Foreign Policy Concerns with Second Tier (Developing) Actors, Classified by Issue Sectors	

Note: Boldfaced issues are archetypal focus cases given extended treatment

Sector	Contemporary and Foreseeable Policy Issues
Geopolitical	**Gulf War Aftermath** Future of global power Future world order
Military	**Peacekeeping in Bosnia (see also Chapter 8)** New demands for peacekeeping, peacemaking, and nation building Implementing START arms control with Russia Solving strictly second-tier conflicts (civil and inter-state wars)
Economic	**Potential Rise of China** and other future superpowers or major competitors
Societal	**Illegal Immigration** Serious and tense intermestic politics Future composition of the U.S. polity
Environmental	**Sustainable Development** What is a fair share of aid? Appropriate technologies Resource dependencies: Oil and other strategic materials

former nationals and descendants now in the United States. Notable issues for both the short and long terms include the future world order of power distribution and governance. Issues examined in this chapter, summarized in Table 15.1, are organized according to the five activity sectors of geopolitical, military, economic, societal, and environmental contexts of U.S. foreign policy in the post–Cold War era. We examine focus cases typical of each sector in some detail.

According to the definitions introduced in Chapter 13, the Second Tier consists of World Bank low-income and lower-middle income states. (See Table 13.2 and the associated discussion.) This group is characterized by tremendous diversity in per capita incomes, resource endowments, population densities, population growth rates, governmental systems ranging from democracy to dictatorship, economic systems from conservative capitalist to doctrinaire Marxist, and homogeneity varying from relatively unified states to those riven by strife between religiously and ethnically based nationalisms. Although some members of this group—including China and India, notable because of their great size—were developing rapidly by the 1990s, the Second Tier as a whole is becoming richer more slowly than the First Tier. Most analysts see this, in itself, as a problem for the entire world. Many Second Tier leaders and scholars perceive fundamental incompatibilities of interest between their countries and the First Tier, and especially with the United States as the most influential First Tier state.

The United States today and in the future faces quite different policy issues with Second Tier states than First Tier states, even though almost all our foreign relations have been profoundly affected by post–Cold War changes in the global policy environment. Second Tier states typically lack the economic, military, and (consequently) political weight of First Tier powers. As we see in more detail in the military sector focus case later, through at least the early years of the twenty-first century most of the world's violence likely will continue to occur within and between Second Tier states. For the United States, Iraq and Haiti may represent two extremes on a continuum extending from rapid and intensive intervention to hesitant and limited action. In the longer term, there are concerns about preventing the development of weapons of mass destruction by the more ambitious developing states. Issues about encouraging, supporting, protecting, and restoring democracy arise far more frequently in the Second Tier than the First. Economic issues more often involve aid than competition, although not in every case over the long term. Societal issues for the United States and other First Tier powers include the impacts and control of immigration, whereas for Second Tier states they include national divisions and the societal impacts of foreign penetration and development. Environmental issues center on sustainable development and appropriate types and amounts of aid from the developed world.

ARCHETYPAL FOCUS CASES

Five focus cases are examined in this chapter, each selected as typical of its tier and issue sector:

- In the *geopolitical sector*, persistent problems with Iraq years after the 1990–91 Persian Gulf War raise serious questions about policy failures, the difficulty of reigning in pariah states and would-be regional hegemons, and global failures to develop broadly successful mechanisms for ensuring security.

- In the *military sector*, the end of the Cold War removed some important constraints against new internal wars and regional conflicts, often ethnically based, that threaten others in their regions and draw in greater powers. Thus far, this need for First Tier states to promote peacemaking in such regional conflicts has been seen most intensely in Bosnia (see Chapter 8).

- In the *economic sector*, rapid growth in such states as China and India has given rise to concerns about (1) whether new economic and military superpowers may arise early in the twenty-first century, and (2) whether the United States should take steps to discourage such developments. Continuing serious balance-of-trade issues surround the growth of new producers, such as China.

- In the *societal sector*, immigration, particularly illegal immigration, raises important questions about the future composition of the U.S. polity. This is a polarizing issue and has been seen before in American history, which may seem surprising for what is traditionally considered a nation of immigrants. Many citizens fear loss of jobs to industrious newcomers willing to work for low wages and even lower benefits. Some fear social and cultural change; others struggle to support immigrant rights and prevent oppression. Echoes of these struggles are found in other First Tier states.

- In the *environmental sector*, we seek appropriate technologies to help promote sustainable, rapid, and efficient development while discouraging developing states from following more polluting paths previously trodden by now-developed economies. Issues for First Tier states often center around their dependencies on Second Tier resources. For Second Tier states, receiving effective development aid in equitable amounts is a critical issue.

Some additional contemporary and foreseeable issues are discussed following the geopolitical, military, and environmental focus cases.

GEOPOLITICAL SECTOR FOCUS CASE: THE AFTERMATH OF THE PERSIAN GULF WAR

We began Chapter 1 by asking who won the Persian Gulf War. Most U.S. citizens quickly answer that the United States won by decisively defeating Iraq's military forces and liberating Kuwait in 1991. To be sure, within four months after Iraq invaded Kuwait on 2 August 1990, the United States had organized and led a coalition of more than thirty countries, and itself sent over a half-million troops, its largest foreign military action since the Vietnam War. In mid-January 1991 the coalition began an intensive five-week campaign of aerial bombardment of Iraq and its forces in Kuwait. This was followed by a spectacularly quick land campaign in which a substantial portion of the Iraqi military was crushed, Kuwait freed, and a cease-fire announced in only a hundred hours. This was an undeniably significant military victory, which President George Bush hailed as a great triumph and the harbinger of a vague "new world order."

Whether we achieved an equally great political victory was disputed immediately, and negative answers have only increased with the passage of time. U.S. actions on behalf of Kuwait and the other Gulf oil states dramatically improved Washington's subsequent relations with the Arab world. In turn, this gave the United States greater influence in promoting a Middle East peace. Agreements between Israel and the Palestinian Liberation Organization during the 1990s, particularly the 1993 agreement signed on the White House south lawn, undoubtedly constituted a win for the entire world, with Palestinian Arabs and peace-minded Israelis the particular winners. Nonetheless, hard-liners on both sides continued to oppose the peace process. Arab extremist terror bombings were met with extreme Israeli reprisals, continued building of Jewish settlements in nominally Palestinian territory, and the election of conservative Likud bloc candidate Benjamin Netanyahu as prime minister in May 1996. Thereafter, with various fits and starts, the peace process ground to a near halt. Beyond direct U.S. interest in Middle East peace—which is examined in detail in the military sector focus case of Chapter 16—most Arab citizens and governments perceived the United States as strongly biased toward Israel and unwilling to pressure the two sides equally to maintain progress toward peace. Consequently, by the fall of 1997, the post–Gulf War surge in America's political stock with Arab governments was only a memory.

Part of the coalition's political victory in the Gulf War was an unprecedentedly strict set of UN sanctions including a special commission empowered to supervise and verify

Iraq's destruction of weapons of mass destruction and programs for their development and manufacture. The focus of control efforts was upon weapons of mass destruction. Conventional weapons used by Saddam Hussein's regime to crush rebellious Kurds in the northwest and Shiites in the southeast were left essentially unchallenged except for limited "no fly" zones to limit Iraqi air operations. Under terms of the cease fire, Iraq was ordered to allow inspectors from the United Nations Special Commission (UNSCOM) and the International Atomic Energy Agency (IAEA) freedom of movement and access to locate and supervise the destruction of all weapons of mass destruction and facilities for their construction. Iraq also was ordered to cooperate in those efforts, including providing lists of weapons, factories, and development facilities. Proscribed items included missiles, chemical and bacteriological weapons, nuclear weapons, and facilities for their production. The prohibitions and enforcement measures went far beyond any seen since the end of World War II and the much later origin of the concept of weapons of mass destruction. In principle, they set precedents that might be followed in some future, more general disarmament agreement.

It would be a massive understatement to say that Iraqi cooperation has been limited and conditioned. Numerous and varied obstacles repeatedly have been posed to UN inspectors, using such means as denying the existence of facilities, hiding plants, relocating production equipment, moving or destroying documents, shuffling weapons from location to location, organizing mass demonstrations against inspections, training antiaircraft guns on inspection helicopters, vandalizing equipment, and physically blocking access to suspect facilities and limiting inspectors' ability to remove documents.

One of the most unpleasant surprises of postwar inspections was the discovery of how little of Iraq's nuclear weapons program had been destroyed. On 1 November 1993, the head of the IAEA said that, after 21 missions in Iraq, his agency had concluded that Iraq's nuclear development program had been mapped and either destroyed or neutralized. On 31 January 1994, President Clinton told Congress that that program had been essentially ended (Katzman, 1994, 2). Nonetheless, only widespread and continued intrusive inspection can prevent future reestablishment of such a program. Knowing that nuclear weapons are possible tells would-be nuclear powers at least half of what they need to know, and Iraq retains accumulated equipment, nuclear expertise, and motivation to become a nuclear power. By 1994, U.S. and UN officials had concluded that only a comprehensive, intrusive, and long-term monitoring plan could prevent eventual Iraqi success, and monitors needed to follow the activities of Iraqi scientists capable of contributing to weapons programs.

Such a program of inspection is far more complex and detailed than any previously undertaken. It requires a level of intrusiveness down to the level of individual activity that would be difficult for the most cooperative of states and peoples to endure, let alone a reluctant regime like that in Baghdad, which really does have things to hide. Table 15.2 clearly indicates that Iraq consistently hid and underreported its development programs and stocks of all classes of weapons of mass destruction. Combining weapons of mass destruction with effective long-range delivery systems such as advanced strike aircraft and ballistic missiles raises very great concerns, which are heightened by Iraq's history of using such weaponry. UN Security Council Resolution 687 requires the destruction of all Iraqi ballistic missiles having ranges greater than 150 kilometers (about 93 miles). In January 1993, a UNSCOM team began daily inspections at the Ibn Al Haytham facility outside Baghdad, suspected of being dedicated to research and development of prohibited

TABLE 15.2			
Iraq's Programs for Weapons of Mass Destruction			
Class of Weaponry	**Concerns**	**Iraqi Admissions**	**UNSCOM and IAEA Discoveries**
Nuclear	Widespread and multifaceted program uncovered after the 1991 war.	Inspections impeded by varied means. All agreements reluctant, including identification of major suppliers.	3 uranium enrichment programs; laboratory-scale plutonium separation; conclusive evidence of nuclear weapons development program. Believed destroyed or neutralized by end of 1993.
Biological	Known research program and supplies purchases imply weapons capability.	Initial denials. Biological research program admitted August 1991. In December 1992, Kurdish groups produced document said to indicate that Iraq possessed battlefield biological weapons.	39 tons of nutrient medium known to have been purchased by Iraq, but only 22 have been accounted for; Iraq claims the remaining 17 tons were destroyed during the 1991 war.
Chemical	Used against Iran in 1980–88 war, and against Iraqi Kurds; greatly feared during 1991 war.	April 1991 initial declaration: 10,000 chemical warheads; 1,500 chemical bombs and shells; 280 tons mustard gas; 75 tons Sarin; no Tabun	140,000 rockets, artillery, grenades, etc. for chemical warfare seized in 1991. UNSCOM found 525 tons mustard gas; 138 tons Sarin; 68 tons Tabun. Destruction believed complete by end of 1994.
Ballistic Missiles (For use as delivery systems)	Scuds used against Israel and coalition forces in 1991; more advanced types known to be under development, could threaten entire region. U.S. press and intelligence reports suggested Iraq was hiding up to 200 of the 819 ballistic missiles provided by the USSR.	Initial declaration of 52 Scud or Scud-variant missiles surviving the 1991 war.	In 1991–92, UNSCOM destroyed or verified Iraqi destruction of 151 such missiles; 19 mobile launchers; 76 chemical warheads; 28 operational fixed launch pads; dual-use missile production equipment; and a 350 mm (and components for a 1,000 mm) supergun. No hidden missiles found.

Source: Extracted from Katzman, 1994, and updated from news reports, including Safire, 1995.

ballistic missiles. In February 1993, another team found information at another site, not previously disclosed by Iraq, which led them to suspect Iraqi work on prohibited ballistic missiles (Katzman, 1994, 4).

By 1999 the Gulf War seemed to have changed little in Iraqi political life. Saddam Hussein continued his oppressive rule from Baghdad. The UN-sponsored trade embargo continued to keep Iraqi oil underground (except for modest sales that allowed the funding of essential medical and humanitarian imports). Saddam and his supporters still enjoyed relative luxury while the living conditions of ordinary Iraqi citizens had plummeted. Even highly educated Iraqis were reduced to selling their personal possessions to buy food. The United States still maintained troops, ships, and aircraft in the region, trying with little success to limit Saddam's oppression of his people, particularly the Kurds and Shiites. Iraq continued to be Iran's only serious competitor for regional hegemony, a fact appreciated (however quietly) by governments from Tel Aviv to Washington.

By failing to dislodge Saddam from power or destroy his most important military forces, the coalition left the seeds of protracted political-military confrontation and years of continued involvement in the region. All the factors reviewed here began to come together in a major Iraqi political initiative begun on 29 October 1997, designed to exploit rekindled Arab resentments against the United States, split the UN Security Council, and yield a lifting of trade sanctions. Claiming that American members of the UN Special Commission (UNSCOM) carrying out weapons inspections were actually spying on their country, top Iraqi authorities announced that U.S. citizens would be barred from future UNSCOM activities and those already in Iraq would be expelled in one week. The Security Council quickly reiterated its authority to proceed without Iraqi hindrance. However, among the council's veto-wielding permanent members, China, France, and Russia indicated reluctance to authorize a response by force. Cynics noted that French and Russian firms held or anticipated lucrative contracts with Iraqi firms if trade sanctions were lifted. Soon Iraq threatened to shoot down American U-2 spy planes flown on behalf of UNSCOM. The UN sent three top diplomats to Baghdad to present a letter restating UNSCOM's authority while denying that they were negotiating at Iraq's bidding. While the diplomats were in Iraq, Baghdad announced a brief reprieve on expelling Americans, and UNSCOM announced a delay in U-2 flights. The diplomatic mission yielded no progress, U-2 flights were resumed, and the American members of UNSCOM were expelled on 13 November, after which UNSCOM withdrew most of the remaining inspectors.

Early in 1998, UN Secretary-General Kofi Annan brokered a deal in which Iraq readmitted UNSCOM inspectors, who were to be accompanied on their visits to so-called sensitive sites such as presidential palaces by individuals drawn from the corps of foreign diplomats in Baghdad. In July 1998 Iraqi officials instigated a new emergency, demanding that UNSCOM declare Iraq already disarmed and ordering the inspectors out when that demand was rejected. Although that dispute was papered over with little real improvement, UN inspectors were again ordered out in October 1998. Iraq backed down and promised unfettered access to inspections only when the United States was within fifteen minutes of launching several hundred cruise missiles against suspected weapons sites and other targets in Iraq. Within a month this new Iraqi promise was broken, all remaining inspectors were withdrawn, and the United States began air strikes. Air strikes in themselves cannot guarantee access to inspectors, of course, and by 1999, nobody expected UNSCOM to ever return to Iraq.

STAKES AT ISSUE

Both Iraq's 1997 "no American inspectors" stand and its 1998 expulsion order seriously and directly challenged UN authority. Within days of the 1997 action, UNSCOM and U.S. officials announced fears that their limited available information suggested even ten days without inspections had allowed the Iraqis to move and hide some critical biological weapons manufacturing equipment. Even in the short term, Iraq's actions threatened to undermine the authority of both the UN and the United States, the most important party to the Persian Gulf War and the ensuing inspection regime. Over the long term, an Iraq ruled by Saddam and equipped with weapons of mass destruction is a formidable prospect, one of the scarier instances in which a Second Tier state could pose severe security threats to First Tier states that are much stronger powers by conventional reckoning. This is a serious direct concern for the United States and every other country, either First Tier or regional neighbor to Iraq. Indirectly, Iraqi success in limiting international inspections and retaining weapons of mass destruction encourages other governments to acquire such weapons, and undermines international efforts to limit their proliferation. (See also the introductory case in Chapter 16 on nuclear proliferation.) While it may be impossible to prevent all proliferation of weapons of mass destruction, it is far easier and far less costly in lives and treasure to stop such proliferation early.

RELEVANT U.S. POLICY THEMES

Direct military action against Iraq raised old images of U.S. interventionism and tendency to rely on force rather than peaceful diplomacy. Success in fully eliminating Iraq's weapons of mass destruction, however, would establish precedents for much more stringent international arms control than ever before and promise more effective future management of threats from rogue states that challenge international behavior norms.

PERCEPTIONS HELD BY OTHER ACTORS AND THEIR RELATIONS WITH THE UNITED STATES

Other governments, including most American allies, were notably less willing than the United States to consider armed force against Iraqi noncompliance in either the 1997 or 1998 incidents. The Clinton administration was considered to be much closer to air strikes against Iraqi targets early in 1998, shortly before Secretary-General Annan's deal with Iraq, than during the following summer. By that time, President Clinton was deeply embroiled in a sex in the White House scandal. This led to widespread perceptions at home and abroad—and perhaps most significantly, in Iraq—that the president no longer could persuade others to cooperate with his policies. Meanwhile, Saddam's government stressed how damaging the continuing international trade embargo and other sanctions were to the Iraqi people, which had some resonance with other governments because it was true.

AVAILABLE ALTERNATIVE ACTIONS AND POLICY TOOLS

This case involves an interesting mix of options for direct U.S. actions, such as air strikes against Iraq, and U.S. involvement in international cooperative actions, primarily through the UN. Of necessity, UNSCOM operations had always relied heavily on a certain degree of Iraqi tolerance, if not cooperation. Formally, the UN Security Council had since 1991 required Iraq as a UN member state to cooperate with the inspection and weapons destruction program, under penalty that the foreign trade embargo and other sanctions would not be lifted until UNSCOM finally certified that Iraq had destroyed its NBC weapons and missiles and their development programs. Neither the United States nor any other state contributing weapons inspectors to UNSCOM had many credible and reasonable options to force Iraqi compliance, particularly in the short run. Congressional calls for bombing missed the point that punishment raids could not apply the type of force needed to get the inspectors into Iraq and then into the various sites they needed to examine. To accomplish that by force would require sufficient troops on the ground with armaments adequate to face down or prevail over any Iraqi military force or organized mob likely to oppose the inspectors' free movement and access to factories, government buildings, and military installations. No such numbers of troops or amounts of armor had been available in the region since the U.S.-led coalition withdrew in 1991. That is why previous Iraqi violations, such as air raids beyond the UN-declared no-fly zone against the Kurds, had been met with air strikes rather than ground actions. Air strikes could be an appropriate response if Iraq fired on U-2 or other aircraft flying in support of UNSCOM operations, but they still would not get inspectors into suspect facilities on Iraqi territory. Calls from various analysts, including *New York Times* foreign affairs columnist Thomas Friedman (1997c), to use air strikes to take Saddam himself out at least suggested a believable, if improbable and difficult, use of force.

FUTURE PROSPECTS AND CONCERNS

By 1999 U.S. air strikes and continued Iraqi intransigence had convinced almost all knowledgeable observers that UNSCOM inspectors would never return. Indeed, Clinton administration officials clearly understood this before ordering air strikes. With neither domestic nor allied support for sending ground troops to achieve definitive inspection and control, the administration settled for an indefinite program of "degrading" Iraq's NBC weapons capabilities. If Iraq prevails in the long term, it threatens the rest of the world not only by the direct acquisition of NBC weapons of mass destruction, but by undermining the promise of a more effective United Nations and more stringent international norms of behavior in the post–Cold War world. Removing Saddam from power by whatever means, whether by fomenting a coup (unlikely) or by direct military force, offers the possibility of a stable Iraq that, although still no democracy, could stand as a natural counter to Iranian ambitions to dominate the region. Even having Iraq fragmented into its three major nations and leaving the field for Iran to become the regional hegemon might appear preferable to Saddam's government armed with weapons of mass destruction. Unfortunately, using U.S. force against Iraq could worsen the prospects for Arab support of Israeli-Palestinian peace, unless it were accompanied by considerably greater U.S. pressure on Israel to grant concessions. In a television interview on 10 November 1997, Secretary of Defense William Cohen allowed as how "it would have been better" if the United States had gone after Saddam in 1991 (Cohen, 1997).

Other Geopolitical Issues

Whereas U.S. geopolitical concerns with First Tier states revolve around future relative standing, issues with Second Tier states center more on the future distribution of global power and the nature of the new world order that the Bush administration found so hard to define. As the Persian Gulf War with Iraq and the long and difficult struggle to restore democracy in Haiti demonstrate, the world has few standing arrangements and essentially no standing forces to counter aggressions and ensure the security of new democracies. By the latter 1990s demands for UN peacekeeping significantly exceeded members' willingness to provide military forces, let alone financial support. Within the United States, a conservative fringe worried about conspiracies under which fleets of black UN helicopters would descend across America to impose world government and suppress individual liberties. More conventional conservatives sought a new "isolationism" in which U.S. foreign commitments would be scaled back dramatically. Those in the political mainstream worried about budget deficits and opportunities to reduce defense spending after decades of Cold War.

President Clinton's efforts early in his first term to offer a new grand vision of "enlargement" of the sphere of market-economy democracies (examined in the opening case of Chapter 13) failed to convince governing and policy elites, let alone the general public. The geopolitical sector particularly strongly demonstrates the costs of failing to settle on a new grand strategy for the post–Cold War era. Nonetheless, about two thirds of citizens, and all but some 2 percent of elites, continued to favor continued U.S. international engagement, about the same fractions seen over the previous two decades.

MILITARY SECTOR FOCUS CASE: NEW INTERNAL WAR AND PEACEKEEPING IN BOSNIA

The Bosnian civil war is a particularly tragic case of nationalistic divisions run amok, in which the efforts of numerous well-meaning outside powers over several years were largely ineffectual in ending or even minimizing a brutal struggle rooted in centuries of ethnic divisions. Bosnia and Herzegovina (hereafter, Bosnia) is one of the republics of former Yugoslavia whose peoples were a complex ethnic mix and that fragmented in 1991–92. Bosnia's three major ethnic groups or nations were Muslims (44 percent), Serbians (31 percent), and Croatians (17 percent). The Bosnian parliament declared sovereignty and independence from Yugoslavia 15 October 1991, an act confirmed by a referendum on 29 February 1992 (boycotted by the Bosnian Serb political party) and by recognition from the United States and the European Union on 7 April 1992. Later that same month Serbia invaded Croatia, using Bosnia as a launching point, and initiated civil war. With Serbian support and amid fierce three-way fighting among the major ethnic groups, the Bosnian Serbs launched a program of so-called ethnic cleansing, killing or expelling non-Serbs and destroying or seizing their property. Despite charges of atrocities on all sides, the Bosnian Serbs quickly gained the upper hand, controlling some 70 percent of Bosnian territory and besieging the capital, Sarajevo, and other Muslim population centers.

Serbian support for the Bosnian Serbs was substantial and decisive. Through the decades he led Yugoslavia on a communist course independent of the Soviet Union, Marshal Tito (d. 1980) had feared attack from both east and west and thus ordered the building and stockpiling of enormous quantities of arms. As the dominant ethnic group in the Yugoslav army, Serbs gained control of much of that weaponry upon Yugoslavia's breakup. Most outsiders were unaware just how many heavy weapons that meant. With only about half as many soldiers as the Muslims, the Bosnian Serbs were able to use artillery to great advantage in pinning down the Bosnian government (Muslim) army and

Force (IFOR) enforced separation of the combatants but did little to disarm them. Day-ton also promised political reunification of the country to the Bosnian Muslims. Although some local and regional elections were held under the watchful eyes of enforcement troops, ethnic hatreds were so intense that true political reunification was unenforceable and would collapse immediately if foreign troops departed. Issues about how long such troops would be required surfaced rapidly. Having casually promised in 1995 that the op-timistically named IFOR would only be needed for about a year, the United States and NATO pulled IFOR out only as they rotated other troops in to form a new Stabilization Force (SFOR). In turn, SFOR was scheduled to be pulled out by June 1998, but by the fall of 1997 trial balloons about the need for a successor force already were being floated in Washington and European capitals. In 1998 a new successor force was declared. Few honest observers foresee any lasting peace in Bosnia without permanent partition and probably a permanent peacekeeping force.

Regrettably, Bosnia appears to be typical of the new internal wars we should expect for the indefinite future. First Tier states, at least pending the rise of China to that status, share democratic governance, good rates of economic growth, and peace. In the future, if some Second Tier states gain NBC weapons of mass destruction and the capabilities to direct them against First Tier states, that situation will change. For now, however, and ex-tending at least a few years into the twenty-first century, it appears we can expect almost all the world's violence to remain within and between Second Tier states. The problem of new internal wars is far worse than most Americans realize; by the mid-1990s, about 35 to 40 such wars were underway in any given time (Snow, 1997, 195). Most of these were in the poorest states and those least known among First Tier peoples. Our collec-tive experience in Bosnia through the latter 1990s does not offer great hope that more ef-fective means of resolving new internal wars will be devised soon.

Other Military Issues

Another military sector arena of particular concern is arms control. We consider prob-lems of horizontal nuclear proliferation to additional states, terrorism involving weapons of mass destruction (NBC weapons), the global abolition of land mines, implementing the global ban mandated by the Chemical Weapons Convention, and a comprehensive nuclear test ban in Chapter 16. A particular concern of the United States during the 1990s was ratification and implementation of the Strategic Arms Reduction Treaties (START I and II) with Russia, and we consider the ongoing issue of U.S.-Russian strate-gic nuclear arms control on pages 580–581.

∍ONOMIC SECTOR FOCUS CASE:
∎ POTENTIAL RISE OF CHINA

The phrase "1.2 billion Chinese" was heard repeatedly from both American and Chinese officials when President Jiang Zemin visited the United States in October 1997. China's huge population long had been seen as both its greatest resource and its greatest claim to major power and potential superpower status. Once the Beijing government turned to market-based economics during the 1980s and GNP started to rise 10 percent or more annually, observers around the world began considering the Chinese economy's potential

---

besieging such Muslim population centers as Sarajevo. Attempts by NATO and the UN to embargo arms shipments into Bosnia thus worked mainly to disadvantage the Bosnian Muslims, and a UN Protection Force of peacekeepers (UNPROFOR) was ineffective in preventing Bosnian Serb attacks.

By mid-1995, many knowledgeable observers expected foreign powers to wash their hands of the Bosnian war and withdraw UNPROFOR forces. Instead, after some months of waffling, the Clinton administration brought leaders of all the major factions together for a carefully sequestered peace conference on the grounds of Wright Patterson Air Force Base outside Dayton, Ohio, where a fragile peace accord was reached in Novem-ber 1995. The Dayton accords provided for a Peace Implementation Force of NATO and Russian troops reporting to a U.S. commander. Several factors made the Dayton accords easier to reach than they would have been a year or two earlier. Every Bosnian faction had suffered terrible losses; Croatian military forces had made major advances at the expense of the Bosnian Serbs, who feared worse to come; and Bosnian Muslims realized that they would never get the lost half of Bosnia back. Until Dayton, however, many observers ar-gued that no outside powers had consistent Bosnia policies—not the United States, nor the UN, nor NATO, nor the EU.

STAKES AT ISSUE

U.S. stakes in the Bosnian civil war include humanitarian concern over the loss of life, fear that the war could spread throughout the region, worries about costs to the United States of a potentially long-term involvement, and apprehensions about how actions in Bosnia might impact Russia's relations with the West. Russia's history of supporting the Serbs raised fears that the United States and other European states might become involved di-rectly or indirectly in conflict with Russia, or at least face dramatically worsened relations with Russia. Failing to resolve the Bosnian civil war also would bode ill for the prospects of resolving other such conflicts.

The Bosnian civil war clearly exemplifies the problems of what Donald Snow (1997, Chapter 8) has termed **new internal war.** By this he means the wave of post–Cold War conflicts within Second Tier states, seen first in the early and mid-1990s in Bosnia, Soma-lia, Rwanda, and Liberia. Other examples include Russia's 1996 war against secessionist rebels in Chechnya, and fighting throughout the early 1990s between the former Soviet republics of Armenia and Azerbaijan over the province of Nagorno-Karabakh, an enclave in Azerbaijan with a majority population of ethnic Armenians. These new internal wars lack the ideological component common to many civil wars during the Cold War period, when nominally anticommunist governments used Western help to fight nominally com-munist insurgents assisted by the Soviets. In many cases, internal war erupts when an old authoritarian regime—such as those imposed over Eastern Europe by the Soviet Union and by Marshal Tito over Yugoslavia until his death in 1980—has collapsed but not yet been replaced by some new and stable political system. Bosnia and Somalia are prominent examples of failed states, in which anarchy follows the collapse of a central government. Arguably, when people's old political reference points are stripped away, they tend to re-vert to older ethnic and religious self-identifications.

Such new internal wars promise to be a sadly significant feature of the post–Cold War era. When failed states are well armed before their collapse, as Yugoslavia was, the resulting internal wars can be extremely intense. Many such conflicts occur in locations

PHOTO 15.1
U.S. assistant secretary of state Richard Holbrooke (right) talks with French deputy
assistant secretary-general Jacques Blot after the Bosnia peace agreement known as the
Dayton accords (1995) was negotiated. Holbrooke, a notable in-and-outer and special
negotiator, later moved to Wall Street investment banking. He was recalled to government service several times to address Balkan conflicts, including the Kosovo crisis in
1999. After more than a year's delay, the Senate confirmed him as U.S. Ambassador to
the UN in August 1999.
AP/Wide World Photos.

little known even to U.S. and world policy elites, making it hard to bring much expert
knowledge to bear on solutions and persuade politicians and the general public to support American or NATO or UN intervention. All the difficulties of peacekeeping, peacemaking, and nation building we examined in Chapter 9 apply. As the U.S. Army found
in Somalia, it may be difficult or impossible to find solutions that even professional soldiers consider affordable. Nonetheless, interventions are encouraged if we grow frustrated viewing the effects of ethnic violence without being able to do much about it.

RELEVANT U.S. POLICY THEMES

Intervention in foreign wars or to forestall expected conflicts, although not always practiced, long has been a theme in U.S. foreign policy. Peacekeeping and related activities,
both by the United States alone and multinationally, usually through the UN, has been an

important post–World War II theme. Many peace agreements have been accompanied by
U.S. aid packages to sweeten the pot (see, for example, Chapter 10 regarding the Israeli-
Egyptian Camp David peace accords).

PERCEPTIONS HELD BY OTHER ACTORS AND THEIR RELATIONS WITH THE UNITED STATES

Many foreigners noted U.S. reluctance during the Bush and early Clinton administrations to become involved in Bosnia, even as we engaged in peacekeeping and nation-
building operations in Somalia. The reason for that reluctance was transparent: fear that
Bosnian operations would be a tar baby from which we could not extricate ourselves.
Prior to the Dayton accords, that U.S. reluctance was the cause of some friction with
America's European friends and allies. Concern about Russian relations with the West
was noted earlier.

AVAILABLE ALTERNATIVE ACTIONS AND POLICY TOOLS

Traditional tools for dealing with Second Tier civil wars include external intervention on
one side or another, peacekeeping or related activities, diplomatic "good offices" to broker peace agreements, and—often sadly—neglect and hope that somebody else will deal
with the problem. The United States has sometimes preferred to deal directly in inte[r]
ventions and peacekeeping, as initially in Somalia (see Chapter 7) and late in Haiti (
the introduction to this chapter). At other times, and increasingly during the 1990s[,]
United States has handled such actions through the UN (e.g., late in Somalia), or [N]
(e.g., in Bosnia after Dayton). An important Clinton administration policy annou[n]
1993 (see opening case of Chapter 13) was to rely more heavily on cooperation[
keeping. Thus far, new internal wars have created peacekeeping needs that s[u]
exceed the capabilities of the UN to manage, leading some observers to pr[
application of benign neglect. In a world of steadily increasing economic[
ethnically based wars atomize countries into inefficient and unproductive [
Optimists suggest that increasing economic returns to scale will help c[
ants that peace is far more profitable than war and state fragmentati[
that the victims of new internal war will drop off the edges of worl[
nomic maps.

FUTURE PROSPECTS AND CONCERNS

Although primarily military, new internal war also is about so[
So, too, are peacemaking and nation building. Unfortunate[
ten stop the fighting without addressing the underlying c[
level conflict. In effect, the 1995 Dayton peace accords f[
character of that conflict by promising mutually exclus[
The Serbs and Croats, who had won the military cor[
of Bosnia-Herzegovina into regions that ethnic clea[
mogenous. U.S.-led NATO and Russian troops c[

to become the world's largest by perhaps the year 2025. By mentioning population, those Chinese and U.S. officials drew attention to China's long-range global power potential and short- to medium-term market potential. Within a year after Mao Ze-dong's death in 1976, Deng Xiaoping had returned to power and begun a revolution in Chinese economic policy. Over the next decade per capita output doubled, setting an all-time world record. According to World Bank purchasing power parity (PPP) estimates, China's 1994 GDP of just under $3 trillion made it the world's second largest economy after the United States. According to a 1995 RAND Corporation study (Wolf, 1995, 5–8), China's GDP should reach $11.3 trillion in 1994 PPP dollars by the year 2010, compared to $10.7 trillion for the United States, $4.5 trillion for Japan, $3.7 trillion for India, and $2 trillion for a reunified Korea (Kim, 1997, 247). Although some analysts challenge the PPP measures, these are indeed heady figures that suggest burgeoning economic superpower status.

Such predictions of China's rising status raise a series of interconnected questions. What are China's economic, military, and great power potentials? How do the Chinese government and people answer these questions? What U.S. policies are appropriate for the new conditions created by China's growing power? In Table 15.3, China is compared with several other states on a number of indicators of great power standing; some support the notion that China is a great power; others do not.

Against the optimistic assessments of China's global standing and prospects based on the economic measures already summarized, other analysts raise concerns about limits. These move beyond economic problems to include military shortcomings, building programs intended to address them, and political concerns about whether Chinese political-economic actions today are consistent with international expectations of great powers. China's rapid economic growth has come at the cost of vastly increased integration into the global capitalist economy, making it ever more vulnerable and sensitive to that economy. Total output quadrupled from 1978 to 1995, and foreign trade increased from $21 billion to $280 billion. Over the same period, however, external trade dependence (that is, the sum of imports and exports as a percentage of GNP) rose from less than 10 percent to more than 56 percent. Rapid development in the southeastern coastal provinces with good Pacific Ocean shipping access led to significant unrest in the less rapidly developing interior. For the first time, large numbers of urban dwellers, perhaps 15 million or more, fell below the poverty line without benefit of a state welfare safety net. By 1997 some 100 million rural Chinese had uprooted and moved to the cities in search of work, which was not always available (Kim, 1997, 247).

Robert Dujarric, an analyst at the conservative Hudson Institute, argues, "there is no way for China to modernize itself without increasing its economic and social intercourse with the capitalist world," thus further undermining present institutions (Pfaff, 1997). To encourage more foreign investment and trade, China needs to move much further toward establishing what westerners term the **rule of law,** under which contracts are honored and violators—whether individuals, firms, or government agencies—are held accountable by legal institutions. Violation of intellectual property rights such as copyright in computer software and music CDs has been a particularly sore point in recent years, on which limited progress has been made. Moving away from a command economy while maintaining a one-party state, China lacks even most of the conceptual foundations for the rule of law. Indeed, some analysts question whether it is possible in the long term to maintain an open market economy in a single-party state.

U.S.-RUSSIAN STRATEGIC NUCLEAR ARMS CONTROL
A Major Cold War Issue Survives

U.S.-Soviet controls on their central strategic weapons systems have precursors as far back as negotiations in the late 1950s about a ban on nuclear weapons tests, which resulted in the Limited Test Ban Treaty of 1963. Superpower strategic arms control took a quantum leap upward with the Strategic Arms Limitation Talks (SALT I) Treaty negotiated between 1969 and 1972. Despite many ups and downs over the intervening years, SALT I began to institutionalize an arms control process that continues to this day. START I (for Strategic Arms Reduction Talks), signed in Moscow on 31 July 1991 by President Bush and President Gorbachev, pledged reductions of strategic offensive arms by about 30 percent, from roughly 10,000 thermonuclear warheads per side, in three phases over seven years. This was the first treaty to mandate major reductions in intercontinental nuclear and thermonuclear weaponry by the superpowers. (Previously, their 1987 Intermediate-Range Nuclear Forces (INF) Treaty brought about the complete elimination of that class of weapons.) START I has a fifteen-year duration, extendable in five-year increments by agreement among the parties.

Within months of signing START I, Gorbachev was nearly overthrown in a failed coup attempt that precipitated the breakup of the Soviet Union at the end of 1991. By the time the U.S. Senate ratified START I on 2 October 1992, the Soviet Union was no more. Boris Yeltsin was president of the Russian Federation, largest of the former Soviet republics and successor to most Soviet international positions, including its permanent seat on the UN Security Council. The United States scrambled to extend START I to the other three former Soviet republics holding strategic nuclear weapons on their territory: Belarus, Kazakstan, and Ukraine. They agreed in principle in 1992 to transfer those weapons to Russia and ratify START I. The Russian Supreme Soviet ratified on 4 November 1992 but decided not to provide the instruments of ratification until the other three republics each ratified START I and acceded to the Nuclear Nonproliferation Treaty (NPT), thus promising not to acquire new nuclear weapons to replace the ones they would transfer to Russia. Belarus and Kazakstan had met these conditions by late 1993. After some maneuvering between its president and parliament, which saw nuclear weapons as its trump card in dealings with Russia, Ukraine ratified START I in February 1994 and acceded to the NPT later that year. In late 1996 Belarus joined Kazakstan and Ukraine in eliminating its nuclear weapons.

In any continuing series of negotiations and agreements, concerns raised by one party or another at one stage may be addressed through agreed modifications—termed *protocols* when they revise a treaty—and in the next stage of agreement. Even as START I was being extended to Soviet successor states, negotiations proceeded in 1991 and 1992 toward a more ambitious START II treaty, which Presidents Bush and Yeltsin signed on 3 January 1993. It called on both sides to reduce their long-range nuclear arsenals to about one third of then-current levels within a decade. Perhaps even more importantly for long-term stability, START II promised to eliminate multiple-warhead land-based missiles. During the 1980s the growing numbers and ever-increasing accuracy of such missiles raised fears

(continued)

(continued)

that they offered a cost-benefit ratio favoring a first strike to shift the balance of forces, because one missile could destroy two or more of an opponent's missiles. Generally, START I did not call for destroying missiles, but START II did, notably including the complete elimination of heavy ICBMs such as the Russian SS-18. The new treaty set ranges for some of the central limits on strategic weapons in two timed phases. In phase 1, to be completed seven years after START I entered into force on 5 December 1994 (thus 2001), each side was to reduce its total of deployed strategic nuclear warheads to between 3,800 and 4,250, including warheads on ICBMs, submarine-launched ballistic missiles (SLBMs), and heavy bombers with nuclear missions. Allowed sublimits included 1,200 warheads on multiple-warhead (MIRVed) ICBMs, 1,700 to 1,750 warheads on deployed SLBMs, and 650 on deployed heavy ICBMs. Phase 2 was to be completed by the year 2003, or 2000 if the United States could help finance weapons elimination in Russia. By that time, no MIRVed ICBMs would be allowed, and total deployed strategic nuclear warheads were to be reduced to between 3,000 and 3,500.

Because START I called for all formerly Soviet strategic weapons to be transferred to Russia, START II required ratification only by the U.S. Senate and the Russian legislature. U.S. ratification came on 26 January 1996, but Russian ratification was caught up in political infighting between President Yeltsin and the Duma (lower house of parliament), which was dominated by the resurgent Russian Communist Party, conservatives, and nationalists. Worse yet, because many Russian conservatives saw START II as giving up their biggest strategic bargaining chip, by 1996 ratification had become linked with resentment over President Clinton's push to expand NATO into Eastern Europe. (See the geopolitical sector

focus case in Chapter 14.) At their March 1997 summit meeting, Presidents Clinton and Yeltsin signed a protocol to START II (also subject to ratification) stretching out the deadlines for phase 1 to 31 December 2004 and for phase 2 to 31 December 2007. They also committed to begin negotiating a follow-on START III treaty in which they would seek limits of 2,000 to 2,500 warheads as soon as START II was ratified. These and other, related agreements were formally signed the following September. Still, START II languished in the Duma. A new ratification push stalled in the spring of 1999, over Russia's objections to U.S.-led NATO bombing in Kosovo (Hoffman, 1999).

Russian ratification and both sides' continuation of the START process have profound long-term ramifications. If the strategic arms control and reduction regime institutionalized over more than three decades is continued and strengthened, global nuclear arsenals and their attendant risks will be dramatically reduced. Eventually, U.S.-Russian strategic nuclear arms will be reduced to levels at which both sides feel impelled to broaden the regime to include other powers. At a minimum, these would have to include Britain, China, and France, all of which had some long-range nuclear and thermonuclear strike capability before 1990. By the latter 1990s China's rate of military modernization heightened such concerns. U.S.-Soviet and U.S.-Russian agreements already have reversed their vertical proliferation in numbers of thermonuclear warheads and missiles. Broader agreement among the already significant nuclear powers to limit and reduce their arsenals could strengthen the chances for more effective measures to limit horizontal nuclear proliferation to additional states. (See also the cross-tier military sector discussion in Chapter 16.)

TABLE 15.3
China Compared with Other Major States on Selected Indicators of Power Standing

Indicator	China	Germany	Japan	Russian Federation	United States
GNP (1994, in billions)	$630	$2,076	$4,321	$393	$6,737
GNP per capita (1995)	$620	$27,510	$39,640	$2,240	$26,980
Human Development Index (1994 World Rank)	108	19	7	67	24
Strategic Nuclear Warheads (1996)	275	none	none	6,758	8,111
Military Expenditures (1995, in millions)	$31,731	$41,815	$50,219	$82,010	$277,834
Arms Exports (1995, % of world total)	2	4	1	10	49
International Currency Reserves (1995, in millions)	$80,288	$121,816	$192,620	$18,024	$175,996

(continued)

The Chinese Communist Party and bureaucracy are among the world's most corrupt. Ownership of factories and land remains unclear. Sixty-three percent of peasant farmers do not know the duration of their land rights. Only 11 percent of GDP is raised in taxes, and there is no effective tax system. As in the former Soviet Union, many of the 13,000 medium- and large-scale enterprises owned by the state are highly inefficient. President Jiang Zemin has talked of selling more than three quarters of them, but it is unclear whether his notion that they would go into "public ownership" means much more than shifting blame for almost inevitable downsizings and failures away from the central government (Pfaff, 1997). Many analysts argue that making purchasing power comparisons of the sorts discussed here greatly exaggerates China's actual economic and productive strength. Others point out that further opening China to global financial flows while maintaining state-directed, authoritarian, crony capitalism invites the same sorts of failings that befell the Asian "tigers," Indonesia, South Korea, Malaysia, and Thailand, by the latter 1990s (Friedman, 1997b). Weaknesses masked by rapid growth can become glaringly evident at the first economic slowdown, and China has many of the same weaknesses as the tigers: misallocation of foreign investment into pet political projects, weak financial regulatory institutions, banks virtually bankrupt from lending to failed state enterprises, real estate overbuilding, rampant corruption, and a weak watchdog business press.

STAKES AT ISSUE

China has become a major market for and supplier to the United States. It also threatens to become a major competitor economically and perhaps militarily. China's sheer size besieging such Muslim population centers as Sarajevo. Attempts by NATO and the UN to embargo arms shipments into Bosnia thus worked mainly to disadvantage the Bosnian Muslims, and a UN Protection Force of peacekeepers (UNPROFOR) was ineffective in preventing Bosnian Serb attacks.

By mid-1995, many knowledgeable observers expected foreign powers to wash their hands of the Bosnian war and withdraw UNPROFOR forces. Instead, after some months of waffling, the Clinton administration brought leaders of all the major factions together for a carefully sequestered peace conference on the grounds of Wright Patterson Air Force Base outside Dayton, Ohio, where a fragile peace accord was reached in November 1995. The Dayton accords provided for a Peace Implementation Force of NATO and Russian troops reporting to a U.S. commander. Several factors made the Dayton accords easier to reach than they would have been a year or two earlier. Every Bosnian faction had suffered terrible losses; Croatian military forces had made major advances at the expense of the Bosnian Serbs, who feared worse to come; and Bosnian Muslims realized that they would never get the lost half of Bosnia back. Until Dayton, however, many observers argued that no outside powers had consistent Bosnia policies—not the United States, nor the UN, nor NATO, nor the EU.

STAKES AT ISSUE

U.S. stakes in the Bosnian civil war include humanitarian concern over the loss of life, fear that the war could spread throughout the region, worries about costs to the United States of a potentially long-term involvement, and apprehensions about how actions in Bosnia might impact Russia's relations with the West. Russia's history of supporting the Serbs raised fears that the United States and other European states might become involved directly or indirectly in conflict with Russia, or at least face dramatically worsened relations with Russia. Failing to resolve the Bosnian civil war also would bode ill for the prospects of resolving other such conflicts.

The Bosnian civil war clearly exemplifies the problems of what Donald Snow (1997, Chapter 8) has termed **new internal war.** By this he means the wave of post–Cold War conflicts within Second Tier states, seen first in the early and mid-1990s in Bosnia, Somalia, Rwanda, and Liberia. Other examples include Russia's 1996 war against secessionist rebels in Chechnya, and fighting throughout the early 1990s between the former Soviet republics of Armenia and Azerbaijan over the province of Nagorno-Karabakh, an enclave in Azerbaijan with a majority population of ethnic Armenians. These new internal wars lack the ideological component common to many civil wars during the Cold War period, when nominally anticommunist governments used Western help to fight nominally communist insurgents assisted by the Soviets. In many cases, internal war erupts when an old authoritarian regime—such as those imposed over Eastern Europe by the Soviet Union and by Marshal Tito over Yugoslavia until his death in 1980—has collapsed but not yet been replaced by some new and stable political system. Bosnia and Somalia are prominent examples of failed states, in which anarchy follows the collapse of a central government. Arguably, when people's old political reference points are stripped away, they tend to revert to older ethnic and religious self-identifications.

Such new internal wars promise to be a sadly significant feature of the post–Cold War era. When failed states are well armed before their collapse, as Yugoslavia was, the resulting internal wars can be extremely intense. Many such conflicts occur in locations

PHOTO 15.1

U.S. assistant secretary of state Richard Holbrooke (right) talks with French deputy assistant secretary-general Jacques Blot after the Bosnia peace agreement known as the Dayton accords (1995) was negotiated. Holbrooke, a notable in-and-outer and special negotiator, later moved to Wall Street investment banking. He was recalled to government service several times to address Balkan conflicts, including the Kosovo crisis in 1999. After more than a year's delay, the Senate confirmed him as U.S. Ambassador to the UN in August 1999.

AP/Wide World Photos.

little known even to U.S. and world policy elites, making it hard to bring much expert knowledge to bear on solutions and persuade politicians and the general public to support American or NATO or UN intervention. All the difficulties of peacekeeping, peacemaking, and nation building we examined in Chapter 9 apply. As the U.S. Army found in Somalia, it may be difficult or impossible to find solutions that even professional soldiers consider affordable. Nonetheless, interventions are encouraged if we grow frustrated viewing the effects of ethnic violence without being able to do much about it.

RELEVANT U.S. POLICY THEMES

Intervention in foreign wars or to forestall expected conflicts, although not always practiced, long has been a theme in U.S. foreign policy. Peacekeeping and related activities, both by the United States alone and multinationally, usually through the UN, has been an important post–World War II theme. Many peace agreements have been accompanied by U.S. aid packages to sweeten the pot (see, for example, Chapter 10 regarding the Israeli-Egyptian Camp David peace accords).

PERCEPTIONS HELD BY OTHER ACTORS AND THEIR RELATIONS WITH THE UNITED STATES

Many foreigners noted U.S. reluctance during the Bush and early Clinton administrations to become involved in Bosnia, even as we engaged in peacekeeping and nation-building operations in Somalia. The reason for that reluctance was transparent: fear that Bosnian operations would be a tar baby from which we could not extricate ourselves. Prior to the Dayton accords, that U.S. reluctance was the cause of some friction with America's European friends and allies. Concern about Russian relations with the West was noted earlier.

AVAILABLE ALTERNATIVE ACTIONS AND POLICY TOOLS

Traditional tools for dealing with Second Tier civil wars include external intervention on one side or another, peacekeeping or related activities, diplomatic "good offices" to broker peace agreements, and—often sadly—neglect and hope that somebody else will deal with the problem. The United States has sometimes preferred to deal directly in interventions and peacekeeping, as initially in Somalia (see Chapter 7) and late in Haiti (see the introduction to this chapter). At other times, and increasingly during the 1990s, the United States has handled such actions through the UN (e.g., late in Somalia), or NATO (e.g., in Bosnia after Dayton). An important Clinton administration policy announced in 1993 (see opening case of Chapter 13) was to rely more heavily on cooperation in peacekeeping. Thus far, new internal wars have created peacekeeping needs that substantially exceed the capabilities of the UN to manage, leading some observers to propose broad application of benign neglect. In a world of steadily increasing economic globalization, ethnically based wars atomize countries into inefficient and unproductive economic units. Optimists suggest that increasing economic returns to scale will help convince combatants that peace is far more profitable than war and state fragmentation. Pessimists fear that the victims of new internal war will drop off the edges of world political and economic maps.

FUTURE PROSPECTS AND CONCERNS

Although primarily military, new internal war also is about societal and political security. So, too, are peacemaking and nation building. Unfortunately, military interventions often stop the fighting without addressing the underlying causes of what actually is a two-level conflict. In effect, the 1995 Dayton peace accords for Bosnia finessed the two-level character of that conflict by promising mutually exclusive results to the different parties. The Serbs and Croats, who had won the military conflict, were given de facto partition of Bosnia-Herzegovina into regions that ethnic cleansing had made fairly ethnically homogenous. U.S.-led NATO and Russian troops of the 1995–96 Peace Implementation

Force (IFOR) enforced separation of the combatants but did little to disarm them. Dayton also promised political reunification of the country to the Bosnian Muslims. Although some local and regional elections were held under the watchful eyes of enforcement troops, ethnic hatreds were so intense that true political reunification was unenforceable and would collapse immediately if foreign troops departed. Issues about how long such troops would be required surfaced rapidly. Having casually promised in 1995 that the optimistically named IFOR would only be needed for about a year, the United States and NATO pulled IFOR out only as they rotated other troops in to form a new Stabilization Force (SFOR). In turn, SFOR was scheduled to be pulled out by June 1998, but by the fall of 1997 trial balloons about the need for a successor force already were being floated in Washington and European capitals. In 1998 a new successor force was declared. Few honest observers foresee any lasting peace in Bosnia without permanent partition and probably a permanent peacekeeping force.

Regrettably, Bosnia appears to be typical of the new internal wars we should expect for the indefinite future. First Tier states, at least pending the rise of China to that status, share democratic governance, good rates of economic growth, and peace. In the future, if some Second Tier states gain NBC weapons of mass destruction and the capabilities to direct them against First Tier states, that situation will change. For now, however, and extending at least a few years into the twenty-first century, it appears we can expect almost all the world's violence to remain within and between Second Tier states. The problem of new internal wars is far worse than most Americans realize; by the mid-1990s, about 35 to 40 such wars were underway in any given time (Snow, 1997, 195). Most of these were in the poorest states and those least known among First Tier peoples. Our collective experience in Bosnia through the latter 1990s does not offer great hope that more effective means of resolving new internal wars will be devised soon.

Other Military Issues

Another military sector arena of particular concern is arms control. We consider problems of horizontal nuclear proliferation to additional states, terrorism involving weapons of mass destruction (NBC weapons), the global abolition of land mines, implementing the global ban mandated by the Chemical Weapons Convention, and a comprehensive nuclear test ban in Chapter 16. A particular concern of the United States during the 1990s was ratification and implementation of the Strategic Arms Reduction Treaties (START I and II) with Russia, and we consider the ongoing issue of U.S.-Russian strategic nuclear arms control on pages 580–581.

ECONOMIC SECTOR FOCUS CASE:
THE POTENTIAL RISE OF CHINA

The phrase "1.2 billion Chinese" was heard repeatedly from both American and Chinese officials when President Jiang Zemin visited the United States in October 1997. China's huge population long had been seen as both its greatest resource and its greatest claim to major power and potential superpower status. Once the Beijing government turned to market-based economics during the 1980s and GNP started to rise 10 percent or more annually, observers around the world began considering the Chinese economy's potential

TABLE 15.3					
China Compared with Other Major States on Selected Indicators of Power Standing (continued)					

Indicator	China	Germany	Japan	Russian Federation	United States
Official Development Assistance (1994, in millions) (*Received*)	*($3,521)* *	$1,623	$14,489	*($2,358)* **	$7,367
UN Budget Assessments (1995–97%)	0.74	9.06	15.65	4.27	25.0
IMF Voting Power (1996, % of total)	2.28	5.54	5.54	2.90	17.78
World Bank Voting Power (1996 %)	2.03	6.97	10.76	0.26	14.98
Influential Patents (World Rank)	†	17,649 (3)	76,984 (2)	†	104,541 (1)

Notes:
*Amount received from donors in 1995
**Amount received from donors in 1994
†Not ranked among the top 15 "patent powers"
Source: Kim, 1997, 250.

gives international meaning to issues that would pass with much less notice in any other state, including human rights issues such as the imprisonment of political dissidents and the exploitation of prison labor to manufacture export goods. Chinese exports to America soared during the 1990s, leading to a mushrooming trade surplus with the United States, up from $10.4 billion in 1990 to $30.0 billion by 1994 (Post and Strasser, 1995, 40). Although many American businesses have been eager to tap the China market, China has penetrated the American market much more deeply, aggravating our trade deficit. Indeed, by 1998 the U.S. trade deficit with China exceeded that with Japan in certain months. Some authorities argue the need for removing market impediments similar to some found in Japan, although the lack of rule of law institutions and practices is a more severe problem. Others argue that China's huge exports should give the United States substantial leverage to bring about change, not only in business practices and supporting legal structures, but also through linkage to human rights. Still others argue against penalizing China because of American dependence on that huge flow of Chinese goods. Industries as diverse as textiles, tools, and toys had been deeply pervaded by Chinese goods by the 1990s, as visits to relevant retail outlets will confirm.

By the latter 1990s many observers began to discern a new movement to develop a serious capability for military force projection beyond China's borders, which would give

China the military means to become at least a regional hegemon. This is a major departure for the People's Liberation Army (PLA), which always had been configured and equipped as a garrison army for internal control. Its limited capabilities for operations outside the country were clearly demonstrated in its ill-fated 1979 invasion of Vietnam. Although China long had a modest strategic nuclear weapons program intended primarily to deter Soviet attack, building highly mobile forces with state of the art weaponry will depend heavily on continued economic success and thus, indirectly, on U.S. cooperation. Reporting to the Senate Intelligence Committee about a study in which some two hundred books and journal articles by mostly mid-level Chinese military officers were translated, Pentagon analyst Michael Pillsbury spoke in September 1997 about "a common theme in PLA views of future warfare—America is proclaimed to be a declining power with but two or three decades of primacy left." The Chinese view, he told the committee, is that "U.S. military forces, while dangerous at present, are vulnerable, even deeply flawed, and can be defeated with the right strategy" (Associated Press, 1997). Although Chinese forces are decades behind U.S. technology, the study suggested that a rapid catch-up was possible through the use of such power leveraging weapons as highly accurate cruise missiles and torpedoes. Because of China's great distance from the U.S. mainland, navy task forces, lengthy supply lines, and logistics bases all could be vulnerable to the right technologies. (See the discussion of strength-versus-distance functions in Chapter 8.)

RELEVANT U.S. POLICY THEMES

Dealing with China as we move into the twenty-first century confronts the United States with practical policy decisions about whether and how we implement wide-ranging and fundamental political values that include promoting business, encouraging global stability, deterring regional conflicts, supporting human rights, encouraging the spread and strengthening of democracy, and protecting allies (most notably Taiwan, in this instance). The degree of emphasis to be given each of these themes and the best ways to implement them remain in dispute as the struggle to form a coherent post–Cold War grand policy continues. Interventionism of the sort practiced for a century before World War II seems out of the question, although direct Chinese attack on Taiwan well might provoke a U.S. military response. The rejection of a deliberate single superpower strategy, as discussed in the military sector focus case of Chapter 14, sets important constraints on how the United States will respond to China's future military development.

PERCEPTIONS HELD BY OTHER ACTORS AND THEIR RELATIONS WITH THE UNITED STATES

Perceived global standing is important in Chinese politics and society, partly because China's rich civilization has a history going back for millennia. From its first treaties with the West in the 1840s until the 1949 communist victory after years of civil war, China was dominated and partly colonized by the West and Japan, and development was retarded by what the Chinese called the "century of humiliation." Restoring China's rightful place in the world has been a central policy goal ever since. Establishing an effective policy for development, however, was subject to tremendous policy fluctuations and reversals for decades after the communists came to power. Chinese leaders perceived their country isolated and contained by the United States and its allies through the Korean and

Vietnam Wars, and turned aside by a Soviet Union that was willing to provide development aid only at the unacceptable price of political control. China's development through the 1970s relied almost entirely on internal effort. Only after the end of the Vietnam War was the United States, which began opening diplomatic relations with China in 1972, willing to relax its political, military, and economic resistance. Thereafter, Japan and other American allies were free to assist in Chinese development.

U.S.-Chinese relations soured after the 1989 Tiananmen Square massacre and countrywide crackdown on political dissidents, an event the United States deplored but could do little to reverse. Through most of the 1990s, Beijing argued that the United States kept China from assuming its rightful place in world affairs by actions as diverse as barring China from hosting the year 2000 Olympics, encouraging Taiwanese independence, and blocking Chinese membership in the World Trade Organization. Beijing's leaders strongly resisted U.S. attempts to link China's internal human rights practices to improvements in relations, and most American leaders were reluctant to push those issues very hard. A focal point in the 1990s was annual battles between the president and Congress over renewal of China's most-favored-nation (MFN) trading status. Broadly, liberals argued for demanding human rights progress before continuing to offer standard trade terms. Conservatives and presidents of both major parties argued that MFN protected American economic interests and would yield greater long-term progress through productive engagement with China.

Some analysts argue that despite rapid economic growth, thermonuclear weapons, and potential regional force projection capability, China will not truly be a great power until it begins behaving more like one. Part of their argument is that China is an economic taker that does not pay its fair share in world affairs. Having asked in 1973 to have its UN assessment raised from 4 to 5.5 percent as a demonstration of its prowess, China reversed course in 1978 by requesting aid from the United Nations Development Program (UNDP). In 1979 Beijing asked that its assessment rate be lowered based on its own "complete national income statistics" (Kim, 1997, 249–50). That rate was lowered to 0.79 percent, and today stands at 0.72 percent, which is surpassed by such Second Tier states as Brazil (1.62 percent), South Korea and Saudi Arabia (0.80 percent), and Mexico (0.78 percent). China today is the world's largest recipient of World Bank multilateral aid, at about $3 billion annually. Samuel Kim and others argue that these behaviors are inconsistent with what the rest of the world considers great power action. These and some related indicators are summarized in Table 15.3.

AVAILABLE ALTERNATIVE ACTIONS AND POLICY TOOLS

The extremes of possible U.S. overall policies toward China, which would impact economics, human rights, military strength, and global standing, are encapsulated in the terms *containment* and *engagement*. Containment would operate somewhat similarly to Cold War anti-Soviet policy and could include embracing the already rejected single superpower policy. Containing China, a policy that appeals to essentialists, almost certainly is impracticable due to its sheer size, the general economic appeal of its huge market potential, and global perceptions that threats to major powers have been fundamentally reduced in the post–Cold War era. Moreover, considering the enormous cost of containing the Soviet Union throughout the Cold War, the United States today probably would want major support from allies. **Engagement** is a cyberneticist strategy that refers to strengthening ties by emphasizing areas of present and potential agreement while pushing gently for changes we would prefer and hoping that long-term forces inherent in increased international interactions will promote constructive change within China. Thus, for example, China's need for even more foreign investment to promote economic growth encourages the development of rule of law and of Western-style financial institutions and practices. Some analysts argue that engagement is not a policy but a fact, stemming from U.S. involvement in the global economy. An intriguing and longer range instance of engagement is related by Thomas Friedman (1996c), reporting a conversation with President Clinton after his brief meeting with Chinese President Jiang Zemin at the United Nations. The president told Jiang,

> The greatest threat to our security that you present is that all of your people will want to get rich in exactly the same way we got rich. And unless we try to triple the automobile mileage and to reduce greenhouse gas emissions, if you all get rich in that way we won't be breathing very well. There are just so many more of you than there are of us, and if you behave exactly the same way we do, you will do irrevocable damage to the global environment. And it will be partly our fault, because we got there first and we should be able to figure out how to help you solve this problem.

Somewhere between containment and engagement lies deterrence, an undoubtedly mechanist perspective. In this view, American and Chinese interests may diverge more than the proponents of engagement hope, and we should be less optimistic and more prepared to take strong action if warranted.

FUTURE PROSPECTS AND CONCERNS

By the latter 1990s successive American administrations had maintained some degree of engagement with China, although a substantial minority in Congress and the public questioned Chinese behavior, particularly on human rights, and sought a stronger policy of deterrence or even containment. Many issues with China occur in less intense form with other, smaller powers, and likely will be encountered around the globe. As of this writing, no clearly dominant U.S. policy has emerged.

SOCIETAL SECTOR FOCUS CASE: ILLEGAL IMMIGRATION

The United States has a long, complex, often uplifting but often troubled history regarding immigrants. We frequently have been called a nation of immigrants because all but Native Americans trace their ancestry to people who came from other lands. In 1996 an estimated 24.6 million Americans or 9.3 percent of the population were foreign born. Immigrants come increasingly from Second Tier states. That fact, coupled with divergent birthrates among different ethnic groups, contributes to projections that the non-Hispanic white population of the United States will decline from 73 percent in the mid-1990s to 53 percent by the year 2050. Immigration is a highly intermestic foreign policy issue and a societal security concern because it influences the living and working conditions of immigrants and citizens as well as the overall cultural, ethnic, and racial composition of American society. Particular concerns have been raised over the impact and potential control of illegal immigration.

The United States received about 60 percent of the world's total immigrants from 1820 to 1930. Pushed by a great population explosion in the then-developed countries, encouraged by transportation companies utilizing new technologies for quicker and easier passage, and pulled by the lure of free land to homestead and plentiful jobs during a period of rapid industrialization, huge numbers of people traveled to these shores to establish new permanent residence. Despite often severe discrimination against new ethnic groups, and notwithstanding immigrant tendencies to settle in ethnically homogeneous communities, most came to stay, make new lives here, learn English, and settle in to build a new nation by "becoming Americans." U.S. limitations on immigration often were based on race or nationality, and restrictions existed against entrance by diseased persons, paupers, and others considered undesirable. The first permanent quota was passed in 1924 and provided for national origins quotas to begin five years later. The 1952 McCarran-Walter Act abolished race as an overall barrier but kept other forms of national bias. National origins quotas were abolished in 1965, after which immigration rose substantially, and the 1980s saw the highest levels since the first decade of the twentieth century. Nonetheless, immigration long has been offered preferentially to persons with high levels of education and skills, likely to contribute quickly to the U.S. economy, and persons with family in the United States or sponsors who guarantee to cover their expenses. The Immigration Act of 1990 raised the total quota and reorganized the preference system for entrance. Annual limits in fiscal years 1992–94 were set at 700,000, reduced to 675,000 in 1995, and subject to some adjustments. In addition to these totals, refugees are allowed in numbers announced annually.

The ability of a mature economy to absorb large numbers or immigrants is debatable, and from an early date the labor movement welcomed some groups of immigrants while it accused others of lowering wages and living standards. Such concerns are compounded when immigrants enter illegally. Because illegal immigrants are reluctant to complain to authorities, they are easy prey for exploitative employers who may offer low wages, long hours without overtime, limited or no benefits, poor accommodations, and, in extreme conditions, enslavement. In 1986 Congress passed legislation seeking to limit the numbers of undocumented or illegal aliens living in the United States, threatening stiff fines on employers who hired them and offering legal status to many aliens who already had lived in the United States for some years. Those measures have not stemmed the flow, particularly across the rather porous U.S.-Mexican border. Many Mexicans see greater wealth close at hand in America, even in low-wage jobs.

STAKES AT ISSUE

Concern about illegal immigration is greatest in those regions closest to entrance points, notably the southwestern states and major ports. Many laborers and labor unions worry about wage depression. Immigrant rights groups are troubled by exploitation and abuse. Employers used to hiring illegals, particularly migrant workers, fear that crackdowns will cost them money. Many citizens worry that illegal immigrants will become dependent on welfare programs, draining public coffers and raising taxes. That fear did much to spur passage of California Proposition 209 in 1996, under which many public benefits were cut off even for legal immigrants. Most programs to curtail illegal immigration have been marginally successful at best. Some political conservatives call that failure to control U.S. borders a fundamental loss of sovereignty. Political liberals express greater concern about immigrant and worker rights.

RELEVANT U.S. POLICY THEMES

Welcoming huge numbers of immigrants made obvious sense while the United States was an infant state and throughout the period of westward expansion, consolidation, and industrialization. Subsequently, as we noted earlier, U.S. immigration policy has varied widely. Broadly, we long have sought to welcome immigrants who will contribute to American strengths.

PERCEPTIONS HELD BY OTHER ACTORS AND THEIR RELATIONS WITH THE UNITED STATES

U.S. immigration policies, for all their problems, are considerably more generous than those of many other states. Japan, for example, has a much more homogeneous society and discourages immigration of non-Japanese. The ongoing problem of illegal immigration long has been a sore point in U.S.-Mexican relations.

AVAILABLE ALTERNATIVE ACTIONS AND POLICY TOOLS

Possible actions range from absolute enforcement of borders and entrance laws to the opposite extreme of declaring open borders and immigration. Most analysts consider the former impossible and the latter undesirable. Fully controlled borders are rare. The most successful modern instances include the Iron Curtain and the inter-German border during the Cold War, hardly politically appealing examples to emulate. However, open immigration today raises serious questions about how many people the mature U.S. economy can absorb, despite the general prosperity of the 1990s.

FUTURE PROSPECTS AND CONCERNS

Immigration, whether legal or illegal, has raised serious political, economic, and humanitarian questions for at least the last century. Lasting and comprehensive solutions are nowhere in sight. Unfortunately, severe actions to control both legal and illegal immigration are quite consistent with a post–Cold War neo-isolationist retreat from globalism as advocated by some citizens and domestic interest groups.

ENVIRONMENTAL SECTOR FOCUS CASE: SUSTAINABLE DEVELOPMENT

What do you see when a forested hillside is clear-cut (completely logged)? The most efficient harvesting of logs to be turned into timber, paper, and bark products, to be followed by replanting and eventual reharvesting, obtaining maximal resources from land ideally suited to such production? Or the creation of an eyesore, destruction of wildlife habitat, and production of erosion and runoff hazards, to be followed by more species extinctions and replanting with a single tree species, reducing biodiversity and disease resistance?

What do you see when farmland near a city is developed for new suburban homes, shopping malls, factories, or airports? New and better housing for a growing population, new jobs, increased production with increased value added, and improved transportation? Or a boring redundancy of tract houses ever further from city centers and civic and cultural attractions, longer commutes between home and work, tasteless strip malls that divert ever more shoppers from already crumbling downtowns and make urban decay a certainty, increased pollution and waste, and the diversion of more of the world's most productive farmland from production, diminishing America's greatest natural advantage in international production and trade?

These two sets of divergent images illustrate how greatly opinions divide on a broad topic of concern to all states, but especially to those in the Second Tier and to First Tier states in their relations with the Second: *sustainability* or **sustainable development.** These terms, which came into widespread use during the 1980s and 1990s, label a major concern for the United States both in our activities at home and in our policies for development in the Second Tier. The precise application of sustainability, however, is disputed. As Jessica Tuchman Matthews (1991) observed, when politicians as diverse as Albert Gore, Jr. (vice president in the Clinton administration), Margaret Thatcher (conservative British prime minister from 1970 to 1990, first woman to hold that post, Reagan admirer during the 1980s, dubbed the "Iron Lady"), and Alan Greenspan (rather conservative chair of the Federal Reserve Board under Presidents Reagan, Bush, and Clinton) use the term *sustainability*, quite different positions are implied. When the word appears in phrases with such starkly different implications as "sustainable development," "sustainable growth," "sustainable societies," and "sustainable yield," we must wonder whether it has become what Baudrilllard (1993) calls a "floating-signifier" that masks underlying disagreement, functions differently in varying contexts, and may lose all relevance to real policy choices.

STAKES AT ISSUE

For the United States, sustainable development is a core issue in future development policy and challenges many of the approaches we have used in the past (discussed in Chapter 13). At home, this is an issue of values; abroad, it will be central to our relations with developing states. In the long term and at the global level, sustainability presents lifestyle and survival issues for the United States and every other member of the global environmental common pool.

RELEVANT U.S. POLICY THEMES

Support for development worldwide has been a fairly important U.S. policy goal since World War II. Since 1990 it has been linked with support for democracy and market economies abroad, even if that support has been underwhelming and has favored selected states. American failure thus far to assign top importance to such goals (noted in Chapter 3) is part of our general failure to develop post–Cold War grand policy.

PERCEPTIONS HELD BY OTHER ACTORS AND THEIR RELATIONS WITH THE UNITED STATES

Sustainable development is a sufficiently new issue that few governments in either the First or Second Tier have settled on broad policies. Without reaching consensus on sustainability at home, the United States is unlikely to adopt consistent policies abroad. To the extent that the search for sustainability may cause the United States and other First Tier powers to encourage slower development or more expensive technologies, they should expect opposition and requests for aid and technical assistance from Second Tier states. These may become wedge issues between the developed, largely First Tier, North and the developing, mostly Second Tier, South in the new century.

AVAILABLE ALTERNATIVE ACTIONS AND POLICY TOOLS

Setting appropriate policies for sustainable development is difficult without settling the issue of what "sustainable" means. In his introduction to a 1997 reader entitled *Flashpoints in Environmental Policymaking*, Robert O. Vos distinguishes three major competing approaches to sustainability: (1) the economists' view, held by free market advocates; (2) the biologists' view, held by ecological-science advocates; and (3) the philosophers' view, held by deep ecologists. Each approach implies radically different policies, although these three approaches actually are ideal types or stereotypes. We may never find any individual who follows any single approach exclusively, but these three views capture important dimensions of the sustainability debate. The roots of each go back long before sustainability emerged as an issue in the economic, political, and scientific study of the environment. Because those roots lie in different disciplines, many scholars tend to ignore work outside their fields and talk past one another in policy debates.

The approach favored by some economists and political scientists in the public choice tradition has led to an entire school of thought, sometimes termed *free market environmentalism*. It is the latest of the three approaches reviewed by Vos to embrace the concept of sustainability. Neoclassical economists long considered sustainability and steady states of economic systems in terms of a capacity for continual growth. They thus tend to look to inefficiencies caused by externalities as potential reductions in an economy's growth capacity. **Externalities** are costs created by a producer but borne by others (e.g., acid rain caused by atmospheric chemical processes or sulfur dioxide sent up smokestacks by coal-burning power plants). Free market environmentalists view nature as a *resource or object of human use* and seek benevolent forms of adaptation to the environmental problems thus generated. No inherent limits are perceived on either the rate or potential scale of development. Technology is embraced as offering solutions when correctly applied. For example, acid rain may be significantly reduced or eliminated by burning low-sulfur coal or using wet scrubbers to remove sulfur dioxide from smokestack gases, although a different problem of using or disposing of the removed sulfur then results. Free market environmentalists expect market forces to resolve choices regarding equitable distribution of costs. Under current U.S. law, for example, firms may purchase rights to emit certain quantities of pollutants, based on the scientific understanding that airsheds and watersheds can absorb and disperse certain quantities of pollutants without long-term damage. Thus a national, and potentially global, market in pollution rights has been created. Free market environmentalists encourage privatization and deregulation of industries to remove impediments to the free working of such markets.

The concept of sustainability originated, however, with the biologists' view. Biologists long have dealt with the rates at which renewable resources like trees and fish can be harvested and restocked—or damaged by pollution—without threatening collapse of their ecosystems. Population biologists originated the important and controversial concept of **carrying capacity,** meaning the number of a given species that can be sustained in a particular ecosystem without degrading the required resource base and producing a population decline or crash. (See, for example, Garret Hardin [1968] and the discussion of the tragedy of the commons in Chapter 12.) Those taking this view of sustainability consider nature as an *object of study* and emphasize the dynamic equilibrium or stability of ecosystems. (See also the discussion of living systems in Chapter 4.) Both the rate and scale of development are seen as limited, although the limits are difficult to define. Technological solutions are embraced only with some skepticism. The late Buckminster Fuller, perhaps best known as the inventor of the geodesic dome, may have been an exception, however. Fuller generally held that the answers to incorrect uses of technology lie in better technologies correctly used so that environmental problems are solvable through objective scientific management. Nonetheless, environmental biologists express serious concerns for human survival and well-being, even in the near future, and usually identify overpopulation and overconsumption as the leading causes of environmental degradation.

Vos's third approach is that of the deep ecologists, who emphasize the need for an appropriate ethical and moral framework for humankind's relationship with nature. That framework usually is seen as directly linked to social structure and normative political theory. Nature is viewed as *fragile*, and there is strong concern for the futures of all species. The deep ecologists are highly skeptical of technology and hold that nature must be taken into account in deciding equity and distribution questions. They hold that environmental degradation stems from an ethical crisis in which human futures were divorced from nature following the eighteenth-century Enlightenment. Deep ecologists see the solution as lying in social learning and the adoption of new values that replace today's focus on growth and development with greater emphasis on attaining human well-being through a spiritually satisfying relationship with the natural world.

The huge and enduring problems of planning and carrying out development that can be sustained over the long term without exhausting planetary resources and poisoning the environment for our descendants are linked to the need for technologies appropriate to developing states' levels of existing technology, education, and worker skills. Sometimes newer technologies offer opportunities for states to leapfrog over stages of development through which the present First Tier states have passed. For example, modern satellites can extend communications and educational television into the most remote regions of states such as India without requiring massive investment in stringing land lines. Of course, some investment is always necessary in both infrastructure and training. The more rapidly developing states—typically those with abundant natural resources—may be able to afford much of that investment. Still, a continuing issue area is what division of effort and wealth is appropriate and equitable between the already developed states and those still developing. By the mid-1990s, calls from the 1970s and 1980s for a new international economic order (NIEO) in which rich states would commit 1 or 2 percent of GDP to poorer states had largely given way to calls for further foreign investment in building market economies.

FUTURE PROSPECTS AND CONCERNS

Although it has important implications for economic and societal security around the world, sustainable development clearly is an environmental security concern, especially for Second Tier states and for their most feasible and likely benefactors, the most highly developed First Tier states. U.S. policy on sustainability remained unresolved as we entered the twenty-first century. One possible resolution of the great differences between the three major views or approaches set out earlier is the increasingly frequent distinction between *growth* and *development*. Scholars making that distinction seek to reconcile (1) the desire to express human freedom through continual change or improvement with (2) the understanding that there are real limits to economic growth. As Vos (1997, 15) summarizes,

> Scholars argue that in ceasing to expand sources and sinks of the economy (i.e., "to grow") we need not cease to improve the quality of life in terms of aesthetic production, better relationships among human beings, and human comfort through specialized services (i.e., "to develop"). Thus, while there are limits to quantitative growth, there are no limits to qualitative development.

Concrete examples of the political difficulties of implementing sustainable development by solving environmental problems may be found in the environmental sector focus cases of Chapters 14 and 16, dealing with ozone depletion and global warming, respectively.

Other Environmental Issues

The United States and most other First Tier states remain heavily dependent on Second Tier natural resources and somewhat dependent on Second Tier markets for their produce and manufactured goods. Additionally, as economic globalization accelerates, they become increasingly dependent on Second Tier labor markets. Supply dependencies extend far beyond the well-publicized need for petroleum to include more than two dozen strategic materials without which a modern industrial economy cannot operate. (See, for example, the discussion in Chapter 9 of the political lengths to which the United States was driven during the 1970s by its need for chromium ore.) In coming decades these greater First Tier dependencies may give increasing political and economic leverage to Second Tier states seeking the wherewithal to accelerate their own development. Provided that neo-isolationist views do not prevail in the United States and cause us to ignore development needs around the world, this may substantially shift prevailing views of what types and amounts of development assistance are appropriate.

SUMMARY

This chapter covers issues the United States faces primarily in its dealings with developing states and other actors interested in development and is organized according to the five sectors of geopolitical, military, economic, societal, and environmental contexts of U.S. foreign policy in the post–Cold War era. According to the definitions introduced in Chapter 13, the Second Tier consists of World Bank low-income and lower-middle-income states, an extremely diverse group. Although some members of this group were developing rapidly by the 1990s, the Second Tier as a whole is becoming richer more slowly than the First Tier. Most analysts see this, in itself, as a problem for the entire world.

The United States today and in the future faces quite different policy issues with Second Tier states than First Tier states, even though almost all our foreign relations have been profoundly affected by post–Cold War changes in the global policy environment. Through at least the early years of the twenty-first century most of the world's violence likely will continue to occur within and between Second Tier states. In the longer term, there are concerns about preventing the development of weapons of mass destruction by the more ambitious Second Tier states. Issues about encouraging, supporting, protecting, and restoring democracy arise far more frequently in the Second Tier than the First. Economic issues more often involve aid than competition, although not in every case over the long term. Societal issues for the United States and other First Tier powers include the impacts and control of immigration, and for Second Tier states they include national divisions and the societal impacts of foreign penetration and development. Environmental issues center on sustainable development and appropriate types and amounts of aid from the developed world. Profound differences and incompatibilities of interests are perceived in many activity sectors between the developed First Tier North and the developing Second Tier South, as illustrated by the clear policy rift evident at the 1997 Kyoto global warming summit (see Chapter 12).

Focus cases given extended treatment in this chapter include dealing with Iraqi weapons of mass destruction after the Persian Gulf War, new internal war and peacekeeping in Bosnia, the potential rise of China to superpower status, illegal immigration, and sustainable development. The Gulf War case illustrates how long-term political defeat may be snatched from the jaws of military victory. The coalition obtained an unprecedentedly strict set of UN sanctions including a special commission (UNSCOM) empowered to supervise and verify Iraq's destruction of weapons of mass destruction and programs for their development and manufacture, but that effort had been brought to a standstill by the end of 1998. UNSCOM inspectors always had to rely on a certain degree of Iraqi tolerance, and cooperation was grudging at best. Beginning in October 1997, Iraqi authorities stepped up their noncompliance with UNSCOM inspections, first barring American inspectors, and later barring any inspections of new suspected weapons sites. Neither the United States nor any other state contributing weapons inspectors to UNSCOM had many credible and reasonable options to force Iraqi compliance, particularly in the short run. Congressional calls for bombing missed the point that punishment raids could not apply the sort of force needed to get the inspectors into Iraq and then into the various sites they needed to examine. By 1999, UNSCOM inspectors were out of Iraq, the U.S. had settled for air strikes to limit Iraq's weapons capabilities, and nobody expected an UNSCOM return to Iraq. In the long term, Iraq threatens the rest of the world not only by likely building NBC weapons of mass destruction, but by undermining the promise of a more effective United Nations and more stringent international behavior norms for the future.

U.S. involvement in peacekeeping and peacemaking in Bosnia under the terms of the 1995 Dayton peace accords clearly exemplifies the problems of new internal war. This wave of post–Cold War conflicts within Second Tier states lacks the ideological component and East-versus-West political polarization common to most civil wars during the Cold War. Although primarily military, new internal war is also about societal and political security, as are peacemaking and nation building. Unfortunately, military interventions often halt violence without addressing the underlying causes of what actually are two-level conflicts. Regrettably, Bosnia appears to be typical of the new internal wars we should expect for the indefinite future. Optimists suggest that increasing economic returns to scale will help convince combatants that peace is far more profitable than war. Pessimists fear that the victims of new internal war will drop off the edges of world political and economic maps. Experience in Bosnia through the latter 1990s offers little hope that more effective means of resolving new internal wars will be devised soon.

China has become a major market for and supplier to the United States, but also threatens to become a major competitor economically and perhaps militarily. China's sheer size gives international meaning to issues that would pass with much less notice in any other state, including human rights issues such as the imprisonment of political dissidents and the exploitation of prison labor to manufacture export goods. Moreover, by the latter 1990s, many observers began to discern a new Chinese movement to develop a serious capability for military force projection abroad, which potentially could make China a regional hegemon or even a global power. The extremes of possible U.S. overall policies toward China, which would impact economics, human rights, military strength, and global standing, are encapsulated in the terms *containment* and *engagement*. Many issues with China occur in less intense form with other, smaller powers, and likely will be encountered around the globe.

The United States has a long, complex, and troubled history regarding immigration, which is a societal security concern because it influences the living and working conditions of immigrants and citizens, as well as the overall cultural, ethnic, and racial composition of American society. Welcoming huge numbers of immigrants made obvious sense while the United States was an infant state and through the period of westward expansion, consolidation, and industrialization, but the ability of a mature economy to absorb such numbers is questionable. Particular concerns have been raised over the impact and potential control of illegal immigration. Possible actions to control illegal immigration range between absolute enforcement of borders and entrance laws to declaring open borders and immigration, but most analysts consider the former extreme impossible and the latter undesirable. Lasting and comprehensive solutions are nowhere in sight.

Although it has important implications for economic and societal security around the world, sustainable development clearly is an environmental security concern, especially for Second Tier states and for their most likely benefactors, the United States and other highly developed First Tier states. Sustainable development may be viewed from any of three major competing ideal types or stereotypes: (1) the economists' view, held by free market advocates; (2) the biologists' view, held by ecological-science advocates; and (3) the philosophers' view, held by deep ecologists. One possible resolution of the tremendous differences between these approaches is the increasingly frequent distinction between *growth* and *development*, seeking to reconcile (1) the desire to express human freedom through continual change or improvement with (2) the understanding that natural, physical systems impose real limits on economic growth. For the United States, sustainable development is a core issue in future development policy, and challenges many of the approaches we have used in the past, discussed in Chapter 13.

KEY TERMS

Carrying capacity	New internal wars
Engagement	Rule of law
Externalities	Sustainable development

SELECTED READINGS

Carment, David, and James, P. eds., 1997. *Wars in the Midst of Peace: The International Politics of Ethnic Conflict.* Pittsburgh, Penn.: University of Pittsburgh Press.

De la Garza, Rodolfo O. 1987. "U.S. Foreign Policy and the Mexican-American Political Agenda." In Mohammed E. Ahari, ed., *Ethnic Groups and U.S. Foreign Policy.* New York: Greenwood Press.

Isbister, John. 1998. *Promises Not Kept: The Betrayal of Social Change in the Third World*, 4th ed. West Hartford, Conn.: Kumarian Press.

Kamieniecki, Sheldon, George A. Gonzalez, and Robert O. Vos, eds. 1997. *Flashpoints in Environmental Policymaking: Controversies in Achieving Sustainability.* Albany: State University of New York Press. An excellent collection summarizing major issues regarding types of sustainability and how they might be achieved.

Moffett, George D. 1994. *Global Population Growth: 21st Century Challenges.* Headline Series 302 (Spring). New York: Foreign Policy Association.

Third World Quarterly. 1994. "The South in the New World (Dis)Order." Special Issue, 15 (March): 1–176.

CHAPTER 16

CROSS-TIER ISSUES

⊕ FACING THE CHALLENGE OF NEW NUCLEAR POWERS

On the afternoon of 11 May 1998, India exploded three nuclear devices underground at its Pokharan test site in the Thar Desert near the Pakistani border. With those blasts, the world's worries about nuclear arms proliferation took a quantum leap upward. Two more explosions at a nearby site followed on 13 May. Despite President Clinton's pleas for restraint, India's archenemy, Pakistan, responded with five underground nuclear tests on 28 May, and a sixth two days later. Twenty-four years earlier, in 1974, India had exploded one nuclear device underground. In a neat bit of casuistry, it was carefully labeled a "peaceful nuclear explosive," but its political-military significance was not lost on Pakistan, which turned during the 1980s to developing a countering "Islamic bomb." For decades, nuclear nonproliferation experts had considered India a "threshold state," a country that did not possess nuclear weapons but could produce them relatively quickly. When new Indian prime minister Atal Bihari Vajpayee assumed office in March 1998, he and his party promised to pursue a nuclear weapons program. Nonetheless, the May 1998 tests surprised most governments, including that of the United States. Subsequent reports indicated the Indians had worked hard to conceal their impending tests from U.S. spy satellites by moving people and equipment in and out of the test sites at night and conspicuously preparing for missile tests on the other side of the country to divert attention from the Thar Desert. This was a distinct American intelligence failure.

For the United States and the world, the May 1998 tests raised the specter of a nuclear arms race or war on the Indian subcontinent. Indeed, within weeks both sides were engaged in artillery duels over the disputed Kashmir region, over which they previously had fought several wars. Worse yet, the tests raised worries about whether other threshold states would be encouraged to follow India's and Pakistan's examples, and whether more than thirty years of global efforts to limit nuclear proliferation might be undone. Vertical nuclear proliferation, or growth in the sizes of existing nuclear arsenals, long has been almost universally seen as bad. With the end of the Cold War came real reductions in U.S. and Russian nuclear arsenals during the 1990s, so that vertical proliferation by the greatest nuclear powers no longer seemed likely. Horizontal nuclear proliferation, or the spread of nuclear capability to additional states (or, worse yet, nonstate actors) appears much more serious. Moreover, it raises the prospect that the long established middle-range nuclear powers, Britain, China, and France, might feel compelled to increase their arsenals to compensate for the new capabilities of regional nuclear powers such as India and Pakistan. Finally, any horizontal proliferation threatens to encourage more, particularly by rogue states such as Libya, Iran, Iraq, and North Korea.

The centerpiece of world efforts to control nuclear proliferation for more than thirty years was the **Nuclear Nonproliferation Treaty** of 1968, or **NPT.** Strongly promoted at the outset by Britain, the Soviet Union, and the United States, the NPT is highly unusual because it permanently divides the world into two classes of sovereignties. Acknowledged nuclear weapons states (the United States, Russia, Britain, France, and China, in the order they gained nuclear capability) promise not to support horizontal proliferation in any way, directly or indirectly, and to work toward their own nuclear disarmament. Non-nuclear weapons states promise not to acquire nuclear weapons directly or indirectly, although peaceful nuclear activities such as power plants and research reactors are allowed. The NPT was opened for signature on 1 July 1968, when the three promoters and 59 other governments signed. By 1998 over 180 non-nuclear weapons states were parties to the NPT. China and France did not join until 1992. In 1996 Belarus joined Ukraine and Kazakhstan in removing the last former Soviet nuclear weapons from their territories, transferring them to the Russian Federation, and joining the NPT as non-nuclear weapons states. Brazil, a state long thought to have a nuclear program, signed in 1997. More than 170 governments sent representatives to the 1995 NPT Review and Extension Conference in New York, and in a major foreign policy win for the United States, extended the NPT indefinitely and without conditions (Fellowship of American Scientists, 1998a, 1998b).

As with other common pools, the NPT has faced the problem of nonsignatory defectors or holdouts. Admitted nuclear powers China and France waited more than two decades before signing, saying they needed additional nuclear tests to avoid being relegated to permanent second-class status. Israel, India, and Pakistan have never joined the NPT. Israel, widely believed since 1975 to have up to several hundred nuclear weapons, has neither admitted its possession nor signed the NPT, although it did sign the Limited Nuclear Test Ban Treaty of 1963. Arguably, this is an ideal foreign policy position for Israel, since it obtains the benefits of nuclear deterrence against its enemies, without formally admitting to having developed weapons of mass destruction. One issue at the 1995 NPT Review and Extension Conference was whether the nuclear weapons states had done enough toward disarmament, although that concern had lost potency after real U.S. and Russian nuclear reductions began. Another issue was whether Israel should be required to join, presumably under U.S. pressure, for the NPT to be continued. However, it is doubtful whether the United States could compel Israeli compliance and nuclear disarmament, and perhaps it is questionable whether we would wish to do so.

By the time of the 1995 conference, India was asking for some new formulation that would bring the three "de facto nuclear" powers, Israel, India, and Pakistan, under the NPT framework. Amending the treaty to declare them full-status nuclear weapons states would only reward their having held out, and could encourage other holdouts and weaken any future international efforts to pressure holdouts to accede to the NPT. Instead, some authorities proposed building a new "nuclear restraint regime" outside the NPT that would not "discriminate" against India and other non-NPT nuclear weapons states. This might be done through such mechanisms as (1) a universal inspection and verification regime for all nuclear installations, similar to procedures under the Chemical Weapons

Convention; (2) prohibiting all future manufacture of nuclear weapons; and (3) imposing a comprehensive ban on all nuclear tests. (See, e.g., Subramanyam, 1993.) Of course, no inspection and verification program is entirely free of loopholes, as we already have seen in Iraq.

India's and Pakistan's 1998 tests represented the most serious horizontal nuclear proliferation yet seen. Beyond the threat that it would encourage additional states to go nuclear lurked the threat of international nuclear terrorism. The bottleneck to building nuclear devices has always been obtaining enough fissionable nuclear material. Just knowing that nuclear bombs work is virtually half of what one needs to know to design one, and important details of at least primitive nuclear weapons have long been available in print. Numerous authorities agree that a competent graduate student in physics could design a nuclear bomb that would explode. By the early 1960s, specialists argued that perhaps ten states could build nuclear devices within three years if they launched crash programs, and up to thirty states could within a decade. Given these predictions, international efforts to limit horizontal nuclear proliferation must be seen as fairly successful to date. After the breakup of the Soviet Union, many experts feared the leakage of nuclear technology and materials from former Soviet republics or even the theft or sale of complete tactical nuclear weapons. Although there has been some success in forging international agreements to prevent such transfers, any horizontal proliferation only multiplies the number of points from which leakage could occur. Horizontal nuclear proliferation thus poses several interrelated problems for the United States and the world: limiting further proliferation; preventing regional nuclear wars or even attacks on greater powers; and preventing the spread of nuclear capabilities to international political terrorists.

Another major problem is technology and equipment transfers that facilitate the eventual undermining of the treaty by encouraging the spread of nuclear manufacturing capabilities. In 1981, Israel mounted a precision bombing attack that destroyed a French nuclear reactor under construction at Osirak, Iraq. Had it been completed, that reactor would have been capable of enriching uranium to produce plutonium for nuclear bombs. Given information about the breadth and depth of Iraq's nuclear weapons program uncovered by UN arms inspectors after the Persian Gulf War, the Osirak reactor appears even more ominous, and we well may see the Israeli attack as a humanitarian act. Why, then, did the French government ever agree to the reactor sale? It comes down to money, and the political favor of a major Arab oil exporter.

Although the United States is not without options to act alone, nuclear proliferation problems are more likely to yield to cooperative cross-tier efforts, carried out with the help of other First Tier powers, especially those that are NPT nuclear weapon states. India's and Pakistan's tests notwithstanding, diplomacy as expressed in the NPT has been moderately effective for more than thirty years. There is no confirmed instance of a signatory government transferring nuclear weapons technology or unsafeguarded nuclear materials to non-nuclear weapons states. However, some non-nuclear weapons states, such as Iraq, have been able to obtain sensitive technology and equipment from private parties in signatory states. Under the Nuclear Proliferation Prevention Act, signed by President Clinton in 1994, severe economic sanctions must be imposed on any previously undeclared nuclear state that conducts nuclear tests. The act requires that within thirty days nearly all aid be suspended, U.S. banks be prohibited from making loans to the offending government, and the U.S. government oppose aid from the World Bank and the

NewsToons

CARTOON 16.1

During the early Cold War years, "duck and cover" drills were commonplace in U.S. schools. Although such nuclear safety drills are not practiced today, major worries continue into the twenty-first century about attacks from emerging powers and rogue states that can or will control missile systems and weapons of mass destruction.

Reprinted with special permission of King Features Syndicate.

International Monetary Fund (IMF). This last condition could be particularly onerous for India, the World Bank's largest borrower. Yet both India and Pakistan appeared to have anticipated and discounted such sanctions. Bringing them into the NPT regime in the ways suggested here seems rather unlikely, given widespread fears that doing so would create a precedent for similar demands from other holdout powers. It seems wildly unlikely either that the United States would act militarily against Indian and Pakistani nuclear facilities or that other states would join in imposing nuclear inspection measures of the type ordered by the UN against Iraq after the Persian Gulf War.

Once the knowledge base, resources, manufacturing facilities, and development work for nuclear weapons have been brought together, it is almost impossible to stuff the nuclear genie back into the bottle. Prime Minister Vajpayee announced that one of India's tests involved a thermonuclear device (hydrogen bomb). Experts stated that both state's tests appeared to place them close to having "weaponized" nuclear devices capable of being mounted as warheads on their ballistic missiles, already tested to ranges nearing 1,000 miles. Thus India's and Pakistan's nuclear status appears to be a fait accompli. If so, the United States and other NPT adherents might best concentrate on preventing regional nuclear wars and on limiting further proliferation to additional states and the leakage of nuclear materials and technology to terrorists. One way to accomplish those goals would be to share technologies, highly developed over decades of Cold War by the United States and USSR, for safeguarding nuclear weapons to prevent theft or unauthorized use. Horizontal nuclear proliferation is not a problem for which we have many good policy options, and it threatens to extend to additional states and even nonstate actors in the future.

SOLVING CROSS-TIER PROBLEMS

This chapter is devoted to issues that bridge between the First and Second Tiers either by unavoidably involving the entire world or by linking powerful and influential developed states to less powerful and less influential developing states. The profound post–Cold War changes in the global policy environment have led to many new cross-tier problems, by removing the former focus on U.S.-Soviet confrontation and increasing the numbers of significant independent states in each tier. Solving cross-tier problems requires the United States to interact with states in both the First and Second Tiers. Among the many such problems are arms control focused on conventional (non-nuclear) weapons and of NBC (nuclear, biological, and chemical) weapons of mass destruction, local and regional peacekeeping, most global environmental problems, ensuring needed resource supplies while minimizing the effects of their unequal distribution around the planet, and promoting the most appropriate technologies to simultaneously maximize economic development while minimizing environmental impact. Issues examined in this chapter are summarized in Table 16.1 and organized according to the five activity sectors of geopolitical, military, economic, societal, and environmental contexts of U.S. foreign policy in the post–Cold War era. Focus cases typical of each sector are examined in some detail. The shading of the cell for environmental issues reflects the fact that, although this area is not as traditionally primary to U.S. foreign policy as geopolitical, military, and economic issues with First Tier states (see Tables P4.1 or 14.1), it already was receiving increasingly serious attention by the 1990s.

In Chapters 14 and 15 we argued that the United States today and in the future faces quite different policy issues with First Tier states than Second Tier states. Some cross-tier problems addressed in this chapter involve U.S. interactions with states from both groups, and the remainder require joint action with other First Tier states to deal effectively with problems in the Second Tier. Many environmental issues, like global warming, occur in common pools connecting rich and poor states in ways that require common action if any solutions are to be found. Dealing with the threat of terrorism, whether by conventional means or by weapons of mass destruction, is a cross-tier problem because both great and small states may be targets. The same is true of rising Islamic radicalism. Problems that are sufficiently widespread and require massive resources to resolve are much more likely to yield to joint action with other First Tier states than to unilateral American initiatives. Examples include worldwide promotion of democracy, market economies, and economic development.

ARCHETYPAL FOCUS CASES

We examine five focus cases in this chapter according to the five-point framework used earlier: stakes at issue, relevant U.S. policy themes, perceptions held by other actors and

TABLE 16.1	*U.S. Foreign Policy Concerns That Cross the Tiers* *(Classified by Issue Sectors)*

Note: Boldfaced issues are archetypal focus cases given extended treatment.
Shaded areas denote traditional areas of primary U.S. concern.

Sector	Contemporary and Foreseeable Policy Issues	
Geopolitical	**Promoting Democracy and Human Rights** Does democracy promote peace? Resource supply and distribution	Relations with Russia and Eastern Europe Islamic radicalism Korean security and unification
Military	**Middle East Peace** Arms Control (e.g., land mines, nuclear proliferation, chemical weapons, comprehensive nuclear test ban)	Terrorism (esp. nuclear, biological, chemical) Helping failed states
Economic	**Promoting Development (See also Chapter 13)**	Do market economies promote the right types of development?
Societal	**Humanitarian Political Asylum**	
Environmental	**Global Warming (See also Chapter 12)** Distributing solution costs Species extinctions	Deforestation (also linked to global warming)

their relations with the United States, available alternative actions and policy tools, and future prospects and concerns. Cases given extended treatment in this chapter include the following:

- In the *geopolitical sector*, the United States and its major developed allies have yet to agree on how, and how vigorously, to promote the spread of democratic governance, market economies, and economic development. These concerns are central to American political theory and ideology. Yet they are notoriously difficult to implement and often are subjugated to narrower and shorter term interests.

- In the *military sector*, regional peacemaking that links between the tiers is most notably seen in the still unsettled Middle East. Such regional peacemaking was motivated during the Cold War by fears that regional fighting would escalate into superpower war. Today's motivations are less self-interested and therefore more difficult to sell.

- In the *economic sector*, many issues remain unresolved about how best to promote development, using appropriate mixes of the strategies sketched in Chapter 13.

Questions persist about whether market economics, despite its global political ascendancy during the 1990s, promotes forms of development that are best for Second Tier states.

- In the *societal sector*, calls for political and economic asylum have continued or increased since the end of the Cold War. Driving forces have included new internal wars and dislocations caused by economic globalization.

- In the *environmental sector*, intense and long-lasting global issues occur in common pools that link all states. Biophysical systems link global warming, as discussed in Chapter 12, to deforestation and species extinctions.

Some additional contemporary and foreseeable issues are discussed following the geopolitical, military, and environmental focus cases.

GEOPOLITICAL SECTOR FOCUS CASE: PROMOTING DEMOCRACY AND HUMAN RIGHTS

The troubling case of slow but ultimately effective U.S. action to restore Haiti's first democratically elected president to power was explored in the introduction to Chapter 15. Taken under UN auspices, that action stretched out over three years following the 1991 military coup which ousted President Jean Bertrand Aristide. Haiti exemplifies an important class of political problems likely to confront the United States and other First Tier powers fairly frequently in their dealings with developing states. It does not bode well either for future efforts to succor fledgling democracies or for assigning such efforts high priority in post–Cold War U.S. foreign policy. The broad policy decision to be made is how widely and strongly we will promote democracy and human rights abroad. Action in Haiti clearly received much lower priority than did the Persian Gulf War, which ended only six months before the coup.

STAKES AT ISSUE

Analysts including policymakers and commentators have argued that the United States should support transitions to democracy worldwide in order to help create a world that is more peaceful and more compatible with U.S. values. In that world, the likelihood of political stability is increased, support for market economics enhances the prospects for development, and basic human rights are more widely respected and guaranteed. These goals would receive high political priority under American democratic and economic theory. They also are supported by the **democratic peace hypothesis,** the widely supported belief that democracies rarely go to war against one another. Thus, promoting the spread of democracy around the globe ostensibly would produce a more peaceful world. Promoting democracy is also supported by realist political perspectives, at least where stability is concerned. In each instance, however, democracy is an intermediary goal to be pursued because of its anticipated end results. Some analysts, such as Robert L. Rothstein (1991), have challenged whether the democratic peace hypothesis is likely to apply as well to Second Tier states as it does to the First Tier. His argument challenges those who would extend the notion that democracies tend not to fight each other beyond a world in which the majority of the democracies are developed states to a potentially evolving world of mostly democracies, many of which will be weak and potentially unstable. Many Second Tier states have considerably greater restrictions on individual liberties and greater freedoms for ruling elites, making the choice of war easier. Economic resource issues may be more intense and help stimulate war, particularly if resource bases are eroding. Finally, democratic procedures may make internal conflict easier in highly polarized societies.

RELEVANT U.S. POLICY THEMES

U.S. promotion of democracy abroad has been the subject of an intense debate about post–Cold War foreign policy. (See, for example, Diamond, 1992.) During the Cold War, the United States often supported authoritarian regimes because they claimed to be anticommunist (i.e., the enemy of my enemy is my friend, or he's an SOB, but he's *our* SOB) or out of a belief that economic development would lead to later political development, and that authoritarians could better enforce the sacrifices needed to push their societies to the takeoff stage. Today, neither rationale makes great sense. Additionally, some analysts have suggested it can be ineffective to support transitions to democracy if we do not also provide substantial financial and other development assistance to the often weak and heavily burdened fledgling democracies. Thus support for the spread of democracy may become closely linked with economic development policy. (See Chapter 13 and the economic sector focus case later.)

PERCEPTIONS HELD BY OTHER ACTORS AND THEIR RELATIONS WITH THE UNITED STATES

Although Second Tier states are extremely diverse, relatively few would turn down every type of development assistance. (See Chapter 13 for discussion of the many types possible.) Although the latter 1990s saw some severe international economic upheavals, the considerable majority of Second Tier states appeared to have embraced market economics. Whether they were nearly as wedded to American notions of democratic governance, and just how we might best promote such governance, was more problematic.

AVAILABLE ALTERNATIVE ACTIONS AND POLICY TOOLS

What, then, is to be done? Many studies of opinions held by the general public (hereafter, GP) and by policy-making and opinion-leading elites (EL), such as the quadrennial surveys conducted for the Chicago Council on Foreign Relations (CCFR), find relatively little enthusiasm for promoting the spread of democracy and human rights. Of even greater concern is the fact that they show diminishing support since the end of the Cold War. Consider some possible U.S. foreign policy goals, which CCFR respondents were asked to rate as "very important," "somewhat important," or "not important." Asked about *"helping to bring a democratic form of government to other nations,"* over the full 1974–1998 span of the CCFR surveys elites have lower percentages than the general public rating the promotion of democracy as "very important" and as "not important." The consistent tendency of elites has been toward consensus on the middle option of "somewhat important." Similarly, both groups register significant declines from 1990 to 1994 in support of "*promoting and defending human rights in other countries,*" with support rebounding only slightly in 1998. GP support for this as a "very important" goal peaked in 1990, probably as an artifact of the Bush administration's campaign to use the Iraqi regime's well-documented human rights abuses to justify the Persian Gulf War.

FUTURE PROSPECTS AND CONCERNS

Taken as a group, the patterns of both elite and general public responses to these potential foreign policy goals do not bode well for the Clinton administration's attempt to promote a new grand policy of enlargement, under which the United States would seek to expand the number of states with democratic governments and market economies (see the opening case in Chapter 13). Announced in a coordinated series of public speeches by President Clinton and three of his top foreign policy advisers in September 1993, enlargement policy envisioned four components, including strengthening core states, fostering new democracies and market economies, isolating "backlash" (rogue or pariah) states, and pursuing a humanitarian agenda (Lowenthal, 1993). The CCFR survey results amply demonstrate that the administration has been unsuccessful in selling this new post–Cold War foreign policy agenda either to elites or to the general public. Little can be found since the 1993 speeches to demonstrate any serious attempt by the administration to promote a coherent and consistent global policy of promoting democracy and human rights, although the stakes remain high in both the short and long terms. If that consistent policy is to be adopted, the debate will have to be taken up again.

Other Geopolitical Issues

The grandest geopolitical issues as we move beyond the Cold War era well may be clashes between the forces of integration and disintegration. This is equally true at state, regional, and global levels. First Tier and Second Tier states, along with other actors, are linked in ways that make it difficult for the United States to act alone, if it is to act at all. Within many contemporary states, integrative forces such as outside pressures to join in economic globalization clash with internal disintegrative forces. A disruptive international environment frequently produces appeals to ethnic and nationalistic identifications, which can lead to new internal wars as we discussed in the military sector focus case of Chapter 15. Often, as seen early in Bosnia, no single First Tier state is willing or able to take effective action. Thus far, no adequate international regime capable of managing such conflicts exists. Although freed from Cold War East-West polarization, UN responses to new internal wars always are ad hoc. The world body lacks any standing peace force, and demand for peacekeeping, peacemaking, and so on, exceeds supply. When the United States decides to act, it must lead and recruit assistance, as with NATO in Bosnia. Similar limitations affect global capabilities to maintain regional peace and security, as seen when ethnic violence spread in waves through Rwanda, Burundi, and Zaire in 1994–97. Only in some regions, such as the European Union, did the forces of integration appear be to winning over the forces of disintegration as the twentieth century wound toward its close.

The contest between integrative and disintegrative forces takes on additional facets at the global level. To the problems of dealing with struggles in multiple regions are added the problems of coordinating—or simply being able to undertake—simultaneous action in many places. With thirty-five to forty new internal wars underway in any given year during the 1990s, the United States is unlikely to act alone in more than a few situations. Practical political decisions usually reduce to which cases demand collective action, let alone U.S. unilateral involvement. Inaction may be excused on the grounds that no crucial U.S. interests are involved and others do the short-term suffering. Nonetheless, inaction is unfortunate for the United States in at least the medium and long term, beyond the notion that peace is desirable on humanitarian grounds and because of the democratic peace hypothesis. Still, it usually is difficult to encourage new democratic institutions in any state or region currently at war.

The nurturing of democracy in Russia and the other republics of the former Soviet Union is particularly critical and intimately connected with their difficult and fitful conversions to market economies. Russia's only pre-1991 experience with democratic governance involved less than eight months of experimentation after the czar's overthrow in 1917. Although Soviet economic restructuring began in the latter 1980s under Gorbachev, conversion from more than seventy years of centrally dictated command economics has been difficult. Many members of the old communist elite profited handsomely as state enterprises were sold off while ordinary Russians suffered major declines in their standards of living. As Russians struggled to reorganize enterprises to make them competitive in a market economy, some struggled to make ends meet; others became fabulously rich. At various times during the 1990s, major groups including coal miners and soldiers threatened strikes if their months-delayed wages were not paid. Tax collections lagged while a new mafia grew to shake down merchants who prospered in the new free markets. By 1997, however, some signs of growing stability could be discerned. *Forbes* magazine reported that 5 of the world's 500 richest people live in Moscow. Massive capital exports since 1991 had begun to reverse, with Switzerland becoming the leading foreign investor state in Russia (Powell and Matthews, 1997). The summer of 1998, however, saw massive economic upheavals in Russia.

The eventual fate of democracy and market economics in Russia, exceedingly important to the United States and at least the rest of the First Tier states, is unlikely to be solved by America alone. Russia's importance is reflected in such political signals as acceptance into the G-8 despite economic troubles, as we discussed in the economic sector focus case of Chapter 14. It may also be discerned in the great attention paid by top NATO and Clinton administration officials, all the way up to the president, to Russian unhappiness about NATO's eastward expansion. Nonetheless, President Clinton apparently decided that NATO expansion would go forward regardless of Russian opposition because Russia was not powerful enough to stop it; see the geopolitical sector focus case of Chapter 14 for discussion of other reasons behind that action. The Russian Federation remains the world's largest state, roughly comparable to the United States in nuclear power and blessed with abundant natural resources. It possesses a skilled and educated population nearly 60 percent as large as the U.S. population, plus the political cachet of having been near the pinnacle of world power throughout the Cold War.

Compared to the optimism immediately following the demise of the Soviet Union, Western expectations about future relations with Russia were notably muted by the latter 1990s. Barely three months after the Soviet breakup, the G-7 announced a one-year $24 billion program of aid, including $4.5 billion from the United States (Rosenthal, 1992). More quietly but perhaps more importantly, the United States set up a half-billion-dollar program to help keep former Russian nuclear scientists gainfully employed and reduce their temptations to take on building weapons of mass destruction for rogue states like Iran, Iraq, or Libya.

Yet by the mid-1990s, as Boris Yeltsin's presidency and democratic governance appeared ever more threatened, Russia's internal power struggle began to take precedence over cooperation with the United States. Conservatives and ultranationalists played to public discontent over the dislocations of economic conversion by preaching the retaking of the Russian "near abroad" and restoration of great power status. On 15 March 1996 the Duma, lower house of the Russian parliament, cast a nonbinding vote calling for reconstituting the USSR and branding the actions of Yeltsin and others to disband the USSR illegal. Signals were mixed, however. Over the first weekend of that same March, Russia became the fifteenth state of Eastern Europe or the former USSR to join the Council of Europe, which required acceding to the Universal Declaration on Human Rights. We should anticipate that relations with Russia will continue to be important, demanding, challenging, and subject to intense political infighting and rapid event swings.

Islamic radicalism grew rapidly enough during the 1990s to be considered a major geopolitical movement both in its global distribution—from the Afghanistan in the east, across the Persian Gulf states and Middle East, and through North Africa to the west—and in the profound political shifts sought. Although there are important state-to-state differences, political radicals who claim to find their answers in Islam generally seek to establish truly Islamic governments under Koranic law, end rule by leaders they consider corrupt, unjust, and "unislamic," and eliminate foreign—especially American—interests and influence. Islamists present several different faces, and no individual presents all of them. Religious Islamists seek to make society more "just," as they define just, through personal piety, prayer, preaching, and conformance to Islamic law as set out in their holy book, the Koran. Reformist Islamists seek to use democratic, electoral means to change state and society from within. If elected, however, many then would deny rights and freedoms seen as conflicting with the Koran. Extremist Islamists believe that only violent confrontation and destruction of existing states can establish a new Islamic world order.

Part of the impetus for the Islamist movement may arise from the same individual search for stable sources of societal and political value that leads people in failed states to turn to ethnic and nationalistic self-identifications. Reaction to external political and economic pressures, such as those imposed by economic globalization, provides additional impetus. Islamist anger is particularly easy to focus on the United States and other First Tier states because they lead the global political and economic movements that evoke considerable fear among Second Tier states. Finally, America's long support of Israel plays into the hands of Islamic radicals, particularly when Middle East peace processes show little progress. As the twenty-first century approached, the Islamist movement showed far more signs of strengthening than of weakening. It remained a problem for many First Tier states and other actors, notably including multinational corporations, and few effective solutions appeared to be in the offing.

Korea remained an important flashpoint for global politics in the 1990s. The peninsula's arbitrary division at the 38th parallel by the victorious Allies in 1945 led to prolonged contention between the communist North and capitalist (and often only nominally democratic) South. By the latter 1990s there still was no peace treaty after the devastating 1950–53 war. Tensions rose and fell severely along the tense demilitarized zone, ugly military incidents occurred sporadically, and North Korea remained perhaps the contemporary world's most truly isolated state. When the North Korean government threatened to terminate International Atomic Energy Agency (IAEA) inspections under the Nuclear Nonproliferation Treaty, fears of a nuclear weapons program soared. With much uneasiness, a solution was developed to restore inspections and provide the North Koreans with new nuclear reactors less capable of making weapons-grade fissionable materials. At the same time, international food aid programs were arranged to help alleviate widespread famine brought about by a combination of multiple natural disasters and chronic poor management. All these programs went forward in an extremely tense atmosphere, with much fear and bad feeling on both sides. Nonetheless, there appears to be a widespread Korean desire for eventual reunification, founded in shared nationality no doubt as strongly felt as that in divided Germany during the Cold War, and some tentative reunification talks have occurred. In the terminology of Chapter 10, these have been stage 1 contacts, very preliminary talks about holding more serious negotiations. Optimists hope that food aid, together with economic and energy assistance, will stimulate more cooperation and further moves toward unification. Nonetheless, many analysts continue to fear that the Korean peninsula poses a greater danger than almost any other region of stimulating a new regional war.

MILITARY SECTOR FOCUS CASE: MIDDLE EAST PEACE

The Middle East comprises the states of Southwest Asia and Northeast Africa that lie west of Afghanistan, Pakistan, and India. Thus defined, it includes Cyprus, the Asian part of Turkey, Syria, Israel, Jordan, Iraq, Iran, Lebanon, the states of the Arabian Peninsula (Saudi Arabia, Yemen, Oman, the United Arab Emirates, Qatar, and Bahrain), and Kuwait and Libya. Some analysts use the term culturally to include the group of predominantly Islamic states in that region, which adds Afghanistan and Pakistan plus the remaining North African states (Tunisia, Algeria, and Morocco). The history of this vast region goes back thousands of years, and many authorities believe the earliest human civilizations arose there. Throughout the millennia, wars and other conflicts have swept over it, scattered and regrouped its nations, reorganized alliances, and redrawn the borders of its states. Today it remains divided by manifold economic, political, and religious fault lines across which violence still flares periodically. The Persian Gulf War of 1990–91, examined in some detail in Chapter 1, was a classic geopolitical war for treasure and influence. Religious conflicts include the divide between Sunni Muslims, such as those who control the holiest places of Islam (Mecca and Medina in Saudi Arabia), and Shiite Muslims (as in Iran). Typically, the Shiites are more aggressively religious and more likely to promote movements toward rule under Islamic law, as discussed earlier. Conflicts and potential conflicts dividing the Middle East—almost all of which have some repercussions for the United States—are diverse and numerous enough to make us wonder whether the phrase "Middle East peace" is an oxymoron.

   The Middle East conflict most likely to come to most minds in the United States, Europe, and the Middle East itself, undoubtedly is the long-running dispute between Israel and its Arab neighbors, particularly the Palestinian Arabs. They are divided by religion, nationhood, and territorial claims going back thousands of years. We can identify a Jewish nation dispersed around the world centuries before the establishment of the modern state of Israel in 1948, and a dispersed Palestinian Arab nation that claims rights to much of the same territory as Israel and may yet achieve some form of statehood with sovereignty over the West Bank and Gaza.

The most important roots of the contemporary conflict trace to the early part of the twentieth century. After some four centuries of Ottoman rule, Britain took Palestine in 1917. In the Balfour Declaration of that year, Britain promised to support a Jewish national homeland in Palestine, as sought by the Zionist movement dedicated to restoring the Jewish state that had flourished there two to three thousand years earlier. A British Palestine Mandate was recognized in 1920, and the land east of the Jordan River was detached in 1922. Jewish immigration had begun late in the nineteenth century and swelled in the 1930s with European refugees fleeing from the Nazis. Heavy Arab immigration from Syria and Lebanon also occurred during this period, and Arab opposition to Jewish immigration turned violent at several times during the 1920s and 1930s. As the liberation of Europe proceeded during the last years of World War II and the world learned about the horrors of the Holocaust, the Nazi program to exterminate the Jews and other racial minorities of Europe, refugee flows and pressures for a secure Jewish homeland grew. The UN General Assembly voted in 1947 to partition Palestine into an Arab and a Jewish state.

Britain withdrew from Palestine in May 1948, and Israel declared independence on 14 May 1948. The Arabs rejected partition, and Egypt, Iraq, Jordan, Lebanon, Syria, and Saudi Arabia invaded but failed to destroy the new Jewish state, which gained more territory than it lost. Separate armistices brokered by the UN were signed in 1949. Jordan occupied the West Bank and Egypt occupied Gaza, but neither granted Palestinian autonomy. The UN partition plan had failed, and the biggest losers were the Palestinians, who did not gain autonomy anywhere. Cynics argued that Arab governments were willing to exploit Palestinian grievances in their conflict with Israel, but not to cede any territory or power to them, preferring to keep many of them bottled up in enclaves like the Gaza Strip and the West Bank. Many Palestinians then became members of a nation dispersed around their region and the world.

STAKES AT ISSUE

Although this case has a strong military component and already has involved several wars, its broader geopolitical aspects seriously impact U.S. relations throughout the region, and indirectly with Europe. (Recall extensive treatment of the 1973 Yom Kippur War in Chapter 15.) With the disappearance of Cold War fears that a war in the Middle East could escalate into direct U.S.-Soviet conflict, the major motivating factors behind continued active U.S. involvement in the region are de facto alliance with Israel, support for Israel's democracy despite its discrimination against Arabs, fear that general regional war could endanger oil supplies, and humanitarian desire to see peace in the long-troubled Middle East.

RELEVANT U.S. POLICY THEMES

The United States was an early and lasting supporter of Israel because of belief in the justice of the Zionist cause (especially after the Holocaust) and in Israel's democratic governance. Increasing American dependence on imported oil has been a powerful pressure toward seeking Mideast peace, and, in turn, has encouraged a more evenhanded approach toward the Arabs. There is also an important intermestic element at work. As we noted in Chapter 4, there are strong connections between the facts that (1) U.S. policy has long been dominantly pro-Israel in Middle East conflicts, (2) there are far more Jews than Muslims among the American populace, and (3) Israel's leaders have learned effective ways to lobby the U.S. government directly and to enlist major American Jewish organizations in pressuring the U.S. government to support Israel's policies. Some analysts credit President Truman's prompt recognition of Israeli independence as a major factor in helping him win election in 1948.

PERCEPTIONS HELD BY OTHER ACTORS AND THEIR RELATIONS WITH THE UNITED STATES

Israel long has depended on strong U.S. financial and military aid and political support, but remains fiercely independent, frequently ignoring American wishes and political pressures. Arabs, and particularly Palestinians, long have faulted the United States for tilting toward Israel. Many other governments, including American friends in Europe, often have joined in those reproaches. Criticisms were somewhat reduced after the United States began pressuring Israel for a peace agreement, and the high point of American-Arab relations was reached in 1991, shortly after the Persian Gulf War. After Israeli prime minister Netanyahu was elected in 1996 and stalled the Israel-PLO peace process promised in the 1993 Oslo accords, U.S.-Arab relations deteriorated. By the latter 1990s, even moderate Arab regimes were again suspicious of the United States.

AVAILABLE ALTERNATIVE ACTIONS AND POLICY TOOLS

Israel's war of independence was followed by major wars with various groupings of its neighboring states, notably Egypt, Syria, and Jordan, in 1956, 1967 (the Six Day War), and 1973 (the Yom Kippur War). The last of these wars began to shift official U.S. thinking toward achieving some lasting regional settlement. The resulting process has been lengthy and difficult, filled with changing interpretations of U.S. evenhandedness. The United States brokered two partial Israeli withdrawals from the Sinai during Richard Nixon's presidency. Intensifying the momentum of the peace process, President Carter mediated the Camp David agreements that led to a formal peace treaty between Israel and Egypt, signed 26 March 1979 (see the introductory case in Chapter 10). Under those agreements, the rest of the Sinai was returned to Egypt in 1982, but Israeli-Egyptian relations still remained frosty through the 1990s. The Persian Gulf War significantly improved U.S. standing with Arab governments, which, coupled with improved U.S.-Soviet relations, helped make possible a joint U.S.-Soviet peace effort. Launched with a general conference in Madrid in 1991, that peace process has seen many fits and starts and has required continued U.S. promotion. Yet a major breakthrough with little U.S. input was achieved in 1993, with mutual recognition between Israel and the Palestine Liberation Organization and moves toward Palestinian self-rule in Jericho and the Gaza Strip (see the introductory case in Chapter 8). Important pressures encouraging that agreement included Israeli domestic politics, international problems of the PLO in the aftermath of their support for Iraq in the Persian Gulf War, and fear of the threat of rising Islamic fundamentalism.

FUTURE PROSPECTS AND CONCERNS

In the aftermath of Cold War, some analysts question how much more time and treasure the United States should commit to Middle East peace. The outlook after the signing of the Israeli-PLO accords in 1993 appeared more encouraging than in many years. Yet much of that momentum was lost over the next several years, driven by events such as the assassination of Israeli prime minister Yitzhak Rabin by a Jewish extremist on 4 November 1995, the election of conservative Likud Party politician Benjamin Netanyahu as prime minister in 1996, hard-line negotiating tactics, and the continued building of Jewish settlements in predominantly Arab areas. Netanyahu's election and some subsequent repressive Israeli moves were stimulated in part by suicide bombings in Jewish population centers by Palestinian extremists determined to sabotage the peace process. By 1997 the peace process seemed mired in stalemate and enmity. The depth of feeling and division of polities within the region was reflected in one survey reporting that 28 percent of Israeli youth believed that Rabin's assassination was correct. Netanyahu's defeat and Ehud Barak's election as prime minister in 1999 was hailed by Palestinians and peace-minded Israelis, but resulted partly from internal divisions between secular and religious Israelis.

In this situation, some observers have called for a hard-line U.S. approach to both sides, backed up by threats to withdraw political and financial support unless Israel moderates its stands on settlements and treatment of Arabs and the PLO acts effectively to curb extremist terrorism. Nonetheless, a continuing U.S. role seems likely, both as a facilitator of negotiations and as an international fund-raiser. Many hurdles remain before a comprehensive peace is achieved, and its accomplishment would send important signals around the world about the feasibility of resolving deep-seated and prolonged disputes elsewhere.

Other Military Issues

Military concerns that link between the tiers range from threats which could subject even the most powerful states to devastating attack, to optimistic developments suggesting we are moving toward a new world order in which many of the great threats of the Cold War years and the recent past will be brought under control. Notable threats include nuclear proliferation and terrorism involving weapons of mass destruction (WMD), that is, nuclear, biological, and chemical (NBC) weapons, particularly when combined with missiles or supersonic aircraft for medium- or long-range strike capability. So-called vertical nuclear proliferation, in which present nuclear powers acquire additional weapons, has been substantially reversed under the U.S.-Soviet and U.S.-Russian SALT and START agreements, as discussed in Chapter 15 and in the introductory case of this chapter. The greater global concern today is horizontal nuclear proliferation, in which additional states acquire nuclear weapons capabilities. Contemporary concerns about nuclear proliferation center on the WMD programs of rogue or pariah states believed willing to defy international behavior norms. Potential biological and chemical weapons capabilities only compound those fears. Iraq demonstrates the difficulties of controlling such weapons, as discussed in the geopolitical sector focus case of Chapter 15. Worse fears yet are evoked by the possibility of NBC terrorist attacks, sponsored either by rogue states or autonomous groups.

Biological and chemical weapons generate even greater worries than nuclear weapons, simply because they are far easier to make than nuclear devices. Such concerns were intensified after Iraq's 1997 expulsion of American personnel on the UNSCOM weapons inspection teams. Jonathan Alter (1997) quotes Daniel Goure, former Defense Department official and WMD expert, to the effect that "a two-bedroom apartment could take you through the whole process" of making poison gas, "from cooking up the stuff all the way to weaponization." He also notes that UNSCOM found more than a hundred anthrax bombs in Iraq in 1991, plus development programs for botulism and gas gangrene weapons. The root problem is that such weapons are far simpler and cheaper for rogue states or terrorist groups to develop and deliver than nuclear devices, even while most of the world is moving to ban and destroy such weapons.

Optimism in the military sector centers around arms control agreements, which have accelerated in pace and number and deepened in impact since the end of the Cold War. Such agreements are enormous and complex undertakings involving many actors, extending over decades, and subject to serious holdout problems. Scrupulous attention to agreed details and careful monitoring or "verification" of compliance are essential to ensuring long-term success and producing accurate forecasts for policy planning. Important arms control agreements and negotiations of the 1990s included the **Chemical Weapons Convention (CWC),** the **Comprehensive (nuclear) Test Ban Treaty (CTB),** and negotiations toward a worldwide ban on antipersonnel land mines. Agreeing to control most of these areas would have been unlikely during the Cold War, although agreement by today's major powers still does not solve the problem of holdout states.

The Convention on the Prohibition of the Development, Production, Stockpiling, and Use of Chemical Weapons and on Their Destruction, commonly known as the Chemical Weapons Convention, or CWC, was opened for signature in Paris on 13 January 1993, following negotiations that trace back to the UN Eighteen-Nation Committee on Disarmament in 1968. The United States signed immediately but did not ratify until the spring of 1997, mere days before the convention was scheduled to enter into force. Indeed, the potential political embarrassment of having the convention enter into force without U.S. ratification was used as an administration argument before the Senate. The CWC has been called the most comprehensive disarmament treaty ever negotiated. It calls for all "states parties" to destroy any existing stocks of chemical warfare agents within ten years and forgo all preparations for offensive chemical warfare, including in-kind deterrence and retaliation, subject to elaborate verification measures (SIPRI, 1997). Difficulties in defining chemical agents and anticipating future developments are solved by banning the general purposes for which chemical warfare agents might be employed.

Negotiations toward a Comprehensive (nuclear) Test Ban Treaty (CTB) trace back decades and were seriously proposed as early as the Carter administration in the latter 1970s. The Limited Nuclear Test Ban Treaty of 1963 already prohibited all nuclear explosions on land, at sea, in the air, and in outer space. Only underground tests were allowed, and their sizes were later restricted. Banning all nuclear tests is intended both to limit future qualitative improvements in weapons and to degrade confidence in the performance of existing weapons, thereby reducing the chances that they will be used. The five nuclear weapons states recognized under the NPT, Britain, China, France, Russia, and the United States, all signed the CTB on 25 September 1996. Despite considerable diplomatic pressure, India held out. Less than two years later, India was to explode five nuclear weapons, as we discussed in the introductory case in this chapter. The CTB does not take effect until all forty-four states that have some type of nuclear program—most of them not weapons programs—accede, which may take many years (Kempster and Peterson, 1996).

Negotiations toward a worldwide ban on antipersonnel land mines, and on the removal and destruction of those already in place, moved forward rapidly during 1997, driven by desires to end the maiming of innocent civilians that was so widespread in Southeast Asia, even years after the Vietnam and other regional wars, and in Bosnia. The United States, however, was a notable holdout, driven by concerns that the defense of South Korea required some additional years' use of conventional mines. This was argued for technical reasons because U.S. antitank mines were too easily disarmed unless protected by nearby antipersonnel mines. The anti-mine movement is yet another instance of worldwide humanitarian concerns driving a development that would have been unimaginable during the Cold War.

ECONOMIC SECTOR FOCUS CASE: PROMOTING DEVELOPMENT

We examined eleven general strategies for encouraging economic development in Chapter 13: industrialization, rapid accumulation of investment capital, mobilization of underemployed workers, centralized planning by an economically active state, direct foreign aid in forms ranging from grants through loans to military assistance, foreign trade, foreign direct investment, technical assistance, self-development in isolation, regional integration, and commodity producer cartels.

STAKES AT ISSUE

Most available strategies for assisting development involve inherently cross-tier and increasingly multilateral processes. For the United States, the most important questions are how much will be given to what programs where, and how much we will do directly and how much through multilateral agencies. A new issue for the late twentieth century and beyond is how our assistance contributes to or impedes sustainable development (see the environmental sector focus case in Chapter 15). Additionally, as we noted in the geopolitical sector focus case in this chapter, there is a moral question whether promoting democracy requires assisting the resulting states through at least the most difficult period of the democratic transition.

RELEVANT U.S. POLICY THEMES

Foreign aid and development assistance have been important themes in U.S. foreign policy since the end of World War II. Both direct U.S. aid and multilateral efforts, usually organized through the United Nations, have contributed to substantial development progress. Unfortunately, foreign aid rarely has been popular in the United States. In the Chicago Council on Foreign Relations (CCFR) surveys mentioned earlier, the foreign policy goal of *"helping to improve the standard of living of less developed nations"* shows dramatic decreases in support from both elites and the general public over the 1974–94 period, with some increase in 1998. The percentage of elites (EL) rating this goal as "very important" has exceeded the general public (GP) percentage in every survey year except 1990, when the two groups tied at 42.4 percent. That percentage peaked at 64.1 for EL in 1978, but its GP peak was in 1990. Both groups show highly significant change long term and highly significant drops in support to 1994, when "very important" ratings were given by only 27.6 percent EL and 24.7 percent GP. In the long term, elite support as "very important" has shifted from nearly two thirds in the 1970s to less than one third by 1994, rising to 36 percent in 1998. A long-term consensus shift away from U.S. aid programs may be starting to reverse.

PERCEPTIONS HELD BY OTHER ACTORS AND THEIR RELATIONS WITH THE UNITED STATES

Many Second Tier states have argued for some time that First Tier powers have moral obligations to assist their development, and some have raised questions about whether the available types of assistance have promoted appropriate types of development. Others have questioned why many other states, notably in Western Europe, contribute higher percentages of GNP to foreign aid than the United States and have been more willing to forgive the debts of the poorest states. Fundamental incompatibilities in worldviews underlie these arguments.

AVAILABLE ALTERNATIVE ACTIONS AND POLICY TOOLS

Unfortunately, there is no single magic bullet for development. Advantages and disadvantages of each of the general strategies listed here were considered in detail in Chapter 13. Realistic policies likely will involve combinations of several of these strategies, selected to be appropriate to the human and material resources and the current economic structures of particular states.

FUTURE PROSPECTS AND CONCERNS

As economic globalization sweeps around the world, it should provide not only pressures to develop and join the global economy but opportunities to utilize new international ties to facilitate development. This is an optimistic view, of course. Pessimists see widening global economic divisions. Nonetheless, it seems clear that already developed states have a number of options to employ in facilitating development around the globe if they choose that policy goal, which is supportable on grounds of equity, humanity, and practical politics. Whether the United States and other high-income First Tier states can work together to promote development worldwide, and whether we will give such a goal high priority as we enter the twenty-first century, remain to be seen.

SOCIETAL SECTOR FOCUS CASE: HUMANITARIAN POLITICAL ASYLUM

Asylum refers both to the process of granting hospitality and protection to a fugitive and the place where such refuge is offered. Its usage traces back to the granting of sanctuary in temples and churches in ancient and medieval times. Under modern international law, a state's sovereignty includes the right to grant asylum on its territory to refugees from other lands. States decide either categorically (for example, the United States took in all refugees from Castro's Cuba during the early years) or on an individual, case-by-case basis whether to grant asylum. Refugees have no right to demand it. Because most states belong to extradition treaties providing for the mutual return of fugitives from justice, granting asylum can be contentious. Thus states tend to grant asylum primarily to political refugees and in cases of apparent discrimination and intolerance. As we noted in Chapter 10, the territorial status of embassies and legations sometimes leads to their becoming places of refuge in times of conflict and disorder. Most states discourage this form of asylum except in cases in which a threat to life is apparent because the removal of persons from the embassy or legation across the territory of the host state is sensitive and must be negotiated. High-level political defections, although rare, can be embarrassing, and states often negotiate prominent cases. Occasionally, particularly notable political refugees are allowed to move by agreement, as in the release of imprisoned Chinese dissident Wei Jingsheng and his immediate travel to the United States in November 1997. For face-saving reasons (casuistry), neither side openly discussed the fact that Wei's "parole for medical treatment because of his illness" was arranged as part of the deal for Chinese president Jiang Zemin's state visit to the United States the previous month.

STAKES AT ISSUE

As we noted in the societal sector focus case in Chapter 15 on illegal immigration, all forms of immigration have raised serious political, economic, and humanitarian questions in the United States for at least the last century. Asylum may be granted to protect freedom of political expression or to make a political point abroad. Granting asylum to whole categories of people, for example political refugees from a particular government, can lead to substantial numbers of immigrants, with societal and economic impacts here. The strongest arguments for asylum often are moral and humanitarian.

RELEVANT U.S. POLICY THEMES

Throughout its history, the United States has accepted large numbers of immigrants but discriminated against some racial and ethnic groups, as noted in Chapter 15. During the twentieth century, numbers of immigrants accepted fluctuated, but generally were reduced from earlier levels, although the discrimination was greatly lessened toward the end of the century. Typical immigrants to the early United States came for economic opportunity and for political and religious freedom. Later, the imposition of immigration quotas encouraged the development of special procedures for humanitarian and political asylum.

PERCEPTIONS HELD BY OTHER ACTORS AND THEIR RELATIONS WITH THE UNITED STATES

Resettlement of Vietnamese boat people after the 1973 Vietnam peace agreement and 1975 communist victory provides a poignant example of how intermestic considerations tend to work against large programs of refugee resettlement, even when a strong humanitarian case for political asylum exists. Many Vietnamese who had cooperated with America and the Saigon government fled in fear for their lives, often traveling at great risk on overcrowded boats only to be interned in refugee camps in other Southeast Asian states such as Thailand. Few states in the region wanted to absorb so many foreigners, and many believed the United States had a moral obligation to help these unfortunate people who had sided with our ultimately losing cause. Many Americans agreed, and substantial numbers of refugees were accepted outside normal immigration quotas. In several unfortunate cases, however, government moves to resettle groups of the Vietnamese refugees in particular communities evoked ugly protests from local citizens who feared losing jobs to industrious newcomers willing to work hard for low wages.

AVAILABLE ALTERNATIVE ACTIONS AND POLICY TOOLS

Lasting and comprehensive solutions are nowhere in sight. Unfortunately, severe actions to control both legal and illegal immigration are quite consistent with the post–Cold War neo-isolationist retreat from globalism advocated by some citizens and domestic interest groups. Notable problems in the latter 1990s included changes to U.S. immigration procedures permitting Immigration and Naturalization Service personnel to decide immediately at entry points whether particular individuals were likely to qualify for asylum. Previously, asylum seekers were allowed to remain free in the United States after making a brief claim at entry, pending a full hearing and status determination by an immigration judge. Opponents of the new procedure charged that it made it easy to refuse and return inarticulate asylum claimants who could face torture and death in their home countries.

FUTURE PROSPECTS AND CONCERNS

Political asylum requests show no sign of decreasing in frequency since the end of the Cold War and will continue to prove vexing. Indeed, the increase in new internal wars such as the Bosnian civil war of 1992–95 may only increase the number of refugees, as did U.S.-led NATO bombing in Kosovo in the spring of 1999. If serious political efforts at reform are to come, they may be triggered by publicity about some particularly egregious individual case or group situation.

ENVIRONMENTAL SECTOR FOCUS CASE: GLOBAL WARMING

We examined the structure and development of the United Nations Framework Convention on Climate Change (hereafter, the convention or UNFCCC) and its associated global warming regime in some detail in Chapter 12. They are reviewed here because the UNFCCC is an important instance of the U.S. government working across the tiers with the majority of other states around the world in building a new regime to deal with an important problem in the common pool that is the global environment.

The UNFCCC was developed through several years of negotiations in multiple intergovernmental bodies and adopted at the June 1992 United Nations Earth Summit in

Rio de Janeiro, Brazil. Faced with scientific consensus that global warming is a real threat, but with many unknowns about its severity, timetable, and possible solutions, the parties committed in 1992 only to a framework convention in which they agreed to do something sometime in the future, and they set up procedures for working out what and when. The convention indicates broad international recognition that a serious problem exists and establishes expectations that detailed procedures will be developed to deal with that problem. It sets the "ultimate objective" of stabilizing "greenhouse gas concentrations in the atmosphere at a level that would prevent dangerous anthropogenic (human-induced) interference with the climate system." This nonspecific objective recognizes that it may take another decade of scientific work, another generation of supercomputers, and a good deal of political-scientific bargaining to resolve current uncertainties. Nonetheless, the convention's objective remains meaningful regardless what atmospheric concentration of greenhouse gases is ultimately accepted as dangerous. It directs that "such a level should be achieved within a time-frame sufficient to allow ecosystems to adapt naturally to climate change, to ensure that food production is not threatened and to enable economic development to proceed in a sustainable manner" (UNFCCC, 1977b, 3).

STAKES AT ISSUE

Dealing with climate change involves interactions among science, technology, and politics as they jointly influence a very large and highly complex natural system, in the sense of "system" discussed in Chapter 4. Because the natural system involved spans the globe, complex and difficult international politics are unavoidable in dealing with global warming. Earth's climate is an obvious and enormous common pool in which global warming affects each of us and is affected by the sum of all our individual actions, regardless of our awareness or desires. Curing such problems also involves mixes of science, technology, and politics. The answers to how much and how quickly we can reduce global warming hinge on the concrete details that negotiators can accept, so the devil truly is in the details.

RELEVANT U.S. POLICY THEMES

Global warming is seriously impacted by U.S. economic activity and development, which long have been major themes in domestic and foreign policy. American actions alone cannot end warming, and solving global warming appears to require coordinated international cooperative action. Fortunately, such cooperative action in other arenas has been an increasing theme in U.S. foreign policy since World War II.

PERCEPTIONS HELD BY OTHER ACTORS AND THEIR RELATIONS WITH THE UNITED STATES

Human activities, particularly the production of so-called greenhouse gases by the burning of fossil fuels, have grown in scope to have significant long-term effects planetwide. The physical processes by which greenhouse gases contribute to global warming are discussed in Chapter 12. Carbon dioxide seems clearly to be the most important greenhouse gas resulting from human actions, notably the burning of fossil fuels and all other combustible materials. Manifold political problems face those trying to deal with global warming, partly because the physical processes take many years and their effects persist far beyond the terms in office, or even the lifetimes, of politicians and bureaucrats. The physical system has significant time lags, and even if we could drastically cut greenhouse gas emissions immediately, the warming trend would continue for centuries. Climate models predict that changes would continue for centuries after atmospheric gas concentrations stabilized, and it is estimated that emissions would have to be cut to perhaps 30 percent of present levels for concentrations to stabilize eventually at double the present level. Even small increases in global average temperatures can create serious problems for people in many regions of the world. By the latter 1990s a scientific consensus was emerging that global warming is likely to run between 1.5 and 4.5 degrees Celsius (2.7 to 8.1 degrees Fahrenheit) over the next century.

As with many other physical systems that have serious impacts on humans, the science of global warming is disputed. Scientists have genuine disagreements and many individuals, firms, and governments have huge stakes in maintaining business as usual—a classic case of exploiting an endangered common pool. Uncertainty about the likely extent of global warming parallels uncertainties in the temperature increase estimates. Moreover, the underlying climatological/ecological system is so complexly interconnected that almost any change causes further changes elsewhere, often in unforeseen ways. Weather almost certainly will be affected as rainfall and evaporation patterns change. In turn, these affect freshwater resources vital to individuals, industry, and agriculture. Farming seems likely to suffer some regional dislocations that easily could lead to food shortages in some areas. Rising sea levels threaten not only extensive coastal flooding, but possible increases in severe storms. Economies, settlements, and health seem likely to experience numerous impacts, both direct and indirect.

AVAILABLE ALTERNATIVE ACTIONS AND POLICY TOOLS

Like many environmental problems, global warming has such tremendous impact on so many ordinary citizens, businesses, governments, and other actors that many initiatives will be taken to deal with its manifold aspects. Governments took dramatically different stands on what greenhouse gas reductions the 1997 Kyoto agreement (under the framework convention) should mandate, depending on their diverse state interests and their expectations regarding anticipated climatic and other impacts of warming. Comparably diverse positions are held by different interest groups within every country. In October 1997 President Clinton announced a U.S. bargaining position for Kyoto proposing that greenhouse gas emissions be reduced worldwide to 1990 levels by 2010 and that developing states be required to bear a share of the burdens of accomplishing those reductions. Most environmentalists termed the proposed reductions wholly inadequate, whereas advocates of industry termed them ruinously excessive and announced plans for an advertising campaign aimed at U.S. abrogation of the previously ratified convention. Advocates for developing states denounced the burden-sharing requirement as unfair and too great a restriction on their legitimate aspirations for higher standards of living.

FUTURE PROSPECTS AND CONCERNS

After serious fears that no agreement on cutting greenhouse gases would be reached at Kyoto in 1997, the United States retreated significantly from its earlier position.

Thirty-eight developed states agreed to cut their aggregate greenhouse gas emissions to 5.2 percent below 1990 levels between 2008 and 2012. That overall target would be met by cuts varying among states, including the European Union, 8 percent; United States, 7 percent; and Japan, 6 percent. No agreement was reached for emissions reductions by developing states, and working out details for possible trading of emissions rights was left for a November 1998 conference. Supporters called the agreement an historic, significant, and necessary step on the long path to limiting global warming, although numerous environmentalists called the planned emissions reductions woefully inadequate. Opponents decried U.S. concessions and doubted our national capability and willingness to make the sacrifices needed to meet the 2012 target. The Kyoto agreement still required ratification by the United States and other signatories, and prospects for early Senate action were not encouraging.

The solution of global warming, like its onset, may be almost instantaneous on geological time scales while still protracted in ordinary human and political time. Ultimate global political and physical outcomes, the arrangements accepted, and their physical result all remain in doubt. Action will be multifaceted and incremental, and overall success will require that enough initiatives be taken around enough of the world to reach the critical mass impact needed to halt and reverse this class of environmental degradation. Rather than suggesting delay and further study, the huge scope and long time scale of the problem mandate that solutions begin immediately. The stakes for everyone—as both local and global citizens—are enormous, however, and the politics somewhat new, quite fascinating, and well worth following as the climate change regime develops.

Other Environmental Issues

Although a host of environmental problems confronts the entire planet, the United States has a special role, both as a political leader and as the world's largest economy. Numerous environmental problems arise directly from the activities of the United States and others. Those include pollution caused in the extraction, movement, and use of oil; global warming from fossil fuel burning; deforestation; desertification; and ozone depletion from CFCs. Yet the United States and other developed economies are taking a significant part in some solutions, such as catalytic converters for automobile exhaust and phasing out of chlorofluorocarbon (CFC) production. Although developed economies suffer numerous problems because of excessive dependence on a variety of scarce natural resources unevenly distributed around the world, Second Tier states often seek rapid development at the cost of both resource depletion and severe pollution, effects seen in both Eastern Europe and the Southern Hemisphere. And, in 1991, the Persian Gulf saw deliberate Iraqi ecological warfare in the form of enormous oil spills and the torching of oil wells.

Environmental problems involve U.S. interactions with First Tier states, with the Second Tier, and often in cross-tier links that unavoidably affect the entire world. Thus varied but interconnected environmental problems have received attention in several earlier chapters. Environmental policy problems occur because of natural physical processes in common pools that unavoidably link different polities. Thus they require cooperative action and are subject to holdouts usually driven by short-term incentives to exploit a natural resource. Achieving universal action usually is far more difficult and time consuming than reaching scientific consensus on what action is needed. As we saw earlier, arguments often rage over how monetary, technological, development, and lifestyle modification costs are to be allocated.

Deforestation and species extinction, which also demonstrate these characteristics, could not be considered solved as the twentieth century wound down. In such states as Brazil and Indonesia, vast tracts of old growth rain forests had been flattened, usually more to create new farmland than to harvest the timber. Resulting farmland typically proved marginal and prone to erosion, and trees usually were burned. This seriously aggravated global warming because it produced heat and carbon dioxide and removed trees capable of absorbing unwanted CO_2 and releasing needed oxygen. Additionally, massive amounts of particulates were released as smoke, contributing to severe air pollution. When monsoon rains normally counted on to extinguish such fires failed to come on schedule to Indonesia in the fall of 1997, much of Southeast Asia was blanketed by smoke thick enough to shut down airports and cause severe respiratory problems. Pressures from First Tier states to stop deforestation have yielded little, although financial incentives appear more promising. Species extinctions are closely linked to deforestation because an enormous number of as-yet-uncatalogued species exists in tropical rain forests and many extinctions have been demonstrated in recent years.

SUMMARY

This chapter is devoted to issues that bridge between the First and Second Tiers either by unavoidably involving the entire world or by linking powerful and influential developed states to less powerful and less influential developing states. The profound post–Cold War changes in the global policy environment have led to many new cross-tier problems by removing the former focus on U.S.-Soviet confrontation and increasing the numbers of significant independent states on both tiers. Examples of such issues include arms control focused on conventional (non-nuclear) weapons and on NBC weapons of mass destruction, local and regional peacekeeping, most global environmental problems, ensuring needed resource supplies while minimizing the effects of their unequal distribution around the planet, and promoting the most appropriate technologies to simultaneously maximize sustainable economic development while minimizing environmental impact.

Some problems addressed in this chapter involve U.S. interactions with states from both First Tier and Second Tier states, and the remainder require joint action with other First Tier states to deal effectively with problems in the Second Tier. Many environmental issues, like global warming, occur in common pools that connect rich and poor states in ways that demand common action if solutions are to be found. Dealing with the threat of terrorism, whether by conventional arms or weapons of mass destruction, has this character because states both great and small may be targets. The same is true of rising Islamic radicalism. Other problems that are sufficiently widespread and require massive resources to resolve are much more likely to yield to joint action with other First Tier states than to unilateral American initiatives. Examples include promoting democracy, market economies, and economic development worldwide.

Cases given extended treatment in this chapter include promoting democracy and human rights, Middle East peace, promoting development, humanitarian political asylum, and global warming.

CARTOON 16.2

A decade after the end of the Cold War, the United States had not yet developed a consensus for a grand policy to guide its foreign relations in the twenty-first century. In the new millennium, however, foreign policy concerns and confrontations will be more numerous, more varied, and more globally distributed. Threats (including nuclear proliferation) will come from other states and from international terrorists who certainly will make the already complex economic, military, and environmental demands more challenging than ever before.

Toles © 1992 *The Buffalo News*. Reprinted with permission of Universal Press Syndicate. All rights reserved.

AFTERWORD: THE MOST IMPORTANT TYPES OF FOREIGN POLICY PROBLEMS

A few combinations of development tier, activity sector, and time frame (see Part IV introduction on page 491) allow us to summarize the classes of foreign policy problems that are most critical for the United States. Many of those problems are entirely new, or have assumed increased importance, since the profound changes in the international policy environment brought about by the end of the Cold War about 1990.

During the Cold War years, major U.S. attention was devoted to geopolitical, military, and economic problems primarily involving highly developed (First Tier) states, with economics gaining in importance after the mid-1970s. Time horizons were almost always immediate and middle range. Today the United States is unable to carry out as many unilateral actions as it did during the height of the Cold War, which has increased the need to coordinate our actions with other governments and international actors. Driven by rapid world economic changes and globalization since the mid-1970s, the need for such coordination, particularly intense in the economic sector, is reflected in the creation of such bodies as the G-8 and APEC. Many problems that once might have involved the United States alone dealing with developing (Second Tier) states now often involve coordinating with other First Tier states in cross-tier actions. Examples include the major international currency bailouts of the late 1990s, such as those to Mexico in 1996, South Korea in 1997, and Indonesia in 1998. In those instances, loan packages from the United States alone or together with the still U.S.-dominated International Monetary Fund were insufficient, and numerous other governments needed to sign on to build sufficiently large funds. The degree to which the United States would involve itself directly in promoting democracy and market economics in the Second Tier remained unclear as the twentieth century wound to a close. In the 1990s, however, environmental problems began receiving major international attention. Their inherently common pool nature makes them unavoidably cross-tier issues.

LOOKING FORWARD

How shall we, as individuals, respond to the world changes and foreign policy problems facing the United States as we enter the twenty-first century? In every sector of global activity—geopolitical, military, economic, societal, and environmental—the United States and the world are moving into new and imperfectly charted waters. Whether we like it personally or not, each of us is moving with them. Our first great individual choice is whether to be active or passive participants in the process. I hope the principles and approaches developed and discussed throughout this book will help each of you improve your (1) understanding of U.S. foreign policy processes, and (2) ability to predict their outcomes. Over time, perhaps you will decide to play an active role in those processes.

In making that individual choice, you stand at a difficult but fascinating point in history. The end of the Cold War allowed contradictory developments in global politics and U.S. foreign policy. The simplifying lens of East-West competition was removed, freeing perceptions to embrace important policy concerns in other sectors beyond the previously dominant arena of military security. Removing the pressure of superpower competition allowed new issues to arise. Some American citizens believed the post–Cold War era— notably defined by what it was not—allowed them to retreat into a neo-isolationism that permitted decreased attention to world affairs. In reality, the old world order driven by fears of superpower nuclear confrontation has been replaced by a new world order, still neither fully defined nor fully understood. It is already clear, however, that foreign policy concerns and confrontations in the new era will be more numerous, more varied, and more widely distributed around the world. Threats that nuclear and other weapons of mass destruction will spread to additional states and to international terrorists are but one example. Nearly a decade after the end of the Cold War, *New York Times* foreign policy columnist Thomas Friedman (1999) wrote that the new post–Cold War international system was globalization, and he meant it in more than simply the economic sense. As we enter the twenty-first century, it promises to be extremely challenging and interesting.

Not everyone will welcome those challenges, but they will occur. Friedman (1999, xviii) noted that

> . . . I feel about globalization a lot like I feel about the dawn. Generally speaking, I think it's a good thing that the sun comes up every morning. It does more good than harm. But even if I didn't much care for the dawn there isn't much I could do about it. I didn't start globalization, I can't stop it—except at huge cost to human development—and I'm not going to waste time trying. All I want to think about is how I can get the best out of this new system, and cushion the worst, for the most people.

Recall that when people in stability-loving Chinese society expressed the wish, "May you live in interesting times," it was meant as a curse. For optimists, however, the challenges ahead offer fascination and tremendous opportunity.

KEY TERMS

Asylum
Chemical Weapons Convention (CWC)
Comprehensive Test Ban Treaty (CTB)

Democratic peace hypothesis
Nuclear Nonproliferation Treaty (NPT)

SELECTED READINGS

Barnet, Richard J., and John Cavanagh. 1994. *Global Dreams: Imperial Corporations and the New World Order.* New York: Simon & Schuster.

Bitzinger, Richard A. 1994. "The Globalization of the Arms Industry: The Next Proliferation Challenge." *International Security* 19 (Fall): 170–198.

Brown, Seyom. 1995. *New Forces, Old Forces, and the Future of World Politics.* New York: Harper-Collins.

Gaddis, John Lewis. 1992. *The United States and the End of the Cold War: Implications, Reconsiderations, Provocations.* New York: Oxford University Press. One of many early post–Cold War pieces by the historian Gaddis, who called the Cold War the "Long Peace" and described its ending as producing "tectonic shifts" in the global political order.

Gaddis, John Lewis. 1998. *We Now Know: Rethinking Cold War History.* New York: Clarendon Press and Oxford: Oxford University Press.

Gardner, Hall. 1994. *Surviving the Millennium: American Global Strategy, the Collapse of the Soviet Empire, and the Question of Peace.* Westport, Conn.: Preager.

Harkavy, Robert E., and Stephanie G. Neumann, eds. "The Arms Trade: Problems and Prospects in the Post–Cold War World." *The Annals* 535 (September): 1–244.

Kennedy, Paul. 1993. *Preparing for the Twenty-First Century.* New York: Random House.

Petras, James, and Morris Morley. 1995. *Empire or Republic? American Global Power and Domestic Decay.* New York: Routledge.

Toffler, Alvin, and Toffler, Heidi. 1995. *Creating a New Civilization: The Politics of the Third Wave.* Atlanta: Turner Publications.

APPENDIX

ABBREVIATIONS AND ACRONYMS

Abbreviations play many roles. They save time and space when items must be referred to frequently, and this is no less true for the U.S. government. Although people often find them oppressive, abbreviations do provide an effective shorthand for referring to the government's myriad departments, bureaus, and operating units, as well as to their many programs, products, and procedures. Psychologically, abbreviations demonstrate that users are "in the know," that they are informed and engaged in the political and policy process.

Abbreviations are so commonly employed in Washington that people oftentimes have trouble operating without them. In this book, abbreviations help you understand the references to not only departments and programs, but also to government papers, official reports, public statements, journalistic writings, policy think tank analyses, and the works of academics focused on foreign policy. As difficult as it may be to believe, the number of abbreviations used here has been kept to a minimum. The following list is provided for convenient reference.

ABM Anti-ballistic missile.

ACDA United States Arms Control and Disarmament Agency.

AFL-CIO American Federation of Labor–Congress of Industrial Organizations; large umbrella organization of most U.S. labor unions.

AID Agency for International Development. AID is a semi-independent agency functioning as part of the U.S. International Development Cooperation Agency (IDCA).

APNSA Assistant to the president for national security affairs, commonly referred to as the NSA (not to be confused with the National Security Agency).

CBO Congressional Budget Office.

CCFR Chicago Council on Foreign Relations, sponsor of an important quadrennial national survey (since 1974) of opinion regarding U.S. foreign policy. CCFR surveys are particularly valuable because they include separate studies of general public opinion and the opinions of elites (opinion leaders to whom most people look for policy guidance and officials who make and execute policy).

CFCs Chlorofluorocarbons.

CFE Conventional forces in Europe. The 1990 CFE Treaty led to significant reductions.

CIA Central Intelligence Agency.

COP Conference of the Parties; formal negotiating meeting of the parties that have signed a treaty or other agreement. In Chapter 12, it refers to any of the conferences of governments that have signed the United Nations Framework Convention on Climate Change (UNFCCC).

CRS Congressional Research Service.

CTB Comprehensive [nuclear] Test Ban Treaty.

CWC Chemical Weapons Convention, properly the Convention on the Prohibition of the Development, Production, Stockpiling, and Use of Chemical Weapons and on Their Destruction.

DCI Director of Central Intelligence; also heads the Central Intelligence Agency (CIA).

DDCI Deputy Director of Central Intelligence.

DFI Direct foreign investment.

DIA Defense Intelligence Agency.

DMZ Demilitarized zone. In Chapter 12, it refers to the demilitarized zone created along the Iraq-Kuwait border after the Persian Gulf War that was supervised by the United Nations Iraq-Kuwait Observation Mission (UNIKOM).

EC Economic Community; successor to the European Economic Community, or EEC.

EEC European Economic Community, initially consisting of Belgium, France, (West) Germany, Italy, Luxembourg, and the Netherlands, founded under the Treaty of Rome, signed in March 1947. The EEC later became the Economic Community or EC, still later the European Union (EU).

EU European Union.

FOIA Freedom of Information Act.

FSO Foreign service officer, in the Department of State.

G-7 Group of Seven, an organization of the finance ministers of the major democratically governed market economy states (Canada, France, Great Britain, West Germany, Italy, Japan, and the United States), intended to strengthen multilateral surveillance of the world economy. Organized in 1986, the G-7 soon began taking stands on broader political issues. See also the Group of Eight (G-8).

G-8 Group of Eight; the Group of Seven (G-7) plus the Russian Federation. In 1998 full formal membership was offered, creating the G-8 and giving Russia equal status with the major developed democracies, except on issues of international finance.

GAO General Accounting Office.

GATT General Agreement on Tariffs and Trade. From 1947 until 1994, extending through some eight rounds of protracted negotiations, GATT was the primary international trade organization. In 1995 GATT was succeeded by the World Trade Organization (WTO).

GDI Gross domestic investment.

GDP Gross domestic product. Total value of the goods and services produced by a state's economy over a specified period, usually one year.

GNP Gross national product. Quantitative measure of a state's total economic activity: gross domestic product (GDP) plus income earned by domestic residents through foreign investments minus the income earned by foreign investors in the domestic market.

GRIT Graduated Reciprocation in Tension Reduction; through a sequence of highly publicized unilateral moves by each side, the sequence being continued as long as responsive moves sufficient to avoid any serious disadvantages to either side are forthcoming.

IAEA International Atomic Energy Agency.

ICBM Intercontinental ballistic missile. A missile of intercontinental range—typically 5,000 to 8,000 miles—designed to follow the trajectory that results when it is acted on predominantly by gravity and aerodynamic drag after thrust is terminated.

ICJ International Court of Justice, at The Hague, Netherlands.

IGO Intergovernmental organization. Members are governments of states, and different IGOs deal with economic, functional, political, and security problems.

IMF International Monetary Fund.

INF Intermediate range nuclear forces. The 1987 U.S.-Soviet INF Treaty led to their total elimination.

INGO International nongovernmental organization. INGOs bring groups of individuals, businesses, and other organizations together across government lines to pursue common interests, often lobbying and even taking stands against particular governments.

INR State Department Bureau of Intelligence and Research.

IO International Organization. See IGO; compare INGO.

IPE International political economy.

IRBM Intermediate range ballistic missile. A ballistic missile of intermediate range, some 500 to 1,500 miles. Under the 1987 Intermediate Nuclear Forces (INF) Treaty, the United States and USSR destroyed all their IRBMs by about 1991.

ITO International Trade Organization. Proposed in 1947, it was vetoed by the United States. The gap was filled for decades by the General Agreement on Tariffs and Trade (GATT), until the World Trade Organization (WTO) became operational in 1995.

ITU International Telecommunications Union, one of the many functional intergovernmental organizations (IGOs) that operates under the auspices of the United Nations.

JCS Joint Chiefs of Staff, in the Department of Defense.

LC Library of Congress.

LDCs Less developed countries. Term widely applied in the 1950s to what are today termed *developing states*. Either term also obscures their enormous differences. These states have many different types of economies, from pure market to (rarely, today) pure command and every degree of mix in between. They vary enormously in state and per capita income, patterns of wealth distribution, degrees of development, and future prospects.

LIC Low-intensity conflict; armed action characterized by forces limited but sufficient to achieve overwhelming local superiority, used briefly to achieve limited objectives, ideally with low casualties and a quick, decisive result.

LNOs Limited nuclear options.

MAD Mutual assured destruction.

MFN Most-favored-nation trading status; essentially the standard tariffs on international trade that the United States offers almost every state.

MITI Japan's Ministry of International Trade and Industry.

MNC Multinational corporation.

MX Originally, Missile Experimental. Ten-warhead U.S. ICBM, dubbed "Peacemaker" in 1984 by President Reagan.

NAFTA North American Free Trade Act, which created a free trade area encompassing Canada, Mexico, and the United States. It was ratified by the United States in 1993 and took effect in 1994.

NAM National Association of Manufacturers.

NASA National Aeronautics and Space Administration.

NATO North Atlantic Treaty Organization.

NBC Nuclear, biological, and chemical weapons. See also *weapons of mass destruction* (*WMD*).

NEC National Economic Council; created as an executive branch advisory body by an executive order signed 25 January 1993 by President Bill Clinton. The NEC was intended to parallel the NSC in importance, coordinating national economic policy in the same way the NSC seeks to coordinate foreign and security policy.

NFIB National Foreign Intelligence Board.

NFIC National Foreign Intelligence Council.

NGO (International) nongovernmental organization; see also *INGO*.

NICs Newly industrializing countries. Notable examples include Singapore, South Korea, and Taiwan, which have enjoyed rapid and sustained growth in recent decades.

NIE National Intelligence Estimate.

NIEO New international economic order. Proposal advanced by a large group of developing states, under which developed states would devote 1 percent of GNP to development assistance.

NIO National intelligence officer.

NPT Nuclear Nonproliferation Treaty of 1968.

NSA Properly, National Security Agency, the U.S. government's supersecret agency of cryptanalysts, code breakers, and electronic spies. Also common Washington usage for the national security adviser to the president, more correctly called the assistant to the president for national security affairs, or APNSA.

NSC National Security Council.

NTR Normal trade relations. In 1997's annual debate over renewing "most-favored-nation" (MFN) trade status for China, the Clinton administration attempted to defuse the issue by substituting the phrase "normal trade relations," or NTR, which is more accurate, because all but a half-dozen states have MFN status.

ODSs Ozone-depleting substances.

OMB Office of Management and Budget, in the Executive Office of the President.

OPEC Organization of Petroleum Exporting Countries.

OSCE Organization for Security and Cooperation in Europe.

OTA Office of Technology Assessment (b. 1972, d. 1994).

PAC Political action committee; a source of relatively unregulated campaign funds.

PAE Office of Program Analysis and Evaluation, in the Office of the Secretary of Defense.

PLO Palestine Liberation Organization.

PMA State Department Bureau of Political-Military Affairs.

PPBS Planning, programming, and budgeting system, introduced to the Defense Department in the early 1960s by Robert S. McNamara, secretary of defense under Presidents Kennedy and Johnson.

PPS Policy planning staff, in the Department of State.

SALT Strategic Arms Limitation Talks between the United States and the Soviet Union, begun in 1969. They yielded treaties and executive agreements in 1972 (SALT I) and 1979 (SALT II). Although the United States never ratified SALT II, both sides generally followed its terms, which set precedents followed in the later START treaties of the 1980s and 1990s.

SDF Strength/distance function.

SDI Strategic Defense Initiative, a controversial Reagan administration program launched after a surprise 1983 Reagan speech. SDI involved a many-faceted program to intercept Soviet nuclear missiles and their warheads in flight, perhaps in part through use of space-based interceptors. It was dubbed "Star Wars" by supporters and opponents alike. Major doubts persisted about whether much of what had been proposed was technically feasible. By the latter 1990s, the large-scale and space-based aspects had been replaced with new plans for limited missile defense by ground-based interceptor missiles.

SIOP Single integrated operational plan for military operations.

SLBM Submarine-launched ballistic missile.

SOP Standard operating procedure.

SSBN Nuclear-powered ballistic missile submarine.

START Strategic Arms Reduction Talks between the United States and the Soviet Union, begun in 1982; succeeded the SALT negotiations. The acronym START was chosen by the Reagan administration to emphasize its political break with the SALT process. START I was signed by the United States and the Soviet Union in 1991. After the USSR's breakup, START I was extended to include Belarus, Kazakstan, and Ukraine, and further extended by START II in 1993, leading to deep cuts in intercontinental strategic weapons.

UN United Nations.

UNFCCC United Nations Framework Convention on Climate Change.

UNIKOM United Nations Iraq-Kuwait Observation Mission.

UNSCOM United Nations Special Commission; set up to locate and supervise the destruction of Iraq's weapons of mass destruction after the Persian Gulf War.

UPU Universal Postal Union; one of the many functional intergovernmental organizations (IGOs) that operate under the auspices of the United Nations. The UPU works to promote mutual recognition of postage and acceptance of international mail.

USIA United States Information Agency.

WEU Western European Union.

WMD Weapons of mass destruction. See also *NBC* weapons.

WTO World Trade Organization; entered into force in 1995.

GLOSSARY

Abrogate To cancel agreement and withdraw from a treaty, usually on the (real or pretended) ground that continued observance would threaten "supreme national interests." Although the right to abrogate is grounded in international law, it has become common practice in recent decades to specify that right explicitly in treaties.

Accommodationists (or **Idealists**) In Wittkopf's analyses (1990, 1994, 1995) of belief structures, accommodationists are "selective internationalists" who support cooperative internationalism (CI) and oppose militant internationalism (MI). Thus they accept conciliation, negotiation, and cooperation while rejecting the use of force.

Actual Power Power attributes that are immediately available. Examples include active duty military forces, diplomatic weight sufficient to sway a vote in the UN, or economic strength sufficient to manipulate an international currency market. Compare with *potential power.*

Aggression An unprovoked attack too severe to be justified by any prior provocation (e.g., Japan's attack on U.S. naval forces at Pearl Harbor, Hawaii, on 7 December 1941).

Allison Models Three conceptual and analytic models of government decision making, each at a different level of analysis. They are the government as a whole (Model I, "rational actor" or unitary government); the organizations within that government (Model II, "organizational process"); and individuals within the government (Model III, "governmental politics").

Armed Peacekeeping Mission First employed in the Sinai in 1956, such peacekeeping missions generally are authorized to fire only in self-defense, partly because they almost always are outgunned by the parties they monitor.

Arms Transfers Sales, aid, and gifts from producer states to recipient states. Additionally, and increasingly in recent years, they also comprise licensed production in consumer states under authorization from the developer states.

Asylum The process of granting hospitality and protection to a fugitive; also the place where such refuge is offered. Its usage traces back to the granting of sanctuary in temples and churches in ancient and medieval times. Under modern international law, a state's sovereignty includes the right to grant asylum on its territory to refugees from other lands.

Back-Channel Negotiations Negotiations conducted through unusual contacts, usually well outside public view, and outside whatever formal negotiations may be underway between the same parties over the same issues. Back-channel negotiators may be of either higher or lower rank than the officials conducting the formal negotiations.

Background When officials speak with journalists "on background," reporters can use the information but may not name their source. Readers must rely on the correspondents' reputations and draw their own conclusions.

Bargaining The third stage of negotiation: actual substantive negotiations. This follows preliminaries and process talks.

Bargaining Chips Goods or powers acquired with the specific intent of bargaining them away later in return for offsetting concessions. Their biggest problem arises directly from bureaucratic politics: as products of government programs, bargaining chips acquire their own constituencies and become difficult to give up.

Belief Structures The sets of key ideas and core values people hold and the structure of relationships between them. These should be understood in the general sense of systems examined in Chapter 4.

Bilateral Two party. In diplomacy, state-to-state talks between two governments. Contrast with *multilateral.*

Black Programs Government programs considered so sensitive that they receive no publicity and are kept out of published budgets, with details revealed only to a few select members of Congress. Examples include the budgets and programs of the CIA and NSA, certain covert actions abroad, and some advanced military developments (the F-117 "Stealth" fighter aircraft during the 1980s).

Brief In Washington usage, a verb meaning to present a summary of pertinent information, usually in person. Secondarily, a document presenting such a summary.

Bureaucracy   Hierarchical structure of bureaus and subagencies with responsibility and authority funneling up through many levels of increasing scope of responsibility. Although it has many problems, this system helps overcome the limited span of control of any one individual. The executive branch of the U.S. government is a great bureaucracy that carries out most foreign policy actions, with authority channeled from the president down through cabinet secretaries and undersecretaries.

Carrying Capacity   Number of a given species that can be sustained in a particular ecosystem without degrading the required resource base and producing a population decline or crash.

Cartel   National or international producer group formed to fix prices and allocate export (or domestic market) quantities.

Casuistry   Masking negotiating concessions by appealing to general principles; subtle but misleading or false reasoning; creative lying; "spin doctoring." Casuistry is based on the principle that whoever controls the language controls the debate. In an era when policymakers and citizens all suffer from information overload, the shorthand description of a policy proposal strongly shapes popular perceptions.

Charter   Legislative grant of authority specifying the general functions that a government agency is to perform. Responsibilities are usually divided among *offices;* within each office, *programs* are developed; and within those programs, *procedures* are devised to carry out desired functions. See also *standard operating procedures.*

Chemical Weapons Convention (CWC)   Treaty properly entitled the Convention on the Prohibition of the Development, Production, Stockpiling, and Use of Chemical Weapons and on Their Destruction. The CWC was opened for signature in Paris on 13 January 1993, following negotiations that trace back to the UN Eighteen-Nation Committee on Disarmament in 1968. The United States signed immediately but did not ratify until the spring of 1997, mere days before the convention already was scheduled to enter into force.

Choice   One of the five fundamental axioms of rational choice. A rational actor always chooses the highest ranked alternative. See also *consistency, decisiveness, ranking,* and *transitivity.*

Classified Documents   U.S. government documents, typically about policy or intelligence, to which access—or even knowledge of their existence—is restricted to those officially believed to have a "need to know." There is a many-level hierarchy of levels of classification.

Client States   States dependent on another, allied government for economic, military, or political support. Although degrees of dependence and of policy subservience vary, notable examples of client states include Cuba (dependent on the Soviet Union until the late 1980s) and Israel (dependent on the United States). Supporting states may act out of perceived duty to support the like-minded, and may receive economic or other benefits from having clients.

Coalition Making and **Alliance Building**   Fundamental and widely used grand policy under which governments gain strength through agreements to act together with others under either broad or narrow conditions. Both formal and informal agreements are possible, and many forms of cooperation exist, including political, economic, and military types. Examples include collective security pacts, military alliances, common markets, and secret understandings (ententes).

Coercive Diplomacy   Coercive diplomacy extends from peaceful diplomacy to limited war, overlapping and including both. Its one indispensable prerequisite is that *usable and believable options to use force must exist,* although coercion need not always require military force.

Cognitive Misers   Individuals who use their older or more general information to interpret newer or more specific information because of their limited capabilities for dealing with new information. This model, said to apply to everyone, comes out of the cognitive psychology literature. As applied to foreign policy, it resolves the major question of how people who are poorly informed about the facts of foreign events may nonetheless take positions logically consistent with their political values. When confronted with some new foreign policy development salient enough to attract their attention, they can gather limited new information and interpret it consistently with their core values and general policy postures.

Cold War   The period (roughly 1947–90) of intense global polarization and confrontation between a "Western" democratic capitalist bloc led by the United States and an "Eastern" communist bloc led by the Soviet Union.

Collective Action Problem   Any problem in which governments try to limit and coordinate their citizens' individual activities so society as a whole—the collectivity—benefits. Typically, as in the tragedy of the commons, such problems can be solved only by coordinated collective action.

Collective Security Agreement   Regional or even global cooperative undertaking to protect the military security of some number of states either by waging war or by taking military steps designed to prevent war.

Colonialism   The seizing and ruling of territories; the most extreme form of interventionism.

Command Economy   Economy in which central planners dictate what is to be produced, in what quantities, where, by whom, and how it is to be distributed.

Common pool   Distinct physical system, within which individuals are unavoidably bound together in a collectivity, so the actions of any person affect everyone else. An example is Garret Hardin's (1968) story of grazing cattle on Boston Common; see the introduction to Chapter 12.

Comparative Advantage   Theory asserting that all states should export those goods they produce most efficiently and import goods they produce less efficiently. In a two-party trade, both can benefit even if one is absolutely less efficient in producing all the types of goods traded.

Comprehensive Test Ban Treaty (CTB)   Treaty to ban all nuclear weapons testing, thereby helping to limit horizontal proliferation, limit future qualitative improvements in weapons performance, degrade confidence in the performance of existing weapons, and reduce the chances that they will be used. (The Limited Nuclear Test Ban Treaty of 1963 already prohibits all nuclear explosions on land, at sea, in the air, and in outer space.) The five nuclear weapons states recognized under the NPT, Britain, China, France, Russia, and the United States, all signed the CTB on 25 September 1996. However, the CTB does not take effect until all forty-four states that have some type of nuclear program—most of them not weapons programs—accede, which may take many years.

Conditional Viability   Condition in which a state could be absorbed or destroyed as an independent decision-making center; its opponent then is said to be dominant. See *viability;* compare *unconditional viability*, *secure conditional viability*, and *insecure conditional viability*.

Congressional Budget Office (CBO)   Youngest of the congressional support organizations, created by the Congressional Budget Act of 1974. In a town in which assured access to information carries significant political power, the CBO guarantees Congress its own budgetary and economic information, regularly used in making policy and in challenging executive branch numbers. Like the Congressional Research Service (CRS) and the General Accounting Office (GAO), CBO helps make Congress independent of the administration's experts, forecasts, and interpretations.

Congressional Oversight   Broad process of supervision to ensure that actions by the president and executive departments follow the laws of the land. Specific legislation has established oversight procedures for intelligence management and the use of U.S. troops abroad.

Congressional Research Service (CRS)   Oldest and second largest of the congressional support organizations, housed both physically and organizationally within the Library of Congress (LC). Its sole purpose is providing information and policy analysis to the Congress. The CRS thus has a broad mandate to prepare and analyze policy alternatives, evaluating them by whatever criteria its analysts may propose. Like the Congressional Budget Office (CBO) and the General Accounting Office (GAO), CRS helps make Congress independent of the administration's experts, forecasts, and interpretations.

Consistency   One of the five fundamental axioms of rational choice. Faced with the same set of alternatives, a rational actor always makes the same choice. See also *choice, decisiveness, ranking,* and *transitivity*.

Containment   U.S. Cold War policy to block further Soviet expansion by all means short of major war. Based on an assertion that a Soviet Union prevented from imperialist expansion would eventually fail because of the internal contradictions of its own political-economic system.

Contingency Planning   Systematic evaluation of "what could we do if . . ." Contingency planning can keep adverse developments from being crises by eliminating surprise. Unfortunately, it seems impossible in principle to anticipate every contingency.

Convertibility   Arrangement under which a government permits the free exchange of its currency for that of other states. Gold was used internationally for convertibility until 1971, when the United States terminated the practice. Since then, some major trading groups, such as OPEC, have used baskets of several major currencies to price their sales.

Cooperative Internationalism   One of the two major dimensions of foreign policy belief systems found in the research of Wittkopf (1990, 1994, 1995). Involves activism emphasizing economic aid, diplomacy, multilateral action in cooperation with others, and support for international cooperation through strengthening international cooperative institutions such as the UN. The other major dimension Wittkopf found is termed *militant internationalism.*

Corps of Diplomats   Set or body of diplomats accredited to any one particular state.

Covert [Military] Operations   Foreign operations by U.S. and/or friendly personnel, concealed or disguised from examination by our own or the world's media, formally disavowed in the world of international politics. In practice, an operative bureaucratic criterion for covert operations often has been their plausible deniability.

Crisis   Unanticipated situation with high stakes and a short time in which to decide on appropriate action.

Crisis Management   Means of controlling crises, keeping the decision making as normal as possible, maintaining or even improving lines of communication, and limiting the escalation of violence.

Cybernetic or **Cyberneticist**   View holding that we may be able to evoke desired responses from adversaries by carefully sending appropriate signals calculated to appeal to leaders (or that faction within a government) willing to work with us. One of three views on the role of ideology in shaping foreign policy behavior as described by William Zimmerman (1974), this view assigns the least importance to ideology. Compare with *essentialist* and *mechanist* views.

De Facto Recognition   View that diplomatic recognition implies only our realization that a particular government does wield power and we need to be able to carry on business with that government. Recognition is not believed to express approval of that government or of the way in which it came to power. Contrast with the opposing *moral approval* position.

Debt Rescheduling   Rewriting loan terms to allow smaller payments over a longer time.

Decisiveness   One of the five fundamental axioms of rational choice. Faced with a set of alternatives, a ra-

tional actor always is able to make a choice. See also *choice, consistency, ranking,* and *transitivity.*

Default   To cancel or be unable to repay debt.

Defectors   Free riders or holdouts who decline to cooperate, typically in some common pool situation that calls for collective action.

Democratic Peace Hypothesis   Assertion that democracies rarely go to war against one another. Thus promoting the spread of democracy around the globe might help produce a more peaceful world. Data tend to support this hypothesis, although some authorities argue it fits First Tier states better than Second Tier states.

Detecting or **Evaluating**   In the systems theory of policy control, the process of measuring the results achieved. Second of three steps that include directing or guiding and effecting or controlling. Also see Dunsire, 1985.

Détente   French term for relaxation of tensions; said of joint U.S.-Soviet diplomatic and strategic arms control moves in the early 1970s.

Deterrence   Strategy intended to convince an opponent that the costs and risks of aggression or other actions contrary to our desires outweigh any benefits likely to be gained. Although often thought of as a product of the nuclear age, deterrence is an ancient political-military-economic concept.

Deterrent Deployment   Form of peace enforcement that involves strategically placing military forces to signal their ability and intent to counter some threatened aggression.

Devalue   Reduce the supported value of one's currency against foreign currencies. Traditionally, devaluation promotes exports by making them less expensive in foreign currencies, and discourages imports by making them more expensive to your own citizens.

Diplomacy   Process of conducting international relations, especially communication between governments and other international actors. Above all else, it is a process of signaling others regarding the issues we care about, how much we care, and what we are prepared to do about it.

Diplomatic Immunity   Doctrine granting diplomats exemption from search, arrest, or prosecution by the governments to which they are accredited. They are to be allowed communications and transportation without interference, a practice with deep roots in history and almost universally recognized as essential for diplomats to properly carry out their duties without fear of reprisals. See also *exterritoriality*.

Directing or **Guiding**   In the systems theory of policy control, the process of goal setting and policy determination. First of three steps that include detecting or evaluating and effecting or controlling.

Divided Government   Situation in the United States in which one major party holds a majority in Congress while the other party holds the presidency. This has occurred frequently over the last generation, with surveys often indicating strong public support, suggesting the emergence of a new element added to the constitutional system of checks and balances.

Economic Security   Involves the access to natural and financial resources and to markets necessary to maintain acceptable levels of individual welfare and state power.

Effecting or **Controlling**   In the systems theory of policy control, the process of adjusting and revising policy to more closely approach targeted outcomes. Third of three steps that include directing or guiding and detecting or evaluating.

Embassy   Official residence or offices of an ambassador in a foreign state. See also *legation*.

Engagement   The 1990s term for globalism or internationalism: deliberately playing a major world role, consciously shaping and maintaining the world order.

Enlargement   Broad new grand policy, proposed by the Clinton administration in 1993 with little concrete policy follow-through, but clearly intended to succeed the Cold War grand policy of containment. Under enlargement, the United States would seek to expand the number of states that are democratically governed and have market economies.

Environmental Security   Involves maintaining local, national, and planetary biospheres as the vital life support system for all human endeavors.

Escalation   Controlled increase of action severity over time, with results monitored by feedback, until a level sufficient to accomplish policy goals is reached.

Essentialist   View assigning great importance to official and formal ideology as a shaper and predictor of an adversary's actions. Thus essentialists described Soviet foreign policy behavior as "flowing logically from the nature of totalitarianism," so "it is not what the country . . . does but what it is that is the source of conflict" (Zimmerman, 1974, 91). One of three views on the role of ideology in shaping foreign policy behavior as described by Zimmerman, this view assigns the greatest importance to ideology. Compare with *mechanist* and *cybernetic* views.

Executive Agreement   Formal, written accord between the executives or heads of government of two or more states. Often considered as treaties in all but name, executive agreements usually are not formally ratified like treaties. A notable exception for the United States is that Congress passed legislation over President Nixon's veto requiring that all arms control agreements be approved by Congress. The tremendous growth in international functional arrangements since World War II has led to a concomitant increase in numbers of executive agreements.

Executive Privilege   Constitutional doctrine that a president is entitled to strictly confidential consultations with close advisers.

Exit Strategy   Plan for graceful withdrawal from a policy, particularly used to refer to a plan for bringing troops home from some foreign deployment.

Externalities   Costs created by a producer but borne by others. For example, acid rain is an externality caused by atmospheric chemical processes on sulfur dioxide sent up smokestacks by coal-burning power plants. In turn, the acid rain creates international political problems, as between the northeastern United States and southeastern Canada.

Exterritoriality   Diplomatic principle of exempting diplomats, along with their families and staffs, residences, and archives from the jurisdiction of the states in which they reside and to which they are accredited (Freeman, 1994, 140). To allow diplomats to operate independently and effectively, these aspects of jurisdiction are temporarily suspended. In theory, such suspensions can be lifted, although this is rare in practice because diplomacy relies so heavily on mutual respect and mutual extension of such privileges.

Failed State   State that has suffered major collapse. Instances are (fortunately) few, and typically occur either because (1) the central government has lost its ability to control the countryside and anarchy or civil war has broken out, or (2) the economy has collapsed and has no serious chance of recovery without massive restructuring and outside help. Prominent examples in the 1990s include Somalia and former Yugoslavia.

Feedback   Process in which, in our foreign policy system, some input information concerns measures of how well policies are working, so those policies can be adjusted to more closely approach the desired outcomes.

First Tier   Set of developed states. See also *First World*.

First World   During the Cold War, the developed states with market (capitalist) economies. Today's best examples are the G-7 states, but the First World certainly includes the United States, Canada, Western Europe, Scandinavia, Japan, Australia, and New Zealand. Compare with *First Tier*.

Foreign Policy Perspective   General view that concentrates on the decision-making process within a state and the domestic influences on it. Contrast with the *international politics perspective*.

Fourth World   During the Cold War, some authors distinguished within the Third World a Fourth World of states having very limited development and even poorer future prospects. Sometimes termed the *least developed states*, they lie primarily in a band across equatorial Africa, plus some of the more physically isolated states in southern Asia, including Afghanistan, Nepal, Bangladesh, and Laos. See also *Second Tier*.

Framework Convention   Agreement to do something sometime in the future, and establishing procedures for working out what and when. The United Nations Framework Convention on Climate Change (UNFCCC) is a notable example.

Free Riders   Defectors or holdouts who hope to benefit by taking advantage of the collective action of others in some common pool situation.

Free Trade Area   Area within which two or more states agree to allow goods and services to move freely without tariffs. A notable example is the North American Free Trade Area or NAFTA, which after 1993 included Canada, Mexico, and the United States.

Freedom of Information Act (FOIA)   The 1966 act that requires government agencies to make information available on request unless it falls within one or more of nine stated exempt categories. Agencies still may censor the released information, but may choose to release records even though they are covered by an exemption.

Functional Activities   Activities that almost everybody agrees need to be regulated to ensure the necessary infrastructure and procedures for international communication, travel, commerce, and so on. Typically they are regulated by autonomous specialized intergovernmental organizations (IGOs) or international organizations with their own memberships and organs. Functional IGOs usually are affiliated with the UN through formal relationships or working agreements. Most functional activities are so widely understood to be necessary that they have relatively limited political salience and controversy and usually receive little public attention.

Functions   Every system operates so as to perform certain tasks or produce certain outputs. This is one of Rapoport's four criteria for recognizing and describing a system. See also *members, relationships*, and *predictability*. The foreign policy system has a wide range of products or functions or actions taken, ranging from diplomatic messages sent or received to formal policy announcements to the waging of war.

G-7 or Group of Seven   Economic policy organization of the world's most highly developed (First Tier) market economy states: Canada, France, Great Britain, West Germany, Italy, Japan, and the United States. In 1975 heads of their governments held the first of what unexpectedly became a continuing series of annual summit meetings focused on both economic and political issues. In 1986 the conferees agreed to create a Group of Seven (G-7) made up of the participating states' finance ministers, intended to strengthen multilateral surveillance of the world economy. The European Union (formerly the European Community) has been represented since 1977, as a less-than-equal partner. See also *G-8*.

G-8 or Group of Eight   Economic policy organization of the world's most highly developed (First Tier) market economy states, Canada, France, Great Britain, West Germany, Italy, Japan, and the United States (the G-7 states), plus the Russian Federation. The former G-7 was renamed the G-8 when Russia was offered full membership status at the 15–17 May 1998 summit. The former G-7 states, however, remained free to meet without Russia in certain circumstances, as when the primary focus was global finance. See also *G-7*.

Game of Strategy   Situation or interaction structure with the following necessary characteristics: (1) Two or more players are involved in an interaction. (2) Each player must choose from among two or more possible alternative actions. (3) The outcome of their interaction is jointly determined by the choices of all the players. (4) Every outcome has certain pay-offs—costs and benefits—to each player. The pay-offs may favor one player and penalize another, but no single player can determine the outcome. The prisoners' dilemma is no doubt the most widely studied game of strategy because it occurs in so many real-world situations.

General Accounting Office (GAO)   Nonpartisan agency of the Congress, created by the Budget and Accounting Act of 1921 to "investigate, at the seat of government or elsewhere, all matters relating to the receipt, disbursement, and application of public funds. . . ." Like the Congressional Budget Office (CBO) and the Congressional Research Service (CRS), GAO helps make Congress independent of the administration's experts, forecasts, and interpretations.

Glasnost   Literally, openness. Russian term for a broad set of political reforms launched by Soviet leader Mikhail Gorbachev in 1987 to bring democratization and expanded freedom to participate in the political process and criticize government. See also *perestroika*.

Globalism or **Internationalism**   Grand policy of deliberately playing a major world role, consciously shaping and maintaining the world order. Motivations may include both "global interests" and "national interest." Globalism first became consistent long-term U.S. policy toward the end of World War II.

Good Offices   Assistance and facilitation in negotiation, often provided by individual governments or intergovernmental organizations (IGOs). They may call on the parties to come together, provide a meeting place and other logistical support, offer suggestions for settlement, proffer peace inspection and enforcement forces, supply economic and military aid and other enticements as rewards, and engage in considerable arm-twisting to encourage agreement.

Governmental Politics   Allison's Model III, which emphasizes the interplay between key individuals, each with his or her personal history, goals, priorities, past policy stands, and network of connections —both positive and negative—to others throughout government. Compare with Allison's *unitary government* (Model I) and *organizational process* (Model II) models.

Grand Policy   Broad policy guidance, intended to influence foreign policy goal setting and responses to many specific problems over a considerable span of time. Also referred to as programmatic policy or

long-term policy themes. Notable examples include containment of Soviet and communist expansionism during the Cold War. Contrast with *specific policy*.

Grants   Foreign aid gifts of funds for specific purposes and projects, which may include such diverse purposes as training and educational facilities and programs, demonstration projects, dam and road construction, and so on. Unlike loans for similar purposes, which are much more common, no repayment of grants is expected. However, grants often come with conditions, for example, a requirement that American funds to buy tractors be spent in the United States.

Greenhouse Gases   Naturally occurring or human-made gases that help absorb and trap surface infrared radiation in much the same manner as greenhouse windows. The most important are carbon dioxide (CO_2), methane (CH_4), and nitrous oxide (N_2O). Occurring naturally, they make up less than one tenth of 1 percent of earth's atmosphere, which is mainly oxygen (21 percent) and nitrogen (78 percent). Yet, although fairly rare, the greenhouse gases are crucial to life as we know it. Without them, the earth's surface would average about 54 degrees Fahrenheit colder than today.

Gross National Product (GNP)   Total value of all goods and services produced in a state's economy during one year.

Groupthink   Phenomenon in which the desire for consensus in a group that must concur on policy makes it difficult for group members to challenge the first reasonable proposal raised, even if that proposal is not optimal (see Irving Janis, 1972).

Hard Power or **Command Power**   Ability to coerce and compel others, bending them to one's will, usually by using tangible power resources such as military and economic might. See Nye, 1990, 267; compare with *soft power*.

Hard-liners (or **Realists**)   In Wittkopf's analyses (1990, 1994, 1995), "selective internationalists" who oppose cooperative internationalism (CI) and support militant internationalism (MI). Thus they accept the coercive use of force but reject conciliation, negotiation, and multilateral cooperation.

Head of Government   Effective leader of a state who proposes and shapes policy by directing an executive branch that carries out existing policies and proposes new ones. The U.S. president is both head of state and head of government.

Head of State Highest leader of a state, whether an actual ruler or ceremonial chief official such as the constitutional monarch of Britain.

Hegemon State that leads or dominates on the world scene, as the United States did particularly in the years immediately following World War II.

Holdouts Defectors or free riders, who decline to cooperate, typically in some common pool situation that calls for collective action.

Horizontal Nuclear Proliferation Spread of nuclear capability to additional states (or, worse yet, nonstate actors), a threat still growing in the aftermath of the Cold War. Compare with *vertical nuclear proliferation*.

Human Intelligence Intelligence gathered by agents in place (spies), as opposed to such means as electronic intercepts and satellite imagery. Also abbreviated *HUMINT*.

Humanitarian Relief Missions typically involving provision of food, shelter, medical services, and other supplies after wars and natural disasters. May include assisting in the repatriation of prisoners and displaced peoples.

In-and-Outer Hilsman's (1967, 541–44) term for an individual whose career history involves a number of alternations between periods working in government and times working in academia, business, or policy think tanks. They may build up considerable expertise and policy influence (see zone 2 of Figure 4.2).

In-Person Services In Robert Reich's (1991) classification, work that cannot be performed without direct customer contact to deliver a product or service. Like routine production services, they involve repetitive and standardized operations. Such jobs comprise the rapidly growing service economy. Compare with *routine production services* and *symbolic-analytic services*.

Incrementalism Decision-making mode in which governments modify existing policy as little as possible and only in response to problems which have grown severe enough that they no longer can be ignored. Under incrementalism, policy movement over time will almost surely be a series of fits and starts, proceeding jaggedly from point to point rather than smoothly from start to eventual goal. Compare with *satisficing*; contrast with *optimizing*.

Industrial Policy State policy of sponsoring economic programs in which the public and private sectors coordinate their efforts and investments to develop or promote new industries and technologies, and ex-

ports generally. Thus, for example, Japan's Ministry of International Trade and Industry (MITI) coordinates policy between industrial combines to promote Japanese penetration of foreign markets.

Insecure Conditional Viability The state could be absorbed or destroyed, and that attack would "pay off" for the dominant government, but the dominant government still refrains. See *viability*; compare *unconditional viability*, *conditional viability*, and *secure conditional viability*.

Information In the intelligence community, unevaluated material or raw information. Compare with *intelligence*.

Infrastructure Fundamental systems on which growth and development depend. Traditionally, these include such systems as transportation, energy generation and transmission, and communications.

Institutional Design Structure of members and relationships established in a system, such as the U.S. foreign policy system, by the Constitution, legislation, executive orders, and case law.

Intelligence In the intelligence community, the product after received information has been processed.

Intelligence Community Large, functionally defined group of analysts and officials in a number of executive branch agencies and departments with overlapping interests and global reach. From the perspective of the foreign policy system as an information processing system (see Figure 4.1), the intelligence community is one of its most important subsystems.

Interests Section Section within an embassy that represents a third state that has no diplomatic relations with the host state and government. For example, since the United States broke relations with Castro's Cuba in 1960, Switzerland has run a U.S. Interests Section in its embassy in Havana. In other cases, Interests Sections often are staffed by nationals of the third state, by permission of the host government.

Intergovernmental Organizations (IGOs) Organizations with governments of states as members. Examples include the United Nations, NATO, and the Organization for Security and Cooperation in Europe. Different IGOs deal with economic, functional, political, and security problems.

Intermediate-Time Feedback Information about policy results from actors involved in the policy process and sources built into that process, which takes some while to become available, but may be at hand soon enough to influence current policies. Examples include congressional oversight hearings and investigative journalism. Information does not always remain within the institutional structures of government, and several intermediate-time feedback channels require making information public. Compare with *real-time feedback* and *post hoc feedback*.

Intermestic Policies   Policies influenced strongly by both international and domestic forces. Because foreign policy has impacts both at home and abroad, all foreign policies actually are intermestic (with varying mixes).

International Law or **the Law of Nations**   Body of rules considered legally binding in international relations, comprising both the customary rules and usage to which states have given express or tacit consent, plus the provisions of ratified treaties and international conventions.

International Nongovernmental Organizations (INGOs or **NGOs)**   Organizations with individuals as members, often having state organizations and local chapters. Examples include Greenpeace and Amnesty International. Frequently they operate as interest groups raising individual consciousness and pressuring governments on behalf of broad international goals such as limiting practices that threaten species extinction, ending nuclear testing, and terminating human rights abuses worldwide.

International Political Economy (IPE)   Broad area in which politics and economics intersect, or the politics of economic issues.

International Politics Perspective   General view that concentrates on interactions between states and other international actors. It leads us to examine the structure of the international system for its patterns of interaction and for the external influences on government decisions. Contrast with the *foreign policy perspective*.

International Regimes   Created by treaties and actions; may include specialized intergovernmental organizations (IGOs). Regimes combine law, regulation, and the actions of interstate and international organizations and individual state governments to create international norms and thereby influence and manage selected behaviors. Examples include the formal international regulation of whaling and the informal international consensus after the 1995 Dayton peace accords for Bosnia to prevent further fragmentation of former Yugoslavia.

International Security Regimes   Arrangements to preserve international order and the safety and security of individual states and governments. See also *international regimes*.

Internationalists   In Wittkopf's analyses (1990, 1994, 1995), individuals who support both cooperative internationalism (CI) and militant internationalism (MI), accepting an active international role compounded from both conciliatory and coercive strategies. This position is exemplified by the bipartisan foreign policy paradigm widely held from World War II until the Vietnam War.

Intersecting Negotiations   Negotiations intersect when parties bargain about more than one topic simultaneously, creating opportunities to trade concessions in one set of talks for offsetting concessions in another. In domestic legislative politics and ordinary committee meetings we know this as *logrolling*.

Interventionism   Forcible interference in locations abroad, typically involving military and/or economic actions to direct or influence the affairs of others. Interventionism is more likely to be a tendency in specific policies than a grand policy. Its duration varies from brief incursions to prolonged rule, sometimes (and arguably) done for the benefit of those influenced or ruled. Its extreme form is *colonialism*, the seizing and ruling of colonies.

Iron Triangle   Term applied to the politically potent Cold War combination of military forces, defense contractors, and Congress members. The military services needed Congress to provide funding and contractors to develop and build weapons systems; defense contractors needed business and could provide attractive postretirement jobs to reward cooperative military officers; and Congress members wanted military bases and contracts to provide jobs for their voters.

Isolationism   Strictly, a grand policy of minimizing all foreign ties. Examples include Japan before its opening to the West in 1854, Cambodia under Pol Pot and the Khmer Rouge from 1975 to 1979, and North Korea for the entire second half of the twentieth century. Isolationism is commonly but incorrectly used to refer to U.S. policy in the early postindependence years and between World Wars I and II. Successful true isolationism is aided by many conditions, including the following: economic self-sufficiency; social self-sufficiency; a diffuse structure of world power (no concentrated pressures); physical or geographical isolation; and an absence of external threats.

Isolationists   In Wittkopf's analyses (1990, 1994, 1995), individuals who oppose both cooperative internationalism (CI) and militant internationalism (MI), thus rejecting most forms of active international involvement, as the United States did shortly after achieving independence.

Law of Nations   See *international law.*

Leak   Deliberate sharing of restricted or classified information outside official channels in hopes of changing policy. Since the Vietnam era, leaks have become an important channel of Washington politics.

Legation   Permanent, foreign-posted diplomatic ministers with supporting staff.

Legislative Veto   Ruled illegal by the Supreme Court in 1983, such vetoes occur when Congress provisionally authorizes the president to take action, subject to ultimate legislative approval. The War Powers Act of 1973 runs afoul of that ruling because it grants the president authority to deploy troops but reserves a congressional right to reverse such deployment decisions.

Level of Analysis   When we begin to analyze any system, we choose some appropriate level of analysis, essentially the smallest independent member of the system. For many systems, we can make more than one such selection, so we effectively choose a viewpoint to take on the system. The three Allison models span three different levels of analysis.

Liberals or **Idealists**   In contrast to realists, liberals recognize international anarchy but stress the growing ability of international institutions and regimes to constrain governments' freedom of action, and the resultant opportunities to craft win-win outcomes. Compare with *realists.*

Limited War   Armed conflict limited in any or all of the following: goals, area of military operations, amount of force used, and types of military force and weaponry employed. The Korean (1950–53) and Vietnam (for the United States, roughly 1963–73) Wars are examples of limited wars. Contrast with World War II, to which few limitations applied.

Living System   In the sense used by James Miller and other researchers in the Society for General Systems Research, a system itself has many of the properties of a living organism. The system by which U.S. foreign policy is made and carried out is such a living system, composed of individual human beings and organizations. Miller identifies seven levels of living systems, each of which consists of multiple systems that are subsystems of the next higher level: cell, organ, organism, group, organization, society (in our terminology, nation), and the supranational system (in our terminology, the international or global system).

Lobbyists   Individuals hired to represent and advocate special interests. The term originated in the 1830s, based on the tendency of such advocates to populate the lobbies of Congress, the White House, and executive branch offices in hopes of buttonholing officials and legislators.

Mechanist or **Mechanistic**   Traditional realist or power balance political view. Foreign policy behavior is perceived not to be based on ideology and declaratory policy, but on the interests of a government as a world power. One of three views on the role of ideology in shaping foreign policy behavior, as described by William Zimmerman (1974), this view assigns only moderate or limited importance to ideology. Compare with *cybernetic* and *essentialist* views.

Media   Channels for widespread dissemination of news, interpretation, and opinion, which include newspapers, magazines, radio, television, and, increasingly, the Internet. Their direct and indirect roles in influencing U.S. foreign policy grew dramatically after World War II.

Members   Any system is composed of a set of components or parts or elements or members. One of Rapoport's four criteria for recognizing and describing a system. See also *relationships*, *functions*, and *predictability*. The U.S. foreign policy-making system is a complex social and political system comprising individuals as well as groups or organizations.

Mercantilism   Policy of maximizing exports and minimizing imports, so as to generate the largest possible trade surplus. Almost all states pursued mecantilism until the midnineteenth century.

Militant Internationalism   One of the two major dimensions of foreign policy belief structures found in the research of Wittkopf (1990, 1994, 1995). Involves strongly activist and sometimes unilateral policies around the world, including alliances, military aid, use of American troops abroad, and foreign interventions.

Military Security   Traditional focus of security studies, embracing not only the interplay between states' armed offensive and defensive capabilities, but also their perceptions of each other's intentions.

Mission See *legation*.

Moral Approval Recognition The view of diplomatic recognition, often avowed by the U.S. government, which holds that it implies at least some degree of approval. Consequently, recognition becomes a good for which a political price may be extracted.

Multilateral Many party; that is, more than two. In diplomacy, state-to-state talks between three or more governments. Contrast with *bilateral*.

Nation Group of people distinguished primarily by their shared sense of being a distinctive single group. Nations typically share a common ethnic, linguistic, and religious heritage and identify with some piece of territory, although they may not occupy it. They may or may not be formally recognized by others; compare with *state*.

Nation Building Actively working to create new political, social, and economic infrastructures in a target area. May be part of a comprehensive program including either peacekeeping or peace enforcement to maintain stability.

Nation-State State with only one significant national group. Under the most extreme form of nationalism, every nation would have statehood.

National Intelligence Estimates (NIEs) Documents that embody the intelligence community's current knowledge about the situation in some specific country or region, or about a particular topic, along with estimates of projected future developments. The director of Central Intelligence (DCI), as the president's principal foreign intelligence adviser, is officially responsible for each NIE, which is supposed to reflect the DCI's judgment about the known (and knowable) facts and probable developments.

National Security Usually refers to what properly should be called state security. Decision makers regularly invoke national security but rarely define the concept at all, let alone with any precision. It was a catch phrase of the Cold War period and of political realism.

National Security Council (NSC) Under the National Security Act of 1947, the NSC consists of only four people: the president as chair, the vice president, and the secretaries of defense and state, plus several statutory advisers and additional temporary and permanent members added based on presidential preferences and the issues under consideration. In recent decades the NSC staff has rivaled the State Department as a source of policy planning and influence.

Nationalism Drive of nations to attain independence as recognized states. The intensity of that drive grew dramatically during the latter half of the twentieth century, often fragmenting existing states.

NATO Expansion Movement to expand the sphere of NATO security guarantees by inviting some newly democratizing Eastern European states to become NATO members. In their July 1997 Madrid Summit, NATO leaders invited the Czech Republic, Hungary, and Poland to begin accession talks; other new memberships were deferred for later decision. The U.S. Senate ratified this expansion in 1998. Previous NATO membership included the United States, Canada, and fourteen Western European governments (Belgium, Denmark, France, Germany [initially West Germany]), Great Britain, Greece, Iceland, Italy, Luxembourg, the Netherlands, Norway, and Portugal, Spain, and Turkey.

Natural Power Attributes Power attributes or capabilities involving strengths that actors possess by fortunate accident of location, such as a rich resource endowment or a protective geography. Compare with *synthetic power attributes*.

NBC Weapons Nuclear, biological, and chemical weapons, collectively considered to be weapons of mass destruction (WMD).

Neoisolationism Grand policy of post–Cold War U.S. nonalignment, called for by some analysts who prescribe increased attention to domestic problems and increased reliance on others and international cooperation to deal with foreign policy problems.

Neocolonialism Policies that, deliberately or not, tend to keep former colonies economically tied to their previous ruling states.

Neoimperialism System under which developed states control and seriously retard the economic development of weaker states, by using unfair trading practices and exploiting the weakness of controls over international business corporations. One form of neocolonialism.

Neutrality Strictly, noninvolvement in other states' wars. Neutrality may be a grand policy applied broadly to all conflicts, as by Switzerland, or a specific policy for a single conflict. In the 1950s neutrality in the Cold War was used to mean nonalignment with the superpowers.

New Internal Wars   The wave of post–Cold War conflicts within Second Tier states, seen first in the early and mid-1990s in Bosnia, Somalia, Rwanda, and Liberia. The term was originated by Donald Snow (1997, Chapter 8). These new internal wars lack the ideological component common to many civil wars during the Cold War period. They often occur in failed states, in which anarchy follows the collapse of a central government.

Nonalignment   Fundamental and widely used grand policy under which governments choose to not form alliances with other states. Nonalignment may be applied either broadly, to all states, or narrowly. It was first used (c. 1950) to mean not siding with either superpower. The "nonaligned movement" actually is a coalition of developing states.

Noninterference   Diplomatic principle that diplomats should be allowed to conduct their business in host countries without obstruction.

Normative considerations   Views about what is to be considered "good," and exactly whose good we should consider. The foreign policy stands that individuals and governments take depend crucially on their fundamental values or belief structures, including views about the nature of international politics and of the country's appropriate world role.

Nuclear Nonproliferation Treaty (NPT)   The 1968 treaty, subsequently signed by more states than any other arms control agreement, permanently dividing the world into nuclear weapons states (the United States, Russia, Britain, France, and China, in the order they gained nuclear capability) and non-nuclear weapons states.

Optimizing   Decision-making model or process in which every possible option is examined and the one best option is picked. Practical considerations of time limitations, changing options, and so on, make all political decisions tend away from optimizing and toward satisficing; contrast with *incrementalism.*

Organizational Process   Allison's Model II, in which it is assumed that government actions are organizational outputs arrived at through competition for leadership group approval. Available options provided by programs and standard operating procedures strongly constrain all government actions. Compare with Allison's unitary government (Model I) and governmental politics (Model III) models.

Ozone-Depleting Substances (ODSs)   Any of a series of related chemicals that contribute to the destruction of ozone in the upper atmosphere. ODSs, such as chlorofluorocarbons (CFCs), when released at the surface eventually migrate to the upper atmosphere. Removing upper atmospheric ozone reduces the natural filtering of harmful ultraviolet (UV) rays from sunlight.

Peace Enforcement   Moves beyond the limitations of peacekeeping by involving military operations of many types designed to impose peace on would-be combatants. Often this must involve disarming the combatants, thus bringing about peace by removing the wherewithal to continue making war.

Peacekeeping   Confidence-building measures that aid wary states or factions in defusing potential new hostilities and building toward eventually living in peace, provided all parties want to keep the peace. Operations may involve unarmed military observer missions or armed peacekeeping missions.

Peacemaking   Process of negotiating agreements to accomplish such ends as stopping armed hostilities, defusing a threatened military clash, repatriating displaced peoples, addressing the root causes of sustained disagreements, and laying the groundwork for a more amicable future.

Perestroika   Literally, restructuring. Russian term for a broad set of economic reforms launched by Soviet leader Mikhail Gorbachev in 1987 to bring market-like mechanisms designed to overcome chronic shortages and inefficiencies. See also *glasnost.*

Persona Non Grata   Literally, unwelcome. Said of a diplomat ordered out of a country, nominally for abuse of diplomatic privileges.

Plausible Deniability   Situation in which officials can claim, either in their own right or on behalf of the U.S. government, to have no knowledge of a covert operation or other potentially embarrassing matter, and reasonable people can say that the disclaimer might be true.

Police Actions   Military actions of diverse types undertaken to enforce international law or treaties. May range in size from brief actions by small units up to fairly sizable and prolonged wars.

Political Party Leader   Official viewed as the chief spokesperson for a political party, by virtue of public elected office held or party choice. The U.S. president is generally considered a party's titular leader by virtue of being its highest elected public official. In parliamentary systems, leadership of the majority party usually leads to election as prime minister, the head of government. Compare also *head of state*.

Political security   Concerns the organizational stability of states, including their systems of governance and the ideologies to which they appeal for legitimization.

Post Hoc (or After-the-Fact) Feedback   Information about policy results from actors involved in the policy process and sources built into that process, which becomes available only well after the relevant events have transpired, but still may be useful in assessing the quality of policy making. Compare with *real-time feedback* and *intermediate-time feedback*.

Potential Power   Power attributes that require time, after which they may or may not be actualized. Examples include mobilizing reserve troops, converting a civilian economy to wartime production, developing a highly trained modern work force or a new technology, and exploiting a previously untapped natural resource. Compare with *actual power*.

Power Attributes   Those things that cause us to consider their possessors, whether states or nonstate actors, to be "powerful"; see *natural power attributes*, *synthetic power attributes*, and *social-psychological power*.

Power Projection   Movement and use of military force abroad.

Precedence   Diplomatic standing based on seniority, to avoid arguments over whose government is more powerful, more important, or better liked by the host government. Thus the dean of the corps of diplomats in any particular host capital is the ambassador who has served there longest.

Precommitment   Locking oneself into a strategy announced in advance. This strengthens one's bargaining position by limiting flexibility, leaving the other party the last clear chance to reach agreement or avoid escalated conflict by backing down.

Predictability   We can use our knowledge of the structure and past functioning of a system to gain insight into its likely future performance. This is one of Rapoport's four criteria for recognizing and describing a system. Arguably, this criterion is redundant and already implied by the combination of his other three criteria: members, relationships, and functions. Systems analysts use the term *state of the system* to refer to a snapshot describing all the significant variables, essentially everything important about the membership, connections, and functioning of the system at one instant. If we know the system's structure and its state at one moment, we should be able to predict its state at any future time.

Preliminaries   The first stage of negotiation: contacts about deciding to negotiate. Precedes process talks and bargaining.

Prisoners' Dilemma   Situation or game of strategy in which individuals who pursue goals intended either to maximize their individual benefit or to minimize their individual risk end up worse off than if they had cooperated with others.

Process   The second stage of negotiation: working out the procedures for conducting negotiations. Follows preliminaries and precedes bargaining.

Protectionism   A system of policies designed to protect domestic producers from foreign competition. Tariffs are the major example, but there can be important *nontariff barriers* to trade.

Ranking   One of the five fundamental axioms of rational choice. Alternatives are ranked by preference or indifference; that is, given any two alternatives A and B, either A is preferred to B, or B is preferred to A, or each is considered equally desirable, so the chooser is indifferent between them. Any number of alternatives may be ranked in this manner by making pairwise comparisons, adding one alternative at a time to the ranked list. When the process is complete, either a single alternative or a set of two or more tied alternatives heads the ranking. Different individuals may have different preference orderings over the same set of alternatives. See also *choice*, *consistency*, *decisiveness*, and *transitivity*.

Real-Time Feedback   Information about policy results from sources built into the policy process and immediately available, primarily to qualified officials formally entitled to access. Examples include diplomatic messages and trade statistics. Compare with *intermediate-time feedback* and *post hoc feedback*.

Realists   Those who see states as the most important actors in a fundamentally anarchical international system. States thus need to maximize their power relative to all possible opponents, on all dimensions of power, including military, economic, and diplomatic or political influence. The contemporary variant on this view often is termed *neorealism*. Compare *liberals* or *idealists*.

Realpolitik   Original German term for realism. See *realists*.

Relationships or **Connections**   Any system has a network of relationships or connections between its members, which binds them together into a functional unit. This is one of Rapoport's four criteria for recognizing and describing a system. See also *members*, *functions*, and *predictability*. Relationships in the foreign policy system are connections between human individuals and groups, organizations, and governments, which include legal, organizational, political, and personal ties.

Routine Production Services   In Robert Reich's (1991) classification, work involving repetitive or similar steps that yield a stream of identical or similar products, whether made from metal, plastic, fabric, or data. This includes both blue-collar labor and assembly-line work, and many white-collar jobs, including most clerical positions and routine supervisory jobs. Compare with *in-person services* and *symbolic-analytic services*.

Rule of Law   Condition under which contracts are honored and violators—whether individuals, firms, or government agencies—are held accountable by legal institutions. Rule of law has become a key phrase in U.S.-Chinese relations because its absence or primitive condition in China raises major obstacles to the greater economic interchange sought by both governments.

Salami Tactics   *Tacit bargaining* tactic of endlessly pushing just a bit beyond what the rules allow, and, if not stopped, pushing just a bit further. The logic behind the term is that what is lost at each step is only a tiny slice of the salami, and seems not worth fighting over, although eventually the whole salami is gone.

Salience   Property of being noticeable, prominent, conspicuous, or standing out from the rest. Political salience can be defined as political impact, noticeabilty, or effectiveness.

Salient Points   Points arrived at in bargaining because of their obviousness or because they appeal to equity norms. Examples include 50-50 division between two parties, and the drawing of state boundaries along lines of latitude or longitude, or along the middles of rivers.

Satisficing   Decision-making model or process in which only some options are examined and the first option that meets a given set of criteria for minimal acceptability is adopted. Practical considerations of time limitations, changing options, and so on, make all political decisions tend toward satisficing; compare with *incrementalism* and contrast with *optimizing*.

Schema   Concept derived from the cognitive psychology literature. A *problem schema* consists of information about a class of problems to which it applies and information about their solutions. Within a policy domain, beliefs are then expected to show a vertical structure from core values to general policy stands to specific policy positions, a proposition backed up by a good deal of empirical research.

Second Tier   Set of developing states. See also *third world*.

Second World   During the Cold War, the developed states with command economies, generally considered to include the Soviet Union and Eastern Europe, particularly East Germany, Poland, Czechoslovakia, and Hungary, the most developed Soviet satellite states. With the breakup of the Soviet Union at the end of 1991 and moves toward the adoption of market economies throughout the region, the Second World effectively ceased to exist.

Secure Conditional Viability   Condition in which a state could be absorbed or destroyed, but it would not be advantageous for the dominant government to do so. See *viability*; compare *unconditional viability*, *conditional viability*, and *insecure conditional viability*.

Security   State or sense of safety or certainty, and of freedom from anxiety, danger, doubt, and so on. There is an important distinction between the physical state or condition of being secure and the psychological perception of feeling secure.

Severity   Intensity of an action, or how much available power will be utilized, from the least manageable bit to everything obtainable.

Shuttle Diplomacy   Negotiations in which third parties serve as mediators or brokers who propose solutions and carry ideas and responses back and forth between parties otherwise too deeply estranged to negotiate formally across a conference table.

Side Payments   Casuistic political science term for bribes, because they occur outside the formal framework of negotiated exchange.

Social-Psychological Power Attributes   Important subclass of synthetic power attributes, which includes such aspects as charismatic leadership or the ability to command the political allegiance of allies and citizens.

Societal security   Concerns the maintenance of national cultural, ethnic, linguistic, and religious identity and traditional practices, presumably with some allowance for necessary evolution and adaptation to external conditions and developments.

Soft Power or **Cooptive Power**   Ability to attract rather than command others, persuading them to join one in seeking the same goals. Compare with *hard power* or *command power.*

Span of Control   Number of individuals whom one person can supervise effectively. Limitations on span of control are a primary reason why large organizations manage through many-level hierarchies.

Specific Policy   Applied policies that deal with single problems at specific points in time. Contrast with *grand policy.* For example, an early specific policy component of the Cold War grand policy of *containment* was to fight the 1950–53 Korean War to reverse North Korea's invasion of South Korea.

Stability   Usually some notion of stability is associated with a systems viewpoint. The system is expected to achieve more or less of an equilibrium and to function in much the same way over time.

Standard Operating Procedures (SOPs)   Detailed operating procedures developed by agencies to ensure that all their employees carry out needed functions correctly. SOPs are imperative for large organizations that must ensure their operations are performed consistently, frequently, and in many places.

State   Legal entity that has a government, has sovereignty under international law, is identified with some piece of territory, typically has at least de facto control over that territory, and usually is formally recognized by other governments. Canada is a (binational) state; compare with *nation.*

Strategic Planning   Planning of large-scale programs to achieve long-range goals. Strategic planning is analogous to grand policy, and contrasts with tactical planning.

Strength/Distance Function   The manner in which usable power, for example military or economic strength, declines with distance from one's homeland because of risks and time and transport costs that increase with distance. The viability of states derives from the different rates at which usable power changes with distance; see also *unconditional viability,*

secure conditional viability, conditional viability, and *insecure conditional viability.*

Structure   Members of a system and the set of relationships between those members are sometimes called the structure of the system. In the foreign policy system, structural changes typically are accomplished by legislation or executive order, and represent changes to the institutional design of the system.

Subsystem   Systems tend to be made up of subsystems, and themselves to be subsystems of larger systems. For example, parts of several cabinet departments are included among the elements of the subsystem that deals with foreign trade agreements.

Summit Meetings   Meetings between heads of state or heads of government. Although occasionally venues for substantive negotiation over issues that can be settled only at the highest level, summits normally are ceremonial gatherings at which leaders sign and formally recognize agreements worked out in advance by negotiators within their administrations.

Superpowers   The United States and the Soviet Union (USSR), from the end of World War II in 1945 until the end of the Cold War in about 1990 and the breakup of the Soviet Union at the end of 1991. So called because their power—especially military and political strength—greatly exceeded that of any other state.

Sustainable Development   Development that can be sustained indefinitely because it relies on renewable resources in quantities which can be renewed indefinitely.

Symbolic-Analytic Services   Most creative of what Reich (1991) calls the "three jobs of the future." Symbolic analysts deal in problem identification, problem solving, and strategic brokering of many types. Their products are ideas, solutions to problems, and brokered agreements, represented as manipulations of symbols, which may include streams of data, writings, design drawings, logical and legal arguments, systems of equations, and the like. Compare with *in-person services* and *routine production services.*

Synthetic Power Attributes   Power attributes or capabilities involving strengths that actors can acquire only by choice, such as a large army or a loyal voting bloc in intergovernmental organizations. Synthetic power often requires natural power attributes for support, as, for example, natural resources that underlie and help support a developed economy. Compare with *natural power attributes.*

System Entity defined by Rapoport's four criteria of members, relationships, functions, and predictability. U.S. foreign policy is made and carried out by such a system, composed of many individual human beings, groups, and organizations (see *subsystems*). See also *living systems*.

Tacit Bargaining Negotiating through actions and the reciprocation they evoke rather than through formal talks. In tacit bargaining, we allow our actions and public statements to communicate what we seek and what we are willing to do to obtain it.

Tactical Planning Planning of procedures for dealing with specific problems and fighting specific battles. Tactical planning is analogous to specific policy, and contrasts with strategic planning.

Tariff Union Agreement to eliminate tariffs and other trade restrictions between member states while establishing common tariffs on imports from nonmembers. Examples include the European Economic Community (EEC; later the European Union or EU) and the North American Free Trade Agreement (NAFTA). See also *free trade area*.

Terms of Trade Problem Over the long term, prices of manufactured goods usually inflate slowly; agricultural and raw material prices fluctuate widely because suppliers enter or leave the market, new oil or mineral deposits are discovered, or crop yields vary with rainfall cycles and weather extremes. States whose one- or two-product economies are tied to exports of agricultural produce and raw materials thus face the dilemma of importing manufactured goods at slowly increasing prices while their export incomes ebb and flow and do not necessarily average out to long-term increases.

Think Tanks Not-for-profit, nominally (although sometimes decreasingly) nonpartisan centers, foundations, or organizations dedicated to full-time policy analysis and advocacy. They often provide jobs to in-and-outers during their out-of-government periods.

Third World During the Cold War, all states not in the First World or Second World, lumped into the otherwise largely undefined category "developing states." See also *Second Tier*.

Timing In power considerations, timing refers to the availability of options, many of which require advance planning (see Chapter 8).

Tragedy of the commons Garrett Hardin's (1968) term for an archetypal situation in which a common resource can be destroyed unless collective action prevents its overuse. See also *collective action problems* and *common pool*.

Transitivity One of the five fundamental axioms of rational choice. It is assumed that among any three alternatives A, B, and C, if A is preferred to B, and B is preferred to C, then A is preferred to C. This property is necessary to prevent preference cycles (A preferred to B, B preferred to C, but C preferred to A) that would not leave a clear best choice. (A classic problem in democratic voting theory, formally proved by Kenneth Arrow (1963), is that a group voting by majority rule among three or more alternatives may not have a transitive group preference even though every individual member's preference ordering is transitive.) See also *choice*, *consistency*, *decisiveness*, and *ranking*.

Treaty Formal agreement between the governments of sovereign states or intergovernmental organizations of states; the source of most international law.

Trial Balloons Announcements of potential policies intended to gauge reaction before they are put into force. A proposed policy that evokes significant protest may be disavowed within days, and often some scapegoat waits in the wings to be sacrificially fired for being "responsible" for the "mistaken" policy announcement.

Unarmed Military Observer Mission First employed in the Balkans in 1947, such peacekeeping missions can help keep a cease-fire peaceful by overseeing and reporting on the conflicting parties' behavior and helping resolve violations before they escalate into local battles.

Unconditional Viability Condition of a state that could not be absorbed or destroyed as an independent decision-making center. See *viability;* compare *secure conditional viability*, *conditional viability*, and *insecure conditional viability*.

Understanding or **Entente** Relatively informal and often unwritten agreement that may guide serious policy for years. An example is the de facto alliance between Israel and the United States, no part of which was reduced to writing until the early 1980s; compare with *treaty*.

Unitary Government or **Rational Actor** Allison's Model I, in which it is assumed that governments can be treated as undivided (or unitary) rational actors which optimize policy choices. If we meet all the assumptions, this model works well in assessing the impacts of global-level government-to-government interactions, but it cannot answer questions about effects at lower levels of analysis within the government. Compare with Allison's *organizational process* (Model II) and *governmental politics* (Model III) models.

Verification   Institutionalized process of confirming that another party is abiding by the terms of an agreement. Although publicized particularly in the context of strategic arms control agreements, verification is applicable to many types of agreements.

Vertical Nuclear Proliferation   Growth in the sizes of existing nuclear arsenals. It is no longer a problem for the major nuclear powers, nor for some of the minor nuclear powers. Compare with *horizontal nuclear proliferation.*

Viability   Set of conditions concerning whether or not a state could be absorbed or destroyed as an independent decision-making center during a conflict. As originated by Kenneth Boulding (1962, 58–59), this concept has several important variants. From most to least secure, they are as follows: unconditional viability; secure conditional viability; conditional viability; and insecure conditional viability.

War Powers Act of 1973   Controversial legislation passed with the intent of limiting the president's ability to commit U.S. troops abroad to combat without congressional approval. Critics charge that it gives the president a 60- to 90-day blank check for exactly such actions.

Weapons of Mass Destruction (WMD)   Weapons of extremely great destructive capacity. Generally considered to comprise nuclear, biological, and chemical (NBC) weapons.

Whistle-Blowers   Government employees or others who expose illegal activities, often to media or congressional investigators, in hopes of changing policy.

World Bank   Common shorthand for the International Bank for Reconstruction and Development.

BIBLIOGRAPHY

Albright, David, William M. Arkin, Frans Berkhout, Robert S. Norris, and William Walker. 1995. "Inventories of Fissile Materials and Nuclear Weapons." In the (Stockholm International Peace Research Institute) *SIPRI Yearbook 1995: Armaments, Disarmament and International Security* (pp. 317–33). Oxford: Oxford University Press.

Allison, Graham T. 1971. *Essence of Decision: Explaining the Cuban Missile Crisis.* Boston: Little, Brown.

Alter, Jonathan. 1995. "Confessing the Sins of Vietnam." *Newsweek,* 17 April: 40–54.

———. 1997. "Why This Is Not a Drill." *Newsweek,* 17 November: 34.

Amnesty International. 1996a. "About Amnesty." http://www.oneworld.org/amnesty/ai_info.html (2 April 1997).

———. 1996b. "International Community Failing to Take Responsibility for Massive Human Rights Violations in 1995." http://www.oneworld.org/amnesty/press/annreport_june18.html (2 April 1997).

———. 1999. "How to Contact Amnesty International in Your Country." http://www.amnesty.org/aisect/contacts.htm (30 May 1999).

Anthony, Ian, Pieter D. Wezeman, and Siemon T. Wezeman. 1995. "The Trade in Major Conventional Weapons." In the (Stockholm International Peace Research Institute) *SIPRI Yearbook 1995: Armaments, Disarmament and International Security* (pp. 491–509). Oxford: Oxford University Press.

Arrow, Kenneth J. 1963. *Social Choice and Individual Values,* 2nd ed. Yale University. Cowles Foundation for Research in Economics. Monograph 12. New York: Wiley.

Aspin, Les. 1992. *National Security in the 1990s: Defining a New Basis for U.S. Military Forces.* Address before the Atlantic Council of the United States, January 6. Reprinted by the Committee on Armed Services, U.S. House of Representatives.

———. 1993, 1 September. *The Bottom-Up Review: Forces for a New Era.* Washington, D.C.: Department of Defense.

Associated Press. 1997. "China Sees Weakness in U.S. Military." By John Diamond. 19 September.

Axelrod, Robert. 1984. *The Evolution of Cooperation.* New York: Basic Books.

Bacchus, William I. 1983. *Staffing for Foreign Affairs: Personnel Systems for the 1980's and 1990's.* Princeton, N.J.: Princeton University Press.

Baker, Peter. 1997. "Washington Wins War of Words." *Washington Post,* 15 September: A1.

Baldwin, David A. 1993. "Neoliberalism, Neorealism, and World Politics." In David A. Baldwin, ed., *Neorealism and Neoliberalism: The Contemporary Debate* (Chapter 1, pp. 3–25). New York: Columbia University Press.

Barton, John H., and Lawrence Weiler, eds. 1976. *International Arms Control: Issues and Agreements.* By the Stanford Arms Control Group. Stanford, Calif.: Stanford University Press.

Baudrillard, Jean. 1993. "The Evil Demon of Images and the Precision of Simulacra." In T. Docherty, ed., *Postmodernism: A Reader* (pp. 194–99). New York: Columbia University Press.

Baugh, William H. 1989. "On the American-Soviet Strategic Nuclear Balance." In Edward A. Kolodziej and Patrick M. Morgan, eds., *Security and Arms Control. Vol. 2: A Guide to International Policymaking* (Chapter 3, pp. 57–84). Westport, Conn.: Greenwood Press, 1989.

———. 1995. "Structure and Polarization of Public and Elite Opinion on Foreign Policy Issues." Paper presented at the annual meeting of the American Political Science Association, Chicago, 31 August–3 September.

Binnendijk, Hans A., and Patrick L. Clawson, eds. 1997. *Strategic Assessment 1997: Flashpoints and Force Structure*. Washington, D.C.: National Defense University, Institute for National Strategic Studies.

Bliss, Howard, and M. Glen Johnson. 1975. *Beyond the Water's Edge: America's Foreign Policies*. Philadelphia: J. B. Lippincott.

Blum, James L. 1992. "The Congressional Budget Office: On the One Hand, On the Other." In Carol H. Weiss, ed., *Organizations for Policy Analysis: Helping Government Think* (Chapter 12, pp. 218–35). Newbury Park, Calif.: Sage.

Boulding, Kenneth E. 1962. *Conflict and Defense: A General Theory*. New York: Harper & Row.

Breckinridge, Scott D. 1986. *The CIA and the U.S. Intelligence System*. Boulder, Colo.: Westview Press.

Brown, Harold. 1980. *Department of Defense Annual Report, Fiscal Year 1981*. Washington, D.C.: U.S. Government Printing Office.

Brown, Seyom. 1994. *The Faces of Power: Constancy and Change in United States Foreign Policy from Truman to Clinton*, 2d ed. New York: Columbia University Press.

Brzezinski, Zbigniew. 1987. "The NSC's Midlife Crisis." *Foreign Policy 69* (Winter): 80–99.

Burt, Richard. 1978. "The Scope and Limits of SALT." *Foreign Affairs 56*, 4 (July):751–70.

———. 1980. "Study Says a Soviet Move in Iran Might Require U.S. Atom Arms." *New York Times*, 2 February: 1, 4.

Buzan, Barry. 1991. *People, States and Fear: An Agenda for International Security Studies in the Post–Cold War Era*, 2d ed. Boulder, Colo.: Lynne Reinner.

Cannon, Lou. 1983. "President Seeks Futuristic Defense Against Missiles." *Washington Post*, 24 March: A1, A13.

Carson, Nancy. 1992. "Process, Prescience, and Pragmatism: The Office of Technology Assessment." In Carol H. Weiss, ed., *Organizations for Policy Analysis: Helping Government Think* (Chapter 13, pp. 236–51). Newbury Park, Calif.: Sage.

Carter, Janelle. 1997. "Georgian Diplomat Gets 7 to 21 Years in Fatal Crash." *Associated Press*, 19 December.

Carter, Jimmy. 1982. *Keeping Faith: Memoirs of a President*. New York: Bantam.

Chayes, Abram, and Jerome B. Wiesner, eds. 1969. *ABM: An Evaluation of the Decision to Deploy an Antiballistic Missile System*. New York: New American Library.

Chernow, Barbara A., and George A. Vallasi, eds. 1993. *The Columbia Encyclopedia*, 5th ed. New York: Columbia University Press.

Church Committee. 1976. *U.S. Congress, Senate. Final Report of the Senate Select Committee to Study Government Operations with Respect to Intelligence Activities. Report 94-755. Book I, Foreign and Military Intelligence*. Washington, D.C.: U.S. Government Printing Office.

Churchill, Winston. 1954. *The Second World War, Vol. 6. Triumph and Tragedy*. London: Cassell.

Cohen, Roger. 1995. "France to Rejoin Military Command of NATO Alliance." *New York Times*, 6 December: A1.

Cohen, William. 1997. Newsmaker interview by Jim Lehrer on the PBS television series *Newshour*, 10 November.

Converse, Philip E. 1964. "The Nature of Belief Systems in Mass Publics." In David Apter, ed., *Ideology and Discontent*. (Chapter vi, pp. 206–261). New York: Wiley.

CQ. 1998. *Federal Staff Directory 1998/Winter V.1*. Alexandria, VA: CQ Staff Directories, Inc.

Crutsinger, Martin. 1997. "U.S., Japan Resolve Shipping Dispute, Avoid Port Showdown." Associated Press.

Daniels, Jonathan. 1946. *Frontier on the Potomac*. New York: Macmillan.

Davis, Otto A., M. A. H. Dempster, and Aaron Wildavsky. 1966. "A Theory of the Budgetary Process." *American Political Science Review 60*: 529–47.

Department of State Bulletin. 1985. Mr. McFarlane's Interview on "Meet the Press." *Department of State Bulletin*, 85: 33.

Deutsch, Karl W. 1967. "On the Concepts of Politics and Power." *Journal of International Affairs 21*, 2: 232–41.

Diamond, Larry. 1992. "Promoting Democracy." *Foreign Policy* 87: 25–46.

Drell, Sidney, and Uri Dan. 1979. "Untold Story of the Mideast Talks." *New York Times Magazine*, 21 January: 20 ff.

Druckman, Daniel. 1995. "Situational Levers of Position Change: Further Explanations." In Daniel Druckman and Christopher Mitchell, special eds., *Flexibility in International Negotiation and Mediation. The Annals of the American Academy of Political and Social Science*, Vol. 542 (pp. 61–80). Thousand Oaks, Calif.: Sage Periodicals Press.

———, and Christopher Mitchell. 1995. "Flexibility in Negotiation and Mediation." In D. Druckman and C. Mitchell's *Flexibility in International Negotiation and Mediation. The Annals of the American Academy of Political and Social Science*, Vol. 542 (pp. 10–23). Thousand Oaks, Calif.: Sage Periodicals Press.

Dumbrell, John. 1990. *The Making of U.S. Foreign Policy*. Manchester: Manchester University Press.

Dunsire, Andrew. 1985. "A Cybernetic View of Guidance, Control and Evaluation in the Public Sector." In Franz-Xaver Kaufmann, Giandomenico Majone, and Vincent Ostrom, eds., *Guidance, Control, and Evaluation in the Public Sector: The Bielefeld Interdisciplinary Project* (Chapter 15, pp. 313–25). Berlin and New York: Walter de Gruyter.

Durch, William J. 1993a. "Introduction." In William J. Durch, ed., *The Evolution of UN Peacekeeping: Case Studies and Comparative Analysis* (pp. 1–14). New York: St. Martin's Press.

———. 1993b. "The Iraq-Kuwait Observation Mission." In William J. Durch, ed., *The Evolution of UN Peacekeeping: Case Studies and Comparative Analysis* (Chapter 15, pp. 258–71). New York: St. Martin's Press.

Dye, Thomas R., and L. Harmon Zeigler. 1989. *American Politics in the Media Age*, 3d ed. Pacific Grove, Calif.: Brooks/Cole.

Dyson, Freeman J. 1984. *Weapons and Hope*. New York: Harper & Row.

Economic Report of the President, February 1999. Washington. D.C.: U.S. Government Printing Office. [DOCUMENTS/HC/106.5/.A272]

E-FOIA. 1996. Freedom of Information Act and Electronic Freedom of Information Act Amendments of 1996. 5 U.S.C. 552, as amended by Public Law No. 104-231, 110 Stat. 3048.

Elliott, Michael. 1995. "America Is Back." *Newsweek*, 9 October: 44–45.

Environmental Management Bureau. 1994. *The Ozone Layer*. Quezon City, Philippines.

European Commission. 1997. *Central and Eastern Eurobarometer* 7 (March).

Fain, Tyrus G., Katherine C. Plant, and Ross Milloy, eds. 1977. *The Intelligence Community: History, Organization, and Issues*. New York: R. R. Bowker, Public Documents Series.

Fellowship of American S]cientists. 1998a. Nuclear Non-Proliferation Treaty [NPT]. http://www.fas.org/nuke/control/npt/index.html (6 August 1998).

———. 1998b. Nuclear Non-Proliferation Treaty [NPT] Chronology. http://www.fas.org/nuke/control/npt/chron.html (6 August 1998).

Feshbach, Murray, and Alfred Friendly, Jr. 1992. *Ecocide in the U.S.S.R.* New York: Basic Books.

Findling, John E. 1989. *Dictionary of American Diplomatic History*, 2d ed. New York: Greenwood Press.

Freeman, Chas. W., Jr. 1994. *The Diplomat's Dictionary*. Washington, D.C.: National Defense University Press.

Friedman, Thomas. 1995a. "New Mexico (Life after the Peso Bomb)." *New York Times*, 15 March: A25.

———. 1995b. "The G-Who?" *New York Times*, 28 May: Section 4, p. 11.

————. 1996a. "China's Leaders Won't Go over the Brink, Will They?" *The Register Guard*, 12 March: 11A.

————. 1996b. "China's Nationalist Tide. (A Dissident's Views on How the U.S. Can Ride It)." *New York Times*, 13 March: A19.

————. 1996c. "Gardening with Beijing." *New York Times*. 18 April: A23.

————. 1997a. "China, Part III. (U.S. Business Should Wake Up)." *New York Times*, 10 March: A15.

————. 1997b. "Have I Got a Deal for You. (China's Economy May Eventually Founder in the Way That Thailand's and Malaysia's Are Doing at Present.)" *New York Times*, 20 October: A17.

————. 1997c. "Head Shot." *New York Times*, 6 November: A31.

————. 1999. *The Lexus and the Olive Tree: Understanding Globalization*. New York: Farrar Straus Giroux.

Gaffney, Frank J., Jr. 1989. "Disarmament and Distortion." *Wall Street Journal*, 2 February: A2.

Garthoff, Raymond L. 1987. *Policy versus the Law: The Reinterpretation of the ABM Treaty*. Washington, D.C.: The Brookings Institution.

Gates, Robert. 1998. *Global Challenges to American Foreign Policy*. Address to a conference on "Two Images of a Future American Foreign Policy," University of Washington, 23–24 April.

Gelb, Leslie. 1983. "Why Not the State Department?" In Charles W. Kegley and Eugene R. Wittkopf, eds., *Perspectives on American Foreign Policy*, (Chapter 18, pp. 282–98). New York: St. Martin's Press.

George, Alexander L. 1991. *Forceful Persuasion: Coercive Diplomacy as an Alternative to War*. Washington, D.C. : United States Institute of Peace Press.

————, David K. Hall, and William E. Simons. 1971. *The Limits of Coercive Diplomacy; Laos, Cuba, Vietnam*. Boston: Little, Brown.

Gersh, Debra. 1990. "General Fired for Talking to the Press." *Editor & Publisher 123*, 38: 22.

Gilbert, Felix. 1961. *To the Farewell Address: Ideas of Early American Foreign Policy*. Princeton: Princeton University Press.

Gilpin, Robert. 1975. *U.S. Power and the Multinational Corporation*. New York: Basic Books.

Glastris, Paul. 1997. "Multicultural Foreign Policy in Washington." *Newsweek*, 21 July: 33–35.

Goshko, John M. 1991. "Iraq Accepts UN Terms to End Gulf War." *Washington Post*, 7 April: 1.

Graham, Daniel O. 1982. *High Frontier: A New National Strategy*. Washington, D.C.: High Frontier.

Hafner, Katie. 1993. "Does Industrial Policy Work? Lessons from Sematech." *New York Times*, 7 November: F5.

Haggard, Stephan, and Beth A. Simmons. 1987. "Theories of International Regimes." *International Organization 41*, 3 (Summer): 491–517.

Hajnal, Peter I. 1995. "The G-7 Summit and Its Documents." *http://www.usask.ca/library/gic/v1n3/hajnal/hajnal.html* (4 November).

Halperin, Morton, with the assistance of Priscilla Clapp and Arnold Kanter. 1974. *Bureaucratic Politics and Foreign Policy*. Washington, D.C.: The Brookings Institution.

Hardin, Garrett. 1968. "The Tragedy of the Commons." *Science 162*: 1244.

Havens, Harry S. 1992. "The Evolution of the General Accounting Office: From Voucher Audits to Program Evaluations." In Carol H. Weiss, ed., *Organizations for Policy Analysis: Helping Government Think* (Chapter 11, pp. 201–17). Newbury Park, Calif.: Sage.

Hebert, H. Josef. 1995. "Radioactive Waste Cleanup May Cost $350b, U.S. Says." *Boston Globe*, 4 April: 16.

Heilbrunn, Jacob. 1998. "Playing Defense." *The New Republic*, 17 & 24 August: 16–17.

Hermann, Charles F. 1972. "Some Issues in the Study of International Crisis." In Charles F. Hermann, ed., *International Crises: Insights from Behavioral Research* (pp. 3–17). New York: Free Press.

Hillenbrand, Martin J. 1994. "An Assessment of the Future." In Pierre-Henri Laurent, ed., *The European Community: To Maastricht and Beyond. The Annals of the American Academy of Political and Social Science 531* (January): 168–77.

Hilsman, Roger. 1967. *To Move a Nation.* Garden City, N.Y.: Doubleday.

Hinckley, Ronald H. 1992. *People, Polls, and Policymakers: American Public Opinion and National Security.* New York: Lexington Books.

Hoagland, Jim. 1998. "Holbrooke's Prophetic Memoir" *Washington Post*, 9 April: A25.

Hoffman, David. 1999. "Russian Moves Toward Ratifying START II." *Washington Post.* 17 March: A24.

Holloway, David. 1984. *The Soviet Union and the Arms Race.* New Haven: Yale University Press.

Hoopes, Townsend. 1969. *The Limits of Intervention: An Inside Account of How the Johnson Policy of Escalation in Vietnam Was Reversed.* New York: D. McKay.

Hopmann, P. Terrence. 1995. "Two Paradigms of Negotiation: Bargaining and Problem Solving." In Daniel Druckman and Christopher Mitchell, special eds., *Flexibility in International Negotiation and Mediation. The Annals of the American Academy of Political and Social Science*, Vol. 542 (pp. 24–47). Thousand Oaks, Calif.: Sage Periodicals Press.

House Armed Services Subcommittee. 1978. U.S. Congress, House, Committee on Armed Services, Subcommittee on Intelligence and Military Application of Nuclear Energy, Staff Study. *Land-Based ICBM Forces Vulnerability and Options*, 95th Cong., 2nd Sess, 5 October, HASC Report No. 95-69.

Huntington, Samuel P. 1993. "The Clash of Civilizations?" *Foreign Affairs* 72, 3 (Summer): 22–49.

Huntley, James Robert. 1998. *Pax Democratica: A Strategy for the 21st Century.* New York: St. Martin's Press.

Hurwitz, Jon, and Mark Peffley. 1987. "How Are Foreign Policy Attitudes Structured? A Hierarchical Model." *American Political Science Review 81*, 4 (December): 1099–1120.

Inderfurth, Karl F., and Loch K. Johnson, eds. 1988. *Decisions of the Highest Order: Perspectives on the National Security Council.* Pacific Grove, Calif.: Brooks/Cole.

Janis, Irving L. 1972. *Victims of Groupthink: A Psychological Study of Foreign-Policy Decisions and Fiascoes.* Boston: Houghton Mifflin.

Jervis, Robert. 1976. *Perception and Misperception in International Politics.* Princeton. N.J.: Princeton University Press.

———. 1985. "Improving the Intelligence Process: Informal Norms and Incentives." In Alfred C. Maurer, Marion D. Tunstall, and James M. Keagle, eds., *Intelligence: Policy and Process.* Boulder, Colo.: Westview.

Johnson, Loch. 1983. "Seven Sins of Strategic Intelligence." *World Affairs 146*, 2 (Fall): 176–204.

Kahn, Herman. 1965. *On Escalation: Metaphors and Scenarios.* New York: Praeger.

Kamen, Al. 1990. "Americans Held in Iraq Described as 'Restrictees.'" *Washington Post*, 15 August: A1.

Katzman, Kenneth. 1994. *Iraqi Compliance with Cease-Fire Agreements.* Washington, D.C.: Congressional Research Service, The Library of Congress, Issue Brief IB92117 (3 February).

Kaufman, Burton Ira, ed. 1969. *Washington's Farewell Address: The View from the 20th Century.* Chicago: Quadrangle Books.

Kempster, Norman, and Jonathan Peterson. 1996. "U.S. Signs Nuclear Test Ban Treaty." *Los Angeles Times*, 25 September: 1A.

Kennan, George F. 1947. "The Sources of Soviet Conduct." [Written under the pseudonym "X"]. *Foreign Affairs 25*, 4 (July): 566–82.

Kennedy, Paul. 1987. *The Rise and Fall of the Great Powers: Economic Change and Military Conflict from 1500 to 2000.* New York: Random House.

Kent, Sherman. 1966. *Strategic Intelligence for American World Policy.* Princeton, N.J.: Princeton University Press.

Kim, Samuel S. 1997. "China as a Great Power." *Current History 96*, 611: 246–51.

Kissinger, Henry A. 1979. *The White House Years.* Boston: Little, Brown.

Knight, Jerry. 1993. "Hard Lessons Learned at State and Defense: Will Inman's Difficulties in Business Prove Valuable as Pentagon Chief?" *Washington Post*, 20 December: 1A.

Knorr, Klaus E. 1956. *The War Potential of Nations*. Princeton, N.J.: Princeton University Press.

Krasner, Stephen. 1983. "Structural Causes and Regime Consequences: Regimes as Intervening Variables." In Stephen Krasner, ed., *International Regimes* (pp. 1–21). Ithaca, N.Y.: Cornell University Press.

Lairson, Thomas D., and David Skidmore. 1993. *International Political Economy: The Struggle for Power and Wealth*. Fort Worth, Tex.: Harcourt Brace College Publishers.

Latham, Robert. 1995. "Thinking About Security After the Cold War." *International Studies Notes* 20, 3 (Fall): 9–16.

Lewis, Anthony. 1995. "Which Side Are We On?" *New York Times*, 7 April: A35.

Lovell, John P. 1985. *The Challenge of American Foreign Policy: Purpose and Adaptation*. New York: Macmillan.

Lowenthal, Mark M. 1992. *U.S. Intelligence: Evolution and Anatomy*, 2d ed. Westport, Conn: Praeger.

———. 1993. *The Clinton Foreign Policy: Emerging Themes*. Washington, D.C.: Congressional Research Service Report 93-951 S.

Lutz, William. 1989. *Doublespeak : From "Revenue Enhancement" to "Terminal Living." How Government, Business, Advertisers, and Others Use Language to Deceive You*. New York: Harper & Row.

Mann, Jim. 1993. "Taiwan Thriving Four Decades After CIA Predicted Its Fall." *Los Angeles Times*, 6 November: A3.

Marquis. 1977. *Who's Who in Government*. Chicago: Marquis Who's Who.

Masland, Tom. 1994. "For Sale: Nukes." *Newsweek*, 29 August: 30–32.

Matthews, Jessica Tuchman. 1991. "Introduction and Overview." In Jessica Tuchman Matthews, ed., *Preserving the Global Environment* (pp. 15–38). New York: W. W. Norton.

McNamara, Robert S. 1995. *In Retrospect: The Tragedy and Lessons of Vietnam*. With Brian VanDeMark. New York: Times Books.

Mead, Walter Russell. 1990. "On the Road to Ruin: Winning the Cold War, Losing the Economic Peace." *Harper's* 280, 1678 (March): 59–64.

Michener, James A. 1996. *This Noble Land: My Vision for America*. New York: Random House.

Middleton, Drew. 1980. "U.S. Stressing Expansion of Ability to Put Units in Iran to Fight Soviets." *New York Times*, 3 February: 10.

Millar, Alistair. 1998. NATO Enlargement. Council for a Livable World Education Fund, Arms Control Briefing Book. 105th Congress, Second Session. March 1998. *http://www.clw.org/pub/clw/ef/acbb/bbnato.html* (29 May 1999).

Miller, James Grier. 1978. *Living Systems*. New York: McGraw-Hill.

Moore, James D. 1996. *Gulliver in the Gulf: The United States and the End of Realism*. Paper presented at the annual meetings of the International Studies Association—West, University of Oregon, Eugene, 10–12 October.

Morris, Richard B., ed. 1965. *Encyclopedia of American History* (updated and revised). New York: Harper & Row.

Mueller, John. 1988. "The Essential Irrelevance of Nuclear Weapons: Stability in the Postwar World." *International Security 13*, 2 (Fall): 55–79.

Neustadt, Richard E. 1990. *Presidential Power and the Modern Presidents*. New York: Free Press.

New York Times. 1954. Text of Dulles' Statement on Foreign Policy of Eisenhower Administration. 13 January: 2.

———. 1993. "Who's in Charge of Curbing Arms?" 21 April: A22.

Nimmo, Dan, and James E. Combs. 1992. *The Political Pundits*. New York: Praeger.

Nitze, Paul H. 1989. (with Ann M. Smith and Steven L. Rearden) *From Hiroshima to Glasnost: At the Center of Decision; A Memoir*. New York: Grove Weidenfeld.

Nixon, Richard M. 1978. *The Memoirs of Richard Nixon.* New York: Grosset & Dunlap.

NSC (National Security Council). 1950. *A Report to the National Security Council, NSC-68*, April 14, 1950. Declassified on 27 February 1975 by Henry A. Kissinger, assistant to the president for National Security Affairs.

Nunn, Sam. 1987. Interpretation of the ABM Treaty. *Congressional Record—Senate.* 11 March, S2967-S2986; 12 March, S3090-S3095; 13 March, S3171-S3173; 20 May, S6809-S6831.

Nye, Joseph S., Jr. 1990a. *Bound to Lead: The Changing Nature of American Power.* New York: Basic Books.

———. 1990b. "Against Declinism." *The New Republic,* 15 October: 12–13.

———. 1992. "What New World Order?" *Foreign Affairs,* Spring: 83–96.

Office of the Federal Register. 1993. *The United States Government Manual 1993/1994.* Washington, D.C.: Office of the Federal Register, National Archives and Records Administration. DOCS SUDOCS Y4.G74/9:S.prt.102–116

———. 1998. The United States Government Manual 1998/1999. Washington, D.C.: Office of the Federal Register, National Archives and Records Administration. DOC-LC JK 421.A3.

Osgood, Charles. 1962. *An Alternative to War or Surrender.* Urbana: University of Illinois Press.

Pastor, Robert. 1980. *Congress and the Politics of Foreign Economic Policy.* Berkeley: University of California Press.

Pfaff, William. 1993. "The Economic Powers Are Western, Not Eastern." *New York Times,* 26 July: B7.

———. 1997. "Obstacles to China's Development Often Neglected." *Register-Guard.* 19 September: 13A.

Pike Committee. 1975. *Select Committee on Intelligence, Hearings: U.S. Intelligence Agencies and Activities. Part I: Intelligence Costs and Fiscal Procedures.* Washington, D.C.: U.S. Government Printing Office. 31 July, 1, 4, 5, 6, 7, 8 August.

———. 1976. *Select Committee on Intelligence, Hearings: U.S. Intelligence Agencies and Activities.* Washington, D.C.: U.S. Government Printing Office. 26 January.

Plamondon, Ann L. 1994. "A Comparison of Official Secrets and Access to Information in Great Britain and the United States." *Communications and the Law* 16, 2 (October): 51–68.

Post, Tom, and Strasser, S. 1995. "No Free Lunches Here." *Newsweek.* 20 February: 39–40.

Powell, Bill, and Owen Matthews. 1997. "Moscow on the Make." *Newsweek,* 1 September: 36–38.

Prados, John. 1986. *The Soviet Estimate: U.S. Intelligence Analysis & Soviet Strategic Forces.* Princeton, N.J.: Princeton University Press.

Puchala, Donald, and Raymond Hopkins. 1983. "International Regimes: Lessons from Inductive Analysis." In Stephen Krasner, ed., *International Regimes* (pp. 61–91). Ithaca, N.Y.: Cornell University Press.

Quill, The. 1991. "How to File an FOIA Request." 79, 8 (October): 45–46.

Randall, J. G. 1969. "George Washington and 'Entangling Alliances.'" In Burton Ira Kaufman, ed., *Washington's Farewell Address: The View from the 20th Century* (pp. 82–88). Chicago: Quadrangle Books, 1969.

Reich, Robert B. 1991. *The Work of Nations: Preparing Ourselves for 21st-Century Capitalism.* New York: Knopf.

Resor, Stanley R., and John B. Rhinelander. 1993. "Keep Arms Control a Separate Agency." *New York Times,* 3 May: A14.

Richardson, Lewis F. 1960. *Statistics of Deadly Quarrels.* Edited by Quincy Wright and C. C. Lienau. Pittsburgh: Boxwood Press.

Rielly, John E. 1991. *American Public Opinion and U.S. Foreign Policy 1991.* Chicago: Chicago Council on Foreign Relations.

———. 1995. *American Public Opinion and U.S. Foreign Policy 1995.* Chicago: Chicago Council on Foreign Relations.

———. 1999. *American Public Opinion and U.S. Foreign Policy 1999.* Chicago: Chicago Council on Foreign Relations.

Risen, James. 1995. "2 CIA Officers Ousted over Guatemala Scandal." *Los Angeles Times,* 30 September: 1A.

Robinson, William H. 1992. "The Congressional Research Service: Policy Consultant, Think Tank, and Information Factory." In Carol H. Weiss, ed., *Organizations for Policy Analysis: Helping Government Think* (Chapter 10, pp. 181–200). Newbury Park, Calif.: Sage.

Rosenthal, Andrew. 1992. "West Tags Billions for Russia." *New York Times,* 2 April: 1A.

Rostow, Walt. Whitman. 1960. *The Stages of Economic Growth: A Non-Communist Manifesto.* Cambridge: Cambridge University Press.

Rotella, Sebastian. 1998. "Degrees of Progress at Environmental Summit; Global Warning: Delegates Set Compliance Deadline. U.S. Hails Shift in Developing Nations' Attitude." *Los Angeles Times.* 15 November: A17.

Rothstein, Robert L., ed. 1991. *The Evolution of Theory in International Relations: Essays in Honor of William T.R. Fox.* Columbia, S.C.: University of South Carolina Press.

Rowen, Henry S. 1975. "Formulating Strategic Doctrine." In Commission on the Organization of the Government for the Conduct of Foreign Policy, ed., *Adequacy of Current Organization: Defense and Arms Control,* Vol.4, Appendix K (p. 220). Washington, D.C.: U.S. Government Printing Office.

Safire, William. 1984. "Somebody Is Lying." [Column on mining of Nicaraguan harbors]. *New York Times,* 25 May: A23.

———. 1995. "Hussein Still Hiding Powerful Pestilential Weapon." *New York Times,* 14 April. (*Register Guard,* 14 April: 11A).

Sanger, David E. 1995. "Clinton Offers $20 Billion to Mexico for Peso Rescue." *New York Times,* 1 February: A1.

———. 1997a. "Mexico Repays Its Debt." *New York Times,* 19 January: Section 4, page 2E.

———. 1997b. "Agency Orders U.S. Ports to Bar Japanese Ships." *New York Times,* 17 October: A1.

Sansbury, Tim. 1998. "Deregulation Monitors Face Reshuffling at FMC." *Journal of Commerce.* 8 October: 1A.

Schelling, Thomas C. 1960. "An Essay on Bargaining." In *The Strategy of Conflict* (Chapter 2, pp. 21–52). Cambridge, Mass.: Harvard University Press.

Schneider, William. 1997. "The New Isolationism." In Robert J. Lieber, ed., *Eagle Adrift: American Foreign Policy at the End of the Century* (Chapter 2, pp. 26–38). New York: Longman.

Schwarzkopf, General H. Norman. 1992. *The Autobiography: It Doesn't Take a Hero.* Written with Peter Petre. New York: Bantam.

Scowcroft, Brent. 1981. Transcript of a panel discussion among Scowcroft, David Aaron, Barry Blechman, Leslie Gelb, William Hyland, John Kester, Philip Odeen, and Peter Szanton. In Lawrence J. Korb and Keith D. Hahn, eds., *National Security Policy Organization in Perspective.* Washington, D.C.: American Enterprise Institute.

Sen, Amartya. 1983. "Presidential Address: Development: Which Way Now?" *Economic Journal 93* (December): 745–62.

Sestanovich, Stephen. 1997. "The Collapsing Partnership: Why the United States Has No Russia Policy." In Robert J. Lieber, ed., *Eagle Adrift: American Foreign Policy at the End of the Century* (pp. 163–77).New York: Longman.

Seymore, Bruce II, ed. 1992. *International Affairs Directory of Organizations: The ACCESS Resource Guide.* Santa Barbara, Calif.: ABC-CLIO.

Shapiro, Walter. 1990. "Prolific Purveyor of Punditry." *Time,* 12 February: 60–64.

Shoemaker, Christopher C. 1991. *The NSC Staff: Counseling the Council.* Boulder, Colo.: Westview.

Simon, Herbert A. 1956. "Rational Choice and the Structure of the Environment." *Psychological Review 63,* 2: 129–38.

————. 1987. "Satisficing." In John Eatwell, Murray Milgate, and Peter Newman, eds., *The New Palgrave Dictionary of Economics* (Vol.4, pp. 243–45). London: The Macmillan Press Limited.

SIPRI (Stockholm International Peace Research Institute). 1997. "Entry into Force Fact Sheet: The Chemical Weapons Convention." http://www.sipri.se/projects/eiftext.html (23 April 1997).

Sloan, Stanley R. 1991. *The U.S. Role in a New World Order: Prospects for George Bush's Global Vision.* Washington, D.C.: Congressional Research Service Report 91-294 RCO.

Smeloff, Ed, and Fred Branfman. 1998. "Kyoto, Global Warming and the 21st Century: A 'Global Warming Central' Perspective." Http://www.law.pace.edu/env/energy/perspective.html (13 January 1998).

Smith, Gerard, and Michael Krepon. 1993. "A Face Lift for ACDA." *New York Times,* 3 May: A14.

Smith, James Allen. 1991. *The Idea Brokers: Think Tanks and the Rise of the New Policy Elite.* New York: Free Press.

Snow, Donald M. 1986. "Crisis Instability and Deterrence Breakdown." In Peter C. Sederberg, ed., *Nuclear Winter, Deterrence, and the Prevention of Nuclear War* (pp. 67–80.) New York: Praeger.

————. 1997. *National Security: Defense Policy in a Changed International Order,* 4th ed. New York: St. Martin's Press.

————, and Eugene Brown. 1994. *Puzzle Palaces and Foggy Bottom: U.S. Foreign and Defense Policy-Making in the 1990s.* New York: St. Martin's Press.

Sollenberg, Margareta, and Peter Wallensteen. 1995. "Major Armed Conflicts." *SIPRI Yearbook 1995: Armaments, Disarmament and International Security* (pp. 21–25). Oxford: Oxford University Press.

Specter, Michael. 1994. "Mother Russia, Your Bill Is Overdue." *New York Times,* 25 September: E2.

Stanglin, Douglas. 1992. "Toxic Wasteland." *U.S. News & World Report,* 13 April: 40–46.

Starling, Grover. 1984. "Evaluating Defense Programs in an Era of Rising Expenditures." In G. Ronald Gilbert, ed., *Making and Managing Policy: Formulation, Analysis, Evaluation* (Chapter 18, pp. 289–308). New York: Marcel Dekker.

Steele, Karen. 1991. "Ground Water Effect 'Very Serious.'" *Oregonian,* 10 March: A1, A10.

Steigman, Andrew L. 1985. *The Foreign Service of the United States: First Line of Defense.* Boulder, Colo.: Westview Press.

Subramanyam, K. 1993. "An Equal-Opportunity NPT." http://www.bullatomsci.org/issues/1993/j93/j93Subramanyam.html (6 August 1998).

Talbott, Strobe. 1988. *The Master of the Game: Paul Nitze and the Nuclear Peace.* New York: Knopf.

Tharoor, Shashi. 1997. *India: From Midnight to the Millennium.* New York: Arcade.

Tonelson, Alan. 1998. *Another Image: Minding Our Own Business in Foreign Affairs.* Address to a conference on "Two Images of a Future American Foreign Policy," University of Washington, 23–24 April.

Tower Commission. 1987. [John Tower, Edmund Muskie, and Brent Scowcroft]. *Report of the President's Special Review Board.* Washington. D.C.: U.S. Government Printing Office.

Tullock, Gordon. 1965. *The Politics of Bureaucracy.* Washington, D.C.: Public Affairs Press.

Tyler, Patrick E. 1992a. "Pentagon Imagines New Enemies to Fight in Post–Cold-War Era." *New York Times,* 17 February: A1.

————. 1992b. "7 Hypothetical Conflicts Foreseen by the Pentagon." *New York Times,* 17 February: A8.

————. 1992c. "War in 1990's? New Doubts." *New York Times,* 18 February: A1.

————. 1992d. "U.S. Strategy Plan Calls for Insuring No Rivals Develop." *New York Times,* 8 March: A1.

————. 1992e. "Excerpts From Pentagon's Plan: 'Prevent the Re-Emergence of a New Rival.'" *New York Times,* 8 March: A14.

————. 1992f. "Lone Superpower Plan: Ammunition for Critics." *New York Times,* 10 March: A12.

————. 1992g. "Senior U.S. Officials Assail Lone-Superpower Policy." *New York Times,* 11 March: A1.

———. 1992h. "Pentagon Drops Goal of Blocking New Superpowers." *New York Times*, 24 May: A1.

United Nations Climate Change Secretariat (UNFCCC). 1997. "A Brief History of the Climate Change Convention." http://www.unfccc.de/fccc/conv/hist.htm (31 March 1997).

———. 1997. "Understanding Climate Change: A Beginner's Guide to the UN Framework Convention." *http://www.unfccc.de/resource/beginner.html* (30 May 1999)

USIA Electronic Journal. 1997. "Negotiations Background and Calendar: A Fact Sheet Released on the Climate Change Convention." http://usiahq.usis.usemb.se/journals/itgic/0497/ilge/gj-9.htm (16 July 1997).

U.S. Bureau of the Census. 1975. *Historical Statistics of the United States, Colonial Times to 1970, Bicentennial Edition.* Washington. D.C.: U.S. Government Printing Office.

———. 1998. *Statistical Abstract of the United States: 1998*, 118th ed. Washington. D.C.: U.S. Government Printing Office. [DOC-LC/HA/202/118th ed./1998]

U.S. Central Intelligence Agency. 1994. *Handbook of International Economic Statistics, 1994.* Washington. D.C.: U.S. Government Printing Office.

U.S. Department of Energy. 1998. *Annual Energy Review 1997.*

[UNIKOM]. 1994. "United Nations Iraq-Kuwait Observation Mission." http://ralph.gmu.edu/cfpa/peace/unikom.html (27 June 1997).

[UNEP] United Nations Environmental Program. 1994. *1994 Report of the Technology and Economics Assessment Panel for the 1995 Assessment of the UNEP Montreal Protocol on Substances That Deplete the Ozone Layer.* Kenya: UNEP.

United States Department of State. 1993. *Dispatch*, Number 49. ACDA Celebrates 30th Anniversary. 88.

[UNRes687]. 1991. Gopher://gopher.undp.org:70/00/undocs/scd/scouncil/s91/4 (27 June 1997).

[UNRes689]. 1991. Gopher://gopher.undp.org:70/00/undocs/scd/scouncil/s91/4 (27 June 1997).

Verdier, James M. 1992. "The Congressional Support Agencies: Comments." In Carol H. Weiss, ed., *Organizations for Policy Analysis: Helping Government Think* (Chapter 14, pp. 252–55). Newbury Park, Calif.: Sage.

Vos, Robert O. 1997. "Introduction: Competing Approaches to Sustainability." In Sheldon Kamieniecki, George A. Gonzalez, and Robert O. Vos, eds., *Flashpoints in Environmental Policymaking: Controversies in Achieving Sustainability* (pp. 1–27). Albany: State University of New York Press.

Watson, Bruce W., Susan M. Watson, and Gerald W. Hopple. 1990. *United States Intelligence: An Encyclopedia.* New York: Garland.

Weiss, Carol H. 1992. ed., *Organizations for Policy Analysis: Helping Government Think.* Newbury Park, Calif.: Sage.

Wieseltier, Leon. 1983. "The Great Nuclear Debate." *The New Republic*, 10 and 17 January (combined special issue nos. 3547 and 3548): 7–38.

Wittkopf, Eugene R. 1990. *Faces of Internationalism: Public Opinion and American Foreign Policy.* Durham: Duke University Press.

———. 1994. "Faces of Internationalism in a Transitional Environment." *Journal of Conflict Resolution 38*, 3 (September): 376–401.

———. 1995. *Faces of Internationalism Revisited.* Paper presented at the annual meetings of the American Political Science Association, Chicago, 31 August–3 September.

Wolf, Charles Jr., K. C. Yeh, Anil Bamezai, Donald P. Henry, and Michael Kennedy. 1995. *Long-Term Economic and Military Trends, 1994–2015: The United States and Asia.* Santa Monica, Calif.: RAND Corporation.

Woll, Peter, ed. 1984. *American Government: Readings and Cases*, 8th ed. Boston: Little, Brown.

Woodrow Wilson School. 1988. Undergraduate Policy Conference Report: *The United States Intelligence Community.* Princeton, N.J.: Princeton University, Woodrow Wilson School of Public and International Affairs.

World Almanac. 1998. *The World Almanac and Book of Facts 1998.* Mahwah, NJ: K-III Reference Corporation.

World Bank. 1997a. *World Development Report 1997: The State in a Changing World.* Washington, D.C.: The World Bank.

———. 1997b. *World Development Indicators 1997 on CD-ROM.* Washington, D.C.: The World Bank.

York, Herbert F. 1973. *Arms Control: Readings from Scientific American.* New York: Freeman.

Zimmerman, William. 1974. "Choices in the Postwar World" In Charles Gati, ed., *Caging the Bear: Containment and the Cold War.* (Chapter 6, pp. 85–108). Indianapolis: Bobbs-Merrill.

INDEX